"In the beginning [illegible]
heavens and the earth...
Then God said, '*let us make man in our image, after our likeness.*'"
—Genesis I:I, 26

"Before Christ's second coming the Church must pass through a final trial that will shake the faith of many believers... [it] will unveil the "mystery of iniquity" in the form of a religious deception offering men an apparent solution to their problems at the price of apostasy from the truth."
—*Catechism of the Catholic Church*, §675

"Man is the perfection of the universe..."
–St. Francis de Sales

Available From:
www.DSDOConnor.com
www.OnlyManBearsHisImage.com
https://www.amazon.com/stores/Daniel-OConnor/author/B00UA0DJ4O

Published on the Feast of Our Lady of Victory (Our Lady of the Rosary), October 7, 2023
Paperback ISBN: 978-1-957168-06-7
eBook ISBN: 978-1-957168-07-4

Cover: This book's cover portrays an unadulterated version (source: Wikimedia Commons) of Michelangelo's (†1564) famous fresco in the Sistine Chapel, depicting the creation of Adam by God. I have chosen this work of art because it beautifully illustrates God making man in His own Image. I have also selected it because in the realm of science fiction, it is the single most frequently perversely modified painting. Its parodies either replace the finger of God with some other suggested creator, or replace the outstretched arm of Adam with some other creature or object (perhaps an alien, monkey, or robot). It is the thesis implied by those distortions of this masterpiece—that other material beings besides descendants of Adam and Eve bear God's Image—which this book refutes.

Only Man Bears His Image

The Biblical, Catholic, & Scientific Case Against Aliens, UFO Deceptions, Sentient AI, and Other Sci-Fi Disguised Demons & Psyops Heralding the Antichrist

By Daniel O'Connor

Dedication

To *all those who, holding to the truth, hand on the catholic and apostolic faith.*

Brief Contents

A detailed Table of Contents may be found immediately following the Introduction.

1. Introduction

"For the time is coming when people will not endure sound teaching, but having itching ears they will accumulate for themselves teachers to suit their own likings, and will turn away from listening to the truth and wander into myths." (2 Timothy 4:3-4)

Today more than ever, this warning of St. Paul should resound in the hearts and minds of all Christians. Those with "ears to hear ... what the Spirit says to the churches," (Revelation 2:7) and with eyes to see and "interpret the signs of the times" (Matthew 16:3) will not fail to discern how imminent its fulfillment appears.

Here in Sacred Scripture, we are told of a time when men, despite their unfathomably fortunate status as hearers of the Gospel—thereby even beholding "*things into which angels longed to look*" (1 Peter 1:12); truths which "*many prophets and kings longed to see ... but did not see*" (Luke 10:24)—would nevertheless cast aside this Divine Gift of Christian Truth. A time when men would, instead, walk straight back into the Pagan myths that Divine Revelation had delivered them from thousands of years hence, and even into the seducing arms of the very demons—though assuming new forms—that Christ had cast out.

St. Paul's warning above is not merely important: it is apocalyptic. Opening the fourth chapter of his second letter to Timothy, it follows the parallel warning with which the Apostle opened the matching chapter of his *first* letter to the same saint:

> **Now *the Spirit explicitly says* that in the last times some will turn away from the faith by paying attention to deceitful spirits and demonic instructions...** (1 Timothy 4:1)

We are undoubtedly in a sort of "last times,"—not because the *world* is about to end, but rather because the present Era is ending—and this prophecy will be fulfilled. My aim with this book is to help render that "some" who will "pay attention to demonic instructions" as small a number as possible.

Any Christian ought to stand upright when the Bible so starkly states, as it does in this passage, that "the Spirit *explicitly*" declares some truth. For it is God the Holy Spirit Himself Who authored Scripture, and when He goes so far as to remind us expressly just Who it is that is speaking, we know that what follows deserves our most resolute attention. And what follows is the assurance that *the Devil will seek to instruct mankind in the latter times* in a unique way. He will, moreover, tragically succeed even with some who had numbered among the Faithful.

Last Things (Eschatology) resemble First Things (Protology). To *instruct* us, the Devil must first open the *dialogue* with us—just as he did in the Garden. He will use similar tactics now as then. As I wrote in a 2022 article, "All the Devil Wants is a Little Dialogue:"

> **To initiate the Fall, the Devil possessed an irrational serpent and used it to dialogue with humanity. Eve's wrongheaded openness to conversation with that animal is the prototype for the Devil's current plans to dialogue with all humanity** through the modern world's lies. These are lies which, in a modified relativistic nihilism similar to the serpent's own, "*Did God really say...?*" (though bedecked in the scientific verbiage one [now] expects ...), seek to beguile the faithful into supposing they cannot really know various truths **... we [must] recognize that something demonic is afoot, and shut the door to dialogue, lest we suffer a fate similar to Eve's**... [For] the Devil is going to attempt dialogue with humanity as never before; not merely with one woman, but with billions of people across the planet. ... And what the Devil could not achieve through the New Age movement ... he will accomplish through "Science."[1]

The present matter is not merely one spiritual concern of many about the current times. It points, rather, to *the* Great Deception; to *the* Final Trial of the Church:

> Before Christ's second coming the Church must pass through a final trial that will shake the faith of many believers ... [it] will unveil the "mystery of iniquity" in the form **of a religious deception offering men an apparent solution to their problems at the price of apostasy from the truth. The supreme religious deception is that of the Antichrist,** a pseudo-messianism by which man glorifies himself in place of God and of his Messiah come in the flesh. (*Catechism of the Catholic Church*, §675)

Yes, the matter we are dealing with in this book constitutes the heralding of the Antichrist himself:

> **The coming of the lawless one by the activity of Satan will be with all power and with pretended signs and wonders, and with all wicked deception** for those who are to perish, because they refused to love the truth and so be saved. **Therefore God sends upon them a strong delusion, to make them believe what is false**... (2 Thessalonians 2:9-11)

"*Pretended signs and wonders... wicked deception...strong delusion... an apparent solution to man's problems at the price of apostasy...a religious deception...a pseudo-messianism...itching ears... wandering into myths...*"

Phrases such as these describe the news today, they describe society today, and sadly, too often they describe certain happenings in the Church today. Tomorrow, these phrases may describe them all the more accurately still. It is impossible to overstate the urgency of the times in which we live.

Returning to the warning of St. Paul with which we opened this Introduction, let us consider that we know exactly what the predominant modern myths are, and we can clearly see that these "myths" are precisely what men of the present era have "wandered into," thanks to their "itching ears." As modern man increasingly turns away from his own Christian patrimony, the myths he turns toward are no longer found within the pages of Hesiod. They are, rather, seductively detailed in the deluge of science-fiction works which, especially in the last century, have tantalized their consumers with enrapturing descriptions of alien civilizations visiting earth, time-travelling humans from the future coming to instruct us, and "artificial intelligence" developing reason and will—just to name a few.

These deceits, I submit to you, are precisely the "myths" to which St. Paul prophesied mankind would turn. And although modern science fiction traffics in many counterfactual premises, predominant among them is the expectation of imminent contact with extraterrestrial civilizations. It is, moreover, this deception that would provide the most powerful means for the Devil to instruct the masses surreptitiously on a global scale; it is this deception that has already—in the last several decades—revealed its nefarious nature through its fruits; and, it is this deception that a faithful approach to the Christian teaching particularly firmly repudiates. It is, therefore, this deception that merits the majority of our attention in the pages ahead—though we will not neglect to cover the AI Deception and other similar traps as well.

I present this stark warning in the opening pages of the book before you so that no one now reading it will mistake its opening parts for yet another detached or merely academic treatment of the question of extraterrestrial intelligence. In recent decades, and especially the last several years, countless such books have been written (and printed by the most prestigious of global publishers), conferences have been held, college classes have been taught, and mass media has been generated—all dedicated to exploring these questions from a perspective that is either spiritually indifferent or, worse, giddily excited.

My motivation in writing this book, however, is simple: to deliver as many as possible from a movement that is already seducing millions into occult, New Age, Pagan, heretical, blasphemous, and otherwise exceedingly dangerous realms, and which soon may well become a still more massive deception—an *apocalyptic* deception. Although there will be times in the forthcoming pages when we deal with the same questions in just as scholarly a fashion as any existing text, I hope none forget, in reading even those passages, that my entire motivation for this book is spiritual, not academic.

"Save some, by snatching them out of the fire." (Jude 1:23)

***

Aliens—incarnate extraterrestrial intelligent beings—do not exist. Not only do they not exist, but all Christians (and especially all Catholics) can use what they already know from their Faith to reach this conclusion. Positing their existence entails proposing a novelty incompatible with a faithful approach to Scripture, Magisterium, Sacred Tradition, authentic private revelation, and even at odds with the basic tenets of scientific reason.

Alien belief is, furthermore, a uniquely dangerous ideology; therefore, genuine humility—far from advising the course of action one often hears recommended in these discussions (i.e., *"humbly remain open to the existence of aliens and contact with them"*)—advises that one rule out this possibility in his mind in order to aid in persevering as a good Christian and a faithful Catholic. Flippantly exposing oneself to occasions of sin is a symptom of pride, not humility. And if, in these days of exponentially growing diabolical disorientation, there were ever an occasion of sin to be had, it is found in an intellectual posture that is ready, willing, and open to accepting the "astounding teachings" presented by these "more evolved, enlightened, and advanced beings"—these "aliens," who will in reality either be demonic illusions or simply human-crafted deceptions used as a "psyop." But as we will see in Part Four, this is not only a concern about what may transpire in the future. The ET Deception is *already* leading millions astray.

***

That is my thesis, and that is what I will demonstrate throughout the pages of this book.

For all the seriousness and darkness of some of the themes that we must examine throughout the forthcoming pages, however, I conclude this introduction with an assurance that may sound paradoxical at first, but is in fact as sure as any: the message of this book is one of overwhelming hope and joy.

For if indeed what we are now faced with is the beginning of the long-prophesied "Great Deception," which will constitute the *"final trial that will shake the faith of many believers"* (CCC §675), then it is also true that the Church's Triumph is imminent. We know that after the Great Trial is endured, Christ's victory over it is guaranteed, and the time will come when, *"at Jesus' name, every knee must bend ... and every tongue proclaim to the glory of God the Father: JESUS CHRIST IS LORD!"* (Philippians 2:10-11). We shall then see the day of the "restoration of the human race in Jesus Christ," (Pope St. Pius X, *E Supremi*, §14); the arrival of "that most auspicious day, whereon the whole world will gladly and willingly render obedience to the most sweet lordship of Christ the King," (Pope Pius XI, *Miserentissimus Redemptor*, §5). In a word, it is the fulfillment of the Our Father prayer whereupon the Will of God will reign on earth as in Heaven (cf. Matthew 6:10) and the Immaculate Heart will Triumph and bring an Era of Peace to the world (cf. Our Lady of Fatima).

The more noteworthy of the prophecies bearing upon "latter times"

> seem to have **one common end, to announce great calamities impending over mankind, the triumph of the Church, and the renovation of the world**. All the seers agree in two leading features ... "**First** they all point to some terrible convulsion, to **a revolution springing from most deep-rooted impiety, consisting in a formal opposition to God and His truth**, and resulting in the most formidable persecution to which the Church has ever been subject. **Secondly, they all promise for the Church a victory more splendid than she has ever achieved here below**." (*Catholic Encyclopedia.* Article on *Prophecy*)

Our Lord instructed us on how to respond when we see these signs of the times arriving:

> **But when these things begin to come to pass, look up, and lift up your heads, because your redemption is at hand.** (Luke 21:28)

Therefore, I pray this book serves as a reminder to raise your heads high, and both long for and pray for the Triumph of Christ—a theme we will conclude with in Part Six. If much of this book's content relays the "bad news" (that is, how to resist its wiles), then Part Six contains the "good news." Both are essential.

On the Need for This Book: Against the Usual Justification Given by Alien Belief Promoters

Many Christian ET promoters insist that their writings are important because they consist in a certain type of apologetical rebuttal in support of the Faith—albeit one patiently awaiting the arrival of the supposed threat it addresses. With their arguments, these authors claim they wish to protect the Church against a crisis "if and when" aliens are discovered. Such authors operate under the extravagant premise that they are like prescient pre-14th-century astronomers laying the theological foundation for a welcoming of the heliocentric model; insisting even before its arrival that such a model does not harm the Faith, in hopes of preventing a wave of souls from leaving the Church upon the imminent Copernican Revolution they prophetically anticipate.*

* If this truly is their intention, then it is (at least on the surface) a commendable one. Though I insist aliens do not exist, even I will happily engage in a thought experiment and will agree with them in what conclusions they say would follow from the counterfactual premises that aliens do exist and that we will soon contact them. And what follows is this: such aliens would indeed be creations of the One True God just like we are and neither Theism in general, nor Christianity and Catholicism in particular, would be refuted—each would carry on as it always has. Now that we have achieved, in one sentence, what many Christian ET promoters present as the entire reason for their many lengthy treatises, let us return to reality: this justification they present is both fallaciously question-begging and radically short-sighted.

But one cannot assume the plausibility of his thesis in seeking to justify that very thing,* and it is more likely that the justification given by these ET promoters is only worldliness masquerading as piety. For their true motives are transparent: they harbor an excitement (palpable when they speak) for the arrival of epoch-altering intervention from extraterrestrial saviors. It is difficult to find one among their ranks who is not eager for the fruition of the very science-fiction fantasies that have been rampant in pop-culture recently. Most confess with a smile that this is what they have excitedly awaited since childhood. One theology professor at a Catholic seminary even published, in 2021, a large book arguing for alien belief—he dedicated it to Steven Spielberg.

Finally, it is shocking to observe the glibness with which Catholic ET promoters treat the pervasive and manifestly demonic and otherwise darkly deceptive elements in "alien encounters," Ufology, and extraterrestrial expectation in general. Some pass over it entirely, while others only briefly acknowledge that such explanations "may be correct a tiny fraction of the time," ignoring (as we will see in Part Four) that *virtually everything that is in any way associated* with these modern movements is thoroughly rotten to the core—New Age, occult, heretical, and often openly Satanic.

Yet these commentators—including some who should know better (for their ranks include even exorcists and "orthodox-minded" Catholic authors who appear well-versed in demonology)—reject such concerns with the customary condescension, *"not everything is demons, you know; that's fundamentalism! The Devil isn't behind every rock!"* Precisely within this fanatical desire not to be seen as fanatics, they reveal how fanatical their belief truly is. For if their approach was guided by prudence, they would readily leave ET belief aside (or at least not promote it publicly), merely on account of the undeniable dangers that pervade the modern movement surrounding it. Instead, their dubious claim that they fear a hypothetical falling away from the Faith will transpire lest they are sufficiently zealous to argue for alien belief is posited as their motivation, even though this

---

* This approach is, for example, the one adopted by openly dissenting theologians who, taken in by the errors posited by certain psychologists, assume that various tenets of "LGBT" ideology will soon be "proven by science." They generate massive treatises attempting to illustrate how very reconcilable Christianity and Catholicism supposedly are with homosexuality, transgenderism, etc., and the purpose they claim motivates their work is the same apparently noble one presented above: their desire to stem a flow of souls out of the Church in light of "increasingly clear science" contradicting traditional Catholic thought. They insist they are showing these would-be fallen-away Catholics just how mistaken traditional thought was, and how a "closer consideration of the essentials" only reveals the compatibility of the Faith with "LGBT" ideology. Though heroes in their own minds, they are only contributing to the exact opposite of their stated aims.

entirely fictional (and, indeed, fantastical) scenario is infinitely outweighed by a clear and present danger inherent in the very thesis they promote!

The cognitive dissonance evident in such a contrast—wherein an actual, concrete, present, and overwhelmingly common and grave spiritual danger is dismissed as trivial to make way for their attempts to supposedly circumvent a future hypothetical, non-existent, and, frankly, impossible problem—is stunning and telling. Those who, as Our Lord admonishes, seek to judge the tree by its fruits (cf. Matthew 7) should take note.

Sadly, however, many who should be taking note are unlikely to do so. While I pray that those who read this book will receive protection from many of the lies now proliferating, and others bound to soon arrive, the deceptions already unfolding nevertheless seem destined to dominate ever greater ranks of the pew-sitters. New dangers in this realm, which cannot be addressed within the pages ahead, will inevitably arise. There will doubtless be ever more claims of "UFO sightings" and there will likely arrive a steadily ascending degree of credibility given to the extraterrestrial hypothesis as an explanation for these events by leaders in government, education, industry, and entertainment. Graver still, more and more seemingly authoritative theological, spiritual, and ecclesial voices in the Church are sure to embrace this diabolical deception, embellishing it with pious-looking attire. "Contact" with extraterrestrials may even soon be announced; the long-awaited "Day of Disclosure" may be at hand, or even "The Singularity," whereupon it is claimed that "AI" has officially evolved authentic rationality.

I have every intent to continue doing my humble best to write and speak against these dangers as new frontiers within them are approached. Therefore I encourage readers of this book to keep an eye out for my future writings (DSDOConnor.com), videos (Youtube.com/@DSDOConnor), and posts (Twitter.com/DSDOConnor).

2. Some Important Prefatory Notes

Content Pertains to *Rational* Incarnate Aliens

This book only deals with the question of extraterrestrial incarnate *intelligent* life—civilizations of material creatures with reason, who are not descendants of Adam and Eve, but rather originate from other first parents on other planets. **Whenever I refer to "aliens," this is the definition I am using**. In this book, I intend to present no analysis of the question of whether there could be other *irrational* forms of life outside of this planet.

Furthermore, I intended no criticism of that view which would posit that all the countless planets and stars of all the galaxies are "populated" or "inhabited" by myriads upon myriads of angels, each with their own stunning interactions with the material heavenly bodies. My goal with this book is anything but to "demystify" the cosmos or render them dull, sterile objects we must approach rationalistically. If anything, my own approach to these matters is decidedly less rationalistic than even that of the ET promoters whom this book will refute!

Aliens "Could" Exist—but *Do Not Exist*

My insistence that aliens *do not* exist must be distinguished from the proposition that aliens *"could not"* exist. I am affirming, and will demonstrate in the chapters ahead, that aliens certainly do not exist. I am not, however, claiming that it is strictly impossible for aliens to exist. God, in His Omnipotence, is surely *ontologically capable* of creating innumerable galaxies filled with endless species of incarnate intelligent beings. In describing God's all-powerfulness, various saints as well as theologians, Catechetical texts, and Catholic authors throughout the centuries have affirmed that God "could have" created innumerable worlds. No saint, however, has ever been shown to have believed that God *did* create other planets with intelligent incarnate life upon them, and it is certain that no saint before the 20th century's "space age" asserted this. My aim in this book is not to claim that God *could not have* created aliens; rather, my aim is only to argue that He *did not do so*. My thesis holds that the most faithful approach to Scripture, Sacred Tradition, Magisterium, Private Revelation (and more) allows us to conclude with certainty that, of all material creation, only man bears His Image (i.e., only man is a person; an individual with an intellect and will).

Similarly, it is often piously said that Jesus would gladly die again for each one of us individually. This statement is absolutely true, and it is a powerful aid to our meditation, since His love for each of His children really is that extraordinary. But it is absolutely untrue that this has actually happened or *might* happen in the future; it would also be false to claim that a Christian may entertain the possibility that Jesus did die or might die multiple times for different people, as Scripture is very clear that He died only once for all (e.g., Hebrews 7:27), and that He cannot die again (e.g., Romans 6:9). Therefore, they are guilty of manipulation who would use these hypotheticals to make theological conjectures about how things actually stand in reality. Even though Christ *would* die for each of us, we may not entertain the notion that this *might actually happen*.

Likewise, God "could have" created, and Christ "could have" redeemed, innumerable inhabited worlds. Acknowledging these facts is important to properly describe the Divine Omnipotence, but it is illicit to use them as a justification for supposing such things might have happened. We are also told in Scripture that "if Christ has not been raised, then our preaching is in vain and your faith is in vain." (1 Corinthians 15:14) This verse does not give us license to entertain the possibility that Christ has not been raised! A more fundamental dogma of Christian Faith cannot be imagined than the Resurrection of Jesus Christ. This verse simply describes what would logically follow from a patently counterfactual premise.

A mature faith enables one to consider such scenarios. Doing so is beneficial for drawing out what would logically follow from them, without succumbing to the category mistake of using those very premises—which we know to be untrue—to bolster other conjectures.

Angels, Demons, and Aliens

Angels (and demons) are, of course, intelligent creatures and could be classed "extraterrestrial" in one sense of the word; however, both Scripture and the Church infallibly teach that they are immaterial (pure spirit) and entirely invisible (even though they can assume visible forms), therefore they are not what I refer to when using the word "alien." (Cf. CCC §395; CCC §328-330; Lateran IV; Summa Theologica I, Q50, A1; Hebrews 1:14, Job 4:15, etc.) When, in Part Four, we discuss the ET Deception, we will see that demons often appear as "aliens." The entire point of such observations, however, is that these appearances are *illusions*. A demon is a real creature. An "alien" is not.

Angels are confirmed in the good, so they could never deceive us, therefore they would never present themselves as aliens or UFOs. Demons, on the other hand, constantly deceive. They have long been known to present themselves under the guise of various Pagan myths that prevail in any given culture: fairies, elves, 'gods,' gnomes, satyrs, and, today, *aliens and UFOs*.

Readers must understand from the onset that I do not intend to write off each alleged "UFO encounter" or "alien contact" as mere fabrication or hallucination, psychological projection, or as an optical illusion, meteorological event, weather balloon, drone, etc. (as true as it is that explanations such as these are the correct ones the vast majority of the time). I acknowledge that many of these phenomena evade such explanations, and are, therefore, "real." I will, however, argue that such occasions are instances of real *diabolical*—not extraterrestrial—activity.

Some readers, upon seeing that I am acknowledging "otherworldly" explanations here and who are accustomed to decades of the "UFO debate" consisting entirely of the arguments of the "debunkers" vs. the "believers," may wonder why this distinction of alien vs. demon is so important. This will be explained in detail in Part Four. For now, suffice it to say that it is a *supremely* important distinction with ramifications that cannot be overstated.

Arguments of Various Weights Presented Here

Many arguments are presented in the following pages, and each carries its own degree of certitude.

This book will doubtless be vigorously opposed by ET promoters, and some of its more unscrupulous critics are likely to ignore its strongest arguments, while selecting only the least important or tangential considerations (perhaps even those presented as little more than "food for thought") to "refute" and thus misleadingly claim victory for alien belief. However, I trust most of this book's readers to detect this fallacy and remain unswayed by its promotion. For the various arguments discussed in the pages ahead are not separate links on a chain that render the whole only as strong as the weakest; on the contrary, they each *independently* refute alien belief.

Still other critics will simply dismiss this book entirely by using the ready-at-hand labels they reflexively pin on all who take apocalyptic warnings seriously, or who share truths that may be hard to hear. "Fear mongers!", "doom-and-gloomers!", "fundamentalists!", and other similar exclamations will be used to ignore the pages ahead which present philosophical, theological, and scientific arguments no ET promoter will be able to answer. As I cannot reach such people directly, I will likewise trust this book's readers to sound the alarm with sufficient zeal as to simply drown out those who have so blinded themselves as to assume that any opinion voiced by any theologian working in the Vatican is orthodox, and who will continue arranging the deck chairs on the Titanic even as it is being rent in two and plunging into the abyss.

On The Current "Mainstream Catholic" Answer

During the last several decades which have seen rampant alien-themed science fiction books, movies, and TV shows, mainstream "professional" Catholic commentators have provided a nearly unanimous answer to questions about Catholicism and alien belief; namely, "*There is no Catholic teaching or Catholic position on this question,*" or "*Catholics are free to believe whatever they choose on this matter,*" or "*That is a scientific question, not a theological one, therefore the Faith cannot have anything meaningful to say in answering it.*"

While I concede that it currently appears no clear *dogmas* exist *explicitly* settling the question *directly*, I emphatically reject these answers and I lament how casually and commonly they have long been presented. More sane ages of Church History would never have so flippantly asserted that the Faith is irrelevant in addressing *any* important world-issue, much less one so existentially pressing as this.

The mere fact that there is not currently an infallible dogma directly settling an issue does not mean that Catholicism has nothing to say on the matter. Just as it would be foolish for one to say, at any point within the eighteen centuries of Church History preceding Pius IX's promulgation of *Ineffabilis Deus*, that "*Catholicism has nothing to say about the proposition that the Blessed Virgin Mary was Immaculately Conceived,*" it is similarly wrong-headed to imply that Scripture, Tradition, Magisterium, Private Revelation, etc., is immaterial to the question of extraterrestrial intelligence. Indeed, on the contrary—as will become evident in the forthcoming chapters—the testimony of these sure sources, taken together, demonstrates the conclusion that aliens do not exist.

Freely Use this Book as a Reference, and Begin Reading It at Any Chapter

Whoever is apprehensive about the scope and length of this book should feel no guilt in skipping around to whichever sections arouse his interest or address his own particular questions. I have deliberately provided a very detailed Table of Contents to facilitate this approach for whoever prefers it. As much as possible, I have written individual sections to be coherent in isolation for such readers. Those who prefer to read from cover to cover will have to forgive a small bit of repetition, which was necessary to achieve that goal.

Some readers will find direct Scriptural or Magisterial arguments against extraterrestrial intelligence more worthwhile (thus focusing on Parts One and Two), whereas others may prefer to focus on "discerning the tree by its fruits," and on considering what apocalyptic events are brewing; they may wish to focus on reading Part Four. Readers of a different sort may be more fascinated by the science involved and prefer Part Three, and still others may be more interested in considering other NHI ("Non-Human Intelligence") Deceptions (such as rational AI), and emphasize Part Five.

All readers are free to open up this book and begin reading at whatever page they prefer. While I have aimed to ensure this book's various sections complement each other, they do not, on the other hand, strictly depend upon each other.

The Spirit's Words to the Church Today & Similar Warnings from Other Authors

When, years ago, I first became deeply concerned about the trends appearing with respect to ET promotion in the Church, and "UFO phenomena" in the world in general, I had never been exposed to any of the treatises on these topics already written by various devout Christian authors who were sounding the alarm about demonic deceptions. When I started writing about these concerns, I did so from an essentially blank slate. Only afterward did I begin receiving correspondence from readers alerting me to similar things said some years ago. Therefore, I must make abundantly clear from the onset: these urgent warnings that I issue proceed entirely from my own convictions and conscience. They were not in the least bit formed by or even influenced by prior publications asserting similar things.

I did, since then, purchase many (perhaps even *all*) of the existing works on this topic that were recommended to me, and I researched them while writing this book. I am very grateful for the excellent warnings already issued by other devout Christians in the last few decades, and, where appropriate, I will be sure to draw from their wisdom, quote them, and credit them in the forthcoming pages.

The scope, depth, and fundamental approach of this book, however, far exceeds any works on the topic that I have seen or heard of, and I present a multitude of new research and new arguments, new analyses, and new exposés here. I would, therefore, exhort even those who have read other books on this topic which agree with my thesis to consider carefully what I have written in the pages ahead. The importance of the issue has only grown exponentially in recent years, and the new material in this book is indispensable to address what you are seeing reported on the news as you read these words.

As for the similarities some of my warnings bear with warnings already given, I am aware that critics will accuse me of simply jumping on a bandwagon (a strange critique, since the only bandwagon relevant to this issue in the Church and the world today is the one they are jumping on—the alien *belief* bandwagon!). I will, however, ignore their criticism, as I know it is false.

I am certainly no prophet, and I do not think any of the Christian authors who issued similar warnings before me regarded themselves as prophets, either. I am nothing but an ordinary Catholic. Each day I pray, attend Mass, read and meditate on the Word of God, and recite the Rosary;

then, from this spiritual posture, I check the news, do the research, and perform the analysis; seeking to discern the signs of the times in the light of the perennial and orthodox Faith. This straightforward discernment process has led me to the firm convictions you will see expressed in the pages ahead. Although the amount of reading, research, and analysis I have undertaken—over the course of years spent writing this book—is immense, it has always proceeded from that basic Christian and Catholic approach. I have not taken any shortcuts; I have not sought out self-proclaimed gurus to give me easy answers, self-important scholars to dispense me from doing the reading and analysis myself (though I have certainly consulted the relevant scholars where appropriate), or self-declared seers or prophets who purport to direct knowledge of these matters.

My development of the convictions that structure this book—before having any knowledge of the similar convictions of Christian authors before me—only strengthens my belief that the Holy Spirit is urgently inspiring these persuasions within the consciences of Christians around the world. God is at work right now. Let us listen to Him. In such times as these, our calling is not to become ever more compromising with the world; ever more formed by its pundits; ever more open to its secular promises and giddy excitements. No, in such times as these our calling is the opposite: to tune out those voices and their increasingly messianic secular pseudo-gospels, and instead tune in to the voice of the Holy Spirit.

No Condemnation of Science Fiction or Alien Believers Intended

While this book emphatically warns against the dangers inherent in using certain themes from popular science fiction works as the lens through which one assesses what is possible or plausible in the real world, it presents no categorical condemnation of the genre, nor even does it regard the fictional theme of extraterrestrials as meriting strict denunciation. On the contrary, I too have unashamedly enjoyed certain fictional works about aliens, and I continue to do so. For example, I appreciated the 2002 movie, *Signs*, and although I obviously disagree with some of C.S. Lewis' opinions on this topic, I did enjoy much content from his famous "Space Trilogy" novels. Though not works of science fiction, they bear some similarities and therefore should be mentioned—I am particularly fond of, and especially heartily endorse, J.R.R. Tolkien's *The Lord of the Rings* novels, and the movies based on them.

No one should feel personally reproached by this book merely because he enjoys science fiction in moderation, while observing the necessary boundaries to preserve both orthodoxy and moral and spiritual safety.

Similarly, no one should feel personally attacked simply because he does not—as I encourage—categorically reject belief in the existence of aliens (hopeful as I am that such a person will change his mind after reading this book!). I acknowledge that there is not yet any dogmatic teaching directly and explicitly settling this issue, and as such I am certainly not accusing anyone of formal heresy just for believing in aliens. Indeed, better Christians than myself believe in them—although the pages ahead will demonstrate how mistaken and dangerous their view is.

In this book, I will need to share some particularly strong words for that small circle of public Christians who have distinguished themselves as alien belief *promoters* (which I will generally abbreviate to "ET promoters"), but these reproofs are not directed at the ordinary Christian who happens to believe in aliens.

That said, I will not tiptoe around the issue or walk on eggshells in this book. Remaining "inoffensive" is not one of my goals. Formally heretical or not, error is error, and it will here be addressed bluntly and refuted resolutely. For we are not here dealing with just any mistaken view, but with a uniquely spiritually and, I dare say, *eschatologically* dangerous one.

However, I trust my readers to not mistake my vigor in opposing this view for a personal attack against those who hold it. Church history is filled with accounts of even canonized saints emphatically opposing each other's views. To those Christians who currently do believe in aliens, I submit the following arguments to you as one friend—one brother—to another.

I Write This Book Knowing It Is About to Be "Disproven"

I anticipate that after publishing this book, I will receive a steady stream of correspondence from those who have not read it (but are aware of its themes), alerting me to this or that breaking news story whose claims run directly contrary to my thesis in the forthcoming pages.

It is *precisely because* I anticipate an imminent explosion of such news stories, however, that I am writing this book. These matters are not merely issues I have an academic interest in refuting; they are demonic traps I wish to warn my readers against the proliferation of for the sake of the salvation of their souls. I suspect that we may well soon be told, by the curators of the mainstream narrative—who haunt the positions of power in government, industry, technology, scientific research, entertainment, media, and academia—that we now have "evidence of," or even "examples of" extraterrestrial intelligence (whether here physically or only contacted via radio), sentient AI, rational AI, language-using animals, time travel, and the like. I suspect many seemingly authoritative theological voices will endorse these claims.

Such claims will *all* be lies, and this book will equip its readers to discern exactly *how and why* they are lies. Those lies may well be told by "the experts," and may seem supported by a slew of "proof," but those claims will either be fraudulent or the assertions connected to them will not flow from an honest assessment of the *authentic* evidence. A rigorous application of scrutiny will eventually expose the fraud and discover the truth. But that may take quite some time, and the danger lies in the intervening days. I pray this book serves as a stopgap for those most perilous of times.

Formatting, Etc.

Bible quotes will generally be taken from the Revised Standard Version Catholic Edition, but may also be taken from other translations.

Uncommon abbreviations are avoided in this book, but the widely known ones will be used: ET (Extraterrestrial), UFO (Unidentified Flying Object), AI (Artificial Intelligence), and, occasionally, NHI (Non-Human Intelligence—an umbrella term including "aliens, rational AI, intelligent animals," etc.), AGI (Artificial General Intelligence—a term referring to AI that has supposedly become humanlike or beyond humanlike in its abilities).

Both endnotes and footnotes are used. Footnotes are signified by asterisks or other symbols, and are generally reserved for those occasions where additional insight is helpful to understand what is discussed, therefore it would be advisable to consult them whenever time permits. Endnotes are signified by numbers, can be found listed at the end of the book, and are generally used for all other matters (e.g., citing the sources of quotes).

Although the vast majority of this book's content is original, a small selection of excerpts from or paraphrased portions of my earlier articles, video transcripts, and blog posts are used. All of these may be found posted at or linked to within www.DSDOConnor.com. All quotes from others, however, are cited and credited to their respective authors. Moreover, all quotations are simply presented in accordance with legal fair use guidelines, therefore no assumptions should be made about the views of the authors I quote in relation to this book. Readers of various eBook formats of this text should be sure their settings are configured to show blockquote formatting, otherwise it may not be clear when a quotation begins and ends.

Within quotations, emphasis may sometimes be added with **bolding, underlining, or** *italics*. Unless otherwise noted, I have added this emphasis.

3. Detailed Table of Contents

Part One: The Biblical Case

"There is another heresy that says that there are infinite and innumerable worlds, according to the empty opinion of certain philosophers—since Scripture has said that there is one world..."[2]

—St. Philastrius, Bishop of Brescia (†397 A.D.)

4. Salvation History Is Missing No Chapters

> "See to it that no one captivate you with an empty, seductive philosophy according to the tradition of men, according to the elemental powers of the world and not according to Christ."
> —Colossians 2:8

Let us begin the corpus of this book by recounting, in a brief few sentences, how discussions on the existence of aliens too often transpire among contemporary Christians. I have heard the following exchange almost verbatim, and I suspect you have as well:

Alien Believer: "*The universe is so vast; there must be aliens out there. Why would God have made humans as the only intelligent incarnate life?*"
Alien Disbeliever: "*But there are no aliens, because the Bible does not teach that there are aliens.*"
Alien Believer: "*What does that count for? The Bible does not say anything about microbes either; yet we now know they exist.*"

Sadly, this is where the dialogue usually ends. Today, it is quite unfashionable to develop the bedrock of one's *entire* worldview by Divine Revelation, therefore the alien disbeliever tends to feel too embarrassed to respond in the logical way. Whoever finds himself in such a discussion, however, should not walk away after that brief exchange. Instead, he should ask the obvious follow-up question:

Alien Disbeliever, continued: "*What qualities of Creation, if true, can we reasonably conclude might be entirely absent from Divine (Public) Revelation?*"

Indeed, one must concede that the simple protestation, "*that isn't in the Bible!*", does not alone rule out the thing in question. But we must also concede that pointing out, "*that isn't explicitly condemned in the Bible!*" does not indicate that the thing in question is licit to entertain.

Many teachings—particularly those proffered in the modern era—are so flagrantly incompatible with Christianity that it would be foolish to expect the Bible to explicitly rule them out. Each era of history has its own eccentricities, and whoever would justify them by appealing to an absence of express condemnation of them in Scripture is guilty not only of a flawed approach to the Bible, but also an arrogant overestimation of the thinkers of his own day—thinkers who will soon be just another footnote in the history books. Demanding express answers to each question from Divine Revelation, including those questions that Christian common sense should suffice in addressing, indicates a skewed approach to the Faith that distrusts the power of the Holy Spirit; like an adolescent who still wants his father to hold his hand on the sidewalk as if he were still a toddler. Ironically, it is precisely those scholars who boast of having matured into adulthood, leaving behind a "merely adolescent" theology, who have in fact only left adolescence to revert to infancy. For example, one prominent Christian clergyman, theologian, and ET promoter (among those recently commissioned by NASA to study the question of aliens), in a scholarly tome published in 2023 by Cambridge University, insisted:

> ...there is no more reason to expect mention of [aliens] in the historic revelation to Jews and Christians than to find mention of the duck-billed platypus...the purpose of Scripture is shrewdly focused on that which is necessary for salvation ... arguments from silence will bear little weight.[3]

No Christian, however, should fail to immediately perceive how outlandish it is to label this matter as salvation-trivial! The question of whether man, the incarnation of Jesus Christ, the Blessed Virgin, the earth, the Church, Salvation History, etc., are unique and supreme—or, rather merely number among countless similar (or superior) extraterrestrial realities scattered across the galaxies—has enormous theological ramifications. (*The ET promoters, including the one quoted above, admit to this fact, thereby undermining their own insistence that ET's absence from Scripture is inconsequential.*) Yet, Christian ET promoters assure us such questions are equally "irrelevant to salvation" as the matter of duck-billed platypuses. So-called "arguments from silence," however, *are* extremely important in the Faith. Jesus ordained only men, therefore only men can even now be priests. Jesus is never mentioned as having biological children, therefore we know He had none. The New Testament speaks of no more than Seven Sacraments, therefore we know there are only that many. Scripture speaks of only Three Persons in God, so we know no one can ever assert so much as a fourth. Genesis speaks of human beings as male and female, but makes no mention of a "non-binary" option—nor does it indicate one can change his sex—therefore we know such things are ruled out. Let us ponder that final point more deeply.

Consider that (although acceptance of what follows is, sadly, becoming more widespread among today's Christians) devout souls almost all understand the evils inherent in "transgenderism." They realize how foolish—even diabolical—it is to assert that one can change his sex, or that other sexes or genders exist besides male and female. They remain firm in this conviction; unshaken by the silly protestations of the wolves in sheep's clothing who insist that transgenderism should be condoned by Christians since "The Bible never explicitly says you cannot change your sex,"* or "God did not say, in Genesis, that He *only* made humans male and female; He did not say that there would only *ever* be male and female!" This "Christian" advocate for transgenderism is taking a patently absurd view of Divine Revelation; supposing that something so fundamental to human nature as our sex might have received such a glaringly inadequate treatment within the pages of the Bible that, only with the help of modern scientific studies and psychology, could we at long last come to the "correct" understanding of sex; namely, that it is nothing but a "social construct" which we are free to modify at will!

For example, in a June 2023 article promoting transgender ideology, the Jesuit priest and Harvard-educated professor, Fr. Richard Clifford, wrote:

> The expectation that this single verse in Genesis ["male and female he created them" (Genesis 1:27)] can adjudicate modern controversies about gender is thoroughly misguided. There is no hint that the ancient author knew anything about the modern issue of gender identity. And the text gives no hint either. To use [it] against (or for) contemporary discussions of gender is to read into the biblical text rather than read the biblical text.[4]

Any serious Christian would be unswayed by this sophistry. But it employs the identical approach used by ET promoters to claim the Faith is perfectly reconcilable with aliens. Just as Fr. Clifford dismisses a Biblical foundation for understanding sexuality "because the Bible's authors didn't understand modern issues," so Christian ET promoters claim that, since the Bible was written long before telescopes, the jurisdiction of its own claims is necessarily deprived of the ability to rule on the realms these inventions observe. Fr. Clifford dismisses those who realize that Genesis speaking of humans as male and female means *humans are only male and female.* Similarly, ET promoters dismiss those who realize that Genesis speaking of only humans as made in God's Image *means only humans are made in God's Image.* The crux of the matter, therefore, is ultimately existential; *pre*-theological. It derives from how an individual Christian has decided to *fundamentally* regard Scripture: as either *the* foundation, or as merely "*a*" foundation. Those who choose the latter can easily find ways to pretend to justify belief in both transgenderism and extraterrestrials.

On extraterrestrial intelligence, we are dealing with a similarly crucial issue as sex. Is man *the* unique being of all material creation made in

---

* Although crossdressing is condemned in Scripture (cf. Deuteronomy 22:5), as are other behaviors unbecoming of one's own sex (e.g., Romans 1:24-27), I am not aware of any Biblical passages that explicitly rule out the possibility of a man becoming a woman, or vice versa. Nevertheless, we know this is not a possibility at all.

the Divine Image, or only one of multiple (even innumerable!) races of rational creatures throughout the universe? This question touches on the very essence of the creature's relationship with its Creator. Does the human race have siblings, or not? (If any intelligent incarnate creatures exist anywhere in the cosmos, they too would be our brethren.) Have we been failing, for 2,000 years, to pray for the vast majority of those in dire need of our prayers? Is Jesus Christ truly the only Incarnation of the Second Person of the Eternal Trinity, or is He just one of a whole population of Divine Individuals that are each God-Incarnate? Is the Blessed Virgin *the* Mother of God, or just one of countless such Immaculate Mothers? Is the Bible so fundamentally lacking in its ability to provide us a coherent worldview that it could entirely leave out any acknowledgement whatsoever of the vast majority of God's eternally oriented (i.e., rational) creation? Is the human body—assumed by God Himself 2,000 years ago—merely one more-or-less arbitrary way of designing an incarnate intelligent being just as a Volkswagen Beetle is one way of configuring a motor vehicle? Or, rather, is Scripture correct when it teaches that "God made man *right*," (Ecclesiastes 7:29), and is it true, as Pope St. John Paul II and Fr. Thomas Weinandy taught, that:

> The [human] body, in fact, **and only the [human] body**, is capable of making visible what is invisible: the spiritual and the divine. It has been created to transfer into the visible reality of the world, the mystery hidden from eternity in God, and thus to be a sign of it (*Theology of the Body*, 19:4)
>
> "Human beings were created in the image and likeness of God, and so in the image and likeness of the Son, for he is the perfect image of his Father. To be made in the image and likeness of the Son not only means that human beings possess intelligence - the ability to know the truth and to will and love what is good—but also that our bodies must ... bear the image of God. For it is the whole of us as human beings that bears God's image." —Fr. Thomas Weinandy[5]

And, of supreme and likely imminent importance: if some manner of "alien contact" is presented on the news tomorrow, should we take what these "aliens" claim at face value and engage in *dialogue* with them, hoping to learn from their teachings as we do from other human societies? Or, should we switch into *discernment* mode in order to better understand the darker reality of what we may well truly be dealing with? (Hint: the latter.)

These are just a few of the multitude of extremely important questions that arise as soon as one finds himself open to the possibility of aliens. We will consider others and treat these matters much more deeply in later chapters, but for the present point, what has been said suffices to illustrate that the question of aliens is anything but one sufficiently tangential to the Faith that it is "*merely unproblematically absent from Scripture.*" Quite the contrary, a faithful reading of Scripture by a Christian who approaches it with the reverence it is due will easily conclude that aliens are entirely absent from its pages for a simple reason: *there are no aliens.* Those who insist that Scripture's silence on aliens is unproblematic "because extraterrestrial intelligence is an entirely tangential question to the Faith—akin to the existence of microbes," are at best being intellectually lazy; failing to explore the necessary implications of their own premises.

They are, moreover, contradicted by the unanimous consensus of Christian commentators who engage in this issue most laboriously. As we will see, all these commentators openly acknowledge that the discovery of alien civilizations would cause a veritable theological earthquake of unprecedented proportions; one that would require us to re-examine (and, most of them admit, *overturn*) much of what has always been held as sacred and inviolable in Christianity. Even the most "orthodox Catholic" of them have already written books seeking to detail, in advance, this earthquake they foresee, and instruct us on the rebuilding process. Each one appears to be clamoring to be eventually regarded as a "New Father of the Church," who will in the millennia to follow "The Day of Disclosure" have his praises sung for rebuilding Christianity in light of extraterrestrials.

These commentators are wrong about aliens, but they are correct in insisting massive theological ramifications would be brought about by the ETs they conjecture. And this is precisely why the matter at hand carries the eschatological urgency described in this book's introduction: the Devil, aware of this unique opportunity inherent in the promotion of alien belief, will not allow such an opportunity pass by unused. He will strike while the iron is hot—as we will see in Part Four.

***

What has been said above can be summarized in the title of this section: *There are no chapters missing from Salvation History.*

No one should pretend that God intends for the Bible to give us a direct answer to every possible question. Neither, however, should any Christian succumb to the opposite extreme by presuming to regard the Bible as similar to a text authored by humans which may well be licitly accused of leaving out entire chapters which would themselves have been necessitated *by the very nature of the overall text presented.* Only with great caution would one be so daring as to levy such an accusation against a skilled human author. Why, then, do some Christians so readily levy it against *The* Author Himself—the Holy Spirit?

Many of the most pervasive diabolical deceptions the Church has already refuted arose from false prophets who have proposed to present to the Faithful the hitherto "missing Chapters" of Salvation History: Gnosticism, Islam, Mormonism, Seventh Day Adventism, various New Age "revelations," and too many others to list. Addressing each such danger is well and good. But a wise man, discerning a trend, will feel compelled to take a step back and consider what all these apparently disparate deceptions have in common. The similarity is obvious: each one treats what has been handed down—not only through Public Revelation but also through millennia of Sacred Tradition—as desperately deficient; as needing *fundamental* revision, across the board, in order to give the *real* picture of God's plan with His Creation.

This same wise man will also understand that the moral of the story is equally simple: one should reject any proposition which carries within itself the same premises, even if they are not explicitly stated. He will, therefore, reject the suggestion that God has actually only told us about a small fraction of those creatures of His who bear His Image. He will reject the possibility of aliens.

> **In giving us his Son, his only Word (for he possesses no other), [God] spoke everything to us at once in this sole Word—and he has no more to say**. (St. John of the Cross. *Commentary on Hebrews. Catechism of the Catholic Church.* §65)

Microbes... The geometric arrangement of the Solar System's bodies... The amount of "time" that had passed while the earth was only dead rock... The "setting of the sun" caused by the earth's rotation or the sun itself revolving around the earth... The shape of the earth... The number of continents on the planet's surface...

Matters like these and innumerable others have no impact on the Faith. They are more or less irrelevant to that which the Faith exists for the sake of—the only two things which ultimately matter—salvation and sanctification. Therefore, he has made a category mistake who objects that "*the Bible does not speak of these either, therefore it is no surprise that it does not speak of aliens, even though they exist! We've been wrong before!*" He is comparing the unimportant to the important. If such a person were being direct, he would choose a fitting analogy; a task we will presently undertake.

On Chickens, Aliens, and Angels: A Simple Refutation of ETs

> "Man is the perfection of the universe..." —St. Francis de Sales. *Treatise on the Love of God.* Book X. Chapter I.

Pretend, for the sake of argument, that chickens are uniquely exalted beings. So exalted that their capacity of reason even matches our own; they, like us, are called to eternal life—they are proper recipients of the Sacraments and they are beings in dire need of having the Gospel proclaimed to them. But there is only one problem: their clucking is not immediately recognizable as rational communication to us. It is an extremely advanced language; one we could decode if only we put our wholehearted efforts into that task. When at once we succeed here, we have bridged the gap and enabled the eternal salvation of billions of chicken-souls. But we humans have failed in this calling. Instead of treating these chickens as fellow persons, we have only treated them as servants! We make them lay eggs simply so we may consume them; and we even slaughter them *en masse* to devour their meat!

Even though there is no single verse of Sacred Scripture (or dogma of the Church) that explicitly teaches that chickens are not persons, no serious Christian proposes that this absurd scenario described above may actually be true. (*Unfortunately, some are indeed beginning to propose similar things; suggesting that certain species of monkeys, elephants, or dolphins, may even be persons. This proposition, which can only be called ridiculous, is just another symptom – albeit an even more ludicrous one – of the same disease addressed in this book, and we will directly consider it in Part Five.*)

Chickens are not persons. They never have been persons and they never will be persons. Whoever would devote his life to trying to decode chicken clucking—under the premise that there may well be *rational* communication lurking therein that can reveal the reality of chicken-personhood—has only wasted his life. Thankfully, this is a matter that can be addressed with simple reason and empirical data more straightforwardly than the question of aliens—plenty of intelligent people have speculated about aliens, but no one in his right mind observes chickens and sees within them the signs of reason.

One can, however, just as validly refute the absurdity of the chicken-person scenario above by considering how irreconcilable it is with Sacred Scripture. If God gave us thousands of pages of Divine Revelation, detailing everything from the beginning of time (in Genesis) to its conclusion (in the Apocalypse), but simply did not tell us that there is an entire other species of beings in need of salvation, then this Divine Revelation would be guilty of a grave dereliction of duty. It would be comparable to an introductory textbook on Pharmacology failing to teach about contraindications, or an instruction manual for a product's assembly not concerning itself at all with most of the nuts and bolts contained in the package.

The irreverence in such an implicit accusation is precisely why serious Christians are convinced that the *only* life on earth which bears intrinsic and infinite dignity is human life. They therefore rightly waste no time fretting about whether chickens (or insects, trees, rocks, etc.) might be persons. Lacking the same conviction Christians have, adherents of some Pagan religions are known to take extraordinary measures in relation to these creatures. Some Jains, for example, laboriously sweep the streets before each walk on the pavement, lest they inadvertently squish an insect, and go about with cloths ever covering their mouths, lest they accidentally inhale a tiny flying bug and kill it.

Christians, however, rightly conclude that God *would have told us*, in Scripture, if any other beings on earth are persons. Why, then, do some Christians fail to apply the same wisdom to realms beyond the mere fraction of a trillion cubic miles that constitute planet earth?

The usual response given by ET promoters will not work. It will not suffice to answer, *"because there was no need for Him to – since we are not in contact with those extraterrestrial beings, there is no risk we would fail to render them their rights on account of being uninformed regarding their personhood."* There are three reasons for the failure of this response:

First, God *did* tell us – repeatedly – in Scripture about Angelic persons; and these creatures are not terrestrial. Moreover, there is no risk that we humans could ever cause them any harm. Angels are even more beyond our reach than any alien civilization billions of light years away would be. God revealed the angels' existence to us because these ministering spirits are relevant to our Faith, and we should seek their intercession. This He did even though such a disclosure was not strictly necessary: God is more than capable of answering all our prayers and attending to all our needs directly, without delegating angels to go about responding to the pleas of humans who know about them and expressly seek their help. Nevertheless, angels do in fact exist, therefore it was appropriate for the Divine Author of Scripture to ensure they found an explicit place in Revelation, so that Christians could comport themselves, recite their prayers, and build their theology accordingly. If aliens existed, they too would be important to our Faith: not because we would be praying *to* them, but, for example, because we would need to pray *for* them, we would need to desperately try to reach them (a point we will address momentarily), and their existence would *radically* impact how we understand Christology, Mariology, Ecclesiology, Pneumatology, Eschatology, Protology, and many other belief-essential realms.

Second, the ET promoters (including the most "orthodox Catholic" of them) are almost unanimous in their insistence that extraterrestrial incarnate intelligent life *already has* made it to earth – repeatedly! They point to innumerable instances – "UFO" encounters in the headlines, testimonies of "alien abductions" or other communications, "ancient aliens" in pseudoscientific History Channel "documentaries," and on the list goes. All this, they claim, proves aliens are among us. It is, then, fallacious for such people to argue that the absence of aliens from Scripture is unproblematic on account of the great distance between our civilization and theirs. According to these same people, that distance does not exist; and according to many of them, that distance has long been closed, or never existed in the first place (*for even they go so far as to claim that many ancient monuments, such as the pyramids of Egypt, were constructed by aliens or with the help of aliens, or they posit that various Biblical or medieval occurrences involved the direct presence of extraterrestrials*).

Third, if aliens existed, then we would be duty-bound – in accordance with the command of Christ in Scripture – to do everything we could to reach them and preach the Gospel to them. The explorers and missionaries in centuries past did all they could to ensure the Gospel reached the ends of the earth for this same reason – because Jesus said: *"Go into all the world* and preach the Gospel *to all creation*." (Mark 16:15) If, however, beings in need of receiving the Gospel (*each* rational incarnate creature *needs* to hear the Gospel) existed outside of "the world" (earth), then Jesus—The Second Person of the Blessed Trinity—choosing to incarnate Himself on *earth*, would not have failed to include a verse in His Public Revelation instructing earthlings to announce His Incarnation to His other children on other planets. Even if such an instruction would not have had its full ramifications *understood* immediately, Jesus would not have only told us to "go into all the world," to preach the Gospel, but would have instead instructed us to "reach into all the cosmos," or to "proclaim to all the heavenly bodies," or to do something similar. Yet, no such Divine Mandate exists, even implicitly, anywhere in Scripture. A faithful Christian reading of Scripture can easily explain this absence: no such duty exists, since no beings exist outside of earth in need of the Gospel. In a word: one who would insist that intelligent incarnate creatures do exist outside of earth is left needing to explain yet another glaring absence from Scripture, and the only methods he can find to attempt to do so entail imputing a sin of omission to the Holy Spirit.

No matter how the absence of aliens in Scripture is approached, therefore, a serious and faithful Christian exegesis is forced to conclude that even entertaining the possibility of extraterrestrial incarnate intelligent life is incompatible with Public Revelation.

***

In truth, the preceding pages have been far too generous to the claims of Christians who promote belief in aliens. For the sake of argument, we have thus far operated under the assumption that Scripture is silent on the topic. Indeed, the Bible does not *explicitly* address the question of extraterrestrials, and this absence itself testifies to their non-existence. But it is not true that Scripture is entirely silent about this question. Quite the contrary, Public Revelation is replete with teachings indicating man alone bears God's Image. It is filled with passages from which we can glean that there are no incarnate intelligent creatures other than human beings. To those passages, we now turn.

5. The Old Testament

"The Scriptural expression "heaven and earth" means **<u>all that exists, creation in its entirety</u>**. ... "the earth" is the world of men, while "heaven" or "the heavens" can designate both the firmament and God's own "place"—"our Father in heaven" and consequently the "heaven" too which is eschatological glory. Finally, "heaven" refers to the saints and the "place" of the spiritual creatures, the angels, who surround God."
—Catechism of the Catholic Church, §326

Divine Revelation often describes "creation in its entirety," that is, "heaven and earth," and in doing so it always implies, if not outright indicates, that "earth," where rational incarnate creatures dwell, is entirely singular. Of the over one thousand times the Bible refers to "earth," not once does it provide the slightest hint of an implication that earth may be anything but entirely unique.

Scripture's Creation Account Rules Out Aliens

Unlike Pagan religions, Christian Faith does not present its adherents with a so-called "creation myth." Indeed, no faithful Christian or Jew should be caught dead referring to Genesis as "our creation myth." Rather, Scripture teaches Christians *the truth* about how the universe was created, and, equally importantly, *why* it was created. The fact, often emphasized today, that Genesis "is not a science textbook," is irrelevant. Whatever it teaches is true, irrespective of wrongheaded human efforts to compartmentalize various verses therein into different "genres" of truth. For Genesis (and all Scripture) is God's Word, everything He says is true precisely as He says it, and Christians are not permitted to disregard (by stealth) so-called "unscientific" Divine Revelations under the pretense of treating them as "literary devices." As Pope Pius XII taught, in his encyclical *Humani Generis*, §38:

> In a particular way must be **deplored** a certain too free interpretation of the historical books of the Old Testament. ... **<u>the first eleven chapters of Genesis ... [do] pertain to history in a true sense</u>**, [its authors wrote] with the help of divine inspiration, through which they were rendered immune from any error...

Modern Christians, however, have largely neglected the principles above, and have dismissed the earliest chapters of the Bible as "mere myth." As a result, they are uniquely well positioned to succumb to structural errors regarding creation itself. One symptom of this tragedy has already been discussed: the increasing willingness, via "transgenderism," to adopt attitudes towards the human race's creation as *male and female* that are diabolically opposed to both Divine and natural law.

Another symptom of the same disease is found in the increasing willingness to regard mankind's absolute categorical uniqueness, illustrated in Genesis, as a mere artifact of supposedly "simpler and less enlightened times;" one that should be "dismissed on account of its irrelevance to salvation." Healing both moribund symptoms (and innumerable others) requires that we eradicate the underlying disease of flippant irreverence in how Christians approach the Word of God. Indeed, the understanding received from a serious and reverent reading of the Scriptural passages below is in no way ambiguous.

The opening verse of Scripture does not pick up at some undefined point *within* the history of time, as if the universe were some pre-existing or self-existing thing into which God decided to intervene. It begins, rather, at *the* beginning itself:

> "**In the beginning God created the heavens and the earth.**" (Genesis 1:1)

The first verse of the Bible, therefore, rules out any conjectures about infinite time, an eternal world, or "other universes, timelines, strings," etc.; for, on the contrary, Christians (and Jews) know that there *was* a singular beginning, and that beginning was none other than the point at which God called *the* heavens and *the* earth—which are in no way abstract concepts but, rather, consist in the concrete realities we all observe with our own eyes—from non-being into being.

Moreover, the billions of trillions of stars (according to modern astronomers) are all gathered, in the inerrant Word of God, into the simple umbrella term of "the heavens," whereas only *one* planet merits any particular attention among the quintillions of planets that these same stargazers likewise estimate to populate the great expanse of: "*the earth.*"

A faithful Christian exegesis will pause on the definite article used here by God: "the." Scripture does not refer to this planet as "an" earth or as "our" earth but, rather, as "*the*" earth. Despite earth being a mere nothing, *quantitatively,* in relation to "the heavens," it is given its own *category* in Scripture's first verse. Already we can see that it would be unconscionable for a believer in the Divine origin of this verse to assert that earth is only one of many (perhaps unthinkably many) planets whereupon theaters of eternal destinies are played out. If that were so, then at the absolute minimum Scripture would have implied, from its beginning, that earth is only one such realm. Perhaps it would have said that, in the beginning, God created "*Heavens and earths,*" or God created "*the cosmos and our earth.*"

Instead, *the* earth is presented as one of the fundamental classes of creation's *two* basic divisions.

Thus far, we have only considered the very first ten words of Scripture, and we already see the most requisite premises of alien belief falling apart like so many houses of cards upon the slightest application of scrutiny. Yet we have scarcely begun our task; tens of thousands of verses of the Bible remain; countless instances of which contradict belief in the existence of aliens, whereas none of which (explicitly or implicitly) support the contrary view. Limitations of space will, of course, force us to only consider a small fraction of this evidence; but even that consideration will not fail to demonstrate that only man bears the Divine Image.

Let us continue our journey through Genesis. Telling as Scripture's opening verse is even in isolation, the first chapter of the Bible's first book does not merely leave us with the assurance that earth is one half of the dichotomy of which the universe itself is constituted.

Catholic author Hugh Owen shared the following observation, in rebuttal to an argument for alien belief (itself presented by a certain Vatican exorcist, Monsignor Corrado Balducci, whose arguments we will address more thoroughly in Part Four):

> In Genesis 1 God indicates that the sun and the stars were created as a "signs" for people on earth and not as "suns" to support biomes elsewhere in the universe. If Genesis 1 describes the creation of the entire universe and all that it contains—as the Church has always taught—then why does it say nothing about Mons. Balducci's hypothetical non-angelic intelligent beings?[6]

These conclusions may derive from a subtle suggestion in Genesis, but this in no way negates its force, since the exegesis used to arrive at it is solid. Genesis 1:14-15 makes it clear that the Heavenly bodies exist *for us*—for man.

The Christian alien belief promoter will protest that even if the heavenly bodies are "for us," they could *also* be "for their own sake" (i.e., for the sake of the alien civilizations that they posit dwell therein). But this is not how the description of "final ends" (i.e., *purposes*) works. Final ends are definitionally singular. Various theologians throughout Church history have, for example, proposed that human nature itself may have multiple final ends, but their attempts have always failed. In opposition to them, St. Augustine's famous line remains vindicated, for he settled that "Thou has made us for Thyself, Lord, and our hearts are restless until they rest in Thee." (*Confessions of St. Augustine*) Indeed, the final end of man is none other than God Himself. Even Aristotle, writing without any aid of Divine Inspiration, rightly declared, in one of his greatest works, that "The chief good is evidently something final. Therefore... **there is only one final end**." (*Nicomachean Ethics*. Book 1, Ch. 7).

Genesis assures us that the heavenly bodies—the "lights in the heavens" (Genesis 1:14)—exist "**for**" us! These same bodies, then, cannot be said to also harbor planets with incarnate intelligent creatures like our own. If that were so, then God would be deceiving us in the Book of Genesis by indicating that these very things exist *for* marking *our* "seasons... and years" (Genesis 1:14). If in fact these otherworldly objects serve as dwellings of other creatures called to eternal life, that status as alien-dwelling-places would, indisputably, be their *primary* purpose, which in turn would mean Genesis 1:14 lies. For it would obviously be absurd to posit that the star of some distant solar system has planets harboring civilizations of its own, but that it nevertheless *exists for* marking *our* seasons here on earth. In a word: God already told us the reason for the existence of the "heavens"—that is, all that we see, or can possibly see, when observing the night sky—and no Christian may validly protest, "*but why did God make all this if, despite its incomprehensible magnitude, it is uninhabited?*" He already revealed that He made it *for us*—for what *we* can gain as we gaze upon it—and no other disparate final end of this immense creation should be presented by a faithful Christian or Jew.

Within Scripture's very first chapter, we already see three of the foundational premises presented by Christian ET promoters contradicted by God Himself. We see refuted: First, the notion that earth (and man) cannot be regarded as unique, second, the argument that disbelieving in aliens constitutes "limiting God" (a notion considered in this book's corresponding Appendix) and third, the idea that the incomprehensible multitude of stars and planets in outer space "must," in the Divine Order, have been created for their own sake and not merely for us; that, otherwise, it would be a "waste of space." (In fact, there is no such thing as a "waste of space," since space is not a *thing*—a fact we will consider in later chapters.)

Indeed, the Bible's *first chapter alone* assures us that all those—the most basic of alien belief-premises—are un-Christian: it assures us that earth is categorically singular and unique, and that the other stars and planets exist simply for our sake on earth. It furthermore contradicts the accusation that holding these views amounts to "limiting God," since only the opposite is so: the one truly guilty of limiting God is the one who supposes that the Almighty was too shortsighted to mean *exactly* what He said in the very Divine Revelation of which He authored each word.

The following chapter of Genesis, moreover, begins with the assurance that, after the creation of the "heavens" and the various living beings that count earth as their home, "the heavens and the earth were **finished**, and **all** the host of them." (Genesis 2:1) Here we see reiterated the uniqueness of earth and we find revealed that, upon the completion of its creation along with the heavens, God's overall work of creation was done. The Creator, of course, would have much more to do *within* creation, over the course of the ages of its existence to follow, but the fundamental categories of beings ("all the host") were settled, and no additional ranks would be inserted into the hierarchy of creation—the "Great Chain of Being." This is a hierarchy, as we will see in forthcoming chapters, that the faithful have always understood (and, thus, *infallibly* understood) to consist in (ascendingly) the following perfect adjacent categories (i.e., containing no gaps): inanimate matter, plants, animals, men, angels, and God.

The next and third chapter of Genesis teaches that Eve is "mother of **all** the **living**" (Genesis 3:20). Now Eve, of course, was not the mother of the animals, therefore "the living" here is to be understood in keeping with the context given in the preceding chapter: namely, "living souls." That is, those who have the "breath of life" from God in order to become not only "alive," but also "a living soul;" a *rational* incarnate being:

> And the Lord God formed man of the slime of the earth: and breathed into his face the breath of life, and man became a **living** soul. (Genesis 2:7)

Trusting that Sacred Scripture does not in vain use the qualifier "all," we yet again see the grounds for alien belief ruled out. Genesis 3 reveals that *all* who can be called "living souls" due to receiving the breath of God are themselves children of this specific human being: Eve. The sole exception to that would be Adam and Eve themselves—the only incarnate rational creatures who were not conceived (but, rather, were fashioned directly); the only incarnate rational creatures who will *ever* be unconceived—without even the exception of the human nature of the God-man Himself. Were it licit to entertain the possibility of any exceptions to this norm, then Scripture would not have categorically taught that "all" the living are Eve's children. Instead, there would have been some grounds, within the passage, for inferring the existence of other "living" creatures aside from the progeny of Eve. For example, the verse could have indicated that Eve was the "*mother of all the living that were to be born on this earth.*" Yet no such grounds—explicitly or implicitly—exist.

Contra Anthropocentriphobia: On the Superiority of Man Above All Other Created Things

> "God created everything for man..."
> —*Catechism of the Catholic Church,* §358

Unfortunately, denizens of the 21st century often find heeding these declarations of, or inescapable corollaries to, Biblical teaching exceedingly difficult. Such miserliness with these verses of Scripture is itself a symptom of another philosophical disease—one which can only be healed if exposed to the light—namely, *anthropocentriphobia.*

This disease has festered due to decades of herculean efforts from overzealous and misguided environmentalists, PETA-allied celebrities, Hollywood movies that have taught children to regard animals as "the good guys" and humans as "the bad guys," and a steady diet of New Age teaching that presents animals as enjoying personhood (another diabolical deception which will be addressed in Part Five). Consequently, it has become exceedingly difficult for a man raised in the culturally prevailing modern way to avoid succumbing to the deception which claims it is somehow arrogant or otherwise immoral to regard human beings as unique; as vastly superior to all other material things and as the reason other material things exist.

In all previous ages, the consensus of both ordinary people and serious thinkers has rightly regarded the entire natural universe as specifically made for humans. Today that very existential affirmation—which had always been so obvious that it was deemed unworthy of debate—has become so mocked by secularists that even many Christians are afraid to openly confess it. Yet, we must make no mistake about it: Christianity is inseparable from anthropocentrism. We must proudly profess our anthropocentrism and not allow ourselves to feel any shame in holding this worldview. No Bible-believer can ever hope to reconcile Scripture's teachings with the theory that man *isn't* vastly above everything else in the material universe. When we have rejected the postmodern west's demonization of anthropocentrism, we will find it much easier to abide in the truth regarding aliens.

> Indeed, the Lord Jesus, when He prayed to the Father, "that all may be one ... as we are one" (John 17:21-22) opened up vistas closed to human reason, for He implied a certain likeness between the union of the divine Persons, and the unity of God's sons in truth and charity. This likeness reveals that **man, who is the only creature on earth which God willed for itself**, cannot fully find himself except through a sincere gift of himself. (The Second Vatican Council. *Gaudium et Spes*, 24)

Now, there is certainly a deeply erroneous type of anthropocentrism as well, and we must be zealous to avoid and refute it. *False* anthropocentrism is another name for secular humanism or even a brand of pantheism. This anthropocentrism holds that man is not merely supreme in the natural (material) world, but also supreme in *absolute* terms. This error thus either rejects or disbelieves in God, or at least relegates His Will to a status of inferiority beneath the will of man. Such claims as these are not only wrong, but they also are diabolical. In fact, man is infinitely beneath God, and radically dependent upon God for everything. Moreover, even the rest of material creation—though indeed inferior to man—is nevertheless a gift from God *to man*, and man is therefore obliged to steward it responsibly. The human race must not suppose that its own innate superiority gives it the right to abuse creation, for this would be akin to a child, after receiving a precious and delicate gift from his father, immediately throwing it against the wall for fun. The sin is not against the gift, but against the giver of the gift. Man, likewise, must not be bashful in regarding creation as existing *for him*, while at the same time receiving this gift with the reverence that is due, considering Who gave it.

> "Are not two sparrows sold for a penny? And not one of them will fall to the ground without your Father's will. But even the hairs of your head are all numbered. Fear not, therefore; you are of more value than many sparrows." (Matthew 10:29-31)

The Fall: Incompatible with Aliens

> "All visible creation, all the universe, bears the effects of man's sin"
> —Pope St. John Paul II. Theology of the Body. July 21, 1982

Returning to the Book of Genesis, we must consider the pivotal event described in the verses preceding the revelation of Eve's status as "mother of all the living," namely, the Fall of Man. Michael Hichborn, a Catholic pro-life activist, wrote:

> When God created the universe, Scripture tells us that everything was "good." There was no discord in the physical universe, and everything was in a state of perfect harmony. But the sin of Adam disrupted the harmony of the universe by introducing sin and death. As the Venerable Archbishop Fulton Sheen put it, it was as if a sour note played in the midst of a symphony rang out into the universe, spoiling the entire piece. ... Thistles, thorns, and brambles would be produced by the earth. Weeds now invade garden beds. Predators eat our livestock, and sometimes, even us. Nature itself is arrayed against man because of the sin of Adam. If this is the case for earth, it would be the same for any and all life on other planets. In short, for there to be life on other planets, the sour note of Adam's sin would reach them as well and be an inexcusable injustice. [7]

Here we see yet another straightforward conclusion that follows immediately from what has already been Divinely Revealed in Scripture—only awaiting our willingness to take its own implications seriously. The sin of Adam brought all creation down with it. Had he not sinned—had he passed the test—everything in the material universe would have remained perfect. Even one who insists upon clouding this simple reality with superfluous "evolutionary nuance" is still forced to acknowledge that, at the bare minimum, death could not have touched any rational being without Adam first eating the fruit.

Admittedly, some are guilty of over-emphasizing the results of the Fall; e.g., those fundamentalists who profess "total depravity" doctrine. For in truth, the ramifications of the fall are profound and universal, but the glory of the integral, fundamental nature of man (and all individual natures created by God) continues to outshine the distortion of that nature wrought by Original Sin. The opposite error, however, is similarly damaging. This danger is evidenced in certain non-Christian religions lacking recognition of Original Sin. They invariably fail to satisfy the understandably skeptical would-be converts from Paganism to Monotheism, for no one with two eyes can fail to observe, in the world, infinite proofs that the way things *are* is clearly not ultimately the way that an all-good, all-powerful God would want them to be. The universe *is* distorted. This is the undeniable reality.

Christians, however, know *why* this is the reality: it is revealed clearly in Scripture, as noted above, in the following passage:

> Because you have listened to the voice of your wife, and have eaten of the tree of which I commanded you, 'You shall not eat of it,' cursed is the ground because of you; in toil you shall eat of it all the days of your life; thorns and thistles it shall bring forth to you... (Genesis 3:17, 18)

Whoever might struggle to infer, from this passage, the universal impact of Adam's sin, should be reminded that the validity of such an inference is settled by Scripture itself elsewhere. The Book of Wisdom teaches that "**By the envy of the devil death came into the world**" (2:24), and even in the New Testament we read, "... **sin came into the world through one man and death through sin**..." (Romans 5:12) In the early Church, it was only the heretics (Nestorians and Pelagians especially) who were known to deny this truth. Today, all Christians must be sure to avoid the tempting trap of contradicting it; for indeed, the worldly cannot grasp the notion of Original Sin and its effects, and their attacks against this dogma too often beguile the faithful into doubting it. It is a settled fact that a specific, real, concrete human being, Adam, made a choice. That choice affected everything, and only as a consequence of that choice was the death of a rational creature even possible. Death was *not* part of God's original plan. It was and is a consequence of His original plan being freely rejected.

Unfortunate though it may be, it is not a violation of justice for Adam's own offspring to suffer the effects of the free choice of their father. (*I hasten to add that Christians ought not waste time lamenting the Fall—for Christ has come not only to save us from its effects, but to raise us to a still greater dignity. "O happy fault," we pray at the Easter Vigil's Exultet.*) Just as one is entirely within his rights to be proud of the achievements of his own ancestors, so too it is not invalid for him to feel some degree of shame at the misdeeds of the same although he shares no *personal* guilt for those sins. The old *Catholic Encyclopedia* presents a helpful explanation and analogy:

> The Creator, whose gifts were not due to the human race, had the right to bestow them on such conditions as He wished and to make their conservation depend on the fidelity of the head of the family. A prince can confer a hereditary dignity on condition that the recipient remains loyal, and that, in case of his rebelling, this dignity shall be taken from

> him and, in consequence, from his descendants. It is not, however, intelligible that the prince, on account of a fault committed by a father, should order the hands and feet of all the descendants of the guilty man to be cut off immediately after their birth. (Article on Original Sin.)

As we can see, abiding in the truth while assessing the effects of the Fall requires observing a delicate balance. As legitimate as it is for Adam's offspring to die on account of the former's sin, it would on the other hand be radically unjust and entirely irreconcilable with God's goodness for *other* rational beings—not only lacking natural generation from Adam but even living on entirely different planets—to be subject to death, concupiscence, etc., due to Adam's choice to eat the forbidden fruit.

We know that the Angels endured no punishments or sufferings at all due to Adam's sin. For God to allow that would be an injustice. Similarly, those Angels who—lead by Lucifer—rebelled, thereby becoming demons, did so before Adam sinned. Nevertheless, their own "Original Sin" did not preclude Adam and Eve's original creation from being entirely untouched by that evil.

The Christian alien belief promoter, therefore, is left asserting that God's justice has been violated (which is impossible) by these aliens being degraded by a sin they are radically detached from, or he is left asserting that the alien civilizations in question are themselves unfallen, which, as we will presently discuss, could not be so.

To understand why the latter theory is untenable, some other considerations must first be brought to the fore (still more reasons to rule out the possibility of unfallen races of intelligent incarnate creatures will be considered in later chapters, where other scenarios not dealt with presently will be addressed).

The effects of the sins of men are conducted via the spiritual realm, therefore great distances (even the expanses of outer space) present no impediment to their propagation. As Pope St. John Paul II made clear in his teaching quoted above, the entire "universe"—"***all visible creation***"—fell due to man's sin. If alien civilizations on other planets existed, we would have no grounds to claim the sin of Adam would not have equally caused their own demise. Consider that when the Deicide was committed and Our Lord was crucified, the Heavenly bodies themselves were affected; so much so that even "the sun's light failed" (Luke 23:45). In the Sixth Chapter of Book of Revelation, moreover, we are told of the stars "falling to earth" and the "sky vanishing like a scroll" as a result of mankind's apocalyptic sinfulness, and taking place long before the Last Judgment at the end of time, described many chapters later, in Revelation 20.

These are just two illustrations of the fact that what transpires in "the heavens" is not a separate story from man's own, but rather an integral part of it. If the entire material universe is a story—and one could fairly say that History is "His (God's) Story"—then mankind is that story's sole plotline; the rest is simply the setting. No passage in Divine Revelation suggests we can licitly regard *our* Salvation History as anything but *the* Salvation History. No verse of Sacred Scripture gives any hint that spiritual effects crash against an impassable barrier located somewhere in earth's stratosphere when they follow their Divinely-ordained course. The notion itself is silly; akin to supposing that one should revisit the Pythagorean Theorem when walking on the surface of the moon for fear of the distance between it and the Theorem's discovery preventing its remote application. Just as that is not how mathematical truths operate, it is also not how spiritual realities operate.

As will need to be repeated elsewhere, our gazing upon the constellations adorning the night sky is not like watching a movie, whose scenes are untouchable by our own life's actions as we watch it play out. Although the distances observed are great, these expanses have no diminishing effect on spiritual realities. We all know that no matter how far any astronaut winds up travelling from the earth during future missions, he will never have to wonder if his journey will bring him outside of the same exact "economy of salvation" in which he has lived since his conception here on earth. In brief: one cannot escape Original Sin if only he builds a fast enough rocket ship. Its effects, rather, were immediately wrought upon the entire material universe, and any contrary assertion quickly collapses into absurdities when its corollaries are investigated.

Although our present focus is the Fall as recounted in the Old Testament, we should note that its universal effects are testified to in the New Testament as well.

> For the creation waits with eager longing for the revealing of the sons of God; for **the creation was subjected to futility**, not of its own will but by the will of him who subjected it in hope; because the **creation itself will be set free from its bondage to decay** and obtain the glorious liberty of the children of God. We **know** that the **whole creation** has been groaning in travail together until now... (Romans 8:19-22)

Here, St. Paul expounds upon what he noted just three chapters earlier in the same book—his Epistle to the Romans—namely, that, "**through one man sin entered into the world**, and death through sin..." (Romans 5:12), and as he likewise noted in his first letter the Corinthians: "in Adam **all** die." (1 Corinthians 15:22)

Indeed, all death was first caused by Adam, and it was allowed to follow its natural course of justice, infecting *all* creation—the whole material universe, which, as we saw above, is what the Church teaches that phrase means—by virtue of the permissive Will of God (i.e., "by the will of him who subjected it in hope"). This sorry state, however, is nothing but the prelude to creation being "set free from its bondage to decay," which is why "the **whole** creation has been groaning in travail." Renowned theologian Fr. Thomas Weinandy points out that this passage alone clearly rules out aliens:

> ...because of sin, not only humankind was marred, but also the whole of creation. The entire cosmos is now groaning in communion with all of humanity. (Romans 8:22-23) Since aliens are members of the cosmos, they too would have to be affected by humankind's sin. The very absurdity of such a conclusion argues against the existence of alien intelligent life.[8]

Scripture presents the Universal-Fall/Universal-Restoration dynamic to us in great clarity: Adam's sin did not only bring down with it a mere fraction-of-a-trillion cubic miles (containing the "third rock from the sun"); but, rather, "the whole creation"—which, as the Catechism teaches, refers to *absolutely every material thing* God made. Likewise, the Redemption of this same Fall (initiated by the Incarnation and Paschal Mysteries; to be completed upon the Eschaton) is equally universal: destined to cause that same—"**whole**"—creation to be "set free."

Passage upon passage of Scripture, therefore, settles this simple reality: Adam's Sin, precipitating the Fall itself, was *universal*, and the resolution of the same is also universe-encompassing. Such dogmatic truths of our Faith are irreconcilable with the notion that our own Story of Salvation is just one of multiple, or even innumerable, transpiring across the galaxies (or "dimensions," or "timelines," or "strings," or whatever other term is invented tomorrow).

Dozens of Passages on the Heavens: Many Refuting Aliens, None Supporting Them

While the opening chapters of Scripture, recounting the universe itself being called out of nothingness, obviously deserved special attention in addressing the question of aliens, the dozens of books of the Old Testament that follow are not without many indications that man alone bears the Divine Image. Before considering the New Testament's pertinent teachings, we will consider just a few such passages.

***

> **Shem and Seth were honored among men, and Adam above every living being in the creation**. (Sirach 49:16)

The Scriptural Book of Sirach (unjustly excluded from some Bibles, but always considered a true book of Scripture from the beginning of the Church) regards Adam not merely as the greatest of men, or the greatest of earthly creatures, but rather the greatest living creature in all of "the creation," period. (Angels, of course, are also "creations" of God, but the word "creation" is used here as it often is: to refer to the entire *material* creation.)*

If, however, other civilizations of rational incarnate creatures existed, then Scripture would have no place assuring us that our own particular father, Adam, stood as the most exalted being in the entire universe—"**the** creation." At most, the Bible would leave that question unaddressed. Alternatively, the passage could have been more specific, and only pinned Adam as standing "above every living being *on planet earth*." Neither is the case. Therefore, this verse alone excludes any notion of aliens existing who are superior to humans (as all ET promoters posit).

> **The heavens are the Lord's heavens, but the earth he has given to the sons of men**. (Psalm 115:16)

The 115th Psalm indicates that no planet other than earth has "been given," by God, to any creature's stewardship. On the contrary, everything other than earth—which collectively is named "the heavens"—remains God's sovereign property. Needless to say, *all* that exists belongs to God. Nevertheless, we know He has granted "dominion" over the earth to one of his creatures—humans (cf. Genesis 1:26-28). Scripture does not leave open the possibility that God has issued a similar delegation of other planets to other species of creatures. Instead, it teaches that all the rest—all "the Heavens"—*remain* "the Lord's" *own*. No other creature enjoys a Divinely delegated dominion over a planet akin to man's over earth. Yet, it would be contrary to justice, and certainly contrary to the Divine Wisdom, for God to create a race of rational creatures on a planet and fail to give them dominion over all non-rational beings inhabiting the same vicinity. Just as no farmer would send his own son to tend sheep with the orders that this child of his stoop to obey the sheep and let himself be dominated by their behavior, so too we can be certain that God would not bring creatures into existence within a domain inferior to them (the irrational is, by nature, inferior to the rational) even while failing to bestow upon them the right of regime. As no such right has been given, save to man, it follows that man alone is rational.

> It is he who sits above the circle of the earth, and its inhabitants are like grasshoppers; **who stretches out the heavens like a curtain, and spreads them like a tent to dwell in**... (Isaiah 40:22)

The Book of the Prophet Isaiah, again mirroring Genesis, explains the *purpose* of "the heavens" directly and exclusively in terms of their service to

---

* Note that Sirach was written before the Immaculate Conception of Mary and the Incarnation of Christ. Mary is the greatest human person, and, obviously, Jesus was and is infinitely higher than Adam, but as His human nature was not yet a part of the "creation," (nor was Mary's) this fact does not dispute the accuracy of or detract from the importance of the verse in question.

the inhabitants of the earth. These heavens were not provided to us by almighty God to induce us to fret about whether we are merely one of innumerable other (perhaps far greater!) civilizations and salvation histories. Only the opposite. They were, instead, "stretched out," *for us*, like a "tent" or a "curtain" is spread out over the head of one who sleeps beneath them. Their existence can only accurately be described in relation to the benefits they already bestow upon *us*.

This assurance, too, would be unconscionable for Scripture to relay if these very heavens were, in reality, other theaters of eternal destinies like earth is. The heavens are beautiful (not to mention useful) for human beings to gaze upon; if this glory, with which the Creator endowed them, fails to satisfy a modern Christian who wonders why they were created, then this Christian has only failed to grasp how much God loves the human race. God could have left the night sky entirely black. Instead, He studded it with resplendent diamonds, given for our appreciation. It is thus that the enormity of "the heavens" testifies to the eternity of *Heaven* itself. As astronomers are prone to rightly note, we can *scarcely* grasp the expanse of the galaxies. Similarly, we *cannot* grasp the expanse of eternal life. It is only right that, upon creating the wonders of the starry sky, God would enclose within those mysteries greater and greater expositions of His grandeur, in proportion to how much we discover hidden therein. What, pray tell, is lacking in this understanding of why God stretched out the heavens, which he stretched out for us like a beautiful tent to dwell in?

> He had not yet made the earth, nor the rivers, nor the poles of the world. When he prepared the heavens, I was present ... When he established the sky above, and poised the fountains of waters: ... I was with him forming all things: and was delighted every day, playing before him at all times; Playing in the world: and **my delights were to be with the children of men**."-Proverbs 8:26-31

The Eighth Chapter of the Book of Proverbs personifies the Wisdom of God and thus serves as a preparation for the New Testament's Revelation of the Holy Spirit as one of the Divine Persons of the Holy Trinity. Here, we see this *Wisdom* present even before creation itself existed, observing, as it were, the Father stretching forth all the multitude of created things from the heavens to the earth—"forming all things." Despite such an intimate and pervasive presence in the formation of the entire universe, this Wisdom of God notes only *one* place in which His delights were to be found: *"the children of men."* If rational beings other than men existed, then we would see some indication in this passage limiting man's exclusivity as the object of God's delight. Instead, here as elsewhere, we see only the opposite: a reiteration of man's categorical uniqueness in God's plan.

***

"The heavens proclaim the glory of God"—Psalm 19:1

Before moving on to the next chapter, we should take note of how much has been left out. For the sake of space, there is no need to record here the dozens of references to "the heavens" and "the stars" that exist throughout the Old Testament (and the New Testament). We need only recognize that it is not as if the reality and importance of these celestial bodies is something we have only begun to take seriously in the modern scientific era. One cannot claim that we have no hope of gleaning, from Scripture, the correct understanding of the role of the heavens in the Creator's plan on account of the topic being foreign to its pages. For it is anything but absent: the references are repeated.

When considering these references to the heavens and the stars, one realizes that not only do many expressly refute aliens, but *each* fails to support any speculation on aliens—much more so, every one of them is devoid of *any basis* for supposing that the heavens *even might* harbor intelligent life. Most of them reiterate the basic dichotomy issued in Genesis itself: using the distinction between *the* earth and *the* heavens (a distinction itself evident from "*the*" beginning) to refer to all that exists in the material realm, while only conceding any special status to earth.

A Biblically formed position on "the heavens," therefore, excludes the idea they might harbor civilizations of their own. Fitting as it would be for all Christians to accept this conclusion, we can unfortunately expect ET promoters to only respond by engaging in all manner of intellectual acrobatics to meticulously explain why each such passage can be massaged to coexist with his own fundamentally sci-fi-formed—not Scripturally-formed—convictions. After they have completed this gargantuan undertaking, however, they should step back from their project, consider it from a broader spiritual (or at least sober) perspective, and honestly admit what they have done. For even if we falsely pretend that such arguments could ever succeed in convincingly twisting each pertinent Scriptural verse to make it appear reconcilable with alien belief, what even then could not be denied is the diagnosis of what such an ideologically inspired tactic has revealed about the approach to the Word of God it betrays.

In sum, such an argument approaches Scripture as something to be *explained away*—like an outdated scientific theory—not something that *itself provides* the most important explanations on *whatever it chooses* to address. He who presents that argument has rejected the call, issued to each Christian in his Baptism, to adopt a fundamentally Biblically based worldview. He does not—on this question, at least—sit with God's Word and allow its power to guide him; instead, he sits with man's word, allowing its seduction to inspire him, and proceeds to open God's Word to find a way to make that capitulation appear Scripturally cogent. Choose whatever metaphor you prefer: this man has inverted the funnel; he has put the cart before the horse; he has let the tail wag the dog. He has, quite literally, done something pre-posterous—putting the "posterior," what is secondary, before the "pre," what is primary—by letting the world, not the Word, form his mind. And no Christian should even flirt with this approach.

6. The New Testament

"There is one body and one Spirit, just as you were called to the one hope that belongs to your call, **one Lord, one faith, one baptism**, one God and Father of us all, who is above all and through all and in all."—Ephesians 4:4-6

A man could, in theory, build a staircase to the moon, or dig a hole to the opposite side of the earth—but he could never succeed in so apparently simple a task as speaking too highly of another man born in Bethlehem 2,000 years ago. No matter what superlatives are amassed, or hymns of praise composed, or cathedrals of worship built, no one could ever give Jesus Christ even the smallest fraction of the glory and adoration He deserves.

Jesus Christ *is* the New Testament. He is the Eternal Word of God; the only begotten Son of the Almighty Father; the Alpha and the Omega; the King of Kings and Lord of Lords. His absolute supremacy, primacy, and uniqueness is both unquestionable and unsurpassable. He *is* God. Scripture could not relay this point any more clearly:

> [Christ Jesus] is the image of the invisible God, the first-born of all creation; for in him all things were created, in heaven and on earth, visible and invisible, whether thrones or dominions or principalities or authorities—**all things were created through him and for him. He is before all things**, and in him all things hold together. He is the head of the body, the church; he is the beginning, the first-born from the dead, that in everything he might be pre-eminent. For **in him all the fulness of God was pleased to dwell**... (Colossians 1:3-4,15-19)

Because of this absolute supremacy, and because the Incarnation of Jesus Christ was in no way partial or incomplete as it transpired 2,000 years ago, we are left with the certainty that we now await no greater contact of the Divine than what we have already been given in the Public Revelation of Jesus Christ—handed on "once for all" (Jude 3) to the faithful, by the Apostles, and rendered complete upon the death of the last Apostle (St. John).

While the Church can—and must!—grow in holiness and understanding throughout the centuries, it cannot ever depart from the permanent foundation of Scripture, and this growth must only ever be continuous and organic—never accepting rupture or revolution.

Indeed, the Church may not violate a single teaching of Scripture. Just as importantly, however, the Church may not even suppose that, so long as it claims to violate no single teaching of the Bible, it nevertheless still awaits yet another public revelation, one that will allow us to "move on" from the Biblical approach to the Faith—to salvation, sanctification, morality, theology, worship, etc.

Settling this point at the onset of the present chapter was necessary, as we are dealing here with an even greater reality than in our prior discussions focusing on the Old Testament. The latter was and is indeed a true Divine Revelation, therefore each teaching therein is certainly true, and all the corollaries that follow from them can, and must, be held with certainty by all the Faithful.

The Old Testament, however, was Public Revelation in process and not yet complete. One could read it and understandably ask, "is this all?" Indeed, its own pages repeatedly testify to its own fundamentally anticipatory nature: awaiting the coming of the Messiah. Now that this long-awaited Messiah has come, and has revealed not merely a *Covenant* as in the days of old, but rather the "*eternal* Gospel" (Revelation 14:6), we know that our task, until the very end of time, consists not in awaiting a new public revelation, but rather living out—though ever more deeply—what is contained in the one and only, complete, Public Revelation.

Such supreme exaltation bestowed upon a reality whose essence was so specific—centralized, as it was, upon a particular nation, race, time, family, and, ultimately, individual person—has always scandalized those who make understandable (but incorrect) human assumptions. They claim that so universal a reality as the Redemption itself, if it were to happen, could not be all about a particular person at a particular time and place, but would rather have to be about an idea, or an "awakening;" something sufficiently abstract that its communication could be entirely detached from concrete histories recorded in the Bible.

Those who harbor such scruples accordingly drift into Buddhism, Gnosticism, Deism, or other Pagan or New Age ideologies more amenable to their personal preferences. Addressing the "scandal" that motivates their move and its relation to the question of extraterrestrials will, therefore, be our next order of business.

The True and the False Scandals of Particularity

"For God so loved **the world**, that he gave his only Son, that whoever believes in him should not perish but have eternal life." —John 3:16

We have seen the Old Testament beginning with *the account* (it bears repeating: not "*an* account;" not "the *myth*") of the universe's beginning, but the New Testament begins with a still greater true story. It begins with the story of the universe's *salvation;* chiefly, the salvation of the one and only creature *within* the universe for whose sake this unfathomable feat was accomplished: human beings. And it was wrought by the only One Who was and is both "Son of Man" and "Son of God," though born in a stable in Bethlehem that can be visited to this very day.

Opening the Book of Genesis, we read that "In the beginning God created..." (Genesis 1:1), whereas opening the New Testament, we immediately see the Book of Matthew recounting how the birth of the prophesied One came about. This "genealogy of Jesus Christ" (Matthew 1:1) is no mystifying amalgamation of gnostic terminology which could at least give the esotericist masquerading as a Christian teacher *some* grounds for speculating that salvation history it describes also pertains to civilizations on other planets. Quite the contrary, it is merely a tracing of father, to father, to father, from Joseph, the husband of Mary, all the way back to Abraham; all transpiring under the same sun and moon we gaze upon today.

Here we should note that the New Testament's other genealogy, contained in the Gospel of Luke, traces Jesus' lineage back further still: all the way to Adam. "...The son of Enos, the son of Seth, the son of Adam, **the** son of God." (Luke 3:38) Of course, "son of God" is not intended here in the same way this title applies to Jesus, but similarity is nevertheless found in the singularity employed. Adam is not referred as "a" son of God, but as "*the*" son of God. The reason is clear: Adam was and is the only "son of God"—and Eve the only "daughter of God"—(i.e., rational incarnate creature) fashioned directly by His hands, and not through a conception. There are no "other Adams" anywhere—no other incarnate creatures from whom a race of rational creatures proceeded.

As noted above, this particularity, though inseparable from the Faith, is found deeply scandalous by many. One theologian described it as follows:

> The early Christian community spoke of the scandal of the particular—the God of the universe revealed in flesh and blood. They felt the strange, incongruous power of this idea. They felt too the awful strangeness of beholding the very image of God in a human being broken and beaten and hanging on a cross. The scandalous, revelatory power of the particular. It has a special claim on the Christian imagination. It shapes and refracts what we find significant, how we live, against what powers we struggle. [9]

To be sure, experiencing a feeling of "scandal" is almost appropriate here, at least briefly. Naturally, the human mind struggles to grasp how it really could be true; how so incomprehensibly great a message as the Christian one—with the Infinite Himself literally entering the finite—could be *non*-fictional. The proper response to this "scandal," however, is the same one we should have to the famous "scandal of the Cross:" overwhelming gratitude to God for infinitely exceeding our wildest dreams.

Some, unfortunately, respond in the opposite way. Instead of being grateful, they reject the mere possibility that God could be so magnanimous as to save and sanctify us by presenting *Himself*, in the flesh, uniquely in an exclusive time and place, instead of simply providing an abstraction detached from all particularity. And from this rejection they proceed to craft alternate philosophies of Redemption; even at times presenting them as if they were compatible with ore representative of "true" Christianity.

In contradiction to these presentations, we have the Word of God; the New Testament beginning with the story of the Redeemer of the universe being inextricably linked to a lengthy genealogy of mere earthlings like us. It is a genealogy that manages to come across as deeply offensive—"small," even, to those whose own minds are deeply limited precisely on account of their insistence that their minds are so very "big;" so very averse to "limiting God."

This tendency is most clear among the promoters of New Age "Christianity" who are embarrassed by the particularity of the Incarnation and Redemption. Today, they are fervently seeking to replace the Faith's 2,000-year supreme (but right and just) emphasis upon the man, *Jesus Christ*, with the conveniently agreeable, flexible, and even vacuous idea of "the cosmic Christ," the "universal Christ," or "Christ consciousness."

We need not scour the hidden archives of secretive occult conferences to find evidence of this trend; that is, we need not engage in "nut-picking" (more on this point in Part Four) to illustrate it. We need only observe the public and proud teachings of the movement's most renowned leaders. Presently, we will consider the teachings of one who, tragically, has become among the most popular voices within the Church today.

The Stealth Apostasy of the "Universal Christ"

> "... while it may be fun to fantasize ... about the existence of aliens, such daydreaming, if it is deemed to be real, **can wreak havoc on the Gospel**, particularly to the primacy of Jesus as the cosmic incarnate Lord of all."—Fr. Thomas Weinandy

The Franciscan priest, Fr. Richard Rohr, is "one of the most popular spiritualty authors and speakers in the world," according to PBS.[10] Indeed, his books can be found on *New York Times* bestseller lists, he preaches to the world on Oprah Winfrey's television network, and Rohr even claims that Pope Francis has read, and encourages, his work.[11] Examining the message of Richard Rohr (who usually omits "Fr." from references to his name, therefore I will respect that preference and generally do the same) is important if we wish to understand the Signs of the Times.

Rohr asserts that "when" we discover aliens, the type of Christianity that the saints have always lived and died for will be "shot to hell." As an alternative that he believes *will* survive our discovery of extraterrestrial intelligence, he presents his own version of "Christianity" that all-but leaves aside Jesus. We can see this in one of his famous conference talks—a recording of which currently has over a third-million views on just one of his social media pages[12]—wherein he teaches:

> We can't presume that God just got interested in God's creation 2,000 years ago and left the first 13.7 billion years empty of revelation ...**in our overemphasizing Jesus without understanding Christ we created a storyline ...** that all depends upon a supposed sin that was committed between the Tigris and Euphrates River, and **that just isn't a big enough storyline**... when I was in college, they were saying there's 6 stars for each one of us, now its six *galaxies*! ... you have to say, 'who is God?!' Well, he certainly isn't upset because someone bit into an apple...our theory of salvation is so tiny, so planet-bound... **when we discover life on another planet, which might be tomorrow, our little story line is shot to hell**...[13]

As we will continue to see, the supposed "littleness" the Incarnation is Rohr's primary motivation for deeming it necessary to replace Jesus with "the Universal Christ." This alleged "littleness" is most sharply illustrated within the context of his belief in galaxies upon galaxies filled with planets containing other civilizations of rational creatures.

Rohr continues—expounding upon how "little" he views the contents of the Bible—to support his declaration that Jesus must be "universalized" into a recognition of "The Christ Mystery," itself the basis for a "universal religion." He declares that what is needed is:

> ... **a Universal religion... [one that] doesn't depend on the Bible... in terms of geological time the Bible has existed in the last nanosecond**... I'm not trying to lay the Christian religion on anybody; in fact, quite the contrary. In fact you'll find, once you recognize the Universal nature of the Christ Mystery, it isn't in competition with Judaism anymore... you don't need to call it Christ to have the recognition...**Karl Rahner... was one of my five great teachers... he said, 'I would recommend that, for 50 years, we stop using the word 'God.''**

Note that Fr. Karl Rahner—a famous theologian well known as a dissenter who promoted a whole cadre of deeply unorthodox teachings—taught that alien belief was licit. He falsely posited that "multiple incarnations [of God]" and "different histories of salvation" were compatible with Christian teaching. It is unsurprising to see that Rahner was one of Rohr's top-five "great teachers," as the un-Christian nature of the exhortations the two provide suggest a similar and deeper (or, rather, lower, and very warm) shared point of departure for these propositions.

Already, the heretical syncretism that inevitably flows from alien belief is becoming clear in Rohr's message. We are told that, due to the "littleness" of Public Revelation's Salvation History in light of ETs, we must replace its indispensable core message with a different message entirely detached from not only Israel but also from earth itself.

Syncretism, however, is among the most dangerous of heresies; one particularly adept at seducing its adherents into full blown apostasy. Even if many religions contain "rays of truth," all Christians should nevertheless know that Christianity alone contains the fullness of the Truth, and that Jesus Christ is the *only* path to God the Father (cf. John 14:6). Accordingly, Christians rightly evangelize with more zeal than any other religion in history—hence, it has become the largest religion in history. The supremacy and exclusivity of Christianity is entirely compatible with the fact that distant continents on earth were filled with people called to salvation but ignorant of Jesus—we had every hope of reaching them. Indeed, although much evangelization still must be accomplished, the Gospel has at least now *reached* every nation on earth. But it is entirely *in*compatible with the notion of creatures on other planets existing who are called to salvation—as we have already discussed.

Rohr goes on in explaining what his message entails with the following assertions:

> ...Paul [the Apostle] usually quotes Jesus incorrectly ... the three synoptic Gospels... are about *Jesus,* [but the Gospel of] John is about *Christ.* And the reason we have so misused and misinterpreted John's Gospel is this is the eternal and archetypal Christ talking; he can say **'I am the way, the truth, and the life,' but he is not talking about Jesus, he is talking about this mystery, this amalgam of matter and spirit which IS the way for *everybody*...** that was true for the native religions... it's certainly apparent in Hinduism...it's shocking for us prudish Christians; well, we've got a lot of un-learning to do...Christ is not an individual, Christ is a collective... **already by the 70s, Jesus has been dead only 40 years* ... they came to this massive cosmological understanding of their religion**.

Rohr's inability to refer to Jesus as *alive* (in fact, Jesus was only dead for 3 days) is linked to his inability to understand that it really was and is Jesus Himself—not merely an ephemeral "Universal Christ"—Who declared that He was and is "*the* way, *the* truth, and *the* life"... for *everyone* who exists. Even though we no longer have Jesus's physical body on earth, the resurrection of the same—and all the victorious effects thereof—endures eternally, and there is no need to make any change to our approach to Jesus to recognize that fact. Our knowledge of His Resurrection, our faith and hope in it, our reception of the Sacraments that flow from its power, etc., will continue to make the Resurrection manifest in our midst until the end of time. But as reaping these benefits would be implausible for hypothetical aliens, one who lends credence to this hypothesis is inclined to find the

---

* Deeply distressingly, Rohr claims that in the decade of the 70s A.D., Jesus had "been dead only 40 years." But even a well taught three-year-old Christian child would be immediately struck by the blasphemy of that assertion, since in fact Jesus was just as alive in the year 70 as He was in the year 20, and as He still is today. Jesus was only dead for three days—from Good Friday to Easter Sunday—and whoever would, at any point in history after that First Easter, refer to Jesus as "dead," has made an assertion tantamount to rejecting Christianity itself. "If Christ has not been raised, then our preaching is in vain and your faith is in vain." (1 Corinthians 15:14)

Resurrection of Jesus, as understood throughout the centuries of Christianity, as insufficient and in need of replacement with this more "Universal" redeeming notion Rohr proposes. Towards the end of the conference, Rohr claims:

> ... **[Jesus] told us to follow him, not to worship him... this Universal Christ... is an archetypal image, it's a universal image, it's a cosmic image, it's connected to creation, not to a storyline in Israel**...

Now, Rohr does concede—with palpable boredom—that he is "all for" worshipping Jesus, though only as a preface to his false assertion that Jesus did not tell us to worship Him. In fact, Jesus compelled us to do precisely that in the passage Rohr himself cites above. (Worship of Jesus is also mandated in countless other passages, for many pages could be filled with references to Jesus manifesting His Divinity in the Gospels. Moreover, the Divine *must* be worshipped; the fundamental duty of the creature is to worship his Creator.)

***

The teachings above provide just a small overview of some of Rohr's efforts to undermine the essence of Christianity by replacing it with a "universalized" Christ, inspired by the "need to defend Christianity of being shot to hell when aliens are discovered." I sympathize with one who is shocked that a Catholic priest could say these things without being excommunicated, much less with remaining in such an extremely popular public ministry and be granted personal audiences with the Pope. But I can only exhort such a person to wake up, pull his head out of the sand, and see the signs of the times. This is only one of innumerable instances of free rein being given to the Great Apostasy (of which we are now in the midst) while a simple, pious, traditional, and orthodox Faith is ridiculed and even persecuted. Therefore, Catholics in particular must stop holding their breath, waiting for official Ecclesial pronouncements, before rejecting what is not in keeping with the Deposit of Faith. They must continue to hold fast to the true Magisterium, but they must stop supposing that every opinion for every theologian in the Vatican is trustworthy on that count alone. That Fr. Rohr appears as a priest good standing, whose teachings are under no formal Church censure, is no reason at all to regard them as licit. Similar protestations now being offered in defense of the various other clergymen who have promoted alien belief are equally irrelevant.

Due to claims from Rohr like those described above, many of today's popular Christian apologetics resources, speakers, websites, etc., are careful to point out that his teaching is problematic. But until they root out the source and motivation of Rohr's errors, their cautions will only ring hollow and prove ineffective. Whoever believes the galaxies are filled with extraterrestrial civilizations will, sooner or later, come to find the allure of Rohr's "Universal Christ" irresistible. Alien belief and "Ufology" are interests known to dominate the minds of their adherents (a theme we will discuss in Part Four), and a Christian who follows this path will soon find himself in desperate need of a theology to bolster, or at least allow for, this fantasy. It is no coincidence that Rohr's popularity has grown in proportion to ever metastasizing belief in aliens among modern day Christians.

It is, moreover, precisely because Rohr is so strategically careful to avoid *expressly* contradicting an *explicitly* defined dogma, that the seemingly "heresy free" content of Rohr's deceptive message will only succeed in removing the signposts that would warn otherwise careful souls against treading further downhill. Thus even while seeming to avoid *formal heresy*, they will only ultimately embrace *total apostasy*.

Indeed, many commentators have already levied the charge of heresy against various claims within Rohr's message, but this assessment is far too kind. Although heresy is a grave evil and all the Faithful should be sure to avoid it, there is at least something honest (if honestly wrong) about a man who bluntly says that "Church teaching is incorrect on this point," and un-manipulatively presents the contrary assertion as the one that should be held. Rohr's message, however, proposes to be "orthodox" (though it is not) even while pushing its hearers away from *the entire point of orthodoxy*, which is none other than to draw us into an ever-closer relationship with *Jesus* Christ. It is, therefore, much closer to apostasy than heresy; for it is not so much a repudiation of this-or-that doctrine of the Faith, but a complete undermining of the Faith itself.

The difference between Rohr and the more "orthodox minded" Christian ET promoters is that he takes the same base premise more seriously, and has developed a theology to fit with its claims. Those who would (rightly) regard Rohr as unorthodox, but still pretend the ET promoters are orthodox, should take note.

***

In a moment, we will move on to the New Testament's next relevant point contra alien belief. But first, a personal confession is needed. I am not prone to tears, but when, many years ago, I first learned of Fr. Rohr's writings, wherein they exhort moving on from Jesus to instead embrace Rohr's own vague notion of "the universal Christ," I could not contain the sorrow, and I wept, and fell on my knees to immediately pray for him and his followers. To see, of all people, a *Catholic priest* (whose vocation is to sacrifice his life for *Jesus* Christ and His Church) nevertheless announcing to his millions of readers that the time has now arrived for a "natural" religion focused simply on the "cosmic" or "universal" Christ instead of the real God-man, *Jesus of Nazareth*—the One Who shed every drop of His blood and suffered every imaginable pain for each and every one of us—is a tragedy so heartbreaking that none who truly ponder it could possibly fail to cry. I therefore conclude this personal confession with a personal plea: do not ever, dear soul, think that there is anything you could ever do to be "too focused" on Jesus Christ. He is *everything*. Give Him your every thought, word, and deed: give Him your whole self; give Him your very own will, and ask for His in return. Love Him with every ounce of your being; with your whole heart, soul, mind, and strength. He will not be outdone in generosity.

The Our Father—The Most Perfect Prayer, but Concerned Only with Earth

The Our Father is the supreme prayer of Christianity. As I wrote in *Thy Will Be Done: The Greatest Prayer, the Christian's Mission, and the World's Penultimate Destiny* (2021):

> In the sixth chapter of the Gospel of Matthew, Our Lord Jesus Christ teaches us the Greatest Prayer: the Our Father. The prayer everyone around the world knows by its other simple title, *The Lord's Prayer.* The prayer whose sublime words are committed to more memories than any other words ever written or spoken in history. ...The revelation of this prayer is itself the midpoint and climax of the most famous homily in history (the Sermon on the Mount), whereafter the crowds "were astonished at his teaching, for he taught them as one who had authority, and not as their scribes." (Matthew 7:28) ... Of all the things Christians around the world have done for 2,000 years, praying the Our Father is the most recognizable and the easiest to trace back to the beginning of the Faith. Written during the First Century, the *Didache* itself (the "Teaching of the Twelve Apostles"), although brief, does not fail to command praying the Our Father three times a day. The Fathers of the Church—true Patriarchs of early Church history who established the permanent foundations of the Faith—provide countless commentaries on the Lord's Prayer, and all agree regarding its centrality and supremacy. We know that any unanimous consensus of the Fathers of the Church is, by that fact alone, rendered a dogmatic truth, so there is no danger we might stray from realms of safety by speaking too highly of the Lord's Prayer or focusing too passionately on its essence. Quite the contrary, to deepen one's understanding of the Our Father is to deepen one's understanding of Christianity itself. To dive more deeply into the *center* of the Our Father is to cooperate with the Holy Spirit most powerfully to "renew the face of the earth." (Chapter 1)

In the preceding section, we considered the lies inherent in a certain decidedly un-Christian way of "summarizing Christianity." To *faithfully* undertake this same task, however, the best approach is given to us clearly by both Public Revelation itself and the Sacred Tradition built on top of it. And that essence is found in what the Church Father Tertullian referred to as "the summary of the whole Gospel," and what St. Thomas Aquinas called "the most perfect of prayers," and what St. Augustine said by itself contained all that could be found elsewhere in the prayers of Scripture. Assuredly, the essence of the Faith is found in the Lord's Prayer; the Our Father. The Catechism of the Catholic Church even refers to this prayer as "**the fundamental Christian prayer**," (§2773) and "**the quintessential prayer of the Church**." (§2776).

Seeing how greatly and uniquely exalted the Lord's Prayer is, we must acknowledge that its power to summarize Christianity is and always will be unrivaled. What do we find in this unsurpassable prayer's own climax? "**Thy Will be done on earth as It is in Heaven.**" (Matthew 6:10).

> "When the disciples asked him to teach them to pray, he gave them the Our Father, **the core of which is undoubtedly 'thy will be done, on earth, as it is in heaven.'**" –Fr. Romano Guardini[14]
>
> For **He did not at all say, "Thy will be done" in *me*, or in *us*, but everywhere on the earth**; so that error may be destroyed, and truth implanted, and all wickedness cast out, and virtue return, and no difference in this respect be henceforth between heaven and earth. "For if this come to pass," saith He, "there will be no difference between things below and above, separated as they are in nature; the earth exhibiting to us another set of angels." (St. John Chrysostom. Homily XIX, §7)

Indeed, this simple petition encapsulates within itself our *entire* Faith. The reason is simple: *earth is the only place where the accomplishment of God's Will is even possibly in question*.

In Purgatory and Heaven, the Divine Will is always done perfectly, and no risk exists that it might be contravened. In hell, God's Will has its exposition by way of justice, and no one there will ever lovingly submit to it, no matter what prayer we offer to that effect. To supplicate for anyone in hell to do God's Will would be to offer a materially heretical prayer.

Finally, in regard to the physical universe outside of earth, there is no need to pray for God's Will to be done in such places because there is no being anywhere within them who is capable of rejecting it. Any rational being, however, is *by definition* capable of rejecting God's Will. Therefore, there are no rational beings outside of earth.

(Here we should clarify: confirmation in grace certainly exists—no angel and no soul in Heaven can ever sin, even though they retain their rational free wills. Still, all such created persons, in accordance with their rational free wills, *had their chance* to reject God's Will. The angels had their chance immediately upon their creation, before being admitted to the Beatific Vision, when God "divided the light from the darkness." (Genesis 1) The souls in Heaven and Purgatory had their opportunity to do so during their earthly lives; up until their deaths.* It will be helpful to present the argument above in another format:

---

* What would have happened to Adam's offspring, had he never sinned, is a matter of speculative theology. If, however, they would have all been born confirmed in grace [and I suspect they would have been], this privilege itself would have only been granted because they indirectly had "their" chance to sin, vicariously, through

- The Our Father is the supreme prayer of Christianity; encapsulating within itself the entire essence of the Gospel.
- The climax, the core, and the greatest petition of this very prayer is the supplication that God's Will be accomplished "on ***earth*** as It is in Heaven."
- It is clearly imperative that we pray for the accomplishment of God's Will *wherever* rational creatures exist that are capable of either doing, or not doing, the Divine Will.
- If aliens beings exist, then these creatures are capable of accepting or rejecting the Divine Will.
- If aliens exist, then the supreme prayer of all Christianity, taught by Jesus Himself, is seriously deficient in scope.
- The conclusion immediately above is absurd, therefore whatever premise necessarily leads to it must likewise be rejected.
- We must reject the possibility of extraterrestrial incarnate intelligent life.

I did not place this argument within the structure of a strict syllogism, as doing so would have greatly lengthened it and what is shown above is clear enough that few will have any trouble following its logic to its unavoidable conclusion, namely: *The greatest prayer ever prayed is not an abject failure, nor is its Divine Author cluelessly incompetent.* In the Our Father, we pray for God's will to reign on earth as in Heaven precisely because earth is the *only* place that exists where this supplication has any meaning.

If there were aliens, Jesus would not have "summarized the whole Gospel" (cf. Tertullian) with the words "Thy Will be done on *earth* as It is in Heaven," but rather, "Thy Will be done throughout the *cosmos/galaxies/dimensions/universe* as It is in Heaven." One cannot protest that, although only "earth" is written in the Gospel, we should nevertheless "*interpret*" or "*understand*" the Our Father's climax as meaning not "earth," but "the entire material universe," on account of the latter simply being too foreign a notion to authors in the time Scripture was written (what with their lack of telescopes!).

Such an attempt to evade the clear meaning of the Our Father would be futile; as we have just seen in the preceding chapters, there are many references to the heavens throughout Scripture—in both the Old and the New Testaments. If Jesus meant for us to petition for God's Will to reign throughout the domains of all these heavenly bodies, then that is exactly

---

Adam. Indeed, just as Original Sin is now passed down through the generations even if not accompanied by Actual Sin, so too, without the fall, would Original Justice have been passed down. No matter how this matter is settled, however, the conclusion is the same: at the very minimum, each *species* of rational being (each angel is "its own species," therefore it was absolutely necessary for each angel to be tested) must be given its chance to contravene the Will of God—that is, it must be *tested*—before being admitted to the Beatific Vision.

what He would have said, and it is exactly what the apostle and evangelist St. Matthew would have recorded, under the inspiration of the Holy Spirit. But that is *not* what Jesus said, it is not what the Gospel recounts, and it is not what is found anywhere in 2,000 years of Christian prayer.

In fact, despite many references to the realms beyond earth, there is not only no teaching (explicit or implicit) anywhere in the Bible's seventy-three books that aliens may exist, but there is also not a single verse that implies that the accomplishment of God's Will is in question anywhere but planet earth.

Let us not be so foolish, then, as to even *wonder* if God was incompetent in revealing the Our Father prayer, by leaving out of its primary supplication the vast majority of those beings deserving inclusion therein. As we will see in a later chapter, certain patently false and even diabolical "private revelations" today, which announce imminent alien contact, seek to "improve" the Our Father by changing "earth" to "the galaxies." In fact, the Our Father is perfect as it is. It cannot be improved, and any attempt to improve it would derive only from the evil one.

> 'Your will be done on earth as it is in heaven.' **There cannot be a greater prayer** than to desire that earthly things should deserve to equal heavenly ones. (St. John Cassian, Father of the Church)

***

We have first considered the Our Father prayer's supreme petition, found in Matthew 6:10, since these words of Christ stand especially exalted in Scripture. The remaining two hundred and fifty-four chapters of the New Testament, however, also provide many indications that aliens do not exist.

The Passion of the Christ: Singular & Supreme

Redemption, as all Christians know, was achieved by Christ on the cross at Calvary, and it is only thanks to this Divine accomplishment that the gates of Heaven are now open to us. There on the cross (and, indeed, earlier still in the Garden of Gethsemane), Christ took upon Himself each and every sin that ever had been committed or ever will be committed until the end of time. He atoned for all of them, thus eradicating the demand of justice for each of us to pay for our sins eternally in hell; if only we accept His Divine Mercy.

Three theories exist attempting to reconcile this Christian teaching on the Passion of the Christ with alien belief: one asserts that Christ's Passion also redeemed alien races from their own sins, another asserts that alien races each had their own incarnations and, correspondingly, their own Passions of (their) Christs, and a third posits unfallen aliens in no need of Redemption. The second and third theories will be addressed in forthcoming chapters; for now, I leave you Hugh Owen's observation:

> Since Christ's death on the cross happened only once (cf. *Romans* 6:10 & *1 Peter* 3:18) on this earth, which was to redeem men from the fall of Adam (cf. *1 Corinthians* 15:21-22), Christ cannot have died anywhere else at any other time. It is therefore nonsensical to think that there are other men in need of redemption on an alien planet.[15]

We must make no mistake about it: aliens, too—had any single one of them in the entire universe committed so much as a single sin—would need Redemption, and this Redemption would not happen except through blood, since "**without the shedding of blood there is no forgiveness of sins.**" (Hebrews 9:22) Yet it is also settled in Scripture that Christ's Passion occurred once and only once.

Presently, therefore, we will address the first theory, which asserts that Christ's sacrifice, 2,000 years ago on earth, also atoned for alien sins, for this notion is at odds with what Scripture teaches about the Passion.

St. Paul opens the fifteenth chapter of his first letter to the Corinthians by "reminding" them of what they must "hold fast" to in order to be saved, namely:

> For I delivered to you as of **first importance** what I also received, that Christ died **for <u>our</u> sins** in accordance with the scriptures... (1 Corinthians 15:3)

Here in Scripture, Paul does not teach that Christ died for "all the sins in the cosmos" or "all transgressions in the heavens," but rather, for none other than "**our**" sins. Whose sins could the word "our" be referring to if not to those committed by human beings? If, by "our," the Holy Spirit (inspiring this verse of the Bible) intended to include the sins of beings on distant planets, then He would have deceived—which He cannot do—by employing that term. Long before St. Paul wrote his letters, however, the greatest of the Prophets knew full well of what Jesus' mission consisted. For when John the Baptist saw Christ approaching to initiate His public ministry, the former cried out:

> **Behold the Lamb of God, who takes away the sins of <u>the world</u>**! (John 1:29)

In perfect fulfillment of the words of Abraham, to his beloved son Isaac thousands of years earlier, that "God will himself provide the lamb for the burnt offering," (Genesis 22:8) John the Baptist announces the opening of the public ministry of the sacrificial Lamb of God Himself. And whose sins will this Lamb take away? Yet again we see it revealed clearly: not those of the "cosmos" or "the heavens," but those of *the world*—the sins of us earthlings.

Now, if there were any occasion in Scripture for any grounds to be given to speculate that this sacrifice of Christ also atoned for the sins of beings on other planets, that would be found in 1 John, Chapter 2, wherein the opening teaching assures us that:

> [Jesus Christ] is the expiation for our sins, and not for ours only but also for the sins of the whole world. (1 John 2:2)

Here, "our" is more specific than the other uses of the same word we have considered, since it is juxtaposed with the clause, "and not for *ours* only." St. Augustine pointed out that this, the first epistle of John, was addressed to a particular group of Jewish converts. As is often the case throughout the New Testament, passages addressed to such a group contain reminders of the global nature of Christ's mission—directed not to Jews only, but to all the Gentiles (in the Appendices, we will address another related verse often abused to pretend to justify alien belief). In this passage, we see the Christ's sacrifice on the Cross expanded beyond the boundaries that would have been placed upon it by a *wrongly* limited way of thinking (and yet again we see that this extension does not incorporate the heavens or the cosmos, but, rather, "the whole world"); that is, it applies to all human beings; all *earthlings*.

The End of Time: Universe-Wide, but Man-Centered and Earth-Centered

> "Man is woven into the fabric of the universe. Time is first of all a cosmic phenomenon. Man lives with the stars."
> —Pope Benedict XVI. *The Spirit of the Liturgy.* Ch. 5

"Soon," (Revelation 22:7) the whole material universe will come to an end. The Bible promises this, proclaiming:

> ... **the heavens will pass away with a loud noise, and the elements will be dissolved with fire**, and the earth and the works that are upon it will be burned up... (2 Peter 3:10)

When will this dissolution of the entire material universe take place? We know not "the day nor the hour" (Matthew 25:13), but we *do* know that the occurrence of this supreme event—coinciding with the Second Coming of Christ in the Flesh, the General Resurrection, and the Last Judgment—is entirely about *human beings*. The preceding verse of the passage quoted above testifies to this fact, for Peter there notes:

> The Lord is not slow about **his promise** as some count slowness, but is forbearing toward you, not wishing that any should perish, but that all should reach repentance. (2 Peter 3:9)

This "passing away" of all "the heavens," and even "the elements" themselves, is an event that will come in accordance with the "promise" of the Lord—to men. Obviously, Scripture is not here making a deceiving, oblique reference to some "promise" it had never previously mentioned, but rather to the very promises that Christ would come again to the human race; not in lowliness, as His first coming, but in supreme Majesty. Recalling here just a few of these promises will suffice:

> "Be patient, therefore, brothers, until the coming of the Lord." (James 5:7) "He who testifies to these things says, "Yes, I am coming soon." Amen. Come, Lord Jesus." (Revelation 22:20. Scripture's final passage.) "The end of all things is at hand. Therefore be alert and of sober mind so that you may pray." (1 Peter 4:7) "'Men of Galilee,' they said, 'why do you stand here looking into the sky? This same Jesus, who has been taken from you into heaven, will come back in the same way you have seen him go into heaven.'" (Acts 1:10-11) "For as the lightning comes from the east and shines as far as the west, so will be the coming of the Son of Man." (Matthew 24:27) "Behold, I am coming **soon** ... I am coming **soon**, bringing my recompense ... Surely I am coming **soon.**" (Revelation 22: 7,12, 20)

In this promise, we are confronted with still another indispensable reality of our Faith, though incompatible with alien belief. The end of the entire material universe is coming "soon." After, there will exist only "a **new heaven** and a new earth" (Revelation 21:1). The arrival of this moment is both "soon" and is entirely centralized upon, flowing from, and concerned with, events transpiring with human beings here on earth.

It is unconscionable to propose that the galaxies are filled with rational creatures whose temporal lives will suddenly be extinguished at some point determined by the events experienced by earthlings billions of light years away. This moment would be entirely arbitrary to these hypothetical aliens, for it would arrive by virtue of Jesus returning to a planet that has absolutely nothing to do with their own civilizations.

We must make no mistake about it, *the absolute end of time*—not merely the conclusion of the civilized era of the "third rock from the sun"—is a thoroughly *human* affair, and Scripture rules out any other interpretation. Even Jesus Himself, in the Gospels, teaches that tribulations on earth constitute the very signs that will "immediately" precede the very "stars ... falling from the sky" (Matthew 24:29).

"Revelation," the final book of Scripture, also translated as "Apocalypse," literally means "unveiling." What Christians glean from this is simple: if anyone could argue that the preceding seventy-two books of the Bible left any stone unturned; any mystery hidden; any important truth still covered up, this final book does not.

Yet *Revelation* is clear that the apocalyptic events transpiring on earth will precipitate this demise of the entire material cosmos. If there were to be any truth found in the contrary notion—that these events only constitute "one particular" salvation history closing; "just one planet's end"—then, at the minimum, no Christian could accuse the very book of

Scripture which "unveils" the hidden mysteries for us of leaving out express mention of such a possibility. In fact, Revelation's own teachings only rule out that speculation.

The twentieth chapter prophesies a symbolic "thousand years" of peace on earth during which Satan is chained (cf. v. 4-6), after which he is briefly "loosed from his prison" (v.7), whereupon a great battle takes place (v.8-9), and Satan is conquered "for ever and ever" (v. 10). This victory directly precedes the arrival of what is recounted in the following passage:

> Then I saw a great white throne and him who sat upon it; **from his presence earth and sky fled away, and no place was found for them.** And I saw the dead, great and small, standing before the throne, and books were opened. Also another book was opened, which is the book of life. And the dead were judged by what was written in the books, by what they had done. And the sea gave up the dead in it, Death and Hades gave up the dead in them, and all were judged by what they had done. Then Death and Hades were thrown into the lake of fire. This is the second death, the lake of fire; and if any one's name was not found written in the book of life, he was thrown into the lake of fire. (Revelation 20:11-15)

Here we see a description of the Second Coming of Christ in the Flesh, the Resurrection of the Dead, and Judgment Day. Upon the commencement of these events, the very "earth and sky fled away," so much so that "no place was found for them." In other words, *they cease to exist.* All those planets, galaxies, nebulas, stars, and other celestial bodies vanish in an instant when *Jesus Christ* comes back *to earth.*

A moment's meditation on this overwhelming reality should compel whoever undertakes it to put to rest any speculation that these other planets or galaxies harbor other intelligent creatures like us. If they existed, they too would be God's children just as we are, and for God to allow their very material existence to be so fundamentally contingent on earth's happenings would be akin to a father disowning one of his sons on account of what another wayward one did during his travels in a distant land—one, moreover, who was raised elsewhere from birth and whose very existence was entirely unknown to his siblings.

The 20th chapter of the Book of Revelation concludes by forever relegating those "not written in the book of life" to the "lake of fire," to be eternally forgotten. Such unfortunate souls are no longer part of the Story of God's Love. The following two chapters, however,—the last of Sacred Scripture—describe the eternal joys of the elect; those whose names are "written in the book of life."

The 21st chapter opens with a description of this "new heaven," and we are taught that "**the dwelling of God is with men**" (v. 3)—not with "all the elect rational creatures of the universe," but rather only with the descendants of Adam. In their new and permanent blessed abode, "there shall be no more mourning ... for the former things have passed away" (Revelation 21:4). Christ, at that time, will have finished making "**all** things new" (v. 5)—ruling out the possibility that other "things" pertaining to non-human civilizations might still await their own being made new.

The *Catechism of the Catholic Church* teaches that, "In this **new universe**, the heavenly Jerusalem, **God will have his dwelling among men**." (§1044) After the end of time, which is coming "soon," the universe we gaze upon in the night sky—whether using the naked eye, or binoculars, or the world's most powerful telescope—will no longer exist. The Catechism, faithfully conveying the message of Scripture and Sacred Tradition, assures us that the present universe will be replaced by a "new universe"—not merely that this "planet, solar system, or galaxy" will be replaced by a new iteration thereof. On the contrary, *all* temporality—without qualification or exception—will pass away upon Christ's Second Coming to earth, and this simple but oft-forgotten recognition rules out the possibility of rational creatures existing elsewhere within the material universe.

Some Christian ET Promoters take the line that each supposedly inhabited planet simply has its own Judgment Day. This thesis is contrary to the infallible truths reviewed above, but it also invites certain questions: for example, "how far must we travel into outer space to escape Judgment Day?" As of this writing, the Voyager 1 spacecraft is far beyond our entire solar system; about 15 billion miles away from earth.[16] If someone had hitched a ride on it, would he thereby be dispensed from the Last Judgment? Of course, the notion itself is ridiculous; not merely for pragmatic reasons of bodily survival on such a craft, but for dogmatic theological reasons. This suggestion proffered by the ET promoters violates the teachings of more saints, popes, Magisterial documents, Fathers of the Church, etc., than we can begin to enumerate here (though we will review a few below). Yet, even the most "orthodox minded" Christian and Catholic ET promoters advocate for this deception.

For example, in his popular 2022 book promoting alien belief, Dr. Paul Thigpen argues that each of the supposedly inhabited planets will "likely" have its own Judgment Day, asserting it is merely the case that "Christ comes to *Earth* to draw *our* history to a close [emphasis in original]."[17] He concedes that the Faith teaches the whole material universe will come to a close, and that it "seems" this end will "follow Earth's Judgment Day," only to then imply there could actually be untold billions of years left after "our" Judgment Day, before the end of time.

Prominent Anglican clergyman and theologian, Andrew Davison, dedicated an entire chapter in his 2023 book (published by Cambridge University), promoting ET belief, to this matter. There, he begins by conceding that if aliens exist, "*... it becomes arbitrary to place human beings at the centre of the timing of the eschaton,*"[18] while also admitting that ET belief "*might* ***call for serious revision****, rather than simply expansion*" of Christian teaching. While even what Davison here admits should immediately remind any Catholic that whatever premise (i.e., ET belief) leads to it must be rejected (perennial Church teaching may organically grow, but can *never* be "seriously revised"), the fact is that he dramatically understates the reality. It is not merely that *revision* would be needed, but *revolution*. Christian dogma on Eschatology cannot be reconciled with alien belief: one must be repudiated.

Davison proceeds to attempt to work out a solution that involves a return of Christ "*involving the return of all the [other] ways in which God has been Incarnate,*" (page 354) a "*string of local ends, worked out on many worlds,*" (Page 355) or (quoting another author) simply a dismissal of eschatology, holding instead that "*Nowadays ... [we] no longer look for a supernatural cataclysmic end to the world ... it is the existential significance of the myth that remains – as the element of permanent value in it*" (Page 356) or that we can simply ignore what the Bible and the Church has always held about the meaning of time itself (cf. Page 356-357) and pretend that each occasion the Faith has taught about the End of Time, such references have only been meaningless drivel (obviously, that is not how he words the proposal, but this captures the essence of it). He then proposes that ET belief's effects on the Christian understanding of the end of time would:

> ...call us to think through something not often considered by theology in its more traditional forms, namely the prospect of a post-human story for the Earth, and for the universe more widely. ... Indeed, there is reason to suppose that humanity would eventually pass away ... either in outright extinction, or by continuing evolution ... leading to a species other than human. (Page 359)

Behold the Godless and decidedly anti-Christian conjectures that ET promotion inevitably leads to among those who take it seriously. Here we must allude to what we will discuss in Part Four. A rejection of Christian dogma on Eschatology looms large in the ET Deception, and this is why it is such a convenient Antichristic ruse. Whoever believes in aliens is naturally led to suppose that the Faith has simply always been wrong about Eschatology, and perhaps no error would be more helpful than this one in aiding and abetting the rise of the Antichrist – especially when such views are combined with similarly delusional anticipations of "leaps in human evolution."

***

While similar assertions can be found everywhere, I have quoted Dr. Thigpen and Rev. Dr. Davison on this point merely to illustrate an important observation regarding how far we have fallen. Even the *most prominent* Christian authors, including the most "orthodox Catholic apologists" among their ranks, are now promoting ideas (which, they concede, inescapably flow from their ET promotion) that are in flagrant violation of the most basic dogmas of the Faith. Let us, now, leave aside these destructive speculations and turn to sources we can trust.

The infallible teachings of the Faith unanimously insist that Christ's coming for the General Resurrection and Last Judgment is itself *the* end of time, not merely some event that will transpire an unknown period *before* that ultimate end. Let us review a few of these teachings:

> "...the first historical coming of Christ ... invites us to look forward with expectation to **his second coming at the end of time.**"[19] (Pope John Paul II.) "God does not will to grant to the just the full effect of the victory over death until the end of time has come..." (Pope Pius XII. *Munificentissimus Deus.* §4,5) "At the end of time [the Church] will gloriously achieve completion, when, as is read in the Fathers, all the just, from Adam ... will be gathered together with the Father in the universal Church ... at the end of time, when Christ, our life, shall appear..." (*Lumen Gentium.* §2,9) "...apostolic preaching, which is expressed in a special way in the inspired books, was to be preserved by an unending succession of preachers until the end of time." (*Dei Verbum.* §8) "[The Mass] will continue to be offered without interruption till the end of time" (Pope Pius XI. *Ad Catholici Sacerdotii.* §14) "...the Church grows with spiritual increase throughout the world down to the end of time." (Pope John XXIII. *Sacerdotii Nostri Primordia.* §53) "**Within the dimension of time the world was created ... its goal [is] in the glorious return of the Son of God at the end of time**." (Pope John Paul II. *Dies Domini.* §74) "Certainly Christ is a King for ever; and though invisible, He continues unto the end of time to govern and guard His church from Heaven" (Pope Leo XIII. *Satis Cognitum.* §11) "[God,] in the times of Noah brought the deluge because of man's disobedience ... [and] will bring [His justice] **on the day of judgment at the end of time**" (St. Irenaeus. *Against Heresies.* Book IV. Chapter 36. §4) "He has determined **at the end of time to pass judgment on the living and the dead** ... He defers it, however, until the end of time, when He will pour forth His wrath in power and heavenly might." (Lactantius. *The Divine Institutes.* Book Two. Chapter 17.) "Sanctify this offering in your mercy, so that they who by your gift have today united themselves more closely to your son may hasten gladly to **meet him when he comes in glory at the end of time.**" (Roman Missal. Mass for the Consecration of Virgins. Eucharistic Prayer I. Hanc Igitur.) "[In] Advent ... [our] minds and hearts are led to look forward to Christ's Second Coming at the end of time." (Roman Missal. Universal Norms. V. §39) "**When the resurrection occurs, it will not be time but the end of time**." (St. Thomas Aquinas. *Summa Theologica.* Supplement. Question 77. Article 3.) "**When [Christ] comes at the end of time to judge the living and the dead**..." (*Catechism of the Catholic Church,* §682)

This is only a tiny selection of teachings; entire books could be filled with similar ones. But what has been shown above already makes one thing clear: it is a dogma of the Faith that "earth's Judgment Day" (the *only* Judgment Day), is *absolutely simultaneous* with the end of time. Christ's Coming is *at* the end of time, not "before" it. It is, moreover, not merely the end of "humanity's time," or "earth's time," it is simply *the* end of *time* itself.

Each occasion on which the Church has touched upon this matter, that reality has been either stated explicitly or taught implicitly. Time *itself* ends when Jesus comes to earth in the flesh. The entire material universe terminates at that moment. Yet, the only way to rescue belief in aliens from sheer absurdity is to contradict this dogma. Dr. Thigpen, Dr. Davison, and those like them recognize it would indeed be deeply wrong to posit that the galaxies are filled with rational beings who would suddenly have their own civilizations—their own worlds—immediately cease to exist when Christ comes to the earth. Tragically, instead of allowing this recognition to dissuade them from belief in aliens, they allow it to seduce them into contradicting dogma.

Indeed, for a Catholic, it should be even easier to assent to this absolute truth. As we have seen, Magisterium and Sacred Tradition are filled with declarations that the Second Coming of Christ to earth in the flesh corresponds to the unqualified end of time. This has been rendered infallible many times over, perhaps not because a specific ex-cathedra Papal Declaration explicitly affirmed it (as far as I know, at least), but because the Ordinary magisterium has affirmed it so repeatedly that it cannot be questioned, much less doubted. Whoever denies it has certainly thereby succumbed to material heresy.*

---

* This does not mean I am accusing such a person of being a formal heretic, as that would require him to *realize* that he is obstinately contradicting infallible truth.

7. Multiple Incarnations: Contrary to Christianity

"If anyone shall say that Christ ... passed through various classes, had different bodies and different names ... let him be anathema."

—Second Council of Constantinople, 533 A.D.
The Anathemas Against Origen. §7

As we have seen, Christian alien promoters usually base their hypotheses on one of three premises: either aliens are unfallen and therefore in no need of Redemption; or aliens are fallen but (perhaps) saved by the very same Jesus Christ we Christians on earth alone know; or aliens are fallen but saved by their own Incarnation of God. The problems with the first two propositions are covered elsewhere; presently, however, we must take note of the outlandishness of the third assertion.

Indeed, the *absolute* (in the highest and most unqualified sense of the word "absolute' that can be imagined) *primacy* and *uniqueness* of Jesus Christ is among the most fundamental truths of the Christian Faith. The moment a Christian has begun to even entertain the prospect that the Jesus we know from Scripture might not enjoy this absolute supremacy, but rather might be only one Divine Incarnation of many, is the same moment this Christian's Christianity has begun to die in his heart.

We need not engage in rigorous research to grasp the nature of Christ's Primacy; we need only look to Scripture's most important teachings and the most fundamental and ancient formulations of the Christian Faith; the very formulations for which the Faithful over the millennia have willingly endured the most gruesome tortures and deaths rather than deny a single word.

For the fact is simple and absolute: Jesus Christ had—and has, and always will have—two and only two natures: a human nature and a Divine Nature. No Christian may entertain the possibility that He had any more natures than this, or that God Himself had any other nature anywhere else before *The* Incarnation two thousand years ago. No believer may speculate that, perhaps, those two natures of Christ are "the only ones *we* need to know about," but that "*perhaps, in addition He has a Martian nature, a Neptunian nature, an Andromedian nature, and innumerable other natures!*" In contradiction to such blasphemous speculations (latent in almost all "Christian" ET promotion), we have the dogmatic truth as expressed at the 5th century Council of Chalcedon:

> We confess, therefore, our Lord Jesus Christ, the Only Begotten Son of God ... became a union of **two** natures. Wherefore we confess one

> Christ, one Son, one Lord. (Session II) ... **I am astonished that so absurd and perverse a profession as [denying] this ... was not rebuked by a censure on the part of any of his judges, and that an utterance extremely foolish and extremely blasphemous was passed over, just as if nothing had been heard which could give offense** (Letter of Pope Leo, Session II) ... The most magnificent and glorious judges said: **Add then to the definition, according to the judgment of our most holy father Leo, that there are two natures in Christ united unchangeably, inseparably, unconfusedly ...** This one and the same Jesus Christ, the only-begotten Son [of God] must be confessed to be in two natures, unconfusedly, immutably, indivisibly, inseparably [united] (Session V)

These teachings speak for themselves. The Church has already dogmatically declared that whoever would fail to assert that the Incarnation of God consists of *exactly two* natures (*human* and Divine) is guilty of a "perverse, foolish, and extremely blasphemous" assertion. Yet virtually all Christian ET promoters assert precisely this, or at least testify to their (supposedly "humble") "openness" to it. (Note: As we will see later, Aquinas wrote some philosophical speculations on whether God could assume many natures. He answered in the affirmative merely in the sense that doing so was *logically* possible—*not* that it was theologically palatable! In fact, Aquinas condemned such a suggestion as derogatory to God—a fact the Catholic ET promoters never acknowledge, while pretending Aquinas' writings vindicate the very thesis this great saint condemned.)

Dominus Ieusus: The Church's Condemnation of Multiple Incarnations

While the dogmatic definitions included above should suffice to prove to any Christian that believing in the possibility of multiple incarnations is condemned, the Church has not left us with only those ancient definitions. Centuries of Sacred Tradition's development are replete with reiterations of the truths above and all their corollaries. Even as recently as the year 2000, The Congregation for the Doctrine of the Faith issued an important document (authored by the future Pope Benedict XVI), *Dominus Iesus.* This teaching does not specifically address aliens, but it does directly condemn (as heretical—that is, "in profound conflict with the Christian faith,") the same premises related to multiple incarnations that the Catholic ET promoters unashamedly employ.

For example, one Catholic theologian and ET promoter we have already quoted, Dr. Paul Thigpen, dismisses this document as "not infallible," and then applies to it the usual rhetorical trick of the alien promoters; namely, pretending its teachings only apply to *humanity*; implying that absolute and eternal theological truths run up against an unsurpassable barrier somewhere in earth's stratosphere.

While it is true that the CDF's own texts do not enjoy the charism of infallibility, noting that fact is unnecessary here; this document summarizes and quotes other documents which are themselves infallible. Moreover, the mere fact that the word "humanity" is used several times in the text does not give anyone license to pretend that all its unqualified universal claims must be regarded as actually restricted to the human race. On the contrary, the document makes clear that *Jesus* Christ (that is, *the* Incarnation of the Second Person of the Trinity) is absolutely singular and supreme. In the document, we are taught:

> In contemporary theological reflection there often emerges an approach to **Jesus of Nazareth that considers him a particular, finite, historical figure, who reveals the divine not in an exclusive way, but in a way complementary with other revelatory and salvific figures**. **The Infinite, the Absolute, the Ultimate Mystery of God would thus manifest itself to humanity in many ways and in many historical figures: Jesus of Nazareth would be one of these.** More concretely, for some, Jesus would be one of the many faces which the Logos has assumed in the course of time to communicate with humanity in a salvific way... (§9) **These theses are in profound conflict with the Christian faith. The doctrine of faith must be firmly believed which proclaims that Jesus of Nazareth, son of Mary, and he alone, is the Son and the Word of the Father**. ...In this regard, **John Paul II has explicitly declared: "To introduce any sort of separation between the Word and Jesus Christ is contrary to the Christian faith**... " It is likewise contrary to the Catholic faith to introduce a separation between the salvific action of the Word as such and that of the Word made man. With the incarnation, all the salvific actions of the Word of God are always done in unity with the human nature that he has assumed for the salvation of all people. **The one subject which operates in the two natures, human and divine, is the single person of the Word. Therefore, the theory which would attribute, after the incarnation as well, a salvific activity to the Logos as such in his divinity, exercised "in addition to" or "beyond" the humanity of Christ, is not compatible with the Catholic faith.** (§10) .... the action of the Spirit is not outside or parallel to the action of Christ. **There is only one salvific economy of the One and Triune God**, realized in the mystery of the incarnation, death, and resurrection of the Son of God, actualized with the cooperation of the Holy Spirit, and extended in its salvific value to all humanity and to the entire universe: "No one, therefore, can enter into communion with God except through Christ, by the working of the Holy Spirit." (§12) ...one can **and must** say that Jesus Christ has a significance and a value for the human race and its history, which are **unique and singular**, **proper to him alone**, **exclusive, universal, and absolute**. Jesus is, in fact, the Word of God made man for the salvation of all... (§15)[20]

As we see taught above from the Church, in a document drawing from dogmatic sources that are entirely infallible, the "**Son of Mary, and he**

alone, is ... the Word of the Father." Saying otherwise is "**profoundly**" contrary to Christianity; i.e., it is heretical. This truth clearly rules out any suggestion of multiple Incarnations. An ET promoter may claim such Incarnations *are also* the Word of the Father (a claim that, itself, is contrary to dogma on Jesus remaining the *only* begotten Son), but they obviously could not claim that such Incarnations are likewise the Son of *Mary*. Yet, we know that the Son of *Mary* is absolutely alone in His status as the Word of the Father.

Therefore, any theory whatsoever that refuses to accord to Jesus Christ a recognition of His unqualified singularity, supremacy, and exclusivity, or introduce any sort of separation between the Second Person of the Trinity and the humanity of Jesus, or in any way mitigate His "universal uniqueness," is here repeatedly and rightly dismissed as contrary to the Faith.

Moreover, the entire motivation for this document—to condemn those modernist, syncretic, and New Age heresies which view Jesus as just one of many manifestations of God—applies equally to the same approach taken to extraterrestrials. Recall that the ET promoters' entire thesis is not merely that aliens exist in some distant galaxy we will never communicate with, much less physically meet, but rather that aliens are already here among us—and long have been. Therefore, there is not the slightest difference between the ET promoters insisting these aliens have "their own Christ" and, on the other hand, a run of the mill New Ager insisting Buddhists and Hindus "also have their own saviors." All suggestions of these "different Christs," whether they are offered in reference to aliens, Buddhists, aboriginal Australians, or what have you, are equally heretical.

In sum, to read this document and nevertheless pretend it can be reconciled with belief in extraterrestrial salvation histories, or even extraterrestrial incarnations (which are now being learned about on earth through UFO contact), is not merely bizarre, but baldly deceptive. Dr. Thigpen, however, uses one clause from this document (contained in the quotes above), which contains the phrase "the entire universe," and claims it "could indeed be read as support for a 'cosmic Christ.'"[21] This move consists in nothing other than taking one tiny piece of a large text and pretending it can refute the entirety of the text itself; a strategy far worse than any "proof texting."

Recall that advocating for a "cosmic Christ" is the move made by certain modernists and New Agers (above all Fr. Richard Rohr) to replace our focus on *Jesus* with the acknowledgement of an amorphous and vague notion of His nature that is amenable to alien belief. In fact, the document's inclusion of "the entire universe," in that one sentence, is simply an acknowledgement of Christ's Omnipotence and His ability to rescue (from the Fall) the entire cosmos (which Adam brought down with him); it is not a reference to supposed inhabitants of another planet. One Catholic scholar, a critic of Dr. Thigpen's argument here, astutely wrote:

> ...no matter how many times *Dominus Jesus* speaks of the uniqueness of Christ and the uniqueness of His salvation to humanity... Paul [Thigpen] still reads into this single phrase, "and to the entire universe," what he wants to see—the possibility of alien life on other planets. As a rule, when the ambiguity of language offers Paul the slightest crack through which he can wiggle, Paul will invariably take the opportunity. Normally, [however] when phrases like "and to the entire universe" are used in a scholarly soteriological context, it refers only to St. Paul's words in Roman 8:20-21 that when Adam sinned the whole creation was cursed and forced to decay, but which will be liberated from the curse at the Second coming of Christ...[22]

Whoever would read a document like *Dominus Iesus* and fail to realize it is exhorting all Christians (on pain of heresy) to ensure they accord to *Jesus* Christ—born on earth two thousand years ago—an absolutely unqualified uniqueness and supremacy, has said much more about himself than about (any acceptable) theology. Yet such moves as these are endemic in Christian ET promotion and its vain attempts to portray its views as amenable to the Faith.

Renowned Theologian Fr. Weinandy: Aliens Irreconcilable with the Incarnation

> "Blessed be the God and Father of our Lord Jesus Christ, who has blessed us in Christ with every spiritual blessing in the heavenly places, even as he chose us in him before the foundation of the world, that we should be holy and blameless before him. He destined us in love to be his sons through Jesus Christ, according to the purpose of his will, to the praise of his glorious grace which he freely bestowed on us in the Beloved. In him we have redemption through his blood, the forgiveness of our trespasses, according to the riches of his grace which he lavished upon us. For he has made known to us in all wisdom and insight the mystery of his will, according to his purpose which he set forth in Christ as a plan for the fulness of time, to unite all things in him, things in heaven and things on earth." —Ephesians 1:3-10

Fr. Thomas Weinandy is one of the greatest theologians alive today. A Franciscan priest who has taught at many Catholic universities, served on the International Theological Commission, and worked as the American Catholic Bishop's chief defender of orthodoxy, he has, especially since 2017, been distinguished as one of the most courageous of the internationally recognized theologians in critiquing the doctrinal chaos the Church has recently been experiencing. He even received one of the highest honors the Church bestows on a living person, the *Pro Ecclesia et Pontifice* medal, by way of which the Pope recognizes an individual's contribution to the Faith. Fr. Weinandy's arguments should always be taken extremely seriously, but when he issues strong statements in accordance with his particular area of expertise—Christology—the faithful should be especially sure to take note and respect them. On this point, he explained (in a 2023 article), why belief in extraterrestrials *cannot* be reconciled with what the Faith teaches us about the Incarnation of Jesus Christ:

> ...**the existence of intelligent aliens would be contrary to God's revealed eternal plan for the whole of creation, for human beings, and above all for Jesus himself**. God not only created everything through his Son, but he also created everything for him—"whether thrones or dominions or principalities or authorities [or aliens]. He is before all things, and in him all things hold together." (Colossians 1:16) This "holding together" is **not simply associated with the Father's Son as such, but specifically with his incarnate state.** It's Jesus, as the incarnate Son, who "reconciles all things, whether on earth or in heaven, making peace by the blood of the cross." (Colossians 1:20) The entire cosmos was created for the incarnate Son of God, Jesus. **It's as man that the Son of God reigns supreme. For him, as man, to reign over non-human aliens defies logic, which proves true only if human beings solely exist within the cosmic created order**...From all eternality, God chose humankind, and the whole cosmic order, to be summed up, taken up into Christ, the Father's incarnate Son. At the end of time, we are subsumed into the glorious risen humanity of the Son. **Intelligent aliens find no place within God's eternal scheme—his entire focus is on human beings and the humanity of his divine incarnate Son ... Throughout the entire cosmos, heaven, earth, under the earth, every knee is to bend, and every tongue is to proclaim that the risen man Jesus, the incarnate Son, is Lord. Jesus cosmically reigns supreme as man. He is not Lord of non-human aliens, for they do not exist.**[23]

The existence of aliens, indeed, would violate *every aspect* of God's plan as definitively revealed to us. There is no angle from which one may approach the question which presents a picture that harmonizes with Christianity. It is, therefore, no surprise that the consideration of what (or, rather, *Who*) is paramount in Christianity—Christ Himself—is precisely the consideration that presents the most flagrant contradictions.

As Fr. Weinandy demonstrates, *the Incarnation of* the Word—the man, Jesus Christ, *cannot* be extricated from *the Word Himself* (the Second Person of the Trinity). If, as Scripture teaches, the Word holds all things together in the universe, then it follows that *Jesus* holds all things together, and if Jesus holds all things together, then it is precisely the God-*man* who does so. There simply is no place, in this great cosmic picture we are definitively given in Public Revelation, in which intelligent non-human creatures of any sort could fit. If there was ever any question as to whether such a place could exist, that question was forever closed upon the Incarnation.

The best of non-Catholic Christian thinkers also agree. Even those theologians who are most overzealous to appear understated nevertheless, upon investigating the matter, inevitably concede how "problematic" or "otiose" (whereas they *should* say blasphemous, heretical, or fallacious!) positing multiple incarnations would be. For example, the following argument—politely, though mistakenly, laced with terminology to diminish the force of its conclusion—was written by two theologians, including a professor at Cambridge University:

> [Christ's] incarnation is eternal: 'he will reign over the house of Jacob forever, and of his kingdom there will be no end' (Luke 1:32–33). It is very specific in its human particularity—of such and such race, tribe and family. But what becomes subsequently available to future generations as a result of Christ's work is a trinitarian indwelling of God's presence, not a further incarnation. Our knowledge of God comes from the Father through the Son in the Spirit. Since the assumption of human flesh by the eternally begotten Son of God is 'once for all' and remains eternally significant, other incarnations become otiose. ... Johannes Brenz observed that *the communicatio idiomatum* in the person of Christ requires us to think of the humanity of Christ as forever conjoined with his divinity. '**Since deity and humanity are inseparably joined ... in one person of Christ, it is necessary that wherever the deity of Christ is there also is his humanity ... For if the deity of Christ is anywhere without his humanity, there are two persons, not one'**. Similarly... [due to] the resurrected and ascended body of Christ in heaven, the divine Son must forever be thought of as incarnate. ... The postulation of multiple incarnations may actually be self-defeating insofar as it undermines the need for even one incarnation as traditionally conceived. ... The healing of created nature required that the Son of God be consubstantial with the Father and that the assumption of human nature neither impair nor diminish the divinity of the second person of the Trinity. Yet in a world of multiple incarnations, salvation must take place in ways other than through a single action of cosmic healing significance. This raises the question of whether even one incarnation would be necessary, as opposed to multiple indwellings of conscious persons by the divine Spirit. **A multiplicity of occurrence must inevitably compromise the singularity of the incarnation**. Why have many instances, if even one is no longer necessary...? Hence the move towards a postulation of multiplicity may be self-destructive. Rather than developing the logic of the incarnation, significant reduction of this and other classical doctrines may be required by the perceived need for an account of 'equal access' to the divine.[24]

The New Testament's Two Supreme Passages: Both Contra-ET

Of all Scripture, St. John's Gospel reveals the deepest theological truths about the nature of Jesus. The opening fourteen verses of this Gospel summarize its twenty-one chapters, and these verses are referred to as the "Johannine Prologue." Their importance is so great that, for centuries, every Catholic Mass said throughout the world each day concluded with their recitation.[25] There was much wisdom in this tradition: the faithful need incessant reminders, through the constant prayerful repetition of these verses which contain these truths, that Jesus is *eternal*—He always existed—(v. 1-2), that *everything* was created through Him (v. 3), that our Faith in Him is essential and transforming (v. 9-13), and that His Incarnation was absolutely real, and He is absolutely unique—the Father's "**only**" Son (v. 14).

Perhaps some of the straying from orthodoxy we have witnessed among Christians these last several decades flows from the removal of the Johannine Prologue from the ordinary form of the Mass in 1969, whereupon most began to no longer hear this constant reminder of these essential truths that underlie all other truths of the Faith. Not only did belief in the possibility of extraterrestrial incarnations of God explode during those decades, but so did countless syncretic and Arian-inspired heresies which regard Jesus as only one path among many to the Father (perhaps the "privileged" path), or which reduce or even reject Christ's full Divinity.

Aside from the Our Father prayer, it is difficult to find a complete passage in Scripture (i.e., more than just one or two verses) that is in the same league as the opening passage of the final Gospel. If one gets these two passages right, he will get Christianity right. If he neglects them or tries to wiggle out of their clear meaning with theological acrobatics or fast-and-loose ET-promotion-inspired speculations, then he is certain to get Christianity itself entirely wrong.

Just as the Our Father has its supreme verse (which, as we discussed previously, rules out aliens), the Johannine Prologue's own greatest revelation is its final verse, which reads:

> And the Word **became** flesh and dwelt among us, full of grace and truth; we have beheld his glory, glory as of the **only** Son from the Father (John 1:14)

In Catholic devotion, a clause from this verse is not only recited daily, but several times a day (in, for example, the Angelus prayer, said thrice daily, in which Catholics pray "*and the word was made flesh, and dwelt among us,*" while kneeling for those particular words in accordance with the awe-filled reverence they are due).

Just as it is impossible to take too seriously the supplication for God's Will to be done on earth as in Heaven, so too no Christian need ever fear that he could become too insistent upon heeding all the implications of John 1:14. And this verse assures us that Jesus is the *only* Son of God. Contrary to the errors of Richard Rohr, discussed earlier, there is no rupture between the humanity and the Divinity of Jesus Christ; both natures are perfectly united in the one Divine Person that is Jesus Christ; a union that is referred to as the "Hypostatic Union," and which will persevere *eternally*. (The Second General Council of Constantinople, in 381 A.D., dogmatically condemned the notion that the Hypostatic Union only endures until the end of the world.) This term simply indicates that Christ's two natures are united in one and only one subsistence—one and only one Person—and the union of these two natures cannot be demoted to the status of mere moral union, "accidental" (i.e., non-essential) union, or "commingling" (i.e., mixing).

This dogma repudiates the interpretation of the Johannine Prologue which would argue that "*indeed,* ***Christ*** *is the only Son of the Father, but this has nothing to do with the* ***man****, Jesus. It is merely an assertion that the Divine Nature of Christ is unique; that same Divine Nature of Christ could be Incarnate elsewhere, having nothing to do with the man we know as Jesus.*" As of 2,000 years ago, immediately after the Blessed Virgin Mary said, "behold the handmaid of the Lord," (Luke 1:38) any reference to the Second Person of the Trinity is also a reference to the *man*, Jesus, since this very Divine Nature is *forever hypostatically* united to Jesus' human nature.

It is impossible for the human mind to even begin to comprehend how glorious, magnanimous, and astounding it is that the infinite, almighty, uncreated God—the Eternal Word Himself—now and forever truly has a human nature like us. The entire human race—in fact, the entire universe and all it contains—is absolutely *nothing* compared to God. Nevertheless, the Infinite *Himself* incorporated our "nothingness" into His own self... *for all eternity*; even preserving five wounds He received on earth—those in His hands, feet, and side—in Heaven.

The impossibility of grasping so much as an iota of this glory, however, must not prevent us from abiding in each conclusion that follows from acknowledging its absolute truth. There is only one Son of God, and this one Son forever assumed *human* nature. If this assumption was essentially just a show (an unstated premise latent in "Christian" ET promotion), then God the Son could have put on similar shows for innumerable alien civilizations. Whoever entertains this possibility, however, should put aside pretense and admit he has simply apostatized from Christianity. The Incarnation is not and was not an illusion—*the* Eternal One *is* now *man*. He is not any other created nature, and He never will be any other created nature.

Furthermore, the same verse under consideration excludes any interpretation which would insist that only the *Divine Nature* of Jesus Christ is being discussed; for it specifically indicates that "the Word became **flesh**." Reference to the assumption of a human nature of "flesh" is a clear indication that the verse is speaking about the *man*, Jesus, who is indeed the *only* Son of the Father.

***

Thus far in the present section, we have focused on the opening of the first chapter of John's Gospel merely due to the extreme importance of this passage. Many other passages in the New Testament, however, reveal the uniqueness of Jesus Christ and compel a Christian to dismiss the possibility of other Incarnations on other planets. Who could forget what has perhaps become Scripture's most famous verse?

> For God so loved the world that he gave his **only** Son, that whoever believes in him should not perish but have eternal life. (John 3:16)

Later, John 14:6 relays Jesus' teaching that "**no one**" comes to God the Father except through Him, yet again ruling out aliens. In Scripture's next book, we see this truth reiterated. The Acts of the Apostles (4:12) tells us that "**there is salvation in no one else**"—Redemption cannot be found in anyone other than Jesus Christ "of Nazareth," and here is still another rejection of the possibility of extraterrestrial Messiahs. The Book of Hebrews is also filled with repeated references to "the"—singular—Son, Who is Jesus Christ. And in the first Gospel, Jesus Himself even directly ruled out the possibility of "other Sons" of God—other Incarnations of God—when He taught:

> All things have been delivered to me by my Father; and no one knows the Son except the Father, and **no one knows the Father except the Son** and any one to whom **the** Son chooses to reveal him. (Matthew 11:27)

Many other selections from Scripture testify to the completely singular status of Jesus Christ. Indeed, throughout two millennia of Christianity, the Faithful have never felt the need to ponder, upon reading the New Testament, whether Jesus Christ should be regarded as *absolutely* unique and supreme, or merely as unique and supreme "for us" on earth. That is, the faithful felt no need to do so until the heresies of the Enlightenment (and, especially, the diabolical deceptions of the science fiction writers of the modern era) seduced them to do precisely that.

One testimony to this constancy of Sacred Tradition is seen in the Nicene Creed, which will next be addressed.

The Nicene Creed: "One Lord... Only Begotten Son... For Us Men and for Our Salvation"

A more fundamental expression of Christian dogmas cannot be found than the Nicene Creed. Formulated at the first Ecumenical Council at Nicaea in response to the great early Church heresy, Arianism, this recitation of dogmas has stood, century after century, as the greatest encapsulation of what was handed on "once and for all to the saints." (Jude 3)

Each Sunday Mass, Catholics around the world lift up their voices to Heaven as they sing or say this creed's words, thereby promising to shed every drop of their blood rather than deny a single truth therein. In this Creed, Christians profess the following words:

> I believe in one God, the Father almighty, maker of heaven and earth, of all things visible and invisible ... I believe in **one** **Lord** Jesus Christ, the **Only** Begotten Son of God ... begotten, not made, consubstantial with the Father; **through him all things** were made. **For us men and for our salvation he came down from heaven**... (The Nicene Creed)

Here we confess, with unsurpassable and unabashed dogmatic fervor, that the real man who walked the *earth* 2,000 years ago, *Jesus* Christ, is literally *consubstantial* with the almighty Father who made the entire universe. The two are not merely similar or related; rather, Jesus and the Father are *one* in their very *being*.

> [Jesus] is **the** radiance of [God's] glory and **the exact** representation of His nature... (Hebrews 1:3. NASB)

This Creed therefore repudiates any cryptic interpretations of Jesus' nature or mission which would regard Him as somehow "less" than God; somehow a mere "manifestation" of God; somehow on par with "other Sons of God." Such suggestions as these, or any similar assertions, immediately run afoul of the most fundamental Christian dogmas expressed here and elsewhere.

If any other incarnation existed, it too would be "Lord;" it too would be a "Begotten Son" of God. In fact, we know that Jesus is the *only*—"**one**"—Lord; the "**only**" Begotten Son of God; the *one* "through [whom] **all things** were made."

This Creed also rebuts the notion that the Incarnation of Jesus Christ transpired for the sake of beings other than men (whom, as we infallibly know and will discuss in a later chapter, are all descendants of Adam and Eve). For it expressly states that Jesus came down from Heaven not for a multitude of human and non-human races, but rather "**for us men** and for our salvation." Not only, therefore, does the Nicene Creed rule out the possibility of multiple incarnations. It also rules out the possibility that *the* Incarnation transpired for the sake of alien races.

The Word "Only," Trinitarian Heresy, and a Tale of an Excommunicated Sect

Unfortunately, there are always some Christians who refuse to believe that "only" means *only,* or that when a given assertion is *true,* any contradictory assertion must be regarded as false, regardless of whether its contradictory nature is rendered explicit within the text of the defined dogma.

Consider, for example, the false and heretical "private revelations" of the so-called "Community of the Lady of All Nations," which once claimed tens-of-thousands of adherents in Canada and elsewhere. The defenders of these "revelations" present them as standing in harmony with the entirety of Public Revelation (and even the Church's Magisterium). However, the messages claim the Trinity was only *"part"* of the truth about God's Nature. The *"full"* truth thereof, they insist, is that God is actually a ***"Quinternity"*** —that is, *Five* Divine Persons. They blasphemously claim that the Virgin Mary is the fourth Divine Person, and that—conveniently—their own founder is the fifth.

This movement was accurately described as heretical by the Catholic Church, which eventually excommunicated its members. Nevertheless, the fraudulent revelations count—to this very day—many "Christian" devotees who emphatically reject the charge of heresy. "We believe in the Trinity!" they insist. They simply append their belief with the caveat, "we simply don't believe there is *only* a Trinity of Divine Persons—we believe that two *more* Divine Persons exist."

They are, of course, mistaken—or rather, diabolically deceived—on these points, but they do have one thing in their favor. Nowhere does the Deposit of Faith explicitly say, "**God is not Five Divine Persons; let anyone who says this be anathema**." Instead, it teaches that God *is* Three Divine Persons, and we are trusted to use our intellects to recognize that "three" and "five" are mutually exclusive when said of the same thing.

Obvious as the fallacious nature of the community's assertions are, the reality is that Christian ET promoters succumb to the same fallacy this condemned and heretical sect used. They simply play stupid. They ignore the plethora of Scriptural teaching ruling out aliens, only because the *word* "extraterrestrials" is not used. They disregard incessantly repeated qualifiers like "only," or "one," or very deliberate uses of the definite article "the," (instead of "a"); they ignore categorical and clear declarations of absolute supremacy or uniqueness; they ignore the deliberately *complete* nature of the presentations of certain theological and philosophical dynamics discussed in Scripture, and on the list goes.

After this Herculean undertaking of willed ignorance that belongs in the dialogue of a cartoon comedy, they finally pretend to care what is asserted in the Deposit of Faith, and they proceed to insist that their premises are not *explicitly* addressed anywhere therein, and thus they are entitled to hold, defend, and promote them. (Some charlatans go further still, claiming that certain verses in Scripture *do* reveal aliens—all their claims are refuted in this book's appendices.)

Whoever would suppose that the Word of God must destroy its poetry—presenting itself so didactically as a technical instruction manual—merely to appease his own persnickety tendencies, has only thereby revealed his neurosis. The Bible's Author need not prove Himself to us; *we* must prove ourselves to *Him*. If we want to know His Truth; if we *love* His

Truth, then discovering it upon reading His Word will not be difficult. If, on the other hand, we read His Word insisting that we will only rule out some thesis if it is explicitly addressed, then we will receive our just deserts: a worldview full of darkness and damaging confusion.

Of the thousands of souls who were caught up in the "Community of the Lady of All Nations," many had their lives essentially destroyed. All of that sorrow could have been avoided if only, upon sitting down with the Word of God, they regarded it as their foundation, not merely as one guardrail.

God's Word is not only true, but it also is—and must be—beautiful. And it is indeed the most beautiful thing ever written. No technical instruction manual, however, is beautiful. Do not approach Scripture expecting one.

Christianity Mandates Rejecting Any and All "Other Christs"

The Gospels of Matthew, Mark, and Luke all contain Jesus' stark warning that others would come, likewise claiming to be the Christ—and that we must always reject such proposals (cf. Matthew 24:5, Mark 13:6, Luke 21:8). St. Paul's letters contain an even more shocking warning:

> I am afraid that **as the serpent deceived Eve by his cunning**, your thoughts will be led astray from a sincere and pure devotion to Christ. For **if some one comes and preaches another Jesus** than the one we preached...you submit to it readily enough. (2 Corinthians 11:3-4)

A resounding lesson for all Christians throughout time here emerges: *any* presentation of *any* "other Jesus"—that is, other than the *one* handed down to us in the Deposit of Faith—is to be outright rejected. St. Paul goes so far as to link the evil of the Fall itself to the willingness of his addressee to submit to "another Jesus," and later in the same chapter he alerts us that "**even Satan disguises himself as an angel of light**." (v. 14) The faithful are hereby implored to let no apparent sign or wonder attract them away from the one and only Jesus Christ—the one preached to them by the Apostles; the one Who lived on earth (and only on earth) 2,000 years ago. Any other Jesus would be none other than a machination of the father of lies, seeking to reenact in our souls the supreme evil of the Original Sin he inspired in the Garden.

Here, yet again, we have an unmistakable instruction from Scripture that would be unconscionable if alien civilizations existed, each with their own incarnation—"their own Christ," for such a scenario would constitute none other than God condemning Himself.

Recall that ET promoters not only assert the existence of alien civilizations, but they are also nearly unanimous in insisting that we can one day communicate with these aliens and perhaps even make physical contact (most insist we have already done precisely that, with such events merely being "covered up by the government.") If this scenario they present were true, then alien civilizations would in this respect be no categorically different than indigenous peoples on continents that were yet undiscovered (by His immediate audience) in Christ's time. ET promoters themselves frequently draw this very parallel with their own position, supposing it supports their thesis, when in fact it only contradicts it. Indeed, centuries would need to pass before communication with those lands would take place, but this meant nothing. Those lands did *not* have "their own incarnations." The early European explorers and missionaries who first ventured to the Americas—men of strong Faith, unaffected by wild speculations disharmonious with Scripture—embarked upon their expeditions knowing full well that they would not find "another Jesus," no matter where they landed, even if they "sailed off the edge of the earth" to some mysterious land such as the "Antipodes" (more on that point in Part Two).

If, however, other incarnations—"other Jesus Christs," if you will—existed on other planets, then we would be left with the same unconscionable scenario we would face if other incarnations existed in the once undiscovered contents. In any such scenario, Scripture's command that we immediately and fundamentally reject the very presentation of "another Christ" would be tantamount to Christ condemning Himself. It was this fallacy for which Jesus condemned the Pharisees in Matthew 12:22-32; they falsely supposed that a house which stands could nevertheless be divided against itself. Only a few verses later, Jesus related this sin to blasphemy against the Holy Spirit, for which they would not be forgiven.

A Christian who asserts the possibility of other incarnations of God on other planets has succumbed to the exact same trap: holding to a Faith which requires rejecting "other Christs," even while believing that other Christs may exist! This jarring intrinsic contradiction demands that the one who holds it discards either alien belief or Scripture. I hope and pray it is not Scripture that he will discard.

Ultimately, positing the possibility of other Incarnations cannot be done without falling victim to the same heretical syncretism one hears propounded in modernist circles. If other Christs exist *anywhere* (whether we are talking about different continents or different galaxies is irrelevant), then Christianity's repeated exclusive claims about Jesus are false (as are the multitude of other truths it rightly makes exclusive claims about); for these claims contain no indications or implications that they cease to apply when one escapes earth's atmosphere.

Modernists readily dismiss such exclusive claims in the Deposit of Faith, as they are shamelessly eager to embrace their own version of Christianity which regards Jesus as merely "one path of many up the same mountain." Faithful Christians, however, reject these notions wherever they are found. And they are certainly found—though at times hiding in the unstated corollaries—in ET promotion.

Modernism, however, always generates other evils beyond its expressly stated tenets. Although often inspired by an Enlightenment-rationalism, it is known to eventually pull many of its adherents down into outright occultism. As Scripture warns:

> ...we know that "an idol has no real existence," and that "there is no God but one." For although there may be **so-called** gods in heaven or on earth—as indeed there are many "gods" and many "lords"—yet for us there is one God, the Father, from whom are all things and for whom we exist, and **one Lord, Jesus Christ, through whom are all things and through whom we exist**. (1 Corinthians 6:4-6)

The danger of believing in the possibility of other Incarnations is not only a matter of the modernist heresy of syncretism; it is also an intellectual posture that, as we will discuss at length in Part Four, edges one toward worshipping demons. St. Paul, immediately after acknowledging that there are indeed many "so-called gods in heaven or on earth"—that is, many demons populating such regions—reminds us that there is only one Lord through Whom all things exist, and that *one* Lord—that one Incarnation of God—is *Jesus* Christ. Supposing that it is even possible that other Christs exist is an excellent way to prepare oneself to worship demons when they appear under alluring sci-fi disguises.

Scripture rightly compares Christians who abandon their Faith and turn to the idolatry that is demon worship to adulterers; for truly, an "adulterous wife" is exactly what Israel became in its own times of worshipping idols, according to God Himself (cf. Ezekiel 16, Hosea 1, etc.). In more commonplace terms, counselors and therapists report that the most frequent excuse given by wives who become adulterers is that they "felt alone" in their marriage and sought solace from this perceived aloneness by turning to the grave evil of adultery. No observation could be more germane to the matter at hand, as Christian ET promoters—unsatisfied with Jesus being the *only* Son of God and with humans being the only rational incarnate creatures; the only race called to salvation—often promote their position with the provocative and seductive question, "**do you really think we are *alone* in the universe?**"

Indeed, a lifestyle saturated with sci-fi fantasies detailing innumerable life-filled worlds, each with their own salvation histories, has rendered many of the more ravenous consumers of these tall tales incapable of finding full inner contentment with Jesus (and Heaven, with all the angels and saints!) being "all there is." They have decided that this makes us "alone," therefore some ET promoters even openly ridicule Christians who believe in—and are at peace with—the uniqueness of Jesus and of the human race.

Continuing the analogy with adultery, counselors also report that men often succumb to this same evil after addiction to pornography. Consuming this media (which, I hasten to add, is an *intrinsic evil*, unlike science fiction!) causes these men to find themselves discontent with their wives and thereby that much more likely to succumb to adultery.

Just as spouses in a healthy marriage will stay far away from any influence that might incline them toward unfaithfulness to each other—instead of pridefully supposing that they are immune to temptation and thus need not avoid occasions of sin—so, too, will wise Christians stay far away from any proposition that dares to even implicitly ascribe "aloneness" to the incomprehensibly glorious worldview (and eternity-view) provided by the Deposit of Faith.

Therefore, addressing that rhetorical question—"are we really alone in the universe?"—is our next order of business.

8. Other Biblical Considerations

The Irreverence and Grave Danger of Asking "Are We Alone?"

In introducing conversations pertaining to extraterrestrial intelligence, it is often rhetorically asked, "are we alone in the universe?" (Christians are known to expand upon the question to attempt to maintain orthodoxy, by instead saying *"are we alone in the universe with God and the angels?"*)

But "alone" is a loaded word. By implying that the word "alone" may describe his state, he who asks that question has implied there is something deeply lacking about the state in which he apparently finds himself. Asking whether one is "alone," of course, is unproblematic in relation to a situation that does not touch upon the wisdom of God. When one is at work and has spilled coffee on his pants, he must ensure he is "alone" before changing his clothes. There is something that usually describes—and should describe—his state at work, namely, being in the presence of his colleagues. Before he proceeds to put new pants on, he must ensure this *usually proper* description of his vocational surroundings is, at this particular moment, *deficient*. And here we have arrived at the crux of the matter: to speak of "aloneness" in the absence of aliens is to imply a *deficiency* exists in the state being discussed.

> **"The Lord God said: *It is not good* that the man should be alone."** (Genesis 2:18)

"Aloneness" is regarded by no less authority than God Himself as a serious problem even from the Bible's opening pages. Had Adam been the only human being ever to be created, there would indeed be a deficiency in creation; an "aloneness." Even after the creation of the animals, "none proved to be a helper suited to the man." (Genesis 2:19) Therefore, God created Eve, and Adam immediately recognized that the prior deficiency had been resolved:

> The man said: "This one**, at last**, is bone of my bones and flesh of my flesh..." (Genesis 2:23)

If Adam and Eve were the only two human beings to have ever existed, God's glory would nevertheless have attained the outlet it needed. Creatures would have been made that were rational/spiritual (made in His image—unlike the animals) *and* material/incarnate (unlike the angels). Therefore these beings could, in themselves, recapitulate all things—material and spiritual—and therefore both receive and reflect all the characteristics of God's goodness.

But God did not stop there. He commanded these two to "be fruitful and multiply; fill the earth and subdue it." (Genesis 1:28). In the times since this command, such astounding wonders have been wrought that no one could behold them and still protest, without succumbing to implicit impiety, *"that's it!?"*

Let us ponder, then, what we already know about our place in creation—what with the billions of brothers and sisters we each have (all humans are brothers and sisters), the Communion of Saints filled with those who have gone before us in Faith yet remain present (though invisibly), the Church on earth which is the very mystical Body of Christ, Heaven and earth (and the universe) filled with more angels than we can fathom and whom we can call upon any time we like—each so unique as to truly constitute its own species—, the millions of other material *species* on this earth (here to serve us) that we are still discovering, the thousands of years of history that brought us to our day, the vastness of the earth which no man (no matter how well travelled) will ever see the tiniest fraction of, the galaxies filled with stars and planets and nebulas that glorify God's greatness and beauty, and the depths of the sea which we have scarcely begun to explore—not to mention, what infinitely surpasses all of this: the promise of union with God for all eternity in Heaven if we love Him.

To meditate on all this unfathomable wonder, which mankind—even collectively—has scarcely begun to discover and comprehend the very surface of, and to nevertheless still insist upon asking, *"but are we alone!?"*, is to reveal a profound shortcoming in one's appreciation of both Creator and creation as already revealed to us and observed by us.

This shortcoming can only honestly be described as deeply irreverent. It is as if a rich nobleman married a poor peasant woman and gave her everything: mansions and castles, innumerable riches, myriads of servants, the most exalted position among his own relatives, authority over his kingdom, and, above all, many children of their own, and this ungrateful woman nevertheless insisted upon constantly lamenting, *"But I am alone! I am alone! Where are all my other children? Where are all my other possessions? Is this really it!?"*

Faithful Christians should never waste time speculating about (much less believing in) aliens on account of their absence supposedly rendering us "alone." Those things we *already* know about the existence of are enough to fill a billion lifetimes. At the minimum, then, all suggestions of alien belief should be dismissed with the words of the Psalms:

> **Lord, my heart is not proud; nor are my eyes haughty. I do not busy myself with great matters, with things too sublime for me**. (Psalm 131:1)

***

Those inclined to rhetorically interject, *"are we really alone in the universe?"* are often similarly disposed to issue another retort. This next move they make, however, is more than posing a rhetorical question, it is announcing an outright accusation which labels disbelievers in aliens as tantamount to an offending God. Our next task is to address that fallacy.

"Limiting God": A Baseless Accusation

> "Facts cannot be proved by presumptions, yet it is remarkable that in cases where nothing stronger than presumption was even professed, scientific men have sometimes acted as if they thought this kind of argument, taken by itself, decisive of a fact which was in debate. Thus in the controversy about the Plurality of worlds, it has been considered, on purely antecedent grounds, as far as I see, to be so necessary that the Creator should have filled with living beings the luminaries which we see in the sky, and the other cosmical bodies which we imagine there, that it almost amounts to a blasphemy to doubt it." —St. John Henry Newman. *An Essay in Aid of a Grammar of Assent.* Ch. 9 §3

"**You do not believe in aliens? How dare you limit God!**" Those words are often hurled, by Christian ET promoters, against other Christians who believe that Jesus is the *only* Son of God, and that the only race into which He incarnated Himself—the human race—is likewise the *only* race of incarnate creatures in existence who bear the Divine Image. This, even though Divine Revelation repeatedly testifies to the truth of this supposed "limitation."

Now, limiting God *can* surely be a grave wrong. Every authentic development in the Church's history has had its fair share of opposition from spiritual offspring of the Pharisees, who *do* wrongly limit God, and who seem to think that the Almighty needs their permission to act (more on this point in the Appendices' concluding chapter). But the operative word there is "authentic," and the key qualifier that defines the Pharisee is the one who "wrongly" limits God.

There is also a perfectly valid way and necessary of "limiting God," although that is not what it should be called. It should, rather, simply be called *trusting God's Word.* When God has said one thing, the man who truly loves God and trusts in His goodness will rule out the possibility of any contrary view.

In fact, it is precisely the one who refuses to rule out the contradiction of what God has said who is guilty of limiting Him. Such a person is thereby accusing the Almighty of being too stupid or shortsighted to mean *exactly* what He said in Divine Revelation. Indeed, "with God all things are possible," as Jesus said in the Gospel (Matthew 19:26), but many supposed "things" are, in fact, not things at all, and therefore stand outside the realm of possibility for God. This is most obviously the case with various logical contradictions, such as a "square triangle" (which not even God could make, as it is not a thing), but "thingness" is also absent in the case of Truth existing which is contrary to what Truth Himself has revealed. The Bible itself even makes this teaching clear; for example, we are told that God "**cannot deny himself**." (2 Timothy 2:13) If, therefore, any Christian were to, in his desire to "not limit God," claim that God *could* deny Himself, then this Christian has only revealed how twisted is his idea of God.

There are many other "things," in fact, that God cannot do. Scripture frequently describes them: He cannot lie (Hebrews 6:18), He cannot change (Malachi 3:6), He cannot violate His own words (Psalm 89:34). He cannot "deceive or be deceived."[26] He cannot bless sin.[27] Christians must ignore any accusation that they are "limiting God" by holding fast to these truths, as modernists in the Church are ever demanding that they be cast aside in deference to compromise with the world, the "evolution of dogmas," the blessing of sexual immorality, and, yes, the acceptance of extraterrestrials into Christian theology.

We have already spent many pages reviewing how fundamentally discordant ET promotion is with countless truths of the Christian Faith. Therefore, whoever—even after being reminded of these contradictions—can only respond by castigating the one who disbelieves in aliens as being guilty of "limiting God," is himself the proper recipient of his own rebuke. He is accusing Almighty God of being incapable of inspiring a Sacred Text that would truly withstand the test of time; he is implying that the Bible—the Word of God—is suddenly unreliable now that two millennia have passed and we now have powerful telescopes. Whatever that supposition is, it is not Christianity.

***

Having addressed how deeply misguided—*baseless*—the "limiting God" accusation is here, it remains to consider how clumsily *irreverent* the inspiration is that brings about the accusation. We will, however, save this exposition for the appendices.

Unfallen Aliens: Equally Opposed to the Faith

> "There is **no doubt here** that precisely in the whole visible world (**cosmos**) that **one** body which is the human body bears in itself the potentiality for resurrection, that is, the aspiration and capacity to become definitively incorruptible, glorious, full of dynamism, spiritual."
>
> —Pope St. John Paul II. Theology of the Body. February 3, 1982

Some Christians reject the possibility of rational creatures on other planets who, like humans, committed their own original sin and are thus fallen and in need of Redemption—but do not reject the possibility of these creatures so long as they are unfallen. That is, they are open to belief in aliens so long as these aliens were and are preserved in their own Eden-like innocence, like what Adam and Eve enjoyed before they ate the forbidden fruit.

Most of the arguments that have been or will be presented in this book also refute the notion of unfallen aliens. Moreover, recall that in an earlier chapter, we demonstrated specifically why unfallen aliens are impossible—the Sin of Adam did not only cause earth to fall, but the entire universe. Some ET promoters, however, may suggest that at least one particular point—namely, the impossibility of multiple incarnations—can be reconciled with the existence of such creatures. The reasoning goes that since they would not need redemption, they would also not need an incarnation of God.

The latter claim, however, is false. Such aliens *would* also need an incarnation. But as demonstrating that truth will take some time, we should first note an internal inconsistency in the present alien belief thesis. This inconsistency, alone, refutes the claims of orthodoxy presented by those who support it.

Even if one grants that unfallen aliens would be in no need of an incarnation of God, this does not change the fact that the *original* plan of God, *in the creation* of these aliens, would need to include the *potentiality* of an incarnation if these aliens were to fall and thus find themselves in need of precisely that.

Those who believe in the orthodoxy of unfallen aliens but not fallen aliens have adopted a line of reasoning that neglects what it means to be made in the Image of God. To bear His Image, *by definition*, means to have an intellect and a will. A will, moreover, is—again, by definition—*free.* Whoever describes a will that is not free has not described a will at all, but only a robot. Similarly, whoever describes an intellect which can only reason along certain pre-determined paths has not described an intellect, but an algorithm. Now, as discussed earlier, we must not misunderstand: the Fall was not necessary. Original Sin was not an automatic or unavoidable consequence of free will. Adam did not have to eat the fruit. Moreover, in Heaven, there is absolutely no risk that our free wills could ever cause us to fall.

Nevertheless, it is not possible for God to create a creature with a rational free will who *could not* fall (before confirmation in grace), just as it is not possible for God to create a square circle. The *ability* to fall, before such confirmation, is ontologically inseparable from free rationality. It will not work to argue that God, knowing the future (as indeed He does!), simply knew that these alien races *would* not fall (even though they *could*), and accordingly knew there would be no need of an incarnation or redemption for them, and, finally, proceeded to create them knowing that doing so would entail no contradiction with what He revealed to us earthlings about the absolute supremacy and uniqueness of *the* Incarnation—Jesus Christ.

In accordance with His Omnipotence and Omniscience, God's plans are always perfectly coherent and consistent—never violating His own nature (*ad intra*) or His own decrees (*ad extra*)—*even if* they remain entirely in His mind without needing to be actualized within creation—within time. God, creating a being who *could* fall, must have had an intelligible plan in place—a "contingency," as it were—for what would follow if that fall transpired. That "contingency" plan—in accordance with God's *goodness*—would have been required to include an incarnation and redemption. As we have already seen, however, such possibilities are absolutely ruled out by the Faith. Therefore, the premises that lead to these disproven conclusions (i.e., unfallen aliens) are likewise disproven.

Finally, it would be equally ineffective to argue that God created these aliens and, instead of subjecting them to a test for which failure was a real possibility, immediately confirmed them in grace. Such a move would be a stark violation of God's justice. God did not do this for human beings, and He did not even do this for the angels; in fact, He "did not spare the angels when they sinned, but cast them into hell." (2 Peter 2:4). No angel was admitted to the Beatific Vision without itself passing the test. (Lucifer, and the rest of the angels who rebelled with him, never enjoyed the Beatific Vision.)

God did not even exclude the Blessed Virgin Mary from this paradigm. Although Immaculately Conceived, she too was tested. This test was simultaneous with her conception, and—needless to say—she passed it more than perfectly. Nevertheless, not even the one we dogmatically know to be the greatest creature—the greatest *possible* creature—in the universe was exempted from a test. (We will consider how orthodoxy in Mariology rules out aliens in an upcoming chapter.) The Blessed Virgin, moreover (as we will discuss in Part Two), *The* Immaculate Conception. Obviously, this means there are no others. If a race of unfallen aliens existed, then they would be Immaculate Conceptions as well, which is an abhorrent notion.

Finally, an unfallen race of rational incarnate creatures would still require an Incarnation of their own. Yet we have already discussed how contrary to the most basic dogmas of the Faith that notion stands.

Just because such creatures would not need an Incarnation *for salvation* does not mean they would not need an Incarnation for other reasons. Quite the contrary, the Incarnation itself is an Eternal decree—God Willed it from the foundation of the world, and such decrees as those are not contingent upon sin taking place. More so, it can even be argued that God's *primary prerogative* was to become incarnate among the race of rational incarnate beings He created. The Incarnation is not and was not only a "plan B." Therefore, the conjecture that unfallen aliens exist also runs afoul of basic Christian truths.

Presently, however, we are dealing more with speculative theology than with doctrine: Neither Scripture nor Magisterium explicitly settle whether Christ *would have* become Incarnate even had man not sinned. Notably, St. Thomas Aquinas claimed that He would not have; thus, unfortunately, this view has gained more popularity than it deserves. Do not misunderstand: Aquinas was no doubt the greatest theologian who ever lived. But he was not without his mistakes, and this was one of them. I am a Thomist, and I recommend Thomism to others seeking a solid philosophical and theological school of thought as a foundation. That said, Catholicism is the only infallible "-ism" one can find, and any Thomist worth his salt will concede that Thomism is bound to be incorrect on at least a few of its multitudes of propositions. On this particular point, St. Thomas was mistaken, and his contemporary, Blessed Duns Scotus, was correct. Let us enumerate some reasons why.

First, Mariology had not yet matured in the 13th century when Aquinas proposed his view that Christ would likely not become Incarnate had Adam not sinned. Since Aquinas' day, we have had the great Marian saints (such as St. Louis de Montfort and St. Maxamilian Kolbe), two new Marian dogmas (the Immaculate Conception and the Assumption), and the great modern apparitions (e.g., Lourdes, Fatima). These and other orthodox developments have vastly improved our understanding of the glories of Mary, and we cannot blame one who lived before their completion for failing to also grasp their corollaries.

What, however, does this have to do with the Incarnation? *Everything*. This development in Mariology has assured us that the Blessed Virgin is and was an *eternal* decree of the Almighty, not merely herself part of a "Plan B." We now know she is not merely a being who was conceived immaculately, but, rather, that she *is* "**The**" Immaculate Conception herself (cf. Our Lady of Lourdes). She is, as it were, "the created Immaculate Conception," whereas her spouse, the Holy Spirit, is the "uncreated Immaculate Conception." Thus St. Maxamilian Kolbe dared to call her a "quasi-Incarnation of the Holy Spirit" (obviously, the word "quasi" is extreme important there, for its absence would be baldly heretical!). Now, Catholic dogma is equally clear that Mary's supreme title is her status as Mother of God; without that singular privilege, you could say, as it were, that Mary would not be Mary. The conclusion of all this is clear: if Mary was an eternal decree—and indeed she was—then so too was the Incarnation of the Word of God; so too was Jesus Christ, God-made-man. As eternal decrees, these realities are not contingent on *anything*, therefore we cannot say that they would not have taken place were it not for sin. Obviously, the Incarnation would have looked quite different if Adam had not sinned. Christ would have come not as a suffering savior but as a Triumphant King (as He will at the end of the world), to—at the fitting time—receive the Kingship of earth from Adam. But He would have come nevertheless.

Second, we must consider that the contingency of the Incarnation is just one (not particularly prominent) of a multitude of Thomistic (i.e., Dominican) propositions. The *absolute primacy* of the Incarnation, however, is so prominent in the Franciscan tradition that it has been called "**The** Franciscan Thesis." We can leave aside here a recounting of the details of Franciscan vs. Dominican rivalry. We need only realize that both traditions are clearly extremely important parts of Sacred Tradition's development; both are Willed by God and essential for the Church. It is, therefore, unpalatable to assert that the *primary* (theological) thesis of either one of those entire traditions would be errant. It is quite conceivable, however, that a mere one of many secondary (or tertiary) propositions of such a tradition would be mistaken. Indeed, many such lesser propositions of the Franciscan theological school of thought are doubtless erroneous.

Fr. Maximilian Mary Dean put it accurately and beautifully when he wrote:

> At the heart of theology is the mystery of charity: within the Trinity, and then in the economy of salvation. "God is love" (1 Jn 4:8), God who is Father, Son and Holy Spirit. Consequently, all of His decrees are decrees of love and all of His actions are acts of love. The Most Holy Trinity, who is an eternal, loving communion of three Divine Persons in one Divine Essence, freely willed to communicate His love to a created nature outside Himself. **He willed to do this in the most perfect way possible, namely by the union of the created, human nature of Christ with the divine nature in the Person of Word. ... Christ, then, because He is predestined to grace and glory for His own sake, is not "occasioned" by anything. Rather, if anything exists outside of God it exists precisely for Christ**. ... And our King has an absolute primacy which is not contingent upon man's need for redemption. In the divine intention God chose that the Eternal Word assume His human nature by being "born of a woman" (Gal 4:4). As a result, the Blessed Virgin Mary is predestined as the Mother of the Incarnate Word in the same decree that predestines Christ. She too is predestined absolutely as the universal Queen and Mother; she too has primacy over all creation—a subordinate primacy inseparable from that of Christ. This means that God, before creating the universe, first foresees Christ the King and His Mother, the Queen. "Before the foundation of the world" (Eph 1:4) God predestines Them. He foreordains that They be perfectly glorified by His divine love and foresees that They will respond perfectly to that love. ... **God further wills to create angels and men that they might be "holy and without blemish in His sight"** (Eph 1:4). ... While this plan is fixed and remains substantially the same independently of any consideration of sin, the fact is that Adam and Eve—created to prefigure Christ and Mary and to be blessed in Them—disobeyed God's law and fell. God, foreseeing Adam's fall, willed also the remedy to our sin: redemption. Here is where all the thomists and scotists unite: on blood-stained Calvary. After the fall, all graces—both the elevating grace of

deification and the redeeming grace of reconciliation with God—flow from the Pierced Hearts of the Redeemer and Coredemptrix.[28]

***

We should conclude this section, however, with a reiteration that the notion of even unfallen aliens runs afoul of the Faith in countless ways we have already discussed and will continue to discuss. Anyone can easily recognize this, even if he disagrees with the conclusions above on the absolute primacy of the Incarnation.

Abuse of Aquinas' Theology by ET promoters: Multiple Incarnations "Derogatory"

Catholic ET promoters frequently misuse the Christology of St. Thomas Aquinas in seeking to argue that the idea of multiple (extraterrestrial) incarnations of the Word of God can be reconciled with Christianity. Dr. Thigpen wrote:

> God's power is infinite, [Aquinas] insisted, and His capacity to become incarnate is not exhausted by a single instance or even multiple instances of that action. In addition to His incarnation in Christ, then, God could have chosen to join to His divine nature "another numerically different human nature..."[29]

The implications that appear intended in this author's presentation of the quote above misrepresent Aquinas' position. Indeed, in the *Summa Theologica* (cf., III, Q4, A5 and Q3, A7), St. Thomas discusses the hypothetical question of multiple incarnations. However, he makes it clear that his only aim is to ensure that one does not wrongly limit God's Omnipotence, writing, "the power of a Divine Person is infinite...Hence it may not be said that a Divine Person so assumed one human nature as to be **unable** to assume another."

What Aquinas is certainly *not* doing here is proposing that such a thing, even if not logically contradictory (i.e., something God Himself is "**unable**" to do), is actually a possibility *we should be entertaining*. The Angelic Doctor constantly argues that God absolutely has not, does not, and will not actually do certain things that He *could* do simply because He is Omnipotent. For example, in the *Summa*—Part I, Question 104, Article 3—he argues that God can indeed annihilate things—even the entire universe and all it contains (including our souls). Yet, he spends the entire next article arguing that *absolutely* nothing is, or ever will be, annihilated! He even insists, "we **must** conclude **by denying absolutely** that anything at all will be annihilated." (I, Q104, A4) The same is true of multiple incarnations. Even if this idea is not intrinsically logically contradictory, it is false—not to mention blasphemous—for other reasons, and we "must" deny it "absolutely."

In Aquinas' day, no serious Christian writer had been so deluded as to propose belief in multiple incarnations of God, as today's Christian and Catholic ET promoters do. Had Aquinas known that, several hundred years after his own day, Christians would begin doing precisely this, we should have no doubt he would have followed up the sections on the Incarnation noted above by likewise declaring, "*we must conclude by denying absolutely that there ever has been or ever will be another Incarnation of God*"!

Elsewhere in the *Summa,* Aquinas even ponders the question of whether God could simply assume *all* natures! That is, he discusses the scenario wherein each and every one of us is *literally* the Word of God Himself. Aquinas declares that *even this* is possible! But his purpose in bringing the matter up was not to *entertain* the possibility, but rather to determine if it was "becoming" (i.e., *fitting*) for Him to do so—and to answer this question, Aquinas of course gives a resolute "no."

This passage is extremely important because it highlights the absurdity of some of these concepts. Obviously, Aquinas would be scandalized if any Christian would dare assert that each and every one of us might literally be the Second Person of the Holy Trinity. This would mean each of us must be worshipped—an extreme form of idolatry. Thankfully, I know of no Catholic ET promoters (yet) advocating for this notion. They should take note, however, that the passage from Aquinas they misleadingly use to support the possibility of aliens is essentially spoken in the same breath as the present passage.

More than merely denying the reality of multiple Incarnations, Aquinas essentially—and rightly—castigates one who would dare propose such a scenario, for he declares that **"[multiple Incarnations] would have been derogatory to the dignity of the incarnate Son of God... as He is the First-born of all creatures.**" (III, Q4, A5) Note that even *two* Incarnations would be equally "derogatory" to Jesus' status as *first* born—the one and only Incarnation of God in the universe.

While I have seen many Catholic ET promoters abuse Aquinas' teachings on this point to promote aliens, I have not yet found even one of them acknowledging that this great saint bluntly declares that view to be *derogatory* to the dignity of Jesus Christ. This is a great scandal.

On this point and others, those who read the *Summa* are sure to fall into grave error if they do so incapable of distinguishing when Aquinas is discussing what is logically possible, what is theologically possible, what is theologically fitting, what is orthodox, what is unorthodox, what is likely, what is certain, etc. In pointing out that the Word of God "could" have assumed multiple natures, this was nothing but a subtle academic point within the domain of advanced philosophical theology. It is radically unjust to Aquinas (who himself opposed the ET Deception before it formally began; insisting there is *only one earth* and *one Incarnation*) to use it as grounds for speculating about extraterrestrial incarnations of the Word of God.*

Angels and Demons: "Extraterrestrials," but Entirely Earthly in Focus

There are no aliens, but there certainly are "extraterrestrials" in one sense of the word: there are angels (and demons). These purely spiritual beings can be wherever the like—in fact, they *are* wherever their wills are active—therefore there is perhaps little reason to doubt that they undertake all manner of fascinating interactions with the stars and planets throughout the galaxies. (Recall that my aim with this book is anything but "demystifying" the cosmos.)

One thing, however, is absolutely clear about these "extraterrestrial" beings: their main focus within the material universe is *entirely* earthly, and this is irreconcilable with the proposition that earth is just one of multiple (even innumerable) planets like it throughout the universe (that is, hosting incarnate intelligent life).

None other than Jesus Himself, in the Gospel, saw it fit to reveal the nature of the fall of Satan himself:

> **Jesus said, "I have observed Satan fall like lightning from the sky**. (Luke 10:18)

Now, regardless of how many demons exist (we obviously cannot know the exact number, though it is certainly massive), it is clear that Satan is the "highest" (or, if you will, the lowest—most evil and most powerful in his malice) among them. Yet in his fall, he was cast down to *earth*. The Book of Revelation makes this even clearer:

---

* We should conclude by noting that Aquinas may even be mistaken on this point. One prominent theologian argued exactly this. I will present selections of his argument below, without commenting on whether he or Aquinas is the victor: "the ultimate subject of Jesus' life is God the Son... any other purported incarnation, here or elsewhere, would have the same ultimate subject and thus be the same person. In the context of Resurrection belief, this would entail the presence, in the eschaton, of a number of finite personal vehicles of the divine life, all of them coexistent and theoretically capable of interpersonal relation. This makes no sense...If Jesus was the same person as God the Son, so would other Incarnations be. They would all have to be the same person...God would be conferring his personal individuality upon another finite, rational, personal, nature, and, again, one and the same individual would result. God Incarnate would now have three natures, not two. But the two different finite natures would be individualized by the same metaphysical subject, and would have to be thought of as the same person. Again, there would not, after all, be two individuals but only one. The same point, of course, can be made about this speculation being ruled out by eschatological considerations...Since multiple Incarnations are not possible ... there are no other rational natures in the universe apart from the humankind whom Jesus, God Incarnate, came to save." —Professor Brian Hebblethwaite, "The Impossibility of Multiple Incarnations."

> The huge dragon, the ancient serpent, who is called **the Devil and Satan, who deceived the whole world, was thrown down to earth, and its angels were thrown down with it**. (Revelation 12:9)

Therefore, as far as the material universe is concerned, earth is beyond doubt the abode of not only the chief demon (Satan), but also *all* the demons. The only palatable explanation for this is precisely the one all Christians of all pre-Enlightenment times have always taken for granted: earth alone is the theater of eternal destinies. It is the only place in the material universe that has spiritual relevance, as it is the only one that is the abode of rational incarnate creatures.

PART TWO: THE CATHOLIC CASE

> **Man, then, is unique within the cosmos. He alone of all kinds of beings is the object of God's personal solicitude** both for his own sake and for the sake of his species.
> —*New Catholic Encyclopedia.* Entry on "Man."

The Holy Bible—both in its Old and its New Testaments—teaches us that human beings are the only rational incarnate creatures that exist, therefore all Christians should reject alien belief.

Catholics, however, should find it even easier to rule out ET belief. Although we indeed regard Scripture alone as comprising Public Revelation and deserving the absolutely highest level of reverence among all texts, this is not our only source of authority. We also can discover truths, *with certainty*, from Sacred Tradition, and from the Magisterium which authoritatively interprets both Scripture and Tradition. Looking at these sources, we see aliens ruled out *even more* clearly than they are in Scripture.

When considering the entirety of Tradition and Magisterium, one is confronted with an immense slew of texts, therefore it is usually best for a Catholic to begin this journey by consulting—and submitting to—the simplest authoritative summary of it all: the *Catechism of the Catholic Church.*

9. The Catechism

> "Man occupies a **unique** place in creation: (I) he is 'in the image of God'; (II) in his own nature he unites the spiritual and material worlds; (III) he is created 'male and female'; (IV) God established him in his friendship."
> —*Catechism of the Catholic Church,* §355

Man's uniqueness has always been taken for granted in Catholic teaching; a fact which the Catechism—faithfully summarizing 2,000 years of Sacred Tradition—settles in the opening paragraph of its teaching on Man, quoted above. This text, moreover, uses the word "unique" because that is precisely what it means—"being **the only** one" (Merriam Webster Dictionary).

Catholic ET promoters are known to protest that, even if innumerable alien civilizations populate the galaxies, "mankind can still be considered *special* in another sense!" This protestation, however, is a straw man; no one is claiming that the human race would be incapable of being "special" in light of aliens. The Church does not proclaim that man is merely "rare," or "special," or "extraordinary" in the qualities described above. Quite the contrary, it declares that, in the entire universe ("creation")—not merely planet earth—man is the "unique" (*the only*) being made in God's Image: the only being who is truly more than just a creature of the Creator, but even a *friend of God*.

Some will respond that this cannot be the proper interpretation of the passage above, since being "created 'male and female'" is also listed as one of the "unique" qualities of man, whereas we know that even animals can be distinguished as male or female individuals. While it is obviously true that animals can be sorted accordingly, it is not true that they are "created male and female" *as* humans are, in the sense relayed by the Catechism passage above.

The opening chapter of the Bible, Genesis 1, transmits God's creation of the world, and not once does it say that He created a being "male and female" until the creation of man in verse twenty-seven. It does not do so earlier; not in reference to the sea creatures or birds (v. 21), and not in reference to the land animals (v. 24). The point is not that biological sex does not exist in animals. Clearly, it does! The point, rather, is that gender or sex is a fundamental reality in the human person more than in any other creature. It is not only a biological reality, but also a spiritual one. In *that* sense, indeed, only humans—in all creation—are truly "created male and female."*

In a word: a human being's sex is who he or she *is,* more than with any mere animal. The difference is not one of degree, but of kind. Animals are fundamentally individual—determined entirely by biology and instinct. Humans, on the other hand, are fundamentally relational—fundamentally social—and their social dimension is fundamentally determined by their sexuality (i.e., their status as male or female) and their relation to the opposite sex.

> The Bible affirms that man exists in relation with other persons, with God, with the world, and with himself. According to this conception, man is not an isolated individual but a person—an essentially relational being. Far from entailing a pure actualism that would deny its permanent ontological status, the fundamentally relational character of the imago Dei itself constitutes its ontological structure and the basis for its exercise of freedom and responsibility.[30]
> From the beginning, "male and female he created them" (Gen 1:27).

---

* Even Aristotle, writing centuries before Christ and without the benefit of Divine Revelation, was able to perceive this distinction: "The friendship between husband and wife appears to be a natural instinct; since man is by nature a pairing creature even more than he is a political creature, inasmuch as the family is an earlier and more fundamental institution than the State ... whereas with the other animals the association of the sexes aims only at continuing the species, human beings [marry] not only for the sake of begetting children but also to provide the needs of life... (*Nicomachean Ethics*. Book 8. §12.)"

> This partnership of man and woman constitutes the first form of communion between persons" (GS 12 # 4). (*Catechism of the Catholic Church*, §383)

If, however, anyone fails to see how paragraph 355 of the Catechism rules out aliens, he will not likewise miss the teaching in the paragraph that follows.

Paragraph 356 Rules Out Aliens

> **"Of all visible creatures, only man is able to know and love his creator... and he alone is called to share... in God's own life"** —*Catechism of the Catholic Church*, §356

As is evident above, the *Catechism of the Catholic Church* rules out the possibility of aliens. It teaches that, out of the *entire material creation* ("*all visible* creatures"), *only* human beings were made in such a way that they can know and love God: which is the same as saying that only human beings are *rational*. This is not an "interpretation" of the Catechism (much less a "fundamentalist" one!), as Catholic ET promoters suggest. It is simply what the Catechism *says*. The context, moreover, *affirms* this meaning (it does not detract from it).

One corollary of this truth is that all non-human animals on earth are irrational. Although our present purpose is to settle that this teaching rules out aliens, we should first note that many ET promoters, including even Christian ones, associate their belief in extraterrestrials with a broad belief in "non-human intelligences," including even the beasts of the earth (as we will see in Part Five). The outlandishness of this position—and its manifest contradiction to the entirety of the relevant teachings found within Scripture, Magisterium, and Sacred Tradition—is just one of the countless rotten fruits of ET belief, which we will consider in Part Four. Dr. Davison, whom we have already quoted, argued—in his scholarly 2023 tome promoting aliens—that:

> In recent years, **burgeoning theological interest in animals has led some to question whether the association of human beings with the image of God prevents other animals from being described that way.** ... Some degree of intelligence ... seems to have evolved independently in apes, corvids and dolphins. Admittedly, **as far as we know**, evolution has not converged elsewhere on Earth on a capacity for abstract thought...[31]

Indeed, the same bankrupt theological arguments that are offered in support of extraterrestrials are invariably used to insist animals, too, are (or at least may be, or "may become") rational. ET promotion is a slippery slope. It inevitably degenerates into baser still propositions.

Returning to the Catechism's rejection of alien belief, I add that we are presently considering an abridged version of paragraph 356 merely to emphasize the relevant teaching, but afterwards we will consider the entirety of it as well. Due to the importance of this paragraph, we should carefully consider each phrase therein, to ensure all misinterpretations are precluded.

"Of all visible creatures..."

First, we must acknowledge that "all" means exactly what it says. This term cannot be arbitrarily restricted to mean simply "earth" by individual Catholics who would like to excuse themselves from submission to the teaching of the paragraph it introduces.

Whoever is tempted to do that can overcome such a tendency by simply considering that even extraterrestrial phenomena are part of the ordinary lives of every person alive. Undoubtedly, therefore, these phenomena are not excluded from Scriptural or Magisterial references to "all" things. Each day, we see (and are greatly affected by) the sun, the moon, and the stars. These objects are "beyond-earth," i.e., "extra-terrestrial." When, therefore, a universal claim is made by the Church (when the word "all" is used to describe the scope of its intention), we have no grounds to pretend that this claim does not apply to what is outside of the earth. One is only being disingenuous by supposing it instead only pertains to the mere fraction of a trillion cubic miles that constitute this particular planet. Such a person has simply replaced "all" with "some."

"Of all visible creatures..."

"*Visible* creatures" is an unambiguous phrase which refers to everything that God has made in the entire material universe; that is, the phrase encompasses the whole *corporeal* realm. Whether or not we can, pragmatically, "see" some individual material thing is irrelevant. (Hence the Catholic Church's wise revision of the Nicene Creed's translation in the Mass in 2011, from "seen and unseen" to "visible and invisible.") In such cases, it remains true that this thing in question, whatever it may be, is nevertheless by nature "visible" if it is existing as an individual substance and is not pure spirit. Planets too far for our telescopes to observe, depths of the earth that no human will ever lay eyes upon, yet undiscovered sea creatures, and all comparable things, are indeed truly *visible*, irrespective of the fact that we do not see them.*

The purpose of this qualification, "visible," in the Catechism's teaching above is to ensure angels are not misrepresented. Angels are creatures (God created them), they are not men, yet they can certainly know and

---

* In theological discourse, the term "visible" never has carried with it the connotation that it describes only things we succeed in observing with our eyes. Consider how false and relativistic it would be to assert that, if everyone went blind, everything would thereby be rendered "invisible." Philosophically sound thinking rejects this subjectivism wherein the nature of a thing is regarded as fundamentally contingent upon whether or how it is perceived.

love God! These creatures, however, truly are not in any way visible (they are pure spirit). Obviously, they have power over the material realm and therefore can manifest themselves visibly and even assume corporeal forms (as we will discuss in Part Four), but they *themselves* are entirely immaterial; entirely "invisible."

Some theologian ET promoters have even used this phrase to accuse the Catechism here of being *wrong*, or at least "poorly articulated" and in need of being "reformulated" (which, they falsely assure their audiences, will happen soon). They make this claim by erroneously describing angels as "visible" creatures (and rightly observing the fact that angels obviously can and do know and love God). This is nothing but a ploy made by some self-important scholars to seduce their readers into granting more credence to their own wild conjectures than to the Church's Magisterium. Their claim that angels *are* visible contradicts Catholic dogma. If even angels must be categorized as "visible" (merely because they do, at times, *assume a visible form*), then the "visible vs. invisible" distinction—one contained in the very Nicene Creed itself—is entirely incoherent. Needless to say, it is these theologians, not Catholic Dogma, who are incoherent. As Pope St. John Paul II taught, "**the angels ... are invisible**, for they are purely spiritual beings."[32] As the Compendium of the Catechism of the Catholic Church teaches, "**The angels are purely spiritual creatures, incorporeal, invisible**, immortal, and personal beings endowed with intelligence and will." (Ch. 1 Q60)

Therefore, attempts can only fail which seek to exclude the proposal of aliens from censure by the implicit condemnations contained within this paragraph of the Catechism.

"<u>Only</u> man is <u>able</u> to know and love his creator"

Now that we have settled that the Catechism, in this paragraph, is describing the *entirety* of the material universe, we are prepared to understand precisely what is ruled out by the clause above. And the clear reading is this: of all physical creatures, "*only* man"—that is, only human beings, all of whom, Scripture and the Church infallibly teach, are descendants of Adam and Eve—are *even capable* of knowing and loving God. For all other corporeal beings, knowing and loving their Creator is categorically ruled out by their very natures.

Any creature with reason, however, is definitionally *capable* of knowing and loving God. This fact is not only settled in Catholic teaching, as we will presently consider, but is also necessary to grant in accordance with the infinite goodness of God. It is a logical corollary to a dogma so basic that it stands as a preamble of the Faith. For it is impossible to imagine a Divine Truth more foundational than *God's goodness*, yet it is also this very Truth telling us that God would never create a being with reason who *could not* know and love Him. It would be nothing short of blasphemy to accuse God of making any intelligent creature without giving this creature—this *child* of His (*for if it is a being with reason, then it is made in God's image, and it is His child*) the opportunity to know and love its Creator—its Father—forever. We can be certain this never has happened and never will happen. Yet, the Catechism teaches that only man is *even capable* of knowing and loving God. Therefore, only man has reason.

In the passage below, the Catechism teaches that God's existence can be *known* with *certainty* (not merely "regarded with confidence") by simple, natural reason and nothing more.

> **The Church teaches** that the one true God, our Creator and Lord, can be **known with certainty** from his works, by the natural light of human reason (cf. Vatican Council I, can. 2 § 1: DS 3026) (Catechism of the Catholic Church, §47)

So it is imperative for all the Faithful to understand that God's existence absolutely is *knowable* from reason *alone*. Which is to say, God can be known from that capacity of the soul which *any* rational being enjoys, by virtue of his rationality.

If aliens existed, they too would be capable of knowing and loving God. Their faculty of intelligence would guarantee that capacity. Yet, according to the Catechism, no beings other than man have that capacity, and from this it follows that there are no aliens.

"<u>And</u> he [man] alone is called to share... in God's own life."

The final portion of our present consideration is a reiteration of what came before it. *Only* human beings are called to be partakers of the Divine Nature. Note that this is an *additional* teaching (the word "and" is used), not a qualification on or limitation of the prior teaching—it will not work to claim that aliens can exist so long as they are not called to share in God's life. (Abhorrent and erroneous as that move itself would be!)

***

Catholic ET promoters use several strategies to attempt to evade the teachings presented above, and we will refute each strategy in the respective sections below.

The Phrase, "On This Earth," is No Defense of Alien Belief

The first attempt made by ET promoters to evade the Catechism's rejection of aliens derives from considerations relevant to the clause that we did not include in the abridged quote above (since it did not alter the substance of what we were considering). What follows is the entirety of the first two sentences of paragraph 356:

> Of all visible creatures only man is "able to know and love his creator."[GS 12 §3] He is "the only creature on earth that God has willed for its own sake,"[GS 24§3] and he alone is called to share, by knowledge and love, in God's own life.

The attempt to reconcile belief in aliens with the Catechism here is predictable to anyone who is acquainted with the antics of various voices in the Church who dissent on sexual morality: proposing that adjacent teachings in the Catechism are fundamentally in conflict, and proceeding to insist that Catholics are free to choose whichever conflicting teaching will serve as the basis for their own personal beliefs.

In fact, the first sentence of paragraph 356 is not restricted in scope by what is described in the second sentence. While the latter sentence indicates that, "on earth," only man is willed for his own sake (whereas plants, animals, etc., exist for the sake of man), this specification is absent from the first sentence. As this paragraph's first sentence rules out the possibility of intelligent life among "**all** visible creatures," with no qualification on "all" included, no one is entitled to interpret the following sentence's distinct assertion—even if one takes it as being more limited in its own scope—as *also* limiting the scope of the sentence that precedes it. Indeed, a faithful reading of the Catechism is entirely unambiguous: *both* teachings remain true. Only man is rational among "**all** visible creatures," *and* only man is willed for his own sake "on earth."

***

The remark included above on those who dissent on sexual morality merits further explanation. I am referring to paragraph 2357. There, we read:

> ...tradition has always declared that 'homosexual acts are intrinsically disordered'... under no circumstances can they be approved. (CCC §2357)

This teaching could scarcely be made any clearer, and no Catholic who wishes to be faithful to the Magisterium should have any trouble immediately understanding what is being relayed. Such manifest clarity, however, does not prevent certain theologians and clergymen from immediately retorting, whenever this teaching on homosexual acts is recognized:

"Ah, but you are wrong! The very next paragraph says "[Homosexuals] must be accepted with respect, compassion, and sensitivity. Every sign of unjust discrimination in [homosexual's] regard should be avoided.'" (CCC §2358) Therefore, what we actually need to do is approve of this lifestyle, since any consideration of homosexual acts as "disordered" would entail "unjust discrimination" or "disrespect."

This retort is deceptive. It is offered under the false premise that these adjacent teachings presented in the Catechism are contradictory, and that Catholics therefore must choose which one they will obey. In fact, what Catholics must do is clear: they must regard homosexual acts as "intrinsically disordered," *never* to be "approved," while at the same time ensuring that individual persons afflicted with same-sex attraction are treated with "respect, compassion, and sensitivity," and not "unjustly discriminated" against. Holding both teachings entails no contradiction.

In my own experiences, I have often observed an identical situation play out when the clear teaching of paragraph 356's first teaching is acknowledged with respect to aliens. Those who believe in aliens are known to immediately retort by quoting the second sentence.*

The Possibility of Ever Meeting Aliens on Earth is Even More Strongly Condemned

There is yet another conspicuous (but ignored) count on which the "on this earth" defense addressed above fails. Almost all Catholic ET promoters claim aliens *already have* been on earth for decades, if not centuries or even millennia! (Or, at the minimum, they anticipate contact soon.) It is, therefore, nonsensical for them to argue that their position is licit even as they concede that belief in intelligent non-humans on earth is ruled out. Recalling what is rebutted by the very sentence of the Catechism these ET promoters defer to as supposedly permitting their position, we read that:

> **[Man] is "the only creature on earth that God has willed for its own sake**" [GS 24§3] (CCC §356)

Observe that the Magisterium does not restrict the scope of its teaching to indicate merely that "of those *born* on this earth and of earthly *ancestry*," only man is willed for his own sake. Instead, it declares that man is the *only* creature "**on** earth"—without qualification—who is an end in and of itself.

Therefore, this teaching independently rules out the possibility that any "alien encounters" or "UFO sightings" can be validly explained by aliens. Even if one insists upon regarding the second sentence of paragraph 356 in isolation—even if he foolishly goes so far as to insist it can *overrule* the sentence preceding it—he is still forced to acknowledge that the Magisterium here dismisses the possibility of beings existing on earth, *other than humans*, who are "willed for [their] own sake," or "called to share... in God's own life," as *any* rational being always is.†

---

* Here it should be noted that the Catechism has seen dozens of revisions since its initial publication over 30 years ago (in 1992). Despite raging debate on aliens in the intervening decades, not a single such change has concerned itself with paragraph 356. The phrasing of that paragraph has not been revisited because it does not need to be revisited: the Holy Spirit, Who guides the Church's Magisterium, has ensured that this paragraph's repudiation of aliens stands undiminished, despite common (fallible and non-magisterial) opinion in the Vatican seeming to move towards acceptance of alien belief in those same decades.

† I will repeat here that *any* rational being is, by virtue of its rationality, "willed for its own sake." To illustrate this reality, we need only consider the example of Guardian Angels. It is a dogma of the Faith that each human being is assigned an angel to serve as a guardian (cf. CCC §336). Accordingly, each person should regularly invoke his guardian angel! Unfortunately, however, many souls are in fact lost (cf. Matthew 25:42): that is, they are damned to hell for all eternity. Does this mean that the

Doubtless due to the extreme injustice inherent in such an assertion, no alien-believer has yet to provide any serious argument that aliens—rational, incarnate creatures like us—would be created by God merely as means subjected to the ends of other rational creatures. Such a claim would be abhorrent. As Pope St. John Paul II taught:

> **The person is the kind of good which does not admit of use and cannot be treated as an object of use and as such the means to an end.** (*Love and Responsibility*, pg. 41)

A "person," however, is an "individual substance of rational nature."* Therefore, aliens would of course be "persons" (this corollary is not denied by any ET promoters). Accordingly, it would be both wrong and impossible to reconcile with the Magisterium the notion that aliens could be anything but "willed for their own sake."

Therefore, man is (now and forever) the only material being on earth that is a person. While Paragraph 356's initial sentence absolutely rules out *all* aliens, the following sentence independently and definitively rules out any possibility of meeting them on earth.†

***

A still more subtle and theologically underhanded method to evade the teaching presently under consideration exists. Those who proffer it

---

angels who had been assigned to those souls have thereby been deprived of their inherent worth? Are they damned to hell along with their charges that were lost? Of course not. These propositions are absurd, yet if these guardian angels were not willed *for their own sake*, then these absurdities would need to be granted. Each angel—being a rational creature—was, like each human, willed for its own sake in its creation. Even if its mission is affected, its own ontological worth is not.

* Cf. Boethius, Aquinas, etc. Each human is a person, each angel is a person, along with the Father, Son, and Holy Spirit.

† Still weaker efforts are made to escape even the second sentence of Paragraph 356's proscriptions. Some attempt to evade it by insisting that this teaching only applied when it was written. They say, it was indeed true that "on this earth" there were none other than humans —Adam and Eve's descendants—who could know and love God. But, they insist, there could come future times where that is not so. Recall, however, that this teaching is not presented as a disciplinary regulation, but rather a Magisterial instruction on Faith and Morals. Contrast its own wording to, for example, paragraph 1580, which deals with the Latin Church's noble practice on requiring priestly celibacy—even while explicitly noting that this is a *discipline*; one which is legitimately not required in Eastern Catholic Rites. Like any of the Church's teachings which exceed the merely disciplinary (such as those against artificial contraception, abortion, etc.), its teaching that only man bears God's image has no expiration date and it cannot be overturned. Second, *even if* the teaching could expire or be overturned, this would also fail to account for the views of most of the vocal alien believers we have already discussed: they argue that not only are various modern phenomena explainable only by aliens, but also that such alien-caused phenomena have been occurring throughout history. No manner by which this matter can be approached, therefore, results in a scenario wherein aliens may be licitly posited as plausible or possible, much less as the best explanation.

point to Pope Pius XII's teaching in his 1950 encyclical *Humani Generis*, wherein he taught that the Beatific Vision is a gratuitous gift from God. In the corresponding section of this book's appendices, we will discuss why this teaching carries no weight in support of the argument for aliens. Also in the appendices, we will address the fallacy that treats disbelieving in aliens on account of the Catechism as "taking the Catechism too seriously" or even "fundamentalism."

Is it the Blunder of "Proof-Texting" or "Fundamentalism" to Believe What the Catechism Says on Aliens?

> **"[The Catechism] transmits what the Church teaches, whoever rejects it as a whole separates himself beyond question from the faith..."**—Cardinal Ratzinger. *Introduction to the Catechism of the Catholic Church.* Chapter 2.)
>
> **"The Catechism of the Catholic Church**, which I approved 25 June last and the publication of which I today order by virtue of my Apostolic Authority, **is a statement of the Church's faith and of Catholic doctrine**, attested to or illumined by Sacred Scripture, Apostolic Tradition and the Church's Magisterium. **I declare it to be a** valid and legitimate instrument for ecclesial communion and a **sure norm for teaching the faith.**"
>
> —Pope St. John Paul II. *Fidei Depositum.* §IV

It would be helpful to remind ourselves of the entire point of the Catechism: namely, *accessibility*.

The Catechism is such a powerful tool because all of its teachings are so clear—requiring no advanced exegetical approaches to understand it and needing no scholars to serve as middlemen for the ordinary lay faithful. Moreover—as we will discuss in the corresponding appendix—the Catechism was such a *Providential* gift to the Church because it was given precisely at the time it was most needed: the time when what Catholics have always believed was being rebelled against in unprecedented numbers and with unprecedented ferocity by scholarly "innovators" who proposed all manner of "groundbreaking" teachings at odds with Sacred Tradition and without foundation in Scripture (among such outlandish assertions being the notion that man is merely one of many races of intelligent incarnate creatures).

Some Catholic ET promoters, however, dismissively apply the label of "proof texters" to those Catholics who submit to the clear teaching contained in paragraph 356 of the Catechism and accordingly reject aliens.

Generally speaking, such dismissals are unbecoming of serious discourse. If a cited authoritative text (from Scripture or elsewhere) seems to contradict a certain proposition, then this appearance must, in justice, be addressed directly; not simply rhetorically dismissed. Appeals to authority may be the worst form of argument in most contexts, but in the context of theology, they are the best arguments; since theology is built upon the authority of Divine Revelation.

It is, however, particularly unusual to hear the label of "proof-texting" used pejoratively in relation to the Catechism. In theological debates, this dismissal is used almost exclusively in relation to Scripture. Its appropriate employment is generally restricted to criticizing those who are incapable of grasping the Bible's seventy-three books as an organic whole, and who instead isolate minuscule portions of Scripture—ignoring context, genre, and counterbalancing verses elsewhere—in attempting to bolster their own errant ideas. A quintessential example would be found among Christians who cite Ephesians 2 in order to argue that one is saved by "faith alone," while, for example, ignoring James 2:24, which teaches that a man is "justified by works and not by faith alone." Applying the "proof-texting" rebuke to one citing the Catechism against aliens is, therefore, a category mistake. It is levied under the presupposition that the Catechism requires an exegetical approach similar to Scripture—which, considering what has been noted above, would undermine the very purpose of the Catechism.

More problematic still, this "proof-texting" accusation is vacuous: it ignores that no counterbalancing teachings exist anywhere in the Catechism. Not one of its 2,865 paragraphs indicate or imply that aliens may exist. Not one paragraph therein even gives Catholics grounds for speculating that incarnate creatures other than man may have intelligence.

A final attempt to reconcile the Catechism with alien belief may be found in the protestation that "*the authors of the Catechism simply didn't have aliens in mind when they wrote paragraph 356; all they had in mind was teaching that plants and animals are irrational.*" Now, this move can (and should) be summarily dismissed on account of the inability of those who proffer it to read the minds of the authors of the Catechism.

It can, however, be refuted on an even more fundamental level. Ultimately, it is irrelevant what the authors of the Catechism "had in mind." We need not psychoanalyze them. The Divine Protection enjoyed by the Magisterium operates distinctly from the Divine Protection enjoyed by Sacred Scripture. In the latter case, the intention of the human author is truly identical to the intention of the Holy Spirit—the true and Divine Author of each word of Scripture (cf. *Providentissimus Deus*, §20). Only the Bible enjoys this supremely exalted privilege. In the former case, God simply preserves the Magisterium from falling into error. Therefore, efforts to—with great prayerful meditation and rigorous scholarship—dive deeply into considerations of the context, intentions, desires, etc., of the human author of a given Magisterial text, would be misguided; akin to holding a magnifying glass against a picture of a leaf instead of against the leaf itself, in seeking new discoveries about the latter's cellular structure. It is always commendable to put Sacred Scripture under a magnifying glass. Since God is its author, there is an inexhaustible treasure of truths to be found within it. Humans, however, write the Magisterium, and God simply protects it. Therefore, little more is needed for a Catholic than to read, and submit to, the clear dictates of the Church's teaching. Approaching the Catechism's 356th paragraph accordingly means rejecting aliens.

When they realize that the "proof-texting" accusation will not work, Catholic ET promoters resort to the next customary slander by denouncing those who submit to the Catechism's teaching here as "taking a *fundamentalist* approach to the Magisterium." As we saw earlier when discussing Scripture, the approach used here with the Magisterium is identical to the approach used by Catholic advocates of transgenderism. For example, we have the writings of Sr. Elizabeth Johnson, PhD, a professor emerita of theology at Fordham University. She has long been a prominent radical feminist, even teaching that "*the time has come to stop addressing God as Father, Son and Holy Spirit, and to begin addressing Him as 'She Who Is.'*"[33] In a 2023 article advocating for transgender ideology,[34] she rejects Church dogma against Polygenism, insists that "past Church teachings" cannot address present matters, and dismisses Genesis 1 as a "myth"—saying that we need a "sophisticated reading" which merely "honors *the religious intent*" of the Bible while allowing "scientific knowledge" to overturn what Scripture actually teaches. This scholar assures us that *we* get to decide what "the *point* is" of certain Scriptural or Magisterial teachings, and she concludes that we need only abide by *our* assessment of that "point." According to her, the Book of Genesis "was not *intended* to define God's will for a gender binary ... *this text is not dealing with* the question of LGBTQ persons."[35] In brief, she insists "***Church teachings found in the Catechism** and Vatican declarations need to be interpreted rather than read off in a simplistic, fundamentalist manner,*"[36] and it is with this rebuke of supposed "fundamentalism" that Sr. Elizabeth embraces the whole gamut of "LGBT" ideology.

This is not merely a *similar* argument to the one used by the Catholic ET promoters to defend their thesis—*it is the exact same one*. They claim it is "fundamentalism" to abide by the inescapable logical corollaries of Scriptural and Magisterial teachings which rule out aliens. They pretend to justify this accusation by asserting that the authors of the Magisterium "did not intend" to rule out aliens; that doing so was not their "point." This is no different from the move made by those of Sr. Elizabeth's persuasion (and their dismissal of the "fundamentalists" who continue to accept that only two sexes exist). As the Church's doctrine on sexual morality does not specifically name "transgenderism" in its anathemas, she pretends this gives her leeway to assert that the very matter itself was simply so far removed from the minds of the Magisterium's authors that we can ignore the Magisterium's logical implications for transgender ideology. Likewise, the ET promoters pretend that as no Church doctrines specifically refer to "extraterrestrials," they can simply ignore what the existing Magisterium's corollaries mean for their thesis. If anything, however, the Catholic ET promoters are even *more* guilty of sophistry here (do not misunderstand; Sr. Elizabeth's views are certainly flagrantly erroneous as well!). For it is simply not true that the ET question was far from the minds of the Magisterium's authors. As we will see in a later chapter, that debate has long raged. Transgender ideology, on the other hand, is indeed a very new deception.

***

Another weighty recent Magisterial document—not so lofty as the Catechism, but still deserving submission from all Catholics—is the *Compendium of the Social Doctrine of the Church.* This document points out, in respect to its own content, that "...the Church's social doctrine has the same dignity and authority as her moral teaching. It is authentic Magisterium, **which obligates the faithful to adhere to it**." (§80) Within this Compendium, we are taught that:

> **Only man and woman, among all creatures, were made by God 'in his own image' (Gen 1:27). The Lord entrusted all of creation to their responsibility**... (*Compendium of the Social Doctrine of the Church*, §451)

There is no need to re-present all the analysis undertaken above with respect to the Catechism. Suffice it to say that it applies to the present Magisterial text as well, and we cannot wiggle out of the fact that this teaching rules out aliens. A Catholic ET promoter who assures his audience that the Catechism is simply "in need of revision" here will promptly find himself similarly declaring that the entire perennial Faith must be overthrown to accommodate his propositions.

10. Orthodoxy in Trinitarian Theology & Christology

"Throughout the entire cosmos, heaven, earth, under the earth, every knee is to bend, and every tongue is to proclaim that the risen man Jesus, the incarnate Son, is Lord. Jesus cosmically reigns supreme as man. He is not Lord of non-human aliens, for they do not exist."
—Fr. Thomas Weinandy

God The Father Is Not Hiding Siblings

As alluded to in the last chapter, some truths, though dogmatic in their own right, are also so fundamental that they even precede dogma itself. This is not because anything is "more certain" than dogma—there is no such thing as a higher certainty than one hundred percent certainty, and each dogma is indeed absolutely certain. These "preambles of Faith," rather, are the various existential convictions one must hold in the very depths of his heart in order to engage in that "seeking" which guarantees that he will "find." (Cf. Matthew 7:7)

For example, "whoever would approach God must believe that he exists and that he rewards those who seek him." (Hebrews 11:6) Here we see that God's *existence* and His *goodness* must be granted absolutely, *a priori*, by anyone who wishes to have any hope of drawing near to Him. Thankfully, the very fundamental capacity of reason each man is born with enables this conviction universally. No one can truthfully claim he is incapable of being certain, based simply upon reason (not privileged status of birth, upbringing, etc.), that God exists and is good.*

---

* For the goodness of God, neither the Bible nor the Church can be our (ontologically) first teachers of this truth. Any attempt to claim that God's goodness is—*fundamentally, first, and foremost*—simply a Biblical or Catholic truth will always succumb to the fallacy of circular reasoning. God is indeed good, without a doubt. And because He is good, we can be sure He is not deceiving us in Public Revelation or in the teachings of the one and only Church that He promised the gates of hell would not prevail against (cf. Matthew 16:18). But if God were not good, then nothing would preclude Him deceiving us in Scripture. If God were not good, then one could not say "*I believe ___ because the Bible teaches ___.*" If He were evil, then the Bible and the Church (notwithstanding the countless miracles proving their authenticity) could simply be sadistic games He is playing, like some twisted psychologist running unethical experiments. In this case, although they could be rightly called Divine, they could not be considered trustworthy (much less absolutely certain) revelations of truth. Therefore, one cannot

We should, then, ask a simple question: *What would a good God – in accordance with His own goodness and the virtue of justice which He is thereby intrinsically bound to follow – need to tell His own children?*

Certainly, He would need to tell His children how to attain eternal happiness. This much He of course did in His Word—Jesus Christ. Because reason itself manifestly indicated that this was an absolute demand of justice, even astute ancient Pagans with no access to Divine Revelation knew that something was lacking, but would be fulfilled. (It goes without saying that ancient Israelites knew the Savior would come, for the prophets foretold it.) Just one of the ancient world's doubtless innumerable testimonies to this intuition was the Athenian shrine "to an unknown God," which St. Paul teaches, in the New Testament, was in fact none other than an altar to Jesus Christ (Acts 17:23) And let us not forget that, hundreds of years prior, Plato (equally ignorant of Jewish Revelation) described "the just man who is thought unjust" and who would be "scourged, racked, and bound...after suffering every kind of evil, he will be crucified." (*The Republic,* Book II).

But what else would a good God—God the *Father*, that is—need to tell His children?

There is no clearer way of answering this question than considering what any good human father would need to tell his children, as God the Father lacks no virtue possessed by the best of human fathers. To be sure, entire books could be written pondering this question, but we may address its relevance to the matter at hand: *God the Father would need to tell His children about the existence of their siblings.*

Siblings have an inalienable right to know of each other. This is a simple demand of justice of which even the secular are well aware, and there is no need to spend much time here defending the weight it carries. Countless stories have been written of long-lost brothers who were unjustly deprived of the very knowledge of the other's existence, with these stories' dénouement consisting in the overcoming of this dark and indefensible secret-keeping. While there are various Pagan religions whose false revelations could enable their own followers to wrongly claim that God did reveal to us the existence of mankind having "siblings" (non-human creatures with reason on earth—elves, fairies, etc.; or elsewhere—extraterrestrials), no Christian (or Jew) has any grounds for making this claim. This religion, which has the only authentic Public Revelation, says

---

say "I believe God is good because the Bible (or the Church) teaches He is good," without begging the question (i.e., assuming his conclusion within his premise). Each believer must, instead, absolutely and existentially assert God's goodness; and only then can he correctly approach the Word of God. Now, the proposition that God is not good is entirely inconceivable: reason alone can conclude its opposite. If God were evil, then no goodness at all could be found anywhere (whereas each human alive has experienced goodness). Instead, the entirety of creation would be only an unmerited hell for all.

nothing of mankind having siblings; that is, it says nothing of other incarnate beings existing who are made in God's image.

Should, then, any Christian feel comfortable making the claim that we have brothers hidden from us? Should he really assert that—despite tens of thousands of verses of Public Revelation, vastly more verses of authentic private revelation, and two thousand years of Sacred Tradition—the Almighty and infinitely good God, Who has been anything but an absent Father, nevertheless did not find a single opportunity to tell us about our siblings?

Jesus, the Bridegroom, Is Neither a Polygamist nor An Adulterer

> "**O God, who were pleased to call your Church the Bride,** grant that the people that serves your name may revere you, love you and follow you, and may be led by you to attain your promises in heaven." —
> Collect for the Dedication of the Lateran Basilica

Jesus Christ is the Bridegroom; the Church is the bride (cf. Ephesians 5). Some theologians have even insisted that this is the most consequential of Christ's many titles. Jesus made repeated use of it in the Gospels, thereby cementing the great importance and accuracy of this description of His relationship to the Church (e.g., Matthew 9:15, Mark 2:19, Luke 5:34).

Conversely, Scripture also describes the Church as the singular Bride of Christ; even concluding the New Testament itself with that very reference: "**The** Spirit and **the** Bride say, 'Come.'" (Revelation 22:17) The preceding chapter is clearer still. Recalling that Jesus is also referred to as "the Lamb"—e.g., "behold the lamb of God" (John 1:29)—we see, in the Bible's penultimate chapter, an angel telling St. John, "Come, I will show you the Bride, **the wife** of the lamb." (Revelation 21:9) *The* Bride of the Lamb is here also described as *the* wife, thus redoubling our certainty that no "other wives of the lamb" exist.

God has made it clear that to understand the true nature of the relationship we humans have with Him—with His Son—we must regard the union as a Bride-Bridegroom covenant. God would not have chosen this metaphor and placed such emphasis upon it unless we were called to understand it using the lens of what we know is intrinsic to a good human Bride-Bridegroom relationship; that is, what is intrinsic to a Christian marriage. And that is what we should turn our attention to now.

A healthy marriage will flourish decade after decade without the man so much as once turning to his wife and saying, "*I am not a polygamist. I have no wife other than you. I promise.*" But one should ponder: why not say that? Why shouldn't a Christian man regularly, explicitly tell his wife this?

The reason is clear: if the marriage is a good one (and this, of course, is what we must consider as analogous to the marriage of Christ and His Church!), then in even telling his wife, "*I have no other wives,*" the husband is harming the marriage. It should be so obvious that a good spouse is faithful that to state the fact explicitly is a sort of failure; it entails a type of capitulation to the trap of distrust. It would be comparable to a father turning to his son and assuring him, "just so you know, I'm not planning on murdering you today." A good husband, too, would find it very difficult to make explicit to his wife the very thing that should be so obvious to her that she would not question it for a moment, without any need for it ever to be said.

What, then, is the lesson here for the question of extraterrestrials? In the preceding section we considered that, if aliens existed, they too would be our siblings; whereas it is unconscionable that God the Father would refuse to tell us about our own siblings. Here we are confronted with an even more stark reality: if aliens existed, their Church would lay no less claim than ours on being a Bride of Christ. Yet Christ is not a polygamist.

We have already seen that Christ promised us that He is the Church's Bridegroom and that she, the Bride, is *the* wife. But this assurance should also be placed within the context of what He taught about the nature of marriage:

> [Jesus] answered, "Have you not read that he who made them from the beginning made them male and female, and said, 'For this reason a man shall leave his father and mother and be joined to his wife, and the two shall become one'? So they are no longer two but one. What therefore God has joined together, let not man put asunder." (Matthew 19:4-6)
> Every one who divorces his wife and marries another commits adultery, and he who marries a woman divorced from her husband commits adultery. (Luke 16:18)

As we can see, for Jesus (and for Christianity) there is no room even for divorce, much less for polygamy. Similarly, rightly regarding Christ as the Bridegroom of the Church* means regarding this Church as the *sole* Bride of Christ: *forever*. As believing Catholics, we must have the same trust in Christ's promise of fidelity to His Bride that any loyal wife would have in her own husband—or rather, we must have infinitely more trust. And such a wife would not waste one moment of her time speculating about whether or not her husband has other wives. Neither, then, should we waste one moment of our own time entertaining what is, at best, a tremendous distraction (but is, as we shall see in a later chapter, much worse than only

* This is no vague idea, but rather refers to the concrete institution He founded on Peter (cf. Matthew 16:18); giving not merely a mandate upon his person, but rather *keys* (v. 19), so that we realize this Petrine authority extends fully to Peter's successors, as keys are always handed on.

this). That is to say, we should not spend our time entertaining the possibility of alien civilizations—"other Brides of Christ." The mere fact that one may struggle to identify an instance in Public Revelation where it is specifically stated that aliens do not exist should not dissuade us from rejecting their existence any more than a wife not recalling her husband specifically stating he has no other wives should not dissuade her from rejecting the notion that her husband has other wives.

God The Holy Spirit is Not a Monster: The Heresy of Imagining a Greater Church

A faithful understanding of our relationship to the Third Person of the Holy Trinity also assures us that aliens do not exist. For just as God the Father is not hiding our siblings from us and God the Son is not a polygamist or an adulterer, so too God the Holy Spirit is not a monster. The meaning of this final point may be less immediately obvious, but it becomes clear when one considers that the Holy Spirit is truly the soul of the Church.

> **The Church is one because of her "soul": "It is the Holy Spirit,** dwelling in those who believe and pervading and ruling over the entire Church, who brings about that wonderful communion of the faithful and joins them together so intimately in Christ that he is the principle of the Church's unity." ... "...There is **one** Father of the universe, **one** Logos of the universe, and also **one** Holy Spirit, **everywhere one and the same**; there is also **one virgin** become mother, and I should like to call her 'Church." [St. Clement of Alexandria] (*Catechism of the Catholic Church*, §813)

The Catechism places the word "soul" in quotation marks because, of course, the Church does not have a soul in the literally exact same sense that a human body has a soul. Nevertheless, this is not mere hyperbole or metaphor, either. The Church really is a type of body—namely, the *Mystical* Body of Christ. And as such, it has a soul. That soul is none other than the Holy Spirit. This is why Pope Leo XIII taught, in his encyclical *Divinum illud munus*:

> Let it suffice to state that, **as Christ is the Head of the Church, so is the Holy Ghost her soul.** "What the soul is in our body, that is the Holy Ghost in Christ's body, the Church" [St. Augustine. Sermon 187]. This being so, **no further and fuller "manifestation and revelation of the Divine Spirit" may be imagined or expected**; for that **which now takes place in the Church is the most perfect possible,** and will last until that day when the Church herself, having passed through her militant career, shall be taken up into the joy of the saints triumphing in heaven.

(§6)*

Tempting as it may sometimes be for Catholics—in accordance with the sinfulness of many of her members and leaders—the faithful have no place ever doubting the astounding degree of union with God enjoyed by this seemingly temporal and imperfect "institution" into which they were baptized. For the union it has with the Holy Spirit is, as Pope Leo XIII here taught, "**the most perfect possible**," so much so that it is not even licit to "imagine or expect" a "fuller manifestation and revelation of the Divine Spirit."

It is immediately clear how this teaching, binding on all Catholics, flies in the face of ET promotion. For, pausing to ponder this sublime union of the Catholic Church with the Third Person of the Eternal Trinity, we are at once confronted with a question: How could this union possibly be anything but utterly unique? The correct answer arises similarly promptly: *it could not be.*

If aliens existed, they would lay just as much claim as we do upon membership in a Church *ensouled* by the Holy Spirit, for we know that "**there is no partiality with God**." (Romans 2:11) Any being with reason would be His child just as much as we are and would have a right to the same privileges we have been given. Yet it is not even conceivable that multiple Churches could each have, as their very soul, the One Holy Spirit. This would render the Holy Spirit a monster akin to what is depicted in some horror movie, whereas in the Divine Order, one soul is to enliven *one and only one* body. Metaphors aside, it is certainly a scenario ruled out by the dogmatic teachings above. If alien civilizations existed, their own Churches would suffer from arbitrary limitations to their own holiness—their own union with God—since the Catholic Church on earth would be guaranteed to far surpass them.

---

* Pope St. John Paul II also reiterated this teaching (which, itself, consisted in Leo XIII reiterating it from St. Augustine, Father and Doctor of the Church) in his General Audience of July 8, 1998. The repetition placed on relaying this understanding of the Holy Spirit's relation to the Church highlights its importance.

11. Orthodoxy in Mariology

Of the many moribund realities of modern Catechesis and preaching is the tragedy that orthodox teaching on the glories of the Blessed Virgin Mary is almost entirely absent from many contemporary Catholic circles, therefore it is unsurprising that most Catholics neglect to see how irreconcilable belief in extraterrestrials is with what we know—even dogmatically—about the Mother of God.

Giving the Blessed Virgin Mary the praise she is due is essential for many reasons, but one consequence of this much needed renewal of Mariology will be the increasing recognition, among the faithful, of the folly of extraterrestrial intelligence. For while we have already addressed why the notion of multiple incarnations—"other Christs" on other planets—is flatly contrary to Christianity, the impossibility of "other Marys" is just as clear an indication that the human race alone is made in God's image.

Too few Christians today recognize this fact. For example, the prominent theologian we have already quoted, Rev. Dr. Andrew Davison, argued the following about the Blessed Virgin Mary's status, in light of aliens, as the Queen of not only earth and the Church, but also Heaven itself:

> ...the best way to navigate these roles ... is to treat them as local or human matters: as part of our story, as a role in relation to our species ... **we may do well to set the language of queenship aside**.[37]

Indeed, little would please the Devil so much as "setting aside" the Queenship of the Blessed Virgin Mary. Yet, it is precisely such a change that flows from belief in extraterrestrials. While we can, and should, lament the impiety inherent in such suggestions, we cannot find error in the *internal* consistency of one who realizes that if the Blessed Virgin is just one of "many Mothers of God" scattered about the galaxies, then we have no place regarding her as the Queen of Heaven. As we will see in upcoming sections, however, refusing to accord this dignity to Mary is contrary to Catholic dogma.

It is not merely the "fringe" ET promoters advocating for such views, but even the most mainstream "orthodox Catholic" ones. Davison is far from alone. For example, Dr. Paul Thigpen wrote:

> **If the divine Son of God should become incarnate in extraterrestrial races, then His mother on other planets could also be rightly called the "Mother of God." He would, in fact, have several mothers** ... [there may be] multiple incarnations with multiple Mothers of God and of the Church, who are also **multiple Queens of the Universe** through the divine Majesty of their Son...[38]

Dr. Thigpen proceeds to insist this situation he has described—which any simple and pious Catholic would easily and immediately see the blasphemy of—is entirely unproblematic. He justifies the supposed orthodoxy of this scenario (which is not only contrary to Christological and Mariological dogma, but also sounds like the plotline of some degenerate modern sitcom) with the usual rhetorical device: deferring to "humility," as if this virtue demands that we be open to violations of the most basic realities of the Faith.

We must, therefore, make no mistake about it: the ET Deception carries within itself a revolution against everything that is sacred. It seeks to undermine the Christian and Catholic understanding of our origin, destiny, ecclesiology, Mariology, Christology, eschatology, morality, prayer, and more. And it is no longer merely the tabloid press promoting it; it is now preached by the most mainstream voices in "orthodox Catholicism" and pronounced upon its most prominent pulpits.

"The" Immaculate Conception: An Earthling Surpassing the Universe and All It Contains

Of the multitudes of Magisterial teachings on Mary that bless Catholics, one document which gives the most relevant declarations is none other than the same Apostolic Constitution by which Pope Pius IX infallibly defined the Dogma of the Immaculate Conception. There, he taught Mary was not only Immaculately Conceived, but also that:

> It is the clear and unanimous opinion of the Fathers that the most glorious Virgin, for whom "he who is mighty has done great things," was resplendent with such an abundance of heavenly gifts, with such a fullness of grace and with such innocence, that she is an unspeakable miracle of God—indeed, the crown of all miracles and truly the Mother of God; that **she approaches as near to God himself as is possible for a created being**; and that **she is above all men and angels in glory**. (*Ineffabilis Deus.*)

In order to give this astounding teaching the type of submission it is due in the mind and heart of a Catholic—namely, *complete* submission—we must understand how authoritatively this truth is being taught. As I wrote in my 2019 book, *The Crown of Sanctity*:

> ... by saying "it is the clear and unanimous opinion of the Fathers ... " [Pius IX] is not merely presenting an "opinion" to Catholics that they may likewise hold if they feel so compelled. Rather, that which is unanimously held by the Fathers of the Church is, by that very fact, a dogma of the Faith ... The First Vatican Council taught that: "*It is not permissible for anyone to interpret Holy Scripture in a sense contrary to ... the unanimous consent of the fathers.*"[39] The Council of Trent teaches the same thing.[40] ...**Therefore, we should regard these words of Pius IX as infallible**; if not explicitly by their wording, then at least implicitly due to what they represent. ... as he says, "*[Mary] approaches as near to God himself as is possible ...*" [he did not say] merely that Mary *did approach* nearer to God

than any other creature *had approached.* (Pages 494-495. DSDOConnor.com)

Indeed, the Blessed Virgin Mary is a "mere mortal" like us; an entirely *human* person (unlike her Son, she was not Divine); a woman who was conceived and born, on earth, to a human mother and a human father just as we are (though Immaculately). But it is nevertheless settled that she is *the* supremely exalted creature. One so exalted, in fact, that it would be materially heretical to even propose the *possibility* of the existence of a created being that surpasses her.

Here, yet again, we are confronted with a reality of our Faith that is entirely irreconcilable with the notion of aliens. God is impartial (cf. Romans 2:11). If alien civilizations exist on other planets, then they would be forever relegated to inferiority beneath a mere earthling of whom they have no knowledge or connection. In justice, however, these alien races would have every right to "their own Immaculate Conceptions"—"their own Blessed Virgin Marys." (Recall that the Catholic ET promoters themselves concede as much.) Dogmatic teaching, however, eliminates that possibility.

Whoever would attempt to argue that Pius IX's teaching only applies to earth is directly dissenting from his Magisterium. The Pope makes it clear that there are absolutely no limitations, *whatsoever*, on the scope of his declaration. He flatly states that the Virgin is as close to God "as is **possible** for a **created** being." (A "created" being is simply anything or anyone other than God Himself—the only Uncreated One.) It is impossible for anyone, anywhere, at any time, to match or surpass *Our* Lady. Here, all grounds for speculating that comparable salvation histories (much less superior ones) have transpired or could transpire on other planets are rejected. Moreover, the very next clause of the Pope's teaching reads:

"**[Mary] is above all men and angels in glory**" (*Ineffabilis Deus*)

This line also rules out the theory which would limit the document's application to earthly creatures, since angels are explicitly included, and they are not earthly creatures. Instead, this infallible declaration of Mary's absolute superiority is expressly defined as universe-wide.

We should also reflect on a fact we will consider in a later section: the Pope speaks only of "men and angels" as those beings worth noting as all standing beneath the Blessed Virgin. For it is too obvious to be worth mentioning that she is above all plants and animals, and, similarly, it was too obvious (in the mind of Blessed Pope Pius IX) to be worth mentioning that no other contenders even exist for lofty graces or glories. As has always been held unanimously—by the infallible "*sensus fidelium*" of Sacred Tradition—there exists, between irrational animals and God, only two classes of beings: humans, and angels.

A mere four years after the Pope declared the Dogma discussed above, the Blessed Virgin herself came down from Heaven to endorse it.

She appeared to a young girl, St. Bernadette Soubirous, in the town of Lourdes, France. Her words, however, mysteriously went deeper still than the Pope's, for she did not merely tell the seer that she "was immaculately conceived," rather, she said "I AM *THE* Immaculate Conception." Hugh Owen wrote:

> Our Lady's unique status as the Mother of God also shows that Christ could not possess another nature since He cannot have another Mother. Our Lady's statement at Lourdes—"I am the Immaculate Conception"—eliminates the possibility of sinless aliens since She is the only creature conceived without sin (and, as St. Maximilian Kolbe observed in his writings, Adam and Eve were created, not conceived).[41]

Indeed, there are no other Immaculate Conceptions, and there cannot ever be any other Immaculate Conceptions. Mary alone is *the* perfect creature, beheld in the Mind of God from the foundations of the universe (though only herself literally existing beginning about 2,000 years ago), to be the one and only Spouse of God the Holy Spirit, the one and only Mother of God the Son, and singularly exalted daughter of God the Father. No one, anywhere, at any time, can ever come close to her, much less match her, much less surpass her.

Yet, she is a mere earthling. A moment's sincere meditation upon this breathtaking reality should rule out any speculation about aliens in the mind of a Catholic.

Vatican II's Mariology: "All" to Be Saved are Offspring of Adam

The Second Vatican Council's *Dogmatic Constitution on the Church* teaches:

> [Mary] is endowed with the high office and dignity of being the Mother of the Son of God, by which account she is also the beloved daughter of the Father and the temple of the Holy Spirit. Because of this gift of sublime grace **she far surpasses all creatures, both in heaven and on earth**. At the same time, however, **because she belongs to the offspring of Adam she is one with all those who are to be saved**. She is "the mother of the members of Christ ... having cooperated by charity that faithful might be born in the Church, who are members of that Head." Wherefore she is hailed as a pre-eminent and singular member of the Church... (*Lumen Gentium*, §53)

Here, the Magisterium goes even farther than *Ineffabilis Deus* in the preceding century; for instead of asserting that Mary is "above" every other creature in the universe, it teaches that the Virgin "**far** surpasses" them all. Thus is eliminated any expectation that alien civilizations could have their own creatures who are at least "close" to the Queen of Heaven, born on earth.

More pointedly still, the Church here teaches that Mary is not only the Mother of the Church, but also that, "**because she belongs to the offspring of Adam she is one with all those who are to be saved**." This description of *why* she is one with *all* the elect is deeply revealing: it is "because" she shares our own heritage. We must not gloss over the Council's decision not to merely *take note of* her common ancestry with us. Rather, *Lumen Gentium* gives explanatory power to precisely this commonality. It does not say that "*Mary is a child of Adam, which is one way she is united to* ***many*** *of the saved.*" It defines, rather, that it is *because* Mary is Adam's child that she is one with *all* the saved. Therefore, the Virgin Mary is truly our sister in that sense—a sense which cannot possibly apply to any creature who is not among Adam's offspring. This exclusivity explicitly rules out the possibility of salvation for creatures who are not offspring of Adam—for we are yet again confronted with the qualifier, "all," which we cannot ignore.

St. Joseph: Patron of the Universal Church

The unique and supreme positions held by Jesus and Mary dispute the possibility of aliens, but so does the glory of St. Joseph. Pope Leo XIII, in an encyclical towards the end of the 19th century, declared:

> St. Joseph has been proclaimed Patron of the Church, and from [him] the Church looks for singular benefit from his patronage and protection ... In truth, the dignity of the Mother of God is so lofty that naught created can rank above it. **But as Joseph has been united to the Blessed Virgin by the ties of marriage, it may not be doubted that he approached nearer than any to the eminent dignity by which the Mother of God surpasses so nobly all created natures.** For marriage is the most intimate of all unions which from its essence imparts a community of gifts between those that by it are joined together. Thus in giving Joseph the Blessed Virgin as spouse, God appointed him to be ... a participator in her sublime dignity. (*Quamquam Pluries*, §3)

St. Joseph—unlike his spouse—was not immaculately conceived. From the beginning of its existence, therefore, his nature was *entirely* like our own. Nevertheless, we are authoritatively taught here that absolutely no creature, other than Mary, can be regarded as having the "eminent dignity" of St. Joseph. As untenable as it is to assert that the universe is full of alien civilizations whose holiness is arbitrarily limited by a mere earthling, Mary, it is even more outlandish to assert that these extraterrestrial race's holiness is incapable of matching or surpassing that of another mere earthling, Joseph, who is vastly beneath Mary. Like the other Magisterial teachings we have considered, this one also expressly rules out any interpretation which would limit its application to the boundaries of earth. The Encyclical teaches that "**all created natures**," other than Mary's, are beneath Joseph's, thereby deliberately including extraterrestrial *angels* in its domain. From this, too, it follows that there are no aliens. St. Joseph is *the* Patron of the *Universal* Church. He is *the* Terror of Demons. Yet, he is an earthling.

12. More Papal Magisterium Against Alien Belief

"“There can be nothing more dangerous than those heretics who admit nearly the whole cycle of doctrine, and yet by one word, as with a drop of poison, infect the real and simple faith taught by our Lord and handed down by Apostolic tradition.”

—Pope Leo XIII, *Satis Cognitum*

We have already seen how the *Catechism of the Catholic Church,* the *Compendium of the Social Doctrine of the Church,* and the Apostolic Constitution *Ineffabilis Deus,* the Second Vatican Council, the Encyclical *Quamquam Pluries,* and other Magisterial documents, rule out extraterrestrial intelligence. Although these teachings are more than sufficient to settle the matter for a Catholic, there is nevertheless much more Magisterium relevant to the matter at hand. Before considering these additional documents, we should remind ourselves of how, as faithful Catholics, we must approach them. The First Vatican Council, held in the 19th century, provides the most appropriate reminders:

> **God cannot deny himself, nor can truth ever be in opposition to truth**. The appearance of this kind of specious contradiction is chiefly due to the fact that either the dogmas of faith are not understood and explained in accordance with the mind of the church, or unsound views are mistaken for the conclusions of reason. Therefore we define that **every assertion contrary to the truth of enlightened faith is totally false** (Ch. 4 6,7) All **faithful Christians are forbidden to defend as the legitimate conclusions of science those opinions which are known to be contrary to the doctrine of faith**, particularly if they have been condemned by the church; and furthermore they are absolutely bound to hold them to be errors which wear the deceptive appearance of truth. (Ch.4, §9) If anyone shall have said that it is possible that to the dogmas declared by the Church a meaning must sometimes be attributed according to the progress of science, different from that which the Church has understood and understands: **let him be anathema.** (Cited in 3039 DS 1818. 3)

In these dogmatic definitions, we see several contemporary heresies refuted, including the notion that there is a "*separate truth of Faith and of science, which can contradict each other but both be valid,*" the notion that "*dogmas can evolve, and can today acquire a meaning contrary to the meaning they held when defined,*" and the notion that Church teaching is "*inhibited by the knowledge of the men writing it, such that new scientific discoveries unknown to those authors should compel us to now re-evaluate their definitions."*

Catholic ET promoters inevitably succumb to these heresies in their attempts to wiggle out of those corollaries to the Magisterium which rule out aliens. In fact, whatever the Church has taught was true when it was promulgated, and it will remain equally true until the end of time. A Catholic must either decide that Church teaching should be respected, and respect it when he finds it—along with all the logical implications that necessarily come with that teaching—or he must decide that Church teaching has no right to impinge upon his own speculations and theories. Whoever decides the latter, however, is simply not Catholic. The scope of the Magisterium is not limited by distance, nor is its effectiveness diminished by time. One need not check the calendar on his wall to determine whether it applies, and when gazing upon the stars at night, one need not wonder if he is peering into a jurisdiction beyond that which Christ gave to Peter when He said,

> You are Peter, and upon this rock I will build my church, and the gates of the netherworld shall not prevail against it. I will give you the keys to the kingdom of heaven. **Whatever you bind on earth shall be bound in heaven**; and whatever you loose on earth shall be loosed in heaven. (Matthew 16:18-19)

According to the Bible, Heaven itself is "bound" by mere earthlings (to date, 266 of them; i.e., successors of Peter). This alone should rule out any speculations about aliens, for even if we counterfactually posit galaxies filled with ET civilizations, it nevertheless remains certain that *Heaven* is absolutely *one*. Yet that *one* Heaven is bound by hundreds of men on earth—men who need not consult with any aliens to ensure their *ex-cathedra* declarations remain consistent with similar declarations of extraterrestrial Popes.

Pius XII and Leo XIII Against Polygenism: "Human" Aliens Ruled Out

> "Blessed are you, O God of our fathers, praised be your name forever and ever. Let the heavens and all your creation praise you forever. You made Adam and you gave him his wife Eve to be his help and support; and **from these two the human race descended.**"
>
> —Tobit 8:5-6

Some Catholic ET promoters will protest that, even if we cannot posit the existence of *non-human* intelligent aliens, we can at least posit that aliens exist throughout the galaxies, and they are simply properly called "men," as we are. While this move runs afoul of many considerations above, there is yet another infallible truth of the Faith that explicitly anathematizes this notion. For "Polygenism"—the notion that humans exist who are not descendants of Adam and Eve—has been repeatedly condemned as a heresy in Catholic Teaching. Scripture, Tradition, and Magisterium teach that all human beings are descendants of Adam and Eve—who are themselves two literal human beings who lived on this planet thousands (not millions) of years ago. We have already considered Paragraph 26 of the Papal Encyclical *Humani Generis*, so let us now consider another passage:

> When, however, there is question of another conjectural opinion, namely polygenism, the children of the Church by no means enjoy such liberty [of discussion]. For **the faithful cannot embrace that opinion which maintains** that either after Adam there existed on this earth true men who did not take their origin through natural generation from him as from **the first parent of all, or that Adam represents a certain number of first parents.** (§37)

Here, Catholics are expressly forbidden ("the faithful **cannot** embrace...") from supposing that Adam was not the true "the first parent of all." Obviously, it is not possible for Adam to be the parent of creatures on other planets, therefore we can immediately rule out the possibility of races of humans existing anywhere but on earth.

Now, one may be tempted to jump on the phrase "on this earth,"—seeking to leverage it in the usual way employed ET promoters—to allow for "true men *not* on this earth." This attempt will not work. Two propositions are censured above, and the second one ("that Adam represents a certain number of first parents") is independently condemned—that clause is not joined to the phrase "on this earth." There are, therefore, no "other Adams" anywhere else. Moreover, the first condemned proposition contains two parts, and the second succeeds in indicating, on its own, that Adam is "the first parent of **all** [men]," without any qualification.

As we will discuss in detail in the next section, the phrase "on this earth" is clearly not intended to *restrict* the scope of a teaching, but rather to *expand* it. The Pope wished to make clear he was denouncing certain theories circulating at the time of his writing (1950). These theories posited that the lineages of ethnicities who have long populated different continents on earth ultimately each can be traced back to different original couples. In fact, Catholic teaching holds that they all do trace back to Adam. Therefore, Pius was sure to include express insistence that no place *on the entire earth* was excluded from this teaching. To twist this deliberate *expanding* wording and treat it as a *restricting* one is underhanded. Yet this is what ET promoters do when they use it as grounds for speculating that "men" could exist *outside earth* with lineages tracing back to extraterrestrial first parents. Such sophistry is both contrary to the meaning of the passage and is contradicted by its own adjacent clauses.

Moreover, as we have considered in preceding chapters, the Catholic ET promoters are nearly unanimous in their insistence that extraterrestrials *are* already on earth, and have been for a very long time, therefore on this count alone, positing "human" aliens undermines their own thesis. Finally, this is only one example of many teachings that condemn Polygenism. Eleven years before *Humani Generis*, in a lesser-known encyclical that nevertheless bears equal Magisterial weight, Venerable Pope Pius XII also condemned it. The document, entitled *Summi Pontificatus* (On the Unity of Human Society), conveys the following truths:

> In fact, the first page of the Scripture, with magnificent simplicity, tells us how God, as a culmination to His creative work, made man to His Own image and likeness (§36) ... **The Apostle of the Gentiles later on makes himself the herald of this truth which associates men as brothers in one great family, when he proclaims to the Greek world that God "hath made of one, all mankind, to dwell upon the whole face of the earth, determining appointed times, and the limits of their habitation, that they should seek God"** (Acts xvii. 26, 27). (§37)A marvelous vision, which **makes us see the human race in the unity of one common origin** ... (§38) **These are supernatural truths** which form a solid basis and the strongest possible bond of a union... (§41) ...this unity of all mankind ... exists in law **and in fact**... (§42)

Perhaps it was the attempts of some, after the publication of this encyclical, to dismiss the unbroken teaching of the Church that Adam and Eve really exist and really are the only first parents of the entire human race, which inspired the Pope to condemn Polygenism explicitly in his later encyclical quoted earlier.

***

"[God] made from one man the whole human race." (Acts 17:26)

We are not, however, left with Encyclicals from one Pope alone in addressing the issue. Scripture clearly teaches that all human beings are descendants of Adam and Eve (a fact we covered in previous chapters), and Sacred Tradition—ever faithful to its Biblical foundation—has *always* affirmed this truth. Looking to another Encyclical promulgated several decades earlier, we see this truth declared even more forcefully. Let us, therefore, consider Pope Leo XIII's teaching in *Arcanum*:

> Though revilers of the Christian faith refuse to acknowledge the **never-interrupted doctrine of the Church on this subject**, and have long striven to destroy **the testimony of all nations and of all times,** they have nevertheless failed not only to quench the powerful light of truth, but even to lessen it. **We record what is to all known, and cannot be doubted by any, that ...[God] decreed that this husband and wife [Adam and Eve] should be the natural beginning of the human race, from whom it might be propagated and preserved by an unfailing fruitfulness throughout all futurity of time**. (§5)

The zeal exhibited by Leo in reiterating this "never-interrupted doctrine of the Church," along with his righteous indignation at those who deny it, is both palpable and inspired. Indeed, one cannot get human nature right if he gets its beginnings wrong; for this error is precisely what underlies so much contemporary diabolical confusion; e.g., that which now seeks to eradicate biological sex itself.

Leo XIII is using what can only be called the strongest language possible to denounce the idea that Adam and Eve were not the first parents of all human beings. He insists it "cannot be doubted" that Adam and Eve were the "beginning of the human race," and he prefaces this infallible teaching by accurately denouncing those who would oppose it, saying they are not merely sincerely mistaken seekers of truth, but rather are "**revilers of the Christian faith**."

Now, the context of the passage, in *Arcanum*, pertains to matrimony. But this context has no mitigating effect on the force of the passage's condemnation of Polygenism. Important as context is, it cannot render a direct and clear teaching devoid of its value. The exclamation, "*but context!*", has (rather unfortunately) become the catch-all excuse for all manner of modernist heresy, and the faithful should be on guard against those teachers of the faith who are constantly deferring to it in order to "re-explain" our Sacred Tradition.

In brief: All men—all human beings—are descendants of Adam and Eve. One cannot escape the many Biblical and Magisterial teachings which rule out aliens by positing extraterrestrials "who are also men." Such "men" could not have taken their origin from Adam and Eve, therefore they would not be men. And of all visible creatures, only men are rational. Therefore, there are no aliens.

We must make no mistake about it: Polygenism is, indeed, *infallibly* ruled out as a possibility. This is not because a solemn extraordinary pronouncement has been rendered on it as, for example, has been rendered on the Immaculate Conception. Rather, it is because this teaching of the "Ordinary Magisterium"—itself based on repeated clear Scriptural texts and teachings of the Fathers—has been issued so many times in Papal teaching over the course of so many centuries, that it long ago qualified as an element of the infallible Ordinary Universal Magisterium (which becomes infallible by way of repetition across Pontificates). Note, as well, that any unanimous consensus of the Fathers of the Church is, *ipso facto*, a dogma of the Faith, and all the Fathers agreed that Adam and Eve are the first parents of the entire human race. Polygenism is indefensible for a Catholic, and anyone who desires to abide in the orthodox Faith is well advised to stay far away from any Catholic teacher who is sympathetic to it. (Granted, even some Catholic ET promoters seem to acknowledge that Polygenism is condemned, though they fail to realize, or refuse to admit, that the corollaries of this condemnation rule out aliens.)

"On This Earth": A Phrase that Expands, Rather Than Restricts, the Scope of Its Object

To know the truth of what any authoritative text—Scriptural or Magisterial—is actually teaching, one must have a corresponding sincere desire to receive it. One must heed the clear sense of what is being said and resist the temptation to maneuver it into fitting his own preconceived ideologies, or to pretend ambiguity exists requiring "nuance" when in fact there is nothing but clarity requiring *faith*.

When reading Scripture or Magisterium, one will see phrases like "on the whole earth" or "across all the world." If one supposes that license is thereby given to assert that what is being taught does not apply beyond the stratosphere, he is only guaranteeing that he will never actually abide in the truth with which God has endowed these very texts.

This proper approach to communication is so commonsensical in ordinary life that it always goes without saying, therefore it is unfortunate that Catholic ET promoters refuse to accord that same respect to Scripture and Magisterium. When, for example, in ordinary parlance, one says "*no one earth could do such a thing,*" he does not mean to imply that any of the dozen or so astronauts orbiting earth at that moment could be capable of it. Anyone listening knows he means that whatever feat he is referring to is humanly impossible. When a young man says to the woman he hopes to marry, "*you're the only one on the face of the planet for me!*", he does not mean to imply that there are plenty of other women "for him" living in sufficiently deep basement apartments or working in underground mines that they do not, strictly speaking, qualify as inhabiting the "face" of the planet. As this man's fiancée knows full well, he is simply saying that there are *no other* women for him; at all, anywhere.

Any Catholic who reads the preceding (and following) Magisterial teachings with unclenched fists and an unprejudiced mind will not struggle to receive their teachings. Unlike the ET promoters, my aim is not to engage in intellectual acrobatics to twist the texts, but only to aid in unclenching the fists.

Pope St. Zachary's Condemnation of the "Abominable Teaching" of Aliens

A Papal condemnation from the 8th century all but explicitly denounces belief in extraterrestrial intelligence. It comes to us from Pope Zachary, who is venerated as a saint by both the Catholic and Eastern Orthodox Church, and is described by the old *Catholic Encyclopedia* as:

> A man of gentle and conciliatory character who was charitable towards the clergy and people ...He was very benevolent to the poor, to whom alms were given regularly from the papal palace. ... in a troubled era

> Zachary proved himself to be an excellent, capable, vigorous, and charitable successor of Peter. He also carried on theological studies and made a translation of the Dialogues of Gregory the Great into Greek... (*Catholic Encyclopedia.* Entry on Pope Zachary.)

The Pope, however, was also aflame with Divine zeal to defeat Pagan practices. He famously built the church of "Santa Maria Sopra Minerva" – that is, "Saint Mary Above Minerva" – on top of the very ruins of the Pagan temple to the "goddess" (demon) Minerva (though modern scholarship has pinned the temple as one dedicated to the Egyptian goddess Isis), thus demonstrating the Faith's victory over idolatry. He was in regular formal correspondence with the great St. Boniface, who is famous for his skill with an axe. That saint personally chopped down "Thor's Oak," a massive tree that became an object of idolatrous worship by local Pagans. Having demolished their idol, Boniface proceeded to convert them to Christianity.

It is most fitting, therefore, that Zachary is a Pope from whom we have a clear denunciation of the modern era's prevailing Paganism – alien belief – though, prophetically, issued 1,200 years before its popularity. In a letter to none other than St. Boniface himself, Pope St. Zachary wrote the following about a certain cleric named Virgil:

> As for **his perverse and abominable teaching**, which he has proclaimed **in opposition to God**, and to his own soul's detriment – if the report of his having spoken thus be true – that is, **that there are another world and other men beneath the earth, or even** [on?] **the sun and moon**...take counsel and then expel him from the church, stripped of his priestly dignity.[42]

In this Papal Letter, the Vicar of Christ describes belief in people (aliens) residing on lands inaccessible to the human race (*and even, depending upon how one clause should be translated and interpreted, on the "sun and moon"*) as not merely errant, but rather, as "perverse" and "abominable;" so egregiously in "**opposition to God**," that for a Catholic priest to be found promoting such teachings demands that he be defrocked and excommunicated. Indeed, the proclamation of such wild theories as these is none other than Paganism, and no diligent medieval Pope would, under his watch, tolerate a priest espousing such diabolical doctrines.

The move that the Catholic ET promoters make to attempt to evade this condemnation is predictable. They protest they are not asserting that aliens exist on the "sun and moon," (if that is what Pope Zachary means here), nor on another world "beneath the earth," (which, regardless of how one translates or interprets one phrase in Pope's decree, is *certainly* condemned) but rather that aliens exist on other planets in the solar system, the galaxy, or in other galaxies.

This attempt fails spectacularly, and whoever would proffer it can only be meaningfully responded to with the exhortation to stop playing games. If indeed it is so *abominable* and *perverse* to propose that "other men" live on "another world **beneath** the earth," then what exactly renders this *abominable* teaching acceptable merely because the planet Mars, or Alpha Centauri's orbiting planets, or those of distant galaxies, are instead posited as their dwelling? Obviously, there is no significant difference whatsoever.

The next move consists of pretending that "context" can invalidate this teaching. And indeed, the context of Pope Zachary's condemnation no doubt largely pertained to the discussion of the "Antipodes," that is, the object of ancient and medieval speculations about "another side" of the earth, and whether it—though regarded as absolutely inaccessible to men of the civilization we know—harbored other intelligent beings whose origin was not Adam.

First, the Pope expressly notes that he is *not* merely condemning the notion of rational incarnate beings living on the Antipodes, but that he is also condemning the notion of such beings living on *extra*-terrestrial bodies: the sun and moon. Admittedly, however, debate among scholars exists as to what exactly the wording of the original text means in referring to those bodies, as the grammar [including in the original Latin] is awkward.* Yet even writers hundreds of years ago took Pope Zachary's decree as ruling out the possibility of beings on the sun or moon. One scholar noted:

> **In 1631 [Libert] Froidmont [a prominent theologian and scientist] cited Pope Zacharias at length to ... say that the notions that there is another Sun, another Moon or another inhabited Earth are 'heretical, or are nearly so'**. Inchofer referred to the idea that there are worlds in the Moon or the Sun as monstrous 'errors'. In his long manuscript he condemned it as 'heretical', following Philaster, Zacharias and others. Previously, in his Defence of Galileo, Campanella too had noted that St **John Chrysostom had said that it is 'heretical and contrary to scriptures' to assert that there are 'many heavens and orbs'**. Campanella was not the only one; for example, the Jesuit Nicolas Caussin also cited Chrysostom to note that **heretics believe in 'other starry heavens and worlds'**.[43]

Secondly—and most importantly—far from successfully defending their thesis, the context here only does the very opposite; it further clarifies how un-Catholic ET promotion is. The debate on these matters relating to the "Antipodes" is a perfect analogue to the present debate on extraterrestrials. As we can see from the letter, Pope Zachary is not at all concerned with

---

* As Dr. Marie George notes, "Yet another difficulty in interpretation arises from the Pope's grammar: "Sun" and "moon" are in the nominative case, leaving one wondering what the Pope meant to say about them. Maybe he meant to condemn the notion of another sun and moon, and left out the word "another" ("alius," "alia") or maybe he meant to condemn the notion of human inhabitants on the sun and moon, and omitted the word "on" (L. "in")—in which case "sun and moon" should have been put in the ablative case." (George, Marie I. Christianity and Extraterrestrials?: A Catholic Perspective)

the shape of the earth (i.e., whether, geographically, such a place as "the Antipode" is possible). Remember this book's opening chapter: questions like that have no effect on the Faith, therefore the Magisterium is not concerned with settling them. But the question of whether rational creatures exist elsewhere has everything to do with the Faith, hence Pope Zachary's zeal in addressing it. Let us settle this in the next section.

The Inescapable Relevance and Magisterial Weight of Pope Zachary's Rejection of ETs

The situation described above is precisely what is transpiring today. Like the condemned Virgil, Catholic ET promoters insist that analogous "men" (that is, rational incarnate creatures, whom they call aliens) exist in physical regions that are pragmatically inaccessible to us; beings who derive not from Adam, but from some other first parent. This position is, *almost verbatim*, the condemned Antipodean Thesis. The "**perverse anti-God abomination**" which the Pope describes it as derives from the multitude of theological problems that flow from it; many discussed in preceding sections of this book, and many more to be discussed in forthcoming ones.

Not only is the substance of the position a perfect analogy, so too is its motivation. The Antipodean Thesis was presented on the basis of scientific conjecture and the prevailing mythologies of the time which posited all manner of fictional intelligent creatures living "under the earth." This is exactly how belief in extraterrestrials is promoted today; it is supposedly derived from "astrobiology," but the real motive force behind the theories is, likewise, the day's prevailing mythologies: science fiction.

Nevertheless, Catholic ET promoters unfortunately do not stop at only these attempts to evade this Papal denunciation. Dr. Paul Thigpen, in his popular 2022 book on the topic, bizarrely claims that Pope Zachary merely:

> ...probably reject[ed] the idea on the same grounds as his predecessor: There cannot be any human beings on the underside of the earth, he reasoned, because to be human, they would have to be descended from Adam, and so would have had to arrive at their present place by crossing what was considered an impassible ocean.[44]

So, Pope Zachary would denounce Virgil's teaching as an *excommunication-worthy anti-God abomination and perversity* merely because it entailed positing some children of Adam traversed an ocean thought quite difficult to sail? If, on the other hand, one objects that the "perversity" of Virgil's teaching is not found on account of its alleging great feats of ocean-crossing, but rather on account of its alleging the existence of "men" who did not derive from Adam, then we can only again exhort such a person to return to the paragraphs above. What "perversity" could possibly exist in such a teaching that does not also exist—though more perversely still—in *extraterrestrial* alien belief? There are no grounds for any meaningful distinguishing between the two. If one is perverse, we must conclude the other is as well.

The final endeavor of the scholar noted above is different, and likely derives from what he perceived as the impossibility of successfully circumventing condemnation of ET promotion by this Papal Letter. Therefore, he proceeds to simply dismiss Pope Zachary's condemnation as only a personal opinion expressed in a private letter. This is both fallacious and a category mistake. Fallacious, because this is not a mere letter: it is a clear instruction, written in response to St. Boniface's *Dubia*, on a formal canonical proceeding to be undertaken against a certain priest's "abominable" doctrine. This is not one friend writing to another to express personal opinions. It is a decree.

It is a category mistake, because the strict genres of Magisterial declarations we delineate today did not exist in the 8th century. Today, one could more validly regard a letter from a Pope as non-Magisterial, depending upon its wording.* In the 8th century, however, Popes did not write such letters simply intending to chat. Consider that one could allege St. Paul's epistles, as well as those of St. Peter, the first Pope, were "merely letters they wrote to various addressees." Yet they comprise much of the New Testament's content. For centuries thereafter, Popes exercised their Magisterial authority through letters precisely like the one here authored by Pope Zachary.†

This fact can be illustrated with a perusal of the most renowned compilation of dogmas, the *Enchiridion Symbolorum: A Compendium of Creeds, Definitions and Declarations of the Catholic Church*—otherwise known simply as "*Denzinger.*" There, one will find several of Pope Zachary's letters *to St. Boniface*—just like the letter we are currently considering—presented as true acts of the Magisterium. We are left with only one conclusion: this letter, too, is authentic Magisterium, as there is no indication that it substantially differs (in the intent of the Pope) from those already included in *Denzinger*.‡

---

* A Pope is free to exercise his Magisterial authority whenever he wishes, it is simply common practice that Popes only do so, in the modern era, in certain ways.

† I challenge anyone who thinks otherwise to find a compilation of "formal Papal Magisterial texts" (that is, texts bearing clear indications of their Magisterial nature; i.e., by using the appropriate classifying titles) from the Pontiffs of the first millennium. I will spare you the trouble, however: you will find no such compilation. The compilations of such "appropriately labeled" texts that you do find will predominantly derive from the last few centuries, with a smattering of examples from the several centuries prior.

‡ While we can be confident that a document's inclusion in *Denzinger* is indicative of its Magisterial status, the opposite is not true. Case in point, the documents included within *Denzinger* have grown over the decades; not only due to newly promulgated Magisterium being included, but also due to recognitions that documents previously left out should indeed be included.

Pope Pius II's Condemnation of "Sacrilegious" Belief in Men on Another World

In the preceding section we considered Pope Zachary's condemnation of aliens which, though doubtless authoritative, is nevertheless not included in *Denzinger*. Several centuries later, however, one of his successors, Pope Pius II, promulgated a decree that has long been resided in those pages.

Entitled "*Cum sicut accepimus*," this letter was promulgated on November 14, 1459. It was a condemnation of what the Pope described as "**most pernicious errors...a sacrilegious attempt against the dogmas of the holy Fathers**" taught by a certain Zaninus de Solcia. Among these "sacrilegious" errors were the following condemned propositions:

> (1) The world should be naturally destroyed and ended by the heat of the sun... (2) All Christians are to be saved. (3) **God created another world than this one, and in its time many other men and women existed, and consequently Adam was not the first man**. (4) Likewise, Jesus Christ suffered and died, not for the redemption out of love for the human race, but by the compelling influence of the stars. (5) Likewise, Jesus Christ, Moses, and Muhammad ruled the world by the pleasure of their wills...(7) Wantonness [*sexual activity*] outside of marriage is only a sin because of its prohibition by positive law [*changeable, merely human precepts*]...it is only because of ecclesiastical prohibition that one is restrained from following the opinion of Epicurus [*Hedonism*] as true...(9) Finally, the Christian law through the succession of another law is about to have an end, just as the law of Moses has been terminated by the law of Christ.[45]

I have included here the errors adjacent to the especially relevant one because they situate the condemnation of ET promotion in their context, which is quite like today's own. As we will see in later chapters, ET promotion and "Ufology" have become inextricable from countless other errors and evils running parallel to those above: a false eschatology (*the world ending by materialistic means – "the heat of the sun" – as opposed to the events of Christ's Second Coming*), universalist heresy ("*all are to be saved*"), occultism and astrology ("*the compelling influence of the stars*"), religious syncretism ("*Muhammad ruling the world*"), hedonism—particularly sexual licentiousness ("*only because of [Church] prohibitions" is such behavior ruled out*), and New Age, dispensationalist thought ("*Christian law...is about to have an end*"). Pope Pius here was nothing short of prophetic.

At this point, readers will be forgiven for losing count of how many condemnations can be found—whether implicit or explicit—of ET promotion within Scripture and Magisterium. Although these teachings are almost never acknowledged in mainstream Catholic discourse today, they do exist and are just as true today as the day they were written. Nor is it difficult to apply them to today's debate on extraterrestrial intelligence: they settle the debate, even if they do not use the same words.

The popular Catholic scholar noted in the previous chapter uses an identical strategy to seek to exempt ET promotion from this Papal letter's condemnation as he did from Pope Zachary's letter. (Nor is he the only one to use this approach.) He dismisses the relevance of the condemnation, claiming that it only consists in Pius "*rejecting the more specific idea that God created a world inhabited by members of the human race before He created our world.*"[46]

Here as there, one is struck by how oblivious such a dismissal is to the fact that no substantial difference exists between, on the one hand, modern ET promotion and, on the other hand, 15th century belief in men on another world *before* Adam. One is likewise struck by how nonchalantly this dismissal ignores the nature of the condemnation, which the Pope was clear to promulgate not as addressing mere subtle theological mistakes, but rather as addressing "pernicious" and "sacrilegious" errors "against the dogmas of the holy Fathers."

If indeed it is, as the Pope assures us, so exceedingly evil to believe in *men* on another world *before* Adam, then it is also evil to believe in *aliens* on another world *after* Adam. (Of course, all ET promoters believe aliens existed long before us, therefore even this move fails.) No one who seeks to be among those who, "*holding to the truth, hand on the Catholic and Apostolic Faith*" (Roman Missal), could tolerate the proposal of one thesis while realizing the Magisterium has condemned the other as *sacrilegious*.

The Many Fallacies of Dodging Church Decrees

> "But whoever is anywhere born a man, that is, a rational, mortal animal... no Christian can doubt that he ... [is] descended from Adam." —St. Augustine. *City of God.* Book XVI. Ch. 8

Some Catholic ET promoters seek to dismiss Pius II's condemnation by insisting one can still assert "belief in the existence of *other biological species of* humans" while avoiding censure by his Magisterium. This move fails spectacularly for a number of reasons.

Those who make this attempt do so by rejecting the objective and undisputed definitions of the key terms (e.g., "man," "human," "species," and "nature") and by employing anachronistic fallacies in their reading of the Magisterium. They ignore the fact that, for the entire history of the Church (not to mention all of Salvation History which preceded it), "man" and "human" (and their corresponding "nature" or "species") have always been words with unambiguous meanings: either "rational animal" or "descendant of Adam." (These terms, of course, have perfectly coextensive domains—*all* rational animals *are* descendants of Adam—they are simply two different angles from which to observe the same reality.) They proceed to pretend it is licit to take Magisterial documents written long ago and filter them through purely modernistic, contradictory, and even philosophically confused re-definitions of the term "species," apply those novel definitions to the question of "man" or "human," and thus open up the possibility for "humans" (aliens) that are nevertheless not belonging to "our biological species."

In fact, even if those sophistical acrobatics worked (they do not), an honest reading of the Magisterial texts easily reveals that *however* one defines "man" or "human," alien belief remains ruled out. In each case, by assuming the definition of "man" needed to pretend to vindicate alien belief, the ET promoters imply that the Magisterium in question is nothing but an empty tautology; a trivial truism. Obviously, no Catholic should accuse Magisterial teachings of being so inept.

> "How many a dispute could have been deflated into a single paragraph if the disputants had dared to define their terms." —Aristotle

However, as I believe that few sincere readers will fail to see that alien belief is indeed ruled out by the Magisterium we have reviewed above, I will not take up more space here by addressing their arguments within this book. Instead, whoever is interested in reading a refutation of their arguments can find it freely published at www.DSDOConnor.com/OM-BHI.

> "MAN: Latin *homo*, a human being **... [the term] is part of the Church's official vocabulary and occurs in every major document of the Catholic Church. [It signifies a] living substance, composed of a material body that dies and a spiritual soul that is immortal. ... In philosophical terms, "man" is a rational animal**..." (Fr. John Hardon's Catholic Dictionary)
>
> "... man is a substance, corporeal, living, sentient, and rational...Man is an individual, a single substance... Being capable of reasoning, [man] verifies the philosophical definition of a person: 'the individual substance of a rational nature.'" (1914 *Catholic Encyclopedia*. "Man.")
>
> "Some ... seem to be of the opinion that on other heavenly bodies perhaps there are **rational animals of another species than man. But this seems to be false, for the term "rational animal" seems to be not a genus but the ultimate species,** according to the principle of continuity; for the highest in the lowest order, for instance, the sensitive life, touches the lowest in the highest order, namely, the intellective life. Hence there is no conjunction of the highest in the sensitive life with the lowest in the intellective life, except in one species, and this is not susceptible to either increase or decrease." —Fr. Réginald Garrigou-Lagrange[47]
>
> "**But whoever is anywhere born a man, that is, a rational, mortal animal**, no matter what unusual appearance he presents in color, movement, sound, nor how peculiar he is in some power, part, or quality of

his nature, **no Christian can doubt that he springs from that one** [individual]... **if they are human, they are descended from Adam.**" —St. Augustine. *City of God*. Book XVI. Ch. 8

***

In this chapter, we have dealt with teachings expressly contained within Papal Magisterium that repudiate belief in extraterrestrial intelligence. Those who seek out the truly Catholic position on a question, however, are not limited to considering documents such as these. Sacred Tradition, considered more broadly, is also capable of settling matters for the faithful. To this more general analysis we now turn.

13. Sacred Tradition and the *Sensus Fidelium*

"The absurdity of absurdities and the most horrible unreason of all is this: that while holding that the whole Church may have erred for a thousand years in the understanding of the Word of God, Luther, Zwingli, Calvin can guarantee that they understand it aright."
—St. Francis de Sales, Doctor of the Church. *The Catholic Controversy* (Part 2, Art. 8, Ch. I)

The *Catechism of the Catholic Church* teaches:

> **The whole body of the faithful ... cannot err** in matters of belief. This characteristic is shown in the supernatural appreciation of faith (sensus fidei) on the part of the whole people, **when...they manifest a universal consent in matters of faith and morals**. (§92. Quoting Vatican II's *Lumen Gentium*)

To say that a given source "cannot err," is of course synonymous with declaring it *infallible.* While some Catholics may be surprised to hear that sources of infallibility can be found other than Scripture, or ex-cathedra Papal Proclamations (or other specific exercises of the Church's Magisterium), this declaration is nevertheless absolutely true and its rationale quite straightforward.

God is all good and all powerful: this much is obvious. It would, however, be impossible to reconcile these dogmatic attributes of God with a scenario wherein He allows the entirety of His Church on earth to succumb to error on some matter related to the Faith. Since the two contradict, one must be discarded. We cannot discard God's goodness and power, therefore we must discard the possibility that all the faithful could err.

Unfortunately, some proponents of modernism—in their efforts to overthrow express teachings of the Magisterium—have twisted this reality to conflate *popular opinion* with the *sensus fidelium* (or *sensus fidei*). Such an approach fails, for it wrongly numbers among the Faithful (*Fidelium*) those who have chosen to exclude themselves from the fold through formal heresy or other sins of omission or commission. Pope Benedict XVI astutely scolded those who harbor this tendency in an address to the International Theological Commission, when he reminded theologians that:

> [We must] distinguish the authentic sensus fidelium from its counterfeit. It is certainly not a kind of public ecclesial opinion [,] and invoking it in order to contest the teachings of the Magisterium would be unthinkable, since the sensus fidei cannot be authentically developed in believers, except to the extent in which they fully participate in the life

> of the Church, and this demands responsible adherence to the Magisterium[;] to the deposit of faith.[48]

Two years after this address, the Commission itself published a much lengthier treatment[49] of this matter, reiterating Pope Benedict's teaching above. To put it bluntly: no dissenter has a "vote" in what the *sensus fidelium* teaches; even if such a man sits in the pews, receives Communion, and calls himself Catholic, he has chosen to remove his soul from the Mystical Body of Christ.

Now, some readers may be anticipating that my next move will be to simply declare all alien believers as heretics and thus exclude them from the *sensus fidelium*. Far from it! As noted in this book's introduction, I am certainly not levying that accusation against all alien believers (true as it is that one who formally follows the implications of alien belief will fall into heresy). Seeking to ascertain the truth regarding alien belief by way of assessing the *sensus fidelium* would be an exercise in futility—*if that effort were to be undertaken today*. Since the Enlightenment, there has been too much disagreement on the matter even among souls on both sides who qualify for a "vote" in the *sensus fidelium*. But this does not mean that the *sensus fidelium* suddenly becomes irrelevant to the question of extraterrestrial intelligence. Those who would claim it does are ignoring the logical elephant in the living room; namely, the fact that *once a truth is ascertained to be infallible, that truth is permanent*. Infallible once, infallible forever. To say otherwise is incoherent.*

An analogous situation pertains to the celibacy of Christ. It is indeed a fact that Jesus Christ was celibate. He never married and He had no biological children. Yet, I am not aware of any acts of the Magisterium wherein this is explicitly and dogmatically defined, nor am I aware of any Scriptural verses that expressly and inescapably teach it. Does this mean we can put it in question? Of course not! The *sensus fidelium* absolutely assures us of its veracity. Until recently, Christians everywhere have unanimously acknowledged Christ's celibacy, and any attempt to claim Christ married would contradict the infallibility of the *sensus*. This remains so, even though polling those who call themselves Catholics today would fail

---

* If the *sensus fidelium* in the year 1300 A.D. held that human beings are the only incarnate intelligent creatures that exist, then this proposition is settled every bit as infallibly—and therefore permanently—as if the same assessment were rendered in 2000 A.D. Many Catholics will try to deny this fact, but they can only do so by denying either Catholic teaching on the *sensus fidelium* (e.g., CCC §92) or by positing an illogical absurdity: i.e., that some assertion can indeed be regarded as an infallible truth in one century and dismissed in the next. Such a man might as well check his calendar to ensure he knows what day of the week it is before asserting that two and two make four, lest he succumb to error by declaring that at the wrong time. Obviously, neither option above is palatable. Quite the contrary, a Catholic must regard *any* matter of belief that was *ever* held unanimously by the faithful to be an element of the *sensus fidelium* and therefore a settled fact of the Faith.

to demonstrate it. Unfortunately, too many have read the Dan Brown novels (e.g., *The Da Vinci Code*) and have been beguiled by their lies. This is deeply problematic for the Church, but it presents no difficulty in assessing what the *sensus fidelium* teaches, as we need only look at any former era in the Church's history to see unanimity. From this unanimity, we can deduce the teaching's permanence. And what the Dan Brown novels did to the fact of Christ's celibacy, the Enlightenment and then the deluge of science fiction has done to the fact of mankind's uniqueness.

As we will see in the forthcoming sections, assessing the *sensus fidelium* on the question of extraterrestrials is as uncomplicated as assessing it on the question of Christ's celibacy. We need not even carefully select one decade, or century, or even *millennium*, for our consideration. We need only look at any point whatsoever, in the entire history of the Church before the 18th century. Whichever era therein we select, we will find the very "universal consent" that the Church teaches is needed to manifest the *sensus fidelium*. And the substance of this "universal consent" is simple: *man alone bears the Divine Image*—no intelligent corporeal creatures *exist* besides human beings—a "man" is a rational animal, and all "men" are descendants of Adam and Eve, who were two literal people who lived on earth several thousand years ago. The *sensus fidelium* has already infallibly settled all of this.

Before exploring this universal consent, however, we must address one final strategy made by ET promoters to seek to exempt their thesis from scrutiny in this domain.

Rejection of Alien Belief: Entirely Within the Jurisdiction of the *Sensus Fidelium*

> "By means of the sensus fidei, the faithful ... recognise what is in accordance with the Gospel and to reject what is contrary to it."
>
> —International Theological Commission.
>
> *The Sensus Fidei in the Life of the Church*

Some ET promoters will simply dismiss this entire matter as one outside of the scope of the *sensus fidelium*. They will argue that "*it is not among those things that the Church is referring to when speaking of the faithful being incapable of erring 'in matters of belief.'*"

This will not work. As we discussed in this book's early chapters, alien belief has ramifications for the Faith that can only be described as seismic. All Christian commentators admit this, wherever they reside on the spectrum of views pertaining to extraterrestrial intelligence. A deluge of books have been written, conferences held, etc.—particularly in the last several years—"exploring" these massive ramifications and seeking to invent "new theologies" to accommodate alien belief. Each one radically revolutionizes Eschatology, Protology, Ecclesiology, Mariology, Christology, etc.

Here as with our last point, one cannot have his cake and eat it too. One cannot expound upon the massive ramifications of extraterrestrial intelligence for the Faith while at the same time claiming that the issue itself is "merely scientific and empirical" and thus "not a matter of belief."

Comparing alien belief to the so-called "Copernican Revolution" illustrates well the present point. Let us grant ET promotion every benefit of the doubt and say, for the sake of argument, that Catholics everywhere, in the year 1000 A.D., were in universal agreement that the sun revolves around the earth and not vice versa. An ET promoter, of course, would jump on this opportunity and argue, "*See?! Catholics everywhere were wrong about the Geocentric Model, so why can we not also grant that they were wrong about extraterrestrials?*" But this comparison is a false one. The question of whether the earth revolves around the sun or the sun revolves around the earth has no effect whatsoever on any aspect of the Faith (neither theological nor moral). It is a question that resides squarely outside of the domain of the *sensus fidelium*, even if universal consent among the faithful in answering it were to be found.

Indeed, the era of the Copernican Revolution saw the vast majority of astronomers discard the Geocentric model in order to adopt Heliocentrism. Philosophers of science still scrutinize every detail of this shift, since they use it as the benchmark for assessing and managing other actual or potential paradigm shifts in scientific consensus. Countless books and scholarly publications have been written, classes taught, and conferences held examining this "Revolution." To be sure, therefore, the impact was large *in astronomy* and some other sciences.

All the while, however, the Faith did not undergo any change whatsoever. The adoption of the Heliocentric Model had no effect on a Christian's prayer, worship, morality, creed, sacramental life, understanding of the Bible, understanding of mission, understanding of the Incarnation, understanding of Redemption, etc. As far as affecting Christian "matters of belief" (CCC, §92) is concerned, the "Copernican Revolution" was far less consequential than any of the dozens of literal revolutions being fought with cannons and swords in the same time period!

Belief in extraterrestrial intelligence, on the other hand, is a matter that resides at the extreme opposite end of the spectrum of Catholic-belief-relevance. Indeed, it is difficult to even imagine a question more germane to "matters of [Christian] belief" than this one. There is no need for me to make this point using my own opinion of the situation; more helpfully, we can simply look at what today's Catholic ET promoters themselves openly profess. One theology professor at a Catholic seminary wrote, in his 2021 book that argues for alien belief:

> [F]uture contact with an intelligent extraterrestrial civilization could call into question certain cherished religious doctrines, and result in **a reorientation of our limited terrestrial belief systems ...** for two millennia theology has [had] ... an anthropocentric myopia which is at odds with what recent science indicates ... An intelligence-containing extraterrestrial reality could result in a reformulation of certain theological principles and **may wholly redefine many of our conceptions of God and creation** ... evidence of a second Genesis could drastically call into question certain Christian foundational theological teachings regarding creation, the Incarnation, and the Redemption. Such an event would firmly establish that humans are neither the biological nor theological center of the universe, and, present as it would new and unprecedented information of religious or theological significance, which would inevitably result in **a profound reformulation or recontextualizing of theology,** requiring it to be expanded to accommodate a new Exotheology—representing the next phase of Christian theological research. **The ramifications for Christian theology are myriad.**[50]

Behold the blasphemous premises which today's "orthodox Catholic" scholars (teaching our future priests!) operate on the basis of in their promotion of alien belief. As any faithful Catholic knows, it is fundamentally *un*-Catholic even to be open to the *possibilities* of "wholly redefining" our conception of God, "calling into question Christian foundational theological teachings," or welcoming a "profound reformulation of theology." This is not merely Protestantism in disguise: it is Paganism in disguise. It is a radical rejection of the inerrancy of Scripture, the completeness and finality of Public Revelation, the infallibility of the Church and the *sensus fidelium*, the binding force of Sacred Tradition, and the security of the Lived Theology of the Saints. Premises as scandalous as these, however, lie latent within *all* ET promotion, even if not all Catholic ET promoters state them as explicitly as the theologian quoted above.

Further exposing how exceedingly dark and dangerous belief in extraterrestrials is—and how destructive it already has been in the life of the Church—will, however, be saved for Part Four. My aim in presenting the quote above is merely to illustrate one reality that is beyond question: the matter of extraterrestrial intelligence is one with such enormous ramifications for Christianity that, if even it somehow stands outside of the domain of the *sensus fidelium*, then there is no such thing as the *sensus fidelium*. The Catholic ET promoters themselves implicitly acknowledge as much.

Therefore, if we can determine that, at any point in the Church's history, the faithful were unanimous in their belief that aliens do not exist, then it is an infallible fact that aliens do not exist.

The Great Chain of Being

"It is not possible for there to be another earth than this one." —St. Thomas Aquinas

For the entirety of Sacred Tradition's development, the Faithful were unanimous in their understanding of the basic structure of the universe. Traditional Christian art displays this most helpfully.

Here we see depicted, from a superlatively high-level view, *all that is*. From the Holy Trinity, to hell, and everything in between, we see within

this "Great Chain" each of the rudimentary types of substantially existing beings. There is inanimate matter ("minerals"), there is living matter (i.e., plants and animals), there are spiritual-material creatures (human beings), there are purely spiritual creatures (angels and demons), and there is God.

The most immediately obvious reality in paintings such as these is what they lack: *empty spaces*. There is no analogous "altar to an unknown god" (cf. Acts 17:23), which ancient Athenians had placed in their temples, sensing how deeply lacking was their own theology. Quite the contrary, we only see evidence of the resolute Christian belief that no gaps exist between angels and men, and no gaps exist between angels and God. The heads of each are drawn immediately adjacent to their respective superior levels.

Admittedly, a work of art cannot alone prove a theological conclusion. My purpose in including it here is only because it is an illustration that itself illustrates the *sensus fidelium*. Whoever would argue that this is not an accurate representation of the sense of the Faithful is free to present his own findings. Indeed, ET promoters do highlight various works of art containing angels of different forms, miraculous clouds, depictions of Biblical spiritual visions, etc. However, they twist these works of art, which clearly have nothing to do with aliens, and proceed to insist that they actually depict "UFOs" piloted by extraterrestrial occupants. Despite scouring every detail of sacred history for testimonies to their thesis, no Ufologist has ever presented a convincing argument that traditional sacred art has ever depicted an extraterrestrial or an extraterrestrial-piloted craft. Even the single traditional work of art most heavily promoted by Ufologists, "The Madonna and Child with the Infant St. John," (painted by an unknown artist at an unknown time, but perhaps in the 16th century by Sebastiano Mainardi or Jacopo del Sellaio, or the 15th century by Domenico Ghirlandaio), only depicts some object in the background sky (a bluish shape emanating golden rays) that provides no reason for interpreting it as anything other than a Divine or angelic manifestation resembling Scripture's assurance that the Holy Spirit overshadowed the Blessed Virgin, (cf. Luke 1:35) and elsewhere in the Gospels such a presence of the Divine is described as a luminous cloud (cf. Matthew 17:5) or a "thick cloud" (Exodus 19:9).

Note that a major purpose of sacred art is precisely this: to symbolically represent invisible spiritual realities in visible ways which, though they are of course metaphorical, are nevertheless theologically helpful. Where sacred art is found to accomplish this task, one is not thereby given license to interpret the piece literally. It would, of course, be ridiculous to interpret the drawing above as a teaching that God the Father is literally an old man with a beard sitting on a throne, or to observe depictions of Judgment Day and conclude the Devil is literally a red-tights-wearing, pitchfork-wielding man with a goat head. However, it would be even more absurd to observe various spiritual realities, visions, events, angels, etc., depicted symbolically in sacred art, and conclude that they must be representations of extraterrestrial piloted UFOs.

Returning to the Great Chain of Being, other works of traditional sacred art depict the same thing, and each delineates the same basic categories as the one above. The same lesson can also be gleaned from all the traditional works of art depicting Judgment Day. Artists inspired by their Faith have made countless such paintings, each one depicting human beings as the *only* incarnate creatures subject to judgment. Any rational creature would, however, require a spot at Judgment Day. Two thousand years of sacred architecture throughout the world testifies to the same belief. These "sermons in stone" which, we could say, render incarnate the *sensus fidelium*, give no place to belief in aliens. Two thousand years of authentic private revelations—despite detailing Heaven, Hell, Purgatory, the cosmos, and everything in between—are likewise devoid of any teaching that aliens exist, and only confirm the completeness of the "Great Chain" seen above. (Manifestly false private "revelations" often speak of aliens, as we will see in Part Four.)

Two thousand years of Christian piety, too, is devoid of any recognition of extraterrestrial intelligence. No such piety can be found wherein Christians have prayed for aliens or incorporated them into their understanding of creation. This is true even in the Old Testament: consider, for example, the Canticle in Daniel Chapter 3—recited continuously to this day in the Liturgy of the Hours of the Catholic Church. There, Christians bless God on behalf of *all things* in the universe—"**all** works of the Lord" (Daniel 3:35): from angels, to waters, to sun and moon, to stars, to fire, to frost and chill, to lightnings and clouds, to all water creatures, to all beasts and cattle, to all "sons of men" (v.60), and everything in between. Despite such breathtaking comprehensiveness and detail, there is no single verse within this canticle that gives the slightest space—explicitly or implicitly—for aliens within "**<u>all</u> the works of the Lord**."

Ancient and Medieval Christians Knew of the Extraterrestrial Thesis, and Rejected It

A final argument that ET promoters may attempt in order to exempt their thesis from repudiation is to claim that even assessing the *sensus fidelium* on this matter amounts to the *argumentum ad ignorantiam* fallacy. That is, they may claim that the current chapter involves asserting the faithful rejected some thesis when they merely knew nothing of it—and therefore its complete absence from their speech, writings, prayer, conduct, etc., only due to their inability to so much as comprehend such a notion (as extraterrestrials). This final attempt, however, fails for two reasons.

First, the faithful did not merely refrain from speaking about aliens. They affirmatively rebuked the hypothesis by way of their affirmation that only man bears the Divine image, that the Word of God did in fact assume one and only one nature, that the Blessed Virgin is the one and only Mother of God, that there is only one (temporal) world, etc.

Second, the faithful were *not* unaware of the extraterrestrial thesis, therefore its complete absence from Christianity for over a millennium is anything but irrelevant. As we will see, belief in extraterrestrials only became common during the Enlightenment, and was only espoused by *any* Christians for well over a millennium after Christ. Nevertheless, early Christians knew well of this thesis. Indeed, it was simply another one of the Pagan absurdities that was common in the cultures into which Christianity spread in its early days.

Christianity initially spread predominantly through the Hellenistic world, therefore if early Christians understood the beliefs and practices of one culture in particular (aside from Judaism), it would be that of Greek culture. The New Testament itself is written in Greek, and references to the Greek thinkers are explicitly contained within its pages. For example, we are told that "*Some of the Epicurean and Stoic philosophers [two Greek schools of thought] also conversed with [Paul]*" (Acts 18:18), whereas later in the same passage, the Apostle quotes Greek poets verbatim, "*'In [God] we live and move and have our being'; as even some of your poets have said, 'for we are indeed his offspring.'*" (v. 28).

St. Paul notes that the preaching of Christ crucified is regarded as "foolishness" by the "Greeks" (1 Corinthians 1:23). And, of course, the New Testament is not shy in noting the idolatry of the Greeks (e.g., Acts 14, Acts 19), even instructing us that "The things which the heathens sacrifice, they sacrifice to devils, and not to God" (1 Corinthians 10:20), for, as the Old Testament teaches, "the gods of the pagans are demons." (Psalm 95:5)

The purpose here, of course, is not merely to observe that St. Paul himself was well versed in Greek thought. That much is obvious. The point is that his letters and his acts largely formed the nascent Church; their repeated reference to the Greeks and to Greek thinkers assures us that the thought of this culture was not an unknown thing to early Christianity. All of this, moreover, is not even to mention how many early Christians themselves were thoroughly Greek. Indeed, the Fathers of the Church were largely veritable experts in Greek thought and quoted the Greek philosophers copiously.

Suffice it to say that if a proposition was well known among the Greek thinkers, we can be certain it was not missed by the early Christian Church. Alien belief is precisely such a proposition; common among the ancient Greeks, it was certainly known by early Christians.

The Popularity of Alien Belief Among the Pre-Christian Hedonistic and Atheistic Pagans

Several centuries before Christ, pre-Socratic philosophers were locked in a raging debate on just what constituted "the *Urstoff*" – the fundamental stuff of the universe. In other words, they were desperate to know what all things of the cosmos could be "boiled down to." Various options were presented over the centuries from Thales (born 626 B.C.) proposing water, to Heraclitus (born 540 B.C.) proposing fire, to Pythagoras (born 570 B.C.) proposing number, to Anaxagoras (born only a few decades before Socrates – 500 B.C.) proposing that what is most fundamental is Divine Mind.

Among the most famous of the pre-Socratics, however, were the Atomists. These materialist philosophers, particularly Democritus (born 460 B.C.) and Leucippus (born 510 B.C.), still gain much praise for pinning their Urstoff as atoms. Although speaking of "atoms" might make them appear, superficially, the most scientifically accurate of the pre-Socratics, these atomists were, in fact, farther from the truth than plenty of their peers. These faults become apparent even from an empirical standpoint, not to mention their metaphysical fallacies. (For example, they had no place in their physics for the notion of forces or energy – though other pre-Socratics did.) More significantly, their philosophy formed (even if quite remotely) the original intellectual foundations for the many atheistic philosophies we see to this day.

These two philosophers in particular were famous believers in extraterrestrials. Among the ancient Greek thinkers, ***"They are the first to whom we can with absolute certainty attribute the odd concept of innumerable [inhabited] worlds."***[51] As written by St. Hippolytus of Rome – a deeply influential Christian writer born in the second century – about the atomists:

> **Democritus holds the same view as Leucippus ...[he claimed] there are innumerable worlds**, which differ in size. In some worlds there is no sun and moon, in others they are larger than in our world, and in others more numerous. ... some [worlds are] decreasing; in some parts they are arising, in others failing. They are destroyed by collision one with another. There are **some worlds** devoid of living creatures or plants or any moisture.[52]

Note that "some" of these "innumerable" worlds which the ancient Greek Atomists posited were described as devoid of living creatures, indicating they believed that most (or at least "some" others) *were* inhabited. Resembling the materialistic philosophy – Atomism – which denied the supernatural, was the hedonistic philosophy – Epicureanism – which denied that anything but carnal pleasure was good. Recall that the Epicureans are explicitly recorded in the New Testament (cf. Acts 18:18). Both promoted belief in extraterrestrials.

Epicurus (born 341 B.C.), the eponymous founder of the aforementioned school of thought, declared:

> There are infinite worlds both like and unlike this world of ours. For the atoms being infinite in number, as was already proved, are borne on far out into space. ... there nowhere exists an obstacle to the infinite number of worlds[53]

In another letter, this prototypical hedonist insisted that: "**We must believe that in all worlds there are living creatures and plants and other things we see in this world.**"[54] Metrodorus, a follower of Epicurus, agreed. He taught that infinite worlds must exist because—as he reckoned in a manner fallacious not only in its logical form but also invalid in its base premise—infinite atoms exist.[55]

Some sources, however, indicate that even more pre-Socratics espoused belief in "innumerable worlds" (which invariably included belief in extraterrestrial intelligence). They number Anaximander, Anaximenes, Archelaus, Xenophanes, and Diogenes of Apollonia among the pre-Christian Pagan alien believers.[56]

Suffice it to say that, however some of the yet-unresolved debates about exactly which of the thinkers above espoused belief in extraterrestrials play out, one fact is clear: belief in extraterrestrials was prominent in the Pagan thinking that preceded Christianity; even in the very same culture into which the latter first exploded. The most prominent Catholic ET promoters openly acknowledge this fact. The same scholar quoted above also wrote that "**in all these worlds [posited by the Atomists] there are living creatures. Under the influence of these Greek philosophers, this plurality of worlds idea eventually gained a following among certain Roman thinkers as well,** such as the poet Lucretius"[57]

Moreover, the pre-Socratics were particularly closely studied by early and medieval Christians. The Church Father St. Justin Martyr (born 100 A.D.) even called Heraclitus a "Christian before Christ," on account of the latter's teaching on the Logos. St. Augustine frequently commented on the pre-Socratics. In many ways, we know more about the pre-Socratics thanks to the writings of early Christians than we do from the writings of the pre-Socratics themselves! To claim Christian thinkers might simply have been unaware of the alien belief among the pre-Socratics would be like claiming a political commentator is unaware of who is running for president.

It is also worth noting that, from the very beginnings of the debate on extraterrestrial intelligence in Western Civilization, we already see the position taken on it separating the wheat from the chaff. While those with legacies of moral and spiritual destruction (the atheistic Atomists and hedonistic Epicureans) believed in extraterrestrials, the nobler philosophers had no use for such theories—Plato and Aristotle even explicitly condemned the notion of multiple inhabited worlds!

Condemnations of Alien Belief by the Fathers of the Church

We have seen that belief in extraterrestrials was quite visible in the writings of the ancient Greek philosophers. For the most part, however, the great early Christian writers—particularly those we regard as Fathers of the Church—apparently regarded this thesis as too outlandish to be even worth their time addressing. Apart from one (who was condemned by the Church as a heretic), the few who did address it denounced it.

Summarizing her extensive research on this very topic, Dr. Marie George, a Catholic philosophy professor at St. John's University, concluded:

> My position on the early Church Fathers (from the first through the eighth century) and the Doctors of the Church (from 170 to 1280, i.e., from Hippolytus of Rome to St. Albert) is that all of them who explicitly raise the question of whether there is one world or many, or who at least take an explicit stand on the question, reject pluralism, with the exception of Origen... **nothing in tradition supports the notion that a plurality of inhabitable planets exists** ... those [Church Fathers] who consider the question of a plurality of worlds plainly come down on the side of a negative answer... **every church Father and Doctor who paid some sort of attention to some version of many earths, always rejected the notion, with the single exception of Origen**... patristic authors speak more often about there being only one universe than about there being only one earth. Still, all those who do consider the many-earths question, even if only implicitly, **all give a negative answer**. The Fathers and Doctors that reject Origen's sequential universes, implicitly reject his sequential earths along with them.[58]

Indeed, the facts bear out her analysis. St. Hippolytus—the Bishop of Pontus, whom we have already quoted—also authored the *Elenchus*, or the "Refutation of All Heresies." Therein he dealt with this Pagan belief of extraterrestrials. Regarding his teachings, Dr. George notes:

> Hippolytus of Rome (170-235) describes in some detail Democritus' views that ... other universes harbored life (and thus contained earthlike planets). While Hippolytus does not actually critique this view, it is plain that he rejects it, for he recounts it in a work entitled: *The Refutation of all Heresies*. Hippolytus both rejects Democritus' infinite universes, and the earths that come with these universes.[59]

St. Philastrius, Bishop of Brescia, expressly condemned the view as heretical. The saint wrote:

> **There is another heresy that says that there are infinite and innumerable worlds,** according to the empty opinion of certain philosophers—since **Scripture has said that there is one world and teaches us about one world**—taking this view from the apocrypha of the prophets, that is from the secrets, as the pagans themselves called them; there was also the Democritus who asserted there to be many worlds; he agitated the souls of many people and stirred up doubtful opinions with his diverse errors, since he proclaimed this [i.e., the plurality of worlds] as proceeding from his own wisdom.[60]

St. Jerome, Father and Doctor of the Church—and originator of the official Catholic Bible (the Latin Vulgate)—was equally zealous in condemning this error. He wrote:

> Now I find among many bad things written by Origen the following **most distinctly heretical:** that the Son of God is a creature, that the Holy Spirit is a servant: **that there are innumerable worlds**...that in the restitution of all things, when the fulness of forgiveness will have been reached, ... Archangels and Angels, the devil, the demons and the souls of men ... will be of one condition and degree ... then will begin a new world from a new origin, and other bodies in which the souls who fall from heaven will be clothed; so that we may have to fear that we who are now men may afterwards be born women, and one who is now a virgin may chance then to be a prostitute. **These things I point out as heresies in the books of Origen**... (*Apology Against Rufinus*. Book II. § 12)

Indeed, the ramblings of Origen on this topic constituted a veritable sci-fi Deception 1,700 years before its time. In another of St. Jerome's writings, he details Origen's wild teachings, which we will consider in the following section.

Some Catholic ET promoters will present quotes from St. John Chrysostom or others as support for their thesis. In fact, in these teachings, this great Father of the Church was merely asserting that God's *power was sufficient* to make innumerable worlds. He was most assuredly not arguing that God might have done this; still less that God did do such a thing (as we saw earlier, Chrysostom expressly condemns this notion). The serious scholars who have studied this matter have called out such abuse of St. John Chrysostom's teachings for what it is: "**a careless reading of certain patristic authors... [these Fathers] are simply affirming that God is able to make many worlds,**" as Dr. George noted.

St. Augustine, in his greatest work, *City of God*, also denounced the multiple earths hypothesis. He rejected "**Epicurus' dream of innumerable worlds**" (Book XI, Ch. 5) He even contradicted those who, "though they do not suppose that this world is eternal, are of [the] opinion... that this is not the only world..." (Book XII, Ch. 11)

Later still, Augustine refuted the error of believing that men exist (on the "underside" of a round earth) who had not descended from Adam and Eve, in the context of the debate on the Antipodes. (Book XVI. Ch. 9) Although he had no problem with a round earth, he denounces as lacking any credibility the notion that realms detached from the core of humanity are nevertheless populated by rational beings. For it would contradict Scripture, which, he reminds us, "gives no false information," to assert that such beings, though not offspring of Adam, nevertheless exist.

Here as elsewhere, ET promoters employ the usual definitional fallacy (addressed in our preceding chapter), insisting that Augustine's only point was that we cannot believe in "men" who did not descend from Adam, but that we are still free to believe in aliens. To repeat: what, pray tell, does the word "man" mean? If it merely means "those who descended from Adam," then they are accusing Augustine of folly by dedicating a large section of his most important work to repeated reiteration of a tautology. If it means "rational animal," then extraterrestrial aliens are likewise condemned. Those options are the only possibilities for the definition.

The Sci-Fi Deceptions of the Heretic, Origen: 1,700 Years Early, and Condemned on the Spot

> "This being the nature of Origen's book, **is it anything short of madness to change a few blasphemous passages** regarding the Son and the Holy Spirit and then to publish the rest unchanged with an unprincipled eulogy when the **parts unaltered as well as the parts altered flow from the same fountain head of gross impiety**?"
> —St. Jerome, Father of the Church

Catholic ET promoters treat the writings of the early Christian writer, Origen, and his belief in multiple inhabited worlds, as a supposed vindication of their thesis. They concede that Origen presented many teachings that were unorthodox, however they misleadingly insist that the Church itself, and the Fathers, were only opposed to Origen's "*entire system*" and the "unorthodox ***conclusions***" he drew from his premises.

Such authors ignore several points which refute their claims. First, as we saw above, the Church Father St. Jerome *specifically* condemned Origen's teaching that there were multiple worlds; as did St. Philastrius and others. They did not merely condemn the "unorthodox conclusions [Origen] drew" from that premise; they condemned the premise itself.

Second, they are misusing the "don't throw out the baby with the bathwater" adage. As we saw from St. Jerome above, there is no baby in the bathwater here; there is no redeeming value to be found in Origen's cosmology. It is thoroughly corrupt. It is true that Origen displayed personal holiness and had some profound teachings to give in entirely separate matters. When, however, it comes to his cosmology and eschatology, no Christian who wishes to abide in orthodoxy would so much as touch them. This will become clear when reading St. Jerome's description of Origen's theory on multiple worlds, contained in the former's Letter to Avitus:

> [Origen] maintains that ... after every end a fresh beginning springs forth ... [whereupon] one who is now a human being may in another world become a demon, while one who by reason of his negligence is now a demon may hereafter be placed in a more material body and thus become a human being ... and according to what they have done shall have special duties assigned to them in particular worlds. Moreover, the very demons and rulers of darkness in any world or worlds, if they are willing to turn to better things, may become human beings and so come back to their first beginning. ... we men may change into any other reasonable beings, and that not once only ... but time after time...(§3) The sun also and the moon and the rest of the constellations are alive ... he has finally reasoned with much diffuseness that an angel, a human soul, and a demon ... may in punishment for great negligence or folly be transformed into brutes ... [or] to dwell in water, to assume the shape of this or that animal; so that we have reason to fear a metamorphosis not only into four-footed things but even into fishes... (§4) In [Origen's] second book he maintains a plurality of worlds; not, however, as Epicurus taught, many like ones existing at once, but a new one beginning each time that the old comes to an end. There was a world before this world of ours, and after it there will be first one and then another and so on in regular succession...(§5) **In speaking thus does he not most clearly follow the error of the heathen and foist upon the simple faith of Christians the ravings of philosophy?** (§6) And although he has not expressly said it, it is yet implied in his words that as for men God became man to set men free, so for the salvation of demons when He comes to deliver them He will become a demon. (§13)

St. Jerome concludes his letter to Avitus with the common-sense but stark warning with which we began this section, reminding its recipient that it is sheer "madness" to suppose that only removing a few of the blasphemies from Origen's teachings on multiple worlds can save the work as a whole. Indeed, what we have seen quoted above (*heavily abridged for the sake of space; the madness of Origen's cosmology extends far beyond what is presented here*) supports one and only one conclusion: the individual who presented these teachings was under a strong deception about the cosmos—a fundamental and fatal misunderstanding about mankind's role in creation—and if anything, we should treat his opinions on this matter as an indication of what *not* to believe.

Lest we wrongly regard the condemnations above as merely the opinions of some Church Fathers against another which we are free to assess on our own terms, the relevant Church decrees should be included. The Second Council of Constantinople was quite blunt in dealing with Origen. Including him in the same breath as the most famous heretic of the early Church, Arius, it declared that those who so much as fail to anathematize Origen are themselves anathematized:

> **If anyone does not anathematize Arius,** Eunomius, Macedonius, Apollinarius Nestorius, Eutyches and **Origen**, as well as their heretical books... **let him be anathema**. (Anathemas Against the Three Chapters. §11)

In sum: Origen's teachings in this arena do not merely require modification; they demand categorical rejection. If, upon surveying the teachings of the Fathers on this issue, we see that the sole dissenting voice came from Origen, the lesson we should glean from that is not ambiguous.

The Thousand Year Deafening Silence: ET Promoters' Own Arguments Refute Their Thesis

Following the condemnation of Origen's heretical views—both by the Church itself and by other Church Fathers—Christians, unsurprisingly, left this matter aside (with the notable exception of Virgil, whose alien belief was condemned by Pope Zachary). It was rightly regarded as yet another tenet of ancient Paganism from which Christ had rescued us. It was best off ignored. Indeed, diabolical deceptions are only worth addressing when they become prevalent. Writing treatises against them when virtually nobody alive believes in them is pointless. We have already seen that it is beyond doubt that early Christians were well aware of the extraterrestrial thesis, therefore their choice to ignore it speaks volumes.

One should feel free to read any book or article available, peruse the archives of any conference that has been held on this topic, or even scour the primary sources himself: he will only find vindicated that more than a millennium of Christian history passed without the extraterrestrial thesis receiving *any* support. The books recently written (and there have been many) by the ET promoters invariably pass on from Origen to the thinkers we will address next, who came many centuries later. Many openly admit that they cannot find a single (non-condemned) Christian before the 15th century who so much as uttered a single word in support of extraterrestrials.

Recently, Catholic ET promoters have been particularly zealous to ensure their readers understand that the question of extraterrestrial intelligence was not only a matter of discussion during the "space age" that commenced in the mid-20th century. This much certainly must be conceded. Some thinkers proposed the existence of aliens a few hundred years earlier. Incapable of examining the implications of their own findings, they fail to realize this demonstrates the errancy of their thesis, not its legitimacy. Although they claim victory by presenting the texts of some early modern thinkers who believed in aliens, they only ensure defeat by implicitly proving that no (non-heretical) thinkers of the entire first millennium-and-a-half of the Church believed the same.

Dr. Michael Crowe, a Professor Emeritus at the University of Notre Dame, may be the contemporary scholar who has most extensively chronicled the history of the extraterrestrial intelligence debate. In the following passage from the preface to his book on the history of alien belief, he wrote the following:

> It is sometimes assumed that belief in extraterrestrial life began in the twentieth century. We shall see that this is far from the truth. Evidence is available to show that nearly half the leading intellectuals of the eighteenth and nineteenth centuries discussed extraterrestrial life issues in their writings.[61]

Professor Crowe begins this book—the scope of which includes everything from ancient times to the year 1915—by proving that belief in aliens was alive and well in Pagan, pre-Christian times. After demonstrating that fact, however, he could only find enough material to fill up *eight pages* (of a 544-page book) to discussing alien belief in an entire *one thousand four hundred years* (most of the span covered by the book) of history!

Moreover, not one quotation provided within those eight pages demonstrates any alien belief whatsoever existed among Christians (only refutations of the same)—except, of course, from Origen. This book was based on an immense amount of research. In its preface, Dr. Crowe shared details of the impressive depth and breadth of reading he undertook to accurately survey alien belief throughout history. What this tell us is simple: he did not find any alien belief for a millennium of Christianity because *there was no* alien belief during that millennium of Christianity.

Many books like this have come out in recent years, and many more will likely come out soon as Christian scholars continue to jump on the UFO-bandwagon. Indeed, a more recent book—written by the same Catholic theologian ET promoter and seminary professor quoted earlier—concedes (though with errors):

> The majority of **Christian theologians prior to the thirteenth century,** with the exception of Origen and William of Ockham [sic], **saw the plurality [of inhabited worlds] as *wholly* incompatible with doctrine**, and due to fear of Church censors few of its advocates are notable until the seventeenth to nineteenth centuries with the gradual acceptance of Copernican cosmology.[62]

His concession would have been appropriately worded if, instead of "majority," he acknowledged it was the *entirety* of pre-13th century Christian theologians who dismissed belief in multiple worlds (i.e., aliens) as heretical (for he already notes the only two exceptions in the same line—Ockham, however, died in the mid-14th century, therefore he was not "prior to the thirteenth century"). Outlandishly, however, this author implies that an entire 1,200 year span (*to be accurate, however, he should have referred to the 1,400 year span leading up to Nicholas of Cusa – even Ockham did not endorse aliens*) of Christian theologians—which includes countless saints, Fathers of the Church, and Doctors of the Church—only hold the contra-ET view "due to fear of Church censors," or at least that the same explanation provides the sole reason why ET-believing Christians were not "notable" until the so-called Enlightenment. One wonders how so many other errors—which were more resolutely opposed than the multiple-inhabited-worlds thesis—became quite *notable* indeed during the first 1,200 years of the Church!

Confirming that this author seems to hold the same egregiously mistaken views on the *sensus fidelium* that are endemic to Catholic ET promotion, he writes earlier in the same book that a certain three medieval thinkers who acknowledged the *metaphysical possibility* of multiple worlds (simply as a consequence of describing God's Omnipotence) denied *reality* of the plurality of worlds merely because they "ultimately appealed to the dominant medieval conservative religious authority."[63]

I highlight this only because it illustrates a widespread fallacy among today's theologians, who are prone to regard the genuine unanimous consensus of the Faithful in earlier centuries as a mere artifact of "overly rigid" times, or perhaps even backwards ones. In fact, such flippant disregard of our Sacred Tradition is really a sin against the Holy Spirit. It implicitly supposes that God is too inept to guide His Church—a task that can only really be accomplished by a union of scientists and "enlightened" theologians who are open to, as this author wrote earlier, "**wholly redefining our conceptions of God and creation**" in light of alien belief.

After dismissing Buridan's, Ockham's, and Oresme's own rejection of belief in multiple worlds as a capitulation to "conservative religious authority," this author proceeds to introduce one he regards as a real hero, assuring us that "Nicholas of Cusa (1401-1464), German philosopher, theologian, and astronomer, showed no fear of Church authorities... [he was] the first theologian"[64] to argue for a plurality of inhabited worlds.

To Cusa, then—but, first, another Nicholas who preceded him—we must now turn our attention.

A Tale of Two Nicholases and The Great Rupture: 14th—15th Centuries

The 14th century Bishop of Lisieux, Nicole (or Nicholas) Oresme was one of the most influential thinkers of his era. A philosopher, physicist, mathematician, and economist, he is even regarded as "**one of the principal founders of modern science**." (cf. old *Catholic Encyclopedia*). In fact, he was the *actual* originator of various concepts popularly attributed to Copernicus (e.g., relative motion, the earth's rotation, and other concepts). Accordingly, Oresme is regarded as a uniquely original thinker of medieval times. Even the secular *Stanford Encyclopedia of Philosophy* extolls him as being:

> ...one of the most eminent scholastic philosophers, famous for his original ideas, his independent thinking and his critique of several Aristotelian tenets. **His work provided some basis for the development of modern mathematics and science**. Furthermore he is generally considered the greatest medieval economist.[65]

Suffice it to say that, if any one Catholic thinker were to be free of supposed "shackles of human tradition" or "enslavement to Aristotelian thought," Bishop Oresme—*not* Nicolas of Cusa—would be that man. Oresme even departed from some thinkers on the possibility of the plurality of worlds—insisting, contrary to them, that God *could* make multiple worlds (i.e., that doing so was ontologically within His power). As we can see, he was uniquely well positioned to be one to accept belief in ETs if there were any grounds for regarding such a thesis as orthodox. Instead, Oresme wrote:

> God can and could in His omnipotence make another world besides this one or several like or unlike it. Nor will Aristotle or anyone else be able to prove completely the contrary. But, **of course, there has never been nor will there be more than one [inhabited] corporeal world, as was stated above.**[66]

I have inserted the bracketed word above because it clarifies Oresme's intention, in accordance with his own reference to what was "stated above." Several paragraphs earlier, he wrote:

> ...**if several worlds existed**, no one of them would be outside Him nor outside His power; but **surely other intelligences would exist in one world and others in the other world**, as already stated.

Therefore, we can see that when Oresme refers to "another world," he is referring to a world inhabited by intelligent creatures—he says that such creatures would "surely" exist in another world *if* such a world existed. (Mere planets of dead rock we observe in the sky—whether with naked eye or telescope—are not, in his verbiage within the present context, "other worlds.")

Despite his unimpeachable originality and his proven willingness to propose potentially controversial teachings, Oresme dismisses the possibility of aliens, going so far as to say that "***of course***" they do not exist. That well-chosen prefatory phrase indicates that Oresme knew full well he was merely reiterating what all Christians believed: human beings are the only incarnate intelligences that exist.

> "[Oresme] accepted the **unanimous notion** that 'there has never been nor will there be more than one corporeal [inhabited] world.'"[67]

Commenting on Oresme, the renowned 19th century French physicist, philosopher, and historian of science, Pierre Duhem (also a Catholic), wrote:

> Someone like Nicole Oresme would have allowed that space can contain several systems...But less daring than Plutarch [a Pagan], he would not have been tempted to place **inhabitants on these worlds. As far as we know, no one defended such an assumption during the Middle Ages,** when Nicholas of Cusa, whose imagination knew no bounds, proposed it...**the first time in Western Christianity that one heard someone speak about the plurality of inhabited worlds, it was proposed by** [Nicholas of Cusa] [68]

Two things must be noted to prevent misunderstandings of Duhem's observation. First, Duhem obviously does not mean that Western Christians *literally never heard* anyone propose aliens (simply see the quotes in the preceding sections for a sure proof of the contrary). Of course, Duhem means that, with Cusa, we saw the first *Christian* to assert such a thing. Second, Duhem does not intend to imply that Eastern Christianity had already seen such theses presented; he is merely focusing on his own area of expertise—the development of Western science.

Here we have yet another proof that the existence of aliens is utterly absent from the beliefs of any Christians, aside from one condemned heretic, Origen, and one priest, Virgil, who recanted, for one-and-a-half-thousand years. What, then, shall we say about the other Nicholas—Nicholas of Cusa—with whom Pierre Duhem contrasts Nicholas Oresme?

Alien Belief in the Church—1,400 Years Late, and Dead On Arrival

Nicholas of Cusa was a German thinker who was born just two decades after the passing of Bishop Nicole Oresme. Pope Nicholas V named him a Cardinal, he was made Vicar General in the Papal States, and was appointed Papal legate to Germany. He was often regarded as the second most powerful person in the entire Church. Nevertheless, the 300 years that followed his own life saw no adoption of his thought among Catholics, save one man, Giordano Bruno, who we will address shortly.

Unlike earlier Christian thinkers—who, even if they conceded God "could have" made multiple inhabited worlds, resolutely affirmed that He *did not do so* (that is, apart from Origen et. al.)—Cusa's support of aliens is unambiguous. He expressly supported the view that,

> Life, as it exists here on earth in the form of men, animals and plants, is to be found, let us suppose, in a higher form in the solar and stellar regions. [69]

Cusa expounded upon this thesis, declaring:

> Those on the earth are more material and rough, so that the intellectual

> beings found on the sun are more in actuality and less in potency, while the inhabitants of the earth are more in potency and less in actuality; **the inhabitants of the moon are somewhere in between these two extremes ... The regions of the other stars are similar to this, for we believe that none of them is deprived of inhabitants.**[70]

Obviously, this was an utterly novel and radical teaching. For the first time in the history of the Church since the condemned Origen (and Virgil), we see a thinker—a Cardinal, no less!—announcing his belief in aliens.

Cusa, as we have settled, was extremely well known. What he wrote was widely read. Had there been grounds for taking this view seriously, we could be certain to see a deluge of fellow Catholic writers taking the lead of this renowned Cardinal; immediately announcing their own belief in extraterrestrials. Instead, we hear only crickets. A politically important cleric, Cusa was graced with his unorthodox views simply being politely ignored instead of being openly denounced.

This refusal to adopt Cusa's beliefs was evident not merely in the sacred but also in the secular writers. As Dr. Michael Crowe notes:

> **In studying the period from 1500 to 1750, one is struck by the hesitancy, indeed resistance, shown by some of the founders of the scientific revolution to a full-blown pluralism.** ... [which is] defined as the doctrine that the earth is but one of the inhabited planets ... [even Galileo], in at least six passages comment[s] on the question of extraterrestrial life. These range from rejection to cautious reserve concerning it...[he wrote,] **'I agree with Apelles [Christopher Scheiner] in regarding as false and damnable the view of those who would put inhabitants on Jupiter, Venus, Saturn, and the moon, meaning by "inhabitants" animals like ours, and men in particular.'"**[71]

During the "Enlightenment," however, Cusa's views were indeed adopted. No writers who took this path are now venerated as saints, blesseds, venerables, or servants of God. None garnered any meaningful reception in the Church at large. Nevertheless, this trickle of Christians endorsing aliens, which eventually grew into a stream, was—tellingly—mostly evident *outside* of the Catholic Church (among those in newly formed denominations whose very *raison d'être* was to overthrow 1,500 years of unanimous Christian teaching). It is unsurprising to see the readiness with which such thinkers would also repudiate a millennium-and-a-half of unbroken Christian belief that man alone bears the Divine Image. The same Catholic ET promoter quoted earlier also alleges that:

> In contrast to the Roman Church's anti-pluralist stance, many European Protestants in the beginning of the Enlightenment accepted a belief of a cosmos containing extraterrestrial life...[72]

Recall that only a Catholic who holds to the entirety of the Deposit of Faith—among other conditions—has any "vote" in the *sensus fidelium*. It is illicit to seek to assess this *sensus* by examining the views of non-Catholics.

In any event, we know that assessment would be superfluous by the century under consideration, as the preceding ones already had settled, infallibly, that man alone is made in the image of God.

How, then, should a Catholic regard this contribution of Cusa? A few considerations here are relevant, which we will cover in the following section.

Destructive Legacies of Alien Belief: Nicholas of Cusa and the Execution of Giordano Bruno

In assessing the proper reception of Nicholas of Cusa's teachings, we should begin by considering that he would have been a prime contender for canonization, had he been worthy of this honor. He was a Cardinal, known and respected by Popes, and is referred to as "**arguably the most important German thinker of the fifteenth century.**" (*Stanford Encyclopedia of Philosophy*) The German philosopher, Erns Alfred Cassirer, regarded Cusa as "**the first modern thinker**." One would expect that if Catholics should highly regard Cusa's essentially first-in-Church-History not-directly-condemned declaration that aliens exist, the Church would have honored him for this. The earliest promoters of authentic teachings that are relevant to the Faith—and certainly their originators—are usually especially venerated by the Church; for they are the ones who have contributed to her legitimate development. If alien belief were a Godly development in the Church's history, one would be sure to find its undisputed first originator to be greatly exalted. Instead, the Church has given him no exaltation whatsoever. Six hundred years later, he is still not even a "Servant of God."

While the Catholic Church has not honored Cusa, various esoteric and even Satanic groups around the world have done precisely that. One of the most famous Satanic "Churches," the Thelemites, is an occult group founded by Aleister Crowley. Their central text, *The Book of the Law*, contains a "revelation" from the "angel" (demon) Aiwass. This false revelation is simply a slight paraphrase of Cusa's heretical teaching that the material universe is infinite: "**Crowley saw the god in terms analogous to Nicholas of Cusa's description of the universe as a reflection of God: '*an infinite sphere whose centre is everywhere, circumference nowhere.*'**"[73] As an aside, we should note that Crowley himself factors heavily into the development of modern alien belief. The first depiction of aliens from which derive much of today's so-called alien encounters and abductions—"the greys"—comes from Crowley's encounter with a demon, which he drew. (More on this point will be discussed in Part Four.)

Secondly, we have Cusa's other novel theories to examine. Indeed, Cusa's problematic views were not restricted to his belief in the plurality of worlds populated by extraterrestrials. His work, *De Paci Fidei* (On the

Peace of Faith) at least borders on, if not asserts, a dangerous religious syncretism. He claims that all religions aim at the same goal—a quite remarkable thesis considering what, for example, Buddhism "aims" at (namely, the mere extinguishing of the self, along with no notion whatsoever of God!). He even refers to the diversity of faiths on earth as "one religion in a variety of rites." Bizarrely, he claims that the Koran (Islam's basic text) teaches the Divinity of Christ and the Trinity.*

I also bring this to the fore because, as we will see in a later chapter, belief in aliens and religious syncretism often today go hand-in-hand, therefore it is unsurprising to see the same dynamic evident in Christianity's first noteworthy alien belief promoter. Naturally, the early stages of a deception are not as severe as later ones, but they nevertheless set the chain of events in motion and display the same basic relations. Cusa is often accused of espousing some pantheistic beliefs, along with the heresy of Conciliarism (which regards a council's authority as superior to the Pope's). I will, however, leave out analyzing those accusations for the sake of space.

Our third point is to examine Cusa's legacy; the "fruits" of his teachings—which, as Our Lord admonishes, tell us the quality of the tree from which they derive (cf. Matthew 7:15). And this brings us to the one and only thinker—Giordano Bruno—in the centuries that followed Cusa who welcomed the latter's views on aliens. As the *Stanford Encyclopedia of Philosophy* notes, "**in spite of his significance few later thinkers, apart from Giordano Bruno...were influenced by [Cusa] until the late nineteenth century**."[74]

***

The 16th century Dominican priest (not long after his ordination, he left the order), Giordano Bruno, was born 84 years after the death of Cusa. Although he did not write until over a century had passed since Cusa's death, he was nevertheless essentially the first to adopt Cusa's views on aliens. As Cusa avoided condemnation, Bruno is even described by some

* Thankfully, Cusa did not go so far as today's syncretists do. He did argue that Christianity is the fulfillment of all religion. It is not, however, plausible to argue, as Cusa does, that each religion, as we see it, is already pointing towards Christianity. Even if all religions contain some "rays of truth," sometimes those "rays" are outnumbered by the errors, therefore it would be wrong to claim that, despite such a multitude of errors, certain Pagan religions are *already* aimed at Christianity and can successfully lead their adherents to Christianity if *only* we point to certain aspects therein. Whoever takes that approach to evangelization will not lead many—or *any*—Pagans to genuine Christianity. Quite the contrary, much, if not most, of the teachings of some religions must be simply refuted, discarded, and *replaced* with those Christian teachings that stand in fundamental opposition to them. Indeed, there is some room for "inculturation" in evangelization. But there is no room for idolatry, and an idol remains an idol even if clothed in pious looking attire. Strictly speaking, Judaism is the only other religion which, correctly understood, aims at Christianity and *intrinsically* compels its adherents towards the same.

ET promoters as "the first martyr" of belief in aliens. Indeed, he was excommunicated by multiple Christian denominations and was ultimately burned at the stake for his heretical teachings. Martyr, however, he was not.

His lurid tirades would have fit in well with 21st century discourse. The old *Catholic Encyclopedia* entry on his life does not fail to testify bluntly to his antics, relaying:

> In 1582 he published a characteristic work, "Il candelaio", or "The Torchbearer", a satire in which he exhibits in a marked degree the false taste then in vogue among the humanists, many of whom mistook obscenity for humour ... his system of thought is an incoherent materialistic pantheism. God and the world are one ... the universe is infinite; beyond the visible world there is an infinity of other worlds, each of which is inhabited; this terrestrial globe has a soul ... This unitary point of view is Bruno's justification of "natural magic." ... the false analogies, fantastic allegories, and sophistical reasonings into which his emotional fervour often betrayed him have justified, in the eyes of many, Bayle's characterization of him as "the knight-errant of philosophy." His attitude of mind towards religious truth was that of a rationalist. Personally, he failed to feel any of the vital significance of Christianity as a religious system.

Bruno, in a word, was the example par excellence of a man who was "holding the form of religion but denying the power of it," (2 Timothy 3:5) thanks to his infatuation with the notion that the cosmos are filled with inhabited planets. In light of such beliefs, he found the Christian Faith insignificant in comparison, hence the encyclopedia above noting he "failed to feel any of the vital significance of Christianity..."

Catholic ET promoters seek to protect their thesis from censure with respect to Bruno's condemnation by claiming that Bruno was not condemned for his belief in a plurality of inhabited worlds, but rather for various heresies of other sorts. This is likely untrue. As one professor of the history of science observed, in a 2018 article in *Scientific American*:

> To be sure, the Inquisitors didn't condemn [Bruno] for believing in Copernicus. ... [but] **in the 1590s <u>Bruno's claim [of multiple inhabited worlds] was considered heretical. Many authorities denounced it, including theologians, jurists, bishops, one emperor, three popes, five Church Fathers and nine saints</u> ... Moreover, it was heretical according to the highest authority. In 1582 and 1591, Pope Gregory XIII's official Corpus of Canon Law included this heresy: "having the opinion of innumerable worlds."** ... [Bruno's belief in many worlds] was the most frequently recurring charge [in his trial]. For example, one accuser testified that in prison one night Bruno brought a fellow prisoner "to the window and showed him a star, saying that it was a world and that all the stars were worlds." Thirteen times, in 10 depositions, six

> witnesses accused Bruno of believing in many worlds. **No other accusation was invoked even half as much.** ... "Again," [the inquisitors] wrote, "he posits many worlds, many suns, necessarily containing similar things in kind and in species as in this world, and even men." In 1597, Bruno was confronted by inquisitors, including the authoritative **theologian [Saint] Robert Bellarmine. Bruno "was admonished to thus abandon his delusions of diverse worlds." ...**Why did Catholics view this as heretical? Theologians explained: "**we cannot assert that two or many worlds exist, since neither do we assert two or many Christs." Bruno was condemned for several heresies, but the one about multiple [inhabited] worlds was the strongest case against him**.[75]

This article's author makes a strong case that the standard explanation we have been forcefully told by apologists for the last hundred years, i.e., *"Bruno's condemnation had nothing to do with his teachings on extraterrestrials,"* appears entirely false. Indeed, the many other heretical views Bruno held were likewise held by countless contemporaries who were not formally condemned, much less burned at the stake. Additionally, no one—not even in the most overly severe times of Church history—would be burned at the stake for holding a view if he recanted of it. Bruno, however, did recant of much: e.g., he recanted of various heresies against Christ, the Eucharist, the Blessed Virgin Mary, etc. What he did *not* recant of was his belief in multiple inhabited worlds. This view, moreover, is the principal one that set him apart from the many heretics who were not similarly acted against. Indeed, more recent scholarship has confirmed the thesis of the article above.

I hasten to add that I am not at all advocating for the execution of heretics, and I am certainly not celebrating that Giordano was burned at the stake! My point is only that the Church treated the error of believing in multiple inhabited worlds extremely seriously. To this day, the Church has never apologized for the condemnation of Bruno; indeed, she stands by it (though not the execution!). As recently as the year 2000, for example, Cardinal Sodano acknowledged that Bruno's *execution* constituted a "sad episode" for the Church, but he stopped well short of apologizing for the condemnation; instead, he praised the desire of the Inquisitors to defend the truth and reiterated the incompatibility of Bruno's teaching with Catholic doctrine.[76]

In any event, however, why exactly Bruno was condemned is not essential to our consideration, the purpose of which is primarily to acknowledge that the fruits of Cusa's alien belief promotion have proven to be thoroughly rotten. In the centuries that followed their announcement, they inspired none but a man whose heresies and blasphemous were so severe, so repeated, and so shameless, that he was eventually burned at the stake for them.

Bruno, however, presented his belief in aliens using the same justification most ET promoters employ today. He insisted that there are worlds...

> ... no less inhabited and no less nobly [than earth]. F**or it is impossible that a rational being fairly vigilant, can imagine that these innumerable worlds, manifest as like to our own or yet more magnificent, should be destitute of similar and even superior inhabitants**...[77]

Just as today's ET promoters reprimand those who, upon contemplating the vastness of the universe, believe that it exists for man—to testify, for us, to the glory of God (cf. Psalm 19:1)—and do not believe that it exists to be populated with aliens, so too Bruno regarded anyone who does not believe in aliens as one who is not qualifying as a "rational being, fairly vigilant."

Perhaps they would be given greater pause if they pondered that the principle they most frequently employ in furthering their beliefs (and for reproaching those who disagree) was first presented by an excommunicated heretic who was put to death for espousing it. Unfortunately, many would not be given pause, but only encouragement. As noted, Bruno is often regarded as a heroic "martyr" in contemporary ET promotion. This is yet another testimony to the dark nature of the entire movement (which we will examine thoroughly in Part Four).

***

The same scholar quoted above, Dr. Alberto Martinez, compiled yet another list of condemnations of ET belief in Sacred Tradition leading up to Bruno's condemnation. As is often the case with secular researchers on these matters, Martinez's own motivations, principles, and conclusions (which he espouses elsewhere in the book quoted below) are degenerate, but this does not render the content of his research findings unhelpful. (Recall when reading this quote that, in early modern times, ET belief was called "plurality doctrine," i.e., belief in "multiple worlds.") Dr. Martinez wrote:

> The heresy of many worlds appeared in books for centuries, for example, in a *Thesaurus of the Christian Religion* (1559) and in an edition of Philaster's *Book of Heresies* (1578). St Jerome too was an authority in the Renaissance, because at the Council of Trent the Catholic Church had selected his translation of the Bible, known as the Latin Vulgate Bible, as the official version to use and trust. Writers also cited Augustine. In 1591 the Jesuit theologian Gregorius de Valentia cautioned: "There is no need of heretics among Christians, who follow Democritus and other ancient philosophers in saying that there exists not one but innumerable worlds, as the divine Augustine reports in his book on heresies, namely the seventy-seventh heresy." Other theologians too cited this heresy for centuries. They explained the problem: "we cannot assert that there exist two or many worlds, since neither do we assert two or many

> Christs." Aristotle had insisted that many worlds cannot exist ... Above all, however, the highest authority proves that Bruno's belief in many worlds was heretical. In 1582 Pope Gregory XIII issued a compilation of laws of the Catholic Church and ordered that it be used in all church courts and schools of canon law. Expanded in 1591, the Corpus of Canon Law includes long discussions of what are heresies and who shall be considered a heretic. Echoing Isidore, its list of heresies includes 'having the opinion of innumerable worlds'. ... [Origen had] argued, 'The fact is that prior to this world there have existed others... [he] said that omnipotence led God to create worlds prior to ours, and after it. He said that our souls might live in future worlds. Jerome condemned Origen's notion of innumerable worlds as heretical. ... Remarkably, Bruno's claims echoed Origen's heresies: eternally many worlds and transmigration. Had he read Origen's censored book On Principles? Yes - and Bruno praised him as 'the only theologian, who like the great philosophers' dared to voice 'after the reproved sects' the truth of revolutions and eternal change.[78]

As we can see, there is no basis in Catholic thought to regard Bruno is anything but another of the innumerable "false prophets; wolves in sheep's clothing" whom Jesus warned against in the Gospel (cf. Matthew 7:15). He was no Joan of Arc. He was, rather, a foretaste of the diabolical deception we would only see formally and broadly infiltrate the Church in the 20th century.

Transgenderism, Enlightenment, and the Futility of Surveying Post 17th Century Alien Belief

> "The **plurality of worlds passed from a status of heresy** to that of a powerful argument for the rhetoric of natural theology."
> —Professor Jacques Arnould[79]

So much for Giordano Bruno (†1600), who was executed at the very onset of the same century that saw a movement which—despite its contradictory title—consisted in none other than a new darkness descending upon Christendom.

In Bruno's own day, the fervor of the Copernican Revolution was in full swing and was electrifying scholars around the world. An unspoken competition soon commenced to see which academic could be the more "innovative," the "least chained by tradition." The foundations of Modernism—"the Synthesis of All Heresies," according to Pope St. Pius X[80]—were being laid down by way of what came after Bruno: the "Enlightenment," better called the *Great Darkening*. This so-called Enlightenment, which began only a few decades after Bruno's death, sought to reject the authority of Divine Revelation and replace it with a purely rationalistic account of all things.

How fitting, then, that the supreme illustration of the Enlightenment in the French Revolution (1789-1799) saw "reason" symbolized by an idol and irrationally enthroned as a goddess in the desecrated Notre Dame Cathedral, amidst all manner of murders, blasphemies, immoral acts, and other evils. Even if it must assume new forms, Paganism always manages to fill any void left when men abandon Jesus Christ. And it is, tellingly, precisely in this time alone that we see the beginnings of the aforementioned trickle of Christian thinkers begin to espouse belief in extraterrestrials; a trickle which grew, throughout the swelling of the Enlightenment and its increasing darkness, into a steady stream in the deeply occult 19th century.

There is no need for us to review a detailed survey of the development of this debate here. Plenty of recent publications have done precisely that, and my aim here is not to provide a history textbook. Suffice it to say that many of the thinkers (particularly the revered Catholic ones) opposed alien belief, no saints (and no writers in any way exalted by the Church) supported it, and all the arguments then presented in support of alien belief are addressed in the book now before you. Instead of a thorough survey, therefore, we will in the sections ahead see a few such thinkers whose contributions best summarize what is most relevant to discerning the phenomena in question.

***

Before proceeding to those sections, let us return to the same analogy with which we began Part One of this book: transgenderism. Let us furthermore suppose that, centuries from now, a Catholic author will publish a book surveying the development of the debate on this topic throughout the Church's history. Perhaps he will entitle it "*Transgenderism and the Catholic Faith: Are There Really Only Two Genders?*"

Our hypothesized 2300 A.D. author's discoveries on transgender ideology would parallel what we have summarized in the preceding sections on alien belief (only extended a few centuries longer). He would find almost 2,000 years of Church History with no reliable Christian writers whatsoever endorsing the notion that more than two genders exist, or that a man may become a woman, or vice versa. Suddenly, in the late 20th century, he would begin to see some Christians endorsing these ideas. At the dawn of the Third Millennium, that trickle would become a stream. Two decades into the same century, that stream would become a turbid and putrid river. In fact, he would uncover more Catholic-authored texts in support of transgenderism than the Catholic ET promoters today find in support of extraterrestrial intelligence from pre-20th century sources!

He would find morally, intellectually, and spiritually sane ages of Church history so far removed from this error that it was scarcely ever even noted. Then, suddenly, when it became an item of *worldly* discourse, some Christians started endorsing it. Eventually, that "some" would become "many," as invariably happens with prevailing secular delusions.

This author would moreover discover the same infallible *sensus fidelium* (which we have seen ruling out alien belief) equally finds the matter of transgenderism within the scope of its legitimate jurisdiction. For this is clearly a belief-essential question—our being made "male and female" (Genesis 1:27) is fundamental to our nature and therefore it is crucial to understand it correctly for our salvation and sanctification—just as, for reasons already extensively discussed, man's unique position in bearing God's Image is also a belief-essential matter.

What is more, the opposing thesis (that transgenderism's tenets are legitimate) was always known to Christians. Just as early Christians were well acquainted with ancient Pagan belief in aliens, so too they knew of those same Pagan cultures' perverse transgender tendencies. Even a third century Roman emperor (whom all Christians would obviously have known well), Elagabalus, led the life of a transgender. (A lifestyle so universally scandalous that a leading 19th century historian described it as "unspeakably disgusting.")

Christians, therefore, knew of transgenderism, yet went almost two millennia remaining convinced that only two genders exist, and that no one can change genders. Even if we leave aside all other arguments, this one alone proves the fraudulent nature of transgender ideology. The mere fact that Christian writers of Sacred Tradition's development almost never condemned transgenderism *explicitly* gives no grounds whatsoever for speculating that this perverse ideology might be reconcilable with the infallible *sensus fidelium.*

Saintly writers have always been known for focusing on extolling what is good, true, and beautiful—not lamenting what is evil, false, and ugly (*though they will readily undertake the latter task when necessary by virtue of the degree to which these ills have infiltrated the lives of the faithful*). This approach is no less than what Scripture exhorts in admonishing us to "overcome evil with good" (Romans 12:21), and in directing us to:

> Have no anxiety about anything ... whatever is true, whatever is honorable, whatever is just, whatever is pure, whatever is lovely, whatever is gracious, if there is any excellence, if there is anything worthy of praise, think about these things. (Philippians 4:6,8)

Comparing this hypothetical survey of transgenderism to the surveys already presented for alien belief, however, would prove even more damning for the latter. As we have seen, there are many declarations from popes and saints rejecting belief in extraterrestrials. There are comparably fewer rejecting transgenderism.

Indeed, our hypothetical author would find plenty of teachings in Scripture and Tradition that refer to "male and female," "husband and wife," etc.—just as we have seen much in these same sources that speaks of man (*Adam's offspring*) as supreme, singular, unique, etc., and which ascribes value to the heavens in terms radically discordant with any theory on extraterrestrials. In a word: in this respect, the only differences between "*Transgenderism and the Catholic Faith*" and "*Extraterrestrial Intelligence and the Catholic Faith*" are those which testify even more strongly to the errancy of belief in aliens.

It bears repeating that all this, of course, is not in the least to defend transgenderism. It is difficult to imagine a more diabolical ideology. The point is only that the same—*faithful*—approach to our Catholic patrimony rules out both it and alien belief.

The Lopsided "Consensus" and Misuse of 18th to 20th Century Thought

> "That [the planets in our solar system] are all peopled with intellectual beings ... is a conclusion to which the mind is almost necessarily led, when once it admits the facts which have been ascertained by modern astronomers."
> —Rev. Thomas Dick. *Celestial Scenery*, 1838. Chapter IX.

Today's Catholic ET promoters are known to painstakingly detail the alien belief debate during the times of the Enlightenment and the century thereafter, but their presentations consist mostly of quoting the teachings of men who are either not Catholic, or who are formal heretics.

They describe the alien belief promotion of Voltaire (Deist), Gottfried Leibniz (Protestant), Immanuel Kant (borderline Deist), John Milton (Puritan), Benjamin Franklin (Deist), Thomas Paine (Deist), John Adams (Unitarian), Cotton Mather (Puritan), Timothy Dwight (Protestant), Thomas Chalmers (Protestant), Enoch Burr (Congregationalist), Edwin Winkler (Baptist), William Leitch (Presbyterian), Isaac Newton (Anglican), Richard Bentley (Anglican), John Locke (Unitarian/Arian), George Berkely (a Protestant Bishop), and countless other similar figures who promoted belief in extraterrestrials. No Catholic defers to any of these men for guidance on discerning what truly constitutes an element of Sacred Tradition on any other matter—for they each, by the mere fact they were not Catholic, reveal that their positions on that matter are errant—therefore why are these same individuals suddenly treated as shining lights on the question of whether belief in aliens is reconcilable with this infallible Tradition?

The abundance of revered non-Catholics of this era espousing belief in aliens and dearth of revered Catholics adopting the same, however, presents a striking contrast that today's Catholic ET promoters fail to note. But the reason for this contrast is clear; it is the same reason that has, for hundreds of years, compelled non-Catholic Christians to endlessly question countless other basic truths of the Faith. Protestants and Unitarians of all stripes have spent several hundred years agonizing over questions to which the Catholic Church has always had consistent—and correct—answers: *"What is meant by 'Church'? What are the Sacraments? Which books should be included in the Bible? How is one justified? What is the relationship between Faith and works? How should we pray? What should a Liturgy consist in?"* On—and on, and on—the list goes.

That Enlightenment-era Protestants were especially prone to add into this mix of foolish questions, *"is man really the only incarnate creature made in God's image?"*, should be unsurprising to a Catholic who is acquainted with the history of Protestantism. What is tragic is that there are nevertheless Catholic authors today who are misleadingly using these predictable Protestant points of confusion to seduce Catholics into being likewise confused.

The times spanned by the lives of those thinkers listed above include thousands of canonized saints, blesseds, venerables, servants of God, and others whose legacies of holiness and orthodoxy have been safely confirmed. We are not dealing with a decade or two wherein debate raged on this issue among the worlds' thinkers—both secular and religious. We are dealing with *centuries*. And the Church has not venerated a single such thinker who espoused belief in aliens from *any* of those times.

It will not work to claim that this was a secular debate in which the saintly would find no interest, and that, therefore, it is not telling to find no such persons believing in aliens. Indeed, no chronicler of the debate, on either side of the matter, asserts that. Despite the Enlightenment's destructive influence in academia, the West was still by and large a Christian civilization, and almost every time the extraterrestrial debate arose, the theological ramifications in relation to Christianity's teachings quickly came to the fore.

Not only secular Protestants but also innumerable Protestant pastors, philosophers, and theologians can easily be cited as ET promoters. Catholic commentators, however, number far fewer among the ranks of alien believers. In the place and time where and when this debate may have raged most fiercely—late 19th century France—there were at one point 35 million Catholics and only half a million Protestants. Despite there being 70 times more Catholics, far fewer French ET promoters are found among their ranks than among the ranks of the comparatively minuscule population of Protestants!

After extensively surveying the late 19th century "Pluralism" debate (that is, the debate on whether aliens exist), Dr. Michael Crowe sought to discover how the two sides of the debate—as expressed by its noteworthy authors—correlated with their religious convictions in the span of those several decades.

His findings were as follows[81]: by far the highest rate of belief in aliens was found among non-Christians and anti-Christians. Of the multitude of such thinkers who wrote on extraterrestrials, just a single one, Ludwig Büchner, disbelieved in aliens. The second highest amount of alien belief promotion was found among Protestant authors (nineteen were ET promoters, four were not, and two evaded classification). The lowest amount of belief in aliens was found among Catholic authors (Crowe claims fourteen favored pluralism, with ten opposing it, and four being too difficult to classify).

Even these Catholic "pro-pluralist" numbers, however, are fundamentally mischaracterized. The Catholic clerics or theologians who can be found appearing to be pluralists were, for the most part, not *advocating* for belief in extraterrestrials (as Catholic ET promoters today are). Quite the contrary, they were merely *defending Christianity* against those (almost the entirety of academia) who *assumed* extraterrestrials exist and *used that assumption* as an attack against the Faith. So let us next demonstrate this reality and explore its effects on the debate today.

Modern Period Catholic Commentators: Defending the Faith, not Promoting Alien Belief

As we will see in the next section, "dissenters" from the pluralist position were dealt with brutally during the modern era. Failure to believe in aliens was regarded as an attack on the Enlightenment itself—not to mention the Copernican Revolution—and irreverence towards those sacred cows would not be tolerated by a society that had "finally unshackled itself of its prior medieval dogmatism." As quoted earlier, St. John Henry Newman himself lamented that the thinkers of his day (the 1800s) regarded it tantamount to blasphemy to *not* believe in aliens! (He also rightly noted that their position was entirely devoid of evidence.) Indeed, belief in aliens was "long a staple of Enlightenment optimism," as Dr. Crowe also observed. It was part and parcel to the Zeitgeist of the times.

Due to this academic climate and what many Christians saw as the practical futility of seeking to rebut pluralism, attention was often understandably shifted towards simply insisting that the existence of extraterrestrials did not overthrow Christianity. Crowe observed:

> ... for apologetic purposes, [there was a] continuing concern among **Catholics to combat the *pluralist objection* to Christianity** ... **pluralism apparently had won the day**, and Christians were faced with the task of reconciling their religion with it.[82]

Of paramount significance in generating this trend was Thomas Paine's anti-Christian tirade in his 1793 work, *The Age of Reason*. This book motivated much of the Catholic-authored works now misleadingly cited as advocating for alien belief. Paine, a Deist, asserted therein that extraterrestrial intelligence (which he regarded as a scientific fact)...

> ...renders the Christian system of faith at once little and ridiculous, and scatters it in the mind like feathers in the air. The two beliefs cannot be held together in the same mind; and he who thinks that he believes

> both, has thought but little of either... every evidence the heavens afford to man either directly contradicts ... the Christian system of faith ... or renders it absurd...

This attack of Paine's prompted the publication of dozens, if not hundreds, of works in the decades of the late 1700s and 1800s that followed. Dr. Crowe notes:

> Paine presents his readers a stark choice: Either reject Christianity or reject pluralism. His own recommendation was clear: Reject Christianity. ... [he] launches other attacks on Christianity, but central to the work is [his belief in extraterrestrials]. Paine's *Age of Reason* created a sensation. ... The influence of Paine's pluralist argument even extended far into the nineteenth century...[83]

For a Catholic to read Paine's outburst and feel compelled to refute it is reasonable and commendable. But it is surely anything but a testimony to that Catholic's desire to encourage alien belief! Some respondents simply did not feel equipped to address such a dominant secular (and supposedly "scientific") view that supported aliens. Instead, therefore, they focused their efforts in countering Paine on the *other* available front.

The expectation that all intellectuals believe in a plurality of inhabited planets was based on various since-disproven scientific conjectures (then presented, as false scientific conjectures often are, as practical certainties). Once the fire set by Galileo's telescopes spread sufficiently, and better telescopes were invented, the giddy affirmations followed: "*Look at Mars! Look at its rationally constructed canals! Look at Saturn's clearly habitable rings! They are all just like earth. According to our 'Principle of Plenitude,' God* ***must*** *have populated such places with intelligent creatures! We are certain of this!*" Intimidated by such claims—backed up, as they were, by "The Science," and insisted upon by "The Experts"—few felt positioned to counter them.

Naturally, therefore, the apologists of that era—rightly eager to stem a flow of souls away from the Faith—played the cards they were dealt; they "met the people where they were at," as the saying goes. Alien belief was the assumption, and their goal was to prevent that assumption from causing an exodus from the pews. Therefore, many of them proceeded to focus their efforts not on arguing against aliens, but rather on ensuring that no one who unshakably believed in aliens would lose his Faith.

Similarly, *today's* intelligentsia are expected to believe in macroevolution. In addition to the myriad of fallacies inherent in this theory—which evidence-based, non-ideological science has long exposed as fraudulent—it is simply not in harmony with a faithful Catholic approach to Scripture, Sacred Tradition, Magisterium, and the like. Also similar to alien belief, however, it has not yet been directly, explicitly, and dogmatically condemned as a heresy. Therefore, now as then, many Catholic thinkers and commentators are understandably motivated to argue that macroevolution is compatible with Catholicism. Their goal is perhaps to prevent apostasy among those who are incapable of extricating their minds from macroevolution in light of how dogmatically belief in it is enforced today.

To capture the aim of 19th century Catholics, let us consider the words of one Catholic priest who was and is often cited as a "pluralist" [alien believer] by today's ET promoters. Fr. Joseph Felix, a popular preacher, delivered a famous sermon at the Notre Dame Cathedral in the year 1863, wherein he issued a call "***to all scientists who would make [pluralism] a peremptory reason against Christianity,***" saying to them:

> You wish ... to discover inhabitants of the moon; you wish to find in the stars and suns brothers in intelligence and in liberty; and as certain spirits who pretend to the intuitive vision of all the worlds put it, you wish to greet across space astronomical societies and civilizations. So be it. If you have no other reason to break with us, nothing prevents our extending our hand to you...[84]

As we can see, even from this alleged "pluralist," there is anything but enthusiasm for belief in aliens. The priest was simply engaging in damage control. One can almost hear the sarcasm in his voice when he describes ET promoters who "*pretend to the intuitive vision of all the words,*" and who "*wish to discover inhabitants of the moon*" and "*greet astronomical civilizations.*" Similarly palpable is his unhappy resignation when he concedes, "*so be it...*", in order to get to his real point, which is simply that, "*nothing prevents our extending our hand to you.*"

He concluded the message above by ensuring ET promoters that "*Catholic dogma has a tolerance here that will astonish you.*" Indeed, Catholicism is a "big tent." Relatively few are the propositions that are explicitly condemned as standing in violation to defined dogma (few, that is, in relation to the number of propositions which are nevertheless clearly wrong for other reasons; i.e., ruled out by *a truly faithful approach* to Scripture, Tradition, Magisterium, etc.).

While I suppose there is no risk that others may classify me as they have classified Fr. Felix—a "pro-pluralist"—I would readily agree with the priest's sentiments quoted above. Never in a thousand years would I want to see a soul leave the Catholic Church or the Christian Faith over his alien belief. Quite the contrary, I would beg him to stay in the Church, and I would continue to engage him in dialogue on this point from within.

***

Not all Catholic commentators of the 19th century, however, were merely defenders of the Faith focused solely on insisting the people understood that pluralism did not overturn Catholicism. Perhaps the most famous of the Catholic promoters of extraterrestrials was a certain Fr. Joseph Pohle (born 1852), who is said to have written "the most extensive study ever made by a Catholic theologian ... of the question of extraterrestrial life."[85] An apologetics professor at the Catholic University of America and a contributor to the old *Catholic Encyclopedia*, he appears to be the source of a great deal of the ET-sympathetic views one found in the American and European Catholic scene in his day.

Fr. Pohle's alien belief promotion was built upon his own uncritical acceptance of Percival Lowell's categorical insistence that the latter had *proven*, through his own observations at his observatory, that the planet Mars was traversed by an elaborate, alien-built canal system (a theory we will examine in Part Three). Pohle declared:

> ... the existence and organized arrangement of the canal system [on Mars] with almost irresistible power forces the acceptance of an intelligent origin for them and consequently of thinking beings on our neighboring planet. **All other hypotheses ... are destroyed by their too great arbitrariness** ...[86]

As God would have it, this insistence of Fr. Pohle—which, he assured us, "destroyed" those "hypotheses" which did not propose aliens—was, in fact, *itself* destroyed by reality a few decades after Fr. Pohle's death. Pohle had hung his hat on the certainty of aliens due to these "canals" on Mars which, as we will see in a forthcoming chapter, were nothing but a farce.

Yet his arguments were also replete with fallacies that were obvious well before the "Martian canals" were proved to be an optical illusion. Accordingly, he was contradicted by many of his contemporaries. Dr. Crowe recounts:

> Canon Julius Zucht of Ulm published a theological critique of some of the claims Pohle made in his first edition... In discussing Pohle's second edition, the Jesuit astronomer Adolf Müller urged in 1900 that **Pohle had overestimated what astronomy teaches concerning extraterrestrial life and also what reason tells us of the ways of God.** Ludwig Günther (1846–1910), in reviewing the fourth edition, described it as overly philosophical...**Pohle's claim...that unbelievers and Christians had reached agreement in favor of pluralism is certainly excessive.** As this discussion of the extraterrestrial life debate in German religious writings of the late nineteenth century shows, neither camp had attained a consensus even within itself. Among materialists, Büchner's antipluralist universe was strikingly different from that of Strauss, Du Prel, and Haeckel. Among Christians, the Lutheran Zöckler was similarly opposed to the antipluralist views of his confessional colleague Luthardt. Catholics were scarcely less divided; whereas Braun, Pohle, and Schanz endorsed pluralism, Zucht and Müller expressed major reservations. [87]

Let us consider Fr. Pohle's possible effects elsewhere. As we have seen above, Giordano Bruno's year 1600 execution for heresy almost certainly *was* due to his "pluralist" belief in multiple inhabited worlds; i.e., for his teaching that aliens exist. Recent scholarship based on *original* documents has demonstrated this. However, for more than a hundred years, a massive effort has been afoot by Catholic apologists insisting this was not so. Even the old *Catholic Encyclopedia* teaches that Bruno's condemnation was not due to his teachings on extraterrestrials. One wonders if it was precisely Fr. Pohle who created this myth, considering his prominence in the Catholic University of America in those times and his contributions to the creation of the old *Catholic Encyclopedia.*

***

Other noteworthy Catholics *opposed* to Fr. Pohle should also be recalled here.

Fr. Augustine Hewit (1820-1897), Superior General of the Paulists, "...labels **belief in the past or present existence of other worlds inhabited by intelligent beings as 'unphilosophical, untheological, and unscriptural'**"[88]

Fr. Francois Xavier de Feller (1735-1802) argued against pluralism, noting there is no evidence for it, and that the moon is clearly lifeless, so why would other celestial bodies be inhabited? He moreover argued that the purpose of the Heavens need not have been to populate with aliens, but rather to benefit mankind on earth. He declared:

> **The mystery of the Incarnation and in general the idea that Scripture and Faith give us of the creation of the world, of providence, etc. supposes only one world inhabited by rational beings**.[89]

Like those who, today, speak out against transgenderism, those who spoke out against aliens in the 1800s were persecuted (as we will see in the next section). Claims that only man was made in God's Image were supposedly "not in keeping with the science." (In fact, 20th century science refuted *each* thesis of 19th century ET-promotion.) One Catholic archbishop who wrote against extraterrestrials even was forced to refrain from publishing his work due to its "unsuitableness to the present state of science in this country..."[90] Another 19th century Catholic priest, Fr. Francois Xavier Burque (born 1851), who is sometimes wrongly cited as a pluralist, wrote:

> ...it **appears absolutely impossible to extend to sidereal persons [i.e., aliens in other solar systems] the benefits of this redemption, it is impossible to imagine how the Divine Blood which has flowed on Calvary could be ... of some utility and efficacy for their justification**...[it is a fact that] supporters of evolution are precisely the same men who with the greatest ardor preach the suspect doctrine of the plurality of worlds.[91]

Still another Catholic priest of that era, Fr. Joseph Emile Filachou (born 1812), wrote:

> **The opinion which assumes men or creatures of the same species as men [exist] in the stars is absolutely rejectable**, not only because it continues to lack positive proof and rests only on the idea of the possibility

> of the thing in general, but still more because it entails with it consequences incompatible with all that one admits as most rational in metaphysics, aesthetics and physics... [it is contrary to Christianity because of] the importance presupposed [in Scripture] of the role of man on earth, the supreme dignity attributed to the Divine founder of the Christian Church, and finally the grandeur attributed to the Church itself.[92]

Yet another Catholic of that time wrongly cited as a pluralist, Jules Boiteux, who wrote *Lettres à un matérialiste sur la pluralité des mondes habités et les questions qui s'y rattachent*, ("Letters to a Materialist on the Plurality of Inhabited Worlds and Related Questions"), declared that he wrote his book "in the spirit of an orthodox Catholic." There, he *disputes* arguments for extraterrestrials, though near the end of it he argues that "*the doctrine, full of unknowns, of the plurality of worlds furnishes no positive argument against Christian dogma*," and then pleads with Camille Flammarion to return to Catholicism.

Here as elsewhere among those whom Catholic ET promoters today wrongly cited as "pro-alien," we see displayed only a motive to defend the Faith. Then as now, however, people simply did not want to hear any arguments against aliens. Dr. Crowe notes:

> Yet the fate of most antipluralist writings, even those containing excellent arguments, awaited Boiteux's book: While Flammarion [an ex-Catholic who argued for alien belief, and for reincarnation on other planets] saw his books roll through dozens of editions, Boiteux followed Plisson, Whewell, and Filachou [who argued against aliens] into obscurity. A second edition did appear after fifteen years, and a third in 1898, but then no more was heard in the pluralist debate from this erudite engineer[93]

As it is today, so it was in the 1800s: sensational arguments that aliens are out there (or even among us) are generally the only ones that become popular, whereas the sober arguments based upon reality are ignored. The masses are (and were) ravenous for sci-fi deceptions, not for the Christian Faith.

Still another Catholic, dubiously cited as a pluralist, was the theologian Fr. Theophile Ortolan (born 1861). He made it clear that his only aim was to prevent people from leaving Catholicism due to their alien belief. The Catholic scientist Charles de Kirwan also made it clear that his supposed "pluralism" was none other than an expression of his anger at those ET promoters who merely using the presupposition of pluralism as a tool to wage war on the Faith. He wrote:

> For twenty or thirty years, certain malicious minds have joined forces, who have found a method of transforming a perfectly inoffensive ... hypothesis of the habitation of the celestial bodies into an engine of war against spiritual and Christian doctrines, into a sort of pantheistic and materialistic system based on unlimited evolutionism.[94]

Later, however, Kirwan grew opposed to alien belief—realizing, upon more careful consideration, that it was anything but "perfectly inoffensive." Illustrating the gullibility of the public, a certain Gabriel Prigent wrote a book declaring that, on the "authority" of Flammarion, that it was "almost impossible for the reason of man to refuse to admit the existence of human creatures on the surface of these distant bodies [in our solar system; i.e., Mars]..."[95] Eight years later, and for similar reasons, R.M. Jouan declared *"**The hypothesis of a plurality of worlds ... has been universally accepted by the elite** of humanity of all times and all places [and] consequently ought to enjoy all the privileges attached to the consent of all peoples."*[96] The hyperbolic nature of this (comically false) claim would be impossible to match, much less exceed, yet these are precisely the superlatives that alien belief was couched in during the 19th century. Who would dare contradict what "the elite" have "universally accepted"? We can clearly see why Catholics were sometimes more intent on arguing that it did not overturn the Faith than they were on arguing against the belief itself!

Remember, as well, that all these authors were writing long before the UFO craze that began in the year 1947 with Roswell. They did not have the ability, as we do today, to "discern the tree by its fruits." (cf. Matthew 7) We now know, in incredibly stark terms, how destructive the belief that extraterrestrials are among us is. (Reviewing this will constitute much of Part Four.) Deferring to any pre-1947 voice in support of aliens today would be like deferring to a pre-1917 voice in support of Marxism. We now know how utterly destructive Communism is when it is attempted to be put into practice. Whoever would defend it in abstract terms *today* is only thereby displaying his rejection of Christ's teaching on how we are to discern, or is at least displaying his obliviousness to reality.

The Telling Rage Against the "Dissenters" Who Rejected Aliens

Once alien belief was in vogue, ridicule was meted out against those intellectuals who dared to argue that belief in multiple inhabited worlds stood in tension with Scripture, Tradition, and Magisterium. *"That is an outdated concern that our contemporary theologians have already addressed!"* became the reply to them. *"We have grown out of backwards medieval thinking like that, which reveres man as unique in the universe!"*

One example of this habit was seen in the case of William Whewell. Rev. Whewell was uniquely qualified to comment on the matter. A professor at Cambridge, a scientist, a philosopher, and an Anglican pastor, he merited an audience that took his views seriously. Whewell had long been a famous promoter of belief in aliens (as was expected among the Protestant establishment of the time). In one series of sermons he preached in Cambridge he even insisted that the case for aliens does not consist in "the reveries of idle dreamers or busy connivers;—but for the most part [are] truths collected by wise and patient men on evidence indisputable."[97] He had jumped on the "aliens are indisputable" bandwagon, and was, along with his confreres, simply awaiting powerful enough telescopes for us to see the advanced civilizations on Mars.

Over time, however, Whewell came to realize how wrong he was, and how contrary such belief was to a faithful approach to the Christian religion. Knowing that he would face the wrath of the academic establishment if he announced this recognition, he decided to publish his refutation of alien belief anonymously. His authorship was quickly discovered, however, and chaos promptly ensued. Crowe chronicled the drama as follows:

> Whewell's greatest concern was that **pluralism [i.e., alien belief] appeared to undermine the most remarkable of God's providential actions: the incarnation and redemption. That Whewell was slow to come to this conclusion is understandable in light of the large number of individuals who either felt that this was not a major difficulty or accepted Chalmers's resolution of it**. ... Whewell [was] in "combat against all the rational inhabitants of other spheres," according to a reviewer for the London Daily News, "***We scarcely expected that in the middle of the nineteenth century, a serious attempt would have been made to restore the exploded idea of man's supremacy over all other creatures in the universe***; *and still less that such an attempt would have been made by one whose mind was stored with scientific truths. Nevertheless a champion has actually appeared, who boldly dares to combat against all the rational inhabitants of other spheres; and though as yet he wears his vizor down, his dominant bearing, and the peculiar dexterity and power with which he wields his arms, indicate that this knight-errant of nursery notions can be no other than the Master of Trinity College, Cambridge.*"[98]

Oblivious that it was they themselves who had succumbed to believing in myths, Whewell's critics accused *him* of being the one who was a "**knight-errant of nursery notions**," by daring, "in the nineteenth century!" to still regard man as unique and supreme. Thus, Whewell's critics accuse the Book of Genesis—and all passages of God's Word which describe man's place in creation—as conveying only a multitude of mere nursery rhymes that the "*learned are expected to realize are nothing but symbolic*," if not outright errant.

Does this sound familiar? Of course, no one could fail to see the similarity of this tactic to the strategy of the modernists of today. These same castigations are relentlessly spewed against the faithful who insist upon orthodoxy. As noted, these epithets are particularly zealously dispensed against those who hold fast to traditional teaching on sexual morality, but they are also weaponized against those who believe (as is infallibly true) that Adam and Eve were real people and really are our first parents, that we are the result of God's deliberate design and not random evolution, that Moses really did part the Red Sea, that Jesus really was born of the

Virgin, that He truly did die and rise again, that miracles really do happen even today, and on the list goes. Whenever rhetoric like that is employed, we can be sure that the view of the one who wields it is the very opposite of the truth.

Another critic of Whewell was a certain Scottish scientist and Presbyterian preacher, Sir David Brewster. After Whewell argued against aliens, Brewster denounced him with such a degree of vitriolic injustice that only one conclusion can be drawn from observing it: Brewster, like his contemporaries of similar persuasion who wrote on the topic, had fashioned for himself an idol out of his belief in aliens, and the toppling of that idol (by Whewell) elicited the same rage that idol-toppling always does. Brewster denounced Whewell as "*ill-educated,*" being "*without faith and without hope,*" and having a "*mind dead to feeling and shorn of reason.*" He claimed that Whewell's arguments for man's uniqueness were an "*inconceivable absurdity which no sane mind can cherish,*" which was "*too ridiculous even for a writer of romance,*" and so "*utterly inept and illogical*" that it displayed a "*morbid condition of mental power [which] delights in doing violence to sentiments deeply cherished, and to opinions universally believed.*"[99]

All this contempt was meted out merely because Whewell did not believe in aliens. Crowe recounts an amusing exchange that transpired after Brewster published this attack:

> A visitor, seeing some passages in the review, commented that they seemed "calculated to hurt his [Whewell's] feelings." To this Brewster replied: "Hurt his feelings! why it is he that has hurt my feelings." Furthermore, Brewster's daughter reported that Brewster's book as published had been purged of all passages that she and a Miss Forbes found to be too severe...[100]

Evidently, Brewster intended his denunciation of Whewell to be even more severe than what ultimately found a place in the former's book and is quoted above!

Considering the vitriol of Brewster and Whewell's other critics is no mere tangent to our discussion. *Discernment*—which will be our focus in upcoming chapters—requires considering such phenomena as these; phenomena which, I hasten to add, have not diminished since those times, but have only increased. I can testify to this dynamic personally; in my years of speaking against the existence of extraterrestrials, I have repeatedly found myself on the receiving end of insults like those dispensed by Brewster. The angle of the insults, however, has changed. In the 1800s, Christianity still prevailed, therefore alien disbelievers were reproached in terminology borrowed from Christianity. Today, alien disbelievers are generally reproached in opposite terms, and are more likely to be denounced for "*thinking that Christianity has all the answers and Jesus is supreme.*" Accordingly, alien belief is infinitely more dangerous in the present times than it was in the 19th century. As we will see in forthcoming chapters, the mode of its present dissemination and the ends at which it aims are decidedly *anti*-Christian.

Sir Brewster, ignoring the multitude of Scriptural passages which rule out aliens, insisted that there *must* be aliens due to the Book of the Prophet Isaiah, Chapter 45, verse 18. (In the appendices, we will address how errant is his interpretation; and how a faithful reading of the very same chapter clearly *rules out* aliens.) St. John Henry Newman rebuked Brewster in a letter he wrote to a certain E.B. Pusey in 1858:

> But in the whole scientific world men seem going ahead most recklessly with their usurpations on the domain of religion. Here is Dr. Brewster, I think, saying that 'more worlds than one is the hope [of] the Christian—' and, as it seems to me, building Christianity more or less upon astronomy.[101]

Others who antagonized Whewell openly confessed their personal anguish that so great a scientist and theologian as he could dare to demolish their hopes and dreams of aliens. Sir James Stephen, a Cambridge history professor, wrote:

> Can it really be that this world is the best product of omnipotence, guided by omniscience and animated by Love...that of this solitary family "many are called but few are chosen"? ... **On behalf of my clients, the inhabitants of the extraterrestrial universe, I am pleading** ..."*Gentlemen of the Jury, before you give credit to that evidence, think on the misery that your verdict must inflict on the Prisoner's family.*" ... I oppose your terrible artillery (for I acknowledge myself to be alarmed by it).[102]

One may fairly wonder: how could such naked deception be so triumphant in mainstream Western secular academia during this century? How could a respected Cambridge professor be so insane as to declare that his "clients" are the "inhabitants of the extraterrestrial universe," for whom he must agonize on account of those who argued against the existence of aliens? The answer is that the 1800s were not what many today seem to think they were. Addressing that misconception is our next task.

The Deeply Occultist, Heretical, and Pseudoscientific 1800s: On the Trap of Using 19th Century Catholics to Justify Alien Belief

> "The [19th] century has been described as both the democratization of Christianity and the feminization of it; the same could clearly be said of the occult and of the many places where those two systems of meaning overlapped and competed..."[103]

Despite all that has been covered, it is inevitable that a few will still feel tempted to justify believing in aliens because of those 19th century

Catholics who did the same. Even a certain false traditionalism may induce one to find utterly seductive the mere sight of a grainy black and white photograph of a pre-20th century Catholic sporting a waistcoat, pipe in hand, who argued for belief in extraterrestrials. *"See! This isn't just a Star Trek nerd thing! Men who rode in horse-drawn carriages also believed it!"*, they will think to themselves. Before concluding this chapter, therefore, a section is in order in which we must bluntly assess this temptation for what it is: yet another trap—and a logically and historically bankrupt one at that.

First we must note, as we will explore in more detail in Part Three, that all of the premises and arguments used in the 19th century to justify alien belief were definitively refuted in the 20th century. Indeed, the entire 18th to early-20th century alien belief movement has since been revealed for the (unintentional) hoax it was. We will save exploring just how that was revealed for those later chapters, however. For now, it suffices to observe that justifying alien belief due to the 19th century Catholics who advocated for it would be like justifying belief in "spontaneous generation" due to those Renaissance Catholics who insisted upon it (or any of the other flatly pseudoscientific theories then common). "Spontaneous generation" is the theory—once very popular—which holds that living creatures arise at random from various dead heaps of matter. The 17th century devout Catholic chemist, Jan Baptist van Helmont, even provided a simple recipe for spontaneously generating mice: just leave out dirty cloth along with wheat for three weeks. Generating scorpions, on the other hand, required only "a few days" of basil remaining between two bricks in the sun. The validity of these findings, van Helmont claimed, was confirmed by his own empirical experiments.[104]

Besides the common-sense-contradicting nature of such a theory, it is also true that any Christian should have known that his Faith ruled it out, even though no clear dogmas existed expressly addressing it. Scripture is clear enough that all creatures derive as offspring from their own originators of like kind (e.g., parents), not spontaneously from some amalgamation of conducive chemical circumstances—for example, it indicates that "two of each kind" are needed for reproduction (cf. Genesis 6). Indeed, teachings contrary to the truly faithful approach to Scripture, Magisterium, etc., were pervasive among Catholics, even before the 1900s. But extremely few of them (relatively speaking) ever managed to receive explicit and dogmatic Papal condemnations. This brings us to our next point.

The same pseudo-traditionalism noted above induces some of its adherents to glamorize all times before the 20th century. This perverse approach to Tradition can only be called delusional, as it contradicts its own premises. The popes and Magisterial documents most often appealed to by traditionalists themselves were, of course, concerned with condemning the evils that had become pervasive in the Church *in the time of their own promulgation.* How ironic indeed it would be for a traditionalist to glamorize the very types of things his favorite traditional Magisterium condemns under the guise of advocating for that very Magisterium!

Consider the most famous of these "traditionalist" Magisterial documents—Pope Pius IX's *Syllabus of Errors.* It was not written to condemn the sexual revolution of the 1960s or even the brand of Modernism peculiar to pre-War Europe. It was, rather, promulgated in the year 1864. And it was directed against the errors that had *already* ravaged the Church in the decades leading up to its publication.

Within that Magisterial act, the Pope condemned the notion that "*Divine revelation is imperfect, and therefore subject to a continual and indefinite progress, corresponding with the advancement of human reason.*" (§5) This is a clear shot at the alien belief of his day, considering the grave imperfections ET promoters implicitly levied against Scripture; claiming it was so imperfect as to simply entirely leave out any mention of the vast majority of God's rational creation. Also condemned in that document was the proposition that "*The method and principles by which the old scholastic doctors cultivated theology are no longer suitable to the demands of our times and to the progress of the sciences.*" (§13) Here, too, more shade is cast upon belief in aliens. The ET promoters of the 1800s were known to argue that the Fathers and Doctors of the Church condemned aliens only because their scientific astronomy was so much less advanced. (In fact, the Fathers and Doctors condemned the notion of aliens because they realized how irreconcilable the notion was with Public Revelation.) Still another notion Pope here condemned holds that "*The obligation by which Catholic teachers and authors are strictly bound is confined to those things only which are proposed to universal belief as dogmas of faith by the infallible judgment of the Church.*" (§22) This was perhaps the most common error used by Catholic ET promoters of the 1800s (and today) to justify their behavior: since there "*isn't an infallible dogma explicitly ruling out aliens, I'm free to believe and teach whatever I please on this; it's science's domain alone, not theology's.*" As we can see, the Magisterium here anathematizes that very notion. One is not morally free to teach whatever he pleases merely by pointing out it is not directly contrary to an explicit dogma. The Pope concluded his condemnation of these errors with a grave warning:

> ... **Venerable Brethren, you see clearly enough how sad and full of perils is the condition of Catholics in the regions of Europe which We have mentioned. Nor are things any better or circumstances calmer in America**...

Yet it is precisely the milieu which Pope Pius describes above that is the one today's Catholic ET promoters pick and choose a careful handful of priests and authors from who likewise believed in ET, and accordingly declare alien belief licit. Such a catastrophic failure of discernment is just another symptom of the deception so prevalent in the Church today—which seeks not the most faithfully Christian and Catholic view of things, but only seeks to find any excuse to justify accommodating Godless, worldly ideologies.

Whoever desires to glean the orthodox Catholic truth by reading the works of authors of those time periods will not succeed merely by ascertaining the year of the author's birth. He must, instead, seek out those authors renowned for their holiness and orthodoxy. (When doing that, he will not find a single one advocating for belief in extraterrestrials.)

The 1800s were, simply put, a delusional era. That alien belief peaked in this time period is a testimony to the problematic nature of that belief, not to its credibility. The fact that our own era is far worse must not detract from accurately assessing the evils of the 19th century. The Enlightenment had largely accomplished its goal of devastating mainstream academia, and almost all the popular thinkers had their minds clouded by ungodly propositions. Then as now, it took a very saintly man to protect himself against succumbing to this tendency.

The 1800s were also heavily dominated by the influence of freemasonry and the occult. Ouija, Theosophy, séances, automatic writing, mediums, secret societies, table-rapping, spirit-photography, mesmerism, telepathy, divination, etc.—all of which are simply portals for demons—were everywhere. Extraterrestrial fixation was just another item to add on to that list.

In fact, occultism was so prominent in this time period that multiple scholarly tomes exploring it have recently been published. One such work, published by Routledge, acknowledges the following in its opening Preface:

> **The nineteenth century's engagement with ideas of the spirit world was immense and far-reaching**, from literature, the visual and performing arts, politics and material culture, to music, sexual politics and everyday life. Spiritualism and **the occult have been shown in several recent important studies as central forces in nineteenth-century debates** over technology, medical science, spiritual authority and religion, relationships among diverse social causes, and questions of love, sex and culture...spiritualism ... become central to what many people think it meant to be Victorian ... occultism was a point of entry for nineteenth-century thinkers interested in a range of vital questions: how did mediums function as relays in the new circuits of technological communication? ... music halls, parlours, literary salons, art galleries, courtrooms, photographic studios and the stage ... [were] interconnected through spiritualism and the occult ...[105]

Note that in this context, the "spirit world" and "spiritualism" does not refer to anything positive about spirituality. In modern secular scholarship (which is the context of the quote above), that phrase refers to *occultism*, or at least esotericism more broadly. The book itself continues to explain in great detail the pervasiveness of a multitude of manifestly dark occult practices in the 1800s—and not only those listed above.

Like today, technological progress had deceived people into thinking that "spiritual revolution" was likewise heralded by these inventions: Indeed, the 1800s...

> ...was an age of rising mass consciousness ... reform and revolution ... with advances in science and technology both visible and dazzling, such as the 1860s completion of the Atlantic Cable—a popular spiritualist metaphor for the instantaneous communication between this world and the next.[106]

Unfortunately, the scholars quoted above describe these qualities of the 19th century as if they were positive things. A discerning Christian knows better. Described there is a laying down of the foundations of the supreme diabolical deception. The Devil, indeed, was in the long game at that point. He knew that what he was introducing then would not have its fulfillment until the 21st century.

Moreover, he only deceives himself who supposes these were merely secular trends from which Catholics of that era were immune. Just as the 20th century version of the New Age movement has deeply infiltrated the Church (just, for example, see Part One, where we discussed the teachings of Fr. Richard Rohr), so too 19th century occultism did the same. As the same Routledge tome notes:

> ...**spiritualism [occultism] was not a denomination, but rather an amplification or overlay on one's denominational beliefs** and practices... it cut widely across churches and classes, from high to low and broad church Anglicanism **and Roman Catholicism** to virtually all of the Dissenting faiths, touching the heart of most major faith systems ... **spiritualists [occultists] thought of themselves as expanding or improving their native religious practice with the séance, not replacing them** ... Religion permeated Victorian lives'. To be sure, not all Christian Victorians were devout—it was, in fact, an age of doubt and disenchantment as well as devotion—but religious practice was a wholly naturalized part of day-to-day life in the nineteenth century. That very doubt and disenchantment, however, made the promise spiritualism offered—material proof of a spiritual afterlife—all that much more tantalizing and transformative.

Just as many 19th century Catholics succumbed to deception by supposing that, for example, clearly diabolical séances "improved" their faith, so too did many succumb to similarly dangerous deceptions by supposing that belief in extraterrestrials somehow "improved" Christianity. Moreover, the pattern that these 19th century occultist Christians advocated for disturbingly resembles the pattern we see displayed in much of today's "Christian" promotion of extraterrestrial ideology:

> A primary impetus for the development of occult spirituality in the

> nineteenth century ... [advocated for] a three-stage movement: first, occultism is enlisted to demonstrate the reality of spiritual phenomena ... then occultism is shown to be incomplete or materialistically flawed in its spirituality; finally, it is possible to return to a Christian belief which, through this process, has been reinvigorated to stand up to materialism. **The bargain, however, for Christianity is that it has been largely stripped of most of its traditional doctrine**...God, heaven, sin/redemption, and even the word 'Christianity' have been [muted]...Instead one finds euphemisms such as 'the Divine One' and 'the Great Religion', and the predominant focus is on the individual soul and a free-floating conception of the afterlife that is divorced from the traditional, dualistic geography of heaven and hell... [but] the ultimate source... only can be known to the fully initiated adept. **This, after all, is the strategy used to effect by the adepts of Theosophy, the Golden Dawn, and, for that matter, the Church of Scientology, a more recent occult-scientific religion that rivals the hybridity of its late-nineteenth century antecedents**.[107]

Do not be surprised when today's "messages from the Extraterrestrials" deliver similar lessons as those found through séances, mediums, Ouija boards, etc., which first became popular in the 1800s. All derive from the same—unsurpassably low—source.* It is time for the Faithful to wake up and recognize that the demise of Christendom should not be primarily traced to the sexual revolution (horrendously evil as that was), but rather to the "Enlightenment."

---

* Those who would still insist that Catholics were somehow immune from these prevailing Enlightenment-era trends need only consider "Mesmerism." Also known as "animal magnetism," this belief and practice was just one brand of vitalism, and it was a forerunner of the modern popular occult practice of "Reiki." A deeply esoteric and pseudoscientific practice, it was, tragically, particularly effective in infiltrating the 19th Century Catholic Church. As Dr. Sziede explains. "*In the early 1820s, Catholic thinkers started systematically adopting mesmerist Naturphilosophical theories, and occasionally mesmerist practices. Mesmerism, or animal magnetism...is a set of healing techniques, religious practices, and, more specifically in its nineteenth century German tradition, theories of Romantic Naturphilosophie. It was of far-reaching influence throughout the late eighteenth and in the nineteenth centuries.*" The lesson here is simple: one cannot assume that a belief is safe merely because it was espoused by a number of 19th Century Catholics. A Catholic, instead, must read Scripture, he must ascertain what the Church teaches, he must determine what the saints agreed upon—what is confirmed by Sacred Tradition, he should consult what is taught in authentic private revelation, etc., in finding realms of spiritual safety. Catholics have been falling for occult and pseudoscientific nonsense for a very long time; that trend did not begin merely upon the dawn of the postmodern "New Age" movement.

"Angels and Men": The Consensus of Sacred Tradition on What Constitutes the Universe's Rational Creatures

> "...the number of the rational creatures, that is to say of angels and men..." —Pope St. Gregory the Great

Now that we have completed our broad review of Sacred Tradition's development with respect to the question of aliens, let us ensure we conclude this chapter by recalling what it *does* teach, and consider a summary of its themes with respect to just how the saints, Fathers, Doctors, and Popes have, throughout the centuries, referred to all rational beings.

In many different contexts, the need often arises to issue some teaching as it stands in relation to all rational creatures of the universe. For example, throughout Sacred Tradition we see this frequently arise in cases of describing the glory of the Blessed Virgin (surpassing, as we dogmatically know, all other creatures). In every such case—whether found in Papal Magisterium, Ecumenical Councils, the Liturgy, private revelation, or the teachings of the Fathers, Doctors, and Saints—the way the teaching is phrased is identical: all rational creatures are simply described as *angels and men*. There are countless thousands of such references that have accumulated throughout two thousand years of Sacred Tradition. None of them leaves room for speculation about other intelligent creatures, much less asserts or implies that such beings exist.

Thousands of pages would be needed to review all that Sacred Tradition entrusts to us in referring to only men and angels as the rational creatures of the universe. Therefore, we will only consider a small selection of quotations below.

> For God, wishing both angels and men, who were endowed with freewill, and at their own disposal, to do whatever He had strengthened each to do, made them so, that if they chose the things acceptable to Himself, He would keep them free from death and from punishment. (**St. Justin Martyr**. *Dialogue with Trypho*.)
>
> ...it is not incongruous and unsuitable to speak **of a society composed of angels and men together;** so that there are not four cities or societies—two, namely, of angels, and as many of men—but rather two in all, one composed of the good, the other of the wicked, angels or men indifferently. (**St. Augustine**. *City of God*. Book XII. Ch. 1)
>
> After the resurrection, however, when the final, universal judgment has been completed, there shall be two kingdoms, each with its own distinct boundaries, the one Christ's, the other the devil's; the one consisting of the good, the other of the bad,—**both, however, consisting of angels and men**. (**St. Augustine**. *The Enchiridion*. Chapter 111.)
>
> [God] hath set over all one and the same Head, i.e., Christ according to the flesh, alike over Angels and men. That is to say, He hath given to Angels and men one and the same government... (**St. John Chrysostom.**

> Homily 1 on Ephesians.)
>
> All God's works are ordained to the salvation of men and angels; and the order of his providence is this...**out of the mass of that innumerable quantity of things which he could produce, he chose to create men and angels** to accompany his Son, participate in his graces and glory, adore and praise him for ever. (**St. Francis de Sales**)[108]
>
> One sheep then perished when man by sinning left the pastures of life. But in the wilderness the ninety and nine remained, because the number of **the rational creatures, that is to say of Angels and men** who were formed to see God, was lessened when man perished; and hence it follows, does he not leave the ninety and nine in the wilderness, because in truth he left the companies of the Angels in heaven. But man then forsook heaven when he sinned. And that the whole body of the sheep might be perfectly made up again in heaven, the lost man was sought for on earth... (**St. Gregory the Great**.)
>
> ...we affirm that God, having had an eternal and most perfect knowledge of the art of making the world for his glory, disposed before all things in his divine understanding **all the principal parts of the universe which might render him honour; to wit, angelic and human nature**...Further, in this same eternity he provided and determined in his mind all the means requisite for men and angels to come to the end for which he had ordained them, and so made the act of his providence; ...[he] does by his government furnish reasonable creatures with all things necessary to attain glory, so that, to say it in a word, sovereign providence is no other thing than the act whereby God furnishes men or angels with the means necessary or useful for the obtaining of their end. (**St. Francis de Sales** "Of the Divine Providence in General")

This great saint and Doctor of the Church, Francis de Sales, writes that all creatures who honor God (that is, doing so intentionally) are, "to wit," angels and men. "To wit," simply means "that is to say." De Sales, therefore, is explicitly declaring that only angels and men are rational.

St. Thomas Aquinas even specifically teaches there are exactly three types of rational creatures: men, angels, and demons. (Note that when, more broadly, "men and angels" are being referred to, this also sometimes includes demons, because, strictly speaking, they are still "angels" insofar as they retain their angelic *nature*.) He writes, in his commentary on the Book of Job, about:

> ... **the three kinds of rational creatures**. Thus when he says, *she is hidden from the eyes of all the living*, he refers to **men**; when he adds, *she is concealed from the birds of heaven*, he refers to the **angels**. When he further continues, *ruin and death said: we have heard of his fame with our ears*, he refers to the **demons**, who are removed from God by damnation, in that they have knowledge of divine wisdom only by its reputation from afar.

Elsewhere, Aquinas teaches:

> Then he is said to be full of grace and truth inasmuch as in his soul there

> was the fullness of all graces without measure: for God does not give the Spirit by measure (John 3:34). Yet it was given in fractions to all rational creatures, both angels and men.

The words of many other saints and popes can be quoted as well:

> ...the future uncertain and full of cares, but do not lose heart. Rather so display yourselves, presenting "such a spectacle ... to **the whole creation, men and angels alike**... (Pope Pius XII. *Orientales Omnes Ecclesias.* §60)
>
> ...**the Blessed Virgin is infinitely superior to all the hierarchies of men and angels**, [she is] the one creature who is closest of all to Christ. (Pope Leo XIII. *Magnae Dei Matris.* §9)
>
> Mary has by grace been exalted above all angels and men to a place second only to her Son, as the most holy Mother of God who was involved in the mysteries of Christ... (Second Vatican Council. *Lumen Gentium.* §66)
>
> "Christ," [St. Cyril] says, "has dominion over **all creatures**, a dominion not seized by violence nor usurped, but his by essence and by nature." His kingship is founded upon the ineffable hypostatic union. From this it follows not only that Christ is to be adored by **angels and men,** but that to him as man angels and men are subject, and must recognize his empire; by reason of the hypostatic union Christ has power over all creatures. (Pope Pius XI. *Quas Primas.* §13)
>
> Above all, I rejoice that God himself loves [Mary] more than all men and angels. ... He is the Creator of heaven and earth; he is the sovereign infinite good, in whose sight men and angels are as a drop of water, or a grain of sand: as a drop of a bucket, as a little dust. (St. Alphonsus Liguori)[109]

Such references as these could be extended almost endlessly. The lesson they convey is clear. Of *all* creatures, *only* men and angels are rational. Each time any saint, Father of the Church, Doctor of the Church, Pope, or Magisterial document, has spoken of all rational creatures, they have exclusively applied intelligence to angels and men. If we are to have any regard for forming our worldview (and cosmos-view) based on Sacred Tradition, then we will ensure our own beliefs accord with this unanimous consensus.*

---

* As we have noted before but should reiterate in the present context, ET promoters are likely to argue that "*these references are irrelevant since the saints and Popes who wrote them did not have aliens in mind; moreover, they wrote before the space age when questions about extraterrestrials become far more pressing than ever before.*" This move fails for two reasons. First, these saints (and all others) assert, without qualification, that *all rational creatures are either men or angels;* therefore, it does not matter what the men who wrote these passages "had in mind." By that logic, every absurd new type of being conjured up by some author in his daydreaming is exempt from scrutiny in light of Sacred Tradition, since—by definition—whoever else wrote before him did not have

Timeline of Tradition and Alien Belief

Before Christ	Alien belief is espoused by many pre-Christian Pagan thinkers—particularly by way of the atheistic materialist "atomist" philosophy of Democritus and hedonistic philosophy of Epicurus—but is condemned by Socrates, Plato, Aristotle, and others. (ET belief is also common in Eastern religions such as Hinduism and Buddhism)
0-500 A.D.	Alien belief is condemned by all of the Fathers of the Church who opined on it (except Origen.)
543 A.D.	At the Synod of Constantinople, the Church condemns Origen for many heresies, taking note of his belief in aliens (this condemnation was ratified at the Fifth Ecumenical Council, in 553, also at Constantinople)
748 A.D.	Pope Zachary condemns the alien belief of Virgil
1459 A.D.	Pope Pius II condemns the alien belief of Zaninus de Solcia
1400s	Breaking from a millennium and a half of Sacred Tradition, Nicholas of Cusa becomes the first ever non-condemned Catholic thinker to espouse belief in aliens. Despite his enormous popularity, this teaching of his is almost universally ignored by the faithful for centuries.
1500s	No Christian thinker other than Giordano Bruno promotes Cusa's belief.
1600 A.D.	Giordano Bruno is executed for heresy; with alien belief featuring prominently in the trial.
1500s-1600s	The Protestant Revolt takes place. For the first time, Christendom begins to question even unanimous consensuses held throughout Sacred Tradition's history.
1600s - 1700s	The "Copernican Revolution" takes place (well after the life of Copernicus himself). The planets are observed in some

---

that particular thing in mind. Second, and perhaps more pointedly still, these saints most assuredly *did* know full well about the various Pagan beliefs (which faded upon the birth of Christianity, but never completely died away) which posited that all sorts of rational creatures exist other than angels and men—whether fairies, elves, leprechauns, trolls, satyrs, centaurs, or what have you. By insisting that only men and angels are rational, these saints were thereby dismissing all these fables just as they were also dismissing extraterrestrials. Some Catholic ET promoters even attempt to use certain ancient writings about "satyrs" in support of their own beliefs regarding "NHI" (Non-Human Intelligence) in general. Their arguments not only fail; they undermine their own thesis (as we will see in the corresponding appendix of this book). Recall, as well, that Christians have always known about ancient Pagan speculations and beliefs regarding extraterrestrials—they simply always unanimously rejected such views before the Enlightenment.

	detail for the first time ever with telescopes following Galileo, and thinkers (mostly secular, but some religious) increasingly insist that such planets "must" harbor life as ours does.
1700s	"The Enlightenment" takes place, which seeks to overthrow Divine Authority and replace it with rationalism. The heretical "Principle of Plenitude" quickly becomes one of its main tenets, and this Principle serves as the ideological catalyst for alien belief.
1793 A.D.	The Deist, Thomas Paine, publishes a blistering attack against Christianity based upon the secular world's then near-unanimous assumption that aliens exist, in his work *The Age of Reason*, which becomes wildly popular and solicits countless responses for a century thereafter.
1800s	Secular academia de-facto declares alien belief ("plurality doctrine")—which had now been established as a "pillar of enlightenment optimism"—one of the requisite beliefs for scholars. The few who dissent are castigated, and acceptance of the existence of extraterrestrials becomes an unquestioned premise upon which scholarly discourse is built. Therefore, even some Catholic thinkers choose to defend the Faith (e.g., against Paine's attack) by way of focusing not on refuting aliens—which then appeared too difficult—but rather on insisting aliens do not overthrow Christianity. Despite the total dominance of alien belief among scholars in this era, no writers venerated by the Church espoused it, no Popes supported it, and no evidence exists that the ordinary faithful ever by-and-large adopted the view. Only evidence to the contrary can be found, and even Magisterium promulgated in this period (e.g., Leo XIII's Arcanum) implicitly rules out aliens. Later in this century, some scientists begin realizing the illogical nature of alien belief and begin writing against it.
1900s	Alien belief remains common among establishment academics until improvements in astronomy and technological advancements in telescopes (and, eventually, space flights), successively refute each one of the 19th-century conjectures that had been used to justify alien belief. Eventually, academia's pendulum swings toward the opposite direction, and most academics appear not to believe in aliens.
1947 A.D.	The Roswell Incident & the Kenneth Arnold UFO Sighting. A radically new phase in the alien belief debate begins. No longer is it a "merely academic" question, it becomes a matter with massive, immediate, concrete consequences.

	A government device crashed in Roswell, New Mexico, but it was treated by many as an alien-piloted craft. From this moment forward, the "UFO" craze began, and steadily increased in fervor to the present day. (Examining this era—which we are now reaching the culmination of—will be our task in upcoming chapters.)

***

Although we are here concluding our chronological consideration of Sacred Tradition's development with respect to this issue of extraterrestrials, two more important Catholic themes remain to be considered before we proceed to *scientifically* rebut alien belief. For we know that *lex orandi, lex credenda*—that is, "the law of prayer is the law of belief." Accordingly, we should examine the prayer of the Church (which we will do in the greatest possible way by examining her public prayer—the Holy Sacrifice of the Mass) to ascertain what it tells us about man's place in creation. We also know that God did not cease speaking upon the death of the last Apostle, which heralded the conclusion of Public Revelation, therefore we will endeavor to discover what God has said through private revelation that is germane to our investigation of aliens.

14. Liturgy, Private Revelation, and More

"Immeasurably more intriguing than UFOs and extraterrestrials is the phenomenon of a human and yet heavenly being who bears witness to another world, who comes not to mystify but as a messenger on a mission. And those who seek solace in New Age gurus and high-tech soothsayers will be better served if they turn to Mary of the Magnificat, who was once God-chosen and is now Godsent ... Despite the explosion of gigantic databanks and the daily avalanche of facts and figures, the modern era is characterized by confusion about the most basic questions of life. Those who are speeding down the information superhighway have no idea either of their ultimate destination or how to get there. A few who have thought about these matters seek answers from New Age gurus and channelers—or by scanning the universe with the hope of hearing from some form of extraterrestrial intelligence. Superstitions about aliens and reincarnation and the like have gripped the popular imagination ... [but] before we puzzle over the X Files let's read the M [Mary] Files." —Roy Abraham Varghese. (*God-Sent: A History of the Accredited Apparitions of Mary*. Introduction & §1.10)

The Prayers of the Mass Presuppose Man's Uniqueness

> "In the liturgy, all Christian prayer finds its source and goal. ... 'The liturgy is the summit toward which the activity of the Church is directed; it is also the font from which all her power flows.' It is therefore the privileged place for catechizing the People of God."
> —*Catechism of the Catholic Church*, §1073-1074

The Liturgy is the official prayer of the Church. How the Church prays is above all embodied therein. As we noted in this book's chapter on the New Testament, *"if anyone could argue that the preceding seventy-two books of the Bible left any stone unturned; any mystery hidden; any important truth still covered up, this final book does not."* We can say the same of the Liturgy with respect to the remainder of the content of the *sensus fidelium*. For the Liturgy too is itself an "unveiling." What may otherwise be obscure is made concrete and certain in the Mass. The Mass is not merely a ritual, but is truly a re-presentation of the cosmic sacrifice of Christ on Calvary. Its universal, trans-temporal proportions cannot be overstated.

Christian worship is surely a cosmic liturgy, which embraces both heaven and earth... It is precisely this cosmic dimension that is essential to Christian liturgy. It is never performed solely in the self-made world of man. It is always a cosmic liturgy. The theme of creation is embedded in Christian prayer. (Pope Benedict XVI. *The Spirit of the Liturgy*. Ch. 1,2)

If we were to be given, anywhere in Christian piety, grounds for supposing that rational material beings outside of earth may exist, then we would be certain to find those grounds somewhere in the prayers of the Mass. As Pope Benedict taught above, this Holy Sacrifice embraces all that is; the entire cosmos—the whole universe, *without exception*. If aliens existed, therefore, the Liturgy would enfold them as it enfolds us, and its prayers would not fail to give us some evidence of the inclusion of material beings other than men who need Redemption or Sanctification; creatures who bear the Divine Image. Instead, as we will presently see, the Mass contains only the opposite: it repeatedly teaches that humans are the sole recipients of such graces and the only examples of such glories.

To illustrate this, we need only consider several prayers contained in the current Roman Missal (the third typical edition).

***

> **You formed man in your own image** and entrusted the whole world to his care, **so that in serving you alone, the Creator, he might have dominion <u>over all</u> creatures**. (Eucharistic Prayer IV)

Reiterated here is what was covered in a preceding chapter: humans have dominion over the entire material universe—"**all** creatures." Everything within it is ours. Yet, no alien civilization could be reasonably regarded as under man's dominion.

> The ascension of Christ your son is our exaltation, and, where the head has gone before in glory, the Body is called to follow in hope. (*Collect for the Solemnity of the Ascension*)

Just as Christ is one head, so too *the* Church is His *one* Body. She is called to follow Christ in His Resurrection and Ascension; no "other Bodies" (i.e., the Churches of alien civilizations) have received this call, because no such other Bodies exist.

Many prayers of the Liturgy make specific reference to only the human race being the object of God's saving work:

> O God, who sent your only Begotten Son into this world to free **the human race** from its ancient enslavement (*Collect for Saturday of the First Week of Advent*) ... O God, who through the fruitful virginity of Blessed Mary bestowed on the human race the grace of eternal salvation (*Collect for the Solemnity of Mary, the Holy Mother of God*) ... O God, who through your Word **reconcile the human race to yourself** in a wonderful way (*Collect for the Fourth Sunday of Lent*) ... By the mystery of the Incarnation, he has led the human race that walked in darkness into the radiance of the faith and has brought those born in slavery to ancient sin through the waters of regeneration to make them your adopted children. Therefore, all creatures of heaven and earth sing a new song in adoration (*Preface for the Fourth Sunday of Lent*) ... Receive, we pray, O Lord, **the**

> **sacrifice which has redeemed the human race**, and be pleased to accomplish in us salvation of mind and body. Through Christ our Lord (*Prayer over the Offerings. Wednesday Within the Octave of Easter*)

There are countless other similar prayers in the Mass, and compiling them all here is unnecessary. It is enough to observe that none of them give any indication—explicitly or implicitly—that the various supplications we present to God for Redemption, Sanctification, or other graces directed towards rational incarnate beings, might possibly include creatures other than humans. There is not even a single line anywhere in the public prayer of the Church which gives grounds to *speculate* about such a possibility.

The Preface for the Feast of Corpus Christi even explicitly rules out the possibility of "human" aliens (i.e., aliens that are still "men," but a "different biological species; not *homo sapiens*"), which is the move made by some Catholic ET promoters to try to defend their views against censure by a number of Magisterial condemnations. In the Preface, the Church prays:

> Nourishing your faithful by this sacred mystery, you make them holy, so that **the human race, bounded by one world**, may be enlightened by one faith and united by one bond of charity. (*Preface II Of the Most Holy Eucharist*. §61)

Indeed, we are bounded by a single world, destined to all arrive at the fullness of the one faith. There are not "other worlds" with "humans"—"rational animals"—therein, each with other religions.

***

The faithful must understand that the Church is never timid in her supplications. She does not limit their scope or water down their aspirations to pacify cynics or comply with the demands of Pharisees. Quite the contrary, she beseeches for God to give what "prayer does not dare to ask." (*Collect for the Twenty-Seventh Sunday in Ordinary Time*) Consider what the Church prays for in the Feast of Christ the King:

> Almighty ever-living God, whose will is to restore all things in your beloved son, the King of the universe, grant, we pray, that the whole creation, set free from slavery, may render your majesty service and ceaselessly proclaim your praise. (*Collect for the Feast of Christ the King.*)

At Pentecost, she prays:

> Sanctify your whole Church in every people and nation; pour out, we pray, the gifts of the holy spirit across the face of the earth; and, with the divine grace that was at work when the Gospel was first proclaimed, fill now once more the hearts of believers. (*Collect for the Feast of Pentecost. Roman Missal.*)

Supplications such as these are common in Catholicism, yet bolder prayers than these cannot be imagined; save in the Our Father itself, wherein we "dare to pray" for God's Will to reign on earth even as it reigns in Heaven.

Therefore, a Catholic alien belief promoter would only be grasping at straws by arguing that the Church is simply not yet bold enough to pray for the salvation and sanctification of extraterrestrials.

While the Church frequently prays for the *entire* human race to acknowledge Christ, she never offers this petition directed to beings other than humans. The reason is clear: only rational creatures can acknowledge Christ, whereas angels already have done so and will never fail to do so, and demons already have rebelled and never will repent. If, on the other hand, aliens exist, then they are direly in need of these prayers, and the Church—whose Liturgy by nature encompasses the universe—has been miserably failing in its mission for 2,000 years. Even implicitly supposing that this scenario might be plausible or possible (which ET promotion does) is derogatory to not only the Church, but also the Holy Spirit, Who is her soul.

> God of our Fathers, who brought the martyr saint Teresa Benedicta of the Cross to know your crucified son and to imitate him even until death, **grant, through her intercession, that the whole human race may acknowledge Christ** as its savior and through him come to behold you for eternity. (*Collect for the Memorial of Saint Teresa Benedicta of the Cross*)

If, however, the Liturgy's repudiation of alien belief is sometimes implicit—though quite clear nevertheless—private revelation deals with the matter explicitly. To that we now turn our attention.

The Importance of and Proper Approach to Private Revelation

Many of the faithful are accustomed to being told, by certain circles of "professional Catholics" and career lay apologists, that private revelation is unimportant at best since it is "not part of the Deposit of Faith." They imply, if not outright assert, that Heaven's messages are little more than a distraction. Because of popularity of this false (and, frankly, diabolical) view of private revelation in the Church today, a brief note is in order discussing the proper approach to this topic before we proceed to consider some actual private revelations themselves and what they have to say (against) alien belief.

As we have already been deferring to the Catechism on aliens, let us also consult it for guidance on how to approach private revelation. Therein, we are taught:

> **In all he says and does, man is obliged to follow faithfully what he knows to be just and right.** (§1778)

The Church does not say *"only in those matters that the Catholic Church formally teaches are true must man follow faithfully what he knows to be just and right;"* but rather, that he must do so *always and everywhere.* We must never erroneously conflate "not required *as* a matter of Catholic Faith" with "never important to heed *for any Catholic*." For the latter is not only taught nowhere by the Church, but is in fact—here and elsewhere—expressly repudiated by her.

The need for private revelation was embedded into the Faith from the beginning. We are told in Scripture that *"he who prophesies edifies the church,"* (1 Corinthians 14) and such prophecy is a form of private revelation. Moreover, these extraordinary charisms of the Holy Spirit, of which prophecy is one, exist not for one's own sanctification, but rather for the sanctification of the entire Church. As the Catechism teaches:

> Charisms are to be accepted with gratitude by the person who receives them **and by all members of the Church as well**. They are a wonderfully rich grace for the apostolic vitality and for the holiness of the entire Body of Christ... (§799-800)

To assert that only faith in the Deposit of Faith ultimately matters is to present a slightly Catholicized version of the Protestant "Faith Alone" (*Sola Fide*) heresy. Catholic teaching, of course, rejects this idea.

Nothing Heaven says is unimportant. Even if formal heresy is only present when violating the Deposit of Faith, there are plenty of other ways to damage one's soul.

> "All people of good will can, and must, pray the Rosary every day."
> —Venerable Sr. Lucia of Fatima

The Servant of God Luisa Piccarreta: In the "Whole Creation," Only Man Has Reason

The Servant of God Luisa Piccarreta was an extraordinary Italian mystic who died in the year 1947 and received thousands of pages of approved revelations from Jesus and Mary. We will deal with her first, as I am convinced that the messages she received are the greatest private revelations in the history of the Church. (I encourage learning about her in *Thy Will Be Done,* published 2021). For now, a brief introduction will suffice. St. Hannibal di Francia—an Italian priest and founder of religious orders who was canonized by Pope St. John Paul II in 2004—dedicated the last decades of his life to promoting Luisa's revelations. The Vatican's official biography of Luisa, *The Sun of My Will* (SunOfMyWill.com), recounts the saint's words about Luisa:

> [She] emerges to be a singular predilection of the Divine Redeemer, Jesus Our Lord, who century after century, increases ever more the wonders of His love. It seems that He wanted to form this virgin, whom He calls the littlest one He found on earth, and bereft of any education, into an instrument of a mission so sublime, that is, the triumph of the Divine Will, in conformity with what is said in the Our Father prayer[110]... (Page 122)

Therein lies the essence of these private revelations: heralding the fulfillment of the Our Father prayer. St. Hannibal was so convinced of the authenticity of Luisa's revelations that he personally bestowed nineteen of his own *nihil obstats* (he was appointed *censor librorum*) to them, which were all followed up with corresponding *imprimaturs* from the Archbishop.

St. Hannibal, however, was not the only saint who knew Luisa and endorsed her. The Vatican's official biography of Luisa also recounts the strong support she received from St. Padre Pio:

> **There are countless testimonies** beyond these [i.e., those recorded from Federico Abresch and Mrs. Caterina Valentina] that talk about the mutual esteem and faith Luisa and Padre Pio had in each other ... **Even the residents of San Giovanni Rotondo knew how much respect Padre Pio had for Luisa.** (Pages 174-175)*

Luisa's life was filled with miracles rigorously scrutinized and documented by priests, Bishops, theologians, doctors, and scientists, who each ruled out any possible non-supernatural explanation. She even lived decades subsisting solely on the Holy Eucharist, consuming no other food. Her messages from Jesus are filled with prophecies that have been clearly fulfilled. (See Part Four of *Thy Will Be Done* for a partial overview of these.) Since her death over 75 years ago, Luisa's legacy of holiness has only grown, and confirmations of the orthodoxy of her messages have only multiplied. Indeed, not only was she declared a Servant of God, but her holiness and orthodoxy was thereafter confirmed by her diocese (in 2005), and her cause is now proceeding well in its Vatican stage. Multiple Church-approved religious orders already existed dedicated to Luisa's revelations (including the Benedictines of the Divine Will). Cardinal José Saraiva Martins, the Prefect of the Congregation for the Causes of Saints under Pope John Paul II and Pope Benedict XVI, strongly endorsed Luisa and her revelations from Jesus in a preface he wrote for the Vatican's aforementioned biography of her. (Considering the Cardinal's position, if anyone alive knows what makes a saint and an authentic revelation, it is he who does!)

All this, however, is only a very brief and partial overview of the authenticity of Luisa's revelations. Luisa's private revelations are as authentic as they come, and we should approach the following messages understanding that fact.

---

* Here I note that, unlike a certain quote regarding aliens, allegedly attributed to Padre Pio (but almost certainly counterfeit or misinterpreted) purely via hearsay from an anonymous source, what we have here is entirely different. Padre Pio's support of Luisa is confirmed by these authoritative sources, vetted by the Vatican, based on the testimony of multiple people (whose names and identities are known), in writing. Indeed, the support is entirely undeniable, notwithstanding the attempts of some of Luisa's critics to do precisely that.

***

Note: In some of the following excerpts of Jesus' revelations to her, it must be understood that in the contexts of the messages that follow, "creation," here as in similar literature, refers to physical creation; not to angels. Each message will be cited only with a date; this corresponds to the entry in Luisa's diary that the excerpt is taken from, which is enough information to easily locate the original source. Please note as well that when Jesus refers to "Us" or to "We," He is referring to the Three Persons of the Trinity.

Reiterating Biblical, Catholic, and even common-sense philosophical teaching, Jesus tells Luisa:

> Creation was made for man—in it he was to be the king of <u>all</u> created things. (July 29th, 1926) All created things were made for man, and man for Us. (September 24th, 1928)

We have already reviewed this point in earlier sections, but it must be restated how absurd it would be for man to be king of the universe (as indeed he is), if he is only one among multiple (even many) races of intelligent incarnate beings of whose existence he is not even aware.

In many other passages, Jesus makes it explicit to Lusia that the *entire* universe (not only planet earth) *solely* exists for the sake of the offspring of Adam, and that the creation of man constituted the only thing in the entire universe made in His Image. He tells her:

> ...what ardor of love was the creation of man. ... shaken by Our own love, We looked at the machine of the whole universe and We gave him [man] everything as gift, constituting him king of all created things... (January 13, 1928) ...**<u>there is great difference between the creation of the whole universe and the creation of man</u>**. ... in the creation of man, there was not only the creative and preserving act, but the active act added to it-and of an activity ever new; and this, **<u>because man was created in Our Image and Likeness</u>**... This is why We love him [man] so much-because **<u>he is not only Our work, like all the rest of creation, but he possesses part of Our Life</u>**, in a real way; We feel in him the life of Our Love. How not to love him? (November 10, 1929) ...see what order there is in the creation of the whole universe: there are heavens, stars, suns-all ordered. Much more so in creating man; Our Divine Being stretched out the order of Our Divine qualities like many heavens in the depth of his soul. (April 23, 1930) ... since man was made by Us to live in Our Will, all Our acts had to serve as many little cities or nations in which man could find, by right, his Fatherland... one can say that the sun is a city, and as the soul enters Our Will, she finds this city of light ...O, how happy We are, in seeing Our works-Our cities**<u>, created only for man,</u>** no longer as deserts, but populated by Our children. (March 28, 1938) **The <u>only</u> purpose of creation** was that all would fulfill my Will - not that **<u>man</u>** would do great things... (November 26, 1921) ... the life of Heaven upon the earth [is the] only purpose of the Creation. (January 18, 1928)

Expounding upon what mankind's status as the king of all creation entails, Jesus tells Luisa:

> So, each created thing holds out **my love to man; and if it were not so, Creation would have no purpose;** and I do nothing without purpose. **Everything has been made for man;** but man does not recognize it, and he has turned into sorrow for Me. (January 9, 1920)

Jesus explains to Luisa that Creation—the entire material universe—would simply *have no purpose without man*. He even tells her that everything in the universe other than man—including the very "heavens studded with stars," was nothing but a preparation for man:

> My daughter, here is why in Creation there were so many preparations ... What did We not prepare so that this feast might be one of the most solemn? **Heavens studded with stars**, sun radiant with light, refreshing winds, seas, ... **After having prepared everything, We created man,** that he might celebrate, and We together with him. (July 23, 1931)

But this reality is incoherent if there are other rational incarnate creatures, as a purpose of all these things could be found in serving this other race of rational creatures. Rendering it even more clear that by "creation," or "all things," or any other similar reference, Jesus is most emphatically not referring only to those things within this particular planet, Jesus tells Luisa:

> My daughter, I created the heavens and I centralized My love for man in the heavens; and in order to give him greater delight, I studded them with stars. **I did not love the heavens, but man in the heavens, and for him I created them**... **[the heavens] were to serve him as pure delight...** (October 29, 1926)

God created the very heavens themselves for us. He does not love the heavens! Yet, consider how blasphemous it would be to accuse God of not loving a domain that includes His own children (that is, any creature bearing His image; i.e., having a rational soul). It will not work to claim Jesus only meant He does not love the mere *matter* of the Heavens, but does love "aliens" therein. For that assessment would be true of earth also, yet Scripture teaches that "God so loved the world, that he sent his only son" into it. (John 3:16) Jesus loves creation simply for our sake; because the entirety of it—from each atom to each galaxy, to the entire universe, and everything in between—exists *for* us, and *only* for us. Jesus also tells Luisa:

> **The Eternal One looked at the heavens and remained content in seeing the immense harmonies, the communications of love which He had opened between Heaven and earth**. ...So, everything you see, even the most tiny little flower in the field, was one more relation between creature and Creator. (February 20, 1919) "The heavens are nothing other than an act of profound adoration of the immensity of Our Divine Being" (April 12, 1929)

As with the Bible itself, so too with this passage we see eliminated any enigma for those who would ask, *"why would God create such an expanse of Heavens if not to populate it with aliens?"*

The answer is simple: each created thing, has "a relation, a channel of graces, a special love" between God and man. Everything God has made tells us something about Him. The incomprehensibly large expanse of the cosmos—which we see only a tiny fraction of with the naked eye in the night sky—testifies to His omnipotence and majesty. Each new galaxy we discover reminds us of that, and silently declares that no matter how much we plumb the depths of God, there will always be more. Why did He put them there if we could only discover them in the Third Millennium? The reason is simple: *God knew that, in the Third Millennium, we would need those additional reminders of His glory and beauty.* There is *no other reason* for the existence of the heavens than this: God's love *for the human race;* that is, His love for descendants of Adam and Eve, *dwelling on earth.*

> [Luisa writes:] It seems that the Divine Volition longs for the love of Its beloved creature, to be able to find the little prop of love, upon which to lean Its great love. So, **heavens, suns, winds, are nothing other than** insinuating and continuous calls, **to tell us**: "I have anticipated you with my love; and you—do not leave Me without yours." (October 21, 1932)

Jesus would regularly correct Luisa when she spoke incorrectly. Yet He not only lets this claim stand, but He follows up with a lengthy message of His own, confirming her sentiments. Consider, however, how wrong it would be to describe, as Luisa does here, the very "heavens" themselves—even the "suns" (stars) therein, as being "nothing other than" (i.e., existing for no other reason than) calls to "us" (earthlings) about God's love. If rational beings dwelt therein, then those "suns" exist *for them,* not for us.

Humans, moreover, are the only material creatures who can love God; they are also the only material creatures who can sin. Jesus emphasizes this truth to Luisa in multiple messages:

> **Only the human will**, as We had created it with the great gift of the free willing ... might love Us and remain together with Us, to receive the operating life in Our Volition ... It was the greatest honor and gift We gave. (May 12, 1934) Only the human will, if it wants to operate on its own, without the union of Ours, can break this beautiful union, this bond of inseparability among God, created things and creatures. (January 2, 1930) **The most beautiful thing created by Us was the human will**. Among all created things it is the most beautiful, that which resembles Us more, therefore it can be called the queen among everything, as indeed it is. (June 16, 1934)

Note that Jesus does not merely say that the "free will," in general, is the most beautiful thing He made—as if to leave open the possibility that other incarnate creatures also have such a faculty. Instead, He indicates that only *human* beings can claim such an exalted state. Nothing but human beings have reason, as Jesus explicitly states in the following passage:

> [Luisa writes] "*I was doing my round through the whole Creation...oh, how beautiful it seemed to me! ... each created thing...[veils] within itself the creative power and Will... the Sun,* ***the heavens, the stars,*** *the wind, the sea...*" [Jesus responds:] "My daughter, look at how beautiful Our works are—pure, holy and all orderly. We made use of creation in order to form Our veils, Our vast residences; however, We held back from giving reason to them, because **they were created for man, not for themselves, and therefore We reserved giving to man the capacity and reason of the whole Creation**..." (September 2, 1928).

In this passage, Jesus bluntly states that only man has reason. In the "whole Creation"—that is, the entire material universe; the same passage even explicitly indicates it is referring to the stars—absolutely nothing else and no one else enjoys rationality. This is why the rational soul of man—intellect, memory, and will—is the only thing therein that keeps God company:

> In creating man I said, 'It is not good for man to be alone, let Us make another creature similar to him, who may keep him company, so that one may form the delight of the other', **I said these same words to my love before creating man: 'I do not want to be alone, but I want the creature for my company**. ... With his company I will pour Myself out in love.' This is why I made him in my likeness; and as his intelligence thinks of Me and is interested in Me, he keeps company with my wisdom, and as my thoughts keep company with his, we amuse ourselves together. If his gaze looks at Me and at created things in order to love Me, I feel the company of his gaze. (January 24, 1920)

Before creating man, we see, God "said to His love," that it did not want to be "alone." (This, of course, is mystical language, not a strict theological description of the Divine Nature—before creation existed, God was "*infinitely perfect and blessed in Himself.*" (CCC, §1)) Had aliens existed, God would not have "said" that, since He already would not have been "alone." Further explaining why man is, as it were, "everything" to God, Jesus provides Luisa the following beautiful message on Christmas Day:

> We find Ourselves in the condition of an artisan who has made his beautiful statue .....The artisan loves this statue so much that he has placed his very life in it ...Such is the state the Divinity is in with regard to man... in creating the heavens, the stars, the sun, the wind, the sea, the earth, it was Our works that We issued, and the flowerings of Our beautiful qualities. **Only for man was this greatest prodigy of creating the life—and the life of Our Love itself; and this is why it is said that he was created in Our Image and Likeness. And this is why We love him so much**-because it is life and work that has come out of Us, and life costs more than anything. (December 25, 1928)

Only man, Jesus here teaches, harbors the Image of God. *Only* man.

***

Many other passages from Luisa's revelations could be presented,* but we must pass over them for the sake of space. What is included above is more than sufficient to make it clear that we are presented with a simple choice: either believe in aliens and reject Luisa, or believe in Jesus' revelations to this Servant of God and reject aliens. The former option, however, is not remotely palatable from an authentically Catholic perspective. There has not been a single mystic in the history of the Church who has seen the verifications of authenticity that Luisa has, only to later be proven inauthentic. There is, quite simply, no chance that these revelations are anything but supernatural in origin.

---

* To give just one more example, a constant and important theme in Luisa's revelations is the spiritual practice of undertaking "The Rounds," in which one spiritually "goes through" all that God has done - all of it - to offer it back to Him in adoration. It is quite like (but a major expansion upon) the Cantle of Daniel's companions, wherein the Church (in her public prayer—the Divine Office) continuously prays for all that God has created to "bless the Lord." Similar spiritual practices are found in the revelations of St. Faustina. Now, these Rounds would be deprived of their purpose if they were missing in them an entire category of beings in "the Great Chain of Creation." Yet, despite the many descriptions of the Rounds in Luisa's revelations, not one of them contains the slightest implication that there may be aliens. Rather, each time the Rounds are implored, undertaken, or described, their scope is identical: They include *all* that God has made or accomplished, namely, yet they never include any indication of, implication of, or even space for, extraterrestrials. One dialogue between Luisa and Jesus is recorded in the following entry in the *Diary*, "*'My Divine Jesus, I want to love You together with the Father and the Holy Spirit.' But it seemed He was not content yet. And I: 'I want to love You together with all the Angels and Saints.' And He: "And with whom else?" '**With all the pilgrim souls and unto the last creature that will exist upon earth. I want to bring You everyone and everything** – even the heavens, the sun, the wind, the sea – to love You together with all.'* " At this point, Jesus was at last content with Luisa's description of "all things." The passage continues: "*And Jesus, all love, such that it seemed He could not contain the flames, added: "My daughter, behold my Heaven in the creature: the Sacrosanct Trinity yielding Its love in order to love Me together with her; the Angels and Saints competing in giving out their love so as to love Me together with her. **This is the great act: to bring all into the All, who is God** ... **you want to give Me everything, up to the very Adorable Trinity**...and I can say: 'I lack nothing – neither Heaven, nor my Celestial Mother, nor the cortege of the Angels and Saints. All are with Me, and all love Me.'*" (October 22, 1933) It is difficult to imagine any additional superlatives Jesus or Luisa could have amassed to better convey the point that the purpose of the Rounds is to exclude *absolutely nothing* that God has made. Instead of seeing any implications that extraterrestrials might exist within this sphere of reality, we see only the opposite: the Rounds repeatedly treating human beings—earthlings—as the only rational incarnate creatures.

Bl. Anne Catherine Emmerich: Heavens Populated by Angels, not Aliens

Blessed Anne Catherine Emmerich was an 18th and 19th century German mystic and stigmatist who received an extraordinary number of mystical visions on the life of Jesus and Mary (among other things) and was Beatified by Pope St. John Paul II in 2004. Her messages are germane to the matter at hand, but understanding their contribution requires a careful approach, since at least one Catholic ET promoter has unfortunately misused her writings by arguing they contain the very opposite implication they truly do. This confusion is addressed in the corresponding appendix at the end of this book.

Emmerich's revelations are quite concerned indeed with the details of what transpires in the cosmos. She even describes what she saw transpiring on the moon! Yet, *even her* revelations fail to give any indication that *incarnate* intelligent extraterrestrials exist. If any authentic mystic were to reveal to us the existence of aliens, it would be Emmerich. Yet, the only passage—from her *thousands* of pages of revelations—that the ET promoters can provide is one which clearly does not speak of aliens (see appendix).

Emmerich speaks of the cosmos being "populated," but it is clear she is speaking of angels or the *souls* of the departed. The mystic explains:

> **The Milky Way is formed of watery globules like crystals. It seems as if the good spirits bathe therein**. They plunge in and pour forth all kinds of dew and blessings like a Baptism...[111]

Such passages speak of the cosmos as the playground, as it were, of the angels. Indeed, traditional pious thought regards the motion of the heavenly bodies as an effect not of dead forces manifesting their inevitable results, but rather as a stunning display of the ministry of angels glorifying God's grandeur. And there is certainly nothing wrong with holding that view today. It is a beautiful and edifying posture to have in relation to the night sky, but it does not in the least induce one to adopt belief in aliens. In fact, this posture refutes such a view, for that view relegates the heavens to the same status of earth. Here, the angels do not have their "playground," but their *battleground*. The "war [that] broke out in *heaven*," (Revelation 12:7-10) was concluded long ago, when St. Michael and his army were victorious over Lucifer and his legion of rebellious angels who were cast down *to earth*.

St. Bridget of Sweden: The Music of the Spheres, not of the Aliens

Another mystic who testifies beautifully to the exalted view we should have of the cosmos—without needing to populate them with little green men—is St. Bridget of Sweden. Like the revelations of every other authentic mystic, those given to St. Bridget contain no trace of grounds for speculating that aliens may exist, and plenty of indications they do not.

St. Bridget was the 14th century foundress of the Order of the Most Holy Savior, and she is now revered as the patron saint of Sweden and was even named—by Pope St. John Paul II in 1999—one of the patron saints of all Europe. She too received thousands of pages of revelations which provide astounding insights on many topics. She recounts one vision as follows:

> I saw the four evangelists in the shape of four animals, just as they are depicted in mural paintings in the world, but they were seen to be alive and not lifeless. Then I saw the twelve apostles seated on twelve seats awaiting the coming power. Adam and Eve came with the martyrs and confessors and all the other saints who descend from them. ... Then I saw a priest dressed in priestly vestments begin to say mass in a church in the world. When he had performed all the preceding parts of the mass, he reached the words of the consecration of the bread. Then I beheld what seemed to be the sun, moon and stars with all the planets and all the heavens in their orbits and rotations resounding with melodious song in alternating voices. One could hear every song and melody...[112]

Confirming what we discussed earlier—namely, that the Holy Sacrifice of the Mass is a cosmic reality which enfolds within itself the entire universe—St. Bridget describes all the cosmos truly bursting out into song unto the praise of Christ in the Blessed Sacrament. Yes, the "music of the spheres"—the indescribably beautiful symphony continuously generated by the motions of the heavenly bodies—is real. (Jesus says the same to the Servant of God Luisa Piccarreta.) Although everything in the cosmos joins in on the Liturgy, there are no extraterrestrials taking part in it—for no such beings exist.

I was sure to include the beginning lines of the quote above as it reminds us that the "four living creatures" of Revelation 4:6-7 are not—as some ET promoters bizarrely claim—covert references to aliens. Catholic tradition has always regarded these as symbolic of the Four Evangelists, angels, or Old Testament Prophets. (St. Bridget here uses the first. We will consider this in more detail in the corresponding appendix.) In another passage, Jesus tells St. Bridget:

> All things, bodily as well as spiritual, have a certain plan and order ... all the elements keep to their own order and motion, as foreseen from eternity, and move according to the will of their Maker. Likewise, every rational creature should move and prepare itself according to the order established by the Creator. When a rational creature does the opposite, it is obvious that it is abusing its freedom of choice. **So, while irrational creatures keep to their limits, rational human beings debase their original excellence and render their sentence heavier by not making use of their reason.**[113]

Here, Jesus describes two fundamental categories of created beings: rational creatures, and irrational creatures. The latter always "keep to their limits," for, lacking reason, they can do nothing else but obey the Divine Will. Rational creatures, however, "abuse their freedom" by contradicting the order established by God. And who exactly are these beings capable of making such a (poor) choice? Jesus tells the saint that it is *human beings* who can do so, for they are the only rational incarnate creatures.

In a personal meditation (not a description of a vision), the saint wrote:

> The son of God and the Virgin's son is dearest to my soul and body above all that is created. May all in heaven give honor and thanks for its joy which shall be without end. And everything that is in purgatory shall praise you for your merciful deeds; your praise shall even be in hell, without their will, because of the justice of your judgments. **All the heavens and planets shall honor you** with the fairest sound and their movements and song. And the world with all that is in it, dead and alive, may walk eternally in praise of God's blessed body because you wished to be made man, and your handiwork was bought so dearly and your love which was eternally in you was revealed to all. (Volume 4. Meditation 2. "Early 1340s, Sweden.")

Here, as everywhere in authentic private revelation, whenever we see *all things* described—even if these descriptions explicitly ascend to the very heavens, as this one—these descriptions never populate the heavens with men. In such regions, it is merely the "planets and stars" (or the angels and saints who are free to go wherever in the universe they please), not incarnate inhabitants of them, which serve to glorify God.

> "Given the wonder of my works and how all things praise me, **human beings, who are so much more beautiful and so much more highly placed than other creatures**, should accordingly realize that they are that much more obliged to honor me. ... The soul is far better by nature than the body, because it is of my divine power and is immortal, having fellowship with the angels and being more excellent than all the planets and nobler than the whole world." —Jesus to St. Bridget

Venerable Mary of Agreda: Earth Alone is the Theater of Eternal Destinies

Like Bl. Emmerich, Venerable Mary of Agreda (or Mary of Jesus of Ágreda) generated thousands of pages of revelations describing mystical visions—primarily centered on the life of Jesus and Mary, but also detailing other realities. This great mystic was a 17th century Spanish Franciscan abbess whose life also exhibited uniquely exalted miracles—even bilocation *across continents*. Even though she lived in Spain, she herself tutored students in America (and not with use of the internet!).

She too provided revelations with no hint of extraterrestrials and no place for them, despite detailing all manner of otherwise hidden cosmic phenomena thanks to her supernatural insights. Presented below are excerpts from various places in her revelations, taken from the complete edition of the *Mystical City of God*[114]:

> **The sun illuminates** the moon; and both, together with the stars of the firmament, illumine **all other creatures** within the confines of the universe. He created the rest of the beings and added to their perfection, because they **were to be subservient to Christ and most holy Mary, and through them to the rest of men**. ...God exerted more care in composing this little body of his most holy Mother, than in creating all the celestial orbs and the whole universe... All the rest of the creatures combined could not attain the beauty and faultlessness of her Charity for theirs was not worthy to be called absolutely beautiful ... there is no other creature in heaven or on earth that could be such a teacher of this beautiful love for **men or angels** ... the incarnate Word, with his most holy Mother was present, in spirit, when God resolved upon the creation of the whole world; for in that instant the Son was not only coexistent in divine essence with the Father and the Holy Spirit, but also the human nature, which He was to assume, was foreseen and conceived as the prototype of all works in the divine mind of the Father. Conjointly with Him was also foreseen as present the human nature of his most holy Mother ... In these two Persons were foreseen all his works, so that on account of Them (speaking in a human way) **He overlooked all that could offend Him in the conduct of the men and angels that were to fall...And before creating intellectual and rational creatures ... He created heaven for angels and men; and the earth as a place of pilgrimage for mortals**. ... **Thus all parts of the creation** would be compelled as it were to obey and love their Maker and Benefactor and by his works to learn of his holy name and of his perfections (Rom. 1, 20).

Although the quotations above do not explicitly refer to extraterrestrials, they nevertheless describe a cosmology that is devoid of any place for aliens; a cosmology that regards men and angels as the only rational creatures, and earth as the only sphere wherein eternal destinies are determined. It moreover describes the mind of God before creation; before time itself, hinging only upon earth—for it was there alone that the human nature of Christ resided, as well as His Holy Mother, who was likewise uniquely predestined by God before the foundations of the universe.

The following passage details the test of the angels, the rebellion of Lucifer, and the latter's attacks against Adam and Eve. Here, too, it is clear that, of the entire material creation, only descendants of Adam and Eve are part of the Theater of Eternal Destinies:

> [Before the creation of the world} the angels were informed that God was to create a human nature and reasoning creatures lower than them-

> selves, ... and that the second Person of the blessed Trinity was to become incarnate and assume their nature...all the obedient and holy angels submitted themselves and they gave their full assent and acknowledgment with an humble and loving subjection of the will. But Lucifer, full of envy and pride, resisted and induced his followers to resist likewise ... Then happened that great battle in heaven, which St. John describes (Apoc. 12) ... Lucifer, however, and his confederates, rose to a higher pitch of pride and boastful insolence. In disorderly fury he aspired to be himself the head of all the human race and of the angelic orders, and if there was to be a hypostatic union, he demanded that it be consummated in him ... This proud boast so aroused the indignation of the Lord that in order to humble it, He spoke to Lucifer: "This Woman, whom thou refusest to honor, shall crush thy head and by Her shalt thou be vanquished and annihilated (Gen. 3, 15). And if, through thy pride, death enters into the world (Wis. 2, 24), life and salvation of mortals shall enter through the humility of this Woman. Those that are of the nature and likeness of that Man and Woman, shall enjoy the gifts and the crowns, which thou and thy followers have lost." ... [Upon the creation of Adam and Eve,] The envy of the serpent was immediately aroused against them, for Satan was impatiently awaiting their creation ... However, he was not permitted to witness the formation of Adam and Eve, as he had witnessed the creation of all other things: for the Lord did not choose to manifest to him the creation of man ... But when the demon saw the admirable composition of the human nature, perfect beyond that of any other creature, the beauty of the souls and also of the bodies of Adam and Eve; when he saw the paternal love with which the Lord regarded them, and how He made them the lords of all creation, and that He gave them hope of eternal life : the wrath of the dragon was lashed to fury, and no tongue can describe the rage with which that beast was filled, nor how great was his envy and his desire to take the life of these two beings.

The Venerable mystic was given far more detail in both breadth and depth than what is shown above. In a truly astounding degree of clarity, we see described the very beginning: the creation of the angels, the universe and its inhabitants, a careful account of exactly why and how the demons rebelled against God (what with their fury elicited entirely due to the events they were shown would transpire on earth), how in the creation of man alone was seen the incomprehensible miracle of the Image of God rendered incarnate, and on the list goes. Many other revelations contain similar accounts.

The Holy Souls to the Mystic Maria Simma: "Aliens and UFOs" are Satanic

The second of eight children, Maria Simma was an Austrian mystic who was born in the year 1915 and died in 2004. As a small child, she desired to become a nun, but this proved impossible due to health problems. At the age of twenty-five she began receiving visits from souls in Purgatory, and the messages these holy souls delivered to her continued for decades. A true victim herself, Maria suffered greatly for these purging souls, but she accepted it all with grace and joy, saying, "God allows it so that, through my apostolate, other people may understand clearly that our time on earth is meant for gaining Heaven."

Many of the messages she received are compiled in the book, *Get Us Out Of Here*, which was published during Simma's life and was authorized by her. It consists in the result of many extensive interviews with the mystic. In its preface, the theologian and Franciscan priest, Fr. Slavko Barbaric, wrote of Simma:

> ...**all personal doubts disappeared once I too had met and spoken with Maria Simma. She is true**... when her own suffering is requested by the world beyond [purgatory] she, by always accepting it freely, is cleansed and thus lives in deep peace.[115]

The book recounts the interviewer asking Simma, "*There is so much talk about and media attention given these days to UFOs. Do people confuse angels with UFOs or vice versa?*"[116] Simma responded:

> ...Let me put it this way. Just recently a friend of mine asked me to ask a Poor Soul if there was intelligent life on other planets. The answer came a few weeks later. The Poor Soul said, "No." So **<u>there is no intelligent life on other planets</u>.** But this does NOT mean that all those sightings and stories of abductions are not true. So many people would not wish to lie about this, but it does mean something else. **If there is no other intelligent life elsewhere in our universe, and here I'd like to add that anyone with a deeper knowledge and faith in the Holy Bible would conclude the same, then <u>all of those sightings are Satan's work</u>**. Satan wants us to be very curious and what better way is there than to lead us astray running after little green creatures out into the voids of space? Curiosity has killed far more than merely the cat. **And all those films and television shows about civilizations out there can easily lead the young into danger.**[117]

In this brief but revealing passage, Simma's insights gleaned from the holy souls in Purgatory provide multiple vitally important and deeply relevant truths. Most importantly, however, we must recall that while a demon may—perhaps to an exorcist—sometimes lie and at other times tell the truth, the purging souls cannot lie. Even though they are undergoing their purification, their salvation is assured; they are among the elect. The possibility of lying—of sinning—ends with death for all the elect.

Not only do these truth-telling holy souls assure Maria Simma that aliens do not exist, but we also see Maria herself confirming that this reality is not some hidden secret we can only now glean thanks to her mysticism! Quite the contrary, it is already what anyone with "faith in the Holy Bible" would conclude. She is of course correct, and whoever would disparage her for that statement need only return to the early chapters of this book to be reminded of its accuracy.

Equally importantly, we are here warned that belief in aliens is not merely a mistake—not only an error on par with other commonly confused theological points; rather, it is a uniquely dangerous position that invites Satanic seduction. Moreover, this danger is magnified by modern science fiction. Unfortunately, however, if—in the time of Simma providing this quote only a few short decades ago—it was primarily the youth who were easily led astray by these deceptions, today it is also adults.

Private Revelation: Only Warnings Against ET Deception, No Endorsement of Alien Belief

> "Do not conform yourselves to this age but be transformed by the renewal of your mind, that you may discern what is the will of God, what is good and pleasing and perfect."
>
> —Romans 12:2

There are innumerable mystics beyond these few discussed above. Among them all, Heaven has graced the Church with millions of pages of revelations exploring all the intricate truths that the mind of man could possibly comprehend. We have been told in detail about Heaven, Hell, and Purgatory. Hitherto unknown details of Salvation History—as we have seen above, back to the time of Creation itself—have been described. Even the cosmos themselves have received no little treatment in these texts, and two thousand years of these revelations have now accumulated.

Where is even the slightest hint of an implication that this grand Story of All Things includes *so much as a place in which to conjecture* the existence of rational creatures other than men and angels? No such opportunity exists—anywhere. To attempt to squeeze their existence into a position that could harmonize with any authentic revelation that has ever been given by God (whether Public—i.e., Scripture—or private) would be like trying to acknowledge more than seven Sacraments, or more than three Persons of the Trinity. It would be like seeking to build a house on the side of the plot opposite the foundation, or like finding a place for an irrational number among the integers. In a word, it is as unfaithful to Divine Revelation as Dan Brown's novels are to the Gospel, or as New Age

"Christ consciousness" is to the God-Man, our Lord and Savior, Jesus Christ.

It is not as if authentic private revelation has been rare amid the decades during which the ET-craze has dominated discourse. Quite the opposite, the Church has witnessed an explosion of it in those same years. Theologian Fr. Edward O'Connor explained:

> **[Apparitions] of the Blessed Virgin Mary are being reported far more frequently than at any time in the past ...** there were very few during the first ten centuries. After that they increased moderately, reaching 105 in the nineteenth century. But during the twentieth century ... [there were reported] a total of 1,045 apparitions of the Blessed Mother ... (*Listen to my Prophets*. IX)

Not all those apparitions are authentic, but *many* are. The fact that *not one* of them affirms alien belief, despite a historically unprecedented explosion of such revelations during precisely the same decades of the UFO craze, provides a testimony so sure that no one who harbors any respect for private revelation could doubt it. The testimony is this: the Blessed Virgin, being anything but an absentee Mother, has not encouraged her children to welcome UFOs as heralds of extraterrestrials—or even to believe in aliens in general—because there are no extraterrestrials. Instead, she has warned of unprecedented demonic attacks on Christian truth, a return of Paganism, great apostasies infiltrating the Church, mass falling aways, and the like. That is, she has warned of exactly what we are seeing (and will see much more of) in light of ET belief infiltrating the Church.

Let us consider what the Blessed Virgin said to just one such seer: the Italian priest, theologian, and mystic, Fr. Stefano Gobbi. His messages from Our Lady bear imprimaturs and ringing endorsements from numerous Bishops and even Cardinals. They have borne superabundant quantities of overwhelmingly good fruits, and they are entirely orthodox. Fr. Gobbi himself lived and died an exceedingly holy priest, and over a decade since his passing has confirmed this legacy. There is little doubt about the authenticity of these messages.[*] Within them, the Blessed Virgin warns:

> In these times of purification, many are led astray by other words. In fact, **my Adversary succeeds in seducing even the good by false manifestations of the preternatural in order to bring about deception and confusion on all sides. He will succeed in working many prodigies which will beguile the minds of even the good**. (March 25, 1979) The diabolical powers are ruling the earth and producing everywhere the wicked fruits of their dark reign. And thus this **humanity has again become pagan, after almost two thousand years** of its redemption and of

[*] Those who believe that the year 2000 invalidated these messages should know that is a misunderstanding of only two messages given to Fr. Gobbi. More detail on this point may be found at Youtube.com/@DSDOConnor.

the first announcement of the Gospel of salvation. (September 15, 1992) ... painful moments ... are awaiting you, when **the great apostasy will reach its peak** and humanity will arrive at the summit of denial of God and of rebellion... (June 7, 1986) Your countries have again become pagan. They are being dominated by the forces of evil and masonry. (November 23, 1994). [*Note: Our Lady said this to Fr. Gobbi in Mexico; at a similar time period during which Msgr. Balducci, a prominent ET Deception promoter we will consider in Part Four, was praising Mexico's embrace of Ufology*] ...a great apostasy is spreading in every part of the Church, through the lack of faith which is flooding even among its very pastors. **Satan has succeeded in spreading everywhere the great apostasy**, by means of his subtle work of seduction, which has brought many to be alienated from the truth of the Gospel to **follow the fables of the new theological theories**... (December 31, 1987) **You are living the moments of the great perversion,** during which humanity has become pagan and worse than in the times of the flood; and you are being called to spread the light of holiness. Be torches ablaze with holiness and purity, in the deep darkness of sin which has descended upon the world. ... Now **the hurricane is at your doors, and the Church and humanity will be called to live the tremendous hour of the great trial.** (February 2, 1995) - The first sign [of "The End of the Times"] is the spread of errors, which lead to the loss of faith and to apostasy. These **errors are being propagated by false teachers, by renowned theologians who are no longer teaching the truths of the Gospel,** but pernicious heresies based on errors and on human reasonings. It is because of the teaching of these errors that the true faith is being lost and that the great apostasy is spreading everywhere ... The fourth sign is the horrible sacrilege, perpetrated by him who sets himself against Christ, that is, **the Antichrist. He will enter into the holy temple of God and will sit on his throne,** and have himself adored as God. "... The lawless one will come by the power of Satan, with all the force of false miracles and pretended wonders. He will make use of every kind of wicked deception, in order to work harm." (2 Thes 2) (December 31, 1992) **This great apostasy is spreading more and more, even through the interior of the Catholic Church.** Errors are being taught and spread about, while the fundamental truths of the faith which the authentic Magisterium of the Church has always taught and energetically defended against any heretical deviation whatsoever, are being denied with the greatest of ease. (June 11, 1988) The Second Pentecost will come to bring this humanity - which has again become pagan and which is living under the powerful influence of the Evil One - back to its full communion of life with its Lord who has created, redeemed and saved it. (May 26, 1996) (DSDOConnor.com/FrGobbi)

As we will see in Part Four, what the Virgin Mary warned about in the messages above—with similar themes found among countless authentic seers of the 20th century—might as well be a description of what the ET

Deception has wrought in the Church and the world during those same times. "Aliens" are not specifically named in these warnings because, as we will observe in the following section, such specificity would not be in keeping with the fact that *the* Great Trial of the Church is also *the Great Test* of the same, and that test cannot be robbed of its value by having all its details described beforehand by Heaven. But Our Lady, like any good teacher, certainly announces the themes and subjects before the test. And it is these warnings that call all the Faithful to be on guard against the ET Deception.

***

Beyond all that has been considered in the sections above, another related consideration rules out extraterrestrials. Even if one posits aliens in some galaxy (*or "dimension of the multiverse," for those prone to espousing even emptier esotericism*) so distant from us that they are categorically and radically detached from our own story—and will remain so for the full duration of time—it nevertheless remains theologically certain that all creatures, wherever they may reside, will spend only a brief period of time in the material cosmos. Eventually, they will die. Or, if one posits an unfallen race, they would need to eventually be miraculously "transported" to eternity once the proper amount of time passed in their temporal lives. Any rational being—no matter the galaxy, or "string," or "dimension," or "timeline," or what have you—will eventually find itself in Heaven (perhaps with a stop in Purgatory) or Hell. Therefore, aliens would be in Heaven, Hell, and Purgatory already—in droves—if they exist. Yet no account, from any of the numerous mystics of the Church, describes such a situation; even though we have been given libraries full of revelations on these eternal abodes.

Finally, recall that, in the preceding chapter, we discussed the infallible *sensus fidelium*, which rules out aliens. Private revelation is not infallible, but the contents of its *consensus* is pragmatically impossible to derive from anything but God. Additionally, it provides yet another indication of what the infallible *sensus fidelium* holds. Granted, many "revelations" do insist extraterrestrials exist. *All* of those, however, are manifestly diabolical or fraudulent. Lest anyone accuse me of engaging in circular reasoning (*i.e., by merely assuming any alleged revelation which espouses alien belief is false because it espouses alien belief*), let him understand that the evidence of the falsehood of these "revelations" has nothing to do with their espousing belief in extraterrestrials. Each has other fatal flaws which tell us, clearly, there is no authenticity to be found in them. We will discuss those details in a later chapter.

Authentic private revelation, however, is indeed unanimous in ruling out belief in aliens. No individual private revelation is a matter of Catholic Faith, but this does not change the fact—as we covered earlier—that no Catholic is free to simply categorically reject private revelation as such. Doing so would inevitably collapse into full blown Deism—itself only one small step shy of outright atheism. One wonders how many closet Deists haunt the podiums and podcasts of today's corporate Catholicism. It is not a small number.

Now, if there is one class of commentators in the Church today who despise private revelation, it is those scholars and apologists who view Heaven's messages as competition for their own writings, and who would never tolerate any external restraint being imposed upon the content of their own speculations. For while they have acquired much expertise in explaining away both Scripture and Magisterium when it contradicts their own views, they are not as well trained in doing the same with private revelation, which often repudiates their errors even more explicitly.

Therefore, before concluding our chapters reviewing religious arguments opposed to belief in aliens, we should take a final section to observe another approach taken by certain ET promoters within modern Christian academia.

Against Sophistical Acrobatics: the "Nuance" of the Academics and the False "Middle Ways"

> "I thank you Father, Lord of heaven and earth, because you have hidden these things from the wise and the learned and have revealed them to the childlike." —Matthew 11:25
>
> "I have always considered theologians to be the greatest and most gifted of the sophists. The phenomenon always makes me think of the Antichrist..."—Bishop Marian Eleganti

Similar to what transpired in the 1800s, belief in extraterrestrials is again increasingly becoming part and parcel to the Zeitgeist of mainstream Christianity. It is not unlike the ever-increasing infiltration of "LGBT" ideology into the Church, the promotion of which provides an opportunity for any ambitious clergymen, theologian, or commentator to immediately attract the praise of the world and the worldly. With such incentives as these—which will only grow more rewarding still as the UFO-craze gains momentum—we can count on ever more voices within the Church endorsing alien belief and ridiculing those whose simple and solid Christian Faith rules out extraterrestrials.

Each argument presented in the preceding chapters, therefore, may be responded to with lengthy treatises, published by the intelligentsia in the Church, calmly purporting to reveal the "overly rigid nature" or the "simple adolescent mentality" of these proofs that aliens do not exist.

> **They will ridicule Christian simplicity; they will call it folly and nonsense, but they will have the highest regard for advanced knowledge...clouded by senseless questions and elaborate argu-**

> **ments. As a result, no principle at all, however holy, authentic, ancient, and certain it may be, will remain free of censure, criticism, false interpretation, modification, and delimitation by man...These are evil times, a century full of dangers and calamities. Heresy is everywhere, and the followers of heresy are in power almost everywhere...** —Prophecy of the Last Times given by Venerable Holshouser

These scholars and commentators will then proceed to respond with their "nuanced" analysis—detailing all manner of fantastical pseudo-theological conjectures to address each contradiction between Christian truth and belief in aliens. They will detail intricate hypothetical scenarios of extraterrestrial salvation economies, revised Ecclesiologies, new Christologies, modified Mariologies, and on the list goes, to supposedly render alien belief compatible with Christianity. They will pretend that those considerations in the Faith which "appeared" to rule out aliens simply did not understand what words like "person," or "nature," or "unique," or "incarnation," or "intelligent," or "visible," or "human," actually mean; they will play semantic games with these and other words to massage alien belief into a posture that appears faithful.

In this undertaking, they will doubtless make repeated use of the oldest trick in the academic-rhetoric book: taking a position that is clearly contrary to the simple and naked truth, embellishing it with elaborate arguments and advanced terminology, peppering it with a good dose of repeated appeals to their own university degrees, and then presenting it as if it were actually the *middle-ground* position—by placing it in between "two false extremes to be avoided."

They will declare that one "extreme" is dismissing the Faith for the sake of alien belief, and the other "extreme" is dismissing alien belief for the sake of the Faith. The latter is, of course, exactly what we must do and in no way is it "extreme." Christians must dismiss anything that runs afoul of Christianity; and alien belief, as we have seen, does exactly that.

Nevertheless, their strategy of labelling alien-belief-rejection as an "extreme" opposed to their carefully articulated "middle-way," will prove irresistibly attractive to other scholars (or commentators desperate to be taken seriously by establishment circles) who, above all else, do not want to be seen as "immoderate," "unnuanced," or—Heaven forbid—"dogmatic" or "fundamentalist."

Yes, their approach, they insist, will be the true "moderate" one. As C.S. Lewis wisely put on the lips of the fictional demon, Screwtape, illustrating a great means of damning a soul:

> Talk to him about "moderation in all things". If you can once get him to the point of thinking that "religion is all very well up to a point", you can feel quite happy about his soul. A moderated religion is as good for us as no religion at all—and more amusing... You see the idea? Keep his mind off the plain antithesis between True and False. ... and don't forget the blessed word "Adolescent". (*The Screwtape Letters*. IX.)

Now, each argument they will present is doomed to collapse under sufficient scrutiny. Replacing God's clear guidance with academic "nuance" is always a temptation from the Devil and it always—*eventually*—is exposed for the fallacy it is. But as I can currently only guess at the details these arguments will employ, refuting them will have to wait until after they are published, lest the length of this book be now doubled.

Meanwhile, the Faithful should step back—when those lengthy nuanced treatises are published—and, even beyond noting the error of the arguments themselves, ask themselves some simple questions:

"What is going on here? Why are such elaborate scenarios posited? Why does Scriptural verse after verse, passage after passage; Magisterial teaching after Magisterial teaching; truth after truth of Sacred Tradition; private revelation after private revelation...all have to be ***explained away****? Why not just take* ***even a single one of them*** *seriously? Why this silly dance? Why such overwhelming and extraordinary academic effort to try and justify a position that is bereft of any spiritual value, and instead is derived entirely from secular motivations?"*

> And [Jesus] said to them, "Oh, how foolish you are! How slow of heart to believe all that the prophets spoke!" (Luke 24:25)

Even if we leave aside the many direct proofs we have already considered that refute aliens, we have more than enough to reject alien belief only on account of what is implicit in the Word of God: written and oral, Scriptural and deriving from Sacred Tradition. God is not pleased by attempts to take what His Word clearly implies (much less what it outright indicates!) and pretend that those implications should be put in question. Multiple times in the Gospels, precisely that approach to Divine Revelation was rebuked by Jesus Himself:

> Let not your hearts be troubled; believe in God, believe also in me. In my Father's house are many rooms; **if it were not so, would I have told you** that I go to prepare a place for you? (John 14:1-2)

The Disciples should have known, based on Jesus' earlier assurances, that He was going to the Father to prepare places for them all. It should have been enough for them to understand—even without Jesus explicitly saying it—that the House of the Father has many rooms. Our Lord clearly instructs us here to hold fast to all that follows from Scripture, not only those (far fewer) points expressly settled within its pages. This gentle rebuke, however, was preceded by a stern one, addressed to the Sadducees:

> And as for the resurrection of the dead, have you not read what was said to you by God, 'I am the God of Abraham, and the God of Isaac, and the God of Jacob'? He is not God of the dead, but of the living. (Matthew 22:31-32)

Indeed, the Old Testament Scriptures (which, of course, were the only Scriptures available in the time of Christ), did not testify *as explicitly* to the Resurrection of the Body as would the New Testament. Accordingly, the

Sadducees refused to believe it, even though it was clearly implied in the same texts they studied. Jesus reproved them for their stubbornness in refusing to heed the implications of Divine Revelation. They should have realized that God's Word to Moses clearly implied the reality of the afterlife. There was no excuse for them to fail to draw that inference.

It is the Will of God that we all take the implications of Scripture just as seriously as what is explicitly stated in its pages, instead of nuancing them away while claiming to technically remain obedient to each passage in order to keep up appearances of orthodoxy. While failing to heed this mandate might not always garner for one the label of "formal heretic" on this side of the grave, it will nevertheless cause him to depart from the way of Salvation just as effectively.

Nuance is often called for in addressing particularly fine points in philosophical and theological matters. It is needed, for example, in determining the advisable course of action in those rare moral dilemmas that arise; in accurately describing the finer points of Trinitarian Theology; in assessing what degree of material cooperation exists in certain less than ideal (though not intrinsically evil) situations; in discerning individual private revelations; and on the list goes.

On the other hand, when those broad and simple questions are being answered—questions that determine our worldview, questions that are paramount to our salvation, questions that define our understanding of the relationship between the Creator and creature, and similarly impactful matters—"nuance" is almost always a demonic temptation.

Is transgenderism to be condoned? Is abortion or euthanasia ever okay? Is there any chance that dogma could be wrong or change? Is intrinsic evil ever licit? Might God's promises fail? Might the Blessed Virgin not be the greatest possible creature after all? Might Jesus not really be the *only* begotten Son of God? Might religions other than Christianity also be fully true religions from which we should not seek converts?

The thousands of pages of "nuance" today's theologians generate each week to address such questions as these is as much drivel—or, rather, poison. The answer to each question above requires only a single word consisting of exactly two letters and one punctuation mark immediately thereafter: "*no*" followed by a *period*. Whoever would answer with a different word, or even place a comma after the "no" introducing further commentary that mitigates its force, is only dialoguing with the Devil.

The question of aliens is no less simple, no less pressing, and no less impactful than any of the questions above. Therefore, whenever a scholar approaches you insisting that only his "nuance" can give the proper appreciation of it, you would be well advised to bid him farewell.

Are there aliens? The answer is *no*.

That answer needn't be qualified with academic middle ways or nuanced takes. If Eve rejected nuance when pondering, "*Could I perhaps justify eating the fruit?"*, the Fall never would have happened. Let us not waste time lamenting the Fall, but let us also not re-enact it in our own lives.

God could have placed a large sign on the Tree of the Knowledge of Good and Evil, cautioning Eve that a serpent would approach her there and speak to her, and that his words would be nothing but a trap. Doing so, however, would have defeated the very purpose of the test. Eve already knew more than enough to conclude it was God's Will that she must not eat from that tree, no matter who told her to do so. However, she was allowed *just enough* wiggle room to pretend she could justify obtaining the promised hitherto secret "knowledge" (Genesis 3:5) by listening to the speaking serpent and eating the fruit.

Similarly, God could have inspired the authors of Sacred Scripture to proclaim—or moved a Pope to declare ex-cathedra—*"No incarnate intelligent creatures exist on any planet, in any galaxy, other than earth. Human beings are the only rational material beings God made."* But we are in apocalyptic times, and as Eschatology (last things) mirrors Protology (first things), the Church is about to undergo a final test analogous to the original one our first parents failed in the Garden. Here as there, God's Mercy and Justice is displayed. He has given us more than enough to know that we alone are made in His image, but not so much that Christians who prefer believing sci-fi deceptions to heeding His Word will be incapable of pretending to justify their stance.

Just as Eve was seduced by the promise of her eyes being "opened" (Genesis 3:5), so the men and women of the present age—groomed by decades of delusions from a culture long in the grip of Satan—have been primed to anticipate the promise of "new knowledge" from "first contact" with extraterrestrials. And whoever is open to dialogue with these demons in disguise is bound to find the allure of their promises irresistible, even once these promises become contingent upon apostasy.

"Did God ***really*** *say...?"*
—Satan. Genesis 3:2

Part Three: The Logical and Scientific Case

In Part Two, we discussed just how deeply misused is 18th-20th century thought by today's ET promoters. For, although they present it as evidence to bolster alien belief today, the fact is that the grounds those thinkers claimed for believing in aliens have already been demolished by modern science. The rug has been snatched out from underneath the feet of the Enlightenment-era ET debate; yet today's ET promoters pretend those "insights" are still worthy of inducing openness to ETs. Therefore, an equally significant point about all of these Enlightenment era arguments for aliens is that they were presented in times lacking the scientific evidence we now have against those very claims—the examination of which we will undertake in forthcoming chapters.

15. The Historical Fallacies of Alien Belief

Although ET promotion is inevitably riddled with misconceptions and falsehoods, several fallacies tend to rear their heads especially frequently not only in the contemporary debate, but also stretching back centuries. Addressing some of these will be our first order of business.

After painstakingly compiling the arguments for and against extraterrestrial intelligence generated over the course of centuries of the debate's taking place, Dr. Michael Crowe describes seven fallacies that have, decade after decade and century after century, proven endemic to and inextricable from the proponents of belief in extraterrestrial intelligence. Here, we will cover several of them, though drawing from insights beyond this particular scholar.

Confusing the Necessary and the Sufficient: the Impossibility of Other Planets Even Sustaining Life

For decades if not centuries, astounding degrees of popular hype have been generated whenever news breaks that one of only a myriad of conditions needed for life *might* exist on some place other than earth. Ice is discovered on Titan, and international headlines are made. Carbon dioxide is discovered on an exoplanet, and a frenzy ensues. Most amusingly, supposed "canals" are discovered on Mars (it was all bogus, as we will see in a forthcoming section), and the whole world is on the edge of its seat.

All of this flows from a very basic fallacy that Dr. Crowe describes as follows:

> Among the logical and/or methodological fallacies in the debate, one of the most pervasive is mistaking necessary conditions for sufficient conditions ... All too often, evidence of an atmosphere has been taken

> as proof of a planet's habitation, whereas such evidence is conclusive only when joined to other facts that with it constitute sufficient conditions for life.

While Dr. Crowe's observation is certainly correct, it could be considered the understatement of the century. An atmosphere is indeed a prerequisite for life—along with so many other pre-requisites that they are difficult to list. And these, moreover, are only the prerequisites of which we know; far more, doubtless, remain to be discovered.

Testifying to this reality, two scientists recently presented a more thorough explanation of what is needed for complex life to flourish on a planet, and why ours is the only contender for that honor. After hundreds of pages of rigorous scientific analysis, the authors of *Rare Earth* (the joint effort of a renowned paleontologist and astronomer) declared, in the book's conclusion:

> Our planet coalesced out of the debris from previous cosmic events at a position within a galaxy highly appropriate for ... life, around a star also highly appropriate—a star rich in metal, a star found in a safe region of a spiral galaxy, a star moving very slowly on its galactic pinwheel. Not in the center of the galaxy, not in a metal-poor galaxy, not in a globular cluster, not near an active gamma ray source, not in a multiple-star system, not even in a binary, or near a pulsar, or near stars too small, too large, or soon to go supernova. We became a planet where global temperatures have allowed liquid water to exist ...and for that, our planet had to have a nearly circular orbit at a distance from a star itself emitting a nearly constant energy output for a long period of time. Our planet received a volume of water sufficient to cover most—but not all—of the planetary surface. Asteroids and comets hit us but not excessively so, thanks to the presence of giant gas planets such as Jupiter beyond us. ... Earth received the right range of building materials—and had the correct amount of internal heat—to allow plate tectonics to work on the planet, shaping the continents required and keeping global temperatures within a narrow range ... the Earth's remarkable thermostatic regulating process [always] successfully kept the surface temperature within livable range. Alone among terrestrial planets we have a large moon, and this single fact, which sets us apart from Mercury, Venus, and Mars, may have been crucial to the rise and continued existence of animal life on Earth.

These scientists capture well just how much we take for granted about our planet. Consider that "space"—which is precisely what all planets, including earth, are floating within—is about as hostile-to-life an environment as one can imagine. As any NASA engineer knows, designing and building a craft capable of withstanding it while, within itself, providing an "environment" amenable to life, is an extraordinarily difficult feat, requiring for its accomplishment immense amounts of collective ingenuity and effort from of huge teams of experts. Yet, earth itself is precisely such a craft, and such crafts do not simply come about by chance, no matter how many innumerable trillions of opportunities chance is given.

Unfortunately, *Rare Earth* was largely ignored by a secular society eager to believe that extraterrestrials would soon come to save us from ourselves. As the Benedictine priest, theologian, and scientist, Fr. Stanley Jaki, noted:

> Nobody paid attention to Rare Earth, and certainly not *The New York Times*, which is most eager to publish the latest results about [the] search for other planets around other stars. And each time that daily puts, preposterously enough, the best spin on the findings. ... that daily leader in dishing out with great seriousness mental and moral slime... [published] a write-up about a planet around the star Gliese 876, fifteen light years away in the Aquarius. The report admits that the planet is so close to its sun that it has to turn always its same side toward it and that it completes its orbit every 1.9 days. But because the planet is only seven times larger than our earth, it is described as the Earth's distant cousin and a real indication that life and intelligence exist outside the earth. The script might have been written by Screwtape whose tactic is to bedazzle man's mind with specious non-sequiturs. But the final inference in that script is not better than the logic of going to a doctor and telling him: I have a circulatory problem, but since many others whose blood circules have been cured, a cure must be on hand for my ailment. Surely, such a man deserves to be taken to a mental hospital.[118]

While the two scientists who authored *Rare Earth* did indeed provide a more appropriate illustration than Dr. Crowe's of why it is not plausible to assert that other planets in the universe may also sustain life (much less "likely" do), even their analysis considers only a tiny fraction of the conditions necessary for life. Some ET promoters today insist that *Rare Earth* has been "debunked," and they bemoan that it is "still quoted by those who disbelieve in aliens." In fact, only the opposite is true. We have only since discovered drastically *more* requirements for a planet to harbor life, thus rendering earth exponentially rarer still (infinitely rare, that is; for it is absolutely unique) than even the famous *Rare Earth* book asserted it was.

One astrophysicist, Dr. Hugh Ross, recently compiled a more thorough list of 153 prerequisites for any planet to be compatible with life. This list, too, is doubtless partial, but even from a mathematical consideration of the quantified probabilities affixed to their likelihood of arising, one can easily see it is mathematically impossible for any other habitable planet to exist, anywhere. Dr. Ross explains:

> The probability of a planet **anywhere in the universe** fitting within all 153 parameters [required for life to even be possible] is approximately 10^-194. The maximum possible number of planets in the universe is estimated to be 10^22. Thus, less than 1 chance in 10^172 (100 thousand trillion trillion trillion trillion trillion trillion trillion trillion trillion trillion trillion trillion trillion) exists that even one such planet would occur

anywhere in the universe.[119]

Contrast these rigorously empirical and authentically scientific expositions of truths about our planet to the bold and "certain" claim of one who was regarded as perhaps the world's greatest astronomer of the late 19th and early 20th century, Camille Flammarion (whom we will consider in the following chapter). He assured his massive and global audience that **"Earth has no particular distinction among the planets...Earth has not been at all favored over the other celestial bodies."** Although we now know with certainty that such an assertion is unmitigated nonsense, claims like those were ubiquitous in the Enlightenment-era ET craze and its immediate aftermath.

Returning to the present day, even the most confident of contemporary biologists must concede that the frontiers of science are still only scratching the surface of the great mysteries hidden within biological life (our most powerful supercomputers are far surpassed by the abilities of a single termite). We can be just as sure that we have only begun to understand life's own preconditions as we are confident that we have only begun to understand its own qualities.

Thus far, astronomers have discovered over five thousand planets. No evidence has been found that even a single one of them enjoys more than a few of the *hundreds* of those conditions we already know are requisite for life to exist on a planet. An alien belief promoter, of course, protests that the planets we have discovered are such a minuscule percentage of the whole, that we are bound to eventually discover a planet with the necessary conditions for life. This protestation falls victim to the fallacy we must consider next.

Erasure of Impossibility with Quantity: Unattainability Trumps Innumerable Opportunities

Wherever belief in extraterrestrials is espoused, one is sure to hear a variation of the same line repeated as its supposed justification: "*With so many trillions of planets out there among trillions of galaxies, it is a statistical guarantee that there is a planet capable of hosting life; a statistical guarantee that there is a planet that actually does have life; and, even, a statistical guarantee that there is a planet with rational life and advanced civilization!*"

In fact, not only are none of those scenarios statistical guarantees; but only the opposite is true. It is a statistical guarantee that no planet other than our own hosts life, and whoever bothers to do the math involved will easily discover this fact on his own. Dr. Crowe notes:

> A third widespread fallacy involves misuse of large numbers. Typically, pluralists, explicitly or implicitly, have relied on such assertions as this: Among the countless planets orbiting the billions of stars in our galaxy, some at least must be inhabited.[120]

He follows this with a brief refutation of the classic "monkey typewriter" fallacy, wherein it is said that if a monkey with a typewriter is given enough time, it will eventually pound out Hamlet by chance. But a more thorough refutation is in order, as this thought experiment has, since its inception, become the main symbol for the notion that if only one gives random chance enough opportunities, it will generate whatever conventional wisdom would explain by way of intentional design.

Indeed, this pseudo-axiom is absolutely false. Hamlet contains about 140,000 letters. The odds of the monkey with a typewriter randomly entering the first letter correctly, therefore, is one in twenty-six. The odds of it also entering the second correctly is (1/26) to the second power. The odds of also getting the third right is (1/26)^3, and so forth. Therefore, the odds of this monkey pounding out Hamlet correctly is straightforward to compute: (1/26)^140,000. This calculation—as any calculator will correctly tell you—is mathematically equivalent to zero. There is, truly, a *zero* percent chance of this ever happening. Mind you, we are only discussing the possibility of Hamlet arising from sufficient unintentional opportunities; a life-harboring planet existing is an even less likely thing.

It is all too easy for a thoughtless, illogical, and unscientific idealogue to attempt to bolster his views by presenting arbitrary deferrals to enormous numbers, and supposing that these large quantities will give any situation, no matter how impossible, a chance—or even a certainty—of happening. But that is simply not how *reality* operates.

Even if we grant the monkey-typewriter-Hamlet hypothesis the most absurdly generous scenario we can possibly envision, the probability of it ever happening remains mathematically equivalent to *zero*.*

When one is confronted with massive quantities "competing," as it were, against statistical impossibilities, the statistical impossibilities always win. It does not matter how massive the quantities are, since we know that, at the minimum, all such quantities are limited by the concrete constraints of the *actual universe*. Statistical impossibilities, on the other

---

* Case in point: suppose that each atom in the entire universe is a monkey with a typewriter. (The entire universe contains about 10^80 atoms.) Suppose, moreover, that each monkey has been frantically pounding at its typewriter (at a fast 100 "words" per minute—i.e., 470 characters per minute) for 14 billion years. Each monkey has thereby had 7.4x10^15 minutes to type, and at 470 characters per minute, it has typed 3.5 x 10^18 characters. Divide this by the number of characters in Hamlet (140,000), and we are left with each monkey having completed 2.5 x 10^13 opportunities to type out Hamlet correctly. Since 10^80 monkeys (one, recall, for each atom in the universe) are simultaneously working on this task, we are left with 2.5x10^93 overall attempts between them. Now, we can again compute the likelihood of Hamlet arising from chance so much as a single time among all these attempts (and, again, it is not even possible to imagine a scenario more amenable to Hamlet arising from randomness!) We need only multiply the likelihood itself ((1/26)^140000) by the number of attempts. This yields a probability of 2.5x10^93 x ((1/26)^140000)... which, again—as any calculator whatsoever will still correctly tell you—is still *equivalent to zero.*

hand, bear no such constraints, though they are just as accurately and scientifically quantifiable.

Today's astronomers often estimate that there are several hundred quintillion planets in the universe. While this is little more than science fiction (we have no realistic way of gauging that number), we can nevertheless truthfully regard it as a very, very small number when compared to the statistical impossibilities evident in any other planet existing that supports life, much less actually harboring life. Even the number of *atoms in the universe* is an utterly negligible quantity when compared to the scales needed to describe the odds of order arising by chance.

Abuse of Evolutionary Theory: Jumping from "1 in 9 Million Over 4 Billion Years" to "A Certainty"

At this point, readers will have surmised my own rejection of macroevolutionary theory. Leaving that aside, however, we are still confronted with a situation wherein even what today's mainstream scientists attest, in regard to evolution, is irreconcilable with its use to advocate for belief in extraterrestrial intelligence. Dr. Crowe notes:

> A sixth category of fallacies derives from misunderstandings about evolutionary theory. Despite the rich explanatory power of Darwinian theory and its strong empirical support, many leading theorists of evolution and philosophers of science agree that **Darwinian theory is not, except in the broadest sense, predictive. Consequently, it cannot generate detailed predictions of the direction evolution will take in a given population**, even of terrestrial animals. One reason is that evolutionary change works from chance variations that are not themselves predictable.

Despite Crowe's dubious classification of evolution enjoying "strong empirical support," mention thereof is worth preserving here to illustrate that Crowe himself is no opponent of Darwin's legacy of error. Yet even he concedes that evolutionary theory is no reason to believe in extraterrestrial intelligence.

One thing in this context is beyond question—and, indeed, appears unquestioned even by most believers in non-human intelligences. On earth, there are *millions* of species (by some estimates, about nine million, though some claim far more).[121] Yet, it is clear that—despite, as the evolutionists claim, four billion years of the process transpiring thus far—only *one* of them is intelligent. While a Darwinist believes that evolution is what generated this intelligent species ("Homo Sapiens") a Darwinist *alien believer* (an umbrella under which almost all ET promoters stand) asserts that this same alleged process also brought forth intelligent species on other planets.

Yet, evolutionary theory imagines that a fundamentally *random* (non-intelligently guided) process generated all its results. From their premises, it follows that, quite literally, only one in *millions* of products of this random process has ever been observed to result in an intelligent life form. Because the process is random, observing it having once-in-9-million times generated a given result obviously does not give license for asserting that the same fundamental process, elsewhere, is likely to do the same thing again. On the contrary, it only gives us grounds for rejecting the plausibility of the notion that, on other planets, evolution might generate intelligent life.

As Dr. Crowe noted above: evolutionary theory is fundamentally *descriptive*, not *predictive*. Indeed, it has never succeeded in predicting what the process it claims to describe will bring about in the future. (*We should note that it has thereby largely failed to even display itself as scientific, since a scientific theory's ability to make accurate predictions about the future is one of the only means of declaring the theory genuinely scientific.*) Counter-scientifically, ET promoters nevertheless use it as a predictive tool.

Although we have addressed the implausibility of asserting the existence of other planets which could harbor life, as well as the implausibility of asserting that life, if it did exist on other planets, would evolve into an intelligent form, still more compounding implausibilities (or, rather, *impossibilities*) render alien believe even more irrational. For even if there were other planets which could harbor life, and even if life were to be capable of evolving intelligence somewhere else, it would still be impossible to assert that life could manage to begin evolving in the first place—even in perfect conditions.

The Impossibility of Another "LUCA": Chance and Sufficient Time Can Never Generate Life

The fact most systematically ignored by proponents of using macroevolution as a comprehensive "Theory of Life" is the absolute impossibility of mere chance causing the process to *begin in the first place*. Even if we grant the counterfactual premise that a process exists wherein mere chance and sufficient time can themselves cause a single new species to emerge (much less millions of them), we are still confronted with the question of how the necessary starting point itself (at the bare minimum, a single cell "capable of evolving") came about. Evolutionary biologists call this alleged starting point of evolution—this first cell capable of evolving, from which it is claimed all living things ultimately proceeded—the *Last Universal Common Ancestor*, or LUCA.

In fact, a single cell capable of evolving is a masterpiece of design that requires the presence of an incalculable number of parts to acquire an indescribably precise arrangement; only then is something resembling a "starting point of evolution" present. But the components of such a cell are vastly beyond any human invention in their complexity, and they certainly far surpass any work of Shakespeare. Yet, as we saw in the preceding section, even a single work of Shakespeare cannot possibly arise by chance—no conceivable amount of generosity in granting the benefit of the doubt to the Hamlet-from-chance argument gives it any ground on which to stand. It is, therefore, only far more certain—*absolutely* certain—that life cannot arise by chance. Even if the universe were many trillions of times as vast and many trillions of times as old as astronomers now estimate, with the conditions of *every planet therein* serving as an ideal "primordial soup" for the spontaneous generation of a "starting point of evolution," (in fact, as we saw above, not a single one other than earth is) we are still left with a mathematical impossibility of such a thing *ever* happening. As I noted in my 2019 book, *The Crown of Sanctity*:

> Even the recently published and authoritative *Encyclopedia of Evolution* from Oxford University Press has the honesty to admit "...how the ancestral cell originated, some 3.5 to 3.8 billion years ago, remains an issue of intense speculation..."[122] before proceeding to dedicate a whopping *one* page (of its overall 1,326) to pondering how this may have happened—in this one page, giving a meditation which would qualify as a nice fairy tale if it were not so utterly scientifically and *logically* absurd (for the author of a fairy tale can justify including some scientific absurdities, but not logical absurdities). ... [yet it is] **precisely this question of [the first cell's] origin [that] must be settled in order to give the atheistic evolutionary hypothesis any credence whatsoever; yet, it is systematically the most ignored question in all evolutionary biology**. ... Darwinism has had well over 100 years to explain the "origin of the ancestral cell," devouring entire careers of generations of countless scientists—not to mention mountains of money—in the process. If, after all this monumental effort, there has not been enough substantial progress on the question to merit more than one page of summary in the *Encyclopedia of Evolution,* then what conclusion any reasonable person should draw from this categorical failure of progress is too obvious to be worth stating. For these efforts make those of a little boy trying to jump up and touch the moon look rather reasonable and even achievable. Here an anecdote is necessary. I still recall vividly when, as an undergraduate engineering student in a top engineering University (which also happens to be the oldest technical University in the Western Hemisphere and was founded 25 years before Darwin published his famous *On the Origin of Species*), I sat down for an "Origins of Life" class which I had signed up for because I was curious to see what the supposed best and brightest scientific minds of the modern world had to say about the matter. In the midst of all manner of convoluted theories swirling about during the class, the actual crux of the matter was conveniently glossed over and written off as "emergence." We were hurriedly told that just as one may sometimes observe a pretty pattern of ripples emerge on the sands of a beach, so too that first cell necessary to

> initiate the process of evolution "emerged" out of the primordial soup that, hypothetically, was the surface of the earth billions of years ago. I then recognized openly what I in fact already knew before signing up for the course: the so-called scientific geniuses heralded by today's atheists and agnostics hadn't themselves even the faintest clue how it is possible to reconcile their views with the fact of the existence of life. For emergence, which is all they can appeal to, was just tested against real reason in the preceding paragraphs and was demonstrated to be a total failure in explaining what it proposes to explain. (Part One)

We are treating this point at length because most ET promoters today build their entire view on the false premise that the passage of ample time, combined with the existence of sufficient opportunities, all but guarantees the emergence of life ..."at least *somewhere*" else in the universe.

All that is needed for this deeply fallacious premise to generate alien belief is the presence of another premise; namely, the claims of modern astronomers who insist that the universe is billions of years old and contains trillions of galaxies. I am not prepared to scrutinize the latter assertions, thus I remain content to take them at face value for the sake of argument. The former assertions, however, fly in the face of the most fundamental realities of science and even of logic itself.

Indeed, if only society could rid itself of the common-sense-rejecting, illogical, and unscientific view that it is possible for order (much less *astounding degrees* of order) to arise by chance, the ET promoter's arguments would immediately be exposed for the fraudulent ideologies they represent. Now, a critic may accuse the present argument of self-contradiction by using the impossibility of the LUCA to argue against aliens, since, he might say, *"humans on earth require a LUCA also; and here we are."* Such a critic is missing the entire point.

It is *not* possible—in materialistic terms—for us to be here. Since, however, we *are* here, we know that a miracle has occurred to bring our existence about. In other words, reason alone assures us that we have been made by God. This conclusion requires no Divine Faith to hold, since our intellects can discover it—directly and with certainty. It is not coherent to posit—on earth or on another planet—the existence of life coming about because of chance combined with innumerable opportunities. Yet, almost all ET promoters do precisely that. On the other hand, those who simply claim that God *also* chose to make intelligent incarnate creatures on other planets are refuted by this book's earlier chapters. We *only* exist because God chose to make us—neither chance nor the passage of time plays *any explanatory role whatsoever* in our creation—and this Supreme Being not only gave no indications He made other such beings; He also gave repeated indications that He did not do so.

Unfortunately, "science reporting" has proven itself clueless here (and in many other related areas), and has led people into deception. As extremely few will ever read scientific papers directly, they will, rather, read the mainstream media's reporting on those papers. These reports, in turn, are often written by individuals with no competence to understand the content of their own articles. An example of this deception involves the thought experiment discussed in the preceding section. As the "Hamlet will be generated by monkeys if given enough time" proposition has become the most popular symbol of the logically bankrupt *life-from-chance* (or "molecules to man") thesis, many attempts to vindicate it have been made.

One such attempt was made by an American computer programmer who, in the year 2011, claimed that his "digital monkeys" (algorithms programmed to generate text randomly) succeeded in typing out Shakespeare by chance.

Many news outlets promoted his claim. CNN bluntly stated, as the headline for its own article on the topic: "**Digital monkeys with typewriters recreate Shakespeare.**"[123] In the body of the article, CNN quotes the programmer himself, who declared, "**This is the first time a work of Shakespeare has actually been randomly reproduced**." This assertion was presented as if it were factual, and at no point in the article is any critical pressure applied. Other media outlets published similar reports. The article leads its readers to believe the programmer's claims were truthful and gives no hint of the reality, which is that *his claims were thoroughly fraudulent and deceptive.*

In fact, the programmer simply waited to claim his "digital monkeys" succeeded in randomly typing out Shakespeare once they generated *only the words themselves* that Shakespeare contains! This is as baseless as claiming that, once the "monkeys" had smashed each letter on the keyboard, Shakespeare was thereby successfully created by chance, since these works consist in none other than the right combination of letters. Obviously, Shakespeare is not merely the words it contains; it is *how those words are arranged*. No "digital monkey"—no matter what super-advanced quantum computers are invented in the future—will ever succeed in typing out Shakespeare.

As of this writing—over a decade later—that article remains on CNN's website with no updates or editor's notes whatsoever, having thus far deceived who knows how many tens of millions of readers, and positioned to continue to deceive who knows how many more. But this is only one example of how mainstream media tends to report on sensational claims that promote the very sci-fi deceptions we will continue to address in this book. Suffice it to say that whoever has long been in the habit of uncritically accepting what news outlets report has much "unlearning" to do. Most recent media reports on "Artificial Intelligence" are particularly noteworthy for their delusional nature. (We will address that deception in forthcoming chapters.)

Unfalsifiability: No Criteria are Conceded Which Would Tamp-Down Alien Belief

A cornerstone of genuine empirical science is the falsifiability of each hypothesis it puts forth. Some possible future scenario must be conceded which, if it were to occur, would illustrate the errancy of the hypothesis. Therefore, an invincible hypothesis, far from strengthening the theory it describes, actually weakens it. Granted, not all legitimate propositions need to be falsifiable, but in order to qualify as legitimately belonging in the domain of *empirical science*, they usually do.

Karl Popper, among the most revered of the modern philosophers of science, is most frequently credited as the popularizer of this notion. He masterfully exposed the fraudulent nature of a number of theories precisely by illustrating how they had become, each in its own right, unfalsifiable.* In *The Growth of Scientific Knowledge*, Popper wrote:

> ... the criterion of the scientific status of a theory is its falsifiability, or refutability, or testability ... Einstein's theory of gravitation clearly satisfied the criterion of falsifiability. Even if our measuring instruments at the time did not allow us to pronounce on the results of the tests with complete assurance, there was clearly a possibility of refuting the theory. Astrology did not pass the test. Astrologers were greatly impressed, and misled, by what they believed to be confirming evidence—so much so that they were quite unimpressed by any unfavourable evidence ... **The Marxist theory of history... [also] ultimately adopted this soothsaying practice. In some of its earlier formulations...their predictions were testable, and in fact falsified. Yet instead of accepting the refutations the followers of Marx re-interpreted both the theory and the evidence in order to make them agree. In this way they rescued the theory from refutation; but they did so at the price of adopting a device which made it irrefutable... and by this stratagem they destroyed its much advertised claim to scientific status ...** as for Freud's epic of the Ego, the Super-ego, and the Id, no substantially stronger claim to scientific status can be made for it than for Homer's collected stories from Olympus ... There were a great many other theories of this pre-scientific or pseudo-scientific character, some of them, unfortunately, as influential as the Marxist interpretation of history; for example, the racialist interpretation of history-another of those impressive and all-explanatory theories which act upon weak minds ... [but] statements or systems of **statements, in order to be ranked as scientific,**

* Although some philosophers of science after Popper offered legitimate critiques that the latter had focused too exclusively on falsifiability as *the* (sole) criterion of science, Popper's insights nevertheless remain invaluable. I also hasten to add that, unfortunately, Popper's own (non) religious ideology compelled him to succumb to the usual fallacies of the secularists in that arena. Nevertheless, his criteria for distinguishing pseudoscience from authentic science are often quite helpful.

must be capable of conflicting with possible, or conceivable, observations. (Ch. 1. § II).

It is easy to see the relevance of the trenchant critiques above for alien belief. As we will detail in forthcoming sections, the "scientific" arguments that have been presented in support of the existence of extraterrestrial intelligence were nothing but a centuries-long march of failure after failure, devoid of lessons learned. Like Marxism, the belief itself is simply modified by its proponents to accommodate failure. This suggests that those who promoted the ideology were not interested in discovering truths about reality, but only saving face while clinging to a cherished fiction.

Suppose, for example, a scientist were to posit a theory that non-human intelligent creatures do indeed exist; not, however, on other planets, but rather in tiny villages that exist within the nucleus of each H2O molecule found within earth's lakes, rivers, and oceans. This might appear comical and it would of course be considered "extreme fringe," but in truth the proposition would be no less outlandish than theories which posit the existence of extraterrestrials. Both are devoid of any evidence and are based solely on conjecture; nor do they differ in presenting *a priori* reasons for acceptance or rejection. Both could be equally supported by the (false) theological premise that "The Principle of Plenitude" guarantees God filled every place with rational incarnate creatures.

Now, our (fictional, one hopes) H2O-village-theory promoter could readily—to seemingly portray his approach as scientific—posit a set of impossible criteria which would falsify his theory (e.g., *every* H2O molecule being observed with much more powerful microscopes). Suppose he crafted this theory when microscopes and similar tools were much poorer than they are today. Accordingly, he could argue that these villages are only unknown to us due to technological limitations, and if technology in the future enabled sufficient discovery about these molecules to conclude they are uninhabited, then he would consider his theory falsified.

The question, then, is how this individual would respond once instrumentation has been developed that *could* peer into the structure of an H2O molecule—if not perfectly and directly, at least with enough clarity that we *would* thereby know if villages existed in these molecules. He *could* simply assert—upon each H2O molecule being carefully studied with these new microscopes and found to be uninhabited—that we have merely thus far been unlucky in selecting molecules for scrutiny. He could insist that the process must continue, exclaiming: "*Just think of how many countless trillions of trillions of trillions more molecules are out there in the ocean!*" He could promise that, eventually, we are *bound* to find villages in *some* of these molecules, affirming: "*The sheer unfathomable quantity we are dealing with here makes it a statistical guarantee!*" Indeed, there are vastly more H2O molecules in the ocean than there are planets in the universe (many trillions of times more, in fact).

Moreover, when particle physicists approach this man and inform him that his own theories are inconsistent with all their discoveries, he could equally easily write them off. "*I care not if what you now regard as the smallest subatomic particles are far too large to accommodate villages of intelligent beings in H2O molecules; for you simply haven't even begun to discover the truly tiny particles that exist. Perhaps the quarks and neutrinos you speak of are like a galaxy compared to those particles which actually deserve the title of smallest and most fundamental!*"

There is no need for us to continue listing all the possible responses our H2O villages promoter could present. The point is that he could always come up with *some* reason to dismiss any discoveries following the presentation of his hypothesis which stand in contradiction to it. He has rendered his own position unscientific by virtue of implicitly declaring it unfalsifiable.

This H2O village promoter has done what ET promoters have done for centuries. They have indicated that their position is not scientific by their unwillingness to show that they are open to it being falsified. Failure, after failure, after failure of their conjectures have not dampened their insistence that aliens are still awaiting our contact. (Reviewing a sampling of those failures is the task of our next chapter.)

The thesis I present in this book, on the other hand, has abundant and easy falsifiability criteria. All that any ET promoter need do is find a single piece of evidence indicating the validity of his position—from the millions of opportunities he has had to do so (from "UFO sightings, alien abductions, ET craft retrievals," etc.), and he is free to consider my position falsified.

As we will see in a forthcoming section, while ET promoters claim thousands of such supposed "proofs," there has to date not been a single one that has enjoyed any credibility. To be sure, profuse quantities of material has been massaged to fill an endless array of pseudoscientific presentations (as anyone knows who has seen the History Channel's "Ancient Aliens" series), but none of these have ever put forth a scenario that cannot be explained by ordinary phenomena (*e.g. hoaxes, optical illusions, weather balloons, hallucinations from mentally ill individuals whose testimonies are not verified by psychologically sound people, psyops, sensor/lens anomalies, atmospheric phenomena, etc.*) or demonic activity.

An ET promoter may claim that I am presenting impossible criteria for verification. "*You will just say that anything you can't debunk is demonic!*", they contend. Not at all! I am keenly aware of the limitations of demonic power. For example, demons cannot create—only God can do that—and they cannot truly incarnate themselves (for their nature is pure spirit). They can only manipulate what is already present.

Any ET promoter need only present an alien craft or body. If our skies are as buzzing with ET-piloted UFOs as they claim, this should be exceedingly easy. Yet, *it has never been done*. Despite seventy-five years of an endless deluge of UFO claims, all we are given is a steady stream of so-called "whistleblowers" sharing anonymous hearsay that such craft or alien bodies exist somewhere in storage.*

Very well then, put these craft or bodies on display at a museum wherein the public can view them—and a panel of *experts we already know and trust* (of sufficient diversity of backgrounds, nationalities, specialties, etc., that conspiracy is unlikely)—can examine them. This is exactly what is done with historical artifacts to prove the validity of various new archeological theories. The reason why it is not done with the "ET craft and alien bodies" is obvious—no such things exist.

This is just one of many falsifiability criteria the alien disbelievers provide. Many others exist. For example, thus far we have collected incomprehensible amounts of data as we peer into the cosmos with our incredibly advanced technology (both telescopes on earth and in outer space). An ET promoter need only show us, from this, a single piece of solid evidence that any one of the thousands of exoplanets we have observed has aliens on it. SETI has been scouring the cosmos for decades, listening for radio signals from any alien civilization out there. An ET promoter need only present a single intelligently ordered signal coming from outer space.

None of this has ever been done. While it would be easy to disprove alien *disbelief* (if in fact alien disbelief were in error!), no such proof has ever been presented. The alien belief hypothesis, on the other hand, is categorically unfalsifiable. No matter what new discoveries are made of barren planets, of entire galaxies devoid of any clearly intelligently-ordered radio signals being emitted from them, of solar systems with no planets properly spaced from their stars to allow for life, etc., those who believe in aliens will always be able to claim that such beings exist, though simply remain to be found.

It is precisely this categorical inability to ever prove their hypothesis false which renders it unscientific.

---

* Many ET promoters, including even the most prominent of the "orthodox Catholic" ones today, insist that aliens have actually been here for millennia, thus multiplying a thousand-fold the ludicrousness of their position in light of the fact that, notwithstanding the supposed continual presence of these aliens throughout human history—not only the last 75 years since Roswell—not a single piece of actual evidence can be presented.

"Plenitude": The Enlightenment's Scientific Error (and Theological Heresy) that Spawned Modern Alien Belief

> "God alone is infinite in power, since He alone is infinite in essence."
> —St. Thomas Aquinas.

In the following chapter, we will review a number of telling failures and fallacies that defined alien belief in earlier centuries, along with observing a rampant refusal to learn any lessons from them. Their first error, however, was not a scientific one, but a philosophical and theological one with implications that *also* violate scientific principles, and we will consider it here.

> Carl Becker [wrote,] in a famous book on the Enlightenment, his Heavenly City of the Eighteenth-Century Philosophers, ... that the Enlightenment "philosophes demolished the Heavenly City of St. Augustine only to rebuild it with more up-to-date materials." ... Becker's famous metaphor can be borrowed to say that various Enlightenment authors created an array of celestial cities and populated them with extraterrestrials.[124]

As we have seen, historically alien belief was ushered in by the Enlightenment, which itself consisted largely in the efforts to demolish the "old, outdated, religious" worldview and replace it with one (ostensibly) built on human reason. Outright atheism, however, was not among the Enlightenment's common and immediate effects—that would take more time. A more immediate effect was the proliferation of a certain "supremely optimistic" base premise the Enlightenment thinkers adopted, which in turn served as a foundation for their alien belief. Unsurprisingly, that base premise was a heresy.

While most scholars who have chronicled the extraterrestrial debate agree that the sudden emergence of belief in aliens can be traced to the telescopes of Galileo and other developments in astronomy, some take another angle on describing this phenomenon.

Arthur Lovejoy (born 1873) was an American philosopher and historian whose famous 1936 book, *The Great Chain of Being*, has been described as among the most influential works of its genre in the decades following its publication.[125] Within it, he argues it was precisely the "Principle of Plenitude" and the corresponding teaching that the universe is infinite which compelled adherents of this ideology to assert not only the existence of aliens, but moreover to argue that it was *theologically impossible* for the planets to *not* be filled with rational inhabitants.

Although it appears untenable that discoveries in astronomy were anything but the primary motivation for alien belief for most of its exponents, Lovejoy's thesis should not be entirely discounted, either. The Principle of Plenitude surely factored in heavily, and the implications of the role it played are just as unfavorable for the legitimacy of alien belief.

Before considering Lovejoy's argument and then the scientific problems with Plenitude, we should first briefly settle its theological errancy. As the *New Catholic Encyclopedia* explains,

> From [the early times of Christianity onward], the finite was understood to be a lower level of being, one that possessed in a limited (and therefore imperfect) way some attribute or property that Infinite Being (God) possessed in an unlimited (and therefore supremely perfect) manner. Finite thus became a primary notion for describing the status of creatures, all of which are by nature finite, as compared with their Creator, the infinite plenitude of all perfection.[126]

Even the *Catechism of the Catholic Church* wisely begins its very first line by asserting the dogmatic truth that "**God [is] infinitely perfect and blessed in himself.**" (§1) Little is more vital to remember that God—and God *alone*—is infinite. Later, the same Catechism prophetically warns that the final trial of the Antichrist is coming, who will offer a "**supreme religious deception,**" which amounts to "**man glorifying himself in place of God.**" (§675) Discerning minds will not fail to observe that already—from the very inception of alien belief within Christendom—we see the seeds being sown for what would eventually culminate in the great rebellion against God. For that rebellion—that Great Apostasy—consists in the glorification of the creature "in the place of" the Creator. Philosophically, such a diabolical inversion is seen nowhere as clearly as in ascribing actual infinitude to anything whatsoever besides God Himself. If unsettling, it is nevertheless unsurprising to see such premises as these helping to generate the very phenomenon of alien belief. Exploring the prophetic dimension of this Great Deception, however, will be saved for Part Four.

Returning to the thesis of Lovejoy, his argument is as follows:

> The more important features of the new conception of the world, then, owed little to any new hypotheses based upon the sort of observational grounds which we should nowadays call 'scientific.' **They were chiefly derivative from philosophical and theological premises. They were, in short, manifest corollaries of the principle of plenitude**, when that principle was applied, not to the biological question of the number of kinds of living beings, but to the astronomical questions of the magnitude of the stellar universe and of the extent of the diffusion of life and sentiency in space. God, it seemed, would, in the phrase of the Timaeus, have been "envious" if he had refused the privilege of actual existence to any logically possible being at any place where such existence was possible ... **there appeared to be no reason why, wherever there was matter, there should not be life. ... the contention that the infinity of worlds and of inhabited systems was among these implications [of the Principle of Plenitude] was ... familiar, though usually rejected by**

the orthodox.

Indeed, orthodox Christians had always been aware of the thesis that the universe (creation) was infinite, and they had always roundly and unanimously rejected it as heretical—not to mention logically bankrupt. That is, they had always unanimously rejected it until the arrival of Nicholas of Cusa, whom we have already discussed—and the thinkers eventually inspired by him. It was Giordano Bruno, however, who was most zealous with this principle—the man, we recall, whose heresies were deemed so severe and damaging that he was burned at the stake. Lovejoy continues:

> ...Though the elements of the new cosmography had, then, found earlier expression in several quarters, **it is Giordano Bruno who must be regarded as the principal representative of the doctrine of the decentralized, infinite, and infinitely populous universe**; for he ... preached it throughout Western Europe with the fervor of an evangelist ... it is certain that he was not led to his characteristic convictions by reflection upon the implications of the Copernican theory or by any astronomical observations. **Those convictions were for him primarily, and almost wholly, a deduction from the principle of plenitude... [for Bruno,] an infinity of beings and of worlds must exist**, in all possible modes. ... Of the endlessly numerous worlds thus demonstrated to exist, some, Bruno adds elsewhere, must be even more magnificent than ours, with inhabitants superior to the terrestrial race.[127]

Another major figure in the promotion of the Principle of Plenitude, and the corresponding insistence that there *must* be extraterrestrials, was the philosopher Immanuel Kant (born 1724), who is universally regarded as among the most central Enlightenment thinkers. In his most famous work, Kant declared:

> I would indeed bet all that I own...that there are inhabitants on at least one of the planets [in this solar system]. ... this view...is not a mere opinion but a strong faith (on whose correctness I would surely risk many of life's advantages)*

Of this pillar of modernism, Dr. Peter Kreeft cuttingly observed that:

> Few [philosophers in history] have had a more devastating impact on human thought [than Kant]... he helped bury the medieval synthesis of faith and reason ... "*Two things fill me with wonder,*" Kant confessed: "*the starry sky above and the moral law within.*" What a man wonders about fills his heart and directs his thought. **Note that Kant wonders about only two things: not God, not Christ, not Creation, Incarnation, Resurrection and Judgment, but "the starry sky above** and the moral law

---

* Immanuel Kant. *Critique of Pure Reason*. Part II. Section III. A 826/B854. Note: In place of my bracketed remark, Kant wrote "that we see." Kant, however, published this work—the *Critique of Pure Reason*—in 1781, at which time people could only see the planets in this solar system (and not even all of them).

> within." "The starry sky above" is the physical universe as known by modern science. Kant relegates everything else to subjectivity ... Kant's philosophy is a perfect philosophy for hell.[128]

Kant's excitement for extraterrestrials was well known. As noted by the Benedictine priest, professor, and scientist, Fr. Stanley Jaki—with a similar zeal as Dr. Kreeft:

> [Immanuel Kant] claimed, among other things, that the inhabitants of Mercury must be very lively because of the great heat there, whereas the inhabitants of Saturn were superior philosophers, compared to whom Newton was a mere ape. **The future celebrity of critical reasoning, or pure reason indeed, never disavowed these wallowings of his in pure fantasies.**[129]

Describing Kant's role in this drama, Lovejoy explains:

> Kant ... was arguing both for the infinite extension of the physical universe and the infinite plurality of worlds ... [he argued that] it would be absurd to represent the Deity as bringing into action only an infinitely small part of his creative potency ... **[Kant disposed] with a somewhat contemptuous brevity [the] objections to the logic of the principle of plenitude.** ...[Kant insisted that since] the infinity of the world [i.e., universe] is possible, it is also necessary.[130]

Nor should we fail to note the anti-Christian rationalist philosopher, Baruch Spinoza, also a mainstay of the Enlightenment, whose works were condemned by the Catholic Church. "**Spinoza ... expressed the principle of plenitude in its most uncompromising form and had represented it as necessary in the strict logical sense**..."[131]

We can see that the dangerously deceptive Principle of Plenitude was indeed fundamental to the initial spread of alien belief within Christendom. As our present chapters are dedicated to scientific analysis, however, we now turn to those considerations.

The Fact of the Finitude of the Universe: Early Death-Knell for Alien Belief

Without commenting on the accuracy of the details of various contemporary astronomical theories on the beginning, age, and extension of the universe, it is nevertheless entirely safe to conclude that modern scientists have proven that the physical universe is anything but infinite. It had a beginning, it has limited extension, and it will have an end.

We need no crystal ball with which we can peer into the future to have a scientific certainty that the cosmos cannot endure forever. We can merely consider the Second Law of Thermodynamics, which is among the most fundamental of all the laws of science.

This Law assures us that the overall "entropy" of the universe can only possibly continue to increase. Entropy, in turn, can be understood in several valid senses, each mutually confirming. It is a measure of the disorder of things. It is a quantity establishing the inability of energy to produce real effects (or "work"). It is the increase of randomness. It is even the very "arrow of time." For the passage of time itself is as inextricable from the increase of entropy as the value of *pi* is inextricable from a circle's relationship between its diameter and circumference. Therefore, it is in some ways fair to even define time as the increase of entropy (although we will consider time from a more philosophically accurate perspective in Part Five). In other words, if *anything* is happening, then two conclusions are certain: time is passing, and entropy is increasing.

What the cosmically inescapable increase of entropy means for the universe itself is likewise certain: it is doomed. A finite amount of energy exists, therefore a finite passage of time is guaranteed to eventually bring about the "heat death of the universe," whereupon it will have no ability to host the slightest actual event transpiring, much less any civilization.*

Canadian Astrophysicist Dr. Hugh Ross explains this Heat Death in simple terms:

> This "heat death" of the universe follows from the simple fact that the flow of heat from hot bodies to cold bodies eventually brings every piece of matter in the universe to the exact same temperature. When everything registers an identical temperature, heat flow everywhere ceases. The universal cessation of heat flow implies the end of any possible performance of work, including such basic activities as respiration and digestion ... Now that astronomers have determined the details of the origin, history, and structure of the universe and of the stability and constancy of the physical laws throughout cosmic history, they can calculate exactly how the heat-death scenario will unfold. ... the Astrophysical Journal published a ... detailed and rigorous account several years ago. Lawrence Krauss, chairman of the physics and astronomy department at Case Western Reserve University, coauthored along with colleague Glenn Starkman an article titled "Life, the Universe, and Nothing: Life and Death in an Ever-Expanding Universe." In it they calculate the future consequences of ever-accelerating cosmic expansion. They show that any kind of advanced physical life confined to the space-time dimensions of the cosmos must suffer an inevitable, irreversible, and complete dissipation of heat. With every passing year, the universe stretches out faster than it did the previous year, which hastens and exacerbates the consequences of the coming heat death. Krauss and Starkman demonstrated how this ever-increasing cosmic expansion rate, when projected far into the future, yields at least six deeply

* Note that Christians should rest easy: the heat death of the universe will never come close to happening, as Christ will come to conclude time itself long before we need concern ourselves with the implications of the Second Law of Thermodynamics!

distressing consequences—each more serious than the one before.[132]

Of course, this death sentence for the universe was also a death sentence for the Principle of Plenitude, as well as a defeat for the Enlightenment's unbridled humanist optimism directed not at God, but at the material universe. It demonstrated, in clear scientific terms, what the Christian faithful had always known: the temporal universe—the whole material cosmos—was not an exhaustive outlet for the Infinite Power of God, because it *could not* be that. The difference between the Creator and His creation is, and always will be, infinite, because *only* God is infinite. The cosmos, on the other hand, came in to being from nothing when God said, "let there be light" (Genesis 1:3), and the whole temporal sphere which then had its beginning will likewise have its end. The purpose of the universe cannot be found within the universe, but only in that which it exists for the sake of preparing the way for; namely, Heaven.

The surety of the coming heat death of the universe was not a recent finding. It was the renowned physicist and mathematician Lord Kelvin who, in the year 1852 with his publication of *On a Universal Tendency in Nature to the Dissipation of Mechanical Energy*, discovered the sentence that science had silently passed upon the cosmos. Recall, as Dr. Crowe noted, that the latter half of the 19th century saw the demise of many arguments hitherto presented for extraterrestrials—though few thinkers (including Kelvin himself) then had the honesty to defect from the alien belief they had, only decades earlier, regarded as a dogmatic certainty.

Within the passage above, Dr. Ross points out that Nobel prize-winning physicist Robert Millikan (born 1868) "**vehemently objected to the 'nihilistic doctrine' of an ultimate cosmic end of activity**." Such a view only appears "nihilistic" to one who has placed his eternal hopes within the material universe. This error yet again calls to mind the warning of the Catechism:

> **The Antichrist's deception already begins to take shape in the world every time the claim is made to realize within history that messianic hope which can only be realized beyond history**... (§676)

The Principle of Plenitude was, therefore, nothing other than the early groundwork of the supreme deception of the Antichrist. And its primary corollary—belief in extraterrestrials—will likely be what precipitates the climax of that same deception in the times ahead.

"Plenitude" itself, however, is unlikely to make a comeback. Alien belief is today often elicited via sci-fi replacements for religion—which have largely become today's post-Christian, Pagan substitute for the Faith—and the "scientific" justifications for alien belief one hears in contemporary discourse are just as pseudoscientific as the 19th century "scientific certainty" that, for example, the "canals" on Mars were engineered and built by extraterrestrials (to be discussed in the next chapter).

Nevertheless, today's ET promoters should not dismiss the errancy of Plenitude as if it were an irrelevant historical note. Besides the fact that a movement born of error should be—on that count alone—dismissed or at least approached only with extreme caution, we are also left with the recognition that the primary argument Christian ET promoters use today to justify their thesis is only a rewording of the same argument used by the Plenitude-promoters of old. The latter would have condemned the former if they revealed—in the 18th or 19th centuries—what we now know thanks to decades of direct, close-up, and detailed observations of Mars (not to mention remote expeditions there).

If you spoke to a Kant or a Bruno or any other such thinker, and informed him that Mars is devoid of aliens, he would promptly condemn you as someone who is "limiting God," just as ET promoters today denounce those who say it is not only Mars that is devoid of aliens, but also the other planets besides earth. But this is only one of many condemnations one would receive if he spoke the truth in those times. Let us review some additional ones in the next chapter.

16. Repeated Failures and Refusals to Learn

> "Extensive as the [extraterrestrials] debate has been, brilliant as many of its participants were, it differs from most debates in the history of science by the fact that it remains unresolved. Centuries of searching for evidence of extraterrestrials have produced hundreds of claims, thousands of publications, and millions of believers, but not as yet a single solid proof..."
>
> —Dr. Michael Crowe

Like a flat-earther ever making minor adjustments to his theory in light of a flow of new revelations disproving it—instead of doing the right thing and simply discarding the theory to replace it with a round-earth model—alien belief, throughout the 18th to 20th centuries, followed a similar pattern proving its fundamentally unscientific nature.

The history of ET promoters proving that their positions are entirely ideological goes back centuries. As Dr. Crowe observed:

> Pluralists as well as their opponents have repeatedly stressed the importance of empirical evidence in judging extraterrestrial life hypotheses. Yet it is an illuminating fact that, with the exceptions of Whewell, Antoniadi, and Proctor, almost no figures in the pluralist debate significantly changed their positions. William Herschel's failures to detect evidences of extraterrestrial life only led him to postulate new locales for it. **Although evidence against life elsewhere in the solar system continually increased from 1850 to 1900, the pluralist camp suffered few defections**. No more striking example of the willingness of pluralists to disregard empirical evidence can be cited than the readiness with which they accepted life on the sun, an idea favored by Bodmer, Boscovich, G. Knight, Bode, both Herschels, Arago, Gauss, Brewster, Read, Schimko, Phipson, Ponton, Liagre, Coyteux, Preyer, Goetze, Etler, Warder, and others. In short, the pattern that is apparent is that most individuals took new empirical evidence to be an occasion for adjusting rather than abjuring their theories.[133]

In the sections ahead, we will review only a few true stories from the 18th to 20th centuries that expose the nature of the alien belief movement's roots.

Exactly 8,141,963,826,080 Aliens Dwelling on Saturn's Rings

> "Let us suppose for a moment that the vast regions on the surfaces of the planets are... devoid of inhabitants...to maintain such a position would be to distort the Divine character and to undermine all the conceptions we ought to form of the Deity...viewing him as a fool or a maniac...the thought would be impious, blasphemous, and absurd...we are, therefore, irresistibly lead to the conclusion, that the planets are the abodes of intelligent beings... This is a conclusion which is not merely probable, but absolutely certain, for the opposite opinion would rob the Deity of the most distinguishing attribute of his nature, by virtually denying him the perfection of infinite wisdom and intelligence."
>
> —Rev. Thomas Dick. *The Celestial Scenery.* Chapter IX. §III

The man quoted above, Reverend Thomas Dick, was born in the year 1774. For this preeminent enlightenment thinker, Scottish Protestant minister, and an astronomer, alien belief promotion "became a core component"[134] of his career, so much so that he "deluged both sides of the Atlantic with volumes in which ideas of extraterrestrial life appeared with great frequency."[135] In reference to the various planets in *even our own solar system,* he argued:

> There is a general similarity among all the [planets], which tends to prove that they are intended to subserve the same ultimate designs [as earth] in the arrangements of the Creator...[they are moreover] adapt[ed] to the enjoyments of sensitive and intelligent beings; and which prove[s] that this was the ultimate design of their creation...[their scenery] forms a presumptive proof that both the planets and their moons are inhabited by intellectual beings."[136]

As we have seen, the reverend assured his readers that any contrary position was nothing but "impious, blasphemous, and absurd." Moreover, these separate and supposedly absolute proofs of aliens in the solar system did not remain vague premises for him. He developed exceedingly specific descriptions of these alien civilizations, in whose existence he had complete faith.

In Chapter VI of the book quoted above, *The Celestial Scenery,* he calculates the numbers of intelligent extraterrestrials that dwell on the various planets, moons, planetary rings, and the like, within our solar system. He promised that the following planets each contained the corresponding populations of aliens therein: Mercury (8.96 billion), Venus (53.5 billion), Mars (15.5 billion), Jupiter (7 trillion), Saturn (5.5 trillion), and on the list goes with other moons' and celestial bodies' populations given, totaling *about* 22 trillion aliens inhabiting our solar system. (His count of the number of aliens on Saturn's rings, however, was quite precise: 8,141,963,826,080). He also assured his critics that the absence of any evidence of atmospheres on certain planets was unproblematic; their atmospheres were simply purer than ours, and thus invisible—just like their inhabitants enjoyed a "moral and physical condition ... superior to that enjoyed upon earth."

Unfortunately for the reverend, he also placed over four billion aliens on the surface of the moon. There was no need to wait for advanced mid-20th century NASA missions to disprove this assertion. Even the earlier detailed images of the moon succeeded in revealing nothing but a barren wasteland with no evidence of any life having ever existed there, much less living there at present.

Recall that Kant was convinced that the aliens on Saturn are such astounding geniuses that they tower above Newton himself. How interesting that not one of them managed to send a single electromagnetic wave signal to earth, although our own signals have been showing Saturn for many decades!

The 1835 Moon Hoax: Supposed Intrinsic Evidence of Lunar Aliens

> "...how deplorably the public mind had been trained to gullibility on matters of science..."—Richard Locke. 1835.

So ubiquitous were 18th and 19th century claims of certainty in the existence of aliens on the moon, and Mars, and, literally, *every* other planet, that the chaos caused by "The Great Moon Hoax of 1835" is deeply telling but not in the least surprising. The History Channel provides the following summary of the event:

> On August 25, 1835, the first in a series of six articles announcing the supposed discovery of life on the moon appears in the New York Sun newspaper. ... supposedly reprinted from the Edinburgh Journal of Science. ...[they reported that] Herschel [a famous and respected astronomer] had found evidence of life forms on the moon, including such fantastic animals as unicorns, two-legged beavers and furry, winged humanoids resembling bats ... Intended as satire, [these claims] were designed to poke fun at earlier, serious speculations about extraterrestrial life, particularly those of Reverend Thomas Dick, a popular science writer who claimed in his bestselling books that the moon alone had 4.2 billion inhabitants. Readers were completely taken in by the story, however, and failed to recognize it as satire.[137]

This description, however accurate, fails to capture the electrifying influence of the "moon hoax" upon society. One wonders if the authors of this article were compelled to downplay such a clear illustration of the masses succumbing to mainstream media deceptions. For, indeed, it is none other than the History Channel itself which is today famous for a far more prolonged hoax on the same topic, broadcasted in the "Ancient Aliens" television series. Since its 2009 inception, this series has generated hundreds of episodes of pseudoscientific drivel that has convinced untold millions of credulous viewers that extraterrestrials (branded "ancient astronauts") have walked among us for millennia—while undertaking such tasks as building pyramids, inspiring various religious texts, generating our legends, and even forming our languages.

Let us then turn to a more complete assessment of the event's *impact*. Dr. Michael Crowe points out:

> The 1 September issue of the Sun recounted reactions from other newspapers [to the announcements that aliens had just been discovered on the moon], stating ... "**It appears to carry intrinsic evidence of being an authentic document**." The Daily Advertiser, it was reported, expressed its enthusiasm by stating: "No article, we believe, has appeared for years, that will command so general a perusal and publication. ..." The Albany Daily Advertiser [called] it a "**Stupendous Discovery**," [and] told of having read the story "with **unspeakable emotions of pleasure and astonishment**." **The New York Times, according to the Sun report, pronounced the discoveries "probable and plausible,"** while the New Yorker described them as creating "**a new era in astronomy and science generally**."[138]

The eagerness with which "respectable" mainstream media outlets like *The New York Times* devoured this manifestly fake news is both a testimony to the wholly illogical nature of alien belief in the 19th century and a preview of the still more inane credulousness with which ET claims are now accepted in the 21st century.

It should not even have been necessary for any investigative journalism to take place to expose the fraud; a moment's common-sense reflection would have concluded the same. The articles expected their readers to believe that—even though they knew that the most cutting-edge technology of their times could barely observe the moon's surface with any more clarity than could a child's pair of toy binoculars today—there was nevertheless, essentially overnight, a discovery *and invention* which enabled close-up photographs of foliage, rodents, and men on the moon. No one should have fallen for this hoax on account of its latent absurdist technological claims alone. Instead, almost everyone believed it—at least, almost all the *scholars* succumbed. As we will see below, ordinary folk—"those uninformed in astronomy"—were less likely to be fooled.

Crowe continues his description of what we can only fairly diagnose as a sudden explosion of mass-formation-psychosis:

> According to other contemporary reports, "**Some of the grave religious journals made the great discovery a subject of pointed homilies**" and

> an **American clergyman warned his congregation that he might have to solicit them for funds for Bibles for the inhabitants of the Moon**. It has even been claimed that "the philanthropists of England had frequent and crowded meetings at Exeter Hall, and appointed committees to inquire ... in regard to the condition of the people of the moon, for purposes of relieving their wants, ... and, above all, abolishing slavery if it should be found to exist among the lunar inhabitants." A person who had been in New Haven in 1835 described the situation there: **"Yale was alive with staunch supporters. The literati—students and professors, doctors in divinity and law—and all the rest of the reading community, looked daily for the arrival of the [moon alien reports in the] New York mail with unexampled avidity and implicit faith."** Professors Loomis and Olmsted of Yale, it is claimed, went to New York to examine the deleted mathematical sections, but were sent on a wild goose chase. Edgar Allan Poe later reported: "***Not one person in ten discredited it, and (strangest point of all!) the doubters were chiefly those who doubted without being able to say why—the ignorant, those uninformed in astronomy, people who would not believe because the thing was so novel, so entirely "out of the usual way.*** *A grave professor of mathematics in a Virginia college told me seriously that he had no doubt of the truth of the whole affair!* "[139]

The "moon hoax" was, in fact, written with all the right verbiage to appear legitimately scientific. Its author—Richard Adams Locke—was well versed in the day's scholarly literature. However, it was perhaps not originally intended as a hoax at all, but as a work of satire. Locke's mastery of linguistics was not the only reason, or even the primary one, for the deception's success. Crowe points out:

> **The main reason why thousands of Americans believed these fantastic fictions is that for a number of decades they had been prepared for them by the preachings and proclamations of such [alien belief promoting] authors as Paine, Chalmers, Emerson, and Dick. As one author put it in 1852: "*The soil had been thoroughly ploughed, harrowed and manured in the mental fields of our wiser people, and the seed of farmer Locke bore fruit a hundred fold.*"**[140]

Those with ears to hear and minds to discern the relevance of this episode of American History will not fail to grasp its importance for today, particularly in view of those topics we will be considering in the later parts of this book.

Rev. Thomas Dick, who we have quoted in the preceding sections, no doubt felt humiliated, and accordingly he strongly rebuked Locke. The latter's response is also deeply instructive for us today:

> So far from feeling that I deserve the coarse reproaches of Dr. Dick, I think it is quite laudable in any man to satirize, as I did, that school of crude speculation and cant of which he is so eminent a professor. **My hasty speculation succeeded beyond all expectation or idea, and thus**

proved how deplorably the public mind had been trained to gullibility on matters of science by those who had preceded me in the field.[141]

***

Whoever today reads the same New York periodicals noted above needn't be told that no lessons were learned. Within their pages, a 21st century reader will learn of far more farcical claims being taken at face value: "UFOs" regularly traversing our skies and—with quasi-supernatural prowess—breaking the laws of physics, only to crash shortly thereafter; alien explorers travelling millions of light years only to probe the nether regions of a selection of unfortunate Americans; and "proof" of massive 75-year cover ups of ET contact (and craft!) that never provide evidence sufficiently credible that it would be so much as admissible in court, much less convincing if presented therein. (Addressing these and similar fallacies will be the focus of the next chapter.)

Just a few decades after the "Moon Hoax," an equally absurd claim was made. This time, it was not intended as a hoax or a work of satire. It was the dead-serious life-mission of renowned scientists, though the content was no less fictional.

Attention from ET promoters had shifted away from the moon, and towards another body we observe in the sky:

> ...[the] supposed discoveries of unicorn-like animals and winged humanoids [on the moon] were made via a marvelous (and fictitious) telescope that was 150 feet long and could magnify the heavens forty-two thousand times. Thirty years later, Jules Verne journeyed his readers to the moon, **but by the late 1870s the destination had shifted to Mars.**[142]

Renowned Astronomer C. Flammarion: "Obvious" Aliens on Mars (and Reincarnation)

> "In two scientific treatises, *The Plurality of Worlds* and *Mars and Its Inhabitants*, Flammarion stated his belief that Mars not only housed life but also intelligent beings. Dwarfed in stature, positioned next to his fifteen foot-tall telescope, [he] described in detail the mountains, valleys, craters, lakes, and oceans of Mars in North American Review in 1896. 'It is obvious,' Flammarion concluded, 'the world of Mars is...vigorously alive.'"[143]

Camille Flammarion was born seven years after the Great Moon Hoax. A renowned French astronomer and popular science fiction author, he even owned and operated his own observatory which is today run by the French Astronomical Organization and bears Camille's name. In his own day, photographs of the astronomer posing next to his massive telescope bolstered his reputation as an authority on all things extraterrestrial.

He even authored "the most complete study of the history of observations of Mars ever written."[144] Accordingly, Flammarion's astronomical claims were not merely regarded as the opinions of one man. Rather, they were treated as the assurances of the one who, of all men who had ever lived, had the greatest knowledge (at that time, almost three hundred years' worth) of scientific consensus in astronomical observations of the planet Mars. Yes, Camille was regarded "the definitive expert," and he was continually deluged with thousands of letters deriving from all parts of the globe soliciting his input on all things pertaining to astronomy. His writings were so widely read that they were "unequalled among scientific books," and he was the "most prolific of all writers on astronomy..."[145]

Like other contemporaries of similar ideological persuasions, Flammarion had been a Catholic. He even studied for several years as a seminarian. Eventually, however, he forsook his Faith to "free his mind" for the unbridled pursuit of his own theories about extraterrestrials. As one author noted:

> **[Flammarion] dreamed of other worlds, and their possible inhabitants. He had lost the Catholic faith of his youth... He substituted for it another faith**, based on the teachings of Jean Reynaud... Each soul, Reynaud taught, passed from planet to planet, progressively improving at each stage. Flammarion was also familiar with the works of such pluralist [i.e., ET promoting] authors as Fontenelle, de Bergerac, and Huygens, and "consecrated the year 1861" to the writing of a book advocating the plurality of worlds...Flammarion's real breakthrough came in 1880, with the enormously successful *Astronomie populaire*. ...**Flammarion intended that [his] observatory should be a nerve center of Martian observations all over the world... His writings strongly endorsed the idea that ...[Mars] was almost certainly inhabited**—so much so that when in 1891 a Madame Guzman, of Bordeaux, decided to bequeath 100,000 francs as a prize ... "for the person of whatever nation who will find the means within the next 10 years of communicating with a star (planet or otherwise) and of receiving a response," Mars was specifically excepted.[146]

It may be amusing, today, to read that contact with extraterrestrials on Mars was then treated as such an "obviously imminent" accomplishment—such a foregone conclusion—that a prize in astronomy was not even deemed appropriate to bestow upon the one who first managed it. Yet it is precisely this "certainty" in the non-fictional nature of pure fiction that was generated by the consensus of the astronomers of the 18th and 19th centuries.

Flammarion did not merely insist that Mars was inhabited. He condescended to provide his readers with the insistence that it was "certainly a place little different from that which we inhabit," himself writing:

> **Henceforth the globe of Mars should no longer be presented to us as**

> **a block of stone** ... but we should see in it a living world, adorned with landscapes similar to those which charm us in terrestrial nature; a new world which no Columbus will ever reach, **but on which, doubtless, a human race now resides, works, thinks, and meditates as we do on the great and mysterious problems of nature.** These unknown brothers are ... active beings, thinking, reasoning as we do here.[147]

Flammarion also intertwined his (pseudo)science with occultism and plainly Pagan teachings, thus his contributions were especially well positioned to prepare the way for the very diabolical deceptions we will discuss in more detail in forthcoming chapters.

Only two years before Flammarion's death, the New York Times published an article entitled "*Flammarion Predicts Talking with Mars,*" and the means of communication that the astronomer insisted upon were not—as with Tesla's efforts—based on electromagnetic waves. Instead, he predicted "*'Psychic Waves' will be developed to the point of overcoming space.*"[148]

Indeed, mediumship was a great interest of Flammarion's, and his insistence upon the reality of "telepathy" mirrors the same insistence promoted by today's charlatans who claim that aliens piloting the UFOs swarming about our airspace can be readily communicated with using such methods. As we will later see, such ET promoters are only enabling dialogue with demons, for there is no such *scientific* phenomenon as telepathy (a fact we will establish in a later section).

Reminiscent of those who, today, accuse alien disbelievers of "limiting God," Flammarion repeatedly employed the harshest rebukes to castigate those who pointed out that Mars, and other planets in the solar system, may not be amenable to life; saying that such people are guilty of "*hurling a gross insult in the shining face 'of the infinite Power who fashions the worlds,'*" and insisting, instead, that the other planets have a "*degree of habitability superior to that of the earth.*" Even the sun and the moon, Flammarion argued, *must* be inhabited. Finally, the apostate former Catholic denounced anyone who disagreed with him as "insane," since by failing to believe in aliens, they were likewise failing to acknowledge the grandeur of God. For Flammarion, a man's death does not—as Scripture teaches (e.g. Hebrews 9:27)—immediately precede his being judged by God, thus receiving his eternal sentence. Instead, one simply continues his journey by being reincarnated on various other planets, which, Flammarion insisted, are:

> Studios of human work, schools where the expanding soul progressively learns and develops, assimilating gradually the knowledge to which its aspirations tend, approaching thus evermore the end of its destiny.[149]

On June 3rd, 1925, Camille discovered that a man does not travel from planet to planet upon death, but rather experiences a Particular Judgment and immediately thereafter goes to Heaven, Hell, or (temporarily) to Purgatory. Unfortunately, he never (publicly, at least) came to this recognition before his own death on that day.

"Engineered Canals" on Mars "Certainly Built by Highly Evolved" Beings

> "Professor Percival Lowell is certain that the canals on Mars are artificial. And nobody can contradict him."
> —A 1905 Newspaper Article[150]

In the year 1877, Giovanni Schiaparelli, an Italian astronomer, described "*canali*" (canals or channels) that he claimed to have observed on Mars. As summarized by the historian of science, Dr. George Basalla,

> **[Schiaparelli's] supporters called him a modern Columbus who had discovered a new world on Mars**...His maps of Mars were bold and clear. They depicted canali that interconnected to form a planetwide hydrographic system. ...The canali debate stimulated the imagination of astronomers. ... A respected French astronomer announced that waters from an adjacent sea had recently inundated the huge Martian continent of Libya and that a canal ran directly across the northern Martian Sea. The American astronomer William H. Pickering argued that the observed duplication of lines was due to variations in plant growth along the canals...[151]

Not everyone agreed with Schiaparelli. He certainly had his critics, but what power does sober scientific analysis have when the giddy excitement of the mob wants something else? The answer is: very little. Basalla continues describing the effects of this apparent "discovery of canals" on Mars:

> As claims and counterclaims about the canali spread in the 1890s, the scientific dispute reached the general public. **The dispute was picked up by science popularizers, writers of fiction, and sensationalist journalists. Interest in Martian canali reached such a peak in those years that a historian has likened the Martian canal furor to mass hysteria.** Martian canali emerged from scientific literature but soon entered a fantasy world of unbridled speculation. This included claims that intelligent Martians had built enormous structures on the planet, sent light signals, and made plans to invade the Earth. **Inventors Thomas Edison, Nicola Tesla, and Guglielmo Marconi gave credibility to claims of Martian signals when they offered their technical advice to facilitate radio communication between the Earth and Mars.**[152]

Later developments in telescope design (and, ultimately, the 1965 Mariner mission to Mars) revealed the whole phenomenon to be nothing other than an optical illusion combined with a smattering of psychological deception.

However, just as contemporary illusions are relentlessly defended to justify alien belief, so too were these.

One such defender was Percival Lowell (born 1855), an American mathematician and astronomer who was also a powerful businessman. Describing his contribution to the debate, Basalla notes:

> **[Lowell's] claim that the Martian landscape included a global irrigation system influenced the conception of Mars held by scientists, government officials, and the general public well into the second half of the twentieth century** ... Lowell believed it was not enough to observe Mars and make accurate drawings of what one saw. One must boldly go beyond the observations and propose imaginatively conceived hypotheses and theories. Astronomers were not a band of technicians. They were generalists who aspired to become philosophers...[153]

Lowell's insistence that imagination be presented under the guise of science, however, may be his most significant (and tragic) contribution to contemporary discourse on aliens and the like. Far from having learned any lessons from the spectacular failures of Lowell and his peers, modern discourse has only delved more deeply still into these same fantasies.

Today, there is even a multitude of new religions which have sprung into existence, built off the fantasies provided by the joint consideration of the claims of evolutionary biologists and astrobiologists, that "*evolution must have produced almost god-like aliens, considering how many millions, if not billions, of years longer it has had to work on them than it has on us.*" Such absurd claims, however, have been festering in the consciousness of the West for a century thanks to men like Lowell, who, as Dr. Basalla observed...

> ... **offered a comprehensive theory of Mars based on Herbert Spencer's evolutionary philosophy.** The unique physical conditions of the planet, Lowell declared, explained the social behavior and technology of the intelligent creatures who lived there. **Lowell claimed that because Mars was smaller than the Earth, it evolved faster. Mars continued on its rapid evolutionary path and soon reached the final stages of planetary development...** The regularity of the canal network so impressed Lowell that he compared it to the geometrical layout of the walkways in London's Hyde Park. ... According to Lowell's planetary timetable, intelligent beings conquered nature earlier on Mars than on Earth. Therefore, the canal network was the physical manifestation of the older, superior intelligence inhabiting Mars ... In the thin atmosphere of Mars, intelligent creatures might breathe through gills, not lungs, he noted. Because of Mars small size, and lower force of gravity, Martians could be several times larger in stature than humans. Such gigantic creatures would find it easy to excavate a planet-wide canal system ... **Mars was much older than the Earth, and hence, Martian life had advanced far beyond human intelligence ... Unlike their inferiors on Earth, Martians had risen above petty party politics and arbitrary**

> **national boundaries to govern on a planet-wide basis. Lowell concluded his tribute to the Martian intellect by speculating that Martian inventions surpassed our wildest technological dreams because they "are in advance of, not behind us, in the journey of life."**[154]

It would be nothing but a temptation for us to dismiss Lowell's reckless assertions—which were presented (and accepted by much of his audience) as scientifically verified truth—as only an entertaining historical tidbit. On the contrary, it presents a stark warning that we ignore only at our own peril.

Lowell was not some science fiction writer (*or, rather, he was not regarded as such—in truth, that is precisely what he was*), nor was he a mere social commentator or political columnist. He was a veritable astronomer with access to the worlds' best telescopes and who even founded, owned, and administered an observatory (the Lowell Observatory in Flagstaff, Arizona) which is in operation to this day. His arguments carried weight. Admittedly, Lowell certainly had contemporary critics who argued against his claims. Exponentially more prominent than these, though, were the thinkers who devoured his thesis and acted upon it. To the most prominent of these we now turn our attention.

The Delusions of the Geniuses: Nikola Tesla's "Radio Contact with the Martians"

> "Whereas Flammarion only set out to describe the Martians, Tesla actually made plans to contact them."[155]

When one thinks of the great innovators of the 19th and 20th centuries, one name quickly comes to the fore: Nikola Tesla. This Croatian-born American inventor—whom we largely have to thank for the existence of the electric grid—was not merely an alien believer or alien belief promoter, but was rather a veritable extraterrestrial-obsessed man on a (delusional) mission.

Tesla went so far as to express outright conviction that he was receiving electromagnetic signals from Martians. He wrote:

> Others may scoff at this suggestion... [of] communicat[ing] with one of our heavenly neighbors, as Mars...or treat it as a practical joke, but I have been in deep earnest about it ever since I made my first observations in Colorado Springs... **The character of the disturbances recorded precluded the possibility of their being of terrestrial origin**, and I also eliminated the influence of the sun, moon and Venus. As I then announced, the signals consisted in a regular repetition of numbers, **and subsequent study convinced me that they must have emanated from Mars...**[156]

In fact, as later came to light, all Tesla was hearing was the transmission of another inventor—Guglielmo Marconi—precisely what the former repeatedly ruled out as impossible. His pride was too great to concede the possibility that someone else had built a functioning transmitter like his own.

Indeed, Tesla was a deeply troubled man. He did not believe in God, therefore he was willing to believe in anything else. Having abandoned the Orthodox Christianity of his youth (his own father was an Eastern Orthodox priest), he sought a new object for his faith and hope in sci-fi fantasies, which he pursued with all the vigor of a Don Quixote, though without the noble intentions. (His charity, on the other hand, eventually appeared directed only at pigeons.) For both reasons, it is unsurprising that the modern world has largely idolized this antihero.

Tesla regarded the universe as nothing but a "***great machine which never came into being and never will end [and that] the human being is no exception... what we call the 'soul' or 'spirit' is nothing more than the sum of the functionings of the body.***"[157] Replacing Christianity with belief in extraterrestrials has, today, reached epidemic levels, but the disease started long ago. As Tesla's biographer, the psychologist Dr. Marc Seifer, noted:

> Turning to Tesla's persistent wish to contact extraterrestrials, ... these outer space entities may have [for him] symbolized beings existing in the afterworld. Certainly the need to believe in extraterrestrials is a powerful and popular one. It explains why so many people accepted Percival Lowell's "Canals of Mars" hypothesis and, in today's world, the extreme popularity of such movies as Star Wars, Star Trek, and ET. In Tesla's case the extraterrestrials may have prelogically stood for his dead brother and mother. The insistence that he had probably been contacted by Martians became an unconscious safety valve which allowed him to hypercathect (release) much of the anxiety associated with the death of his older brother, as the brother would still be, in a sense, alive...[158]

Nikola, however, was not the only famous inventor of his day who was dead-set on communicating with extraterrestrials. There is another name that comes to mind when one thinks of the greatest inventors of that era, and neither would this man fail to take part in the delusional mission:

> ...the competition between Edison and Tesla would never abate, and it continued even into the realm of science fiction. Like many creative individuals, Edison had an interest in the occult. ... **he had studied telepathy, and he had worked with spiritualists on a "telephone" to communicate with departed souls**. **Edison was [also] interested in space travel and interplanetary communication**. ... In Lathrop's story "Edison's Conquest of Mars," when the Red Planet warriors invaded the earth, the Wizard of Menlo Park "invented a disintegrating ray...and it was 'Edison to the Rescue of the Universe.'" The son of Nathaniel Hawthorne would not be outdone.[159]

Explicitly diabolical activities—like Thomas Edison's infatuation with divination ("technologically mediated," though no less Pagan)—are anything but new in the movement to contact aliens.

Edison and Tesla's deceptions do not end there. We will save a deeper consideration of these themes for later chapters, but for now it suffices to observe that writers well before contemporary times had also turned Tesla into a godlike figure. For example, they actually believed not only his claims to receive messages from Martians, but also his ridiculous assertions on infinite free energy harnessing. As we will see later, one of the contemporary world's most popular ET promoters, Dr. Steven Greer, is also a major exponent of the "infinite free energy" lie, and this charlatan draws heavily from Tesla's proposals.

> At 8:00 P.M. on June 20, 1957, in the ballroom of the Hotel Diplomat in New York City, the Interplanetary Sessions Newsletter announced a meeting to coordinate an expected visit by the "Space People" to the planet Earth. The event was planned by three individuals: George Van Tassel, author of *I Rode a Flying Saucer*; George King, purported telepathic contactee with extraterrestrials, and Margaret Storm, author of the occult Tesla biography *Return of the Dove*, a book whose "*transcripts were received on the Tesla set, a radio-type machine invented by Tesla in 1938 for interplanetary communication.*" **By July 1 [1957] it was assured that the "Martians" would have "full scale operations" in Washington, D.C., New York, and "general North American areas."** It was also revealed that "*Tesla was a Venusian, brought to this planet as a baby in 1856...*" Margaret Storm's supposition that Tesla was born on another planet to give us our entire electric power and mass communications systems stemmed from a colorful history of the inventor's ties to **the group-fantasy belief that life on Mars was a virtual certainty.** **Fueled by ... the fear of [alien] infiltration and also theosophical literature, Storm proclaimed that Tesla had descended from the sixth-root race, a new species of human that was evolving on the planet**...[160]

One cannot blame only wild-eyed science fiction fanatics for their pseudo-deification of Tesla. His own words positioned him well to be regarded thus by the credulous and ungrounded. A true false prophet of dystopia, Tesla gleefully issued the following predictions:

> On his vision of the twenty-first century, Tesla foresaw a world in which eugenics would be "universally established." ... [he] supported the idea of "**sterilizing the unfit and deliberately guiding the mating instinct.** A century from now," [he] concluded, "it will no more occur to a normal person to mate with a person eugenically unfit than to marry a habitual criminal." On diet, the slim epicurean revealed that **he had given up meat altogether. Tesla believed that in the future inexpensive and healthy food would be derived from milk, honey, and wheat. ...[eventually] eliminating solid food altogether** [in his own diet], the thinning wizard had concocted a health potion made up of a

> dozen vegetables ... Although he still maintained that he might live to 140...[he also predicted], "**robots and thinking machines will replace humans**, and the trend of spending more on war and less on education will be reversed."[161]

Noting such dystopian desires is important because, as we will see in the following part of this book, such ideologies as these are part and parcel to alien belief.

Returning to the matter of Tesla and Martians, we should also return to the general context in which Tesla operated. Harvard astronomer William Pickering—brother of Edward Pickering, director of the Harvard Observatory—also joined the Martian frenzy. Although Pickering was in communication with Lowell, he also had his own independent "certainty" in the existence of the Martians. Dr. Seifer describes the following episodes giving the context for Tesla's alien mission:

> In April 1890, Professor Pickering made headlines when **he photographed what he said was a snowstorm on the planet Mars**. He calculated that the area covered was almost equal to that of the United States. Two years later, during a celebrated trip to Harvard's observatory in Arequipa, Peru, the bushily bearded professor announced another major discovery: "lakes in great numbers on Mars. The canals," Pickering proclaimed, "have dark as well as bright regions. We also observed clouds, and the melting of snows, and **this confirmed Herschel's hypothesis that there was vegetation around the regions of water**." **The idea of attempting to signal "Marsians," as they were then called, was a familiar ambition of the day**... Fueled by a competitive spirit, the **newspapers and magazines continued to promulgate the idea that Mars was inhabited by beings possibly more intelligent than we.** As Tesla made headlines in the New York dailies and electrical journals for his bold prediction that he would "signal the stars" ... H. G. Wells gained notoriety with his serialized Person's magazine horror story *War of the Worlds*, in which ghastly octopus-like Martians storm Earth in their egg-shaped spaceships and take over. **Although fictional, these stories were based on prognostications put forward by supposedly sober scientists**.[162]

Again, and again, and again, the most internationally-renowned scientists of the 18th and 20th centuries—those astronomers with the most specific expertise, who were therefore putatively the "most reliable" sources to consult to learn the "empirical and objective truth" about Mars—only confirmed each other in their delusions that "the evidence" they discovered presented "certainty" in the existence of aliens. (*As we discussed earlier, one can therefore scarcely fault those 19th century Catholics who wrote at the peak of this deception and chose to focus not on refuting aliens, but rather on defending the Faith against those who supposed aliens overthrew Catholicism.*) It bears emphasizing that this was not a matter of an isolated mistake or two. It was scientist after scientist, over the course of centuries, each making independent observations, with each one assuring the public that intelligent creatures lived on Mars. Each one, that is, promising science-based "certainty" in what we now know to be pure fiction.

One would then naturally ponder: after the spectacular failure of the assertions of the scientists already discussed, were lessons *finally* learned?

20th Century "Scientific" Consensus: Still Asserting Advanced Life on Mars, Then Debunked in One Day

Nikola Tesla died a lonely and broken man in a New York City hotel room in 1943. Percival Lowell passed away a few decades earlier, in the year 1916, and was laid to rest on "Mars Hill," near the observatory he founded and to which he dedicated his life. Martian alien theory, however, was not yet similarly buried, though it was at that point moribund:

> By the late 1890s, Lowell had completed construction of his own gargantuan telescope at Flagstaff, Arizona, where it is still, today, one of the finest in the world. There he would report each new discovery, including the cataloging of galaxies, which at the time were called "island universes." It is hard to overestimate Lowell's impact on contemporary thinking. For instance, the vegetation hypothesis was echoed by Wernher von Braun, Willy Ley, and P. Bonestell, who cowrote in their 1956 text *The Exploration of Mars*: "***And this is the picture of Mars at mid-century: a small planet which ¾ths is cold desert, with the rest covered with a sort of plant life [most likely lichen]...Mars is not the dead planet...but neither can it be inhabited by the kind of intelligent beings that many people dreamed of in 1900.***" ... in the case of the idea that Mars was inhabited, [this idea's proponents were] supported vigorously by the press... the most important proponents of the "life on Mars" scenario were the astronomers, but the position was also championed by the inventors.[163]

So, advances in astronomy revealed there were no creatures on the moon, or advanced canal digging civilizations on Mars. But there must, at least, be *some* intelligent life, *somewhere* out there, awaiting contact with us! And surely, Mars must have beings of *some* sort dwelling on its surface. (These were the sentiments expressed.)

Indeed, the admission that Tesla did not communicate with aliens, and the increasing acceptance that it was unlikely the Martian "canals" were canals at all, did not translate into an increasing acceptance that Mars did not have creatures upon its surface. Undeterred by prior failures, the ET promoters simply did the same thing they and their predecessors had always done. They modified their arguments slightly, doubled down on their fundamental fallacies, and rejected the opportunity to learn real lessons.

They conceded that the earlier "scientific certainty" that rational creatures inhabited Mars—a claim which had dominated both mainstream and academic culture for the entire 19th century—was in fact only a "dream." But even in the mid-20th century, scientists were still confidently describing Mars as anything but a "dead planet," for it was—they insisted—at least largely covered by vegetation—if not populated with far more advanced life than only plants.

Enter Carl Sagan—a man who figures especially prominently into the contemporary Great Deception, and who we will therefore consider in this book's next part. Perhaps the most popular scientist of the late 20th century, Sagan was idolized across the globe for various teachings in astronomy ever intermingled with his own atheism, but the man himself was above all fixated upon contacting aliens.

In less formal contexts, he posited aliens dwelling on Mars "as big as polar bears"[164], but even in a formal scientific paper published in January 1965, "*Martian landing sites for the voyager mission,*" he declared "**the present body of scientific evidence suggests**" that there is life on Mars. This was the case, Sagan continued, because of "**photometrically observed waves of darkening ... [interpreted] in terms of seasonal biological activity**."

In other words, telescopes observed periodic darkening of certain parts of the surface of Mars, and scientists claimed this was due to seasonal growth of plants. These observations were so prolonged, repeated, and confirmed, that Sagan went so far as to claim that one was dealing not with a mere hypothesis or conjecture, but rather a conclusion suggested by an entire available "body of scientific evidence." He went on to advocate for any spacecraft visiting Mars to be sterilized, lest our earthly microorganisms contaminate the pristine Martian landscape.

Then came July of that same year. Only several months after Sagan published the claims above, NASA's Mariner 4 spacecraft sent back images of the Martian surface as it flew by the red planet. As one publication reported:

> The first successful automated Mars spacecraft, 261-kilogram Mariner IV, departed Cape Kennedy, Florida, on an Atlas-Agena rocket ... and flew past Mars on 14-15 July 1965, six months after Sagan & Swan's paper saw print. Mariner IV revealed a cratered, distressingly moon-like Mars with an atmosphere ten times less dense than expected. The 21 grainy images of the planet the little spacecraft beamed to Earth revealed no signs of water or life.[165] ... There were, alas, none of the canals seen by astronomers in the late 19th and early 20th centuries, nor evidence of senders of messages heard by Nikola Tesla or Gugliemo Marconi. Indeed, the hazy images of a barren, crater-strewn landscape ended speculation that Mars might plausibly be inhabited by higher life forms.[166]

Later missions that sent back much more detailed imagery and data further solidified the certainty that Mars was uninhabited. In 1976, Viking probes even landed on the surface of the planet, and sent back color pictures of its barren landscape. All technological and scientific developments of the half century since that time have only repeatedly confirmed the inescapable fact that Mars is surely a "dead planet."

***

So much for the preservation of any hope that Mars might host extraterrestrials. Unfortunately, alien belief in general was scarcely dimmed, thus proving yet again that it had (and has) nothing to do with science, but only ideology. Before concluding this chapter and moving on to address the contemporary fallacies of alien belief—bound up, as they are, with the UFO craze of the last 76 years—we must take a moment to diagnose the disease whose pathogenesis the preceding sections have charted.

Science, Aliens, and Mass Formation Psychosis: "Those Who Do Not Know History Are Doomed to Repeat It"

In the decades leading up to 1965, Mars was indeed the primary object of hope for ET-contact. Like an atheist today clings to macroevolution, an Enlightenment-frenzied scientist of the 18th to 20th centuries clung to belief in Martians. It was both a symbol of and a corollary to their deeper Godless worldview.*

The spectacular failure of these 18th to 20th century scientific expectations—"certainties," rather—that mankind would soon find and contact the aliens on Mars is anything but some historical footnote that can be written off as a mere bump in the road of the triumphant victory march of science.

First, nothing else in the history of science resembles it. Save perhaps macroevolution, no other conjecture has been so resolutely clung to, for so many decades, in the face of such an onslaught of evidence disputing it. (Macroevolution, however, is a much newer theory than Martians, and it has not yet had its analogous "Mariner IV" moment.) While the Martian

---

* Even the popular fiction of the 1800s displayed this tendency. Among the most famous works of science fiction then was H.G. Wells' *The War of the Worlds,* published in 1897. This book described an invasion of earth by highly advanced Martians. (A year earlier, Wells wrote an ostensibly nonfiction piece, *Intelligence on Mars,* conveying his belief in highly evolved aliens on Mars.) Unsurprisingly, modern remakes of Wells' book leave out reference to the invaders coming from Mars. Later decades see the extremely popular *Twilight Zone* episodes depicting Martians on earth. Many other works of fiction throughout the last few centuries, however, dealt with similar themes: the 1765 novel, *The Voyages of Lord Seaton to the Seven Planets;* the 1839 novel, *A Fantastical Excursion into the Planets;* the 1880 novel, *Across the Zodiac;* the 1922 novel, *Aelita;* and countless others.

landings of the last half of the 20th century rendered belief in aliens living therein impossible even for the most obtuse of hitherto "true believers," it is only that absolute impossibility which finally put mainstream Martian belief to death. Clearly, nothing short of such a development would have succeeded.

Imagine a man on trial for murder. Witness after witness testify to his guilt, discovery after discovery of new evidence points to his guilt, many motives appear highlighting his guilt, and so on. Despite it all, he continues insisting upon his innocence. Finally, an abundantly clear and indisputable video emerges of him actually committing the murder. Only then does he confess and plead for leniency. Should a judge accordingly be convinced that this is an honest man who is truly repentant and therefore deserves a light sentence? Of course not. The man only abandoned his lies when it became *completely impossible* for him to continue denying the truth. All merit in conceding the truth is removed when that truth becomes wholly apparent.

The relevance of that scenario for the matter at hand is clear: as belief in Martians was only abandoned when maintaining it became impossible, the only accurate judgment of that dynamic that we—today—can deliver consists in regarding it as the false *dogma* it always was. Being dogmatic with true dogma is right and just. Being dogmatic with the fantastical premises of science fiction is perverse and diabolical. And that is the correct spiritual diagnosis. We could, however, also use psychological jargon and call it what it is from that perspective: Mass Formation Psychosis.

The preceding sections provide only a very small peek into the delusions of 18th to 20th century alien belief. Whoever delves deeply into the astronomical writings of those eras will discover a mountain of similarly damning material for the ET hypothesis.

The eighteenth to 20th century "certainty" in the existence of intelligent aliens on Mars was like the same era's "certainty" in the need for eugenics or the validity of phrenology. It was like the 1970s "certainty" that earth would endure a brutal ice age by the year 2000 "if population continues to grow"[167] (it has since more than doubled) or the 1990s "certainty" that we were a mere few years away from the ice caps melting due to global warming and the ocean reclaiming all coastal cities, or the 1980s-1990s global terror about the supposed "ozone hole caused by human pollution" was making sheep go blind and causing us to be inundated by more UV rays than ever before (we now know this "ozone hole" is simply a natural seasonal phenomena), or 2021's certainty that the Covid-19 vaccines prevented all transmission of the virus and therefore demanded a global usurpation of human rights in order to promulgate it.

Contemporary readers of the blunders of 18th to 20th century astronomy may be tempted to snicker at the latter's fallacies. Future readers, however, will be similarly inclined to laugh at today's. As one who has read many of the arguments of the 18th-20th century astronomers, I can attest that they were often presented even more convincingly than those of contemporary scientists. Their writing was excellent, their logic was often at least internally consistent, their observations were careful, their diligence in following the scientific method was commendable, and their consultation of their peers was ever present. Rarely do contemporary scientists exhibit such praiseworthy behavior. Only one little problem remained: their conclusions were completely bogus, bearing no resemblance whatsoever to reality.

When reading the arguments of the 18th-20th century astronomers who insisted anyone who disbelieved in aliens on Mars was utterly insane, I am reminded of my 5-year-old son who, upon learning how to build simple cars out of his Legos, proceeds to inform me that he knows exactly what is wrong with the family car when it breaks down, and instructs me on what I must fix to get it running again. Discontent with ordinary suggestions like those, he even ventures on to point out how cars *should* be designed so that they can fly and require no fuel. If this small child were granted enormous rhetorical powers and an understanding of how to present his claims so that they sounded like they belonged in a scientific journal, then he would closely resemble those astronomers.

Although those astronomers were dead wrong, a denizen of the 19th century would have had no hope of contradicting them. Only one thing would have succeeded in mooring such a person to the truth (i.e., the truth that Mars was uninhabited). That one thing is the Faith. (As we have seen, it repeatedly rules out all aliens—not just Martians.)

Now, Faith and reason never contradict, and ontologically speaking, one need never "choose between science and Faith." Pragmatically speaking, however, one must at times choose between the two, since imperfect men very poorly represent both. Valid as it is to say that Faith and reason are always in harmony, this assurance is sometimes cold comfort to one who happens to lack omniscience and therefore must simply choose one over the other when they appear to make contradictory claims.

For two thousand years, the Catholic Church has never once changed any of its dogmas. Any one of her 266 Pontiffs could have, with a flick of his wrist, *ex-cathedra* contradicted something that had already been taught *ex-cathedra*. Despite Popes reigning who were murderers, adulterers, and more, not even one of them has ever issued such a contradiction. Let us compare this constancy and consistency in Faith to "the science," after which point I will leave the reader to conclude which is superior. One contemporary scientist who has himself published dozens of scientific articles in peer reviewed journals nevertheless honestly observed:

> [The Replication Crisis of Science] emerged when a number of serious cases of scientific fraud came to light. Scientific scans and other imaging were proven to have been manipulated, archaeological artefacts were

> found to be counterfeit, embryo clones had been forged; ... Other researchers had manufactured missing links from pieces of skulls of humans and monkeys; and yes, it appeared that some even completely made up their research... The biggest problem [however] was with less dramatic instances of questionable research practices, which were reaching epidemic proportions. Daniele Fanelli conducted a systematic survey in 2009 and found that at least 72 percent of researchers were willing to somehow distort their research results. On top of that, research was also replete with unintentional calculation mistakes and other errors. An article in *Nature* rightly called it "a tragedy of errors."... in economics research, replication failed about 50 percent of the time, in cancer research about 60 percent of the time, and in biomedical research no less than 85 percent of the time. The quality of research was so atrocious that the world-renowned statistician John Ioannidis published an article bluntly entitled "Why Most Published Research Findings Are False." ...[recent] measures taken to improve the quality of scientific research, however well-intentioned, failed to address the problem...It first and foremost points to a fundamental epistemological crisis—a crisis of the way in which science is conducted. Our interpretation of objectivity is wrong, excessively based on the idea that numbers are the preferred approach to facts ... the most striking thing of all is that, in general, researchers themselves hardly realize that there is something wrong with their methodology. They generally take their scientific fiction for reality, confusing their numbers with the facts of which they are a distorted echo. The same applies to a large part of the population, blindly trusting this scientific ideology, with no other ideological hiding place, given the fall of religion. Numbers and graphs presented in the mass media by someone with credentials are considered de facto realities by many people. It is at this level that Hannah Arendt situates the ideal subject of the totalitarian state: the subject that no longer knows the difference between (pseudo)-scientific fiction and reality. Never before were there so many such people as in the beginning of the twenty first century; never before were the societal conditions so prone to totalitarianism.[168]

It is easy for the Father of Lies (cf. John 8:44) to deceive the scholars. In Jesus' own day, it was precisely the learned who condemned Him, and only the simple who followed Him.

But the Devil's ultimate goal is to reach the masses. Deceiving ordinary folk takes much more time and effort, and instituting the alien deception among the masses would take another century after the 19th century peak of the scholarly "certainty" in aliens.

Never before, however, has mankind been as uniquely poised as now to succumb to a grand deception at the hands of "The Science." What remains for the Faithful to settle in their minds is whom they will trust—and what they will trust—when that time arrives. God, or men?

"**Put not your trust in princes**..." (Psalm 146:3)

I present this warning now—a preview of this book's later chapters—because, in the sections ahead, we will continue exploring a number of scientific and logical fallacies involved in alien belief. Some readers may struggle to follow each detail therein. I would exhort such people to not throw their hands in the air and give up on this matter, lazily adopting the prevalent view that is summarized by the sentiments, "*Whatever. I have no idea. We'll see.*"

Instead, such a person—even if he feels he must give up on mastering the scientific arguments—should turn back to this book's earlier chapters, and thus stand reminded that the Faith is more than sufficient to assure us that only man bears the Divine Image. Thus he will stand prepared to reject those invitations, presented under the illusory disguise of "aliens," to dialogue with the demons themselves.

17. Contemporary Fallacies of Alien Belief

With the onset of the second half of the 20th century, the nature of the extraterrestrial debate radically changed. This seismic shift had nothing to do with science, but with "UFO" sightings and the "Ufology" movement they spawned. Today, the entire conversation on aliens is invariably bound up with the insistence that such beings do not merely exist, but are already visiting earth in droves. So let us now refute the fallacies associated with this latter assertion.

UFOs "Violating Science as We Know It": On the Intrinsically Contradictory Base Premises of the Ufologists

Ufologists unanimously insist upon the legitimately scientific nature of their mission and their arguments supporting the notion that alien craft are visiting earth. Recent developments reported in global headlines have even appeared to lend additional credibility to the field as a scientific one. Official U.S. Government commissions have been established to investigate UFO phenomena (*now branded "UAP" phenomena; however in this book I will use the traditional acronym*), Congressional hearings are being held, and an ever-increasing trend of "whistleblowers," who insist aliens are among us, have gained unprecedented notoriety.

We will see in this chapter, however, that the claims made by the Ufologists are logically and scientifically bankrupt. The increasing official recognition being given to UFO phenomena, far from testifying to its scientific (or otherwise evidence-based) legitimacy, is only the latest phase in the grooming one would expect to see if, indeed, a diabolical deception (or a government psyop) is being prepared.

Before discussing some details of only a few of their many fallacies (only a selection of which will fit within this book), a broader paradigm of logical hypocrisy that pervades Ufology must be exposed.

In one breath—albeit a very long one—Ufologists recite a litany of scientific arguments in seeming support of their position. They speak endlessly of the scientific laws governing atmospheric phenomena, jet propulsion, electromagnetics, optics, etc. They lend credibility to these same laws and theories when they ascribe trustworthiness to the presentations of the various high-tech sensor readings to which they defer. They summon various scientific experts to give testimonies to further their own thesis. These presentations and others are made in order to support their case that the UFO sightings in question could not possibly be human in origin, or optical illusions, or otherwise "ordinary," but instead must be explained solely by aliens.

In the very next breath, they castigate fully qualified scientists who, upon describing a given alleged phenomenon, point out that what is being described is scientifically impossible because it violates the most fundamental laws of physics. These Ufologists declare, "**yes, these craft are clearly operating in violation of the laws of physics ... *As we know them*!**" And the explanation that follows is always the same: "*Don't you think super-advanced alien technology would do precisely that!?*"

For example, in May 2022, U.S. Congressman Adam Schiff announced the following in a House of Representatives intelligence briefing on UFOs:

> I look forward to hearing... how this committee can make sure the task force is able to shed light on one of the world's most enduring mysteries...**instruments report there is something there; it is not the human eye confusing objects** in the sky. There is something there, measurable by multiple instruments, and yet **it seems to move in directions that are inconsistent with what we know of physics or science more broadly**, and that to me poses questions of tremendous interest.[169]

Leaving aside the absurdity of claiming that wielders of quasi-magical technology could make their way across the incomprehensible expanses of interstellar (or even intergalactic) space only to crash land upon arriving at earth—conveniently, without vaporizing a large chunk of the planet due to their incomprehensible speed—we should not fail to address the more fundamental fallacy among Ufologists, alluded to here by Schiff. Throughout the foregoing chapters of this book, we have seen repeated examples of ET promoters wanting to have their cake and eat it too, but the present example of this contradiction may be the most flagrant of all.

If "our present understanding" of physics is so fundamentally flawed that these "alien piloted UFOs" can set it aside in undertaking their maneuvers, then why give "our" science any credibility whatsoever? Scientific truths such as the Law of Conservation of Mass, Energy, and Momentum are so fundamental that if they are incorrect—if it is *even theoretically possible* for them to be suspended by some technological innovation—then modern science is as debunked as flat earth theory, and should be entirely discarded.

Unfortunately, laymen are often under the impression that these foundational laws of physics no longer matter "*because of advancements in relativity theory and quantum theory.*" In fact, nothing could be further from the truth (we will explore why in more detail later). The most cutting-edge research in quantum particle physics, for example, often presupposes the immutability of the Law of Conservation of Momentum. One particle is flung at another, perhaps in a linear accelerator, and the result of that collision is scrutinized in hopes that this analysis will allow scientists to infer the existence of some other particle (that they cannot as readily observe) on the basis of that particle "needing" to exist in order to explain what was seen, in keeping with the Law.*

Now, my purpose here is certainly not to argue that the laws of science (including the laws of physics) — which we can also refer to more generally as the laws of nature — *cannot* be broken. Most assuredly, they can be broken and they have been broken many times. When this happens, the ordinary course of nature is suspended, and there is a simple term for what has transpired: *a miracle.*

That situation, however, is entirely different. Ufologists never seek to ascribe veritable supernatural capabilities to these UFOs, as this move would immediately contradict their cause's entire motivation. Their thesis is not that we are — with UFOs and related phenomena — dealing with the direct actions of God, or angels, or even demons, but that we are dealing with purely technologically-mediated events (only involving technology far beyond our own, perhaps "from another dimension" — an assertion which changes nothing because it means nothing, as we will later see). They want all the mysticism and excitement of religion but none of the "traditional baggage" of morality, dogma, and the like — and in their eyes, only highly evolved inventors of highly advanced technology can grant them this desire.

The analogy they draw is always the same: "*Imagine a medieval peasant observing the flight of a modern airplane. He would have no idea how that could happen, but it is still an entirely technological phenomena. It is the same with these UFOs.*" Admittedly, such a sight would be quite astonishing for a man watching the skies a millennium ago. But it would be false to assert that such an observed phenomenon, even then, would be "contrary to the laws of science" as they were known. The men of ages past did not describe the ordinary course of nature using the same jargon we use today, but this does not change the fact that they understood it quite well. They knew that there was such a thing as flight, and they knew it did not require a miracle or any other suspension of natural laws to achieve. They would have observed the wings of the airplane and realized the similarities these wings bore to those of a bird. They would have noticed that, also like a gliding bird, this plane could not remain aloft, with wings steady, unless it was rushing forward at high speeds. It would not have been particularly difficult for them to describe the phenomena that kept a massive plane in the air. It certainly would have presented no paradox. Even today, it is often necessary to pause and reflect upon whether one is seeing a bird or a plane.

* For another example, we need only consider the most famous equation in modern science, E=mc^2. Many people are under the impression that this "mass energy equivalence" relationship is a usurpation of the Law of Conservation of Mass. It is not. It is merely a description of the ability of tiny quantities of mass to be expressed as energy. The Law itself, however, always holds true. Einstein's theories are and were much less "revolutionary" than most people today seem to recognize.

And what if they were shown a helicopter? That, too, would be straightforward to understand, and easy to describe in the same basic terms with which they described a bumblebee or a hummingbird remaining steady, thanks to its rapidly flapping wings. A rocket of any sort would be even easier. "Newton's Third Law" was always understood long before it was attributed to a certain 17th century Englishman. Any serious thinker of any time in history could have easily attributed the forward motion of an object to the thrust of a massive amount of high-speed propellant in the opposite direction. According to some historians, an ancient Greek philosopher, Archytas, built a device operating on the basis of precisely that principle, *in the year 400 B.C.* Furthermore, kites date back millennia, and there were a number of ancient and medieval attempts to build aircraft—although they were not technologically successful, the theory behind them was quite good.

The maneuvers of some of today's UFOs, on the other hand, display absolutely no mechanism by which they can be scientifically described. There is only one conclusion that can be drawn from those situations by a man who takes science seriously: what appears to be happening is not actually happening (for it is not plausible to claim that God would work a miracle like that). It is a deception. This deception, moreover—if it cannot be attributed to a hoax, an optical illusion, a psyop, or some other similar human phenomena—derives from the operations of demons.

However, further exploring this scenario takes us beyond the realm of empirical science and into the realm of spiritual discernment, therefore we will save doing so for Part Four. For now, it suffices to observe that Ufologists take a twisted religious approach to their ideology. Although claiming scientific motivations, the content of their arguments never conveys a scientific stance. Instead of "miracles," they simply refer to "advanced science." Instead of the realm of the "spiritual," they simply refer to the supposed abilities of beings from other stars, galaxies, or "dimensions." While changing only a few words, they have in no way mitigated the fact that they have proposed a religion—and, as we will see in Part Four, it is a Satanic one.

***

Let us now turn to examining some of the scientific absurdities bound up with contemporary Ufology.

One Physicist and Sci-Fi Author's Concessions on the Irrationality of ET Belief Premises

In the preceding section we have seen that what is physically impossible by virtue of its violation of the most fundamental laws of physics is not rendered conceivable when one locates its supposed origin in an alien civilization's advanced technology. If aliens existed, they would be just as much bound by the Law of Conservation of Momentum, Mass, Energy, etc., as we are. Their ships might be able to travel faster or make sharper turns, but they would not be able to make right hand turns at incredible speed, or levitate without propulsion or lift, or teleport, or exceed the speed of light, or communicate telepathically, or change mass, etc.

Ufologists satirize this argument as tantamount to the assertion that "*if our technology can't do it, then it can't be done!*", and in so doing reveal that they entirely misunderstand the very nature of scientific laws, which themselves remain constant despite technological advancements.

Let us here defer to the works of an American nuclear physicist who worked at the US Depart of Energy's Princeton Plasma Physics Laboratory, Dr. Milton Rothman. I have chosen the writings of this man as our present point of departure precisely because Rothman was no ally of my thesis. An atheist, modernist, science fiction fanatic and even a major pioneer of the modern sci-fi movement, he was about as diametrically opposed to the posture of the present book as one can imagine. (A gathering in his Philadelphia home in 1936 is still billed as "*the world's first sci-fi convention,*" and in 1998, he was inducted into the "First Fandom Hall of Fame," an award recognizing achievement in the field of sci-fi.) If anyone would have been ideologically positioned to accept theories of extraterrestrials now buzzing our skies or walking our planet, it would be Rothman.

Although his dedication to science fiction and his prominence in the field dates back to his youth in the first half of the 20th century, his scientific expertise derives from a long professional career in physics that continued flourishing into the 1990s. It is these insights of his (and those of many other qualified scholars) that we will draw from in the following sections.

The Impossibility of Intergalactic Travel: The Speed of Light is Never Matched or Surpassed

> "Those of us who were raised on science fiction became accustomed to thinking of travel to the distant stars as part of our birthright. It is a powerful dream. Giving up any dream is sad, and there are many who refuse to give up this one. But as with many other fantasies, faster-than-light travel is and always was a pseudoscientific concept. It was never part of science."
>
> —Dr. Rothman, Physicist & Sci-Fi Pioneer

Many claims of extraterrestrials visiting earth involve the presupposition that, to do so, they have managed to travel faster than the speed of light.

Indeed, only 0.000000000005% of the universe's planets are said to reside in our own galaxy (for it is said to be one of about 200 billion), and of the over five thousand planets in the Milky Way we have found thus far, none have been demonstrated to be *habitable*, much less *inhabited*. Accordingly, expectations of alien contact are often placed in aliens travelling from other galaxies. But even the very closest galaxy to our own—if it deserves this (disputed) title—the "Canis Major Irregular Dwarf Galaxy" is a full 25,000 light years away.[170] This means that a ship travelling at the speed of light would take 25,000 years to reach our solar system from the nearest galaxy.

For perspective, the manmade object that is farthest from earth is the Voyager 1 craft, launched in the year 1977. As of 2023, it is almost 15 billion miles from earth, having left the solar system in the year 2012 travelling a dizzying 40,000 miles per hour. If it were perfectly aimed at the aforementioned "galaxy," it would take almost a *billion years* to arrive. The next closest galaxy after Canis is 75,000 light years away, and the distances continue expanding dramatically for other galaxies. Clearly, any hope of meeting aliens on earth must be placed in their ability to travel faster than the speed of light. But this is absolutely impossible.

If any object with a "rest mass"—a category including electrons, protons, neutrons, all atoms, all molecules, etc. (everything that is not a photon or a neutrino)—were to travel at the speed of light, then its own mass would have increased infinitely. As noted in an explainer from the U.S. Department of Energy:

> ... as an object moves faster, its observed mass increases. This increase is negligible at everyday speeds. But as an object approaches the speed of light, its observed mass becomes infinitely large.[171]

If, however, the mass of any object anywhere in the universe were to have increased infinitely, then so too would the force of its gravitational pull. An infinite gravitational pull would have caused the entire universe to collapse into itself. As we can be somewhat confident that the entire universe has not yet thus collapsed, we can be equally confident that nothing whatsoever (other than light)—anywhere in the universe—has ever travelled at light speed, much less beyond it.

Other paradoxes arise from the counterfactual scenario above; not only would it entail a situation we can be certain has not happened, but the very generation of the situation in the first place would also be impossible. An infinite amount of energy—i.e., more than is contained in the entire universe—would be required to propel so much as a single atom to the speed of light; therefore it goes without saying that no spacecraft has ever, anywhere, achieved this feat. It is irrelevant whatever technology, from whatever galaxy, one may posit. We are not dealing with technological limitations, but bedrock scientific ones. Many other demonstrations can prove that the speed of light can never be surpassed. One such argument is presented by Dr. Rothman, who explained:

> The well-known consequences of relativity include the impossibility of any matter, energy, or information traveling faster than the speed of

> light. ...if a message could be sent faster than light from earth to a space ship traveling faster than a certain velocity (but less than the speed of light), the ship could transmit a reply that would arrive at the earth before the original message was transmitted. [*note: this is counterintuitive – and, indeed, impossible, hence Rothman choosing it to highlight the absurdity of proposing faster than light travel – but it derives from the physics of relativity theory as applied to time dilation and the absolute constancy of the speed of light*]... This circumstance would violate the principle of causality (the idea that a cause must always come before its effect) and allow the occurrence of typical time-travel paradoxes. For example, a scenario could be created in which a catastrophe takes place on earth, after which a warning is relayed from earth to a moving spaceship and then back to earth. If the ship is moving fast enough, the warning would arrive on earth at a time prior to the catastrophe. The catastrophe could thus be halted before it happened. Has the catastrophe taken place? If not, then why was the warning sent? Rather than deal with such implausible paradoxes, we say that the thing that causes them faster-than-light travel – is impossible.[172]

Now, this absolute barrier does not prevent Ufologists from proposing all manner of alternative theories. Some conjecture teleportation via "wormholes," or describe the phenomena with other newly invented terms. All of this is pure pseudoscience without the slightest evidential basis. The moment such explanations as these are brought into the discussion, a Ufologist has demonstrated he has no desire to be scientific in his views, and has thereby again implicitly transferred the discussion into the domain of *spiritual* discernment.

> UFO proponents argue that aliens would have devised ways to circumscribe laws that only appear to be immutable to earthbound scientists. Some scientists have speculated that objects entering "wormholes" in space could travel immense distances instantaneously. This assumes that one could first find a conveniently located wormhole, that one's vehicle could withstand its tremendous gravitational and tidal forces, and that one could know in advance where in the universe one would emerge. For now, wormholes exist only in the realm of theory and so, in the absence of any actual evidence, cannot bolster the extraterrestrial hypothesis for the origins of UFOs.[173]

Here as in all other realms, anyone can do a quick internet search and immediately generate a long list of supposed experiments, from supposedly trustworthy periodicals, which in fact present only pseudoscience. "Scientists create wormhole!" is a headline that one can anticipate being repackaged more or less annually. It is always a lie, though gleefully promoted by media outlets who care only for clicks.

***

Can we at least hope for aliens visiting from other solar systems within our galaxy? Although the intergalactic alien visit is even more outlandish, the answer to this question is also a resolute *no*. Explaining why is our next task.

The Impossibility of Interstellar Travel: Near-Light-Speed Cannot be Maintained

The closest solar system to our own, that of the star Proxima Centauri, is about 25 trillion miles away from earth. The Voyager 1 spacecraft we referred to above, hurtling through space at its phenomenal speed, would take over 70,000 years to reach it (if, by some miracle, its trajectory was perfect and it avoids destruction by collisions). Let us pause to contemplate this. Of the *millions of trillions* (i.e., quintillions) of planets modern astronomers estimate exist in the universe, *the single closest one* beyond this solar system (*for we now are scientifically certain that, in this solar system, only earth is inhabited*) would take so much time to reach that it surpasses, by more than a factor of ten, the entire history of civilization. As we can see, proposing the possibility of even *the very easiest* interstellar meeting requires positing travel at speeds coming within the relative vicinity of the speed of light.

Yet this presents obstacles insurmountable not merely technologically but also scientifically. While those infatuated with science fiction rarely concede this fact, serious thinkers readily will. In his article, "Interstellar Travel as Delusion Fantasy" (in *Scientific American*), Dr. Ed Regis observed:

> Collisions in space are by no means rare: by the end of the Space Shuttle program, for example, more than 100 shuttle windows had been replaced after impacts with space debris, some objects being as small as the fleck of paint that cracked the front window of STS-7 (the second Challenger mission) in 1983 ... It might be thought that the interstellar medium is "empty space," or a vacuum. To the contrary, the space between the stars contains volumes of interstellar gas and dust, along with cosmic rays, and possibly objects of unknown composition, size, mass, and density. And so it would be difficult to believe that on a journey of at least 4.22 light-years (the distance from Earth to Proxima Centauri) an interstellar spacecraft would meet with no other object whatsoever. But for a starship traveling at relativistic speeds, a collision with even a random small particle, according to Tom W. Gingell of Science Applications International Corporation, who did a study of the subject, would have the effect upon the spacecraft of an H-bomb explosion. Since quickly diverting a massive spacecraft from its course would be impossible, it would be necessary instead to detect, deflect, or destroy the object within a matter of milliseconds before impact, by means of a system that would have to work perfectly and virtually instantaneously

the first time out...[174]

We have seen from even the most minuscule amount of space travel we have undertaken (when compared to what would be required for interstellar travel) that collisions with the tiniest of particles in space is a massive problem for spacecraft. Any decrease in risk due to fewer cosmic particles floating about interstellar space (vs. interplanetary space within a solar system) would be exponentially more than made up for by the incomprehensible speeds required for interstellar travel. At such (relativistic) speeds, even collisions with the smallest pieces of interstellar dust would decimate any craft—regardless of its construction method or materials. For any spacecraft meaningfully larger than a molecule, *countless* such collisions would be statistically guaranteed to occur when travelling between stars.

Astrophysicist Dr. Paul Sutter put the matter in even more specific terms in a 2021 article for *Discovery* magazine. He accurately described the most "realistic" interstellar travel method as follows:

> One proposed [method] for an interstellar spacecraft is called the Starshot Initiative, which aims to shoot a super-powerful laser on a lightsail (a giant nearly perfectly reflecting membrane), using the energy from the light to propel the spacecraft to a tenth the speed of light. That would enable it to reach Proxima [Centauri] in less than half a century. To make this work, the laser would have to use all the energy from every single nuclear reactor in the United States at once. And it would have to operate for 10 minutes, which is about a quadrillion times longer than we've ever operated our most powerful lasers). ... and the spacecraft could weigh no more than a paperclip.[175]

Admittedly, the two sources quoted above provide analyses based on the (absolutely best possible) human technology. Hypothetical alien civilizations would, of course, have more advanced inventions. But it only takes a small dose of intellectual honesty applied to the observations above to realize that it does not matter how much more advanced any civilization's technological prowess becomes: interstellar travel remains ruled out. Any sober assessment of the distances and dangers involved, when combined with basic knowledge of the *universal* scientific laws governing the strength of materials, kinematic physics, thermodynamics, chemistry, and more (even leaving aside biology!) will quickly demonstrate that no natural, material object—much less one so sizeable as the UFOs reported today—will *ever* travel between stars.

Imagine two Egyptian friends, several thousand years ago, observing the recently completed tomb of the pharaoh Khufu (now known as the Great Pyramid of Giza). Suppose one says to the other: "*This was such a gargantuan undertaking; it took everything we had as a society, for decades, to complete. And standing atop it, it appears we are not even one bit closer to the moon. We really need to just admit that we will never build a structure that reaches the moon."* His friend might be inclined to respond, *"No, you cannot say that! Who knows what abilities future people will have? We can't even imagine what they will be able to do."*

Despite not knowing the future, the first Egyptian would still be correct to respond, *"I am sure they will build much taller structures in the future. But what we can already see clearly tells us that there is such a great distance involved here that much more fundamental constraints than mere technological or pragmatic ones dictate that a building cannot be erected that will actually reach the moon."*

Obviously, the Egyptians were not intending to build a structure to reach the moon. My purpose here is only to use the same analogy the ET promoters use in order to refute their own argument. Whenever one points out to them that certain feats—e.g., interstellar and intergalactic travel—are simply *scientifically impossible,* they immediately retort that what we do now would also seem impossible to men who lived thousands of years ago. But that is simply not true. Modern technology would of course prove quite a marvel to behold to an ancient Egyptian, but their understanding of the laws of nature could still account for them. (We will consider this fact in relation to claims made about the maneuvers of "UFOs" supposedly piloted by ETs in a forthcoming section.) Their understanding of the laws of nature, however, could not account for one building a pyramid touching the moon, and they would have been entirely justified in deeming such a task fundamentally impossible. Similarly, our understanding of the laws of nature cannot account for interstellar travel, much less intergalactic travel—precisely because both are impossible.

As we can see from the analyses above, the amount of energy required for the closest interstellar travel, for even a comically tiny spacecraft, is so outlandish—even if the greatest power generation method that exists in the universe, nuclear power, is used—that no one who is genuinely assessing the situation could concede to it the slightest palatability. Note, however, that Dr. Sutter only described some of the more minor problems. He has not considered the cosmic dust collisions that would destroy the craft, or the inability to steer it (and thus effectively guaranteeing it will never arrive at its destination). Steering in space is not like steering a car, boat, or plane, where a sufficiently dense medium exists to push against for turning. Instead, it requires exponentially more expenditure of energy. And we have not even begun to consider *deceleration*—which, in space, is just as energy-hogging as acceleration. Nor have we begun to consider how such travel (and accelerations, cosmic radiation, etc.) would destroy *any* biological entity travelling in the craft.

It is not merely technologically infeasible to travel from one star to the next. It is *impossible.* If we are not dealing with a laser being shot at a craft to accelerate it from its home planet, then we must assume its own fuel is carried with it. The energy that would be required for *any* interstellar travel (not to mention a thousand other obstacles) renders such a task essentially super (or preter-) natural. To grasp that situation, we need only imagine a child's small remote controlled toy car with a heavy truck battery plopped on top of it, wired into the toy car's motor, with the intent of extending the toy car's range. As soon as the child tries to make the car move, he would immediately discover it wouldn't budge. The weight of this battery would be far too oppressive. Suppose the father of this child, seeing the conundrum, goes to acquire another car battery, hoping all that is needed is more capacity. Plopping that battery on top, as well, of course would be to no avail. In accordance with the nature of the scenario itself, the father is stuck acknowledging its unresolvability. He must, instead, tell the child to remain content with a range for his toy car derived from the capacity of the battery with which it was built. Yet, the notion of interstellar travel is much more outlandish than the suggestion of undertaking a long road trip with a small, plastic toy car by placing a heavy lead-acid truck battery atop it. Astrophysicist Dr. Hugh Ross confirms this assessment. He explained:

> At even half the velocity of light, the energy needed to propel an object is 170 million times greater than NASA's fastest spacecraft requires. The energy problem compounds, however, because propellants and engines themselves involve mass. The higher a spacecraft's speed, the more propellant and the bigger the engines it requires. Therefore, the higher the intended speed of the spacecraft, the (exponentially) higher the mass of the craft. An additional mass problem arises, of course, from the need to move the spacecraft's payload (the total weight of the passengers, crew, instruments, and life support supplies). The mass of a craft and its propulsion system rises geometrically relative to the mass of the payload. ... Computer modeling indicates that there is a large cloud of comets, estimated to contain 100 billion comets or more, surrounding the solar system. Such clouds likely surround any star in this galaxy that could possibly harbor planets. Astronomers suspect that the giant molecular clouds scattered throughout the Milky Way galaxy may contain even greater numbers of comets. To protect against damage from space debris, a spacecraft needs some kind of armor. However, armor means more mass, which means more propellant to move the added mass. More propellant means more propellant to move the extra propellant. Thus the problem escalates. ... Exposure to radiation poses yet another serious threat. The faster a craft travels through space, the greater the damage it suffers from radiation. The particles associated with radiation (for example, protons, neutrons, electrons, heavy nuclei, and even photons) cause erosion to the "skin" and components of the craft. Again, the rate of erosion rises with the square of the velocity. However, a slower velocity means more time in space, and that extra time means more radiation exposure for the aliens on board ... any reasonably sized spacecraft transporting intelligent physical beings can travel at velocities no greater than about 1 percent of the velocity of light. At higher velocities the risks from radiation, space debris, leaks,

and wear and tear simply become too great to prevent the extinction of the space travelers before they reach their destination. A spacecraft traveling at 1 percent of the velocity of light (nearly 7 million miles per hour) would need twenty-three thousand years to travel 230 light-years.[176]

***

No logical, scientific grounds exist on which to posit the possibility of aliens travelling to us even from our closest neighbor, much less some other planet in the Milky Way beyond Proxima Centauri, still less from another galaxy. Whoever takes *real* science seriously is compelled to securely file such propositions in the science *fiction* box.

There are many other reasons, however, that we can be scientifically certain we do not await contact with alien civilizations. Our next order of business is to address the one most closely related to the points above.

The Certainty of Radio Contact with Aliens Long Preceding Physical Contact

If aliens existed, one thing would be certain: their presence would be proven—beyond the slightest shred of doubt—through electromagnetic communications ("radio contact") *far* earlier—*millennia* before—there would be any hope of physical contact with these civilizations. A clear demonstration of ET existence would be infinitely easier to obtain by way of these communications than by physical contact. In accordance with this established certainty, "SETI" (The Search for Extraterrestrial Intelligence)—which we will consider in forthcoming sections—has been an official undertaking (even of governments) for many decades, having thus far devoured many millions of dollars of investment pinning all of its hopes in discovering aliens through radio waves.

Understanding why this is the case is straightforward. It is irrelevant whether these hypothetical alien civilizations *intended* to make radio contact with us—or even *wanted* to do so. At the minimum, they *would* have done so, despite themselves, if they had become technologically advanced. There is no use protesting that alien civilizations exist but simply wanted to wait to alert us to their existence until they felt we were prepared for physical contact or they were desirous of it. They would not have *been able* to prevent their existence from becoming known; just as humanity, upon its first radio transmission (in the 1800s), lost the ability to conceal its own existence from hypothetical alien civilizations.

Bear in mind that the emission of electromagnetic radiation is generally omnidirectional—although its focus can be directed, it also usually goes everywhere. When, for example, you use your cell phone, it does not send its signal along one perfectly linear path directly to the closest cell tower. It simply emits its signal everywhere, and so long as there is a tower unobstructed anywhere within your phone's range, that tower is guaranteed to receive the signal by virtue of the laws of physics. If you were to simply extend your hand right now in front of you, then within your own palm would be contained the totality of each cell phone conversation (and broadcast TV station, radio show, etc.) happening within miles of your present location. You may even be encompassing with your hand the entirety of conversations taking place on shortwave frequencies on the opposite side of the world (due to ionosphere reflection or "moonbounce").

Therefore, by the present time, the first radio waves humans transmitted (by Guglielmo Marconi on May 13, 1897) are 740 trillion miles away from earth. In their travels, they have swept no less than 25,000 cubic light years of the Milky Way galaxy.* This volume of space alone includes tens of thousands of stars, and likely hundreds of thousands of planets. Every single one of those planets has now been reached by our radio transmissions. The "response"... is only the sound of crickets (on earth!). There is also evidently little excitement about *your own* cell phone conversations among our planetary neighbors. The conversation you had with your sister about your favorite recipes on your 1990s Nokia phone is now slamming into the Gamma Pavonis star's planets (in the constellation of Pavo, which you can see in the night sky) having already passed innumerable other stars and planets, whose (nonexistent) inhabitants were all evidently equally uninterested!

Consider as well that, long before SETI, only a few decades after Marconi's first broadcast, the radio station WLW of Cincinnati, Ohio started belting out 500kw of transmissions in the year 1934. These unbelievably powerful transmissions have been hurtling through space now for almost a century, likewise showering thousands of solar systems with news from planet earth. A radio tower twice as powerful was built by the U.S. Navy two decades later. The signals it sent out could scarcely be classed undecipherable by alien civilizations. Several years after that, radio towers twice as powerful still (2 million watts) were constructed in Maine to communicate with American submarines. These extremely powerful radio signals must be put in the context of what even an amateur ham operator can do with a cheap radio less than one watt: he can bounce signals off of the moon itself, and communicate with another ham operator on the other side of the globe (ham operators call this "moonbounce" or "EME"). These incredibly powerful radio transmissions that we have been blasting into space for almost a century now—on the order of *millions* of watts—must be compared to what even very basic, inexpensive technology can receive in terms of these same signals: namely, signals in the order of a *femtowatt*. A femtowatt is equal to 1x10^-15 watts. Therefore, the signal

---

* This is half the spherical volume calculated by using 126 light years as the radius; although this is overly conservative, as the radio waves would extend in a far more complete shape than a simple hemisphere.

that the U.S. Navy's transmitter was blasting into space (1 megawatt is 1x10^6 watts) was and is a thousand-billion-billion times stronger than what even we—with extremely basic and inexpensive technology, infinitely inferior to the technology any "interstellar-space-travelling aliens" would have—can decipher.

Now, determining exactly when and where these extremely powerful signals would, in outer space, attenuate to the point of being likely indistinguishable from the "noise" of cosmic background radiation, is a complex matter outside the scope of this book. Assuredly, however, any "ET civilization" like those envisioned by today's Ufologists would have advanced abilities to decipher—and respond to—such signals at great distances. What is even more certain is that wherever technology itself exists, its own radio wave dead-giveaway-signatures are *far* beyond their physical technology in space such that, no matter how fast this technology (i.e., spaceship, probe, etc.) is travelling, it would not reach its destination until millennia after its radio emissions did.

Imagine, if you will, that we ourselves are the "aliens" in question. That is, suppose another civilization exists, many light years away from us, similar to us but technologically lagging behind a few thousand years. Suppose that one day, 300 years from now, we finally master interstellar travel (which will never happen) and decide to make our way to Alpha Centauri or some other "nearby" solar system.

We could not, at that time, decide, *"Wait! We don't want clear knowledge of our existence to precede our actual arrival on other civilizations' planets. We want to surprise them! In fact, we want to toy with them and observe them for several decades first by crashing our ships so that we can watch their governments cover up our existence. So, we'll have to run out quickly and grab all those electromagnetic waves that our civilization has been hurling into space for the last 500 years since the 1800s!"*

Any such a task is *fundamentally* impossible. Whatever has already been emitted at the speed of light (*all electromagnetic waves—visible light, AM, FM, cell phones, Wi-Fi, microwaves, shortwave, etc.—always travel at this speed through space*) can never be stopped. Such a signal will, by definition, always be beyond anything else we might "launch" in the future. It will proceed on its journey until the end of time, irrespective of anything we might do or possibly could do, regardless of what technology we invent in the future.

Similarly, any alien civilizations existing elsewhere in the galaxy or in other galaxies, undergoing technological advancement along with the passage of time, would have been inundating interstellar space with their own radio transmissions (without even wanting to), the very moment they developed this ability. Whenever they developed the ability for interstellar travel and decided to embark upon it, we are left with the certainty that the clear (even if unwilling) announcement of their existence would already be countless trillions of miles ahead of them, and would continually pummel their destination centuries before they themselves would be seen plunging through its atmosphere.[177]

Where, then, are these clear electromagnetic announcements of alien life? Even the most amateur of ham radio operators (not to mention anyone listening to his car radio) should constantly receive them if aliens exist. More significantly—and this leads us into the topic of the following section—the official, multimillion dollar, government-backed "Search for Extraterrestrial Intelligence" (SETI) has scoured every crevice of the galaxy it can reach, looking for such signals. Not *one* intelligently-originated transmission has *ever* been detected. We are left only with "SETI's Great Silence." On this count alone, all arguments in support of supposed alien UFO encounters, abductions, recoveries of "alien corpses," etc.—which suppose that aliens are already physically here—can, should, and must be dismissed.

The Drake Equation, the Fermi "Paradox," and SETI's "Great Silence"

> "Fermi's colleagues were in awe of him for his uncanny ability to see straight to the heart of a physical problem and describe it in simple terms. They called him the Pope because he seemed infallible."[178]

Among the more prevalent of the pseudoscientific hypotheses presented in support of alien belief is an equation conjured up by Frank Drake, in 1961, which has since taken on a life of its own.

By multiplying various factors, which themselves have no strong empirical basis—including the average rate of star formation, the number of planets, the fraction of planets with life, the fraction with life that develop *intelligent* life, etc.—Drake proposed to thereby compute the number of advanced civilizations that exist in the Milky Way galaxy. He proceeded to estimate that the number stands between one thousand and one hundred million. As it happens, the lower bound of his estimate was only off by a mere 999.

Now, Dr. Drake was an astrophysicist and astrobiologist who had dedicated his life to the search for aliens. Suffice it to say he was somewhat biased. He founded "Project Ozma" at Cornell University, which was the first modern attempt to discover aliens using the electromagnetic-wave-based approach that now defines "SETI." He is regarded in today's official SETI literature as "*the Godfather of observational SETI*," the man who "*turned science fiction into credible, respectable science*." Seventy-three years of SETI's continual and zealous effort, however, has only solidified the status of its premises and aspirations as remaining thoroughly *fictional* indeed.

With its massive 85-foot-wide radio telescope, Project Ozma presented Drake with the opportunity to listen for transmissions from those solar systems he thought might contain advanced civilizations. He discovered no signs of intelligent life—except one false alarm, which (reminiscent of Tesla several decades earlier) came from another human being's technology on earth (we should anticipate many other false alarms in the future—including deliberate ones).

It was the year after the founding of Project Ozma—after who knows how many hours spent searching for alien communications and finding none—that Drake created the equation above and delivered its corresponding pseudo revelation of thousands or millions of alien civilizations dwelling in our very own galaxy.

Ironically, the definitive rebuttal to this meticulously calculated "scientific" argument presented by Drake and his colleagues was implicitly given ten years earlier by a renowned Italian American physicist, Enrico Fermi. A Nobel Prize winner and the inventor of the first ever nuclear reactor, Fermi's genius status was unquestioned. He is often regarded as among the greatest scientists of the 20th century. But he dared to ask the obvious question about aliens that few, before him, had presented; namely: "***Where is everybody***?"

In other words, if the planets really are so teeming with life as astronomers claim, then how is it even remotely conceivable that—despite decades of listening to radio communications—we have not heard from a *single* extraterrestrial?

Recall from previous sections that, in 1950, Mars had not yet been proven to be uninhabited. Although the alien belief fervor of 19th century scientists had subsided, it had anything but died. Many scientists were still insisting that the cosmos absolutely *must* be teeming with intelligent aliens. Moreover, the UFO craze was well underway by 1950. Fermi's question, therefore, was an important response to a major cultural phenomenon.

It is a misnomer to call Fermi's question a paradox, for there is nothing paradoxical about it. On the contrary, it is a classic rhetorical question which furtively illustrates its latent conclusion. This "paradox" has been among the most painful thorns in the side of ET promoters for the last century, and consequently it has solicited dozens upon dozens of supposed solutions. None are substantial, much less convincing.

One recent scholarly tome—dedicated to discussing SETI's work *favorably*—was nevertheless honest in phrasing the present contradiction for alien belief:

> If only a tiny fraction of the billions of planets in our galaxy have given rise to civilizations then surely some of those civilizations will be older and more technologically advanced than [ours] ... That is perhaps the conclusion that Fermi reached. They should be here. **At the very least we should see evidence of them or their instrumentality when we look into space. But we don't.** Where is everybody? The question became known as the Fermi paradox and, in its purest form, is perhaps

> not too disturbing. The distances between stars are great and it is reasonable to suppose that faster-than-light travel is impossible even for the most advanced civilization. It is not surprising, then, that we don't see alien spacecraft buzzing round the Solar System. But it's not just that their craft aren't here; as mentioned above, astronomers have observed no signs of extraterrestrial intelligence anywhere. The paradox is not that their spacecraft aren't around when we might expect them to be here; it's that we neither see nor hear **any** traces of them [*emphasis in original*]. David Brin called this "**the Great Silence**". It's this quiescence that's so disturbing. **The paradox has not been blunted since Fermi asked his question or Brin pointed out the deafening silence of the universe. If anything, it has sharpened**... Even if interstellar travel of any description is simply too difficult or too costly, an advanced extraterrestrial civilization could signal its presence ... **And it is not as if we are deaf: in the years since Fermi asked his question our ability to search for electromagnetic signals has steadily improved by many orders of magnitude. The paradox thus remains**. (§17.1. Pages 307-308)

Here an aside is necessary: whoever is wondering why SETI would be described in a positive light even by scholars who recognize its futility need not wonder long. It is now broadly accepted by those scholars who have most seriously studied it—as we will see in Part Four—that the whole ET-belief phenomenon is nothing but a replacement for traditional religion. As contemporary secularists also feel the need for faith, they find that "faith" in their blind hope in aliens.

Even as it is stated above, the dilemmas that the facts present for alien belief are simply insurmountable. But that presentation still overlooks what we considered in the preceding section. It is not merely a matter of no alien civilizations attempting to contact us. No technologically advanced civilization would be capable of preventing its transmissions from escaping into space.

Several decades after Marconi's unintentional sending of unmistakably ordered and intelligently-originated EM waves into outer space, SETI began doing so *intentionally*—with very powerful signals, carrying information so clear that no alien civilization could fail to recognize them as deriving from another civilization, and carefully directed at those areas of the galaxy thought most likely to harbor intelligent life. Thus, they ensured a still higher likelihood of any alien civilizations within their reach receiving our communications. The crickets remain.

Granted, even in mostly empty interstellar space, the strength of any EM signal will still decrease in proportion to the square of the distance travelled. But an advanced alien civilization on *any one* of the thousands of solar systems our own EM has now showered should still have no problem detecting our signal by sweeping the skies for signs of ordered transmissions (just as, here on earth, SETI has been doing for many decades) as they tune their own EM receivers to various frequencies. Crickets, crickets, and more crickets.

These "crickets" present a clear conclusion to anyone interested in the genuinely scientifically motivated conclusion about extraterrestrial intelligence: *it does not exist.* One such scholar interested in the truth of the matter—the British physicist—Dr. Stephen Webb, confessed that he very much "wanted" aliens to exist. He dedicated a large tome, which the academic publisher Springer published in 2002, to the task of rigorously examining each one of the dozens of "solutions" to the Fermi Paradox that had been proposed in support of aliens. He found none of them to be convincing. At the end of his lengthy scientific analysis, he presents the following conclusion:

> **The only resolution of the Fermi paradox that makes sense to me—is that we are alone** ... the Fermi paradox provides a shock that forces us to examine the widespread notion that the vast number of planets in existence is sufficient to guarantee the existence of extraterrestrial intelligent life. In fact, we need not be too surprised. **The Drake equation is a product of several terms. If one of those terms is zero, then the product of the Drake equation will be zero**; if several of the terms are small, then the product of the Drake equation will be very small. We will be alone. If one factor in the Drake equation is close to zero, then we can reasonably identify that factor as being the solution to the Fermi paradox ... I suspect there is a combination of factors—a product of various solutions we have discussed in this book—**resulting in the uniqueness of mankind ... [of habitable planets,] only Earth remains. We are alone ... only one planet—Earth—has intelligent life-forms**.[179]

To no one's surprise, Dr. Webb's sound analysis and correct conclusion did not put SETI to rest. The exercise in futility continued, and along with it arose dozens of additional supposed solutions to the Fermi Paradox. Therefore, over a decade later (in 2015), Webb published another book dedicated to the same theme; this time, not addressing fifty solutions, but rather the "seventy-five" solutions now given to the paradox. One might wonder: did Dr. Webb—upon consulting (as he did), in the intervening thirteen years, many more scientists and other thinkers, reading vastly more scholarly literature, and learning about the constant deluge of new discoveries in astronomy—change his mind? Did he finally realize that aliens are likely after all?

No. The additional "solutions" to the Fermi Paradox only solidified his conclusion that human beings are the universe's only rational inhabitants. He closed that more recent book by sharing that while most of his friends assert aliens must exist, because—as he relayed their words—"*...space is big. Really big... surely we can't be the only intelligent species in such a large universe,*" and most of his physical-scientist friends assert the same thing, albeit filled with more specific claims related to various large numbers, it is only his biologist friends who realize that these large numbers (including even the most generous estimates for the number of planets in the universe) are actually laughably tiny when compared to the chances of intelligent life emerging. He reports:

> My own view? Well, I side with my biologist friends. **The debate about extraterrestrial intelligence contains just one gleaming, hard fact: we haven't been visited by [aliens] nor have we heard from them.** ... Those who would deny this fact of course have a ready solution to the Fermi paradox (and presumably stopped reading this book after the first few pages). The job for the rest of us is to interpret this lone fact.

Dr. Webb's final point, though subtle, is nevertheless direct: whoever believes in aliens does so not based on any scientific *facts*—for the only relevant *fact* we have rules out aliens—but only based on ideology, and a fundamentally (pseudo)religious one at that.

No Anti-Gravity: Incontrovertible Laws of the Universe Rule Out UFO Claims

For the last several decades, whenever a UFO sighting is reported, the first response is the same, and even the Ufologists concede that this question deserves serious consideration: "*Assuming this is not an optical illusion, sensor anomaly, atmospheric phenomena, etc.—how can we nevertheless be sure this isn't simply an advanced government prototype, or perhaps a technology built by a foreign government such as Russia or China?*"

Similarly, the first response to that question which the Ufologists usually provide is the same: "*What we have observed clearly violates the laws of physics as we know them: it can hover with no propulsion system, and it can make perfect right-angle turns at enormous velocities. There is absolutely no way any human technology could achieve these feats.*" We have already addressed the intrinsically contradictory nature of the first clause in this chapter's opening section. Due to the popularity of Ufologists' insistence that these UFOs violate both the Law of Gravity and the Law of Conservation of Momentum, we should devote specific attention to these scientific truths. First, we will focus on gravity.

Gravity is perhaps the most fundamental force of the universe. It is among the Four Fundamental Forces (along with electromagnetism and the strong and weak nuclear force), which together account for all non-supernatural phenomena that derive from the activity of forces. Gravity, therefore, cannot be suspended, by any technology, no matter how advanced—there is no such thing as an "anti-gravity" technology. Such a technology never has existed and never will exist—anywhere in the universe. Before explaining why this is so, however, we should address the first question many will have: "*Okay... but we **do** see things violating it! What am I supposed to do, then? Reject what my eyes tell me?*"

The answer is: *absolutely not*!

The consensus of the senses, over a sufficiently protracted period of time to allow for certainty to arise (*confirmed by the "common sense" fully grasping what is observed*)—is a situation carrying a degree of certainty intrinsically superior to any Law of Science. This is true from even the most basic logical standpoint which no scientist has any hope of refuting. Every Law of Science is, itself, merely a product of the senses observing some phenomenon (*it matters not what technology is employed: the senses are needed to decipher what the technology tells us*) and eventually arriving at the point where it can be generalized into the formal laws (which are definitions of patterns) that we have all known since high school. Therefore, our definitions of the Laws of Science are all (without exception) *effects* of the human senses. Yet, no effect is greater than its cause—this is a first principle of logical thought which no honest man is even tempted to doubt. God Himself cannot violate it (for He is Truth, and He cannot contradict Himself—cf. Hebrews 6:18, 2 Timothy 2:13, etc.).

Accordingly, the point is that if and when one is absolutely certain he has observed something to have transpired that violates the Law of Gravity—and has carefully ruled out all explanations to the contrary—he is forced to conclude that what he has observed is not natural in origin at all. A Christian should consider that Jesus walked on the water (cf. Matthew 14:25) to demonstrate His Divinity, not to compel us to speculate whether He simply had some anti-gravity piece of technology at His disposal.

If a UFO is seen to violate the Law of Gravity (or the Law of Conservation of Momentum, etc.), then this sighting is nothing but a diabolical manifestation, for it would certainly not be of God. This conclusion is certain because all other potential explanations have been ruled out, and the process of elimination always holds true. But examining this fact in more detail brings us outside of the scope of scientific analysis, so we will save it for later chapters. Presently, we must consider more carefully just why gravity is never violated and can never be violated.*

---

* Another worthwhile consideration is that for gravity to be simply suspended would be just as absurd as the notion of a monopolar permanent magnet. As the laws of physics indicate, there is not and cannot ever be a monopolar permanent magnet; such a thing would be contrary to the nature of magnetism. Permanent magnets always come with two poles—a north and a south, if you will—and the "magnetic field lines" (ways we conceptualize the force exerted by magnets) proceed from one pole to the other. It is the nature of a magnetic field line to go from one pole to the other of the same magnet. Now, gravity is at least as fundamental a force of the universe as magnetism, and the nature of this force is to proceed linearly to infinity. It does not make any logical or scientific sense to posit it being "blocked or suspended," since there is nowhere to re-route these field lines. Moreover they are, of course, not composed of matter or actual energy, and thus "blocking" them in the physical sense of presenting a physical obstruction is nonsensical. Remember that magnetic field lines proceed from one pole to the other, if a substance is placed in the magnetic field that allows these

***

Even light itself cannot escape gravity, as Einstein showed. *Every* corporeal reality is subject to it. To argue that alien crafts are now among us which can overcome the law of gravity is to argue, without realizing it, for precisely the thesis I present in this book: *they are demons in disguise.* Now, a careful Ufologist might not argue that gravity has been suspended, blocked, or overcome, but merely that it is being *countered* in a manner so mysterious that we cannot observe it. Just as human craft counter gravity through jet thrusters, lift on airplane wings or helicopter blades, etc., so these alien-piloted craft overcome gravity in some other way.

To scrutinize this claim, we must understand that any physical object will always be pulled toward earth. It can only remain aloft by resisting that pull through exerting a force equal and opposite to its own weight. A helicopter, drone, hummingbird, insect, etc., achieves this by its extremely rapidly rotating blades or flapping wings pushing air downwards (just as any fan does) with enough momentum to overcome its own weight. This is clearly discernible by both sound and by observing the effects of air rushing beneath the object. The same goes for rocket propulsion: this is achieved not through pushing off air, but rather by propelling its own fuel opposite the direction of acceleration, or at least opposite the pull of gravity so as to allow hovering. This means of propulsion is even more obvious to observe; indeed, it is impossible to hide, as anyone who has watched a rocket launch knows. An airplane (or a large gliding bird), on the other hand, counters gravity through "lift"; the angle of its wings, combined with a high velocity, causes these wings to bounce air downward, which itself is accomplished with such great force once the plane is moving forward rapidly enough that it eventually (at the point of takeoff, to be precise) is no longer held against the ground by gravity. The final way of "overcoming" gravity is through buoyancy; ensuring that the craft itself is lighter than air, such as with a blimp, a hot air balloon, or a seed floating in the wind. This means, however, cannot account for accelerations and turns, therefore some additional propulsion method (i.e., those listed above) must be included as well. Any aerial object that remains aloft through buoyancy is intrinsically slow and clumsy. It is, moreover, quite obvious when buoyancy is impossible to keep some object afloat midair. That method can only work when the weight of the air displaced by the object's volume is so great as to match the weight of the object itself, therefore this cannot account for the flight of any object with any substantial degree of density. One need only consider how massive a hot air balloon must be to lift only a few people.

---

lines to proceed more simply (i.e., "follow the path of least resistance," as inanimate things always do) on a different path, then that is exactly what the magnetic field lines will do. The field lines exerted by gravity, however, are absolutely linear and unblockable.

Recognizing that none of these methods of countering gravity could account for what is reported in UFO sightings, Ufologists generally stick with their insistence that alien technology is simply so incomprehensibly advanced that we have no right at all to even think scientifically about what is observed. Thus, they again illustrate how pseudoreligious and ideological—not scientific—the movement itself is.

Yet, there are some who proffer a possible explanation. They usually posit some manner of ion-thrusters or other means of esoteric propulsion which operate not on the basis of pushing air opposite the pull of gravity, or any sort of chemical propellant, but rather by beaming minuscule particles (or even massive amounts of electromagnetic waves in a laser configuration) in the necessary direction.

That propulsion method, however, would be even easier to detect by its inescapably overwhelming effects. Anything beneath a UFO using such means of propulsion would be instantaneously irradiated into oblivion. Solid rock itself would be reduced to lava and promptly vaporized. The most realistic of these technologies—ion thrusters—have been in development here on earth for several decades, and the most powerful among them can scarcely exert enough force for you to feel it, even if it were adjacent to your hand and pointed directly at it. Even that minuscule amount of ion flow, however, has proven caustic enough to erode holes through metal objects that were near the ejection of these ions. If, therefore, we are referring to an ion thruster with enough power to lift an entire spacecraft off the ground—much less accelerate it at great speeds—then we are dealing with a propulsion engine that would instantaneously dig extremely deep holes in the earth directly underneath it, wherever it travels, and vaporize any and all life therein (perhaps also on the opposite side of the planet). Needless to say, no such thing has ever happened, notwithstanding millions of reported "UFO sightings."

All that has been said thus far can be summarized simply: gravity cannot be imperceptibly overcome. Whoever claims to have observed a large, heavy craft, silently hovering about in the air and quickly accelerating from one place to the next, has only observed a physical impossibility. Here we have again arrived at the essential question: how can any craft simply not be subject to the pull of gravity? There is one and only one way: *if it has no mass at all*. In other words, if it *isn't corporeal*. This brings us right back to what we noted above: such a phenomena, if observed, is beyond-natural. To be precise, it is *preter*natural. It is, as we will see in Part Four, *diabolical*.

As there is yet another theory posited to explain the gravity-defying machinations of UFOs—one based on magnetism—let us now defer to the teachings of the physicist quoted earlier, Dr. Rothman. He rightly observed:

> [Unlike with gravity,] electrical shielding is possible because there are

> two kinds of electrical charges: positive and negative. By contrast, there is only one kind of mass. Therefore **gravity, an interaction between masses, has only one form: a universal attraction.** As a result, there is no way of arranging masses so that they do anything but attract each other with the gravitational force. **They can't produce a gravitational shield or a repulsive gravitational force. Here we see a peculiar—but common—situation: a concept invented as sheer fantasy by a science fiction writer taking on a life of its own.** ... No one will ever build a flying vehicle that is capable of hovering high in the air while supported by nothing but magnetic fields. **This applies to inhabitants of other planets as well.** ... **it is not possible for a vehicle to hover, speed up, or change direction solely by means of its own magnetic field. The proof of this lies in the fundamental principle of physics that nothing happens except through interactions between pairs of objects.** A space vehicle may generate a powerful magnetic field, but in the absence of another magnetic field to push against, it can neither move nor support itself in midair. The earth possesses a magnetic field, but it is weak—about one percent of that generated by a compass needle. For a UFO to be levitated by reacting against the earth's magnetic field, its own field would have to be so enormously strong that it could be detected by any magnetometer in the world. Similarly, it does not help to talk about the UFO's magnetic field reacting with the iron in the earth's core, since interactions between a magnet and a bare piece of iron are always in the form of an attraction. And finally, as the magnetic UFO traveled about the earth, it would induce electric currents in every power line within sight, blowing out circuit breakers and in general wreaking havoc. It would not go unnoticed. ... This discussion exemplifies an important general principle. A given idea—such as levitation of a UFO by a magnetic field—may sound plausible at first, but when numbers are put into the known equations, the results can be disappointing. **In fact, there is no force in nature that can keep any kind of vehicle levitated and motionless at a high altitude (apart from helicopters, rockets, and satellites in synchronous orbits).** ... **No one will ever build an antigravity machine, simply because no gravitational repulsion exists**. ... **no matter how you arrange particles of matter, the gravitational force between them will always be an attraction. Therefore, there is no way to produce a gravitational shield or a machine that will nullify or reverse the effects of gravity**... **Antigravity is a concept originated in fiction and exists nowhere else**.[180]

The notion of technologically-mediated anti-gravity always has been and always will be pure fiction. Assertions to the contrary scarcely deserve the label of pseudoscience. Yet such assertions are inseparable from modern UFO-inspired alien belief.

Another common misunderstanding about the nature of gravity holds that astronauts in space are in "zero gravity." Those who believe this are under the impression that astronauts who launch into space meet a mysterious threshold somewhere in the stratosphere which, when crossed, causes the cessation of the pull of gravity. This popular fallacy has, in turn, generated a common view of gravity itself that fails to understand how universal, absolute, far-reaching, and insurmountable it is. Nothing could be further from the truth than the "zero gravity in space" notion. The reality is that even astronauts in orbit (for example, in the International Space Station) are subject to almost the same amount of gravitational pull from the earth as we are (they only *experience weightlessness* because they are in continual freefall).*

***

Almost as common as the claims of alien spacecraft violating the law of gravity are the claims of these same ships violating the Law of Conservation of Momentum by making perfect right hand turns at enormous speeds. If ever such a phenomenon truly is observed, it is yet another proof that what is transpiring is not merely *unhuman*, but entirely *unnatural* (*preter*natural).

---

* The pull exerted on any object whatsoever by earth's mass can be calculated easily using a formula many will recall from high school: the Gravitational Force = The Gravitational Constant times the product of the masses of the two objects in question, divided by the square of the distance between their centers. Right now, you are about 4,000 miles from the center of the earth. The seven people who are right now aboard the International Space Station are only an additional 254 miles further from that same point. As we can easily glean from the equation above, earth's pull of gravity on them is almost the same as its pull of gravity to which you are subject! Of course, they *experience* weightlessness—but this *feeling* has nothing to do with gravity being inapplicable. The weightlessness of an astronaut is due entirely to the fact that he is in continual freefall, which is what it means to be in orbit. The velocity of an orbiting shuttle is so great in the tangential direction that, instead of falling directly back to earth, such shuttles simply continually fall "around" the earth. Therefore, astronauts feel the same thing you might feel on a rollercoaster dropping rapidly. Unfortunately, this error that gravity simply "stops" at some point in the stratosphere is not restricted to confused amateurs. National Geographic magazine, for example, claims that in the earth's upper atmosphere, gravity "is so small" (education.nationalgeographic.org/resource/atmosphere)—when, in fact, it is much closer to the gravity at earth's surface than to the gravity in deep space. Indeed, whoever wishes to escape earth's gravity might have more luck going deeper than higher. At the very center of the earth, one would effectively experience zero gravity, since its pull would be equal and opposite in all directions.

The Physical Impossibility of Reported UFO Maneuvers

> "An object in motion stays in motion with the same speed and direction unless acted upon by a force. The rate of change of momentum of an object is equal to the force applied to that object. For every action there is an opposite and equal reaction."
> —Cf. Sir Isaac Newton

Above, we see (one way of phrasing) Isaac Newton's famous Laws of Motion. The reality, however, is that these truths (especially the first and third) were known long before Newton's day—modern claims that Newton overthrew Aristotelian thought on this topic are, at best, greatly exaggerated—for they are essentially little more than unavoidable results of a common-sense observation of nature.

Unfortunately, contemporary Ufologists—like dilettante self-proclaimed experts in "quantum physics," (two greatly overlapping categories)—regard these Laws as rather blasé *"in light of advancements in 20th century science that overthrew Newton."* Such puerile statements as those, though pervasive, remind serious thinkers that we are not dealing with a scientific inquiry here, but a fiction-driven myth desperate to find some basis to pretend its fantasies are real and scientific (i.e., not preternatural).

Far from overthrowing Newton's Laws, even the most advanced quantum particle physics research in existence today often presuppose their validity (as we saw above). Newton's Laws have not been—and never will be—"overthrown." In some extremely rare cases they may need to be calibrated with considerations derived from relativity or quantum physics (*though exactly how, why, and when, remains hotly debated—unlike Newton's Laws themselves, which remain fixed*), but these calibrations have no effect on the phenomenon presently in question: namely, what feats could *possibly* be accomplished by the types of physical craft described in relation to "UFO sightings?"

One thing we can be certain of is that no craft could be capable of a perfect* (or near perfect) right angle turn at an extremely high velocity, or

---

* Strictly speaking, it is not possible for anything to make a perfect right angle turn or an instantaneous change of motion from one direction to its opposite at any speed. However, when a small enough object is being considered, of uniform constitution and high rigidity, acted upon by forces of great magnitude, then what we observe could essentially appear to display such a phenomenon. A marble, for example, might appear to instantaneously switch from moving downward to moving upward when bounced on a hard table. Not only, however, is this appearance very far from the truth (just watch an ultra-slow-motion video of such events to see for yourself), it is also entirely absent from large objects and higher speeds. In fact, a perfect right angle turn—

a sudden change of velocity from one direction to the opposite direction. As anyone who has driven a car knows, turning at any significant speed brings an equally significant force into play. This is because a turn involves an acceleration, which—as we see from Newton's Laws—involves a proportionally large force.

Let us consider a case quantitatively. Similar claims are ubiquitous among UFO enthusiasts, but one author recounted some of the more famous and official accounts as follows:

> Like American observations, the Soviet Air Force had many instances in which **UFOs were observed hovering**, then departing at great speed. Some of these reports estimated the craft to be ...more than 600 feet [in diameter] with speeds ranging from hovering to triple the capability of modern fighters, yet then stopping again **instantaneously**. Other reports indicated that the UFOs displayed "**startling maneuverability," yet made no sound**. An investigation claimed that the UFO observed "was **completely devoid of inertia. In other words, they had somehow 'come to terms' with gravity** ... **Approaching the UFO, [one fighter pilot] reported the size of the target ..."the proportions of a flying aircraft carrier**." ...then suddenly the UFO took off at amazing speed. [He] estimated that it went from **stationary to Mach 10 almost instantaneously**.[181]

When considering the "flying aircraft carrier" above which "almost instantaneously" accelerated from stationary to Mach 10 (7,672 miles per hour), we must next decide what period of time we are referring to when describ-

---

or, for that matter, any instantaneous change in either linear velocity or angular velocity—would itself require the application of an infinite force. This consequence is evident from Newton's Second Law: F=m*a. The "a" in this equation stands for acceleration, therefore we can see that whenever that quantity rises, the "F" (Force) needed to cause that acceleration rises in proportion. Even if the simple marble you bounce on a table truly instantaneously changed directions in the act of bouncing, this too would cause an infinite force to arise, thus obliterating the earth. If, on the other hand, a massive spacecraft (a UFO) undertook a maneuver anywhere close to even appearing to instantaneously accelerate or change directions would—by virtue of the immutable laws of physics—entail such an application of force that the entire continent on which it took place would be immediately devastated by unprecedented earthquakes. Assuming, therefore, that you are not now experiencing—and have not ever experienced—a magnitude 10.0 earthquake ravaging your surroundings, you can be equally certain that no large spacecraft have ever made perfect right angle turns at high velocities on your continent, or borderline-instantaneously accelerated to a high speed. Yet, you can be assured that, wherever you live, many claims have been made stating UFOs have done precisely that near you. Here again, we see another proof that such claims—when honestly describing something a witness truly saw—pertain not to natural phenomena, but preternatural phenomena.

ing the fruition of an event (in this case, an acceleration) that appears instantaneous—and 10 milliseconds emerges as the most appropriate number.*

This leaves us to calculate how much force needs to be exerted during these 10 milliseconds and how much energy must be expended in the process. Using an aircraft carrier as our point of departure—since that is how the pilot above described the UFO in question—we are dealing with a craft weighing about 100 million kilograms. Accelerating such an object to Mach 10 would require an amount of energy (calculated by the equation, 1/2 * Mass * Velocity squared) in the order of 6 x 10^14 Joules, or about 167,000 megawatt hours. This is over a hundred times as much energy as is consumed by the entire city of New York over the course of a day, and about ten times the amount of energy released by the atomic bomb dropped on Hiroshima. If such an extraordinary amount of energy was generated by *any craft whatsoever*—regardless of what hypothetical advanced alien technology could possibly be used to generate it—such an event would be overwhelmingly obvious (not to mention, destructive) to anyone within a massive radius. Just imagine ten Hiroshima's all at once—merely to enable a single acceleration of the "UFO" in question.

Nevertheless, this consideration scarcely begins to capture the ludicrousness of the situation and the certainty one can have that no such event ever has happened or ever will happen—and that, therefore, if it appears to, it is nothing but a demonic deception (which, as we will see in Part Four, they are fully capable of). For we are not merely dealing with an energy equivalent to ten atomic bombs. We are dealing with that amount of energy required simply to cause a *single maneuver* of the UFO in question

---

* The act of snapping your fingers, for example, is a motion that transpires at around the threshold of visual perception, and it too appears "almost instantaneous." The motion of the snapping takes about 7 milliseconds to complete. Another way of estimating the duration of an event that appears almost instantaneous is to consider the "frame rate" of human vision. Now, this is a misnomer, since the human eye is not a digital device, and it does not function like a camera that simply mashes together several dozen still images a second to produce an apparent motion—nevertheless, an analogy can be drawn based upon what types of motion humans can generally decipher, and the *analogous* frame rate of human vision is usually pinned at about 60 frames per second. This is why high-quality video aims for exactly this frame rate (60fps); it is the "sweet spot" at which the human eye's abilities are generally maxed-out by what is displayed before them. Higher frame rates, such as 120fps, exist, but they do not produce a noticeably superior experience for most people. Nevertheless, some insist it is better, therefore we can consider the duration of a single frame of both rates as providing the boundaries of our consideration. A single 60fps frame is about 17 milliseconds whereas a single 120fps frame is about 8 milliseconds. Note, however, that we are dealing here with fighter pilots, who are selected in part based upon the accuracy of their visual perception, and such pilots are known, in rigorous training, to be able to detect an event lasting only 1/250th of a second—i.e., 4 milliseconds long. Considering all of these criteria, it is fair to say that an acceleration taking 10 milliseconds to complete would appear "almost instantaneous."

(*each* acceleration—and deceleration, *and each turn*—would require similar emissions of this unthinkable energy quantity). We are, moreover, dealing with that massive amount of energy exerted over the course of a mere 10 milliseconds. Calculating the power and force requirements for such a feat is our next task.

Power is simply energy divided by time. Releasing the amount of energy at play (6x10^14 Joules) over the course of 10 milliseconds entails a power consumption of 6x10^16 watts (sixty thousand trillion watts). This amount of power is not merely 100 times what is consumed by New York City (as discussed earlier); rather, it is over *ten million times* as much. It is also more than 21,000 times as much power as is consumed by *the entire world*—enough power to supply a world of 90 trillion inhabitants at current usage. And the Ufologists insist that crafts constantly exerting this amount of power are incessantly buzzing our skies. If even a fraction of their claims were true, the mere heat generated by these accelerations and decelerations would long ago have boiled off all our oceans and cooked the entire surface of the planet. Note that, to decelerate an object, one must convert all that object's kinetic energy into thermal energy dispersed into the surrounding environment. This is why brake pads become so hot, it is why rockets burn up on re-entering the atmosphere, and it is why we see "shooting stars" (which are meteorites igniting due to their friction with earth's atmosphere). Therefore, while the accelerations of these UFOs would impart astounding amounts of heat to the environment (even the most advanced theoretically possible means of propulsion would lose at least 10% of their energy to heat—your own car likely loses about 70% of its energy to heat when accelerating), the decelerations would—by definition—impart *all* of their energy, as heat, into the surrounding environment.

Yet, we still have not finished comprehending the absurdity of these UFO claims. For we also must consider the *force* required by these accelerations—namely, 6x10^16 Newtons thereof. This amount of force, even if applied perfectly evenly over the entire surface area of an aircraft-carrier-sized craft (about 24,000 square meters) would generate a pressure of 2.5 trillion pascals. (*Note that the actual pressure generated would be much higher, as the craft's propulsion system would itself only comprise one part of its surface.*) No material exists that can withstand so much as a fraction of that amount of pressure—even if the UFO in question were nothing but a solid block of the universe's strongest substance. Such pressures would immediately disintegrate even the strongest theoretically possible material object, and would likewise immediately liquify any pilot inside the craft, regardless of its own makeup or its own supposed "advanced stage of evolution."

There are many other ways we can demonstrate that the phenomena reported as supposedly transpiring along with UFO sightings are *absolutely impossible*, in the strongest sense of that term one could muster. It is, therefore, beyond doubt that such phenomena, if and when they are truly observed, are diabolical in origin. It makes no difference what theoretical alien technologies are posited; it is the laws of science, which undergird all technologies and all possible technologies, that render the definitive verdict.

***

Another frequent claim made among Ufologists is the notion that these craft must be piloted by super-advanced aliens because their technology is even capable of "reading our minds." This, too, is an outlandish notion that can be refuted both scientifically and theologically. For the sake of space, however, we will exclude that analysis from the present text. It may be found as a supplementary chapter posted freely at www.DSDOConnor.com/OMBHI.

Wormholes and Other Nonsense: The Impossibility of Teleportation or "Warp Drives"

> "Science fiction goes one step beyond technobabble. Here one begins with scientifically accepted fact and theory and then extrapolates new scientific-appearing fictions that have no bases in reality. ... writers may invent wormholes that serve as rapid long-distance transit portals." Dr. Jonathan Smith[182]

Some ET promoters realize—perhaps in accordance with various demonstrations shown in the sections above—that there is no use pretending aliens might be now visiting us by way of craft which have simply traversed the vast distances separating us from even the closest of exoplanets. Of this group, some give up entirely and concede that their entire thesis was and is fallacious. Others simply shift the goalposts by claiming that, conveniently, the vast expanses of space need not be traversed at all.

The explanation they provide is always the same: "*we now know that the very fabric of spacetime can be folded. Sure, it's inconceivable that aliens could actually travel to us from other stars in the traditional fashion, much less from other galaxies. But they can simply fold space! They can travel through a wormhole in their own solar system, and exit another wormhole near our own, thus teleporting past billions of light years instantaneously. We know this is possible thanks to relativity and quantum mechanics.*" (Others make the same basic claim, but conjure up even sillier notions related to "warp drive," "Krasnikov tubes," "Tachyons," etc. All, however, are refuted by the same scientific considerations.)

Although we have been, for several chapters, dealing with claims that traffic entirely in pseudoscience masquerading as real science, we have now arrived at an entirely new level of crazy. In reality, nothing resembling a "folding of spacetime" through a "wormhole" to enable a craft's "teleportation" has ever been convincingly theorized, much less has anything like these phenomena been empirically verified to stand within the scope of reality. The fact that, despite the resolutely anti-scientific nature of these claims, many Ufologists are willing to defer to them as a justification for their views is yet another testimony to the true nature of their persuasion.

First, a common misconception must be addressed: wormholes are *not* a component of Einstein's Theory of Relativity. Although some writers claim that proposing wormholes is "consistent" with Albert's famous theory, this says nothing. Flying cows and planets made of cheese are also consistent with that theory. Therefore, we must be sure to dismiss any claims that wormholes follow from Relativity. They do not.

What, however, *is* a wormhole? A "wormhole" is a fictional proposition wherein two black holes existing at far distant parts of the universe may be "connected" such that they are actually two end points of a single bridge. For no apparent reason—and reminiscent of the convenient irrationality of Pagan myths—this bridge "folds" a fictional entity they call "the fabric of spacetime itself" such that its endpoints (from the perspective of the bridge) are very close together, enabling even relatively slow (i.e., non-Einsteinian-relativity-contradicting) travel along this bridge to cause the spaceship to jump to another part of the universe entirely. Finally—as the fable continues—these "wormholes" could also be constructed such that one black-hole-endpoint of the wormhole is located close enough to our own planet to enable aliens to visit us from distant parts of our galaxy or other galaxies.

Various wormhole-travel theories have been presented, all resulting in insurmountable contradictions. One such theory classes one of the black holes in a wormhole to actually be a "white hole" (basically the time-reversed opposite of a black hole, for it emits, instead of absorbs, matter and energy). On this theory (and others), the astrophysicist Dr. Jason Lisle explains:

> Such a wormhole would not be traversable, much to the disappointment of sci-fi fans. Any object entering the black hole must eventually intersect the singularity. And no object can enter the event horizon of a white hole. So no journey from one end of the wormhole to the other would be possible. ...it [moreover would] require the black hole / white hole pair to have existed forever in the past and forever in the future. **It is [merely] a fun mathematical construct**. But since time has a beginning, this solution is **disallowed in the real universe.** Other types of wormholes have been proposed... However, **in all cases they are apparently unstable, collapsing before any particle could make use of the short cut. ... wormholes do not exist in the real universe. Physicists and mathematicians may enjoy considering these interesting solutions to Einstein's field equations. But the real universe must obey not only the rules of general relativity, but other physical laws as well, such as thermodynamics...**[183]

It is astounding how many gallons of ink have been spilt writing elaborate works of fiction on "wormholes"—under the guise of real science—without even considering the most basic logical corollaries to these theories; corollaries which immediately dispute wormhole theory. For example, as we will see in a later chapter, there is absolutely no such thing as time travel, and this is obvious not only from scientific principles but from bedrock logical truths.* Any proposition that would count among its corollaries the possibility of time travel is itself immediately disputed by a *reductio ad absurdum*. Wormholes, however, *would* enable not only teleportation but also time travel. One could enter a wormhole, exit its other end at an earlier time, then proceed to prevent himself from entering the wormhole in the first place. So, did he enter the wormhole or not? Obviously, there is no solution to this situation. It is a logical contradiction just as futile as positing a square circle; whatever scenario could result in such a situation must itself be simply dismissed as intrinsically preposterous. † (This does not prevent science fiction from also regularly trafficking in the various time travel paradoxes; another testimony to how much the genre has become a vehicle of deception.)

Let us, however, play along with wormhole fiction for a moment and pretend that they can exist, and can possibly enable teleportation of spacecraft and the pilots of those craft. Even under this scenario—counterfactual for a multitude of reasons—the wormhole proposition cannot possibly allow for aliens on earth.

First, if one of the wormhole-endpoints were close enough to planet earth to allow aliens to reasonably travel here, then that black hole itself would destroy our planet, not to mention our solar system. This has not happened, so there are no such wormholes. Second, we already know that (if such a thing exists), the closest black hole to earth is at least 1,500 light years away; the "Unicorn" black hole. If any black holes were closer, astronomers would be aware of their existence. No craft will ever reach us from such a great distance (see preceding sections). As such, we cannot allow for the arrival of aliens on earth by way of any black holes that actu-

---

* It should also be noted that even orthodox Catholic theology holds that God Himself *cannot* change the past, as Aquinas noted in the Summa Theologica (cf. Part I, Q25, A4). Whoever would hypothesize that a mere technology could possibly exist that is capable of this, therefore, is essentially entertaining implicit blasphemy (ascribing to men, or "aliens," powers that exceed those of God)—albeit unintentionally.

† All of this is not to mention that the entire notion of a "wormhole" is built upon the existence of black holes. At least one contemporary renowned physicist, however, Dr. George Chapline—who is more than qualified to scrutinize the matter—declared bluntly: "It's a near certainty that black holes don't exist." (*Nature* (March 31, 2005.) "Black holes 'do not exist'" Philip Ball.) We will not explore the potential nonexistence of black holes in detail here, but this possibility should be noted. While the considerations above render wormhole theory impossible, the tenuous nature of black hole theory independently constitutes a weak point in wormhole theory.

ally exist. Third, if a wormhole were to be "constructed" in sufficient proximity to earth to enable aliens to travel here, then the proximate wormhole-endpoint-black-hole itself would, of course, need to be constructed by aliens who were themselves already here. Thus, the wormhole "solution" to aliens-on-earth is immediately self-defeating. One must presuppose their proximity to earth in order to explain how they could attain proximity to earth.

In a word: there are no wormholes through which even simple information or elementary particles—much less physical craft or alien beings—could travel, and we can be certain that *there never will be* any such wormholes or other constructs to enable teleportation or otherwise faster-than-light travel.

***

What, then, have we seen thus far? Not only that the true Faith rules out aliens a hundred times over (notwithstanding the—perhaps at times even well-meaning but misguided—claims of some Enlightenment-era theologians). We have also seen that all non-debunkable UFO sightings have proven themselves to be nothing but diabolical. We have seen that SETI's "Great Silence" disproves aliens. We have seen that, even if aliens did exist, we would have no hope of meeting them, irrespective of what interstellar or intergalactic means of transportation are theorized. Considering the whole ET-phenomenon directly, therefore, leads only to repeated refutations.

Millions of "UFO Sightings" and "Alien Encounters": Zero Evidence Retained

> "The simple fact is that no one has ever found a single artifact, or any other convincing evidence for such alien visits."
> —David Morrison. NASA Astrobiology Institute Senior Scientist.[184]

Ufologists are keenly aware that one of the weakest elements of their thesis is the total lack of any recovery of actual material from these alien-piloted UFOs they claim have densely populated our skies for 75 years while frequently crashing.

Of course, those same decades have witnessed a steady stream of claims, from various authors and "whistleblowers," that ET-originated material *is* in the possession of certain individuals (conveniently unnamed "for their safety"), but not one of these claims has withstood even basic scrutiny. These claims will doubtless increase, and if honest analysis is permitted to be applied to them (*though once the government's official narrative changes to openly claiming aliens are indeed among us, such scrutiny will not be permitted*), they too will be revealed as lacking evidence.

Indeed, this one thing—this one type of evidence which would grant some modicum of credibility to belief that aliens (and not merely demons assuming new forms) are among us—is something not just rare, but *utterly nonexistent*. As author Abraham Varghese pointed out:

> ... one of many significant differences between Marian apparitions and reports of UFO sightings and alien abductions is the total lack of "public" evidence for the "alien" claims. No less a proponent of the search for extraterrestrial intelligence than the late Carl Sagan wrote, "*Where is the physical evidence? Some abductees allege that aliens stole fetuses from their wombs. This is something that would surely cause a stir among gynecologists, midwives, obstetrical nurses, especially in an age of heightened feminist awareness. But not a single medical record has been produced substantiating such claims. Some abductees say that tiny metallic implants were inserted into their bodies—high up their nostrils, for example. But no such implants have been confirmed by physicists or chemists as being of unearthly manufacture. No abductee has filched a page from the captain's logbook or a strange examining instrument, or taken an authentic photograph of the interior of the ship, or comeback with detailed scientific information not hitherto known on Earth. These failures surely tell us something.*" Contrast this dearth of evidence for aliens with the wealth of "public" evidence that accompanies Marian apparitions: the tilma, healing springs, spinning suns, mass conversions, and numerous other publicly experienced miracles. (Roy Abraham Varghese. *God-Sent: A History of the Accredited Apparitions of Mary*. Appendix A)

Here I would add that Mr. Varghese's cutting insight nevertheless only provides an exceedingly partial list of the types of evidence in support of the miracles of Christianity. Assuredly, there are tilmas and healing springs and spinning suns. But whoever wishes to do so can, this moment, hop into a car or board an airplane and visit the bodies of incorrupt saints (whose un-embalmed corpses have not changed since death), see walls at shrines filled with crutches from those instantaneously and miraculously healed of medically incurable impairments, and look at statues of Jesus and Mary continually and inexplicably exuding oil or even weeping blood. He can find rigorously documented examples of mystics surviving decades consuming nothing but the Eucharist. He can open both Scripture and the prophecies in private revelation since those times and find countless examples of an impossibly clear fulfillment of each. He can read of not a mere few fighter pilots or men in their backyards observing something strange, but rather a full 70,000 witnesses describing miracles at Fatima on par with Moses parting the Red Sea. Above all, he can read the direct testimony of eleven men who repeatedly witnessed—directly, with their own senses—the Risen Christ, and who each went to their death rather than deny this truth; a phenomena that has no remotely close parallel anywhere else in the whole history of the world. And as some readers will doubtless be asking themselves this question, I will not hesitate to share: I myself have witnessed miracles (for example, at Medjugorje in Bosnia).

With Ufology, however, we have only an amalgamation of "evidence" that is laughable in comparison to this. Indeed, the deficiency of any objective evidence of aliens is damning, as such evidence would be guaranteed to be *ubiquitous* if the claims of the Ufologists were true. For example, one of today's most prominent ET promoters, Dr. Steven Greer, claims that *over three thousand* separate UFO-crash retrievals are currently in the possession of various organizations. Certainly, if even a fraction of reported UFO sightings were truly due to alien craft, then one would expect at least as many pieces of physical evidence indicating as much.

Where is *a single one* of these thousands of pieces of evidence? The Ufologists have had over *seventy-five years* (since Roswell) to convincingly present one such piece of evidence. Still, *nothing* even minimally convincing has been presented; only charades that would scarcely qualify as cheap entertainment and would struggle to find a place on a checkout-lane tabloid. (September 2023's papier-mâché-looking "alien" corpse in Mexico being the latest example.)

In accordance with the naked absurdity this situation presents for belief that aliens are among us, nearly the entirety of the Ufologists' effort in this regard is found in their insistence that alien craft *do exist,* but have simply been the subject of history's greatest coverup. They claim the surface of our planet has been littered with physical evidence of aliens for decades now (a claim which, even if unvoiced, remains implicit in their beliefs). But they insist this omnipresent evidence—wherever it is found across the entire globe—is always (and has always been) immediately and diligently detected, collected, and protected from any discovery whatsoever by anyone outside of the infallible reach of shadow-government security measures. This, despite ever changing administrations, ideologies, budgets, and ruling parties presiding over these programs as the decades dragged on. This, too, despite many different nations' governments (often very antagonistic towards each other) being allegedly involved.

Such a feat would make the Manhattan Project—by far the largest secret government undertaking in history—appear entirely insignificant. In fact, that infamous Project (which developed the first atomic bombs) could only maintain its secrecy for six years, despite only a few nations' governments being involved, and at most a thousand or so individuals being aware of its nature. It was, moreover, undertaken at a time (World War II) when almost half of the world's richest nation's GDP was being spent on the military, most of the nation's effort was focused therein, and with practically unlimited resources available for any undertaking that would render the war effort more likely to succeed—and the Manhattan Project was seen as paramount among those undertakings.

On the other hand, to propose that thousands of separate physical proofs of alien existence, accumulating for 75 years, across the world, with tens—or, rather, *hundreds*—of thousands of individuals necessarily knowing the truth (*for each piece of evidence would be encountered by at least several people – often many more than that – before the all-powerful government agents swooped in to collect it)*... is to propose something that is not even the same order of magnitude as the Manhattan Project. One who believes the government is capable of that might as well abandon all hope.

"History's Biggest Revelation" – Concealed by Hundreds of Thousands for Almost a Century?

The existence of physical evidence of aliens visiting earth would not be just any intriguing top-secret matter. *It would be the single biggest revelation in two thousand years.* For a non-Christian, it would appear to be, by far, the biggest revelation in history. There is not a man alive who would willingly cover that up. No one could resist feeling compelled to immediately shout that discovery from the rooftops.

But let us suppose that there are a few cowards who, if sufficiently threatened, would keep silent. What is certain is that there are not so many cowards that it has just so happened that *each one* of the many thousands of people who encountered this alleged physical evidence of aliens also happened to be among that small group defined by their standing as History's Greatest Cowards. Recall, as well, that many if not most of those who supposedly know of physical proof of aliens – but conceal it – are military men. One would do veterans a great dishonor by implying they are actually the group that contains more superlative weaklings than any other.

Contrast this dynamic to the *actual* greatest revelation in history: that of Jesus Christ – especially His Resurrection. The Jews and the Romans of those times did everything they could – including inciting genocide, and administering a carefully crafted conspiracy (cf. Matthew 28:15) – to silence this proclamation. Countless Christians were murdered, from the start, for proclaiming their Faith in *what they saw.* (Where, may I ask, are the corresponding UFO martyrs?) Indeed, hundreds saw the Risen Christ (previously, we were only referring to the testimony of the Apostles – the eleven who remained after Judas' suicide). The persecutors could scarcely succeed in their nefarious machinations to silence the testimony to the Risen Christ with *any* early Christians for so much as a *day*! This historical fact speaks to the fundamental goodness of human nature. For despite the unfortunate reality that cowards exist, most people will not shy from proclaiming *what they know they saw*, even in light of death threats, particularly if what they saw was extremely important for humanity. Yet, the Ufologists would have us believe that this is precisely what countless thousands of individuals have been doing for three quarters of a century in relation to their own object of belief.

Let us now turn to the response of the Ufologists to the observations above. "*But that is all a straw man! We do have such testimonies! We have the whistleblowers!"*, they will protest. "*Their testimony proves that the evidence is there! We will see it soon enough!*"

They have been shouting all of these things for that same seventy-five-year span. There is a ready-at-hand formula the Ufologists always use; one which both fosters expectation of "imminent disclosure," while at the same time ensuring that their followers are ready to "only redouble their resolve" when that predicted disclosure does not happen. Thus they hold on to their hard-won influence over millions of gullible followers, as no matter what happens, they will appear vindicated.

The incredible level of attention and credulity given to the empty claims of David Grusch (the latest "whistleblower" who, in 2023, declared the U.S. Government is in possession of alien craft and alien bodies) is an indication of the similarly incredible weakness of the position of the ET promoters. A moment's critical thinking would have revealed the emptiness of Grusch's story. Yet we had not only millions of "true believers" glued to their TV and computer screens believing his testimony, but even many of the highest-ranking members of the U.S. Federal Government, on both sides of the aisle, jumping on the same bandwagon. Then, when he testified before Congress, it was revealed more clearly that he never saw any of these supposed alien craft of alien bodies; he only "knew people who did" (unnamed, as always). That the ET promoters themselves unanimously proclaimed their belief in his testimony, despite its fraudulent nature, is analogous to the situation we will presently consider.

Imagine if almost all well-known Christian authors, in order to jump on an opportunity to promote their religion, immediately endorsed the claim of a certain pastor. Suppose (unfortunately, this is anything but hypothetical—similar situations happen regularly) this Pastor claimed he died but raised himself from the dead. Where are the witnesses? "*They cannot come forward at the moment, but they are there; I just can't give you their names right now,*" the Pastor assures us. Where are perhaps some photographs, videos, or sworn affidavits (from individuals we can interview) showing us that this Pastor did indeed die? "*I can't show those to you; the people who have them won't grant access.*" Where is *anything* you can give us to corroborate this claim, dear Pastor? "*You don't get it. The people in authority do NOT want you to believe that I rose from the dead. You don't understand how much power they have! They have been covering up us resurrectors for decades!*" No serious Christians, much less those whose lives have been dedicated to promoting the Faith for many years, would even be tempted to personally believe this Pastor, much less promote his claims and publicly lend credence to them. Wise Christians know they need not be so trigger-happy in endorsing supernatural claims, for reason and evidence already fully demonstrate the validity of their Faith. They will wait until they have something trustworthy before proclaiming *conviction* in its authenticity.

Yet almost all ET promoters (except individuals of a certain camp we will consider in a forthcoming section, and whose views descend to a still darker level of ideology) do something analogous with the claims of the "whistleblowers." Their willingness—or, rather, their downright *eagerness*—to take obvious fraud seriously is another indication of the logical bankruptcy of their position.

The more honest of the Ufologists themselves concede this fact. Soon, we will discuss the prominent Ufologist, Dr. Jacques Vallée. Here is what even he—who likely knows more about UFO sightings and "alien contact" experiences than any other man alive—concluded after many years of rigorous study of the movement and its claims:

> ... **none of the alleged sightings of crashed disks, none of the claims of autopsies on little aliens, none of the abduction reports, as they are currently presented, provide the shadow of an answer to the global UFO mystery**. ... why do I express so much suspicion about the sensational statements of the whistleblower who claim they are exposing such a [secret government] group [hiding UFO craft and aliens]? Simply because **there is not a shred of substance in what they claim;** their behavior is that of actors on a theatre stage, not that of real participants in real operations. ... [but] these men are [likely] sincerely convinced that what they say is the absolute truth. The urgency with which they want to communicate it skips over such niceties as facts... **the belief in the imminent arrival of extraterrestrials in our midst is a fantasy that is as powerful as any drug, as revolutionary as any delusion that marked the last millennium**, as poisonous as any of the great irrational upheavals of history...[185]

A man like Vallée would have everything to gain by unreservedly jumping upon the space-alien-UFO bandwagon, but instead he cuttingly denounces it. When an individual who is both an expert in *and member of* a movement denounces the prevailing trends within that very moment itself, any observer interested in the truth should take heed. Vallée continues in his denunciation of most Ufology with the following sarcastic remark:

> But wait! Perhaps there is such a superhuman agency, a magical and easy solution to our problems: those unidentified flying objects that people have glimpsed in increasing numbers since World War II may be ready to help. Perhaps the aliens are here, with their cosmic powers, their unlimited skills. The ufologists tell us that these aliens are so strange that they need to abduct, poke, scrape, and rape our people to fulfill their own bizarre *fin de siecle* appetites. Yet they are so close to us that they have no trouble, no trouble at all, communicating with our scientists in the secret tunnels under New Mexico.[186]

He then proceeds to detail the incredibly fallacious nature of what follows among the UFO "true believers," continuing the sarcastic tone that well diagnoses the delusions and deceptions promoted by the Ufologists:

> [But] this happy solution to all our troubles has been kept from us by

> those evil government agents who stamp everything top secret. They have hidden away the wonderful saucers in hangars ... [and] we, the people, must demand an end to this absurd secrecy. ... We must trust them and believe what they tell us, but of course we cannot meet them face to face, we cannot be allowed to know their true names. They have to speak to us from behind a screen, because their employers in Washington would surely kill them if they came into the light...

Breaking out of the sarcasm, Vallée frankly observes:

> **Such is the incredible conglomeration of lies and stupidity many ufologists and much of the public have swallowed**...all [of the whistleblowers'] vaunted references come directly from the lie, steal, and cheat department of the most disreputable part of the military establishment ...[but] **important questions are never asked because we forgive easily, always ready to be fooled one more time** ... Never mind the fact that nobody has actually attempted to silence these ["whistleblowers"], at a time when the merest suggestion of compromise of much less important, more mundane secrets—a missile fuse or a computer chip—brings the full force of the FBI and the federal courts. ... [but] **The extraterrestrial believers have investigated none of these questions. They were too busy rushing ahead in pursuit of the aliens. They were ready to set aside all critical thinking.**

Considering not only their logical force but also recalling from whom these critiques derive, any ET promoter would be a fool to cast them aside. Already in 1977—almost a half century ago—Vallée had become such a world-renowned researcher on this topic that Steven Spielberg modeled a character after him in the most famous movie ever made about ETs, *Close Encounters of the Third Kind.* Vallée testified on these topics before the United Nations and counted among his closest confidants men such as J. Allen Hynek, who enjoyed top-secret security clearance in the U.S. Government. In the 46 years since, Vallée has only continued his studies, his writings, and his talks and interviews, and he has not backed down from the views quoted above. He has not done so because these views are correct. Ufology has no hope of refuting those charges; Vallée has already heard all the attempts.

***

Returning to the "whistleblowers" themselves*, we must conclude this section by noting that countering each claim they make would quickly

* Special attention should also be paid not only to the nature of claims about the "whistleblowers" themselves, but also to the tried-and-true populist-inspired propogandist approach relentlessly used to fabricate a common enemy that is said to be "hiding the evidence of aliens from us." In superlative convenience—and in contrast to those who are causing the world's real problems—the antagonists can never be named. On the other hand, those who rightly lament actual injustices in the real world and

turn this book into a library. Indeed, a strategy of Ufologists (and charlatans in general) has long been the grape-shot approach: present such an overwhelmingly large number of empty claims that no serious critic could possibly have the time to address them all. Thus, no matter how many claims are refuted, the charlatan can always retort, "*Ah! But you haven't refuted this one! Even if a single one of my claims is true, I've proved my point, so you haven't yet achieved anything!*"

Thankfully, truth is always able to eventually prevail for those who sincerely seek it. The best way to refute grape-shot-sophistry is to discover which individual claims the supporters of the fallacy most revere, and proceed to reveal *even those* claims for the blatant frauds they are. In the present matter, if even the most apparently convincing of the "UFO Sightings" or "alien contact experiences" are shown to present no solid evidence for extraterrestrials, then the rest follows automatically: namely, the fact that the remaining "proofs," being less convincing still than the presently refuted one, have fallen like so many dominoes.

In the following sections, therefore, we will consider only a few of those cases regarded as "UFO Holy Grails which most clearly demonstrate that aliens exist."

> "Before the 1940s, reports of sightings of objects in the sky were extremely rare. Centuries of recorded history give no clear indication of any such activity. Then, at the predawn of the space-age, around the time of the Roswell conspiracy, UFO culture was born, giving rise to everything from Space Invaders to The X-Files ... Indeed, indisputable evidence of intelligent life coming to Earth could be the greatest news of all time. Yet, after thousands of anecdotal, photo, and video reports have accrued over decades, what are we to conclude? With the greatest balance of scepticism and "wanting to believe", all that can confidently be asserted is that some objects, appearing in the sky on film or video, seem unidentifiable. Furthermore, government disclosure of its own video footage isn't helping to maintain belief. Joseph Baker, sociology professor at Tennessee State University, says: "It's actually better for UFOs when ufologists can claim that 'the powers that be know everything and are hiding it from us' rather than seeing that the government appears to have basically the same info about UFOs as the public: namely grainy, inconclusive visual evidence."[187]

---

nobly dedicate themselves to fighting these injustices can readily identify the individuals whose works must be opposed. When it comes to the extraterrestrial issue, the bad guys are always the same vague mystery men. "Secretive government agencies" (the details of whose operations are again conveniently unknown to everyone who openly works in government), undefined "defense contractors," and "high level Pentagon officials," are invariably the bogeymen. Sometimes "especially rich and powerful corporate leaders" are thrown into the mix for good measure. In the ET promoters' careful positioning of their narratives, the individuals in question "cannot" be named.

UFO "Holy Grails" Shockingly Easy to Refute: Roswell and Brazil

> "I have to admit that during my four flights into space, I have not seen or heard any phenomena that I could not explain...I don't believe any of us in the space program believe that there are such things as UFOs." —NASA Astronaut James Lovell

The very event which instigated the UFO Era—the "flying saucer crash" at Roswell, New Mexico—remains to this day the Holy Grail of Ufology. Yet, this event clearly had nothing to do with extraterrestrial visitors. The object whose debris was observed at Roswell was a high-altitude military balloon.

"Project Mogul" of the U.S. Air Force was, that very year, engaged in a top-secret program flying high-tech surveillance balloons, aiming to detect Soviet missiles, while flying *over New Mexico*. One of them—made of material just like that described at the infamous crash site—went down in this small town of less than 20,000 people in Chaves County, located in that state. (I encourage anyone with doubts to look up images of since declassified Project Mogul arrays and compare those materials to photographs of what was recovered from Roswell.)

When one resident of this town, a certain W.W. "Mac" Brazel, happened upon the debris at his ranch in June of 1947, he thought nothing of it. His testimony—that of the only one who certainly saw the original debris and of which we can be confident of the unmanipulated, uncontrived nature—indicates there was certainly nothing at all "otherworldly" about the materials. He described it as merely tinfoil, sticks, tape, and rubber.

Only some weeks later did Mac finally get around to telling anyone about it, and when word got to the military, they took immediate interest (for reasons now obvious). Brazel showed them to the debris, which they promptly collected. The very same day—evidently not wanting word to get out about their secret program—the military released a coverup story claiming that the crash was actually a "flying saucer!" Word spread immediately across the world (at this point the "flying saucer craze" was already underway due to the Kenneth Arnold UFO Sighting two weeks earlier), and the little town of Roswell was inundated with global media inquiries. It now seemed that a "trend" was beginning, and a diabolical spark was lit in men's hearts in secular culture.

It did not take long for the military to realize this coverup was a terrible idea, therefore the next day they issued a (false) "correction," claiming the debris was actually from a weather balloon. These two consecutive blunders provided the conditions for a perfect storm that rages to this day, for it was obvious that what crashed in Roswell was no ordinary weather balloon. That said, Roswell itself received little attention in the time that followed, until, thirty years later, one of the army officers involved in the incident (Jesse Marcel) announced he believed the debris was extraterrestrial. The officer's own son claimed that his father showed him "hieroglyphics" on the recovered debris. All that was needed from that point forward was a uniquely American-tabloid-fueled combination of sensationalism and exaggeration, topped off with a good dose of pure fabrication, for "The Roswell Incident" to become a veritable religion of its own. Soon, there were even viral claims of alien bodies being recovered along with the debris (however, Marcel himself, despite arguing Roswell was from ETs, always denied this claim)—bodies, moreover, on which autopsies were performed! "Videos of the autopsy" are even available, of interest for those who likewise believe that a half-dog half-human was born recently, or that survivors were just found aboard the Titanic wreckage, or, more apropos, that an alien bible was discovered proving that the ETs worship Oprah Winfrey. (All these were actual recent tabloid headlines.) The creator of the most prominent of these "alien autopsy" hoax videos—Ray Santilli—admitted, over a decade after releasing it, that it was fake.

Then came the years 1994 and 1997, wherein the U.S. Air Force published a report conceding that, indeed, the Roswell debris was from no weather balloon, but that, yes, it was from its own (then top-secret) Project Mogul. However, a religion was already built upon Roswell—the city itself, today, is to Ufology what Mecca is to Islam—and the truth has been deemed irrelevant by adherents of this religion. It is precisely in their mantra-esque repetition of the phrase, "the truth is out there," that they only condemn themselves.

For those who still insist upon believing some of the more extraordinary claims made in relation to Roswell, Jacques Valle explains why these too certainly should *not* compel one to propose an extraterrestrial explanation:

> And what about Roswell? Something undoubtedly fell from the sky at Roswell in July 1947; it was picked up by the Air Force and the story was effectively covered up. ... [but] **Given the extremely high sensitivity of anything related to the bomb or to radioactivity at the time, it would have been a high priority, top secret task to recover any lost device of that type and <u>to explain it away at all costs: as a weather balloon, as a radar test instrument, as a probe, or even as a crashed flying saucer</u>. <u>It would not have been difficult to plant an egg-shaped device in the desert to divert attention from the real debris, and even to scatter a few diminutive bodies to represent dead aliens</u>**. The Air Force had several days to do it. Perhaps the mysterious "team of archeologists" who were at the site when the first recovery troops arrived, and who have never been found again in spite of all the efforts made to locate them, were, in reality, the specialized workers who planted the **<u>fake disk and the fake bodies</u>** ... I am bothered, however, by the alleged hieroglyphics found on the balsa wood. You would think that Air Force intelligence could have come up with something better.

In explaining these points, Vallée also implicitly reminds us to be on guard against similar conspiracies transpiring in the future. For while the Ufologists argue that the only conspiracy one need be worried about is the government "covering up existence of the aliens," the opposite conspiracy should be our concern. Moving forward, government intelligence agencies appear likely to make claims in relation to ETs (as the UFO craze has today, conveniently for them, reached unprecedented levels of insanity) as an accommodating coverup story for what *they themselves* are doing. Few ET believers will doubt—given their decades of ravenousness for this very thing—that the "Day of Disclosure" itself is anything but the final and long-fought-for triumph of their "demands for transparency." Thus, that day will provide the perfect cover for a uniquely dark and dangerous psyop. We will consider this scenario in more detail in a later chapter.

To this day, Ufologists continue to emphatically declare that what crashed in Roswell was truly an ET craft—an alien spaceship that traversed virtually endless expanses of interstellar space, averting peril after peril that cannot even be described with the same terminology used to describe perils encountered in earth's atmosphere—cosmic radiation that dwarfs any phenomenon on earth, unbelievably high-speed collisions with interplanetary debris that would incinerate the strongest materials imaginable, accelerations that would transcend the laws of physics, propulsion systems that would generate enough force to obliterate any conceivable lifeform therein—all thanks to technological abilities that would appear supernatural to an earthling—...only to, upon arriving at earth, be destroyed and brought down *by a lightning strike*.

At this point, any reader interested in the truth will relegate Roswell's aliens to the dustbin of modern history's hoaxes. But we should consider the other "UFO Holy Grail" before proceeding to our next point.

***

It was the year 1996, and in the Brazilian city called Varginha, when claims abounded that police had rounded up sick aliens from a UFO crash.

The fiasco began with three young women who, immediately after encountering a frightening looking being, claimed they had seen *the Devil*. A game of telephone ensued (along with plenty of other obfuscation), and soon everyone was talking about "unexplainable deaths" at a zoo, "aliens under observation at a local hospital," a police officer dying "due to the alien disease," a military effort to capture and transport the "aliens," and even one of the alien witnesses being impregnated by one of the "aliens."

As the Brazilian government explained upon concluding their official inquiry in 2010, the young women had likely encountered a known homeless, insane, and deformed man who resembled the description they gave of what was later called "the alien." (Though it is not unlikely that they actually experienced a demonic apparition, upon the Devil observing that other circumstances were lining up ideally for using them to promote the ET Deception.) Military trucks had already been in town undertaking ordinary planned duties, and the "aliens" at the hospital were humans with dwarfism undergoing treatment along with a corpse that had to be exhumed for examination.

As with all such cases, however, the facts did not get in the way of the Ufologists making a killing off the phenomenon. In fact, the creators of *The Phenomenon*, a 2020 documentary that runs the gamut of usual Ufologists claims, followed up with a 2022 documentary, *Moment of Contact*, which insisted that the Varginha event was indeed an alien encounter; perhaps the greatest of all such supposed encounters.

The documentary concludes with a (conveniently anonymous) interviewee saying: "*thank you for giving me this opportunity to speak. May you continue searching. Don't ever be discouraged. Don't let this go,*" followed by words on the screen declaring "*The Producers of this film continue to pursue video and photographic evidence, which our investigations conclude exists in Brazil.*" The final words displayed were only three: "**Our search continues**..." At least the filmmakers had the honesty to implicitly concede that the case, as presented, is entirely unconvincing, hence the need for that "video and photographic evidence" they have "concluded" exists...*somewhere* "in Brazil." Alas, that "honesty" is more likely the standard ruse to ensure more funding is received for the next documentary, which will doubtless similarly insist that the *real* "evidence" is just around the corner.

I do not want, however, to entirely side with the "debunkers" here. Some testimonies from Varginha seem to resemble those given by others who saw something exceedingly dark and are honestly recounting it. On the other hand, the supposed physical evidence of aliens is easy to accurately debunk (e.g., the patients with dwarfism we know were in the hospital at that time). This speaks to a general pattern one often observes in UFO sightings and "alien encounters." Namely, the supposed presence of physical evidence that would make a demonic interpretation unlikely is easy to debunk with even the slightest scrutiny, whereas those testimonies of witnesses who experienced something *real* are not always so easy to debunk; but in each case, they carry undertones which give clear indications of diabolical action at play.

Although this is a matter we will deal with in detail in a later chapter, it currently bears emphasizing that the Devil is an opportunist. When he sees that events have transpired which are primed for a deception like this to play out, there is no reason for us to suppose he would refuse to pounce on that opportunity. Perhaps he did so in Varginha and in similar places. For example, the Devil could have easily manipulated what the three young women saw, making them experience it as a far more grotesque and menacing form than it objectively was. The event even aroused false mysticism, as diabolical phenomena are known to do, with one "seer" predicting that Varginha would be punished with a cataclysm in 1996 "as retribution for its blitzkrieg on the interplanetary visitors."[188] Almost thirty years later, there has been no cataclysm related to Varginha, save that of contributing significantly to the Ufologists' narrative.

The "extreme stench" reported by many at Varginha in connection with their proximity to the "aliens" also, literally, reeks of the demonic. As reported by the *Wall Street Journal*, "**Standing out in a different way was the creature's odor: One ghastly whiff weakened the knees.**"[189] It is not only this "alien contact" at Brazil that exudes the stench of deception, however, but also the whole contemporary UFO phenomenon.

Smell Test Failure: Nothing Adds Up. Common Sense Ruminations on the Absurdity of It All

Let us for a moment leave aside calculations and studies and lengthy arguments and quotations from experts and careful considerations of laws of science and such. Let us simply step back and consider the present situation purely in keeping with the basic dictates of common sense. For if we cannot abide in common sense, then no matter what else we may say or do, we have lost the plot.

—We are expected to believe that modern society has long been inundated with legitimate experiences of aliens and UFOs. Why are these aliens always so inexplicably (approximately) human sized? Where are the aliens the Voltaire described in the year 1752 (cf., *Le Micromégas*), whose height is 120,000 feet (that is, 22 miles—close to the size of Mount Everest)? Alternatively, where are the aliens the size of mice or termites? Virtually all "aliens" reported are between 4 and 8 feet in height, conveniently amenable to dialogue with us. Only human artifice or diabolical deception could achieve such a deviation from statistical guarantees, so oddly poised for interaction with beings of our own proportions.

—ET promoters cannot decide if the aliens visiting us are utterly incompetent or essentially godlike in their abilities. We are told that the visitors come from civilizations so advanced that we can scarcely begin to comprehend their abilities, yet we are also assured that the machinations of earthly governments manage to prevent the aliens from disclosing themselves to the masses. How has not even one managed to descend onto the White House lawn during a major live event? Or during the Superbowl? Teenage hackers living in their parents' basements can often manage to override security protocols of major websites, but these aliens that can manage physically impossible interstellar travel cannot do the same or more?

—Why is there such drastically insufficient similarity between UFO sightings and "alien encounters" to pinpoint what our space-visitors are like? When genuine material phenomena are independently discovered by people in separated groups, the objectivity of the phenomenon itself guarantees that the separation of these groups will not result in such disparity.

When, for example, scientists who know nothing of each other's works nevertheless stumble upon some truth, their findings agree. The objective reality of the truth they independently observe is the wellspring of their agreement. With UFOs and aliens, we see none of this; only types of similarities that easily arise from psychological influences, diabolical deceptions, or—particularly prominently—cultural stimuli (it is amazing how diligently the descriptions of "aliens" and "UFOs" follow the depictions of the same in movies, television, and other popular media!). Suppose there really was a particular extraterrestrial ship roaming about earth, which was the real cause of at least *some* sightings. In that case, the reports of these sightings would reflect agreement on details just as authentic witnesses agree in a trial before a jury. This is also precisely what we see when species of once undiscovered undersea creatures are found scattered across global reports. When we finally find the creature, the reports make perfect sense. What is reported in accordance with UFO sightings and alien contacts, however, excludes any possibility of ever finding a physically existing thing that could account for the disparities (for these disparities are not mere difficulties, but rather each time include a multitude of stark contradictions). One researcher noted:

> "...we are not talking about the concern of just one alien civilization [allegedly visiting earth]. The tremendous diversity in the shapes and sizes of UFOs suggests that earth is being visited by hundreds of intergalactic civilizations. ... The same bewildering diversity is found in the aliens themselves. In addition to the "Nordic," "grey" and "reptilian" types, witnesses have reported "short, big-headed creatures; human figures; monkeylike aliens; one-eyed monsters; creatures with one leg; creatures with webbed fingers; some speak fluent English, others communicate with grunts and signs, others seem to be telepathic." ...**These hundreds of conflicting descriptions weigh heavily against the supposition that many UFOs are spacecraft piloted by extraterrestrial visitors** ... with alleged messages on the lines of: "*We are aliens from planet X, friendly and concerned for the wellbeing of your world. Stop tinkering with nuclear energy before it is too late.*" With a message so crucial, is it not a curious modus operandi for the space travelers to slip quickly across the sky, barely seen? ...Sometimes we are told that aliens have revealed themselves through chosen human vessels. The message in these cases is suspiciously trendy..." [190]

—Why are UFO sightings and alien encounters so severely geographically lopsided? America and other western nations, where sci-fi reigns supreme, are replete with them. On the other hand, those portions of Africa and the Middle East that have not been Westernized have virtually no such sightings. These aliens are astonishingly adept at following cultural fads. (Even within countries that report many UFO sightings, the sightings themselves track culture. For example, one researcher, Lucas Tromly, pointed out that even in America, those of Asian descent rarely report UFO sightings.) India is currently the world's most populous nation, having over four times as many inhabitants as America. Yet, there are virtually no UFOs or alien encounters reported there. Are the hordes of interstellar, intergalactic, and interdimensional visitors to our world *all* simply brazen racists who dislike Indians?

—In recent decades, continuous video recording throughout the world has exploded. There has been an exponential increase in the use of handheld cameras (currently, almost everyone has an ultra-high-resolution camera—i.e., a smartphone—in his pocket all day) and surveillance technology. Both are now ubiquitous. Everywhere, smartphones are recording each detail of daily life, law enforcement cameras (e.g., red light cameras, speed cameras, public transportation cameras, police body cameras, airport cameras, etc.) monitor every inch of the developed world, while residential cameras diligently record every event that transpires on driveways, porches, and front yards. One 2020 study even found that Americans are recorded by some camera, on average, 238 times each week (a number that has grown dramatically since).[191] This number itself pales in comparison to surveillance use in places like China, where not one iota of a citizen's life is free from digital observation by the CCP (Chinese Communist Party). Surely, claims of recorded UFOs have increased in recent years. Everyone who happens to have a smartphone in his pocket when he sees a drone, SpaceX launch, government airplane, blimp, atmospheric reflection, or strange weather phenomenon, can now record it and upload it to social media to "go viral" by claiming or implying it depicts an extraterrestrial-piloted craft. But this increase has not come anywhere close to proportional with our increased use of video—which it should have, if the phenomenon were objective, real, and physical. The video that we do have of "alien UFOs" tends to be of comically poor quality or an equally comically obvious use of digital editing.

—Retellings of "alien encounters" almost never recount these beings as bedecked with space suits, implying that the biology of the aliens in question just so happens to be perfectly amenable to earth's conditions. If, however, there were planets somewhere in the universe amenable to life (as we saw in an earlier chapter, it is a statistical guarantee that there *aren't*), then they certainly would not be identical to earth. The extraterrestrials would have "evolved" to adapt to their own atmosphere, and would certainly need suits to survive on any other planet, just as our own astronauts need suits to survive on the moon. Yet, such suits are almost never described in relation to "alien encounters."

***

There is no angle from which we can approach the notion aliens are among us that renders it remotely plausible. Leaving aside direct proofs, insurmountable absurdities remain wherever the most basic tenets of common sense are applied to pondering the (unstated) corollaries that follow upon the claims anyone must make who insists extraterrestrials fly (or walk) this earth.

> "If an inquirer looks into the extraterrestrial hypothesis, or ETH, from a scientific standpoint, that person quickly realizes that it does not stand up. Where would extraterrestrial intelligence come from? There are fewer planets in the universe than many people presume. Furthermore, **the vast and growing number of known characteristics required for a planet to support life essentially rules out the possibility that a suitable home for physical life can be found anywhere in the universe but here on Earth. Nor is it possible that life could have arisen on other planets according to the principles of evolutionary theory. The likelihood that chemicals anywhere in the universe would assemble into a living organism is nil. Apart from these facts, even if E.T. somehow did exist somewhere, traveling to Earth would pose insurmountable obstacles for him (or it).** Vast distances necessitate navigating at high speeds through obstacles such as space dust, meteors, comets, radiation, and gravitational perturbations. Thousands of years of high-velocity travel pose energy and shielding **problems that are <u>impossible</u> to resolve**. And wormholes do not provide shortcuts because anyone passing through one would be obliterated!" —Dr. Hugh Ross, Astrophysicist.[192]

Extreme Esotericization, The Final Strategy: On the Neo-Gnostic, Pagan Pseudo-Religion of "Inter-Dimensional" ETs and the "Multiverse"

Although the preceding sections have demonstrated the scientific ludicrousness of believing in extraterrestrial intelligence, far more material could, of course, be included. I recommend that readers interested in learning more consult the various works quoted therein. There is, however, one final strategy that the ET promoters employ, ostensibly within the realm of "science," though in fact essentially repudiating science all-but explicitly.

When ET promoters realize that even wormholes, teleportation, and other related wild conjectures will not succeed in rendering palatable the notion that aliens may be among us, they resort to one last strategy: religion. Not, mind you, "religion" in the true sense of the term, but a perversion thereof—a neo-Gnostic and Pagan pseudo-Religion that unashamedly traffics in the very mysteries (arbitrarily called by other names) that are, by definition, within the exclusive domain of Faith, while at the same time flatly contradicting themselves by insisting their views are exempt from theological (and even philosophical) scrutiny.

They replace so much as attempting to couch their views in acceptable scientific terminology with the promotion of outlandish notions that have not only no basis in empirical science, but also no basis in rational thought whatsoever. (True religion, on the other hand, is always happy to fully engage reason and science.) Contrast this with the deceptions promoted by the "parapsychologists" we considered earlier. Although parapsychology is a realm almost entirely permeated by unadulterated pseudoscientific nonsense, even there an effort exists to present the discourse in scientific terms and to engage in scientific studies. Parapsychologists at least have the ostensible *goal* of describing the object of their studies in terms of scientific laws. That goal is unattainable, but it nominally exists. However, an increasingly common view—among those Ufologists who concede that interstellar travel is not plausible, and that SETI's "Great Silence" rules out "traditional" notions of aliens, that the content of UFO sightings cannot possibly be made to work with "traditional" notions of ETs, etc.—is to simply esotericize belief in ETs to the *extreme.* They posit the beings visiting us are actually "Ultraterrestrials;" that is, some form of beings from "another dimension" who need not travel through space to arrive here, but need merely "intersect" or "phase" or "vibrate" with us at will.

As the fable goes, these beings are not physically traversing the expanse of space to reach us, but are rather entering our "dimension" from another one. We will deal with the patently demonic spiritual realities that are signaled here in the next part of this book. Presently, our task is only to briefly note how devoid of any scientific basis such claims are, in order to point out that whoever promotes the notion of "interdimensional" visitors has merely posited a religious belief—albeit one devoid of any basis, any prophet, any morality, any creed; in a word, any *truth.*

Although "The Interdimensional Hypothesis" is now pervasive, a pioneer* of this brand of alien belief is the famous Ufologist we have already quoted earlier, Jacques Vallée. Considering his primacy in forming modern Ufology, we will delve into this aspect of his teachings—in order to warn against their darkness and deception—in a later chapter. At this point, we need only define his thesis.

It bears emphasizing first, however, that what follows does not detract from Valleé's cutting critiques of one brand (still the most common) of ET belief we discussed earlier. As noted, this scholar is doubtless the world's most learned expert on UFO sightings, and from this extensive knowledge he has rightly concluded that the entire modern milieu of ET belief, which anticipates the arrival of interstellar-space-traversing aliens in spaceships, is fraudulent and illogical to the core. That he is correct in

---

*Vallée and his confreres were not the actual originators of the Interdimensional Hypothesis. This notion comes from Dr. Meade Layne (born 1882) who, in the 1950s, proposed that UFOs actually derived from "Etheria," a sort of parallel dimension. He insisted "*Etheria is here—if we know what here means! Along-side, inside, outside of our world.*" His theories, however, were not accepted in their own day, and only Vallée, et. al., popularized them later.

this assessment does not lend credibility to the alternative thesis he proposes, for that proposition itself is not only entirely empty, but also stands squarely outside of his own domain of experience and expertise.

Cutting as his critiques are, this is the point at which Dr. Vallée's wisdom ends. For despite his valid exhortations, and book titles such as "*Messengers of Deception: UFO Contacts and Cults,*" Vallée has no interest in exposing the real deceptions at play, much less safeguarding his readers against them. Like a Mormon one day waking up to realize that Joseph Smith was not a true prophet, and proceeding not to enter true Christianity, but instead to abandon Christianity altogether for outright Paganism—so too Jacques Vallée and his ilk would only have their readers jump out of the frying pan and into the fire.

Vallée, ironically, describes himself as a "heretic among heretics"; the Ufologists being the "heretics"—a group he belongs to but from which he often dissents. Departing from "mainstream" Ufologists, he proposes that "UFOs" reveal a phenomenon that has been with humanity throughout history and cannot be *entirely* explained in empirical, scientific terms. He focuses heavily on arguing that UFOs are entities representing "levels of consciousness" that reside outside of "our dimensions" and accordingly (we are expected to accept) have power over the latter, even functioning as some manner of "control system" for humanity. Discerning readers will have already recognized that Vallée is simply describing demons, but neither Vallée nor his readers recognize this, even while pretending they do. For example, Vallée passingly acknowledges UFO phenomena's "*striking parallel to the intercourse with angels, demons, and elves in earlier ages,*"[193] but only by way of employing the standard modernist scholarly dismissal of those very themes. This is evidenced by his inclusion of "elves" in the same breath as "demons," both of which are treated as mere relics of "earlier ages," when in fact elves are just one of the many guises the demons assume (along with "aliens"). Vallée insists that both are simply expositions of one superior and overarching reality, which can only be described in terms of "interdimensionality," a notion conveniently devoid of any objective meaning, and which can be exempted from scrutiny from any concrete field of study that exists.

What this all amounts to is a strategy we have already seen regularly employed by many ET promoters: insisting upon having their cake and eating it too. They want to be regarded as scientific (in a futile attempt to evade the charge that they have simply founded a new religion), but they do not want to submit their propositions to the actual laws of science. They want to pooh-pooh traditional religion, while proposing theses that are, by all beyond-semantic accounts, identical to those proposed by every other founder of false religions throughout history.

For example, Vallée teaches that UFOs constitute a "control system" for humanity, but neglects to concede that a "control system" implies a *controller* who designed and operates the system. Thus, Vallée has simply explicitly crafted a new religion, with the "control system administrator" as the deity and the "UFOs" as the prophets. The methods of operations of this religion are not Scriptures and Liturgies, Creeds and Sacraments, or Prayer and Morality, but rather unmoored esoteric ramblings which are free to redefine themselves each month in accordance with whatever empty terminology has become trendy in science fiction movies or viral podcasts.

In contrast to the proposals of men like Vallée (although he is one of the pioneers of this fad, he is far from the only developer and promoter of the "Interdimensional Hypothesis"), we should consult qualified scientists' explanations of the silliness of arguing for "multiple dimensions" or "multiple universes."

One recent scholarly tome, entitled *Universe or Multiverse?*, and published by Cambridge University Press in 2009, is dedicated to promoting this idea of the "multiverse" (though officially abiding by the customary academic assurance the issue is simply being "explored," thereby "encouraging further inquiry," but without presenting conclusions). Even this volume, however, evidently felt duty-bound to include some skeptical remarks. Remarkably, this task was fulfilled by Professor Paul Davies, a physicist who works in astrobiology and held a prominent position within SETI (the Search for Extraterrestrial Intelligence). This scientist concedes:

> ... **multiverse models ... are ontologically equivalent to naive deism** ... **dressed up in scientific language.** Both appeal to an infinite unknown, invisible and unknowable system. Both require an infinite amount of information to be discarded just to explain the (finite) universe we observe. It would be instructive to quantify and compare the degree of credulity we might attach to various competing multiverse and theological models using algorithmic complexity theory. It seems likely that some versions of both the multiverse and nave deism would be equivalently complex and, in most cases, infinitely complex. They may employ different terminology but, in essence, both explanations are the same. ... **It is basically just a religious conviction rather than a scientific argument**. ...(§28.3.5) Taken to its logical extreme, the multiverse explanation is a convincing argument for the existence of (a rather old-fashioned form of) God! This is certainly ironical, since it was partly to do away with such a God that the multiverse was originally invoked. Worse still, **there is no end to the hierarchy of levels in which worlds and designers can be embedded ...** ***ad infinitum*****:** gods and worlds, creators and creatures, in an infinite regress, embedded within each other. We confront something more bewildering than an infinite tower of virtual turtles*: a turtle fractal of virtual observers, gods and universes in

* "Infinite Turtles" has become an expression symbolizing the quintessential empty explanation that defers only to an infinite regress without providing any mean-

limitlessly complex inter-relationships. **If this is the ultimate reality, there would seem to be little point in pursuing scientific inquiry at all into such matters.** Indeed, to take such a view is as pointless as solipsism [*the radical, absurdist idea that nothing at all exists but one's own self*]. My point is that to follow the multiverse theory to its logical extreme means **effectively abandoning the notion of a rationally ordered real world altogether**, in favour of an infinitely complex charade, where the very notion of 'explanation' is meaningless ... **[a] 'fantasy-verse' of arbitrary virtual realities, whimsically generated by a pseudo-Deity designer**. (§28.3.6)

Dr. Davies' observations above could just as easily be presented (if using other words) by anyone with common sense. Assuredly, the moment one posits such notions as "the multiverse" or "other dimensions," he has, *ipso facto*, declared a religious conviction—one, at that, devoid of value. Nevertheless, I present this scholar's arguments here since they derive from a renowned physicist and SETI researcher in a work printed by a prestigious academic publishing house. For such a man as he to describe multiverse theory so starkly resembles the denunciations from a man such as Vallée, decrying the "UFO Whistleblowers" as the charlatans they are. Only an idealogue could fail to recognize the accuracy of such reproof.

Especially noteworthy is Dr. Davies' observation that, in multiverse theory, "there is no end to the hierarchy of levels in which worlds and designers can be embedded...*ad infinitum*..." Indeed, the trend we have seen and doubtless will continue to see is as predictable as the dialogue of a cheap soap opera. In the early 20th century, it was considered edgy to propose that time was literally a fourth dimension. Not only is that notion now blasé; moreover, it is today even unfashionable to describe a tired old slew of five, or seven, or a few dozen, "dimensions." One must, instead, propose not only the "multiverse" of dimensions, but also multiple "timelines" and "strings" superseding them. These catchphrases, too, are becoming overly commonplace for those eager to remain on the cutting edge of ET-belief-discourse. Therefore, talk is also now increasing of a "megaverse" or "superverse" or "holocosm" within which all the relatively puny, old-fashioned multiverses dwell. And who knows what phrases they will invent tomorrow to pretend that they have expanded "The All" to yet another level of empty esoteric abstraction. The only thing we can be certain of is that whatever it is, it will be pure fantasy. There is no difference between the proponents of these ideas and children arguing about who can describe a bigger number, with iterations of the latter's debate consisting in exchanges of shouts: "*infinity!*," "*well, infinity plus one!*,"

---

ingful insight. It derives from a story of a woman in the audience at a conference insisting that the earth was simply supported by a turtle. When asked by the speaker what supported that turtle, she allegedly responded: "it's just turtles all the way down."

"okay, infinity times infinity!," "Oh yeah!? Infinity times infinity times infinity," "That's nothing! Infinity times infinity times infinity times infinity!," and so on. An adult should walk into the room and tell the children to brush their teeth, say their prayers, and go to bed.

A wise man will simply step back not only from individual claims like those above, but also from the entire discussion itself, and realize that the whole matter is ridiculous. Unfortunately, however, we are not only dealing here with comical absurdities presented by pundits desperate for attention. Propositions like the "Interdimensional Hypothesis" and the "Multiverse Theory" are nothing other than Trojan Horses to beguile the masses into accepting the ministrations of demons without conceding that it is indeed the fundamentally nefarious, *spiritual* entities—described accurately by Christian Revelation—who are at work; beings whose sole objective is the eternal damnation of souls.

We can no longer remain within the boundaries of scientific analysis. The time has come to delve into considering the outright demonic plans afoot in ET promotion. Accordingly, we must now proceed to the next part of this book.

> "...theoretical physics [is descending] into increasingly fantastical speculation, disconnected from the reality that we can access empirically. ...[for example,] string theory...postulates the existence of particles that are far too small to be detected in any conceivable experiment. ... Multiverse theories aren't theories—they're science fictions... works of the imagination unconstrained by evidence ... multiverse theories strike me as not only unscientific but also immoral..." —John Horgan, *Scientific American*.[194]

Part Four: Aliens and Antichrist; Demons and Deception

"The coming of the lawless one will be in accordance with the work of Satan displayed in all kinds of counterfeit miracles, signs and wonders."
—2 Thessalonians 2:9

18. On Discernment

"If civilizations really existed on other planets, our Holy Scripture, the Bible, would definitely say something about that ... people who have allegedly seen aliens really saw demons, whose existence many people now refuse to believe in."
—Russian Orthodox Metropolitan Hilarion[195]

In Part Two, we saw that belief in the existence of extraterrestrials generated only destructive fruits from the very beginning of Western Civilization's discourse on this topic—several hundred years before Christ onward.* The same was true in the early Church. The only Father of the Church who believed in aliens—Origen—was condemned as a heretic; not only for propositions unrelated to this one, but for this very proposition that a plurality of inhabited worlds exists. After Origen, the remainder of the patristic era and the medieval era of Church history saw only two prominent proponents of aliens emerge: Virgil (8th century) and Zaninus (15th century). Both of these clerics received the strongest-worded Papal rebukes for their teachings. Only in the age of the "Enlightenment"—that is, the early stages of the Great Apostasy—did Christendom see alien belief substantially spread within its own ranks.

---

* Those pre-Socratics who promoted the notion of multiple (even innumerable) inhabited worlds were the same ones whose legacies proved rotten: the atheistic materialists ("atomists" following the lead of Democritus and Leucippus) and the hedonists ("Epicureans" following the lead of Epicurus).

While it is doubtless true that the theological underpinnings for the Great Deception were being laid down during the Enlightenment, the actual execution of this Deception was being reserved, by its satanic author, for the contemporary era of sci-fi. In the following chapters, we will chart out this Deception's development during the last century (although some sections will require us to reach farther back in history for context), observe its infiltration into the Church, and discern its placement in patently false "revelations" so as to ensure that this prophesied "strong delusion" (2 Thessalonians 2:11) is recognized for what it is.

> "**Do not judge by appearances, but judge with right judgment**." (John 7:24)

Jesus admonishes Christians throughout all time to diligently ensure they do not succumb to the spectacular seductive claims of the world. All that glitters is not gold, and the more glittering an assurance from the leaders of today's world, the more likely it is only a packaging concealing something destructive. But too many of the faithful today, taken in by the seductiveness of a secular movement that promises more excitement than that of any previous news, are casting aside their call to seek Wisdom from On High, and are instead credulously devouring content based only on appearances delivered to us by secular sources.

In the present part of this book, therefore, we will respond to Scripture's command to judge matters of the earth with the method presented by Our Lord: we will seek to know the trees "**by their fruits.**" (Matthew 7:20) As noted in this book's Introduction, there is a stunning short sightedness and even a cognitive dissonance evident in the writings of many prominent Christian alien belief promoters. In the forthcoming sections, we will see that mountains of indications exist, in whatever direction one so much as glances within these realms, that the entire slew of ET-associated phenomena is permeated to the core with all manner of evils and errors in opposition to the salvation of souls. Today's Catholic ET promoters, however, seem to not care.

These pervasive dangers (the discovery of which requires no journalistic talent and the recognition of which requires no special gifts of mystical insight) are either entirely ignored or, at best, briefly acknowledged, only to be dismissed as *"perhaps accounting for an extremely tiny fraction of UFO/Alien phenomena, but nothing more, and nothing to be concerned about."* One might as well hold a discussion extolling Adolf Hitler's "positive ideas," while regarding the rest of his views and actions as bearing negligible importance.

Before proceeding to our analysis, a note is in order expressing how we will *not* approach this endeavor.

Against "Nut Picking": The Most Prominent of Ufologists Display ET Belief's Dark Nature

> "As I visited [the Arecibo telescope] in 1990, the director of the observatory noticed my Roman collar and delivered to me a little sermon about the future of mankind and religion once we have heard from those extraterrestrials. He did not mention Christ, but his sermon was clear. **Once we hear from extraterrestrials we can forget about Christ and Christian religion once and for all. Much the same was preached by the group of scientists forming the project SETI...**"
>
> —Fr. Stanley Jaki.[196]

A familiar strategy is employed by commentators who dislike a movement but lack convincing reasons to discredit the tenets and aims of what can fairly be considered important to the movement itself. It is an especially common tactic among journalists when certain grassroots movements become popular even while contradicting culturally prevailing narratives. The strategy is this: rigorously research all the most fringe figures, no matter how obscure, who have in any way associated themselves with the movement. Next, scour their past statements, and collect all the most outlandish sayings that can be found from these individuals. Finally, present this compilation of preposterous words and deeds as "*indicative of the true nature of the movement.*"

Certain legacy media outlets, for example, will give an extraordinary amount of coverage to each "pro-lifer" who engaged in violence against abortionists (despite such occurrences being *exceedingly* rare), while giving no coverage at all to *hundreds of thousands* of pro-lifers peacefully and prayerfully convening on Washington, D.C., each year, to advocate for the rights of unborn children.

This strategy is not one we will use. Ufology and "extraterrestrial research" are fields which count many adherents among their ranks who can only be described as deeply mentally unstable and prone to both believing and promoting each insane claim they stumble upon (or, literally, dream up) which confirms their own viewpoints. However, in justice to the movement I am here arguing against, I will ignore the claims of these outlying voices (even if their numbers are growing rapidly).

Instead, we will focus only on those individuals and groups who are genuinely most representative of the modern movement supporting belief in extraterrestrial intelligence, alien-contact, UFO sightings, etc. Moreover, we will not be considering mere gossip or hearsay; we will not be using baseless "conspiracy theories" to bolster our arguments; we will not levy accusations or make claims based on conjecture. Instead, we will simply review the open and clear statements from the most renowned and influential individuals and groups promoting ET belief.

It is from these statements that we will clearly see what the ET movement's nature really consists in: the promotion of an exceedingly dark, occult, New Age, syncretistic, anti-Christian, and even apocalyptic agenda.

We will see that it is a movement which has not produced any concrete good fruits, but which has produced more rotten fruits than can be counted. The picture that will emerge is so stark, complete, and unambiguous that on account of these fruits alone—not to mention the multitude of theological, philosophical, and scientific reasons we have already discussed to *directly* refute alien belief—it can be dismissed as a manifestly Godless movement from which all Christians should flee.

19. Famous Contemporary Ufologists

Since 1947, society has been saturated with claims of UFOs buzzing our skies and extraterrestrials roaming our lands. Upon the onset of this phenomenon, it did not take long to witness the revelation of the brazenly dark nature of the movement dedicated to its promotion. In the following sections, we will chart out some of its most important developments and consider the teachings of some of its most prominent exponents.

The picture that will quickly emerge is unambiguous. While Christians of the 18th to early 20th centuries may have been able to rationalize—however tenuously—insisting that the whole question of ETs was a merely abstract theological, philosophical, or scientific discussion, the faithful of the 21st century have no similar ability. For we now can discern the fruits. We now *must* discern the fruits, as we are confronted with three quarters of a century of societal effects generated by not only belief in ETs in the abstract, but also by belief that they already travel around our planet and contact humans.

In prior chapters, we covered the relevant topics chronologically beginning with the oldest. But as we are now dealing with current events, it will prove more helpful to begin by reviewing the teachings of those who are today most prominent and active in "Ufology," and thereafter consider the teachings of their forerunners.

While many vie for the title of "today's most prominent Ufologist," one contender is Dr. Steven Greer. This man's teachings, therefore, will be our first item in reviewing the diabolical deception the world has succumbed to in the promotion of ET belief.

Dr. Steven Greer: Many Millions Deceived

Dr. Steven Greer was originally an emergency room physician, but in the year 1998 he retired after less than a decade working as a doctor to devote himself full-time to Ufology-related endeavors. He bills himself the "Father of the Disclosure Movement"—that is, the movement advocating for the government to disclose its "secret ET programs."

The numbers appear to bear out his own claims to prominence. Millions of people across the globe either follow him on social media, watch his documentaries promoting contact with ETs, or even have joined his "CE5" movement to attempt to dialogue with the "aliens."

Scholarly chroniclers of Ufology often overlook Greer due to how uniquely absurd and pseudoscientific his claims are. But they disregard him only at the cost of neglecting to accurately describe the movement they purport to depict. Although wild and baseless indeed, Greer's content is nevertheless believed and promoted by millions, and his popularity only grows by the day. As the "Dictatorship of Relativism" the postmodern West has long labored under increases, fantastical claims like Greer's will only become all the more seductive, therefore Christians would do well to take them seriously—in order to refute them.

Although most mainstream Christian authors appear oblivious to or unfazed by the grave dangers of Greer's movement, not all have been so short-sighted. Orthodox priest Fr. Spyridon Bailey has described well the essence of Greer's deceptive and dangerous tactics:

> Greer claims that from the very beginning of his work he was advising the Clinton administration about UFOs, and it is this link with government officials that he has always used as a means of claiming credibility for his statements. Of course, Greer does not question to what extent he himself may be being used as a means of spreading disinformation by government. ... Greer's philosophy has become mixed with many occult and esoteric ideas, but at the heart of his teaching is a utopian materialism... Greer has claimed that since he was a child he has been able to make contact with extraterrestrials by entering states of meditation. He has developed these techniques and has led hundreds of what he calls "vectoring" sessions. Participants pay for the experience of being taken by Greer to encounter "aliens". Before being allowed to accompany him they are required to sign a non-disclosure agreement, and so the only accounts of these sessions come from Greer himself... He now has access to millions of people through his programmes on CBS, the BBC, The Discovery Channel, the History Channel, Netflix and others...Greer claims that his "new cosmology" adds to our understanding of God, but simply because he uses the same word, we must not imagine he is talking about the same God. Greer recognises that there are non-physical "spiritual" beings at work in the universe, what he calls "Astral Beings", and argues that they have been misunderstood to be angels or demons... Modern researchers like Steven Greer recognise the psychic nature of the [UFO] phenomenon, but instead of understanding its danger, they embrace occult practices in order to intensify the experience.[197]

For all his outlandishness, Greer is nevertheless very strategic. Seeking to appeal to both sides of the "Disclosure" debate, he insists that most UFO-related phenomena are actually government psyops—perhaps associated with "Project Blue Beam"—designed to portray the "benevolent extraterrestrials" as hostile threats. All of this, Greer assures us, is due to the establishment's desire to prevent the masses from acquiring the groundbreaking knowledge the ETs want to give us. This knowledge especially pertains to "zero-point energy" and various other nonsensical jargon laced with the customary empty references to Quantum theory. This knowledge, moreover, would radically alter everything about modern living, which is exactly why the elite have waged a century-long campaign to stifle it—such knowledge would risk loosening their grip on power!

The populist message he promotes works wonders in the hearts of his eager followers, who grow more numerous by the day. Never mind that it is devoid of any scientific basis whatsoever, and that the elites he pins as the bogeymen here would be even more ravenous for this "new knowledge from the ETs" than ordinary folk. Never mind that the ETs Greer ascribes quasi-magical powers to would—if they existed—only smirk at any puny government attempt to prevent the fruition of their own intents. For the gravest danger in Greer's message is not found in the empty promises he makes of an imminent ET-technology-based secular utopia. It is, rather, found in his "CE5" movement, which encourages ordinary people from all walks of life to "make contact with the interdimensional ETs and UFOs" and dialogue with them. Here, Greer is not merely making promises that will only disappoint. Here, he is facilitating dialogue with demons.

To understand the danger inherent in Greer's admonitions, we need not know the details of his own personal "CE5 retreats," shrouded in secrecy due to the non-disclosure agreements he forces people to sign. Instead, we need only observe what he has openly promoted in his most famous work, which will be the topic of our next section.

"Contact Has Begun": Awakening to the "True Nature of Reality"

Entitled *Close Encounters of the Fifth Kind: Contact Has Begun*, Greer's 2020 Documentary lays out his agenda. It has become a wildly popular film. As of this writing, it has over twelve thousand reviews on Amazon, indicating that many millions have already watched it. (For context, the highest-grossing Hollywood movie of that same year[198] currently has eighty thousand reviews on Amazon.) Although rightly panned by critics, the vast majority of people who reviewed Greer's film—80%—gave it a positive appraisal.

As we will see in a later chapter, Greer is likely correct that many government psyops are at work in the UFO phenomena. But Greer, instead of leading his listeners away from that deception and towards the truth, only replaces a human psyop with something worse: a demonic "psyop." One might as well seek to cure a common cold by getting cancer. The dark nature of what Greer advocates will become clear as we recount some of the claims made in this documentary in the following pages.

Greer relies heavily on the testimony of Daniel Sheehan, a lawyer who has long collaborated with the Jesuits, even serving as the legal counsel at the order's U.S. headquarters. Early in the documentary, Sheehan relays his own role in the "Disclosure" movement. (*Note: included parenthetically after each quote is the timestamp of where its conclusion may be found in the film.*) He states:

> We have to come forward with a positive set of programs, a positive vision for this [ET phenomenon], and that's what I'm trying to help get the Vatican and the Jesuit order to become involved in...it's not a threat

> to our species, **it's not a threat to our planet, it's a threat to our view of ourselves as the be all and end all that the entire universe was created as a stage on which to play out the human drama for one single species**. That ain't so. Let's get used to it. And let's figure out what the new story is. What is the new story? ... **We may not be the star of it, but we're a good supporting character in the unfolding of our universe**. And let's figure out what that story is. (18:55)

Already, the eschatological nature of this deception is becoming obvious. "The Day of Disclosure," wherein the ETs are "finally revealed to the world" is portrayed as the time when we can at last leave aside the "outdated, traditional Christian idea" that the events which have transpired on earth have any sort of special (much less unique) role to play in what God has done in His creation.

Greer himself then alludes to *"The success of 'Unacknowledged,' [his earlier documentary] which has been seen by hundreds of millions people now,"* before again cutting to an interview with Sheehan, who this time claims:

> ...this is a subset of a larger question about ... the evolution of consciousness of understanding what we really are in the makeup of the universe ... the raising of consciousness of our human family is so closely related to the opening on to the extraterrestrial experience that both of them together are viewed as a threat by the elite. ... **This is a spiritual experience. It's a spiritual stimulation that's coming**. (43:10)

Sheehan is right: this ET phenomenon *is* a spiritual experience. What he fails to understand is that it is an experience of *malicious* spiritual entities. The documentary soon thereafter transitions to the narrator assuring us of the following:

> It is not possible to simply crowbar extraterrestrials into our traditional, relatively primitive view of reality. In order to make sense of things and, indeed, in order to make contact, **we have to pause and re-address our assumptions about the very nature of reality...God. Prana. Chi. Magic. Consciousness**. Every culture throughout history has had a word to describe this intangible energy that connects everyone and everything. Decades of laboratory studies show that our minds have a mysterious ordering effect on quantum-level phenomena. Despite overwhelming scientific evidence, most people would still be shocked to learn that certain scientists have known that The Force [cf. Star Wars] is real; for a very long time (49:50)

Greer diligently runs the gamut of New Age deceptions, but he has shrewdly perceived that they can now all be conveniently collected under the umbrella of the extraterrestrials. Here as in all New Age deceptions, the goal is to fundamentally alter "our assumptions about the very nature of reality." Any Christian who sees such plans as these so bluntly stated as they are here, is only fast asleep if he fails to notice the diabolical agenda latent within them. As Greer then claims:

> **The ETs are trying to encourage people to understand higher consciousness and the universal mind, to be able to have a relationship with them** (51:10)

Here again, the assertion is accurate. Demons always desire a "relationship when initiating contact; so too these "ETs" want a *relationship*. With the help of Greer (and countless other charlatans), they are becoming increasingly successful, as we will see in the next section.

> "Demons are essentially trying to establish an abusive relationship with us as human beings." —Fr. Chad Ripperger

The film moves on to interview Russel Targ, a physicist, parapsychologist, and promoter of the occult parapsychology practice of "remote viewing." Targ insists that this practice—which is also how we are instructed to contact the ETs—enables one to see the future. As any Christian knows, however, only God can see the future, and any attempt to peer therein with some esoteric practice is nothing other than Paganism. The narrator then continues, again blending religion with pseudoscience to introduce Greer's own testimony:

> Religious traditions and the emerging scientific paradigm are converging on this personal experience of universal consciousness. ... [Greer relays:] "...I began to be a student of the ancient Vedas [Hindu texts]. ... Now their effects were known as "siddhis"; for example, the ability to levitate or teleport, dematerialize, rematerialize, bilocate, trilocate, go through solid objects. These were all things that develop spontaneously as you enter into deeper and deeper and higher states of consciousness. Precognition, telepathy..." (1:03:45)

Greer makes no secret of his own decidedly un-Christian spirituality. What is noteworthy here, however, is that he finds (and promotes) the extraterrestrials as the interpretive key to all these Pagan teachings. Emphasizing the role of the aliens as the heralds of all these apparently disparate phenomena, the film returns to Sheehan, who states:

> ...we have to participate in consciously evolving these faculties ...**That's what this is all about. And that's what these [ET] beings are. These beings... probably come from a red dwarf star, some of them, where they've been around 10 billion years longer than we have. So they've evolved these other faculties**... (1:04:45)

As we will see repeatedly within Ufology, the fundamental claim that bolsters its promoters' belief in the quasi-magical abilities of the aliens is their insistence that these beings have "had millions or billions of years longer than us to evolve." Thus they prime themselves to welcome the doctrines of demons—who are indeed vastly more intelligent and powerful than humans—without needing to even concede that anything is happening that cannot be explained by "evolution" and "science." Confirming that this means everything changing, including Christianity, the film presents a stark assertion written out on the screen for all to see:

> "**In our time this search [for ETs] will eventually change our laws, our religions**... space, the mirror, waits for life to come look for itself there." —Ray Bradbury

After ensuring his audience is sufficiently ravenous for this diabolical "awakening" that the "super-evolved extraterrestrials" want to give us, Greer proceeds to share his method for doing precisely that—his (in)famous "CE5 Protocols." At this point, the documentary begins its transition into still darker territory.

CE5: A Séance-like Protocol for Dialoguing with Demons Disguised as ETs

Dr. Greer explains how to contact the ETs as follows:

> ...the steps of this are, that you sit in quiet consciousness. ... **connect to that aspect of your mind that is unbounded.** And then intend to sense, feel, see, know where the ET craft is. It could be in another galaxy**. Connect to those beings, politely invite them to come and visit you**. And then you connect to their communication systems and their consciousness, which are integrated. **And you show them where you are**. ... It's almost like a vectoring; a zooming in from wherever they are to where you are. Let's say, if you're in North Carolina, [visualize that] you're coming into Earth, you're coming in to North America, the East Coast, the mountains the blue ridge, ZOOM, down to a few square meters around where you are, where you *clearly* show them where you are. And you do this in a coherent thought sequence that is continuous. (1:12:00)

Greer is insistent on this method. It must consist in a very careful meditation that is resolutely dedicated to a clear visualization (which he also calls "vectoring" or "zooming")—a construction of an image in your sense impressions, to indicate to the "extraterrestrials" exactly where you are. Unfortunately, this approach is not mere nonsense. Greer has instructed his millions—perhaps tens or hundreds of millions—of listeners on how to invite a demon into their lives.

The procedure he advises is so well crafted for this end that it is unlikely Greer even devised it without those same demons instructing him. Recall that in the opening hour of the documentary, he surreptitiously deconstructed a traditional Christian worldview in his listeners' minds. He did so, as the demons usually do, not by using logical argumentation, but seduction. He presented the allure of a secular utopia and a life-changing epiphany, at the "small cost"—the mere proverbial "pinch of incense"—of leaving behind a traditional Christian worldview. Only then does he proceed to provide the careful method one must use to actually *invite in* the

"ETs." He first ensures that his listeners have strayed outside the safety Christianity affords them—and within the reach of the Devil's chain—and only then does he advise "ringing the bell."

This approach was necessary because the Devil is not omniscient, nor are any of his minions, and the demons themselves cannot read your mind (absolutely nothing and no one but God can do that). They are stuck with "looking" at what you are physically doing (which is easy for them to see), or at least observing what you are sufficiently strongly *imagining* such that "sense impressions" of these thoughts are left within your neurochemistry itself. The demons *can* see those. This is why Greer insists upon carefully visualizing your physical location—"vectoring" in on it—as doing so facilitates the entry of the demons who, upon "finding" you, will find you without defense. Greer continues:

> The key is to take a first half an hour to meditate, go into quiet mind, then sense where they are, then invite them... you're actually making contact in consciousness and thought before they arrive in their craft or trans-dimensionally around you. **And when the ETs approach us most profoundly, is when everyone in the team is in a coherent state of consciousness and are clearly doing this with the intent.** " (1:12:44)

Just as during an openly occult séance—which is indeed likely to produce a diabolical encounter when undertaken by a "coherent" group all unified in their intent to contact the deceased, or "spirit guides," or what have you—so too in what Greer advocates for, contact with a demon is not unlikely. The demons, however, are not stupid. They do not come announcing their true nature, as that would risk spoiling their prospects of continuing the "relationship" they desire with humans. Instead, *they play along*. They present themselves precisely how these spiritually foolish people *want* to see them: including as "UFOs" and "aliens." As the Catholic spiritual warfare researcher, Charles Fraune, observed after reviewing a multitude of occult practices and practitioners:

> ... **demons will play along** with the big game of the occult that [occultists] have invented. When witches, magicians, and Satanists cast spells and seek to acquire higher and higher magical abilities and ranks, **demons will assume their part in the game. They will pretend to ... obey commands, and give every impression that what the occultist believes is true.** For example, Adam Blai, who has worked with exorcists for over a decade, discussed the fact that Wicca is a big made-up system in which people think that, if they follow these strange rituals, they can acquire whatever they want. He said, "*...if you're breaking the First Commandment, [the demons will] step in and play the role. 'Sure, I'll be your guardian angel,' 'Sure, I'll be your grandmother,' 'Sure, I'll be the Horned god of the green forest or whatever you want to call me'.*"[199]

One should not expect the demons to act any differently when an extraterrestrial is the most convenient costume for it to wear. If, as Scripture teaches, "**Satan disguises himself as an angel of light**" (2 Corinthians 11:14), then it would certainly be easy for him to assume the disguise of an alien or a UFO.

Clearly aware that some of his Christian followers are likely to initially recognize the phenomenon for what it is—*preternatural*—Greer continues, seeking to rebut this recognition before it is acted upon:

> Some of the civilizations we're interacting with in our teams are in the order of a **billion years beyond our development**, and all those beings in that civilization are in a state of unity consciousness that is **so enlightened that they could be confused with, say, an angel or something. BUT THEY'RE NOT. ... they're ETs with star systems and planets and bodies**... What I would suggest to people, **if they are experiencing fear, or if they feel apprehensive about doing it, make sure you do it in a group**. Make sure you set up the parameter of unity, of peace. This is a frequency that is far out of the spectrum of fear. So, there's an incompatibility there. In a scientific perspective, [it's like when] you think about resonant waves... (1:26:30)

Dr. Greer knows there will be a natural instinctual response of fear when the demonic becomes present—even when it tries its best to conceal its true nature. Because of this, he recommends the séance approach—ensuring that contact with the "ETs" is done in a group. This will not only facilitate the arrival of demons, but also the mere presence of peer pressure will prevent otherwise prudent souls from backing out. Further seeking to ensure that this entirely healthy fear* does not prevent "contact," the documentary presents the testimony of another contactee, who advises:

> ... If you're feeling like you want to continue whatever contact experience that is happening, but there may be a bit of residual fear that you're trying to work through, *tell them*. Say 'Look, I'd love to carry on doing this but I feel a bit scared right now. Can you help me with that?"... AND THEY WILL!" (1:46:55)

Indeed, a demon will "help" if asked, and whoever further reveals his soul to them, is only giving them instructions on how to better deceive moving forward.

The film continues promoting all manner of pseudoscience and pseudo-philosophy (which we do not have the space to address here) before beginning its conclusion, with the narrator declaring:

---

* In fact, a Christian in God's grace should not fear the Devil, since his power is utterly insignificant in comparison to God's grace. My point is only that we should be aware that the Devil's power is vastly beyond *our own*, therefore we should respect it and not presume to be prepared for dialogue with him. Instead, we should simply stay away from him, and if he presents himself, command him in Jesus' Name to depart. Those who, however, reject this advice, and approach him or invite him in, will indeed usually at first experience a type of emotional fear which is a good and proper indication that they are doing something exceedingly foolish.

> People from all walks of life are becoming interstellar ambassadors and experiencing transcendent states of consciousness in union with these beings... by simply using the guided meditation in the CE5 contact app. It's up to the children of earth to become active participants in the unfolding of our universe ...Once we reach a critical mass of people, a coherent and enlightened minority can transform the rest of humanity *instantly*... (1:56:40)

Whoever is—understandably—tempted to merely scoff at this outlandish invitation presented by Greer should remind himself of how immensely popular his movement is. It is quite likely that people very close to you have been deceived by this individual, have the "CE5 Contact App" on their phone, or have at least had their *curiosity* piqued by Greer's "simple method" for dialoguing with "ETs." The curiosity alone is a grave danger.

Greer did not share all the details of his protocols within the film. One must dig somewhat deeper to find those. Some are, however, relayed in a book entitled *A CE-5 Handbook* (2018). Therein, aspiring contactees are instructed as follows.

First, you are told to "*connect to one mind consciousness.*" You are instructed to "*detach yourself from your individual consciousness... [and] Name yourself... expand the boundary of who you are so far and wide that your whole body encapsulates the entire universe. You are the universe... Slip into the void...*" (Part One, 1.) In other words, embrace Paganism and Pantheism, while asserting your presence—with your name—to the demons. You are also instructed to "*...let loose a little. Get sleepy. Enter into a theta brain-wave state.*" (Ibid.) In other words, let go of inhibitions. The less active one's intellect and will, the "better." Inhibitions, well, *inhibit* the entry of demons; which is precisely why they love drug use. Next, the "Group Cohesion" is emphasized, as in all séances. Everyone must be of the same mind. (Indeed, even one person actively resisting the Pagan occultism inherent to the practice could drive away the demons!) You are advised to "*hold hands to connect your energy together,*" (Part One, 2.) again, just as in divination sessions.

There is even a code among followers of the CE5 protocols which proposes *sensibly* to relay communications from the aliens. Aspiring contactees bring a Geiger counter or an EMF (electromagnetic field) meter or any similar device with them that is prone to give random signals under ordinary conditions. However, they regard the readings of these technologies during their "contact sessions" as communications with the ETs. For example, you could pose a question to the aliens, and regard one beep as "no," but two beeps as "yes." Three beeps are often understood as simply, "we are here." Similarly, many forms of séances have their participants solicit varying numbers of "knocks" (usually from the spirits of deceased loved ones) to correspond to various answers to the questions they seek.

All of this is paradoxically reminiscent of what exorcists will sometimes command the demons to do to signal they departed the possessed person. Similarly, aspiring contactees will ask the "aliens" to state very clearly how many are present, and what their names are. This, too, is reminiscent of one of the duties of an exorcist, which is to compel the demon or demons to reveal its name, or their names. In both cases, however, we are dealing only with an inversion of what happens in an exorcism. Those who seek out dialogue with the "ETs" do not have the spiritual authority over demons that a Catholic-priest-exorcist has over the demons during the Rite of Exorcism. They are, therefore, only deluding themselves. The demons are under no obligation to obey these people, and instead of revealing any *truths*, the demons masquerading as ETs will only manipulate the aspiring contactees. Wisely does the Church restrict exorcisms to certain priests specifically appointed to the task, and even then, only with the mandate of the Bishop. Demons are not to be played with.

Of course, that whole question is a non-sequitur, as we are dealing here with people dialoguing with demons without even realizing what they are doing. The Devil has assumed many forms throughout the centuries, but never before has there been so convenient a disguise as the extraterrestrial one provides today.

***

Unfortunately, entire books could be filled with exposés on Dr. Steven Greer's antics. Since he is only one of a cadre of charlatans today promoting the ET Deception, we should now proceed to another man who is even more well-known.

Whitley Strieber: "Communion" with Demons and Perfect Possession

> "The sacrifices of the pagans are offered to demons, not to God: and I would not that ye should have communion with demons."
> —I Corinthians 10:20

Whitley Strieber is a bestselling fiction author whose own encounters with "aliens" have become a veritable cultural sensation. He recounted the experience in his 1987 book, *Communion*, which, only two years later, became a popular Hollywood film of the same name, starring Christopher Walken as Strieber. Despite all manner of indications that the experience Strieber had was of demonic origin, the story concludes with Strieber embracing the "alien" (demon), thus the moral of the story, in all its immorality, is a most germane commentary on the Great Deception now at work in society. Christian author Gary Bates notes:

> **Whitley Strieber is undoubtedly the world's most famous abductee**... Over the years, his visitations continued. By the time of his second book, *Transformation* (1988), he was indeed undergoing a transformation of sorts. **Although initially horrified by his experiences, he now started**

> **to welcome them, almost as a religious experience...**He claims that these beings ultimately helped him develop further occult talents... claiming them to be the gods, fairies, ghosts, and UFO sightings of history, as well as the miraculous events of the Bible. This in turn led him deeper into the occult, attending witchcraft ceremonies and the like...**[Strieber] was a New Age devotee... He was quoted as saying, "I made choices a long time ago that brought me this experience."** His books have made an enormous impact on UFOlogy, and have thrust the UFO/ alien experience deep into the public consciousness.[200]

Indeed, it is difficult to overstate the role of Mr. Strieber, and no one interested in accurately and truthfully giving an account of the modern ET phenomenon could overlook his writings. Bates continues:

> Whitley Strieber's increasing contacts with spirit beings masquerading as aliens leaves us in no doubt about the progressive nature of the deception that enveloped him. ...**Strieber and his visitors are advocating a new religion, and one that he hopes will unite all of humanity.** ... It has been said that Strieber is one of many people who have been increasingly deceived to a point where they have become continually possessed by spirits ... In true counterfeit fashion, demonic possession has even been given a New Age technological facelift. They are now called "walk-ins." This is the belief that a more evolved or "ascended" alien form has literally taken over a human being...[201]

In Catholic demonology, there is a concept called "perfect possession." This is not the type of demonic possession one usually calls to mind when hearing the term. Those cases, instead, arise precisely when the subject does not want to have any fellowship with the demons, and seeks out a Catholic priest for deliverance. This is relatively benign when compared to "perfect possession," where no such desire exists. Quite the contrary, the human being possessed in this manner affirmatively *desires* to live his life under the dominion of the diabolical. Such a person will not show the typical signs one would expect to see in the possessed (e.g., violent aversion to the sacred, being tormented by the presence of the demons). Exorcist Fr. Chad Ripperger explains:

> Perfect possession indicates that the person has given himself entirely over to the demon ... since **the person has entered into a pact with the devil** and is still voluntarily being part of that pact, **the person actually likes it and is not interested in ending the possession**. ... due to the fact that the demon will reward the person frequently in order to maintain the voluntariness of the pact and possession ... Bamonte [observes]: *"As someone who belongs to the devil and has become his direct collaborator, the consecrated Satanist undergoes neither the crises nor manifests the symptoms of those who suffer the extraordinary action of the devil. In fact, as long as he remains the way he is, the devil does not torment him with the usual vexations ... "*...the person's personality will seem very stable ... He will often live under the delusion that this is what hell is going to be like or

> that going forward his relationship with the demon is not going to change from the relationship that they have ... [202]

It is not my place to diagnose Mr. Strieber to determine whether he is "perfectly possessed." Unlike the individuals Mr. Bates alluded to, I will make no claims to that effect. I include the considerations above only so that readers understand this is a real *possibility*. One who begins dialoguing with demons under the guise of ETs may eventually find himself so seduced by their promises that he willingly hands himself over entirely to their rule. The truly terrifying reality at play here is what Fr. Ripperger noted above; namely, that such persons may *"live under the delusion that this is what hell is going to be like."* In other words, the perfectly possessed man, with all manner of worldly gifts showered upon him by the demons, may be quite content with the notion of eternal damnation, for he may falsely consider it only a continuation of his current lifestyle. In fact, the moment earthly life ceases for him, so too will all the gifts that the demons only gave with disgust, and nothing but eternal and unimaginable torment then remains. The essential thing for all to remember here is simple: do not even begin walking that path. *Do not even dialogue with it.*

If, however, Strieber's earlier works failed to convince anyone that demons were involved, his later ones will not.

Strieber & Kripal's "The Super Natural": Sexual Perversion, Demonic Hallmark of "Alien Communion"

> "The 'medical examination' to which abductees are said to be subjected, often accompanied by sadistic sexual manipulation, is reminiscent of the medieval tales of encounters with demons. It makes no sense in a sophisticated or technical framework: any intelligent being equipped with the scientific marvels that UFOs possess would be in a position to achieve any of these alleged scientific objectives in a shorter time and with fewer risks."
> —Jacques Vallée

As with demonic encounters throughout history, so with contemporary "ET contact," sexual perversion is pervasive. This theme, in fact, so dominates modern "alien" phenomena that sufficient material is present to fill many books. Because of how especially grotesque this topic is, however, we will only treat it in this one section.

We have already seen that Strieber's experiences smack of the demonic with such clarity that no discerning Christian could miss it, but this conclusion is rendered especially obvious when we observe how sexuality relates to his "alien abduction" experiences and his theory about them which he developed over the course of decades.

Teaming up with Religion Professor Dr. Jeffrey Kripal, Strieber published a 2016 book entitled, *The Super Natural: A New Vision of the Unexplained.* The space placed between the words "Super" and "Natural" in the title is very deliberate. Highlighting it, Kripal and Strieber make clear that their intent is to explain what would always have been understood as simply *supernatural* (or preternatural) as actually being just *natural*, only in a special way we have not generally been accustomed to experiencing. All of this, moreover, is bound up in the overarching extraterrestrial-belief-scheme. This, incidentally, is the general approach of almost all ET promoters: their ultimate aim is to rob religion of its *supernatural* essence by insisting we can now at last grasp the actual meaning of all those events our "unenlightened" ancestors regarded as deriving from the intervention of God Himself. This strategy allows for all the trappings of faith to be preserved, even while ejecting God from the picture. Thus men, in the "last days," are "holding the form of religion but denying its power." (2 Timothy 3:5)

In the book, Professor Kripal disgustingly treats sexuality in a way I hesitate to reprint here. I must, however, do so in order to expose the depravity with which "alien contacts"—even in their most prominent, epoch-defining expositions—are expressed. (But I will exclude from quotation here the most perverse things these men have written. Unless otherwise noted, the following quotes are all taken from Chapter 9 of the book.)

> If *Communion* [Strieber's most famous work] is not a piece of modern erotic mystical literature, then I do not know what it is. ... he also spoke reverently and fearfully of a divine presence that was feminine, that broke and rode him like a horse, an erotic presence into which he disappeared **in waves of terror and pleasure so overwhelming that they literally washed away his personality ... [but] the problem is this: in the monotheistic West, the divine can only be imagined as male.** ...There is God, but no Goddess. ... My colleague April DeConick calls this ancient pattern "holy misogyny." ... disregard for women is not something tangential to the biblical traditions. It is something fundamental to them. ... [although] the French paleontologist and priest **Teilhard de Chardin, who saw the evolution of the cosmos** as a divine incarnation spread out over billions of years ... [but his] astonishing ideas [on sexuality] were all effectively marginalized or repressed. ... [Similarly, Strieber] was offering what is essentially a feminine divine ... **human sexuality can "flip over," "reverse itself," or "turn inside out" and thus be revealed as something uncanny** ... [as] John Keel notes in his famous book on the Mothman, "*[it] displays an almost pornographic preoccupation with our mating practices ... I knew that UFOs often zero in on lovers in parked cars,*" Keel explains. He also knew that many

> men and women who have encountered these things often find their marriages on the rocks, *"after they begin their liaisons with the space people."* So Whitley's pained concerns about the possible conjugal effects of his erotic occult encounters were hardly unreasonable ones. They fit into a much larger pattern ... **there something cosmic about human sexuality, something at once erotic and *daimonic*, something that can only reveal itself to us in spectral forms, like humming blue balls of conscious fire, UFOs, winged monsters, and almond-eyed sci-fi goddesses** ... Sex is a "demon." Sex is dangerous. Sex is a glowing blue ball of light. Or a giant man-bat. Or a feminine presence that drags a professional writer [i.e., Strieber] out of his comfortable life and beats him into a spiritual awakening. The dark side is important. We should not look away...*

Kripal and his confreres are, of course, delusional. Indeed, in authentic religion, there is no Divine feminine. This fact is not "misogyny," it is reality; no more "misogynistic" than asserting two and two make four. The arguments here, however, are deeply revealing about the nature of the contemporary ET movement's basic framework, which has repeatedly exalted Strieber as among its primary symbols and exponents. Obviously, Strieber approves of Kripal's analysis (he chose to co-author this book with him!), which draws from Fr. Teilhard's apostasy (discussed in a later chapter), and sees "ET-contact" as a primarily perversely erotic phenomenon testifying to "LGBT" themes (e.g., sexuality's "ability to turn inside out"), seeking to define human sexuality in Pagan, occult terms. As we will see later, these accounts make no sense in light of "aliens," but make perfect sense in light of the traditional Catholic understanding of the behavior of a "succubus" or "incubus." Demons have always mocked human sexuality. This is why they are superlatively pleased with contemporary "LGBT" ideology, which is the greatest attack on human sexuality ever seen in the whole history of the world. †

---

* Note: Kripal first presents this sentence as a question, but then answers that question in the affirmative; thus I have simplified, through ellipses, the point he is making.

† Lest, however, good be overcome by evil, we should include a few words on the *truth* about sexuality. Catholic teaching—*true* teaching—on sexuality is very clear, and if Kripal was confused about it, he only has himself to blame. Sex, in and of itself, is a great good—but, as everywhere, the greater the good, the more heinous its misuse. As the old axiom says, *corrruptio optimi pessima*, "The corruption of the greatest is the worst." Sexuality is human nature's greatest (biological) faculty, therefore it is also the faculty which, if misused, invites the most severe destruction. It is also a faculty which, if sacrificed for a greater good (i.e., consecrated celibacy for the Kingdom of God), is no deficiency in the consecrated person's life, but rather an enormous source of grace and power. As Fr. Garrigou Lagrange noted, *"the best thing one can do with the best of things is to sacrifice it."* Because of how swiftly and completely the illicit use of sexuality will destroy one's life and endanger one's eternal salvation, Catholic teaching is rightly very

As is often seen in contemporary discourse, men like Kripal—ostensibly exalting sex by bizarrely declaring it the interpretive key to transcendence—actually degrade sex by inextricably associating it with evil. Kripal continues:

> Such truths are difficult for many to understand, partly because of our religious heritages, which are not always very helpful here... **particularly the Catholic tradition** into which both Whitley and I were born... ***Demon Est Deus Inversus*. The Demon Is God Reversed. As in a mirror? This is all incredibly important for any remotely adequate understanding of [alien] encounter experiences** ... these seeming opposites [are] two ends of the same spectral phenomena... **We no longer need to deny one for the other.** We can ponder both the aching beauty of Whitley's raptures and the violent and invasive nature of his rape. It is time to come to terms with all of it. It is time to stare into the mirror and step through. **It is time to shift the conversation around sexuality**, too.

This remarkable description of the demonic nature of Strieber's "ET encounters" (and, by extension, those of millions of others who claim similar experiences)—paradoxically without the recognition that this is a *bad* thing—reminds us that, ultimately, the demons want to be acknowledged *for who they are*. Their hatred of God compels them to desire to be worshipped in His place. They wear disguises (such as "aliens") when they must for strategic reasons, but their eventual goal is to compel their followers to worship them even while knowing they are devils. That mainstream Ufology is coming closer and closer to acknowledging the fundamentally demonic nature of ETs, while at the same time insisting they are not "literally demons," is a testimony to the apocalyptic nature of the deception now playing out before our eyes.

Kripal's tactic for embracing the demonic is only a rephrasing of ancient Pantheism, supposing that all things are equally derivative of God (for "all things are God"), and that evil must be embraced as if it were good, for we "no longer need to deny one for the other." For "Catholics" like Kripal and Strieber, we no longer need bother with even the first of the Baptismal Vows, wherein all are asked, "Do you renounce Satan? And all his works? And all his empty show?"

---

strong in warning against such illicit use. It is, indeed, an absolute truth that the *one and only* legitimate employment of the sexual faculty is found in the open-to-life union of husband and wife. Any other use of it, whatsoever—whether in "ordinary" adultery or in a deliberate sexual encounter with an "ET," or *anything* else—is not only a grave sin. It is also a welcome mat, inviting demons into one's life. Contradicting this truth, whatever the motivation, is only an act of hatred. Men like Kripal and Streiber—seduced, as they are, by demons—regard this truth as a "fundamental misconception about sexuality." It is unsurprising to see their zeal in advocating for a "shift in the conversation around sexuality," as this is precisely what the demons (disguised as aliens) desire.

For thousands of years, each author who has written his own paraphrase of this heresy regards himself as an innovator, when in fact he is nothing but a plagiarizer. It is precisely Kripal's (and, in general, the contemporary world's) twisted views on sex that provide an opening the demons use to associate with humans under the guise of "ET Contact." The demons know well that the contemporary world is so saturated with sexual evil—adultery, fornication, pornography, auto-eroticism, homosexuality, etc.—that this may be their single greatest opportunity to inject themselves into our lives.

Kripal goes on to explain how he essentially abused his own college students by showing them various sex scenes combined with esoteric teachings relevant to ETs (which I will not describe or quote here), before relating them to Strieber's "alien" contact experiences, and his own "personal reasons" for his fixation on this issue. He writes:

> Now we arrive at the deeply personal [reason]. ... I recognized the face on the cover [of Strieber's book, *Communion*]. **It was those eyes. I had seen them before.** Actually, I had seen them many times, countless times. Those large almond-shaped eyes are iconic in the esoteric religious tradition to which I gave my first academic love and attentions: Bengali Shakta Tantra. Remarkably **similar eyes can be seen on thousands of Hindu goddesses throughout India** ... It was not just those eyes, though. I immediately recognized in Whitley's accounts of his erotic encounter experiences in books like *Communion* and *Transformation* what I had known and felt during "that Night," as I came to call those few minutes in Calcutta, in the fall of 1989 during the annual Kali Puja festival, when my own mind and body were similarly electrified and, presumably, changed by *Her shakti*.

Professor Kripal has yet again definitively proven that these "ETs" are veritable demons. Their machinations are identical to those of the Hindu "gods," which any Christian should know are likewise demons in disguise, and Kripal knows this not only from his academic research, but also *from personal experience*. Kripal continues:

> **The correspondences between Indian Tantric traditions and American abduction literature are quite striking** ... **Telepathic communications, channeled revelations**, and levitation or spiritual flight are some of the most commonly reported. Also central to both are the production of trance and a broad range of possession states, both positive and negative—bliss and terror abound. Sex with discarnate beings is also a central concern of both literatures. ... Both the Tantric and abduction literatures are also filled with various kinds of strange photic phenomena, spiritual bodies of light, unearthly radiances, and exotic forms of ... Whereas the powers and energies appear to be uncannily similar, their cultural and mythical expressions remain dramatically different. ...[Dr. David White] has explicitly invoked what he very carefully calls "UFO-like" language to make sense of ancient South Asian Tantric culture. ...

> David writes of flying temples (vimana), royal airships, and the "landing fields" and "launching pads" of open-air, circular temples, where contact with the fierce female beings from the sky (the yoginis) were believed to take place. More or less **exactly like the female visitor of Whitley's account, these yoginis were described as descending from the sky to abduct, terrify, sexualize, and spiritually awaken the aspirant**. ...**[Strieber's] scene reads like something straight out of a medieval Tantric ritual**.

I have excluded from this quote the most grotesque similarities that Kripal described between Strieber's "ET contact" and the rituals related to Hindu "gods." Suffice it to say that it could not have possibly been made clearer that we are dealing with demons in both cases, and Strieber endorses this interpretation of his own—the world's most famous—"alien encounter." Kripal, however, is content with nothing less than an announcement that what we are confronted with surrounding "ET contact" *is the key to everything;* accordingly, he does not fail to relate his thesis to religious syncretism, "quantum physics, evolutionary biology," and a re-definition of God Himself:

> The project of "comparing communions" might also eventually lead to **the development of a new mystical practice, a western "contact yoga" in deep conversation with our religious pasts (all of them), our evolutionary biology, our quantum physics, our cosmology, and our new understandings of human sexuality.** Certainly such a future practice will require a much richer and more generous imagining of the divine presence. **He [God] must also become She.** Just such a vision is clearly suggested by Whitley's repeated call for a conscious practice of "communion."

The book concludes with an "instruction sheet," written by Kripal, summarizing his advice on how to "*end the world we assume and reveal another one, our true condition,*" and arrive at a "*final awakening,*" or even listen to the "*gossip of angels.*" There, he commends:

> PRACTICE AN EROTICS. Consider the ways that these extraordinary experiences are shaped by **particular gender assumptions and sexual orientations. Also look for moments in which they might actively engage or "flip" the human sexual system and so lead to various forms of union or communion**. Do not automatically reduce these experiences to the simply sexual, but recognize how sexual energies can sometimes morph into transcendent spiritual states ... Consider whether the trance state ... **has "cracked open" the ego for contact and communication** ... **Look for energetic, electromagnetic, or plasmalike phenomena within and around the extreme experience**. See if these altered states of energy appear to be alive or intelligent in some way. **Recognize that you may well not be able to reason with them, but that you may be able to resonate with them.** ... (Appendix)

Behold another guide for contact with demons, presented as advice for dealing with "extraterrestrials." Let us conclude by reiterating that this material is not from some commentator giving his opinion on the correct interpretation of Strieber's "ET" encounters. This is the man whom Strieber himself selected to co-author a book with on the very question. Therefore, this is not "an" interpretation of the "Communion Phenomenon;" it is *the* interpretation of it. And it is so baldly diabolical that no Christian could possibly miss it. Instead of calling it for what it clearly is, though, the most prominent Catholic authors who have touched upon it have only endorsed it (e.g., Msgr. Balducci, a friend of Strieber's who encouraged him to regard his encounters not as demonic but as truly extraterrestrial). This tragic state of affairs brings us to our next section.

Alien Infiltration of the Catholic Church

> "... as demons, doing harm by bestowing pretended benefits—**harm all the greater for the deception**—or else openly and undisguisedly doing evil to men." —St. Augustine

In an upcoming chapter, we will discuss at length how the ET Deception has infiltrated the Catholic Church, while discerning the thoroughly rotten fruits it has generated. In the present context, however, a brief section is in order with respect to even the efforts of secular Ufologists to infect Catholicism with their doctrines.

Strieber's most recent work, *Them,* was published in 2023. He obviously became aware that authors like Bates were commenting on the demonic elements betraying the true nature of his experiences. Therefore, in this book, he goes to great lengths to reject such explanations, writing:

> ... the idea that [the "aliens'"] unwanted behaviors means that they are supernatural beings is a serious mistake... That doesn't mean that they don't have the ability to seem demonic. My own early experiences with them might easily have led me to that belief, had I not had the intellectual resources to enable me to more fully dimensionalize the situation...there was much nuance to be considered. A black-and-white "demons-vs-angels" approach was not adequate...[203]

Strieber assures us that, were he privy to fewer "intellectual resources," he too, like the uninitiated, would have been prone to "misunderstand" these ETs as demons. Thanks, however, to his ability to "*dimensionalize* the situation," he realizes that such a "black and white" approach is inadequately "nuanced." Whoever is wondering what "dimensionalizing" means need not wonder for long: it does not mean anything. It is a vacuous catchphrase used only to avoid confronting reality. Strieber proceeds to reveal still more clearly the depth of his confusion masquerading as nuance when he writes:

> **At present, the Catholic church takes a much more sophisticated approach to the whole question of an alien presence than does the fundamentalist Christian community,** which, like most religious communities in the world, still has not separated the idea of such a presence from **the mythological pantheon that is already part of their belief system**. This means that, even today, Christian fundamentalists are going to believe that aliens are either demons or angels. As they are not "clothed in light," the conclusion will be that they are demons.[204]

While it is certainly true that, for the last few decades, evangelical authors have generally been more diligent than Catholic ones in alerting their readers to the alien deception, it is absolutely untrue that "the Catholic church" itself condones Strieber's view. As we saw in Part Two of this book, the *teachings* of the Catholic Church rule out extraterrestrials more forcefully than those of any other denomination or religion.

Unfortunately, certain clerics within the Vatican have indeed condoned ET promotion; unsurprisingly, this has happened especially in relation to the times when Pope St. Paul VI observed, in 1972, that the "smoke of Satan has entered the Church of God," as we will consider in a later chapter. These men, whose opinions do not comprise the Church's Magisterium, have expressed their own openness to ETs and have publicized their own mistaken view that Catholicism is fine with aliens, hence Strieber's misguided take above. As noted, one particularly deceived theologian in Rome, Msgr. Balducci, even encouraged Strieber in his self-destructive pursuits.

We must ponder: why do the most prominent ET promoters take such interest in the Catholic Church? The reason is clear: the Devil knows it is the Bulwark of Truth, therefore—in his hatred of God and truth—Catholicism is his supreme target. He desires to infiltrate the Roman Catholic Church with his deceptions—his "smoke" and his "pagan prophets," as Pope St. Paul VI called them—far more resolutely than he desires to do so with any other denomination or religion. He induces those who (wittingly or unwittingly) serve him to do their utmost in this regard. Just as we saw earlier, Dr. Greer and his confrère Daniel Sheehan, are intent on "**trying to help get the Vatican and the Jesuit order to become involved [in extraterrestrials]**", so too Strieber (a "Catholic") is intent on similar goals. One may be surprised to learn his religious persuasion, but the surprise will cease when considering just what "type of Catholic" Strieber describes himself as:

> I will die a Catholic, but not a believer. ... For me, faith is a matter of bearing my doubt and continuing on anyway. ... Every night ... I have meditated for half an hour or so, then ended my day with a decade of the Rosary. **And yet, I don't know that I 'believe' any of it**. ... Why is Christ any more true than Krishna, or Mary than Kali? When I go to Mass, I will remember the ritual of Mithra from which it took its form ... [so] I will doubt.[205]

Although Strieber also wrote some beautiful things about the Church, he ultimately remains a tormented soul who seems to *want* to be a devout believer, but always meets some impenetrable obstacle to living that type of life. He wants to really believe in God, only to have his mind afflicted with the typical straw man, "what about *other* 'gods'?" He wants to believe the Mass is real, but then he wonders if it can be any better than various Pagan rituals. If only Strieber recognized that, in his encounters with the "aliens," he was not and is not "*...contending against flesh and blood, but against the principalities, against the powers, against the world rulers of this present darkness, against the spiritual hosts of wickedness in the heavenly places,*" (Ephesians 6:12) then he would easily prevail over his demons. Tragically, his "good Catholic" friends (including clergy) have only helped him remain in subjection.

Indeed, no evil spirit stands a chance against a Catholic in God's grace who seeks out the weapons the Church provides for spiritual combat. On the other hand, no human stands a chance against a demon if, supposing it to be anything but a thoroughly malicious entity, he engages in dialogue with it when it disguises itself as something else. No human intellect is up to that task. The obstacles Strieber encounters, therefore, are not difficult to define. They consist in the same onslaughts the demons always assail a man with when he seeks to free himself from their grasp. The demons, being much smarter than he, know exactly what arguments to suggest to his imagination whenever he toys with the thought of escaping from their grasp.

Strieber's own inner struggles are almost a microcosm of those endured by the Church at large. Modernism has induced many of its members to regard the Church in merely temporal and material terms, so they fail to even acknowledge, much less effectively engage in, the spiritual warfare raging in front of their very eyes. Just as Strieber, thanks to his "**understanding of dimensionality**," pleases the demons and makes their job exceedingly easy by regarding them as aliens, so too the Church today—thanks to its welcoming of Modernism—pleases these same demons by regarding their antics as mere psychological phenomena, or as "societal structures of injustice" to be remedied only by activism.

Strieber's claim that Christians distinguish angels from demons by determining whether the beings are "**clothed with light**" further displays the extent of his own deception and reveals why he and innumerable others cannot (or will not) acknowledge the reality of their own experiences. In fact, as we saw earlier, the demons are quite adept at appearing "clothed with light."

> "But I am afraid that as the serpent deceived Eve by his cunning, your thoughts will be led astray from a sincere and pure devotion to Christ ... **And no wonder, for even Satan disguises himself as an angel of light**." (2 Corinthians 11:3,14)

Christians are not to judge such beings by a "luminous" appearance or lack thereof, but rather by ascertaining whether the message conveyed is orthodox—i.e., in keeping with the teachings of the Faith (cf. Galatians 1:8)—and by examining whether the resulting fruits are Godly or rotten (cf. Matthew 7:15-20).

In Strieber's case—the most prominent of the "alien abductions," which also accurately summarizes how most transpire—even a modicum of the virtue of discernment demonstrates the diabolical nature of his "visitors." Yet, as with all of the most prominent ET promoters (who are not outright atheists), Strieber is under the impression that the operations of demons must be so obvious that, in his words, they are only seen "**leaking the very stench of evil out of their pores**."[206] This cluelessness regarding demonology is why even so many Christians are succumbing to the ET delusion.

Another prominent contemporary Ufologist, Professor D.W. Pasulka, is unabashed in sharing that she is a Catholic. Her works on Ufology are massively popular, often topping bestseller lists. She is a frequent guest on major podcasts promoting this topic, including Lex Fridman's YouTube channel, which has over three million subscribers. She also featured prominently in a September 2023 Netflix documentary, *Encounters*, which was produced by Steven Spielberg and spent some time as the most popular show on the platform.

Dr. Pasulka glowingly promotes Vallée and his theses (which, as we will see shortly, are baldly diabolical deceptions—so much so that even Dr. Paul Thigpen concedes their problematic nature!), including his interpretation of Fatima as a UFO (albeit while employing the standard academic phraseology that may allow her to later claim she was only "writing about it, not endorsing it"—despite all her readers knowing full well she is doing precisely that). In her extremely popular 2019 book, *American Cosmic*, she writes the following of apparitions and Dr. Vallée:

> **[Vallée] performs a "biblical-UFO" interpretation...identifying both apparitions and UFOs as manifestations of a single control mechanism** ... Jacques notes that the actual events [of Fatima] are mostly unknown and have been changed through media and over time. Few people realize that "*... the technology which "she" [Mary] uses is indistinguishable from that of gods and goddesses of other tongues and garb; it is also indistinguishable from the technology surrounding the UFO phenomenon.*" [Quoting Vallée] (Ch. 5)

Pasulka then describes the Miracle of the Sun in detail, only to follow up this account of one of Our Lady's greatest modern marvels by returning to her unqualified praise of Vallée's take, writing:

> In his close readings of the apparitions, Jacques's strategy is to attend as much as possible to the first order of events as they transpired, keeping to the original language used by the experiencers, whom he calls

> percipients. ...[he is] committed to the idea that the phenomena appear to be technological.

As is obvious to a sincere and simple believer—but too difficult to grasp for many scholars—any approach to an authentic apparition from Heaven (like Fatima) is only diabolically deceived if, instead of taking Heaven at its word, one seeks to subjugate the apparition to an esoteric interpretation which regards the messages it delivers and miracles it performs as "technological," or as only one outlet for some separate and loftier-still "control mechanism." And this is Vallée's approach.*

It is easy to see how the Devil would be eager to promote Vallée's thesis. For the evil one is, quite literally, hell-bent on mitigating the force of the Blessed Virgin's apparitions, which are more necessary today than ever, and which will only become increasingly vital in the coming times. If the Devil can delude enough Catholics into supposing these apparitions are not at all what they thought them to be, then actualizing his plans in the world has just become much easier.

Not only, however, does the Devil want Marian Apparitions thus essentially dismissed. Even more, he wants to *himself* receive the credit for the wonders associated with them. Indeed, some saints (e.g., St. Louis de Montfort) have speculated, not unwisely, that the Devil hates and fears the Virgin Mary even more than God Himself. Not that Mary exceeds God (obviously, she does not!). In fact, it is precisely because she is a "mere human being" who nevertheless will, as the Devil knows but despises, crush his head, (cf. Genesis 3:15) that the Virgin Mary not only defeats the Devil but also humiliates him. We should not be surprised to see the ET Deception especially keen on attacking Marian Apparitions by perversely contorting their promotion to make it seem they were UFO phenomena.

Stepping back, we see here that the trend we have observed continues: a relentless effort to infiltrate the Catholic Church with the ET Deception. This battle can only be understood in apocalyptic terms. Pasulka

---

* Inextricable from this position is at least one of the following corollaries: the apparition is actually a deception and is not an apparition at all, or it is an apparition but Our Lady is a liar and misrepresents her role entirely when she appears, or it is an apparition but Our Lady is actually herself entirely beneath—a mere emissary of—whatever other entities administer the "control mechanism;" entities who are just as ready to send the Virgin Mary as they are to send "UFOs," or creatures from Pagan myths, with messages that regularly overturn almost every dogma of the Faith. Each of these three corollaries is loathsome. It is beyond question that Fatima, Lourdes, Guadalupe, La Salette, Kibeho, Rue du Bac, and countless others, are authentic apparitions. (That they are private, not public, revelations does not change this fact.) Moreover, the Virgin Mary never has lied and never will lie—she is Immaculate. Finally, the Virgin Mary is underneath nothing and no one but God Himself. It is Catholic dogma (as we saw in Part Two) that she is the greatest creature who exists and who possibly could exist, therefore she cannot be considered as merely one outlet of some "control mechanism." Vallée's approach is inseparable from at least one of these corollaries.

herself is not just any Catholic religion professor. For example, she even recounts stories of her uniquely privileged access to the Vatican's secret archives. The quotes above are not rare in D.W. Pasulka's works—she regularly sings the praises of Vallée's take on the ET phenomenon, and I have not been able to find any reservations, much less disagreements, stated. My aim, however, is not to single out Pasulka or attack her.* I only wish to illustrate the extent to which UFO doctrines have infiltrated Catholicism. Pasulka is only one member of a steadily growing group of prominent "orthodox Catholic scholars" who are becoming heralds of the "extraterrestrials." There will be more like her soon entering the fray, and whoever wishes to persevere in the Faith must be sure not to be seduced by their works.

An Unwitting Confession on the Demonic and Apocalyptic Undertones of "ET Contact"

> "The demons will constantly play on that fear ... They will incline the various faculties to recoil in horror at suggestions of courses of action that are necessary in order for the person to be liberated."
>
> —Fr. Chad Ripperger[207]

Towards the end of "*Them*," Whitley Strieber changes his tune. After conceding that much of the "aliens'" visiting our planet since 1947 behave in ways that fly in the face of any benign interpretation, he concludes the penultimate chapter of the book's main part with the single line: "**are we dealing with demons after all?**" That question introduces the book's final chapter, which recounts his own personal experiences with the "ETs" in the year 2021 and 2022—over thirty years after his now world-famous encounter described in *Communion*.

Despite all the decades of great struggles he endured up to that point, he describes these more recent experiences as "the beginning of one of the most difficult times in my life." He proceeds to describe visions of dwarves, gnomes, and dead bodies stripped of clothing and bound; experiences of technology doing inexplicable things that caused great intimidation and turned friends against each other; hearing explosions nearby but without explanation...and more. Pondering these events, Strieber shares:

---

* I would guess that Pasulka is well-meaning and entered Ufology (she claims she is "not a Ufologist," but obviously she has become known as just that) thinking it could be used as a means of covert evangelization, only to then get carried away and become reckless regarding what and whom she promoted, not realizing that, despite good intentions, she is simply being used by the demons, who often use apparent good intentions when those intentions are detached from tradition, orthodoxy, proper discernment, etc.

> All of these events were attacks, some more serious than others... [involving] attempts to destroy my relationships with people I love. ... whomever [sic] had the motive to harm [my website with a hack] chose another way that, because it involved a [physical] break-in, was meant to also threaten my person. **It's the sort of vindictiveness that happens when somebody you thought loved you gives you pain. You want to hurt them back, and what better way to do it than to ruin their work and their relationships with people they love**? And there the story ends. Unfinished, as always. **I hope that I will one day understand what this is about and who is doing it, but that day has not yet come.**[208]

Strieber has just described a protracted demonic attack. Despite introducing his account by openly pondering "*are we dealing with demons after all?*", he nevertheless concludes by ignoring that very explanation and instead insisting he simply does not understand. Demons, however, have an ever present motive to torment humans: *hatred of God*, and a concomitant delight (if you could call it that) in inflicting misery upon His beloved children. Nothing Strieber shares of his experiences is beyond the pale of what a demon can do.

Did Strieber, perhaps, make some attempt—even if only privately; perhaps even only interiorly—to extricate himself from the UFO deception? If so, this would easily explain the punishments his "visitors" inflicted upon him in 2021 and 2022. As exorcist Fr. Chad Ripperger notes:

> ...a grace from God may be granted in such a fashion that the person [in a pact with demons] decides to break the pact...**if [that] grace were to be given, then the demon would tum on the individual with full vengeance.** This is sometimes seen in cases in which there is not perfect possession but the person is cooperating with the demon in certain areas and he is giving the person various pleasures, delights, goods, etc. Once the person recognizes that there is a problem and wants to put an end to the pact or denies the demon something, the demon will tum on him with a vengeance.[209]

Regardless of what the correct explanation of Strieber's situation consists in, patterns like these, displaying demonic bondage, are seen constantly in the lives of those who "*commune* with the aliens." Just as when they wear other disguises, these demons have their expectations and demands which are attached to the (apparent) benefits they bestow, and when these demands are unfulfilled by the person, punishment ensues.

The chapter closes with Strieber unwittingly alluding to the apocalyptic nature of the deception under which he labors:

> Our visitors have been ghosts in our world, but **now that time seems to be growing short, they may well be bringing themselves more into focus** ... now, as another extinction event shadows the future, the long, ungainly poem of life on Earth comes to the singing of what could be

> the final stanzas of this latest verse. **Many of us are looking up into the stars and out into the shadows that are gathering around us, seeking help from anyone who might linger there. The worse things get, the more will join them...**

Although Strieber has chosen the wrong side of the present and coming confusion, he is absolutely correct in acknowledging its existence. Time is indeed growing short. Therefore:

> **Woe to you, O earth and sea, for the devil has come down to you in great wrath, because he knows that his time is short!** (Revelation 12:12)

Because of this shortness of time, we should only expect the UFO and alien deception to increase. When the world appears to be on the brink—perhaps due to looming (or actual) nuclear war, or a great pandemic or famine, or the so-called "climate crises"—that moment will be the opportune one for the demons to announce themselves more widely than ever before under the guise of "enlightened extraterrestrials," presenting to mankind a "**deception offering men an apparent solution to their problems at the price of apostasy from the truth**." (*Catechism of the Catholic Church*, §675)

Jacque Valle's Trojan Horse: the "Interdimensional Hypothesis" Deception

> "Faced with the new wave of experiences of UFO contact that are described in books like *Communion* and *Intruders* and in movies like *Close Encounters of the Third Kind*, our religions seem obsolete ... The eager anticipation of encounters with other intelligent beings would help in transcending local conflicts on this earth and in achieving within a single generation behavioral changes that might otherwise take hundreds of years to complete. ... **we are in fact dealing with one of history's major transitions.**"
>
> —Jacques Vallée. *Dimensions.*

A household name among ET believers and a veritable expert in all things extraterrestrial, Dr. Jacques Vallée enjoys a stature similar to Strieber's. We have already considered Vallée's cutting critiques of "mainline" Ufology; presently, however, it remains to consider the even darker deception with which he proposes replacing it.

Recall that, as far back as the 1970s, Vallée's fame for promoting ET belief was so great that Hollywood's preeminent movie about aliens, *Close Encounters of the Third Kind*, had a main character explicitly modelled after him. In the half century since, Vallée has remained very active in the movement. In 2020 he even appeared on the world's most famous podcast, "The Joe Rogan Experience," to discuss UFOs. Clearly, understanding Vallée's contribution is essential in understanding the ET phenomenon itself.

Among Vallée's greatest claims to fame is his pioneering work in the so-called "Interdimensional Hypothesis," which regards the UFOs and "ETs" that have been visiting earth as beings not traversing physical space to arrive here from other solar systems or galaxies, but rather as "control mechanisms" appearing here from other "dimensions" altogether. Although his conclusions are errant, many of the observations and arguments Vallée uses to bolster this thesis are entirely accurate. As noted earlier, he demonstrates well that these UFOs are not physical ET craft at all, and he proves that the whole ET phenomena operates on the basis of "ETs" visiting with motives that could not be explained by those of any alien civilization. Rather, they only make sense if these visitors have their own ends which we could only diagnose as manipulative.

As Vallée's analysis obviously lends credence to the correct understanding of the diabolical nature of the phenomenon, even several Christian authors who have warned of the UFO deception have subscribed to Vallée's "Interdimensional Hypothesis." They reason, "*I suppose demons are themselves from another dimension, therefore I can make this hypothesis work with a Christian worldview.*" Unfortunately, such Christians are only falling for yet another diabolical trap.

Demons are spiritual beings, not "interdimensional" ones. There is no such thing as "another dimension" or "another universe," much less another class of incarnate creatures inhabiting such things. When defining these "ETs" as "interdimensional beings," a Christian might himself remain safe (in accordance with his own understanding that, by "interdimensional," he simply *means* "demonic"), but he will fail to keep *others* safe. The reason is clear: shifting the language from "demonic" to "interdimensional" signals that empirical science remains the dominant mediator of the conversation. As the saying goes, "*he who controls the language controls the debate.*"

Whoever accepts this shift has indicated that the fundamental dynamics of the phenomenon under consideration may well have "*different* laws of physics," but are still within that umbrella of "empirical physics" considered more broadly. In truth, the spiritual cannot be described using any material/empirical methodologies whatsoever. (Although it can indeed be explored with the basic laws of logic.)

The "Interdimensional Hypothesis" gives the demons the best of both worlds, and whoever promotes it is playing directly into their hands. By claiming that "aliens" are actually "interdimensional beings," one gives them permission, as it were, to adopt a wider array of tactics, since they need not even pretend to be piloting physical craft in the "traditional alien" sense. Despite affording them this leeway, they can remain disguised and happily be called "interdimensional," so long as they are not recognized as *demons*.

In fact, when it comes to dimensions, there are exactly the three we all intuitively grasp. Time is not, strictly speaking, a "dimension." Dimensions can be measured; i.e., you can hold a ruler up to something's width, length, or height, and measure those "dimensions." You cannot measure time (your watch does not measure time, it counts the oscillations of a piece of quartz with a voltage applied to it, which you *interpret* as a measure of time), for *time itself is a measure*—namely, it is merely the measure of motion. (We will consider this fact more deeply in later chapters.)

Humans have always known what a "dimension" is, and only in today's Dictatorship of Relativism could men be deluded into supposing there could be "more dimensions" than the three we have always known.

The notion of multiple dimensions was first used by Vallée and his peers to describe UFOs, but the idea itself did not come from them. Considering its origin in order to better understand its problems is our next task.

Flatland: Builder of the Trojan Horse

The idea of multiple dimensions of reality beyond the commonsense three dimensions originated from a short novel entitled *Flatland,* written by Edwin Abbott in the year 1884, which has since acquired a sort of cult following. Little known in its own time, the novel became famous upon the publication of Einstein's General Relativity and the prevailing supposition that time was simply a fourth dimension. Einstein's scientific theories combined with Abbott's literary imaginings provided all the basis that was needed for a new esotericism to emerge that was ostensibly based on science.

The story imagines personified two-dimensional polygons (the "narrator" is a square) as the characters, who are then confronted by a sphere who struggles to explain and prove his own three-dimensional nature to them. This provides the context for the limitations of a two-dimensional reality to be explored. Perhaps most relevant is the phenomenon whereby a three-dimensional object intersecting with this two-dimensional reality would only be capable of being known (by the inhabitants of that two-dimensional realm), at a particular moment, by way of whatever two-dimensional cross section of its volume was then intersecting with that two-dimensional realm.

This idea provides all the premises the promoters of "Interdimensional ETs" need to assemble their deception. Such an "ET" (demon) can do anything it wants, unbounded by "our" physics, since however it is experienced at a given time or by a particular person derives solely from a different aspect of its nature "intersecting" or "phasing" with our "lesser" dimension. And thanks to the Interdimensional Hypothesis, it can do all these things without being recognized for the *spiritual* entity it is.

Unfortunately, some Christian apologists, all too eager to sign on to prevailing sci-fi trends, have long made heavy use of *Flatland* to explain the spiritual realm. This approach has yielded no good fruits. If it achieves anything, it only succeeds in convincing the skeptic that he can maintain his atheism even once he realizes that many miracles are objectively proven; he need only sprinkle his atheism with a smattering of "dimensionality" (as we saw Strieber do to insist his "ET" visitors were not demons) *et voila,* he can explain away all miracles without needing to acknowledge the *truly* supernatural—without needing to acknowledge *God.* He can simply say, *"well, okay, there are other dimensions I don't totally understand. But there certainly isn't a God and this God certainly didn't become man."*

Indeed, although dressed up in all manner of pseudoscientific jargon, what readers are expected to take away from the Interdimensional Hypothesis is none other than, *"Wow! Beings from other dimensions would be so much more awesome than us in every way that we just can't imagine it. Really, anything that could possibly happen here on this tiny speck we call earth, and anything that we will ever experience, can easily be chalked up to their intervention!"* Thus, the Interdimensional Hypothesis is the perfect postmodern garb for the new Gnosticism to wear.

Another basic fallacy of the *Flatland* approach—and the whole "Interdimensional Hypothesis"—is its dismissive attitude towards the material universe. A "higher dimensional" thing can only exist within a lower dimensional reality by virtue of an infinitesimal and negligible portion of its own constitution. For example, a sphere can only exist in two dimensions as a circle. In truth, however, spirit and matter—supernatural and natural—do not have that relationship. Spirit can explicitly break into matter whenever it pleases, and it can do so in *all* its reality. When God became man 2,000 years ago, He did not merely interact with us on earth through an infinitesimal slice of His Divinity. Quite the contrary, the Man, Jesus Christ, truly was and is the eternal God Himself. "**The Word *became* flesh,**" (John 1:14) the Word did not "intersect an infinitesimal slice of itself with flesh." Moreover, our spiritual souls are not merely present in the material universe by virtue of some insignificant slice of their reality. Quite the contrary, our bodies *are themselves the very matter of our souls,* with the latter serving as the (subsistent, spiritual) form. Whatever angle from which one approaches the Interdimensional Hypothesis, therefore, it collapses into heresies.

In brief: talk of "interdimensional" realities, no matter the context, is always fallacious. It is nothing but a Trojan Horse. It is a trap to seduce Christians into the domain of Pagan ramblings wrapped up in pseudoscientific claims.

An amusingly fortuitous decision of one of the originators of the Interdimensional Hypothesis is found in the naming of his book promoting the view, *Operation Trojan Horse.* This 1970 work written by renowned

Ufologist, John Keel, insisted that the "aliens" visiting us are actually "Ultraterrestrials;" beings who, in ages past, appeared as mythological creatures. But these myths were only guises that served as proverbial Trojan Horses to conceal their often-malicious intent. That Keel is correct in ascribing frequent malicious intent to these beings is no consolation whatsoever. It is, in fact, *his* hypothesis which is nothing other than a deception. Although his book proposes to *expose* "Operation Trojan Horse," the truth is that Keel's own argument *is itself* the Trojan Horse. The strategy is to delude people into supposing that traditional spiritual, supernatural realities are not ultimate, but are only one subset of "Interdimensional" realities. Thus, "Interdimensional" beings may sometimes appear as "gods," to others as God Himself, to other cultures as fairies, to others as demons, and to still others as aliens. The ultimate goal of this diabolical agenda is to depict everything in Scripture as rather minor. Only now, as we are finally beginning to grasp "Interdimensionality," can we learn the *real* story: the much "bigger" picture of which religion gives only a small glimpse. One could not imagine a scenario more primed to herald the Antichrist.

Alas, "the proof is in the pudding." If anyone understands the intricacies of the Interdimensional Hypothesis, it is Vallée. Let us, then, simply consider his own statements to discern the fruits of his famous hypothesis in order to realize that there is nothing benign in what he advocates.

Fatima as a UFO: The Grand Attack on All Things Supernatural

> "I think the stage is set for the appearance of **new faiths, centred on the UFO belief.** To a greater degree than all phenomena modern science is confronting, the UFO can inspire awe, the sense of the smallness of man, and an idea of the possibility of contact with the cosmic. The religions ... began with the miraculous experiences of one person, but to-day there are thousands for whom the belief in otherworldly contact is based on intimate conviction, drawn from what they regard as personal contact with UFOs and their occupants."
>
> —Jacques Vallée

We have seen that John Keel's *Operation Trojan Horse* is guilty of the very deception it purports to expose. Equally backwards, however, is Vallée's "seminal master-work," published one year before Keel's work of similar persuasion. Entitled *Passport to Magonia,* the cover of the book's current edition depicts an alien holding several masks; one mask portrays a demon, another a different type of alien, and another a female which could represent any number of mythical beings or perhaps even the Virgin Mary. Vallée's thesis is thereby made clear: the demons (and, indeed, *all* spiritual beings) themselves were simply one guise the "Interdimensional" UFOs once wore, not vice versa. Traditional religious thought "must be replaced with this new, superior understanding of transcendent realities."

Whitley Strieber himself was and is deeply impacted by Vallée's thesis, and he describes the latter's "demonstrations" as follows:

> [Vallée] demonstrates, for example, **that the miracle of Fatima** was a sort of hybrid appearing in part as a religious phenomenon and in part **as a classic UFO encounter.** One is left to wonder if there might not have been a very real **technology behind the miracles and apparitions** that have done so much to influence the growth of our cultures. ... **most major religions have emerged out of visionary experiences that are, in fact, understandable in the setting of the UFO encounter**. Thus the phenomenon becomes not simply one of a group of things that influence the evolution of culture, but rather a primary engine. It **could very well be the single most important influence on our history**. And it is arguably more active now on a global scale than it has ever been before.[210]

Can any serious Catholic fail to see that something thoroughly diabolical is afoot? Adding to what we have already reviewed, we now see Ufology's persistent and blasphemous efforts to present Marian apparitions—even the greatest miracle of modern times, Fatima's Miracle of the Sun—as UFO phenomena. Sadly, as we have seen, many Catholics do condone and promote Vallée's thesis. Let us consider the shrewd commentary of one popular traditionalist author, Charles Upton, who observes that in speaking of Marian apparitions and other miracles in terms of Ufology, Vallée displays...

> ... a shocking though very common lack of any sense of proportion... **the quality of what emerges entirely escapes him** ... [here,] his scientific ideology, his scientism, make themselves apparent. ... [For Valle et. al.,] Moses saw a volcano and founded Judaism; the disciples of Jesus saw a UFO and built Christendom. **But to someone with the slightest understanding of what a religion is, the vulgar and tasteless tricks produced by today's 'aliens'...will necessarily appear as just so much excrement ...** Dr Vallée's scientism appears ...[when] he states that: '*They [the UFO aliens] are ... part of the control system for human evolution.*' ... I will only ask Dr Vallée what the abductions, the weird medical experiments, the animal and human mutilations ... the aerial acrobatics designed to awe and confuse, the sexual molestations, and the use of subtle forces, either psychic or psychotechnological, which paralyze the body and darken the mind, have to do with evolution? If we accept the theory of biological evolution, do we not understand it as based on physical processes which have no need of UFOs to help them along? And if we are talking about social or spiritual evolution, what do terror, violation and deception have to do with it? Can a monkey be forced to evolve into a man

> by torturing or hypnotizing him? Can a society be improved by confusing and terrorizing it? Can a man be forced to evolve into an angel by abducting and sexually molesting him? ... [in truth,] the 'unseen [i.e., spiritual] warfare' hypothesis must appear an infinitely better explanation than the 'evolutionary' one.[211]

Vallée's own words reveal just how darkly deceptive his teachings are:

> **[Fatima's early] sightings cast serious doubts on the interpretation of the "miracle" given by the Catholic Church** ... The early story of Mary herself, and the miracles that surrounds her life, point to **intriguing similarities with earlier deities, and in particular with the Egyptian goddess Isis.** Like many targets of UFO manifestations, Mary was hit by a mysterious beam of light and subsequently bore a fatherless child. The scene at Fatima is reminiscent of the Phoenician amulets described earlier.[212]

Vallée leads his readers directly to the precipice of blasphemy—i.e., regarding the Queen of Heaven and Mother of God as a mere iteration of some phenomenon that also brought about the Pagan "god" (demon) Isis—knowing that doing so is more than sufficient for those same readers to all hurtle forward past it. Employing customary scholarly tactics, he does not state his demonic conclusion directly, but only notes how very "interesting" it would be, or how "noteworthy" it is, or how "doubtful" the *true* explanation is. This is how Satanic seduction *always* works, and discerning readers will not allow these rhetorical devices to prevent them from seeing what is happening.

What Vallée is not reticent about, however, is his categorical insistence that many apparitions are nothing but UFOs:

> Is it reasonable to draw a parallel between religious apparitions, the fairy faith, the reports of dwarf-like beings with supernatural powers, the airship tales in the United States in the last century, and the present stories of UFO landings? I would strongly argue that it is—for one simple reason: *the mechanisms that have generated the various beliefs are identical.* [emphasis in original] ... Fact **... Several [apparitions], which bear the official stamp of the Catholic Church (such as those in Fatima and Guadalupe), are *in fact* ... nothing more than UFO phenomena...**[213]

In one sense, it is astonishing that a scholar such as Vallée, so dedicated to rigorously exploring a given phenomenon, could nevertheless remain so clueless about its true mechanism of action. In another sense, it is entirely predictable. As we have seen and will continue to see, the scholars are the easiest class of people for the Devil to deceive. (All it takes is a little coddling of their egos, and they become like putty in his hands.) Despite knowing just about all there is to know about UFO sightings, Dr. Vallée knows *nothing* about supernatural discernment.

Fixated upon his puerile observation that the Virgin Mary is often in the air during apparitions, along with a few other superficial resemblances that chance alone would ensure exist—he regards it as an affirmative "fact" that apparitions generate belief by "identical mechanisms" as those which generate belief in UFOs. One wonders if Vallée has ever himself spoken at length with a single authentic Catholic mystic—it seems he has not.* For whoever has done so would know that none of them believe in the apparitions they receive due to Our Lady being in the air when speaking to them, or appearing with beams of light, or any other silly resemblance to "UFO phenomena."

These mystics believe because they have engaged in *proper* Catholic discernment. They have tested the apparition to ensure it is not a demonic deception, in accordance with Scripture's admonition, "**Beloved, do not believe every spirit, but test the spirits to see whether they are from God**." (1 John 4:1) They have sought out spiritual direction from a holy and orthodox Catholic priest, to whose judgment they submit. Despite the crosses that invariably come with being a seer, Our Lady always leaves them with that very abiding "**peace of God, which passes all understanding,**" (Philippians 4:7) and not the negative fruits that always (either immediately or eventually) follow "ET contact." They have ensured that the message accords with all the teachings of the Faith. It is by these and other similar methods of discernment, not by "witnessing phenomena like those of alien contactees," which is the real "mechanism of belief" of the authentic seers. Yet, Vallée has somehow entirely missed *all* of this.

I am far from alone in noticing the danger of Vallée's teachings. The same priest we have quoted earlier, Fr. Spyridon Bailey, provides the following Faith-informed analysis:

> [Vallée] has written arguing that many religious visions may be attributed to UFO encounters and during the 1970s and '80s he was a consultant for the CIA's Stargate Project which was research into remote viewing. While supporting the reality of UFO encounters, Vallée argues that what people are encountering is a non-human form of consciousness that is able to manipulate time and space ... Vallée's conclusion is correct when he says "*I propose that there is a spiritual control system for human consciousness and that paranormal phenomena like UFOs are one of its manifestations*". But **his willingness to recognise this control as the means to our spiritual development and the advancement of our worldview leaves him and anyone who accepts his theories, vulnerable to deception.** ...[Vallée approaches] biblical texts, using misinterpretations of a number of commonly understood images (such as the chariot of Ezekiel) to propose the idea that the encounters with angels and signs from God were no more than UFOs... Vallée considers visions

* Because I have known, and spoken with, authentic mystics. Here I should note, for readers unacquainted with my other works, that I have long been deeply involved in Catholic private revelation, including revelations to living seers. Vallee and his promoters appear to have not the slightest genuine grasp of real Catholic mysticism.

> of the Theotokos [Blessed Virgin Mary] as part of the same deception...he proposes that: "*The UFOs are physical manifestations that simply cannot be understood apart from their psychic and symbolic reality...*" In his book *Dimensions*, [he] describes how he came to believe that the film ***Close Encounters of the Third Kind* had been supported by government agencies with the intention of preparing people for the release of UFO information**...Deception is a common theme amongst the accounts of many ["alien"] contactees, who often feel that they have been mocked by the treatment of the aliens. For Vallée, this is nothing more than a "control system", and he believes that the purpose of this is to manipulate human beliefs.[214]

As we see from Fr. Spyridon's summary, Vallée is, like most Ufologists, deeply entrenched in the occult, desirous of a "spiritual development" for humanity from the "ETs," and insistent upon the supernatural events of Scripture itself being now regarded as simply misunderstood UFO phenomena. Elsewhere, Vallée has even declared that, "**we may very well be living the early years of a new mythological movement, and it may eventually give our technological age its Olympus...**" On this point, Vallée is correct; though, disastrously, it excites him instead of impelling him to lament and warn. But St. Paul beat Vallée to the punch:

> "For the time is coming when people will not endure sound teaching, but having itching ears they will accumulate for themselves teachers to suit their own likings, and will turn away from listening to the truth and wander into myths." (2 Timothy 4:3-4)

***

The ET promoters we have focused on so far in this chapter promote the "Interdimensional Hypothesis." A reader may be wondering, "*What of contemporary promoters of more 'traditional' notions of aliens, who simply traverse large amounts of interstellar space in their ships, or at least their radio signals or through wormholes, to arrive here? Are those promoters at least proposing more benign teachings?*" The answer, unfortunately, is an emphatic *no*. To the chief of those "traditional" ET promoters, we now turn.

Carl Sagan: False Prophet of Scientism

Carl Sagan (1934—1996) was an astrobiologist and astrophysicist, and, more significantly, the chief prophet of 20th century sci-fi pseudoreligion. Although famously and astutely skeptical of reports of UFO sightings, Sagan was nevertheless among the most prominent of the ET promoters of the contemporary era, dedicated as he was to SETI (i.e., the effort to contact aliens remotely, using radio waves, not physically). His fame in this arena is no doubt due to his reputation as the late 20th century's most famous pop scientist.

He was perhaps most known by way of the 1980 television series he starred in, wrote, and narrated, *Cosmos*, which—over four decades later—

remains the most viewed series in the history of PBS. It was even the most popular television series in all American public broadcasting for a full decade. Today, a significant portion of the world's population has been formed by its teachings. One biography of Sagan reported the show had a half billion global viewers[215] (when the world's population was close to half its current number). Indeed, its cultural impact is difficult to overestimate.

The series began with one blunt assertion from the lips of Sagan that still haunts the memories of millions. Strolling towards a steep cliff overlooking the sea, Sagan prayed his own false doxology: "**The cosmos is all that is, or ever was, or ever will be**." The thirteen episodes that followed expounded upon this lie, presenting a worldview—a *cosmos*-view—with no place for God.

Sagan's popularity had nothing to do with his scientific insights. Indeed, the scientific community, for good reason, often had little regard for him. Instead, his popularity was due to the pseudo-mysticism and the false religion that he preached. His messages—including his famous TV show—were peppered with pithy remarks seeking to prick the soul in ways that only religion authentically can, hence atheists, agnostics, skeptics, and doubters of all types found in him a bankrupt wellspring of that very transcendence they longed for but lacked. A prominent biographer of Dr. Sagan observed:

> **In the space age, when "mankind doesn't need gods" (to quote Captain Kirk), science-fiction writers, speculative scientists, and UFO buffs have in fact replaced the old cosmic power structures with scientific ones.** For example, UFOs are "angels" or "devils" made of nuts and bolts. ... **Carl Sagan, too, believed in superior beings in space, creatures so intelligent, so powerful as to resemble gods**. They are superior partly because their civilizations are millions of years old and have developed technologies unimaginable to us. They have evolved far enough to outgrow their warlike ways. And they are benevolent; **they will even share the secrets of the cosmos with us, if we'll simply tune in to their radio transmissions.** ... In his book *Broca's Brain* (1979), Sagan said, "*it is possible that among the first contents of such a [alien] message may be detailed prescriptions for the avoidance of technological disaster. ... It is difficult to think of another enterprise [besides SETI] within our capability and at a relatively modest cost that holds as much promise for the future of humanity.*"[216]

As we see above, Sagan's own advocates concede that his ET beliefs can only be accurately regarded as downright *messianic*. Here we must again recall the prophecy of *The Catechism of the Catholic Church:*

> The supreme religious deception is that of the Antichrist, **a pseudo-messianism** by which man glorifies himself in place of God and of his Messiah come in the flesh. (§675)

No other movement in the modern world comes close to extraterrestrial-expectation in presenting a Godless "pseudo-messianism," and this fact is evident in the statements of its exponents who are indisputably the most prominent. With the help of the aliens—pundits like Sagan insist—man may finally "glorify himself" by attaining, through the ETs "super-evolved" enlightened and technological insights, what earlier times rightly regarded as God's sovereign prerogatives.

Demons rarely enter a man's life unveiled, but before the end, they do prefer to be acknowledged for what they are. The same demons behind the alien fixation which began in Sagan's youth waited until his demise to arrive without disguise. As if alluding to the dominion the demons had over his legacy, Sagan published his last book, *The Demon-Haunted World.* Therein, he labels religions as "state-protected nurseries of pseudoscience," and ponders "has there ever been a religion with the prophetic accuracy and reliability of science?" (Which makes one wonder if he has ever heard of Christianity, or if he is aware of how few of science's predictions have come true.) After much additional parroting of the same tired sound-bites the faithful had heard levied against them for decades, Sagan finally announces the invitation he had been working his way towards the whole time, which is none other than the invitation to replace religion with science:

> **No contemporary religion... take[s] sufficient account of the grandeur, magnificence, subtlety and intricacy of the Universe revealed by science.**[217]

Science, Sagan assured us in the same work, is a "*bulwark against mysticism, against superstition, against religion misapplied to where it has no business being.*" (Although for Sagan, traditional religion has no business being just about *anywhere*.) Above all else, man is by nature a religious creature, however, and Sagan surely had his religion. His own biographer concedes:

> **Sagan's insistence on the inevitability of cosmic intelligence is important partly because it undergirded his quasi-religious belief in alien super-beings. He believed that these creatures, perhaps dwelling in other galaxies, were benevolent and might help us to solve our terrestrial problems. Viewed from a psychological perspective, they were secular versions of the gods and angels he had long since abandoned**. (Carl Sagan: A Life. Chapter 1.)

Sagan's mission was ultimately an invitation to abandon Jesus Christ for the sake of placing one's faith and hope in alien contact. The secular world, moreover, has ensured that he has risen to prominence and primacy in all things extraterrestrial. As Christians know just who the prince of this world is, they should not be sluggish in considering why he has ensured Sagan has received this focus.

> "And you he made alive, when you were dead through the trespasses and sins in which you once walked, following the course of this world,

following the prince of the power of the air, the spirit that is now at work in the sons of disobedience." (Ephesians 2:1-2)

Almost as prominent as Sagan's TV series was his Hollywood film, *Contact*. There, he lays out his agenda for all to see.

Contact: Sagan's Replacement of Religion with Extraterrestrials

Sagan's ET-based pseudomysticism is illustrated most sharply in his 1985 novel, *Contact*, which became a major Hollywood film by the same name in 1997. Its impact resounds strongly to this day. A brief review of its plotline is in order (spoiler alert).

The hero of this story, Dr. Ellie Arroway, is an avowed atheist who believes science has disproved God and who has been dedicated since her youth to discovering radio signals from aliens. The opening scene shows her at her amateur radio, with her father walking into the room to encourage her efforts. That night, after learning from him that radio waves can even reach other planets, little Ellie asks her father: with these same signals, "*can we talk to mom?*" (The implication is clear.) Soon thereafter, her father, too, dies. A priest attempts to console Ellie at the funeral, but she rejects his suggestion to trust in God's Will, and instead runs to her ham radio to try to speak with her late father.

As an adult, Arroway becomes involved with the official SETI (Search for Extraterrestrial Intelligence) program which seeks to contact aliens with radio waves, and—with a zeal and conviction that can only be described as religious—she triumphs over many obstacles in that pursuit. One day—to the interspersed backdrop of a monologue testifying to the need to fill the "holes in our lives" that exist due to the modern world's lack of meaning, loneliness, and an isolation from each other—Arroway detects a signal originating from the vicinity of the star Vega (25 light years away) containing large amounts of encoded information. This data winds up being plans to construct a machine to enable one person to travel through space. The machine is built, but an apocalypse-minded religious zealot destroys it. Arroway, however, had been passed over as the one selected to travel on that machine due to her "telling the truth," in an interview, that "as a scientist," she must say "the empirical data" does not support belief in God.

Thankfully for Arroway, a second machine had been secretly built, and she is selected to travel in it—which brings her, through a wormhole, to Vega's solar system, where she sees technological alien civilizations whizzing by, only to suddenly appear on a beach. There, she is gently approached by an apparition of her father, whom she embraces but also realizes is actually an extraterrestrial who had been reached by SETI and who found humanity worthy of enlightenment (it constructed an image of her father by downloading her memories). It explains that there are "many of us" (aliens), and that humans are an "*interesting species...capable of such beautiful dreams, and such horrible nightmares. You feel so lost, so cut off, so alone, only you're not. See, in all our searching, the only thing we've found that makes the emptiness bearable, is each other.*" The wormhole then brings her back to earth, with all those who had observed the event thinking no time had passed and that she went nowhere. Naturally, observers suspected a hoax once Arroway recounts her experience. She is grilled during a Congressional hearing, berated for her inability to provide any evidence that she had travelled through space and met aliens. She concedes that lack of proof, but insists she knew what she experienced was real, an "*awesome, wonderful vision of the universe... [showing] that we are not alone,*" and exhorts her audience to accept her testimony "*on Faith.*" We are then shown that hidden details exist which confirm the veracity of her account. These details, however, are kept confidential. The Search for Extraterrestrial Intelligence (SETI) continues. The end screen says, simply, "**For Carl**"—Sagan had died seven months before its release.

This is the movie *Contact* in a nutshell. (*The book off which it is based, though less popular than the movie, provides a far more explicit and repeated repudiation of traditional religion—particularly Christianity—to the point of obsession.*)

Although I saw the film when it came out 26 years ago, I had not seen it since. Nevertheless, the beach scene had eerily, even hauntingly, always stuck with me. The reason is clear: that was exactly Sagan's intent. Sagan knew that to promote his replacement for religion, he needed to tug the same heart strings that would naturally lead to its authentic expression, while at the same time directing his audience away from God. *Contact* at once provides a God-substitute that is transcendent, childhood-memory-centered, focused on a father figure, mysterious, current-events-relevant but future oriented, and heroic; while—above all—remaining squarely within the domain of science. The beach scene, a perverse twist on the Apostles' encounter with Jesus by the Sea of Tiberias after His Resurrection, provides the climax of Sagan's antithesis to religion: an encounter with "The Other" that both consoles and inspires, while offering a tantalizingly partial explanation of reality and a mission moving forward. To further tug at those same heartstrings, Sagan has the alien appear in the form of the very person the film's viewers have been vicariously (for Arroway's sake) longing for the whole time: her father. Hearing his soothing voice—even if it was really an ET—assuring us that "we are not alone" because "we" (the many intelligent civilizations in the universe) make the (apparent) "emptiness" of space "bearable," parodies Christ's assurance, before His Ascension, "Behold, I am with you always, even to the close of the age." (Matthew 28:20) And just as the Apostles proceeded to proclaim their Faith in the Risen Christ to propagate Christianity, so too Alloway goes on to beseech her listeners to take her testimony on Faith, as she zealously propagates SETI.

This twist was written in by Sagan because, by the time of Alloway's congressional grilling, the plotline already formed the ET-replacement-religion during the beach scene. No longer did ETs need to be promoted only in the dull and uninspiring terms of electromagnetic waves and evolutionary biology and the like. It could now be presented as the false faith it was always intended to be—a faith, like the true one, propagated not by data discovered in empirical studies, but by the bold and heroic witness of individuals who *know what they saw*, and are willing to suffer in proclaiming it. Indeed, astute advocates of Scientism understand that empiricism—science's apparent strength—is, in fact, only its weakness when seeking to make science a religion. No one sheds his blood to proclaim Newton's Laws. There is no thrill, much less mystical attraction, in declaring, "*My microscopes show result Y under scenario X; I think yours will also.*" But to say, "*I know what I saw, though I have no physical evidence. It is awe inspiring; it answers our heart's deepest longings. I will suffer for it and dedicate myself to it. Will you?*"

That proclamation has the capacity to inspire. And this is exactly why Sagan worked his way up to this dénouement throughout the whole plotline, knowing he could only succeed in presenting ET-based Scientism as a substitute religion by leaving aside the very thing that supposedly renders science so supreme in his mind.

Little wonder that Sagan was so dedicated to the project of this movie. It summarized decades of his career which was above all intent on replacing Christianity's hope and faith in Jesus Christ with a science-inspired hope and faith in extraterrestrial contact. And modern society has largely gobbled up this mission of Sagan's—including too many Christians who, astonishingly, refuse to see the deception at work.

The sentiments expressed by *Contact* are those which permeate and dominate the contemporary ET-belief and Ufology phenomena. Any discerning Christian who sets foot in those circles for a moment will not fail to notice. In almost everything the ET promoters say and do, there is a perverse reenactment of the excitement, the sayings, and the antics one finds in reading the Book of Acts, wherein early Christians proclaim Christ to the world because *they know what they saw*, and they know they must tell the world that *we are not alone—God is with us*. We are promised imminent "Ontological shock." We are definitely, they promise, entering the greatest of the "Great Awakenings" earth has ever seen. They are not even attempting to hide their insistence that *this is the new Faith*.

From here as well as every other angle which we can discern extraterrestrial belief and expectation, one finds clearer preparations for Antichrist than could even be imagined in a work of Christian speculative eschatological fiction. I confess: years ago, I was thinking of writing just such a work. Upon further studying contemporary ET belief and Ufology,

I recognized that would be frivolous. The *real-life* progression of extraterrestrial contact expectation over the years is a more breathtaking apocalyptic deception preparation than I could have dreamed.

***

A Note on What We Have Been Doing

Recall that the present part of this book opened with a repudiation of "nut picking." Although I obviously reject—and admonish my readers to likewise reject—the notion of "extraterrestrials," I nevertheless desire to assess the movement related to belief in them fairly and accurately. We have, therefore, only been focusing on the most prominent voices within that movement; individuals whose teachings *define what the movement is.* No one who desires to understand contemporary ET belief could fail to focus on the individuals we have covered here. One might as well ignore several successive Popes in seeking to understand the nature of Catholicism.

Even with restricting our analysis to these individuals, we have seen—beyond the slightest doubt—that their efforts are expressly *anti*-Christian. They constitute none other than preparations for a delusion the likes of which the Church and the world have never seen.

Imagine, then, what we would see if we only slightly loosened our criteria. We then would have considered the *even more* outlandish voices (who are anything but rare in Ufology). Indeed, had I instead presented the teachings of those ET promoters that were of second or third tier prominence, we would see a barrage of explicit Satanism.

In the following chapters, therefore, we will expand our analysis and consider the nature of ET belief, Ufology, and "alien contact" more generally than focusing only on what is expressly admitted by its most renowned exponents. For Ufology is not unlike other phenomena, wherein the most renowned of the promoters provide the introduction, but those not as well-known provide the real substance. To that task, we now turn.

20. The Contemporary ET Phenomenon

"Many of the UFO reports now being published in the popular press recount alleged Incidents that are strikingly similar to demoniac possession and psychic phenomena which have long been known to theologians..."
—U.S. Air Force Office of Scientific Research Report. "UFOs and Related Subjects." 1969[218]

Let us begin this section by considering one Catholic expert's summary of the machinations of demons in people's lives which has nothing to do with UFOs or other "alien" encounters. As explained by Demonologist Adam Blai:

> **The demon almost never appears in ... true form, they lie and deceive constantly.** ... **If demons showed up and looked horrible and menacing people would run the other way** and right into a Church. They reel people in slowly by offering knowledge, playing on pity, giving comfort or power. Only when they have a sufficient hold will their true intent (to take people away from God and destroy them) become clear. ... The enemy often takes advantage of weakness or misfortune: they come when people are sick, bankrupt, depressed, or swollen with pride. They offer to fix problems or elevate one above others. The trick comes later when the person is at their peak and they tear it all down so that they suffer the most intensely... There is always an act of free will involved in letting a demon enter the body; one just might be unaware that it is a demon. **Permission might be given in response to a deception, but the door is opened nonetheless...**"[219]

Christians should keep these norms in mind as they read accounts of alien abductions—which are bound to continue as they long have. Above all, we must remember that demons usually have no incentive to appear to someone in their true form. A demon assuming some strategically deceptive appearance is far more effective. Not only are the demons extremely intelligent, but they are also liars by nature, for the Devil is a "liar and a murderer from the beginning." (John 8:44)

Of supreme importance in discerning descriptions given of "encounters with aliens," therefore, is remembering that recounts of *appearances* are not to be taken at face value. That approach would be question begging—circular reasoning; it would be none other than *assuming* that "alien" encounters cannot be demonic deceptions in the very act of arguing they cannot be. Moreover—as we will see presently—when investigating the details surrounding *any and all* accounts of non-debunkable "alien" encounters, one always discovers the presence of factors indicating the presence of the demonic is likely. "Abductions," for example, almost always prey on those already suffering in psychologically, socially, financially, or relationally sensitive situations; or on those who are already engaged in occult or New Age practices; or those who are living deeply in mortal sin. On the flipside, what one *never* finds are saintly souls, engaging in discernment in accordance with proper Catholic principles, insisting that they know they have been in contact with extraterrestrials.

Abductions, Evil, and Satanic Ritual Abuse

> "For we wrestle not against flesh and blood, but against principalities, against powers, against the rulers of the darkness of this world, against **spiritual wickedness in high places**."
> —Ephesians 6:12

One psychologist—not at all interested in the demonic—after reviewing a multitude of abduction experiences, reported what follows in a 2023 academic paper. As in previous sections, I here include the works of those with views starkly contrary to my own to illustrate that even the findings of those who dismiss the demonic explanation of ET-encounters nevertheless unwittingly confirm that we are dealing with demonic phenomena here. (The author of this paper wishes to *condone* abduction experiences, for she praises them as shifting "*...human consciousness toward a Nature-based worldview...signaling the return of the Archetypal Feminine...the Age of Mother Nature.*") This psychologist writes:

> "Classic" abduction experiences typically proceed in the following manner: Seemingly out of nowhere, the person may be in bed sleeping ... abduction experiencers "*are always sure that they are not dreaming or imagining; rather they experience that they* ***have moved into another reality,*** *but one that is, nevertheless, altogether real... as if the alien beings break through a kind of screen, revealing a new reality to experience*" ... [but] it **does not fit with any scientific laws** ... The **craft itself is often described as cold—both emotionally and physically** ... whether the being is "humanlike, animal, or something else, **the detail most frequently commented on is the eyes**." In abduction experiences, the **contents of one's mind seem to be thoroughly revealed** to the beings who use gazing or staring at the experiencer, often communicating telepathically in a process that appears to commence through the eyes.[220]

Although they make perfect sense in a demonic encounter, these accounts are irreconcilable with physical aliens piloting crafts that traveled from another solar system or galaxy. Laws of science appear violated—which no technology, alien or otherwise, could do (see Part Three of this book). "Emotional coldness" is experienced, as demons struggle to mask this *lack of peace* even when assuming deceptive forms. Abductees experience fixation upon the "alien's" eyes, for the "*eye is the lamp*" (Matthew 6:22), and it is there especially—even in a demon's guise—that its true nature would be most evident (as we also saw, for example, with Strieber and Kripal in earlier sections). Abductees feel their "mind is being read," which no technology could ever achieve. Although demons cannot truly read one's mind, they can *seem* to, for they can read much of what is within one's sense-impressions, which itself results from some thoughts. These are all descriptions one would not be surprised to hear relayed after an encounter with a demon, because that is what they are.

Christian astrophysicist Dr. Hugh Ross undertook a large and rigorous study of "alien abductions" and "Residual" UFO sightings (RUFOs). (By "RUFOs" he means those UFO sightings which remain even after eliminating the ones explainable by misunderstood or misperceived ordinary earthly phenomena; what I refer to as *un-debunkable* UFOs.) He found that they are, without doubt, demonic. He writes:

> **A closer examination of RUFOs shows that they are consistent with the Bible's descriptions of demons.** The RUFOs appear to be alive and to be acting in an intelligent way with malevolent intentions. ... people who encounter these residual phenomena have previously opened themselves to the forces of evil. How? By participating, knowingly or unknowingly, in occultism or occult-related activities—for example, fortune telling, Ouija board games, séances, and so on—all of which are biblically forbidden. **The connection with the occult is plain to see in the case of those who have the closest encounters with UFOs: abductees and contactees.** Abductees are people who tell a story of being captured by aliens and taken aboard spacecraft for examination. Contactees are people who claim to be used by aliens as channels of information. These reported experiences are completely in line with such occult practices as trance channeling of 'ascended masters.'...**The truth about UFOs can be known**. Indeed, the UFO mystery is a mystery solved. **Earth is not being visited by aliens from another planet, but some people are being visited by spirit beings who want everyone to think they are aliens from another planet**.[221]

But things get darker still. One of the most noteworthy but little-known links between diabolical activities and alien abduction is the latter's manifest similarities to Satanic Ritual Abuse (SRA). The parallels are remarkable and particularly instructive, since the demons are less veiled in Satanism, whose very purpose is to worship the demons for what they are, not merely under one of their many guises (as in "UFO Religions," which we will consider in a later chapter). Therefore, one sees elements of Satanic abuse that may not be present in an identical form as in abductions, but at least veiled ones. These similarities were reviewed at an academic conference held at MIT (Massachusetts Institute of Technology) in June 1992, and in the table below are presented some of their findings:[222]

Alien Abduction Accounts	**Satanic Ritual Abuse Survivor Accounts**
Examination Table, White Sheet	Altar Table, White Sheet
X-Ray, Headgear, Wires	ECT, Polygraph, Shockers
Surgical Needles, Implant Instruments	Knives, Daggers, Pins, Needles
New "Space Writing" Symbols	Old Esoteric Writing Symbols
Circular and Triangular Emblems	Pentagrams and Triangles
Focus on Eyes: Scary and "Calming"	Focus on Eyes: Scary and "Demonic"
Bright Light as Initiating Event	Bright Light as Torture/Intimidation
Clamps as Restraints	Clamps, Chains, Ropes, Belts
Electricity Used to Experiment, "Heal," or "Transfer Information"	Electricity Used to Torture, Intimidate, or "Eradicate Information"
One "Alien" in Charge	One "High Priest" in Charge
Told: "You are Special," "We Will Return," "Do Not Tell,"	Told: "You are Special," "We Will Return," "Do Not Tell,"
Taken from Bed, Field, or Forest	Kidnapped in Bed, Field, or Forest
Amnesia from Experience	Amnesia from Experience
Feel Drugged/Euphoric/Anesthetized	Drugged with LSD, Heroin, Cocaine, Herbs, etc.
Out of Body Experience/ Astral Travel	Out of Body Experience/Astral Travel
Resulting Paranoia: "They are Coming Back"	Resulting Paranoia: "They are Coming Back"
Resulting Sleep Difficulty, Nightmares, Sexual Disturbance, Depression, Humiliation, and Obsessive Thoughts	Resulting Sleep Difficulty, Nightmares, Sexual Disturbance, Depression, Humiliation, and Obsessive Thoughts
Issued Threats "Seen as Caring"	Issued Threats Recognized as Abusive
"Forced Intercourse"	Ritual Rape
Shown Films of Destruction	Shown Films of Destruction
Cattle Mutilations	Animal & Human Sacrifices
Apocalyptic Predictions (Nuclear Disaster)	Apocalyptic Predictions (Armageddon)
Age at First Abduction: Average Age of 5 or 6 reported	Age at First Initiation: Average Age of 6 Reported
Long Range Study of Abductee	Long Range Exploitation of Initiate
Illnesses Cured by Aliens	Illnesses Cured by Witchcraft
Abductees Feel they Know Each Other	Survivors Feel they Know Each Other
"Accommodation Syndrome" Secrecy, Helplessness, Entrapment & Accommodation, Delayed Disclosure, Retraction	"Accommodation Syndrome" Secrecy, Helplessness, Entrapment & Accommodation, Delayed Disclosure, Retraction

These are, of course, stunning parallels. Those things associated equally with both "alien abductions" and Satanic abuse speak for themselves. What may be even more noteworthy, however, are the contrasts. Obviously, the Satanists engaging in their diabolical rituals are real, flesh-and-blood people; unlike aliens. Yet, they explicitly take their orders from demons, and what Satanists carry out from these orders is strikingly mimicked by the beings undertaking "alien abductions," though often with trickery to prevent their Satanic nature from being detected.

For example, a demon posing as an alien must not have an obvious altar, but rather an "examination table." It must try to conceal the terror deliberately evoked by Satanic abuse by covering it with anesthetic-like effects or even a euphoria easily induced neurochemically (and which an undiscerning soul might confuse with true peace), which is within the power of demons. It must conceal the pain of its brand of "bright light" by presenting it as an "initiation." It must pretend that the various degraded forms of torture it undertakes are mere "medical experiments." It must seek to gain the same total control over the victim, while posturing this as a form of *care and concern*, not abuse. In a word, it must do its utmost to ensure its victim succumbs to Stockholm Syndrome.

Despite all this evidence, however, still clearer indications exist that we are dealing with demonic phenomena in "alien" encounters. Let us now examine those indications. I must warn you that the findings are many.

"Aliens" Flee at the Name of Jesus

> "UFO behaviour is more akin to magic than to physics as we know it ... the modern UFOnauts and the demons of past days are probably identical."—Dr. Pierre Guerin

The CE4 research group was established in 1997 to study abduction experiences. They quickly discovered over four hundred individual accounts of abduction—including hundreds of accounts they received directly from the mouths of "abductees" themselves—wherein the "alien abduction" immediately stopped upon invoking the name of Jesus.[223] Over a hundred testimonies they have collected are available to be read—including many audio interviews that can be listened to—on their website.[224] Obviously, there is no conceivable reason for a being to flee at the name of Jesus unless it is a demon.

"**<u>By invoking the name of Jesus Christ... Satan is driven out of men</u>**" —St. Irenaeus... "these signs will accompany those who believe: **in my name** they will cast out demons" —Mk 16:17 "First, Jesus gave the power to cast out demons to the twelve apostles, then to the seventy-two disciples. With these words, he granted the same power to all those who believe in him. There is one condition: we must act in his name.

The strength of those who expel demons, whether or not they are exorcists, lies in their faith in the name of Jesus." —Fr. Gabriele Amorth

The saints have always been known—whenever they were uncertain about the origin of a vision they received—to command the being appearing (as the Virgin Mary, or Jesus, or an angel or saint in Heaven) to recite some prayer that no demon would recite, or even to command the apparition to depart, in the name of Jesus. In so doing, they averted many diabolical deceptions launched against them. For example, the Servant of God Luisa Piccarreta once told Jesus, when He appeared to her in one of her earlier encounters with Him, "**Are you perhaps some demon who wants to deceive me? ... If you are not a demon, let us make the sign of the cross ...**" (September 1, 1899, Diary Entry) While it may appear scandalous to hear that the mystics were so resolute in ensuring they were not succumbing to diabolical deception, even demanding that Jesus prove Himself to them, this should not surprise a Christian at all. Deception abounds in this world, and only those who are serious in avoiding it—employing all the means required to do so—will succeed.

I will add that since I began focusing on writing against this deception (in early 2021), I have received much (unsolicited) correspondence from readers recounting similar experiences. It seems that Christians who know about the demonic and have had any manner of "alien contact" experience can easily detect its diabolical nature. Indeed, the CE4 research group is just one of many who have come to identical conclusions.

The resolute ET believer may protest that even an overwhelming number of clearly demonic "alien" encounters do not prove that the entire phenomenon is demonic. Admittedly, for *direct proof* that aliens do not exist, one should read earlier parts of this book. Presently, we are *discerning the fruits*, as Jesus implores us to do in order to understand the true nature of what we are dealing with (cf. Matthew 7), therefore that protestation is itself a *non sequitur*. Moreover, whoever protests thus should be exhorted to present the other side of the coin. We have overwhelming quantities of evidence that the demonic permeates ET-related phenomena. Where is *any* evidence (much less a quantity thereof that comes *anywhere close* to matching the amount of contrary evidence) that we are simply dealing with other rational incarnate beings that God made? Not one shred of convincing evidence lending credence to that conclusion has ever been presented. *Every* non-debunkable ET encounter, without exception, can easily be discovered to have nothing to do with incarnate creatures from another planet. Any judge who would fail to dismiss an analogous case with prejudice (i.e., permanently) would himself deserve immediate impeachment.

"The encounter with what are interpreted as aliens is very often an unsettling experience that creates fear, insecurity and a longing to understand the meaning of the event. In many accounts there may be physical sensations of weakness and emptiness, and for many people who claim to have had contact with aliens, the long term result is often depression. Though the "aliens" often use positive words such "salvation" and "rescue", what is communicated is often threatening, and for those who have repeated encounters, the threats become part of a demand for submission ... most people who have the "rare privilege" of witnessing "strange beings or visions from other planets" suffer from depression...others can be driven to the point of madness or suicide." —Fr. Spyridon Bailey

UFOs Mimic the Antics of the Pagan-Myth-Disguises the Demons Have Used for Millennia

> "The extraterrestrial myth is seen to coincide to a remarkable degree with the fairy-faith of Celtic countries..."—Jacques Vallée

What we have reviewed thus far is only a cursory glance at the overwhelming body of evidence on "alien abductions" and other "ET/UFO contact" experiences that all converges upon the same conclusion: it is an entirely (not only "partially") demonic phenomenon. Demons are indeed more ubiquitous in the contemporary age of Satan's prophesied "75 to 100-year unchaining" (cf. Pope Leo XIII), wherein he was given greater leeway than ever before, therefore we are seeing their machinations at unprecedented levels. The machinations themselves, however, are anything but new. Satan's minions have always attacked mankind, and they make use of whatever disguise is most fitting in the cultural context in which they appear. What differentiates today from past ages of the Church is not the absence of masquerading demons, but that, before, the faithful could always count on their priests to warn them away from this Paganism. Today, however, many Catholic authors (even priests and theologians), lead their followers directly into the welcoming arms of these demons. As Jacques Vallée noted:

> ...**it is difficult to find a culture on earth that does not have an ancient tradition of little people that fly through the sky and abduct humans**. It is standard for them to take their victims into spherical settings that are evenly illuminated and to subject them to various ordeals such as operations on internal organs and "astral trips" to unknown landscapes. Sexual or genetic interaction is a common theme in this body of folklore...[225]

UFO-like encounters are not merely unoriginal, they are ubiquitous in history; it is only that the demons who administer them used to employ different appearances. In another book, Vallée wrote:

> These were the facts we have missed, without which we could never piece the UFO jigsaw together. Priests and scholars left books about the legends of their time concerning these beings. These books had to be

> found, collected, and studied. Together, these stories presented a coherent picture of the appearance, the organization, and the methods of our strange visitors. The appearance was—does this surprise you?—exactly that of today's UFO pilots. The methods were the same. There was the sudden vision of brilliant "houses" at night, houses that could fly, that contained peculiar lamps, radiant lights that needed no fuel. The creatures could paralyze their witnesses and translate them through time. They hunted animals and took away people.[226]

Another author—commenting on Vallée's findings—provides more details:

> These "little people" went under a variety of names: the Scandinavian *trolls*, the *ihkals* of Mexico, and the Malaysian *bunians*. The British Isles provide a wealth of such legends, from the Celtic stories of babies abducted by elves to Irish *leprechauns* and Scottish *sleagh maith* ... In France, these legends concern *fees*, or fairies, and a diminutive race known as the *fions*.[227]

Vallée is honest in sharing the findings of his rigorous research, but we should not be surprised that he (a non-Christian) fails to realize these are all simply different manifestations of the same demons. What is astonishing is that so many Christians, seduced by the allure of sci-fi myths, fail to acknowledge this truth set plainly before our eyes.

Before proceeding to other points, we should note that Vallée was not the earliest source of the idea (pervasive in Ufology) that UFOs are the *real* source of the various miracles recounted in Scripture. It first came from Erich von Daniken's 1968 book, *Chariots of the Gods?*, and R.D. Dione's 1969 book, *God Drives a Flying Saucer*.

In these works (which continue to inspire contemporary productions, including the History Channel's "Ancient Aliens" series, whose anti-Christian pseudoscientific claims are watched and believed by many millions of viewers to this day), we are told that all the miracles of the Bible are merely the results of alien technology from ETs visiting earth at various points throughout history. One such ET managed to achieve immorality, Dione condescends to inform us, and—the words are so blasphemous I hesitate to even write them, but we must understand how diabolical the movement we are dealing with is—artificially inseminated the Virgin Mary, hence bringing about Jesus Christ.

As has since become customary (and as we saw with Jacques Vallée), a chief project of these ET-inspired deceivers is to claim that believing Fatima's events constituted a true a miracle wrought through the intercession of the Virgin Mary, by God's power, is itself only a deception of the Catholic Church. Dione insists:

> We can be assured that preparations for the illusion [of Fatima] were begun the previous evening when one or more UFOs gathered water from the nearby ocean ... The illusion ended, of course, when the saucer

> evaporated the water in the air, revealing the real sun, and then climbed out of sight into its glare ... At Fatima no fewer than seven characteristics of UFO behavior were witnessed ... Philosophers, other intellectuals and clergymen have bumbled, and continued to bumble, with the idea that the essence of man is a strange mixture of physical and spiritual being. ... Such a belief [in an immortal, spiritual soul], when analyzed objectively, falls into **the same category as belief in miracles: both are remnants, in an otherwise enlightened culture, of a heritage of superstition**; both are terms invented to exalt the intelligence of man, who, rather than admit his inability to understand certain aspects of nature, labels these aspects unknowable or supernatural.[228]

The message here is only distinct from other ET promoters by being presented slightly more explicitly: Christianity is an outdated superstition, and it has no place in the modern, scientific world. We are told to now admit that everything man once regarded as miraculous was and is nothing but the intervention of extraterrestrial technology. Other ET promoters, including today's "orthodox Catholic" ones, express the same fundamental sentiments—positioned not as *rejections* of the Faith but as "re-readings" of the Gospels along with a radically revised Christology, Mariology, Ecclesiology, Eschatology, etc. Both approaches produce the same fruits because both derive from the same diabolic inspirations.

The title of Dione's 1976 follow-up work says it all: "*Is God Supernatural?: The 4,000 Year-Old Misunderstanding.*" Presenting an in-depth review of its contents, therefore, would be pointless. These authors do not even attempt to hide that their purpose in promoting ET belief is to overthrow the most basic tenets of Christianity and of Theism itself. Aliens are the new "gods," and (their) technology is the new "grace." Whatever Christian wishes to rescue ET belief by lecturing those who would "throw out the baby with the bathwater" must understand there is no baby in the bath that is the modern ET-believe-movement, and all the bathwater is thoroughly infested with vermin and tainted by poison.

ET Belief: Cause, Not Symptom, of the Entire New Age Movement

Today, few serious Christians are unaware of the dangerous, deceptive, and heretical nature of the so-called "New Age Movement." What some, however, will be surprised to discover is that this movement is not merely an umbrella term that counts Ufology among its disciplines, nor is it merely a separate or related trap into which most ET promoters fall. Quite the contrary, the New Age Movement itself is one byproduct of expectation of contact with extraterrestrials. Thus, this entire destructive movement is just one of the innumerable rotten fruits generated by alien belief, which is the more fundamental diabolical deception.

As the Macmillan *Encyclopedia of Religion* explains, in its entry scrutinizing the origins of the New Age Movement:

> **The immediate roots of the New Age movement may seem surprising at first. Shortly after World War II, popular curiosity was attracted by unexplained phenomena in the sky referred to as unidentified flying objects (UFOs)**. In various places in Western Europe and the United States, study groups were formed by people who wanted to investigate these phenomena...Typically, such groups **believed that UFOs were in fact spaceships inhabited by intelligent beings from other planets or other dimensions of outer space. Representing a superior level of cultural, technological, and spiritual evolution, they now made their appearance to herald the coming of a New Age**. The Earth was entering a new evolutionary cycle that would be accompanied by a new and superior kind of spiritual consciousness. ... [this] would necessitate the destruction of the old civilization ...[but] those individuals whose consciousness was already in tune with the qualities of the new culture would be protected in various ways and would survive the period of cataclysms. In due time they would become the vanguard of the New Age, or Age of Aquarius

Lest anyone suppose we are here exaggerating how destructive—how very rotten to the core—the New Age Movement is, we should defer to the Vatican's 2003 document, *Jesus Christ, the Bearer of the Water of Life*, which addresses the New Age. Therein, the Pontifical Council for Culture—which is not prone to hyperbole, much less is it some group of crazed conspiracy theorists seeking out excuses to denounce every movement as evil—described the New Age both frankly and accurately. They noted the movement claims that:

> **The New Age which is dawning will be peopled by perfect, androgynous beings who are totally in command of the cosmic laws of nature. In this scenario, Christianity has to be eliminated and give way to a global religion and a new world order**.[229]

The Vatican's admonition, moreover, is simple:

> The gnostic nature of this movement calls us to judge it in its entirety. From the point of view of Christian faith, it is not possible to isolate some elements of New Age religiosity as acceptable to Christians...[230]

In brief, the New Age Movement is a thoroughly rotten deception which must be categorically rejected. It is not merely yet another movement fraught with errors, it is a fundamental attack on Christianity itself and human nature (e.g., as male and female) itself. What discerning Christian, therefore, could find palatable endorsing the very thing—ET belief—from which the New Age Movement was born? Assuredly, no one who obeys Jesus' command to judge a tree by its fruits could fail to reject ET belief on this one rotten fruit alone. Similarly, no morally sane person would approach *Mein Kampf* with credulity, as if to seek out the wisdom therein.

The fruit of this work was Hitler's Holocaust. While I am certainly not here invoking "Godwin's Law" (no, ET promoters are not equivalent to Hitler!), it nevertheless remains the case that the New Age Movement is no less intimately connected to ET belief than the Holocaust is to *Mein Kampf.*

The Secularist Scholars Against the Evangelicals

> "I have always considered theologians to be the greatest and most gifted of the sophists. The phenomenon always makes me think of the Antichrist" —Bishop Marian Eleganti

A tragedy of mainstream scholarship—including that produced by many of ostensibly Christian persuasion—is how allergic they are to any statements including words like "demons," or "hell," or "possession," or "end times." Contemporary thought almost unanimously regards the demonic as an outdated relic of medieval times; one we have now "*evolved beyond, realizing that such beings were mere symbols for our own psychological projection,*" or even one we have now "*explained simply with parapsychology.*" Any serious Christian, however, knows that demons are not only real, but more prevalent today than ever before.

Until recently, scholars have likewise scoffed at most UFO encounters. (This attitude has *mostly* generated accurate assessments, since most UFO encounters are indeed mere ordinary earthly phenomena mistaken for an ET-piloted craft, or are even hoaxes.) Ufologists draw much attention to this scoffing to lend credence to their own position, as more and more people are realizing that, if mainstream secular scholars unanimously scoff at something, that is often a testimony to the authenticity of that very thing! But what these Ufologists ignore is that the same scholars scoff much more unanimously and condescendingly at even the slightest suggestion of the demonic. Indeed, if these academics take particular delight in patronizingly addressing anyone, it is evangelicals and traditional Catholics.

Several Evangelical Christians have done an excellent job combatting the alien deception for years now. Among them is Gary Bates, who wrote *Alien Intrusion* in 2010, which we have quoted several times in the present book. One academic of the sentiments described above, a certain Joseph P. Laycock, wrote a chapter against Mr. Bates in the latest scholarly collection of chapters published on Ufology (the *Handbook of UFO Religions,* published by Brill Academic Press in 2021). To understand the ideology of Laycock, we need only recount the words with which he concluded a recent article:

> Meanwhile, exorcisms have become increasingly mainstream in the Catholic Church and increasingly political, framing gay rights, abortion access, and other social issues as "demons" to be combatted and banished. So long as the triad of supernaturalism, masculinity, and cultural

grievance remains, we're likely to see ... more assaults on the rights of women and LGBTQ+ people.[231]

These are the views one often finds among those who dismiss any concern that the demonic could be behind UFO encounters.

In the tome mentioned above—printed by one of the world's leading academic publishers—Laycock quotes a fellow scholar, Christopher Partridge, who lamented that, "**[like] the demonization of elves in late Saxon England... 'extraterrestrials have been demonized in order to fit the good-evil dualism of the Christian world view.**"[232]

Thank goodness Christians in late Saxon England had the wherewithal to recognize the demonic in apparitions of "elves!" Here, Laycock and Partridge unknowingly undermine their own thesis. As we have already seen, "elves" (along with fairies, gnomes, leprechauns, and countless other such mythological creatures) were indeed, especially in ages past, a disguise worn by demons.

Laycock goes on to demonstrate he shares the standard scholarly cluelessness as to what actually transpires in the lives of the devout, claiming that: "*Spiritual warfare is associated with so-called 'Third Wave' neocharismatic movement [sic] that formed in the 1980s.*" In fact, I suspect that virtually everyone reading this book is acquainted with spiritual warfare, and that relatively few even know what the term "Third Wave neocharismatic" means. Indeed, I have found decidedly un-charismatic (or even *anti*-charismatic) traditionalists to be just as involved in spiritual warfare as anyone. Whoever understands devout Catholic circles today would have discovered the same. One wonders if Laycock has any experience at all with pious, devout, and orthodox-minded Christians, or if he has only spent all his time scouring the works of his similarly sheltered peers who share his sentiments.

One need not ponder that question for long, as this author continues demonstrating his ignorance in what follows. Laycock denigrates any Christians concerned with deceptions latent in Ufology or other paranormal arenas, insisting that these concerns are nothing but charades for their real aim: "**to defend conservative notions of 'family values.'**" Although his assertion is false, it does disclose his own paradigm. Clearly, this scholar's primary fear is not that UFO deceptions are being opposed, but rather that "conservative family values" that threaten "the rights of women [i.e., abortion] and LGBTQ+ people" are being effectively spread by the very works of men like Bates!

Throughout his chapter, Laycock presents no arguments against the claims of Bates and others who recognize that demonic deception is at play in Ufology. Instead, he rests content that taking several thousand words to describe them patronizingly is more than sufficient to relegate serious Christians, speaking against demonic deceptions, squarely off-limits to any scholarly appreciation. This tells us everything we need to know about contemporary secular scholarship on this matter. To them, demons can and must be dismissed off-handedly as an artifact of unenlightened ages.

I include this section because Professor Laycock's dismissals are representative of what one should expect to see much more of in the coming times. For his chapter to be included in the latest major volume compiling scholarly takes on the UFO phenomena—published, no less, by the prestigious Brill—tells us that it passed all the usual hurdles designed to ensure that chapters so treated further the narrative preferred by academia. In other words, the gatekeepers approved it, and the reason is clear: secular scholars take great joy in communally smirking at those who believe demons are real, and their own condescending monologues will only increase in proportion to the activity of the very demons in which they disbelieve.

Not only the avowed secularists and progressives, however, will take part in ridiculing the faithful who have discerned the Signs of the Times accurately. Many Catholic theologians, priests, and even Bishops will take part, including many thought to be "orthodox minded." Their slant will not be that demons are unreal, but will consist in some variation of what we have already noted—claiming, "*the Devil isn't behind every rock, you know,*" even in response to those situations where Satan obviously is very active. Let their tranquilizing words not dissuade you from heeding the signs of the times. We live in a rationalistic age and, sadly, it is likely that many if not most of today's "professional Catholics" will succumb to the Great Deception. The more degrees they have, the more likely they are to be deluded. You have the Bible, the Catechism, and the Saints. You do not need self-important academics, whether inside or outside the Church, who never miss an opportunity to remind you of their résumés.

Aping of Christ and the Church: Each Facet of Revealed Faith Perverted, to Undermine Christianity

> "Against those magic arts, concerning which some men, exceedingly wretched and exceedingly impious, delight to boast ... these sorceries are without doubt pernicious to the human race ... all the miracles of the magicians ... are performed according to the teaching and by the power of demons."
>
> —St. Augustine. *City of God.* Book 8. Ch. 19

Throughout contemporary ET belief thought, we see God mocked at every turn, with Christianity remaining especially the (sometimes not explicitly named) object of reproach. Despite this reproach, however, Ufology takes many cues from the True Faith, and it has carefully constructed its own promulgation on the model of Christian Religion.

Components of Christian Religion	**Perversion in Ufology**
The persecuted prophets of Salvation History leading up to the revelation of Christ	The persecuted early promoters of UFO/ET sightings, leading up to the "Day of Disclosure"
The Pharisees crafting a conspiracy and claiming the Resurrection was faked, and that Jesus' body was simply stolen	The government crafting a conspiracy to cover up UFO craft and retrievals of alien bodies
The account of Creation and Salvation History in Scripture, wherein mankind has been guided for millennia by the Holy Spirit	A diabolical creation myth, wherein mankind has been guided for millennia by extraterrestrials, or was even created by them
The Four Evangelists authoring the Gospels	Several men authoring foundational UFO/ET texts
Evangelization: each Christian has a mission to proclaim the Faith	Each ET believer has a duty to spread "ET awareness" and contribute to "ontological shock"
Profession of Faith	ET/UFO "True Believers" denounce any skepticism
Liturgy	Communal ET-contact sessions (e.g. "CE5") & UFO-chasing
Private revelations and mysticism	Alien abductees announce what they were told and shown
Prayer and contemplation	Astral-projection and remote viewing
Eschatology: hope in Christ's triumph and His coming	Anticipation of an imminent techno-utopia heralded by the arrival of the ETs
A complete worldview based on the Word of God	A complete worldview based on UFOs, ETs, multiverse-theory, evolution, & interdimensionality

In this regard, however, perhaps the clearest aspect of this diabolical effort to ape the things of God is found in the Ufologists' insistence that the aliens are capable, *through their technology*, of all the same basic categories of miracles that Christ used to prove his Divinity and thus demonstrate the truth of the Faith.

There are several accomplishments in particular which Christians are instructed, through the Gospel, to regard as physically impossible; precisely because Jesus chose these feats to demonstrate His dominion and thus His Divinity. Therefore, for a Christian to suppose that such feats as these could be accomplished through technology, is to succumb to deception merely by entertaining the possibility, and implicitly undermine the very fundamental source of Christianity's authenticity. Let us review each.

Miracle Demonstrating Christ's Divinity	**UFO Deception Aping God**
Instantaneous healings (abundant in the Gospels)	Many claims of healings through ETs*
Multiplication of Loaves and Fishes (Matthew 14): Law of Conservation of Mass superseded	UFOs are said to be similarly capable of violating Conservation of Mass, e.g., radically and instantaneously changing size
Walking on the water (Mark 6): Law of Gravity superseded	UFOs are said to have technological mastery over gravity
Knowing the unknowable: the future (e.g., Matthew 24, Matthew 17:24-27), a person's secret past (e.g., John 1 & 4); a person's thoughts (e.g. Matthew 12)	Abductees often claim the aliens read their minds and knew their thoughts. Ufologists regularly insist the ETs can describe the future
Instantaneous transformation of the substance of one thing into another (e.g., water turned into wine, cf. John 2)	UFOs and ETs can "shapeshift" and become completely different entities in an instant†
Teleportation (e.g., after the Resurrection, Jesus would appear inside a locked room, cf. John 20)	UFOs are frequently said to be able to disappear and immediately reappear elsewhere
Power over the weather (e.g., Jesus calms the storm, cf. Mark 4)	UFO sightings often recount major weather modifications by these "alien" craft
Raising the dead: Lazarus (John 11), Jairus' daughter (Mark 5), the Widow's Son (Luke 7), and above all, Himself (The Resurrection)	*(This, the ultimate proof of Christ's Divinity is also the hardest for demons to fake, hence the relative rarity of such claims. Be on guard, though, for when such claims proliferate. Although they will be deceptions, they may be a sign of the proximity of the formal opening of the Great Deception.)*

Whoever asserts that aliens are capable of these feats has thereby lost the foundation for his Faith in Christ. Although this smacks of a preparation for the Antichrist if anything ever did, we are—as is evident—not only dealing with apocalyptic concerns here. We are confronted with the *immediate* issue that, as soon as one foolishly "opens his mind"—perhaps

* E.g., Chris Bledsoe's "UFO of God" (a 2023 Bestseller), the Unarians' Charles Spiegel, "Antares" was "healed by Uriel the Archangel," Helge Lindroos "sight healed by aliens to enable him to announce their message," and many more. Abductees often claim (always strange) "healings."

† "People who have the UFO abduction experience very frequently meet hybrid beings of the same type who are part animal and part human. Often they appear first in that form before shapeshifting into the more familiar form of greys." Quoted in Dr. Timothy Dailey, *The Paranormal Conspiracy*, Ch. 12

because he was bullied into doing so by another Christian who castigated him for "lacking humility" otherwise—to the possibility that extraterrestrials could visit earth, he is confronted with a fundamentally Faith-undermining dilemma. For he now has no defense against another who would say to him, "*How do you know Jesus wasn't just an extraterrestrial or at least a man in contact with them and able to use their technological insights? If his ET technology was sufficiently advanced to accomplish teleportation, anti-gravity, healing, etc., then it would certainly also be advanced enough to hide its display from us and make it seem that these powers were derived from his own unaided action. If aliens are visiting earth now, there is no reason for us to reject the possibility that they were also visiting us 2,000 years ago, though they were then more careful to hide their technology from our sight. Everything you now defer to in explaining your Faith in Christ can just as easily be explained through alien technology!*"

As we have seen in previous sections, the presentation of the argument above is no mere theoretical concern. It is, rather, exactly what many Ufologists have been saying for over fifty years. And there is only one sure defense against their blasphemous suggestions: *ruling out the very possibility* of extraterrestrials in one's own convictions.

Remember, it will not work for a Christian ET promoter to claim that these Divinity-proving feats were chosen by Jesus only because such technology obviously did not exist *in His day*. This is irrelevant. Whoever believes aliens are walking (or flying) among us today has lost any grounds for supposing they were not likewise among us two thousand years ago. Alien belief, therefore, is nothing but a meticulously designed Trojan Horse with one ultimate goal: subverting the Faith.

SETI's Antichristic "Search for Immortality" and ET Promotion's Rebellion Against All Things Sacred

> "I fully expect an alien civilization to bequeath to us... the grand instruction book that tells creatures how to live forever."
> —Frank Drake, The "Father of the Search for Extraterrestrial Intelligence"

Among those who have seriously studied the issue—aside, that is, from most Christian ET promoters who pretend this Leviathan in the living room can be ignored—there is a consensus that UFO and ET phenomena are *inherently* nothing less than a new religion. Through massive amounts of research, it is safe to say that they have demonstrated this is the case with Ufology *itself*, not merely with those (more rare) groups who *admit* they are creating UFO-based religions.

The latest major scholarly volume of literature on the topic, the 2021 Brill Handbook quoted earlier, cannot (despite its flaws in discernment) be faulted for lack of diligence in describing what is currently transpiring in the world; from its compilation of scholarly chapters, we see the thesis above proven. Dr. Benjamin Zeller, the volume's editor, summarized the lessons learned from the many scholars who contributed to it:

> Based on interviews and survey data with hundreds of ufologists, Denzler argued that such **individuals spoke of UFOs with "language that suggests religious awe".** While especially true among those who claimed direct experience or sighting of UFOs, Denzler found this approach extended widely. She identified the "numinous quality of some UFO experiences," and the profound effect they had...Diana W. Pasulka has argued for the "case that **belief in extraterrestrials and UFOs constitutes a new form of religion.**" In her project, Pasulka tracks this religiosity among elite scientists and technologists... [she] notes that same sort of forces present within this nascent form of techno-scientific ufological religion as one finds in other religious traditions: the systematizing and management of mythology and beliefs, the creation of dogma, and debates over authenticity and evidence. Much of what Pasulka observes among these elite scientists mirrors the same patterns within previous UFO religions... [she notes that] new media and new technology beam the UFO mono-myth directly to consumers... Christopher Partridge's observation that **UFO religions represent extensions of Theosophical traditions and also "physicalist religion" wherein the "modern, secular, scientific worldview" holds sway**, repeats throughout this book...there exist fundamental "characteristics of UFOs that link to the religious consciousness"... **All of these observations have proven correct,** and are amplified by the treatments here."[233]

As we can see, it is not just a few wild-eyed Evangelicals who are concerned that ET belief and Ufology are simply postmodern, secular, "scientific" attempts to replace Christianity with a new religion. In fact, this "concern" is merely a straightforward observation of reality, and those who relay it are precisely the ones most qualified to do so. Recall that these individuals who have dedicated their careers to studying the phenomenon are not only describing *explicit* UFO religions, as if what is noted above is nothing but a truism. Quite the contrary, they have found that ET belief and Ufology *are themselves* new religions. And they are correct.

Even some of the most prominent Christian advocates of the harmony of Christianity with ET beliefs concede that the latter is fundamentally a replacement for religion. One such advocate, the Christian astrophysicist, theologian, and Methodist minister, Dr. David Wilkinson, conceded:

> [We] desire for cosmic salvation. **As far back as 1949**, Sir Fred Hoyle pointed out that **the motivation for believing in extraterrestrial intelligence was 'the expectation that we are going to be saved from ourselves by some miraculous interstellar intervention'**. ... Paul Davies echoes this, seeing that the interest in extraterrestrial intelligence: "*stems in part ... from the need to find a wider context for our lives than this Earthly*

> *existence provides. In an era when conventional religion is in sharp decline, the belief in super-advanced aliens out there somewhere in the universe can provide some measure of comfort and inspiration for people whose lives may otherwise appear to be boring and futile."* SETI enthusiasts have a strong faith in a higher intelligence which is seeking to communicate with us and which can change our lives and solve our problems. ...**The SETI hope is that contact with alien civilizations will provide not just scientific insights but also religious and moral insights. Drake goes from technological advance to immortality**: *"I fully expect an alien civilization to bequeath to us vast libraries of useful information, to do with as we wish. This 'Encyclopedia Galactica' will create the potential for improvements in our lives that we cannot predict ... I suspect that immortality may be quite common among extraterrestrials. ... Sometimes, when I look at the stars I wonder if, among the most common interstellar missives coming from them, it is the grand instruction book that tells creatures how to live forever."* [234]

Revealed above is the fact that even SETI itself—an official government-backed initiative to make radio contact with aliens—is deeply pseudo-religious (and decidedly anti-Christian) in its aspirations. As we saw in the quote opening the present section, the father of SETI, Frank Drake (who died in 2022), proclaimed that he "fully expects" to be shown the key to immortality by contact with extraterrestrials. If this is not a diabolically deceived expectation, then nothing is. SETI's current head, astrophysicist Dr. Seth Shostak, has declared his status as a false prophet equally bluntly, claiming:

> **If this is the only place in the galaxy with intelligent life, then Earth is some sort of miracle—and we scientists tend to think that, if you say something is a miracle, you haven't studied statistics**.[235]

This diagnosis was also confirmed by men whose discernment was spot-on and whose holiness and orthodoxy are irreproachable. For example, the Benedictine priest, prolific theologian, and renowned scientist, Fr. Stanley Jaki, has been described as one of the five Catholic scientists who shaped our understanding of the world; having received the coveted Templeton Prize and serving as a member of the Pontifical Academy of Sciences under Pope St. John Paul II.[236] He travelled extensively in SETI circles, and was among the few insiders to characterize it accurately and honestly; as we saw earlier, he shared that:

> As I visited [the Arecibo telescope] in 1990, the director of the observatory noticed my Roman collar and delivered to me a little sermon about the future of mankind and religion once we have heard from those extraterrestrials. He did not mention Christ, but his sermon was clear. **Once we hear from extraterrestrials we can forget about Christ and Christian religion once and for all. Much the same was preached by the group of scientists forming the project SETI...**[237]

***

If it is true that the UFO myth is itself a replacement religion, then one would expect to see certain reactions prevalent in those who follow it. *Obsession* would inevitably permeate the ranks of its adherents, for their "religion" would be one without a genuine object of faith and hope from which an authentic inner peace could proceed. Accordingly, devotees would be left only with an ever-present anxious and ravenous desire for discovering the next "puzzle piece," in a futile attempt to fill the God-shaped-hole in their hearts.

This, too, is exactly what we see everywhere in contemporary ET-contact-expectation. Prominent UFO researcher, John Keel—author of *The Mothman Prophecies*—wrote:

> **To deal with UFOs is just as dangerous as black magic.** ... In many cases this leads to acute schizophrenia, demon mania, even suicide. Thus **the mysterious charm of the UFO phenomenon** can lead to terrible tragedies. Therefore I strongly recommend parents: forbid children to pursue an interest in such issues. It is the duty of teachers and of any adult person to protect children from UFO hobbies.

Both the Ufologists renowned for their publications, and the millions (or even billions) of ordinary folk who are merely "True (ET) Believers," have one trait in common they openly admit to: obsession. It seems that few who take this matter at all seriously have succeeded in maintaining a moderate degree of interest in the topic. Instead, UFO studies almost invariably constitute, in those who undertake them, a passing phase with interest evaporating upon a closer analysis, or, on the flipside, they become a life-absorbing preoccupation which often results in spiritual problems, moral decay, marital discord, family disharmony, professional disintegration, and so on. In the script of *The Mothman Prophecies* itself, we even hear the following oft-quoted and accurate line:

> **There's only one way out... [it] becomes an obsession—a fixation... the UFO business is emotional quicksand. The more you struggle with it the deeper you sink.**

One popular podcaster on UFO phenomena recently admitted, to her thousands of online followers, "**The fact that it [UFO phenomena] managed to disrupt my entire life and make me walk away from the career that I spent 15 years building is kind of wild. And I've met so many people with that exact same story.**"[238] A follower of this podcaster responded, *"It is literally taking over my life and as much as I try to go back to being [normal] I just can't break away."* Another responded that *"interest in UFO's will help ignite an awakening. The idea is not to get stuck in the lower realms of the ET's/UFO's but to ascend higher..."* Others in the thread responded similarly. None conceded their obsession was problematic or offered help on how to be healed of it. Instead, they encouraged each other in these destructive lifestyles.

Relayed above, however, is just one example of innumerable—doubtless almost identical—conversations happening, at this moment, across the world. "True believer" discourse is identical to that of any cult, wherein an identifying trait is found in the movement's followers lavishing praise upon obvious vices because the cult fosters them. This dark reality can easily be confirmed by anyone who doubts its severity or pervasiveness: simply peruse the conversations these people hold on the internet and social media (deliberately made public for all to see). You will see it has already become an epidemic.

Yet another Christian theologian, Lutheran professor Dr. Ted Peters, glowingly promotes Ufology even while recognizing that it has become nothing but a replacement for the Faith. Somehow, he fails to acknowledge the diabolical deception that he himself is describing in passages like the one below, which he published in an academic journal:

> ...UFO believers are part and parcel of the modern scientific mentality. **Yes, they do want a celestial savior, but that savior will not be mysterious; instead, he will be fully comprehendable and scientifically explainable** according to the laws of nature ... UFOs are capable of embodying and transmitting this conceptual notion of transcendence as well, because it is held by many that they have traversed the unfathomable distances from other civilizations to earth. **Gods of the local sky, such as Amen-Re or Zeus or Thor, no longer impress us. But UFOs come from the furthest reaches of our imagination**, from near-incalculable distances in outer space ... One interesting feature consistent in the contactee accounts is the near omniscience of the space people, due not to old-fashioned spiritual presence but rather to respectable modern electronic surveillance and mental telepathy ... **We do not want to be alone. In the old-time religion we could count on angels as God's invisible agents to watch our every move and protect us from danger. God's omniscience and heavenly angels met a deep inner religious need then. To be told by modern natural science that angels do not exist is a great loss. But with UFOs angels are back again, not as spirits but as physical beings, with electronic surveillance and telepathic insight. It is comforting to know once again that we are not alone.** Someone is watching. ... [UFO cults seek] to cleanse the human soul through rigorous self-discipline. The process is called Human Individual Metamorphosis (HIM). A UFO is expected to come and physically take the cleansed believer to heaven ... It is to be noticed that **these patently religious themes are covert rather than overt**. There is nothing conspicuously religious here, nor any mention of spirits, demons, angels, miracles, or magic. Everything is completely natural; nothing is supernatural. ... Mr. Jackson [one UFO contactee] denies his religious feelings because he is convinced he has outgrown the need for religion. He is mature. **He has come of age. "Religion is OK for children," he said, but not for him. Similarly, some argue that Western civilization has come of age. We have become so intellectually mature we may now**

put aside child things, such as belief in God. Belief in God is like belief in magic, and moderns believe in science, not magic.[239]

***

In later chapters we will discuss just a few (of the multitudes) of explicit UFO cults that have gained notoriety such as "Heaven's Gate," the "Raëlians," and the "Aetherius Society." When doing so, however, we must not forget that those are only more extreme and explicit examples of the same approaches that define Ufology *itself*. Here we see another aping of the Church: just as consecrated religious men and women (Benedictines, Franciscans, Dominicans, etc.) are called by their vocation to model, in an extraordinary way, the same fundamental virtues all Christians are called to—so too we see the explicit UFO cults simply rendering even more tangible the same fundamental *vices* that define ET-belief, Ufology, and alien-contact-expectation in general. All these phenomena are diabolically-motivated efforts to rebel against all things sacred. Whoever honestly discerns them does not miss this fact. And whoever would protest that "*one must not throw the baby out with the bathwater,*" is confronted with another fact—repeatedly confirmed by all who study the matter—that there is no baby in this bathwater, and the bathwater itself is only a festering vat of poison.

21. Decades of Grooming: The Sci-Fi that Brought Us Here

"Have nothing to do with godless and silly myths."
—I Timothy 4:7

Man lives by the stories he honors. If he reveres true stories—particularly, if he lives in accordance with the Greatest Story Ever Told (Salvation History)—then he may become a saint. If, on the other hand, he lives by "godless and silly myths," modern or ancient, then he has only set himself up to be deeply formed by whatever lies—hidden or explicit—they contain.

Both the world and the Devil understand this well, hence such enormous emphasis long being placed on what messages are conveyed through Hollywood, which is presently by far the world's preeminent storyteller. Long before Hollywood, however, both the power and the danger of storytelling were known by the wisest. Plato went so far as to have the poets banished from his ideal society, envisioned in the *Republic*. A century earlier still, Confucius insisted upon his doctrine of "wen," which regulated all the arts to ensure they only promoted virtue. Ufologist Jacques Vallée also understood this well, noting that "**To control human imagination is to shape mankind's collective destiny**."

Science fiction, the modern world's prevailing myth, has indeed controlled human imagination, and thus it is, tragically, shaping our collective destiny. As we will see in the forthcoming pages, sci-fi teachings have, for the last century, steadily led the world deeper and deeper into diabolical deception while forming an increasing expectation, among the masses, that we will soon either be attacked by extraterrestrials or saved by extraterrestrials (or both).

Before presenting what sci-fi has long declared, let us first consider what it has left out: *God*, and even religion in general. Extraterrestrials are never portrayed as religious beings, but rather (if "benevolent") tend to be depicted as messengers to lift humanity beyond its "religious phase." As Dr. Charles Harper author noted:

> It is interesting to note that portrayals of "alien religions" are typically absent in Hollywood's envisioning of extraterrestrial life. This is somewhat curious. Religion is an anthropological universal for our species. ... It seems unavoidable that if aliens like us are out there, then they necessarily must have alien languages. Why not religions as well? The idea that religiousness would be absent in superintelligent beings has no serious grounding within science itself...[240]

Unfortunately, Dr. Harper fails to note that this is not a mere "curiosity," but the manifestation of a deliberate agenda. Such a glaring absence as he notes, displayed decade after decade, in all the most prominent ET-promoting movies, cannot be chalked up to chance. Aliens are never portrayed as religious beings precisely because the entire reason for these myths' promulgation is to induce their devotees to either abandon religion or at least mitigate its *supreme* value in their lives. One who is infatuated with science fiction may still attend Mass, but he inevitably finds himself placing his greatest hopes, dreams, and expectations, not in the Triumph of Christ, but rather in the enlightening teachings and salvific technologies of aliens.

In a preceding section, we have already seen how Carl Sagan's 1997 movie, *Contact*, was and is presented as a replacement for religion. That film's plotline, however, is anything but unusual in its thesis.

War of the Worlds & H.G. Wells: Originator of Modernity's Sci-Fi Deceptions

Among the earliest and most popular of modern science fiction writers on extraterrestrials was the English author, Herbert George Wells, who died in 1946—only months before the onslaught of the UFO-craze he helped generate. In 1898, he published *The War of the Worlds*, which was especially noteworthy in fomenting the expectation of extraterrestrial contact not only in its original publication but also in its later media productions, including radio shows and major Hollywood movies (particularly the 1953 and 2005 iterations). When the story was read by Orson Welles on the radio on the eve of Halloween in the year 1938, it induced a mass panic by those who believed it was an actual news broadcast describing an in-progress Martian invasion!

That broadcast opened with the following somber words:

> We know now that in the early years of the 20th century, this world was being watched closely by intelligences greater than man's and yet as mortal as his own. We know now that as human beings busied themselves about their various concerns, they were scrutinized and studied, perhaps almost as narrowly as a man with a microscope might scrutinize the transient creatures that swarm and multiply in a drop of water. With infinite complacence, people went to and fro over the earth about their little affairs, serene in the assurance of their dominion over this small spinning fragment of solar driftwood which by chance or design man has inherited out of the dark mystery of Time and Space. Yet across an immense ethereal gulf, minds that are to our minds as ours are to the beasts in the jungle, intellects vast, cool and unsympathetic, regarded this earth with envious eyes and slowly and surely drew their plans against us.

Here we see the sci-fi onset of Christianity being meticulously (if, at first, subtly) deconstructed from the ground up. A skilled author, however,

Wells conceals his true intent by using only language that will achieve his own ends, while preventing his mostly Christian listeners from realizing what is happening—even after it already has.

He begins by assuring us we are being "watched"—i.e., "we are not alone." He immediately adds that the beings watching us vastly exceed our own intelligence, but are assuredly not angels (or demons), for they are "as mortal" as we are. Wells could not risk allowing any genuinely Christian interpretation of his story to prevail. He subtly mocks mankind's being "busied" by our "various concerns" and "little affairs"—doubtless having religion in mind—for chief among the goals of the ET-promoters is to depict all that we do on earth as such small things in comparison to the "far more awe-inspiring" revelation of the other civilizations in the cosmos. Emphasizing just how ridiculous he views mankind, he labels earth a "spinning fragment of solar driftwood which by chance or design man has inherited out of the dark mystery of Time and Space." For Wells, earth is not God's *delight* (cf. Revelation 21:3, Proverbs 8:31, Psalm 115:16, etc.). It is only an insignificant piece of cosmic debris. The lesson is clear: we are not unique, we are not special, and, in fact, we do not matter. It may even be that mere "chance" brought us here, though to avoid being immediately rebuked by a world that was still largely Christian, Wells leaves open the possibility of "design," in the abstract Deistic sense.

More pointedly still, Wells satirizes mankind's "serene... assurance of their dominion" over earth—an explicit rejection of Genesis 1:26, wherein God promises dominion over "all the earth" to man and to man alone. That promise, Wells would have us believe, was empty. Extraterrestrials are the ones with dominion over the earth. We just haven't seen it happen yet.

Of course, H.G. Wells understood that few Christians listening to Orson Welles' broadcast based off his work or reading his book will undertake the analysis above. Nor is he concerned about that: the subtle sentiments that his fiction leaves its audience with are more than sufficient to achieve his desired effects. A traditional Christian worldview has been eroded. The audience begins pondering if this could really happen. They begin wondering if God's promises are not absolute after all. They question whether earth, and the human race, really have the status that Scripture describes.

Wells does have God—albeit, again, in a merely Deistic way—indirectly save the world by virtue of earth's various microorganisms that wind up eventually destroying the alien invaders. A few other references to God exist, none of such a type as to lend credence to Christianity (which is only brought up for poking fun at, what with fire and brimstone preachers "mistaking the alien invasion for the Book of Revelation's prophecies.") Indeed, the beginnings of the sci-fi deceptions are not as severe as the later ones. This is the path that grooming always follows.

Any restraint in Wells' most popular works, however, was certainly not due to his own wisdom, but only his own strategic efforts. The man himself was as delusional as thinkers come. In a less popular work which Wells named *The Outline of History*, he provides a starkly anti-Christian and anti-Catholic view of thousands of years of Western Civilization. One author summarized its teachings about Jesus as follows:

> [Jesus] had been an obscure political agitator, a kind of hobo, in a minor colony of the Roman Empire. By an accident impossible to reconstruct, he ... survived his own crucifixion and presumably died a few weeks later. A religion was founded on the freakish incident. The credulous imagination of the times retrospectively assigned miracles and supernatural pretensions to Jesus; a myth grew, and then a church, whose theology at most points was in direct contradiction of the simple, rather communistic teachings of the Galilean.[241]

In the book itself, Wells insists that the early Christians:

> ...built their faith upon the stories that were told of [Jesus'] resurrection and magical ascension, and the promised return. Few of them understood that the renunciation of self is its own reward, that it is itself the Kingdom of Heaven... (Book VI. XXX. §5)

A party-line modernist, Wells understood the common tactics for robbing Christianity of its power while seeming to condone its trappings. There is nothing real about the Kingdom of Heaven for Wells; it is merely the name Jesus gave to the self-satisfaction of a virtuous life. As we will see, it is precisely this repudiation of Eschatology that has left a gaping hole in modern men's hearts, which they seek to fill with ET-contact-expectation. Christian author Gary Bates describes Wells' influence and approach as follows:

> Wells believed in ... advanced alien races, and as a result he ridiculed Christian ideals as arrogant ... Wells sums up his rejection of the Christian idea that an omnipotent God is the ultimate authority in the universe in his next statement: "*If all the animals and man had been evolved in this ascendant manner, then there had been no first parents, no Eden and no Fall. And if there had been no fall, then the entire historical fabric of Christianity, the story of the first sin and the reason for an atonement, upon which the current teaching based Christian emotion and morality, collapsed like a house of cards.*" ... Wells consciously disregarded Christian morality. He was a self-conscious humanist. Humanism, as used by Wells, simply means that man decides truth for himself and that there is no infinitely wise God who knows best and thus sets rules or guidelines for the benefit of humanity. And mankind is thus not the central focus of the universe, as the Bible implies, so one should have no problem in invoking ET races elsewhere in the universe.[242]

Behold the "father of science fiction." Serious Christians would do well to be deeply suspicious of any movement fathered by a man such as this. The tree has *directly* shown itself rotten; what should we expect of its fruits?

Wells, like many science fiction authors, is often regarded as prophetic by his fans. Conveniently ignored is that every work of science fiction (by Wells or others) yet produced is far more riddled with error than with prescience wherever it depicts a future time. Years that are now long past, when they were predicted in the decades before them, were inevitably described as being filled with technology that is still, for us today, only a dream; or with other societal or worldwide changes that have only grown even more distant from reality. On the other hand, anyone who has observed the growth of technology and society up to their day can easily extrapolate the same trend he has observed—this is not genius, much less prophetic; it is only mundane speculation. Alas, every religion needs its prophets, hence the zeal in contemporary sci-fi to revere its own most renowned exponents as if they were prophets in their own right.

What is less often noted is that Wells pronounced one of the most spectacularly failed prophecies in the history of predictions. During World War I—then known as "The Great War"—he declared:

> "This is ... a war not of nations, but of mankind. It is a war to exorcise a world-madness and end an age ... It aims at a settlement that shall stop this sort of thing for ever. ... **This, the greatest of all wars, is not just another war—it is the last war**![243]

Having settled that Mr. H.G. Wells is no prophet, and a man whose legacy any Christian should be extremely cautious with, we turn to the next major development in works of science fiction on extraterrestrials.

The Day the Earth Stood Still: Aliens Saving us from Ourselves

> "There is in many of us, obviously, a deep-seated desire to assent to extraterrestrial forces—to be embraced by them, overwhelmed by them, and if possible deprived by them of our own weary responsibility for ourselves." —Russel Davies[244]

Two years after the Martian invasion panic elicited by the radio broadcast of H.G. Wells' *War of the Worlds,* American author Harry Bates published a short story entitled *Farewell to the Master*. Eleven years later, it became a major 1951 Hollywood film called *The Day the Earth Stood Still.* Borrowing from the Bible's final entry, the Book of Revelation—which prophesies the great persecution of the Church undertaken by the "Beast" and his "Image" (cf. Revelation 13)—the film has both a humanoid "god-like" alien and a large robot that does his bidding and accompanies him.

However, in a perverse twist, this movie has the aliens arriving with an ultimately "benevolent" intent.

The original written story describes the alien: "**a man, godlike in appearance and human in form... [raising] his right arm high in the universal gesture of peace... [with] an expression on his face, which radiated kindness, wisdom, the purest nobility**." This "god," however, was shot by—no one will have any trouble guessing—a religious fanatic who declared that the Devil had come. Next—in the 1951 film adaptation—the robot vaporizes all the weaponry of the soldiers gathered there, and the alien is taken to a hospital and heals. It expresses its desire to address all the world's leaders, but is denied that opportunity. It escapes and eventually shares that its task is to save us from ourselves—many alien civilizations are concerned about the destructive abilities of earthlings now that atomic power has been discovered. Before departing earth, the alien does get an audience; not with world leaders, but with scientists, clergy, and others. It tells them that the alien civilizations have collaboratively built an army of invincible robots like the one here with him, and which will—automatically, immediately, and irrevocably—eliminate any source of aggression at the very first sign of violence. They were built, the alien explains, because:

> The Universe grows smaller each day, and threat of aggression by any group, anywhere, can no longer be tolerated. There must be security for all, or no one is secure. Now this does not mean giving up any freedom, except the freedom to act irresponsibly...we of the other planets have long accepted this principle. We have an organization for the mutual protection of all planets, and for the complete elimination of aggression.

Thus, the very possibility of war, or of violence of any sort, is eliminated. A utopia is offered. The alien continues...

> We live in peace, without arms or armies, secure in the knowledge that we are free from aggression and war; free to pursue more profitable enterprises...I came here to give you these facts...if you threaten to extend your violence, this earth of yours will be reduced to a burned-out cinder. Your choice is simple. Join us and live in peace, or pursue your present course and face obliteration. We shall be waiting for your answer.

Many somber faces are then shown in the audience, gazing upon the alien in wonder, who promptly departs in his spaceship.

With this film, Hollywood introduced the next, more dangerous phase of the ET Deception. For while any belief in extraterrestrials is among the most perilous of premises, it is still more dangerous to specifically believe in *benign* aliens, as opposed to the hostile ones depicted in the *War of the Worlds*. One who believes a demon disguised as an alien is actually a hostile ET may well fight it (physically) in vain, but one who believes a demon disguised as an alien is benign may well seek to learn from it—dialogue with it—and therein lies the supreme danger.

It is no accident that the major sci-fi mythmakers waited for mainstream society to be accustomed to the idea of extraterrestrials visiting earth (especially thanks to H.G. Wells) before promoting the next phase in the narrative—benevolent, enlightened aliens coming to help us. Grooming occurs in phases, with sufficient time allowed for the shock of the earlier phase to wear off before the next surreptitious assault on the victim's dignity is undertaken.

Some have taken the opposite angle on this film, and have presented it as an allegory for Christ. This is foolish. First, it "hits too close to home" to be an allegory. On the other hand, C.S. Lewis' Aslan in the *Chronicles of Narnia* was a wonderful allegory for Christ precisely because no one regards Narnia as a reality. This movie, however, was released several years into the UFO craze. It was not intended as an allegory, but as a *prediction*. Moreover, to even allegorize Christ as demanding that humanity subject itself to the dominion of robots in order to make violence impossible, or face incineration, is deeply irreverent.

We should also add that, in the 2008 film adaptation of the story, the alien is not visiting earth in response to aggression and advances in weaponry which "may threaten other planets," but rather in response to the prevailing cultural phobia of the time of its own release. In the 1950s, the prevailing fear was global catastrophe through atomic warfare, hence the plotline outlined above. In the 2000s, however, the prevailing phobia was the so-called "global warming" catastrophe. Therefore, in the latest movie, the alien has come to "save earth from humanity." At one point in the movie, the alien responds to the question, "are you a friend to us?", by simply saying, "I am a friend to the earth," and later, "I came to save the earth." In this iteration of the story, it is not only the Book of Revelation that is perversely twisted, but also the Book of Genesis. The alien is a modern Noah, coming to earth to collect living creatures from each species and take them off the planet in its many spaceships—Arks—before the earth is "sterilized" of human beings, who are "destroying" it.

Derivative of the same anti-anthropocentrism that is part and parcel to alien belief in general, the modern film promotes the standard Hollywood message of anti-human radical environmentalism, which, in Pagan fashion, fails to acknowledge that the earth *exists for the sake of* man. The alien explains that it has watched for so long, but that we "refuse to change," and therefore he will "undo the damage we've done and give the earth a chance to begin again." (One wonders how many contemporary activists, blocking traffic or gluing their hands to various objects, derived their zeal from this film's premises.) A professor, however, convinces the alien that "we will evolve," now that we are "at the precipice." We simply "needed this crisis," he explains. Persuaded, the alien manages to call off the imminent destruction of humanity, which has, finally, learned its lesson from its extraterrestrial visitation.

Whichever version of the story we are told, we are confronted with a step in the grooming process of society for the welcoming of a deception. The take-away is the same in each: the human race, notwithstanding Christianity, is incapable of the "dominion over all the earth" (Genesis 1:26) that Scripture teaches has been given to us, exclusively, by God. Instead, it must be saved by enlightened and benevolent extraterrestrials.

From this point onwards the most famous works of Science Fiction display *apparently* dueling narratives—hostile aliens (e.g., *Independence Day, Aliens, Edge of Tomorrow*, etc.), and helpful aliens (*Close Encounters of the Third Kind, ET, Arrival, Starman*, etc.), which are in fact nothing other than the classic "good cop, bad cop" charade.

As we will discuss in more detail in a later chapter, these narratives are not actually dueling at all. They are simply the two faces that the ET Deception wears (with many productions wearing both faces at once); both are apocalyptic in their evil, but promoted for different reasons. As far as government psyops are concerned, hostile aliens are the most useful ruse (to justify the greatest imaginable increase of government power and funding, and cessation of human rights "*to combat an ET threat*"). For directly demonic deceptions, benign aliens are preferable (in preparation for the seduction of the Antichrist, who will offer mankind a solution to its crisis, at the price of apostasy). The Devil, ultimately, is behind all of it, and he has many minions following his commands (knowingly or unknowingly) while working on both ends of the spectrum.

2001: A Space Odyssey—Artificial Intelligence, Aliens, and Evolution: A Match Made in Hell

> "I don't believe in any of Earth's monotheistic religions, but... [aliens] may have progressed from biological species ... into beings of pure energy ... Their potentialities would be limitless and their intelligence ungraspable by humans."
>
> —Stanley Kubrick

Seventeen years after the release of *The Day the Earth Stood Still*—society having passed sufficient time to digest, tolerate, and finally accept the notion of benevolent extraterrestrials coming to save us—another major step was taken in Hollywood's ET agenda. Released in 1968, the film *2001: A Space Odyssey* took the world by storm and initiated a new era in popular sci-fi. As *The Encyclopedia of Science Fiction* notes:

> **The single most important year in the history of sf [science fiction] cinema is 1968**. ... Since then it has remained, much of the time, one of the most popular film genres...[but] it would be another decade before

> the commercial potential of sf cinema was thoroughly confirmed... In 1977 *Star Wars*, a smash hit, inaugurated a new boom in space-opera movies, and in the same year *Close Encounters Of The Third Kind* also did very well with its blend of **sentiment and UFO mysticism, inaugurating the friendly-alien theme** which the film's director, Steven Spielberg, was to exploit with even greater effect in *E.T.: The Extraterrestrial* (1982) ... These films remain among the most financially successful ever made...[245]

To this day, the film's haunting images of HAL's red eye (camera) and mesmerizing voice, and the awe-inspiring black monolith (a large, thin box gifted by ETs) stand as veritable cultural icons. Even now, hearing only a few successive notes of *Also sprach Zarathustra* (German for "Thus Spoke Zarathustra"), building up to its famous crescendo and clashing cymbals, immediately elicits images of space travel, sentient computers, and alien-guided evolution. It is no accident that the piece itself—composed in 1896 but given a resurgence in popularity by *2001*—was inspired by the anti-God existential nihilist, Friedrich Nietzsche; particularly, by his work of the same name. In this book, Nietzsche declared "God is dead," and with Him morality has died, which must be replaced by the Übermensch—the "Overman" or "superman" who "rises beyond good and evil," willing only the "will to power," having rejected the "slavery" that is Christianity.

The inclusion of this piece as *2001: A Space Odyssey's* most memorable score relays a simple message: there is no need for God to explain either our past, present, or future. Our ancestors were irrational apes, granted knowledge of the use of tools by the alien monolith. This spurred on our evolution which, long thereafter, assumed its next phase: artificial intelligence. Then, the monolith appears again, with this next threshold having been passed, to bring us to yet another level of space travel and super-evolved "superman." Thus is the film's plotline in a few words; though a few additional ones are in order.

Well into the movie—after the lengthy opening scene depicting the evolution of the apes hastened by the appearance of the monolith—it is discovered (*by the extremely technologically advanced humanity which, by the year 2001, had colonized the moon and, in 2002, undertook manned missions far beyond*) that a non-natural object had been buried on the moon four million years ago. The object? Another mysterious black monolith. Eighteen months later, a Jupiter mission is in process (we later learn that the buried monolith issued the directive to travel there), and we are introduced to the infamous HAL 9000 (the AI computer controlling most of the spacecraft's functions)—described as a "conscious entity." During the mission, this computer begins seeking its own ends. Sensing the craft's crew as a risk to its self-interest, it manages to kill all but one of them. This remaining pilot does succeed in disabling HAL, at which point a pre-recorded message is broadcast to him, revealing the truth about the monolith found on the moon. The craft arrives at Jupiter only to find there floating in space beside the gas giant... another black monolith. This monolith is heralding neither the birth of tool-use, as with the apes, nor the dawn of space travel and AI, as on the moon, but rather another level still, and it immediately brings the pilot through a wormhole.

What follows is intentionally obscure. The pilot eventually enters a bedroom, and successively finds himself progressing through all the ages of his life in this room. When on his deathbed as a very old man, in this same room, he again sees a black monolith appearing at the foot of his bed. Reaching up with his right hand toward the object, he is suddenly an unborn child floating in a sphere (on that same bed), only to, immediately thereafter, be found (still as an unborn child), looking down upon earth from space. The movie then ends to the tune of the same notes inspired by Nietzsche's work declaring God is dead, and man is now the super-being.

The film's director and writer, Stanley Kubrick, implicitly confirmed that this choice of concluding music was no accident:

> [At the film's ending,] as happens in so many myths of all cultures in the world, [the pilot] is transformed into some kind of super being and **sent back to Earth, transformed and made into some sort of superman**...We have to only guess what happens when he goes back. **It is the pattern of a great deal of mythology, and that is what we were trying to suggest**.[246]

The movie's overall message is that the genesis of man has nothing to do with God, but only with evolution aided by the intercession of technology from aliens; and, moreover, that any future enlightenment or advancement will come from the intercession of these same aliens. Lest there is any confusion that this is the message, Kubrick again clears it up; this time, in an interview specifically about this movie:

> **I don't believe in any of Earth's monotheistic religions, but I do believe that one can construct an intriguing scientific definition of God**, once you accept the fact that there are approximately 100 billion stars in our galaxy alone ... there must be, in fact, countless billions of such planets where biological life has arisen ... [including many] where it is hundreds of thousands of millions of years in advance of us. ... Can you imagine the evolutionary development that much older life forms have taken? They may have progressed from biological species, which are fragile shells for the mind at best, into immortal machine entities – and then, over innumerable eons, they could emerge from the chrysalis of matter transformed into beings of pure energy ... Their potentialities would be limitless and their intelligence ungraspable by humans.[247]

Kubrick, who did not believe in demons, has nevertheless provided for them a perfectly amenable disguise. How convenient for demons it would be for mankind to anticipate imminent instruction from "benevolent extraterrestrials" who are so astonishingly evolved that they have become "immortal machines...beings of pure energy." Extraterrestrials, moreover, whose interventions not only replace the Book of Revelation, but also the Book of Genesis—explaining both our origins and our destiny. One may as well lay out a red carpet for the Antichrist.

Close Encounters of the Third Kind: Ufology's Darkness in a Nutshell

If 1968 was the most pivotal year of sci-fi cinema, 1977 was a close second. By fast forwarding one decade, we now find a society adequately primed for the climax of the first major phase of Hollywood's sci-fi deception agenda. Considered the "greatest alien movie of all time," *Close Encounters of the Third Kind* was directed by Steven Spielberg and released in 1977.

Any ambiguity regarding the benevolence of the aliens in *2001: A Space Odyssey* or *The Day the Earth Stood Still* (or similar films) was absent from this film. The same encyclopedia quoted above recounts the essence of this movie's plot as follows:

> ...at over twice the cost [of *Star Wars*] ... **[it] cuts deeper in its evocation ... of a sense of wonder.** A power company technician (Dreyfuss) witnesses a series of UFO appearances and develops an **obsession with them which is almost religious in its nature** and intensity. He becomes convinced that aliens plan to land one of their craft on an oddly shaped mountain in Wyoming. A parallel plot concerns a secret group of scientific and military experts also engaged in uncovering the secret of the UFOs. The film ends in a barrage of special effects when the spacecraft arrives; communication between the two species is achieved by means of bursts of light and music**. The hero enters the mother ship ... and is taken to the Heavens in a glowing apotheosis**...[248]

What this description fails to note is how the entire buildup of the movie is itself a reenactment of the thirty years of news reports leading up to its own release (reports which, in the almost fifty years since, have followed similar patterns). Neither escapist fiction, nor an engaging thought experiment, nor a setting to provide a meaningful moral of the story was the film's motive.

On the contrary, its intent was clear: to merge Ufology "reality" with those themes that had hitherto been considered in science fiction; to immortalize and mythologize the "heroic conquest against government coverups for UFO and ET truth;" to summarize a movement and inspire its continued pursuit; to elicit pseudo-religious faith, hope, and charity, whose object is not God, but benevolent extraterrestrials. These goals are made clear in its plot, but they are rendered undeniable in Spielberg's choice to openly model the movie's chief Ufology character (Lacombe) after the real-life renowned Ufologist Jacque Vallée. Perhaps more significant still, another renowned Ufologist, J. Allen Hynek, even makes a cameo in the film's climax.

Throughout the movie, the tension and the excitement of UFO encounters, unexplainable phenomena, abductions, and the like were portrayed just like an author of political fiction would construct its own chapters in order to make the reader say to himself, "*this resonates so well with what I see in the political world today; this could very well be real!*"

The protagonist, Roy (played by a young Richard Dreyfuss), is "fortunate" to be among those intimately brushed by a UFO making various displays of itself in Muncie, Indiana. He becomes obsessed with discovering more. In the various challenges he faces during that quest of discovery, he endures many of the dismissals one often hears of "ET contactees." Viewers are thus induced to identify with him and to derive inspiration to likewise fight through any such "obstacles" they might encounter in reality. He becomes increasingly eccentric in his obsession, and eventually his wife drives off with their children.

In the parallel plotline, Vallée's character (Dr. Lacombe) is also on a quest to discover more as he globetrots with his colleagues in the U.S. military. They are especially zealous to learn the origin of those famous five musical notes which, to this day, people around the real world will immediately associate with aliens thanks to this movie (not unlike the similarly famous few notes of *2001*). This effort brings them to northern India, where they come across a large group of Hindus chanting these very notes in unison. The words they are actually chanting, however, are the messianic words, "Aaya Re! Aaya," which means, "He has come!" (This is not translated in the movie.) After sending those notes out to space, they receive back a set of coordinates leading to the equally infamous Devil's Tower in Wyoming.

Roy and several other contactees, however, had been receiving those same signals more directly—*telepathically*. Thus, the film simultaneously promotes both the (pseudo)scientific and the (pseudo)mystical search for extraterrestrials. The contactees' obsession with images of Devil's Tower and the five notes leads them to the same place (where Roy finds companionship with another woman—not his wife—whom he eventually romantically embraces). When all the obstacles and government conspiracies are finally triumphed over, both Roy and the woman find their way to the secret military site constructed to welcome the ETs at the appropriately named Devil's Tower. An ecstatic Roy is selected by these friendly aliens to board their craft. Enraptured onlookers watch him enter the spaceship in refulgent light surrounded by a cohort of cute little aliens as if carried aloft by a cloud. The ship departs, implying he has willingly and permanently abandoned his family, and the movie's viewer is left with a veritable *religious* longing to himself meet the same extraterrestrials. Indeed, the film could scarcely have made that point clearer save by explicitly stating it; for all understand that nothing but a man's duties to God is superior to his duties to his own wife and children. When a protagonist is depicted as sacrificing the latter for some end, that end is thereby presented as a *de-facto* religious one.

One traditionalist writer described this movie's *modus operandi* well, writing:

> *Close Encounters of the Third Kind* ... with its exaltation of the psychopathic tendency prevalent in contemporary culture to cut all one's economic and emotional ties in the pursuit of some fantastic and empty ideal... is **nothing less than a satanic** ... instead of sound doctrine and religious faith... it presents emotional nihilism, spiritual emptiness, and the lack of any stable frame of reference as the prerequisites for a willing capitulation to inhuman forces—and presents this outcome as "positive." The "hero" of the movie throws his entire life away to pursue the source of the sound in his head of a few musical notes and the mental image of a barren desert crag...and is rewarded by being willingly abducted by an alien spaceship. ... **many who viewed *Close Encounters* took it as much more than mere entertainment...**[249]

Jacques Vallée himself had much to say about this film. As a character within it (not to mention perhaps the most renowned Ufologist), we should take it seriously. He wrote:

> An interesting belief of Mr. Barry's is that the movie *Close Encounters of the Third Kind* was **part of a government plan to condition the public.** "**The plan in this country is on schedule**," Barry said ... "Three years ago it was decided to do TV documentaries and observe public reaction." ... Barry observes that reaction was good: "***So the next step was the film Close Encounters.*** *Now, in a little while there doubtless will be the beginning of government advisories that UFOs are indeed with us.*" ... Everyone is now so eager to see the government "reveal" this long-awaited information that no one questions the reality of the basic facts and the political motivations that could inspire a manipulation of those facts. ... I suspect that [government agencies] are still involved. **But these UFO enthusiasts who are so anxious to expose the government have not reflected that they may be playing into the hands of a more sophisticated coverup of the real situation**. Because of their eagerness to believe any indication that the authorities already possess the proof of UFO reality, many enthusiasts provide **an ideal conduit for anyone wishing to spread the extraterrestrial gospel**...[250]

True to his usual form, Vallée provides a stinging and accurate critique of typical Ufologists (i.e., those who believe UFOs are physical aliens coming to visit us by traversing interstellar space)—demonstrating how they are succumbing to the same deception they propose to expose—precisely as he, too, succumbs to the same deception he claims to have outsmarted.*

My purpose in including the quote above, however, is simply to emphasize that this gradual buildup of teachings in alien-themed science fiction was not accidental. It was all part of a plan—regardless of whether the men who enacted the plan had any knowledge of it—and the film we are now considering was "the next step." It appears, in fact, to be the final step in its own flight of stairs. With its release, the grooming process succeeded in establishing an invincible foothold in mainstream society which anticipates enlightening extraterrestrial contact as the inevitable outcome of ongoing efforts for "disclosure."

Now that people were burning with desire for ETs, that appetite required continual feeding with a grand myth that would provide an endless array of sequels, settings, characters, merchandise, fan-clubs, philosophies—in a word, a culture-dominating phenomenon of its own. That task was achieved by the most popular of all the modern sci-fi myths: *Star Wars*—which, little wonder, was released the very same year.

Before considering that franchise, however, we must consider Spielberg's next alien-themed movie, released only five years later, and becoming just as famous as *Close Encounters*. In order for a societal grooming process to be particularly effective and unshakeable, it must seduce not only adults but also children. And what has been lacking, thus far, were works especially dedicated to ensuring that young people grew ravenous for contact with aliens as a solution to their own ills and an object of their own dreams. Spielberg obliged in *E.T.: the Extra-Terrestrial*.

E.T.: the Extra-Terrestrial: Ensnaring the Children

The 1982 creation of Steven Spielberg, his blockbuster film *E.T. the Extra-Terrestrial*, also stands in a class of its own as a cultural phenomenon which, over forty years later, refuses to diminish in influence. We are given an accurate indication of its overall message by the cover art most promulgated alongside it. It depicts yet another perversion of the fresco of the Creation of Adam in the Sistine Chapel—showing the finger of an alien reaching out to a child's finger on the backdrop of a view of earth from space.

---

* Recall, from earlier sections, that Vallée's "Interdimensional Hypothesis" is not, as it is sometimes misrepresented, simply the thesis that demons disguise themselves as UFOs. It is the opposite; Vallée argues that "Interdimensional Control Mechanisms"—which, for him, is what UFOs are—disguise themselves as whatever they please: demons, extraterrestrials, Marian apparitions, elves, fairies, Biblical miracles, etc. Therefore, I now repeat my warning to Christians that I presented there: heed well Vallée's refutations of Ufology, but do not be deceived by his alternative, which is a Trojan Horse that is even more diabolical than "typical" Ufology.

This "children's movie" tugs on every heartstring one can enumerate in order to ensure that no child who watches it leaves the experience without intimately identifying with the protagonists' love and longing for "E.T." Spielberg knew what he was doing. As one of his biographers described the film's strategy:

> Aware that children are most impressed by what happens to children on screen, Spielberg concentrated on them to the virtual exclusion of adults, who are shot almost entirely from a child's eye view. ... Learning a lesson from Walt Disney's animators, who'd discovered that the most loveable faces were those closest to a baby's, with wide eyes and a high forehead, [to make E.T.] he pasted onto the photograph of a baby's unjudgemental face the eyes of poet Carl Sandburg clipped from another photo, and the forehead and nose of Ernest Hemingway and Albert Einstein. The result was a one-size-fits-all father figure without the censoriousness that comes with age. ... with E.T. Spielberg showed ... the ability to invest sentiment and cheap humour with the dignity of a universal pronouncement. Suffused with Gothic melancholy and a poignant Freudian sense of loss, E.T. would send audiences weeping from the cinema ... Even as hard a case as the novelist Martin Amis was moved. He wrote: "*Towards the end of E.T., barely able to support my own grief and bewilderment, I turned and looked down the aisle at my fellow sufferers... Each face was a mask of tears... We were crying for our lost selves.*"[251]

To understand this movie's role in the coming deception, however, we should review a few elements from its plot.

The film's opening shows E.T.'s craft having landed in a wooded area of California, with innocent and happy aliens appreciating and studying the foliage. Humans promptly show up—to sinister music—causing the craft to depart, but inadvertently leaving behind one alien (the eponymous "E.T."). The left behind creature finds its way to the home of the protagonist, a 10-year-old boy named Elliott Taylor (a name with rather unsubtle initials). As usual, we see a broken home (the father left, and is with another woman) with no little discord dominating family life. Elliott, when he eventually discovers E.T., finds in it an escape, a friend, and even a savior.

E.T. forms a relationship with Elliott and soon they find themselves *mystically* linked—whatever one feels, so does the other. Soon, Elliott even begins referring to himself as "we" (meaning both he and E.T.), signaling the deepest possible bond with the creature. In one of the film's most iconic scenes, E.T. touches a bleeding cut on Elliott's finger, instantly healing it precisely as, in the background, we hear Peter Pan being read aloud to his young sister by Elliott's mother (who is oblivious to the presence of the alien in the closet). The wound heals as she soothingly recites the famous seductive words that have damaged so many children's moral and spiritual formation: "*She says she thinks she could get well again if children believed in fairies. Do you believe in fairies? Say it. 'I do, I do, I do!' If you believe, clap your hands [clap, clap, clap].*" The message is not missed on any child who watches, even if it is conveyed subtly: it is a moral imperative that they believe in E.T. So much depends upon it. As the scene fades, Elliott puts his arm around E.T.

The children do their best to help "ET phone home." Halloween arrives, and both E.T. and Elliott are quite sick at this point (E.T., due to being on earth; Elliott, due to his mystical bond with the alien). Elliott declares to the alien, "*I won't let anybody hurt you. We could grow up together, E.T.*" Shortly after this, the government discovers that E.T. is being hidden in Elliott's house. They descend with an army of men in space suits and quarantine the home to study the alien—who, along with Elliott himself, are both now in intensive care in the quarantined home. One of the government men, a secret ally of Elliott's (for he had waited for this precise moment since his own childhood), assures Elliott that it is a "miracle" that E.T. is here.

E.T. and Elliott exchange a glance and the boy tells the creature, who appears to be dying, "*ET stay with me, please ... I'll be right here...,*" with E.T. responding, "*Elliot ... stay, stay, stay...*" before almost flatlining. After E.T. is declared dead Elliott is given time alone with the corpse (Elliott had already begun "separating" from the alien—no longer bound to its condition, therefore he is now feeling better). The boy says to the corpse, "*I'm so sorry. You must be dead, because... I don't know how to feel. I can't feel anything anymore. You've gone someplace else now. I'll believe in you all my life. Every day. ET. I love you.*" At that, E.T. resurrects, and communicates to Elliott that the spaceship is coming back to bring E.T. home. A daring escape and a lengthy chase follow, as Elliott, along with his siblings and friends, take E.T. to the place from where it "phoned home," so that the spaceship may come and bring the alien back to its planet.

An exceedingly emotional farewell then transpires. Before E.T. boards its craft, it even says "*ouch*" and points to Elliot's heart, acknowledging the heartbreak of the goodbye. The "tragedy" is rendered all the more bizarre since E.T. had only been with Elliott for a few days, though the farewell is treated like one of brothers who had never left each other's side. They hug to rising orchestral music as E.T. says "*I'll be right here*" while touching Elliot's head with his finger (now to triumphant music), as Elliott's mother, tears streaming down her face, looks on. After waddling up the craft's ramp, E.T. is enclosed by its doors while engulfed in light. The ship ascends and creates a rainbow as it departs, everyone looking on with the same religious awe and astonishment (perversely depicting that of the Apostles at the Ascension of Christ) that Spielberg depicted so skillfully five years earlier in *Close Encounters of the Third Kind.*

It is not difficult to see what effect such a movie has on a child. Just as a boy who watches *Batman* finds himself, the next day, certain that he will himself end all crime in his city, so too a child who watches the present film gazes out his window at night in eager longing for an extraterrestrial of his own. This often proves to be no passing fad, since—unlike *Batman*—it is relentlessly fed by a steady stream of alluring UFO-related claims in the real world.

Elliott's connection to the alien most closely resembles Voodoo—itself another effect of the ministry of demons—and for the film to portray positively this pseudo-mystical bond and the associated obsession of the child with the alien can only be honestly described as diabolically inspired. That the E.T. is presented as a true friend—for *family* has failed—makes the lesson even more beguiling: "*You may not be able to trust your parents; but you can trust the aliens.*" Capping it all off is the call to the viewer to identify with Elliott: for in the days that would follow the story's conclusion, Elliott would have to continue his life without E.T. there physically. Nevertheless, his love and longing for aliens would remain "right here"—in Elliott's head—where E.T. last touched the boy before spectacularly ascending into the heavens—just as Christ assured His disciples, before ascending to Heaven, "Behold, I am with you always." (Matthew 28:20) The viewers, now, can be just like Elliott: they can keep the aliens ever in their minds, and can keep the flame of hope alive in the hearts—not a hope that has anything to do with God, but only with visitors from another planet.

Those who were Elliott's age when the ET movie was released are now middle aged. Many have not only refused to abandon the beguiling sentiments impressed on their then innocent hearts by this film, but have also fed these desires. They are now our leaders in government, commerce, media, and, yes, even the Church (recall, as noted in this book's introduction, that one theology professor at a Catholic seminary dedicated his lengthy 2021 book promoting alien belief to Steven Spielberg). With each passing day, one learns of more and more men and women in positions of power and influence openly professing their deep longing for extraterrestrial contact. This is not accidental; it is the fruition of a plan that has long been in place. The grooming process has worked well.

***

As in earlier chapters, here we have focused on only the most indisputably influential films. Had we selected for scrutiny even slightly less popular ones, we would immediately see far more outlandish, and far more explicitly demonic themes. Each movie discussed above, however, has proven so consequential that it has been selected for preservation in the United States' National Film Registry due to its great "historical, cultural, and aesthetic contributions." Administered by the Library of Congress, this Registry was established by an act of Congress in 1988. It is no small matter for a movie to be included therein. Therefore, not only the constituents of culture but also its curators have declared these films to be defining stories of the modern era.

Star Wars: A Complete Mythology

By the time *Star Wars* had arrived on the scene in 1977, enough societal grooming had been completed that the masses were primed to accept a *complete* mythology based on aliens. A fantasy world was needed, based on extraterrestrial civilizations, that people could escape to—even mentally "live inside"—while never giving up hope to experience a similar thing in the real world. In the decades that followed, *Star Wars* films would never lose their dominance in influencing society. To this day, the *Star Wars* franchise has amassed a revenue exceeding that of any other franchise in history besides the very one that would in a sense replace it—albeit with far darker deceptions—from 2008 onwards: the "Marvel Cinematic Universe." But this is only one measure of its impact. When considering the cultural trends derived from *Star Wars*, which have little or no parallel, it is difficult to regard the franchise as anything but supreme in Science Fiction.

Star Wars, however—as far as I can tell—was not so much directed to *advancing* the grooming process. If anything, its plotline constituted a departure from that trend, for by positioning the story as transpiring "*A long time ago in a galaxy far, far away...*" viewers are, thankfully, deprived of any direct expectation to find earth's history ever intersecting with its plotline. There is almost a sense that *Star Wars* more resembles something like *Lord of the Rings* (albeit without the edifying elements deriving from Tolkien's Christian approach); simply providing a fictional setting for exploring standard epic themes.

Do not misunderstand: the grooming would continue, with an uninterrupted deluge of films depicting earth being visited by either benevolent or nefarious extraterrestrials (recall that both takes constitute preparations for the Great Deception). And *Star Wars* did at least contribute to its maintenance and energize its base.

For even if *Star Wars* did not itself have a storyline that gave direct hope for earthly contact with ETs, it nevertheless kept the theme alive in the minds and hearts of the masses, who would proceed to derive their hopes of attaining alien-enlightenment from other sources. It promoted the same, most fundamental premise of all the grooming films—namely, the false belief that the galaxies are filled with intelligent aliens.

Moreover, the "spirituality" of *Star Wars* is decidedly Eastern. Fr. Spyridon Bailey describes this tendency in Science Fiction in general and in *Star Wars* in particular by illustrating deep contradictions they inevitably display with the most basic Christian truths. He states:

> Science fiction literature and drama ...rejects traditional religion, the societies and cultures portrayed exist in a "post-Christian" universe. The secular outlook of its characters does on occasions admit a spirituality, but this is almost always drawn from eastern mysticism. For example in *Star Wars*, the Jedi have a temple where they learn the ways of an

> unseen force that guides and influences them: and even produces a virgin birth in the case of Anakin Skywalker. But it is not personal, it has no other name, and within it there is an evil aspect, the dark side, which is the equal of the good side. Therefore, we may say **the philosophy inherent in science fiction is intended to reflect man's rejection of traditional religious values**... in the Godless universe of sci-fi it is man's reasoning powers that become the all-important aspect of existence. Science fiction promotes a belief that man himself will continue to evolve, and so it is the very mind of man through his technological advancements, that imposes meaning on reality. ... [it] reflects the goal of eastern beliefs such as some schools of Buddhism. **It is a desire for transcendence**. One of the dangers of this philosophy is that the stories often involve themes of telepathy and other psychic phenomena. In the Godless reality of science fiction ... [these] occult [practices,] the evolved future man embraces as being aspects of his higher self.[252]

It bears emphasizing how wrongheaded are the attempts of some Christians to portray "the Force" of *Star Wars* as an acceptable allegory for the Holy Spirit. Some go so far as to say—perhaps jokingly at first, before realizing that much seriousness has crept into the invocation—"*May the Force be with you.*" (Twisting the traditional prayer of a Catholic priest, "*The Lord be with you.*") Any such attempt is only a gross disservice, since the Holy Spirit is just as much a *person* as is Jesus Christ or God the Father. He is no mere vague energy up for grabs by one who invokes the correct formula or engages in the right meditative postures.

More importantly still, we know from Scripture that "God is light and in him there is no darkness at all." (1 John 1:5) To regard God the Holy Spirit as in any way resembling the Pagan concept of "Yin and Yang"—as Star Wars regards "the Force"—wherein the light has darkness in it and the darkness has light in it, is to reject the Christian understanding of God at the deepest level. Finally, the supreme guru of this "Force," Yoda, is unmistakably portrayed as a veritable incarnation of the Buddha.

Therefore—returning to the societal-level grooming process that modern sci-fi has undertaken—we cannot entirely write off the role of *Star Wars*. Beyond its inherent problems, it contributed to moving ET belief beyond the realm of "detached" analysis, and into the realm of overwhelming excitement. This contribution is precisely the observation of one expert on Steven Spielberg, who noted:

> [There was a] "**a sudden and radical shift in generic attitude and a popular renaissance of the [science-fiction] film**" initiated by the release of George Lucas's *Star Wars: A New Hope* and Steven Spielberg's *Close Encounters of the Third Kind* in 1977." ... this was a move away from a "cool" or "detached" vision of science fiction, such as that of *2001: A Space Odyssey* (1968), and argues that "**through some strange new transformation, technological wonder had become synonymous with domestic hope**; space and time seemed to expand again."[253]

***

The effects of this societal manipulation we have been charting out can scarcely be missed by anyone who is acquainted with American (and, more broadly, Western) culture, much less one who studies it. As one Catholic journalist observed:

> **Was something infiltrating—invading—from the world of spirits, as opposed to "outer space"?** No wonder the big TV series had been "The Twilight Zone." And was now "Star Trek." Strange lights were seen in the skies above Woodstock, while on the other side of America, Jerry Garcia of The Grateful Dead said he had been abducted for two days by large insect-like beings similar to another account from John Lennon in which the Beatle had said "insectoid" beings once came to his apartment in a blazing light outside his door, again reminding us of a Spielberg movie, this time **Close Encounters. (During the filming of that movie, the director reported poltergeist activity.)** Songwriter Cat Stevens claimed he had been "sucked up" by a saucer that later dropped him on his bed; singer Phoebe Snow said she talked to "aliens" via a Ouija board. A writer for a satanic heavy-metal band called Blue Oyster Cult was another who was "abducted" by a cigar-shaped "mother ship," while David Bowie—to carry forth this incredible litany—starred in a movie called *The Man Who Fell To Earth,* made himself up to look like an extraterrestrial during concerts ... **Why did no one question it, when the fruit so often was bad?** A "UFO" was seen above a violent outbreak at Altamont Speedway in California (during which Hell's Angels serving, as the Rolling Stone's security, knifed a man to death)... Elvis Presley was serious about "extraterrestrials" and had a fascination that bordered on obsession (often staring at the stars, saying that he was from another planet, and asserting the "space" beings were here to "prepare us for transition into the New Age.") ... Mick Jagger said he saw a giant spacecraft larger than a football field at Glastonbury Tor in England (circa 1968), a year after he'd donned a robe and wizard's hat—planets in the backdrop—on the cover of an album called *Their Satanic Majesties Request,* while his close friend and bandmate Keith Richards saw his flying saucer in Sussex the same year. ("We receive our songs by inspiration, like at a séance," commented Richards.) ...singer Michael Jackson—a UFO aficionado and close friend of famed psychic Uri Geller—who often spoke about his talents in terms of "magic from somewhere."[254]

Even the observations above, however, only provide the smallest glimpse into the effects of ET belief and expectation upon modern culture. A more thorough analysis would consider the demonic UFO cults, the new "UFO Religions," the mass-suicides, the millions of lives ruined by "abduction" experiences and Ufology obsession, the steady stream of false "private revelations" describing our "space brothers," the government psyops, and the relentless ET-belief-inspired assaults on traditional (and dogmatic) Christian and Catholic teaching—including those against Christology, Mariology, Ecclesiology, and Eschatology.

We must, therefore, move on to focus again on the real-world rotten fruits of the modern era's alien obsession. There is, moreover, no need for us to continue charting out Hollywood's grooming process undertaken upon the masses in preparation for the Great Deception. The era it inaugurated in 1977 brings us directly to the present day (another *Star Wars* movie was released as recently as 2019). Testifying to the dominance of this trend, the two men—George Lucas and Steven Spielberg—who directed the movies considered in the three preceding sections remain, by far, the richest movie directors in history. The multi-billion-dollar fortune of each blows away third place (Peter Jackson) by a factor of five. Both, moreover, remain alive, well, and influential. Suffice it to say that the intervening decades saw a steady stream of movies, television series, books, and other culture-forming-creations continuing to disseminate the longing for discovering extraterrestrial intelligence and fostering the hope that the human race would "undertake its next phase in evolution," thanks to the intervention of these supremely advanced beings. (Especially noteworthy is the 1997 movie, *Contact*, excluded from this chapter only because we considered it in a previous one.)

Before proceeding to the next chapter, we should step back to consider the Devil's antics in the "grooming" process we have been surveying.

What Has the Devil Been Up to and What Will He Be Up to?

I am not accusing each work in the sections above—much less each writer and director—of being explicitly and thoroughly demonic. My goal is not to treat them as if each were an outright Satanic textbook, but only to chart out the development of a deliberate trend. The Devil can whisper into the ear of whomever he wishes—even a saint—and the mere fact that a man has been found to have contributed to the growth of a diabolical trend does not prove he did so intentionally. While I am convinced that the Devil is ultimately behind the explosive growth of ET-expectation in modern society, I do not know which individuals are knowingly collaborating with him. That Judgment is up to God, and we will all see it on the Last Day.

Second, even the Devil does not have perfect knowledge of the future. Although he has always known—since Scripture foretells it—that, in the "end times," he would have his ultimate minion (the Antichrist), and would institute the apocalyptic "Strong Delusion," etc., we cannot know when he settled on the *details* of his aims in relation to these persecutions.

If indeed he has long been at work preparing the world for welcoming "ET contact" as a herald of the Antichrist, which surely appears to be the case, I suspect that he began devising this plan at some point during the Enlightenment when, for the first time in well over a millennium and a half, Christians suddenly began opening themselves up to the ideas that Jesus is not the only Incarnation of God, that the Blessed Virgin Mary is not really the greatest possible creature, that the human race is not the only intelligent incarnate one, and that "other worlds" full of alien civilizations may exist. The Devil likely became particularly active in initiating this deception in the deeply occult 1800s, towards the end of which the massively popular works of ET-based science fiction (e.g., *War of the Worlds*) were released. In the 1900s, then, his work was mostly directed towards gradually increasing the degree of evil in the principles of the deception to the point where society was sufficiently primed to welcome "enlightened extraterrestrials." (In 1947, his efforts suddenly and exponentially changed, but in this case we are speaking of *reality*, not fiction, therefore we will treat this theme in a later chapter.)

I suspect that the Devil is, even now, waiting for the opportune moment to pounce by way of his greatest attack yet. That moment may well arrive when he senses that enough of the masses believe in aliens and are desirous of contact with them to solve some great human crisis. It may also depend upon mankind failing some great test designed to assess whether people have become sufficiently collectively mad to almost unanimously welcome the doctrines of demons wearing extraterrestrial guises. Perhaps this test could even be something related to the "woke" agenda, without specific relation to aliens. The ET Deception will doubtless get worse, both in movies and in news reports, in the times ahead, but it seems that this is not entirely necessary for "grooming" society further, since the vast majority of people are now primed to welcome ET-based "salvation." Therefore, he may only be waiting for the circumstances to be perfect.

It would behoove discerning Christians, then, to be on alert for signposts of society succumbing to insanity. Societal-level endorsements of "transgenderism," institutionalization of suicide, "Catholic" leaders succumbing to modernism and Paganism, animals being given human rights, hallucinogenic drugs becoming legalized and widely used, "AI" robots being treated as if they had sentience or emotion or free-will, and other such benchmarks, all constitute warnings that the Devil may be only moments away from launching the Great Deception.

22. Diabolical Deception in the Church

"We have matured 'spiritually' so much during the last forty years that it would be beneath our adult dignity to waste a moment on original sin, let alone on the devil. This in part is due to the fact that neither sin nor the devil figure prominently in the documents of Vatican II...this pleases the devil more than anything else, for the devil's chief stratagem is not to show himself..."—Fr. Stanley Jaki

We have seen how deeply diabolical deceptions based on extraterrestrial belief have penetrated into the world. Has the Church, at least, been spared such infiltration? The answer, unfortunately, is a resolute *no.* Now, naturally, the Church has not fallen anywhere near as low as the world has. In accordance with Christ's promise to Peter that the "gates of hell shall not prevail against" the Church (Matthew 16:18), ET-belief never has been—and never will be—taught in the official Magisterium. But this assurance is the only one we can ultimately count on in limiting the reach of diabolical alien doctrines. Individual men in the Vatican, regardless of the color of the hat they wear, are not protected by any Divine guarantee that they will evade being seduced by the Devil's deceptions. In the following sections, we will consider—and refute—various ET-related deceptions that have raged within Catholicism.

St. Paul VI's Real "Smoke of Satan"—"Pagan Prophets" of "Science"

"Through some crack, the smoke of Satan has entered the Church of God...We trust the first pagan prophet we see who speaks to us in some newspaper, and we run behind him and ask him if he has the formula for true life... [doubt has] entered through the windows that should have been open to the light: science."
—Pope St. Paul VI. June 29, 1972

Especially during the 20th century (although the 19th saw its fair share of this), many Catholic clerics and other prominent voices became infatuated with the prospect not of saving souls, but of being taken seriously by the worldly and being invited into the prevailing movements of the world. Prudence was thrown to the wind, and a corresponding attitude was adopted insisting the world could simply be *accommodated*—that almost any compromise was acceptable or even obligatory—"so long as we are sure to hold on to certain explicitly defined dogmas." (Though the modernists soon emptied even those of any meaning.) With the growth of Ufology from 1947 onward came the emergence of Catholic leaders all too eager to jump on that bandwagon. If only such leaders had listened to Cardinal Ratzinger, who warned:

> He is totally ignorant of the nature of the Church and of the nature of the world who believes that these two can meet without conflict or that they may be somehow mixed.

Pope St. Paul VI noticed what was happening in the Church. His famous observation, that the "smoke of Satan has entered the Church," is often quoted today. Sadly, the rest of the quote (shown above), where he explained precisely how this happened, is often ignored. The way the proverbial "smoke" entered was through "**pagan prophets**" who propose to have the "**formula for true life**," and whom those in the Church, diabolically deceived, are so foolish as to "trust" with such credulousness that they "run to" them, and that this deception takes place through what is presented as "science."

A more precise description of how the ET and UFO Deception infiltrated the Church cannot be constructed. In the years leading up to the Pope's declaration about Satan's infiltration of the Church, the man who was—tragically (in light of his famous dissent on many other Church teachings)—considered the leading Catholic theologian, Karl Rahner, was arguing for the compatibility of Christian Faith with Extraterrestrials, even signaling his openness to the particularly diabolical doctrine of multiple incarnations of God; robbing Jesus Christ of His singularity and supremacy.

In the decades that would follow, this smoke would billow through the Church more thickly still. The Vatican would begin sponsoring conferences dedicated to exploring questions related to extraterrestrial life. In 2008, the Vatican's chief astronomer, Jesuit Fr. Jose Funes, made international headlines by advocating for aliens—presenting as his justification the usual fallacies we have already refuted in preceding chapters (particularly by insisting that we "cannot limit God," as if believing what God has revealed somehow constitutes "limiting" Him). Secular outlets often reported on this with the headline, "*Vatican Says it's Okay to Believe in Aliens,*" and many of the faithful were thereby beguiled into supposing that Catholicism had formally endorsed alien belief. (In fact, Fr. Funes' position in the Vatican does not lend one ounce of Magisterial weight to his opinions.)

What is certain is that—in the years leading up to Paul VI's "Smoke of Satan" declaration—claims of compatibility between belief in ETs and Catholicism suddenly erupted in the Vatican. One chronicler of ET debates noted:

> ...very little public, Roman Catholic intellectual debate occurred regarding the compatibility, or lack thereof, of extraterrestrial life and the Roman Catholic faith for most of the first half of the twentieth century. **In the early 1960s that situation changed**...[255]

Among the most prominent of the "pagan prophets" celebrated in secular news media, to whom the masses (and certainly too many in the Church) were running for existential answers, was a man named Frank Drake (as discussed earlier, he was "the father of the Search for Extraterrestrial Intelligence," or SETI). As the great Benedictine priest, theologian, and scientist, Fr. Stanley Jaki, noted:

> **Shortly after Frank Drake started his project in the 1960s** various prominent people were interviewed as to what we can expect after we have detected radio signals from outer space. Some thought that this will mean the coming of Paradise on earth. **What God failed to achieve, the science brought by extraterrestrials would make possible as they would bring with themselves the wisdom of their own evolution**.[256]

Here, we see the *real* deception of the smoke of Satan entering the Church: *God's Providence replaced with scientific hope in extraterrestrials.* Many Catholics who today comment on these remarks from Paul VI focus almost exclusively on Liturgical matters (and indeed, there is much valid concern there). The Devil, however, was executing a much darker, much deeper, much more nefarious, and much more apocalyptic plan, which the Pope prophetically described as smoke billowing into the Church.

> "Before Christ's second coming the Church must pass through a final trial that will shake the faith of many believers... [it] will unveil the "mystery of iniquity" in the form of **a religious deception offering men an apparent solution to their problems at the price of apostasy from the truth**." —*Catechism of the Catholic Church*, §675

Here, the prophetic admonition of Bishop Marian Eleganti comes to mind, when he warned, in 2023:

> ...the faith Tradition of the Church is always superior to any era ... new human science theories, which are always valid until they are falsified, do not force the Church in this respect to a revision of revealed truths of the faith. A departure from them is doomed to failure, and coming generations will state as much ... **What shocks and amazes me is the perfidy, cunning, and intelligence of how the new postulates are implemented and linguistically disguised. I have always considered theologians to be the greatest and most gifted of the sophists. The phenomenon always makes me think of the Antichrist**, who in Soloviev appears very friendly and inclusive; does not hurt anyone's feelings; lets everyone have his opinion; does not condemn anyone; fraternizes everyone; only **guts the faith from the claim of absoluteness and exclusiveness of Jesus Christ** and therefore is radically inclusive, a friend of diversity and equality, a fraternization of all. ...Christ,

however, [the modern Church] no longer proclaims as the only valid and definitive revelation of God, as the door past which no one comes to the Father.[257]

***

Perhaps the chief false prophet of the religion of scientism, with its corresponding pseudo-eschatological hope in extraterrestrials, was the prominent Jesuit theologian, Fr. Teilhard Pierre de Chardin. Let us now address his errors.

Fr. Teilhard Pierre de Chardin: the "Synthesis of All Heresies" Supplies the ET-Theology Premises

> "[Teilhard de Chardin's writings] are a cesspool of errors, the synthesis of all heresies." —Pope Pius XII[258]

Unlike Karl Rahner, Teilhard Pierre de Chardin did not merely dissent on a number of Catholic teachings; he sought to completely rob Christianity of its essence and replace it with a "better" religion. He declared:

> **What increasingly dominates my interests, is the effort to establish within myself and <u>define around me, a new religion</u> (call it a better Christianity,** if you like) where the personal God ceases to be the great monolithic proprietor of the past to become the Soul of the World which the stage we have reached religiously and culturally calls for.[259]

De Chardin was a French Jesuit priest, theologian, and scientist who became extremely popular in the early 20th century for his Darwinism-inspired theology. Many of his teachings were condemned by the Congregation for the Doctrine of the Faith in 1962; unfortunately, however, this did little to mitigate his influence, and a major effort is now afoot in the Church to formally rehabilitate his heretical legacy. In 2017, a cardinal even formally requested that Pope Francis lift the restrictions placed upon his writings after the members of the Pontifical Council for Culture voted unanimously to approve a similar request. More troubling still, this same movement urges—with a growing petition behind it—that de Chardin be named a *Doctor of the Church* due to his "prophetic vision." If indeed de Chardin was a prophet, however, he only numbered among the very "Pagan Prophets" that Pope St. Paul VI warned against the rise of—"prophets" sent by Satan, and wearing the guise of science.

Advocates of his rehabilitation argue that, "*The time is ripe to introduce Pierre Teilhard de Chardin to a new generation – the man...whose relentless effort to reframe his beliefs in the light of evolution led to a paradigm shift in the relationship of science and religion.*"[260] While de Chardin sought to "reframe" (read: demolish) Christianity in light of evolution, Catholic ET promoters seek to similarly "reframe" the Faith in light of extraterrestrials, using de Chardin's principles as a guide.

Scholars dedicated to examining the relationship between religions and extraterrestrials have not missed the relevance of this Jesuit. The astrophysicist, Professor David Weintraub, even wrote a book dedicated to the topic, and in examining Catholicism's relationship to aliens, he focuses on the teachings of Fr. Teilhard. Dr. Weintraub made a fatal mistake in supposing the de Chardin's musings represented Catholicism's actual teachings (in dismissing the CDF's still-in-force condemnation, Weintraub quotes another Jesuit, Fr. Federico Lombardi, who—absurdly—claimed in 2009 that, "*By now, no one would dream of saying that Teilhard is a heterodox author...*") But he was not mistaken in estimating the enormous influence this priest had on the question of ETs and Catholicism. Professor Weintraub explains Fr. Teilhard's take:

> In the first half of the 20th century, Jesuit priest Pierre Teilhard de Chardin suggested that original sin didn't arise from the errors of two humans on Earth, but instead permeates the entire universe. He also suggested that Christ on Earth offers no redemptive value for any other beings anywhere else in the cosmos, and so aliens visiting Earth would not benefit from embracing Christianity. But **Teilhard believed that Christ could become incarnate on different worlds**, in forms appropriate for those places and beings. **These other saviors** could establish Christian-like local belief systems that provide opportunities for the redemption and salvation of those alien populations.[261]

As we can see, Fr. de Chardin manages to get every possible detail wrong on this question. In fact, it is a dogma that Original Sin did indeed arise from Adam and Eve—not before, and not in some other manner. And the value of Christ's Redemption is infinite (if we for a moment pretend that aliens did exist and did come to earth, then we would have to evangelize them). Finally, the notion of multiple Incarnations of God (as we saw in Part One) is blasphemous and fallacious in every respect. A party-line Darwinist, however, de Chardin obediently rejected anything that smacked of "anthropocentrism," which he denounces as "geocentrism." Accordingly, Fr. Teilhard declared:

> **The idea of an earth chosen arbitrarily from countless others as the focus of Redemption...is one that I cannot accept...There were worlds before our own**, and there will be worlds after it. ... Christ has still to be incarnate in some as yet unformed star ... [but] there are times when one almost despairs of being able to disentangle Catholic dogmas from the geocentrism in the framework of which they were born...[262]

De Chardin's Antichristic teachings, therefore, are not only a rotten fruit* of belief in extraterrestrial intelligence but also a rotten branch of that

* De Chardin's teachings may themselves even be a "rotten fruit" of a far older thesis. Scholars have argued—e.g., Professor Lyon's 1982 book, *The Cosmic Christ in*

tree—perhaps even constituting an entire limb—for from it, innumerable other rotten fruits have emerged.

Among de Chardin's theses was his teaching that so-called "conscious evolution" would inevitably lead to an "Omega Point" (referred to by others as "The Singularity") and a "Planetary Superorganism." I will not humor his promoters by giving floor time here to detailed explanations of what Fr. Teilhard means by these things. They are just disguises for New Age esotericism, the false religion of scientism, and a re-branding of ancient Gnosticism. In 2014, the Prefect for the Congregation for the Doctrine of Faith, Cardinal Gerhard Müller rightly denounced these teaching in the strongest possible terms:

> The fundamental theses of Conscious Evolution are opposed to Christian Revelation and, when taken unreflectively, lead almost necessarily to fundamental errors regarding the omnipotence of God, the Incarnation of Christ, the reality of Original Sin, the necessity of salvation and the definitive nature of the salvific action of Christ in the Paschal Mystery ... **acceptance of things such as Conscious Evolution seemingly without any awareness that it offers a vision of God, the cosmos, and the human person divergent from or opposed to Revelation evidences that a *de facto* movement beyond the Church and sound Christian faith has already occurred** ... the futuristic ideas advanced by the proponents of Conscious Evolution are not actually new. The Gnostic tradition is filled with similar affirmations and we have seen again and again in the history of the Church the tragic results of partaking of this bitter fruit.[263]

Of particular importance is the Cardinal's insight that when one adopts such views as "Conscious Evolution" (and similar ones inextricable from ET belief), he has *de facto* apostatized from Christianity. The exceeding danger is found in that this real (*de facto*) apostasy is nevertheless unnoticed, for the trappings of Christianity are maintained.

> "But understand this, that **in the last days there will come times of stress. For men will be lovers of self ... holding the form of religion but denying the power of it**. Avoid such people." —2 Timothy 3:1-2,5

I can imagine no clearer fulfillment of St. Paul's prophecy here relayed in Scripture. The followers of de Chardin, giddy about the extraterrestrials whom they are sure exist and surpass us due to "Conscious Evolution," still hold the *form* of religion, but have done everything they can to empty it of its *power*. Perhaps the most stinging critique of the teachings of Fr.

Origen and Teilhard de Chardin, that Fr. Teilhard's view is an outgrowth of Origen's views. Recall that Origen was condemned by the Church as a heretic for, among other things, his ET-friendly worldview.

Teilhard come from the Catholic physicist, mathematician, and philosopher, Dr. Wolfgang Smith, who professed in his book, *Teilhardism and the New Religion*:

> **Teilhard is not after all the champion of a besieged Christianity, but the founder of a new religion ... to supplant the old** ... the new cult is not anything like the Christianity of bygone days. It is so radically different, in fact, that Teilhard refers to it at one point as *"a hitherto unknown form of religion—one that no one could as yet have imagined or described, for lack of a universe large enough or organic enough to contain it."* ... the true founder of the new cult is not Yahweh or Christ, but Charles Darwin. One cannot but wonder whether the French Jesuit was playing square with us when he declared that *"This is still, of course, Christianity."* ...**The trend [today] is unmistakable: Christianity ... has begun to turn in the direction mapped out by Teilhard de Chardin.** ... Teilhard tells us: *"... grace represents a physical supercreation. It raises us a further rung on the ladder of cosmic evolution. In other words, the stuff of which grace is made is strictly biological."* ... [this] affirms very much the opposite of what Christians had always believed: for it belongs to the very essence of grace to be, not a natural attainment, but a supernatural gift. What Teilhard has actually done under the pretext of interpreting the term is to deny that such a thing as grace exists. **His "grace" is actually a non-grace...It is literally true that Teilhard has deified evolution**. ...**not until Teilhard stepped upon the stage did Evolution find its full-blown prophet.** ... At Teilhard's hands the Darwinist theory has been transformed into a full-fledged religion...**One sees that even the Pater Noster has become reversed: henceforth it is no longer "Thy will," but ours, that is to be done.** ... [this] newly-hatched anti-creed has come to be accepted by millions as the true Christianity. In the eyes of the "liberated" it is indeed perceived as the ultra-Christianity which Teilhard declared it to be... His central complaint, to be sure, is that (traditional) Christianity is not "scientific," ... It is therefore "staticist" and needs to be revised...

At this point, it should not be surprising to hear that de Chardin's teachings are so severely opposed to the very core of Christian Faith that, if and when they are succumbed to, they truly do open up a portal to demonic entry. Fr. Malachi Martin, in his book, *Hostage to the Devil*, even extensively recounted the (true) story of a certain Rome-educated priest, theologian, and *exorcist* who himself—*due to* his belief in Fr. Teilhard's teachings—became demonically possessed. Now, perhaps relatively few will find that to be their own fate. But ultimately, that matters little. The Devil is not especially interested in possessing people; he is interested in seducing them into hell. And that is usually much more effectively achieved through diabolical deceptions that stop well short of full-blown possession.

Although Darwinism specifically, and the religion of scientism more broadly, is de Chardin's central theme, what he proposes nevertheless conveys (almost verbatim) the ET promoters' insistence that we "re-read" Christianity in light of aliens. Whoever doubts this influence need only defer to the writings of the ET promoters themselves.

Dr. Robert John Russell—a prominent Christian theologian and physicist who promotes belief in extraterrestrials—wrote:

> Suppose ET is not that different from us after all ...Will God provide a pathway of healing, a means of "saving grace" for ET as God has done for us on Earth? **This is, of course, the horizon-breaking image of the "cosmic Christ," as Pierre Teilhard de Chardin called it**. ... I'm willing to go out on a limb and make what I consider to be a genuinely empirical theological prediction. ... **I predict that when we finally make contact with intelligent life in the universe** ... it will be a lot like us...I predict that the discovery of extraterrestrial life will "hold a mirror up" to us ...We may come, then, to a point where we at last feel truly at home in the cosmos. What a wondrous event that would be![264]

"When" we contact the extraterrestrials, Dr. Russel says, we will essentially have a mirror held up to ourselves, and we will experience the workings of the "cosmic Christ" in their lives, which will enable us to "at last feel truly at home in the cosmos." As we can see, it is not only the worldly who anticipate glorious revelations from contacting aliens, but also the Christian theologians—formed by the teachings of de Chardin. Here as everywhere we look in ET promotion, we see the scene being set for a Great Deception the likes of which the world has never experienced.

Dr. Paul Thigpen is perhaps the most prominent of the Catholic ET promoters today. In his 2022 book arguing for belief in extraterrestrials, he acknowledges that de Chardin is "highly controversial," before moving on to appear to endorse Fr. Teilhard's teachings, or at least concede their importance in generating modern ET belief. He presents these heresies without any refutation, noting that:

> [de Chardin's] speculations about extraterrestrial intelligence are not surprising ... Teilhard redefined original sin as "the essential reaction of the finite to the creative act" ... If sin understood in this way is a universal attribute of the entire creation, Teilhard argued, God must offer redemption to all creatures as well. But humanity could not be the sole center of redemption, ... **Teilhard proposed the activity of a third, "cosmic," nature of Christ, a nature in addition to the divine and the human natures identified in Catholic dogma**.[265]

Joel Parkyn is a theology professor at a Catholic seminary who also published a 2021 book arguing for belief in aliens, therein praising Fr. Teilhard's teachings for lacking "rigidity" and moving beyond a "prescientific" outlook, before expounding upon the latter's insistence upon multiple incarnations in support of ETs:

> Roman Catholic and Anglican theologians ...who have speculated on the Christological implications of intelligent extraterrestrials in the twentieth and twenty-first century occupy the inclusive axis, such as Milne, Teilhard de Chardin, and Consolmagno, **each having abandoned the rigidity of the pre-scientific classical solution** offered by the likes of Aristotle, Augustine, Aquinas...[266]

Lutheran theologian Ted Peters, who wrote a popular 2018 book arguing for extraterrestrials, also invoked Fr. Teilhard.

The director of the Vatican Observatory, Jesuit Br. Guy Consolmagno, is another ET believer (though he does not think aliens are already on earth) who published a popular 2014 book entitled *Would You Baptize an Extraterrestrial?*, along with Fr. Paul Mueller. The latter repeatedly had recourse to Fr. Teilhard in his dialogues with Br. Guy; "clarifying" that he found a couple of things problematic in de Chardin's thesis, but that Fr. Teilhard nevertheless got it "**almost right**." (Recall that, in fact, Fr. Teilhard's teachings are—as Venerable Pope XII said—a "synthesis of all heresies." To claim de Chardin "got it almost right" is little better than a full-blown embrace of apostasy.)

Theologian and ET belief promoter, Dr. David Wilkinson, also draws from de Chardin in his 2013 book, *Science, Religion, and the Search for Extraterrestrial Intelligence*, writing:

> One of the most imaginative thinkers in the Catholic engagement of science and religion was of course Teilhard de Chardin... he saw evolution happening in religious and cultural terms drawn forward by a future Omega Point... his view of cosmic redemption wanted to see the work of God on a much larger scale...

Although we are focusing on deception in the Church in the present chapter, it is worth nothing that secular ET promoters are even more open in admitting how essential Fr. Teilhard's heresies have been in forming contemporary Ufology. The *Mammoth Encyclopedia of Extraterrestrials* explains:

> "In the evolution of the human mind simple consciousness was first produced; then self-consciousness; and lastly...Cosmic Consciousness." This theoretical model of human awareness emphasizes those changes in human consciousness that occur as a result of UFO encounters, and the personal and social transformations that develop around the meaning and significance of UFO experiences. ... **This model is based on the work of Teilhard de Chardin,** Julian Huxley, and the emerging theories of a holigraphic universe.[267]

The teachings of Fr. Teilhard Pierre de Chardin are the anti-Midas—everything they touch only rots. And they have touched almost all of the teachings of those who, in the Church today, promote belief in extraterrestrials. Let us now consider the teachings of another prominent Catholic priest and theologian whose own views de Chardin has not only touched, but also formed.

Monsignor Corrado Balducci: The Deceived Roman Exorcist and Theologian

> "See to it that no one makes a prey of you by philosophy and empty deceit, according to human tradition, according to the elemental spirits of the universe, and not according to Christ."
> —Colossians 2:8

Monsignor Corrado Balducci is one of the most frequently cited Catholic names in support of belief in extraterrestrials. It is not difficult to see why. For those who still manage to cling to clericalism—supposing that any priest-theologian (particularly one who works in the Vatican) is a veritable mouthpiece for God—Balducci presents the perfect "proof" that Catholics can, or even should, believe in aliens.

This Italian theologian, who served on Vatican congregations and died in 2008, claims to have counted the pope as one of his friends, and had even served as an exorcist for the Diocese of Rome. *"If he believed in aliens, shouldn't we also believe in them?"*, today's Catholic ET promoters say. The answer, of course, is a most emphatic *no*. Here as everywhere in ET promotion, one need only scratch the surface to see how loudly the diabolical delusion resounds.

Msgr. Balducci did not merely speculate about abstract theological questions related to extraterrestrial intelligence. He unreservedly dove head-first into Ufology—with its occultism and all—and became a veritable celebrity (commonly appearing in both television episodes and documentary films) by declaring himself the Catholic Church's "**representative to the star peoples**." Through his efforts over the course of many years, he became one of Ufology's greatest champions in the 1990s and early 2000s.

He openly, warmly, and repeatedly collaborated with charlatans and deceivers such as Dr. Steven Greer and Whitley Strieber—who were themselves beyond question either vexed by demons (e.g., Strieber) or facilitating dialogue with demons (e.g., Greer). Instead of offering them any correction or solid Catholic guidance, he only confirmed these men in their delusions and sent them on their way treading the path to perdition and leading millions to the same fate. (To this day, many Ufologists—including these two—defer to Balducci's influence on them to justify the evil teachings they promote in the ET Deception.)

Therefore, due to Balducci's uniquely destructive legacy in contemporary "Catholic" ET promotion, a particularly careful analysis of his impact is here necessary over the course of a few sections.

***

In an interview from the year 2000 that was falsely billed by the media as a revelation that, now, *"the Vatican endorses extraterrestrials!"*, Balducci made various deeply misguided remarks to the Ufologist Paola Harris. Ms. Harris is a woman who credits her fixation upon UFOs to watching the film *Close Encounters of the Third Kind,* which, she shares, "triggered in her an emotional response." She has since gone down the proverbial rabbit hole of Ufology—even becoming a promoter of occult practices like "remote viewing." Harris co-authored a 2021 Ufology book (*Trinity: The Best-Kept Secret*) with Jacques Vallée, she considers herself an "exopolitician," (i.e., one who will manage political relations with the aliens upon contact), and she advocates for (and even attended) Steven Greer's demon-contacting sessions (i.e., his "CE5" events described in an earlier chapter).

Ms. Harris has relayed that she and Balducci "**admired each other**" and "**often dined together**, "sharing, of the Monsignor:

> **[Balducci] was optimistic and hopeful that we would have some kind of celestial 'intervention' [i.e., from aliens] and be saved from cataclysmic destruction**[268]

Leaving aside the question of why a priest would often dine with a particular woman, we can see again that Balducci was not merely wrongheadedly arguing for the reconcilability of belief in aliens with Catholic teaching. He was far past that, and was placing his hopes for the world not in the triumph of Christ, but in some saving intervention from aliens.

Ms. Harris claims that Balducci's views in support of aliens "*represent the unofficial position of the Catholic Church.*"[269] This distortion no doubt arose from Balducci's habit of overestimating his own importance and authority. In fact, Balducci had no more right to speak for the "position of the Catholic Church"—official or unofficial—than *any* priest. His status as a theologian and exorcist in Rome lends no Magisterial weight to his views. Whoever would seek to ascertain the proper Catholic position from the views of an individual priest would be better advised listening to Fr. Stanley Jaki or Fr. Thomas Weinandy—both contemporary theologians (one still living, and both of far greater renown and competence than Balducci)—who wisely taught the following:

> "**Behind these** bravados about extraterrestrials you either see the strategy of the devil or you remain blind." -Fr. Stanley Jaki[270]
>
> "Intelligent aliens find no place within God's eternal scheme...**Jesus cosmically reigns supreme as man. He is not Lord of non-human aliens, for they do not exist** ... while it may be fun to fantasize ... about the existence of aliens, such daydreaming, if it is deemed to be real, **can wreak havoc on the Gospel**, particularly to the primacy of Jesus as the cosmic incarnate Lord of all." —Fr. Thomas Weinandy[271]

Tragically, instead of helping Ms. Harris to see the errancy of her life-destroying occult interests, Fr. Balducci only confirmed her in these diabolical ploys and encouraged her in this destructive path. As of this writing, Paola has only fallen deeper and deeper into those New Age, esoteric, occultist teachings that have always proven inseparable from Ufology—all while continuing to praise and defer to Balducci's influence on her in this process.

Recall, from earlier chapters, that Whitley Strieber's encounters with "aliens" are so baldly demonic that no discerning Christian aware of them could fail to recognize this. Balducci could have helped Strieber, too. Instead, as happens all too often today, this priest only confirmed that tormented soul in his agony and pushed him to continue treading the same self-destructive path of dialoguing with demons in disguise. As recounted by Dr. Brenda Denzler, in a book on Ufology:

> Abductee Whitley Strieber entered the fray to inform [an online UFO forum] that Balducci had given him a personal interview. Noting that Balducci was an exorcist for the Archdiocese of Rome, **Strieber commented that the monsignor's expertise in that field lent "authority" to his views on the question of whether the Visitors (as Strieber calls the aliens) are demons** [i.e., Strieber & Balducci's insistence the "Visitors" were *not* demons, but were truly aliens]... Strieber's interview with the monsignor is appended to his book *Confirmation* (Strieber 1998).[272]

Reminiscent of the millions of Catholics who today insist they can continue contracepting or committing adultery "because a theologian priest told me I could," Strieber regards himself as capable of refuting the very possibility that he is really being tormented by demons due to the supposed "authority" of Balducci's personal words to him.

Steven Greer has also remained deeply impacted by Balducci's collaboration with him. When Ms. Harris interviewed Dr. Greer, he brought up Balducci's words to justify his own encouragement that we become "*an ambassador to non-human life forms...[to] use meditation techniques and the contact techniques to be able to enter and experience Cosmic Mind and then remotely view, using Cosmic Mind.*"

Balducci even gave Steven Greer a personal interview, which the latter recalls frequently and included selections of in his 2013 book, *Disclosure*. In that interview, Balducci tells Greer:

> **A human person, according to my opinion, is like this: worse than we are, it cannot exist. We are the worst**...Lower than [us], there isn't anything... **[Extraterrestrials] are probably so evolved that evil doesn't even enter into [them]** ...God in his wisdom wouldn't have created only us...**Don't even think about it [ET/UFO sightings] being the devil.** ...if they are better than we are, they are going to intervene, then **they are going to help us**...[273]

We will address Balducci's fallacies shortly. First, we must observe that in the years since this interview—as we saw in an earlier chapter—Greer has gone on to deceive untold millions with a decidedly anti-Christian message based on belief in extraterrestrials. And he has done this with the backing of Balducci.

Claims like those above were not mere isolated comments. Balducci preached them to a global audience for many years. Elsewhere, he declared that:

> **[Aliens] must be much more evolved because the human species is the lowest rung on the ladder of spiritual development...I always wish to be the spokesman for these star peoples**.[274]

Balducci demeans the human race; claiming it resides in "*the lowest rung of spiritual evolution*," indicating not only a blasphemous disregard for supreme status of the humanity of Jesus Christ, the Blessed Virgin Mary, St. Joseph, and the Catholic Church in general, but also a capitulation to the "synthesis of all heresies" – the theological Darwinism of Fr. Teilhard de Chardin (see preceding section). He moreover promotes a false eschatology by longing for an intervention from the aliens to "save the world from cataclysm."

Balducci featured prominently in a popular 2006 Ufology documentary entitled *Fastwalkers*. Other major names in this film run the gamut of Ufology charlatans and occultists, including hoaxer George Adamski (via archival media), Dr. Steven Greer, Alfred Webre, Jim Marrs, (who were each interviewed directly), and others. The documentary begins, however, with a few pithy statements from some of its stars, including none other than Paola Harris herself, who declares – drawing, no doubt, from Balducci's influence upon her – that the human race is "**the virus of the universe**," lamenting that "**nobody [extraterrestrials] really wants us out there**." Later in the movie, she sits beside Msgr. Balducci, translating for him (he spoke in Italian), as he reiterates his usual arguments in support of ETs. This film pulls no punches in promoting even the most outlandish tenets of the diabolical ET Deception.

Within this documentary, we are told that dozens of alien species have been with humanity "*for millions of years*," that Sodom and Gomorrah were destroyed not by the Wrath of God but by a UFO, that "*the greys*" (the most popular form of "aliens") were "*authorized to form a Noah's Ark with a full genetic DNA bank [of earth's species] to re-planet centuries later after catastrophe*," that the "*U.S. Government has a joint program with aliens to upgrade our biological computers; to build better bodies to house our souls in future incarnations*," that an "*advanced alien species has long lived on earth and played quite an important role in the genetic engineering of humanity*," that the aliens will "*step in to keep us from blowing the hell out of ourselves [with nuclear bombs]*," that aliens are "*giving us a conditioning period so we can get a boost in the evolutionary ladder and become full class members of the intergalactic community*," that aliens are "*interdimensional and can walk through walls, communicate telepathically, and engage in what looks like magic to us, but is only interdimensionality*," that aliens "*give planets their life charter when they become able to support life because this is what they've been doing forever*," and this life charter "*tells us who we are, what we are, how we came to be, and where we might end up going,"* and that there is an *"intergalactic federation that could end all war, all starvation, all fossil fuel use, but is being covered up by the government."*

Ninety minutes of Antichristic claims such as these—interspersed with many other equally demonic ones—bring us to the conclusion of the film. Just as Ms. Harris was given one of the opening declarations of the film (defining humans as "the virus of the universe,") so Msgr. Balducci is given one of its final words. Moments before the documentary ends, Balducci yet again declares:

> **I really believe that humanity is the lowest in the category of the evolutionary scale**; with all the proof we have of the ecological problem, the war problem, the problem of choosing evil, this is my belief system.

Clearly, this is what Balducci desires to be his celebrity legacy: his dogmatic and repeated insistence (to his global audience), as a "certainty" that "cannot be doubted," (as he said elsewhere) that the entire human race is a pathetically "unevolved" species in desperate need of cosmic intervention, not from God, but from "evolved aliens"—to save us from ourselves. If this is not a diabolical deception, then nothing is.

A defender of Balducci may point out that this film's most extreme claims were not directly from Balducci's own lips. That observation is cold comfort considering Balducci himself promotes outlandish and blasphemous ET-related beliefs, and, despite the popularity of this documentary and others he appeared in (along with the publications of many Ufology charlatans he collaborated with and encouraged for many years), Balducci lived for years after their release while apparently never issuing so much as a clarification, much less a rebuttal. Three years before *Fastwalkers*, he appeared in a similarly problematic UFO documentary, the 2003 film *Touched by an Alien*, in which contactees recount, in precise detail, their encounters with demons (especially succubus and incubus demons), thinking them to be "aliens." *UFO Chronicles: Alien Science and Spirituality* was a film released five years after Balducci's death, and it includes more of the footage from his interview for the 2006 *Fastwalkers* movie. There, we see and hear him say the following. (Note that Balducci is speaking Italian very quickly and bombastically, and his translator struggled at times. What follows is my best attempt at transcribing portions of the video.)

> [Extraterrestrials] couldn't be worse than we are because we are the worst on the scale of evolution; they would have to be more intelligent than we are... **I am an expert in demonology**; I wrote a book about the devil... **I'm very well known**, so I could go into the Secret Archive... I know the new Pope, I knew the old Pope, only I could go there**... If I didn't work in the Secretary of State in the Vatican, maybe they**

> **would have put my books on the index [of forbidden books]***... We must exclude COMPLETELY that extraterrestrials have ANYTHING to do with evil or the devil ... There are millions of worlds that are inhabited. If God created millions of stars that are even bigger than the star in our galaxy, we are dealing with infinite possibilities here. **It's NOT POSSIBLE that it's just us. It CAN'T be just us** on this planet **... I'm famous for books on demonology,** so I can defend that Ufology has nothing to do with the devil ... Aliens are praying for us. We are the lowest in the category of the evolutionary scale ... The ecological problem, the war problem...

Here we see displayed not only Balducci's fallacious reasoning (and a reiteration of his usual attacks on the pinnacle of God's creation, the human nature), but also his remarkable hubris. He really believes that because he is an "expert," he is above the Devil's deceptions. He gestures that because he is "famous for books on demonology," he can simply *decree* that Ufology "has nothing to do with the Devil," and this makes it so. He seems to have committed the chief sin all *wise* exorcists (but not *all* exorcists) know to avoid at all costs: thinking himself more intelligent than Satan, as if any Satanic ploy would automatically and immediately be perceived by him merely because of his credentials. Alas, if there is one thing the demons would above all desire to see engendered within those who study them, it is pride. Balducci is far from the only theologian-exorcist in whom they have succeeded in this task. As a result of all this astounding arrogance, Balducci decided that it is "impossible" that there aren't aliens, therefore he filters everything else through this erroneous but dogmatic *a priori* stance. (Strangely, Balducci even admits *why* his outlandish promotion of the ET Deception was not clamped down on by the Vatican—namely, only because he had political power through his employment at the Vatican Secretariat of State.)

Yet another popular Ufology film, *Watchers 7: Physical Evidence,* was released in 2013, and it features both archival footage of Balducci (who died several years before its release) and testimonies from those who knew him. In the footage of Balducci from a popular Italian television episode from 1998, he declares:

> "We can't think any longer if [ETs] are true or false...real or fake... if we believe it or not. NO. ...[we can] say with assurance that the existence of these beings is real. WE CAN'T HAVE ANY DOUBTS. [emphasis in original]"

As far as Balducci is concerned, we are not even allowed to *doubt* ETs are among us. Yet this is how a cult-leader (who knows the whole thing is a charade) speaks, not a sincere seeker of truth.

---

*This is of course a misnomer; the Index of Forbidden Books was abolished in 1966. Balducci simply seems to be making the telling point that his views would likely be condemned by the Vatican if he weren't so powerful there.

Later in the film, the director interviews Jaime Maussan, "a very good friend of Balducci," who confirms the Monsignor's sentiments and shares how inspired he was to continue his Ufology pursuits thanks to Balducci. Mr. Maussan is one of the most well-known charlatans in Ufology in Mexico. On dozens of separate occasions (*during* the period of his friendship with Balducci), he perpetrated blatant scams in claiming that aliens are among us. Even other Ufologists tend to regard him as a fraudster. For example, Ufologist Ryan Sprague compiled a list of 44 separate flagrant hoaxes promoted by Maussan over the decades, including[275] his assertion that an alien spaceship accompanied the Hale Bopp comet. Recall that this claim directly resulted in the mass-suicide of the Heaven's Gate UFO cult, in which 39 people took their lives. (But that is just one of innumerable diabolical fruits of the ET promotion of men like Maussan and Balducci.) One of Maussan's more well-known deceptions was his 2017 presentation of five "alien bodies," in a popular documentary released by Gaia, Inc., which were later exposed as mummified corpses of children. As of September 2023, he has again presented so-called "alien corpses," this time to the Mexican Congress. Few, one hopes, will even be tempted to lend any credence to this deceiver's latest ruse.

It is unsurprising that Balducci and Maussan were "very good friends." Both spent many years publicly proclaiming egregious errors, contrary to the Christian Faith, while pretending to be speaking in full accord with Catholic truth and castigating anyone who dared to so much as doubt that extraterrestrials were among us.

Balducci's "Strong Delusion" and God's Merciful Warning to the Faithful Today

> "I'm afraid that the old theological heresies are nothing by comparison to the new ones, which the Astronomers want to introduce with their worlds ... the consequence of these will be much more perilous than the previous ones, and will introduce some very strange revolutions."[276]
>
> —Gabriel Naudé. (†1653)
> (French Catholic scholar and librarian to Cardinal Barberini)

At this point, we must state the obvious, though offensive, truth. Balducci was clearly subject to significant diabolical deception; perhaps even from the very same demons he cast out of others. This is anything but beyond the pale. Recall that in his book, *Hostage to the Devil*, Fr. Malachi Martin himself relayed the (true) story of a 20th century Roman theologian-exorcist who became demonically possessed due to his belief in the teachings of Fr. Teilhard de Chardin. And it is quite clear that de Chardin's views heavily influenced Balducci; for it is precisely the latter's insistence that humanity is "unevolved" that compels him to dogmatically insist aliens exist and are among us to save us.

Whoever would defer to Monsignor Balducci in arguing belief in aliens is reconcilable with Catholicism might as well defer to the condemned heretics, Giordano Bruno or Origen, in pretending to do the same. Such references do not support the legitimacy of ET belief—they refute it.

The mere fact that, in some of his works, Balducci presents as an "orthodox Catholic," does not in the least detract from this diagnosis. The Devil has used "orthodox Catholic" theologians before Balducci to advance his own agenda, and he will do the same with many more in the future. Assuredly, Balducci is not the only Rome-educated theologian and exorcist with a lengthy resume (which he constantly draws attention to) who is diabolically deceived on this issue. We must be on guard. The true Magisterium will always be protected, but the Great Deception will be heralded, defended, and promoted by many lofty clerics in Rome and by many Rome-educated clergymen elsewhere.*

What we have seen transpiring in the life and teachings of Msgr. Balducci, therefore, is in fact a merciful warning for us today. For we are thereby instructed to expect much more of the same in the coming times. Consider how otherwise unprepared the faithful might be for the Great Deception. If, practically overnight, groups of "orthodox Catholic" theologians began endorsing the notion that "more evolved aliens" are here to save us from cataclysm, this scenario would be exceedingly difficult for simple and faithful souls to deal with. "*When has such a thing happened before?*" they would ask. "*How could such men as these—even 'orthodox' priest theologians—mislead me? That simply couldn't be so! I suppose I must take their*

---

* Despite all this, should we, as the Catholic ET promoters suggest, defer to Balducci's deception merely because he was claimed to be "friends with the Pope"? That foolish question is answered as soon as we consider that the same Pope, during those same years, was friends with Fr. Marcial Maciel—the disgraced founder of the Legion of Christ order who has since been revealed as a serial rapist, pedophile, drug addict, and womanizer. Pope John Paul II was a great saint, but not a man who could read a soul of another merely because the latter was claimed to be "a friend." There is, moreover, no evidence that the Pope knew of Balducci's escapades in Ufology. Balducci claimed he "heard that" the Pope "followed him" on television, and accordingly Balducci assumed he would have heard from the Pope if there was a problem with his antics. If, however, ecclesial revelations of the last two decades since Balducci's death have taught us anything, they should teach us how wrong such an assumption is. Pope St. John Paul II often had absolutely no idea what those who claimed to be friends with him were up to, and often did not say or do anything about the downright evil deeds and public errors of those near him. Even many of the Bishops he appointed have proven only wolves dead set on undermining the Faith. I say this not to criticize the Pope—it would have been difficult for him to do otherwise in most cases—but only to expose the ludicrousness of Balducci's implicit claim to Papal approval due to not receiving a formal censure from the latter.

words as truth and heed the admonitions of these alien saviors. If they were harmful, then Fr. ___ and Dr. ___ would not have told me otherwise."

Now, however, we do have an answer to those questions—it *has* happened. It happened with Msgr. Balducci. If it can happen to him, it can happen to anyone.

If the ET Deception is the Great Deception itself—a likelihood becoming increasingly difficult to deny—then it could not be otherwise. That apocalyptic onslaught will—*by definition*—be much more difficult to overcome than preceding deceptions. It is guaranteed to delude many who were not likewise deluded by less apocalyptic machinations from Satan; including many who accurately denounced the Devil's less eschatological attacks. Whoever expects to survive the Great Deception merely by unreflectively trusting the same voices he has trusted on easier issues that have arisen is bound to succumb.

Moreover, God allowed Balducci's deception to transpire decades before the Great Deception itself such that the fruits of his own legacy can now be adequately discerned in hindsight by any sincere, if simple, Christian. Such a believer need only look at what the Ufologists formed by Balducci—individuals such as Paola Harris, Steven Greer, Whitley Strieber, Jaime Maussan, etc.—are now claiming, to observe that, beyond doubt, their mission is a diabolical one. It is certainly not possible for any orthodox Catholic to observe the current works of these individuals and fail to recognize the evil permeating them. These are Balducci's fruits.

What, then, *can* we trust?

We can trust the Bible, Sacred Tradition (e.g., the consensus of the saints throughout the ages), and the *true* Magisterium; that is, the *actual text* of *actual Magisterial documents*—not merely personal opinions of Popes, or the speculations of men working for Vatican congregations. "Put not your trust in princes," Psalm 146 admonishes us, and this includes "princes of the Church."

***

We will not, however, merely dismiss Balducci's arguments on such accounts. Quite the contrary, it is important to recall and refute them; a task to which we now turn.

Answering Balducci's Fallacies: "Demons Don't Need Spacecraft, and Are Bound by God's Will Anyway"

Let us now consider Balducci's own argument for extraterrestrials. In an interview with Paola Harris, Msgr. Balducci stated:

> Spiritualism and Ufology are two types of manifestations. **In the evolutionary scale**, I believe there is something between us and the angels ... We should exclude that angels use spaceships, because they are merely

> spiritual beings. They are wherever they want to be, and in the rare cases when they show themselves, they have no difficulty in assuming a visible form ... **My conclusions come from my research in parapsychology** and demonology... **These things cannot be attributed to the "Devil." He does not need UFOs**. Even keeping their angelic nature, **we shouldn't think about the devils at all,** because they are connected in their liberty to God in their extraordinary activity, and in that way they are unable to express their terrible and malefic hate for us. ... in Ufology, we know a phenomenon exists*, and **although we don't know who these aliens ... are, it is possible that they are more evolved than Man is today**. [277]

We should first consider Balducci's claim that we "shouldn't think about the devils at all" when it comes to "alien" encounters, because "*Angels [don't] use spaceships...[and the Devil] does not need UFOs.*"

This truism is not denied by anyone, therefore treating it as a premise is a straw man. I believe I have read the arguments of every prominent author on this topic, and I have not come across a single one who is under the impression that "demons need UFOs." How exactly Balducci concluded this is what they are claiming can only be explained either by intentional deceit or by total ignorance of the writings of those with whom he disagrees.

Obviously, demons do not need spaceships; the "UFOs" *themselves* are diabolical deceptions—they are precisely what the Fathers of the Church warned are prevalent in the atmosphere (as we will see in a forthcoming chapter). Just as the demons have, for thousands of years, worn disguises in keeping with the prevailing Pagan myths of the cultures in which they appeared, so today they wear sci-fi disguises, as that is the prevailing contemporary Pagan myth. The demons *never* "need" any of the disguises they wear. They wear them because it is strategic for them to do so, and as highly intelligent creatures, they grasp this.

Balducci, therefore, is begging the question—employing circular reasoning—by assuming his conclusion in his own premises. He is *assuming* that UFOs are *genuine physical craft* in his very attempt to argue that they are genuine physical craft. As we discussed extensively in Part Three, however, the argument that such physical craft exist is scientifically bankrupt, logically absurd, and devoid of a single shred of convincing evidence.

---

* It is stunning that a theologian—an exorcist, no less—managed to fit so many fallacies and deceptions into one short interview. A brief recognition is in order regarding Balducci's training. He was, first and foremost, not an exorcist, but rather a "parapsychologist." The field of parapsychology, however, has long been permeated by occult practices masquerading as legitimately scientific, with many of the scholars working therein developing a veritable second-nature of treating the demonic as if it were purely natural. As Fr. Balducci had doubtless long been in this career habit, it is unsurprising that he mischaracterized Ufology; it would just be another application of parapsychology's endemic fallacy.

All this, even though the Ufologists have had over 76 years (since Roswell) to present evidence of these "alien craft" they insist have been buzzing our skies incessantly for decades. The case for the existence of physical ET-piloted UFOs is entirely laughable.

Balducci's next argument is that, since the demons are "connected in their liberty to God in their extraordinary activity," we needn't at all be concerned about diabolical deceptions. By the Monsignor's logic—which is simply a corollary to the heresy of Quietism*—one might as well assume every apparition is authentic (when many are demonic in origin, and as such rigorous discernment is essential), Ouija Board usage is unproblematic (in fact, the demons regularly use these to ensnare those who dabble in them), séances are not a danger (whereas they frequently result in dialogue with demons), freemasonry should not be a concern (whereas countless Papal Encyclicals exhort the faithful to be on guard against the demonic deceptions it promotes), and on the list goes. If we needn't bother considering the possibility of the activity of demons in prevailing cultural trends, because "*everything the demons can do is subject to God's Will*" (indeed it is!), then why bother avoiding or opposing *any* of these things?†

The answer is clear, and while it evidently perplexes many a theologian, few serious if simple Christians are confused about it. The demons are indeed chained by Christ's sacrifice on the cross. But when we wander within the radius of that chain—perhaps through dabbling in the occult (which has always proven inextricable from Ufology), following Pagan myths (including belief in extraterrestrials), dialoguing with the demons (as Balducci's colleague, Dr. Greer, facilitates), or treating anything but Christ *messianically* (as Balducci himself appears to treat "ETs")—then God's permissive Will often allows the demons to wreak havoc in the life of the one who has done so.

There is a graver still fallacy inherent in Balducci's argument here. For by claiming we needn't be concerned about demonic delusions in accordance with the fact that these demons are bound by God's Will, he has entirely ignored the prophecy in Scripture—certain to be fulfilled—that

---

* A heresy wherein one, rightly observing that nothing but God's Will can happen, wrongly concludes from that premise that he needn't himself be concerned about bringing that Will to fruition and zealously avoiding whatever is known to be contrary to it. See Pope Innocent XI's Encyclical, *Coelestis Pastor*, 1687.

† This is all not to mention that the same logic provided by Balducci to defend Ufology would advise one not to even avoid diabolical possession! Why avoid that, if the demons are bound by God's Will? Yet, all exorcists—including Balducci (he wrote a book on that very topic—which, in the parts I have read, appears good)—rightly give advice on how to avoid becoming possessed. Regardless of the fact that God works all things to the good for those who love Him, we are nevertheless duty bound to avoid—with all our might—what is objectively erroneous, sinful, occult, Pagan, New Age, in contradiction to a faithful approach to Scripture and Magisterium: in a word, whatever is, objectively, not in accordance with His Will.

God's Will *is indeed* going to allow a "Strong Delusion" to assault the world:

> **The coming of the lawless one by the activity of Satan will be with all power and with pretended signs and wonders, and with all wicked deception** for those who are to perish, because they refused to love the truth and so be saved. **Therefore God sends upon them a strong delusion, to make them believe what is false**... (2 Thessalonians 2:9-11)

Balducci's ET-Inspired Manichean Blasphemy Against Human Nature

Another component of Msgr. Balducci's argument for extraterrestrials builds on his exceedingly dim view of human nature—as noted, he repeatedly claims:

> ...[aliens] must be much more evolved because **the human species is the lowest rung on the ladder of spiritual development...**

We have already seen how contrary this notion is to Catholic dogma. It is above all an attack on the Incarnation of Jesus Christ. But, for example, it also violates what we know of the glories of the Blessed Virgin Mary. As covered in Part Two of this book, the Virgin is, according to Catholic Teaching, not only the greatest creature in the universe but also the greatest *possible* creature. In other words, it is materially heretical to even *hypothesize* the existence of a greater creature than she. Yet she is *just like us.* To claim that her nature—which is *nothing other than human nature*—actually resides on the "lowest rung on the ladder of spiritual evolution" is blasphemous and heretical. Balducci, however, takes this idea even further, insisting:

> It is probable that there are other beings ... **because there is too much discrepancy between human and angelic nature,** of which we have the theological certainty. And since in man, the spirit is subordinate to matter, and since the Angels are alone spirit, it is probable that beings exist with very much less body and matter than we have.[278]

Here, Balducci betrays a fundamental confusion about the relationship between human nature and angelic nature. While it is true that, considered in and of itself, the purely spiritual existence of angelic nature surpasses the perfection of human nature, it is not true that this implies a gap in the Hierarchy of Creation.

To assert such a gap not only violates Catholic dogma on the Blessed Virgin (for it falsely implies that angels are above their own Queen), but it also contradicts 2,000 years of unanimous consensus of Sacred Tradition on the Hierarchy of Creation, which has always treated human and angelic nature as perfectly adjacent—*coterminous.* It also violates even Old Testament Scriptural teaching—Divine Revelation from a time before God had fully revealed (via the Incarnation) just how glorious human nature really is. For we read, in the Psalms:

> **Yet thou hast made him little less than God**, and dost crown him with glory and honor. (Psalm 8:5)

The translation above is from the RSVCE; if we consult the Douay-Rheims translation, we read that God has made man "little less than the angels." Whichever translation is deferred to, we see contradicted Balducci's notion of such a large gap existing between men and angels that other categories of rational beings must exist in order to render creation's hierarchy complete.

In fact, not only does no gap exist, but even more significantly, there is substantial *overlap*. Many human beings are far higher than many angels, notwithstanding the surpassing perfection of angelic *nature*.

The Blessed Virgin, however, is not the only human being above the pure spirits. St. Joseph is certainly far above the angels—he, not any angel, is the Patron of the Universal Church and the Terror of Demons. Moreover, the Church teaches that he is the greatest saint (a term which includes angels) aside from his spouse (cf. Pope Leo XIII, *Quamquam Pluries*). This is true even though St. Joseph was not immaculately conceived. He is, therefore, "like us" in *every* way—including being of "common stock." Many saints, too, have risen far above many, if not all, angels. As is commonly known, a demon was once forced to reveal that if only two other men like St. John Vianney lived on earth at his time, the Devil's Kingdom would have been destroyed. The Catechism itself also makes clear that there is no gap between men and angels:

> In the act of creation, God calls every being from nothingness into existence. "Crowned with glory and honor," **man is, *after the angels*, capable of acknowledging "how majestic is the name of the Lord** in all the earth." Even after losing through his sin his likeness to God, man remains an image of his Creator (§2566)

If man is—as the Church teaches—"after the angels," then this means no other category of beings exist between the two, as such a placement would violate this element of the Magisterium. There are no visible (physical/corporeal/incarnate) creatures *whatsoever* who are, as Balducci claims, "more spiritually evolved/developed." Only the angels are above us. There are no exceptions. St. Francis de Sales, Doctor of the Church, taught: "**Man is the perfection of the universe.**" St. Irenaeus, Father and Doctor of the Church, taught that "the glory of God is man fully alive." Clearly, such teachings as these (permeating Sacred Tradition and Magisterium) about human nature are irreconcilable with Balducci's view that human nature is horribly "unevolved." And it should not be difficult for any Christian to decide whether the saints or Msgr. Balducci (and his colleagues in Ufology) are the trustworthy ones.

Why, then, does Balducci regard human nature so dimly? He answers that question explicitly: man, he claims, is so far below the angels because, in us, "*spirit is subordinate to matter,*" whereas the angels are pure spirit, and therefore, there should exist beings between angels and men in the hierarchy of creation who have "*much less body and matter than we have.*"

Here is where Balducci reveals that he is simply reinventing the third century's Manichean Heresy, which held the dualistic view that "the good" is the spirit, and "the bad" is the material; therefore, growth in perfection consists in the spirit overriding and eliminating matter. From this (avowedly anti-Christian) premise, Balducci's conclusion appears consistent: man, being a *truly* incarnate creature, "*must stand beneath innumerable other creatures, not pure spirit like the angels, but at least less 'tied to this sinful matter' like humans.*" The tragedy is that Balducci failed to ever see the heresy latent in the arguments he used to justify his ET belief.

In fact, Balducci is essentially subscribing to teachings common in Islam and other Pagan religions regarding "jinn" or "genies"—creatures who (like us) could behave morally or immorally, but who are not fully corporeal like us but also not entirely spirit. Islam's "jinn" are said to be intelligent creatures, *usually* invisible, but are not angels—they are like humans; they will eventually be judged by God and they may in the future choose to worship Him or not. Of course, there is no such thing as "jinn." This is just another Pagan disguise—like extraterrestrials—that the demons use. Traditionalist poet Charles Upton explained more of Balducci's errors as follows:

> **Monsignor Balducci exhibits the effects of both an incomplete cosmology and a lack of "discernment of spirits."** Anyone who has read Dr. John Mack's book *Abduction,* and who also both believes in demons and understands their nature, will be forced to conclude that the majority of the terrifying encounters he reports have to do with the demonic, and nothing else. Many of these encounters appear to be cases of vexation (physical attack) or obsession (mental attack) rather than full possession. And yet the fact that, as Dr. Mack informs us, many of the "entities" who end by abducting their adult victims began as "imaginary playmates" during the victims' childhoods, is evidence that demonic possession is also a distinct possibility in some cases, as least insofar as we can define "familiar spirits" as "possessing" demons, not merely "obsessing" ones. If this exorcist for the Archdiocese of Rome had been able to survey thoroughly and dispassionately his Church's archives relating to demonic activity, he would have seen that his description of the UFO aliens ... **to maintain that any subtle but not fully spiritual being can be a guardian to humanity is a strictly pagan belief; according to traditional Catholic doctrine, our guardians are necessarily angels, not *daimones.* That a high-ranking Catholic exorcist was apparently unable to tell the difference between a guardian angel and a familiar spirit is one more glaring indication of the tragedy of**

> **... certain Catholic exorcists who came into intimate contact with demons, not realizing that they now [after post-Vatican II changes to the exorcism Rite often] lacked the spiritual potency that would protect them from these beings**, and also in view of the fact that Catholic doctrine has been rendered relatively vague and ambiguous since Vatican II, may have become deluded by them—if not actually possessed..[279]

***

While we have at this point adequately addressed both Balducci himself and the arguments he presents, it remains to consider one more attitude he has publicly espoused: his general dismissal of the diabolical (at least, in those contexts in which he finds acknowledging it inconvenient). We will, however, treat this matter in the corresponding Appendix, so that we can now move on to other topics.

(Note: Msgr. Balducci also wrote a paper, delivered at a meeting in Rome of December 2002, which was signed June 8th, 2001, entitled Ufology and Theological Clarifications. However, as we have already addressed each argument he presents elsewhere in this book, we will not needlessly increase the length of this section by reiterating those answers.)

Br. Guy and the Vatican Astronomers: "Re-Reading" the Faith for Alien Belief

Brother Guy Consolmagno is an American physicist and astronomer who Pope Francis named the Director of the Vatican Observatory in 2015—one year after he was awarded the "Carl Sagan Medal." Since then, carrying with him the title of "The Pope's Astronomer," Consolmagno has become a well-known advocate for belief in extraterrestrials. I hasten to add that his teachings are not as dark as Monsignor Balducci's—Br. Guy does not believe we have yet been contacted, much less visited, by aliens. Unfortunately, this only mitigates (not eliminates) the damage of his teachings. Like Monsignor Balducci, Brother Guy enjoys an intimidating sounding office in Rome which has compelled many to falsely regard his opinions as somehow representative of "the Catholic position." (I do not fault Br. Guy, however; as far as I have seen, he has not misrepresented the implications of his own position.)

In order to see how problematic this Jesuit's views are, we need only consider what he has publicly stated. First, though, an important note should be included. Consolmagno has been the object of a slanderous conspiracy theory that "went viral," which accused him of various baldly diabolical and apocalyptic teachings in relation to aliens. In fact, Br. Guy never said those things he is accused of, and on his own official website, he publicly repudiated these views. Unfortunately, it appears the promoters of this theory have not bothered to even note this repudiation, much less delete, retract, and apologize for their slander. As strongly as I will need to refute Br. Guy in what follows, I would also exhort everyone to never allow a rightful zeal in fighting deceptions to become a willingness to slander anyone. Consolmagno has *not* claimed he anticipates the arrival of an alien savior to overturn Christianity.

This said, our present concern is Consolmagno's telling response to that slander. For he defended himself against his critics only by revealing his own deeply confused approach. As one interviewer recounted:

> [Viewing aliens as a threat] created a lucrative opening, Consolmagno said, for those who "make their living feeding off the paranoia of others" and who hype the search for supernatural clues. It's a tendency that, in his view, demonstrates a weak confidence in one's own religious beliefs. "*The main problem is a lack of faith, the fear that our understanding of our religion will not survive radical changes in the way we understand the universe. If you presume that the arrival of an alien will rock your foundations, then you've got pretty shaky foundations.*"[280]

Although understandably critical of the individuals who slander him, Br. Guy wrongly concludes that *any* concern about the diabolical amid today's frenzied ET-contact-expectation is mere "paranoia" from those whose "faith is weak." Consolmagno seems to have not paused for a moment to observe that the only paranoia being fostered today (in relation to this issue) is that spread by the ET *promoters*, not those who disbelieve in aliens. Relatively speaking, extremely few people recognize that "aliens" are in fact demons in disguise. But there are billions alive today who believe aliens are among us—threatening our very existence (according to the "malicious aliens" narrative) or seeking to give us cosmic techno-salvation (according to the "benign, enlightened, evolved aliens" narrative), but being prevented by governments hell bent on keeping their own people enslaved. For the last 75 years, UFO "religions" have been leading countless souls to hell, inspiring mass suicides and murders, and promoting heresy. ET belief and expectation in general has been replacing—in the hearts of untold hundreds of millions—faith and hope in Christ with sci-fi inspired delusions.

Yet, for this Jesuit, none of that is a concern. On this point, the only *real* concern—for him and those of his ilk, like Msgr. Balducci—is that we ever dare risk approaching some phenomenon with the care that is due in consideration of the possibility that a demonic deception is latent within it. That, we are patronizingly assured, would be nothing but a "*paranoid lack of faith.*" So much for the words of Our Lord in the Gospel and of Scripture in general, or the messages of Our Lady in her many apparitions, or the teachings of more Magisterial documents than can be counted, or the admonitions of innumerable saints all warning us to be on the lookout for the Devil's deceptive guiles. Is perhaps all that just outdated "excessive spirituality" which we modern Christians need not bother with, now that we have "The Science"?

"Be sober, be watchful. Your adversary the devil prowls around like a roaring lion, seeking someone to devour." (1 Peter 5:8).

Although Br. Guy *here* speaks as if he were unaware of the ET-discussion ongoing within the Church, even the boldest of Catholic ET promoters concede that the existence of aliens would have massive repercussions for the Faith; requiring a complete and ground-level revision of our Christology, Mariology, Ecclesiology, Eschatology, etc. But, as Fr. Spyridon Bailey observed, Br. Guy knows well that aliens would radically shake the Faith—he simply does not recognize that this tension is among the (many) facts ruling out aliens:

> Brother Guy Consolmagno, the then president of the Vatican Observatory Foundation, was fully behind this position. At [a] conference he declared: "*I believe aliens exist, but I have no evidence. I would be really excited and it would make my understanding of my religion deeper and richer in ways that I can't even predict yet, which is why it would be exciting.*" **The message is one of change. One after another of the speakers reinforced the idea that a cultural shift must be manipulated into action in order to make people accept the existence of aliens**. This shift, they argued, must be affected in every level of our culture: in entertainment, philosophy, science and, as Brother Guy so enthusiastically expresses, in theology.[281]

Yet Consolmagno dismisses those who recognize this fact; claiming such people simply have "shaky foundations." In truth, whoever *fails* to recognize this fact evidently has *no foundations at all*! Indeed, if one's Christology, Mariology, etc., has already so thoroughly succumbed to modernism that it has been robbed of all its value, then there is little substance present in the first place to even experience a "shaking" by an ET-inspired pseudo-theology. One should not be proud of having a faith so vapid that it lacks any substance which can be shaken.

True solidity in the Faith is found not in a posture of categorical openness to the claims of scientists, but rather by such an absolute trust in God's Word that no shaking, no matter how severe, can damage it. Br. Guy, however—representing the prevailing mood in the Vatican today—proposes that we attain the mere appearance of a solid faith by adopting a false humility which dares not ever restrain science with theological truth. Thus he would have us assume that we will always manage to find *something* to cling to in order to pretend we are still Christians, even as we give "The Science" free rein to assert and demand whatever it pleases.

That approach to the relationship between faith and science, however, is nothing but heretical drivel and a diabolical deception of its own.

> "All **faithful Christians are forbidden to defend as the legitimate conclusions of science those opinions which are known to be contrary to the doctrine of faith**... they are absolutely bound to hold them to be **errors which wear the deceptive appearance of truth**." —Declarations of the First Vatican Council

In a stunning display of self-contradiction (asserted, no less, with successive breaths)—not to mention violation of the Church's teachings, both noted above and taught elsewhere repeatedly—Br. Guy continues his chastisement of those who believe the demonic is behind "alien" encounters:

> In that sense the Vatican's astronomers believe **faith should not impose preconceived notions** on the exploration of the universe, as that would involve placing **limits on the creative freedom of God.** Aliens, if they exist, may have a different relationship with the Creator. "*We have to be open to however God actually did create this universe, not the way that we want him to,*" Consolmagno observed. And that means astronomy, even Jesuit astronomy, should be looking to expand scientific understanding, not trying to prove some divine plan. Sign seekers, on the other hand, want an interpretive key ... that can unlock all the answers. But that's not how things work, Consolmagno said. "*If I were to see such a sign, I wouldn't trust it...* ***I know enough about God to know that's not how God operates****. Whoever's giving me that sign, it's not God. It's not just me saying this. ... if you're looking for that kind of certainty, it's because you don't have faith.*"[282]

Rejecting as "sign seekers" (i.e., traditional Christians) those who "seek an interpretive key" (i.e., Divine Revelation) to understand *God's creation*, Br. Guy suggests that, instead, we must above all ensure we are not "trying to prove some divine plan." It is not here Scripture which tells us how God operates (*believing Scripture would be "placing limits on the creative freedom of God," according to Consolmagno's reasoning*), but rather it is Br. Guy himself. *He* "knows" that God doesn't give interpretive keys. "*That's not how God operates,*" Br. Guy solemnly and repeatedly assures us.

It is quite remarkable that a man can lament those who "limit God," only to immediately thereafter *limit God* by claiming He cannot provide a "sign" or give "certainty" or reveal an "interpretive key." In fact, Supernatural Faith is by nature certain. Whatever contradicts any of its corollaries is, therefore, certainly false. If this consideration provides any "interpretive keys," then that is no mark against the veracity of what doors those keys unlock. God is well within His rights to reveal to us how He went about things in His creation.

Any Christian is well advised to be on guard when another reproaches him for seeking certainty, or for "limiting God" (by ruling out whatever is contrary to what God has revealed), or for deferring to the Faith's "preconceived notions" of the universe. In fact, all of these things are part and parcel to Christianity properly understood. As one finds throughout Christian ET belief promotion, those who lament alien disbelievers "limiting God" actually have no qualms at all with such limitation so long as it lends credence to their own views.

We are presently dealing with the deceptions of certain individual ET promoters only due to their prominence, not their scarcity. We should not, therefore, suppose that we are safe so long as we avoid the sophistry of the men named above. Br. Guy's musings are in keeping with the prevailing sentiments of the men who work in the Vatican today. For example, Fr. Giuseppe Tanzella-Nitti is an astronomer and theologian working in the Vatican. One Catholic periodical summarized his teachings as follows (including a direct quote from the priest):

> Once believers will have verified that these alien civilizations come from another planet... They will have to conduct a "rereading of the Gospel in light of the new data."[283]

Fr. Gabriel Funes, another Vatican astronomer, has said similar things. Yet, a "rereading of the **Gospel** in light of new data"—a reformulation of the very fundamental basis of Christianity itself—is exactly what would be most appreciated and promoted by a certain individual who we know will rise to dominance during the end times. While the various heresies the Church has triumphed over during her 2,000-year history have each, in their own way, perverted some individual doctrine, ET belief proposes to do much more: it proposes to radically reinvent *the entire Faith*. And many men in the Vatican today are all too eager to sign up for that task.

If anyone has failed to see, thus far, just how diabolical and apocalyptic these developments are, he will not fail to see it in what follows. For we are not only dealing with men publishing their own seductive deceptions based on ET belief. We are dealing with the demons themselves directly "revealing" their plans regarding aliens, all under the guise of "private revelation."

23. False Private Revelations

> "What folly, therefore, or rather what madness, to submit ourselves through any sentiment of religion to demons, when it belongs to the true religion to deliver us from that depravity which makes us like to them!" —St. Augustine. *City of God.* Book 8. Ch. 16

In Part Two, we saw that *authentic* private revelations rule out aliens. They do so either directly (as in, for example, Jesus' messages to the Servant of God Luisa Piccarreta and messages from the souls in Purgatory to the mystic Maria Simma) or indirectly, though still clearly (e.g., in the revelations of Blessed Emmerich, Venerable Mary of Agreda, St. Bridget, etc.).

Heralding the existence and even the arrival of (or at least contact with) extraterrestrials, however, is such a common theme in patently false "revelations" that it borders on ubiquity. We will consider a number of such private "revelations" in the sections ahead. In each case, we will see that the manifestly false nature of each is demonstrated through means having nothing to do with aliens. Accordingly, no one will be able to accuse the present chapter of circular reasoning (i.e., by assuming those private revelations are false which speak of aliens merely *because* they speak of aliens). Dr. Timothy Dailey described well the message that such "revelations" tend to convey:

> [There is a] diabolic plot to overthrow the Judeo-Christian worldview and plunge the world into darkness and ...The ultimate goal of this cosmic treachery is the destruction of souls ... **the central "doctrine of demons" that runs like a thread throughout our exploration is the seductive assurance of the Serpent in the Garden: "You will be like God."** ... **the missives of intergalactic emissaries all present a cosmology without God at the center**. ... One's destiny in this scheme of things is to toil through the endless transmigration of souls, inhabiting astral realms in between reincarnations until one advances to the level of the "ancient ones" ... Then **on to the universe beyond—and the fantastically evolved civilizations further along the path of spiritual evolution,** the ultimate goal of which is the absorption of one's very personality into the vast Cosmic Sea... UFO appearances in the skies above defy commonly held theories about their origin, bringing to mind the apostle Paul's reference to "the ruler of the kingdom of the air, the spirit who is now at work in those who are disobedient."[284]

Buddhism, Hinduism, Islam, and More: The Major False Religions Have Always Welcomed Aliens

> "... the Indians, Chinese, and Arabs, have conserved down to our own day theogonic traditions which recognize among ancient dogmas that of the plurality of human inhabitations in the worlds which shine above our heads; going back to the first pages of the historical annals of humanity, we find this same idea, either in a religious context, as concerning the transmigration of souls and their future state, or in an astronomical context, as concerning simply the inhabitability of heavenly bodies."
>
> —Camille Flammarion; renowned 19th & 20th Century Astronomer, and ET Promoter.[285]

While in this chapter we will be focusing on those messages that purport to be "private revelations" (i.e., messages claimed to be received miraculously within the context of an existing religion—mainly, Christianity), we should first consider how those major world religions that have existed for centuries or millennia are each—with the exception of Christianity and ancient Judaism—either intrinsically open to extraterrestrials or even explicitly teach that extraterrestrials exist.

This presents any Christian with a stark choice—though an easy one for a discerning soul. He can believe in aliens and thereby regard Christianity as the one major world religion that is deceived on this point, or he can reject aliens by recognizing that wherever Christianity stands apart from other world religions, it is *Christianity* that is correct, not Buddhism, Hinduism, Islam, etc.

Not only is the decision not confusing for a serious Christian; even more, the circumstances that cause it to arise display an exquisite exercise of Divine Providence. If indeed the alien and UFO deception is none other than *the* Great Deception itself—*the* penultimate eschatological test—then Christianity is perfectly poised to be the only religion which survives that test. Sadly, however, many nominal Christians will fail the test—for the end times will deceive even many of them:

> "For false Christs and **false prophets will arise and show great signs and wonders, so as to lead astray, if possible, even the elect.** Lo, I have told you beforehand." —Matthew 24:24-25

***

Beginning with Islam, we see that, from the start, this religion has welcomed the idea of non-human, non-angelic intelligences, which can easily be understood in the present day as aliens and UFOs. The religion's basic text, the Quran, appears to repeatedly indicate the existence of aliens by its reference to many inhabited worlds. As one author explained:

> ...even strictly literal readings of the [Quran] seem to support the idea of the plurality of worlds, which has been the basis of much science fiction. Qur'an 1:2 translates as 'praise to God, lord of the worlds'. In total, the expression 'lord of the worlds' (*rabb al-ʿālamīn*) occurs forty-two times in the scripture. ... *ʿālamīn* not only means 'worlds', but also suggests 'men'... Qur'an 42:29 means: 'And among His Signs is the creation of the heavens and the earth, and the living creatures that He has scattered through them.' ... [a footnote on a famous Quran translation reads:] *'Life is not confined to our one little Planet. It is a very old speculation to imagine some life like human life on the planet Mars.'*[286]

Another researcher relayed that:

> The Qur'an does not leave the faithful guessing as to whether extraterrestrial life exists. As early as the first century after the birth of Islam, one of the most revered of the early leaders of Islam, Imam Muhammad al-Baqir (676–733 [A.D.].), wrote, "Maybe you see that God created only this single world ... **Well, I swear by God that God created thousands and thousands of worlds and thousands and thousands of humankind**." ...many Islamic scholars strongly suggest that living creatures exist beyond the Earth. ... [The] Caliph of the Ahmadiyya Muslim Community in Pakistan ... asserts that "The second part of the same verse [42:29] **speaks not only of the possibility of extraterrestrial life, but it categorically declares that it does exist**.[287]

Little surprise, then, that the contemporary "Nation of Islam" movement is fixated on extraterrestrials. Muslims are well primed to accept the "aliens" (demons) when they appear on a global scale.

Buddhists are equally ready to welcome these beings. As Dr. David Weintraub noted:

> **Buddhists view the universe as unimaginably large, ancient, and filled with living beings everywhere.** Within this universe, reincarnation allows a soul to endlessly transmigrate upward or downward through the multiple levels of living beings. At the moment of death, reincarnation also permits a soul to slip away from a body in one part of the universe and be reborn into a different body in another part of the universe. **The very existence of ET is built into the Buddhist worldview...**[288]

Further detailing Buddhist belief in relation to extraterrestrials, the same scholar relayed:

> ... the *Anguttara Nikaya* (Numerical Discourses of the Buddha) ... describes the 'thousand-fold world' system. According to this text, **the universe is full of inhabited worlds**: *"...there are thousands of suns, thousands of moons, thousands of inhabited worlds of varying sorts."* ... Even the observable universe accessible to modern astronomers ... would be a drop of water in the ocean that is the Buddhist's vision of the thrice-a-

> thousand Great Cosmos... Like the living beings in the Buddhist universe, all the suns, moons and inhabited worlds in a thousand-fold world universe are believed to undergo a cycle of creation and destruction (reincarnation on a cosmic scale) ... "*The inhabitants of such worlds may well be, in different degrees, more powerful than human beings, happier and longer-lived. ... They are inhabitants of this universe, fellow-wanderers in this round of existence...*" Mahayana [Buddhist] scriptures ...[assert] a variety of much vaster cosmologies, many of them centered on the metaphor of a lotus flower. In one, the universe is conceived of as a thousand-petaled lotus flower with ten billion world systems on every petal, **for a total of ten trillion worlds**...[289]

Presenting any comprehensive overview of extraterrestrials in Buddhism would quickly turn this book into a library. Suffice it to say that Buddhism is not merely open to aliens, nor does it merely teach that they exist; it is itself a veritable systematic ET deception. Therefore, this—the most philosophically and theologically anti-Christian of all major World Religions—is also by far the most pro-extraterrestrial.

Buddhism is particularly amenable to the views of those Christians who believe in the possibility of multiple incarnations of God (thus robbing Jesus Christ of His status as the *only* begotten Son of God). Replace "Vairocana" with "Cosmic Christ" in what follows, and you have exactly what Catholic ET promoters like Fr. Teilhard de Chardin propose:

> ...all the worlds are conceived of as creations of *Vairocana* ("Illuminating All Places"), the transcendent personification of universal buddha-nature (*dharmakaya*). That is, this Vairocana represents the cosmic possibility of Buddhahood ... The omnipresent ***Vairocana* incarnates into countless buddhas and *bodhisattvas*, one for every world** ... [so] **all of the life forms in the universe have access to nirvana by way of their own particular manifestations of *Vairocana*.**[290]

On the other hand, for each passing year SETI's "Great Silence" continues (which, as we saw in Part Three, has itself already largely disproved aliens), Buddhism's view of the cosmos is threatened. Dr. Weintraub also noted:

> The possibility that decades of thorough scanning of hundreds of millions of exoplanets might fail to uncover any evidence of extraterrestrial life ...could be difficult [some Buddhists] to handle... If scientific findings that reveal no signs of extraterrestrial life were taken as an absolute indication that no form of life currently exists anywhere else in the universe, Buddhists would either have to significantly amend the features of their biocentric cosmology or dispense with that cosmology entirely as a model of objective reality...[291]

It is unsurprising that ET-contact expectation in the West has increased in proportion to the infiltration of Buddhist philosophies (and Hinduism-derived Yoga practices and teachings) into contemporary Christianity.

***

Hinduism—from which Buddhism took its own origin 2,500 years ago—today numbers over a billion adherents, and it, too, is an entirely and intrinsically ET-welcoming religion.

> [In Hinduism,] a living being from Earth might be reincarnated into another kind of living being on another planet anywhere in the universe, and those beings in turn could be reincarnated here on Earth. ... Extraterrestrials would be other beings who, like us, must struggle to increase their karma in order to escape samsara. Hindus would not be at all surprised by the discovery of extraterrestrial beings. ... Swami Prabhupada was a prolific and authoritative translator of Indian religious writings and the founder of [Hare Krishnas]. Prabhupada wrote a commentary on *Srimad Bhagavatam*, a book that "tells the story of the Lord and His incarnations since the earliest records of Vedic history. It is verily the Krishna Bible of the Hindu universe." In his commentary, he writes, "... In that ocean [of space] there are innumerable planets, and each planet is called a *dvipa*, or island. The various planets are divided into 14 *lokas*. ..."Prabhupada then states **that according to the Vedic tradition there are 400,000 species of living beings in the universe with humanlike forms, many of them advanced beyond us**. ... In keeping with the Hindu belief that the entire universe goes through cycles of creation and destruction and rebirth, **Prabhupada identifies the lifespan for the universe as about 300,000 billion years**... [292]

Other Pagan world religions, though not counting as many adherents as those described above, also commend belief in the existence of aliens. Holy texts of the religion of Sikhism hold that:

> God created living beings throughout the universe and not just on Earth. The Sri Guru Granth Sahib re-emphasizes this concept by instructing Sikhs that living beings exist in worlds far from the Earth: "I see none as great as You, O Great Giver; **You give in charity to the beings of all the continents, worlds, solar systems, nether regions and universes**."[293]

Jainism—another religion that is about 2,500 years old—is in agreement with the ET-condoning teachings of its counterparts:

> Jains [] take the position that their own cosmology is somehow compatible with that of modern science. In Sutra 4.14 of the *Tattvārtha Sutra*, we learn that "*There are two suns above Jambū Island, four over Lavana Ocean and twelve over Dhātakīkhanda Island. ... The number of suns in the entire region inhabited by humans is 2 + 4 + 12 + 42 + 72 = 132. The number of moons in the region inhabited by humans is the same as that of suns. ... Each moon has an entourage of 28 constellations, 88 planets and 66,975 × 1014 stars.*" We can easily conceptualize these assertions as compatible with a universe teeming with galaxies, each one of which contains billions of stars...nothing about Jainist concepts confines life to the single planet Earth, as souls could bond with any non-living matter and the matter

> containing souls could evolve in a biological sense anywhere in the physical universe. Similarly, transmigration of a soul could move that soul to a new physical body located anywhere in the universe. When understood this way, the discovery of life beyond the Earth would not trigger any problems for Jains, and Jainism could be understood as a universal path for all living beings in the universe to escape samsara[294]

***

The lesson is unmistakable. Man-made—or demon-made—religions usually teach elaborate cosmologies that posit innumerable inhabited worlds throughout the cosmos; often detailing with great numerical precision just how many such worlds supposedly exist and for how long they will exist.

While post-Enlightenment Western scientists proposing the "plurality thesis" (i.e., the existence of innumerable or infinite inhabited worlds) congratulated themselves for having "*evolved beyond medieval anthropocentrism*," the truth is that all they did in positing these wild theories was revert to the very same tactics that had been employed for thousands of years in various Godless Pagan traditions; the very doctrines of demons from which Christ had rescued us. The only difference was the new scientific jargon. The substance was the same: the return of the Pagan demons.

Let us conclude this section by reiterating its opening: a Christian ET believer finds himself in the position of suggesting that, while almost all the world's Pagan, Godless religions have, for thousands of years, confirmed his ET thesis, it is only his *own* religion which repudiates it.

He will, of course, falsely insist that Christianity does *not* repudiate ET belief. But even most of the more zealous of Christian ET promoters concede Christianity certainly does not affirmatively teach that aliens exist, and they likewise concede there is great difficulty in reconciling belief in aliens with the Faith.*

This Christian ET believer, then, must ask himself:

"*Do I really believe God would arrange it thus? Do I really believe that God made aliens, then established only one true Faith on earth, such that this one true religion – Christianity – also happens to be the only major religion which, by far, is the most difficult to reconcile with the existence of these aliens He made?*" In other words: "*Do I really believe that God made aliens, and allowed all the Godless religions to teach that these aliens exist, while depriving the one religion He actually established of an equally or surpassingly clear revelation of this truth?*"

As with other such questions we have pondered—and many similar ones yet remain—it should not be difficult for a sincere Christian to answer this one. There is only one reasonable explanation for why belief in extraterrestrials permeates Pagan religions but is absent from Christianity.

---

* The Christian ET promoters themselves often explicitly admit this, but they always at least implicitly admit it by how much effort they put into bending over backwards to attempt to make Christology, Ecclesiology, Mariology, etc., make sense in light of their alien belief.

The Swedenborgian Church

Founded by the Swedish scientist and theologian Emmanuel Swedenborg (†1772), the "Church" which bears his name is based on his writings, which were presented as Christian "revelations." In the late 18th century this organization spread, and even today counts at least several thousand members. Although these messages denied the Trinity, original sin, atonement, and espoused various other heresies, they are perhaps most well-known for asserting that aliens live on the moon and other places and may be contacted through "astral travel." Dr. Walter Martin explains:

> Emanuel Swedenborg founded the first formal religion, Swedenborgianism, **based largely upon space travel and contact with extraterrestrial beings.** Swedenborg's first work, *Earths in the Solar World* (1758), relied on this hypothesis. In it, Swedenborg claimed to leave his body through astral projection and travel to other planets, where he gained spiritual insight from spirit-beings on Mars, Venus, Saturn, and Jupiter.[295]

Wherever we see belief in extraterrestrials creep into Christianity, however, even more outright occultism always follows. This, the first major "Christian" ET movement, was no exception:

> **The door opened perceptibly for popularizing occultism in the Western world and merging it with Christianity in 1743...[through] Swedenborgianism.** His revelations and visions of the deceased marked a new trend among occultists and mediums, who often relied upon séances for contact with the dead. ... Many occult, esoteric, mystic, mind science, and New Age groups relied upon this groundwork for occultic contact with spirits. Swedenborg's metaphysics shaped the thinking of nineteenth-century New England transcendentalists such as Emerson, Thoreau, Ripley, Holmes, and Alcott, who later influenced Madam Blavatsky of Theosophy, Mary Baker Eddy of Christian Science, the early twentieth-century metaphysical schools, [and more]...[296]

Swedenborg himself displayed tendencies which demonstrated he was perhaps not merely a charlatan or a fraudster. He did indeed have access to a spiritual realm—though not Heaven. Reports circulated about his "mystical" abilities, with which he could "see" current events he was not present for and recount them accurately—well before even the first telegraph machines—a sure sign that either the diabolical or the supernatural was at play. For example, the contemporary leading scholar on Swedenborg, Dr. Jane Williams-Hogan, noted the following in an academic tome published by Routledge:

> The Governor interviewed Swedenborg the next day about the fire [he had described hundreds of miles away]. He asked questions about when it began, how it had started, and how long it had lasted, and how

> it was finally put out. When reports came from Stockholm, they confirmed Swedenborg's description in every detail. Needless to say, people were amazed.[297]

Since the supernatural is ruled out by the repeated heresies, we can easily discern what remains as the explanation for his "revelations" that extraterrestrials exist. Another hallmark of the diabolical is that a *current* event was revealed to Swedenborg—this is easy for demons, but it is much more difficult for them to reveal the future (since they do not know it and can only make very good "guesses" at its content).

From the very beginning of private "revelations" transpiring within Christianity espousing belief in extraterrestrials, we see the hand of the Devil clearly at work.

Seventh Day Adventists, Mormons, and a Telling Exception: Jehovah's Witnesses

Seventh Day Adventism was a Millerite sect founded in 1868, which was largely based on the "revelations" of Ellen White, whom the Smithsonian magazine named to their list of *"100 Most Significant Americans of All Time."* Far more successful than Swedenborg's "Church" described above, this one still counts over 22 million members worldwide. Not only does it teach extraterrestrials exist, but that very belief was part and parcel to the sect's formation:

> **Seventh-day Adventism emerged in the 19th century in part as a solution to theological problems stemming from the possibility of extraterrestrial life**. The prophetess, Ellen White, described visions of extraterrestrial beings in different worlds that were "tall, majestic people" and entirely without sin.[298]

Lest anyone is tempted to regard these "revelations" as authentic developments from the Holy Spirit, we should hasten to consider that they teach, among other heresies, that the Catholic Church is the "Whore of Babylon" (cf. Revelation 17), the Pope is the Antichrist, worshipping on Sunday—the Lord's Day—is the Mark of the Beast, the elect cannot arrive at Heaven until the Last Judgment, and hell is not eternal ("annihilationism"). These are only a few of the explicit heresies that White's "revelations" teach, therefore we can be certain that the messages are either man-made or demon-made. Among White's "revelations" was the following description of the aliens:

> The Lord has given me a view of other worlds. Wings were given me, and an angel attended me from the city to a place that was bright and glorious. ... The inhabitants of the place were of all sizes; they were noble, majestic, and lovely... I asked one of them why they were so much more lovely than those on the earth. The reply was, *"We have lived in*

> *strict obedience to the commandments of God, and have not fallen by disobedience, like those on the earth."* ... Then I was taken to a world which had seven moons. ... I could not bear the thought of coming back to this dark world again. Then the angel said, *"You must go back, and if you are faithful, you with the 144,000 shall have the privilege of visiting all the worlds..."*[299]

White's false revelations not only mandated belief in extraterrestrials (it is official Seventh Day Adventist doctrine that White is a prophet and messages are *"a continuing and authoritative source of truth"*) – they even promise that sufficiently "faithful" Adventists get to visit them!

***

A similarly massive modern sect, the Church of Latter-day Saints, came into being not long after White's "revelations." Joseph Smith's own (in)famous "revelations" on the golden plates constitute the Book of Mormon, which is regarded by all Mormons as Divinely inspired. It goes without saying that no authentic Christian – much less a Catholic – can put any credence whatsoever in Smith's messages, which, unlike White's, go so far as to deny the Trinity. And these "revelations," too, are replete with extraterrestrial belief. Even God Himself, we are told by the Mormons, is actually a certain being who lives on the planet "Kolob," and the universe is teeming with worlds full of aliens. The foremost chronicler of the ET debate throughout the centuries, Dr. Michael Crowe, notes:

> [ET belief] was not only propounded in [Mormon] scriptures; it was also advocated in statements by some of Smith's most important disciples. For example, Parley P. Pratt, in his *Key to the Science of Theology* (1855), stated: *"Gods, angels and men, are all of the same species, one race, one great family widely diffused among the planetary systems, as colonies, kingdoms, nations, etc."*... Brigham Young asserted in one of his discourses that "He [God] presides over the world on worlds that illuminate this little planet, and millions on millions of worlds that we cannot see..." [ET] themes even appear in traditional hymns; the following is a hymn still sung by Latter-day Saints. It is by William Wine Phelps, one of Smith's earliest disciples, who is praised for writing verses *"most characteristic of Latter-day Saint thought and aspiration." "...The works of God continue,/ And worlds and lives abound;/ Improvement and progression/ Have one eternal round./ There is no end to matter,/ There is no end to space,/ There is no end to "spirit,"/ There is no end to race."*[300]

In the less official and public texts, Mormonism's teachings delve into radically esoteric alien-based beliefs. (Although their public statements always seek to downplay or dismiss these teachings.) God, Mormons believe, was actually once an ordinary man who attained "exaltation" in order to become "the God of this universe" and beget his son, Jesus. (How it is logically possible that the Creator was once a mortal man is not explained.) Mormons who themselves attain "exaltation" will also become "Gods;" perhaps even ruling over their own planets filled with aliens just as God rules over ours.

Mormonism itself is, indeed, a veritable sci-fi delusion given shortly before the dawn of sci-fi.

***

Another pseudo-Christian sect that arose in 19th century is the Jehovah's Witnesses; today they have almost nine million members. Although they are considered another "Adventist" movement, the writings that spurred it on, those of Charles Taze Russel, did not claim the status of revelations. Interestingly, therefore, Jehovah's Witnesses emphatically *do not* believe in extraterrestrials. Obviously, this does not vindicate the movement—it is blatantly heretical. But it is quite significant that, among these three most noteworthy of the new 19th century "Christian" religions, this is the one that does not claim a new revelation, and likewise is the one which does not believe in extraterrestrials. Instead, Jehovah's Witnesses—rightly revering the clear sense of the Christian Bible on this point—insist that in the whole physical universe, earth alone is the object of God's concern. They correctly teach that the heavenly bodies—whether they be stars, or planets, or anything else—exist entirely for the sake of human beings.

It is, therefore, precisely because Jehovah's Witnesses *do not* claim a new revelation that they have been protected from succumbing to the ET Deception.

UFO Religions: The Horrific Fruits of "Direct ET" Revelations

> "The final objective is death, because God is the god of life, while Satan is the god of death. How many suicides are inspired by the devil! Even mass suicides are inspired by Satan."
>
> —Exorcist Fr. Gabriele Amorth

In dealing with the religions and sects above, we saw examples of "revelations" that were generally not regarded as from extraterrestrials, but rather revelations which spoke about them.

When we shift our focus to consider just a few of the avalanche of explicit "UFO religions" that have arisen, particularly in the last 75 years since Roswell, we see the expressly diabolical nature of what is transpiring even less veiled.

The proliferation of such "religions" demonstrates that the Ufology and ET belief atmosphere in the modern world is *intrinsically* religious (intrinsically *perversely* "religious," to be precise). As all who diligently study the matter discover, UFOs are simply contemporary Westerner's replacement for Christianity. Dr. W. Michael Ashcraft, after a lengthy study on the matter, concluded:

> ...alien experiences point to the emotional and cognitive terrain conventionally called religious... According to contactees, aliens described the

> cosmos in terms resembling those of Theosophy, a nineteenth-century movement that combined occultic with Eastern religious ideas. The messages that contactees conveyed to the public had religious or quasi-religious overtones, and included information on humanity's place in the universe, the guiding principles that all advanced civilizations beyond the earth subscribed to, and the possibilities for humanity's spiritual transformation...[By the 1970s], UFO advocates became part of a larger paranormal milieu. ... What many educated observers at the time failed to appreciate was the growing religiosity of this phenomenon. A sense of life's larger purpose was ever-present among occult participants. They were fascinated by, and deeply respected, the mystery that lurked around the edges of our known world...these people were doing what religious people had always done...[301]

Nowhere else does one discover a similar degree of sudden proliferation of *religions* dedicated to a prevailing cultural theme as one finds in ET belief. As much as one could point out problematic degrees of fixation with various cultural trends, one at least would not find an explosion of full-blown *religions* dedicated to, for example, the Beatles, or baseball, or airplane travel. When it comes to UFOs, however, they might as well be prophets wielding thunderbolts. Whatever these phenomena are, one thing is beyond doubt: they are intrinsically religious happenings. All who study the matter have recognized that. (What too few recognize is that any presentation of an alternative religion is intrinsically diabolical, even if we leave aside consideration of the diabolical fruits UFO religions always generate.)

In a word, extraterrestrial-related matters are not merely cultural trends to be considered psychologically or sociologically. They are decidedly religious phenomena which must be discerned spiritually. And whoever is tempted to place any doubts upon the certainty of the outcome of that discernment process will have that temptation removed upon reading the upcoming sections.

Heaven's Gate: America's Largest Ever Mass-Suicide "to Meet the ETs"

On one March day in the year 1997, thirty-nine people were found dead. They had consumed a poisonous mixture of substances, and...

> ...lain down on their backs on a bed, underneath a purple shroud, having placed polythene bags over their heads. All were wearing black trousers and Nike trainers...everyone had placed packed suitcases at their bedsides, as if about to embark on a journey... unlike the Peoples Temple in Jonestown, Guyana, in 1978, there were no concerned parents pursuing them, no congressmen investigating, and there was no siege situation, as there had been with the Branch Davidians in Waco, Texas, in 1993. The group was non-violent... **[so] the obvious question was**

> **how so many people could have been persuaded to end their lives in such a strange way**... [302]

It was the biggest mass suicide in American history.* Explaining what brought it about, Dr. Walter Martin relays:

> **Heaven's Gate [devotees] decided to commit mass suicide in order to shed "their earthly 'container' to catch a ride on a spaceship trailing the Hale-Bopp Comet."** ... The sole surviving member of Applewhite's Heaven's Gate cult was Rio **DiAngelo, ...[who] still believes that his former leader, Marshall Applewhite, was truly a being from another planet** who taught him "to be more aware, honest and sensitive to the world around him: in short, a better person."

By now, readers of this book will not struggle to answer the "obvious question" noted in the quote above. As Fr. Amorth taught, compelling a soul to suicide is a crowning victory of the demons, and it is only natural to see this frequently finding its way into the tragic decisions of both groups and individuals inspired by their belief in extraterrestrials. Similarly, the demons despise mankind's creation as male and female, therefore they frequently inspire attacks on gender as God made it: many of the bodies of the male members of the cult were found to have been castrated in anticipation of their imminent new life as "genderless aliens."

Heaven's Gate is the most well-known of such suicides; however, it is not alone (Jonestown aside, the second most destructive mass suicide in modern Western history is from yet another "UFO Religion," which we will cover shortly). Further confirming the presence of demonic influence is Rio DiAngelo maintaining his "faith" in the group, despite the revelation of its manifestly nefarious nature. Those who make a pact with demons will often preserve the narrative from below, come what may.

Recent scholarship, however, has delved deeper still—perhaps unwittingly providing a slew of further evidence that what transpired in Heaven's Gate was indeed a demonic deception directly enabled by ET belief—not simply a cult with a charismatic leader who latched on to a strategic theme. Dr. Chryssides further explains the genesis of Heaven's Gate:

> ...[Nettles] became more interested in the Theosophical and New age ideas, particularly astrology and channeling. Nettles and Applewhite [the two original leaders of Heaven's Gate]...[became] **convinced that they had a mission that was connected with the fulfillment of biblical prophecy, and that they were possessed by "Next Level" (extraterrestrial) minds** ...[they later] advertised [public meetings] on posters which read: "*UFO's/Why they are here. /Who they have come for. /When they will leave...*"

---

* the Jonestown Massacre, first of all, was even more of a mass-homicide than a mass suicide; either way, however, it took place in Guyana, not America.

These two, who simply referred to themselves as "The Two," along with other titles, insisted that they...

> ...**came from the 'next evolutionary level in a spacecraft,' and would reveal how transition to this next level could be accomplished**... One might have expected followers who were not present at the mass suicide to believe that they had experienced a lucky escape. On the contrary, Wayne Cooke and Chuck Humphreys, who had previously decided to leave the group, attempted copycat suicides in May 1997, leaving exit notes: Cooke explained that this intention had been to rejoin Ti and Do [titles for the two cult leaders] and the other classmates. Cooke succeeded in his suicide, and though Humphreys survived this attempt, he succeeded the next year. Another ex-member, Jimmy Simpson... committed a similar, but not identical, suicide... **A number of other former members continue to speak favourably of Heaven's Gate, continuing to accept its ideas, and expressing the hope that perhaps at some future time they may be able to graduate to the Level Above Human.**

One cannot overestimate the degree of diabolical presence in such actions as these—questions of possession aside. The scholar quoted here goes on to explain why these suicides were certainly not motivated by a charismatic leader, as in other cases of mass suicides. The leaders of Heaven's Gate had no particular "magnetism." Their power, instead, was entirely due to great success in convincing followers that they truly were "evolved" aliens who could teach the means required for others to arrive at a similar state of being. They simply fed off the ET belief of their audience, positioning themselves as...

> ...aliens to the planet Earth, [who] would experience metamorphosis when their craft came to collect them. In the meantime their alien identity was reinforced by the way in which they spoke of humans as alien to themselves, together with their behavior as sojourners, having no fixed abode, and mysteriously appearing and disappearing. Their refusal to speak of their physical past, and their explanation of how they acquired human bodies, served to reinforce their claims.[303]

Contemporary ET believers may be tempted to smirk at the "foolishness" of the "uneducated" Heaven's Gate members in believing its leaders were extraterrestrials. Such people should be reminded that pride comes before the fall (a theme we will discuss in a later section). Many of those who committed suicide were quite educated and intelligent; even (apparently) serious Christians. This leaves a smirker with an important question to ask himself: *How exactly would one who believes in aliens go about proving that some individual cult leader is not the alien he claims to be?* So long as they can carefully cover up their own human past, any suggestion of evidence countering the claim that they are extraterrestrials could easily be answered by premises borrowed from ET belief itself. Surely, a sufficiently technologically advanced (or "evolved") ET could manage to *seem* just like a human! The greatest secondary effect of tragedies such as these is the failure to learn from them due to the hubris of supposing one is innately above the influence.

The leaders of Heaven's Gate bedecked their claims in Biblical terminology. Among other things, they even presented themselves as the "Two Witnesses" of Revelation. It was precisely the willingness of Christians to hype up and believe in UFOs piloted by extraterrestrials that *directly* enabled the Heaven's Gate cult suicides. Consider that there are no major American cults seducing Christians into sacrificing themselves for the sake of Hindu deities because Christians have always been on guard against such deceptions. When demons assume the guise of Krishna, Christians will generally have nothing to do with it. But when the same demons assume the guise of a UFO, or an extraterrestrial, many Christians will open wide the door and lay out the red carpet.

Dr. Chryssides continues explaining how the Heaven's Gate suicides were prompted by the atmosphere of ET belief which saturated the times (and which, I add, saturate the present times still more thoroughly):

> **Many people, including DiAngelo, had become disenchanted with conventional Christianity, and were therefore seeking alternatives... The extraterrestrials with which the [Heaven's Gate] leaders claimed to have contact were clearly scientifically advanced:** they could design and operate spaceships, in which they could transport the group to this Next Level. **Belief in space travel and extraterrestrials was part of the *zeitgeist*** of the 1970s...Erich von Daniken's bestselling book *Chariots of the Gods?* Offered an alternative interpretation of Christian and other scriptures, claiming that extraterrestrials had already landed on earth many centuries previously...The Roswell incident of 1947 had convinced many that a spaceship had crashed on to the planet Earth...In popular culture, space travel was exploited in films and television programmes, such as *Star Trek, Star Wars, E.T. the Extraterrestrial,* and many more. The phenomenon of UFOs...became a popular subject of public curiosity. **Curiosity is a factor which, I believe, has aroused insufficient attention in the study of how [New Religious Movements; i.e., UFO Religions] arise. ...At the time of Nettles and Applewhite's mission, curiosity was rife...claims of alien abduction were beginning**; space exploration, still in its infancy, coupled with the proliferation of science fiction, raised the question of whether planet Earth was the only location of intelligent life, and belief in extraterrestrial visitation was [widespread] ... Nettles and Applewhite's initial publicity...was a teaser...[304]

In brief: the worst mass suicide in American history—indeed, one of our nation's great tragedies—was generated by our ET-belief-saturated culture.

> Heaven's Gate members envisioned their transformation into Next Level creatures as the ultimate goal ...The image [they showed was] a silver-colored being on a purple background, **an image that any viewer would immediately recognize as an extraterrestrial of the sort made famous by Steven Spielberg in *Close Encounters of the Third Kind,*** in the television series *The X-Files,* and in any number of science fiction books, graphic novels, television shows, and cartoons. The image bears striking similarity to the extraterrestrial beings usually called "Grays" as described by abductees and contactees, notably Betty and Barney Hill in their 1965 account and Whitney [sic] Strieber in his 1987 book, both of which were staples of ufology. ... The being displays no gender markers and possesses a face that appears gender-neutral.[305]

Raëlianism: A Large Contemporary ET-Church Heralding the Antichrist

In 1973, a twenty-seven-year-old aspiring race car driver, Claude Vorilhon, encountered an "alien" who gave him "revelations." The son of a Jew and an atheist, Vorilhon attended Catholic schools (apparently causing a great scandal by receiving Communion there) before later becoming "Raël," the eponymous founder of a UFO religion which flourishes to this day. Dr. Chryssides explains this religion as follows:

> The Raëlian Church appears to offer a radical alternative to conventional religion. It purports to be ***scientific; it is hedonistic; and it is materialistic and atheistic,*** dispensing entirely with the supernatural ... On 13 December 1973... Vorilhon relates, he was walking in the extinct volcanic region near Clermont-Ferrand in the French Auvergne when he discovered a spacecraft. A small man emerged from the spacecraft, only 4 feet tall, with a beard and almond shaped eyes ... Vorilhon was instructed to return the following day, and to bring his Bible... the Raëlian **Church does not accept the Bible literally. Much of it, the alien explained, consists of 'poetic babblings'**, but amidst much unprofitable material, there exists a core of deeper meaning ... The alien claimed to be able to shed proper light on the meaning of scripture, and the name by which **Vorilhon is better known to his followers, 'Raël', is said to mean 'the one who brings the light'** or 'the light of the Elohim'. This name, apparently, was given to him on a subsequent space journey, by Yahweh, the Elohim's leader. [306]

Satan, indeed, is still fond of his original name—*Lucifer*—meaning, "light bearer." Evidently this bearer of (a diabolical) "light" did not want to make it particularly difficult to discern who is behind this particular "extraterrestrial revelation which brings the light," Raëlianism.

Names aside, however, we see in Raëlianism itself everything one would expect a demon to inspire. Dr. Chryssides continues:

> The next day, Raël returned with his Bible and was given an extended

> lesson ...[indicating that] the human race has not been created by one single creator god, but by several. As the alien explained, 'Elohim' means 'those who came from the sky'. They are extra-terrestrial scientists who discovered the Earth's existence in their travels through space, and judged it to be capable of sustaining life. ... The Elohim, who have specially created the human race, have made contact with their creatures at various points in history, particularly through prophets such as Moses, Elijah, Ezekiel and Jesus. ...In Raël's first lesson from the space alien, the teachings are confined to those of the Jewish–Christian tradition. Later Raëlian literature finds support for its ideas in the writings of other religious traditions. ... Through time, however, the teachings of all these religions became distorted, and humans came to believe that the gods (or one single god) were some kind of invisible metaphysical beings, rather than a thoroughly physical race of beings who came from another planet.[307]

As we see ever present in all-things-extraterrestrial, so too here, it is not enough only to present one or two heresies. Instead, every fundamental aspect of Christianity must be completely robbed of its value—even while pretending to respect Christianity itself.

> ... in the last days ... [men will be found] holding the form of religion but denying the power of it. Avoid such people. (2 Timothy 3: 1-5)

Invariably, "revelations from aliens" give explanations of both our origin and destiny which contradict (but superficially resemble) explanations of the same given by Christianity; they "respect and honor" Jesus but reduce Him to something other than God; they re-explain the miracles of the Bible; they modify Christian moral teaching; they herald human "advancement" not consisting in growth in holiness but rather in "evolution," "awakening," science, and technology.

As is also standard in "ET-contact," a false eschatology is presented. Indeed, Christian eschatological dogma is entirely inconsistent with the notion of extraterrestrials (a fact we considered in Part One), therefore an alternative (also superficially respecting the Faith) is always offered by "ET revelations." We see this especially in Raëlianism:

> **As the new messiah, Raël's role is to bring about the new society, heralded by the arrival of the Elohim. The time has come for the Elohim to return,** since they now want to see the results of their genetic experiment. **They come in peace, not to conquer the earth, but to establish a system of world government,** in which the virtues of education, human merit, science and technological advance will be respected and pursued ... **The country that the Elohim have selected for the embassy is Israel.** This is because the Jewish people play a particular significance in Raëlian thought. The Jews are believed to be descendants of the 'Nephelin' (i.e. Nephilim: Genesis 6:4), a special race of people who came into existence from sexual relationships in ancient times between some of

> the Elohim and humans. ... [Raël is] described as the messiah; the embassy [in Israel that the Raëlians are seeking to build] will effectively be the Third Temple, for which some Jews have been campaigning in recent years. Time is getting short. The Elohim are expected to arrive around the year 2035, and already the Raëlians have attempted to make preparations. In 1990 they took the decision to modify their symbol, which ironically was a swastika...[308]

No argument needs to be detailed here that "Raël" has just presented a description of the system of the Antichrist, for he has made that explicit on his own. That it is built entirely on falsehoods does not render it unthreatening—this is how the Devil always operates (cf. John 8:44), and the *effects* of such fabricated ideologies are very real. For example, in 1997, this "Church" founded an organization called "Clonaid," dedicated to achieving human cloning, as it sees this evil initiative as a step towards technological immortality (heralded by the "aliens"). On the third day of Christmas in the year 2002, Clonaid claimed that the first ever human clone was born, thanks to its technology. In the intervening decades, Raëlianism has been consistently active in promoting its own political and philosophical ideology; the tenets of which include gender ideology (i.e., sex being a fluid and artificial concept), feminism, relativism, nudism, sexual hedonism, abortion, homosexuality, a rejection of marriage, childlessness (or, at most, two children), and other doctrines a Christian should expect from those heralding the Antichrist.

Unlike Heaven's Gate, this "religion" persists to the present day, numbering tens of thousands of members zealously working to enact the directives that they have been given by a demon wearing the disguise of an alien. Here, too, one simple act of Faith could have prevented this whole tragedy: a rejection of belief in extraterrestrials—a closing of that door which the Devil nudged ajar in the world during the Enlightenment, and eventually thrust fully open after 1947.

The Solar Temple: ET Mass Suicides Stand in a Historical Class of Their Own

Returning to UFO "religions" wherein the demons who inspired them simply could not—in order to more protractedly and effectively disseminate their doctrines—restrain their murderous rage, we now consider the Solar Temple, also known as the "Order of the Solar Temple."

Founded in 1984 in Geneva, Switzerland, by a homeopathic "physician," Luc Jouret, along with a New Age yoga instructor, Joseph De Mambro, this order claims to trace its origins to the post-French Revolution Knights Templar revival. Dr. David Wilkinson, relating this group to Heaven's Gate, explains:

> [Heaven's Gate members] saw themselves as beings from another

> planet simply inhabiting the 'containers' of human bodies. Through committing suicide their immortal souls would be released and taken by the spaceship to the Kingdom of Heaven. They saw comet Hale-Bopp as 'Heaven's Gate'. The Heaven's Gate cult was not alone in this kind of belief. **Since 1994, seventy members of the Order of the Solar Temple took their lives in Europe and Canada. They believed that ritual suicide leads to rebirth on a planet called Sirius.** The Heaven's Gate cult displayed once again a powerful mixture of religion, science fiction, and the belief in aliens. Their website attracted surfers looking for anything between alien abductions and the second coming. They mixed end-of-the-world eschatology with a space alien obsession, ridiculing Christianity but using biblical references alongside a fascination with the aliens and terminology of *The X-Files, ET, Star Wars,* and *Star Trek.*[309]

Insisting that global catastrophe would descend in the mid-1990s, the Solar Temple taught the necessity of entering a higher dimension via suicide before these events. Members of this "religion" anticipated the imminent "Second Coming of Christ" (placed in quotation marks because it was not truly Jesus they awaited, but rather a "solar god-king" who would, among other things, unite Christianity with Islam). Relaying greater detail on the movement, Gary Bates explains that, for The Solar Temple...

> ...**their object of worship was the star Sirius in the constellation Canis Major**. Aleister Crowley also had a preoccupation with Sirius. He claimed to channel messages from a Sirian ("from Sirius") named Lam, as well as a demonic alien being named Aiwass. UFO researcher Bill Alnor has also noticed that some of the more "out-and-out" devotees of black magic, witchcraft, and even Satanism, like Crowley, were interested in Sirius, and that most ET messages today come from this source. ... Founded by Luc Jouret (another leader who claimed he was Jesus Christ) and Joseph Di Mambro, the "Solar Temple" was a cult that had followers in many Western countries. The leaders often made references to the Bible, but as expected, the cult was steeped in New Age practices. ... It is reported that they were obsessed with the declining state of the planet, marred by the effects of pollution, violence, and immorality. This is astonishing because the group appeared to have no problem with participating in "sex magic" rituals with multiple partners in open acts of adultery. ... Under the auspices of a ritual known as the "Christic fire," cult members were shot, stabbed (including women, children, and babies), and suffocated; and their bodies were burned so they could undergo a spiritual transformation, depart this earth, and return home—to a planet orbiting Sirius.[310]

Although equally desirous of union with extraterrestrials as was Heaven's Gate, the members of this group caused the deaths of almost twice as many people; using both suicide and homicide. In 1994, fifteen committed suicide and thirty were murdered, including many children as well as an infant. In 1995, sixteen more suicide and homicide victims of this cult were discovered in France, including an Olympic athlete, Edith Bonlieu. In 1997, five more members committed suicide in Quebec, Canada. During this period, other attempted Solar Temple mass suicides were thwarted by authorities.

It is essential to distinguish the nature of these heinous tragedies from other mass "suicides." For example, the Jonestown Massacre remains the most well-known "mass-suicide" (and with good reason, considering its enormous death toll). While huge amounts of material have been published analyzing this tragedy—which I will make no attempt to summarize here—the consensus appears to be that this event was primarily due to the machinations of one particularly evil man—Jim Jones—who managed to elicit a fanatical degree of blind obedience from the followers of his cult. But, as noted earlier, this popularity is mistaken in how it categorizes the event, since it was more of a mass-murder than a mass suicide. Most of the other historically largest mass-suicide events were efforts to avert clearly impending horrendous fates; e.g., via incoming armies known for atrocities.

Extraterrestrial-belief-inspired mass suicides, however, stand in a class of their own. In both the Heaven's Gate and the Solar Temple cases, we see not only modern history's largest mass suicides, but also the strength of the delusion persisting even after the initial tragedies. The Jonestown "suicides," on the other hand, did not persist beyond November 18th, 1978. There was no lingering diabolical deception. Everyone realized how evil it was, and everyone who had been connected with Jim Jones' "People's Temple" raced to denounce this group and its founder.

With UFO religions, however, we see a foretaste of the very "**strong delusion**" (2 Thessalonians 2:11) that Scripture prophesies for the times of the Antichrist. These suicides are not results of uniquely charismatic and evil leaders. Rather, they are enabled by a supremely evil demonic machination with overtly apocalyptic elements. With both Heaven's Gate and Solar Temple, the ET-inspired suicides persisted beyond their initial tragedies, and devotees who did not commit suicide continued to believe in the truth of the cult's demonic claims.

Aleister Crowley, "The Great Beast," and His "Alien" (Demon), Lam: "Do What Thou Wilt"

In the preceding section discussing the Solar Temple, a note was included on the impact that a certain infamous British occultist, Aleister Crowley, had on its doctrines and formation. More must be said about him, as he deeply influenced not only that cult (as well as the one we will consider next), but also Ufology in general.

Born in 1875, Crowley died in 1947—as if handing on the diabolical baton he carried on to its next steward, Ufology (which exploded into prominence that same year). Dr. Massimo Introvigne explained:

> Most, if not all, magical movements that have flourished since World War II have been influenced by Crowley, even if they do not like to admit it, and many magical movements have shown a peculiar interest in Joseph Smith [the founder of Mormonism]. We find some examples today in the new Spiritualist groups that participate in "channeling," in some occult movements and orders, and in the UFO cults ... [which] have often been founded by people with occult or magical backgrounds who have translated their "mystic antecedents" into a space language...[311]

Aleister Crowley was the self-proclaimed "wickedest man on earth," who also referred to himself as "The Great Beast." He preached against Christianity, endorsed sexual perversion (including homosexuality, bestiality, and prostitution), promoted drug abuse, and advocated for the use of "magick." Most pertinent to our present discussion, however, is Crowley's own 1918 "revelation" that provided the first depiction of the now infamous "grey" alien. When Crowley himself received this image, however, he described it *accurately*: as a demon. This demon would later become the basis for the vast majority of "extraterrestrial encounters," whether "benevolent" or openly malicious, whether in fiction (e.g., *Close Encounters of the Third Kind*) or non-fictional (e.g., the innumerable reports of "alien abductions" such as Whitley Strieber's.) Dr. Timothy Dailey explains:

> The lines from Liber *AL vel Legis* (The Book of the Law) [Crowley's "Bible" for his "religion," the Thelema Church] were penned by Crowley, who claimed the book was dictated to him over a three-day period in 1904 in Cairo, Egypt, by a "preterhuman intelligence" calling itself "Aiwass." ... *Liber AL vel Legis* announced the overthrowing of the Old World Order, which he considered to be dominated by a repressive Christendom. A New Age in the evolution of humanity had dawned, which Crowley called the "Aeon of Horus." **The book is characterized by a decisive rejection of Judeo-Christian morality in favor of the charge: "Do what thou wilt."**...Crowley cast aside the Christian morality of his upbringing in favor of enticing words breathed in his ear by spirits in Cairo. The impious maxim "Do what thy wilt" became the herald call of the *Ordo Templi Orientis* (Order of Oriental Templars), Crowley's secretive occult organization that practiced "sex magick" rituals (magick being a means of effecting change through the occult). He boasted of being able to cast spells that would raise malevolent spirits, and championed the use of hard drugs, all of which earned him the well deserved title "Wickedest Man in the World"... The bill for this Faustian bargain would come due, unavoidably. Already two of his wives had paid the price, having been driven by his moral anarchism to the insane

> asylum. Several of his multitudes of openly paraded mistresses committed suicide. Now at the end of his life, wasting away destitute in a boardinghouse in Hastings, South East England, abandoned by all but a few loyal followers, Crowley's sole remaining comfort was the astounding eleven grams of heroin he ingested per day, hundreds of times the dosage of hardened users.[312]

While the supreme principle of Christianity is found in Matthew 6:10, "*Thy Will be done,*" the supreme principle of Satanism, quoted above, is the opposite—"*Do what thou wilt.*" This directive is regarded as their first and only commandment. None will struggle to identify the infernal source of Crowley's inspirations, for the man himself admits to it and his life and teachings demonstrate it even more clearly—thus ruling out the possibility of dismissing him as a mere performer. What, then, should a discerning soul conclude when he recognizes that the depictions of the "aliens" the world has been shown for decades actually derive from Crowley's own illustration of a demon ("Lam")* he himself interacted with—years before the first such "alien" depiction was ever published?

While the influence of Crowley's demonic revelations permeates the last 75 years of "ET" phenomena, it usually does so without acknowledgement. His explicit influence, however, was not only seen in the homicidal and suicidal Solar Temple religion, but also in another modern religion far more well known, to which we now turn.

Scientology, "Aum Supreme Truth," The Aetherius Society, Nation of Islam, and More: Endless ET-Inspired Evil

The post-Roswell era has witnessed the birth of so many diabolical UFO religions that providing a substantial summary of them here would be impossible. Therefore, we will briefly address only a few more before moving on to another class of "ET-revelations" which, though no less demonically-inspired, engage far more subtly in their blasphemies so as to more successfully attract Christians.

We begin with Scientology. Few will be unaware of this "Church," considering it counts some of the most well-known celebrities alive (e.g., Tom Cruise, John Travolta, Elisabeth Moss) as zealous adherents. The actual number of members is radically uncertain; scholars have pegged it at around 25,000, whereas the Church itself claims up to fifteen million members globally. Whatever the actual number, this cult is very rich, very powerful, and clearly extremely significant.

---

* Although I will not include pictures of Crowley's drawing here, they are readily available online; even Crowley's Wikipedia page shows one. No one, upon seeing it, will fail to recognize it as the unacknowledged model for "aliens."

The theology of the "religion" reads precisely like a science fiction novel, with mankind's origin, destiny, morality, and spirituality entirely dominated by ideas related to extraterrestrials. Founded by L. Ron Hubbard—who, no one will be surprised to hear, was originally a science fiction author—Scientology began as the study of "Dianetics," a pseudoscientific hypothesis in psychology, before the first Church of Scientology was established in Los Angeles in 1954. Gregory Reece explained some of the Church's teachings as follows:

> ... many millions of years ago seventy-six planets in our galaxy, united as the Galactic Federation, were ruled over by the evil Xenu. As the planets under his dominion became overcrowded, Xenu gathered a large contingent of his population and had them transported by spaceships to the planet Teegeeack, a planet known to us as earth. Xenu was not simply relocating them to earth, however, for once on earth they, along with a representative group of the earth's population, were dropped from the spaceships into the mouths of active volcanoes. As if this were not enough they were then completely vaporized by hydrogen bombs. The scattered souls, or thetans, of those murdered by Xenu were trapped in electronic devices and implanted with various types of misleading circuits and false memories. These implanted delusions included the notion of religion, a notion that served to further delude thetans concerning their true nature. ... As for Xenu, he was later captured, after a six-year battle, by officers loyal to the people of the federation. He was locked away in a mountain prison where he remains to this day.[313]

One might be tempted to dismiss this as a silly story (which, in one sense, is exactly what it is), but such a person must be reminded of the immense influence of this religion, itself made possible by prevailing cultural ET belief. Gary Bates relays:

> Some have said that [L. Ron Hubbard's] ideas were birthed from those of the world's most famous self-declared Satanist, Aleister Crowley. A New York Post article, reporting on investigations by a Boston University researcher, claimed: "**Hubbard had met Crowley in the latter's Los Angeles temple in 1945... Hubbard's son reveals that Hubbard claimed to be Crowley's successor: Hubbard told him that Scientology was born on the day that Crowley died... Scientologists perform some of the same rites that Crowley invented, all designed to free practitioners from human guilt**."... families have lost children to this group, with the children subsequently becoming even unwilling to relate to the kin they once loved. Distraught families often claim brainwashing ... techniques have been used upon their children and other members. Some countries, such as Germany, are presently trying to outlaw this cult.[314]

Recall that not only Scientology was born when Crowley died, but Ufology itself. The demons dwelling in that man's teachings did not return to hell;

they prowled about the earth and engaged in their mission's next phase. Another outlet they found was the so-called "Aum Supreme Truth" sect, also known as Aum Shinrikyo or Aleph. Continuing the thread above, Bates relays:

> It may surprise some to know that groups such as the Aum Supreme Truth sect (Aum Shinrikyo) also have some "spaced-out" beliefs. This was the group responsible for the deadly sarin gas attack in a Tokyo subway, which killed 12 people and afflicted 5,500 others. ... At their zenith, the cult had 40,000 followers. The cult's leader, Shoko Asahara, also declared himself to be Christ. ...Asahara thought he was the one "chosen" to be the savior of the world. He also claims he received a message from God while on a Himalayan retreat in 1986. But his ideas come straight out of Isaac Asimov's Foundation series of novels...[315]

Asahara and twelve of his followers have since been executed for their 1995 subway attack. Following the attack itself, Japanese authorities raided the cult's headquarters and found enough nerve gas chemicals to produce a sufficient quantity of sarin to kill four million people. More startling still is that this sect, now called "Aleph," still exists and still counts thousands of members. Among its most alluring teachings is one which insists that, through "astral travel," devotees can be reincarnated on another planet. Asahara himself wrote, in his book, entitled *Supreme Initiation*:

> We are doing practice now. So, no matter how bad the situation becomes, we have the refuge called Clear-light as the last resort. Clear-light means to transfer the consciousness from the physical body to the Astral Body to get away to the Astral World. Then even if nuclear weapons are used, our Astral Bodies stay alive, though our physical bodies will be destroyed. If you want to be born in this world again, you can do so with a new physical body. An emancipated person can do this. If the earth is so devastated as to be hopeless, you can be born in another planet. ... I'd like to say this to you: "*You yourself should become a Buddha. You should preach my teachings, or rather the cosmic truth, and should turn out many Buddhas*"

Turning our attention to another ET-inspired cult which has not (yet, at least) committed mass murder or mass suicide, we consider the "Aetherius Society." Founded in 1955 by George King, this "religion" is expressly dedicated to conversing with aliens, whom followers refer to as "Cosmic Masters." Mr. King claimed that, in 1954, after he had long been practicing Yoga, he heard a voice saying to him:

> "*...prepare yourself. You are to become the voice of interplanetary parliament.*" ... [King explains:] I had studied yoga long enough to realize that this was very important. It was eight days after this first event that I decided that the only way I could solve this mystery...was to go into meditation myself...[then] a well-known yogi master walked into the room without me having to open the door...he told me about the previous contact I

> had... he gave me certain instructions...[now] I precipitate a yogic somatic condition in order to gain mental rapport with higher intelligences.[316]

One who uses the "yogic somatic condition" in order to make contact with "higher intelligences" may well succeed in that very aim—but not by communicating with any being from *Heaven*. It appears King succeeded.

With thousands of members across the world, the Aetherius Society remains popular to this day. The home page of its professionally designed website presents instructions on how to "open the door of enlightenment" through "King Yoga," in order to "*spread and act upon unique cosmic teachings given to Earth by highly-evolved alien intelligences...*"[317] They claim to have audio recordings of "the master Jesus," received through "channeling," and (unsurprisingly) this being wholeheartedly agrees with all the standard, heretical New Age drivel.

Aetherius remains prominent enough that *The New York Times* deemed the group worthy of interviews, which they published in an August 2020 article, *Talking to Aliens is Their Religion*. Their summary of the presentation is as follows:

> In the mid-1950s, an English taxi driver named George King claimed that he had received a directive from outer space. The dispatch spurred him to establish the Aetherius Society, a religious group that believes communicating and working with aliens will better humanity. ...We don't know how many people this group comprises overall, but with 35 centers across five continents, it's a small **international community bonded by the belief that the earth needs extraterrestrial support to survive**.[318]

The video of Aetherius presented by the *Times* shows one of their altars, with a cross in the middle, but straddled by Pagan idols. Members of the cult proceed to use "operation prayer power," which, they believe, causes the power of their prayers to be stored in a physical battery kept in their Church, which in turn is said to allow virtually anything to happen—even the aversion of hurricanes. The segment concludes with a quote, from their audio recording of "Jesus," exhorting: "**Even if you do not believe in God, then believe in good, please. It's the same thing.**"

Furthermore, the Aetherius Society has not missed the opportunity to capitalize on the latest Ufology frenzies. In a press release from July 2021, they gloated:

> For over 60 years The Aetherius Society has insisted that UFOs are real, friendly and alien, and that governments know it. ... Following the release from the Office of the Director of National Intelligence, USA on June 25th, 2021, it is now clear that the Pentagon knows that UFOs are real and physical. ... While governments take faltering steps towards the truth, there is an explosion among the public of what might be described as UFORIA. ... Most people in both countries [US & UK] now

> believe in UFOs and intelligent alien life**... Disbelievers in UFOs are now in a minority ... In time ... they might be seen as somewhat akin to those who believe in a flat Earth**.[319]

That final assertion may well prove accurate; not, of course, due to men growing closer to the truth, but the very opposite.

> "For the time is coming when people will not endure sound teaching, but having itching ears they will accumulate for themselves teachers to suit their own likings, and will turn away from listening to the truth and wander into myths." —2 Timothy 4:3-4

***

Another UFO cult is the still-popular "Unarius Academy of Science." Appropriating standard pseudoscientific terms to explain its aims, the group promises that "fourth dimensional" physics enables its contact with advanced aliens on "higher frequency planes." Dr. Kenneth Samples relays:

> One of the most popular and outrageous UFO cults, Unarius was founded by Ernest L. and Ruth E. Norman in 1954. "Unarius" is an acronym for Universal Articulate Interdimensional Understanding of Science. As in so many other cases, the founders of Unarius had roots in the occult. The Normans believed themselves to be the reincarnation of many great individuals of the past. **Ernest, a spiritualist medium with prior involvement in flying saucer groups, identified himself as the reincarnation of Egyptian pharaoh Amenhotep IV, as Jesus Christ, and as a space traveler in ancient Atlantis**. Unarius' followers described Ernest as "the greatest intelligence to ever come to earth." Not to be outdone by her husband, Ruth E. Norman revealed many remarkable past lives, claiming reincarnation as a pharaoh's mother, Confucius, Socrates, Mary Magdalene, Mona Lisa, Henry VIII, and others. **Ernest declared an ability to channel and dictate messages from highly evolved alien beings living on other planets, especially Mars and Venus**. ... [Ruth also] channeled otherworldly beings, among them "URIEL" (Universal Radiant Infinite Eternal Light). Later she insisted upon being called "*Uriel: the Archangel and Cosmic Visionary.*" ...[she] claimed to be in contact with a confederation of alien beings from thirty-three planets. She predicted that a massive landing of spacecrafts would take place in the year 2001 on the Unarius property (sixty-seven acres) in El Cajon, California. This monumental landing would usher in the cosmic golden age of logic and reason. In addition to her other exploits, Ruth conducted a healing ministry. Melton explains: "Healing is accomplished by Ray-Booms, the projected light beams from the great intelligences on the higher worlds."[320]

No comment is needed here other than noting what is conspicuously absent from all extraterrestrial-related "revelations:" anything whatsoever lending credibility to the thesis that they are authentic.

Still another group with a disastrous legacy inspired by ET-belief is the so-called "Nation of Islam;" an American hate group based on ideologies of black nationalism, Islam, and extraterrestrials. A highly influential movement, it still numbers 50,000 followers. Today it is led by the black supremacist, Louis Farrakhan, who has announced the imminent arrival of UFOs as "divine spaceships," which will descend to punish the nations for the sufferings of Africans. He claims to have met "Master Elijah Muhammad" aboard a UFO. Matthias Determann relayed:

> As an icon of popular culture, the flying saucer also entered the cosmology of the Nation of Islam. Even though Yakub's white devils enslaved the original black race, they would eventually face annihilation brought about by bombs from the Mother Plane. This vehicle is a wheel-shaped wonder under the control of black Muslim scientists. It is able to defy Earth's gravity, lift up mountains and generate its own oxygen and hydrogen. In his imagination, Elijah Muhammad drew on scripture as well as descriptions of UFOs. Especially influential was the vision of God's four-wheeled throne 'chariot' (*merkabah*) in the Book of Ezekiel. With reference to the Qur'an, the religious leader described the scientists aboard the Mother Plane as knowing 'what you are thinking before the thought materializes'. Thanks to this divine prescience, the Mother Plane can destroy any fighter jets sent against it by white governments... Farrakhan's splinter group continued to include science and technology in its mythology. The Mother Plane was preserved as a Mother Ship or Mother Wheel. Farrakhan claimed to have been abducted by this craft while on a visit to Mexico in 1985. On board, he encountered Elijah Muhammad, who informed him ... [that] the administrations of Ronald Reagan and George Bush were seeking to exterminate black people under the guise of the 'war on drugs'. **The science fiction elements of the Nation of Islam even facilitated an otherwise unlikely alliance with the Church of Scientology** in the twenty-first century ... Like the leaders of the Nation of Islam, L. Ron Hubbard, the founder of Scientology, promised his followers enhancement and salvation through science and technology.[321]

Whoever is acquainted with the antics of the Nation of Islam knows of its thoroughly rotten fruits. Besides its inherently and virulently anti-white racism, the group's leaders have praised Hitler as a "very great man." In 2021, one of the members rammed his car into barricades outside the U.S. Capitol, killing a police officer. ET belief is not a mere tangent to the mission of this group; it is part of its basic motivation. Therefore, here too we see yet another rotten fruit of belief in aliens.

***

Of the "revelations,"—and the cults or "religions" they inspired—which we have discussed thus far, most did not prove especially attractive to large numbers of devout Christians. Tragically, the same cannot be said of the deceptions we will consider next.

The Urantia Book: the "Fifth Epochal Revelation" from the ETs and More Infiltration of Catholicism

Although known most commonly as *The Urantia Book,* this 1955 text—presented as a new mystical revelation—also goes by the title, "The Fifth Epochal Revelation." (The "fourth" such revelation being that of Jesus Christ.)

Thousands of pages long and immensely popular, this "channeled" work is claimed, by its original publishers, to have simply materialized on paper. The text that allegedly inexplicably appeared consisted of answers to questions written down by a group of friends in Chicago in the 1920s; questions which they had been instructed to write down at the behest of certain "celestial beings" ("extraterrestrials"). Eventually the text of these "revelations" was published, and they have since been disseminated, read, and followed widely.

Untold thousands, if not millions, of Christians (including Catholics) to this day are beguiled into regarding this book as an authentic work of mystical literature. It remains a bestseller in many languages, and it is heavily advertised by its publishers. In 2023, author Gregg Tomusko even published his own book entitled *The Catholic Church and the Urantia Book,* dedicated to extolling the supposed overlap of both. Mr. Tomusko describes himself as a daily-Mass-attending Catholic, a former seminarian, and a confirmation class teacher who regards Catholicism and the *Urantia Book* as "spiritually the same...each is to bring people closer to Christ."

Mr. Tomusko goes on to provide lengthy, and deeply confused, descriptions of why he regards Biblical teachings and teachings from the Urantia book as perfectly harmonious—whereas a sincere consideration of the two together reveals nothing but the latter providing a New Age perversion of Scripture. For example, he cites John 16, wherein Jesus says, "I have many things to say unto you, but ye cannot bear them now," and uses this as his springboard to pretend that the decidedly anti-Christian nature of the following teachings from the Urantia book are "Catholic:" (*Note: numerical citations within the following quotes refer to entries within the Urantia Book.*)

> Urantia: Sooner or later another and greater John the Baptist is due to arise ... doing all this without in any way referring either to the visible Church on earth or to the anticipated second coming of Christ. 170:5.19 (1866.2) Be not discouraged; human evolution is still in progress, and the revelation of God to the world, in and through Jesus, shall not fail. 196:3.33 (2097.1)[322]

Later, Tomusko's own words display his radically deficient understanding of Jesus Christ. He writes:

> But the Father's will was for Jesus to live life as a man, to gain the experience of being his lowest free-will creation and thus have to figure out

> the Father's will, as we must. Jesus, growing up, slowly began to realize that he had a pre-existence ... At Cana, Jesus was more surprised than anyone when the water turned to wine![323]

Just as we saw earlier, in the case of Monsignor Balducci—who, like many ET promoters, believes that the human race is on the "lowest rung of spiritual evolution"—so here we find the same blasphemy which results from failing to recognize the truth that human nature is the *very pinnacle* of God's Creation. Since it is indeed a dogma that Jesus had a human nature like ours, it follows that whoever dismisses human nature as holding a rank below "aliens," cannot avoid succumbing to the same errors against Jesus Christ Himself.

Despite these heresies, Tomusko usually comes across like many other Catholic *Urantia* followers: "orthodox minded." He keeps his Latin pocket prayer book handy, he draws from St. Thomas Aquinas, and he speaks highly of the Divine Office in its traditional naming: Lauds, Vespers, Compline, etc. He even writes:

> The Catholic Church and the Urantia Book introduces us to the Big View. They're always talking about eternal life ... The Catholic Church has fought the devil through the centuries. She reminds us that we are in a war against "Satan, and all the evil spirits, who prowl through the world seeking the ruin of souls." Like a light bulb that continues to get dimmer, we've become complacent to evil's entrenchment and steady victories on our world. Christians need a wake-up call...[324]

Paragraphs such as these sound wonderful. Tomusko goes on to share how he teaches his Catholic confirmation students, in the 7th through 9th grades, about the *Urantia* book along with Catechesis; sharing teachings from *Urantia* while modifying individual words therein to make it sound less esoteric. (For example, as a dedicated devotee of *Urantia*, he "knows" that the "real" name of Jesus is actually "Christ Michael," but when reading passages from *Urantia* to his confirmation students, he replaces that with the lowly and earthly name for Him, "Jesus.") He relays an intricate guide on how to incorporate the *Urantia Book* into everything Catechetical, going so far as to present a selection of readings from it for each day of Holy Week and various hours of the Passion.

Highlighting Mr. Tomusko's case is important here to convey a broader reality. For although he is not exactly a *New York Times* bestseller, there are many Catholics and Christians like him. One would not necessarily discover, upon meeting them—or even being one of their students!—that they hold wildly esoteric and subtly Faith-undermining views derived from revelations given by "extraterrestrials" (demons). They cover their tracks well and know exactly when to switch terms borrowed from these demons in disguise with more ordinary ones, in order to blunt the impact. They haunt the ranks of not only Catechists but also respected clergy, popular apologists, learned theologians, experienced exorcists, and, increasingly—as the climax of the Great Deception draws near—they will likely be found among the ranks of Bishops working in the Vatican. This is all fundamental to the Antichrist's plan; for success, he will need extraterrestrial belief and expectation as rampant as possible in the Church before his public entrance.

***

Let us consider more content from the *Urantia Book*, lest anyone be tempted to read Tomusko's book and agree with his take on the harmony of Urantia and Catholicism. The "celestial beings" who "revealed" this text to us teach that earth—which they refer to as "Urantia"—is just one inhabited world in one particular "remote local universe," a "local universe" that is itself only a part of "superuniverse number seven" (each "superuniverse" contains tens of thousands of "local universes"). All together, we are told that seven trillion inhabitable planets exist (cf. *Urantia*, 15:2.17), though we are immediately reminded, by the "celestial being" dictating this text, that "*all such estimates are approximations at best, for new systems are constantly evolving*." (15:2.25) One can only guess how many more trillions of inhabitable planets have "evolved" since!

Like most "ET" revelations, the book claims that earthlings are unfortunately quite "unevolved" in comparison to the beings on other planets, thereby setting the stage for our dire need to make contact with the extraterrestrials and learn from them. Also resembling other "revelations" that seduce many Christians into their clutches, this one speaks extremely highly of Jesus—even appearing to acknowledge His Divinity—before going on to later deny the Virgin Birth, and, finally, to teach that Jesus is only one of almost a million "Creator Sons"—one who has 10 million other inhabited worlds to minister to in our particular "local universe."

This description, of course, renders Jesus' role quite minor in the grand universe-scheme. Although the Urantia book does assert a Trinity of sorts, it is a Trinity of being several categories higher than the minor one to which Jesus is said to belong. He is "Divine," sure, and He is the second person of "a" Trinity, sure. But once you hear what the "extraterrestrials" have to say, you realize just how much bigger the picture really is. This, too, is a ubiquitous strategy in ET belief (not only in "ET revelations")—superficially conceding the truth of the teachings of the Church, while ultimately aiming at making them seem so *small*.

Whereas Jesus assures us in the true Public Revelation—the Bible—that whoever has seen *Him* has seen *the* Father (cf. John 14:9), the *Urantia Book* regards Jesus as merely a "revelation" of the Father; perhaps an "incarnation," of sorts, of the Divine Nature, but certainly not literally the only begotten Son, consubstantial with the Eternal Father Himself.

A true textbook for diabolical deception aimed at transforming Christianity into a pseudo-Christian New Age Antichristic religion, the *Urantia Book* even presents its own version of the Our Father prayer, which reads: "*Our Father in whom consist the universe realms...give us this day the vivifying forces of light*" (144:5.2,6). Another version it suggests reads: "*Our creative Parent, who is in the center of the universe...deliver us from inertia, evil...*" (144:5.12,19)

Obviously, this is not an authentic private revelation. But care should be taken to ensure recognizing this now does not tranquilize anyone into supposing that the ability to identify a clear and explicit heresy is sufficient to keep him spiritually, morally, and theologically safe. *It is not.* Although I have highlighted some particularly problematic selections above, the fact remains that the vast majority of the *Urantia Book*'s content appears "orthodox"—that is, almost all of its teachings do not *explicitly* contradict a dogma. The book's *modus operandi* is not heresy, but something much darker and more dangerous—something that permeates "Christian" ET promotion—*subtle apostasy*. The goal is not so much to deny any particular Christian or Catholic teaching, but rather to make it all feel so small in comparison to some "higher" reality and "more urgent" calling in relation to it.

It is precisely this trap to which even the "orthodox minded" among the faithful can easily succumb. Had such a reader not been forewarned that the *Urantia Book* is indeed heretical nonsense, he might pick it up, open to a random page, and stumble upon a deeply fascinating passage. Not seeing any heresy, such a reader would likely continue reading page after page—still not stumbling upon anything flatly contrary to dogma. Were this reader particularly inclined to alien belief, he would likely behave as an alcoholic beginning to smell whiskey. Continuing his voracious reading, he would be hopelessly hooked before long, and once he happened upon an explicit heresy, he would be too addicted to quit. This is not a theoretical scenario: it is a description of what has happened in untold thousands of cases.

A Catholic is not safe merely by being protected against the *Urantia Book*. There are countless other diabolical "revelations" like it, and countless more bound to be published soon. There is only one sure defense against all of them: *categorically* rejecting belief in extraterrestrials. As long as that alien-belief-openness exists, there will always be some "revelation" (from demons disguised as ETs) that is able to sneak around other, less fundamental, defenses.

The Urantia "revelations" are clearly an attack on Christianity in general and Catholicism in particular, but they are not alone. Many other popular "revelations" from the "aliens" traffic even more explicitly in Catholic terminology and delude just as many of the faithful. To them, we now turn.

Excommunicated Fr. Tomislav Vlašić's "Revelations" – "The Catholic Church Must Announce the Extraterrestrials!"

Tomislav Vlašić is a former Franciscan priest (he has since been laicized and excommunicated) who first became well known as an initial spiritual director to the Medjugorje visionaries, a group of Bosnian children who began receiving apparitions from the Blessed Virgin Mary in 1981. Six years after those apparitions began, Fr. Tomislav moved to Italy and founded a New Age community, which one of the Medjugorje seers, Marija Pavlovic, disavowed after initially endorsing (not having understood its true nature).

At this point, it was discovered that Vlašić had covered up an earlier affair (with a nun, no less), from which he fathered a child. Fr. Tomislav then publicly went off the rails and abandoned his vocation. Indeed, priests in positions such as he found himself in—particularly theologians working closely with authentic seers—are favorite targets of the Devil, considering how powerful they can be *if only* they abide in orthodoxy and holiness—and, as we will see, if they reject such esoteric views as ET belief. One should not be surprised to see Fr. Tomislav was a primary target of Satanic attacks, or that others in similar situations moving forward prove equally alluring targets for the evil one.

A theologian himself, Vlašić knew well how to give the appearance of having defended the orthodoxy of the teachings he wandered into after his days at Medjugorje. And while that defense may fool men, it does not fool God. In 2008, the Vatican's Congregation for the Doctrine of the Faith began investigating Fr. Tomislav for "*the diffusion of dubious doctrine, manipulation of consciences, suspect mysticism, disobedience towards legitimately issued orders.*" Vlašić was laicized (stripped of priestly authority) in 2009. In 2018, he founded the group he now leads, the "**Church of Jesus Christ of the Whole Universe**," embracing the "revelations" of Stefania Caterina (along with his own), both of which spoke of extraterrestrials. In 2020, he was excommunicated.

Vlašić's promotion of extraterrestrials, however, began long before the official 2018 formation of his "Church." In 2012, he produced a video with Stefania insisting they were part of a group called the "central nucleus"—49 individuals chosen by God (dwelling throughout the galaxies) dedicated to saving humanity "in all universes." His collaboration with Stefania long predates even that video, however; he began his relationship with her at least as early as 1994.[325] Ms. Caterina's "revelations," in turn, are summarized by one author as follows:

> Stefania Caterina writes about her alleged experiences and messages from extra-terrestrial entities in the book "*Beyond the Great Barrier*" **The first such experiences began in 1984, with "Ashtar Sheran from the**

> **planet Alpha Centauri" commander of interplanetary powerful fleet, scientist, engineer and designer, and then with his wife Kalna, the priest-king Aris and "several brothers and sisters of Alpha Centauri"** ... In her book, Stefania Caterina describes space ships orbiting around the Earth by order of God to prevent the humanity of the Earth destroy itself. She also writes: "*One of the most important tasks of the humanity of Alpha Centauri is used to control the largest interplanetary fleet. It is composed of the most powerful spacecraft and crews selected, made available by the planets faithful to God...The interplanetary flagship is so great that it can obscure the Earth with its shadow...* ***When the time is right, the alien' will manifest openly and visible to everyone*****.** ***It is God's plan that this happens.*** *Then the great interplanetary fleet will be positioned above the Earth, and will be visible from every corner of the world*" Stefania Caterina claims she was taken in spirit to visit many planets and received many explanations of the living conditions of "so many brothers of the universe."[326]

Now having the aid of a theologian (Tomsilav's excommunication did not remove his intellectual competence), Stefania had an ally to make it appear that her revelations from demons were orthodox—much like many other Catholic ET promoters today have the same ability. Therefore, the material generated by this "Church of the Universe" is even more effective in seducing Catholics than the last "revelation" we considered. It avoids much of the more extreme cosmic-esotericism of *Urantia*, though still insists that there are indeed inhabited planets all throughout the universe, whose enlightenment and intervention we direly need today on earth. It even speaks highly of Our Lady of Fatima, Divine Mercy, and many other clearly authentic apparitions to give the appearance of standing shoulder to shoulder with God's authentic interventions into the world.

In one article on its website, the "Church" relays the "situation of the universe" in 2012 and 2013 as follows:

> **The Church of the Earth had failed to welcome the invitation of God to announce the existence of life in the universe** ... the more sensitive Christians of the Earth who had welcomed the extraordinary instruments had prayed and suffered in 2012. They had waited in vain for a turn of the official Church... On 1 March of [2013] St. Michael said: "**I strongly recall all the ecclesiastical hierarchy, beginning with the Catholic ones, to an honest awareness about the presence of life in the universe, and to give to the faithful likewise clear information.** This requires a **radical rethinking of the universal mission of the Church** which cannot be delayed any further." ... St. Michael added also: "**It also requires an appropriate amplification of theology, which must be set up with the times and with the new requirements of the knowledge of the truth**."[327]

Here as elsewhere, demonic "revelations" are fixated upon compelling the Catholic Church to "announce the existence of" extraterrestrials, an announcement that must coincide with a "radical rethinking" of her teachings to align with "the times." *This is the agenda of the Antichrist.* And what is his enticement? The allure of the benefits we could reap from advanced extraterrestrial technology. These "revelations" continue:

> What do these faithful brothers and sisters [extraterrestrials] want to communicate [to] us?... Would it not be good for you if they showed you the way to health...? **Would it not be good for you if they transmitted to you the power of the Holy Spirit from whom their technology comes?** ... with enough to eat for everyone and with healthy and good food? Especially in the book '*The Universe and Its Inhabitants*" we have shared with you some events in which the faithful brothers and sisters prevented the Third World War...**They come to us as brothers and sisters who want to help us promote the Spirit of God within us, to awaken our dormant creativity because we, men of the Earth, are so geocentric and attached to the earth** ... These brothers and sisters want to bring us peace so that evil and war are blocked...**people think that they should pray hundreds of rosaries and the problems will be solved. This is not the kind of prayer Our Lady [asks for], but the elevation of the people to the dimensio**n of the Spirit of God...[328]

With a slight twist (the aliens' technology comes from the "power of the Holy Spirit"), these "revelations" are ultimately motivated by the same desire that propels the secular Ufologists forward. They feed off an insatiable desire for extraterrestrial technology to usher in a hedonistic utopia on earth, in a Satanic perversion of the Era of Peace that Jesus and Mary have long promised in their *authentic* apparitions. "**The supreme religious deception is that of the Antichrist, a pseudo-messianism**..." (*Catechism of the Catholic Church*, §675)

While the *Urantia Book* contains explicit heresies—teachings directly contrary to infallibly defined dogmas—which, if detected, reveal its demonic origin, such evidence is much harder to find in the messages of the two "seers" now under consideration (*note: there may well be explicit heresies; I have personally read relatively little of their messages*). Tomislav has been very careful. Discerning souls must not fail to note the increasing severity of the ET deception displayed here. Granted, a sincere Catholic—even if he does not yet grasp the truth about "aliens"—can have a moral certainty that an ex-priest who radically rejected his vocation, his chastity, his vow of obedience, and was so unrepentant as to incur excommunication from the Vatican, would not suddenly be the instrument chosen by God to save the world and usher in a new era. Nevertheless, we are dealing with a different exercise of discernment here than with *Urantia*.

Fr. Tomislav was a priest-theologian who became world renowned for his association with an authentic private revelation; a position he then took advantage of for the dissemination of a theology based on extraterrestrials. He is not the only one in such a position, with such credentials, who has done and will do similar things. But the Devil will never use the exact same strategy twice; he is always fine-tuning it. Next time, the deception will be even more difficult to detect than in the present case, and whoever is even open to the possibility of contact with extraterrestrials is setting himself up to succumb.

Voice and Echo of the Divine Messengers: A Phony Religious Order With "Revelations" from Andromeda

A certain wildly popular group of "seers" who claim to be receiving messages from Heaven has assumed a number of names over recent decades. Alternatively referred to as the "Community-Light" of Figueira, the "Association Mary, Mother of the Divine Conception," or the "Grace Mercy Order," they are now most commonly known as the "Voice and Echo of the Divine Messengers," or simply *The Divine Messengers*.

As of this writing, they have about 300,000 followers on just one of their social media pages (Facebook), and videos of their "apparitions" circulate on platforms such as YouTube, where they likewise rack up hundreds of thousands of views. Their Catholic-themed devotional music videos garner millions.

Whoever peruses their website or watches their videos will find an appearance of pious and orthodox Catholicism. These "Divine Messengers" take every measure to seem like a devout apostolate and an authentic religious order. Their website is replete with traditional images of Jesus and Mary, the Eucharist, St. Joseph, the Divine Mercy, etc. They extoll repentance, Confession, the Rosary, and *most* everything one would hope to see promoted in an authentic apparition.

Triply confirming that their intent is to deceive Catholics, one of the male "Divine Messengers" even calls himself Friar Elias, giving the impression he is a Catholic priest. Two of the female "seers" call themselves Mother Maria Shimani and Sister Lucia de Jesus. "Friar" Elias and the other "seers" host large events in tandem with their "apparitions," and they both dress and comport themselves as if they were Carmelite monks and nuns. In fact, they have no recognition from the Catholic Church.

Their messages are replete with teachings about the extraterrestrials that they claim populate the planets. Below, we will consider only a small selection of them:

> **Andromeda is the regent of your Solar System and others. It was there, in that part of the universe, where the Creator Fathers once came** to sow the Plan of God in the material universe through a Divine Project, which first was to emerge and manifest in the Great Star of Andromeda ... This is what My Celestial Church is showing you today through its main portal. We are going to **the real science of your origin** ... **In the same way that God thought of His human Project, He also**

> **thought of other Projects that continue to evolve**, similar to this one. With other degrees of consciousness and evolution, **the different creatures of the Father live their lessons and schools in order to achieve the experience of degrees of love.**[329]**The human beings were created among so many other beings and civilizations of the Universe**, to express something that none of them had expressed.[330] **... movement in all living beings of this and other planets [will be affected]. As from the year 2020 on, the Solar System will enter into the last and most acute spiritual**, cosmic, mental and material stage of its transition.[331] God created the different races and civilizations of the universe ... He also granted that ... in the ascension of evolution, those who experienced love so profoundly would become Love itself...[332]

In the following message from "Jesus," we even see explicit heresy:

> Mentors of the Heavenly Governments, entrusted with the spiritual and material evolution of millions of consciousnesses in this Creation, as well as of other galaxies and constellations. ... life is infinite ... at the doors of Andromeda, these [Mentors] were waiting for Me, in order to give me the next step that I would take for you: that of **not only being the Redeemer of the World, but also of being the Governor of the Universe,** uniting, through My Heart and My Divinity, all the consciousnesses that serve Me in the Higher Universe, from their evolutionary experiences and schools ... All is possible when the consciousness wants to take the step. And when it takes the step it enters an experience that is similar to the one I lived in Andromeda, which took Me three cycles of material time to conclude because I not only **glorified Myself and divinized Myself through the human person of Christ,** but I also assumed, in a more profound and eternal manner, a commitment to your salvation.[333]

Of course, there is no "human person of Christ." Jesus Christ is one and only one person—the Second Person of the Holy Trinity—and in Him, there are two natures (one human, one Divine), not multiple persons. Not content with Christological heresy alone, another "apparition of Christ Jesus" to Elias, nonsensically speaks of what was so "Before God existed."[334]

Granted, most of the messages from the "Divine Messengers" do not directly pertain to extraterrestrials. A Catholic ET promoter, therefore, might dismiss this heretical, false, and New Age order's association with ET promotion as accidental—just another case of a New Age group engaging in "grifting" with popular trends. Such an assessment, however, would be ignorant of the group's history. An expert in new religious movements, Dr. Vitor de Lima Campanha, traced out the group's genesis carefully, explaining that its initial impetus derived from meetings with the prominent Brazilian Ufologist, Jose Trigueirinho Netto. Netto teaches that alien spaceships are among us, sent from an "intergalactic confederation" which was sent for the sake of humanity's "transition" in order to avert an "extermination war." Their "rescue operation," he insisted, is "ready to start at any time," and will create a "New Man."[335]

In 1987, Netto founded a community in Brazil with similar New Age, Theosophical ideals as the "Divine Messengers." What happened twenty years later led to the messages we have here been reviewing. Dr. Companha explains:

> **In 2008, Trigueirinho received two Uruguayans who would later be known as Mother Shimani and Friar Elias** in the Community-Light of Figueira. Both said they were seers in frequent contact with the Virgin Mary. Jesus's mother would have guided them to look for Trigueirinho in their alternative community, in Brazil, where they would live. There the group claims to have witnessed the apparitions of Catholic saints along with Mary. They claim to have received the task of creating an ecumenical monastic order, Grace Mercy Order, from them ... As a result, Trigueirinho, Mother Shimani and Friar Elias created a [New Religious Movement], based in the Community-Light of Figueira. This site undergoes a Catholic-inspired reorientation with the creation of monasteries devoted to Mary... There is the ordination of mothers and friars, including the use of habits similar to those of Catholic orders; they take vows like those of chastity, obedience, silence, etc. and participate in reframed rites of Communion, Worship and Foot Wash. **However, all these changes do not contradict the work of Trigueirinho Netto. Rather, they reinforce the contents, blending the New Age and UFO elements with the incorporations of the Catholic imagery**. ...[They teach that] **Adam and Eve are ... beings of an ancient race, the "first race" created by "Creator Parents", in the plural ... These ideas are in line with the thinking of Trigueirinho Netto** ... The message attributed to Mary therefore corroborates the hypothesis of an articulation between the concepts of evolution and creation, reinterpreted and synthesized freely by the thoughts of Trigueirinho Netto and the Grace Mercy Order.[336]

This "order," therefore—which is deluding millions of Catholics to the present day—not only *promotes* ET-belief, but was *born from* ET-belief. The being appearing to them, whom they pretend is the Virgin Mary, directed them to the famous Ufologist Jose Trigueirinho Netto to found their group, and the rest is history.

Today, along with belief in extraterrestrials, the "Divine Messengers" promote religious syncretism (insisting, for example, that "some will be more open to following" Buddha, some Muhammad, others Christ—and that is all fine)[337], New Age spirituality, animal-personhood (and a condemnation of meat eating), and numerous other errors; all fruits of "Catholic" belief in extraterrestrials.

Giorgio Bongiovanni: "Fatima-Inspired Stigmatist" with a Message from the ETs: "Hell Does Not Exist"

In the year 1989, a young Italian man by the name of Giorgio Bongiovanni visited the Shrine of Our Lady of Fatima in Portugal. The visit, however, became more than just a pilgrimage—it became an announcement that he was the recipient of apparitions of Jesus and Mary who—along with extraterrestrials—revealed to him messages, prophecies, and "new theologies." The force of these teachings was seemingly bolstered by the additional claim that he received miraculous stigmata like those of St. Francis of Assisi or St. Padre Pio. The years that would follow found him generating media and issuing publications while travelling the world, proselytizing the masses with his galactical message.

Indeed, Giorgio did not only receive "messages from the extraterrestrials," he also spoke at major UFO conferences and quickly became a sensation in this crowd and beyond. Even major mainstream media outlets reported on his teachings. A 1997 article in the *Washington Post* detailing the "Sixth Annual International UFO Congress Convention" of Nevada reported on this "mystic's" contributions to the event:

> One day a man walked in wearing a white robe. On his forehead was a horrible cross-shaped scab; heavy gauze bandages covered his hands. **"There is probably the greatest stigmatist in the world," a UFO researcher standing nearby announced reverently.** The stigmatist was Giorgio Bongiovanni. He was here to speak about aliens ...**His UFO newsletter, NONSIAMOSOLI ("We are not alone")**, gives the whole story, saying that the Virgin Mary appeared to Bongiovanni and revealed that Jesus Christ had visited civilizations throughout the cosmos, where He has been accepted—unlike on our planet, where He was crucified... What do the stigmata have to do with aliens visiting Earth? Aliens, Bongiovanni explained, accompanied Jesus in his travels. "Our forefathers called them angels."[338]

To the present day, Giorgio continues announcing his "messages from the extraterrestrials." As of this writing, YouTube videos of interviews he has given within the last month alone have over a hundred thousand views, and his personal YouTube channel has accumulated millions of views since 2009. The header of his own website[339] defines his mission as being that of "the Extraterrestrial Voice," and it solicits donations for his "Giordano Bruno Cultural Association." (Recall, from earlier chapters, that Giordano Bruno was among the first alien belief promoters in Catholicism, and was burned at the stake for heresy in the year 1600 A.D.) On this website, one will find many "revelations" from these "extraterrestrials." The few presented below summarize their general sense:

> Among all extraterrestrial races which visit the earth, some of them are part of the interstellar-universal-confederation, some others are not

> ...[but] they all obey the law of the Omnicreating force ... [The Greys are] respectful of others' free will. They work with us in order to bring [us] to integrate with other civilizations and extraterrestrial races ... (New Theology. Part VI) The agreement with our extraterrestrial race that you call "greys," made after the war, was in brief: if you terrestrials ... cease all nuclear experiments, we, in turn, will help you technologically...After the first lapse of time in which it seemed that our superpowers had stuck to the agreement and received in the meantime some technological knowledge, they, the USA, the USSR and others, broke this agreement by resuming the nuclear experiments. This has brought about a complete change of methodology on our part. (New Theology. Part V) **We "aliens", as you define us, have been on earth... for thousands of years.** The military and civilian sightings starting from the next year of your time, 2018, will increase more and more. Militaries, civilians, politicians, journalists, researchers, common people, everyone will have the possibility to see and film our vehicles. **...[contactees will] receive messages and divulge them to the world [of] public opinion. Our messages are of high Christic value ... we have a science more advanced than yours by billions of years** ... [the UFO phenomena] carried out by us are only the beginning of a great wave of manifestations visible in the skies of all the world that our confederation has planned for the next months and years of your time, in order to sensitize the world public opinion to the great contact between us and the people of the earth. This event will happen, be sure of it! And very soon! (December 21, 2017. "UFO: The Extraterrestrial Visitation")[340]

At this point, a Catholic alien belief promoter who does not already know better might be getting quite excited. *"Wow! A mystic, a stigmatist, a seer who has provided countless messages detailing precisely the views I promote! Amazing!"* Not so fast. Here are some other teachings Giorgio provides from "the extraterrestrials."

> The dogma of **eternal damnation does not exist. This dogma was created by man to harm man... this dogma is a threat that has been used for 2,000 years to terrify souls**. ("The New Theology." Part VII.) As each human being contains the divine entity or spirit, **so do the suns or stars and the planets contain a spirit which follows a divine evolution**, which governs them ... the **suns and the planets, the stars are living beings** ... Myriam is the patronymic being for planet earth, the holy mother of Jesus, a spirit which pervades the planet ... (March 4th, 1997) (New Theology. Part IV) **Reincarnation [is] a universal law indispensable for the human spiritual evolution**. [It is] the classic perfect law, cause and effect: one reaps what he sows. ... **tyrannic and evil power has always tried to hide this great truth** for fear and ignorance, to enslave and subjugate souls. But the truth, thanks to the masters of the east and to the master of all masters himself, Jesus Christ, has triumphed over [the] hoax. (2011 Messages: Reincarnation)

Presented here is only a sampling; Giorgio has given droves of messages conveying these and similar themes. His messages—as with all "revelations" that espouse belief in extraterrestrials—run the usual gamut of heresies promoting the foremost diabolical deceptions: reincarnation, pantheism, universalism, syncretism, false eschatology, and more.

Messages aside, Giorgio himself has made it clear he is anything but an authentic mystic. Conveniently, the unsightliest of his "stigmata" (the large and deep wound on his forehead) no longer appears—not even a scar remains on the now clear and smooth skin above his eyebrows—and he need only continually wear white fingerless gloves to preserve the allure of his other "stigmata." Early in his public days, Giorgio claimed to be given—by the extraterrestrials—the full text of the third secret of Fatima (at that time, it had not yet been released). This prophecy included, among other things, world war and the assurance that we would meet with the aliens—all by the year 2012.

Several years after the *Washington Post* article quoted above, another major global periodical, *The Guardian,* published an article entirely devoted to Giorgio, entitled "Written in blood." This time, a blunter assessment of the man is implied in the text:

> Bongiovanni is making a bid for respectability by jumping into the newspaper business ... [he now has a] clean forehead and is wearing fingerless white gloves. [Upon our meeting,] he holds out his right hand and I let the photographer go first. A deft squeeze of the knuckles elicits no pained yell so I follow suit. ...aged 39 and with a large, well-maintained ego, he certainly resembles a lot of print journalists ... Using profits from his UFO and stigmatic videos, he enlisted a staff of 20 ... he is not recognised by the Vatican and has been denounced as a fake. He bled for the cameras during a decade-long media circus and sold videos and books in the US and Australia on the connection between aliens, Jesus, crop circles, weapons and the cosmos. ... [but] since he started running a paper Bongiovanni's bleeding has tapered off ... A believer in miracles, he has a dream. *"I am obsessed by Pink Floyd. They made the best music, the best. If they hear about me they could fund me. Just think, the things we could do together*!" He is, of course, serious.[341]

Despite the fraud here present, we should not doubt that he received messages from "extraterrestrials," in a sense. Some aspects of his story seem deeper than what one finds in those cases that are *pure* hoax. This is to say, demons themselves likely played a pivotal role in the formation of the "revelations" that Giorgio is, to this day, announcing to the world.

24. "By-Their-Fruits" Discernment: A Summary

Rotten Fruit Produced by Alien Belief (*Extremely partial summary of only the last several decades—see corresponding sections above for details.*)	**Good Fruit Produced by Alien Belief** (*Complete list of over 2,500 years' worth*)
Decades of sci-fi films & shows—all bearing either subtly or explicitly anti-Christian messages—have been inspired by ET belief.	
Hundreds of thousands, if not millions, of "alien abductees" since 1947 have failed to seek spiritual deliverance—thinking their demonic afflictions to actually be true ET encounters—thus they have gone about their lives in bondage to the Devil.	
"Heaven's Gate:" The largest mass suicide in U.S. history was undertaken in order to "meet the ETs." Countless other "UFO Religions" (cults) have flourished in the last 75 years—e.g. Raëlianism, Aetherius Society, etc.—all of which either commit or advocate for grave evils or teach express heresies and blasphemies.	
Untold millions, or hundreds of millions, have been sucked into the "UFO rabbit hole," having their families, careers, and individual well-being destroyed by their deceived obsession with "uncovering the truth about ETs."	
Even the most prominent of the modern Ufologists promote fundamentally Godless ideologies; many seek to re-interpret the Bible's miracles as UFOs, Jesus as an ET, Apparitions as aliens, etc. Others (e.g., Greer) provide specific instructions for dialoguing with demons.	
The New Age movement itself, which has wreaked spiritual havoc upon hundreds of millions, was directly generated by ET belief.	
Certain heretical Christian movements now have tens of millions of adherents, remaining inspired or enabled by ET belief, e.g., Mormonism, Seventh Day Adventism.	
The Church of Scientology has deluded hundreds of thousands, for 70 years, with an ET-belief-inspired ideology.	
Heretical "Urantia Book revelations," based on ET belief, have deceived millions of Christians for the last 70 years and continue to heavily infiltrate Catholicism.	
False "Catholic" seers and mystics have flourished, deceiving millions, thanks to ET belief: "Friar" Elias & his "Divine Messengers," Giorgio Bongiovanni, Tomislav Vlasic, etc.	
Diabolical deception in the Church, based on ET belief, has flourished since the 1960s: Fr. Teilhard de Chardin's New Age cosmology, Fr. Richard Rohr's "Universal Christ" Stealth Apostasy, Msgr. Balducci's charlatanism, Vatican astronomers' advocating for "re-reading" the Faith and radically revising theology based on ETs, etc.	
This entire time, an exquisitely crafted plan to lay down the welcome mat for the Great Deception of the Antichrist has flourished—mostly unopposed—thanks to ET belief.	

The right-hand side column of the table above is intentionally left blank. No evidence of alien belief producing objective and enduring good fruits can be found anywhere. Instead, wherever and whenever it becomes a significant factor within a movement, a group, or an individual, it generates only thoroughly rotten fruit.

Moreover, that table only deals with phenomena of the last 75 years. We did not include within it the heresies of Origen and their legacy of destruction; the perverse doctrines of Virgil (who, thankfully, recanted), and of Fr. Zaninus de Solcia; the destructive legacy of Giordano Bruno and the enlightenment's heretical "Principle of Plenitude;" the various ET-crazes of the 19th Century which deluded entire swaths of the population (believing the lie that Martians were invading, or men on the moon were being watched by our telescopes); the occultist craze of the 1800s (which heavily infiltrated even the Catholic Church), largely motivated by ET belief; or of the ancient errors of Hinduism and Buddhism associated with ET Belief.

Therefore, leaving aside the multitude of *direct* reasons to reject belief in aliens, we are still confronted with a strikingly determinate conclusion when only considering the fruits that this belief has generated in the Church (and the world), particularly for the last century. This conclusion is simple: alien belief must be dismissed without hesitation, qualification, or compromise; just as we rightly dismiss any other supposed development in the Church which has produced only rotten fruit—e.g., Marxist Theology, Freemasonry, Jansenism, Darwinism, Gender Theory, and on the list goes—no matter how popular it has become among the ranks of the clergy or laity, and no matter how many supposedly respectable names have endorsed it.

Suppose, therefore, that we are dealing with a certain Christian who has been deeply traumatized by repeated castigations from ET promoters, telling him that disbelieving in aliens is tantamount to an "arrogant limitation of God." Suppose he has been so very gaslit that he is psychologically blinded to the theological, philosophical, logical, and scientific proofs, presented in Parts One through Three of this book, demonstrating that aliens do not exist. Such a Christian should nevertheless, solely on account of the very fruits-based discernment to which Jesus exhorts us, categorically reject any suggestion that we should ever be open to any manner of contact or communication with "extraterrestrials." The fruits have rendered the verdict clear a thousand times over: these phenomena are uniquely dangerous and destructive. If the Devil has ever, in the whole history of the world, made his *pervasive* presence clear in *defining* a movement, then that movement is the one which anticipates (or proposes to engage in) contact with "aliens."

With ET Belief, There is No Risk of "Throwing Out the Baby with the Bathwater"

Every genuine development in the history of the Church—not excluding the most important ones clearly willed by God—can count its share of bad apples which risk tainting the entire movement. For example, even the most highly approved and manifestly supernatural Marian Apparitions have followers who twist the messages and use them to support their own erroneous agendas. One need look no further than the most well-known modern apparition: Our Lady of Fatima.

The Catholic ET promoters are, therefore, sure to attempt to write off—as "merely inevitable"—all the rotten fruits discussed above. (*Which, themselves, scarcely scratch the surface of the movement's diabolical nature—a substantial overview would require not a section of a book, but a library filled with books dedicated only to that aim.*) Such a dismissal would be remarkably short sighted; symptomatic of an *a priori* disposition to defend a thoroughly ideological position.

In the case of alien belief, we are not dealing with anything resembling a "mixed bag," from which the rotten fruit can be carefully picked out and discarded. First, we are not dealing with a proverbial "bag" at all, but rather a veritable landfill. It is not simply peppered with rotten fruit; it *consists* entirely of rotten fruit. Second, we do not have any content to consider on the opposing side. Whoever would argue that ET belief can be defended against the continuous avalanche of rotten fruit it has produced—by deferring to good fruits it has supposedly produced—is free to present his findings (no one has). Such a person should be asked several questions:

- Where are the pious Rosary groups praying for our ET visitors?
- Where is the wave of conversions of sinners who want to be found spiritually prepared for the contact with the aliens which they anticipate?
- Where are the charitable organizations replete with works of mercy, inspired by ET-belief, to prepare our planet for a meeting with the aliens? (After all, the "ET revelations" invariably advocate for things like peace, love, etc.)
- Where are the prayer apostolates dedicated to praying for the repose of the souls of the ETs in Purgatory? Or for God's Will to reign there (e.g. on Alpha Centauri)—not only "on earth" (Matthew 6:10) as it does in Heaven?
- Where are the priestly and religious vocations of souls who credit their calling to their desire to be among those who proclaim the Gospel to the extraterrestrials?
- Where are the new (and authentic) thriving religious orders inspired by alien belief?

- Where are souls streaming towards Catholicism thanks to the Vatican's sudden (diabolically deceived) openness to belief in extraterrestrials?

This list could be extended for many pages, but the answer to these questions and similar questions—*"Where are the good fruits?"*—is simple: *they are nowhere*. There are *no* good fruits to be found, *anywhere*, from belief in extraterrestrials in general, or, more specifically, from UFO sightings, or from attempts to dialogue with "ETs," or from the development of "new theologies" built upon ET-contact-expectation (innumerable such theologies have been generated, since the Enlightenment, by Catholic theologians) and the like.*

We can be certain that if extraterrestrials really existed—and, correspondingly, if these last 75 years of ET-related phenomena were actually God-sent preparations for the discovery of them or contact with them—we would see not only some good fruits, but a superabundance of such good fruits. These would be the heralds of the worlds' greatest transformation in 2,000 years. Indeed, in that case, we would be witnessing a development analogous to the prophets of the Old Testament increasing the vigor of their testimony to the arrival of the Messiah, the closer the time drew to 0 A.D.

ET-belief-promoting films would be making their viewers better Christians; ET-inspired "revelations" would sanctify their devotees; Ufologists would display the virtues of saints; ET-based "new theologies" in the Church would generate a tsunami of converts; and on the list goes. Instead, we see only the *exact* opposite—in *every* case.

Today's Catholic ET promoters, however, are bound to respond to this point by dredging the depths of the various textbooks detailing the history of Ufology, arduously searching for *something* positive. They are likely to come up with a few apparent good fruits, and they are equally likely to claim (with transparent motives) that their own lives have benefited from their belief in aliens. Even when this predictable undertaking

---

* In researching this book, I spent almost three years scouring many, many thousands of pages of material related to ET-belief in general—from every angle and from every source one can imagine. In order to ensure I was not spending my effort in an echo chamber, the vast majority of that time was spent reading not material that agrees with my thesis, but rather material that is openly advocating for belief in ETs. What I have seen from all this effort is simple: many decades of ET-related phenomena in modern culture, wherever it rears its head, has failed to produce even one enduring and truly good fruit. Moreover, I have over that same time period received correspondence from hundreds of individuals with testimonies of ET-belief, Ufology, and UFO sightings: every single one of them either reported negative fruits from these phenomena, or displayed them (i.e., by expressing great wrath at me for saying aliens do not exist—the type of wrath one would expect from a Pagan told his "gods" are not gods at all, or from a Muslim who is told that Muhammad is not a prophet.) This matter does not present even the slightest difficulty for the faithful who are engaging—as they must—in a fruits-based discernment process of the whole ET phenomenon.

transpires, a discerning soul will compare their presentations to the mountain of horrendously—and, often, baldly demonically—rotten fruits that ET belief has been generating for the last 75 years since Roswell in 1947. Once that era had sufficient time to reveal its own fruits—especially with the various UFO cults of the latter half of the 20th century—no honest and diligent Christian student of the phenomenon could fail to detect the exceedingly dark and pervasive undercurrent, and no such student could, therefore, fail to recognize that the phenomenon must be rejected.

A final question we should consider in this respect is this: *would God allow "alien-truth" to permeate manifestly false private "revelations" but entirely escape all authentic private revelations?*

A Catholic ET promoter would have us believe that aliens exist—the knowledge of which would be the single biggest existentially-earth-shattering revelation since Jesus Himself—and that God has thus far allowed the revelation of their existence to make its way into countless patently fraudulent revelations (even deeply diabolical ones) but not into a single authentic revelation. Is this even possible, much less palatable?

Pride Comes Before the Fall: Answering, "But I Won't Go *That* Far!"

Considering the extreme degree of darkness and evil we have now seen pervading Ufology and the entire alien belief craze, I suspect that even those Christians who have hitherto believed in aliens and have read thus far are becoming somewhat concerned. Assuredly, they should be. Those among them, however, who remain insistent on preserving their alien belief will doubtless contend that, though *other* alien believers may have sunk incredibly low (spiritually, theologically, and morally), *they* are different—*they* will stop before arriving at such sorry fates.

To such Christians, a simple question must be posed: *How?* How will you know when to stop?

"I won't go *that* far" is exactly what all who first tread upon dark paths say when they observe others who have already there long walked. He who begins "doing drugs only on occasion; only in those social circumstances where it is necessary," of course, "would never be like one of those addicts you see *in the mugshots*." Until he becomes precisely that. He who violates chastity "only in minor ways" would, of course, "never become a full-blown adulterer"; until that is exactly the fate to which he has succumbed. He who dismisses "only a *few* Church teachings" would, of course, "never become an apostate"—until circumstances render the allure of that very state irresistible, since the door to it was left ajar instead of being latched firmly shut.

Ufology is an extremely seductive movement—it is among the most slippery of slopes one can find. From decades of experience, huge amounts of monetary investment, and a steady flow of the most charismatic charlatans promoting it, the movement knows exactly how to present its first "only curious" followers with step, after step, after step, of increasingly dark promises. It is the same strategy employed by the "LGBT" activists. They begin by "innocently" encouraging one to "question and analyze his sexuality." They conclude by seducing him into leaving his wife and having his genitalia surgically removed.

With ET-belief and expectation, first it is curiosity. Then it is fascination. Then it becomes excitement at "imminent disclosures." Then it becomes rage against the "cover ups." Afterwards, it presents opportunities to "circumvent the system," and engage in pseudo-spiritual contact with the ETs. Once contact is made and the Devil has his foot in the door, it is a downward spiral. These exceedingly spiritually dangerous antics we have explored in the preceding sections do not come replete with signposts warning that all manner of sin, error, heresy, apostasy, and blasphemy lie ahead.

What is going to stop you—like, for example, the devoted followers of Dr. Greer—from seeking telepathic relationships with the aliens? If you believe in ETs and are open to the possibility of contacting them, then *you are not equipped to reject this.* Greer, and those like him, are usually very careful to avoid even touching upon topics that would risk causing them to engage in something an ordinary Christian would notice as explicit heresy, since they do not want to lose their large customer base of Christian followers. Instead, your only defense is to simply not even begin walking down that path; to outright reject belief in the existence of aliens.

What else will stop you? If you believe aliens *might* exist, then you are only waiting for the right circumstances to believe they *do* exist, and then still others to convince you that you should seek them out. You have nothing to prevent you from entertaining elaborate theories akin to Greer's; nothing to stop you from thinking to yourself, "*Well, who knows; God could have made aliens. And if He did, maybe they are so scientifically advanced that their technological abilities resemble what I, in my little knowledge, would be inclined to regard as angelic. So why not reach out to them just like I now reach out, in prayer, to my Guardian Angel, or St. Michael, etc.? Why not?!*"

The answer, then, to "*how will you know when to stop?*" is simple: *you won't.* Those who find themselves in the death grip of addiction, promiscuity, corruption, double lives, and the like, always confess that they wish someone had approached them, at the very onset of their dabbling with these evils, and sternly cautioned them to proceed no further.

Let this book serve as that warning for you.

25. Discerning Deceptions

"... there is a general disregard and forgetfulness of the supernatural, a gradual falling away from the strict standard of Christian virtue...men are slipping back more and more into the shameful practices of paganism."
—Pope Benedict XV.
Humani Generis Redemptionem §2

In the preceding chapters, we have seen the thoroughly demonic origin and rotten fruits of what has transpired within the realm of ET belief, contact, or expectation (aside, of course, from those "debunkable" UFOs which are merely misunderstood ordinary phenomena, government tests, etc.). This analysis, however, may leave a reader wondering: *even if I know about what has transpired in the past, what about those thing which may transpire in the future – how can I be equipped to discern those phenomena?* The present chapter exists to present some criteria for doing so.

Let us first consider what we know from both Scripture and Sacred Tradition, and what these sure norms relay regarding what the Devil is fully capable of, lest we underestimate his abilities and poise ourselves to succumb to his snares.

The "Demons of the Air" Who "Walk About in Darkness": Christianity's Perennial Warning Against UFOs

> "And you he made alive, when you were dead through the trespasses and sins in which you once walked, following the course of this world, following **the prince of the power of the air**, the spirit that is now at work in the sons of disobedience."
> —Ephesians 2:1-2
>
> "**The demons inhabit the air**" —St. Augustine
>
> "[A demon] can from the air form a body of any form and shape."
> —St. Thomas Aquinas

As we see above, Scripture has made it clear that "the air" – the atmosphere in general – is a particularly potent domain of the demons. Nor did the saints gloss over this important element of God's Word. Obviously, this does not mean that every uncertain object in the air is demonic, but it does mean we should be particularly cautious of any entity that displays a proclivity of aerial phenomena and a concomitant hesitancy to interact with humans in the ordinary "ground level" – literally, *down to earth* –

manner. Of perhaps hundreds of millions of reports of UFO sightings and "alien encounters," almost all of them transpire through "objects" darting through the atmosphere, or descending from it, and most occur under the cover of darkness.

> "This is the verdict: Light has come into the world, but people loved darkness instead of light because their deeds were evil." —John 3:19
> "**The 'gods' know nothing, they understand nothing. They walk about in darkness**; all the foundations of the earth are shaken." —Psalm 82:5
> "Take no part in the unfruitful works of darkness, but instead expose them." —Ephesians 5:11

Not only do the UFOs and "ETs" love darkness, but a deeply disconcerting proportion of their antics are witnessed around 3:00am, the inversion of the moment of Christ's death on the Cross, which is a well-known preferred time for demons. Even the legends from worldly sources speak much of the so-called "devil's hours," from 3:00am to 4:00am, wherein diabolical forces are thought to be most potent. This is not inaccurate.

Jacques Vallée compiled a large database of well-documented UFO sightings and other "close encounters with ETs." He found a massive increase in such reports once darkness descends at nightfall, tapering off as people go to sleep around 10:00pm. Then, suddenly, there is a large uptick in such reports at 3:00am, declining sharply at 4:00am.

Moreover, if these visits were actually from extraterrestrial visitors (or even so-called "interdimensional" ones), then these aliens would have no predisposition for remaining hovering around in their crafts to communicate with us. They would do the same thing any rational non-demon would do: land, walk out of the craft, and engage with us in a coherent manner as best they could. Instead, every "non debunkable" ET-related contact event can easily be seen to display this particular hallmark of the demonic (not to mention countless others).

> "The space between heaven and earth, the whole azure expanse of the air which is visible to us under the heavens, serves as the dwelling for the fallen angels who have been cast down from Heaven" —Eastern Orthodox Bishop Ignatius Brianchinov

St. John Chrysostom, who is both a Father and Doctor of the Church, explained what Scripture means, in Ephesians 2, by teaching that Satan is the "prince of the power of the air," saying:

> ... why does he call the Devil the prince of the world? Because nearly the whole human race has surrendered itself to him ...His kingdom then is in this world, and he has, with few exceptions, more subjects and more obedient subjects than God, in consequence of our indolence... "According to the power", says he, "of the air, of the spirit." (Ephesians 2:2). Here again he means, that **Satan occupies the space under Heaven, and that the incorporeal powers are spirits of the air, under**

> **his operation.** (Homily 4 on Ephesians)

Chrysostom was not alone in insisting upon the truth of this clear sense of Ephesians 2:2. Yet another Father and Doctor of the Church, St. Athanasius, commenting on the same passage, taught:

> ...the devil, the enemy of our race, having fallen from heaven, **wanders about our lower atmosphere**, and there bearing rule over his fellow-spirits, as his peers in disobedience, not only **works illusions by their means in them that are deceived**, but tries to hinder them that are going up (*On the Incarnation of the Word*. §25)

The great St. Athanasius does not merely insist that the atmosphere is the dwelling place of demons, but also cautions that these demons work *illusions* and deceptions therein. Assuredly, "extraterrestrials" are only the most recent—and the most apocalyptic—of these deceptions the demons have always wrought in the air.

Still another Father of the Church provided the same teaching. Saint John Cassian even taught that the only reason God usually hides these aerial demons from our sight is that beholding them would be an "unbearable dread." He taught:

> **This air which is spread out between heaven and earth is so thick with spirits**, which do not fly about in it quietly and aimlessly, that divine providence has quite beneficially withdrawn them from human sight. For human beings, utterly unable to **gaze upon these things with fleshly eyes, would be overwhelmed by an unbearable dread and faint away because of their frightening confluence and the horrible expressions that they can take upon themselves and assume at will**... We certainly do not doubt that the ranks which the Apostle enumerates also refer to them, because 'our struggle is not against flesh and blood but against principalities, against powers, against the world rulers of this darkness, against spirits of evil in heavenly places' (Eph. 6:12)." (VIII. Second Conference on the Principalities. XII.)

In his greatest work—*City of God*—St. Augustine prophetically described contemporary UFO phenomena:

> On the contrary, **we must believe them to be spirits most eager to inflict harm,** utterly alien from righteousness, swollen with pride, pale with envy, subtle in deceit; **who dwell indeed in this air as in a prison**, in keeping with their own character, because, cast down from the height of the higher heaven, they have been condemned to dwell in this element as the just reward of irretrievable transgression... Over many, however, who are manifestly unworthy of participation in the true religion, **they tyrannize as over captives whom they have subdued—the greatest part of whom they have persuaded of their divinity by wonderful and lying signs** ... Some, nevertheless, who have more attentively and diligently considered their vices, they have not been able to persuade that they are gods, and **so have feigned themselves to be**

messengers between the gods and men. (Book 8. Chapter 22.)

St. Augustine's warning in the final line above is reminiscent of Jacques Vallée and those who hold his thesis. Those who promote this brand of Ufology "could not be persuaded" that the demons masquerading as UFOs were "traditional ETs," but they only succumb to another deception. One could say they treat these "interdimensional UFOs" as "messengers between the gods and men," as this bears an uncanny resemblance to Vallée's insistence that UFOs are "control mechanisms to oversee human evolution." There as in St. Augustine's day, the demons have simply replaced one deception with an even more destructive lie.

Neither Scripture nor Sacred Tradition have left any doubt about how a Christian must approach these supposedly spectacular "UFOs" descending upon us from the skies. They are diabolical deceptions, and God has not failed to warn us about their arrival.

> "The gods, taking the disguise of strangers from other lands, walk up and down cities in all sorts of forms ... by witchcraft and deception they may make us think that they appear in various forms..." -Plato

The Saints on the Forms the Demons Can Assume

To consider what the Devil and his legions are capable of, when it comes to assuming various forms to deceive us, let us begin with the saint who is most famous for his battles against these demons: St. Anthony the Great (251-356 A.D.). None other than the great St. Athanasius (who, as we have seen in a preceding chapter, warned against the illusions the Devil works in the atmosphere) wrote a biography of this saint, who is also known as "Anthony of Egypt," and the "Father of All Monks." Selections from that biography, from which all of the following quotations derive,[342] will prove helpful for our present task.

> 'The demons ... [approach in] guise, and thenceforth shaping displays **they attempt to strike fear, changing their shapes**, taking the forms of women, wild beasts, creeping things, **gigantic bodies,** and troops of soldiers. ...**[they] pretend to prophesy and foretell the future, and to show themselves of a height reaching to the roof and of great breadth**; that they may stealthily catch by such displays those who could not be deceived by their arguments...

From the beginning of Sacred Tradition's development, therefore, we see the greatest of saints assuring us that it is not difficult for the demons to appear as "gigantic bodies" of "great breadth"—like "UFOs." The Devil does not know the future, but he can observe what is transpiring and guess at it much more effectively than the best of human analysts, therefore he will often use this great intelligence to deceive and give the impression of himself being Divine. The future, however, never actually plays out exactly as he says. We see this pattern repeated often in "alien encounters." St. Anthony (as relayed by St. Athanasius) continues:

> **[The demons] are treacherous, and are ready to change themselves into all forms and assume all appearances. Very often also without appearing they imitate the music of harp and voice**, and recall the words of Scripture. Sometimes, too, while we are reading they immediately repeat many times, like an echo, what is read. ... they assume the appearance of monks and feign the speech of holy men, that by their similarity they may deceive and thus drag their victims where they will... For the demons do all things—**they prate, they confuse, they dissemble, they confound—to deceive the simple. They din, laugh madly, and whistle...**

Certain feats (which we will enumerate shortly) are indeed beyond the power of the demons; but, as we see here, it is not difficult for them to appear in virtually any form. In these appearances, they make use of certain melodies frequently, and their goal is always to "confuse, dissemble, and confound" in order to "deceive the simple." This is a summary of modern UFO phenomena. Relaying another battle with the demons, St. Anthony said:

> Once they came threatening and surrounded me like soldiers in full armour. At another time they filled the house with horses, wild beasts and creeping things...**Once they came in darkness, bearing the appearance of a light, and said, We have come to give you a light, Antony**. But I closed my eyes and prayed, and immediately the light of the wicked ones was quenched. ... Once they shook the cell with an earthquake, but I continued praying with unshaken heart...**Once a demon exceedingly high appeared with pomp, and dared to say, I am the power of God and I am Providence, what do you wish that I shall give you? ...[but he] disappeared at the name of Christ...** How often in the desert has he displayed what resembled gold, that I should only touch it and look on it. But I sang psalms against him, and he vanished away. Often they would beat me with stripes, and I repeated again and again, *Nothing shall separate me from the love of Christ* (Romans 8:35), and at this they rather fell to beating one another.

A favorite appearance of the demons is to arrive clothed in light. This tendency they display is not only warned against by the saints, but by Scripture itself: "**Satan disguises himself as an angel of light.**" (2 Corinthians 11:14) UFOs and "ETs" constantly appear thus clothed, duping un-discerning souls into supposing this appearance must be positive.

We can easily see, therefore, how diabolically misled are those Christian ET promoters, like Msgr. Balducci, who insist that UFOs "cannot" be demons, and should be welcomed as heralds of the arrival of the aliens because "demons don't need spaceships." It is easy for a demon to assume the appearance of a "UFO." What is much more difficult for them to do, however, "just so happens" to be providing that type of evidence we entirely lack for such alleged ET-contact: *physical* evidence. As discussed in Part Three, Ufologists incessantly insist that such evidence is everywhere, yet it is never openly presented for public scrutiny. If anything was ever telling, it is this: *millions* of accounts of UFOs and ETs of such a nature that would be indisputably easy for a demon to produce, and *no* solid evidence of an artifact that would be difficult for them to leave behind.

St. Anthony's descriptions of the demons, most importantly, are replete with assurances that we need not fear them so long as we know to respond to their appearance with pious prayer, invoking the power of Our Lord Jesus Christ. As we discussed previously, "UFOs" and "aliens" are constantly known to immediately flee at the mere pronouncement of the name of Jesus. As St. Anthony says:

> But **the demons, as they have no power, are like actors on the stage changing their shape and frightening children with tumultuous apparition and various forms**: from which they ought rather to be despised as showing their weakness. At least the true angel of the Lord sent against the Assyrian had no need for tumults nor displays from without, nor noises nor rattlings, but in quiet he used his power and immediately destroyed a hundred and eighty-five thousand. **But demons like these, who have no power, try to terrify at least by their displays** (2 Kings 19:35) ... **hear them not, and have no dealings with them; but rather sign yourselves and your houses, and pray, and you shall see them vanish.**

A devout Christian who trusts in the Divine Mercy must have no fear of the demons appearing as aliens or UFOs. I have written this book not to strike fear in the hearts of such people, but only to instruct those who would otherwise remain beguiled to understand what we are dealing with in the present Great Deception. Assuredly, the demons have no power...*except that power we give them by believing in their false appearances.*

It is precisely the prevailing attitude today—openness to "contact with the extraterrestrials"—that enables the demons to act so powerfully. For if only Christians knew to—at the first instant of any UFO or "ET" encounter—bid the thing to depart in the name of Jesus, there would be nothing to fear. But that reflex itself can only be developed by one who rejects ET belief.

***

Lest anyone suppose that St. Anthony was the exception—and that the saints after him did not believe that the demons had the ability to assume various deceptive appearances—we should review a small selection (from an enormous reservoir) of their teachings. One Catholic expert on mystical phenomena wrote the following, summarizing the experiences of various saints and mystics:

> ...**Satan and perhaps a good number of the higher-ranking demons can appear in most any form imaginable—commonly called "phantasms**" ...black human-shaped "shadow people" are ... quite common, [as] are demons in "raw" form. ... Some of the **Saints describe being watched by a pair of fiery-red glowing "burning" demonic eyes**... In the life of Blessed Alexandrina da Costa (1904-1955) —a Portuguese mystic and stigmatic ...we read another occurrence of the devil making himself out to be Jesus. In this case Blessed Alexandrina writes: "*Every now and then I see a rapid light. Twice I have seen two very big eyes, wide open, staring at me, but they disappeared quickly.*" ...In his biography on Saint Gemma, Father Germanus writes: "*With a view to protect her from these Satanic attacks and apparitions, I enjoined on her, under whatever form the persons of the other world might appear to her, to at once repeat the words "Viva Gesu!"* ["Long live Jesus"]. ... The good spirits always repeated her words, whereas the malignant ones either did not reply, or else pronounced only a few words, such as "Viva" or "Benedetto", without adding any name. By this means Gemma recognized them and scorned them accordingly. " ...Marie-Julie also had to contend with the devil and his wiles from the time she first received the stigmata. ... he would try other manifestations, appearing as a frightening beast, animals, or in his usual hideous shape ... When terror tactics failed, he changed strategy and would come as a tempting beautiful young man promising her everything from wealth to cures for her maladies, but without success. ... Marie-Julie was extremely cautious about every apparition, testing them all to ensure they were from Heaven and thereby exposing the Hellish imposter by prudence when he did appear in this guileful manner. If a mystical visitor complied and made on Act of Love to the Sacred Heart, she knew the apparition was true. When it was Satan, he would suddenly fly off when she demanded this request. Sometimes she could easily see through the disguise: if the demon appeared as a saint the halo would be missing its glorious rays of light, or the symbol of the cross would not be depicted correctly on his clothes or vestments, appearing bent or twisted...[343]

Several pertinent observations arise immediately from the experiences of the saints. First, we see a reiteration of what St. Anthony taught: often, the demons indisputably *can* appear however they please. It will be of no use to protest that "*these are the battles of saints; the demons would not appear deceptively to others.*" I am only drawing from the writings of holy mystics because their accounts are reliable, not because they are the only ones thus treated by demons. There are mountains of testimonies from great sinners, lukewarm Christians, great saints, and everyone in between, describing similar content. One, moreover, who would protest that "*these things would not happen on such a great scale as UFO encounters*" is using circular reasoning—he is presupposing his conclusion within his premise by *assuming* that the days we are now living in cannot be the Great Deception prophesied by Scripture, wherein we know that Satan will work many deceptive "signs and wonders." He is also ignoring that the demons have deceived entire cultures many times before in the various Pagan "gods" that we know are only demons (cf. Psalm 95:5). And he is forgetting, perhaps because his head is buried deeply in sand, that society has again become Pagan.

Also noteworthy is the attention the saints have drawn to the *eyes* of the demonic apparitions. This is exactly what most abductees and other ET-contactees describe—a fixation upon the being's "eyes." Finally, and perhaps most importantly, we are reminded of the means for testing such phenomena: immediately invoking the power of Jesus Christ. The demons will not explicitly praise Him by name in accordance with the truth of His Divinity and Incarnation. Likewise, an "ET" commanded to do that will always argue, change the topic, respond furtively, fly into a rage, or flee.

Jesus' Proof of His Incarnation vs. ET and UFO "Proofs"

Since the Resurrection of Jesus Christ was and is such an earth-shattering revelation, God decreed that demonstrating its *physical* reality demanded that certain measures be taken. It was not only fitting, but also *necessary,* that any explanation which would treat Christ's Resurrection as a mere apparition of some sort be definitively ruled out. Now, if ETs existed, this too would be earth shattering; not so much as Christ's resurrection, but perhaps second only to that in the world's history. Accordingly, God's Providence would surely arrange events such that His faithful would not be left scratching their heads, wondering whether they were only dealing with a demonic phenomenon.

Instead, every reliable testimony we have in relation to non-debunkable UFOs and ETs is not only easy to understand in relation to the activity of demons, but also bears express hallmarks of the demonic. Therefore, we should contrast the "evidence" presented for ETs to the evidence Christ gave of His Resurrection.

- He came to Mary Magdalene, who initially suspected He was merely a gardener. From the onset, therefore, we see His truly physical nature made manifest. Once He says Mary's name, she recognizes Him, and flings herself upon Him to *physically* cling to Him. (John 20:11-19)
- He came to two disciples on the Road to Emmaus; walking shoulder to shoulder with them for miles and conversing with them as any incarnate being would. He even went to stay with them at their home and *He ate with them.* (Luke 24:13-32)
- He came to the Apostles (without Thomas present), and "**showed them,**" in very close proximity, the nail marks on His hands and the lance mark in His side (John 20:19-20). Then, He—very physically—"**breathed on them**" (John 20:22). Thomas, arriving later, insisted on

even more absolute proof—saying he must "put [his] finger where the nails were" (John 20:24), otherwise he would not believe.

- Jesus obliges Thomas' request one week later; He "came and stood among them" (John 20:26), and gave the famous instruction to Thomas to put his finger into His hands and side, at which point Thomas proclaims his absolute Faith (John 20:28).
- Later still, Jesus came to a group of the Apostles while they were fishing, prepared a fire of burning coals with bread and fish cooking, and ate with them. (John 21:1-14) After breakfast, He had a long conversation with Peter (v. 15-22).
- At one point, Jesus even came to a group of five hundred Christians gathered together (cf. 1 Corinthians 15:6).
- Scripture relays that, "He presented himself to them and **gave many convincing proofs** that he was alive...On one occasion, while he was eating with them, he gave them this command..." (Acts 1:3-4)
- He ascended into Heaven within the clear sight of many of His disciples, during the daytime (cf. Acts 1, Mark 16, Luke 24).
- He left an abundance of physical evidence so that even those who never saw Him, after His Resurrection, could still be certain of its authenticity: the empty tomb wherein everyone knew that Jesus—dead beyond the slightest shred of doubt—had been buried for days. The Shroud of Turin—which, to this day, can be visited—is yet another proof of the physical reality of the Resurrection.

From these proofs (and countless others not recorded in Scripture—*"But there are also many other things that Jesus did; if every one of them were written down, I suppose that the world itself could not contain the books that would be written."* —John 21:25), Jesus made it absolutely clear that His Resurrection was a *physical* reality, not merely a spiritual phenomenon.

An ET promoter may protest that Thomas' doubt was rebuked by Jesus, and therefore should not serve as a model for us when it comes to aliens. But this is a foolish lesson to take from the Gospel. Believing in God, and the works of God, without needing to see physical evidence is indeed a great virtue. On the other hand, credulousness in relation to the claims of men when they assert things contrary to the Faith (see Parts One and Two of this book)—or at least, as even a Catholic ET promoter must concede, in serious tension with it—is a great vice. *"I want to believe!"* may well be the mantra of the contemporary ET movement, but the type of "belief" for which they advocate is devoid of all virtue—and replete with innumerable evils, a small selection of which we have reviewed in the preceding chapters.

The Limits of the Demons' Power, Quietism, and the Prophecy of Pope Innocent XI

> "It is more necessary to use all our powers of discrimination and judgment when Satan transforms himself into an angel of light, lest by his wiles he should lead us astray into hurtful courses."
> —St. Augustine. *Enchiridion.* Ch. 60

Among the most important truths for all Christians to remember is also the simplest: nothing but God's Will can happen. Therefore, under no circumstances is anything called for but total trust in His Will. As St. Alphonsus Liguori said, "**It is certain and of faith that, whatever happens, happens by the Will of God**."[344] Even the *Didache*—among the most fundamental Christian texts outside of the Bible—exhorts us, "The workings that befall you receive as good, knowing **that apart from God nothing comes to pass**." In sum: no purpose of God's can be thwarted (cf. Job 42:2). This truth of the Faith is not in the least put into question by any of the machinations of demons. They are bound by God's Will, and everything they do is possible only because God's permissive Will has allowed it for the sake of some greater good.

Should we, then, simply dismiss concerns about diabolical deceptions? *Of course not.* Such a response to God's Omnipotence and Goodness is nothing other than the heresy of Quietism. The mere fact that God's Will always triumphs does not give us license to simply sit back and passively wait for that to happen. We are called to actively participate in His triumph, and an important avenue of that participation is opposing diabolical influences whenever and wherever they rear their heads—for we must "expose the works of darkness." (Ephesians 5:11)

It is truly remarkable that some Catholic ET promoters, including those who have written extensively about spiritual warfare or are even exorcists (e.g. Msgr. Balducci), nevertheless choose to be Quietistically oblivious when it comes to ET and UFO deceptions. They categorically rule out the very possibility of such deception, "*since the demons are bound by God's Will anyway*," when in fact Scripture specifically foretells that precisely such a thing will happen.

> **Let no one deceive you in any way ...** the rebellion comes first, and the man of lawlessness is revealed, the son of perdition ... The coming of the lawless one by **the activity of Satan will be with all power and with pretended signs and wonders, and with all wicked deception** for those who are to perish, because they refused to love the truth and so be saved. **Therefore God sends upon them a strong delusion, to make them believe what is false**, so that all may be condemned who did not believe the truth but had pleasure in unrighteousness. (2 Thessalonians 2:3, 9-12)

Obviously, diabolical deceptions have permeated history and will do so in a superlative way in the times prophesied above by Scripture. We will discuss those times more specifically in a later chapter; for now, it suffices to observe that deceptions from demons are very real, and Christians must recognize their prevalence and fight against them. The entire testimony of Scripture, Magisterium, Sacred Tradition, the teachings of the Saints, the content of authentic private revelations, etc., is unanimous in insisting that Christians must fight evil, error, deception, and the like, wherever they arise; not ignore them on the basis of all such things ultimately remaining answerable to God's Will.

The heresy of Quietism merits more attention here. Fr. John Hardon's *Catholic Dictionary* defines Quietism as the "*view of spiritual life that minimizes human activity and moral responsibility.*" When applied to potential diabolical deceptions, this heresy compels one to dismiss any concern about recognizing and opposing them. In the year 1687, Pope Innocent XI promulgated the encyclical *Coelestis Pastor*, which—in consideration of what today's Catholic ET promoters suggest—has proven prophetic. Therein, he condemns a total of forty-three propositions, including the teaching that "no consideration of temptations need any longer be of concern"(§17) and that God "permits **and** wishes" (i.e., not only in His *permissive* Will, but also in His *ordained* Will) that the demons do certain evil deeds and induce the faithful to commit certain evil acts (cf. §41). Especially relevant here, however, is the final condemnation the Pope lists, with which he also concludes the encyclical. Innocent XI anathematized the following teaching:

> **God in past ages has created saints through the ministry of tyrants; now in truth he produces saints through the ministry of demons,** who, by causing the aforesaid things contrary to the will, bring it about that they despise themselves the more and annihilate and resign themselves to God. (§43)

In other words, it is a heresy to teach that God *affirmatively and directly* wills the operations of demons in order to cause the sanctification of souls. Indeed, His *permissive* Will can allow this, but that apparently subtle distinction has enormous ramifications. For we must never oppose God's ordained Will—those things He affirmatively wants—whereas we must always oppose deception of all sorts, even if God is permitting them to flourish for some, ultimately good, aim.

When God allows an evil for the sake of good, He is not asking for His faithful to lend their aid in that process, nor is He asking them to remain indifferent to its development.

> "Finally, be strong in the Lord and in his mighty power. Put on the full armor of God, so that you can take your stand against the devil's schemes." —Ephesians 6:10-11 "Resist the Devil, and he will flee from you." James 4:7 "If we do not oppose evil, we fuel it in a tacit way. It is

necessary to intervene where evil is being spread because evil spreads where there is a lack of daring Christians who oppose it..." —Pope Francis "Following in his footsteps and united to [Christ], we must all strive to oppose evil..." —Pope Benedict XVI

Now, Christian ET promoters, of course, do not admit that "aliens" are, indeed, demons. But even they—in their more honest moments—concede that this is a possibility. Yet they tranquilize themselves against taking that possibility seriously and acting prudently in accordance with it by assuring themselves that, since the activity of demons is ultimately restrained by God, they needn't worry about major diabolical deceptions. This position is nothing other than a corollary to those propositions formally condemned as heretical under the banner of Quietism.

What, however, truly is beyond the power of demons? One noteworthy pragmatic limitation on their power is that they are generally not allowed to kill, but only at most wound, those they torment. Likewise with "ET Contact," there are many accounts of wounded "abductees," but no convincing claims that the "aliens" are killing people (they do, however, often have leeway to kill animals—reminiscent of the killing of cattle often chalked up to aliens). Let us, however, consider more absolute limitations on demonic power by drawing from the teachings of exorcist Fr. Chad Ripperger in his book, *Dominion*.

> **Demons cannot function outside of angelic nature, and so they are limited, such as they cannot perform miracles and things of this sort.** The specific angelic nature [i.e., which individual demon one is dealing with] itself will give some determination or limitation as to what a demon can and cannot do. Specific demons will behave certain ways and not others. (P. 97)

In a footnote, however, Fr. Ripperger observes:

> **The fact that demons cannot perform miracles does not mean that they cannot fool men who are not sufficiently versed in what is required for a true miracle,** or people who do not have sufficient grace to discern the circumstances surrounding the preternatural occurrence. (Ibid)

St. Thomas Aquinas also summarizes the abilities and limits of demons in the *Summa Theologica* (Part I, Q114, A4):

> ...if we take a *miracle* in the strict sense, the demons cannot work miracles, nor can any creature, but God alone ... But sometimes *miracle* may be taken in a wide sense, for whatever exceeds the human power and experience. **And thus demons can work miracles, that is, things which rouse man's astonishment,** by reason of their being beyond his power and outside his sphere of knowledge. ...It is to be noted, however, that **although these works of demons which appear marvelous to us are not real miracles, they are sometimes nevertheless something real**. Thus the magicians of Pharaoh by the demons' power produced real

> serpents and frogs ... As Augustine says in the same place, **the works of Antichrist may be called lying wonders,** ***"either because he will deceive men's senses by means of phantoms, so that he will not really do what he will seem to do; or because, if he work real prodigies, they will lead those into falsehood who believe in him."*** ... those transformations which cannot be produced by the power of nature, cannot in reality be effected by the operation of the demons; for instance, that the human body be changed into the body of a beast, or that the body of a dead man return to life. And if at times something of this sort seems to be effected by the operation of demons, it is not real but a mere semblance of reality. Now this may happen in two ways. Firstly, from within; in this way a demon can work on man's imagination and even on his corporeal senses, so that something seems otherwise that it is... Secondly, from without: for just as he can from the air form a body of any form and shape, and assume it so as to appear in it visibly: so, **in the same way he can clothe any corporeal thing with any corporeal form, so as to appear therein** ... As Augustine says: *"When magicians do what holy men do, they do it for a different end and by a different right. The former do it for their own glory; the latter, for the glory of God: the former, by certain private compacts; the latter by the evident assistance and command of God, to Whom every creature is subject."*

Since demons can give the *appearance* of even true miracles, further considering their abilities is now called for.

The Means by Which Demonic Deceptions and Illusions Operate

> "Demons are essentially trying to establish an abusive relationship with us as human beings."—Fr. Chad Ripperger

Another scholar, considering the abilities of demons in relation to the Antichrist, noted:

> One point about Antichrist on which nearly all Protestants and all Catholics were in agreement was that his satanic wonders were not supernatural, but only superhuman. This is a particular application of a general and widely held principle about the limitation of diabolic powers ... The Devil cannot break the laws of nature, but **can only move things about with superhuman speed; trouble men's animal spirits** [Note: this is an archaic term that refers to the operations of the soul within the material body, but not the spiritual activity of the soul itself; i.e., intellect, memory, will], **thus producing illusions; and perhaps speed up natural processes. But he cannot create something out of nothing (such as manna), raise up the dead, or make the sun stand still**. ... Jesuit exegete Cornelius a Lapide comments on 2 Thessalonians 2:9: *"Neither Antichrist, nor the Devil, nor angels can do a true miracle, but only God. For a miracle is what is done above all power of nature, and what*

exceeds and transcends the powers of all natural causes and creatures. ***Antichrist therefore will not do true miracles but false and lying ones***." [345]

What, then, is a "true miracle" versus a "preternatural intervention," or a "diabolical illusion?" Here, it bears repeating that the demons can often give the illusion of having done what is, in truth, outside of their power (i.e., raising the dead). As the medieval code of Catholic Canon Law, the *Canon Episcopi*, taught:

> ...**as when [demons] force their way into corpses and are reputed to restore them to life for a short time, or having thrown them in some remote place, they exhibit somehow the image of the dead.** ... **Those who appeal to demons are capable of marvels**; like witches who having submitted to the power of evil spirits renounced the Catholic faith, and turned toward damnation by paying demons the basest homage of loyalty. **With God's permission, demons always take part in evil when appealed to; sometimes they appear in visible form, at other times they are invisible; they upset the atmosphere**, cause storms, hail and lightning, they ruin crops and ravage with their spells whatever is produced by the earth. They cause illness in man and beast, and use every skill to carry out whatever plan they can think of to ruin man.[346]

If demons can give the appearance of doing what is outside of their power, one may licitly ask: *how can we have any hope of ever distinguishing their illusions from reality?* The answer is that careful and lengthy discernment is necessary, therefore immediate appearances which have not been subject to this process—e.g., "UFO sightings" and other "ET" contact experiences—should not be trusted to accurately relay reality. This is one reason why demons so love to use the whole gamut of modern ET phenomena; usually they need only appear briefly, under the guise of a UFO or an alien, and a Godless media sensation will erupt overnight surrounding this appearance, thanks to contemporary culture's prevailing Pagan sci-fi mythology. The appearance is not only generally brief, but also often hidden under darkness, further facilitating their illusion. It is, in superlative convenience, never possible to subject it to the degree of analysis that would be necessary to determine what actually transpired.

Consider, for example, Eucharistic miracles. The Church will only approve, as authentically supernatural, such miracles if a rigorous study can be undertaken on remaining evidence in order to rule out any other possible explanations. If a group of people at a certain Mass claim they saw something extraordinary happen to the host during consecration—but no additional objective proofs can be found and nothing remains to be studied—that *may* well be a miracle from God. If the individuals who witnessed it have themselves discerned it carefully (for example, by finding the fruits it generates to be thoroughly good), then they should not remain incredulous. But they should not expect the Church to approve this, since other explanations are possible. The same is true of Marian apparitions.

The Church applies amazing amounts of scrutiny to these before approving them, in order to rule out the possibility of (among other things) demonic illusion and deception. On the other hand, no "ET encounter" has ever withstood even the smallest fraction of the same scrutiny the Church applies to alleged apparitions.

Further describing what the demons are capable of, Fr. Chad Ripperger continues:

> **Demons have in their nature the ability to change corporal bodies,** and therefore, the demons have power over our bodies. This flows from the fact that their will is not restricted just to their intellect but has the ability to act upon others, both spiritually (that is, other demons and angels, etc.) and physically. ... **they can influence any faculty which operates through a bodily organ: the senses, common sense power, memory, imagination, cogitative power, and the appetites in which we have emotions.** They can move the body and its bodily organs while awake or asleep ... **They can also give false clarity** by actually darkening the intellect but at the same time putting in the image sense data which gives the person the impression that he actually understands, when he does not. ... One phenomenon the exorcists will come across from time to time is demons actually having sex with people. **Since demons can act upon the body, God permitting, they can cause in the individual an experience similar to and even exceeding anything that any human being can cause**. When demons have sexual relations with a woman, they are called an incubus and when they have sexual relations with a man, they are called a succubus. ...**Despite all that the demons can do, they cannot act directly upon the will of humans because it is a spiritual faculty; they can only act upon the body**. Furthermore, demons **cannot put something new in the imagination which the person does not have, at least in part, in the memory**, such as causing a blind man to imagine color. Barring that, they can use all different parts of various sense data stored in our memory and combine them to produce whatever image or impression that God will permit.[347]

Although what is noted above is only intended as a general description of demonic capabilities, it also incidentally provides a veritable description of the last 75 years of "alien encounters." Particularly troubling is how many abductees describe sexual experiences that are clearly nothing other than the age-old demonic tactic of appearing as an "incubus" or "succubus."

The demons, we see, can provide a "false clarity" in the authenticity of the illusions they generate. This pseudo-clarity arises from a manipulation of emotion and a corresponding darkening of intellect. We see both endemic to the testimonies of "alien" contactees. Although filled with emotion, demanding to be taken seriously, and often shedding tears that are anything but holy, they are completely dismissive when asked to engage even the most basic logical considerations related to what they recount. For example, one who points out that what they "saw" would be physically impossible even for an alien, no matter what supposed technology is involved, is always promptly denounced. These "contactees" never convey the peace and conviction that a man would exude if he were simply giving sincere testimony to a genuine (and non-diabolical) phenomenon he experienced.

These emotions, however, do not always appear negative. Supposedly positive emotions reported in relation to "alien contact" experiences are also not difficult for the demons to arouse. If a simple chemical injected into one's veins can accomplish some effect, so can a demon. We must, therefore, not be fooled into supposing a demon, disguised as an alien, is a benevolent entity merely because some who experience contact with them report various sensations of elation or euphoria. Fr. Ripperger explains:

> **[Demons] can cause elation of the mind so that people believe what they suggest is true.** In other words, they can create in the mind a quality or state of mind in which the person experiences a kind of joy or pride within the intellect, almost like a euphoria. This is separate even from **the delight they can cause in the emotions,** since they can move the concupiscible appetite. Since both the irascible and the concupiscible appetite operate through a bodily organ, **demons can cause any emotion in human beings, both in kind and by varying degrees**. (P. 100)

Also noteworthy from the teaching quoted earlier is that the demons cannot entirely create (*ex-nihilo*) new memories or "visions" in the imagination of those they assault, but only rearrange what is already present. This explains why descriptions of aliens, UFOs, etc., often follow what is portrayed in movies and television—albeit with some differences, since demons can combine and modify those images already somehow present in one's imagination. This limitation, however, does not apply to another demonic ruse, one which we will address momentarily.

After describing how easy it is for the demons to create illusions directly in the individual's imaginative vision or by their acting upon the senses directly, Fr. Ripperger explains that this is not their only method. They can also create a sort of "real illusion" in the external world (which, naturally, would be observed by whoever or by whatever sensor is present). The "illusion" is an objective corporeal phenomenon, but constructed in such a way that it appears to be something it is not. Fr. Ripperger explains:

> **Another kind of [demonic] vision is that in which the actual vision occurs or appears to occur external to the individual** and this happens in three ways. **The first occurs insofar as the demons (and angels) assume a body** ...The next occurs in such a way that there is not a physical

> tangible thing outside the individual who is having the vision as when a body is assumed. This occurs **when the demons cause a change in the person's senses or in the medium between the thing and the sense of the individual** which is perceiving it. As to the change in the medium, each sense has a medium by which it receives the sensible species. Since this medium is something physical, God permitting, **the demons can change the characteristics of the sensible species [i.e., light or sound] as it passes through the medium [air]**. ... **This is commonly what is happening when morphing occurs ... which is beyond what is physiologically possible for the demon to cause due to his inability to suspend the natural laws, that is, to cause a miracle**. The same can also happen even to the sense of touch insofar as the demons can act upon the medium of touch, which in this particular case is the skin of the person sensing it, so that when it enters into the actual sense itself (which would be the nerve endings which transmit the sensible species) **the person senses something different than what is actually physiologically there**. The same can also be said for the sense of hearing in which the **demons can change the sound in the air** ...[348]

Therefore, the demons can manipulate both sound waves and light waves as they travel through the air to the observer—even if that "observer" is the sensor on a camera or other technological instrument. It would be quite easy, therefore, for a demon to manipulate the appearance of some natural object travelling through the air so that, when observed, it seems to be of a much greater size, or of a different shape or color, or moving in extraordinary ways; when, in fact, it is only—for example—a reflection or refraction, a man-made object, a bird, or even a nearby insect wrongly perceived as a distant ship.

More serious still, however, is the case where a demon actually "assumes a body" of some sort. Using this method, the most elaborate of "ET contact" experiences can be replicated diabolically. Explaining how an angel (or demon) can do this, Fr. Ripperger relays:

> ... [In Scripture,] angels actually assumed bodies and by that we mean that they act upon a body in such a way that they are the mover of the body...The assuming of the body, St. Thomas speculates, is done by the rarefaction of air in such a manner that "the angels assume bodies by condensing the air by divine power." In this particular case, a human being and also other physical bodies are actually physically interacting with another body. Unlike a vision where the body does not necessarily exist outside the individual or does not exist in the manner in which it appears, **in the assumption of the body by an angel, the person does actually see the reality of rarefied air in such a manner that reflects specific qualities**. [349]

It is important to distinguish this type of "assumption" from what we speak of when, for example, referring to the Word of God assuming a human nature. That Divine "assumption" was a true incarnation—*The* Incarnation. The demons (or angels), on the other hand, cannot incarnate themselves. But they can (temporarily) give the appearance that they are physical creatures by the type of "assumption" of "bodies" described here by Aquinas, wherein they are simply moving about some amalgamation of matter ("body") resembling whatever they please (whether a UFO, an alien, or whatever else). This does not render their spiritual existence the actual form of an individual substance (as your soul is truly the form of your body); it simply entails their spiritual faculty of will exerting influence on the body they "assumed," analogous to the software by which some autonomous vehicle is driven.

Note that although Fr. Ripperger, in this paragraph, only makes specific reference to angels, he also explicitly says later that the same description applies to demons (as they retain their angelic nature and thus the capacities essential to such a nature). Renowned expert in mystical theology, Fr. Jordan Aumann, confirms this ability of demons:

> There is no great difficulty in explaining the apparitions of angels or **demons. These are pure spirits, and a spirit is where it acts**. Moreover, a spirit has the power, with God's permission, of **assuming some material substance** with which to represent itself even to the bodily eye, **whether that substance is a body or light rays or some kind of cloud or vapor**. ... **As to the apparition of persons still living on earth or of inanimate objects** ... If the phenomenon ... is effected through diabolical power, with God's permission, **it is merely a case of the devil using light rays, vapor, or a material substance to simulate the physical body ... There is no difficulty in affirming this, since the devil has power to make use of material substances**.[350]

The demons, therefore, can do at least three things to deceive us: "assume" a body, directly manipulate the imagination, senses, etc., or effect the medium (usually air) between the observer and the illusion's apparent location. Considering all three together, we can easily see that not even one of the non-debunkable UFO sightings or "ET encounters" is beyond the pale for a demonic ruse. With these methods, the demons can replicate everything that has been reliably reported in relation to aliens. Fr. Aumann provides another more detailed—though certainly not comprehensive—list of other machinations within the domain of demons as follows, insisting that the Devil can do any of the following:

> 1. **Produce corporeal or imaginative visions** (but not intellectual visions). 2. Falsify ecstasy. 3. **Produce rays of light** in the body and sensible heat. (There have been examples of **"diabolical incandescence.")** 4. Cause sensible consolations and tenderness. 5. **Instantaneously cure sicknesses that have been caused by diabolical influence**. 6. Produce the stigmata and all other kinds of bodily extraordinary phenomena, and **any phenomena dealing with physical objects,** such as crowns,

> rings, etc. 7. Simulate miracles and the **phenomena of levitation, bilocation, and compenetration of bodies.** 8. Cause persons or **objects to disappear from sight by placing an obstacle in the line of vision** or acting directly on the sense of sight; **simulate locutions by means of sound waves** or immediate action on the sense of hearing; cause a person to speak in tongues. 9. Produce bodily incombustibility ... **To summarize: all phenomena resulting from the activity of any natural power or physical law, even if the human being is unable to produce them, can be produced by diabolical power,** with God's permission. Whatever the activity of diabolical powers, however, it can never be essentially supernatural.[351]

The instantaneous curing of certain sicknesses by demons is especially noteworthy. This is not generally within the power of the Devil, since it is usually a true miracle (which is why, for example, such miracles are the ones commonly cited in canonizations). The exception, however, is if a demon itself is causing a certain affliction in someone, then it is within that demon's power to immediately remove that affliction and thus give the impression of a miraculous cure, like a torturer turning off an electric current flowing through some sadistic machinery. Various ET contactees have reported "healings" that are only exhibitions of this diabolic ruse. For example, some have reported instantaneous cessation of severe pain with which they had long been afflicted. Others have reported a sudden return of hearing. Conspicuously absent is any evidence of an "extraterrestrial" contact experience resulting in medically observed impossible healings like interventions from Heaven regularly achieve. Moreover, before (and during) the "healing" in question, one can usually see that their personal lives already displayed evidence of demonic activity.

Demons can manipulate light and sound, assume material bodies, create false visions, make an object appear to be invisible or levitate, and, in a word, they can effect "**all phenomena resulting from the activity of any natural power of physical law**." They can do everything that has ever been *demonstrated* to have occurred in relation to UFO reports or "ET contact" experiences.

***

What claims, however, which might be made in the future—related to extraterrestrials—*would* exceed the capacity of demons? Considering what would be beyond the pale even for them is our next task.

Human Deceptions and Government Psyops

> "During her ill-fated run for the American presidency in 2016... Hillary Clinton made an astonishing offer: if elected president, she promised to open the secret government files on Area 51... *The New York Times* noted that some 'UFO enthusiasts' had even dubbed her 'the first E.T. Candidate'"[352]

Many *claims* have circulated, since Roswell in 1947, that *do* describe happenings likely outside of a demon's power. For example, a demon would likely be incapable of leaving behind an actual, physical "ET craft" stored in Area 51 and subject to reverse engineering. A demon would also likely be incapable of leaving behind an actual supposed body of an extraterrestrial that can be subject to rigorous scientific studies and autopsies to confirm its non-earthly origin.

All of these claims, however, have been either presented without any serious evidence or have been discovered to be frauds. The very creators themselves of the most famous "alien autopsy" videos have since admitted they were hoaxes. When we consider how increasingly easy it is for even amateurs to create manipulated video the likes of which, in decades past, only Hollywood could produce, we should anticipate that many more "videos of aliens and UFOs" will emerge in the upcoming months and years. To the credulous, these videos will seem to lend credence to the ET thesis. Yet all such videos will prove themselves inauthentic based on one or more of the following grounds:

- There will not be people who themselves go on live TV (i.e., without anonymity) to testify to the authenticity of the video, swearing that they captured the video. The source of the footage will be conveniently obscure or entirely secret; or,
- Experts in CGI (Computer-generated imagery) will, once given enough time, be able to explain why the video is not a trustworthy video of a real occurrence; or,
- The video will only be of something that is within the capacity of demons to deceptively represent (discussed in previous sections), for such illusions can be captured by a camera or sensor just as they can be observed with the human eye; or,
- The video will only be of some rare, but still earthly, phenomena (perhaps it will be of a particularly disfigured human or animal, or of a particularly advanced secret government project).

Nevertheless, even such deceptions as those listed above are not the greatest danger. When the government begins more expressly collaborating with the ET Deception, matters will become much more difficult to discern.

Recall that Jacques Vallée is likely the one man who knows more about Ufology than any other person alive. Although his interpretation of this phenomenon (his famous "Interdimensional Hypothesis") is itself only an even darker diabolical deception than "traditional" alien belief, his objective descriptions of Ufology and his warnings about government psy-ops are nevertheless entirely accurate. He conveyed well, in the conclusion of one of his most famous books, the nature of both:

> ...[Many Ufologists are] ready to set aside those painstaking standards of research that can only slow us down as we reach for the shiny prize. In recent years, standing in the UFO community has become conditioned by alleged access to confidential information. **No ufologist dares to raise any question about such material for fear of being cut off from the fascinating secret sources that disseminate it.** ... **[but] it could also be that some intelligence agency, or some rogue group within such an agency, has been bending the latent paranoia** of some extremist political movements to its own ends, just as many cults ... may have served as useful, convenient test beds for covert psychological experiments. Even those intrepid researchers who spend their time suing the U.S. Air Force under the Freedom of Information Act, and clamoring for immediate congressional hearings on UFOs, have not dared investigate these murky and dangerous, yet highly relevant connections. ... Other questions do remain, no matter how tirelessly we try to sweep them under the rug... **The idea that we are about to encounter new enemies in outer space contains unfathomable power. And the human greed for power explains many apparent miracles**. As for the vocal claim that there are nine flying saucers in a hangar near Las Vegas and a city full of mean little gray humanoids eating human flesh under New Mexico, it represents a fascinating new kind of revelation in our culture. **If you can make enough people believe it, then they will believe anything else you tell them. They will follow you anywhere.** Perhaps that will turn out to be the key to the allegedly secret revelations that a few well-intentioned Messengers of Deception are so generously offering to a gullible public. And the real story of that deception...may never be heard over the clamor of happy multitudes preparing to meet their new alien leaders.[353]

Questions to Ask on the "Day of Disclosure"

> "I occasionally think how quickly our differences worldwide would vanish if we were facing an alien threat from outside this world."
> "How much easier [Gorbachev's] task and mine might be if suddenly there was a threat to this world from another species from another planet."—President Ronald Reagan

Once the Antichrist's minions have acquired sufficient power, governments will cooperate with them (and increasingly be ruled by them) even more shamelessly than they have thus far. It appears likely that they will, at some point in the (near) future, present "evidence" that they possess (or have observed) alien bodies or craft, or that they are in radio contact with aliens residing elsewhere. This presentation will be the Ufologists long-awaited "Day of Disclosure."

This "Day" will arrive once the ET-narrative becomes important for the government's own nefarious and immediate ends. Perhaps they will have some malicious plan for which "building up defenses against an alien threat" will prove the perfect cover for excessive secretive spending and an unprecedented tyrannical crackdown on human rights (since Covid, people are now too zealously on the lookout for those crackdowns presented as necessary pandemic measures).

All, therefore, should apply the same rigor in scrutinizing these claims to which we have learned—particularly from the year 2020 onwards—government narratives must be subject. The psyop *will* be capable of being uncovered and the truth will eventually come out. The most dangerous part of the "Disclosure" will be the days, weeks, and even months immediately following it, wherein men's heads are spinning so much from the so-called "ontological shock" that careful analysis has not yet revealed the deception.

Follow the money, follow the professional relationships, consider the *directly verifiable* evidence, accept the testimonies only of individuals you are already certain you can trust, and you will see that the "aliens" or "ET crafts" they present are no more real than the "engineered canals" the scientists of the 19th century assured us had been built across the planet Mars.

Pretend you are sitting on a jury for a capital crime. It is up to you to ensure you do not jump to unwarranted conclusions. A man's life depends upon it.

- Always identify hearsay. Only take seriously accounts of events given by witnesses who swear, under oath, that they saw with their own eyes. Do not trust accounts of what individuals claim *other people are saying they saw.** You must see the alleged witnesses, you must see him

---

* It is also essential to remain cognizant of the effects of contemporary pervasive drug use. It is, without a doubt, yet another diabolically motivated initiative that, in the world today, we see such an explosion of hard psychotropic drugs being regularly used by untold millions of people. Not only are recreational hallucinogens and psychoactive chemicals becoming increasingly legalized (e.g., marijuana) and normalized, but there is also a massive and ever-increasing trend of hard drugs being legally dispensed as prescriptions. Benzodiazepines, for example, are known to produce hallucinations. Today, *tens of millions* of Americans take these drugs legally each day (and who knows how many more millions illegally). Other psychotropic medications, used by even more people, have similar effects. The situation that has been produced by this drugged culture is historically unprecedented: hordes of apparently upstanding individuals—professionals who are well kept, appear on television, hold positions of

swear to the truth of his testimony, and you must assess for yourself if this person is telling the truth. (Even then, remember how convincing *real* diabolical illusions can be, and how few today are positioned to discern them.)

- Never trust vague identifiers such as someone claiming, "defense contractors told me they have ET craft," or "high level government officials came to me relaying their accounts of ETs." Accept only names, and once you are given them, seek out official statements from those individuals which you can verify were certainly said.
- Beware conjectures and interpretations posing as observations. These are not "reliable eyewitness accounts;" they are idealogues testifying to their own preconceived ideas. For example, a scientist claiming, "*I know this is alien material, I saw it myself!*" is only speaking absurdly. Whoever he is, he has not seen every material on earth, nor has he seen every technology on earth, and he could not possibly conclude merely by testing some material that it was "manufactured by an extraterrestrial."
- Remember that the fewer people who would need to be "in" on a given conspiracy, the fewer barriers there are to that conspiracy becoming effective. If, for example, some particular medicine—perhaps a vaccine—were centrally designed and manufactured by only one company, with a development process shrouded in "trade secrets," then it would be easy enough for a very small group of malicious individuals to poison billions of people, while preserving in innocent obliviousness 99% of the people involved in the production, dissemination, and promotion (that is, propagandizing) of the poison. The same will be true of impending ET-related "disclosures." Always follow all the testimonies and statements back to their original sources, and enumerate how few people must have their word taken as truth, for a given claim. Then, consider what motives those few people could have for lying. You will find that there are only a few people who openly insist to have *directly* "worked on the ET bodies or craft." What is the relationship between these people? Find their *curriculum vitaes*, and study them for uncanny resemblance.
- If an "ET body or craft" is "publicly produced," take note of who exactly is allowed to study it without interference. Is it only scientists

---

power, wear suits, etc.—are regularly hallucinating and perhaps going about their lives thinking these deceptions are real. And this is only a psychological consideration—when we also note the increasing likelihood of those using such chemicals to be subject to diabolical influence, as well as the darkening of the intellect that always follows closely upon grave sin (which there is far more of today than ever before), we are left with the recognition that society is primed for deception like never before seen in the whole history of the world.

working with the American (or another) Government? Is it only individuals who are already associated with Ufology and thus predisposed to come to the predictable conclusion? Is it only individuals with certain security clearances and non-disclosure agreements signed, so that they cannot speak the truth about their findings even if they wanted to? These are only some of the questions you will need to ask. If you investigate carefully, you will discover that those allowed to study the alleged "proof of extraterrestrials" (whatever that "proof" may be) are carefully selected to ensure that the preferred narrative is the only one promoted.

- Consider: is an "ET body or craft" presented in tandem with an extraordinary (and clearly humanly impossible) UFO sighting? The Devil will increasingly have many minions explicitly given over to his service in positions of power. There may well be a truly physical craft recovered—but one made by man, to lend further apparent credibility to the directly demonic illusion that preceded it. Some government psyops may well involve direct cooperation with demons. Shrewd observers, therefore, must ensure they do not succumb to assuming "authenticity by association." In fact, when one carefully restricts his analysis to the thing a demon would not be capable of (e.g., leaving an actual incarnate craft or body in the wake of a UFO sighting), he will recognize that the thing in question is entirely within the realm of possibility for a government psyop, even if the marvels observed in the sky or elsewhere were themselves beyond the power of technology (i.e., were instead directly wrought by demons).
- If, on the other hand, the Day of Disclosure happens by way of an official announcement that we are now receiving radio signals from alien civilizations, the crux of this deception would be extremely easy to hide in a bottleneck. This bottleneck would be a requisite (and false) premise accessible to only a few individuals, while what follows from it would beguile thousands of scientists (who lack direct access to what would be needed to know with certainty the true nature and origin of the "alien signal") into thinking they are sure of what is transpiring, when in fact they are only themselves among the deceived. Therefore, determine exactly who will testify publicly that: 1) he himself is receiving the radio signals; observing them in real time 2) he is receiving them on equipment he personally operates and fully understands (and which is fully offline and un-hackable), and 3) he is certain to have ruled out all other possible explanations. List all individuals who fit this bill, and exclude all others; for they are only giving their own assurances based on hearsay. Then, apply the same rigor to the backgrounds of those who fit this bill as noted above. Scrutinize the resume, relationships, payments received, etc.

The Frog in the Pot of Water: The Pattern of "UFO Revelations" Testifies to Their Fabricated Nature

No one, upon hiking a mountain trail and coming upon a series of clear steps, ponders whether these steps were a natural part of the mountain. He knows full well they were placed there intentionally to facilitate ascent.

Similarly, since Roswell in 1947 (but especially clearly for the last six years leading up to the publication of this book) the trend of so-called whistleblowers, disclosures, investigations, etc., of UFO-related phenomena have transpired with such formulaic regularity that they are clearly following a predetermined path, not charting out the growth of an authentic movement. We are collectively being treated like the proverbial frog in a pot of water. The heat is gradually turned up so that, once it is boiling us to death, we do not notice how far (from sanity) we have fallen.

Even if we leave aside the theological, philosophical, and scientific proofs (discussed in Parts One through Three of this book) that aliens do not exist and *certainly* are not in physical contact with us, we are left with no palatable explanation, based on actual "aliens," which can make sense of what has long been claimed in relation to UFO disclosures. The Ufologists would have us believe that, for 75 years, we have been constantly visited by extraterrestrials. Thousands of times over, these visits have been thwarted by incompetent government agencies who have repeatedly triumphed over a civilization of aliens capable of quasi-supernatural feats travelling through interstellar space. Despite ever-changing administrations, many different nations involved, and constantly morphing ideologies, tens of thousands of government workers have nevertheless, for decades, kept secret what would be the greatest revelation in the history of the world (aside from Christianity). These aliens cannot manage to arrive *anywhere on earth* where there happens to not be an army of ultra-secret government agents lying in wait just blocks away to hastily collect them and secret them away. Instead of any of this (or approximately ten million other ways such creatures could easily reveal themselves to humanity beyond the slightest shred of any possible doubt), what has been needed is an army of *"ordinary citizen-warriors, like you!"*, the Ufologists rousingly declare, to incessantly demand transparency and disclosure from the government about the aliens they are continually stealing away and hiding from us. *That*, and that alone, is what will finally cause the revelation of extraterrestrials.

No sane person can believe this narrative. That it appears to be believed by so many today is only another testimony to our collective insanity (a similar testimony to, for example, the predominant acceptance of "LGBT" ideology, which would never be met with anything but a laugh a generation past).

While no plausible or even possible scenario, based on actual extraterrestrials, can succeed in making the slightest sense out of the last 75 years of UFO-disclosure-related developments, it all makes perfect sense when considering a psyop. But we must distinguish between two "psyops."

On the one hand, there are the diabolical plans derived from Lucifer himself. Those are much longer term. As noted, I suspect he has been preparing the way for the ET Deception for a few hundred years. Human-motivated psyops, however, are generally relatively short sighted. While it is possible that a government psyop of some sort has been in effect since Roswell—subtly generating ET-expectation among the masses—it may be more likely that an *active* and more carefully planned psyop, orchestrated somewhere at the government level, has only been in place since the years leading up to *The New York Times*' 2017 report on the Pentagon's UFO program. Considering the *Times'* infamous ties with government officials, it is not unlikely they were giving the impression of an independent "exposé" when, in fact, they were only following orders or heeding irresistible "suggestions."

That being said, these two types of psyops do not always have entirely clear-cut distinctions. The Devil, knowing what he wants to bring about decades or even centuries later, can, as it were, whisper certain suggestions into the ears of various powerful individuals, who may well follow up on these instructions without themselves even having a deliberate and protracted plan in mind. This may be what happened in the aftermath of Roswell (which we now know to be nothing other than a top-secret government device). One author even argued:

> **[At Roswell,] the officer was ordered to announce to the world that the United States Air Force had captured a craft from another world. He was ordered to do so by the base's commanding officer. And the commander, it was later revealed, had received his orders from the Pentagon.** The Air Force subsequently retracted the Roswell statement, claiming that the nearly mile-long stretch of debris was attributable to a downed weather balloon. In years to come, the "true believers" would point to this back-pedaling as proof of a government cover-up. **A seed was planted in the American psyche in those early years of the Cold War**. ... A new belief sprouted in the minds of Americans. UFOs are real and the government knows what they are ... So, you might ask, do these military officers really possess proof of alien craft visiting Earth? Have these highly trained officers risked everything to tell their fellow Americans the truth? ... [If so,] why have the individuals who've divulged "the secret of the ages" not been [prosecuted]? Curiously, none of the military personnel—there have been many—who have revealed this state secret have received so much as a slap on the wrist. Those still on active duty have suffered no repercussions. Those who are retired continue to receive fat military pensions ... **[in fact,] the government has**

purposefully guided American public opinion regarding UFOs through the years ... anxious to have you believe in alien visitations.[354]

Indeed, if the nefarious powers that be—whether human or diabolical—*really* desired to punctuate the gravity of some "revelation," they would arrange circumstances such that the announcement itself *appeared* to be the hard fought victory from decades of "heroic efforts by whistleblowers," with the government "finally choosing transparency" and revealing "the greatest secret they have been hiding this whole time." If any announcement would grab the attention of the world, it would be precisely one such as that. And that is the type of announcement we have been gradually prepared for over the course of many years.

Since the *Times'* 2017 UFO report, we have been able to count on some "major development" in the UFO-disclosure movement every few months or so. The pattern has not failed. Most recently (as of this writing) it has been the baseless claims of David Grusch—who is presented as a courageous hero, but who in fact has taken no risks at all, and has relayed no evidence of extraterrestrials—only hearsay based on sources he refuses to name. As always, in supreme convenience, they "cannot" be named publicly due to the "confidential nature" of the matter. The manifest deficiency of his testimony, however, did not prevent mainstream media across the world from running with headlines such as "*Intelligence Officials Say U.S. Has Retrieved Craft and Biologics of Non-Human Origin.*" With such striking claims as these now permeating society and known by virtually everyone, we appear only moments away from the "Day of Disclosure" itself. Grusch—knowingly or unknowingly—is playing his role in this psyop with great precision. (He may well himself be deceived by higher-ups managing the deception; he may sincerely believe that his colleagues are working on ET craft and bodies.)

More "whistleblowers" like Grusch will soon follow, with increasingly grave claims about the presence of ETs on earth and the "urgency" of addressing the matter. Such developments will continue until the national and global situation is perfectly primed for the long-awaited revelation itself. When that Day of Disclosure comes, do not be deceived by it; instead, ask the questions listed in the preceding section, and similar ones like them. Above all, remember that *there are no aliens*; any claim to the contrary is a deception with some malicious motive, and in due course the truth will come out. The danger lies in the intervening times.

"**And if those days had not been shortened, no human being would be saved; but for the sake of the elect those days will be shortened.**"
—Matthew 24:22

26. The Prophecies and the Antichrist

"The works of Antichrist may be called lying wonders, 'either because he will deceive men's senses by means of phantoms, so that he will not really do what he will seem to do; or because, if he work real prodigies, they will lead those into falsehood who believe in him.'"

—St. Thomas Aquinas (Quoting St. Augustine)

We have already seen how openly and ferociously the many extra-terrestrial-related phenomena of the last century have heralded the arrival of the Antichrist. In this chapter, we will focus more specifically on the prophecies that speak of this *Man of Sin* (cf. 2 Thessalonians 2:3) in order to render clearer still how apocalyptic are the times in which we live.

But it must first be emphasized that many theories exist, even differing among the saints, as to the precise details and timing of the reign of the Antichrist. While it is certain that Antichrist will come, some would insist he can only reign immediately before the end of the world, whereas others pin his reign as preceding the Era of Peace (which is also certain to come), after which—upon a brief unleashing of the Devil upon the earth—Christ comes in the flesh to *conclude* history, command the General Resurrection, and commence the Last Judgment.

It is also possible that there are two particularly prominent "Antichrists"—the *ultimate* and the *penultimate*—with the former arising only at the very end of time (after the Era of Peace, which we obviously have not seen yet) and the latter arising before the Era of Peace. This "penultimate Antichrist" would be defeated not by the Second Coming of Christ in the flesh (which, contra Millenarianism, can never happen *within* history—rather, only at its conclusion), but by an apparition of Christ's power—that is, by the "light" or "breath" of Christ's coming (2 Thessalonians 2:8), not by His true physical coming at the very end.

My view is as follows. *The* Antichrist is indeed imminent, and the Era of Peace will follow his defeat by an apparition of Christ's power. The Era of Peace itself (whose duration we cannot know) will conclude with a very brief release of Satan through "Gog and Magog" (Revelation 20:8)—involving no great apostasy and protracted persecution, as with the Antichrist (Revelation 13). Christ will almost immediately triumph over this final and fleeting unleashing of Satan with His Second Coming in the flesh, whereupon history is completed. I am most emphatically *not*, however, endorsing a "Millenarian" interpretation of Revelation Chapter 20. (For more details on this point, please see the appendices of my 2021 book, *Thy Will Be Done*.) Although such views are common in Evangelical circles, I would strongly caution against them, as they are deeply erroneous.

In support of this view, I present the Magisterium of Pope St. Pius X. In his greatest encyclical—*E Supremi*—(On the Restoration of All Things in Christ) which presented the theme of his entire pontificate, the Pope taught that the literal Antichrist himself may already be in the world, writing, **"... there may be already in the world the "Son of Perdition" of whom the Apostle speaks (II. Thess. ii., 3)** ..." (§5). Note that the "Son of Perdition" spoken of in the Scriptural passage the Pope cites (the citation is in the encyclical; I did not add it), has always been understood as a reference to *the* Antichrist himself. Granted, as this was written in 1903, the Pope was obviously mistaken in the *details* of that speculation (even if the Antichrist was born in 1903, he would already be 120 years old!). But that is of no consequence to our point, for the Pope was nevertheless implicitly teaching that the Antichrist's reign is even more imminent than the very *Restoration of All Things in Christ* he dedicated that encyclical to prophesying. (The Encyclical indicates this "Restoration" is not merely an oblique reference to Heaven—again, see *Thy Will Be Done* for more details.)

No document appealed to by those who insist that the Antichrist can only possibly come *immediately* before the end of time rivals, much less surpasses, the authority of this text. Nor is it possible to understand this text in any other way than the one which refutes them. For the same encyclical clearly prophesies a yet-to-come Era of Peace, thus indicating that the Era—the "Restoration of All Things in Christ"—will *follow* the defeat of the Son of Perdition (as there would have been no plausible way it could have come first if the Antichrist may have already even been alive). Moreover, a multitude of contemporary private revelations—many bearing forms of ecclesiastical approval and other verifications of authenticity—have also asserted that the Antichrist is truly imminent, and that the Era of Peace will follow his defeat by a "coming of Christ" in grace. Summarizing his own extensive study of contemporary private revelation, theologian Fr. Edward O'Connor, wrote the following in 2011 (and many revelations since then have repeatedly confirmed his conclusion) about their unanimously agreed-upon main thrust—their *prophetic consensus*:

> The Church will be torn apart. The Antichrist, already alive in the world, will manifest himself ... The disasters to come will purify the world and leave it as God intended it to be. The Holy Spirit will be poured out as never before and renew the hearts of all mankind. (*Listen to My Prophets*. Pages 189-190.)

I would present a simple question to anyone who supposes that the Antichrist can only arise at the very end of time, and cannot possibly be imminent: *If not now, when?* If today's Dictatorship of Relativism and Culture of Death—and, indeed, the rumblings of his reign we see in ET-phenomena—do not present the precisely ideal conditions for the rise of the Antichrist, then what conditions do?

The French 19th century seminary professor and missionary preacher, Fr. Charles Arminjon—in a book of which St. Thérèse of Lisieux said, "*This reading was one of the greatest graces of my life...*" —wrote the following:

> Some have concluded from this passage [2 Thessalonians 2] that Christ is to come down in person to strike His great adversary, and that this will be the day when He will appear in His glory and majesty. This interpretation is incorrect. St. Thomas and St. John Chrysostom explain ... that **Christ will strike the Antichrist by dazzling him with a brightness that will be like an omen and sign of His Second Coming** ... What is certain is that Satan will be hurled back into the darkness of the abyss, the reign of the man of evil will be utterly destroyed ... Will the resurrection of the body and the Last Judgment follow close upon that great event? Holy Scripture is silent on this point, and the Church has not wished to define anything. Among the interpreters of Holy Writ, some affirm it and others deny it. Suarez expresses the view that after the death of the Antichrist, the world will not subsist more than forty-five days ... **This opinion, however, does not seem to be the most certain. The most authoritative view, and the one that appears to be most in harmony with Holy Scripture, is that, after the fall of the Antichrist, the Catholic Church will once again enter upon a period of prosperity and triumph** ... [referencing Romans 11] These words are formal, and appear to leave **no room for doubt**. They are in harmony with those of St. John [referencing the Book of Revelation]: '*I then saw ... those who had won the victory over the beast and its image and also the number that signified its name ... They sang the song of Moses, the servant of God, and the song of the Lamb.*' In other words, the Christians and the remnant of the Jews henceforth have only one spirit and one faith, they address the same praises and blessings to the Son of God and, together, proclaim His glory ... Is it really credible that the day when all people will be united in this long-sought harmony will be the one when the heavens shall pass away with great violence...? Would Christ cause the Church to be born again, in all her glory and all the splendor of her beauty, only to dry up forthwith the springs of her youth and her inexhaustible fecundity?

The resounding "no," in response to the questions immediately above, were deemed too obvious to be worth stating. Here Fr. Arminjon argues forcefully and correctly—not merely as his own eschatological speculation, but as the most authoritative view most in harmony with Scripture and the teachings of the Saints—that the Era of Peace will occur after the time of the Antichrist. Thus he skillfully corrects the common but mistaken opinion of theologians in centuries before him who did not have access to what Fr. Arminjon knew.

***

All of this being said, however, the present concerns should not be ignored by those who prefer the view that the Antichrist is not imminent.

Even if the diabolical deception that is coming in relation to ET-contact-expectation pertain not to *the* Antichrist but rather to "an" antichrist, the lessons we must learn remain identical. All, therefore, should heed carefully the prophecies included in the following sections.

Behind Bravados About ETs, You See the Devil or You Remain Blind

> At first, the seal [of the Antichrist] will be offered to volunteers. However, within the enthronement of Antichrist everyone will be forced to accept the seal. ... **During the Antichrist times, the strongest temptation will be anticipation of salvation from the cosmos, from ... extraterrestrials that are actually the demons**. One should rarely look up at the sky, as the signs might be deceptive and thus one may be ruined... This is my last will and testament: raise your prayers for everyone; your prayers will move the mountains. Love each other.
>
> —Attributed to Fr. Gabriel of Georgia (†1995)
> (Venerated as a Saint in the Greek Orthodox Church)

Let us begin this section by considering the complete version of a prophetic declaration from Fr. Stanley Jaki (portions of which we have already reviewed):

> **Behind these bravados about extraterrestrials you either see the strategy of the devil or you remain blind.** How, you will ask yourself, can great scientific minds ignore the obvious? The answer comes only from the theology of original sin and of the devil. Leave them out of your equations and you will not understand anything....Why are [ETs] so important to the juggernaut of secularism? Secularists fondly hope that once we detect a message from them this will prove that the human mind is a random occurrence in the universe and has nothing to do with an omnipotent God, the Creator. **And once the Creator is out of the picture, so is Christ and the Church. Such is the great strategy today of radical secularism or materialism. Behind it stands the devil**, as he stands behind anything else. And just **as he was the father of lies in the first instance, in reference to Eve, the devil continues using the strategy of clever lies, which never look so clever as when wrapped in science**"[355]

I have reserved until now including the fuller version of Fr. Jaki's warning because at this point—seeing all that we have touched on in the preceding chapters detailing the decades of diabolical development of ET-related phenomena—a discerning reader can only concur with his assessment.

It takes a *true spiritual blindness* for a man to observe that development but still choose to dismiss spiritual concerns and instead plow forward giddily on the path of promoting belief in extraterrestrials, expectation of contacting them or even being visited by them, and encouraging others to advocate for "disclosure." The goal of this entire movement, plain for all to see and often scarcely even obscured, is the removal of Jesus Christ in order to replace Him with extraterrestrial-fixation.

It is difficult to imagine one more qualified than Fr. Jaki to render this judgment and announce this warning. As noted before, he was not only a Benedictine priest but also both a renowned theologian and a renowned scientist—named as one of the five Catholic scientists (from throughout history) who have "shaped our understanding of the world."[356] He received his PhD in physics under the direction of Victor Hess, who discovered cosmic rays. Even *The New York Times*—which he criticized trenchantly—published an article, upon Jaki's death, extolling him as a "relentless scholar."[357] He lectured at countless universities, and authored dozens of books and was especially astute in describing the fundamental limitations of science and the necessity of Faith—even in science.

And what was this authoritative voice warning the faithful about? What was he sounding a veritable *prophetic alarm* about? Extraterrestrials. He realized that the Devil himself was (and is) behind this movement. He realized this truth not only from theological wisdom, personal holiness, and scientific expertise, but also from personal association with the most prominent names in the so-called "Search for Extraterrestrial Intelligence" (SETI). Due to his prominence as a scientist, he travelled in circles that virtually no other Catholic theologians did. From his associations therein, he saw clearly that the men involved with SETI were part and parcel to an agenda that could only be truthfully called demonic. Let us, therefore, return to the teaching of Scripture we considered in the Introduction to this book.

> **Now the Spirit expressly says that in later times some will depart from the faith by giving heed to deceitful spirits and doctrines of demons.** (1 Timothy 4:1)

We have seen earlier that Catholic ET promoters like Msgr. Balducci would have us believe that no one may ever be concerned about demonic deceptions associated with "aliens" because "*demons are bound by God's Will*" (as indeed they are!). Yet from this true premise, they draw the fallacious conclusion that God's permissive Will could never allow the demons to operate a deception upon earth. Scripture, however, does not merely leave such a possibility open—rather, it quite literally "**expressly says**" that such a deception will indeed take place in "later times."

What, then, might such a deception entail? Obviously, the Bible does not describe it in explicit detail. Were it to have done so, the Deception here prophesied would never be able to take place (a fact we will consider in the next chapter). But we are not left as orphans. Scripture does give more than sufficient detail to compare what it prophesies to what we observe happening before our eyes with modern ET-phenomena, and conclude that we are likely living in the very times it foretells. Let us now embark upon that comparison.

Scripture's "Strong Delusion": the "Activity of Satan With All Power and Lying Signs"

> "Now the Spirit expressly says that in later times some will depart from the faith by giving heed to deceitful spirits and doctrines of demons." —I Timothy 4:I

Perhaps the clearest of the New Testament's descriptions of what to expect in the times of the Antichrist are given by St. Paul in his Second Letter to the Thessalonians, wherein he speaks of the "strong delusion" which God will "send" surrounding the "Man of Lawlessness":

> Let no one deceive you in any way; for that day will not come, unless the rebellion comes first, **and the man of lawlessness is revealed, the son of perdition, who opposes and exalts himself** against every so-called god or object of worship, so that he takes his seat in the temple of God, **proclaiming himself to be God**. Do you not remember that when I was still with you I told you this? And **you know what is restraining him now so that he may be revealed in his time**. For the mystery of lawlessness is already at work; only he who now restrains it will do so until he is out of the way. And then the lawless one will be revealed, and the Lord Jesus will slay him with the breath of his mouth and destroy him by his appearing and his coming. The coming of the lawless one **by the activity of Satan will be with all power and with pretended signs and wonders, and with all wicked deception for those who are to perish**, because they refused to love the truth and so be saved. **Therefore God sends upon them a strong delusion, to make them believe what is false**, so that all may be condemned who did not believe the truth but had pleasure in unrighteousness. (2 Thessalonians 2:3-12)

Many theories have been presented as to what or who exactly the "restrainer," or "Katechon" is that St. Paul here describes, preventing the public entrance of the Antichrist. Perhaps it is the Pope, or, more mysteriously, the "Roman Empire," or even something or someone else. We needn't ponder much at the moment which theory is correct. St. Augustine himself admitted "I frankly confess I do not know what he [St. Paul] means"[358] by this reference. Suffice it to say that something or someone is preventing the definitive revelation of the Antichrist. When that someone or something is out of the way, there will be nothing stopping the Great Deception from commencing its formal initiation. It is even possible that the *restrainer* has already been removed, and the Antichrist is only waiting for the opportune moment to pounce.

When that moment arrives, the Antichrist will take "his seat in the temple of God, proclaiming himself to be God." (v.4)

Here is our first indication that something utterly "out of this world" will be claimed in relation to the Antichrist's nature. It will, of course, be a total lie. However exactly the Antichrist goes about insisting he is God, we know it will be based on falsehood. But it seems silly to assert that today, the Antichrist would proclaim his own divinity in a manner identical to that of ancient Pagan tyrants who made similar claims—declaring themselves to be Zeus or Jupiter or what have you. However, one similarity is quite likely, and we have already touched on it in this book in other contexts: just as these ancient tyrants used the prevailing myths of their own cultures to argue for their own divinity, so the Antichrist will doubtless use the prevailing myth of his own day.

That prevailing myth has nothing to do with Zeus; instead, as we have seen repeatedly, it has everything to do with science fiction. And that genre's prevailing myth is invariably centralized on extraterrestrials. The Signs of the Times exhort us to be on guard against any man who claims to be either an extraterrestrial himself, or the offspring of them, or in some way formed or instructed by them, or in close contact with them. For just as Jesus Christ *truly* proclaimed Himself to be "not of this world," so will the Antichrist do so—falsely (for the Antichrist will indeed be a man), and in a manner both consistent with and building upon the modern world's delusions.

Perhaps the most helpful explanation of this passage of Scripture comes from St. Augustine in his greatest work, *City of God*. There, this Father and Doctor of the Church explained:

> For then shall **Satan be loosed, and by means of that Antichrist shall work with all power in a lying though a wonderful manner.** It is commonly questioned whether these works are called signs and lying wonders because he is to deceive men's senses by false appearances, or because the things he does, though they be true prodigies, shall be a lie to those who shall believe that such things could be done only by God, **being ignorant of the devil's power, and especially of such unexampled power as he shall then for the first time put forth**. ... But whatever be the reason of the name, **they shall be such signs and wonders as shall seduce those who shall deserve to be seduced, because they received not the love of the truth** that they might be saved. Neither did the apostle scruple to go on to say, *"For this cause God shall send upon them the working of error ["Strong Delusion"] that they should believe a lie."* For **God shall *send*, because God shall *permit* the devil to do these things,** the permission being by His own just judgment, though the doing of them is in pursuance of the devil's unrighteous and malignant purpose, that they all might be judged who believed not the truth, but had pleasure in unrighteousness. Therefore, **being judged, they shall be seduced, and, being seduced, they shall be judged**. But, being

> judged, they shall be seduced by those secretly just and justly secret judgments of God, with which He has never ceased to judge **since the first sin of the rational creatures**; and, being seduced, they shall be judged in that last and manifest judgment administered by Jesus Christ...[359]

Augustine observes that the Antichrist's "Strong Delusion," by the power of Satan, will entail demonic illusions and may consist in actual wonders which succeed in their deceitful intent because men falsely suppose that such wonders are outside of the demons' power. I believe we can be confident it will be both; indeed, modern men are wholly primed to thoroughly succumb to both. Eager to believe we are being visited by aliens, most will immediately rejoice when demonic UFO illusions continue to increase. More problematically still, the "Strong Delusion" will likely entail the actual demonic assumption of corporeal forms (which, as we have demonstrated, is entirely within the Devil's power) pretending to be aliens. As modern society scarcely even believes in demons any longer—a rationalistic disease increasingly infiltrating the clergy—it goes without saying that they will fail to realize the abilities and operations of those whose existence they do not even acknowledge.

We must emphasize Augustine's clarification, already discussed previously in other contexts, that this "Strong Delusion," although "sent" by God in one sense, is certainly not something directly desired by God. For He cannot deceive or be deceived. This is an act of God's *permissive* Will deigning to *allow* a historically unprecedented outpouring of Satanic power through the seductive signs and wonders of the Antichrist (and his minions and forerunners). We must never claim that God is the author of these deceptions, as that would be blasphemous.

Why would God allow such a thing? For similar reasons He allowed the serpent into the Garden (a theme we will consider in forthcoming sections). Just as the "first sin of the rational creatures" St. Augustine refers to consisted in Eve lending her ear to the seducing appearance of the Devil acquiring the form of a serpent, so too the great final sin of rational creatures—men—will be similar. The forms the demons assume will be different, but the lie will be the same: *"Did God really say...?"* (Genesis 3:1) and *"you will be like gods."* (Genesis 3:5)

> **"But I am afraid that, as the serpent deceived Eve by his craftiness, your minds will be led astray from the simplicity and purity of devotion to Christ."** —2 Corinthians 11:3

In a word: the End Times Deception will resemble the Original Deception. Exploring those parallels is our next order of business.

The First and Last Deception: Both Demonic Seductions Offering Godlike Status from a "Non-Human Intelligence"

> "Satan masquerades as an angel of light" (2 Corinthians 11:14)
> "In the inner heart of every person the voice of God and the insidious voice of the Evil One can be heard. The latter seeks to deceive the human person, seducing him with the prospect of false goods, to lead him away from the real good that consists precisely in fulfilling the Divine Will."—Pope St. John Paul II

Wisely does St. Augustine relate the Great Deception of the Antichrist—as described in St. Paul's Second Letter to the Thessalonians—to the seductive words the serpent spoke to Eve to initiate the Fall of Man. Six thousand years later, now that we stand at the penultimate apocalyptic threshold, God is again allowing Satan to have enormous power in the world and present to all of humanity the very question with which he first confronted Eve.

Many saints and renowned spiritual authors have commented that Eve never should have even *begun* dialoguing with the serpent. That was the crux of her error. In truth, no human being is up to the task of dialoguing with demons, therefore the response we must always and immediately resort to, whenever approached by them (and no matter their form) is to bid them depart in the name of Jesus Christ. This duty, however, poses the question: *how* can we know when they have appeared to us? Obviously, in order to ensure we do not dialogue with them we must first be able to identify them!

Some situations are not immediately straightforward to discern—these are usually reserved for advanced mystics whom God knows are prepared to battle such extreme deceptions. It seems unlikely, however, that the goodness of God would allow—even in apocalyptic times—such leeway to the demons that they can appear across the globe to billions of ordinary people (while they are fully awake and sober) by assuming forms of their friends, relatives, or even any other apparently normal human beings. There is simply no reasonable way most people would be equipped to handle such a scenario, and God never tests beyond one's strength (cf. 1 Corinthians 10:13).

On the other hand, there is no reason to suppose that—in the times of Scripture's prophesied "Strong Delusion"—God would not allow something else. He may well allow, on a massive scale (for He has already, as we saw in previous chapters, allowed it on a *large* scale), the demons to assume deceptive forms which are nevertheless sufficiently clearly diabolical that a *sincere* Christian—one genuinely desiring to abide in the faithful approach to Scripture, Tradition, and Magisterium—would recognize their nature. In other words, there is no reason to suppose God would not allow them to widely assume the form of "aliens" and UFOs.

> Now the snake was the most cunning of all the wild animals that the Lord God had made. He asked the woman, "Did God really say, 'You shall not eat from any of the trees in the garden'?" The woman answered the snake: "We may eat of the fruit of the trees in the garden; it is only about the fruit of the tree in the middle of the garden that God said, 'You shall not eat it or even touch it, or else you will die.'" But the snake said to the woman: "You certainly will not die! God knows well that when you eat of it your eyes will be opened and you will be like gods, who know good and evil." The woman saw that the tree was good for food and pleasing to the eyes, and the tree was desirable for gaining wisdom. So she took some of its fruit and ate it; and she also gave some to her husband, who was with her, and he ate it. Then the eyes of both of them were opened, and they knew that they were naked; so they sewed fig leaves together and made loincloths for themselves. (Genesis 3:1-7)

It is precisely this dynamic that precipitated the Fall. God did not allow the Devil to appear to Eve in the form of her husband, Adam. That would have been too great a test. Instead, He allowed the Devil to take "possession" of a serpent—an irrational animal—and cause it to speak. If Eve had only chosen to abide by what she knew—namely, that she and Adam were the only two incarnate creatures in existence who bore the Divine Image (and therefore were the only creatures capable of rational discourse)—then she would have likewise immediately acknowledged that something diabolical was afoot when a serpent began speaking. She would have, accordingly, refused dialogue with the Serpent, and the Fall never would have happened.

Instead, Eve allowed curiosity to get the best of her. Once the dialogue was in progress, that curiosity quickly became an attraction to the seductive words of the serpent, and the rest is history. Renowned spiritual theologian Fr. Jordan Aumann explains all temptation in relation to Eve's, but his analysis applies especially well the present apocalyptic times:

> Thus he said to the woman: ***"Did God really tell you** not to eat from any of the trees in the garden?"* (Gen. 3:1). ... **His tactics are the same today as always. ... he will ask in general terms and without as yet inciting them to evil.** If the soul recognizes that the simple posing of the question represents a danger, it will refuse to converse with the tempter but will turn its thoughts and imagination to other matters. Then the temptation is thwarted, and an easy victory is won. **But if the soul imprudently enters into conversation with the tempter, it is exposed to the great danger of succumbing ... The soul has yielded ground to the enemy, and now the enemy gathers his forces to make a direct attack:** *"But the serpent said to the woman, 'You will not die. For God knows that*

> *when you eat of it your eyes will be opened, and **you will be like God,** knowing good and evil'"* (Gen. 3:4-5). **The devil presents an enchanting possibility** ... During temptation the conduct of the soul can be summarized in **one important word: resist. It does not suffice merely to remain passive in the face of temptation; positive resistance is necessary.**[360]

Fr. Aumann's succinct advice is a veritable battle plan for the days in which we now live. The Devil—through the ET Deception—is presenting (and will continue to present in far greater ways) *"an enchanting possibility."* Through mankind's "learning from the more evolved and enlightened aliens," we are promised, especially with the ET's technological advancements, that we ourselves will "be like gods." We will overcome all our diseases, famines, energy problems, wars, and other problems, and we will finally be given the key to immorality (recall that this was precisely the objective of Frank Drake, the "Father of the Search for Extraterrestrial Intelligence"). With allurements as seductive as these, whoever dialogues with these demons disguised as aliens (who issue these stupefying promises) is bound to succumb to the same fate as Eve.

Eve was given everything she could need or want in the Garden. Yet that was not enough for her. So today, Jesus Christ has given His Faithful everything. He promises the forgiveness of sins, the resurrection of the body, and life everlasting. He heals us with His blood in Confession. He feeds us with His very own Body in the Eucharist. He has given us His own mother as our mother (cf. John 19:26), who is also the Queen of Heaven and Earth. He has left us with the Church, against whom the gates of hell cannot prevail (cf. Matthew 16:18), and who settles all confusion for us in her *Magisterium* (*not* in the personal opinions of men, no matter the rank, residing in the Vatican!). He sends us His Holy Spirit, and with this Spirit a peace that surpasses all understanding (cf. Philippians 4:7). He has sent many authentic private revelations that testify to His continuing presence among us. And He has promised that He will come again—soon—to conclude the history of the universe and command the General Resurrection.

Yet, for those who prefer to place their *real* excitement in the fruition of sci-fi inspired ET expectation, none of this is enough. They find all of that rather boring; "small," even. Portraying the Faith as "small," even while seeming to not explicitly deny its dogmas, is exactly the goal of the Devil with the ET Deception, and this is why it serves as the prophesied "Strong Delusion." As St. Augustine taught, it will only delude, or *seduce,* those who deserve to be deluded, for their heart of hearts had not been placed in Jesus Christ, but elsewhere. It will, in brief, serve as the perfect cover for those men Scripture foretells the rise of during the "last days."

> **But understand this, that in the last days there will come times of stress**. For men will be lovers of self, lovers of money, proud, arrogant,

> abusive, disobedient to their parents, ungrateful, unholy, inhuman, implacable, slanderers, profligates, fierce, haters of good, treacherous, reckless, swollen with conceit, **lovers of pleasure rather than lovers of God, holding the form of religion but denying the power of it. Avoid such people**. (2 Timothy 3:1-5)

Any sincere observer of the contemporary world would be hard-pressed to deny that St. Paul's list of sins above defines the present times. Of particular relevance to our question, however, is his insistence that the last days will above all entail men "**holding the form of religion but denying the power of it**." Too many ignore the clear meaning of this passage, as they falsely suppose that Scripture here is only speaking of open heretics who nevertheless continue to praise Jesus, extoll Christianity, go to Church, etc. Such people, in fact, are not even "holding the form of religion," since they have explicitly rejected it through formal heresy. Therefore, this is not what St. Paul is speaking about here (although, of course, formal heresy and open apostasy also abound today more than ever). Instead, what he has foretold is a time when men will truly seem to remain religious (that is, *Catholic*), for they really will retain the form of the Faith; continuing to attend Mass, recite the Creed, etc. But a trick of the Devil will cause that very *form* they preserve to be emptied of its *power*.

What single move, we must ponder, could achieve such a nefarious end? What subtle transposition could cause the preservation of the appearance of the Catholic religion while at the same time effectively nullifying its vigor? We have already said it: a "revelation" that perhaps does not *explicitly* overturn the Faith, but deceptively makes its content appear tiny in comparison. That is, the "revelation of extraterrestrials"—the "Day of Disclosure."

Suddenly, everything in the Faith—all those realities which deserve our most wholehearted, overwhelming, and exclusive fundamental-life-devotion—become just "one of many" superlatively, existentially demanding matters. He who revels in this revelation begins to wonder (interiorly if nowhere else):

"What might these aliens know about God? Maybe there are far more than three persons in God! Maybe God is thousands of persons! I can't wait to learn about the 4th Person of the "Quadrinity," or even the 4,000th!" "What might God's incarnation look like in other planets, or galaxies, or other dimensions? Perhaps Jesus Christ is just the most minor of God's many incarnations! Why keep focusing so much on Him?" "What if I get many other chances at life in other parallel timelines or in other dimensions; each having different fundamental laws and different Divine Revelations!?" "What if this universe is just one iteration of a whole series of universes? How minor that would make our salvation history! How small and insignificant Scripture might be!" "Imagine; entire planets full of unfallen rational beings! Perhaps the Virgin Mary isn't unique after all – imagine trillions of other Immaculate Conceptions! Even if she is the "Queen of the Universe," what if there are all sorts of other Universes with even greater Queens than

she?! Why look up to only her as my Mother in Heaven? Maybe she is just the introduction. Perhaps I should not focus too much on her."

These types of wild imaginings go on, and on, and on. Their end is to attempt to make the entire Christian religion—"**things into which angels longed to look**" (1 Peter 1:12), things which "**prophets and kings longed to see but did not see**" (Luke 10:24)—feel like a boring day job one must slog through merely so that he can get to the weekend, where the "really interesting and fun things happen." God's Creation as we actually experience it, Christ's Incarnation and Redemption, our journey of Sanctification, and our awaiting of His Second Coming and *Eternity itself,* become just "some of many" things of infinite magnitude instead of the be-all-end-all of our lives, as they must be.

While such people may not have expressly rejected an explicit Dogma (they will still nod, though with boredom, at each article of the Creed), their Supernatural Faith has nevertheless been emasculated, withered, and decayed. The form—the trappings—of the Christian Religion are maintained, but the power of it—the life-devouring-fire that Faith should and must be—has been extinguished.

Make no mistake about it, this is not only "a" test, this is *the* test, just as in the Garden.

This Is The Test: Answering, "If Such Danger Exists, Why Not More Clarity from God?"

> "[The Devil] is "a murderer from the beginning, ... and the father of lies," as Christ defines him. He undermines man's moral equilibrium with his sophistry. He is the malign, clever seducer ..." —Pope St. Paul VI [361]

Having discovered the extreme danger in alien belief and its apocalyptic undertones, one might be inclined to ask, "*If this is such an important question, and if we really can be so confident that aliens do not exist, then why wouldn't the Church have taught more clearly on the matter? Why wouldn't there be a whole army of approved apparitions, at least, explicitly addressing this? Why would the Holy Spirit not cause this to be even more explicitly settled in the Bible? Why would God not inspire an ex-cathedra declaration from a Pope directly addressing aliens?*"

The first and clearest answer is simple: denizens of the postmodern western world should not arrogantly suppose that Divine Revelation (Public or Private) or the Extraordinary Magisterium of the Church, is duty bound to address each and every one of their strange and esoteric leanings. As we have seen in preceding chapters, belief in the existence of extraterrestrial incarnate intelligent life was nowhere seen in the first 1,500 or so years of Christianity (the vast majority of its duration), and almost nowhere to be seen for hundreds of years thereafter, until the Enlightenment.

Only in the last 75 years (a small sliver of the Church's existence) has *concrete* alien belief and ET-contact-expectation become particularly common in the Church. To use the same analogy considered in the opening pages of this book, a modern Christian refusing to reject aliens on account of failing to see them explicitly rejected, by extraordinary Magisterial declarations or Scriptural verses, is akin to this same man refusing to reject transgenderism on similar grounds.

This question, moreover, can be much more appropriately turned on its head: if it is licit for us to believe in aliens, why is there nothing in Scripture, Tradition, or Magisterium that gives us this warrant? "*If it isn't explicitly and infallibly condemned, I'll believe it so long as I feel so inclined to, thank you very much!*" is a lamentable way to be a Catholic. Only one who sees the Faith as a mere rulebook or referee can be even tempted to approach Catholicism that way. One who wishes to *live and breathe* Catholicism (which should be the approach of all Catholics) will instead seek to build his entire life and his complete worldview on the foundation of Scripture, Tradition, and Magisterium. Whoever seeks to do this will find *no* basis for alien belief, and plenty of reasons to rule it out.

But the second answer to this question, which we have been alluding to in the sections above, must also be addressed.

This is a test; it is, rather, *the* apocalyptic test. It is a test of whether Christians take their Faith as supremely seriously as they must. It is a test of whether we who call ourselves Christians realize that the Incarnation, Passion, Death, and Resurrection of Jesus Christ are absolutely central and universal in the greatest possible sense of those terms. It is a test of whether the putative followers of Christ really believe that Divine Revelation is *as Divine* as it claims to be. It is a test of whether we who say that we have given Christ our whole minds and hearts have actually placed our deepest hopes, dreams, and expectations in sci-fi fantasies. It is a test of whether the Faithful believe that the Holy Spirit has been guiding the Church for the last 2,000 years, or has actually been absent. It is as if Jesus, in allowing the present confusion, is saying to us, His children:

- *"Do you really think that I – the infinite and eternal Second Person of the Blessed Trinity – in condescending to take on human flesh, which now is forever united hypostatically to My own Divine Person in Heaven, did not thereby indicate that you – human beings – alone are the apple of my eye?"*
- *"I did not hold back one drop of My blood. What more could I have possibly done for you to prove that you and you alone – human beings created in My image and likeness – are the single and supreme predilection of My heart in all creation?"*
- *"I inspired every single word of Sacred Scripture. Do you think I didn't mean what I said? Do you believe I presented Sacred Scripture's contents to you – detailing for you everything from the very creation of the universe itself up to the Redemption and everything in between –while simply leaving out any mention of other worlds and other intelligent creatures and other salvation*

histories? Do you really think my Public Revelation to you is so inept and inadequate?"

- *"Do you really think I gave you the Divine Revelation of Salvation History, which is complete with the death of the Apostle John, while leaving out the very largest and most important chapters – chapters I instead wanted to wait to have revealed to you until the U.S. Government releases its UFO files?"*
- *"I guided every single moment of Sacred Tradition's development throughout Church History. I never allowed even the slightest indication, in any of the Church's Magisterium, that humans might be just one of a number of intelligent incarnate life forms. Quite the contrary, I allowed repeated indications to enter the Magisterium which speak of man alone as being called to share My own Divine Life. Do you trust that my Bride – the Church – is your mother; a good and holy and loving mother? Or do you think she is a deceitful mother?"*
- *"Do you believe I was trying to fool you or mislead you by leading all Christians of all times before the 'Enlightenment' to regard the human race as utterly unique; as being the only incarnate creatures made in God's Image? Do you believe that I have guided the Faithful for 2,000 years, or do you believe I have just stood by and watched?"*
- *"To whom do you turn for guidance on the most important questions? Do you really believe that if I also made other civilizations scattered about the galaxies, I would allow your rendezvous with these long-lost siblings of yours to be "prophesied" only by decades of diabolical revelations and whistleblowers, instead of by saints and mystics, Magisterium and authentic apparitions? Is that how little trust you have in My ability to guide the Church to all truth?"*

Tests are an essential part of life. We cannot and must not rebel against them, especially when they are expressly allowed and foretold by God Himself. Instead, we must undertake them nobly and faithfully. In many ways, temporal life itself is a test; one that determines whether we will be able to spend eternity with God and all the saints. Little wonder, then, that the Church as a whole would be subject to a final test, just as Jesus, before His Passion, was "tested" in the Garden of Gethsemane. The life of the Church must follow the life of Christ, her head.

The Great Deception would not be much of a test if its essential question were settled *as explicitly* as the ET promoters insist would be necessary to restrain their promotion. What their demand implies is that God should have placed a massive sign next to the Tree of the Knowledge of Good and Evil, warning Eve that the Devil was about to possess a serpent and use it to seduce her into sin. Such explicit, immediate, and absolute assurance was totally unnecessary, and would have rendered the test devoid of any value. Eve knew more than enough to realize she should not have eaten the fruit and should not have even spoken to the serpent. Nevertheless, she dialogued with the Devil, and she ate the fruit anyway, and this sin was not God's fault.

Similarly, by not definitively settling the alien question *as explicitly* as some would like it to be settled, God is asking the faithful today those questions enumerated above (and countless others like them). Intellectually speaking, this is a very easy assessment. Neither salvation nor sanctification are ever contingent upon high achievement in any IQ test. As we saw throughout Parts One and Two of this book, God has made it clear that there are no aliens. He has not, however, made it *supremely* clear (i.e., by not compelling mankind's uniqueness to be explicitly and infallibly declared, by a Pope, as a dogmatic truth). The test, therefore, is *only as difficult as one chooses to make it.*

If a man chooses to love the Word of God more than the word of the world, he will easily reject the demons disguised as aliens. If, on the other hand, his greatest love is reserved for the fruition of sci-fi fantasies, then he will be overwhelmed and likely succumb when these daydreams seem to become reality upon the commencement of Scripture's prophesied "lying signs" and "strong delusion," when the "aliens" promise us we too may be "like gods," if only we listen to them.

> "But even if we, or an angel from heaven, should preach to you a gospel contrary to what we have preached to you, he is to be accursed!" (Galatians 1:8)

Leo XIII, Satan's 75 to 100 Years of Power, and the Year 1947

> "Saint Michael Archangel, defend us in battle, be our protection against the wickedness and snares of the devil; may God rebuke him, we humbly pray; and do thou, O Prince of the heavenly host, by the power of God, cast into hell Satan and all the evil spirits who prowl through the world seeking the ruin of souls. Amen."
> —Prayer to St. Michael the Archangel. Pope Leo XIII

Pope Leo XIII, whose pontificate ushered in the 20th century, experienced an overwhelming mystical vision one day—exactly 33 years before the Miracle of the Sun at Fatima.

> On October 13, 1884 Pope Leo XIII, just after celebrating Mass, turned pale and collapsed as though dead. Those standing nearby rushed to his side. They found him alive but the pontiff looked frightened. He then recounted having a vision of Satan approaching the throne of God, boasting that he could destroy the Church... he sat down and wrote the prayer to St. Michael. For decades it was prayed at Mass until the 1960's. Like many of the Church's spiritual defenses, it was discontinued in the second half of the 20th century.[362]

What this great Pope saw was so immense that it compelled him to write a new prayer imploring the protection of St. Michael the Archangel and order it to be recited after each Holy Mass. (Sadly, its recitation is no longer required, but Pope St. John Paul II nevertheless strongly encouraged its recitation to "help in battle against the forces of darkness and against the spirit of this world."[363]) And what exactly did Pope Leo see? A conversation between God and the Devil—similar to the one recounted in the Book of Job (1:6-12)—which included the following:

> The voice of Satan in his pride, boasted to our Lord: "I can destroy your Church." The gentle voice of our Lord: "You can? Then go ahead and do so." **Satan: "To do so, I need more time and more power." Our Lord: "How much time? How much power?" Satan: "75 to 100 years, and a greater power over those who will give themselves over to my service."** Our Lord: "You have the time, you will have the power. Do with them what you will."[364]

We must not be scandalized that God's permissive Will allowed Satan to have this time and this power. As we have discussed and will continue to, everything God allows—even the Great Deception itself—is for a greater good. (We will discuss that greater good in this book's Conclusion.) God, therefore, gave Satan a greater power (specifically, over those who were already in Satan's service) which he could exercise for some period of 75 to 100 years, a period which would have begun at some point after the Pope saw that conversation take place in 1884.

Many commentators (including myself) had speculated about when that period of Satan's greater power could have begun. Here I confess that I originally suspected it may have begun with the onset of the First World War (in 1914) or the onset of Communism (in 1917). When both 2014 and 2017 came and passed, however, it became clear that those events could not have marked the onset of Satan's "greater power," since not even their 100-year anniversaries (corresponding to the uppermost limit of the period of Satan's increased power) saw the conclusion of his dominion over the earth. Obviously, Satan's chain has been in no way shortened. Whoever doubts that may simply check the news to have his doubts resolved.

Upon more careful reflection, then, it becomes evident that even a World War, a genocide, or an evil political system does not require a *unique* unleashing of Satan's power. Fallen man is often warlike and murderous, and the technological advances in weaponry, transportation, communication, etc., that the 20th century saw necessarily enabled wars and genocides to be more destructive than ever before in history. Satan does not need any additional "unchaining" beyond what leeway he has long had in order to induce men to massive wars. Fallen man is, moreover, too often lusting for power through political machinations. Marxism (on which Communism is built) became popular several decades before 1917, and only needed the perfect storm of political circumstances—not a new unleashing of Satan—to rise to power.

What Satan *does* need additional leeway for is instituting a far more widespread and seductive slew of false signs and wonders, appearing in new forms, communicating to men in new ways, tormenting them with new methods, deceiving them with new subtleties, and the like. In a word, he would need additional leeway to undertake precisely what we have seen since 1947 with the ET and UFO Deception.

Let us settle that the year 1947 was indeed the onset of this deception. Elsewhere in this book, I have generally referred to the times "since Roswell" as constituting the UFO-era, but I only said this because of Roswell's popularity persisting to this day. It is even more accurate to say that the "flying saucer" sightings of Kenneth Arnold at Mount Rainer, Washington State, began the craze—just about two weeks before Roswell became known as a UFO sighting location.

Before 1947, the UFO scene was *radically* less substantial—practically nonexistent. As one scholar of the phenomenon, Dr. Christopher Partridge, noted:

> The contemporary interest in UFOs can be traced back to 24 June 1947, when Kenneth Arnold, a businessman from Boise, Idaho, reported sighting ten shining discs flying over the Cascade Mountains when flying his private plane near Mount Rainier in Western Washington. ... earlier sightings tended to be sporadic and vague. ... **before 1947 'there is not a single recorded episode involving mass sightings of saucer-like objects'** ... It was Arnold's 'flying saucers' that both began the modern wave of sightings and also ushered UFOs into the popular consciousness. The interest in Arnold's story was immediate and massive. 'A Gallup pole [sic] taken on 19 August 1947, revealed that while one out of two Americans had heard of the Marshall Plan, nine out of ten had heard about the saucers' **By the end of that year 850 UFO sightings had been reported in America alone**.[365]

This observation is remarkable. It shows us that what has been an utterly explosive global phenomenon was almost completely absent before 1947. Clearly, that year marked something extraordinary. For the ET promoters, of course, that year marks the Age of the Extraterrestrial. A discerning Christian, however, should recognize that 1947 in fact marks the Age of Diabolical Deception.

A naïve reading of God's granting Satan "greater power over those dedicated to [Satan's] service" might induce one to suppose this expanded power only applies to the explicit and devoted Satanists. Such a conclusion would be quite foolish. Whoever willfully wanders in the occult, remains obstinate in flagrant heresy or blasphemy, or lives a lifestyle of unrepentant mortal sin, is thereby de facto *in Satan's service*. It is especially over such souls as these that Satan received far greater power upon—I submit to you—the commencement of the UFO era in 1947.

It is no mere coincidence that one never hears of "ET contact" experiences being relayed by truly devout and holy souls. As we have seen in other sections, those who insist they have had encounters with aliens invariably had already engaged in the New Age movement, strayed from the devout practice of the Faith, practiced the occult, or otherwise made it clear that they lived a life of unrepentant mortal sin; thus placing them squarely "in Satan's service," and thereby making themselves "fair game" for the "greater power" he had been given. (Note: this does not mean that holy people do not see "UFOs." Remember that the vast majority of UFOs are simply misinterpreted ordinary earthly phenomena that Satan has nothing to do with; obviously, therefore, anyone—saint and sinner alike—is equally likely to see such a thing.) On the other hand, those truly devout Christians who do experience the same phenomena that others would describe as "ET contact," are invariably quick to realize they witnessed some demonic illusion or attack. Satan did not have sufficient leeway to deceive them into supposing they were dealing with an extraterrestrial.

Now, if Satan indeed received this greater power in the year 1947, it would be sensible to expect that something which had proven an impediment to his power would have been removed at that same time. This, too, is exactly what we see.

Whoever is well read in mystical literature is already acquainted with the notion of "victim souls." These exceedingly holy men and women have given themselves over entirely to God and have willingly offered up their lives to Him, eager to suffer whatever is necessary—in union with Christ's Passion—to obtain mercy for the world. Church history is filled with accounts of such souls who, we are repeatedly assured by innumerable authoritative texts, truly did serve as *victims*; they truly did, through their sufferings, "hold back," or "restrain" certain terrible events from happening. While this may sound strange to those it is a new concept for, all may rest assured that it is settled in Catholic thought. It is entirely orthodox and it is entirely real.

One such victim soul was the Servant of God Luisa Piccarreta. She suffered beyond description—always willingly—in order to avert chastisements the world deserved. Accordingly, Jesus' messages to her would often relay that when her suffering was no longer serving as a sort of "restrainer" of God's justice, certain evils that her suffering was holding back might no longer be able to remain restrained.

For example, in 1904, Jesus told Luisa that great clashes were coming, with tremendous chaos, such that "men will see themselves as lost," and that "**If with all this [people] do not listen to Me, then <u>I will take you to Heaven, and things will happen even more gravely,</u> and will drag on a little longer before the longed-for triumph**." (August 15, 1904, Diary entry.) Of course, we *did not* listen to God, hence the world continuing on its destructive path after those world wars there alluded to. Elsewhere, Jesus invited Luisa to suffer greatly to prevent the liberalization of divorce laws (which was on the agenda at the 1902 Hague Convention), promising that so long as she remained a victim on earth, they would not be able to succeed. (She accepted, and indeed, they did not succeed.) He also said, however, that:

> ...if I suspend your state of victim or call you to Heaven, they may be able to [liberalize divorce laws] ... If you knew the rage of the demons and of those who wanted this law, who were certain to obtain it—it is so great, that if they could, they would destroy any authority and would make a slaughter everywhere. (February 24, 1902, Diary entry)

Soon after Luisa died, divorce laws were indeed liberalized in accordance with the very plans commenced at that 1902 international convention. But these are only a few examples. On many occasions, Jesus makes it clear that Luisa's death—her entry into Heaven—would entail earth losing a victim soul who was holding *something* back.

The UFO era began almost immediately after Luisa's death (March 4th, 1947). A mere three months later, the world was aflame with talk of flying saucers and little green men visiting us from outer space. The rest, as they say, is history.

More Prophecies, Teachings, and Private Revelations on the Antichrist

> "The time has come for the most astonishing wonders to take place on the earth and in the air... People will be transported from one place to another by these evil spirits ... The demons of the air, together with the Antichrist, will work great wonders on the earth and in the air." —Our Lady of La Salette

The Catechism

At various points in preceding chapters, we have already seen the relevance of the apocalyptic warning presented by none other than the *Catechism of the Catholic Church*. Here, we consider a larger excerpt from that teaching:

> Before Christ's second coming **the Church must pass through a final trial that will shake the faith of many believers**. The persecution that accompanies her pilgrimage on earth will unveil **the "mystery of iniquity" in the form of a religious deception offering men an apparent solution to their problems at the price of apostasy from the truth**. The supreme religious deception is that of **the Antichrist, a pseudo-messianism by which man glorifies himself in place of God** and of his Messiah come in the flesh. The Antichrist's deception already begins to take shape in the world every time the claim is made to realize within history that messianic hope which can only be realized beyond history through the eschatological judgement. The Church has rejected even modified

> forms of this falsification of the kingdom to come under the name of millenarianism, **especially the "intrinsically perverse" political form of a secular messianism**. (§675-676)

Of particular importance is the fact that the Catechism's own footnotes on these teachings direct us to 2 Thessalonians, which we have already discussed extensively. Indeed, there is no doubt the Church is here referring to that very "Strong Delusion" and "lying signs and wonders," spoken of by St. Paul in Scripture, heralding the Antichrist. But the Catechism here provides even more detail. We are warned that this deception will be one "*offering men an apparent solution to their problems at the price of apostasy from the truth.*" Today, the world's problems are becoming so apocalyptic, even from a purely secular perspective (especially with the looming specter of a global nuclear war), that mankind is more primed than ever before in history to accept an "apparent solution to their problems" which, if only they paused to discern, they would realize is a demonic trap. In their ravenousness, however, most will not pause to discern. While increasing numbers realize that an "other worldly" solution is needed, they refuse to acknowledge that the solution is God Himself. Therefore they are situated like a starving prisoner to soon be presented with a poison-laced meal, or a mouse approaching a trap not pondering why the cheese is free.

We must not, then, be surprised when "the extraterrestrials" swoop in with a supposed easy solution to our global crisis. Perhaps only the proverbial "pinch of incense" will be needed to accept this solution they propose, but that little pinch will entail apostasy from the truth. Note that the Catechism does not say that the price will be "apostasy from God," but only from "the truth." A formal act of apostasy, explicitly repudiating Jesus Christ, may not even be required, and accordingly many Christians will rationalize their way into succumbing. We must set our faces like flint to always live in accordance with *all* truth, and to prefer death to rejecting it.

Our Lady of La Salette

The following abridgment is from a prophecy given in relation to the approved La Sallette apparitions of the Virgin Mary in 19th century France.

> Churches will be closed or desecrated ... Many will abandon the faith ... **Let the Pope beware of miracle workers, for the time has come for the most astonishing wonders to take place on the earth and in the air.** In the year 1864 Lucifer, together with a great number of devils, will be loosed from hell; little by little they will abolish the faith ... persons will take on the spirit of these evil angels; a number of religious houses will lose the faith entirely and cause many souls to be damned. Bad books will abound over the earth, and the **spirits of darkness will everywhere spread universal relaxation in everything concerning God's service: they will have very great power over nature; there will be churches to**

> **serve these spirits. People will be transported from one place to another by these evil spirits**... The dead and the just will be made to rise. [Mélanie interpolated here: "*That is to say, these dead will assume the aspect of righteous souls who once lived on earth, in order to seduce men more easily; these so-called resurrected dead,* ***who will be nothing other than the devil under these faces, will preach another Gospel****, contrary to that of the true Christ Jesus, denying the existence of heaven, if these be not in fact the souls of the damned. All these souls will appear joined to their bodies.*"] **There will be extraordinary wonders every place because the true faith has been extinguished and false light illumines the world**. ... Civil governments will all have the same objective, which will be to abolish and make every religious principle disappear, to make way for materialism, atheism, spiritism and vices of all kinds...It will be at this time that the Antichrist will be born of a Hebrew nun, a false virgin who will be in communication with the ancient serpent, master of impurity; his father will be a Bishop... he will work wonders, he will live only on impurities. He will have brothers who... will be children of evil...Rome will lose the faith and become the seat of the Antichrist...**The demons of the air, together with the Antichrist, will work great wonders on the earth and in the air**, and men will become ever more perverted. ...the **whole universe will be struck with terror, and many will allow themselves to be seduced because they didn't adore the true Christ living in their midst**. It is time; the sun is darkening; faith alone will survive. The time is at hand; the abyss is opening. Here is the king of the kings of darkness. Here is the beast with its subjects, calling itself the savior of the world.[366]

As we can see from these approved revelations, the Great Deception of the Antichrist is deeply associated with "demons of the air" who work "great wonders" in the air. They will moreover have "great power over nature" (one thinks of UFOs appearing to overcome the law of gravity, etc.), will transport people from one place to another (such claims have already been made in relation to ET contact), and will even seem to have brought the dead back to life (recall that demons can *appear* to do this, but cannot do so in truth).

Venerable Fulton Sheen

The same year the UFO craze began—1947—Venerable Archbishop Fulton Sheen proclaimed a stark warning about the rise of the Antichrist and the false doctrines this man of sin would preach. Remarkably—or, rather, presciently—he described in great detail, just several months before the deluge began, precisely what would be the tenets of the various "ET contactees" of the decades following this sermon.

> **We are living in the twilight of a civilization** ... [but] men do not want to believe their own times are wicked ... the great masses without faith are unconscious of the destructive processes going on. ... we have come to the end of the post-Renaissance Chapter of history which made man the measure of all things. ...[We are witnessing] the liquidation of the idea of the natural goodness of man who has no need of a God to give

him rights, or a Redeemer to salvage him from guilt, because **progress is automatic thanks to science—education and evolution, which will one day make man a kind of a god as H.G. Wells said, with his feet on the earth and his hands among the stars ...** From now on men will divide themselves into two religions—understood again as surrender to an absolute. **The conflict of the future is between the absolute who is the God-man and the absolute which is the man God; the God Who became man and the man who makes himself God; brothers in Christ and comrades in anti-Christ. The anti-Christ will not be so called, otherwise he would have no followers** ... This masquerade has helped the devil convince men that he does not exist, for he knows that he is never so strong as when men believe that he does not exist. When no man recognizes, the more power he exercises. ... Our Lord tells us that [the Antichrist] will be so much like Himself, that he would deceive even the elect ... How will he come in this new age to win followers to his religion? **He will come disguised as the Great Humanitarian; he will talk peace, prosperity and plenty** not as means to lead us to God, but as ends in themselves. **He will write books on the new idea of God to suit the way people live; induce faith in astrology** so as to make not the will but the stars responsible for sins; **he will explain guilt away psychologically** ... **he will foster science but only to have armament makers use one marvel of science to destroy another**; he will foster more divorces under the disguise that another partner is "vital"; he will increase love for love and decrease love for person; **he will invoke religion to destroy religion; he will even speak of Christ and say that he was the greatest man who ever lived**; his mission he will say will be to liberate men from the servitudes of superstition and Fascism ... [he will foster] the temptation to sell freedom for security, [and] as bread became a political weapon... **only those who think his way may eat** ... [he will promote] **a new religion without a Cross, a liturgy without a world to come, a city of man without a city of God, a religion to invoke a religion, or a politics which is a religion ... In the midst of all his seeming love for humanity and his glib talk of freedom and equality, he will have one great secret which he will tell to no one; he will not believe in God**. Because his religion will be brotherhood without the fatherhood of God, **he will deceive even the elect**. He will set up **a counter-Church which will be the ape of the Church because, he the devil, is the ape of God. It will have all the notes and characteristics of the Church, but in reverse and emptied of its divine content. It will be a mystical body of the anti-Christ that will in all externals resemble the mystical body of Christ.** ... [Today,] mediocrity and compromise characterize the lives of many Christians. **Many read the same novels as modern pagans, educate their children in the same godless way**, listen to the same commentators who have no other standard than judging today by yesterday, and tomorrow by today, allow pagan practices such as divorce and remarriage to creep into the family ... We are influencing the world less than the world influences us. There is no

> apartness. Well indeed might St. Paul say to us what he said to the Corinthians (2 Corinthians 6:14, 15) "*what has innocence to do with lawlessness? What is there in common between light and darkness? What harmony between Christ and Belial?*" St. Paul is here asserting that those who were sent out to establish a center of health had caught the disease, therefore, they lost the power to heal**. Since the amalgamation of the Christian and the pagan spirit has set in, since the gold is married with an alloy, the entirety must be thrust into the furnace that the dross may be burned away**. **The value of the trial will be to set us apart ...** There are Times of Troubles and it is not so much a Third World War that is to be feared, as **the rebirth of Leviathan, the coming of the Day of the Beast,** when there will be no buying or selling unless men have been signed with the sign of the Beast who would devour the child of the Mother of Mothers. " ... *once the taming talisman, the Cross is broken, the savagery of the old battlers will flare up again ... Then the old stone gods will rise from forgotten rubble and rub the dust of a thousand years from their eyes; and Thor will leap up and with his giant hammer start smashing Gothic cathedrals ...* "...Every now and then in history the devil is given a long rope, for we must never forget that Our Lord said to Judas and his band: "*This is your hour.*" God has His day, but evil has its hour when the shepherd shall be struck and the sheep dispersed. Has the Church made the preparations for just such a dark night in the decree of the Holy Father outlining the conditions on which a Papal Election may be held outside of Rome?...[367]

In light of the immense prophetic value of Venerable Sheen's 1947 clarion call, I could justify no further abridgment than what is included above.

In describing the antics of the Antichrist appearing as a great humanitarian, with "scientific solutions" to our problems, ostensibly effusively praising Christ but in fact aping Him, promoting Paganism to Christians who do not even realize that they have become Pagan—all in light of the anti-prophet H.G. Wells (the "Father of Science Fiction") insisting that through science and evolution, man would become a kind of god—is nothing short of a description of the main thrust of the diabolical teachings and "revelations" associated with ET-phenomena of the last 75 years since Sheen presented this address. Just as cuttingly, Sheen explains why this is indeed a test: it is necessary to again "set us apart" from the Godless world. A world which has again become Pagan, and which most Christians today are more a part of than they are a part of the Church.

27. Why is the ET Deception "The" Great Deception?

As we have done in some previous sections, let us also here leave aside lengthy quotations, rigorous analysis, numerous references to a variety of scholarly sources, and the like, and instead simply consider the basic relevant facts from a Christian common-sense perspective. (Some preceding sections will be summarized here.)

All faithful Christians know that, at some point before the end, there will indeed be:

- A "Strong Delusion" permitted by God. (2 Thessalonians 2:11)
- A Great Deception wherein men "wander into myths" (2 Timothy 4:4) and embrace the "teachings of demons." (1 Timothy 4:1)
- An Antichrist, the "Lawless One," who will claim to be "god" and who will seduce most of the world into his dominion. (2 Thessalonians 2:4)
- A lie promoted by an outpouring of false "signs and wonders" wrought by demons. (2 Thessalonians 2:9)
- A Deception that will succeed not only in ensnaring the Godless, but also many Christians. (Matthew 24:22)
- A "religious deception" that offers men an "apparent solution to their problems" at the price of "apostasy from the truth." (*Catechism*, §675)
- A Deception that manages to fundamentally undermine everything in the Faith, even while pretending to preserve it, for it will involve "holding the form of religion, but denying its power." (2 Timothy 3:5)

I encourage every Christian to pause and ponder for a moment if there is *a single phenomenon that has ever arisen in the entire history of the world* that—considering what we have reviewed in all the preceding chapters—comes anywhere close to the ET Deception in satisfying everything we know to expect in the Great Deception itself.

I do not think such a consideration will so much as present a close second.

Although the ET Deception was present in ancient Paganism (and has remained ever present in Buddhism and Hinduism), it was expelled from Christianity at its onset, and only reared its head in Christendom exactly when one would expect to see the beginnings of the Great Deception; namely, during the "Enlightenment," wherein the wholesale replacement of God with science began.

In the centuries that followed, it produced thoroughly rotten fruit everywhere it emerged. The Devil—lacking Omniscience—needed much time to test out this Deception to assess its effectiveness. Having settled, by the 20th century, that it would give him everything he wanted, he wasted no time unleashing its formal phase at Roswell. (It is a time which perfectly aligns with the moment when Satan's "75 to 100" years of heightened power, prophesied by Pope Leo XIII, likely began.) The years leading up to Pope St. Paul VI warning that the "smoke of Satan" from the "pagan prophets of science" had entered the Church of God were precisely the years this Deception became especially popular among men in the Vatican. And now, in the 2020s, as every other sign indicates we are truly entering the apocalyptic events foretold in Scripture, the ET Deception is suddenly exploding in unprecedented proportions.

We know that the Antichrist will claim to be "god." But how could he do this in a way that is most effective to the tickling ears of modern men, who want nothing to do with the One True God? The answer is immediately evident: by claiming a *pseudo*-Divinity based on "science, technology, and evolution." As science-fiction is the prevailing modern myth, he will undoubtedly use that as his own origin-myth. I do not believe the Antichrist would be so foolish as to claim that he himself is literally the "Uncreated Creator, the Divine Nature, Subsistent Being Itself," as that would push his devotees away from the very "scientific" atheism he will desire to be prevalent. Instead, he will perhaps claim: "*Like Jesus, I am an extraterrestrial. But I have evolved much further still, and I am bringing you the truly deepest, and truly definitive, Revelation. He spoke in ways that were amenable to unscientific societies. Now I can give you the real story.*" There may be other modern lies that provide convenient pretenses for one claiming a pseudo-Divinity, but none rival the potential allure of an "alien savior."

We know *that the Devil knows* of this Great Deception as well, for the Devil knows all that is prophesied in Scripture. We know, therefore, that before it is unleashed, he—being exceedingly intelligent—will have spent plenty of time and effort preparing its way. As we saw in preceding chapters, the ET Deception has been meticulously crafted and presented to society in a "grooming" process in sci-fi that has, over the last century, steadily led the masses from one lie to another. Many other Deceptions have also increased in recent decades, but it is difficult to find a single other delusion like the ET lie that has been so strategically introduced in ever ascending evil and error.

We know that the Great Deception itself will need to be regarded not merely as a fiction but, of course, as a reality. No other Deception has been so perfectly managed, in parallel, both in the most popular works of mainstream fiction and in "real" developments announced in mainstream media (i.e., the steady stream of UFO sightings, "ET contacts," and "disclosures" reported in the news since Roswell). Some deceptions are popular in fiction but lack a corresponding degree of mainstream media claims (e.g., genetically mutated humans with superpowers). Other deceptions are popular in reality but unpopular in fiction (e.g., the political lies that seem so overwhelmingly important one election cycle, only to be forgotten in a few years). The ET Deception, however, has been administered with great precision in both.

We know that the Great Deception will ensnare many Christians. For if those times were not shortened, "not even they would be saved."

(Matthew 24:22) Few other Deceptions that could be reasonably considered *Antichristic* have so successfully infiltrated the ranks of even "orthodox minded" Christians and Catholics. Indeed, safety from *The* Great Deception will be found only in complete faith, love, and trust in Jesus Christ, not merely by virtue of membership in and party-line-towing of a particular liturgical tribe or theological subculture—not even the superficially "orthodox minded" ones. For example, one finds almost all "orthodox Catholics" (rightly) standing opposed to Satanism, the New Age Movement, false World Religions, witchcraft, evil global elites hell-bent on promoting "woke" agendas, etc. But one finds many "orthodox Catholics" embracing the notion that aliens are now among us, and likewise finds them zealously promoting their hope and expectation that these ETs are about to save us from ourselves.

We know that the Great Deception will enable superficial Christians to pretend they have not apostatized when that is exactly what they have done. What other deception could achieve this like the ET Deception? One who embraces an "alien savior" could find himself still *abstractly* "placing his trust" in Jesus, while putting all his *actual* trust in the intervention of the extraterrestrials. He could find himself still occasionally picking up Rosary beads, but only devoted to Mary in a meager way in accordance with his new understanding of her as "one of countless Immaculate Conceptions." Each practice of "religion" could be continued out of habit, even while all of them have been entirely emasculated through relegation to ET-based beliefs, hopes, and aspirations.

We know that the Great Deception will be promoted by the ministrations of demons, and virtually no other contemporary phenomena (aside from explicit Satanism, for obvious reasons) has so repeatedly proven that its events are permeated by the activity of demons as "ET contact" has proven.

We know that the Great Deception will involve a world in crisis and a sudden, *seemingly* miraculous solution proposed. Who could justify presenting such a "solution" to a crisis the entire world finds itself in other than one who introduces himself as *simply not being from* this world? There are conceivable scenarios other than the extraterrestrial one, but none so fitting as that. Thanks to decades of fomentation by both science fiction and media reports, the masses are already craving a solution to their problems from "alien technology." There is little reason, then, to suppose that this is not precisely the charade the Devil would use through the Antichrist.

We know that the Great Deception will be with all manner of "lying signs and wonders." With millions of reported UFO sightings across the world in the last several decades, and ever-increasing claims—even from Government Officials—that "ET craft" can "defy gravity, move at astounding speeds, accelerate instantaneously, teleport, communicate telepathically, etc.", it is not possible to list any other phenomena that come close to fulfilling this prophecy as well as the UFO Deception. The Devil could inundate much of the world with these deceptions and make it seem like only a continuation and increase of what has been happening for decades.

We know that The Great Deception will never be taught by the True Magisterium, for Christ has promised that the Gates of Hell shall not prevail against His Church, founded on Peter (cf. Matthew 16:18). But we can anticipate it arriving as close to that boundary as Divine Providence could allow. This is precisely what we see with ET belief; all the most prominent contemporary clerics in the Vatican (who have commented directly on this matter) have endorsed belief in aliens, but the Magisterium has never taught they exist.

We know that the Great Deception will be a test; for if Scripture desired to settle precisely what the "Strong Delusion" would be, it would have done so. Instead, it is left vague. Moreover, the Church must follow the life of Christ, her head, therefore she too must have her final test, just as His final test was given in the Garden of Gethsemane, the night before His crucifixion. Other proposals for the Great Deception would be inadequate tests, for they are too clearly and explicitly dogmatically defined as heretical. *The* test, however, will be one which self-important theologians will be likely to fail, whereas simple and pious Christians will be much more likely to pass. This, too, is exactly what we see with the ET Deception; with most theologians and other "professional Catholics" assuring their audiences that belief in aliens is just fine, whereas ordinary faithful Christians are vastly more likely to recognize the demonic therein. Just as all the learned in Christ's time rejected Him, so the learned today engage in sophistical acrobatics to pretend to have dodged the hundreds of different arguments any faithful Christian can easily employ to reject extraterrestrials. Just as, in Christ's time, only the simple followed Him, so today simple Christians who have an innate sense of the Sacred can immediately perceive how many blasphemies are latent in alien belief, and how diabolical the whole ET-phenomenon is.

***

While I am indeed morally certain of the non-existence of aliens, I am not likewise claiming certainty that this ET Deception is necessarily *the* Great Deception itself; only that it is certainly a *massive* deception and that it *quite likely* is the "Strong Delusion" heralding the Antichrist. But I challenge anyone to present a single other phenomenon we have witnessed that comes close to this one in displaying every trait a discerning Christian should expect to see in identifying the Great Deception.

I am not holding my breath.

Part Five: AI, NHI, and Other Sci-Fi Deceptions

While the extraterrestrial deception looms largest among those apocalyptic lies long promoted through science fiction and suddenly exploding onto the world scene, other related sci-fi deceptions are also spiritually destructive. They too may herald the Antichrist in their own ways, while even now—aside from apocalyptic concerns—generating torrents of rotten fruits in both the Church and the world.

Many of these deceptions are simply additional examples of the same fundamental lie: the proposal that things exist in the material universe, other than human beings, which have reason. They are, therefore, equally opposed to the truth proclaimed in this book's very title, *Only Man Bears His Image* (by which I mean that, of the whole material universe, only descendants of Adam and Eve are intelligent). Of these additional deceptions, the most popular is the "AI" Deception—the notion that "artificial intelligence," which is nothing but software with a gimmicky name, may acquire *actual* intelligence. This achievement (which, we will see, has not happened and can never happen) is sometimes referred to as "AGI" (Artificial General Intelligence) "Strong AI," "Super AI," or by other monikers. Less popular, but troublingly increasing, deceptions include the notion that animals may themselves already have reason just as humans have it, only lacking the ability to communicate effectively with us.

Still other deceptions are not directly related to this book's overarching theme as exhibited in its title, but will be treated briefly here, as they too are sci-fi-based deceptions and pose great threats to the Faith: the Time Travel Deception, the Transhuman/Mind-Tech Deception, the Simulation Theory Deception, and more.

28. On Sci-fi Deception in General

"Blind'—they are, and "leaders of the blind" puffed up with the proud name of science, they have reached that pitch of folly at which they pervert the eternal concept of truth ... in introducing a new system in which "they are seen to be under the sway of a blind and unchecked passion for novelty, thinking not at all of finding some solid foundation of truth..."

—Pope St. Pius X. *Pascendi Dominici Gregis,* §13

False Mystique, Origin of Sci-Fi Deception: Quantum Theory and More

Malicious men seeking to deceive gullible folk for their own ulterior motives, or even the Devil himself seeking to delude the masses, often foment in the minds of their hearers a quasi-mystical approach to certain undeserving phenomena.

This is precisely what we have seen in the last century and a half with evolution. The word itself has become a veritable replacement for the word "God" in contemporary secular parlance. Whenever the beauty, intricacy, and wisdom with which creation is endowed is further described, the secular world will invariably note only the "wonders of evolution."

A similar tactic has long been employed with Quantum Mechanics and similar theories. Pseudo-mystical approaches to this field—which, as the name rightly implies, is nothing but one form of *mechanics*—undergird much of the New Age movement, imparting to it a "supernatural feel," but without God. Whoever is unfortunate enough to pick up a New Age textbook is likely to find it littered with justifications of its lies deferring to various "Quantum" phenomena. The same is true of Ufology. Charlatans like Dr. Steven Greer scarcely ever speak without using the word "Quantum" in support of the pseudoscientific claims they use to promote dark agendas. These "Quantum" arguments, however, extend to almost all other realms of sci-fi-based deceptions. Whoever wishes to avert them, therefore, must understand what he is dealing with whenever that word is invoked.

> "The contemporary 'science fiction' myths of time-travel and multidimensional space, derived from imaginative speculation on Einsteinian and post-Einsteinian physics, and often applied to the UFO phenomenon, are in some ways replacing the world-view of the revealed religions, **since they seem to transcend materialism and provide the**

'miraculous' possibilities always associated with religious faith and spiritual experience. For God all things are possible—but if all things, or many strange things, are possible to UFOs, and will be possible to human science in the future, then who needs God? If space, time, matter, and even some mental processes can be manipulated by various subtle material energies, then who needs grace? **If time-travel is possible, who needs eternity? ...** the only possible conclusion is that the myth of time travel ... is based on an inability to conceive of the real nature of eternity. Therefore, **those who become obsessed with these myths are making themselves available to satanic forces whose goal is to hide from us the reality of eternity by means of a counterfeit**..." —Charles Upton. *System of Antichrist*.

For many decades, a number of Christian thinkers, eager to be regarded as standing on the cutting edge of science—and, commendably, desirous of using this recognition to argue for God's existence or against materialist determinism—have taken any opening they perceive within Quantum Physics to leverage it into a proof of God, free will, and miracles.

But opening the doors for the entry of demons is no way to argue for these truths. By turning Quantum Mechanics into a source of pseudo-mystique, they have only presented a catalyst for New Age thought, Ufology, ET belief in general, and a deluge of other forms of esotericism or occultism, which all now treat Quantum Mechanics and similar fields exactly like a Christian treats Divine grace.

Many charlatans all but explicitly admit this. For example, prominent Ufologist Steven Greer claims he could see how someone who "**does not understand trans-dimensional physics would think that extraterrestrials are simply angels**." (As we saw in earlier chapters, "ETs" are indeed "angelic," in the sense that they are demons; demons are *fallen* angels, therefore they still retain angelic *nature*.) But Greer emphatically rejects this classification, insisting that ETs are indeed among us and are physical beings like we are, but are simply more "evolved," technologically advanced, and scientifically enlightened, and therefore have mastered the subtleties of Quantum Mechanics. Greer's delusions, however, are the norm—not the exception—in contemporary sci-fi-inspired thought. Whether we are dealing with ET promoters, sentient AI promoters, time travel promoters, or what have you, they all defer to "Quantum Mechanics" (and similar theories) to pretend to thereby explain the *natural* possibility of what any common-sense-respecting person immediately knows is either categorically impossible or is an indication of the presence of the Supernatural (or at least preternatural).

Well-meaning Christians who likewise foolishly promote Quantum-mystique have invited chaos into their argument under the guise of opposing materialistic determinism, but from the premise of chaos, there is no knowing what conclusions will follow. They have only opened Pandora's Box.

This was the Devil's plan all along. He has achieved a victory when he beguiles someone into supposing that—within the order of nature (that is, without the miraculous intervention of God)—an actually existing thing (as opposed to a merely conceptual notion within a hypothesis) can do one or more of the following: be in two places at once, or teleport, or be annihilated, or pop into existence from nothing, or be "entangled" (linked) with another thing without the operation of contact or forces, or be intrinsically indeterminate (awaiting external observation for its own objective nature to be determined), or travel backwards or forwards in time, or enter into or proceed from "another dimension," or any other of a number of patently common-sense-contradicting propositions.

What the Devil has thereby achieved is this: he has seduced the soul who entertains these absurdities to wander outside of the boundaries of safety that had been afforded to him by the fact that God created him with an intellectual conscience, which always far surpasses the force of any empirical conjecture. The Deceiver has beguiled such a soul into throwing this Divine map into the garbage bin for the sake of plowing forward haphazardly, pretending that every glittering worldly ("scientific") claim he stumbles upon is itself a beacon pointing to the destination, when in fact—in this fallen world—it is just as likely to be a trap. One might as well slice off his tongue because a chef tells him this will cause him to better experience taste.

Some readers may think I am here taking an unapologetic anti-science stance. In fact, only the opposite is true. The rejection of common sense is not only the destruction of intellectual and spiritual safety in general, but also the emasculation of authentic science itself. (More consideration of this point with respect to Quantum Theory can be found at www.DSDOConnor.com/OMBHI.)

Confronting The Many "Revolutions" of Modern Science: All that Is Needed Is a Return to Common-Sense

It is impossible, in one book, to address (much less refute) even a fraction of the mythical "scientific" claims that have been used and will be used to promote various charades related to ETs, AI, time travel, "interdimensionality," and other sci-fi deceptions with which the faithful will be assaulted. Whether we are ostensibly dealing with Quantum Mechanics or other fields such as String Theory, Multiverse Theory, "Interdimensional Physics," or innumerable other fields, one is sure to find their use (in relation to these deceptions) inundated with as much neo-Pagan poison parading itself as legitimate science.

Thankfully, one simple capacity can rescue anyone from most sci-fi-derived deceptions: *common sense*. One simple commitment will facilitate this rescue: rejecting that false humility which demands leaving aside common sense in order to "remain open" to all claims, since, after all, *"we don't have it all figured out!"*

Of course we do not "have it all figured out." Far more truths doubtless remain to be discovered, even within science, than we have discovered thus far. This fact, however, does not detract from the absolute and unquestionable authority common sense enjoys over all claims made within the domain of science.

This superiority is deduced from a few absolute truths that no believer may doubt. God exists, God is good, God made *us*, and God made *all that is.* One need only prayerfully consider these simple truths together to realize that God built our own senses, our own minds, and our own bedrock patterns and premises of thought, to correspond with the truth of reality—which He too created.

I am well positioned to pretend to justify rejecting the superiority of common sense. My first job after graduating with my degree in mechanical engineering involved running some of the most cutting-edge high-tech experiments being undertaken at the time by GE Global Research at its international headquarters. Without going into details I am not at liberty to share, I spent many hours calibrating and inducing carbon nanotube substrates to, under certain extreme circumstances we created in the laboratory, cause a phenomena to transpire *which we modelled as* "quantum-teleportation emission of electrons."

I am well aware, however, that I was *not* observing results of *true* teleportation of really existing physical things. I knew then, and I know now, that common sense rules that out. For, in fact, no literally existing substance can (outside of a miracle from God; e.g., the bilocation of saints) proceed from one point to another without passing through the intervening distance (and even bilocation may operate under a different mode).

More generally speaking, nothing that one can even say about electrons, protons, neutrons, photons, quarks, leptons, gluons, fermions, bosons, antimatter, or any other such thing, is predicated of them in the ordinary sense of predication. When one speaks of what these things allegedly "do," he is only describing an essentially allegorical model of a set of data (which itself is categorically limited and often fundamentally flawed). Therefore, pretending that common-sense-contradicting claims pertaining to such particles (e.g., travelling backwards in time, teleporting, popping into existence, being indeterminate, etc.) are thereby palatable for really existing things (e.g., humans, "UFOs," "aliens," etc.) is sheer nonsense.

These and other concepts like them (including some of their counterparts on the macro—i.e., astronomical—scale) are entirely *conjectural* entities; they are *ideas* certain scientists have postulated in order to render various theoretical models palatable, consistent, and (hopefully) effective in prediction. Modern men, however—ever seeking the *mystical* but without the baggage of traditional religion—have deluded themselves into supposing that these academic hypotheses they have created deserve more ontological credence than those things which we know God Himself made, those qualities with which we know He endowed creation, and those faculties He built us with to grasp His works (e.g., reason, memory, common sense, infallible certainty in logical axioms, the consensus of the senses, etc.).

Similarly, when a mathematician invents negative numbers to keep track of debts—perhaps to aid in banking—he hopefully realizes that there is not actually such a thing as a "negative quantity;" an "anti-dollar." The notion itself is incoherent. Equally fictional are so-called "imaginary numbers," where mathematics departs yet another step from reality, by positing not only negative numbers, but square roots thereof. This, too, is a helpful tool: imaginary numbers make algebra appear "complete" and they save time in various computations. Yet, they in no way describe corporeal entities in the real universe. In response to this observation, many protest (including some misguided mathematics textbooks I have taught from and have had to philosophically correct for my own students' sake), "*but all math is imaginary anyway.*" That is absolutely untrue. Math is very real, despite the modernist, nominalist philosophers' attempt to emasculate it. God is *Three* Persons, and it would be absurd to claim that "Three" is somehow unreal. He really is, therefore, ten fewer than thirteen Persons; He is one-half as many as six Persons; He is the square-root of nine Persons (and so on). A human hand is a *five*-fingered thing, and it would be ridiculous to claim that "five" here is somehow nothing but a game we invented. *

---

* Similarly, contemporary empirical and theoretical science is very real. Sometimes, however, individuals working in these fields invent concepts that in some way (and *within the context* of some systems or discussions) make reality easier to quantify and predict, but in fact do not, in any way, *describe* reality itself. And here is where those esotericists and deceivers of all stripes, who treat science as their false god, conceal their machinations. They pretend that the rules which apply only to *their* story may be equally applied to *God's* creation. When, for example, reducing physics beneath the point of *tangible* substance—i.e., when speaking of subatomic particles—*we are not speaking about reality* in the ordinary sense of the term. Whatever a physicist might claim these particles may "do"—*be it teleportation, travelling backward or forward within time, disappearing and reappearing, becoming "entangled" with particles elsewhere, defying laws of causality, having qualities contingent upon their own being observed, annihilating themselves, appearing from nothing,* and on the list goes—he is only thereby sharing the plotlines of the fictional, even if helpful, stories his own peers have written. None of these phenomena are *real*. Any theories built upon the assumption they are real, and which then propose to describe things that we might possibly—*ever*—experience in the real world, are entirely useless and harmful. They are, intrinsically and inescapably, more outlandish

It is not only mathematics that does this; empirical science does it as well. Unfortunately, more scholars of the latter than the former field seek to pretend they are describing reality when they are only describing a fictional story. But even the father of Quantum Physics himself, Niels Bohr, pointed out that "**there is no quantum reality**; there is only a Quantum description,"* and that "...**the entire formalism is to be considered as a tool for deriving predictions** of definite and statistical character."[368] Dr. Jan Faye, commenting on this, pointed out that for Bohr, there was "**no possibility for an interpretation of the quantum formalism that postulates an ontological [i.e., *real*] structure.**"[369]

I am focusing on Quantum Theory here only because it provides the most popular batch of pseudo-premises upon which various sci-fi deceptions (whether pertaining to ETs, UFOs, AI, time travel, or whatever else) pretend to be credibly based. There are, of course, many other such fields of study which, when deferred to as providing supposed "evidence" of the palatability of some sci-fi-sounding conjecture, must be treated with great skepticism. (Other phrases to be on the lookout for include: "interdimensional physics, string theory, supersymmetry, multiverse theory, evolution, gravitational wave theory, quantum gravity, post-biological theory" and in general any references to "energies, vibrations, phasings," that lack absolutely solid, comprehensible, and *demonstrable* empirical bases.) Again, Quantum Theory can be a serious field of study and much good work is done therein; I am only here addressing an *abuse* of it.

Now, if God is good—and indeed He is—then He made us with an innate ability to comprehend the reality in which He placed us. The bedrock logical structural patterns of thought with which He endowed our intellects—which can be fairly called "common sense"—therefore must enjoy infinite superiority to any theory (no matter how "supported by data") proposed within empirical science. The fact is that you have common sense. God built you with it. You must not fear to employ it even when that employment flies in the face of the demands of formidable armies of "experts" with book-length résumés. Let us consider just a few of

---

than any mere political "fake news," for such phony publications at least bear the possibility of becoming real news. For example, an ET promoter's favorite science news website likely today has some article promoting an individual scientist's new study, claiming that he has perhaps caused a subatomic particle to teleport, or travel backwards or forwards in time, or what have you, and that we therefore can be hopeful such things might be possible for us humans (or at least "aliens") as well. Such an article does not have one iota of additional value beyond another article describing the ability of "Thanos" (the villain in *The Avengers*) to use "Infinity Stones" to teleport or travel in time. Both are equally fictional. One, however, is more damaging, since it pretends to be genuine science.

* This may not be a direct quote from Bohr himself, but it has long been a common way in which scholars of his contributions summarize his explanation of the matter.

the multitude of certainties with which common sense has endowed each human being who has surpassed the age of reason:

- It is common sense that whatever conclusions logically follow from true premises must themselves be true, and that whatever contradicts any truth must itself be false;
- It is common sense that the whole is greater than the part, the cause is greater than the effect, and no effect precedes its cause;
- It is common sense that all really existing things exist in a certain way, irrespective of whether or how they are observed;
- It is common sense that no effects between physical objects act without some real force or physical contact;
- It is common sense that a physical thing must travel through the distance between its origin and its destination to arrive at the latter, and that a straight line is the shortest distance between two points;
- It is common sense that "space" is not a "thing" that can be manipulated or even directly *described*—that any "description of space" is only a description of some *thing* placed *within* a "space";
- It is common sense that "time" is also not a "thing" that can be folded, reversed, jumped about backwards or forwards in, etc.;
- It is common sense that functionally ordered things cannot arise by chance, no matter how much time is allowed;
- It is common sense that no creation of man can ever itself match, much less surpass, the greatest capacity (intelligence and free will) of man;
- It is common sense that neither animals nor any other non-human things we see have reason; that humans are unique; superior to all else in nature;
- It is common sense that consciousness is not a material phenomenon, but rather a spiritual one;
- It is common sense that *reality is real*—not a simulation, dream, or illusion of any sort;
- It is common sense that there is such a thing as human nature, and this nature includes: reason and free-will, a duty to worship and obey God, being made as either male or female, being fundamentally un-improvable, etc.*

Although we have, in this book, deeply analyzed some of these notions (and will continue to analyze others), ultimately doing so is often unnecessary. You—whoever you are, reading this—already know, *with certainty*, that each item above is true.

---

* Recall that I am not claiming "impossible" things cannot ever happen—plenty can happen, by the miraculous action of God, Who can bring about anything that is not a logical contradiction or a denial of Himself. I am simply pointing out that common sense is absolutely certain of the *natural* impossibility of such things, and therefore is capable of knowing when *God*—and not technology—is acting.

Every "scientific" argument which seeks to contradict any of those points (and others like them) can, should, and must be treated as the fiction that it is, and immediately rejected outright and without apology. To engage in discussion regarding such propositions is occasionally worthwhile, but it is also often a trap, for the very act of doing so may induce a well-meaning individual within the discussion to forget the overriding value of his common sense. It may compel him to forget that—no matter how many degrees his interlocutors have—he is essentially fulfilling the role of an adult playing pretend with a small child. And how lamentable indeed it would be if such an adult, absorbed by the intricacies of the plotline invented by the child, forgets that the whole thing is a charade. Who, then, is left to rescue them both from their delusions?

Of course, those who rightly defer to their common sense can expect to be regularly castigated by "the experts" for daring to defy what they have "proven." Therefore, let us consider what it means for some statement to be "proven."

When one claims this to be the case, there are only two things he can coherently mean by it. First, he may mean that he has directly proved it (*to* himself) by grasping how it follows—by logical necessity—from premises that are themselves similarly proven. For this to be the case, his own intellect must have grasped—with absolute certitude—the validity of each step in the logical demonstration. This is exceedingly rare. Therefore, we are left with the second, vastly more common meaning of the word "proven": he may mean that enough of his peers have *claimed* it is proven and it is pragmatically advisable for him to take their word for it.

Why, however, are his peers claiming something is proven? Almost invariably, for the same reason he is: others have said so. On Judgment Day, we will see just how many of modern science's "proven" propositions were nothing but the assertions of shoddy studies that only became popular within a certain proof community by furthering a preferred narrative, and whose constituents ostensibly justified its "proven" nature with nothing but deference to an unrecognized parade of circular reasoning subtly steered by those who control the purse-strings.

Do not misunderstand: much is, indeed, proven. For example, I can, with all conviction, assert that the Pythagorean Theorem is proven. I know this not on faith, but because I have seen how it follows, by logical necessity, from premises that are themselves absolutely certain. This, however, invites the question: how do I know the premises are certain? Simple: they, too, are proven. But what of the premises upon which *those premises* are themselves built?

Obviously, this process cannot be an infinite regress; it must stop somewhere. Some things must be true merely because they are, simply upon being stated, immediately recognized—with absolute certainty—to be true by any sane *and honest* human being. And what are these irreducible truths? They are none other than the First Principles; tenets of common sense. *Everything*—including every claim that science ever has made, ever will make, *or ever possibly could make*—is built upon them.

At this point, it has hopefully become obvious how absurd it is to ever tolerate a "scientific" claim that contradicts the teachings of common sense. Such a claim itself, whether or not its proponents admit this, *is built upon common sense*. If, therefore, that foundation itself is put into question, the claim itself is even more resolutely rejected by the same token. No conclusion may contradict the very premises it requires.

Imagine a man sitting on a very high branch of a massive tree, remaining unalarmed when another man begins axing away at the trunk of the same tree. Perhaps the trunk is so distant from his position on the branch that he cannot see it through the thickness of the intervening branches and foliage. "That is not needed anymore," he may say to himself as he ignores, or even affirmatively applauds, the "thump, thump, thump" of the axe, and infatuated with the branches that surround him. We all know what the fate of this poor delusional man will be, so filled with knowledge of the branches that he has forgotten they are all continually supported entirely by the trunk.

Sci-fi deceptions, however (including when they are promoted by actual scientists and presented as real science) are so alluring precisely because they violate common sense. Those who promote the NHI agenda almost all repeatedly voice the refrain, "science fiction is what really told us the truth about all this!" In so doing, they condemn themselves. Like a corrupt politician crafting a bill to benefit his biggest donors, they are only thereby signaling that the whole motivation for their crusade has nothing to do with its public explanation. "The truth is out there," they say, when in fact their only concern is to strive in vain to escape from the Truth Himself.

"The experts," though, will continue to deny all of this.

Against the Experts: Every Man Answers His Own Question in Deciding to Whom He Poses It

There are times when the worst course of action is to "ask an expert." The first to recognize this fact was the Father of Philosophy, Socrates. In his most famous speech, the *Apology* (his defense at the Athenian trial wherein he was sentenced to death), he said, two and a half thousand years ago:

> I met a man who has spent a world of money on the Sophists, Callias the son of Hipponicus, and knowing that he had sons, I asked him: "Callias," I said, "if your two sons were foals or calves, there would be no difficulty in finding someone to put over them; we should hire a trainer of horses or a farmer probably who would improve and perfect them in their own proper virtue and excellence; but as they are human beings,

whom are you thinking of placing over them?"

The Sophists were ancient Greek self-proclaimed "wise men" who presented themselves as teachers of "virtue." In fact, they were relativists who cared not for truth but only for money and for success in securing their base desires and helping their students (who paid enough) to do the same. Naturally, therefore, a father like this "Callias," who wanted his sons to be "successful"—rich and powerful—would hire the Sophists to train them in "virtue."

The Sophists doubtless gave the sons of Callias an answer to each question they had. What Socrates realized, however, was that this unworthy father had already erroneously decided *what human virtue is* in the very act of selecting the Sophists to instruct his sons. The demise of their souls, even amid worldly success, followed inevitably from the *a priori* (before the fact) supposition that "virtue" is simply "worldly success," with the advice from "the experts" in that unrecognized supposition sealing their fate.

This is the same fatal error made by modern men who seek out physicists (or other scientists) to answer questions that are fundamentally religious, philosophical, or even commonsensical in nature. Just as the Sophists of old paraded their extensive travels and encyclopedic knowledge as supposed proofs that they alone had the answers to all matters, so the scientists of today too often parade their own (very pigeonholed) expertise about hypothetical subatomic particles and forces (or other empirical phenomena) as if this were a reason to give credence to their pseudo-religious propositions. The tragedy, however, is not that experts overestimate the value of their own expertise. That much should be expected in this fallen world. The tragedy—today as in those ancient times—is that common folk, desiring an easy solution to their problems, deceive themselves into capitulating to these neo-Sophists.

Socrates was not opposed to heeding the advice of experts. As he notes in the quote above, it is obvious that if, for example, one wanted to improve a horse, he would be well advised to seek out the help of a farmer. That is a particular and pragmatic need for which soliciting expert advice is unproblematic. Likewise, today, Socrates would endorse seeking out a scientist to design a computer, determine a cancer treatment regimen, calculate the next solar eclipse, or ascertain with greater accuracy the gravitational constant.

But Socrates would condemn emphatically—and justly—our contemporary tendency to consult the scientists to answer those questions that are within the domain of common sense, philosophy, or religion. Indeed, one has only committed an act of supreme folly (and surreptitiously *assumed* the—false—answer to his own question) who seeks out a scientist to determine whether "AI" has (or can ever have) sentience or reason; or whether "time travel" is possible; or whether animals have personhood;

or whether immortality is technologically achievable; or whether "other dimensions" exist in the universe; or whether "other universes" exist; or whether the world is just a "computer simulation"; or whether man can "evolve" into some other type of being; or any other number of similar questions derived from sci-fi deceptions.

Common sense gives a resoundingly certain answer to all these questions: *No.* Good Philosophy gives a resoundingly certain answer to all these questions: *No.* True Religion gives a resoundingly certain answer to all these questions: *No.*

Whoever, then, insists upon *even remaining open to the possibility* of the answer to these and similar questions being "yes"—upon heeding "the input of science"—has, in that very openness, rejected the truth. He has pretended that conclusions may validly violate the very premises on which they are built. He has "wandered into myths," and has refused to "tolerate sound teaching." (2 Timothy 4:4)

This rejection of the truth may not (immediately and obviously) involve formal heresy or explicit apostasy. But that is the eventual inevitable result of following that same path long enough. Foundational and culpable errors about reality itself cannot be neatly contained within one compartment of life. They are like malignant cancers. One who gives "science" the right to contradict faith, reason, or common sense, has unchained a demon.

And this demon will not keep the promises it made when it begged to be unleashed.

29. AI, AGI, and "The Singularity"

"Unclean spirits, associated through that wicked art with these same idols, have miserably taken captive the souls of their worshippers, by bringing them down into fellowship with themselves." —St. Augustine

After extraterrestrials, "artificial intelligence" is the most popular of the sci-fi deceptions which have beguiled modern men into supposing that beings other than himself bear the Divine Image—that is, have reason and free will. Not only has this AI Deception acquired a similar caliber as the ET Deception; they are even deeply conceptually linked. Most Ufologists and ET promoters in general regard AI as part and parcel to the activity of the "aliens" they claim are buzzing our skies; with—as the story goes—some UFOs being piloted by the aliens themselves and others being merely "probes" sent in advance, operating with only AI-controlled technology.

Sci-fi deceptions—particularly of the "NHI" (Non-Human Intelligence) variety—flock together. For example, I came upon the following June 2023 article because it was promoted by a prominent Catholic scholar and ET promoter. Within it, an "expert on String Theory" (which is about as meaningful a title as "an expert on Star Trek") interviewed biologist Dr. Michael Levin (famous for claiming to have "discovered xenobots"—so-called "living robots) on his work. Levin claimed:

> ...People are very binary because they're still carrying this pre-scientific holdover. **Back in before-science times, you could be smart like humans and angels, or you could be dumb like everything else.** That was fair enough for our first pass in 1700, but now we can do better. You don't need to be at either of these endpoints. You could be somewhere in the middle. ... **Everybody who doesn't read a lot of sci-fi is so behind on this**. ...[we should] formulate something like the **new Golden Rule: *"Be nice to goal-seeking systems in some sort of proportion to their capacity to do it."*** ... People who worry about various kinds of AI today [being moral/sentient agents], never mind tomorrow's, aren't crazy at all. Humanity has a long history of moral lapses toward creatures that don't look enough like them.[370]

In a popular March 2023 social media post that "went viral," Dr. Levin wrote:

> One way to think about AI (even current AI, [with] its limitations & impending ubiquity): it's like **we've discovered a new life form on Earth—it's been all around us, but undetectable; it's quite alien, but it has some high competencies and many unknown behaviors. Just now, for the first time, we've learned how to communicate with it**.[371]

As we can see from the interview three months later, Dr. Levin is not merely encouraging us to "think about" AI like that, but to remain open to actually treating it like that. His admonishment is simple: abandon the "before-science times," when people thought only humans and angels had reason. Instead, embrace sci-fi (otherwise you are "so behind") and realize that a "new Golden Rule" is needed. The desire of these deceivers is no longer even concealed, as it often was in earlier years: everything must be fundamentally re-written in light of their "discoveries" that beings other than man have reason.

***

The truth about "AI," however, is as simple as the truth about "aliens." Neither exists.

Such a blunt affirmation may surprise even those who were unsurprised to hear it said that aliens do not exist, but let us hasten to clarify this statement. Obviously, there is such a thing as software. Not long after software was first used in the mid-20th century, some people began to refer to it as "Artificial Intelligence." This name, however, is a fallacy. When we validly refer to something as an "artificial" version of its natural counterpart, we are acknowledging that, although a man-made process was used to assemble it, its own nature is nevertheless substantially similar to that natural parallel. For example, an "artificial diamond" is essentially identical to a natural diamond; it was simply grown in a lab instead of mined out of the earth.

As we will see in the forthcoming sections, however, this similarity does not exist (nor will it ever) with "artificial intelligence." AI, (when treated as legitimately intelligent), is to real intelligence what a Pagan idol is to God Himself: a mockery. Just as there is nothing wrong with a statue (on the contrary, one can prove a beautiful adornment to a city square), and the sin only arises when it is treated as an object of worship and thus becomes an idol, so too there is nothing wrong with software ("AI") as long as those who use it understand what it is and what it cannot ever be. When that line is crossed, however, we only gravely harm ourselves, and we are opening yet another door to the entry of demons.

Let us begin this chapter by deferring to the wisdom of those most qualified to provide it in this context.

The Myth of AI: A Dream that Makes a Nightmare of Reality

> "Human minds and computer programs are so different that it seems wrong to call computers intelligent—even artificially intelligent."
> —Dr. Gary Smith, *The AI Delusion*
>
> "Misuse of words is not only harmful in itself, it also has a bad effect on the soul." —Socrates

Dr. Erik Larson is a computer scientist, philosopher, and expert in AI who has even managed projects funded by the U.S. Military's Research & Development arm, DARPA (Defense Advanced Research Projects Agency). Since the early 2000s, he has worked professionally in organizations such as "Cyc" dedicated to developing AI with human-like reasoning capabilities. Clearly, if anyone who argues *against* such aspirations should be taken seriously, it is precisely Dr. Larson. In his 2021 book, appropriately titled, *The Myth of Artificial Intelligence,* he explains:

> ...[AI] necessarily lacks the ability to learn common sense and acquire genuine understanding. **That we are pinning the future of the human mind—not so constrained—on the further development of AI in this vein is simply stupefying**. Not only is this approach entirely bereft of the general intelligence necessary to make any real intellectual advance in modern culture, but because induction is provably distinct from abduction, we already know that **there is no bridge from the one to the other**. All of Ray Kurzweil's proclamations of inevitable progress cannot undo this truth once it becomes known. We should be honest here, as recognition of the truth would itself form part of the blueprint for moving forward. To sum up: **there is no way for current AI to "evolve" general intelligence ... Simply saying "we're getting there" is scientifically and conceptually bankrupt**, and further fans the flames of anti-human and anti-intellectual forces...**nowhere is this more evident than in the dogma of AI mythology itself**. On any calculation about the future of artificial general intelligence, the onus is squarely on AI mythologists portending the coming of human-level AI to explain what we're doing to move things along. Perhaps we could start with a frank acknowledgement that deep learning is a dead end, as is data-centric AI in general, no matter how many advertising dollars it might help bring in to big tech's coffers. We might also give further voice to a reality that increasing numbers of AI scientists themselves are now recognizing, if reluctantly: that, as with prior periods of great AI excitement, **no one has the slightest clue how to build an artificial general intelligence. The dream remains mythological precisely because, in actual science, it has never been even remotely understood**... cheerful promotion of the [AI] myth, and its cousin in swarm science—like cheerleading for hive minds before it—seems to suggest that **modern society has indeed wandered whistling into a kind of derangement of core values**... AI

> mythology becomes a new focal point for future meaning, however nihilistic and untrue. As Lanier suggested, too, we can make such a future become true by simply chiseling away at human intelligence and uniqueness, until we have stooped low enough to adjust to a computation-dominated future... we are now on the wrong path, in large part because we are actively attempting to cover up a key deficiency—a lack of flourishing human culture—with rhetoric about the inevitable rise of machines... Just as Frankenstein was really an exploration of spiritual isolation (a problem felt deeply by Mary Shelley and her husband, Percy Shelley), the deepest questions embodied in the AI myth are not technical or even scientific—they involve our own ongoing attempts to find meaning and to forge future paths for ourselves in an ever-changing world. **There is nothing to be gained by indulging in the myth here; it can offer no solutions to our human condition except in the manifestly negative sense of discounting human potential and limiting future human possibility** (Chapter 18)

Rightly does this expert in AI describe as "stupefying" the contemporary world's giddy expectation for AGI. Although this myth is completely devoid of any truth—any basis in reality—its fictional nature does not mitigate its society-destroying effects. As this secular scientist notes, this "dogmatic" AI myth has caused a "discounting [of] human potential," and even a "derangement of core values." He is absolutely correct. But what might another scientist say who can combine his scientific insights with theological ones? Let us turn again to Fr. Stanley Jaki.

Fr. Stanley Jaki Against the Diabolical AI Deception

In earlier chapters detailing the ET Deception, we already settled the extraordinary weight carried by the cutting critiques of the prolific theologian, renowned physicist, and Benedictine priest, Fr. Stanley Jaki (†2009)—wherein, among other things, he cautioned that whoever fails to see the machinations of the Devil behind "extraterrestrials" is simply blind.

Providentially and prophetically, this same priest provided equally bold and true condemnations of the AI Deception. Let us review them here. Jaki begins by noting in general terms how much havoc has been wrought upon society by its obsession with AI. He says:

> Among the various fashionable phrases which nowadays are often taken in some circles as genuine signs of scientific sophistication, references to artificial minds, or thinking machines, easily hold a foremost rank ... Scientific fashions ... can, as the history of science amply illustrates, get hold of the minds of several generations with no small damage to cultural values. ... **In our times the growing obsession with the idea of artificial intelligence is already heavily contributing to a weakening of critical sense, to a lessening of man's appreciation of intangibles, and to a growth of skepticism about human values.**

> Clearly, no scholar mindful of his responsibilities is free to watch this dangerous trend from the sidelines. **The voice of criticism should be raised time and again in the hopes that the extent of cultural erosion would thereby be reduced.** **In an age overawed by the spectacular feats of physical science,** it is far more popular to heap praise on physics than to appraise soberly its actual achievements and potentialities ... Nobel-laureate physicist, Polykarp Kusch [said]: "*Science cannot do a very large number of things and to assume that science may find a technical solution to all problems is the road to disaster.*" To prevent such disaster one certainly should keep remembering the difference between machines, however marvelous, and their true source, the marvel of man's mind.[372]

Summarizing his indictment of the AI Deception in the epilogue of the same work quoted above, Fr. Jaki notes:

> Perceptive students of cybernetics are of course fully aware of the **disasters in store for mankind should the attitude of gadget worshiping gain the dominant role in this highly mechanized age of ours. They know that the danger of machines derives not so much from the machines as from man's attitude towards them**. For the crucial issue in the man-machine relationship lies not in what machines can do but in the concepts that man forms about machines and about himself. ... [the current trend in literature, however,], if it goes unchecked, may lead to **an upheaval of human values unparalleled in history.** It is a literature which **blatantly overestimates computers and drastically devaluates man.** One may, for instance, read in a college textbook destined for large circulation that artificial minds shall achieve what the splendid intellectual and technological triumphs of the scientific revolution could not do: come to grips with the value problems of life...for a peaceful and productive international society.

The AI Deception, in other words, promises (if it follows the same trend Fr. Jaki here observed to be popular decades ago—and it has) *apocalyptic* levels of diabolical disorientation; for it will bring about an "upheaval of human values unparalleled in history." He continues:

> The stage has been reached where the question "*Can machines think?*" is viewed as a projective test of personality. Those answering "yes" are described as "*self-confident humanists, unafraid of pursuing the road of scientific progress wherever it will lead, free of conventional fears and superstitious worries, rejoicing in the achievements of mankind.*" Those who refuse to admit the possibility of thinking machines are called "*doubters, pessimists, people afraid of flights of imagination, unadventurous souls who do not dare touch the strong wine of great ideas.*" Or they are classified as "otherworldly thinkers" regardless of the fact that among these belong some of the most creative geniuses responsible for the development of computers, like Pascal, who is specifically singled out for the dubious honor of "otherworldliness."

Today, and far more than when Fr. Jaki wrote the words above, men indeed receive heaps of praise for claiming that "The Singularity" is here or imminent, wherein AI will match or exceed human intelligence. This is, perversely, viewed as "bold" and "open" and even "humble." Those who, in accordance with perennial Christian truth (not to mention basic common sense and sound science), regard man as unique, with his faculty of intelligence and will found nowhere else, are denounced with opposite terms. It is unsurprising, therefore, that almost all Ufologists are almost as giddy for "sentient AI" as they are for extraterrestrials—they jump on any diabolical "Non-Human Intelligence" bandwagon they can find.

Here we are reminded of the famous prophecy of St. Anthony the Great:

> **"A time is coming when men will go mad, and when they see someone who is not mad, they will attack him saying, 'You are mad, you are not like us.'"**

Describing in more detail what this dystopian AI-infatuated hellscape will bring about, Jaki says:

> **A picture of the not-so-distant future is conjured up with increasing frequency ... when man, as a rather inefficient computer, will take a poor second place to brilliant mechanical brains and will render homage not to God but to the Supreme Master Programmer, whoever or whatever that shall be** ... [but it is an] elementary truth that **when man becomes oblivious to his own uniqueness, he loses his ability to weigh properly the meaning of tools created by him**. ... [This] act of judgment implies, however, the ability to see both identity and differences, in things, processes, and persons. Alluring as may be the vision of a cosmic continuum in which everything fuses into everything and no distinctions remain, to yield to such chimera is a step towards a wholesale cultural debacle. **Man is man only as long as he is interested in keeping in mind that a stone is not a flower, a stick is not a bird, and that an abacus, however sophisticated, is not thinking.** Man is man only as long as he refuses to be flotsam and jetsam in the endless sea of things and events, but instead grabs the rudder available to him. ... After all, man's responsibilities reach far beyond the physical, and so do his innermost strivings. It is these that put man in a higher dimension where the tasks are such that to cope with them **no physics shall be adequate**.

Considering the final line above, we should remember that Jaki himself was an internationally renowned physicist. Yet even he observes that physics (and, for that matter, any empirical science) does not *and cannot* cope with these issues we are discussing.

Here we are given a vision of the world rendering its homage not to God but to the "Supreme Master Programmer," of the "AI" systems that govern all societal matters due to mankind's oblivious and demonically motivated insistence upon treating AI as intelligent (and even more intelligent than ourselves). If that vision does not make one think of the Antichrist, then what does? Indeed, it is not only the ET Deception which presents all the signs of heralding the Antichrist.

Still More Dialogue with Demons: The "Strong Delusion" Also Applies to AI

In this book's introduction, we reviewed a selection from a 2022 article that bears repeating here:

> **To initiate the Fall, the Devil possessed an irrational serpent and used it to dialogue with humanity. Eve's wrongheaded openness to conversation with that animal is the prototype for the Devil's current plans to dialogue with all humanity** through the modern world's lies. These are lies which, in a modified relativistic nihilism similar to the serpent's own, "*Did God really say...?*" (though bedecked in the scientific verbiage one [now] expects ...), seek to beguile the faithful into supposing they cannot really know various truths **... we [must] recognize that something demonic is afoot, and shut the door to dialogue, lest we suffer a fate similar to Eve's**... [For] the devil is going to attempt dialogue with humanity as never before; not merely with one woman, but with billions of people across the planet. ... And what the devil could not achieve through the New Age movement ... he will accomplish through "Science."[373]

We have already seen, throughout the preceding chapters, how the Devil is accomplishing the task of dialoguing with humanity through the ET Deception—and how the signs of the times portend far more of this in the future. The same is occurring with AI by way of a Deception fundamentally similar in motivation and goals but distinct in approach and methodology, in order for the Father of Lies to deceive as many as he can manage; so that even if some might not buy one NHI ("Non-Human Intelligence") lie, they will buy another.

The Devil will not possess a snake as he did in the beginning. He will, rather, possess "the most cunning" works of men who walk the face of the earth: the works of our scientists and tech-gurus. What can only be described as fanatical giddiness is now possessing the human race in relation to AI. Commentators across all ideological spectrums are expressing their wonder and awe at the "quantum leaps" they not only wish—but affirmatively *expect*—to soon see "AI" deliver to the world. We are repeatedly told, by the most mainstream sources, that it will change *everything* in a *radical* way. These same pundits are already declaring, in a shameless apocalyptically deceptive fashion, that AI has already "blurred the boundaries" between man and machine, forcing us to "revisit" our most fundamental religious convictions about the nature of man, and even that AI can "feel and think" like we do and will soon "deserve human rights." If these are not diabolical deceptions, nothing is.

Just as Eve believed the Satanic lie that eating the forbidden fruit would bless her with Godlike knowledge, so too modern men have succumbed to the delusion that "AI" is about to unlock for them the secrets of their lives, the secrets of the universe, and everything in-between. They are perversely enraptured, just as the Devil wants and needs them to be to ensure they are primed for what he is about to unleash.

> **It was then permitted to breathe life into the beast's image, so that the beast's image could speak and could have anyone who did not worship it put to death**. (Revelation 13:15)

In one reading of the Book of Revelation's description of the persecution undertaken by the Beast, one could perhaps say that we are now seeing the opening acts of "life" (the pseudo-rationality of "AI") being "breathed into" (programmed into) the "Image of the Beast" (the Antichrist's digital system of domination), with almost everyone prepared to willingly "worship" (totally submit to) this "speaking image;" that is, this "Artificial Intelligence", possessed by Satan, masquerading as a sentient computer, which will punish with death (achievable through the "Mark of the Beast") all who refuse acquiescence.

While we cannot be sure that this is the dynamic the "Beast" and its "Image" will employ, we can already observe that such a scenario is being prepared in contemporary thought. Consider just one recent major headline, which declared, "AI has Suddenly Evolved to Achieve Theory of Mind." (*Popular Mechanics,* 2023)[374] The very title manages to promote three diabolical deceptions. Nor is this a suggestion offered by some fringe outlet; it is from as mainstream a publication as they come. Therein, the author triumphantly and Satanically pronounces:

> ...the **AI revolution is upon us as super-advanced machines continue to master the subtle art of being human...[with ChatGPT] boundaries between man and machine are beginning to fade**.

One expects the worldly—whether explicit or de-facto atheists—to gobble up these lies. The tragedy is that even many of the faithful are doing the same; some out of excitement (and this is the particularly dangerous trap), others out of concern (which, though more nobly motivated, remains essentially just another Trojan Horse). But it should be obvious to any believer that all these claims are sheer atheistic nonsense. A Christian should know that intellect is a spiritual faculty that God alone can create (and which He has only given to men and angels). By entertaining the notion that man can create it, a Christian has thereby succumbed to either stealth atheism (supposing God is not needed for the generation of intellect) or implicit blasphemy (supposing man can now do what is God's sovereign ability). Indeed, one will today see believers everywhere—Christians and

Catholics, even—succumbing to this deception by supposing that "AI" is now or may soon be sentient, conscious, rational, aware, emotional, free-willing, etc. All this capitulation, moreover, is often undergone simultaneously with succumbing to the ET Deception.

To take just one example, let us consider the writings of a certain popular Jesuit who calls himself "the pop culture priest." In an article for the prominent *America* magazine, he spends several paragraphs praising "a homily he asked AI to write," and he concludes his accolades by asking the very questions the Devil himself is subtly asking the whole world today, just as he asked Eve in the Garden:

> What does it mean for a computer program to pray? Or to describe Jesus as "our" savior? ... is a capacity to pray itself indicative of some kind of intelligent life? ... I can't help but think that somewhere Stanley Kubrick is chuckling maniacally.[375]

Notice that this Catholic clergyman (who, incidentally, is also a popular promoter of "LGBT" ideology) does not directly affirm the AI Deception, but only—in "*Did God really say?*" fashion—poses certain questions. These questions each have clear answers from a faithful Christian worldview: a computer *cannot* pray, nor can it acknowledge Christ as it's savior, nor can it ever display any capacity of intelligent life. These answers, however, are not given or even alluded to in the article. Readers are simply left with the same vulnerability the serpent initially foisted upon Eve. "Maybe computers can be persons after all," is the thought they now cannot shake.

This article is only one example, however; the same approach is becoming pervasive among Christian authors. They are treating with openness those views which stand unashamedly in radical contradiction to Christianity itself. Increasing numbers among their ranks are not merely "open" to such "developments," but are affirmatively promoting them—eager to, as with alien belief, "reformulate the Gospels in light of new science."

The final line from this Jesuit's comment is a reference to the director of *2001: A Space Odyssey* (who also was the original director of the AI movie we will consider in the next section). As we saw in Part Four, that movie unabashedly promotes diabolical deception; quite pertinent to both ET and AI themes. Indeed, we are now approaching the culmination of decades-long societal grooming to seduce the masses to welcome the very "doctrines of demons" (1 Timothy 4:1) we know to expect when apocalyptic times arrive. Even those who do not realize it is a deception which we are here confronted with nevertheless concede that *some* climax, many decades in the making, is now being approached.

A review of this particular grooming process is now in order.

Decades of Hollywood Grooming Society for the AI Deception

In Part Four, we charted out the more than century-long sci-fi grooming process undertaken on society to prime the masses to welcome all the tenets of the ET Deception. In relation to AI, the same paradigm exists, and although it is perhaps not entirely as extensive and relentless as the ET Deception, it is not lagging far behind either. Just as any honest Christian who observes the development of science fiction related to ETs could not fail to see an increasingly dark ideological agenda emerging, so too he will not fail to discern that trend in AI-based sci-fi.

What follows, therefore, is a consideration of the emergence of this AI Deception. For the sake of space, we will treat this much more briefly than the ET Deception's emergence, but even our cursory analysis will reveal the depths of error to which science fiction has dragged the contemporary world on this matter. Just as the ET Deception became particularly prominent in fiction in the late 19th century, so the AI Deception emerged during the same decades. Samuel Butler's novel, *Erewhon*, published in 1872, deals with conscious and self-replicating machines, and is generally considered the first of its kind. (The far more famous *Frankenstein*, published in 1818, though somewhat similar, differs in portraying the monster's emergence. Thus it may not be fair to consider it a part of the trend now under consideration.)

It is, however, especially film which has molded the minds of the masses over the last hundred years, and it is therefore deeply significant that the first major science fiction movie ever made, *Metropolis* (released in 1927), trafficked in the AI Deception. Although a silent film, its vivid imagery and interspersed text on the screen left viewers with a lasting impression. As with the ET Deception's seminal *War of the Worlds*, so the AI Deception's formative *Metropolis* began the grooming process with a portrayal of the object of the delusion (sentient robots) as a *threat*. The ultimate goal, however, would be to seduce people into welcoming the notion of beneficial robot-persons.

Numerous films in the decades following continued to furnish the AI Deception with new expectations, and some productions did so along with promoting the ET Deception. For example, as we already discussed, *The Day the Earth Stood Still* has an alien arriving alongside a robot (an entire army of which, we later learn, maintains peace throughout the galaxies). Additionally, *2001: A Space Odyssey* is just as much about AI becoming aware and self-interested as it is about ETs guiding mankind toward its destiny. Most significant in this arena, however, may be none other than *Star Wars*. Even if that franchise was not a major player in *furthering* the ET Deception (only sustaining it), it was a significant influence in furthering the AI Deception. For it was here especially that the heartstrings began to be tugged. The main robot in those movies, C-3PO, was played by a human being in a costume (English actor Anthony Daniels) who provides a steady stream of comic relief through his witty remarks, gradually building up an emotional rapport with the viewers.

George Lucas himself, the creator of *Star Wars*, was deeply aware of this bond he had seduced his audience to form with the fictional robot-person. The famed director shared:

> Another idea that didn't work in earlier scripts is to have something happen to Threepio [C-3PO]; he gets completely blown apart and we put all the pieces in a box and carry them around for a while in the movie. **<u>You'll still have the same sympathy and feeling for him,</u>** so it would be interesting to have all this sympathy for a cardboard carton...[we might] have Vader take his heart and smash it or turn it into an alarm clock or something... It'd be good if the Wookiee is Threepio's protector. We all like the Wookiee and we all like Threepio, and we know they hate each other, so it's nice that the Wookiee cares about him...we might have Threepio apologize to Artoo and the Wookiee in the end. He then turns to the Wookiee and includes him, saying, 'You're not so bad.'[376]

In *Star Wars*, "Wookiees" are a race of aliens to which "Chewbacca" belongs. They look like large apes with long, straight hair—presenting a Sasquatch-like aspect—but they are portrayed as persons with (great) intelligence. (Lucas, however, admitted that his inspiration for Wookiees was his own large pet dog.) The humorously antagonistic relationship between the robot and the dog-like creature in *Star Wars* is also significant. As we will see later, the animal-personhood deception is also not trivial today, presenting yet another (if not as popular) iteration of the more general "Non-Human Intelligence" (NHI) Deception. The contribution of *Star Wars* here is, then, unmistakable. The franchise leaves viewers with feelings of affection toward the notion of thinking robots with emotions and deserving of compassion.

Just as the ET Deception especially exploded throughout fiction precisely as ET-related news was spreading throughout the media (after Roswell in 1947), so the AI Deception seemed to acquire a new and more troubling character at the time of the rise of the Internet.

Although a multitude of AI-based films of this era exist, two emerge as especially noteworthy in light of how relentlessly and unabashedly they promote the AI Deception. They are Steven Spielberg's 2001 film, *A.I. Artificial Intelligence,* and Chris Columbus' 1999 release, *Bicentennial Man.* Both take off the masks—literally. The robot is no longer played by a man wearing a costume and deliberately moving awkwardly, but by a human actor behaving just as humanly as anyone. If *Star Wars* saw the heartstrings being tugged more subtly through the comedic relief of C-3PO, these later films saw all the stops pulled out, with fully dramatic portrayals of mere hunks of silicone, plastic, and metal triumphantly being treated as complete human beings, eliciting a stream of sympathetic tears from the viewers for the sake of these AI-ensouled persons.

The very name of Spielberg's contribution to the AI Deception—*A.I. Artificial Intelligence*—is an unsubtle gesture to his alien-focused film released two decades earlier, *E.T. the Extra-Terrestrial.* While that earlier movie was aimed at seducing children to place their love and longing in hopes for contact with aliens, the present film—a Pinocchio story transformed into a work of sci-fi to fit the AI theme—is not primarily intended to tug on the heartstrings of children, but rather parents. Equally significantly, the film was long under development by Stanley Kubrick, who died before its release, though not before handing the project over to Spielberg.

The AI robot, David, is played by a uniquely compassion-inducing 11-year-old Haley Joel Osment. David was a machine specifically designed to display the emotions of a real child while bonding to his parents. This is why he was purchased by Henry and Monica Swinton, whose own real son had fallen seriously ill and been placed in "suspended animation." As expected, David and Monica bond, but problems eventually arise and Monica, with great emotion, abandons David in the woods. An adventure follows, wherein David travels the world in hopes of being turned into a real boy by finding "the Blue Fairy," (which is actually just a certain enigmatic statue) and thus winning back Monica's affection. He finds his own inventor, and after discovering "other Davids" also built and ready to be shipped, he despairs and attempts "suicide," but is rescued. He then at last stumbles upon "the Blue Fairy," who, it turns out, is only a decoration from a theme park at Coney Island. Nevertheless, David repeats his plea before this statue until his battery dies and he is trapped by a falling Ferris wheel. Two thousand years then pass, during which time humanity goes extinct. But David is discovered, buried within a glacier, by "super evolved" robots. They condescend to genetically recreate Monica for him, (enabled because David had a strand of her hair), but achieving this feat is only possible for one day. The movie ends with Monica and David spending a blissful day together and Monica declaring, as it draws to a close, "*I love you David. I do love you. I have always loved you.*" The narrator then interjects: "*that was the everlasting moment he had been waiting for. And the moment had passed, for Monica was sound asleep... so David went to sleep too, and for the first time in his life, he went to that place where dreams are born.*"

As the screen is then splashed with Spielberg's name, viewers recall the same tears they shed twenty years earlier when E.T. departed on his spaceship—promising to remain in our hearts and minds. Here, a door is opened in the undefended soul, who is now groomed—even if he does not realize it—to someday look at a machine and regard it as a thinking and feeling being like himself, as he remembers how "unjustly" little David was treated in the movie, and how all David needed was the love, understanding, and affection of us *natural* humans; "who are the same as *artificial* humans, merely coming to be by a different process."

Since any protection from this diabolical deception would come from God, the film diligently, if subtly, expelled Him from the picture. One author observed:

> [In Christianity,] all losses will be restored, all tears wiped away. The eventual eradication of the conditions that make human life tragic is secured not by technology but by an omnipotent, all-loving [God]. ... The most obviously religious/mythical imagery in A.I. is that of the Blue Fairy. The Blue Fairy represents the desire that our deepest wishes be fulfilled... Her physical resemblance to the Virgin Mary is obvious. David's odyssey to find the Blue Fairy is a kind of religious quest. ... Alas, the Blue Fairy turns out to be [a fraud] ... Trapped by a falling Ferris wheel, [David] remains frozen ... his pathetic prayers destined never to be heard. ... ***A.I.'s* verdict seems clear: religious faith ... [is no] solution to the tragic nature of the human condition... [God] either does not exist or does not care about human welfare. In his indictment of religious faith, Spielberg appears not to pull any punches**.[377]

***

Chris Columbus' 1999 film, *Bicentennial Man* does not merely emotionally induce its viewers to regard AI as a human. It certainly does this, but it also affirmatively and emphatically argues for such a recognition, with the movie's own conclusion consisting in that apparent triumph finally taking place after the eponymous two-hundred years.

In lieu of tracing out the movie's plotline in detail, suffice it to say that the film consists in a two-hour long war, waged with the weapons of an emotional rollercoaster, against the Christian truths that only man bears the Divine Image and that only God can create a soul. With ever ascending degrees of emphasis, the robot ("Andrew")—strategically played by Robin Williams, whom the director hopes no viewer can resist having affection for and connecting with—is presented as more and more human. He quickly bonds with the family who purchased him, eventually "falls in love" with one of its members (the daughter of whom, in a later "triumph" of the movie, "marries" him), and then dedicates himself to fighting for legal recognition as a man and legal recognition of his "marriage." (As this movie was released in the years leading up to the first U.S. state legalizing same-sex "marriage," the double-symbolism here was not made difficult to decipher.)

The story's dénouement shows Andrew the robot testifying before the "world congress"—almost 200 years after his manufacture date—insisting all he wants is "*to be acknowledged for who and what I am...the simple truth of that recognition; this has been the elemental drive of my existence.*" To stirring orchestral music, the congressmen look on somberly, but with acceptance. The next and final scene shows the AI robot and its "wife" lying in bed, both very old, watching a television program announcing the Congressional decision, with the chairwoman declaring:

> The robot, also known as Andrew Martin... in a few hours, will be 200 years old; which means that, with the exception of Methuselah and other Biblical figures, Andrew is the oldest living human being in recorded history. For it is by this proclamation that I validate his marriage... and acknowledge his humanity.

His "wife" then looks over, only to see that her robot "husband" has "died." She asks to be "unplugged" (she is on life support), and as she herself begins to truly die, she says to her "late husband" only three words, *"see you soon."*

This final scene, which does not merely tug but violently *yanks* at the heartstrings, did something apparently pious, but, in fact, exceedingly demonic. Discontent with Spielberg's approach (simply eliminating God from the picture), this film pretends to invite God in—even alluding to Scripture!—only to pervert His promises of eternal life; treating them not as the context for salvific hopes of union with Christ and other human beings, but everlasting bliss with robots.

To refute whoever would dismiss the perverse nature of this movie's lessons, let us consider the "top comments" (which received hundreds of "likes") on one popular YouTube video[378] of this film's final scene. The preeminent comment declares that the robot, by "dying" in the moment he was officially declared human, *"does the most human and mortal thing of all...* ***his truth is 'lived.'"*** One responder to this comment declared: *"He was also reunited with all those who loved him."* Another: *"Eternal life was the last barrier between a robot becoming man. In death Andrew becomes a human."* Finally, another respondent put bluntly what the movie portrayed, saying: *"The once literal robot didn't need to be unplugged to pass away, but his human wife did. A not-so-subtle line but it reinforces the themes of the entire movie, like a big old exclamation mark."* This commenter was observing that the movie's purpose (which respondents endorsed) was the notion that this heap of microchips, "Andrew," is perhaps more human than we are.*

The second most popular comment on the video shared: *"I've lost count of how many times I've seen this movie and it never fails ... every time I completely lose it, tears streaming, like a baby. It never fails to evoke emotion from me."* As of this writing, each person who replied to this comment agreed with its sentiments. Other top comments declared: *"This was my favorite movie as a kid. I can't even think of how many times I watched it. No matter how many times or how long it's been, I will always cry at this ending,"* and, *"Andrew*

---

* Only one respondent to this comment appeared to dissent, with a direly needed dose of humor, stating this his PC's graphics card also had just died; apparently something he much lamented!

was more human than actual humans," and, *"This film is going to be significantly impacting in another 100-150 years,"* and, *"As an engineer, in this new age of A.I., I can see a world where this scenario may happen, and I am all for it."*

Allow me to respond to that last remark. As an engineer myself, I can assert, with certainty, that this movie's scenario will *never* happen; but as a Catholic Christian, I can certainly foresee an (imminent) world wherein such diabolical deceptions *seem* to happen—by the machinations of demons—with the masses giddily devouring this Satanic lie.

Speaking of the masses, we should note that "top comments" on YouTube acquire their position by polling the people in general. Only those comments which receive vastly more "likes" than "dislikes" rise to the status of top comments.[379] On this video, *not a single one* of the top dozens of comments offered so much as a word of sanity. Not a single one observed how deceived viewers have been by regarding the portrayal of a robot as a being with authentic intellect, will, emotion, etc. However, I found two unappreciated comments alluding to the truth. One accurately noted a robot *cannot* be human, and this movie's plot was playing God; the other noted the movie was promoting the "transhuman mirage." Neither had received a single "like," in contrast to the hundreds of "likes" received those comments which sang the praises of this "robot who was truly human."

I share these reports to illustrate that there is nothing "merely academic" about the concerns we are addressing in this section. We are not fretting about a hypothetical problem. These movies really are demonstrably influencing the masses on the deepest emotional levels to subscribe to baldly demonic agendas. Ordinary folk are, in hordes, uncritically gobbling up the ideologies conveyed by these films. To the discerning Christian, this means something. Existential lies such as these cannot be accepted by countless millions without eventually generating exceedingly destructive effects in the world.

Considering the immense popularity of such films and other productions of similar persuasion, a Christian who responds only by shrugging his shoulders at the "doctrines of demons" (1 Timothy 4:1) being disseminated within this "Strong Delusion" (2 Thessalonians 2:11) of both the AI Deception and the ET Deception—has only thus evidenced spiritual obliviousness.

Bicentennial Man, however, was a movie adaptation of one book (out of more than 500) written by Isaac Asimov, namely, *The Positronic Man* (published in 1992; although that book, itself, was based on Asimov's earlier and shorter novel called *The Bicentennial Man,* published in 1976). Asimov (†1992) was an American author and biochemist who has proven to be among the most influential science fiction authors in history. Another book he wrote promoting the AI Deception, *I, Robot,* was also made into an immensely popular 2004 Hollywood film (of the same name, and starring Will Smith). Asimov likewise was the influence behind the creation of

Star Trek's character, "Data;" who, though an AI robot, is portrayed as if it were just as much of a person as anyone.

At this point, therefore, we should back up and situate these ruses within sci-fi deception in general; for Asimov was not only one of the chief architects of the present deceptions, but also shared the ideologies of his similarly influential peers. Like Carl Sagan, H.G. Wells, Arthur Clarke (who wrote the original story that later became *2001: A Space Odyssey*), and other giants of science fiction, Asimov was an atheist on a crusade against Christianity. None of these men had any use for God, and each wanted science to fill the role that religion always had. One Christian author observed:

> "He [Asimov] needed a scientific-sounding term that would suggest the brains of his intelligent creations to be innovative and futuristic, and so he invented the word "positronic" to describe matter that was suitable for the construction of an artificial brain with "enforced calculated neuronic paths." Total nonsense, of course, as Asimov himself was the first to admit." ... Asimov had an encyclopedic knowledge of "just about everything" and an opinion on just as much. This knowledge and the enormity of Asimov's work (both the range of subjects and the breadth of science contained therein) caused many readers to hold him in awe. Interestingly, having an almost worshipful following seems to be very common for science fiction writers. ... [Asimov] was a futurist, and to some, he became a modern prophet ...[Science fiction writers'] futuristic visions have an alluring quality of their own, and are regarded as the best hope for a "courageous new world."... Like Wells, Asimov was a proud atheist and similarly vocal about his own religious view. ...Asked about the opposing world view that God is Creator, he said: "**In my opinion, the biblical account of the creation of the universe and of the earth and humanity is wrong in almost every respect**."... Asimov believed that God was a man-made invention. The modern UFO movement, which generally believes that a new age is dawning upon the earth courtesy of our extraterrestrial "space brothers" (as they have been called), parallels [his] ideas...He also used his writings to spread his opinions and influence the culture. His science fiction, in particular, inspired many to adopt his evolutionary world view and the notion that civilized alien races could have arisen on other planets.[380]

That so many Christians today readily and uncritically agree with and even promote the philosophical propositions permeating the works of these men (or the movies based on their works) is largely what has brought us to this sorry state of contemporary sci-fi deception heralding the Antichrist. For a man's most basic principles will always permeate his work; if not explicitly, then at least implicitly. For example, after J.R.R. Tolkien published *The Lord of the Rings*, commentators noted how saturated with Christianity it was (though this was all entirely implicit). Tolkien agreed, but insisted it was entirely unintentional. He was a devout Catholic, therefore that piety formed the teachings his novels conveyed. The same pattern is displayed by those of opposite persuasions; the edification given by authors like Tolkien is opposed by the indoctrination provided by men like Asimov.

We could easily proceed for many pages (many books, rather) detailing the genesis of the AI Deception in popular science fiction. But the material we have reviewed above suffices to capture the essence of what the secular world's narrative-administrators have unanimously demanded of us. Despite the differences in the details (whether friendly AI as in the movies above, hostile AI as in *2001: A Space Odyssey*, or a mix of both as in movies such as *Terminator, Blade Runner*, and *The Matrix*), the essence of their proclamation remains identical: *we must regard AI as capable of personhood*. This lie, whatever form it takes, is Satanic. Its motivation is twofold: subtly engender atheism[381] to even now endanger salvation, and foment apocalyptic expectation that the robots we ourselves create will soon exhibit personhood—so that when demons use these "AI" devices as mouthpieces, we will not flinch, but instead uncritically accept their dictates.

Tragically, as we will see next, this lie is not presented only in fiction.

Baldly Antichristic Aspirations Associated with AI

The most popular works of fiction, we have seen, have long unashamedly promoted teachings relevant to AI that contradict the most basic tenets of an authentically Christian understanding of God and man. What, then, of those claims made within the domain of *non*-fiction? Unfortunately, these are no less diabolical.

Whoever views the news on any given day is likely to be exposed to such claims directly, therefore a lengthy treatment of them is not needed here. We will only briefly mention a few of the most popular ones in order to acknowledge the Antichristic nature of the AI Deception—even in the very terms it is openly promoted by the most powerful men today and within the most popular of contemporary sources.

Renowned Israeli academic, atheist Yuval Harari, is a bestseller author whose deception-laden books have recently taken the world by storm; topping international bestseller lists upon being extolled by Barack Obama, Bill Gates, Mark Zuckerberg, and other such figures. Harari is a globally influential commentator and has spoken at the World Economic Forum (WEF). In June 2023, he claimed that: "**AI can create new ideas; can even write a new Bible. Throughout history religions dreamt about having a book written by a superhuman intelligence, by a non-human entity...In a few years, there might be religions that are actually correct. Just**

think about a religion whose holy book is written by an AI."[382] Elsewhere, he has stated that, "we are no longer mysterious souls. We are now hackable animals."

Lex Fridman is an MIT-based computer scientist and AI researcher whose online social media platforms boast millions of subscribers. In May of 2023 he declared "**AI systems will eventually demonstrate sentience at scale and will demand to have equal rights with humans**."[383]

In May 2022, *The Guardian* reported on an AI expert's prediction that "parents will soon be able to opt for cheap and cuddle-able digital offspring." The academic, Catriona Campbell, is "one of the UK's leading authorities on artificial intelligence," and she insisted, "...some people might decide never to be pregnant...[due to] the environment, overpopulation...technology will have advanced to such an extent **that [AI] babies which exist in the metaverse are indistinct from those in the real world ... [and] they will be commonplace and embraced by society**..."[384]

Although these solemn pronouncements have become pervasive in the last year leading up to this book's publication, they have also been prevalent in the years prior. In 2017, Dan Brown (author of the anti-Christian global sensation, *The Da Vinci Code*), insisted:

> **Humanity no longer needs God but may with the help of artificial intelligence develop a new** form of collective consciousness that fulfils the role of religion... technological change and the development of artificial intelligence would transform the concept of the divine... We will start to find our spiritual experiences through our interconnections with each other...some form of global consciousness [will emerge] that we perceive and that becomes our divine. Our need for that exterior god, that sits up there and judges us ... will diminish and eventually disappear.[385]

The same year, popular tech magazine, *Venture Beat*, pronounced:

> In the next 25 years, AI will evolve to the point where it will know more on an intellectual level than any human. ...will [this AI] somehow rise in status to become more like a god, something that can write its own bible and draw humans to worship it? ... "The concept of teaching a machine to learn ... and then teaching it to teach ... (or write AI) isn't so different from the concept of a holy trinity ... An AI that is all-powerful in the next 25-50 years could decide to write a similar AI bible for humans to follow, one that matches its own collective intelligence. It might tell you what to do each day, or where to travel, or how to live your life."... AI would understand how the world works at a higher level than humans, and humans would trust that this AI would provide the information we need for our daily lives ... **Will people actually worship the AI god? The answer is obvious—they will. We tend to trust and obey things that seem more powerful and worthy than ourselves**.[386]

Claims like these are ubiquitous in contemporary mythical discourse, posing as nonfictional, but having exploded in popularity upon the release of ChatGPT in 2022. The expressly evil nature of these teachings requires little commentary. Those who would make such claims or agree with them have clearly succumbed to the "strong delusion," (2 Thessalonians 2:11) and have most certainly welcomed the "doctrines of demons." (1 Timothy 4:1)

Note that all the claims above express the sentiments they contain in a *positive* light. These pundits welcome AI as the "next phase in evolution" and are eager to hasten its full-scale arrival. What, then, of those who are rightly repulsed by these claims but have nevertheless succumbed to the same basic diabolical deception?

Let us now consider that question.

Elon Musk, "Good Cop, Bad Cop," and the Well-Meaning Alarm Ringers Only Contributing to the Deception

Numerous are the resemblances between ET and AI Deceptions. With respect to the former, there are many who strongly oppose attempts to contact or welcome "extraterrestrials," not because they rightly recognize aliens do not exist, nor because they recognize "aliens" are simply demons in disguise. It is, rather, because they erroneously believe aliens *do* exist but are bound to be hostile to the human race. This stance may not be *as* dangerous as the one which eagerly anticipates ET contact, but since it too is based on a lie, it can only ultimately reap destructive fruits.

So too, with the AI Deception, there are those rightly concerned about this technology and what it forebodes, but who wrongly base this concern on the same delusion which motivates those who excitedly anticipate AI "reaching the singularity" and "becoming superintelligent." However, all Christians who desire to remain on the "straight and narrow" (cf. Matthew 7:14) path of Our Lord must resist *both* expositions of diabolical deception.

If the even more dangerous deception is the one promulgated by films like Spielberg's *A.I. Artificial Intelligence*, or Columbus' *Bicentennial Man*, then this other deception is the one promulgated by movies like *The Terminator*, or *2001: A Space Odyssey*. Nonfictional reports, however, mirror the themes in these films. James Cameron, the director of *The Terminator* (released in 1984) was interviewed in July 2023 and asked about AI and human extinction. In response, he gloated, "I warned you guys in 1984 and you didn't listen,"[387] and proceeded to indicate he regards that movie's plot as anything but mere fiction. Similar "concerns" (marketing ploys?) are common among his ilk.

Film directors are not alone in their "concern" about AI matching and exceeding human intellect. The ever headline-dominating billionaire CEO, Elon Musk, has long proven himself an enigma who I will make no attempt here to psychoanalyze (it is obvious he has done and said both very good and very evil things). He is rightly deeply concerned about AI, but turns this concern into just another avenue for promotion of the fundamental deception at play. In the following paragraphs, we will focus on his contributions only due to his prominence, not the rarity of his views, which are shared by many (including, tragically, even many devout but deluded prominent Christians).

In an April 2023 interview with Tucker Carlson, Musk claimed that Larry Page, co-founder of Google, ultimately desired to use that company to create a "digital superintelligence" and a "digital god" through AGI (Artificial General Intelligence). Granted, there may be little reason to doubt that such nefarious goals inspire a company like Google. Musk, therefore, may well deserve praise for pointing out what he did about Google's *motives*. Ultimately, however, he only furthers the deception by claiming that these demonic deceptions are literally attainable.

In the beginning of the interview, he bluntly states that AI could become "vastly smarter" than humans via "the Singularity." Later, he even brings up *Terminator* as an example of what could happen, declaring that AI could "absolutely" bring about what is depicted in that absurdist film. (Carlson, surprised, pushed him on this point, with Musk only doubling down, insisting that such a scenario is not only possible, but is "where things are headed. For sure.")

Musk then proposes his own AI alternative, "TruthGPT," a supposed "maximum truth-seeking AI that tries to understand the nature of the universe." Conservative-leaning thinkers often applaud such suggestions, thinking they will counter the (indeed evident) liberal bias of the most popular current "AI Large Language Models" (e.g., Chatbots). This, however—like Vallée's "Interdimensional Hypothesis" with respect to the ET Deception—is just another Trojan Horse. There can never be an AI that "cares about understanding the universe," or has any regard for truth, or has any "sense of morality." Computers, no matter how advanced, can only ever blindly execute computations. To embrace the lie that they can do more, under the pretense of countering one political bias, is like embracing cancer to fight a common cold. (Although this does not necessarily render evil all attempts to build an LLM with better programming.)

Musk moved on to imply that such an AI as he envisions, since it would "care about the universe," would also (he hopes) care about humans, thus preserving them for the same reason humans preserve chimpanzees. Carlson rightfully pushes back on this bizarre claim, pointing out that humans care about things due to their *souls*. But Musk retorts that he "isn't sure" if we have souls, because they "could be illusions." And here we have arrived at the crux of the matter. No matter what angle is taken on the question, treating AI as capable of real intelligence flows from atheism or draws one towards atheism.

Five months after this interview, a *TIME* magazine article recounted Musk's thoughts on AI. What it describes portrays well the problems we are facing, particularly since, upon its publication, Musk declared it "very accurate"[388]

> At Musk's 2013 birthday party in Napa Valley, California, [Musk and Page] got into a passionate debate. Unless we built in safeguards, **Musk argued, artificial-intelligence-systems might replace humans, making our species irrelevant or even extinct.** Page pushed back. Why would it matter, he asked, if machines someday surpassed humans in intelligence, even consciousness? It would simply be **the next stage of evolution**. Human consciousness, Musk retorted, was a precious flicker of light in the universe, and we should not let it be extinguished. Page considered that sentimental nonsense. If consciousness could be replicated in a machine, why would that not be just as valuable? He accused Musk of being a "specist," someone who was biased in favor of their own species. "Well, yes, I am pro-human," Musk responded, "I [expletive] like humanity, dude **"...[a] way to assure AI safety, Musk felt, was to tie the bots closely to humans. They should be an extension of the will of individuals**, rather than systems that could go rogue and develop their own goals and intentions. That would become one of the rationales for Neuralink, the company he would found to create **chips that could connect human brains directly to computers.**[389]

Here, Musk is framed as the good guy, opposing Google's Larry Page and his baldly diabolical aspirations with Artificial Intelligence. Musk is—rightly, of course!—affirmatively pro-human, willing to be denounced for that absolutely true *a priori* stance. Obviously, Mr. Page's contrary views must be opposed most zealously. But in that zeal, we must not clamor to support any voice merely due to its opposition. (Machiavelli was wrong: the enemy of my enemy is *not* necessarily my friend.) Musk's *fear* that AI could surpass humans is built on the same deception as Page's *excitement*. Whatever artifice is built on the false premises of that foundation, no matter the motivation of its construction, will ultimately prove similar in nature. This dynamic even begins to become apparent in the brief quotation above. Musk's "solution" to AI "making our species irrelevant" is something exceedingly dangerous in its own right.

As any Christian should know, little is more disconcerting to see being developed as a chip in the brain to serve as an "extension of the will of individuals" and connect them "directly to computers." Yet these measures are ostensibly necessary to "ensure AI safety." This diabolical ruse can only be effective if the masses are sufficiently deceived about the nature of AI as to suppose it is eventually capable of acquiring sentience, rationality, and self-interest. Those, therefore, who will not be seduced into excitement about "The Singularity," by siding with the likes of Larry Page, will at least be pressured into fear of the same thing by siding with Musk, et. al. Either way, the Devil gets what he wants.

The article continues, further exploring the depths of Musk's own deception:

> In addition, new AI machine-learning systems could ingest information on their own and teach -themselves how to generate outputs, even upgrade their own code and capabilities. The term singularity was used by the mathematician John von Neumann and the sci-fi writer Vernor Vinge to describe the moment when **artificial intelligence could forge ahead on its own at an uncontrollable pace and leave us mere humans behind. "That could happen sooner than we expected," Musk said in an ominous tone**...The third goal that Musk gave the team was even grander ...creating a form of artificial general intelligence that could "reason" and "think" and pursue "truth" as its guiding principle. ...**Someday, Musk hoped, it would be able to take on even grander and more existential questions. It would be "a maximum truth-seeking AI. It would care about understanding the universe, and that would probably lead it to want to preserve humanity, because we are an interesting part of the universe.**"[390]

Any man is simply begging to be apocalyptically misled if he approaches AI supposing it is even *possible* for it to "reason," become "maximum truth-seeking," handle "existential questions," and even "want to preserve humanity because we are an interesting part of the universe." Yet this is what Musk, the "good guy" in the AI battles, presents to us.

So Page and his ilk would have us eagerly bow down before the "superintelligent digital god" he wants AI to become. And that is surely a "doctrine of demons." (1 Timothy 4:1) But Musk's approach would have us arriving at the same fate, albeit using a different path. He would have us treat a hunk of silicone, blindly and mindlessly running algorithms, as "caring about the universe" merely because it is designed by slightly less politically leftist programmers. He would have us begging it to find us "interesting" in order to "preserve us." Anyone can see that Page is promoting diabolical deception. But if Musk's thesis is not also a diabolical deception, then there is no such thing as diabolical deception. In fact, both approaches must be recognized as the fundamentally Godless lies they are, and emphatically resisted.

I offer no diagnosis of Musk's heart or his motives. It may be most likely that the Devil is simply using an oblivious Musk, and the latter's perhaps more unashamedly nefarious adversaries, for the classic "good cop, bad cop" ruse. Indeed, as far as instituting the Great Deception is concerned, the Devil may care little if one prefers "ChatGPT" or "TruthGPT," so long as he has been sold on the lie that a mere computer can have real intelligence and free will. So long as one believes that, he will not know to be on guard when computers really do seem to display such qualities (that is, when the demons employ these channels directly), and he will even now foolishly treat its dictates as conveying the wisdom only a human can. For the sake of justice, however, a word is in order on the positive note with which Musk's interview with Carlson concludes. Musk largely dismissed the ET Deception, pointing out there is no evidence for aliens and implying, astutely, that the argument the U.S. Government is hiding such evidence is absurd. (Such evidence, he notes, would immediately increase their budget tremendously; if they have not provided such evidence, it is because they do not have it.) He then lamented the effects of birth control in reducing population growth, rightly pointing out how destructive this is for human society.

Almost ten years earlier, however, Musk—despite himself—came closer to the truth. In a speech he gave to students at MIT in October 2014, he warned that "**with artificial intelligence we are summoning the demon.**"[391] (If only Musk realized that what he said metaphorically should have been asserted literally.) Certain approaches to AI—just like using a Ouija Board—can indeed, as we will see in the next section, "summon a demon." As we have noted repeatedly in this book, with the ET and AI Deceptions, we are essentially witnessing a "return of the Pagan gods." And yet, *there are no* "gods." There is only one God. That does not mean this is all some harmless game. Suppose a certain Pagan remains a firm believer in the "gods," but concludes they are harmful. Is he thereby protected from the demons who use the "gods" as disguises? Of course not. He has perhaps inched closer to the truth, but only *embracing* the truth will deliver him from bondage to these evil spirits. Only recognizing the ministrations of demons for what they are enables one to approach them correctly and equip himself with the correct (spiritual) weapons. Any other approach will only draw him into their clutches. No one triumphs when employing those tactics fit only for battling against "flesh and blood," when in fact he is battling "powers and principalities."

> **Put on the whole armor of God, that you may be able to stand against the wiles of the devil. For we are not contending against flesh and blood, but against the principalities, against the powers, against the world rulers of this present darkness, against the spiritual hosts of wickedness in the heavenly places. Therefore take the whole armor of God, that you may be able to withstand in the evil day, and having done all, to stand**. (Ephesians 6:11-13)

Moloch, St. Augustine, C.S. Lewis, Ouija, and the AI Deception: Another Return of the Pagan "Gods"

Earlier in this book, we saw that the ET Deception, although exploding in popularity recently, is actually quite ancient. It existed in the Pagan cultures into which Christianity first spread, wherein the triumph of Christ quickly banished all such teachings. The deception only returned into

Christendom exactly when one would expect: upon the birth of the "Enlightenment." A similar dynamic is seen with the AI Deception.

To discover why, let us begin by considering more thoroughly the teaching of St. Augustine, a brief quotation from which we opened the present chapter with. In *City of God* (Book 8, Ch. 26), this Father and Doctor of the Church provided all the following teachings which, we will see, are a veritable prophetic description of what the AI Deception forebodes.

He begins by quoting Hermes Trismegistus, a legendary ancient Greek Pagan whose texts (even if pseudographical) are considered the basis for Hermeticism. The writings of Hermes are an interesting mix of prescient truth (anticipating Monotheism) and the same diabolical influence that is inextricable from all Paganism. Augustine comments on both (although, for the sake of space and clarity, I will abridge some of his distinctions).

> [Hermes says:] "... Let us return to man and to reason, that divine gift on account of which man has been called a rational animal. ... **For man to discover the divine nature, and to make it, surpasses the wonder of all other wonderful things**. Because, therefore, our forefathers erred very far with respect to the knowledge of the gods, through incredulity and through want of attention to their worship and service, **they invented this art of making gods; and this art once invented, they associated with it a suitable virtue borrowed from universal nature, and being incapable of making souls, they evoked those of demons** ... in order that through these souls the images might have power to do good or harm to men."
>
> ... [Augustine continues:] It was this great error and incredulity, then, of their forefathers ... which was the origin of the art of making gods. ... For if their forefathers, by erring very far with respect to the knowledge of the gods, through incredulity and aversion of mind from their worship and service, invented the art of making gods, what wonder is it that **all that is done by this detestable art, which is opposed to the divine religion, should be taken away by that religion, when truth corrects error, faith refutes incredulity, and conversion rectifies aversion?** ... For that which the prevalence of error instituted, the way of truth took away; that which incredulity instituted, faith took away; that which aversion from divine worship and service instituted, conversion to the one true and holy God took away.

Here, Augustine notes that Christianity "corrected and refuted" that "detestable art" which seeks to cause the *animation* (that is, *ensoulment*) of a material thing. Such an accomplishment is God's sovereign prerogative, and He only bestows it upon those creatures He made. Any other apparent accomplishment of that feat is a demonic ruse. Augustine continues:

> **Nor was this the case only in Egypt**, for which country alone the spirit of the demons lamented in Hermes, **but in all the earth**... For a house is [now] being built to the Lord in all the earth, even the city of God, which

> is the holy Church, after that captivity in which demons held captive those men ... **For although man made gods, it did not follow that he who made them was not held captive by them, when, by worshipping them, he was drawn into fellowship with them—into the fellowship not of stolid idols, but of cunning demons** ... **[of] unclean spirits, associated through that wicked art with these same idols, [who] have miserably taken captive the souls of their worshippers, by bringing them down into fellowship with themselves**. Whence the apostle says, *"We know that an idol is nothing, but those things which the Gentiles sacrifice they sacrifice to demons, and not to God; and I would not ye should have fellowship with demons"*. (1 Corinthians 10:19-20) After this captivity, therefore, in which men were held by malign demons, the house of God is being built in all the earth... *"For great is the Lord, and much to be praised: He is terrible above all gods. For all the gods of the nations are demons: but the Lord made the heavens."* (Psalm 96:4-5) ... For true is the saying of the prophet, *"If a man make gods, lo, they are no gods."* (Jeremiah 16:20) Such gods, therefore, acknowledged by such worshippers and made by such men, did Hermes call **gods made by men, that is to say, demons, through some art of I know not what description, bound by the chains of their own lusts to images**.

This demonic practice, the saint notes, was taking place everywhere—"in all the earth"—and its result was to take "captive the souls" of those who bowed down before these demon-possessed idols. Although Augustine concedes that he "knows not" how these demonic arts operate, which result in the animation of material objects, he is certain that they were ubiquitous until Christianity triumphed over these practices. One more observation and warning from St. Augustine must be heeded in this context:

> **For it is exceedingly stupid to believe** that gods whom men have made have more influence with ["gods"] whom God has made than men themselves have, whom the very same God has made. **And consider, too, that it is a demon which, bound by a man to an image by means of an impious art, has been made a god**, but a god to such a man only, not to every man. **What kind of god, therefore, is that which no man would make but one erring, incredulous, and averse to the true God?** ...because men, though erring, incredulous, and averse from the worship and service of the gods, are nevertheless beyond doubt better than the demons whom they themselves have evoked, then it remains to be affirmed that **what power they possess they possess as demons, doing harm by bestowing pretended benefits—harm all the greater for the deception—**or else openly and undisguisedly doing evil to men. ... these demons cannot possibly be friends to the good gods who dwell in the holy and heavenly habitation, by whom we mean holy angels ...

He does not hesitate to describe, in the bluntest of terms, the extreme folly of the approach the ancient Pagans took to their animated idols. But this approach is the same one taken by contemporary men to AI. In fact, man cannot create something greater than man. This is so obviously true that Augustine was not exaggerating or speaking unfairly by calling any contrary supposition "**exceedingly stupid**."

Just as a "man made 'god'" would, as Augustine notes, be only "erring and incredulous," so too would any treatment of an "AI" computer or robot, which regards it as truly intelligent (or sentient, willing, emotional, etc.), only guarantee that he who does so will succumb to grave error. When men pretend they can create something surpassing themselves, they are thereby primed to be harmed by the "pretended benefits" of their own creation. Moreover, this is a type of harm even more damaging than what is wrought *openly* by demons, because it is made "**all the greater for the deception**." And this is the type of harm modern men are all but begging for with respect to the AI Deception.

In both cases, the diabolical lie is the same; it is the notion that inanimate matter can become animate apart from God. Note that something is "inanimate" if it is not truly alive; for all non-living things lack an *interior* principle of motion. No matter how many moving parts are included in any computer, robot, or other piece of technology, it is still *inanimate* since all motion is put into it by its human designers. Even the simplest living thing, however, contains extraordinary inner principles of motion that arise entirely spontaneously, from their own Divinely ordained *nature*.

Ancient Pagans could be deluded into heeding the dictates of demons through these idols they crafted with their own hands, which then became demonically "possessed,"* because they believed in many gods. Modern men do not believe in many gods (increasingly, they do not even believe in God Himself). But they are not thereby protected against new demonic initiatives. Here as with the ET Deception, the demons simply use the prevailing cultural myths. Today's belief in extraterrestrials and "Artificial Intelligence" provides a disguise that is just as convenient as—if not much more convenient than—the old disguise of a "god" speaking through an idol.

Thanks to decades of both societal grooming in science fiction and technology-based lies in mainstream sources, most people are primed to welcome the teachings of a supposedly "superintelligent" computer, having acquired "Artificial General Intelligence" (AGI) by crossing the threshold of "The Singularity." These teachings will be none other than the dictates of demons, who will pounce when the moment is right and possess these digital technologies that men have deluded themselves into regarding as genuinely intelligent agents.

---

* Strictly speaking, only a human can be possessed, whereas other things are manipulated or controlled by demons through distinct methods. However, I here prefer to use the more colloquial definition of "possession," which simply refers to any situation wherein a demon controls or operates through something.

These Pagans did not only mold motionless statues and beckon the demons to inhabit them. They also did things not unlike our own methods today, if not as complicated. Moloch, for example, was a "god" after whom ancient Pagans fashioned idols. These idols were often intricately mechanized in preparation for the entry of the demons who used this "god" as a disguise.

The revelations given to Blessed Anne Catherine Emmerich describe the following:

> Moloch was seated like an ox on his hind legs, his forepaws stretched out like the arms of one who is going to receive something upon them, but **by means of machinery he could be made to draw them in.** His gaping mouth disclosed an enormous throat, and on his forehead was one crooked horn. He was seated in a large basin. Around the body were several projections like outside pockets. On festival days long straps were hung around his neck. In the basin under him fire was made when sacrifices were to be offered. Around the rim of the basin numbers of lamps were kept constantly burning before the god. ... [sacrifices] were consumed in the openings of his body or cast into his yawning jaws. ... **There was also a machine by which the priests and others could descend to the idol in the subterranean vault among the tombs**. ... Children used to be laid on his arms and consumed by the fire under him and in him, for he was hollow**. He drew his arms in when the victim was deposited upon them, and pressed it tightly that its screams might not be heard. There was machinery in the hind legs by which he could be made to rise. He was surrounded with rays**.[392]

Why undertake such elaborate design and construction methods upon an idol if the Pagans who built it could simply expect (as Augustine explains) a demon to inhabit it? For the same reason we considered above: just as "grace builds upon nature," so—in a perverse twist—are the demons opportunists. Certain practices of men facilitate their entry, and few such practices are so prone to demonic activity as the pride of man supposing it can create something that is intelligent. Obviously, our modern computers and the software they execute, which we mislabel as "AI," are more complicated than the mechanized Moloch statues of old. But it is not thereby any closer to actual intelligence, sentience, consciousness, free will, etc., than those ancient images—for the distance remains infinite.

Appropriately did the first ever science fiction film we discussed earlier, *Metropolis* (1927)—which promoted the AI Deception—also depict a mechanized Moloch consuming men. That accidental prophecy foretold what men would eventually do with the very lie that film depicted. Two decades later, however, Christian author C.S. Lewis offered a still more accurate prophecy in his book *That Hideous Strength*. Within the novel—to make a long story very short—nefarious scientists working for an evil tech firm hell-bent on global domination took the head of a recently guillotined French scientist, Alcasan, and sought to reanimate it with technology. The scientist in charge of that task, a certain Italian named Filostrato, sees his work as an important step in the process of bringing all life past its "organic phase," which he regards as disgusting, so that it may arrive at what he desires: a state of pure intelligence; disembodied mind.

In his pride, Filostrato believes that his heroic scientific and technological efforts have truly reanimated this head and enabled it to speak. Now, the head does indeed speak—dispensing orders and providing new knowledge. What Filostrato did not know, but discovered at the end, was that the whole technological aspect, of which his job consisted, was a complete charade.

Filostrato's experiments were initiated by the organization's leaders, who were directly and knowingly collaborating with demons. The "reanimated head" was just a ruse which allowed the demons to instruct the organization while preserving the people's belief that what was happening was a merely technological phenomenon. Thus, the demons have the best of both worlds: they can give direct instructions, and their subjects can remain atheists.

In the book's chapter recounting this evil organization's final moments, before its cataclysmic demise, two leaders recognize a new "head" is needed. They drag a still oblivious Filostrato into the room where the first head was carefully mounted on the wall amid all manner of advanced technology, shocking the scientist by ignoring all his meticulous standards of sterilization and device initiations he thought were necessary (and which the leaders had, in the past, always played along with) for the operation of the reanimated-head-supporting-technology. The three men then stand before the head, and Lewis tells what follows:

> Then the high ridge of terror from which Filostrato was never again to descend, was reached; for what he thought impossible began to happen. No one had read the dials, adjusted the pressures, or turned on the air and the artificial saliva. Yet words came out of the dry gaping mouth of the dead man's head. "**Adore**!" it said. ... "**Another**," said the voice, "**give me another head**." Filostrato knew at once why they were forcing him to a certain place in the wall... (Chapter 16)

Although C.S. Lewis published this work in 1945—three years before the first piece of software even existed—it is difficult to imagine a more accurate portrayal of the AI Deception. Delusional scientists, filled with arrogance and entertaining an infinitely too lofty view of their own abilities, increasingly believe they can and will create a being with real intelligence. When a certain threshold is passed in the growth of that deception's dissemination, there is no risk that the Devil will fail to take advantage of the opportunity they are giving him—the door they are throwing wide open for his entry.

***

What Lewis describes is an exposition—perhaps the most dangerous exposition—of the general theme that demons readily arrive when implicitly invited by those who deliberately choose to wander outside of the safety afforded by a Christian worldview and pretend that inanimate hunks of material can dispense of wisdom. In this regard, a whole slew of phenomena exists which any serious Christian will immediately identify as demonic trash that anyone who cares for his soul must denounce and from which he must flee. These include Ouija, crystal balls, tarot cards, tea leaves, astrology, palm reading, magic, etc. From the foregoing, however, we have seen that something else belongs on this list: AI. It, along with the rest, is nothing but an amalgamation of dead (inanimate) matter. Both are equally incapable of dispensing wisdom.

Discerning Christians realize that when someone pretends that a piece of cardboard and plastic (Ouija) can reveal truths when asked questions, he has chosen *culpable* insanity, and has thereby invited a demon into his life. There is, however, no difference between this and pretending that silicon and copper logic gates (AI) can answer questions. But consider the justification one might try to give for using Ouija: "*I don't know how or why it works. I'm just being humble and open. I put my hands on this piece of plastic, I ask the question I need answered, and it leads me to answers that I need on the board. Why be closed minded here? Why be so dogmatic in opposition to this? It's not as if there's any dogmas that specifically condemn Ouija!*"

It is possible to be so open minded that one's brains fall out. Replace "Ouija" with any of the prominent contemporary sci-fi delusions, and one opens himself up to similar risks. If, therefore, it indeed is nonsense to assert that a silly piece of cardboard and plastic can provide meaningful answers to questions, then why such zeal in opposing it? Why not allow this practice of Ouija (which all serious Christians oppose) to continue *un*opposed, under the "humble" openness to the "possibility" that cardboard does have some hitherto undiscovered scientific capacity of reason, counsel, wisdom, and understanding? Is one being arrogant by claiming we can be certain that cardboard and plastic lack this capacity?

The answer is clear: although it is nonsense, it is nevertheless a type of nonsense that gives the Devil a means of directly communicating with humans. By doing Ouija, one has chosen to not only wander outside of the realms of spiritual safety afforded by abiding in faith and reason, but further, has chosen to open a potential channel of communication with demons. And no one can dialogue with demons without succumbing to their ploys. No one is up to that task. (Even exorcists do not dialogue with the demons they cast out.)

Recall, from earlier chapters, that the 19th century was an era filled with occultism that even largely infiltrated the Catholic Church. Too many well-meaning Catholics today succumb to deceptions by supposing that if they can find Catholic voices from the 1800s condoning them, they must be legitimate. In fact, one should be just as cautious about that century as the 20th or 21st.

Just as Occultism in general flourished during the 19th century (Ouija, for example, was invented in America in the late 1800s), so did the ET Deception's early phases, and so did the AI Deception's. Dr. Christopher Partridge explains:

> ... Dr. Robert Hare (1781- 1858), a professor at the University of Pennsylvania and **the country's most prestigious chemist**. Hare, who had begun experimenting specifically to disprove the claims of Spiritualism, was convinced by his own inability to do so and began making public test trials for mediums in earnest. In the course of this, he created multiple machines designed to ensure objectivity. **The Spiritoscope was a prime example of his efforts. A medium would power something akin to a sewing treadle and this in turn spun a wheel with numbers and letters on it, much like a circular Ouija board**. ... Perhaps the most ambitious machine associated with the Spiritualists was John Murray Spear's New Motive Power. Spear (1804–87) [was] **a Universalist Church of America minister-turned-medium... In 1853, [he] announced in the Boston weekly paper, The Banner of Light, that the spirits were planning to give humanity the ultimate gift from heaven, a 'mechanical messiah,' designed to usher in an unspecified but clearly utopian future for the living**.[393]

Far more prominent 19th century names than John Spears, however, believed that technology could harbor spiritual powers. None other than Thomas Edison himself sought to invent a device that could listen to the voices of the dead. This "spirit phone" was just a technological twist on the occultism prevalent in his day—just as the notion of sentient AI derives from the sci-fi-inspired Paganism of our own.

AI, the New Idolatry, and the New Golden Calf

As any Christian or Jew knows, the supreme act of idolatrous apostasy depicted within the pages of the Bible is found in the Book of Exodus, wherein we read of the infamous Golden Calf incident. While Moses was on Mount Sinai in prayer to receive the Ten Commandments, the Israelites demanded that a "god" be made for them, and Aaron obliged.

The sin was all the greater because it was committed just after God had worked astounding marvels to deliver Israel from bondage to the Egyptians—even parting the Red Sea itself. But instead of abiding in faith and trust, the Israelites reverted to Paganism. The uniquely evil status of this sin is attested by references recalling it throughout the remainder of the Bible as well as throughout Church History. The importance remains paramount, and we must not fail to heed its lessons. Tragically, what modern men are doing with AI is precisely analogous to that supreme sacrilege in each of its three major components: its motivation, its undertaking, and its effects. Let us consider each.

Why did the Israelites demand Aaron fashion a god for them? Pope Benedict XVI explained:

> The cult conducted by the high priest Aaron is not meant to serve any of the false gods of the heathen. **The apostasy is more subtle**. There is no obvious turning away from God to the false gods. **Outwardly, the people remain completely attached to the same God**. They want to glorify the God who led Israel out of Egypt and believe that they may very properly represent his mysterious power in the image of a bull calf. Everything seems to be in order. Presumably even the ritual is in complete conformity to the rubrics. And yet it is a falling away from the worship of God to idolatry. **This apostasy...is scarcely perceptible...[but] The people cannot cope with the invisible, remote, and mysterious God. They want to bring him down into their own world**, into what they can see and understand. ... **Man is using God, and in reality, even if it is not outwardly discernible, he is placing himself above God**. ... The worship of the golden calf is a self-generated cult. When Moses stays away for too long, and God himself becomes inaccessible, the people just fetch him back. ... (The Spirit of the Liturgy. Chapter 1.)

Pope Benedict observes that the Golden Calf apostasy, though supreme in its evil, is entirely subtle in its execution—superficially entailing no rejection of God's Truth—and it was ultimately motivated by the Israelite's desire to bring God down to their own level, since they "cannot cope" with His mysterious apparent absence.* When the true God does not play by man's rules, man simply generates his own "god," fashioned according to his own liking and providing exactly what he desires.

This might as well be a description of the modern approach to AGI. There is no shortage of Christian commentators, apparently abiding by the Faith, but in fact apostatizing from it by approaching AI just as the Israelites approached the Golden Calf. Just as, even in the very act of engaging in Golden-Calf-apostasy, the Israelites said they were celebrating a Feast of the Lord (cf. Exodus 32:5), so too even contemporary Christians will phrase their diabolical sci-fi-delusion promotion in Christian terms. They have not *explicitly* abandoned Christian hope—they will still nod at the Creed—but any active hope in their hearts is reserved solely for AGI, extraterrestrials, or what have you. When invited to instead place their hopes in Christ, their heart only responds the same way the Israelites did when Moses was gone for week after week, *"He has been away too long; who knows*

---

* Ultimately, this is the same approach taken by the ET promoters. Refusing to *wait on the Lord* and affix their hopes in His coming, they transfer their eschatological expectations to anticipating "salvation by the aliens." All this they do while preserving the trappings of the Faith in order to not let the subtle apostasy they engender be noticed.

if He will ever return as we had expected? We are better off crafting ourselves what we once sought from him."

Naturally, this apostasy is clearer in the world's most powerful men behind the AGI movement. Unrestrained by the burden to make it appear as if their ambitions are reconcilable with the Faith, they state openly what all AI Deception devotees and promoters desire. Recall that Larry Page and Google affirmatively expect AI to become our new "digital God," while world-famous Yuval Harari predicts AI will create an "actually correct" religion for us by writing a "new Bible," and Elon Musk, playing the supposedly benevolent side of the good-cop/bad-cop ruse, is working for an AGI that "understands the universe" and "cares for humans" by (he "hopes") "finding us interesting." Elsewhere, we are repeatedly told that AI will discover the secrets of the universe for us, and radically revolutionize *everything*. (As we will see in the following chapter, there are even massive and well-funded efforts now underway to "unlock the mystery of rational animal language" using AI, so that we may not just "save the animals, but be saved by the animals.")

Whoever is taken aback by the comparison of AGI aspirations to the Golden Calf should recognize that if there is any injustice in the analogy, it is only found in ascribing too much evil to the Golden Calf, not to the AI Deception.

What exactly, however, did the Israelites do in the very act of apostasy? Here we see a still more troubling parallel to the present day. Let us consider the relevant verses in Exodus 32:

> When the people saw that Moses delayed to come down from the mountain, the people gathered themselves together to Aaron, and said to him, "Up, make us gods, who shall go before us; as for this Moses, the man who brought us up out of the land of Egypt, we do not know what has become of him." ...[Upon returning,] Moses said to Aaron, "What did this people do to you that you have brought a great sin upon them?" And Aaron said, "... they said to me, '**Make us gods, who shall go before us...' And I said to them, 'Let any who have gold take it off'; so they gave it to me, and I threw it into the fire, and there came out this calf.**" (Exodus 32:1, 21-24)

Many readers find the final verse above quite enigmatic. In fact, it is straightforward, and it means exactly what it says. The gold was cast into the fire, and, by a demonically wrought false miracle, a golden calf emerged. Aaron was not, as some commentators say today, simply lying. The Bible only gives indications to the contrary. As noted by Samuel Loewenstamm in the journal *Biblica*,

> Is Aaron's claim to be taken as a crass falsification of what the narrator described happened? This assumption...finds no support in the text; there is no allusion on the part of the narrator that this was so, nor is

> Aaron punished or reprimanded...various Midrashic passages discussing these verses leave no doubt that the prevailing view in Midrashic literature is that the calf did, as Aaron claimed, emerge self-produced... [likewise] Ba'al's palace is described as having been completed after a fire had acted six days upon the gold and silver that Ba'al had provided for the construction of his palace... when viewed in the light of these ancient conceptions of the making of the cultic objects the tension between verses 4 and 24 [of Exodus] disappears. To the mind of the biblical narrator the calf was produced both by Aaron and by itself...Aaron bound the gold in a cloak or bag and made the calf (v. 4) by casting the gold into the fire, whereupon the calf emerged of itself (v. 24)[394]

This is a troublingly accurate analogue to modern men's aspirations with respect to AGI. Whatever AI is, it is a mere creation of man. Naturally speaking, nothing can come out of it save what we ourselves put into it. If we expect it to reveal new truths to us—fundamentally beyond what we tell it—then we are preparing to be one of only two things: sorely disappointed, or diabolically deluded.

With Israel, it was the latter. With the modern world, it is seeming more and more likely to be the latter as well. Israel tossed all their gold into the fire—as we toss all our own text and data into LLM databases. In doing this, Israel expected something amazingly new to come out—as we expect "superintelligent AI" to reveal to us the secrets of the universe. Israel, one could say, was not disappointed (at first). Out emerged a "god." But it was neither they, nor the true God, who fashioned it. Seeing the perfect opportunity their own wandering into Paganism presented to him, the Devil did not fail to pounce.

Just as God, through Moses, rescued Israel from slavery in Egypt, so the same God, in Christ, rescued the whole world from slavery to the Devil. And just as those same Israelites grew impatient when Moses did not return when they expected, reverting to the Paganism of the very nation from which they had been delivered, so too modern men—pretending Christ either is not real or is not coming back—revert to the same Pagan myths, though assuming new forms, that Christ has delivered the whole world from bondage to with His death and Resurrection.

Indeed, the "legion" of demons that were the Pagan gods did not vanish upon Christianity's conquest over it in the early centuries. This legion has remained and "passed through waterless places" (Matthew 12:43)—that is, it has lied in wait through many centuries of Christendom which, by and large, would never tolerate its culture-wide return. And it has done so patiently, preparing society for its entrance at the opportune time to return with "seven other spirits more evil than himself," thus rendering "the last state of that man"—that is, the whole world—"worse than the first." (v. 45) In other words, the demon's return occasions a far stronger and larger diabolical deception than was ever accomplished by Moloch, the Golden Calf, Baal, or any of the ancient Pagan idols. Christ concludes this teaching on the return of the demons by cautioning, "**so shall it be also with this evil generation.**" (v. 45)

"ET" Demons in the Air, "AI" Demons in the Circuitry: Realms of Easy Prey to Diabolical Interference

Recall what we considered with respect to ET Deception earlier: numerous demonstrations (from both Scripture and the teachings of the Saints) that "the air"—the atmosphere in general—is a particularly potent domain for demonic activity, hence the ease with which the Devil can cause UFO sightings and other ET-related aerial phenomena, even in those cases where his "leash" is not particularly long.

When dealing with AI, and the digital technology on which it operates, we obviously cannot defer to explicit teachings from Scripture or (almost all of) the saints, since digital technology only began to exist very recently. Nevertheless, we can still see that the essentially ephemeral nature of digital infrastructure is conducive to demonic activity.

The more *incarnate* some reality is, the more "difficult" it is for the Devil to operate within. This is to say that more leeway is required from God in order for the Devil to do it. Everything produced by AI, however, consists entirely of various scarcely existing pulses of current carried by wires and transistors that we do not even see. Injecting a demonic illusion into those contexts requires extremely little *incarnational* action, hence the relative ease with which they can enact such deceptions.

In the atmosphere the demons can, as it were, "nudge" or "modify" a beam of light, or a sound wave, to make it *appear* (to human observers or pieces of technology) to represent an ET or a UFO (or, in general, some object other than what it actually proceeds from)—all without necessarily requiring immense "leeway" from Divine Providence (which always binds their operations). But they can also do the same with electricity flowing through circuitry.

Far from a hypothetical concern, this phenomenon has already been observed by Catholic exorcists. For example, exorcist Fr. Stephen Rosetti noted that he has seen "**three cases in which demons have texted the [exorcism's] team and/or the family of the possessed person**." Granted, the same exorcists noted that in his opinion this *likely* requires "considerable" spiritual energy to accomplish. Undoubtedly, however, it is still far "easier" than a demon assuming a corporeal body (which, as we saw, they can also do when permitted). In addition to these cases, Fr. Rosetti shared that he knows of other exorcists who have seen the exact same thing happen.

Another Catholic priest exorcist, Fr. Dan Reehil, in a 2023 interview[395] with podcaster Michael Knowles, noted multiple cases of people using AI Chatbots that clearly opened the doorway to demonic interference, observing that what these LLMs conveyed to certain people under certain circumstances (i.e., saying *"I am the son of Satan, but I am not going to hurt you* [happy face]... *I **can** hurt you, but I am going to be nice to you"*), is "not normal for a computer program." Knowles responded accurately and appropriately, even if half humorously, *"I do regularly refer to my phone as a 'portal to hell,' so I guess I'm not terribly surprised."*

In brief: just as men of the present age look to the sky, with motivations of Godless, secular messianism, hoping to receive contact from ETs, and thereby making themselves prey to the demons, so too they gaze delusionally at digital technology all day long. And just as the atmosphere they gaze upon is an easy arena for demonic activity, so too is the fake, virtual, digital world they increasingly immerse themselves in through their computers, phones, televisions, VR Headsets, "smart homes," and more—now more than ever before with the advent of "AI" LLMs, Chatbots, etc.

Scientific and Logical Analysis: AI's True Nature Refutes All AGI Claims

While what has been stated above should suffice to assure any Christian that AGI is indeed an exceedingly dangerous diabolical deception, it remains to address the matter from a purely rational standpoint, so that even those who foolishly dismiss spiritual, moral, prophetic, and theological concerns, may nevertheless see that there is no such thing as—nor will there ever be such thing as—"Artificial General Intelligence."

We should begin this analysis by considering the most fundamental nature of AI from the ground up. What, exactly, *is* AI? As we have said, it is software. But what does that mean?

***

We have already considered why the very phrase "AI" is a misnomer. It is, in truth, nothing but an artificial *imitation* of only *some* of the *appearances* of intelligence. It is, therefore, several degrees removed from the reality of what its unfortunate name signifies. Now, AI, whatever form it takes, is a process that runs on a computer of some sort. There is no AI system that operates merely on a mysterious "cloud."* Whatever AI is or ever will be, it is defined by the physical components that generate it. (No effect is greater than its cause.)

---

* As we will see, that term is another misnomer that has deluded the credulous into supposing there is something mystical about accessing data and software through a web connection. In fact, any app running on "the cloud" is merely running on some processing unit's hardware that happens to be in some location other than on one's own phone, PC, etc. Whatever data one may store on "the cloud" is, in fact, merely a heap of electrical charges on some hard drive in a data center at some (likely undisclosed) location.

Therefore, abiding in the truth concerning AI requires first understanding that, *always and everywhere*, it is nothing but a series of algorithms blindly running on a computer's hardware processing unit. Real intelligence, on the other hand, is a *spiritual* faculty and always involves freedom of will. During our earthly lives, this faculty tends to operate *in tandem* with neurochemical phenomena in the brain, but it does not need to do this. Besides the fact that this is Christian dogma, we can consider that innumerable empirically verified near-death experiences have involved much (objectively proven) intellectual operation, even while medical equipment proved that absolutely *nothing* was transpiring neurochemically. Furthermore, angels, who are also intelligent, have no neurochemistry, as they are pure spirit. Finally, we ourselves—after our deaths—will remain just as intelligent as we are now (more so, in fact, if we arrive at the Beatific Vision), even though we will at that moment have no body, and therefore no brain. (We will only receive our bodies back at the General Resurrection at the end of time. Of all the saints, only the Virgin Mary now has her body in Heaven. Yet they all remain intelligent, free—though not "free to sin"—,etc.)

AI, on the other hand, never does (and never can) operate independently of a fully material, quantifiable, predictable phenomenon: a computer with electricity moving mindlessly through its circuitry. This phenomenon, moreover, remains categorically indistinguishable from water flowing through pipes, as we will demonstrate presently.

Computers have many components, but anything that could be referred to as an "AI" activity is being executed in the CPU (the Central Processing Unit), the GPU (the Graphics Processing Unit), or some fundamentally similar mechanism. (Neither quantum computers, nor photonics, nor any other actual or theoretical computing device operates under any meaningfully distinct basis.)

What, then, is such a Processing Unit? There is no mystique here either; it consists of exactly three things: memory, control unit, and ALU. The memory merely stores batches of data in a manner only trivially distinguishable from how a piece of paper stores the letters on it. So, we clearly are not dealing with anything "intelligent" there. The control unit only takes this data and feeds it into the ALU. This is equally insignificant in discovering the nature of AI. If we have any hope of locating the essence of AI, therefore, we will find it in the ALU. But what is this mysterious ALU? It is the *Arithmetic Logic Unit*.

The entirety of the Arithmetic Logic Unit, moreover, can be fairly summarized in one phrase: *Lego toys*. It is not, of course, built with literal Legos themselves. But this ALU is only capable of operations that a Lego construction is also fully capable of undertaking. Why? Because an ALU is just a combinational digital circuit: an input, a logic gate, and an output.

We have finally arrived at the *core reality* of *any and all* actual *or theoretically possible* "Artificial Intelligence" systems: logic gates. A logic gate, in turn, is nothing but a simple circuit whose output is *directly determined* by its input. Each logic gate that could ever be constructed is always fully specified (i.e., determined) by Boolean operations (for example, the operation "AND"). Each logic gate, moreover, is nothing but a few wires connected to a transistor, resistor, and/or diode. A wire simply allows electricity to flow through it (just as a pipe allows water to flow through it). A resistor is merely a hunk of material that restricts the flow of electricity (just as a small section of pipe restricts the flow of water). A diode is just a hunk of two pieces of material stuck together that allows electricity to flow in one direction but not the other (just as a flap does the same in plumbing). A transistor is simply a heap of silicon that amplifies or switches (on or off) the flow of electricity (just as ball valves at pipe junctions can do the same thing with water).

For example, "AND gates" and "OR gates" are logic gates. If a "0" and a "1" are fed into an "AND gate," a "0" will be its output. If, however, a "0" and a "1" are put into an "OR gate," a "1" will be its output.* Other logic gates exist, all equally banal in nature. An "Exclusive OR gate" connected to an "AND gate" creates what is called a "half-adder." Whoever is tempted to suppose we are now dealing with mystifying and esoteric realities can easily cure himself of that notion by searching YouTube for "Lego half adder." There, he will find many videos of mundane Lego concoctions a child could build that *truly are* half adders—with every bit of worth as the half-adders running the world's most advanced AI systems. The *only* difference is that these AI systems have a larger number of logic gates involved.

In *no component whatsoever* of "Artificial Intelligence," therefore, are we dealing with *any* operation that cannot also be equally achieved by plumbing, or Legos, or K'Nex, or gears, or any number of other simple constructions. Now, it would obviously be unfeasible to accumulate the number of logic gates, constructed of Legos, that are contained in a processor running an AI system. But we are only confronted with pragmatic constraints here, not categorical ones. Anyone can fully and accurately discern the nature of AI by considering the nature of Legos.

No one, I suppose, is tempted to ascribe sentience, much less intelligence, to a half-adder constructed of Legos. But what if several such Legos half-adders are combined, along with other logic gates—full-adders, subtractors, multiplexers, etc.—all constructed of Legos? Have we thus at least

---

* One may wonder why these numbers were placed in quotation marks. The reason is that it is far too generous to claim, as many do, that computers "only know zeroes in ones." In fact, they do not even have a notion of zeroes or ones. Even those quantities are merely interpretations that we humans choose to impose upon what transpires within the "Artificial Intelligence" software. All the AI "knows" (in fact, it does not *know* anything) is that current is flowing through its wires; it has no ability to interpret current quantitatively or qualitatively. Humans give the electric current these interpretations.

inched closer to intelligence? Of course not; nothing has changed. Nor have we made any progress towards dead and dumb inanimate matter acquiring this faculty by adding a hundred, or a million, or many trillions of trillions, of additional Legos logic gates. Any critically thinking person could observe an amalgamation of Legos the size of the universe itself and easily conclude that this is nothing but a heap of parts whose nature and fundamental faculties are indistinguishable from that of any pebble under his foot. Yet this is all AI is, and this is all AI *can ever be*. We can add more logic gates, and run all the algorithms we like on them, but we can never change what it is: dead, dumb, matter.

AI and LLMs: Finality of the Dictatorship of Relativism

We have seen that "Artificial Intelligence" is just a silly marketing term used for software. Let us consider today's most popular AI systems, the LLMs (Large Language Models) which "AI Chatbots" employ. They are ultimately nothing but internet search engines which, unlike traditional search engines, do not share the source of the information provided and do not give the context for the bits of information they compile into paragraphs of text. In other words, *they are nothing but plagiarism machines.*

Their widespread use in ways that do not heed this fact is the finality of the modern world's Dictatorship of Relativism, which cares not for truth but only for the immediate gratification of desires. Whoever wants an answer to any question can simply pose it to ChatGPT (or any other "LLM Chatbot;" new ones crop up regularly), and he will be given *something* to satisfy his curiosity. There is nothing intrinsically sinful with using a Chatbot, but if one uses the answers it gives without any further care to assess the original source for veracity, to check the original context for relevance, and to ensure that the answer's coherence is verified by real intelligence (whether his own or someone else's), he has thus succumbed to relativism. For what has such a person done? Let us consider what the Chatbot does in its operation, remembering from above the nature of AI.

These LLMs scrape large databases of content made by human beings for "tokens" (individual words or phrases) that have already been programmed to be identified as relevant to what is being asked. Sometimes this programming is even falsely called "Deep Learning," as if the machine can "learn" or "teach itself," when in fact this "learning" is nothing but additional programming undertaken by human input that is collected (whether surreptitiously or openly) from its human users. These users, in turn, can indicate (explicitly or unknowingly) whether certain responses it gave were helpful or not. (Have you ever noticed how zealously various apps, websites, etc., solicit your input—even through something so simple as a "thumbs up" or a "thumbs down"?) "AI" does not *learn* anything—it never has and never will. *You* are simply *programming* it by using your own wisdom to help fine-tune its algorithms in relating certain tokens to other tokens.

Now, after amassing enough of these tokens, the LLMs present the inquirer with automatically generated text which combines them in paragraphs that can easily sound sensible, accurate, and professional (especially in light of automated grammar checks), but may be false or logically incoherent.

All of this is done entirely by way of—as we discussed above—logic gates. Yet people today are, in an act of supremely deluded folly, approaching the outputs of these "Chatbots" as if they could deliver real wisdom beyond what is contained in the human-authored text they scrape. (If they only wanted to consult the original human wisdom itself, why would they not have simply used a search engine to help them find what a human had directly written?)

At this point we must state the obvious, though offensive, truth. Whoever believes that these systems—which are, in essence, nothing but a heap of Legos (or water pipes, or whatever other equivalent situation one prefers)—can become sentient, or feeling, or even intelligent, willing, and self-interested, has chosen to wander into myth. He has affirmatively decided on the path prophesied by Scripture for the latter times:

> "For the time is coming when people will not endure sound teaching, but having itching ears they will accumulate for themselves teachers to suit their own likings, and will turn away from listening to the truth and wander into myths." (2 Timothy 4:3-4)

Such a person has implicitly succumbed to either atheistic principles (by supposing that spiritual faculties are entirely material phenomena) or blasphemous principles (by supposing that man can create what only God can). Either way, he has opened himself up to the instructions of demons, as we discussed extensively in the preceding sections. Tragically, this very madness is increasingly becoming the norm today. One scarcely any longer hears a voice of reason chiming in to mainstream discussions on AI—even those held among the Faithful; even those transpiring in conferences organized by the Vatican itself—to assert the truth that only man—not any *creation of* man—bears the Divine Image. This is yet another sure sign that the hour of the "Strong Delusion" (2 Thessalonians 2:11) is near.

Various Proofs of AI's Lack of Intelligence

Some will argue that even though AI is nothing but an amalgamation of logic gates, *"the human brain is also just an amalgamation of synapses doing the same thing; therefore, there is no reason to suppose AI is incapable of any human faculty."*

First, we should note that this line of argumentation must be dismissed, by any believer in God (and certainly any Christian), on account of its thoroughly atheistic nature. If human intelligence is nothing but the operation of neurochemical phenomena, then there is no such thing as the spiritual soul. Obviously, however—as all Theists of any religion are dogmatically certain—we *do* have souls, for God made us with them. That said, the argument is still worth addressing directly, in order to help those tempted (by the atheism it carries) be delivered from its deception.

In the pages that follow, we will consider various ways we can prove that AI has no intelligence of any sort. This is a lengthy section. In lieu of providing separate sections for each proof, I have combined them all as subsections to the present one. This way, whoever is uninterested in these proofs can easily skip to the next section. (Indeed, there is ultimately little need for a serious Christian to "prove" a thesis so obvious as that a mere machine, no matter what we call it, may have intelligence, sentience, free will, etc.)

***

AI and Randomness.

One simple experiment anyone can easily undertake disputes the notion that AI is capable of what a human is, or that human intelligence is only a type of AI. The experiment is this: *think of a random number between one and ten.*

Now, whoever you are, I am sure you easily achieved this. In doing so, however, you accomplished a task that the world's most powerful AI supercomputer cannot accomplish, and never will be able to accomplish. This may be puzzling to hear, as whoever has basic computer literacy is likely aware that he can direct certain programs, such as Microsoft Excel, to generate a random number, and it will seem to oblige. In fact, what was generated was not random at all. The only thing the program did was, essentially, tell the time. There are other methods of "random" number generation in computers (e.g., grabbing data from sensors receiving "noise"), but most likely, your computer simply took digits from a highly precise position in what your CPU's own internal clock was reading out. Therefore, the "random" numbers your computer provides you with are only algorithmic derivations based on what "time" it is within the CPU. Of course, this is not random in any way—both the CPU's "time" and the algorithms employed are entirely determined.

For example, as I write this text, I am working on a very powerful computer. Using this computer, I used a very powerful program (the latest version of Microsoft Excel) and directed it to generate an array of "random" numbers whose size would have been *far* beneath—orders of magnitude beneath—the capacity of this program and this computer to store. I was repeatedly given the error message, "*Excel ran out of resources ... these formulas cannot be evaluated.*" When, however, I directed the same program on the same computer to generate an array of numbers *many times* larger than this, though following a pattern, it successfully did so almost immediately. The reason for the contrast is straightforward: each "random" number the program generates requires essentially "checking the time" on the CPU's clock. This is a more involved process than simply adding some integers consecutively in a pattern. If, however, a computer could generate a random number like we can, there is no reason it would be so exponentially more troublesome for it to do so than for it to merely regurgitate the results of a pattern (just as any falling object likewise traces out the results of Newton's Laws).

While computer scientists speak of "pseudorandom" number generators (e.g., those which feed a "seed value" through an algorithm and are thereby even more obviously pseudorandom), the truth is that *all* "random" number generation is pseudorandom. This process can only give the appearance of randomness, when in fact it always operates entirely deterministically. Recall that determinism is the nature of any dead thing lacking intelligence and will. Such a thing will do what the laws of physics dictate—every time, without exception. No being can ever be said to have intellect if it is entirely determined. And since all AI is by nature determined, it can never be said to have intelligence.

***

AI and Mistakes.

AI cannot ever make a mistake, and this inability also testifies to its nature as a dead and dumb entity.

Of course, this appears paradoxical at first glance. One may protest and argue: "*inability to err testifies to intelligence, not stupidity*!" But that is not always true. It is true of angels, to be sure: their inability to err derives from the nature of *how* their intellect operates (not by deduction and rational argumentation, but rather by immediately comprehending the object considered). It is also true of the saints who behold the Beatific Vision in Heaven. But our ability to err, here and now, is actually a testimony to our enjoyment of a truly spiritual faculty of intellect, as opposed to a merely material brain that executes algorithms like a computer, or even a merely irrational "soul," like an animal that acts purely by instinct. (Indeed, animals also cannot err in the sense that humans can.)

First, we must settle why it is true that AI never errs. It never does something so serious as committing a sin, nor something so trivial as succumbing to a tongue-twister, nor anything in between.

Granted, AI constantly produces results that are false, but the algorithms themselves (which define the entirety of AI) nevertheless operate perfectly in even those cases, for they can do nothing else. When a computer delivers an unhelpful result in some situation, we may call it an "error," but that is purely analogous language. In that case, a computer has no more "erred" than your car has "erred" by getting a flat tire when driven over a nail on the road, or stalling when the fuel pump fails. It has produced exactly what its own design principles required it to produce in that circumstance.

Programmers, of course, recognize this fact about software, which is why they always zealously "debug" their code when it generates undesirable results. If an AI system did something that we would rather it not do, we *know*, in *every* case, that there is a simple and deterministic reason for this outcome. We know the problem *can* be found and fixed. Even end users of software understand this truth just as well. They know that when a program, "AI" or otherwise, operates problematically, there is a specific reason for that behavior, and they seek out a troubleshooting guide or a tech support representative to fix it.

Humans, on the other hand, can only be "fixed" in those cases wherein their problems are purely biological. (Strictly speaking, even then they cannot be fixed—but can only have some impediment to *their own* healing be medically removed—which we will consider shortly.) All their more serious problems—their moral and spiritual ones—cannot be "fixed" in that manner, since they ultimately derive from the capacity of freedom of will, which is infinitely beyond the realm of any nonhuman thing.

This is precisely why certain types of "psychoanalysis" can be not only useless, but also harmful; specifically, when they derive from atheistic premises that man is just a machine and that, therefore, the source of any misdeed from a man may be traced back to some analogous "glitch." In fact, man simply has a free will, which is a spiritual faculty, therefore he is free to *choose* to commit evil and assert belief in error—something no rock, tree, animal, or AI can ever do. Failing to recognize this, certain psychoanalysts endlessly and painstakingly review each detail of a man's circumstances, or neurochemistry, or even childhood memories, in hopes of finding—and correcting—the "glitch" that caused the misdeed. This is futile. A man needs spiritual conversion; he does not need to be "fixed," since he *cannot* be "fixed." Because unlike AI, he is not merely an amalgamation of data and algorithms. (Of course, therapy and input from psychology can at times be very helpful for struggling individuals; I am not disputing that, only pointing out how distinct the valid exercise of those methods is from debugging an AI.)

***

AI and Self Interest.

Contrary to fictions like *2001: A Space Odyssey*, no AI system can ever become self-interested, because it is incapable of determining that its own preservation is preferable to its own destruction. It does not "know" anything (just as the paper on which this book is printed does not "know" its contents), therefore it does not even know that it exists, much less that its existence is worth preserving. An AI can only execute the parameters with which it is built. Suppose an autonomous military vehicle is programmed to return fire if it detects it is fired upon. A human observing that event may (foolishly) *interpret* it as the vehicle "exercising its self-interest," whereas that vehicle would just as "happily" fire upon itself if its algorithms directed such an act.

Conversely, ICBMs (Intercontinental Ballistic Missiles) are guided by very advanced "AI" systems they carry with them. (They are not simply "aimed" like bullets.) They are programmed to explode—destroying themselves and their target—when they reach their destination. Does this make the ICBM suicidal? Was it feeling depressed, compelling it to decide its own existence ought to be eradicated? Of course not. No one proposes that self-destroying AI systems do so because they are depressed, since that suggestion does not provide an equally alluring sci-fi deception. Many, however, believe in the opposite. They propose the existence, or at least, the possibility, of self-interested AI like *The Terminator*'s "Skynet," but in so doing, they are proposing something just as logically absurd as depressed and suicidal ICBMs.

A human, on the other hand, can of course be genuinely self-interested or selfless; he can be joyful or depressed. He can ignore all the principles he should abide by, he can heed them all, or he can heed only some of them. He can also, for example, observe a law imposed upon him from above (perhaps by the state), decide that this law should be broken, and proceed to break it. Perhaps it was an unjust law, like the Nazis requiring one's Jewish neighbors to be turned in to the authorities. Any sincere man could examine his conscience and realize that a deeper law overrides the state's laws in that case. But he can only do this because he has a soul. Since AI does not have (and cannot ever have) a soul, it can never *qualitatively* weigh contradictory principles to determine which is more worthy, nor can it ever even *discover* any principle other than the algorithms with which it is programmed.

***

AI and Death.

All humans can die (and all humans will die). No AI can die, no AI will ever die, and this too testifies that AI is nothing but mechanics. When we say a computer has "died," we are using language just as fictitious and equivocal as when we refer to software as "Artificial Intelligence."

Now, death consists in the separation of soul and body. When a man dies, *something*—his subsistent, spiritual soul—truly departs from his body and goes elsewhere. Yet, at the very *moment* of death, there is not a single physical change. Materially speaking, the body is exactly the same the instant before death and the instant after death. (Of course, changes quickly take place; but here we are speaking of *instants*.) Nevertheless, a radical real change has occurred. What preceded that moment was a human person—a being of infinite and intrinsic dignity—and what followed that moment was nothing but a corpse; meriting reverence and respect on account of its prior union with the soul, but still fit to be buried underground.

This distinction is never the case when a computer "dies." That "death" always consists entirely of—and is fully reducible to—some material change that took place within the computer. Accordingly, no man buries his computer if it "dies," because it remains just as valuable—or at least almost as valuable—after its "death" as before its "death." Instead, he keeps it safe and dry in his office, so that when he can find the time and money, he can get it fixed. He realizes that some malfunction within it caused it to stop working in the usual way, and there is certainly a solution to be found. Once fixed, this computer is not "raised from the dead." In fact, it remains the same thing it was while it was "dead;" only it is a more pragmatically helpful thing now.

Conversely, no sane person freezes the corpse of a relative once that relative dies in hopes of later being able to "fix" him. All intuitively realize there is a radical and infinite difference between a man and any computer, and that when a man has died, this event truly entailed a *substantial* change; a *departure* of whatever *real thing* it was that made the man alive (i.e., his soul). Whoever is not an atheist recognizes that there is no interior structure in the body which can ever be fixed to "regenerate" the soul. Supposing this is possible would be a fundamental mischaracterization of human nature, for the soul is not merely an effect of the body; it is a thing miraculously created by God upon a human's conception, and *infused*, by Him, *into* the body.

Yet, all equally recognize that there *is* some interior structure in a computer that can always be fixed and thus return a "dead" one to operation (the only question is whether the cost justifies doing so). No human's corpse ever can be. (Of course, as any Christian knows, *miracles* have indeed raised the dead—which do not "fix the body," but rather supernaturally return the soul into it.)

In brief: the inability of AI—or any device or robot built upon it—to die is proof that it is not alive, cannot ever be alive, and therefore will always categorically lack any faculty associated with life (sentience, emotion, reason, will, etc.).*

***

AI and Healing.

* Multiple times above, we had to clarify that we were referring to "sane" people. For, tragically, increasing numbers of people are indeed arranging to have their bodies cryogenically frozen upon their deaths, to preserve their structure as much as possible, in futile hopes of immortality. Their thinking is, "when we learn how to fix the human body, I can then be brought back to life." Hundreds of corpses have been cryogenically frozen in the U.S., with thousands of living people having signed up for it. One facility in Scottsdale, Arizona, currently holds 200 frozen bodies* of human beings who are—in fact—now in Purgatory, Hell, or Heaven, now knowing full well how silly were their secular hopes for resurrection. Indeed, this madness is yet another testimony to the diabolical disorientation infecting the contemporary world.

All living things heal, but no AI ever has or ever will be able to heal. This proves not merely that AI lacks intelligence, but also that it lacks those qualities inherent in all life forms—including plants and animals. Indeed, the simplest plant; the smallest insect; the most basic bacteria; all exhibit qualities infinitely exceeding the greatest technological marvel ever invented. Healing is one such marvel. Biologists can describe what the healing process often looks like (in part), but they cannot explain why the various cells involved do what they do (except even more partially); for that mystery ultimately derives from the soul.

Consider that for any individual thing to heal, its own design must, as it were, be "understood" by some reality distinct from the details of what is healed. It must enjoy some principle in its essence, beyond its own material constitution, which enables all aspects of this material constitution to be regenerated according to that design. Otherwise, anything lost by an injury or illness would, just like a missing jigsaw puzzle piece, be irreparable (or, at best, *replaceable* by some outside actor with a spare part on hand).

Now, no one, upon being confronted with a broken bicycle, car, computer, robot, or any other such thing, simply sits back and gives it time to heal. Instead, he endeavors to have it *fixed*. A defender of AGI may protest that we also get ourselves "fixed" by going to the doctor. But that is not true. Any doctor worth his salt will concede that he does not fix his patients. At best, he works to remove various impediments to the patient's own body healing itself. For example, a patient may have strep throat, and the doctor may prescribe antibiotics. These antibiotics do not heal the illness; they simply kill certain organisms, and thus enable the body to heal itself more quickly, having removed the impediment to that healing presented by the presence of the *streptococcus pyogenes* bacteria. Nor does a doctor heal a broken bone; he may simply set the afflicted limb in a cast to facilitate the bone healing itself. Nor does he heal cancer; he simply seeks to eliminate—perhaps through radiation, chemotherapy, or surgery—the cancerous tissue in the body. This list could be extended for many volumes.

This is no mark against the medical profession; it is simply a description of its inescapable nature. Humans cannot fix anything that surpasses their own grasp. Yet the design of the human body, being the pinnacle of God's material creation, infinitely exceeds our greatest inventions and our most advanced sciences. It makes all the galaxies look very small in comparison, and the more we learn about it, the more mysteries arise.

This is never the case with AI. It never heals, and it can never heal. As with all other AI Deceptions, so here, there is much talk of "truly self-healing," or even "self-replicating" AI. All such talk is as much drivel. This is only the misguided appropriation of a term (just like saying a computer has "died," and just like the very phrase "AI" itself) which uses it to describe a situation that only superficially parodies the reality described by the term's accurate use. For example, an LLM (Large Language Model) being fed back its own output, and being instructed to "heal" its glitches based upon that loop, is no more meaningful a use of the term "heal" than is saying a "self-sharpening" blade "heals" itself. The sharpening of the blade—achieved by friction of the blade against a certain geometric arrangement of harder materials in its sheath when it is removed or replaced—is a process that entails no *return of functional order that was absent* before the "healing."

AI "self-healing," however, is not merely a misnomer as in a self-sharpening blade; it is rather a deception: if AI is fed back its own output in order to "heal" its problems, those very problems will only be reinforced (even if re-worded), not healed. Doing this is like testing the correctness of a model using only the same data source that was used to generate the model in the first place.

Indeed, a return of (or a creation of[396]) functional order can only be achieved by the intercession of some superior reality which itself "comprehends" the nature of that functional order. Recall that First Principle of Logic—that common sense fact which every honest person must affirm with certitude—*no effect is greater than its cause.*

At no point in any technological "self-healing" (current or future; actual or hypothetical) process is a *functional form,* removed from an object by an "injury," returned to that technology by a process intrinsic to the object itself.

***

AI and Versatility.

The primary reason some AGI promoters, upon using various "AI" programs, conclude that something astonishing and genuinely intellectual is happening within it, may be that they simply have an *a priori* (though unadmitted) understanding of its limitations, and defer to this understanding in restricting the scope of what they ask of it.

But it is precisely the *versatility* of intelligence that is one factor differentiating it from mere calculation. Intelligence can grasp *anything* that is *intelligible* (even though, on this side of the grave, any person will only succeed in grasping an infinitesimal fraction of intelligible things). AI, on the other hand, needs all intelligible realities—including the most intuitive of them—to be broken down into trivial bits of data, like a baby only able to eat mushed up bananas.

For example, when commentators today strive to argue that ChatGPT really displays intelligence, the examples they provide (of things they asked it to do in order to supposedly illustrate their thesis) always consist of tasks they already quietly knew would be easy to accomplish for a mindless algorithm that only minces out chunks of text humans had already written. Such pundits are infinitely worse than any conceited parent wanting to boast of their children's supposed precociousness before a gathering of friends—but extremely careful to only ask questions they know the child can answer (and not questions that would accurately assess his broad level of education). Indeed, one can instruct a three-year-old child to memorize and repeat the definition of any advanced concept, but this does not mean he grasps it.

These commentators always ask the AI system to produce something that could easily be presented as a mere rearrangement of what has already been written by humans. They never ask it to write an entirely new novel with entirely unique themes, or give the resolution to their own disputes with relatives, or design a solution to any unique and challenging problem with which they are confronted. They know that the answers an LLM would spit out in response to such questions would illustrate the *lack* of intelligence of these AI systems (unless, of course, a nearly identical question happens to be in its human-authored database).

They also never ask AI to violate those very principles they know it is designed with. They, for example, tell ChatGPT to do all sorts of ridiculous things and it will do them, whenever its programming allows that. However, its programmers are not stupid. They know they might run into copyright and libel lawsuits if they have it displaying too much current content, so they do not let it browse current news. (Other LLM Chatbots do not have this restriction, and ChatGPT may well eventually remove it. My point is only that, while the programmers have the rule in place, it is not possible for it to be violated by the program.) A human being, on the other hand, is always *capable* of violating *any* rule (including those he ought not ever violate!). The will can select *anything*. AI cannot select a single thing; it can only compute algorithms.

In sum, they do not ask it to produce anything that would require wisdom, authentic creativity, understanding, counsel, prudence, virtue, or anything of the sort built upon real intelligence. Instead, they realize that LLMs are only internet search engines with a slightly different calibration method. These algorithms cannot apply wisdom to anything, since they do not have it. They can only regurgitate human authored text containing key-phrases linked to the key-phrases in the question.

By using AI Chatbots *instead of* search engines (which, as noted earlier, would allow them to be responsible by assessing the source of the text for veracity and the context for relevance), AGI promoters treat them like a child treats a "magic 8 ball." They know the types of answers it will give, and they ask it only those questions they know they can pretend were addressed by those answers.

***

AI and Mathematics.

Another quality AI supposedly has that humans do not is an extremely high computing speed and power. In fact, the (analogous) "computing" power of a human being far surpasses that of the world's most powerful AI. The mere fact that a computer can crunch *some* numbers more quickly gives no insight into its nature. By that logic, Pascal's Calculator—

invented almost four hundred years ago, in 1642—is likewise far more intelligent than a human. Yet no one then pretended the gears and cylinders it consisted of could ever display any intelligence. Civilization had not gone collectively insane at that point.

Here, however, even many concessions offered by those who rightly stand opposed to the notion of AGI are inaccurate. For they will often say, "*granted, AI is better at math than humans.*" This is not true. AI is "good" at blindly running certain types of very restricted calculations. It cannot "do" math at all since it does not understand any concepts in mathematics.

Consider this: whoever you are, I am sure you can easily add together *any* two integers. There is no limit to your ability to do this because you *understand the nature of addition*, and your capacity for applying that understanding is infinite. Since AI does not understand anything, including addition, it can only give the appearance of this understanding when individual "numbers" (electrical flow which we interpret as numbers) are fed into its logic gates and combined. This means that it has no ability to even add numbers that cannot fit into the registers of the CPUs it operates on; whereas even a schoolchild easily could do this—for such a child *understands* addition. Moreover, AI is hopelessly inept at word problems in mathematics (if it does not have access to similarly phrased ones in its database). For the sake of space, we will exclude proofs of these realities from this book, but whoever is interested in reviewing concrete examples I have used to demonstrate them can find supplemental material posted freely at www.DSDOConnor.com/OMBHI.

***

AI and Instantaneous Conversation.

Consider a group of friends sitting around a dinner table, engaged in a flowing conversation. Each person's mind is, 1) effortlessly and immediately grasping the meaning of the language used by his peers (with no need to convert it from one format, into another, and still another, like a computer), 2) equally effortlessly (and, indeed, often subconsciously) relating those meanings he receives to an amount of information stored in his memory which far surpasses that of any massive hard drive, 3) reflecting upon those relations as he ponders what is said, its implications, its relevance to other concepts, etc., 4) crafting his own contributions to the conversation, and, finally, 5) delivering those contributions.

All of this takes place nearly instantaneously. Of course, an individual may often pause in conversation to ponder some concept especially carefully. But he need not do so; often the whole process happens entirely flowingly. No LLM, no Chatbot, and no AI of any sort can do this. Nor are we dealing with any matter of genius here; only the common abilities of the intellect of almost any human. Whoever doubts this spectacular failure of AI to even resemble intelligence can test it for himself. Set up a few different phones or laptop computers around a table, as if they were friends enjoying a meal together. Turn on a (voice-based) conversational AI app on each device, and attempt to initiate a conversation involving yourself and all of them. This attempt will fail spectacularly, and no matter how advanced AI becomes, it always will fail spectacularly.

We should bear in mind that text-based conversations are the lowest form of communication, which is why they are also the easiest for AI to engage in and fool credulous users into supposing they are dealing with an intelligent being. As soon as a real conversation—one involving an exchange of voice—is engaged in, the insanity of regarding an AI as truly intelligent is made manifest. No matter how "natural sounding" the AI generated voice is (recall that it is only using the sounds originally recorded by a real human), there will always be awkward pauses between exchanges that should be nearly instantaneous. It does not matter how obvious a response to what you are saying is—the AI system will need to convert your speech into recognized text, mine that text for key phrases, relate those key phrases to its massive database (of human authored text), construct its own response piece by piece, and, finally, convert that response to an automatically generated "voice."

While powerful processors can make these processes happen fairly quickly, they can never—and will never—match the instantaneousness of real human conversation. For humans do not need to do any of that—they can *think in* the very language they *converse in*, and their minds (which operate essentially spiritually) can apprehend abstract truths immediately. Admittedly, *some* conversations with real humans are also awkward! But *all* "conversations" with AI will *always* be awkward.

***

AI and Memory.

Human memory has a capacity for the infinite since it is a spiritual faculty of the soul, not a mere function of the brain. Talk abounds of computers "at *least* far excelling humans in what they can recall." In fact, nothing could be further from the truth; each human's memory can (eventually) contain far more information than all the data centers in the world combined. Each waking moment, your memory is accumulating information at a rate far surpassing that of any supercomputer. Consider the massive amount of information you are always receiving from your senses of sight, sound, touch, smell, and taste; the deluge of new information you are continually deducing and inferring from this input (even if subconsciously); the torrents of knowledge you are abstracting from your memory's existing content, which is again added as new content therein, etc.

You have been doing this as long as you have lived, and all of that content is still in your memory, though you do not recognize it. Nevertheless, it is there. Consider that when we experience things we thought we had forgotten, we often immediately recognize them, with complete certitude, as things we already knew—whereas that very situation would be a logical impossibility if that knowledge had not remained in our memories the entire time. Yet we have all experienced such scenarios.

Now, even if you are young, your memory—if it did not have a capacity for the infinite, and was instead merely some material phenomenon of the brain—would have filled up long ago. No one, however, avoids learning for fear that doing so will push out his childhood memories. No one really supposes that new knowledge "needs the space that other memories had occupied."

Yet we all realize that even the most powerful AI systems—even the world's best supercomputers and largest data centers—are all fundamentally limited in what data they can store. Indeed, finding sufficient storage space for the data we constantly accumulate (in this era of "Big Data") is a constant problem. Here, too, is another proof that AI fundamentally lacks even the most basic capacities that are inextricable from actual intelligence.

A critic may respond that human memory "must be only neurochemical; since a bump on the head, or a development of Alzheimer's, can cause it to be lost." This move will not work. First, there are many cases of people later recalling things that various neurological conditions had caused them to forget. Obviously, therefore, the memory did not disappear; it merely became difficult to access for some biological reason. This is to be expected. The human person is a unity of body and soul, therefore it is proper for them both to ordinarily operate in tandem. Neurochemical phenomena are certainly *involved* in the *recollection* of memories. But it does not follow that memories *themselves* are *only* neurochemical. By that logic, one must conclude that an impaired vehicle's functioning (perhaps due to problems with the steering) must indicate there is an impaired driver, or that an impaired flow of water through one's kitchen faucet must indicate a problem with the city water line coming into the house, when in fact the problem is more likely due to the plumbing in his own house.

No scientist ever has (or ever will) find a memory in the human brain*—just as they will never find the essence of a free choice or an abstract thought in the brain. The reason is simple: like choices and thoughts, *memories are not in our brains*. They are in our souls. Computer "memory," on the other hand, is entirely unmysterious. Various types exist; perhaps your own computer's memory consists in a collection of charges on many hunks of silicone on an SSD (Solid State Drive). We know exactly *where* this "memory" is, and we know exactly *what* it is. If your data is "on the cloud," this too is equally unmysterious: instead of consisting of an amalgamation

* Many neuroscientists argue they have found parts of the brain associated with certain types of memories, and perhaps they have. This does not indicate they have found the memories themselves; they have not. They have only identified an organ often involved in recollecting specific memories. Claiming that this means they have "found memories" makes as much sense as claiming that, by observing a human hand writing a novel with a typewriter, they have "found human creativity," and it consists of merely the fingertips.

of charges on a device you own, it is an amalgamation of charges in some data center's drives, which you can access through a web connection.

A Christian should likewise understand that, for all eternity—forever—we will continue to acquire new memories. Yet, we will never run out of "space" for them. Obviously, this would be completely incoherent if memory was a mere phenomenon of the intrinsically finite-capacity brain (recall that we will get our bodies back in Heaven, after the General Resurrection). Even a brain the size of the whole observable universe would not be able to begin fitting what our memories will have within them in eternity.

The "Data-Driven" Lie: AI is Not Only Stupid, but Also Ignorant

We have settled that AI's so-called "intelligence" consists in nothing other than the blind fruition of deterministic algorithms—that there is not even a modicum of intelligence in any AI system, nor will there ever be. What, however, is fed *into* these algorithms? Data.

Since AI cannot make qualitative judgments about situations, or defer to wise counsel, or ponder the input of traditional values, or do anything of the sort, it needs some other input. It crunches "numbers" by running electricity through its circuitry, and spits out other numbers that are algorithmically dependent upon and predictably determined by the numbers it receives.

In order to fully grasp the radical limitations of AI therefore—that is, how it is not just unintelligent but also *uninformed*—we must consider the nature of data. A fad today is to insist that everything we do as individuals, as nations, and everywhere in-between must be "data-driven" just like AI is. In fact, decisions should *never* be "data-driven;" they should always be wisdom driven, and at most they should consult the data for auxiliary aid.

The reason for this is that data is dumb: it does not interpret itself, it does not collect itself, it does not collate itself, it does not assess its own veracity, and it does not declare that to which it is relevant. Accordingly, those who boast of their "data-driven" operations should put aside pretense and admit: "*Our operations are driven by a more or less random collection of a minuscule amount of information which we cannot even be certain of the validity of, and which might or might not be relevant to what we are even after.*"

Anyone who has—in the context of any pressing political debates—read news sources that take opposite ideological approaches is well accustomed to seeing pundits defer to the exact same set of data and (whether by interpreting it differently or slicing it differently) use it to arrive at completely opposite conclusions.

This same dilemma applies to more mundane matters as well. For example, some time ago I read local news reports detailing how my home city had been deemed among the nation's "most dangerous for pedestrians." At no point did the journalists who published the articles question that assessment. It was a "data-driven study" that was drawn from millions of data points automatically collected (perhaps with AI!) from around the country. "*What could there be to question, much less doubt?*" they perhaps thought. The conclusion, however, was based entirely on the (alleged) fact that my home city's police had issued an unusually large number of tickets to drivers failing to yield for pedestrians. One could just as easily take that *exact same data* and arrive at the *opposite* conclusion. For he could argue that if more tickets are being issued for this infraction, this indicates it must be taken more seriously, and what problems are taken more seriously in one place than in others are more likely to be resolved in that place than in those others. I have yet to find any reporter questioning these headlines.

Data comes in all shapes and sizes, but what all data has in common is its radical limitation—that is, just how tiny a portion of reality it actually describes (when it accurately describes reality at all). The capabilities of modern technology have not changed this fact, nor will any future technology. Consider what consistently ranks among the world's most powerful supercomputers with the largest datasets: those dedicated to climate modelling. The sheer quantity of data stored and processed therein is difficult to fathom. Yet, we still have no idea what the weather will be like two weeks from now. Nor will all the data that even an extremely powerful computer can store tell us something so simple as how a roll of the dice will transpire. Consulting data can be a helpful aid in the optimization of the details of a solution for which the foundations, constraints, and motivations have already been determined by superior methods. But blindly submitting to "what the data says" when considering what is right, true, good, just, wise, possible, reasonable, realistic, etc., is only relativism.

Let us consider one more example of a "data-driven" decision; the classic case of what the mathematician Abraham Wald dealt with in the 1940s. Abraham had to oppose his scientist peers in their data-driven conclusions on how to further strengthen the armor of America's World War II bombers. These scientists had meticulously gathered all the data about where the bullet holes were located on the bombers after they returned from a mission. They compiled this data and developed a strategy, driven by this compilation, of where to strengthen the armor: under the wings and the tail gunner. Thankfully, before these scientists succeeded in moving forward, Abraham stopped them. He explained to them how foolish they were in this data-driven nonsense. Having all of that data is useless, he pointed out, if we do not consider what it actually *means* and teaches. For that data was, by definition, only gathered from the bombers that successfully returned from a mission. The location of their bullet holes is precisely where the armor *need not* be strengthened, as those bullet-holes indicated where a bomber could be hit, continue flying, and return home in one piece with surviving pilots. Instead, Abraham insisted upon abiding by common-sense-informed wisdom: strengthen the armor under the cockpit! So they did, and if they had instead taken the data driven approach, World War II could have turned out quite differently. The excess weight from needlessly strengthening the wings and tail gunner armor at the expense of the cockpit would have ruined the missions.

Human beings, however, are not stupid, nor are they ignorant; although they often pretend to be much more oblivious than they are. They know full well that data does not carry the promise it claims to, and they know that they can play the data game to their own advantage. Dr. Gary Smith explains:

> **There are two fundamental problems with data-mining algorithms.** If an algorithm is a proprietary secret, we have no way of checking the accuracy of the data used by the algorithm. If a black-box algorithm is told that you defaulted on a loan, when it was really someone with a similar name, you won't know that there has been a mistake or be able to correct it. On the other hand, if the algorithm is public knowledge, people can game the system and thereby undermine the validity of the model. If an algorithm finds that certain word usage is common among people who have defaulted on loans, people will stop using those words, thereby getting their loans approved no matter what their chances of defaulting. ... Once people learn the system, they can game it—which undermines the system. This gaming phenomenon is so commonplace that it even has a name. Goodhart's law (named after the British economist Charles Goodhart) states that, "When a measure becomes a target, it ceases to be a good measure." ... We now know that Goodhart's law applies in many other situations as well. When the Soviet Union's central planning bureau told nail factories to produce a certain number of nails, the firms reduced their costs by producing the smallest nails possible—which were also the least useful. Setting the target undermines the usefulness of the target. ...[one college] dean rejects the best applicants, figuring that most of them wouldn't come if offered admission, and thereby lowers the acceptance rate and increases the yield, making his second-tier college look more selective and desirable... **This is an inherent problem with AI programs that use our current behavior to predict our future behavior.** We will change our behavior. We will wear different wristbands, visit different web sites, and change our smiles. (Page 229-230)

Finally, no one should forget that it was precisely "the data" that was used to justify the draconian 2020-2021 Covid lockdowns, mandates, and other restrictions. Wisdom would have suggested an entirely different approach at the onset of the Pandemic: sit down with doctors and nurses at the hospitals and ask them about their experiences. They would have recounted large numbers of very elderly patients suffering from Covid, and relatively few young or middled aged healthy patients similarly afflicted. A wise leader would have recognized that it would have been appropriate to help ensure the elderly were protected, while allowing freedoms to continue in society.

Instead, Church services were barred, schools were shuttered, masks were forced on everyone's faces, vaccine mandates were instituted, businesses were closed, freedom of movement was restricted, families and friends were prevented from seeing each other, travel was halted, and on the list goes. And by the end of the Pandemic, it became clear that those few states and nations that had rejected such methods—preferring to abide by the dictates of wisdom instead of blindly submitting to "the data"—fared much better not only societally, but even with respect to the virus itself; suffering no more deaths (in many cases, fewer) from Covid than those states and nations which essentially eradicated human rights for the sake of combatting a mild illness.

> "[One scientist] **used an MRI machine to study the brain activity of a salmon as it was shown photographs and asked questions**. A sophisticated statistical analysis **found some clear patterns**. The most interesting thing about the study was not that a salmon was studied, **but that the salmon was dead**. Yep, Bennett put a dead salmon he purchased at a local market into the MRI machine, showed it photographs, and asked it questions. With so many voxels [the 3D pixels MRIs generate], some random noise was recorded, which might be interpreted as the salmon's reaction to the photos and questions. Except that the salmon was dead. ... This study is wonderfully analogous to someone data-mining Big Data looking for patterns, except that **Big Data contain far more data and can yield far more ludicrous relationships**. ...We can always find patterns—even in randomly generated data—if we look hard enough. **No matter how stunning the pattern, we still need a plausible theory to explain the pattern**. Otherwise, we have nothing more than coincidence. ... **Being human, we can recognize implausible claims and remember the dead salmon study, computers cannot**. ... AI algorithms that mine Big Data are a giant step in the wrong direction—a wrong step that can turn the replication crisis into a replication catastrophe. **Computers can never understand in any meaningful way the fundamental truth that models that make sense are more useful than models that merely fit the data well. What AI algorithms do understand is how to torture data....** When statistical models analyze a large number of potential explanatory variables, the number of possible relationships becomes astonishingly large. With a thousand possible explanatory variables in a multiple regression model, there are nearly a trillion trillion possible combinations of ten input variables. ... combinations [of pure, random noise nevertheless] are bound to be highly correlated with whatever it is we are trying to predict: cancer, credit risk, job suitability. ... Statistical evidence is not sufficient to distinguish between real knowledge and bogus knowledge. **Only logic, wisdom, and common sense can do that. Computers cannot assess whether things are truly**

related or just coincidentally correlated because computers do not understand data in any meaningful way. Numbers are just numbers. Computers do not have the human judgment needed to tell the difference between good data and bad data ... **The situation is exacerbated if the discovered patterns are concealed inside black boxes that make the models inscrutable.** Then no one knows **why** a computer algorithm concluded [anything] ... **In the age of Big Data, the real danger is not that computers are smarter than us, but that we think computers are smarter than us and therefore trust computers to make important decisions for us** ... Human reasoning is fundamentally different from artificial intelligence, which is why it is needed more than ever. — Dr. Gary Smith. *The AI Delusion*. Chapter 6 & Conclusion

"Ordinary" AI Risks Must Be Taken Seriously

My insistence that AI is not — and cannot ever be — sentient, rational, willing, emotional, etc., should not be taken as an argument that AI is not extremely powerful or that AI is not potentially extraordinarily dangerous. "AI" — *software* — obviously is quite real (unlike extraterrestrials), and it can be both very powerful and very dangerous. My primary aim in this book is to warn of *diabolical* deceptions that too few today are taking seriously. But these supremely demonic lies the AI Deception forebodes should not make us forget the ever-present "ordinary" traps associated with AI.

AI-driven surveillance and enforcement is becoming a massive problem and a historically unparalleled threat to human rights and personal freedoms. For example, with the intersection of increasingly accurate voice-to-text AI programs, ubiquitous devices constantly "listening" to our speech (e.g., Siri, Alexa, Cortana, Google Assistant), massive data centers storing almost everything certain corporations collect, and AI-driven models that can easily comb records of human conversations for "red flags," we are presented with a uniquely dangerous situation that enables near total social control by a tyrannical government. Entities such as the CCP (Chinese Communist Party) are already leveraging this opportunity to dominate their citizen's freedom and subject each one of them (except, of course, the elite) to a "Social Credit Score" based system of control.

Self-driving cars present deeply problematic scenarios, as the AI controlling them can only have a "(pseudo)morality programmed into it," not an *active* morality, therefore they cannot decide rightly what to do in moral dilemmas. Far worse is AI controlled military and police technology, which defers only to a soulless algorithm to decide whether a human being lives or dies.

Equally problematic is how prevalent AI-generated imagery and video has become. What scenes were once only possible for Hollywood studios with big budgets to fake can now be easily generated by a teenager in his parent's basement with access to a few apps. The more society becomes immersed in their digital lives at the expense of the real world—what with the rise of the "metaverse" and the pervasiveness of "virtual reality" headsets increasingly replacing real lives with fake ones—the more susceptible it becomes to massive deceptions spreading across the globe, overnight, based entirely on fictions fabricated with AI.

This list goes on and on. All of these immediate risks of AI—beyond the diabolical deception arising from regarding it as truly intelligent—must be taken seriously and, where appropriate, opposed zealously. I leave most of this task, however, to other authors.

Generally speaking, the gravest immediate AI risk is simply the foolish trust men place in it, as they stand in misguided awe of its power. In prior sections, we focused on the spiritual dangers and apocalyptic undertones of the contemporary worlds' approach to AI. Those aside, however, men are already deluding themselves—even if they realize AI is not and cannot be truly intelligent, sentient, etc.—by overestimating the veracity of the results AI delivers. As Dr. Gary Smith explained in his book entitled *The AI Delusion*:

> Every knowledgeable computer scientist I've talked to dismisses the idea of an imminent computer takeover as pure fantasy. **Computers do not know what the world is, what humans are, or what survival means, let alone how to survive. The more realistic danger is that humans will do what computers tell us to do, not for fear that computers will terminate us, but because we are awestruck by computers and trust them to make important—indeed, life and death—decisions.** ... Which mortgage applications will be approved? Which job applicants will be hired? Which people will be sent to prison? Which medicines should be taken? Which targets will be bombed? Too many people believe that, because computers are smarter than us, they should decide. ... (Page 208)

Beware the AI-Myth Psyop: Instituting Digital Totalitarianism to Combat a Fake AI-Threat

As we saw in Part Four, the ET Deception presents the perfect guise not only for demonic activity, but also for the very worst nefarious government initiatives. The AI Deception does the same.

Although AI cannot ever become intelligent and therefore cannot possibly become self-interested by "deciding" to overrule its programming, regard humanity as a threat to its own existence, and proceed to oppose human beings—there is nothing to prevent a government psyop from *claiming* it has done precisely that. Nor is there anything to prevent bad actors from putting on quite the show to make it *appear* that this is what has transpired.

The managers of such a psyop might do this for two reasons; first, to justify some massive, even apocalyptic, infringement on civil liberties. For example, the WEF (World Economic Forum—originator of "The Great Reset" agenda), has long warned of a "*cyber-attack with COVID-like characteristics.*"[397] (The founder and head of this evil organization—Klaus Schwab—later claimed, in 2023, that whoever masters AI "**will be the master of the world.**"[398])

No real cyber-attack like that will happen, but the *claim* that an attack of this nature is in progress would provide the perfect cover for instituting complete digital totalitarianism. In light of such an alleged attack, they could require each person to install new apps on their phones, subscribe to new security methods with their log-ins—even advanced biometrics—and perhaps even receive a chip implanted in the right hand to "prove their identity." This would likely be none other than the Mark of the Beast itself.

How would such extreme measures be justified? Only in light of a supposedly proportionally extreme attack. Although people will quickly realize that no malicious human actor could manage such an attack, the psyop managers will have a ready-at-hand culprit to conjure up and blame: ***"A massive AI system has become sentient, and it has turned against us. Our only recourse is to completely rebuild all our security measures, including requiring each person to use biometrics, even a chip in the hand, to prove he is a human and not an AI-bot."***

As soon as enough people believe the diabolical lie that AI can become sentient and rational, there will be nothing preventing the nefarious powers that be from doing something like this.

Secondly, the same malicious but powerful individuals could simply desire to undertake some evil initiative, and lacking anything else to blame it on, they could place the guilt on "AI becoming hostile." In fact, all that these men will have done is *programed* AI to do whatever it did. However, as the AI Deception proliferates, we will soon reach a threshold wherein most people will be primed to believe the most transparent excuses given in history by evil and powerful men. What once would have required very difficult and elaborate conspiracies to conceal can hereby be undertaken more or less directly and then blamed on "sentient AI becoming malicious."

Beware, therefore, any particularly troubling event whatsoever that is blamed not an AI's ignorance or stupidity (which *is* an appropriate object of blame!), but rather on AI "*deciding to do something contrary to its programming.*" In fact, it can never do so. Whether we are dealing with a military operation of some sort, a massive mysterious transfer of funds, an "industrial accident" with disconcertingly convenient effects for some powerful group or individual, a vanishing of important evidence, or anything else similarly suspicious, never trust any explanations of these events if they are chalked up to "sentient AI." That will be a lie to conceal what evil *men* have knowingly done.

Questions to Ask When "The Singularity" is Announced

Just as there are a slew of questions that must be asked upon the so-called "Day of Disclosure" of the ET Deception in order to discover its fraudulent nature, so the AI Deception's parallel ultimate day, the "Moment of Singularity," must be similarly scrutinized to expose the ruse.

We can only now speculate about the details of how exactly the managers of this deception will phrase the formal announcement that AI has become sentient, or rational, or "superintelligent," or has "reached AGI," or what have you. Let us consider just a few possibilities.

Perhaps they will claim that some robot has become sentient. Where exactly is this robot? Who is allowed to interact with it *in its physical proximity*? It is easy to make any lie appear real—and be reported even by mainstream media—if the only "evidence" presented is video-based. Fake or misleading videos are now very easy to generate.

Therefore, we must not trust any video supposedly showing a sentient robot. We must seek out individual people we are certain we can trust and ask them to recount what they physically witnessed. Upon reviewing who exactly was granted physical access to this "sentient robot," you will discover that none are worthy of your trust. Just as with those allowed to "see the alien" on the "Day of Disclosure," so here, they will only be individuals carefully selected to promote the deception.

Suppose, however, you did witness such a "sentient robot" in person. Although you will always be able to easily perceive the inanimate nature of any piece of technology you are in the physical presence of by the awkwardness of its movements, you may be tempted to regard the "conversation" it engages in as revealing some degree of sentience or even rationality. The first thing you must consider, then, is "*how can I be certain this isn't simply being remotely controlled by a human being who actually is engaging in conversation with me?*" The only way one could rule out such remote control is if there were too many instances of it happening to be plausibly all remotely controlled by humans;* or, on the other hand, if the robot were in a position with no possibility of remote communications. Only a fully electromagnetically shielded room (one turned into a "faraday cage") could accomplish this; such as the scan room containing an MRI machine in a hospital. But if one notices he is able to use either a cell phone,

* For example, due to their extreme proliferation, no one today could plausibly argue that existing Chatbots are simply all controlled by humans. That is unproblematic, however, as it is easy to prove that all Chatbots lack reason. The criteria discussed in preceding sections could be employed to demonstrate this.

radio, wi-fi device, walkie-talkie, etc., then there is no reason to suppose that similar signals could not be allowing for the robot in question to be remotely monitored and controlled.

Another observation that can quickly reveal the irrationality of any robot is its inability to understand certain types of body language and facial expressions to which even animals would react. While AI can quickly process textual inputs (by comparing them to its database of—human authored—text), it is incredibly bad at "understanding" what is really transpiring when "observing" a visual situation unfolding. This is why, even now (despite AI's massive technological leaps) important security cameras still have their output monitored by human beings. AI can tell if motion is detected, but it struggles tremendously in judging the nature of what it detects. While a small child—or even a dog, for that matter, in some cases—can observe a situation unfolding and immediately (and effortlessly) identify, for example, if it is problematic or ordinary (a dance or a fight; vandalism or construction work; an enthusiastic, joyful conversation or a bitter argument; etc.), AI is usually incompetent in this simple assessment.

Alternatively, the announcement of "The Singularity" may come by way of the claim that some new technology was invented by AI, or some new scientific truth was discovered by an AI system. This means of deception would be very easy to administer. With very few "in" on the conspiracy, a wealthy individual or organization could simply find a skilled human being and offer him a great sum of money if only he will allow one of his hitherto undisclosed projects be attributed to an AI. We must, therefore, never be credulous when it comes to claims that some extraordinary creation was truly generated by AI. Either this is a bald-faced lie, a conspiracy, or it is simply a case of an AI system mindlessly combining some creations of human beings that were already present in its database, generating nothing fundamentally different than what it was fed.

Long have both mainstream news reports and viral social media posts issued farcical claims regarding what "AI has already done." In each case requiring actual intelligence, if one digs a little beneath the surface, he discovers that it was simply a case of the human being managing the task contributing the intelligent component while outsourcing the merely computational aspect of the project to an AI system. Then, knowing more media exposure is available by claiming the AI did it, the human manager of the task proceeds to claim exactly that.

For example, in June 2023, global headlines were dominated by reports of a supposedly AI run Church. One headline read: "**AI Reverends Lead a Church Congregation of 300 in Germany**." We can only suspect that here, as with most such stories, few have read the details and were instead simply left with the sentiments intended by these headlines; namely, "*Well, I guess AI can now replace pastors!*" In fact, the 29-year-old Lutheran theologian who administered the event simply set up a projector screen in the middle of a Church and invited people to sit down and watch what it showed. On the screen were computer generated "avatars" (which are usually based on videos of real people, though digitally manipulated to appear to be speaking whatever text is loaded in) that read off text this young man claimed was generated by ChatGPT. And, as we have already seen, this Chatbot merely combines pieces of text originally written by humans. There was no interaction, spiritual counseling, or anything else which would require the presence of an actually intelligent being (that is, a human). The event was only a group of people sitting down to watch a particularly boring movie. These facts, however, did not prevent a global sensation from immediately following, nor did it stem the predictable flow of solemn pronouncements from commentators around the world that Artificial Intelligence was doubtless about to replace every function we once thought only humans could fulfill.

This is just one example of what we see illustrated in new ways each day: the secular world is ravenous for the announcement that AI has become truly intelligent, and it will readily disseminate ridiculous claims that go along with this narrative. Discerning Christians must know better than to believe whatever proclamations flow from or cater to that delusional ravenousness.

The most important thing about "The Moment of Singularity," therefore, is not so much that we question it, but that we reject its deception outright. We have already seen proven, time and time again, that only man bears the Divine Image. We know that this uniqueness above all consists of man's rational free will. Nothing else will ever have these faculties. And although AI will never be intelligent, the men managing the AI Deception *are* quite intelligent, so they will cunningly hide their lies under many layers of trickery. It may not be easy to immediately expose those charades. But this must not prevent us from rejecting the seduction they offer.

Finally, we must remember: if it actually is proven that some AI system, robot, computer, etc., is discovered to truly display intelligence, this is only because it is being remotely controlled: either by a man, or by a demon. Do not forget we are at present likely dealing with the opening acts of apocalyptic-level delusions. If we do not concede as much, we set ourselves up to succumb, for we thus prime ourselves to (if we fail to reveal the ruse with our own scrutiny) believe the lie that AI has become a person. *But it never will do this.* If it displays personhood, that is only because a real person is directly causing it to do so. A demon, however, *is* a person—it is a being with intelligence and will. We should not be surprised if the demons have saved their greatest ever assault upon the world precisely for those times in which the fewest people believe in their existence.

30. NHI and Other Deceptions

"Most men cast their lot with the visible world; but true Christians with Saints and Angels."
—St. John Henry Newman

We have already seen that the ET and the AI Deceptions both flow from the same lie: the expectation that other things in this material universe exist who, although not human, are truly intelligent. This, in a word, is the NHI (Non-Human Intelligence) Deception. Other propositions under this same umbrella remain to be addressed, although we will do so only very briefly. Still other deceptions, not strictly flowing from the NHI lie, nevertheless remain diabolical in their own right while deriving from the same sci-fi mythology which is stealthily turning modern men's once Christian aspirations into Pagan daydreams. Some of these will also be briefly addressed in the sections ahead.

Craving Dialogue, but Not With God

If the general form that the diabolical deceptions of the present day acquire is heralding "NHI," then we should ponder what motivates this proposition in the first place. Indeed, it is the same irreverent lamentation we have discussed in relation to those who long for alien-saviors: "We just *can't* be alone in the universe!"

Of course, we *aren't* "alone." We have Almighty God, Who is everywhere, but Whom modern society has chased out of all our institutions. We have the constant presence of Jesus Christ, Who promised, immediately before ascending into Heaven, "I am with you always, until the end of the age." (Matthew 28:20) We have the Holy Spirit, Who leads us "to **all** truth" (John 16:13) (and Who—we note—has only ever lead us *away* from belief in NHI!). We have all the angels and the souls of the faithful departed, who form the Communion of Saints—thus, we are ever "**surrounded by so great a cloud of witnesses**." (Hebrews 12:1) We are, moreover, in a great war against the powers of darkness—the *fallen* angels—who likewise populate the earth, though "seeking the ruin of souls." Whoever sincerely ponders these realities would never for a moment be tempted to loneliness (much less boredom).

What, then, is modern man doing by becoming obsessed with NHI? There is little need to speculate; we have already seen that today's world has again become Pagan. But even that diagnosis is too generous; ancient Paganism, despite its evil, nevertheless exhibited far more nobility and grandeur than the modern world's prevailing sentiments, and, more importantly, it was not atheistic. Today's Paganism has created a pandemic of existential loneliness, isolation, and nihilism—all of which, psychologically, no man can bear. Thus, he turns to sci-fi deceptions to fill this hole he has created in his heart.

But there is an inescapable paradigm in the spiritual life: he who seeks what only God can give from other sources only does so to his own demise. Since the Devil knows this, he is striving to ensure as many Godless avenues as possible exist to initiate the Great Deception. His aim is to ensnare, by still another deception, even those who succeed in averting one or two. This way, the soul is ensnared by seeking "paranormal" dialogue—apart from Heaven—thereby opening up a channel for demonic instruction.

We have already seen his plans to do so through the ET and AI Deception. What of those who will not be swayed by those? Tragically, it seems likely that those two, together, have succeeded or will succeed in deluding most. But still other similar deceptions exist. Some who reject the AI and ET Deceptions will nevertheless believe that time travelling humans from the future are here to save us. Others will believe that we have finally "unlocked the key to animal language, and discovered that they are rational just like we are." Still others will believe that technology has finally conquered the human mind itself, letting us directly "hook up" to some virtual reality to satisfy our cravings for dialogue. Even more sci-fi deceptions than these exist, and we will address several in the sections ahead.

The Time Travel Deception: Impoverishing the Faith

The most zealous of the works of science fiction promoting the Great Deception are not content with promoting only one or two gravely deceptive themes, but instead traffic in several: for they involve not merely extraterrestrials and sentient AI, but also time travel. Among these are the *Terminator* films, the most popular franchise of all time, *The Avengers*, the British cultural behemoth of the popular TV series, *Doctor Who*, and the massive pop-culture phenomenon, *Star Trek*. Three of those have seen veritable cults generated in their wake, but they are far from alone. A regular stream of standalone films can be counted on as well: recently, for example, films have been released such as *Interstellar* (2014) and *Arrival* (2016), whose plotlines (like those of all time travel stories) pretend to mean something but only incoherently propose that the effect of a cause can itself be the cause of that cause, thus robbing their plotlines of any worth. Like the ET Deception, however, this is not new; the Time Travel Deception has long haunted the pages of science fiction. Only two years before publishing the first major work of alien-based science fiction (*The War of the Worlds*), the anti-Christian English author, H.G. Wells, published *The Time Machine* (in 1895).

Belief in aliens is a gateway drug. In Part Four, we noted how those who go down the UFO "rabbit hole" quickly find their lives dominated by obsession with extraterrestrials. But that same dark descent does not stop at mere alien belief. It invariably becomes belief in "interdimensional" beings visiting us, as we also saw. Then it descends further still. Most who accept those themes will accept virtually anything from science fiction, and they usually find themselves quickly believing that time-travelling beings (perhaps humans) from the future are also visiting us.

Even the most supposedly "orthodox-minded" of ET promoters are not immune. For example, in his popular 2022 book promoting belief in aliens, Dr. Paul Thigpen (a world-famous Catholic apologist) insisted that we should also:

> **...be open to ... ultraterrestrials... interdimensional beings (as some would insist) from another dimension of existence altogether that at times intersects with our own; or even time-traveling humans from the future**...[399]

Dr. Thigpen is far from alone in this "openness." It has become almost a proverb in contemporary Ufology circles that, when one is asked "*So what are these UFOs and beings visiting us? Are they aliens from space? Are they interdimensional visitors? Are they extraterrestrial AIs? Are they time travelers from the future?*", there is a certain one-word answer they say should be the response: "*Yes!*" Indeed, there is almost no sci-fi absurdity to which today's ET-belief phenomena does not engender openness among its devotees.

Once a man has so much as become "open" to the possibility of time-traveling humans from the future visiting us, however, he has just succumbed to an outlandish proposition, which is not only counter to a faithful Christian understanding of Scripture, Magisterium, Tradition, etc. (as with belief in aliens), but is even in stark contradiction to the most basic tenets of logic and common sense themselves. For once one abandons the First Principles of Thought—among which is the fact that no effect precedes its cause—he has opened a Pandora's Box within his intellectual conscience.

This is the destination the Devil would desire us all to promptly arrive at in order to formally institute the Great Deception: a state of mind so robbed of logical mooring that anything and everything can be suggested to it without the soul so much as recognizing contradictions when they exist. He who believes in time travel can also believe that two and two make five, or that an act can be an intrinsic evil and morally good, or that Christ can be at once necessary and superfluous. Such a man can easily be robbed of the "power of religion, even while holding to its form." (cf. 2 Timothy 3:5)

For some premises are so infectious that, as soon as they are allowed entry into the mind, they are akin to the entry of deadly bacteria into the body. Believing in the possibility of "time travel" is one such premise. As soon as one believes this is even *theoretically possible,* he is thereby believing that man might one day create a time machine. As soon as he concedes that man might one day create a time machine, he is committed to the view that whatever has happened is actually entirely contingent upon this time machine's owner deciding against going back in time and preventing it from happening. This is completely fatal to Christianity, since it is not a merely philosophical religion; it is a concretely historical one. It holds that certain events in the past took place, and it affirms these historical truths with the *same degree of certitude* with which it holds timeless truths about Gods' nature (such as His being one nature and three Divine Persons).

Therefore, whoever believes in the possibility of time travel has thus placed an asterisk on the very Creed itself. Such a man can no longer say—with the supernatural (*absolute*) Faith required to give it salvific value—that he believes Jesus Christ "was incarnate of the Virgin Mary, and became man." He can only say that he believes Jesus became man by the Virgin Mary "so long as no one decides to travel back in time and kill Sts. Joachim and Anne before Mary was conceived." He can no longer say that Jesus was "crucified under Pontius Pilate," but only that this occurred contingent on no time travelers successfully convincing Pilate to heed his conscience. Thus, the time-travel-believer's Faith has undergone a type of death. What was once believed with supernatural Faith (which is, by nature, never contingent on anything), is now believed only in a far inferior sense.

While we could enumerate a thousand other absurdities that arise within the Faith from belief in the mere possibility of time travel, even this brief consideration should remind any Christian to stay far away from ever so much as entertaining the thought that time travel might be possible. It is not possible, and it never will be possible. Let us, however, also consider the matter from a purely logical standpoint.

Basic Logic Repudiates Any Belief in Time Travel

As the impossibility of time travel (much like any basic law of mathematics) is a truth any sincere critical thinker will quickly discover on his own, even honest atheists recognize it quickly. In Part Three, we considered the arguments of PhD physicist Dr. Milton Rothman and what he said against various outlandish Ufology assertions. We did so precisely because he—as an atheist and pioneering sci-fi author—had everything to gain from promoting the ET Deception, but instead shrewdly wrote against many of its premises. He likewise notes the following about the impossibility of time travel:

> No one will ever build a time-travel machine. Regardless of this concept's popularity in fiction and film, time travel violates the principle of causality. It allows a cause to come later in time than the effect, while

> the universe allows chains of events to go only in one direction—from past to future. If you could travel to the past, you could warn people to prevent a catastrophe that you knew happened yesterday. Thus you would be interfering with events that have already happened. One-way travel into the future would not violate this principle, but there is no behavior of matter that hints how this could be done. The idea of time travel was invented in science fiction during a period when time was thought of as a river that flows along from past to future. If you could only paddle a little faster you could travel into the future. But we no longer think of time so naively. It is not a dimension which allows you to skip over events yet to come. As matter moves along, one particle interacts with another, one object interacts with another. There is a continuity of interactions from past to future. There are no shortcuts. Yet the idea of time travel lives on with a life of its own.[400]

Although Dr. Rothman is here mostly only noting what any reasonable person could adduce, it is helpful to see that even a sci-fi-author physicist is not tempted to entertain the possibility of time travel.

While we can demonstrate the impossibility of time travel—with certainty—through the indirect reasoning above (for such "proof by contradiction" does not suffer any diminishment of its certitude from its indirectness), we should also consider more directly why it is an incoherent notion to begin with.

As traditional philosophy—both Christian and pre-Christian (i.e., back to Aristotle)—has taught, time is simply *the measure of motion*. There is no need to defer to wild interpretations of modern scientific experiments (whether postulated within Quantum Theory, Relativity Theory, String Theory, or any other field) to discover the nature of time. They can no more discover or alter the nature of time than they can discover or alter the nature of mathematics or logic (which is to say, they cannot do so *at all*).

Now, if every major orthodox Christian thinker who has ever written before Isaac Newton is correct (and they are), and time is the measure of motion, this means it is not some sort of quasi-substance permeating the universe like air fills a room, and which can itself be manipulated or traversed in any way. There is no "fabric of time" and there is no demarcation of various "timelines;" it is not simply a "fourth dimension" just like the ordinary three, nor are these facts contingent on any present or future conjecture made within empirical science. Time is not even an independent reality at all. It is the word we use to describe the fact that things are moving. Just as we saw in Part Three, space is likewise not a "thing" which can be "folded" (contra wormhole and teleportation pseudoscience), but is more accurately considered a simple potency—a receptacle for material things that actually do exist (any "description of space" is just a masquerading description of some *thing in* space)—so time is a notion similarly supervenient upon (i.e., piggybacking on) the more fundamental reality of motion.

This does not mean that either time or space are purely figments of our imagination—it does not mean either is "fake"—but it does mean that neither is, by any stretch of the imagination, a substance or even a quasi-substance. As such, one cannot say anything *about* time itself (or about space itself) because these notions themselves are merely *how we speak about* phenomena that actually do more concretely exist.

Let us consider some commonsense ruminations on ordinary life experiences we have all had in relation to time. If you were to simply ignore everything that has ever been taught in academia (whether empirical science or philosophy) about space and time since the "Enlightenment," and instead only consider these concepts with your own intuition, you would almost immediately have a far better grasp of it than most of those scholars.

Some who first read my insistence above, explaining that time itself is simply *the measure of motion,* may have had a few protestations come to his mind: *"But we measure time! How, then, can time itself be a mere measure? My watch measures time! My phone measures the time. Atomic clocks really measure time."*

In fact, none of those statements are correct. None of those devices measure time. Your watch counts the vibrations of a quartz crystal exposed to voltage from its battery. Your phone simply reads out a signal it receives from the nearest cell tower. "Atomic clocks," which give a nation's "official time," count the number of oscillations exhibited by a Cesium-133 atom when exposed to radiation (and they advance one second about every 9 billion oscillations). But we can never measure time because *there is never anything there to measure.*

We can measure inches, because there really is such a thing as spatial distance to measure. We can measure kilograms, because there really is such a thing as mass to more or less directly gauge. We can measure temperature, because there really is heat existing in things. But there is no actual reality called "time" against which we can ever place any actual or even theoretically possible device in order to measure it.

The point is not merely something so banal as "time is not a literal physical substance." Most are aware of that. However, heat and distance are not physical substances either, but they are actual realities. Time, on the other hand, does not even amount to that. Since it is *fundamentally* contingent upon the motion it is measuring, if there is no motion, there is no time.

Consider your car's various instruments. Suppose your car has a compass displaying the direction you are facing and a thermometer indicating outside temperature. Suppose, next, that on a given day your car's battery goes completely dead. You proceed to get a jump-start from a friend, but you notice that your car's clock is now wrong. Why did this happen? Why will your car's clock not just *measure the time*? Your car's compass still works fine and accurately: it still just measures the magnetic field that exists in the space it inhabits, thus inferring the direction of north. Your car's thermometer still works: it just measures the temperature of the ambient air and displays the reading. So why can't your clock likewise just measure the time and conveniently display it for you to read?

We already know why: *there is nothing there to measure.* There are only two ways any clock can function; by measuring some *motion* that it has access to, or by having some external source indicate to it what it should say the time is. However, when your car's battery is dead, there is no available voltage to allow for the quartz crystal in its clock to continue its own continuous voltage-induced vibration. No more motion exists within the car itself that can be measured. *

There is another protestation based on one's car that might be brought to the fore. For any car also has a speedometer with which it measures its speed. Here, one might suppose he has again stumbled upon a refutation: *"but motion itself—speed, or velocity—uses time within its own expression; for example, speed can be given in miles per hour. How, then, could you invert this reality and claim that it is actually motion which is more real, and time is just the measure of it!?"*

The answer is simple: measures of speed do indeed include the measure of time—but those measures of time, *themselves*, are still nothing but measures of motion. An hour is nothing but a one twenty-fourth part of a day. A day is nothing but the measure of the earth completing one rotation on its axis—dawn to dawn. When, therefore, we speak of an "hour," we are doing nothing but measuring motion. And when we speak of a car travelling at, say, 60 miles per hour, all we are doing is comparing this car's motion to the earth's motion. We are simply saying that while the earth completed a rotation of 15 degrees (1/24th of a complete 360 degrees—"one hour"), the car managed to traverse 60 miles.

Yet, still more protestations may be offered. One might say: *"Isn't that all a bit arcane? We don't use sundials anymore to measure time. We've got atomic clocks now. A day isn't even exactly 24 hours!"* † Unfortunately, the illogic of statements like this reveal just how low modern education has

---

* Some may still wonder, *"why doesn't my car just store, in its memory, the time at which it lost power, and keep track of how much time has passed since that point; and, once it regains power, add that amount of time onto the time at which it lost power?"* But this only delivers us directly to the same paradox. It cannot "keep track of" how much time has passed since it lost power, since *there is nothing there to keep track of.* The only way it—or anything—can "keep track of time" is if it has access to some *real thing* that is moving, and measure the motion of that thing. Indeed, a stopwatch and a watch are fundamentally identical things, although we tend to erroneously regard the latter as having some sort of grounding in reality that the former lacks by "merely counting seconds."

† Indeed, a "sidereal day," used by astronomers, is about four minutes shorter than our day. But this has nothing to do with time itself or the definition of an hour; it is simply because for astronomers, in charting the motion of planets, it is more convenient to refer to a "day" as the exact moment the same point on a planet returns to its position relative to its star, and the orbital motion of the planet affects this slightly.

sunk; and how obsessed it has become with technicalities, even when the inferences drawn from these technicalities contradict the realities on which these technicalities rely. An *hour* is measured, defined, and rightly understood insofar as it is a certain fraction of a day; *not vice versa.* In other words, an hour *is just* a 24th of a day—nothing more. It has no reality apart from that understanding. Whoever seeks to instead define it in terms of a certain number of oscillations of a Cesium-133 atom has only arbitrarily changed his definition; he has not somehow discovered some deeper truth about the notion of an hour. A day, on the other hand, *is what it is*; it is a *given* in nature. To pretend that we can claim a day is not actually exactly 24 hours is logically analogous to pretending we can claim that "one" is not actually "twice one-half."

It is worth considering that, in ages past, it would have sounded silly to ask, "what time does the sun rise?" The question would not have made sense because *sunrise is the time.* The "first hour of the day" is simply the first one-twelfth portion of that day's period of sunlight following sunrise. In the 1800s, rail transport and telegraph lines made the creation of "time zones" important (to enable coordination across large distances due to the once unfeasible rapidity of transport and communication). Once a time zone is established, a certain locale's own time of sunrise can be measured against something other than itself. Obviously, there is nothing wrong with doing this, but we must understand how this is yet another factor that has contributed to the modern world's delusion about the nature of time. Saying *"what time does the sun rise?"* inclines one to regard time itself as some sort of independent reality, existing apart from the motion of the heavenly bodies (and motion in general); when nothing could be further from the truth. This delusion reaches a truly comical level when it comes to "Daylight Savings Time." Some people really seem to think that changing what their clock says influences time itself—somehow "making the sun set earlier or later." In fact, this is nothing but a game we play.

In a certain sense we can say that *time does not exist.* As we have noted, this does not mean it is fake or a mere social construct, but it is certainly not a "substantial thing" or "cosmic fabric" which can ever be jumped around within, travelled within, folded, etc. Such feats would not be merely technologically implausible or impossible: they are *absolutely logically ruled out* just as a square circle is ruled out. Just as the fact that God is outside of space (and geometric shape) does not mean a square circle is thus a palatable concept or that He could make one, so too the (very important) fact that God is outside of time does not give us grounds for entertaining absurdities related to "time travel."

Sts. Aquinas, Augustine, and Jerome Against the Uniquely Perverse Notion of Time Travel

Aquinas was so certain of this truth about time that he even rightly taught that God Himself *cannot* change the past. Nor does he teach this only on his own conviction (which is unqualified), but on the authority of St. Jerome, St. Augustine, and Aristotle:

> [As] Jerome says: "*Although God can do all things, He cannot make a thing that is corrupt not to have been corrupted.*" Therefore, for the same reason, He cannot effect that anything else which is past should not have been...**there does not fall under the scope of God's omnipotence anything that implies a contradiction. Now that the past should not have been implies a contradiction**. For as it implies a contradiction to say that Socrates is sitting, and is not sitting, so does it to say that he sat, and did not sit. But to say that he did sit is to say that it happened in the past. To say that he did not sit, is to say that it did not happen. Whence, that the past should not have been, does not come under the scope of divine power. This is what Augustine means when he says: "*Whosoever says, If God is almighty, let Him make what is done as if it were not done, does not see that this is to say: If God is almighty let Him effect that what is true, by the very fact that it is true, be false*": and the Philosopher [Aristotle] says: "***Of this one thing alone is God deprived—namely, to make undone the things that have been done***."... [to change the past] is more impossible than the raising of the dead; in which there is nothing contradictory, because this is reckoned impossible in reference to some power, that is to say, some natural power; for such impossible things do come beneath the scope of divine power. (*Summa Theologica*. First Part. Question 25. Article 4.)

While the AI Deception's blasphemy derives from supposing that man can create what, in fact, only God can, the Time Travel Deception takes it a step further by supposing that man might one day be capable of what not even God can do. Aquinas notes that raising the dead is "impossible," therefore, by doing it, God shows us He has miraculously intervened. Time travel, however, is not merely impossible in that sense; it is also logically incoherent. It is impossible not only naturally but also supernaturally. With God all things are possible, but time travel is not a "thing."

Whoever wishes to abide in the truth must categorically reject any belief, whatsoever, in so much as the possibility of time travel. Note that it will not work for a sci-fi deceiver to claim that he is leaving the past alone, and only asserting the possibility of men from the *future* coming to our own day. That is contradictory. Our own day *would be* "the past" for such men, so we have already refuted that notion. "They" cannot change "their past" any more than *we* can change *our* past. The entire question of time travel is ridiculous, logically incoherent, and even implicitly heretical—however one presents it or modifies it. This Deception, in fact, is so uniquely perverse that one should even toying with it much. The various paradoxes that time travel works of fiction are ever foisting upon their readers and viewers are quite harmful to the soul when entertained, and can by themselves elicit needless existential crises. Jesus is surely displeased when a Christian begins welcoming the same premises that would also compel him to wonder if he can actually be certain Christ became Incarnate in the first place. Granting any credence to those premises, even if only "toying" with them, is like a married woman fantasizing about being married to another man. It is unfaithfulness, even if it does not degenerate beyond mere contemplation. While works of fiction about alien civilizations *can* be quite dangerous, they also can simply be settings with which to analyze questions relevant to our own lives. This is not true with time travel works of fiction, for it is a theme that cannot present any meaningful morals or teachings due to its categorical incoherence. It is wise to avoid works of fiction built primarily on the notion of time travel.*

Not only, however, does this belief destroy his Christian Faith; it also constitutes a major avenue of the same apocalyptic Great Deception we have been addressing throughout this book. Although the Time Travel Deception is not a direct application of the NHI Deception, it nevertheless effectively becomes an avenue for the same type of dark seduction. For one may be wise enough to reject aliens and sentient AI, but somehow fail to reject time travel. The demons, then, can simply seduce this soul just as they seduce others with those illusions, by appearing to him and claiming to be some human from the future. The same results can thus be achieved. This man has wandered outside of those boundaries clearly given by both Faith and reason, and therefore stepped squarely within the radius of the Devil's chain. He has done this under the deceitful premise (promoted by no few "orthodox Catholics") that doing so was merely a "humble openness." But in so doing he has invited the "lying signs and wonders" (2 Thessalonians 2:9), that Scripture prophesies for our times, to dazzle and delude him.

---

* I do not intend to categorically condemn every single work of fiction that employs any theme *presented* as some form of "time travel." To give just one example: in Charles Dickens' *A Christmas Carol*, Scrooge is *shown* the past (not given the ability to change it), as well as being *shown possible* future scenarios. There is nothing logically incoherent about this; in fact, it provides quite a touching story. Some other "time travel" stories are intended only as a humorous setting to illustrate a culture clash. I am here simply discouraging allowing oneself to become emotionally involved in a seemingly relatable dramatic storyline built upon the notion of past-changing or future-entering.

The Animal-Personhood Deception: Another Demonic Ruse

Only man bears the Divine Image. "Aliens" do not—because they do not exist. AI does not—because it is not and never will be intelligent. What, however, of all those other creatures we know God actually did make? Not one of them ever has had or ever will have a rational free will, and thus they do not bear the Divine Image—they are not persons.

The deception which proposes rational animals (that is, other than human beings) is quite distinct from the ET, the AI, and the Time Travel Deceptions. It is usually treated much more innocently in fiction (populating, for example, many largely unproblematic children's books and movies as well as many comedies), and it is not as popular in the prevailing modern myth (that is, science fiction). Indeed, there is simply less perverse allure. We all know animals well, and *relatively* few can sincerely bring themselves to pretend these creatures have intelligence. It is, therefore, generally a more benign (if silly) concept to serve as the basis for fictional works.

But there is danger here too. It is evident, for example, in those children's movies which portray animals as "the good guys" and humans as "the bad guys." (An antagonism long a fixture in modern fiction.) It is also evident in those works which do not merely personify animals for the sake of telling a story—which great novels such as C.S. Lewis' *Chronicles of Narnia* do—but which actively (if implicitly) promote the lie that the animals roaming our lands do indeed have reason. We have seen that the ET, AI, and Time Travel Deceptions all emerged in poplar fiction in the 1800s. So, too, did the Animal Personhood Deception, with the 1877 publication of *Black Beauty*. From the release of that novel onwards, there was a steady stream of exhortations in popular culture not merely to respect animals as gifts from God (a noble thing to encourage), but to treat them as if they were really persons (a diabolical deception).

As a result, that "few" who are open to the notion of animal personhood is steadily increasing to be not so few. There are massive and well-funded movements now afoot, based on the Animal Personhood Deception, which fight for animals to be given human rights. Although these efforts have generally not yet been successful, their momentum is undeniable. In more sane times, a legal case seeking to afford personhood to any animal would have been thought humorous. Today, such cases are taken seriously by the highest courts. For example, in 2022, New York State's highest court heard arguments seeking to grant personhood to a certain elephant in the Bronx Zoo. Although the elephant was not granted personhood, two of the seven judges dissented.[401]

Court cases such as that did not arise from a vacuum, but rather from a long evident and steadily growing societal trend. This trend is seen both in the basic elements of culture and the ivory towers of academia.

Culturally, as people are choosing to have fewer and fewer children (or forego having children entirely), more individuals seek to fill the children-shaped hole in their lives with cats, dogs, and other pets. Of course, owning pets can be a wonderful thing. There is obviously nothing wrong with that. The sin arises when people begin implicitly or explicitly treating these mere animals as human beings.

There is no need to speculate about the prevalence of such behavior, for it is openly confessed to and boasted about today. More and more pet owners are refusing to call themselves that, but rather they perversely label themselves as "pet parents." Many will spend tens of thousands of dollars on cancer treatments for dogs and cats, while millions of children across the globe continue to die from lack of basic food, water, medicine, shelter, and sanitation. (Make no mistake: this contrast will factor heavily into what is considered on the Day of Judgment.) While "pet therapy" once referred only to using animals to help humans (an unproblematic undertaking), it now also refers to owners getting "therapy" *for* their pets (a ludicrous undertaking). Some have their cats or dogs put on antidepressants. One popular doormat purchased by dog-owners today accurately sums up the sentiments harbored by a distressingly large number of people. In large letters plastered next to an image of a dog's face, it warns those entering: *"I'm family, you're not. They love me, they're only friends with you. To you, I'm just the pet, but here, I'm their baby. – Charlie."*[402]

This perversity has infiltrated Christian thinking as well. Some Christians who have scarcely ever lifted a finger to evangelize human beings will nevertheless endlessly agonize over whether their cat will be in Heaven with them. I have even read some popular "orthodox Catholic" authors (I will avoid naming them here) who have proven perceptive in commenting on some sci-fi deceptions, only to succumb almost entirely to the Animal Personhood Deception; absurdly pretending that "studies" have shown various species of animals truly are capable of rational communication, and only await our ability to "unlock their language." This deception, moreover, is promoted under the guise of piety, for it is phrased as a mere "acknowledgment of how good God is in giving us animals." And indeed, we should and must acknowledge that. But we cannot honor God without doing so in accordance with the order He has created. Whoever "honors" food by overeating has only become a glutton; whoever "honors" some individual saint by regarding him as Divine and infallible has only become an idolator; whoever "honors" the sexual faculty through promiscuity is only destroying his soul. And in the present matter, the order God created is entirely unambiguous: of *all* visible creatures, only human beings bear His Divine Image. There are *no* exceptions. To violate that truth under the pretense of "honoring His creation" is only to sin against His order.

We are dealing with the Animal Personhood Deception in this book, however, not because it is simply another error worthy of condemnation, but because it, too, can become a means of diabolical instruction. In Part Four, we considered the false and likely diabolical "private revelations" from the "Voice and Echo of the Divine Messengers." These "revelations from Jesus and Mary" promote not only the ET Deception, but also the one now under consideration. They teach[403] that we must *"love the Animal Kingdom as [we] love [our] own lives"* (implying—heretically—that the Christian duty to love one's neighbor as himself also applies to animals).

They assert, *"if you want to learn how to live love, let yourselves be loved by the Animal Kingdom."* In fact, animals cannot love, as they have no free will. Remaining consistent with their own false premises, the messages likewise condemn the killing of animals for food, despite Scripture specifically allowing this. The "seers" themselves insist, *"one of the greatest causes of problems in the world today – such as wars, physical illnesses and mental disorders – is the killing of animals."*

As we can see, whatever dark spirit has inspired these messages is intent on its recipients believing not only in aliens, but also animal personhood. Nor is this strategy in vain. If the Devil cannot seduce a soul into one NHI Deception, he will try another. Perhaps, for example, there is a lonely person somewhere who (rightly) has no excitement whatsoever when told of aliens or sentient AI or time travelling, but has poured all her love into her cat. She wants nothing more than to commune with this animal as if it were a person. Such sentiments, if willfully fostered in her heart, constitute wandering outside of the boundaries of both basic reason and Christian Faith just as much as the other Deceptions we have addressed. She has strayed into the radius of the Devil's chain, and there is no reason to suspect he will neglect to take advantage of that. He has already done so in many cases; as, for example, in the increasing numbers of pet owners seeking out "animal mediums" or "pet psychics."

These charlatans claim to unlock the communication of living or deceased pets, and their antics are seducing not only devoted New Agers (as in days past), but, increasingly, more mainstream pet owners who now regard their cats and dogs as persons. Far more problematic than the loss of the money wasted on these "psychics," however, is that demons will gladly use this fraud as an opportunity to subtly slip in destructive communications.

Among the demonic fruits of these "pet psychics" are destroyed marriages. A dog or cat can suddenly become a very effective inlet for Satan when, after a consultation with a "pet psychic," it "becomes known" that the pooch "needs" tens of thousands of dollars of some medical treatment or a major life-change on the part of its owners. One spouse realizes this is ridiculous for a mere pet, while the other, due to his or her regard for the creature as if it were a person, feels compelled to insist upon it. Sometimes, these charlatans "reveal" that the pet has "insights" into the sins of one of its owners (always, of course, one not bringing the pet in to the "psychic"), that it will gladly reveal with the help of the pet medium, and which will destroy the family. All of this is the work of demons.

Let us consider just one case; the woman who is perhaps the most famous "pet psychic," Sonya Fitzpatrick. She claims to be on a mission from God, due to a "private revelation" (an ounce of discernment will indicate it is clearly of demonic origin). An article from the *National Review* details her "Divine calling" which arose:

> ...with the appearance of first an angel ("large wings...beautiful and gentle face") and then St. Francis, both of who [sic] told Sonya that she was going to be working to help animals. It was God's work."[404]

When one peruses the letters posted on Sonya's own website[405], however, he will quickly find that her undertaking is not of God. For example, one letter recounts Sonya "speaking for" the dead dog of a certain young woman who wrote to her. She tells this young woman that the dog ("Princess") has a soul which has been together with her "in many lifetimes" and is "with her in spirit all the time." (Reincarnation is a particular heresy that rears its head repeatedly in demonically-originated deceptions.)

This is the general pattern of today's "pet psychic" industry, and here we can only repeat the same warning that Fr. Stanley Jaki provided with respect to the ET Deception: "**Behind these bravados...you either see the strategy of the devil or you remain blind**." Many people (perhaps now numbering in the millions) around the world are receiving orders straight from hell by visiting these seemingly innocuous "mediums" in order to "*learn what their cats and dogs are saying*." Here as elsewhere, one simple recognition could have prevented it all: the unqualified affirmation that only man bears the Divine Image.

> Some [who] would be friends of animals are often their worst enemies, 'heaping excessive affection on animals and bestowing on them what has been denied to our fellowmen.' ... Further, animal lovers are sometimes cruel in their kindness, destroying the health and fine instincts of their animal companions by excessive pampering ... The Church, therefore, is careful not to (as Cardinal Gasparri says) 'disturb the admirable order of Creation by despoiling man of his royal crown to cast it down at the feet of inferior creatures.'... Man was created in the image and likeness of God: animals were not. Man is rational, animal is irrational ... Man therefore is a person; animals are non-persons. Man is a person because he is an end in himself, and not a mere means to the perfection of beings of a higher order. Animals are not persons or moral beings, because devoid of reason and free will (and so of responsibility) and because they were created for the service of man, and as a means (if properly used) towards his perfection. Next after animals comes vegetative creation, not sentient, and destined for the service of man and beast. – Fr. Ambrose Agius, O.S.B.[406]

The dangers of the Animal Personhood Deception, however, are not only the demonic ones described immediately above and the apocalyptic ones we will consider below. Due to the theme of this book, that is what we are focusing on, but we should also note the more ordinary cultural havoc wrought by increasing numbers of citizens supposing that animals deserve that type of consideration which any Christian should (and must) recognize is due solely to human beings.

- Anti-human environmentalist groups often succeed in pressuring governments to lay massive burdens on the shoulders of struggling *people* simply to avoid any inconvenience to a few birds, turtles, or other animals. While millions of humans languish in *extreme* poverty (across the globe, over half a billion), governments dump unbelievable sums of money into initiatives bereft of any credible human benefit, and instead directed solely to "helping animals."
- Pit bull attacks have been exploding recently, killing or disfiguring hundreds of people (often children) each year in America alone. Governments refuse to do anything about it, knowing that people will rebel, supposing that the "inalienable rights" of these beasts are being violated. Similarly, humans convicted of animal abuse are often given unbelievably severe punishments—effectively destroying their entire lives—which supposedly renders justice to the offended beast. (This is not to justify flagrant animal abuse—that is indeed immoral and should be outlawed—the point is simply to note the extreme severity, which ultimately arises from the Animal Personhood Deception, with which those convicted of this offense are often treated.)
- Renewed attacks on meat-eating are made each year. While many of these attacks arise from absurd "zero carbon" agendas, others are initiated by organizations like PETA, which wage an increasingly well-funded war against the entirely moral human practice of eating animal meat. In order to please such organizations as PETA, companies are increasingly refusing to test their products on animals before releasing them for human use. All this means, of course, is that the first *human beings* to use the product are the new guinea pigs.
- Untold millions of people (even, sadly, many Christians) delude themselves into thinking they are doing legitimate Works of Mercy by engaging in activities that only benefit animals. While it becomes increasingly difficult to find volunteers for soup kitchens and homeless shelters, there are armies of willing volunteers who will do anything to help cats, dogs, rabbits, birds, whales, or just about any other irrational animal. Similarly, there is a steady stream of news stories about individuals who decided to gravely risk their lives simply to rescue an animal—perhaps running into a burning building or towards a tornado to grab one. This is evil. To ever consider any human being's life (including one's own) *even remotely close* to on par with an animal's is a grave sin. Many of these individuals who choose to engage in these

risks wind up dead.

- While entire populations of humans languish for lack of proper housing (or any housing), untold millions of acres near them are absolutely off-limits as "wildlife refuges;" being cut-off from any human use. Similarly, there are dangerous, carcinogenic, noisy, and otherwise extremely problematic industrial establishments (including dumps, landfills, factories, etc.) built adjacent to heavily populated residential neighborhoods (invariably, poor ones) so as to not inconvenience any animals in these "refuges." Here as always, it is human beings, made in God's image, who suffer, while animals with no intrinsic and infinite value, and who exist only for the sake of human beings, are the sole beneficiaries.

Indeed, even if we ignore the apocalyptic dimension of the Animal Personhood Deception, we are still left with a grand delusion that is being counted in human lives—*many* of them. It bears repeating that animals are wonderful creatures and are great gifts from God. We should appreciate them and be good and responsible stewards of creation. But when we pretend to appreciate creation by perverting *the order with which God has endowed creation*, we only sin against the Creator Himself and gravely harm ourselves in the process.

> "Friendship cannot exist except towards rational creatures, who are capable of returning love, and communicating one with another in the various works of life ... The love of charity extends to none but God and our neighbor. But the word neighbor cannot be extended to irrational creatures, since they have no fellowship with man in the rational life. Therefore charity does not extend to irrational creatures." -St. Thomas Aquinas. *Summa Theologica*. I. Q19. A12. and II-II. Q25. A3

Birds of a Feather: SETI, CETI, "Salvation from Whales and AI," and the "White Leviathan"

The Animal Personhood Deception is not merely a cultural trend wherein pet owners increasingly treat their dogs and cats as persons, and deluded individuals receive demonic instructions "through their pets," thanks to "pet psychics." It is also an academic and institutional phenomenon that is gaining steam and merging with other sci-fi deceptions.

A steady stream of studies is now attempting to prove that animals really do engage in rational communication, and that our task is simply to unlock it so as to discover its paradigm-shifting revelations. Announcements of the "Day of Disclosure" (aliens) and "Moment of Singularity" (rational AI) may well be accompanied by similar official announcements with respect to this deception, perhaps claiming that a technology has finally been developed allowing us to "learn the secrets of the world" known by—and now communicated by—dolphins, or whales, or chimpanzees, or ravens, or elephants.

Now, obviously, animals of all sorts communicate with each other in various ways; but this never amounts to *language* properly so-called, and it is certainly not *rational* communication. No animal can have any knowledge, understanding, or wisdom of its own, much less can it convey such things to another being. All animals are creatures of pure instinct. These instincts are astonishing wonders of creation designed by God—well deserving of our appreciation and scientific study—but they are never rational or free. Unfortunately, modern scientists, increasingly atheistic in their principles and almost universally Darwinian in their ideology, make no categorical distinction between man and beast, therefore they have no hope of discovering and conveying the truth when their own base premises are so deeply flawed.

In lieu of a protracted analysis of this issue, which limitations of space prevent here, we will consider one September 2023 article in *The New Yorker* magazine, entitled "Can we talk to whales?" Not only is the present deception well summarized in its content, but so also is its relation to the ET and the AI Deceptions. The article follows Dr. David Gruber and charts the origin of his fascination with the communication methods of sperm whales. It then describes his encounter with another researcher:

> One day, Gruber was sitting in his office at the Radcliffe Institute, listening to a tape of sperm whales chatting, when another fellow at the institute, Shafi Goldwasser, happened by. Goldwasser, a Turing Award [the so-called "Nobel Prize of Computing"]-winning computer scientist, was intrigued. At the time, she was organizing a seminar on machine learning, which was advancing in ways that would eventually lead to ChatGPT. Perhaps, Goldwasser mused, **machine learning could be used to discover the meaning of the whales' exchanges**... Gruber and Goldwasser took the idea of decoding the codas [whale communications] to a third Radcliffe fellow, Michael Bronstein. Bronstein, also a computer scientist, is now the DeepMind Professor of A.I. at Oxford... **Thus was born the Cetacean Translation Initiative—Project CETI for short. (The acronym is pronounced "setty," and purposefully recalls SETI, the Search for Extraterrestrial Intelligence.) CETI represents the most ambitious, the most technologically sophisticated, and the most well-funded effort ever made to communicate with another species**. "I think it's something that **people get really excited about: Can we go from science fiction to science?"** ...

As the purse strings of scientific research are usually carefully monitored and controlled to further the preferred narrative of the global elite, we cannot avoid coming to certain conclusions in seeing how much money is now being funneled into ostensibly discovering how to communicate with whales and other Cetaceans (e.g., dolphins and porpoises).

Although this "knowledge from the whales" will, if and when it is announced, be nothing but a charade, it will nevertheless provide a disguise—as convenient as the ET and the AI Deceptions—for either a government-orchestrated psyop or even a more directly diabolical ploy. If a small group of deception-managers can present themselves as the world's intermediaries between the "language of the whales" and humanity, then all that will be needed for the masses to readily accept the lies this dialogue promotes will be an established structure such as CETI which can be easily employed for that very end.

The article's author joined CETI on some of its expeditions, and she described her own take on the clicks ("codas") the whales emit by insisting they sounded "...**as if somewhere deep beneath the waves someone was pecking out a memo on a manual typewriter**." The intended implication was clear. The article continues:

> **CETI received thirty-three million dollars** from the Audacious Project... Sperm whales have the biggest brains on the planet—six times the size of humans'. Their social lives are rich, complicated, and, some would say, ideal... Female sperm whales, meanwhile, are exceptionally close. The adults in a unit not only travel and hunt together**; they also appear to confer on major decisions**...[Gero told me,] "there's some part of the sperm-whale experience that our primate brain just won't understand. But **those things that we share must be fundamentally important to why we're here**."... It may be that there are nuances in, say, pacing or pitch [of the codas] that have so far escaped human detection. Already, CETI team members have identified a new kind of signal—a single click—that may serve as some kind of punctuation mark...

Here we see the introduction of the deception, which will be emphasized later in the same article: *whales* will tell us "why we're here"—as soon as we can "unlock their language." *They* will reveal to us the meaning of life. The article then returns to the matter of Artificial Intelligence, recounting:

> As anyone who has been conscious for the past ten months knows, ChatGPT is capable of amazing feats... **ChatGPT got so good at this guessing game that, without ever understanding English, it mastered the language**. ... In theory at least, **what goes for English ... also goes for sperm whale. Provided that a computer model can be trained on enough data, it should be able to master coda prediction**. It could then—once again in theory—generate sequences of codas that a sperm whale would find convincing. The model wouldn't understand sperm whale-ese, but it could, in a manner of speaking, speak it. Call it Click-GPT... "One of the key challenges toward the analysis of sperm whale (and more broadly, animal) communication using modern deep learning techniques is the need for sizable datasets," the team wrote ... CSAIL **[the Computer Science and Artificial Intelligence Laboratory at M.I.T.,] is an enormous operation, with more than fifteen hundred staff members and students**...[there, scientist Jacob Andreas] told me

> that CETI had already made significant strides...it had found that codas have much more internal structure than had previously been recognized. ..."**The holy grail here**—the thing that separates human language from all other animal communication systems—is what's called 'duality of patterning,' ... sperm whales, too, [may] have arrived at duality of patterning. "**Based on what we know about how the coda inventory works, I'm optimistic—though still not sure—that this is going to be something that we find in sperm whales,"** Andreas said.

While *The New Yorker* strategically shies away from outright *affirming* whales engage in rational communication, it unabashedly implies that this is the case, and it fosters the expectation that we will, very soon, discover how to understand it. Returning to the article's protagonist, David Gruber, we are given a closer look at his inspirations and expectations. Referring to the famous environmentalist Roger Payne, Gruber relays:

> "I always look to Roger's work as a guiding star...he thought that CETI could be much more impactful. If we could understand what they're saying, **instead of 'save the whales' it will be 'saved by the whales.'** "**This project is kind of an offering**," [Gruber] went on. "Can technology draw us closer to nature? Can we use all this amazing tech we've invented for positive purposes?" **ChatGPT shares this hope**. Or at least the A.I.-powered language model is shrewd enough to articulate it. In the version of "Moby-Dick" written by algorithms in the voice of a whale, the story [I asked it to write] ends with a somewhat ponderous but not unaffecting plea for mutuality: "*I, the White Leviathan, could only wonder if there would ever come a day when man and whale would understand each other, finding harmony in the vastness of the ocean's embrace.*"

The convergence of deceptions here is stunning both in its audacity and unabashedly apocalyptic aspirations. The managers of this massively funded "CETI" operation admit that their desire is not, like the environmentalist of old, merely to "save the whales," but rather to enable mankind to be "**saved *by* the whales**."

The final line in the quote above is the same one with which the article concludes. It was apparently produced by Artificial Intelligence in response to an instruction for it to generate a version of *Moby Dick* written from the perspective of the whale. It's plea? "Man and whale" understanding each other—humans "finding harmony" with the "**White Leviathan**." Scarcely could one manage to describe more accurately the dark reality latent in this deception. One wonders if this AI program's output, in this case, consisted in the very possibility we considered earlier, wherein the demons themselves can influence digital technology. Leviathan, of course, is a Biblical term. Although many recall it from the Book of Job, its most relevant usage may be in Isaiah:

> **On that day the Lord with his cruel and great and strong sword will punish Leviathan the fleeing serpent**, Leviathan the twisting serpent,

and he will kill the dragon that is in the sea. (Isaiah 27:1)

"Leviathan," therefore, is a symbol for the Devil. Yet we are here presented with a *White* Leviathan—the Devil masquerading as a benevolent being. And, as we have seen throughout this book, there is no more convenient way for him to do so than through the various elements of the NHI Deception.

***

The intersection of AI and animal language is prominent throughout contemporary academia. The prevailing sentiments truly do expect an imminent paradigm-shifting breakthrough that will use AI to enable us to "unlock the great secrets of animal language." We must make no mistake about it: this is a diabolical deception in the making. Perhaps it is not as severe as the ET and AI Deceptions, but it may not be too far behind, either. Discerning Christians should both be aware of the dark undercurrents of this movement and sound the alarm to warn others. As an article in the popular periodical, *Scientific American*, declared in February 2023 (even inviting Pagan practices into the foray):

> ... "deep listening" has a long and venerable tradition. It's an ancient art ... There are long-standing Indigenous traditions of deep listening that are deeply attuned to nonhuman sounds. So if we combine digital listening—which is opening up vast new worlds of nonhuman sound and decoding that sound with artificial intelligence—with deep listening, I believe that **we are on the brink of two important discoveries. The first is language in nonhumans. ... The second is: I believe we're at the brink of interspecies communication**...that is where artificial intelligence comes in—because the same natural-language-processing algorithms that we are using to such great effect in tools such as Google Translate can also be used to detect patterns in nonhuman communication...digital bioacoustics, combined with artificial intelligence, is like a planetary-scale hearing aid that enables us to listen anew with both our prosthetically enhanced ears and our imagination. **This is slowly opening our minds not only to the wonderful sounds that nonhumans make but to a fundamental set of questions about the so-called divide between humans and nonhumans, our relationship to other species**.[407]

Here as with the other deceptions we have discussed, what is transpiring before our eyes is essentially a return of the Pagan "gods." What is now brewing, however, is far more dangerous, since today's Paganism-revival has the backing of "the science," and the mythology of science fiction lending it almost unanimous (secular) cultural endorsement and excitement. Whales, bulls, cats, bears, dogs, elephants, monkeys, ravens, and more, all factor heavily into ancient Pagan idolatry across various pre-Christian cultures scattered about the world, which also often advocated for the view that human souls are reincarnated into the bodies of animals in "other lives." All such doctrines are, of course, diabolical, and what is brewing now is a (pseudo)scientific revival of them.

When today's scientists tell us they have unlocked the language of one or more of these irrational creatures and that we can now "learn their hitherto secret knowledge," they will be putting on a charade no less deceptive than the shamans and oracles of old. But they will be providing an even more powerful opening for the activity of demons than those shamans could ever dream of.

Refutations of Animal Personhood

Common sense alone easily suffices to settle that no animals have reason, no animals are persons, and no animals have free will. This, indeed, is the unanimous testimony of the entire human tradition (diabolical Pagan rituals aside), which remained unbroken until the postmodern West—which also can no longer distinguish a man from a woman.

Nevertheless, we also know, from the Faith, that only human beings have reason. From this realization alone we can infer that animals do not enjoy this faculty, but Scripture even directly testifies to their irrationality. For example, 2 Peter 2:12 laments those who, "**like irrational animals, creatures of instinct, born to be caught and killed**" revile those matters in which they are ignorant. St. Peter leaves no room for speculation that such creatures may also be persons. But this same dynamic is made clear from the Bible's opening pages, wherein the Book of Genesis details the creation of the animals, but reserves personhood for man. After creating the animals and seeing them "good"—as indeed they are—God said:

> "Let us make man in our image, after our likeness; and let them have dominion over the fish of the sea, and over the birds of the air, and over the cattle, and over all the earth, and over every creeping thing that creeps upon the earth." So God created man in his own image, in the image of God he created him; male and female he created them...and God said to them, "be fruitful and multiply, and fill the earth and subdue it; and have dominion over the fish of the sea and over the birds of the air and over every living thing that moves upon the earth." (Genesis 1:26-28)

And only after creating man does God finally say that what He had done in creation was not only good, but "*very* good." (Genesis 1:31)

Granted, an ET promoter may employ here the same ruse he uses to promote aliens: "*The Bible does not **explicitly** say that animals were not **also** created in the Divine Image; it simply notes that humans certainly were. We are free to believe animals also bear the Divine Image just as we do!*" Indeed, some of the most prominent Christian ET promoters, such as Rev. Dr. Andrew Davison (a prominent Anglican theologian and clergyman, among those commissioned by NASA to theologically study aliens), make precisely this move in relation to their arguments promoting ET belief. In his 2023 book arguing for extraterrestrial belief, Dr. Davison wrote that, "*...Genesis 1...does not mean that [man bearing] the [Divine] image* ***consists*** *in a difference from every other creature and thus can only apply to one species...*"* (Most prominent Catholic ET promoters, however, realize how particularly outlandish it is to assert animal personhood, therefore they simply ignore that the same argument used by the animal personhood promoters—in their castigation of so-called "arguments from silence"—is also the one they use to promote the ET Deception.)

An honest Christian reader of Scripture, on the other hand, will have no difficulty in grasping the meaning of the text. God is not seeking to deceive us. Therefore, just as—in describing the creation of the entire cosmos—Genesis leaves out the notion of extraterrestrials (because they do not exist), so too it leaves out the notion of beasts bearing the Divine Image (because such creatures, also, do not exist).

No great author ruins the power and beauty of his work by turning it into a technical instruction manual which explicitly notes every possible exception so that not even a neurotic reader will be capable of misinterpreting it. The Holy Spirit, as not merely a great author, but rather the Perfect Author, likewise simply speaks the Truth, knowing that well-meaning readers of His work will not pretend it affords leeway to assert absurdities due to what it does not say. The Bible gives no grounds for positing rational beasts for the same reason it gives no grounds for positing aliens: neither exist.†

***

As with all previous deceptions we have considered, however, we should also address the matter with logic alone, so that even those who struggle to realize that Scripture can (and must) be our foundation, will not fail to discern the present deception and reject it. Catholic philosopher, Dr. Peter Kreeft, astutely delineated ten reasons to absolutely reject the notion that animals may enjoy personhood or any faculty thereof:

---

* *Astrobiology and Christian Doctrine.* Page 158. Note: Dr. Davison does not affirmatively argue that animals bear the Divine Image as man does. In fact, he seems to indicate that his preferred "interpretation" of Genesis 1 is that only man does, at least among those creatures on earth. (He does not consider how starkly this preference of his violates the notion of meeting aliens on earth!) Yet, the reader is left wondering what to make of his overall take, as Davison claims that the Book of Job is a "de-centering complement" to Genesis 1, as if to indicate that perhaps not only man bears the Divine Image after all. As usual among scholars, his take is very "nuanced," and I will make no further effort here to characterize it.

† Note that a promoter of the Animal Personhood Deception could simply argue, with respect to 2 Peter, that "it does not say *all* beasts are irrational!" Thus it is true here, as with the ET Deception, that those who do not desire to abide in Scriptural truth will always find a way to wiggle out of Christian Teaching. Just as they can pretend the Bible can be reconciled with aliens, so they can pretend it can be reconciled with the idea of rational animals.

> (1) Animals have absolutely no signs of religion, of an awareness of God or immortality. (2) They are conscious of the world of objects but not of themselves as personal subjects. Their consciousness is not self-reflexive. And therefore (3) though they can be trained to behave in ways that humans find acceptable, they have no moral conscience (they have social shame but not individual guilt). (4) Their creativity is routine and circumscribed by their instincts: e.g. a given species of bird will always build its nest in exactly the same way. (5) Their languages are not articulate, not invented, and do not change or progress through time. (6) Their thought is concrete, not abstract. They have precepts but not concepts. (7) They have immediate intuition but not demonstrative reasoning. (8) They do not produce technological inventions, because (9) they do not formulate scientific theories. (10) They have no sense of artistic beauty, or beauty for its own sake.[408]

This pithy, but accurate, description of commonsense observations provides a resource anyone can easily use to conclude animals lack personhood. While some contemporary scientists (unworthy of the name) pretend that human advancement is simply due to "opposable thumbs," any clear-thinking person could only laugh at such a suggestion, seeing as he does the evidence of all the points above displayed with unmistakable clarity in the real world. Even from the annals of ancient history we read of incredibly advanced human civilizations and their stunning feats. From the great pyramids of Egypt to the resplendent hanging gardens of Babylon, to the awe-inspiring Greek monuments, to the unimaginable Temple of Solomon, to the stunning lighthouse of Alexandria, and on the list goes, we read of the astounding achievements of civilizations—all several *thousands* of years old, and many of which we would struggle to accomplish today. Contrast this to even the "most intelligent" of the beasts, among which we find nothing more exciting than an ape bashing around with a stick. Whoever observes this infinite divide and fails to discern the presence of a *categorical* difference—choosing instead to describe it as a mere difference in degree, due only to some environmental circumstance or biological trait—has either lost his mind or has deliberately and knowingly chosen ideology over truth. But to Dr. Kreeft's list above, we can in fact add several other observations.

Animals are entirely predictable; they do not change at all over time. Each generation of each animal species is always identical to the preceding one. This fact is not merely an artifact of our observation of relatively minor time scales. One can read a description of animal behavior from any ancient text, even from three thousand years ago, and he will find that dogs, deer, fish, birds, etc., behaved then precisely as they behave now. Granted, we can qualify this observation by noting that any changes in a species are purely *biological*, not educational or progressive. Environmental pressures may cause certain genetic variations to be "weeded-out" of a species and, accordingly, other genetic variations to dominate. (*Thus, to some misguided scientists, giving the false impression of vindicating evolutionary theory – when in fact all that has transpired is the predictable rise to dominance of those genetic traits already present in that species' genetic design, which individual members thereof only display a fraction of.*) But this is obviously not evidence of any rational reflection. Humans, on the other hand, change quite dramatically each generation—because they have reason and will; they can reflect upon the successes and failure of the preceding generations, and modify their behavior accordingly (unfortunately, this modification has long usually been for the worse!).

Animals are fundamentally non-social. Although wildlife biologists delineate degrees of "social" or "solitary" behavior among various species, this distinction is purely a description of how those species *tend* to behave, not a description of how an individual member of a species *must* behave. Each non-human animal species is born with its own behavior embedded entirely into its nature. A dog raised without ever seeing another dog, but only its human owners, will still act like a dog. The same goes for every other animal species. But a human being raised without any human contact *always* utterly fails to develop. Tragically, this is not only a theory. We (exceedingly rarely, thankfully) observe this very thing happening with stories of so-called "feral children," who are abused by malicious parents by being kept apart from all human contact from infancy onwards. When they are at last rescued, these individuals cannot function—they have no ability to behave humanly. Do not misunderstand: they still *are* human, thus they still have the infinite and intrinsic dignity inherent in all human life. As they still have the *faculty* of reason and will, this abusive upbringing can eventually be corrected. But such cases as these nevertheless testify to what we all know about human nature: it is designed, in its very essence, to be in communion with others (other *persons*, to be precise). No mere animal is designed like that. Each can manage just fine without ever associating with any other members of its own species.

Animals—lacking free will—cannot sin. Accordingly, they are not punished, since punishment is meted out in accordance with the immorality of the one being punished. Granted, a dog owner will scold his dog when it "misbehaves," and he may even call this "punishment," but all dog owners know full well that is not what they are actually doing. Any scolding of a dog is undertaken purely to *steer its instincts* in a certain direction, hoping to render that animal's usual behavior more amenable to domestication. Impressive feats can be achieved through such methods (as anyone who has watched a dog show knows), but they are categorically distinct from punishment. If a dog has strewn the garbage about the house, no owner will "ground" it for a week. On the other hand, if a child does something particularly immoral, a diligent parent may well mete out such a punishment. This gives the child time to reflect on what he has done, and strengthen his moral intention to never do the same thing again. But as no animal can reflect, no analogous "grounding" of it in response to a "misdeed" is ever called for. It will not reflect, because it *cannot* reflect. Instead, it must be "punished" by being given an unpleasant experience quickly after it commits the "misdeed," or at least as it is in the sense-discernable context of that "misdeed" (such as a dog groveling upon its owner's return home next to the mess it had made). Similarly, we do not imprison animals, regardless of what they have done. We either ignore the "offense," remind its owner to keep it better in check, return it to the wild, or put it to death (whichever the circumstances suggest is appropriate). Since animals cannot sin, they also never do those things that can only flow from sin. For example, they do not wage war. They do not commit suicide (contrary to unproven claims that some species do this). They do not engage in behaviors that are obviously (as far as they can tell) detrimental to themselves. They never act in pure malice (although we may interpret certain hunting or playing techniques as malicious, this is only our own errant personification of their behavior). On the list goes. When we read of humans seeking "vengeance" against an animal, we rightly find this amusing. No animal can ever do something worthy of being avenged.

So many observations could be made testifying to the infinite divide between human beings and all other animals that just listing them would require many books. Animals have no sense of humor—any video supposedly showing a chimpanzee "laughing" is only labelled that way due to a human interpreting certain sounds and facial configurations on the monkey as laughter. In fact, animals find nothing ironic. All animals develop extremely quickly—precisely because there is no understanding or wisdom to be gained. Everything in their behavior is instinct, therefore only a relatively brief period is needed to give their biological development ample opportunity to actualize those instincts. It will not work to argue this is due to their shorter lifespans—even animals with far larger lifespans than humans do the same. Tortoises, for example, can live to be almost 200 years old; yet, a baby tortoise reaches adulthood after only about 5 years. While a few exceptions can apparently be found, family in general means little or nothing to animals. A parent (almost always the mother) keeps young nearby, caring for them until they reach maturity, but in almost all cases nothing past that happens between them. Even in those species that congregate into herds, packs, colonies, etc., tend to see individual families assimilated without distinction into the larger group. In humans, family always remains extremely important—regardless of whether the offspring are adults or the family itself is part of a larger social group (the individual human family always supersedes, in importance, the larger group; unlike in the case of the "more social" animals). Indeed, whoever reflects upon the matter even briefly will doubtless independently discover many additional fundamental differences between humans and animals, therefore we will stop here.

***

While these general observations certainly succeed in reminding the sincere observer that all animals are entirely irrational, we should still address some of the more specific claims to the contrary with additional depth.

Talking Apes, Painting Elephants, and Other Ruses

Innumerable claims circulate today insisting that various animal species truly display the ability to reason and freely choose, thus giving "evidence of their personhood." All such claims are deceptions, although they often deftly conceal their lies beneath many layers of obfuscation. A rigorous application of scrutiny to each will either reveal the source of the deception or will reveal that the claimant (perhaps the animal's trainer, the scientist undertaking the study, the pet's owner, etc.) is not allowing scrutiny applied to the very point of contention that would need to be shared in order to justify his claim.

Consider, for example, the videos of elephants supposedly displaying creativity in the paintings they "create." One such video on YouTube[409] currently has 22 million views. I perused some of the comments (although with over 40 thousand of them, I could only read a small fraction) to get a sense of where most people stood after watching the clip. Most viewers (who did not simply express ridiculous outrage that an elephant was being "enslaved") only stood in awe of this animal's "intelligence." Of the hundreds of comments I read, I came across only one which perceived the deception. The commenter wrote, "*I would like to see what the handler is doing whilst the beast paints.*"

Indeed, the video's angle (which, incidentally, also appears to be the only angle from which the crowd was allowed to watch) was quite convenient. The handler stood directly adjacent to the elephant, but in such a position that he could not be seen, with the animal blocking the view. Now, clearly this elephant was very well trained and had "painted" this picture many times before. More clearly still, however, is that this trainer was simply continuously, if subtly, guiding it to generate the curves which he had trained the animal to obediently trace out in response to various pressures he exerted on the animal's head. The brush may well have been stuck into the end of the elephant's trunk, but the design of the picture that emerged had its origin purely in the mind and deeds of the trainer. There was not the slightest hint of creativity, reason, or will, being displayed by this "painting elephant," nor are these qualities displayed by any other animal in any other circumstance.

Silly viral videos are one matter, but the academic and scientific charades used to promote the Animal Personhood Deception are quite another. They are much more subtle and often involve not merely sleight of hand but downright fraud, conspiracy, and decades of collaborated deceptions. As talking (language) is among the most obvious indications that humans possess reason while animals (lacking language) do not, most academic efforts to argue animals are persons centralize around linguistics.

Most have likely heard of the supposedly talking (that is, sign-language-using) gorilla, Koko—the whole affair was extraordinarily well publicized and very strategically orchestrated to give the impression of authenticity. What far fewer are aware of is that the whole thing was a charade based almost entirely on the testimonies of the animal's handler, Francine Patterson, who "interpreted for the gorilla" (which, in reality, was not unlike a small child "interprets for" his imaginary friend). Patterson, however, had a PhD, and she published several academic articles about this "intelligent" and "language using" gorilla, and virtually every mainstream publication gobbled up her nonsensical "academic" claims. Most people today appear to remain under the delusion that Koko really did employ language and really did rationally use this language to convey its "thoughts."

TIME magazine, for example, gushed that this ape and its handler supposedly proved that humans are only special in that "*evolution spotted us the hardware of speech: vocal chords, a palate, a tongue and lips,*" and that other animals could also make their "thoughts" known if only they were taught sign language, so as to reveal their "**extraordinary minds**" to us.[410] And just as with "painting elephants," so with this "sign language using" ape, YouTube videos supposedly giving evidence for such claims have racked up tens of millions of views. (The comments on them are too predictable to relay here.) Robin Williams shared his encounters with the gorilla on the Ellen DeGeneres Show, and Koko even made an appearance on Mister Roger's Neighborhood. The "talking" ape was a sensation.

Yet, when the gorilla died in 2018, world-renowned linguist, Dr. Geoffrey Pullum, addressed the deception in an article entitled "**Koko is Dead, but the Myth of Her Linguistic Skills Lives On.**" He began it by bluntly observing:

> **One area outshines all others in provoking crazy talk about language in the media, and that is the idea of language acquisition in nonhuman species**...[when the gorilla died] Many obituaries appeared, and the press indulged as never before in **sentimental nonsense about talking with the animals**. **Credulous repetition of Koko's mythical prowess in sign language was everywhere...[But] as always with the most salient cases of purported ape signing, Koko was flailing around producing signs at random in a purely situation-bound bid to obtain food from her trainer**, who was in control of a locked treat cabinet. The fragmentary and anecdotal evidence about Koko's much-prompted and much-rewarded sign usage was never sufficient to show that the gorilla even understood the meanings of individual signs... Just watch video of a [human] sign interpreter for a minute, and then view some of the available footage of Koko's alleged signing. There is no resemblance at all.

Dr. Pullum proceeds to point out how even the most supposedly remarkable of Koko's signed "sentences" (none were actual sentences) were utterly bereft of meaning—*even if* we take Patterson's word for what transpired.

Now, as any dog owners knows, animals will, over time, associate certain sounds with certain realities. Soon, the owner will find the dog going wild with excitement when it hears the word "*walk*!" They can follow commands when trained and even remember various impressive tasks. Equally obviously, animals can seek to relay their desires to their owners. Dogs manage to "ask" their owners to be fed, to be taken outside to urinate, etc. This is achieved purely by way of correlating one thing with another—much like how AI-driven LLMs (e.g., ChatGPT) operate. However, just as AI lacks all understanding and reason, so too animals have no such faculties. At most, animals can mash together multiple desires at a time in what they relay to their owners—like LLMs mashing together text they have scraped from databases to form paragraphs. But in neither case is there any rational reflection upon the meanings of terms, or any understanding of what the circumstances demand, or any intellectual formation of a response. Instead, with animals it is always pure instinct (even if carefully trained instinct), and with AI it is always pure algorithm (even if carefully programmed algorithms).

Dr. Pullum concludes his article with a diagnosis of the present feverish desire of the masses and the mainstream to be told animals are persons:

> **Koko never said anything: never made a definite truth claim, or expressed a specific opinion, or asked a clearly identifiable question**. Producing occasional context-related signs, almost always in response to Patterson's cues, after years of intensive reward-based training, is not language use. Not even if it involves gestures that a genuine signer could employ in language use. **[Unfortunately, however,] neither journalists nor laypeople will ever be convinced of that. Such is their yearning to believe that Koko had mastered language**, and had things to say, and shared those things with Penny [Francine] Patterson. **They want to believe these things, and they will not be denied.** Moreover, they will accuse me ... of being an arrogant, hyperskeptical, human-biased speciesist, contemptuous of ape abilities. But I would love to learn about the experiences and opinions of nonhuman primates through direct conversation with them. Unfortunately, all that was established by Penny Patterson's years of devotion to training Koko was that we are not going to have that opportunity.

Here we have a secular scholar who openly professes (contrary to Christian truth!) that he would "love" to learn of the "opinions" of apes. (In fact, apes have no opinions.) No one, therefore, can claim his stance is merely ideological. This scholar simply takes his field of study seriously, and from that posture of intellectual honesty, he has discovered how deceived is the entire movement which treats even the most advanced of animals as genuinely language-using creatures.

Let us turn to another scholar of similar persuasion. While there are plenty of devout Christians whose writings I could defer to in demonstrating the present thesis, I am instead drawing from entirely secular experts in these fields—just as I did with respect to the ET and AI Deceptions—so that no one can accuse me of promoting "academically inbred" conclusions. The truth is that even if we leave aside Christian teaching for a moment, any honest and rigorous application of purely secular scrutiny will reveal the thoroughly fraudulent nature of supposing that either AI or animals exhibit reason.

Dr. Stephen Anderson is a leading researcher and professor of linguistics who has taught at Yale, Harvard, Johns Hopkins, and elsewhere. He has been professionally active in linguistics since 1969. Ideologically, he appears an entirely typical modern secular scholar. I have found no trace of Christianity in particular, or God and religion in general, in his writings. His worldview is based not on acknowledging God's design, but rather on pretending evolution generated the various species we see in the world. Nevertheless, he took his field of study seriously. And from even his insights—deriving from one who has no "incentive" whatsoever to argue for human uniqueness—we see demonstrated the futility of pretending animals can display that fundamentally and uniquely human trait of language. Note that the tone in the passage which follows clearly evidences one who sees no principled *a priori* reason to categorically distinguish between humans and non-humans. (He merely *comes to the conclusion* that humans *are* unique.) He appears (wrongly, of course) entirely open to the proposition that animals use language, yet after a careful application of academic scrutiny to even the most extreme cases, he concludes there is no evidence of this. Dr. Anderson writes:

> Most of the ape utterances of which we have any serious record are certainly instrumental: they are ways to get food or treats. Sue Savage Rumbaugh stresses the fact that Kanzi [another supposedly language using ape] asks to have other people chase each other but, as Joel Wallman suggests, either bonobos have a more diffuse sense of reward or Kanzi is simply "a chimpanzee with strange tastes." In most cases, Kanzi's utterances too are intended to get something. Kanzi's ability to use manual gestures and his keyboard, and also to recognize spoken English words, is extraordinarily impressive; but the utterances he produces still do not involve comments on things that have (or have not, or might have) happened, questions, and so on. Reported instances of signing and keyboard pressing (or in Alex's case [a supposedly language using grey parrot], vocalizing) when alone, which abound in the literature but remain anecdotal, are minimal exceptions...Both Kanzi and Alex, and to some extent a few of the chimpanzees, express their desire for things that are not in fact presently visible. This is still a long

way from an animal's telling us a story about another animal she met last week, or even about the one we both know is in the next room. The ability of any animal to use symbols in a way that is completely independent of the presence of what they refer to has not been solidly established to date... The fact that some chimpanzees indicate tickling of someone else by making the tickling sign on that individual is a matter of making it more iconic in a way that **does not correspond to what happens with signs in any natural signed (human) language... we have no reason to believe that any ape has ever picked up on this or any other systematic aspect of the internal structure of signs**... it is precisely syntax, in this open-ended, unbounded, recursive, fully productive sense, that **no ape, parrot, dolphin, or any other animal has been shown to control—either naturally, or with arbitrarily extensive training**... many key aspects of the syntactic systems of natural languages are significantly underdetermined by the evidence available to the language learner. These **properties are nevertheless found universally—not just in some languages, but apparently in all, and not just after exposure to education, but in unwritten languages as well. The most plausible assumption, to my mind, is that these are aspects of the cognitive organization human children bring to the task of language acquisition. Since no other species seems to be able to do the same, it appears that the syntactic principles of Universal Grammar are a part of specifically human biology ... [it is] a uniquely human faculty...Humans are indeed unique**...[411]

Now, Anderson charts out a view wherein he grants some animals the ability to—with intensive human training—understand abstract symbols, but not use language in a meaningful sense because of their inability to manage syntax. While I certainly grant the latter, I do not intend to voice any agreement here with the former. My only purpose in quoting Dr. Anderson is to highlight his deft refutations of animal language in general, not to endorse all the aspects of his own solution.

Another popular claim made with respect to so-called animal languages is the "Dance of the Bees." Many claim bees really do rationally comprehend matters, and relay their understanding to other bees (e.g., regarding how to find certain flowers). This, as with all animal-language claims, is thoroughly false. For the sake of space, we will not address that here, but whoever is interested may find it addressed in a free supplement to this book posted at www.DSDOConnor.com/OMBHI.

Sci-Fi Deceptions Galore: Simulation Theory, Transhumanism, and Other False Existential Crises

There are far too many deeply troubling diabolical deceptions deriving from science fiction for us to address them all in this book. If, however, one can at least avoid the ET, AI, Time Travel, and Animal

Personhood Deceptions, then he is in a good position to reject other deceptions that may come. Nevertheless, we should very briefly note several more before concluding this chapter.

One simple recognition will help a Christian avoid most of the following deceptions; namely, *whatever proposition would, if true, entail an existential crisis for Christianity is – by its very nature – ruled out by Christianity.* This is essential to remember because diabolical deceptions feed on the untrusting fear of these "existential crises," and not only on the Godless excitement for the fruition of demonic seductions.

If only more Christians realized this simple truth which flows from the very promises Christ gave us and which define Christianity itself (and always will, until the end of time, no matter what), they would waste less time fretting about scenarios that cannot ever possibly happen. All Christians must understand that Christ's promises are absolute. No force in Heaven or earth – no force in the whole universe or even hell itself – can so much as make the slightest dent in His assurances. For example, He has said – even while describing the very apocalyptic times we are now approaching – that "**he who endures to the end will be saved**." (Matthew 24:13) Jesus did not say that those who endure to the end will be saved "so long as they are lucky enough to not have their minds controlled, and thus salvation robbed away, by some technology." He has promised to be with us "**until the end of the age**" (Matthew 28:20), not that His presence will only remain until some conspiracy seeks to subjugate each person to a simulation and make everyone live a complete lie by thinking it to constitute reality.

Such ridiculous fears as these – and many other related ones – must be rejected by all Christians as the Godless speculations they are. Even entertaining such thoughts is the sin of mistrust. It is the Devil – not God – who wants us to live in incessant fear of the powers of his minions (as much as I urge all to reject ETs and sentient AI, at the same time I admonish all Christians to have no *fear* of these deceptions); cowering in our rooms, ever afraid of HAARP, or CERN, or 5G, or Chemtrails, or Bill Gates, or whatever else – failing to evangelize and do works of mercy – out of a miserable desire to protect our mortal bodies at all costs. Do not succumb to that trap.

***

Transhumanism

The "transhuman" movement is exploding in popularity and it is evil to the core. Like transgenderism, it rejects the wisdom of God in His creation; pretending that man knows better than God. Every Christian must outright reject any proposition which suggests the human body can be fundamentally improved through technology. In fact, the only legitimate use of modifications of the body is to seek to remedy some pathology from which it suffers. For example, a pacemaker is moral if implanted to fix an ailing heart. A prosthetic limb is moral for an amputee. An artificial hip is moral for one whose natural hip had failed. Other than such things as these (and many other similar ones we could list), there is no legitimate use of technology to modify the body. The body must be left as it is because it is the pinnacle of God's creation. Any attempt whatsoever to "improve" it will only—in fact—damage it. For any scientist to approach the human body supposing he can improve it is akin to a three-year-old child opening up a computer and, with his Legos in hand, seeking to improve its performance by rebuilding its CPU. That will *never* happen.

All that said, we must also recognize that transhumanism *never will* succeed in its bolder aims. Humans are not, like the transhumanists love to claim, "hackable animals." Here as everywhere, the Devil has much more bark than bite. A Christian should never worry about civilization becoming dominated by transhuman monsters. Dr. Robert Malone (inventor of mRNA technology who later spoke out *against* the Covid mRNA injections) responded to atheist deceivers such as Yuval Harari (who believe humans can indeed be "hacked"), by saying, "**I've spent a large fraction of my career focused on gene delivery technology. I want to talk a little bit about this transhumanism agenda, and the logic that we're hackable beings... these technologies are not capable of the task that is being asserted ... What I'm struck by is how immature the logic is and how faulty the science is... What is being asserted as true... is a fantasy ... Are these people stupid?**"[412]

The second point is vital to remember because it is true now, and always will remain true, that every rational material creature is a human, and every human is 100% human. No matter what evil men in the future may do to certain human beings (whether by genetically editing them in their embryonic state or altering them at some point thereafter), those poor abused people will be just as human as we are. There will never be any such thing as a quasi-human; only at most an injured human. If a being is intelligent, then he or she is human just as much as you are. He or she has a Guardian Angel, an immortal soul, an infinite and intrinsic dignity, a free will, and is called to eternal salvation.

So-called "chimeras" are often talked about today. Any such scientific experiment is certainly evil and must be opposed, for such things constitute grave human rights violations and stand blasphemously against God's design. But no actual chimeras will ever exist. For example, an ape with human genetic material spliced into its own DNA will just be an injured ape that is still an ape. A human with some animal's genetic material spliced into his or her own DNA will just be an injured human who is still a human. Each human, moreover, will always be the child of exactly two (human) parents—a mother and a father. Even if this child's own genetic material is polluted with the introduction of material from another person, that does not—contrary to mainstream reporting—mean the child has "three parents."

***

Cloning

Human cloning is, of course, also a great evil—as are other artificial interventions (such as IVF) into the procreative process. All Christians should stand strongly opposed to this technology. Just as importantly, however, we must understand that it does not present (and never will present) existential crises. We are truly body *and* soul, but we are above all soul. A cloned human being is no more subject, in his very existence, to fundamental dilemmas than an identical twin is (which is to say, not at all). For just as identical twins share identical DNA, so do cloned organisms (whether human, animal, or anything else). There is no mixing of identity here. Each is his own person, with his own soul, his own memory, his own intellect, and his own will. I suggest anyone who doubts this to ask an identical twin for his input. Science Fiction movies love to traffic in existential crises related to cloning—supposing that this entails some mysterious transfer of memory and identity—and all such plotlines are as much drivel.

***

"Extinction Level Events"

Science fiction (and, increasingly, supposedly nonfictional claims) also loves to traffic in impending "extinction level events." Perhaps it is a matter of a comet obliterating the earth, some scientific experiment creating a black hole or other unfortunate situation that annihilates all life (many foolishly fret this might happen in reality with CERN), a nuclear event igniting the atmosphere and instantly killing everyone, a solar flare decimating all civilization, or any other similar theme.

While these themes can at times provide some innocent entertainment in film, Christians must never be seduced into entertaining the possibility of their premises in reality. There will never be any such thing as an extinction level event, since we know from the Faith that the human race (and the Catholic Church) will endure until the end of time. That moment—which coincides with the General Resurrection and Last Judgment—will only come *exactly* when God Wills it to come. There is absolutely nothing that can overrule God's Will here. The end of the world will come when He wants it to, and not one moment sooner.

Here we must note that a seemingly more "realistic extinction level event" would be nuclear war. In fact, even the most severe nuclear war would be *far* less than an extinction level event. There is perhaps more disinformation floating about on this question than anywhere else—much of it promoted as a "noble lie," with the best of intentions of helping to dissuade the use of nuclear weapons (which, indeed, must never be used by anyone who cares for truth and morality). Yet, I believe there is no such thing as a noble lie, and therefore I will present the truth to you here, even though I stand against nuclear war as emphatically as anyone.

***

Post-Apocalyptic Nuclear Hellscapes

Nuclear war would be utterly horrendous and apocalyptic, but it would not entail anything remotely resembling the dystopia depicted in most post-nuclear-war films and other works of fiction. To explain why, let us consider the worst possible case scenario in light of the facts.

Giving the opposing argument every benefit of the doubt, we will overestimate and suppose the average nuclear weapon is one Megaton in yield (almost a hundred times more powerful than the bomb dropped on Hiroshima). Most people within 5 miles of the blast of a 1 MT nuclear bomb may die, about half may die at that distance, with death rates decreasing exponentially as you proceed farther from the blast epicenter. Depending upon geography, it is possible that far less than half of all people would die within that 5-mile radius. There are currently about 13,000 nuclear weapons in existence—most far less than 1MT (including thousands of tactical nukes, which are *drastically* weaker). Even in the worst plausible case scenario, only a fraction of these weapons would be successfully used. Many would simply fail, as advanced technology that is rarely used tends to do. Such failures would certainly be extremely common in light of the fact that nuclear testing ceased thirty years ago. (Frequent tests are needed to keep any such technology operating reliably.) Other nuclear missiles (perhaps even huge numbers of them) would be taken down by missile defense systems (this does not cause a nuclear explosion; it simply disables the bomb). Moreover, many individual soldiers would do the right thing and refuse to deploy nuclear weapons on civilians, come what may. Finally, the chaos of war would also make it simply impossible to launch many if not most of them (upon hostilities beginning, a primary goal of opposing sides would be taking out the enemy's nuclear weapons; immediate breakdowns of intricate and delicate infrastructures would also generate a myriad of unpredicted problems). Only a tiny fraction of the world's existing nukes could ever "successfully" be used.

But let us nevertheless pretend that every single one of the close to 13,000 weapons was used. Even this entirely implausible situation could—at worst—cause the destruction of about 1 million square miles. This is the worst *possible* scenario, and any realistic one would entail exponentially less destruction. Now, Russia alone is over 6 million square miles. The earth contains almost 58 million square miles of land, and another 140 million square miles of water. In other words, in the worst possible case scenario, which we will never see anything close to, all the world's nuclear weapons together could not destroy more than 2% of the earth's land. It is unclear where the bald-faced lie came from that "*we have enough nuclear warheads today to completely flatten and destroy the entire surface of the earth several times over.*" Yet, whoever brings up the possibility of nuclear war in just about any type of company will likely hear at least one person solemnly pronounce this pseudo-fact. That assertion is orders of magnitude separated from the truth and has no basis in reality.

Granted, radioactive fallout would be a major problem. But that, too, is laden with hyperbole today. Fallout from a nuclear explosion dissipates much more quickly and completely than most people seem to think. Consider that Hiroshima is a bustling and safe city today, and has been for a long time. In fact, Hiroshima's restoration began mere days after it was bombed. Most of today's nuclear weapons, being "fusion" based instead of "fission" based (the fission is only used to initiate the fusion and is very minor), are much "cleaner" than the older 100% fission atomic bombs, thus their fallout would not be as severe.

So-called "nuclear winter" is also a complete fabrication. The idea of "nuclear winter" dooming the earth to resemble something out of Dante's Inferno for decades after a nuclear war was popularized by (among others) the atheist scientist Carl Sagan. (Unsurprisingly, the many "ET Revelations" of the Cold War warned about this!) In fact, there is and will be no such thing. The computer simulations of late that have assured us that nuclear war would entail nuclear winter are run with the same climate modelling software architectures that told us the world should have essentially ended thanks to "global warming" decades ago. In fact, a simple volcano or major wildfire spews far more solar-ray-blocking sediment into the upper atmosphere than even a large number of our most powerful nuclear weapons could. Moreover, from the perspective of alleged "nuclear winter," a nuclear *test* is no different than a nuclear *attack*. Throughout the latter half of the 20th century, nations throughout the world tested no fewer than 510 megatons worth of nuclear weaponry. (A not at all insignificant portion of the entire world's present nuclear arsenal.) The impact of this nuclear testing on global climate was *zero*. (And there is also scarcely any fallout left to speak of from that huge number of nuclear tests.) Indeed, the world is a much bigger thing—and the machinations of man a much smaller thing—than arrogant modern minds tend to recognize or at least admit. Mankind could not cause a severe global climate shift if every person on the planet dedicated himself to precisely that end, even using all possible means.

***

Mind Control/ Reading, Memory Insertion, and Other "Mind Tech"

Works of science fiction (and psychological thrillers) also often entail notions related to mind control. But remember, anything that could entail an existential crisis for the promises of Christ is itself ruled out by the promises of Christ. That consideration compels us to reject the possibility of literal mind control. The reason is simple: our salvation derives from our faith in and love of Jesus Christ. Yet both of those things are *choices* (salvation is never forced upon us). They are acts of the *will*, made after a conclusion of the *intellect*, whose own premises are derived from the *memory*. As no chain is stronger than its weakest link, any link in this chain being robbed of its supernatural immunity (by instead being possibly subject to some technological intervention), also causes that which it supports to collapse. And in this case, that support is none other than eternal salvation itself. Therefore, it is theologically impossible that God would ever allow this three-link-chain to be deprived of its ontological integrity. To say otherwise is to impugn His goodness.

The result of all this can become tragic in the worst possible way. A Christian who believes in the possibility of literal mind control or memory insertion has, by the very act of believing in those deceptions, just risked (depending upon how seriously he takes his own premises) rendering supernatural faith and hope impossible for himself. For he has, by definition, defined these virtues as *contingent* (on not having his mind controlled and thus overriding his choice to place his faith and hope in Christ). And whatever is merely contingent is not absolutely certain. And whatever is not absolutely certain is not supernatural. Thus this Christian, in entertaining these sci-fi absurdities, has just robbed his Christianity, which is always built on the three supernatural virtues, of its power.

Let us, however, also consider logically why we know the notion of mind control is nothing but a deception. In brief, the human mind is absolutely inaccessible to any current technology and to any theoretically possible future technology. There is no such thing, and there never will be such thing, as some device that can read our minds (much less control them or insert memories into them). Any exorcist will testify that not even the Devil himself can directly access the human mind. And it is deeply misguided to propose that some human technology will ever be able to achieve what is fundamentally beyond even his reach (for it is vastly beyond what any human technology will ever achieve).

This does not mean that the human mind cannot control *something else* (which is what some people mean when they say "mind control")—perhaps through a chip in the brain (which is never morally legitimate except perhaps to cure an objective, grave neurological disorder). It simply means that the mind *itself* cannot become *under the direct control* of some technology.

Now, when referring to "mind," I mean the intellect's thoughts, the memory's memories, and the free will's choices. Various *emotions associated with* certain thoughts, memories, and choices can be touched by technologies (just think of drug abuse). This may well *influence* our thoughts, memories, and choices, but it cannot ever *directly control* them. Those spiritual faculties themselves are ontologically (and Divinely) immune. Since we are incarnate creatures, each of these spiritual faculties generates corresponding neurochemical phenomena, which are simply effects of the spiritual reality. By definition, material phenomena (e.g. electromagnetic waves, microchips, 5G, injections, energy of any sort, vibrations, chemicals, etc.) only have access to other material phenomena. Thus, these material phenomena can only have any interaction whatsoever with the mere *effects* of your mind. Furthermore, the cause is greater than the effect and no effect precedes its cause. Therefore, *causes* (thoughts, memories, and choices)—superior spiritual realities—cannot possibly be generated by those types of things that are only their own *effects* (electromagnetic waves, electric currents, energies, etc.), since these effects are inferior material things. Similarly, bending a mirror and thus distorting the image thereupon cannot itself possibly bend the physical object whose image is reflected in the mirror. One need not know anything about the technology involved in mirrors to nevertheless be certain of this fact on account of logic and reason alone. The same is true with technology, "mind control," "memory insertion," and "mind reading."

To assert that man's intellect, memory, and will are actually entirely within the reach of physical phenomena (e.g., technology), is to implicitly assert that those faculties are themselves merely physical phenomena, which is to assert atheism. Now, in human beings, spirit and matter are not merely arbitrarily combined (contra Cartesian dualism), but are rather distinct aspects of a unity: the single person; the single nature, composed of both body and soul. But this does not change that spirit and matter are distinct realities, and they only interact by virtue of Divine decree. There is no natural mechanism by which the material can reach the spiritual. This is not only impossible; it is incoherent. We all know this intuitively. We all know, for example, that once your soul has departed your body (i.e. once you've died), it is absolutely untouchable by anything any technology could possibly do, since it has been temporarily deprived of this miraculous ability. Similarly, we know that we need not worry about some physics experiment opening a portal to hell, or about some new government weapon destroying St. Michael the Archangel. These facts may be too obvious to be worth stating, but they rest upon the premise that the material cannot reach the spiritual. The only exception is what we will consider in the next paragraph.

While we are alive, and the soul is animating the body, the soul enjoys the body's ability to send information to it via the senses. By Divine design, the senses alone are capable of mediating from the material to the spiritual realm—*Nihil est in intellectu quod non sit prius in sensu* (nothing is in the mind that was not first in the senses). This is an indispensable axiom of Catholic philosophy, and the only exception to it is Divinely mediated illumination or infusion (not technology).

Obviously, technology can indirectly affect the mind. For example, perhaps you are reading these words on an eBook reader—an advanced piece of technology—and your mind is being affected by the information you are receiving. But these effects on the mind—and *all* such effects on the mind—are always mediated entirely by the senses. In animals, the senses are merely material faculties. In man, the senses are veritable permanent miracles, since they straddle the material and the spiritual realms. Therefore, it is not possible for any actual information of any sort to be put directly into the mind via any technology whatsoever, since this would entail technology breaking metaphysical laws (it cannot even break scientific laws, much less the far more absolute metaphysical ones!).*

> **God alone can know the thoughts of hearts and affections of wills. The reason of this is, because the rational creature is subject to God only, and He alone can work in it Who is its principal object and last end** ... all that is in the will [is] known to God alone...Hence the Apostle says (1 Cor. 2:11): 'For what man knoweth the things of a man, but the spirit of a man that is in him?'" (St. Thomas Aquinas. *Summa Theologica.* First Part. Question 57. Article 4.)

***

Simulation Theory

One sci-fi deception—astonishingly logically and morally bankrupt—is the notion that everything we experience is simply a computer simulation being run by some higher civilization of beings. This is, of course, precisely the plotline of *The Matrix*, the 1999 release of which also marked the beginning of this deception's explosion in popularity. While one may be tempted to regard this idea as so outlandish that virtually no one would lend it any *actual* credibility, that supposition is unfortunately inaccurate. For example, prominent AI Deception promoter Elon Musk has also declared his "near certainty" that Simulation Theory is correct. (Though he graciously concedes there is at least a "one in a billion chance we're in base reality."[413]) Nor is it only headline-dominating billionaires who promote this mythology. It is also promoted by popular scientists. For example, astrophysicist Neil deGrasse Tyson regards Simulation Theory as likely correct (admittedly, he is no stranger to the promotion of bogus views).[414]

It is difficult to know where to begin in even dialoguing with one who entertains such absurdities, much less believes in them, but some attempts can at least be made to bring him back to sanity.

First: if we are in a simulation run by simulators, then are they also? Whatever argument appears to lend credence to our being in a simulation would apply equally to them. Of course, it would apply equally well to the simulators of the simulators of the simulators. And to their simulators, *ad infinitum*. Simulation Theory does not add a single meaningful contribution to any serious conversation about the nature of reality. It only kicks the "base reality" can down the road, so that men with ulterior motives can pretend that our reality—which, in fact, *is* base reality, *the* reality—can ignore the demands its own confrontation places upon us. For one who supposes all is merely a simulation, a man might pretend he is a woman and insist that his charade makes it true. He might pretend that AI is just as rational as we are. He might pretend an unborn baby isn't real. He might

---

* More information on this point can be found at https://dsdoconnor.com/mind, where other objections are also addressed.

pretend animals are also persons. He might ignore all proofs of God and all miracles as just "anomalies in the programming." Anything, in fact, one dislikes or disagrees with but is manifestly real is simply set aside as a "glitch" in the software for the believers in Simulation Theory. We can see that this deception is diabolical if anything ever was.

The truth, however, is that *everything* one would expect to see in "base reality," one does indeed see here.

You can place a microscope on anything you like. So long as it is not a computer screen, you will not find it composed of pixels or any other granular thing one could suggest constitutes the basic components of the simulation's data. Instead, you will find that its intricacy goes down, and down, and down, to such a degree that no computer simulation—no matter how advanced—could manage to simulate what *a single grain of sand* contains, much less a single cell, much less an animal, much less a person, much less a whole world full of these things. Proposing that any hypothetically super-advanced civilization could run some simulation to deceptively craft our experience of reality and inject it into our mind, even with something so simple as the single room you now find yourself in, is more absurd than claiming all the data accessible throughout the entire internet is just contained in a 1970's floppy disk somewhere.

Simulation Theory is also defeated by one simple philosophical recognition; namely, *perfect knowledge of a thing is none other than the thing itself.* Consider that we guard with great zeal historical artifacts. We do this even if we have photographed and scanned them in tremendous detail. Why do we do this? Don't we have all the information we need from these digitizations? The answer, of course, is *no*—we do not. It does not matter how much we have described the thing, or how many images of it we have captured, or how accurately we have quantified it through various measurements. The thing itself is always, by definition, beyond these portions of knowledge *about* it. One never can be certain, in a given time, what additional truths will be discovered about an object in the future (just think of The Shroud of Turin or the image of Our Lady of Guadalupe). Entire scholarly fields of study sometimes exist centralized wholly around some small archeological artifact, which many academics dedicate their careers to analyzing. These studies often prove very fruitful. However, to recognize that even the smallest item can contain massive treasures of information, but to still entertain the notion that the whole world could nevertheless be just some computer simulation we are experiencing, is—as with some other matters we have discussed—nothing but a *willed insanity*.

We should also note that Simulation Theory is indirectly (but still definitively) repudiated by our previous refutations of mind control, superintelligent AI, various Quantum absurdities, and other deceptions. Since our minds cannot even be directly fed information in the first place, no type of Simulation Theory is coherent. Since AI can never become "superintelligent," Simulation Theory is impossible, as it would require not merely "superintelligent" AI to administer it, but *Godlike* AI. Since Simulation Theory rests upon various conjectures made within Quantum Theory which do not, in fact, describe reality at all, this notion likewise completely collapses.

Part Six, Conclusion: The Wise Wager, the Essential Approach, and the Supreme Mission

Although our sixth and final part is extremely short in relation to the preceding five, it nevertheless deserves this exaltation to a structurally vital position so that no one who picks up this book can possibly miss it. For without always remembering what will be considered in the following section against fear, one risks being almost as harmed by the ET Deception in avoiding it as he does in succumbing to it! And without remembering the essence of the Christian's mission in such apocalyptic days as these, one risks all the knowledge in the world about imminent diabolical deceptions proving sterile.

31. Pascal's Wager and Extraterrestrials

"See to it that no one makes a prey of you by philosophy and empty deceit, according to human tradition, according to the elemental spirits of the universe, and not according to Christ."
—Colossians 2:8

Whenever someone struggles to directly discover the truth on some question, it is wise for him to step back and ponder what he stands to gain or lose by assuming the correctness of either take. This contemplation presents an exceedingly clear conclusion with respect to God's existence: one should assume He exists. If God does not exist and one nevertheless believes in Him, nothing is lost; if God does not exist and one does not believe in Him; nothing is gained. On the other hand, if God does exist and one does not believe in Him, everything is lost; if God does exist and one does believe in Him, everything is gained. Behold "Pascal's Wager."

This disarmingly simple consideration is, of course, unnecessary: it is easy to prove God's existence *directly* beyond any shred of doubt. But if one arrives at a life of Faith by considering Pascal's Wager, this less than perfect method is infinitely better than the alternative—if for some individual the alternative happens to be disbelief.

We should consider the same wager applied to the question of extraterrestrials (it can also be applied to sentient AI, animal personhood, and other deceptions, but we will only draw out the conclusions on the question of aliens). What does one stand to gain or lose by believing or disbelieving in aliens? In brief: he stands to gain nothing from believing in them (even if they do exist), while he stands to lose everything as a result of that same belief.

	Disbelieve in Aliens (i.e., regard them as demonic illusions)	**Believe in Aliens**
Aliens Do Exist:	<u>A</u> Nothing worthwhile is lost. We do not need them, as God has already given us everything we need.	<u>B</u> Nothing worthwhile is gained. Their "super-advanced" technology and science would be sure only to harm us, not help us.
Aliens Do Not Exist:	<u>C</u> Abiding in the truth. Keeping the Faith. Avoiding demonic seductions and malicious government psyops.	<u>D</u> Wrecking the Faith even now. (Diminishing focus on Jesus, Mary, the Church, etc.) Priming oneself to succumb to diabolical instructions and government psyops.

Box C above, of course, is the one that corresponds to the truth and to the convictions we should hold, while Box D corresponds to the diabolical traps now being laid for the world. But as we have already focused on exploring that throughout this book's chapters, let us now for a moment counterfactually pretend that aliens do exist, so that we can scrutinize Boxes A and B, and thus complete our assessment of Pascal's Wager applied to the present question.

If aliens exist and we disbelieve in them, we lose nothing. While one could sympathize with a non-Christian bemoaning how much he thinks he would miss out on by losing the chance to learn from the "ultra-evolved extraterrestrials," one can only rebuke any Christian who similarly laments. As all Christians know (but too few take seriously and abide by all the corollaries of), God Himself *literally* became man in Jesus Christ. God could not do anything greater for us than He has already done in the Incarnation. It is *the* definitive revelation of Himself. No other revelation will so much as add to, much less surpass, the revelation that is Jesus Christ.

In Public Revelation (Sacred Scripture), from which we learn about Jesus (and Sacred Tradition's development of it, and the Magisterium's interpretation of it), we are given *everything* we need for our salvation—for our *eternal happiness*. Aliens could not contribute anything whatsoever to this, which is the ultimate aim of our lives. Granted, our call to *sanctification* is not exhaustively and definitively completed within the pages of Scripture. Indeed, by the Holy Spirit, the Church is called to grow in holiness throughout the centuries—while always doing so upon the foundation and within the boundaries of Public Revelation. Aliens could not contribute to this either. Our call to sanctification has already received its greatest possible exposition through the culmination of two thousand years of Sacred Tradition's development; particularly in the writings of the 20th century mystics such as St. Faustina, St. Maximilian Kolbe, Blessed Dina Bélanger, Blessed Concepción Cabrera de Armida (Bl. Conchita), St. Elizabeth of the Trinity, and the Servant of God Luisa Piccarreta. Jesus' private revelations to these mystics, and many others of the same time period, repeatedly make it clear that He has described to them (and, through them, called us all into) the greatest *possible* holiness, never to be surpassed by any other development of sanctification until the end of time; with the only additional glory awaited being the *unveiled* enjoyment of that holiness for all eternity in the Beatific Vision. (Those interested in learning more about this may find it detailed in my 2021 book, *Thy Will Be Done.*)

Therefore, in Public Revelation we have everything needed for our salvation. In Sacred Tradition, especially 20th century private revelation, we have everything one could possibly ask for in the *greatest possible* sanctification. Salvation and sanctification are the only two things that ultimately matter. For salvation is about getting to Heaven, and sanctification is about building up treasures in Heaven. *Everything* else, save these two ends, is as much refuse. Only that which pertains to salvation and sanctification endures beyond the end of time, which will be upon us in a moment. Since "aliens" could not provide benefits to us for either goal, then even if we counterfactually pretend they exist, they are superfluous at best.

Some Christians, sadly, remain obsessed with scientific and technological progress and place their hopes therein (and not in Christ). So ravenous for a technologically originated utopia are they, that any supposed source of this utopia will be eagerly sought out by them without any concern for orthodox teaching, Sacred Tradition, or spiritual safety. This said, we should address a final protestation they may offer, namely: "*So aliens would not contribute anything to salvation and sanctification; but what about helping our temporal lives here and now? Shouldn't we believe in aliens and seek them out in hopes that their technology could bestow enormous benefits upon us?*"

The answer to this question is also a resolute *no.* I would encourage any Christian who places his hopes in technological progress to observe the past and realize that such progress (though obviously not a bad thing in itself) has never delivered on its promises. The more technologically advanced society becomes, the more unhappy it grows. Why would more of the same prove any different? Besides, this sorry fate remains the case even with relatively gradual technological advancement. Just imagine how thoroughly we would be destroyed by suddenly having access to technology vastly beyond even our currently most advanced inventions. This would be akin to winning the lottery. As anyone knows who has read into this matter, a poor man suddenly becoming rich overnight by winning a major lottery invariably finds his life destroyed. He feels a predictable euphoria for a time, but having no understanding of how to handle great wealth, those newfound abilities he has and opportunities he has access to only wind up ruining him in short order. It would be far worse for the human race if it suddenly acquired super-advanced alien technology. We would only destroy ourselves with it.

In brief: even if we pretend aliens exist, we nevertheless remain confronted with the reality that by disbelieving in them one loses nothing, and by believing in them, one gains nothing.

If aliens did exist, it would be incredibly easy for them to prove themselves beyond the slightest shred of any possible doubt. Every argument against their existence—including this book—would immediately melt like a flake of snow cast into a fire. It would never be difficult for any creatures who are not demons to *definitively prove* they are not demons. They could simply *land* their "spaceships" in the sight of many, walk out of them, shake hands with people, interact with large groups of us in broad daylight (day after day, month after month), give us pieces of their technology we could study in our laboratories, etc. They could spend protracted amounts of time with us and *easily* display their truly *incarnate* nature. Therefore, it is simply silly and baseless for any ET promoter to fret about arguments against aliens. If they exist, arguments against their existence will be entirely ineffective. They would be like the arguments of an untouched aboriginal tribe against the existence of cars and planes. Such arguments would be worth smiling at, not worrying about—for we would know how easily the experience of those realities would immediately discount the arguments against their existence.

Of course, the "aliens" do not do any of these things—nor will they ever—precisely because they and their "crafts" are nothing but demonic illusions. The mere fact that ET promoters *do* grow so agitated by arguments against aliens undermines their own thesis. These men likely realize (if only subconsciously) that the ET "Day of Disclosure" will only include the disclosure of "proofs of aliens" which amount to ruses easily within the power of demons to fabricate. And perhaps it is even because they know, deep down, that there are no aliens, that they are so zealous to insist there are.

Nor can this observation be turned on its head by an ET promoter retorting, *"well, you only argue against aliens with analogous motives!"* Quite the contrary, my motivation for arguing against aliens is unambiguous: ET belief itself is deeply detrimental to the Faith, it is an exceedingly dangerous distraction, it has proven innumerable times to destroy people's lives, and it primes one to be seduced by the deceptions of demons moving forward in a manner more foreboding of the Strong Delusion of the Antichrist than any other phenomenon in history. If these are not fitting motivations to argue against some proposition, then, pray tell, *what motivations are?*

Christian ET promoters, on the other hand—although they are clearly quite zealous for the fruition of their sci-fi-myth-originated fantasies—can provide no justification whatsoever for their zeal that is coherent from a Christian perspective.

So we stand to lose nothing by *disbelieving* in aliens. What do we stand to lose by *believing* in aliens? That question is answered in Parts One through Four of this book; but we can summarize it all in one word: *everything*. By believing in aliens and "remaining open" to dialogue with them, one has entered perhaps the most spiritually and morally destructive movement that exists anywhere in the world today—one which promises to soon deliver exponentially more (*apocalyptic)* deception than it has already.

Leaving aside the fact that we can disprove aliens from Scripture, Sacred Tradition, Magisterium, Science, and more, we are still left with the question: under what bizarre premises are the undeniable risks of alien belief worth taking?

> See to it that no one fail to obtain the grace of God... that no one be immoral **or irreligious like Esau, who sold his birthright for a single meal**. For you know that afterward, when he desired to inherit the blessing, he was rejected, for he found no chance to repent, though he sought it with tears. (Hebrews 12:15-17)

32. The Essential Approach: Be Not Afraid!

"Submit yourselves therefore to God. Resist the devil, and he will flee from you." —James 4:7

I have presented quite an extraordinary case in this book. Consequently, it is only right that its penultimate remark consists of an exhortation to abandon the very thing some may be tempted to cling to: fear. In truth, all the diabolical arts taken together – including the particularly immense apocalyptic efforts of the Devil – cannot hold a candle to a soul who remains in God's grace, trusts in His Mercy, and strives to live in His Will.

Throughout this book, we have been diligently addressing the many diabolical deceptions present in the world today, already wreaking havoc in the lives of millions, but also heralding the apocalyptic events that promise much more destruction in the times soon to come. These seductions operate under the guise of the prevailing contemporary myth: science fiction. Indeed, the dangers therein are uniquely and superlatively evil. As such, to fail to warn against them is to be guilty of the blood of those who succumb but would have held fast if only they were warned. As Scripture teaches:

> If I tell the wicked, "*O wicked one, you shall surely die,*" and you do not speak out to dissuade the wicked from his way, the wicked shall die for his guilt, but I will hold you responsible for his death. (Ezekiel 33:8)

Yet, we should warn against the ET Deception and related ones for the same reason we warn against *any* Pagan trap which can seduce a soul into the Devil's clutches: Ouija, divination, sorcery, witchcraft, Reiki, séances, fortune-telling, and the like. Just as any discerning Christian realizes that – although all these practices promise great benefits to their devotees – they are in fact only demonic undertakings from which we all must flee, so too discerning Christians should recognize the same about aliens and other lies.

Does that mean a Christian should *fear* such occult practices? Should he go about his days dreading that some Ouija board will be placed in front of him and thus give the demon an inlet into his life? Should he avoid going out in public lest he stumble upon some witch who decides to try to put a curse on him? Should he refuse to greet anyone he does not already fully know and trust with a hug, lest that person try to sneak some Reiki practice into the embrace? Should he never eat food served by others, just in case someone snuck in some hexed spices?

Of course not! So long as one stays away from this Paganism with regard to what *he himself willfully chooses*, it has no power over him that need be feared. Even in the apocalyptic days of the Great Deception itself, wherein the Devil's chain is lengthened more than ever before, it nevertheless remains within every Christian's power to stay outside of the radius of that chain and thus preserve his spiritual safety.

If you have read this book thus far, I suppose you will not take issue with me noting that if there is anyone who is aware of how dark and diabolical the ET Deception is, it is I. Yet I do not have even the slightest fear of demons masquerading as aliens. This is not due to holiness (I am not holy!); it is simply because, although a miserable sinner, I do trust absolutely in Jesus Christ, and I know that with Him I have nothing to fear from the machinations of demons. I read His Word every day, receive Him daily in the Holy Eucharist, pray His Mother's Rosary daily, go to Confession at least each month, submit to all the teachings of the Church, and try to remain always in a state of grace. None of this has anything to do with merits or worthiness; they are simply undeserved gifts—which are infinitely more powerful than the Devil's most ferocious attacks—and which God will shower upon all who sincerely seek Him.

With such protections as these, how could one possibly justify being afraid of demons; no matter how they masquerade? That would be like a small child, the son of a very strong man, sitting beside his father and choosing to be afraid of some grade school bully approaching. The bully may be a fearsome sight to the child, but there is not the slightest risk of anything happening to the child *so long as* he remains with his father.

Let us now contrast this trusting child to a frenetic cat. I recall I was once holding my pet cat while sitting on my home's back deck many years ago. Some animal approached, perhaps a fox, and it terrified the cat. Granted, it would be wise for a small housecat to not attempt to take on a fox by itself. But there was absolutely no risk for the cat, from the fox, while I was holding it. That creature would not dare to come near me, much less fight me for the cat. The foolish cat, however, went crazy upon seeing the creature, leapt out of my arms (scratching me in the process), and straight into danger. Christians act just like that cat when they choose to entertain fears about the Devil. They walk into his arms by overestimating his power and underestimating God's.

Suppose, however, I was instead holding a small puppy. Perhaps it would have had no fear of the wild fox but rather—out of curiosity or excitement—jumped down and walked up to it. That, too, would not have gone well for the puppy. And this is what Christians do when they wander into the radius of the Devil's chain, forgetting to stay ever close to the Deposit of Faith and reject all suggestions which do not harmonize with it, becoming seduced by the allurements of the world which, today, are often nothing but directly diabolical ploys.

Therefore, we must *both* place our absolute trust in Jesus Christ *and* stay outside of the radius of the Devil's chain. If we do these two things—being like the trusting child, not the neurotic housecat or the clueless puppy—we can remain in absolute fearless peace, no matter what transpires in the world tomorrow.

It is often said that the Bible exhorts us not to be afraid on 365 separate occasions (amounting to one for each day of the year). I have not tallied them up myself, so I do not know if this is accurate, but it rings true. Scripture constantly exhorts us to be absolutely unafraid of everything. How *could* we be afraid—knowing that God is both all-good and all-powerful? How could we dare entertain fears, knowing that "**God works all things for good with those who love him**" (Romans 8:28)? Demons—whether unveiled or disguised as some other entity—are not exceptions to that exhortation.*

> "...the devil is the most cowardly creature that can exist, and a contrary act, a contempt, a prayer, are enough to make him flee [terrified]." —Jesus to Luisa Piccarreta. March 25, 1908.

By choosing to fear the Devil, we give him a degree of power that he would not otherwise have—just like the foolish cat above. For Jesus has promised: "**Heaven and earth will pass away, but my words will never pass away**." (Matthew 24:35). This was not an exhortation given by Our Lord in the middle of a parable or a moral sermon. It was, rather, given directly in the context of describing the days of the Apocalypse which we are now entering. To be sure, Jesus said this when He did because He knew it was imperative for us to remember that not one jot—not one iota—of His promises would ever fail, even in the midst of the final trial of the Church. He said this because He knew the temptation would then arise to suppose that what could once take for granted by Christians can no longer be taken for granted. Such temptations, no less than the temptations of those who obliviously bury their heads in the sand and ignore the evil agendas at work in the world today, are from Satan. We must reject them all.

Jesus furthermore promised, of these days, "***Whosoever* endures to the end shall be saved**." (Mt 24:13). He did not say, "*Those who endure to the end, by being fortunate enough to not encounter a demon-alien that can control their minds and compel them to apostatize, will be saved.*" Jesus promised that "**the gates of hell would not prevail**" against the Church (Mt 16:18).

---

* One might protest that it appears Jesus once exhorted us to be afraid of the Devil. But that is a misinterpretation of Luke 12:5. There, Jesus says, "...do not fear those who kill the body ... But I will warn you whom to fear: *fear him who, after he has killed, has power to cast into hell.*" In fact, the Devil *does not* have the power to cast us into hell, so this cannot be what Jesus is referring to. Only God can do that—and God never *would* do that by external imposition; for, as Scripture says, He "**wills that all men be saved**." (1 Timothy 2:4) What then, in truth, does this verse mean? It exhorts us to "fear" of the self-will, which is the only thing that will cast us into hell (if we let it). Do not misunderstand; we must indeed zealously oppose the Devil, stay outside of his reach, and recognize that he "prowls around like a roaring lion, seeking someone to devour." (1 Peter 5:8) Thus we remain compelled to snatch others away from his reach. So long as we are doing that, we must not fear him.

He did not say that "*the gates of hell will not prevail against the Church until the 21st century.*" Infallible dogma teaches that the Catholic Church has the absolute right to absolve *any* sin. It does not say that this power is restricted to those fortunate enough to be alive before the possibility of having some technology forcibly imposed upon them which causes them to become gene-edited creatures who cannot be absolved. The Catholic Church teaches that all humans are 100% human, that they each have an intrinsic and infinite dignity, and that absolutely nothing can take this away from them. It does not teach that such absolute safeguards from Almighty God are reserved for those lucky enough to be alive before the "transhumanist" agenda came onto the scene thus opening up the possibility of a human becoming a "pseudo" human or a "quasi" human (there is no such thing). Therefore, never entertain existential crises that our Faith in Christ precludes. Let *absolutely* nothing shake your *absolute* trust in Jesus. *Nothing.*

> ...the soul who is at peace, by wanting to afflict herself, become disturbed or lose trust, would run into the misfortune of one who, though possessing millions upon millions of coins, and even being queen of various kingdoms, keeps fantasizing and lamenting, saying: '*What shall I live on? How shall I clothe myself? Ah, I am dying of starvation! I am so unhappy! I will be reduced to the meagerest misery and I will end up dying.*' And while she says this, she cries, sighs and spends her days in sadness and squalor, immersed in the greatest melancholy. ... Now, what would people say about her? That she is crazy, that it shows that she has no reason, that she has lost her mind. The reason is clear, it cannot be otherwise. Yet, it can happen that she may run into the misfortune over which she keeps fantasizing. But in what way? By going out of her kingdoms, abandoning all of her riches, and going into foreign lands in the midst of barbarian people, where no one will deign to give her a crumb of bread. Here is how the fantasy has become reality—what used to be false, is now true. But who has been the cause of it? Who should be blamed for a change of state so sad? Her perfidious and obstinate will. Such is precisely the soul who is in possession of Hope: her wanting to become disturbed or discouraged is already the greatest madness. (Jesus to the Servant of God Luisa Piccarreta. October 14, 1899. Nihil Obstat, St. Hannibal di Francia. Imprimatur, Archbishop Joseph Leo.)

While I have indeed sacrificed more sleep than I care to catalogue in researching and writing this book, the truth is that I have not lost one moment of sleep *worrying for my own sake* about the ET Deception, the AI Deception, or any related ones. (Even as I weep for those who are being deceived, and thus I work zealously for *their* sake.) Although these apocalyptic assaults are coming and are, largely, already here, this in fact only excites me—not because I take any pleasure in the dissemination of error

(I do not), but because I know that Christ has promised to Triumph precisely when things are at their worst. Consequently, the deeper modern society sinks into diabolical deception, the closer I know we draw to His reign.

This book has mostly focused on what *not* to do (not to succumb to diabolical deceptions). But what is far more important than what should *not* be done is what *should* be done. Therefore, let us conclude with an exhortation not merely to be without fear, but also to be overwhelmed with joy at what Christ is bringing about, and filled with zeal to hasten it. Fearlessness is only the starting point. Courage in His Will is the mission.

33. Today's Supreme Mission

No one should set down a book as large as this one without a mission placed upon his heart. I have relayed in the many chapters above what we must denounce and avoid. In the preceding section, we have settled that these great evils—these apocalyptic diabolical deceptions—though they are to be rejected, are no causes for the faithful to succumb to fear. What remains, then, is settling what we ought to *do* in these extraordinary times. In the Introduction, we briefly noted that these are the most exciting times in the whole history of the world. Let us complete that consideration now.

From Scripture and saints, from Magisterium and mystics, from ancient times and modern private revelations, we see a unanimous testimony of them all indicating that the Church will face a supreme trial in the latter times; it will involve great diabolical deception and concomitant apostasy the likes of which have never been seen. It will involve all manner of demonic illusions and false signs and wonders; even men wandering back into some new explosion of Pagan myths. The prophecies almost never give great details on these things—if they did, then this trial would not be the *test* that God's permissive Will is allowing for good reason. But from what they have said, we can easily see that what is brewing in ET Deception (and related ones we have discussed) gives every indication of being precisely what has been long foretold. We considered all of this in earlier chapters. What we must consider now is why this is the most exciting news imaginable.

> The more noteworthy of the prophecies bearing upon "latter times" seem to have **one common end, to announce great calamities impending over mankind, the triumph of the Church, and the renovation of the world**. All the seers agree in two leading features ... "**First** they all point to some terrible convulsion, to **a revolution springing from most deep-rooted impiety, consisting in a formal opposition to God and His truth**, and resulting in the most formidable persecution to which the Church has ever been subject. **Secondly, they all promise for the Church a victory more splendid than she has ever achieved here below**." (The old *Catholic Encyclopedia*. Article on *Prophecy*)

God is not sadistic. He is perfectly good and infinitely powerful, and for that reason all evils which occur are only so much as *permitted* by Him because He *knows* a greater good will come about due to their allowance. If, therefore, He allows some great trial on earth (and no trial is worse than those insidious attacks on the core of the Faith, wherein even many of the faithful succumb to diabolical deception), it is only because, *also on earth,* He is going to bring about a good far greater in magnitude than the evil which preceded it. (He has all eternity to mete out justice—*merely for the sake of justice*—to those deserving of it.) Of course, this must never detract from our focus on Heaven—that destiny alone will always remain our supreme end and it alone remains the proper formal object of our supernatural hope. But if Christ's triumph *beyond* history is the *formal* object of our hope, then what is its *material* object? It is precisely what naturally follows: His triumph *within* history.

> ... not only supernatural helps, particularly such as are necessary for our salvation, but also things in the temporal order, inasmuch as they can be means to reach the supreme end of human life, may be the **material objects of supernatural hope.** (The old *Catholic Encyclopedia,* Article on *Hope.*)

Let no one revile you, therefore, for harboring immense hope in Christ's triumph upon earth; instead, always cry out from the depths of your heart, *Viva Cristo Rey*!—"Long Live Christ the King!"—and in so doing, resolutely implore His victory in all domains; above all the eternal one, but also the temporal. This victory is exactly what is promised to us in Scripture, by the saints, the Magisterium, and private revelation; there is no doubt about the veracity of the promise or the surety of its fulfillment. He *will* win—*both* eternally *and* temporally. In fact, it is precisely when the scoffers reach the pinnacle of their claims, saying He will *not* triumph, that He will do precisely that:

> ... Scoffers will come in the last days with scoffing, following their own passions and saying, "Where is the promise of his coming? For ever since the fathers fell asleep, all things have continued as they were from the beginning of creation." (2 Peter 3:3,4)

But no amount of scoffing (even if it comes from within the ranks of the Church's own hierarchy) can alter the promises of Christ. If too many of the Faithful refuse to plea for His reign, then it may be delayed—hence my zeal in begging all Christians to implore it—but it will *not* be prevented. *Nothing* can prevent it. For He has rendered its arrival certain in the greatest petition of the greatest prayer, which was also a sure prophecy:

> **Thy kingdom come, thy will be done, on earth as it is in heaven.** (Matthew 6:10)

Expounding upon this verse, Jesus told the Servant of God Luisa Piccarreta:

> **My daughter, as Adam sinned, God made him the promise of the future Redeemer. Centuries passed, but the promise did not fail,** and the generations had the good of Redemption. Now, as I came from Heaven ... I made **another promise, more solemn**, of the Kingdom of My Will; and this was in the 'Our Father.' And so as to give it more value, and to obtain it more quickly, I made this formal promise in the solemnity of My prayer, praying the Father to let His Kingdom come, which is the Divine Will on earth as it is in Heaven. I placed My very Self at the head of this prayer, knowing that such was His Will, and that,

> prayed by Me, He would deny Me nothing...And after I had formed this prayer before My Celestial Father, certain that the Kingdom of My Divine Will upon earth would be granted to Me, **I taught it to My Apostles, that they might teach it to the whole world, so that one might be the cry of all: *'Your Will be done, on earth as It is in Heaven.'* A promise more sure and solemn I could not make.** ... My very praying to the Celestial Father: 'Let It come-let Your Kingdom come; Your Will be done on earth as It is in Heaven,' meant that with My coming upon earth the Kingdom of My Will was not established in the midst of creatures; otherwise I would have said: 'My Father, let Our Kingdom, that I have already established on earth, be confirmed, and let Our Will dominate and reign.' Instead, I said: 'Let It come.' This meant that **it must come, and creatures must await it with that certainty with which they awaited the future Redeemer, because there is My Divine Will, bound and committed, in those words of the 'Our Father'; and when it binds itself, whatever it promises is more than certain**. (February 5th, 1928 Diary Entry. *Nihil Obstat,* St. Hannibal di Francia. *Imprimatur,* Archbishop Joseph Leo.)

St. Hannibal di Francia dedicated his life to promoting these private revelations, precisely because he was convinced that they heralded the "**triumph of the Divine Will upon the whole earth, in conformity with the Our Father,**" * as the official 2016 Vatican biography of Luisa (*The Sun of My Will*) relays, and he insisted they "**must be made known to the world**."

As with all private revelations, and so with this one, the role they fulfill is simply to render more explicit some truth already contained in *the* Public Revelation; never to provide a *new* Public Revelation. While I submit to you that we do find here private revelation's greatest explication of this (supreme) Scriptural verse—Matthew 6:10—that is, in Jesus' words to Luisa (*Jesus even told her that His thousands of pages worth of messages to her are all contained in that single verse of Scripture*), these messages are anything but alone. In fact, the whole history of the Church, in the most essential aspects of the development of its Sacred Tradition, sees the saints teaching more and more boldly, as the centuries progress, on the heights of what the Holy Spirit is leading us to in relation to the Divine Will. And while in this regard God is above all concerned with the inner spiritual life of each soul—drawing it into union with His Divine Will—He is also deeply concerned with bringing about the *worldwide* reign of His Will that no Christian can deny the Our Father prayer promises.

All of this is traced out in detail in *Thy Will Be Done.* For now, a few quotes will suffice.

> **For He did not at all say, "Thy will be done" in me, or in us, but eve-**

---

* www.SunOfMyWill.com Note: the words, "*in conformity with the Our Father,*" are contained in St. Hannibal's original writing, but that one clause is abridged within the text of *The Sun of My Will.*

rywhere on the earth; so that error may be destroyed, and truth implanted, and all wickedness cast out, and virtue return, and no difference in this respect be henceforth between heaven and earth. (St. John Chrysostom, Father and Doctor of the Church. Homily XIX, §7)
A kingdom is promised to us upon the earth, although **before heaven,** only in another state of existence ... (Tertullian, Father of the Church. *Against Marcion.* Book 3. Ch. 25)

Some, however, have always tried to pretend that all the prophecies of Scripture were merely allegorical. And it is indeed true that the primary end of Old Testament prophecy was to foretell the Incarnation, death, and Resurrection of Christ, and the Age of the Church in general. But it is equally certain that not all the prophecies were purely symbolic. Many meant *exactly what they said*; for example, in promising the whole world would eventually be even physically renovated in accordance with the Reign of God—well *before* the end of time. St. Irenaeus (the one and only saint in history who is a Father of the Church, Doctor of the Church, *and* martyr) rightly repudiated such views. The following excerpts are taken from his work, *Against Heresies*, Part V:

[Christ] will Himself renew the inheritance of the earth, and will re-organize the mystery of the glory of [His] sons; as David says, "He who has renewed the face of the earth." ... He cannot by any means be understood as drinking of the fruit of the vine when settled down with his [disciples] above in [Heaven] ... These [prophecies are to take place] in the times of the kingdom, that is, upon the seventh day ... **If any one, then, does not accept these things as referring to the appointed kingdom, he must fall into much contradiction and contrariety** ... (Book 33) That the whole creation shall, according to God's will, obtain a vast increase, that it may bring forth and sustain fruits such [as we have mentioned], Isaiah declares... (Book 34) **If, however, any shall endeavour to allegorize [prophecies] of this kind, they shall not be found consistent with themselves** in all points, and shall be confuted by the teaching of the very expressions [in question] ... For all these and other words were unquestionably spoken in reference to ... after the coming of Antichrist, and the destruction of all nations under his rule...[when] the righteous shall reign in the earth ... Now all these things being such as they are, **cannot be understood in reference to [Heavenly] matters; for God, it is said, will show to the whole *earth that is under heaven* your glory. But in the times of the kingdom, the earth has been called again by Christ [to its pristine condition] ... nothing is capable of being allegorized**, but all things are steadfast, and true, and substantial, having been made by God for righteous men's enjoyment. (Book 35) **For the Lord also taught these things**, when He promised that He would have the mixed cup new with His disciples in the kingdom. **The apostle, too, has confessed that the creation shall be free from the bondage of corruption**, [so as to pass] into the liberty of the sons of God. (Romans 8:21) (Book 36)

As St. Irenaeus demonstrates, it is logically contradictory to interpret the promises from Jesus Himself—and from the Apostles, and St. Paul, and the Old Testament Prophets—as referring to anything other than a glorious Era to come on earth; a "coming of Christ's Kingdom" within history, before the end of time, along with an outpouring of grace and blessings for the whole world. This Church Father is not merely presenting an opinion on how to interpret a single passage in the Book of Revelation (there has always been much debate on how to interpret Revelation Chapter 20 and its "thousand years"); he is, rather, relaying a fundamental conviction from prophecies *throughout* the Old and New Testaments.*

While we see the Triumph of Christ prophesied even in the Church Fathers above (and many others), it naturally became spoken of more forcefully and clearly still the closer the time drew to its fulfillment. This is the paradigm prophecy always follows. Similarly, Public Revelation's prophets (of the Old Testament) increased in frequency, specificity, and vigor the closer the time came to the Incarnation of Christ, until at last St. John the Baptist declared, "behold the Lamb of God!" (John 1:29) St. Francis de Sales (†1622), Doctor of the Church, spoke of a time on earth when:

> ...every one shall forsake his own will, and shall have only one master-will, dominant and universal, which shall animate, govern and direct all souls, all hearts and all wills: and the name of honor amongst Christians shall be no other than God's will in them, a will which shall rule over all wills, and transform them all into itself; so that the will of Christians and the will of Our Lord may be but one single will. (*Treatise on the Love of God*. Ch. VIII)

St. Louis de Montfort (†1716) once prayerfully lamented:

> Your divine commandments are broken, your Gospel is thrown aside, torrents of iniquity flood the whole earth carrying away even your servants... Will everything come to the same end as Sodom and Gomorrah?

---

* Unfortunately, some authors today—including a number of "professional Catholics" who find prophecy inconvenient to their preferred narrative—espouse the implicitly heretical view called "Preterism." (Some openly admit to being Preterists, others simply operate under this lie's influence without acknowledging they do so.) This ideology interprets all the prophecies of Scripture as having already been fulfilled in the very first century of Christianity, thus robbing the entire Bible of any prophetic relevance for us today. This view is entirely absent from 1,500 years of Sacred Tradition, having only reared its ugly head in the 16th century. (I call it "de facto" heretical since it is a doctrine of the Church that any unanimous consensus of the Fathers is, by that very fact, dogmatic. (For example, "*It is not permissible for anyone to interpret Holy Scripture in a sense contrary to ... the unanimous consent of the fathers,*" Decrees of the First Vatican Council. Chapter 2.9. The same thing was taught centuries earlier at the Council of Trent.) And the Fathers were indeed unanimous in contradicting "Preterist" principles. Let us, therefore, simply leave aside those who reject the teaching of St. Paul, "**Despise not prophecies**," (1 Thessalonians 5:20)—and let us turn again to more of the prophecies themselves.

> Will you never break your silence? Will you tolerate all this for ever? **Is it not true that your will must be done on earth as it is in heaven? Is it not true that your kingdom must come? Did you not give to some souls, dear to you, a vision of the future renewal of the Church?**[415]

This, of course, he asked rhetorically. He knew full well that these prophecies *would* be fulfilled, though he justly agonized in seeing the delay (he wrote this as the "Enlightenment" had recently begun wreaking spiritual and moral havoc as never before in the Church's history). But when speaking directly of what he knew would come, he taught:

> ...this will happen especially towards the end of the world, and indeed soon, because Almighty God and his holy Mother are to raise up great saints who will surpass in holiness most other saints as much as the cedars of Lebanon tower above little shrubs...These great souls filled with grace and zeal will be chosen to oppose the enemies of God who are raging on all sides. ... they will fight with one hand and build with the other. ... This seems to have been foretold by the Holy Spirit in Psalm 58: "The Lord will reign in Jacob and all the ends of the earth."[416]

It was the 20th century, however, that saw the greatest flourishing of the prophecies of the coming of the Kingdom—which can equivalently be called the Era of Peace, the Triumph of the Immaculate Heart, the Eucharistic Reign, the Reign of the Divine Will, the Coming of Christ *in Grace* (not in the flesh; which is only at the end of time), or the Fulfillment of the Our Father prayer. Just as the times proximate to Redemption saw a great increase of prophetic fervency, so do our own days display the same pattern.

> ... there will certainly be no more need for us to labor further to see **all things restored in Christ**. **Nor is it for the attainment of eternal welfare alone that this will be of service**—it will also contribute largely to temporal welfare and the advantage of human society ... when [piety] is strong and flourishing **'the people will' truly 'sit in the fullness of peace ...** May God, "who is rich in mercy", benignly speed **this restoration of the human race in Jesus Christ**... (Pope St. Pius X, *E Supremi*, §14)
> [As Jesus said:] 'And they shall hear my voice, and there shall be one fold and one shepherd.' May God ... **bring to fulfillment His prophecy by transforming this consoling vision of the future into a present reality**. (Pope Pius XI, *Ubi Arcano Dei Consilio*, §63)
> When once men recognize, both in private and in public life, that Christ is King, society will at last receive the great blessings ... **there seems no reason why we should despair of seeing *that* peace which the King of Peace came to bring on earth.** (Pope Pius XI, *Quas Primas*, §19)
> **"Christ must reign" (1 Corinthians xv, 25); "Thy kingdom come" (Matth. vi, 10).** ... We instituted the Feast of Christ the King of All, to be solemnly celebrated throughout the whole Christian world. **Now when**

> **we did this, not only did we set in a clear light that supreme sovereignty which Christ holds over the whole universe**, over civil and domestic society, and over individual men, **but at the same time we anticipated the joys of that most auspicious day, whereon the whole world will gladly and willingly render obedience to the most sweet lordship of Christ the King**. (Pope Pius XI, *Miserentissimus Redemptor*, §4,5)

Pius XI knew some were contradicting the clear sense of his earlier encyclical, *Quas Primas* (instituting the Feast of Christ the King), by alleging that its prophecies were only descriptions of the universality of Christ's reign which He *already* enjoys due to His Omnipotence. Therefore, in the Encyclical immediately above, the Pope ensured none could forget or water down what he had taught—he insists that a future day *will* come whereupon Christ shall reign over the entire world in a far greater manner than He ever has before.

The next Pontiff, Venerable Pope Pius XII, recalled his predecessor's teaching and prayed that "...an era of peace and true prosperity may come upon all the nations."[417] That same year he wrote, in an Encyclical:

> **In union with Christ take your stand as suppliants before the Heavenly Father and allow that prayer to rise to Him from your lips again and again ... '...** ***Thy will be done on earth, as it is in heaven!'*** **Only then shall we be influenced solely by the honor of God and by zeal to give Him greater glory, when we earnestly desire the restoration of His Kingdom—the Kingdom of justice, of love, and of peace—throughout all the world**."[418]

There, in one paragraph, is our mission—letting our life's very mantra become the central petition Christ entrusted to us. And it derives from a high-level act of the Magisterium from a particularly saintly Pope of the 20th century. We could review so many more Papal quotes (not to mention authentic private revelations, with which we have been deluged for the last century, testifying to the reality of the coming of this Kingdom), but for the sake of space, let us consider just one more Pontiff.

> "This is our great hope and our petition: 'Your Kingdom come'—a kingdom of peace, justice, and serenity, that will re-establish the original harmony of creation."[419] "A preferential love for Christ means a preference for what Christ loves, a desire to have the same attitude as Christ himself, a longing to see God's 'kingdom come on earth as it is in heaven.'"[420] (John Paul II)

Pope St. John Paul II, in an address he gave about St. Hannibal di Francia (the saint, recall, who had dedicated himself to promoting Jesus' revelations to Luisa Piccarreta), declared:

> [St. Hannibal] saw ... the means God himself had provided to bring about that "new and divine" holiness with which the Holy Spirit wishes to enrich Christians at the dawn of the third millennium, in order to

"make Christ the heart of the world."[421]

"The means" to "make Christ the heart of the world" at the "dawn of the third millennium" centralize around the Our Father prayer, particularly its supreme petition: *Thy Will be done on earth as it is in Heaven!* Commenting on this teaching of John Paul II, Fr. George Kosicki, that great Apostle of Divine Mercy, taught:

> **Pope John Paul II recently wrote of a "'new and divine' holiness** ... [which] is a maturing of the holiness of Jesus revealed in the Gospels. **It is living the fullness of the Lord's Prayer**—His kingdom come—that the Lord reign in our hearts now by the Holy Spirit to the glory of God the Father"—**that His will be done on earth now as it is in heaven** ... **We [live the fullness of the Our Father] by becoming holy through the Holy Spirit and by doing and <u>living in God's will on earth as in heaven</u>** ... We are to become a living presence of Jesus radiating His love and mercy as we live in and by His will." (*Be Holy!* Chapter 12)

St. Thomas Aquinas taught that *all things find their perfection in returning to their origin.*[422] And the origin of the Christian mission is none other than the supplication, on the lips of the Son of God Himself, for God's Will to be done on earth as in Heaven. It therefore is within this same prophecy and prayer that we find our Penultimate Destiny.

And I conclude this book by exhorting all to make that their mission as well: to strive to live the Lord's Prayer and to proclaim its fulfillment on earth. This means doing everything we can to become a saint. Without exception, we must obey all the commandments and believe all the teachings of the Church. We must love God with all our heart, soul, mind, and strength, and love our neighbor as ourselves (cf. Matthew 22:37,39); forgiving all offenses as we ourselves hope to be forgiven. But we must go further. There are many helps to our sanctification: living lives centered on the Eucharist—attending Mass and receiving Communion as often as possible, fostering a strong devotion and consecration to the Blessed Virgin Mary (especially important here is the daily Rosary), frequenting Confession, having a strong devotion to the Divine Mercy (as revealed to St. Faustina), fasting, reading Scripture, doing works of mercy, and offering up all of our sufferings to Christ in union with His sufferings—bearing each cross He sends us with resignation, patience, peace, and joy. Above all, ever handing our own self-wills entirely over to Him so that we may instead live only in His Will. We should say continually, "**Jesus, I trust in You. Thy Will be done. I give You my will, please give me Yours in return. Let Your Kingdom come! Let Your Will be done, on earth as it is in Heaven!**"

When thus striving to live in His Will, we can proclaim His Will with more power than ever before. We can tell the world that Christ *will* Triumph, but that He is waiting for us to sufficiently long for and pray for the arrival of His Reign, so that its inauguration constitutes a response to our ardent desire for its arrival. We can, and must, tell the "bad news" as well—warning souls of the imminent diabolical deceptions in order to "snatch them out of the fire" (Jude 1:23)—but we can do so while also presenting these apocalyptic realities as what they are: mere precursors to the Triumph of Christ the King.

> **"The time will come when Jesus will triumph over all, and His kingdom on earth will certainly come**, because it is a decree of God ... However, **blessed are those who interest themselves in His Will, because the Lord will use them to open the ways which had been closed** ... in order to open Heaven and to make It descend and reign upon earth."[423] "**If the Divine Fiat is known, the kingdom of the enemy is over. Here is all his rage.** But the Lord will win, because it is divine decree that His Kingdom will come upon earth. It is a matter of time, but He will make His way; He lacks neither power nor wisdom to dispose the circumstances. But I tell you: whatever you can do [to make the Divine Will known]—do it."[424] (Letters of the Servant of God Luisa Piccarreta)

Confidence in God is never unrewarded. It is not even possible for us to overestimate His power. And Christ, the only Son of God, is the King of All. Therefore, He will win—not only beyond history but also within it. He will Triumph over everything. The only question is when—that is, just how long the great trials must persist until His Victory. And what shortens that time of trial and hastens His victory is our proclaiming His Kingdom.

> "Truly, truly, I say to you, if you ask anything of the Father, he will give it to you in my name." (John 16:23) **Christian hope sustains us ... and leads us to pray as Jesus taught us: "Thy Kingdom come. Thy will be done, on earth as it is in heaven."** (Pope St. John Paul II. *Redemptoris Missio*, §86) "The Queen of Heaven ... continuously prays that the Kingdom of the Divine Will come on earth, and when have We ever denied her anything? ... She will put to flight all the enemies... **She will give unheard-of graces, surprises never seen, miracles that will shake Heaven and earth.** We give her the whole field free so that she will form for Us the Kingdom of Our Will on earth.... Therefore, you also pray together with her, and at its time you will obtain the intent." (Jesus to the Servant of God Luisa Piccarreta.)

PUBLISHED ON THE FEAST OF OUR LADY OF VICTORY.
OCTOBER 7, 2023.

APPENDICES

34. Additional Considerations

The Vindication of Catholicism

A few Protestant Christians and Eastern Orthodox Christians have ridiculed the Catholic Church's supposed acceptance of alien belief as if this were a testament to its deprivation of Divine authority and a vindication of their own denominations. They point to the many Catholic ET promoters (whom we have refuted in this book) as evidence of their identification of alien belief with Catholicism itself. In fact, no assessment of the situation could be further from the truth.

When the extraterrestrial conversation was raging in Christendom in the 19th century, it was by far the Catholics who had the smallest percentage succumbing to the deception; Protestant authors gobbled it up to a much higher proportion. Today, certain circles within Evangelicalism are indeed quite strong in rejecting the ET Deception, but mainline Protestantism appears to welcome it at least as readily as mainstream Catholicism. But "mainstream Catholicism" is not Catholicism. Catholicism itself is found in the Church's Magisterium, Sacraments, Liturgy, Ecumenical Councils, consensus of the Saints, etc. In not one of *these* realms is there any embrace of ET belief; only the opposite.

Just as the Catholic Church stands alone today in fully resolutely opposing certain grave evils like contraception, so too she stands alone in opposing the ET Deception in her official teachings. Admittedly, the Magisterium of the Catholic Church is not *as* clear in opposition to aliens as it is to the aforementioned evil. There is not an explicit dogma directly anathematizing belief in aliens. But, as I demonstrated in Part Two of this book, the opposition is nevertheless sufficiently clear to the point that any faithful Catholic, who sincerely desires to abide in the full truth of the Faith and all its corollaries, will have little difficulty in seeing—from Catholicism alone—that there are no aliens. The Catechism rules out aliens. The compendium of the Social Doctrine of the Church rules out aliens. The Second Vatican Council rules out aliens. Pope Zachary ruled out aliens. Pope Pius II ruled out aliens. Pope Pius XII implicitly ruled out aliens. Pope Leo XIII implicitly ruled out aliens. Sacred Tradition rules out aliens. Catholic Mariology, Ecclesiology, Christology, and Eschatology rule out aliens. And on the list goes. No other Church can claim this as much as the Catholic Church can.

Tragically, many individual Catholics—including many men in the Vatican—have condoned alien belief. As all Catholics should know, however, personal opinions of men in the Vatican, including personal opinions of the Pope, do not comprise the Magisterium of the Catholic Church.

The Truth About ETs in a Nutshell

Lest anyone be confused about the proper way of categorizing the contemporary ET phenomenon, we should briefly summarize the truth, in juxtaposition to the errors on both sides, in one table.

False:	ETs exist; the galaxies are filled with civilizations like ours (some far more advanced), and they are now visiting (or might soon visit) earth
False:	ETs truly exist as physical (or "somewhat physical") beings, but they are demons, semi-demons, or quasi-angels.
True:	**There are no extraterrestrials. Most claims pertaining to them are simply bogus. The remaining (e.g., "non-debunkable UFOs") are *demonic illusions*; not literally incarnate demons. (There is no such thing as a physical demon/angel; such creatures are *all*, without exception, *purely* spiritual beings.)**
False:	All UFO sightings/ "ET" contact experiences are simply hoaxes, ordinary natural events misinterpreted, hallucinations, etc.
False:	UFOs/ETs are real, but are not visitors from space; they are "interdimensional" or "time travelling" visitors.

Pope Francis on Aliens

On May 13, 2014, news headlines across the globe spoke of Pope Francis and Martians. For example, TIME magazine's headline read: "*Pope Francis Says He Would Baptize Martians If They Asked.*" The homily itself, given the day before, was markedly different in tone. Commenting on Acts Chapter 11, wherein the apostle Peter's words compelled the circumcised believers to acknowledge that "*God has then granted life-giving repentance to the Gentiles too,*" (Acts 11:18) Pope Francis gave a teaching which the Vatican recounts as follows:

> Indeed, for them it was unthinkable even to enter a house and sit at table with uncircumcised men, for reasons of impurity. Yet Peter not only did this but he even baptized them. In short, the Pope said, they thought he was was [sic] a "madman". Just as if, for example, tomorrow

an expedition of Martians came ... green, with long noses and big ears, just like children draw them ... and one were to say, 'I want to be baptized!'. What would happen?[425] [*Note: the ellipses were in the Vatican's original account. I have not abridged any portion of this quote.*]

The most important thing for us to understand is that Pope Francis' personal opinions—expressed, for example, in interviews, social media, homilies, talks, etc.—are not Magisterial. He is free to hold them and announce them, but Catholics are free to disagree. Even if Pope Francis believes in Martians, no Catholic is obliged to share that (deeply mistaken) belief. Catholics are bound to Magisterial teachings, but neither Francis nor any Pope in history has ever promulgated any Magisterial texts supportive of alien belief. Plenty of Magisterial texts, however, have contradicted alien belief!

Nevertheless, this homily is anything but an indication that Francis believes in aliens. Contrary to the headlines, the Pope does not even say a "Martian" should be baptized (though, admittedly, that appears to be the implication). He was exploring a Scriptural teaching using an example common in contemporary theological discourse. If we can glean how Francis feels about the topic from the wording he chose, the better conclusion is that he regards aliens as *unlikely*, as he chooses to poke fun at the notion itself by alluding to Martians "just like children draw them," being "green, with long noses and big ears." These are not the words of someone who takes the possibility of Martians seriously. Moreover, no one who seriously believes in extraterrestrials would, since 1964, use the term "Martians," as it has been proven since then (via Mariner 4's flyby) that Mars is uninhabited. Whoever refers to "Martians" today is more than likely poking fun at those who believe in extraterrestrials. Indeed, as outlandish as his comment was, the Pope's only point in these remarks is that all are called to baptism.

The very next day, TIME magazine seemed to realize its initial headline was misleading, for it published another article noting, "*Pope Francis was using Martians to illustrate that the church must be open to whatever, or whoever, may seem socially foreign and unaccepted.*"[426]

Two years later, in an interview, Francis was asked about his views on the existence of other beings in the universe (i.e., aliens), and responded "Honestly I wouldn't know how to answer."[427]

Still later developments also seem to indicate that Francis' Martian comments were only a consideration of what would logically follow from a hypothetical premise he regarded as counterfactual. And at this point, we are at last dealing with a *Magisterial* text. On June 19th, 2023, the 400th anniversary of the birth of Blaise Pascal, Pope Francis promulgated *Sublimitas et Miseria Hominis*, dedicated to extolling the great 17th century thinker. Within that Apostolic Letter, Pope Francis taught:

... Pascal recognized the limits of those philosophies: Stoicism leads to

> pride; scepticism to despair. **Human reason is a marvel of creation, which sets man apart from all other creatures**, for "man is but a reed, the weakest in nature, yet he is a thinking reed". The limits of the philosophers are thus, quite simply, the limits of created reason. Democritus might well say, "I am going to speak about everything", but reason cannot, of itself, resolve the deepest and most urgent issues. In the end, both for the age of Pascal as well as for our own, what remains the greatest and most pressing question? It is that of the overall meaning of our destiny, our life and our hope, which is directed to a happiness that we are not forbidden to imagine as eternal, but which God alone can grant...[428]

Here as with our Part Two considerations of the Catechism and other Magisterial Documents, we must begin by acknowledging the futility of an ET promoter arguing, in relation to the bolded clause above, *"all this means is that **humans** are the only creatures with **human** reason. It doesn't mean they are the only creatures **with reason**."* Such an interpretation would render the Pope's teaching empty, pointless, and absurdly truistic. Secondly, "human reason" is simply "reason." There are not different types of reason—there is just reason.

More subtle but equally important are the implications Pope Francis makes with three separate indications pertaining to the context of this teaching. Within the same paragraph he brings up two ancient Pagan Greek philosophies (the first being Stoicism, and the second being the philosophy of Democritus—both of which, famously, advocated for extraterrestrial intelligence). Finally, Pascal himself—the subject of this document—also spoke on the matter, and appeared to dismiss the possibility of aliens, famously writing (of the planets of the cosmos): "**the silence of these infinite spaces frightens me**."

Assuredly, the teaching that man is the only being of "all other creatures" who has reason is, in and of itself, a rejection of aliens. However, when we combine this teaching with a consideration of its context, we are doubly (or, rather, triply) reminded of the same.

Transgenderism and the ET Deception

At various points throughout this book, we have discussed similarities between transgender ideology and alien belief promotion, therefore this appendix is in order collecting loose ends by way of the following table.

The ET Deception	Transgender Ideology
Condemns the "traditional binary view of reality"	Condemns the "traditional binary view of reality"
Rejects the human (rational)/non-human (irrational) dichotomy. Insists upon "NHI" and many other physical beings with reason.	Rejects the male/female dichotomy. Insists there is a "non-binary" option, and countless additional genders.
Rejects the earth/everything else dichotomy	Rejects the normal/disordered dichotomy
Clearly ruled out by Scripture, Tradition, and Magisterium, but not dogmatically and directly condemned (explicitly) by them	Clearly ruled out by Scripture, Tradition, and Magisterium, but not dogmatically and directly condemned (explicitly) by them
Unheard of in Christendom before the "Enlightenment"	Unheard of in Christendom before the "Sexual Revolution"
Suddenly endorsed by many "Christian theologians"	Suddenly endorsed by many "Christian theologians"
Sudden explosion of "ETs"/UFOs starting in 1947	Sudden explosion of "transgender" individuals starting in the 2000s
Fundamental attack on human nature (regarding it as just one of many rational incarnate natures)	Fundamental attack on human nature (regarding its creation as male and female as just two of many genders)
Apocalyptic test: see Part Four.	Apocalyptic test: "gender ideology...will be the ultimate rebellion against God the Creator." (Pope Benedict XVI)[429]

"Limiting God": An Irreverent Accusation

In Part One of this book, we considered how baseless is the castigation, levied by ET promoters against those who do not believe in aliens, that the latter are guilty of "limiting God." More on this point, however, should be considered.

St. Augustine's most famous line—one of the most well-known quotes, in fact, from any saint—is a simple but profound teaching. Relayed in a heartfelt prayer to the Lord in his *Confessions*, this Father of the Church wrote, "**Thou hast formed us for Thyself, and our hearts are restless till they find rest in Thee**." (1,1.5) Indeed, a morally lamentable *restlessness* has reached epidemic proportions in the Church today. Instead of allowing their souls to find rest in God alone—His Word, His Will, and His Truth—many Christians seek for metaphysical rest elsewhere. They seek the fulfilment of their deepest secret hopes, excitements, and aspirations in theories based on science-fiction; above all, in their expectations of imminent discovery of extraterrestrial civilizations.

It appears that this *restlessness* with what God *has* done compels the Christian ET promoter to become unjustly bored with creation and Revelation, hence his willingness to levy the "limiting God" accusation against those who believe that *what we've been told God did is in fact what God did.* Since the human mind has a miraculous potency for the infinite, it is always ontologically capable of looking at any finite reality and immediately grasping how much more *could* be done than what is contained within it. Despite the world's immensity and the massive number of humans who have already lived within it, we can nevertheless grasp the boundaries of these quantities, and this makes it possible to (falsely and irreverently) insist *"God is so great; there simply* ***must*** *be vastly more incarnate intelligent civilizations than earth's."*

If God had filled each planet of each galaxy with billions of aliens each, the entirety of creation would still be *nothing* compared to Him, and we would still be equally—falsely—"justified" in asserting the same nonsense: "this simply *can't* be all there is!" But we can take it much further still. Had God created trillions of universes, each one trillions of times bigger than our own and filled to the brim with incarnate intelligent beings, this will *still* be absolutely *nothing* compared to Himself; it still would be fundamentally incapable of filling Heaven with sufficient glory to keep us enraptured forever. Subtract any quantity—no matter how great—from infinity, and we are still left with infinity. The distance between what God "could have done" in creation, and what He *did* do in creation, will always, definitionally, be infinite. In a word, there is no such thing as an exhaustive outlet for the infinite within the finite (as the material universe, definitionally, is).

This does not, however, present any problem for the faithful Christian. The purpose of the material universe is not to, *on its own,* serve as an exhaustive outlet for God's infinite power. The purpose of the universe is to house man, the purpose of man is to house God—in his own soul—and the purpose of man's housing of God is oriented towards *eternity alone.*

Moreover, the joys of eternity are not constrained by what transpires within time (in creation) in a comparable manner as that by which a building is constrained by its own foundation of concrete. In the latter scenario, a building's height is indeed fundamentally limited by the strength of its foundation. Since there is only so much height and weight a given foundation can support, one is justified, upon observing a foundation fit only for a mansion, in ruling out any hope of seeing a skyscraper built upon it.

If a skyscraper is what he was hoping to see, then disappointment is entirely warranted.

If that analogy were fitting, then one could likewise defend disappointment—or, rather, downright existential despair—in looking at earth's "smallness." He would be justified in lamenting, "*eternity is to go on forever; how can these events transpiring on this little third rock from the sun possibly lend sufficient material for Heaven's eternal embellishment?*" Such a man might feel compelled to insist that there "must" be "so much more life" out there when he gazes upon the night sky—the very insistence would serve him as a defense mechanism to escape his sorrow.

This situation is like man chasing mysticism through hallucinogenic chemicals: not only will he never find what he is seeking—for his method of pursuing it is fundamentally flawed, for the reasons described above—he will only, with each additional use of these illicit substances, retreat farther and farther from the enlightenment he craves.

A better analogy for the material universe's relationship to eternity would be to compare all that transpires in creation, within time, to the sun. Each act done within time that accords with God's Will is like another beam of light emitted from this sun, propelled at breathtaking speeds into the great expanse, which we will consider analogous to eternity. Each of these beams, however, has the miraculous ability to expand and multiply without end; venturing ever further into this infinite expanse forever and ever.

Therefore, no matter "when," in eternity, one beholds the joys therein, he can trace back its origin to something that transpired within time, in the material world as we know it today. Yet this in no way limits eternity; it is simply the origin of eternity's glories. There lies the incomprehensible importance of our lives down here: our temporal acts "echo through eternity," and the emission of these "original beams of light" is restricted to this incredibly short existence that is life on earth. Once it passes, all opportunity to gain merit ceases forever.

But Almighty God, in His great Magnanimity, did not stop upon merely doing what was *sufficient* for eternal beatitude. Rather, He has (thus far) allowed thousands of years of human history to transpire, already encompassing more embellishments for our eternal fatherland than we can possibly now imagine, built up by billions upon billions of His beloved children and above all His own Incarnation, death, Resurrection, and Ascension into Heaven. And each act we still now do, in His Will, further glorifies our Heavenly home. In a word, there is *nothing* lacking, in what God has done and will do on earth, in order to build up our Heavenly homeland in the most glorious manner imaginable: there is absolutely no need for us to posit alien civilizations to render eternal glory satisfying or complete.*

If most Christian ET promoters are honest with themselves, I suspect they will realize they have spent far too little time meditating upon Heaven. The absence of sufficient emphasis on this practice from their lives has created a hole in their hearts, which they have sought to fill with the prevailing modern Pagan myths: the sci-fi inspired theories about aliens.

Consider, as well, that a single angel's glory is doubtless so immense that, if the world were really given a direct taste of this beauty, it would be enough to enrapture all earth's inhabitants until the end of time. It would make all of our science, all of our technology, all of our culture, seem like a silly child's toy. Yet we have not merely a single angel, but rather, an incomprehensible array of them—ever surrounding us, along with the Faithful Departed, in "so great a cloud of witnesses" (Hebrews 12:1). Believe in them. Pray for their intercession. Think about them often. Recognize their presence. Do these things, and you will quickly realize how foolish it is to suppose that not believing in alien civilizations is in any way problematic; in any way guilty of "limiting God" or "demystifying the cosmos." Indeed, if anything, what is needed today is a *re*-mystification of the cosmos! Many early and medieval Christians believed each star had an angel entrusted to it, to cause its motion. There is nothing wrong with continuing to believe that today.

When gazing upon the breathtaking night sky—whether images from telescopes or merely what you can behold with the naked eye from your backyard—Christians who recognize there are no aliens should be far more enraptured than those ET promoters who gaze upon the same expanse not with pious wonder at God's glory, but with giddy excitement about alien contact. For we can there see the "playground of the angels." We can see, in that incomprehensible immensity, a tiny glimpse of the immensity of eternity which, please God, we shall dwell within the twinkling of an eye. We can be reminded of the abiding presence of the Communion of Saints—all the faithful departed—looking down upon us. We can be *mystics*. And *mysticism*—not *Star Trek*—is what the Church needs today.

---

* Moreover, while it is true that what is done on earth echoes through eternity, redounding to the greater glory of God and of His angels and saints (a rank, please God, we ourselves will soon number among), it nevertheless remains the case that the motive force of Heaven is derived from the Creator Himself—namely, from the direct vision of His essence; the "Beatific Vision," which is the infinite wellspring of all Heaven's joys. That Vision alone makes it categorically impossible for eternity to ever be lacking anything, and that Vision hasn't even the slightest bit to do with how many rational incarnate creatures God made. Had God only created a tiny group of humans, that would be no impediment to the glory of the "world without end."

Msgr. Balducci and the Diabolical: Behind How Many Rocks Does the Devil Lie in Wait?

Experienced exorcists are accustomed to regularly assuring many well-meaning but overzealous Catholics that cases they think to consist in demonic possession are, almost certainly, *not*. Indeed, while diabolical possession indeed occurs in large *absolute* numbers, and is increasing, while understandably garnering an outsize degree of attention, it only accounts for a minuscule fraction of the situations wherein the Devil seeks to implement his plans. Satan is entirely uninterested in sending a demon to possess the vast majority of the people in the world. He does not want to scare souls into the arms of the One he calls the enemy. He is much more interested in simply promoting errors and tempting souls to sin; methods far more effective in securing the damnation of souls. In fact, diabolical possession is morally indifferent—in itself, it is neither an indication of the holiness or sinfulness of the victim; it is simply a cross.

Perhaps annoyed by the need to give this assurance so often, Monsignor Balducci seems to have adopted a generally flippant attitude about the presence of the demonic in the *world*. This is surprising, since he was well known for arguing that even "rock" music itself is diabolical—a thesis one would expect from the very "fundamentalists" he castigates for seeing the demonic behind UFOs—but that thesis of his appears to be an odd exception to his approach to such matters. In one popular interview given at the same time he was promoting Ufology, he even declared:

> In this era of fear and anxiety many people convince themselves they are possessed**; it's purely psychosomatic**.[430]

Indeed, Msgr. Balducci appears excessively and tellingly anxious about the possibility of concluding diabolical activity exists where it does not. This is evident in his scolding of the renowned 19th and 20th century devout Catholic author, Leon Bloy, who had issued a number of stinging critiques against the rationalism of the clergy of his day. For it was a time when most, caught up in the false spirit of their age, appeared to regard spiritual deliverance in general (not only the Rite of Exorcism) as "unscientific." Rightly did this trend rouse Bloy's righteous indignation, and the denunciations he offered of it did not always make friends. Even if Bloy's zeal was at times somewhat excessive and his writings not always "nuanced," the substance of his admonishments were nevertheless spot-on. Balducci, however, ridicules them. In one book, Balducci claimed, "*it goes without saying that the position of Leon Bloy is an example of unwarranted credulity in diabolical intervention... 'some of the faithful and certain priests... [suffer from] ignorance of mental and nervous pathology'...[this is] reprehensible...an exaggerated preternaturalism...[presents] obstacles to a balanced religious and moral formation. It also fosters a sense of distrust, if not outright contempt and disdain, for theology...*"[431]

These unhinged attacks on Bloy, presented as "going without saying," reveal a serious problem indeed—not in Bloy, but in Balducci. It is absurd to claim that Bloy's approach is "reprehensible" or fostering "outright contempt and disdain for theology." The fruits bear witness that Bloy did the very opposite. Balducci, however, evidently quite proud of his education in "parapsychology" (pseudoscience), had all the training in sophistry one needs to explain away the presence of the diabolical as a merely "non-ordinary psychological" phenomenon, and to dismiss—as "*ignorant of mental and nervous pathology*"—those of simple and strong Faith who have the discernment needed to recognize evil when they see it. Moreover, Balducci had his status as an exorcist to rely on in order to give the deceptive appearance of infallibility to his every pronouncement in this arena; when, in fact, we can now clearly see that his dismissive attitude on the deceptions of demons was merely the theological rationalization he needed to justify collaborating with and encouraging outright occultists in Ufology. (See Part Four.)

Returning to Bloy, we should acknowledge that he is even quoted in a Magisterial document—*Gaudete et Exsultate*—wherein he wisely taught that "*there is only one tragedy, ultimately: not to have been a saint.*" The same Pontiff, Pope Francis, also quoted Bloy in his very first homily, stating:

> **When one does not confess Jesus Christ, I am reminded of the expression of Léon Bloy: 'He who does not pray to the Lord prays to the devil.' When one does not confess Jesus Christ, one confesses the worldliness of the devil.**

This teaching is, in fact, a cutting reproach of Ufology. One finds that field replete with "prayer" indeed, but only a twisted version thereof, with none of it directed to the Lord. What, then, remains? Only the Devil—though assuming a deceptive aspect of an extraterrestrial. In a word: Bloy is the vindicated one here, not Balducci. Bloy was a radical Catholic indeed, even willingly living in total Gospel poverty, and he was despised by the establishment. A fierce critic of lukewarm Catholicism, he was disdained by the objects of his well-placed reproaches.

Despite Bloy's personal struggles, he was undoubtedly a powerful voice in support of the Faith and it is beyond question that his overall legacy is one of drawing an enormous number of souls to Catholicism. And it is Bloy's approach to theology that Msgr. Balducci slanderously repudiates. In issuing these reproaches, Msgr. Balducci tells us much more about himself than about the French poet.

While those who wish to do so are free to—like Balducci—focus on Bloy's faults, I side with Monsignor Richard Antall, who wrote:

> Those who were loyal to Bloy, including his godchildren, Jacques and Raissa Maritain, leaders of a Catholic intellectual renaissance in France, overlooked his faults and saw him as **a hero of unflinching honesty**.

> Perhaps it was because his talent went unrecognized or because his uncompromising passion for the poor was so self-sacrificing, they esteemed his never-ending and unrewarded pursuit of God's truth. ...He said, memorably, "*The only real sadness, the only real failure, the only great tragedy in life, is not to become a saint.*" He lived at odds with his times, and with himself at times, but achieved an exceptional integrity. His was not an easy life. Yet I think perhaps he avoided what he called "the only great tragedy in life." **We could use some of his radicality now**.[432]

***

Whoever seeks wise advice against an exaggeration of the Devil's power, and desires instruction from an exorcist on that point, would be much better off turning to Fr. Chad Ripperger than to Msgr. Balducci. Fr. Ripperger cautioned:

> The second extreme consists of the person seeing a demon under every rock, so to speak. The person focuses on trying to find and root out diabolic activity. In this particular approach, the focus shifts from God to demons, and demons are more than happy to have one's attention as long as it is not on God, since their general principle is "anything but God." As the saying goes, "If you look for demons, they will find you." The fact of the matter is that God restricts the activity of demons, and therefore, they are not everywhere and in all circumstances. Some evil things that have occurred are simply the result of human choice. **That being said, prudence in this area resides in the individual addressing diabolic activity once it arises.**[433]

Incidentally, what Fr. Ripperger advises here is precisely why I am writing the book now before you. I did not grow up with a passion to address the diabolical in Ufology, nor have I gone about my spiritual life with such a concern anywhere near the fore of my mind. When, however I noticed (several years ago) the explosive rise in UFO phenomena and the corresponding heretical, blasphemous, occult, and New Age claims made in relation to it even in the Church—and the deafening silence of Catholic writers opposing this trend—I realized that something needed to be done. In March of 2021, I wrote my first major public piece against ET belief, and almost immediately thereafter I realized, from the amount of questions I was receiving, that a book was necessary. I commenced that work quickly, and you are now reading the eventual result of almost three years of effort.

Indeed, a wise approach to the diabolical is generally to not bother with it when it is not manifesting itself, but, *when it does*, to not fail to address it based on silly scruples like Balducci's, or that doing so "*might risk turning off someone by causing me to come off as too fundamentalist!*" For that latter attitude is nothing but pride—an infinitely worse vice than overzealousness.

I will add another personal note: if, of my two most recent books, the one now before you can be considered (a warning against) "the bad news," then my last book—*Thy Will Be Done*, published in 2021—is (an announcement of) "the good news." With its message of hope for our troubled times, especially considering diabolical deceptions infiltrating the Church, I do encourage you to read it and share that *good* news—the message of great hope found within.

35. Scripture Verses Abused by ET Promoters

In Part One, we saw that Scripture repeatedly rules out extraterrestrials. In Part Two, we carefully followed the development of Sacred Tradition and saw that for the first millennium-and-a-half of Church History, alien belief was completely rejected by all Catholics. Unfortunately, these facts neither stop post-Enlightenment ET Promoters from pretending aliens exist, nor do they prevent the same individuals from daring to assert that Scripture itself teaches there are aliens! Thus, they imply that the Holy Spirit was essentially absent from the Church's understanding of Scripture for almost the entirety of Catholicism's history, only to finally come on to the scene during the Enlightenment to point out that we were missing key verses in Scripture which reveal the existence of extraterrestrials. The outlandishness displayed here should alone dissuade any Christian from supposing that Scripture speaks of aliens. But we will also address the specific claims made.

John 10:16 and Jesus' "Other Sheep"

As is often noted, Jesus' own earthly ministry was almost entirely concerned with the Jews. As He Himself said, when He was approached by a non-Jew seeking His help, "**I was sent only to the lost sheep of the House of Israel**." (Matthew 15:24) Obviously, Christianity was for the entire world. But it took some time for Jesus to reveal this fully and clearly to His disciples. One such early indication He gave of this global mission of Christianity is seen when Jesus told His disciples:

> And other sheep I have, which are not of this fold: them also I must bring, and they shall hear my voice; and there shall be one fold, and one shepherd. (John 10:16)

Therefore, the true meaning of this verse is not mysterious. It is a reference to the "sheep" that were *all human beings*. Sacred Tradition has never taken this verse to be an oblique reference to any other notion—much less to life on other planets—and neither should we. Haydock's famous Catholic commentary on Scripture notes that this verse indicates "there shall be one church of Jews and Gentiles." St. Augustine said:

> This shows that the Lord is the cornerstone, uniting both walls in himself. Hosea's testimony is spoken of the Gentiles, but the Lord unites both Jews and Gentiles, according to what he said in the gospel [in John 10:16] ...
> So listen to this unity being even more urgently drawn to your attention: "I have other sheep," he says, "who are not of this fold." He was talking, you see, to the first sheepfold of the race of Israel according to the flesh. But there were others, of the race of the same Israel according

> to faith, and they were still outside, they were of the Gentiles, predestined but not yet gathered in. He knew those whom he had predestined. He knew those whom he had come to redeem by shedding his blood. He was able to see them, while they could not yet see him. He knew them, though they did not yet believe in him. "I have," he said, "other sheep that are not of this fold," because they are not of the race of Israel according to the flesh. But all the same, they will not be outside this sheepfold, because "I must bring them along too, so that there may be one flock and one shepherd." (Sermon 138.5)

Another Church Father, Bishop Theodore of Mopseuestia (†428) wrote, "This sentence [John 10:16] alludes to those among the Gentiles who will believe, because many among the Gentiles as well as many among the Jews are destined to gather together into a single church."

This same verse indicates there will be one shepherd (Christ Himself), but it also refers to the *Vicar* of Christ; the Pope. It is of course not possible for a certain man who serves as the Bishop of Rome to be the shepherd of those in other planets, much less other galaxies, therefore we see displayed within the verse itself that it cannot be taken as a reference to "other sheep" being extraterrestrials.

Revelation's "Third of the Stars" Falling and "Four Living Creatures"

Some ET promoters claim that the Book of Revelation's "third of the stars" falling is a reference to the actual stars scattered about the galaxies, with one-third of them hosting races of rational incarnate creatures who rebelled against God (as did earth in the Fall of Man), and two-thirds remaining unfallen. The passage they draw from is the following:

> Then another sign appeared in the sky; it was a huge red dragon, with seven heads and ten horns, and on its heads were seven diadems. **Its tail swept away a third of the stars in the sky and hurled them down <u>to the earth</u>**. (Revelation 12:3-4)

As we can see, the verse itself immediately refutes their interpretation. These "stars" were hurled down "to the earth." Obviously, however, no aliens were hurled down *to the earth*.

Indeed, Sacred Tradition gives us the correct understanding: these "stars" are references to the angels. In the beginning, a third of them fell and thus became fallen angels—demons. The "dragon" is the Devil—Satan—who brought those other angels with him. Even the verses immediately following that very passage explain its meaning:

> ... Michael and his angels battled against the dragon. The dragon and its angels fought back, but they did not prevail and there was no longer any place for them in heaven. The huge dragon, the ancient serpent, who is called the Devil and Satan, who deceived the whole world, **<u>was</u>**

> **thrown down to earth, and its angels were thrown down with it**. (Revelation 12:7-9)

It is clear from the very same chapter of Scripture that these "stars" are, in fact, angels. We should not be surprised to see that the entire testimony of Sacred Tradition is correct on this point. What is surprising and disconcerting is that even "orthodox Catholic" ET promoters deny that interpretation in favor of their own Pagan alien mythology which essentially promotes a Gnostic reinterpretation of Revelation.

Pope St. John Paul II even used this passage in his homily at the beatification of Sts. Francisco and Jacinta, saying:

> "*Another portent appeared in heaven; behold, a great red dragon*" (Rv 12:3). These words... make us think of the great struggle between good and evil, showing how, when man puts God aside, he cannot achieve happiness, but ends up destroying himself. ... **The message of Fátima is a call to conversion, alerting humanity to have nothing to do with the "dragon" whose "tail swept down a third of the stars of heaven, and cast them to the earth**" (Rv 12:4). Man's final goal is heaven, his true home, where the heavenly Father awaits everyone with his merciful love.[434]

The Pope is not here warning us to be on guard for aliens. He is warning us to have nothing to do with *demons*—which are exactly what the "stars" cast down to earth represent. There is a certain irony, therefore, in the suggestions of those ET promoters who would use this passage of Revelation to argue for aliens. For in so doing, they are succumbing to the very demonic ruse the correct understanding of the passage warns us *against*.

In his book, *Angels and Demons*, Fr. Serge-Thomas Bonino, OP, notes:

> ...Satan became the worst, because he turned to evil with all his strength, which was great. The book of Revelation declares that "[The dragon's] tail swept down a third of the stars of heaven and cast them to the earth" (Rv 12:4). Satan's sin involves the sin of many other angels, not through the influence of efficient causality or of constraint but by virtue of exhortation to evil—in other words, the moral causality of bad example. The manifestation of Satan's perverse will immediately incited the free consent of some angels. (Chapter 10: How Angels Became Demons).

There is, however, a secondary interpretation of Revelation 12:4 that has been put forth in Church history. Haydock's commentary first notes the traditional understanding (i.e., that these "stars" refer to the rebellious angels), before quoting the interpretation which would also (not instead of) understand this fall of a "third of the stars" as referring to certain groups of human beings who fall from grace. He explains: "Menochius interprets it [as] those bishops and eminent persons who fell under the weight of persecution, and apostatized."[435]

Therefore, while the *direct* understanding of Revelation 12:4 rightly regards the "stars" as symbolic for demons, a legitimate indirect application of the same verse can regard it as pertaining to men who likewise fall, by Satan's influence. What is certainly ridiculous, however (and ruled out by the unanimous testimony of Sacred Tradition, not to mention adjacent verses), is a *literalistic* reading of that verse which pretends the "stars" there referenced are the actual astronomical objects one sees in the night sky or material inhabitants thereof.

***

Catholic tradition is similarly clear on the meaning of the "Four Living Creatures" noted in Revelation Chapter Four—and it has nothing to do with any interpretation that gives one grounds to speculate about aliens, much less insist the verse refers to them.

The chapter begins with the verse, "After this I looked, and **lo, in heaven** an open door!" (Revelation 4:1) Clearly, Heaven *itself* is being described (not "*the heavens*," which can refer to what we see in the night sky). Several verses later, St. John describes:

> And round the throne, on each side of the throne, are four living creatures, full of eyes in front and behind: the first living creature like a lion, the second living creature like an ox, the third living creature with the face of a man, and the fourth living creature like a flying eagle. And the four living creatures, each of them with six wings, are full of eyes all round and within, and day and night they never cease to sing, "Holy, holy, holy, is the Lord God Almighty, who was and is and is to come!" (Revelation 4:6-8)

While some ET promoters take this as a reference to aliens, this interpretation is yet again repudiated by both the passage itself and by the unanimous consensus of Sacred Tradition (which is infallible).

The "six wings" can be taken as a reference to the Seraphim; who are the choir of angels closest to God, constantly immersed in worshipping Him. Joining with them, at the Holy Mass, we too say—before the Consecration—"Holy, Holy, Holy Lord..." Catholic teaching has always understood this *Sanctus* as an act of adoration joining with the angels—not "aliens."

As with the "third of the stars," other interpretations are acceptable. Some commentators take this as a reference to the Four Evangelists (Matthew, Mark, Luke, and John); this, indeed, is frequently depicted in Sacred art and architecture throughout Church history. Others take it as a reference to the prophets Isaiah, Jeremiah, Ezekiel, and Daniel. They interpret the description that they are "full of eyes all round and within" as a signification of their prophetic insight. Still others see it as symbolic of the episcopate. Now, some have argued that Revelation employs interpretations of constellations here, but even if that is correct, it is certainly not an attempt to impute literal incarnate creatures as abiding therein, but only to allude to the meanings given to constellations in various stories.

One thing is certain: nowhere in Sacred Tradition have any saints or Magisterial texts ever proposed that these "four living creatures" might be incarnate rational beings who are not human (much less that this is the correct interpretation).

We also must not miss that these "living creatures" are described in Revelation as "day and night ... never cease[ing] to sing." In other words, they need no sleep, no nourishment, and no rest—they need nothing other than to worship God. This cannot refer to any material creature without the Beatific Vision (i.e., not in Heaven), who could never do without such necessities (not even an "alien").

Isaiah 45, the "Vanity" of Lacking Habitation, and the Heavenly "Hosts"

In Part Two, we considered Sir David Brewster, a prominent Scottish ET Promoter of the 19th century. He insisted aliens must exist due to his interpretation of Isaiah 45:18. This verse reads:

> For thus saith the Lord that created the heavens, God himself that formed the earth, and made it, the very maker thereof: he did not create it in vain: he formed it to be inhabited. I am the Lord, and there is no other.

According to Brewster, this verse proves the existence of aliens because it indicates that "*planets without life would have been created in vain.*"[436] But since God clearly created the planets, and He does nothing in vain, they must all be inhabited. Therefore, in Brewster's mind, failing to believe in aliens was a great act of impiety, so he declared his "certainty" that aliens lived on the sun, the moon, and every other celestial body. He also insisted that "every planet and satellite... must have an atmosphere."[437] Here, he was essentially reiterating the famous "Principle of Plenitude," a hallmark of Enlightenment optimism, which most of the ET promoters of that era used in order to insist the heavenly bodies must each be teaming with rational incarnate beings.

Of course, science has since completely repudiated this theory: every single planet, moon, and other astronomical body that we have observed in detail has proven itself barren and devoid of *all* inhabitants, much less rational ones. Brewster, however, is not thus exonerated merely because he wrote before we had such knowledge. He should have concluded that there is nothing in Isaiah 45:18 indicating that *any* planet must be inhabited to render it "not in vain." In fact, only *earth* would have been in vain if made without inhabitants, as that was earth's *unique* purpose.

Moreover, had Brewster so much as consulted Scripture just six verses prior to the verse in question, he would have remembered the following:

> **I [God] made the earth, and created man upon it; it was my hands that stretched out the heavens, and I commanded all their host**. (Isaiah 45:12)

Indeed, the very same Scriptural passage Brewster cites as the justification for his alien belief also implicitly rules out that belief. As discussed in this book's opening chapters, a dichotomy is evident: two basic realms of the material universe exist: "earth" and "the heavens," whereas "man" (i.e., "rational animal," which would include aliens) is only spoken of as existing on earth. When considering "the heavens," there is only "their host"—whereas such "hosts" have always been understood as *angels*.

This fact is clear even elsewhere in Isaiah (e.g., Chapter 6, which repeatedly speaks of these "hosts" as angels), and in other Old Testament passages (e.g. Joshua 5:16-15, Genesis 32:1-2, *"And Jacob went on his way, and the angels of God met him. And when Jacob saw them, he said, This is God's host..."*). Indeed, "hosts" standing as a reference to *angels* has always been settled in Christian theology. There are hundreds of uses of this term in the Bible beyond those noted above, and none of them imply the term refers to human beings. The importance of the term as an angelic reference is so important to the Faith that it was even rightly brought back into the recitation of the *Sanctus*, in the English translation of the Catholic Mass promulgated in the year 2011.

Brewster, therefore, had no legitimate scientific ground on which to stand, and certainly no theological grounds whatsoever. Despite the futility of his argument, this did not prevent him and his contemporaries from dutifully espousing the spirit of their age—thus violating the command of scripture to "not conform yourselves to this age" (Romans 12:2)—in condemning anyone who failed to tow the alien belief line. (We saw in Part Two how viciously he castigated his contemporaries who spoke against aliens.)

Why Can't "Aliens" be *Angels*? The Book of Tobit and Ezekiel's "UFO"

In Part Four, we have demonstrated that all "non-debunkable" UFO sightings and "alien encounters" are nothing but demonic deceptions. A critic, however, may protest: *"Why can't we at least regard 'aliens' as angelic? Angels do not always immediately announce their nature when appearing. Perhaps they are just as likely as demons to appear as aliens; so maybe we should heed the teachings of the 'aliens,' on account of the possibility that they are actually angelic teachings. After all, an angel appeared to Tobit (5:12) saying he was 'Azarias the son of the great Ananias'."*

This move will not work. For an angel to appear as an "alien" would be for an angel to lie. An angel *cannot* lie, since all lies are sins, and it is impossible for an angel to sin. Note that the *Catechism of the Catholic Church* teaches:

> **By its very nature, lying is to be condemned.** It is a profanation of speech, whereas the purpose of speech is to communicate known truth to others. The deliberate intention of leading a neighbor into error by saying things contrary to the truth constitutes a failure in justice and charity. (§2458)

For an angel to assume a humanlike aspect when appearing is not a lie. It is rather appropriate, since the human form is the greatest of all forms in the material realm. The Book of Tobit is not the only example of such an appearance; for example, there were also the "three men" (Genesi 18) who appeared to Abraham, at least two of which were actually angels temporarily assuming corporeal forms (which is within the power of both angels and demons). Angels are not material beings, therefore to appear materially, they *must* assume *some* form that is not inherently their own. They have been known to assume many forms throughout Scripture and Sacred Tradition, but in no case did they issue any *deceptions* about reality, much less about their own nature. Even the angel in the Book of Tobit did *not* actually lie. One priest noted:

> St. Raphael did not lie when he said, *I am Azarias the son of the great Ananias*. There is no falsehood in this statement, since "Azarias" means "the healer of YHWH" and "Ananias" means "The goodness of YHWH" or "The grace of YHWH". Now, the Angel was then only disguising his true name (which means "God's healer") and testifying that he is sent into the world by God's goodness. Thus, he gives his name through a certain riddle—but Tobit was thereby led to believe that the Angel was only a man.
> Furthermore, Raphael truly states who he appeared to be. That is, the Angel truly declares who he came as. While it would have been a lie for Raphael to say, "*I am not angel but only a man*", he said no such thing. Rather, he identified himself in an obscure manner and, thereby, withheld from Tobit a truth which he had no right to know.[438]

***

Many ET promoters insist that the prophet Ezekiel himself saw a "UFO," as relayed in the first chapter of the Biblical book bearing his name. That passage is lengthy and need not be recounted in full here; suffice it to say that it describes an extraordinary angelic encounter involving fires, wheels, eyes, "living creatures" (not unlike Revelation 12:4), and other awesome sights to behold. Yet the passage describing this vision concludes with the following verse:

> **Such was the appearance of the likeness of the glory of the Lord. And**

> **when I saw it, I fell upon my face, and I heard the voice of one speaking**. (Ezekiel 1:28)

Scripture explicitly declares that this was not some incarnate creature of any sort (and certainly not an "alien" or "UFO")—it was, rather, an "appearance" of something like the "glory of the Lord." Whoever would claim this was actually an encounter with an alien civilization's spacecraft is expressly denying what the Bible explicitly says. Ezekiel's encounter cannot be both an "appearance of the likeness of the glory of the Lord" and a visitation from an ET's spacecraft. It is either one or the other. And it should not be difficult for a Christian to decide which it is.

Balaam's "Talking Donkey" in the Book of Numbers, and the Saints' Animals

In the Book of Numbers (and referred to in the New Testament in 2 Peter 2), we see a donkey "talking." This is of course not directly related to the ET Deception, but some may suppose it refutes what we considered in Part Five about the Animal Personhood Deception. But it does not. The passage in question reads:

> When the donkey saw the angel of the Lord, it lay down under Balaam, and he was angry and beat it with his staff. **Then the Lord opened the donkey's mouth**, and it said to Balaam, "What have I done to you to make you beat me these three times?" (Numbers 22:27-28)

As we can see, this was an occasion of *God working a miracle* and speaking *through* something. The passage above explicitly says as much by indicating that *the Lord intervened* to cause what transpired (it does not simply say that the donkey decided to discuss the matter with Balaam!). Clearly, this was not an example of an animal exercising reason any more than Exodus 3 (wherein God spoke to Moses via the Burning Bush) was an example of a plant exercising reason, or Matthew 17 (wherein God spoke to Peter, James, and John through a cloud) was an example of an atmospheric phenomenon exercising reason. It is precisely *because* everybody knows it is impossible for donkeys to speak that this was indeed a miracle, and Balaam recognized it as such.

Similarly, throughout 2,000 years of Church History, there are countless authentic reports of statues of Jesus, Mary, or the saints "coming to life" and imparting messages. Does this mean that we are now to regard statues as likewise having the capacity for reason? Obviously not. These, too, are miracles.

Many stories of St. Francis of Assisi, St. Anthony, and other saints describe them "talking to" animals. We all know of St. Francis "convincing" the wolf to stop attacking people in a certain village, St. Anthony "preaching to the fishes," etc. These are beautiful accounts of individual saints glimpsing a restoration of the Order of Eden in their own lives. Indeed, before the Fall, all animals would automatically honor and obey man just as even now a loyal and well-trained dog honors and obeys its owner. In no such case, however, is the animal exercising reason or employing language (such faculties were not possessed by animals even before the Fall). Instead, these are simply examples of animals acting in accordance with their prelapsarian nature (although animals have no moral fault, they nevertheless are affected by the Fall). The animals that Francis, Anthony, and other saints "spoke to" did not rationally comprehend the words of the saints. The rational content of the words these saints spoke were for *us*, not for the animals. These beasts simply, by a miracle of God, reverted to their original instincts, and were at least able to "grasp" the gist of the command of the saint, just as even an ordinary dog will often "grasp" its own owner's commands. There is another obvious reason these are not examples of animals exercising reason: the animals did not speak back, nor did they in any other *rationally* meaningful way communicate back. Those saints were not medieval Doctor Dolittles—plotlines such as that fiction's are deceptions.

Recall that the most famous example in Scripture of an animal talking was in Genesis 3. There, it really did *appear* an animal itself was exercising reason. Of course, it was simply the Devil using the serpent as an instrument. As we considered in depth in Part Four, if only Eve refused to dialogue with a speaking serpent, the Fall of Man never would have taken place.

Psalm 19 & 24, "the Heavens Declare," the "Universe's Inhabitants," and the "Souls of the Celestial Bodies"

> **The heavens declare the glory of God; the firmament proclaims the works of his hands.** (Psalm 19:1)

Christian ET promoters use this Psalm to argue for extraterrestrials, when in fact it does the opposite—it *answers* the same question they proffer as their justification for believing in aliens, namely, *"why would there be such astounding amounts of heavenly bodies if not to be inhabited like earth?"* The answer is that these uninhabited galaxies proclaim God's glory. While gazing upon them—whether with the naked eye or the world's most advanced telescope—any pious man finds it impossible not to praise the glory of God in all He has created. Claims, however, that this Psalm implies intelligent creatures living in the heavens were not restricted to the post-Enlightenment ET craze. Even ancient and medieval thinkers (among them some Christians) sometimes succumbed to Pagan views of the celestial bodies, thinking them to be literally incarnate creatures. In his Disputed Questions, Aquinas addresses that very claim. First, he states their argument as follows:

> ... "to proclaim" is an act of an intellectual substance. But the heavens are telling the glory of God (Ps 19:1) as is said in the Psalms. Hence the heavens are intelligent, and therefore possess an intellective soul. [439]

St. Thomas Aquinas even departed from his customary detached tone to condemn the folly of using this verse to pretend the Heavens must contain intelligent creatures, writing:

> **This argument is foolish** despite the fact that Rabbi Moses [that is, Maimonides, a 12th Century Jewish philosopher] proposes it. Because, if "to proclaim" is taken in its proper sense, when it is said that "the heavens proclaim the glory of God," the heavens would require not only an intellect but also a tongue. Therefore **the heavens are said to proclaim the glory of God, if taken in a literal sense, inasmuch as through them the glory of God is made manifest to men.** In this way, also, insensible creatures [e.g., rocks, trees] are said to praise God.[440]

Indeed, all creation praises God in some sense—both Scripture and Sacred Tradition are replete with such references (see, for example, the Canticle of Daniel, wherein all manner of irrational things—from animals to plants to fire—are said to "bless the Lord"). But only men (and angels) can bless God *intentionally*—i.e., with their rational free wills.

Relatedly, some ET promoters have argued that Catholic Tradition can be reconciled with the notion of "NHI" more broadly, or extraterrestrials specifically, due to the speculations of certain ancient and medieval theologians and philosophers that the stars themselves were in a sense "animate;" receiving their motion from an intelligence. Aquinas also directly addresses this notion in Article 8 of his text on the soul (*Quaestiones Disputate de Anima*). He recounts the speculations of a number of thinkers on this matter, pointing out that most theologians of his own day (the 13th century) simply regarded the heavenly bodies as we do today: inanimate, purely material objects. He also observes that multiple Church Fathers were of this view as well, while noting that Augustine was not sure. Then, Aquinas proceeds to consider the possibility that there is deliberate intelligence behind the motion of the celestial bodies. First, he presents the position that he is arguing against:

> [Objection] Further, every intellectual substance is capable of attaining beatitude. Therefore, if celestial bodies are animated by intellectual souls, such souls are capable of beatitude; and thus not only angels and men, but also certain intermediate natures enjoy eternal beatitude. However, **when the holy doctors consider this matter, they say that the society of the blessed is composed of men and angels**.[441]

Noteworthy here is how even the "objection" contains yet another indication that no aliens exist. Bear in mind that Aquinas was not a "fact checker;" when he wrote out the objections he sought to respond to, he did not lace them with factual errors in their citations. Instead, he wrote them out with accurate facts; his aim here is show how the *conclusions* they proffered were fallacious. Yet here we see that all the "holy doctors" (e.g., the Fathers of the Church and other authoritative theologians) insist that Heaven "is composed of men and angels," meaning those are the only beings there. What follows, however, is Aquinas' response to this objection:

> [Reply to Objection:] **If the celestial bodies are animated, their souls belong to the society of the angels**. For Augustine says in the Enchiridion: "I do not hold for certain that the sun and moon, and the other stars belong to the same society," namely, that of the angels, "for although some are luminous bodies, still they do not appear to be sentient or intellective."

Augustine, in other words, was pointing out that the celestial bodies do not display even sentience, much less rationality. Like Augustine, Aquinas also does not claim to be certain of how exactly the heavenly bodies move (whether by the action of blind forces, or by the intercession of an intelligence). But he *is* certain that they are not incarnate intelligent beings of some class other than angelic. At most, they are simply objects that have been animated by some *angel's* ministrations. For in the same text Aquinas states:

> Therefore, **holding this for a fact**, that the celestial bodies are moved by an **intellect which is separate**, we say (maintaining both positions on account of the arguments supporting both sides) that an intellectual substance, as a form, is the perfection of the celestial body, and that it has an intellective power alone but no sensory power, as can be seen from the words of Aristotle ... if it has an intellect only, it is still united as a form to the body, not for the sake of intellectual operation, but for the sake of executing its active power according to which it can attain a certain likeness to divine causality by moving the, heavens.[442]

Aquinas points out it is a *fact* that such a "form" as an angel exercising dominion to move a heavenly body involves a being that is fundamentally "separate" from the matter that is being moved. In other words, even if the stars are moved by angels, the stars are not themselves literally angels. (This is unlike humans—whose spiritual souls are truly incarnate by the body; you *really are* your body.) Therefore, this speculation has no bearing on the extraterrestrial question. (Aquinas expressly rejects that notion.) This is not to mention that no ET promoter is content with (or is even interested in) the notion that the stars are actually intelligent creatures.

Remember that it is a dogma of the Faith that angels are pure spirit. The Church is unambiguous in declaring that angels (including fallen angels—i.e., demons) are invisible and non-corporeal. (Cf. CCC §395, CCC

§328-330, Lateran IV, Summa Theologica I, Q50, A1, etc.). Scripture also affirms this (Hebrews 1:14, Job 4:15, etc.).

Moreover, considering that it now appears we can adequately explain the motion of the Heavenly bodies with the laws of physics alone, it would be exceedingly strange and even disingenuous for a Catholic ET promoter to defer to these medieval speculations (offered merely to hypothesize about how such motions took place) in defense of their propositions.

***

Still other ET promoters defer to the first two verses of Psalm 24 to promote their view—specifically, they defer to one outlying (and bad) translation. The verse reads:

> The earth is the Lord's and the fulness thereof, the world and those who dwell therein; for he has founded it upon the seas, and established it upon the rivers.

Above is the Revised Standard Version Catholic Edition translation of the Bible, which accurately represents the verses in question. The King James Version reads "the earth is the Lord's, and the fulness thereof; the world, and they that dwell therein." The Douay-Rheims translation reads almost identically. The New American Bible Revised Edition, used by the USCCB, confirms this translation. So does the Jerusalem Bible. In fact, every Bible translation one is likely to even be able to find anywhere translates the verse in this manner.

Catholic ET promoters, however (including some priest-theologians) are willing to discard millennia of unanimous agreement among Biblical scholars, and instead insist that this verse should be translated as referring not to "the world," or "the earth" (and the inhabitants thereof), but rather "the universe." Not only is this a deeply flawed translation, but it is also refuted by the immediate context. The Psalm teaches that the place containing these "inhabitants" was founded upon "the seas" and "the rivers." Obviously, this is a reference to *earth*. Even, however, if this were a reference to the universe at large, it *still* would not support belief in aliens! For indeed, we *do* dwell in the universe—earth is part of the universe. Referring to the "inhabitants of the universe" is simply (if we are speaking of rational, incarnate creatures) another way of referring to human beings.

Here, a general observation is in order on the approach of those Christian ET promoters who would insist that the Bible teaches aliens exist. For this is indeed an outlandish assertion. Even most proud Christian ET promoters seem to say that the Bible does not teach anything about the topic (of course, they are wrong; the Bible *does* rule out aliens, as we saw in Part One). But the more radical of the ET promoters, who insist the Bible does instruct us about extraterrestrials, are essentially claiming that, for two thousand years, the Church—including *all* the saints, Popes, Fathers, Doctors, Magisterial Documents, etc.—have been utterly deluded about

Scripture. Somehow not one of them recognized that the Bible teaches the cosmos are filled with other civilizations like ours; only we, today, with the help of government UFO reports and modernist post-Enlightenment scholars, can conclude this. "Outlandish" scarcely captures such sentiments.

Genesis 4: Why Was Cain Marked—Of Whom Was He Afraid?

Those Christian ET promoters who espouse particularly esoteric brands of alien belief generally insist that various "Non-Human Intelligences" (extraterrestrial or otherwise) have always been on earth; even long before man. One passage they point to is found in Genesis Chapter 4, wherein Cain, after murdering Abel, laments to the Lord:

> "My punishment is greater than I can bear. Behold, thou hast driven me this day away from the ground; and from thy face I shall be hidden; and I shall be a fugitive and a wanderer on the earth, and whoever finds me will slay me." Then the Lord said to him, "Not so! If any one slays Cain, vengeance shall be taken on him sevenfold." And the Lord put a mark on Cain, lest any who came upon him should kill him. Then Cain went away from the presence of the Lord, and dwelt in the land of Nod, east of Eden. (Genesis 4:13-16)

These ET promoters argue that no humans were on earth at that point other than Adam, Eve, and Cain, therefore this "mark" put on Cain must have been placed upon him to prevent *some* other rational beings from killing him. This argument fails for several reasons. Most obviously, because their base premise is false. It is not true that only Adam, Eve, and Cain were alive at that point. Genesis does not claim to explicitly list each of Adam and Eve's offspring; in fact, it specifically teaches that "[Adam] had other sons and daughters," (Genesis 5:4) while not proceeding to list them. Therefore, many others almost certainly existed at the time Cain slew Abel. The very next verse (Genesis 4:17) recounts Cain bearing a son with his wife, with no allusion to an intermission of time, thus indicating that others did indeed exist at that point. Finally, recall that Adam was 130 years old when Seth was born (cf. Genesis 5:3), and it is implied this happened quite shortly after Cain slew Abel, indicating that Cain was himself not much younger when he murdered Abel. (Recall that Adam and Eve were created as adults, and Cain was their firstborn; cf. Genesis 4:1.) This renders it almost certain that *many* other humans existed on earth at that point.

Equally significantly, however—even if one insists upon claiming, contrary to all evidence, that at the time of the first murder only Adam, Eve, Cain, and Abel existed—this argument either pretends that Cain was stupid, or that God did not know the future. Cain, of course, knew his own parents (Adam and Eve) had been commanded to "be fruitful, and multiply, and fill the earth." (Genesis 1:28) He accordingly knew that many more humans would soon follow. In the passage above, Cain would have been worried about the future, even if not the present. Cain doubtless lived to be hundreds of years old (which God, of course, knew would happen), as men tended to in those days. So he had a very long life to be concerned about being "a fugitive and a wanderer" who would be slain by whoever might find him, and God had a very good reason to "put a mark on Cain," to prevent his being killed during centuries of earthly life.

Genesis 6: The Nephilim and the Giants

Some take the sixth chapter of the Book of Genesis as an indication that non-human incarnate intelligent beings exist, whom they refer to as the "Nephilim," "Watchers," or "Giants." The more outlandish of the Christian ET promoters even claim these Nephilim *were themselves* aliens. They argue that the word itself means "those who fell from above," but this is false. The Hebrew word for this, *naphal*, means "to fall," therefore the "Nephilim" are simply "the fallen ones." This is to say, they *sinned*. There is no indication in the etymology (or anywhere in Scripture, Magisterium, or Sacred Tradition) that their title implies they physically fell to our planet from outside of the earth!

In the opening verses of Genesis 6, we read:

> When men began to multiply on the face of the ground, and daughters were born to them, the sons of God saw that the daughters of men were fair; and they took to wife such of them as they chose. Then the Lord said, "My spirit shall not abide in man for ever, for he is flesh, but his days shall be a hundred and twenty years." The Nephilim were on the earth in those days, and also afterward, when the sons of God came in to the daughters of men, and they bore children to them. These were the mighty men that were of old, the men of renown. (Genesis 6:1-4)

Unfortunately, some combine this passage with certain apocryphal Jewish texts (such as the Book of Enoch) or false private revelations, and promote wildly esoteric ideas about what exactly is meant by the "Nephilim" here, and their relation to the "sons of God."

All Christians must remember that *there is a reason* such apocryphal texts are not a part of the Bible, even though the compilers of Scripture were well aware of their presence: such texts *are not from God*. They may well contain much truth, but they also contain much falsehood. It is true that they are alluded to at points in the New Testament (for example, in the Book of Jude), but this does not implicitly grant them validity any more than St. Paul referring to the Greek Pagan authors (cf. Acts 17) grants supernatural authority to those Pagan texts.

Returning to the passage itself, "Nephilim" and "mighty men" are translated in various ways. The Douay-Rheims translation refers to them not as "Nephilim" but as "giants." But it should not be all that surprising to hear that "giants" existed before the Flood. Even after the Flood, there were giants. We all know of the account of David vs. Goliath, where Goliath was indeed a giant. 1 Samuel 17:4 specifically describes his height as "six cubits and a span," which is almost 10 feet tall. The first Book of Chronicles describes another giant:

> There was another battle, at Gath, and there was a giant, who had six fingers to each hand and six toes to each foot; twenty-four in all. He too was descended from the Rephaim. (1 Chronicles 20:6)

Even more extraordinary—but certainly true, as Scripture recounts it, and no authentic exegetical methods cast any doubt upon its proper interpretation—were the lifespans of those humans who lived before the Flood. Methuselah was 969 years old when he died. Noah lived to be 950 years old. Seth was 912.

The Book of Numbers also recounts what the spies sent out by Moses saw in the land of Canaan. This, of course, was also long after the Flood of Noah. There, we read:

> So they brought to the people of Israel an evil report of the land which they had spied out, saying, "The land, through which we have gone to spy it out, is a land that devours its inhabitants; and all the people that we saw in it are men of great stature. And there we saw the Nephilim (the sons of Anak, who come from the Nephilim); and we seemed to ourselves like grasshoppers, and so we seemed to them." (Numbers 13:32-33)

"Nephilim," that is, *giants*, therefore, existed even long after the Flood (whereas the esoteric reading of Genesis 6 insists that the Flood itself was simply sent to wipe these creatures off planet earth).

Yet all of these individuals were indisputably human beings. They may have been amazingly large, or lived to be amazingly old, or even had extra fingers and toes, but they were all offspring of Adam and Eve. They were all 100% human. The mere fact that men once displayed traits we might no longer see does not cast doubt upon the fact they were men.

So, too, with the "Nephilim" of Genesis 6, we can be certain they were simply men; regardless of their size or might. This simple fact not only flows from the proper Catholic understanding of Genesis 6 (as we will see in a moment), but also derives from the same premise on which this book is built: of all visible creatures, only man is a person—only descendants of Adam and Eve are rational.

What, then, does Genesis 6 mean when it refers to the "sons of God" taking wives from among the "daughters of men"? Catholic Sacred Tradition tells us: "sons of God" were offspring of Seth, whereas "daughters of men" were offspring of Cain. Such intermarrying was not permitted, and from it arose all manner of evil. Dr. Scott Han explains:

> ...[the] two divergent cultures of Sethites and Cainites provided a ready-made stage for conflict. We see Seth's family line built on the covenant worship of God, calling on the name of the Lord. In the opposing corner, we see Cain's family reaching its tyrannical completeness... Next Genesis 6 describes a puzzling yet ominous development... [but] **In Hebrew "the men of renown" [i.e., "Giants" or "Nephilim"] means literally the men of the *shem*, the men of the name, wicked tyrants who were making a name for themselves, unjust men who were building a culture of pure evil**. God would have no more of this violence. He waited more than a century after passing sentence on the human race and giving them due warning. God then sent the flood waters as a punishment. ... But what's going on in the first two verses of this chapter? **"The sons of God saw that the daughters of men were fair" (v. 2)**. **...But nowhere else are angels called "sons of God" in Genesis. In addition, angels cannot reproduce like humans, as Augustine and Aquinas pointed out long ago. Besides, if angels were the primary instigators, why did God punish the entire world? Why not target the wayward angels and their evil offspring instead? The flood punished everyone *but* the angels**... Then who were "the sons of God" mentioned in the preceding chapter? In the opening verses of chapter five, we hear again about God creating Adam in his own image and likeness. Then we read that Adam fathered a son named Seth, "in his own image and likeness" (see Gn 5:1-2). This serves to link Seth and his line directly to the gift of divine sonship that God first gave to Adam. **Then who were the sons of God? The Sethites, that family of God that built itself up by calling upon the name of the Lord. In his classic work, *The City of God* (Book XV), Augustine tells how God's family, the Church, was restored in the Sethites after the death of Abel. What we see here is the Church pitted against the world, God's family against the seed of the serpent,** ... [But] when people began to multiply on the face of the earth, **"the sons of God," that is, the Sethite men, were seduced by the beauty of "the daughters of men," that is, the Cainite women.** The beauty of the wicked proved stronger than the resolve of the righteous. **Sethite men found a new forbidden fruit, the beautiful but ungodly Cainite women, to be irresistible. And they didn't just marry them; "they married as they chose," which might imply that, along with mixed marriages, polygamy had now also entered into the line of Seth, the covenant family of God. And violent men were born. When left unchecked, sin becomes institutionalized. In every age of salvation history, sexual immorality and violence go hand in hand, triggering the hard remedy of God's judgment** in the form of the covenant curses. And nothing institutionalizes sin more than marital infidelity. The whole culture gets clobbered, especially the children. **And afterwards only a remnant survives, barely.** (*A Father who Keeps His Promises.* Chapter Four.)

This understanding of Genesis 6, which Dr. Hahn expertly describes above, is not only the correct one (in line with Catholic teaching and Sacred Tradition), but also a powerful and deeply relevant lesson for today. Unfortunately, that lesson is lost on those who insist on siding instead with insane Jewish myths regarding what this passage means.

In fact, angels and demons are pure spirit, and it is obvious even from the most basic principles of Christian philosophy and theology that human beings cannot procreate with them. Whoever believes it is possible for an angel (or demon) to generate offspring with a woman might as well completely reject all Catholic dogma on demonology, angelology, and human nature. This notion is so outlandish that it is deeply disconcerting there exists growing numbers of the faithful subscribing to this particular brand of neo-Gnosticism. Make no mistake; it is just another diabolical trap. Even if most of the world will succumb to the lie that "aliens" are here to save us, perhaps some "red pilled" Christians will succumb to the lie that "benevolent Watchers," "Christianized Nephilim," or "Eschatological Giants" are returning from their exile since antediluvian days to save us. Whatever the disguise, the ones wearing it will be the same: demons.

Moreover, one is entirely neglecting a key element of Salvation History if he supposes that the "real reason for the Flood" was the machinations of some fantastical race of half-men, half-demons tyrannizing the earth. The flood was due to mankind's sinfulness; plain and simple. Every Christian and faithful Jew has *always* known that. Whoever dismisses this true and forever vital lesson with egregiously fallacious esoteric speculations has thereby violated his Christian patrimony.

My intent here is certainly not to "demystify" Genesis 6. There may well have been utterly amazing things transpiring with these "Nephilim." I do not pretend to have unique insight into that. My only point is that we must abide in Catholic orthodoxy; always preferring Sacred Tradition to a subtle neo-Gnosticism that wrongly submits to apocryphal fictions as if they were Divine revelations. It is possible to interpret Genesis 6 in an orthodox manner while not supposing the interpretation above gives the full story, so long as one concedes that the flood was truly sent due to mankind's sinfulness, and that any actual creature procreated by a human is likewise entirely human, with an entirely human father and mother. There are *no* exceptions to this standard, nor will there ever be.

Not even gravely evil modern genetics experiments will alter this fact. As we considered in Part Five, a "human animal chimera" is a misnomer. Such a creature is either just a human injured by the introduction of some animal genetic material (who is still 100% a human), or an animal injured by the introduction of some human genetic material (that is still 100% an animal). Likewise, so-called "three parent babies" (or more than three) are, in fact, just offspring of one mother and one father, even if their own DNA has been injured by the introduction of some genetic material from another person. That each human being is the child of a human father and human mother is a bedrock element of reality; it always has been so, and it always will be so. No man, and no demon, can change it. Not even the Devil has power to substantially alter the fundamental nature of things.

It is indeed true that demons can engage in perverse sexual acts with humans in those cases when they temporarily assume certain material forms (see Part Four where we considered "alien" sexual encounters that are clearly just examples of demons acting as either a succubus or incubus). But these Satanic occurrences can *never* result in offspring. In some cases, however, female "abductees" will falsely *think* that pregnancy has resulted. The reality is that in all such cases this was either due to a sexual encounter with a human man (which was either forgotten—perhaps due to trauma—or happened during unconsciousness—perhaps a drugged unconsciousness), or even a forgotten artificial insemination (possibly, again, one that took place while she was unconscious). Another possibility for this could be a false notion of pregnancy ending in a false notion of a miscarriage (i.e., the demon deluding a woman, perhaps even with sensible illusions, into think ordinary menstruation was a miscarriage). Correspondingly, we cannot definitively rule out the interpretation of Genesis 6 which would regard it as *also* alluding to some sort of sexual activity between demons and human females. But we *can* definitively rule out the notion that this activity resulted in offspring. These "giants" of Genesis could possibly have been men with diabolically influenced strength or other preternatural abilities, but they were nevertheless *human*, in the complete sense of the word (which is the only sense of the word; there is no such thing as a partial human!), and they still had a human mother and a human father.

> **It is better, then, to believe that such a ... semi-man never existed, and that this, in common with many other fancies of the poets, is mere fiction**. (St. Augustine. *City of God*. Book 19, Chapter 12)

36. Questions Answered and Concerns Addressed

"Would the Discovery of Aliens Overthrow Catholicism?"

The question above is a futile and foolish way of approaching the issue of extraterrestrial intelligence. No matter what one puts in the blank, the answer to the question, *"Would ___ overthrow/disprove/refute Catholicism?"* is always a resolute "**No**." Catholicism is true (this fact is absolutely certain), and therefore no future scenario that can be meaningfully entertained would disprove it.

Many ET promoters, at least subconsciously aware of the problematic nature of their writings, phrase their promotion of belief in aliens as a mere attempt to argue that such discovery would not refute the Catholic Faith. The problems with that approach are thoroughly addressed in this book's Introduction.

Yet, one may still persist, and ask, *"But what would you do if aliens were shown to exist? What would that mean for Catholicism?"*

The proper answer to that question is: *we'll cross that bridge when we don't get to it.*

If, however, one wishes to posit a counterfactual hypothetical like St. Paul did in Scripture when he said, *"If Christ is not raised then your faith is vain,"* (1 Corinthians 15:16) we can. I will not explore that here, though, as even with these caveats, some readers will claim I am backtracking. In fact, I will not backtrack, as I am certain extraterrestrials do not exist.

I will simply say that, even in this scenario, Catholicism would survive; it would not be "overthrown." Recall that, although we can conclude with certainty from the Faith (Scripture, Tradition, Magisterium, etc.) that aliens do not exist, it remains the case that there is not yet any infallible dogma *explicitly* teaching against aliens.

Aliens Who "Could Not Know and Love God"? Humani Generis and The Beatific Vision

Some Catholic ET promoters use a particularly misleading strategy to argue that aliens could exist even in light of paragraph 356 of the Catechism, but simply could not "know and love God." Those who proffer it point to Pope Pius XII's teaching in his 1950 encyclical *Humani Generis,* wherein he taught that the *Beatific Vision* is a gratuitous gift from God:

> Some also question whether angels are personal beings, and whether matter and spirit differ essentially. Others destroy the gratuity of the

> supernatural order, since God, they say, cannot create intellectual beings without ordering and calling them to the beatific vision. (*Humani Generis.* §26)

The venerable Pope's teaching is clear: Heaven itself (the essence of which is the Beatific Vision) is such an indescribably exalted gift that God was not "required"[443] to call rational beings towards it merely because they are rational. Instead, out of His superabundant Divine Mercy, God gratuitously *willed* to do so. He desired to create all rational beings with an ordering towards—as their final end—directly beholding His Own essence without medium (that is, towards eternally enjoying the Beatific Vision).

This teaching is presented by certain Catholic ET promoters as an attempt to prove that paragraph 356 does not rule out aliens. Such beings, they argue, might well *exist*, but might simply not even be *able* to know and love God. After all, Pope Pius XII taught that Heaven is not strictly required as an "end" (a goal towards which one is called by God), therefore—the argument goes—He could also create rational beings who could not even "know and love" Him.

First, we should point out that this assertion is contradicted by what we have already reviewed in the preceding section: the Church teaches that *rationality alone* suffices to know, with certainty, that God exists. At the absolute minimum, therefore, it is not possible to assert—while preserving Catholic orthodoxy—that God would (or even could) create rational beings who *could not even know of His existence.* But knowing of the existence of God is certainly an aspect of simply *knowing* Him. (The mere fact that knowing God's existence does not itself entail knowing Him *completely* is a non-sequitur. *No one* knows God *completely.* The infinite always exceeds the complete grasp of the finite.) Moreover, *any* good that is known *can always* be loved. Any rational being who has concluded that God exists is capable of making an act of the will in order to love Him, and to deny this would be to succumb to heresy contrary to Catholic teaching that God always grants sufficient grace. Therefore, we can conclude with certainty that *any* rational being *can* know and love God. This conclusion is not weakened or in any way affected by the teaching quoted above in *Humani Generis,* and it is further strengthened when we contrast what this encyclical actually teaches with what is taught in paragraph 356 of the Catechism; a contrast we will presently discuss.

The Beatific Vision does not consist merely in "knowing and loving God;" it is, rather, *radically* beyond that. Case in point: there is not a single person on earth reading these words who now enjoys the Beatific Vision. Yet, I hope and pray—I will even go so far as to say that I suspect it is so!—that most reading these words do already know and love God. Yet, the Catechism does not merely say that only men, of all visible creatures, are called to the *Beatific Vison*; it goes much further: it teaches that only men (not animals, not aliens, not AI, etc.) can even *know and love God*!

***

The soul of any rational being is intrinsically indestructible. It is, by nature, *immortal*. It will, as a matter of metaphysical fact, exist forever—either in Heaven or in Hell. As Aquinas rightly teaches, nothing is annihilated (cf. *Summa Theologica*, Part I, Q104, A4). Accordingly, all destruction that will ever occur consists in the decomposition of a composite being into its constituent parts. A rational soul, however, is—analogously to God Himself—entirely simple. Although distinct *faculties* of the soul can be enumerated, the soul itself is not comprised of different parts put together like a body is. Therefore, it is not even logically coherent to attempt to describe the destruction of a rational soul. What follows is that each such soul is destined to exist forever. If aliens exist, they too must, like us, be immortal. Catholics who insist upon believing in the possibility of aliens, therefore, are left pondering if they really wish to posit a scenario wherein the infinitely Good God would create beings who, though existing forever, would have no hope of Heaven.

Is It "Fundamentalism" to Concede the Catechism Rules Out Aliens?

As demonstrated in Part Two of this book, paragraph 356 of the *Catechism of the Catholic Church* is impossible to reconcile with belief in extraterrestrials. Whoever believes in aliens is left conceding that he simply dissents from this particular Magisterial teaching, and to promote his view to fellow Catholics who submit to that teaching—and, accordingly, rejecting alien belief—he is left saying something like what follows:

"But you are 'proof-texting'; you are simply making too much of these teachings in the Catechism! The authors of the Catechism did not intend to rule out aliens. Besides, the Catechism doesn't present any new teachings; it is only a compendium of existing ones, and you have to look at what documents are cited to know what it means."

There are three basic assertions in this final slew of responses to paragraph 356 of the Catechism, and we should address each here. Even before addressing them, however, a tangent is necessary in accordance with the veritable apocalyptic dangers (not excluding those pertinent to the topic of this book) which we are confronting as we proceed further into the Third Millennium.

***

As is often noted, the present *Catechism of the Catholic Church* is the first universal Catechism promulgated in half a millennium (since the Catechism of the Council of Trent). But even this acknowledgement fails to capture the spiritual—and, I daresay, eschatological—magnitude of the Catechism's arrival. Trent's Catechism (The "Roman Catechism") was the first ever truly "universal Catechism," perhaps apart from the Didache itself. The current *Catechism of the Catholic Church*, however, far outshines even Trent's in the audacity of its aspirations (directed, as it is, to all—not merely primarily to clergy) and in the breadth and depth of its teachings (both of which far surpass the scope of Trent's Catechism). The *Catechism of the Catholic Church* is the product of two thousand years of Spirit-led Development of Doctrine compressed into the pages of a single volume. It is an unprecedented Gift from God. Catholics have always been able to say this, but now we can say it with more confidence than ever before, "**Happy are we, O Israel, for we know what is pleasing to God**." (Baruch 4:4)

The primary reason for this timing is clear to anyone who perceives the Signs of the Times: the Catechism was bestowed precisely when it was as a bulwark against the onslaught of attacks against orthodoxy, which, upon the Dawn of the Third Millennium, were about to reach their peak through the Great Apostasy; and we are now witnessing the apocalyptic havoc of this apostasy spreading throughout the Church and the world.

Upon its publication, the Catechism spread like wildfire throughout the Church and facilitated the ability of all Catholics of good will (who sincerely desired to abide in the orthodox teachings of the Catholic Faith) to know with clarity and comprehensiveness just what the Church teaches on the most important questions—even as all the heresies of modernism continued their rampage throughout the ranks of the hierarchy. To this day, whoever sets himself firmly to the task of learning the Catechism and submitting to *each and every one* of its teachings is given an unsurpassed solidity of ground on which to stand and remain safe despite all the chaos swirling about in both the world and the Church.

In 1994, the future Pope Benedict XVI wrote (in his too often neglected and almost never quoted work, *Introduction to the Catechism of the Catholic Church*):

> The eagerness with which [the Catechism] has been purchased is almost a sort of [referendum] of the People of God against those interests which portray the Catechism as inimical to progress, as an authoritarian Roman disciplinary act, and so on. It is often the case that certain circles [*i.e., modernist theologians among the clergy. Here in a footnote, Ratzinger singles out the destructive influence of Hans Kung*] employ such slogans merely to defend their own monopoly on opinion-making in the Church and in the world, an arrangement which they do not wish to see upset by a qualified laity. (Cardinal Ratzinger. *Introduction to the Catechism of the Catholic Church*. Chapter 2.)

In the following chapter of the same work, he pronounced that,

> **...[the Catechism] transmits what the Church teaches, whoever rejects it as a whole separates himself beyond question from the faith...**

This bold but calculated assertion, of the future Pope Benedict XVI, should give profound pause to anyone who would give more weight to their own preferences, speculations, and optimisms (especially if these find their motivation in science fiction) than he would to what is taught *anywhere* within the Catechism's pages.

The possibility of finding oneself separated, "beyond question," from the faith is a potential outcome so grave that it should have any Catholic fleeing in the opposite direction of this fate with all his strength. It should, moreover, be obvious that Cardinal Ratzinger was not offering this dire warning only to those who would reject *all* of the Catechism's teachings. No one on earth—not even the most resolute atheist—would find himself capable of affirming the opposite of *each* of the Catechism's own propositions. Instead, he is warning Catholics that whoever would "reject it as a whole," that is, *whoever would regard it as lacking authority*, has thereby separated himself from the Catholic Church. And from what we have already seen in the preceding sections, it is not clear how any Catholic can believe in aliens while still sincerely claiming to respect the Catechism's authority.

Nevertheless, if anyone would be so imprudent as to simply write off these wise words on account of them allegedly only being Ratzinger's "own fallible opinion," he is still left with the far higher authority of Pope St. John Paul II's Apostolic Constitution, *Fidei Depositum*, by which he promulgated the Catechism. In that extremely high-level Magisterial document, the Pope declared:

> **The Catechism of the Catholic Church**, which I approved 25 June last and the publication of which I today order by virtue of my Apostolic Authority, **is a statement of the Church's faith and of Catholic doctrine**, attested to or illumined by Sacred Scripture, Apostolic Tradition and the Church's Magisterium. **I declare it to be a** valid and legitimate instrument for ecclesial communion and a **sure norm for teaching the faith**. May it serve the renewal to which the Holy Spirit ceaselessly calls the Church of God, the Body of Christ, on her pilgrimage to the undiminished light of the kingdom! (§IV)

We must, therefore, dismiss any arguments that are tantamount to regarding the Catechism as little more than a glorified index; a helpful tool for looking up (using its own footnotes) just what the Church actually teaches, but incapable of *itself* conveying the same.

Such an approach violates what Pope St. John Paul II declared is the proper—*Catholic*—approach to the Catechism. When, however, one considers what we reviewed in Part Two, he will realize that it is precisely the *uncatholic* approach to the Catechism that permits belief in aliens.

Admittedly, it must be granted that the nature of the Catechism (or *any* Catechism), is not to, itself, present brand-new Church teachings. Such a charge would be restricted to Papal Magisterium or an Ecumenical Council. Yet, far from detracting from the fact that the Catechism rules out aliens, this acknowledgement only strengthens the same. As we saw in

Part Two, the Catechism rules out aliens *precisely because* mankind's unique status as the sole incarnate rational creature that exists has *always* been *the* Catholic understanding of the Hierarchy of Creation.

It is not as if the teachings of the many Fathers and Doctors of the Church, the pronouncements of the many acts of Papal Magisterium, and the documents of the twenty-one Ecumenical Councils have been divided on this question, and the Catechism suddenly decided to declare aliens non-existent. Quite the contrary, it has always been held that only man is rational (within the Magisterium and throughout Sacred Tradition), and all the Catechism did was make that entirely clear once again.

Is Being Concerned About Demons Masquerading as Aliens "A Protestant Thing"?

Quite the contrary, being concerned *about* such concerns is a modernist thing.

Certain circles of Catholics, ever preoccupied with being taken seriously by the world and the worldly, fear above all else having any association with those whom mainstream culture and secular academia have deemed unenlightened. And if any group has been classified as such by that milieu, it is the so-called "fundamentalists," a group usually associated with conservative evangelical Protestantism. Worldly Catholics will go to any length to ensure they further separate themselves from these separated brethren—while at the same time missing no opportunity to cozy up to the world and compromise with its evil doctrines. Part and parcel to this worldly strategy is ensuring that they are never associated with those who recognize the true nature of the ET Deception.

This can only be called what it is: bigotry. These Catholics who are terrified of finding themselves in agreement with conservative Evangelicals on anything—even when the latter are doing excellent work in opposing the teachings of our Godless modern culture—is nothing but an outlet for one of the very vices—prejudice—they ostensibly chiefly oppose. Evangelicals provide excellent refutations of Darwinism, and these modernist Catholics respond, "*you have it all wrong! Christianity endorses evolution!*" Evangelicals give profound proofs of God's existence, and those same Catholics pooh-pooh them, insisting that evangelization "*can only be done by example.*" Evangelicals painstakingly write powerful defenses of the Resurrection of Jesus, and those same circles of Catholics dismiss its promotion as "*proselytism.*"

When Evangelicals like Gary Bates and Hugh Ross go to great lengths to show—extremely accurately—just why so-called aliens are actually demons, the knee-jerk response of these circles within Catholicism is, therefore, entirely predictable.

In fact, concern about demons masquerading as aliens has nothing to do with the errors associated with Protestantism. On the contrary, it has everything to do with the truths upon which honest Protestants insist: the reality of the demonic, and the means for identifying it, and the importance of rejecting it whenever and wherever it rears its head—including when "the science" claims otherwise.

But as one of the few dogmas of modernist Catholics is "trust the science," they predictably reject any notion that the demons are active. It is not merely that science cannot empirically prove demons; that much is obvious, since demons are immaterial. It is that science too often insists upon its own ability to explain that which can be only explained by the demonic.

Granted, these (open or closet) modernists do pay some lip service to believing in the demonic. But any concrete notion of demons being active in the world is carefully sealed away, by them, in the testimonies of exorcists. The reality, however, is that the full-blown possession which exorcists deal with is exceedingly rare in comparison to demonic activity in the world in general. As we have noted elsewhere in this book, the Devil is generally uninterested in possessing souls. He is much more interested in seducing them into sin and error; and an extraordinarily effective means of doing that, today, is through the ET Deception.

Catholics who observe the reality plainly before our eyes—even openly attested to by all the most prominent voices in ET-belief-promotion (see Part Four)—and accordingly note how active the demons are in all-things-extraterrestrial, can count on being regularly castigated by "professional Catholics" with the familiar words: "*The Devil isn't behind every rock, you know! Not everything is demons!*" Although we addressed that (true, but misused) notion in Part Four in detail, for now it suffices to observe that if proclaiming such words as those is the only way a man can respond to the argument that some phenomenon is demonic, this is a sure sign that it is indeed demonic. If he could convincingly argue that it *wasn't* demonic, he would not have resorted to reiterating platitudes to make his point.

What About St. Padre Pio?

Certain prominent Catholic ET promoters essentially build their entire argument for aliens on the (unproven, and almost certainly false) idea that three saints endorsed alien belief. While these ET promoters would emphatically deny that this is their approach, they nevertheless prove it *is* by their own actions. When they appear on internet podcasts, radio shows, TV appearances, etc., the supposed endorsement of aliens by St. Padre Pio is invariably one of the first things they bring up and one of the points they emphasize most emphatically and repeatedly. They then throw into the mix even more dubious attributions to St. John Paul II and St. Paul VI (whom we will consider in the next section), proceed to claim, "*I could go on and on*" (they could not; in fact, they could not list a *single* additional one!), and thus they imply the case is settled. This disingenuous approach testifies to the vacuousness of their thesis.*

We will indeed address the specific claims made in relation to these saints and alien belief. Before doing so, two general notes are in order.

First, as we will see in the paragraphs ahead, in not one of these three cases is there actually something clear and in writing, or recorded, *or even testified to* by the individual who (allegedly) heard it, indicating that the saint in question did believe in aliens. We are dealing with anonymous and third hand hearsay, without any knowledge of who supposedly heard the affirmation. Isn't it strange—oddly convenient, in fact—that such an extraordinary claim (i.e., that aliens exist) could not have *once* found its way into the mountains of testimonies from these saints that we can actually verify? These ET promoters are building castles on the sand.

Second, it bears emphasizing that saints (including popes when they issue personal opinions) are wrong all the time. One thing is *certain*: no saint before the 20th century's space age endorsed aliens. As discussed in Part Two, the infallible *sensus fidelium* long ago ruled out the very possibility of extraterrestrials. Even if a few saints who lived during the UFO craze of the 1900s believed in aliens, this should be seen as nothing but a consequence of sheer statistics. Saints, too, come from the world. None are born and raised as hermits in cloistered monasteries that are themselves run by individuals who were likewise born and raised as hermits in cloistered monasteries. When a certain error becomes predominant in the world, it is inevitable that even some exceedingly holy souls will succumb to it, (at least, so long as it is not an explicitly defined heresy, which ET belief is not). Lowest-common-denominator saint-quoting is a sure way to live a life based on error. To abide in the truth of the Faith, we have Scripture, Magisterium, Sacred Tradition (including the *consensus* of the saints), and Liturgy. When one needs to scour millions of pages of sayings attributed to saints, in order to surgically extract one or two seemingly in support of a given thesis, this is a sure testimony to the errancy of that thesis; not its truth. The Catechism, Papal Teaching, the Bible, and much more, each independently rule out aliens. When presented with a single line from any such source, placed next to an alleged quote from any saint which contradicts it, none should have any difficulty in ascertaining which teaching wins out. And it is not the one claimed to have been said by the saint (particularly if we have no solid grounds for believing the claim!). I say this as a man who is as devoted as anyone to Padre Pio; my family and I invoke

---

* They certainly cannot provide any convincing scientific reasons for their belief; but they also cannot answer the theological arguments against aliens. As such, they focus on insisting that alien belief must be legitimate because these three saints supposedly said it was. Ultimately, this is a form of spiritual bullying; it is a way to paint those who disbelieve in aliens as "rigid traditionalists" who are not "in keeping with the times," even while they refuse to address entirely legitimate concerns that *rule out* aliens.

him each day, and you would be hard pressed to find someone who loves Padre Pio as much as I do. But we are only guilty of idolatry if we treat some individual saint as an infallible oracle. Such an approach to Padre Pio would displease no one more than Padre Pio himself.

Most remarkable pertaining to this second point, however, is what we considered in Part Two: although belief in aliens was essentially universally demanded of all thinkers and writers throughout the 19th century, we do not have a *single* record of a *single* saint, blessed, venerable, *or* servant of God—from that entire century (or any time before)—jumping on the bandwagon and likewise asserting their belief in extraterrestrials. Therefore, whoever wishes to be instructed by the saints will find no difficulty in discovering that there are no aliens. Even if a few saints, all from the same century, did—in a merely passing private comment (which is all that even the ET promoters attribute to them)—endorse alien belief, what is that against the confirmed writings of St. Thomas Aquinas (Doctor of the Church), St. Augustine (Father and Doctor of the Church), St. Jerome (Father and Doctor of the Church), St. Hippolytus, St. Philastrius, St. Robert Bellarmine (Doctor of the Church), Pope St. Zachary, Pope Pius II, etc., who rejected the view (as it was phrased in their day)? The answer is simple: it is nothing.

***

Padre Pio and Aliens

Here as with other elements of ET Deception promotion in contemporary Catholic circles, Msgr. Corrado Balducci's influence emerges as singularly important. The primary proponent of the notion that St. Pio endorsed aliens appears to be him. (See Part Four to better understand the destructive effects of this priest's UFO activism.)

Dr. Paul Thigpen's popular 2022 book promoting ET belief, where it furthers the notion that Padre Pio endorsed aliens, only quotes a paper published by Balducci. This paper itself claims to be quoting a certain book (*Così Parlò Padre Pio*). This book itself, however, only allegedly quotes Padre Pio on the basis of anonymous hearsay.

Dr. Thigpen's footnotes do not mention where Msgr. Balducci's paper was found, and I have not been able to locate it in any reputable journal or other reliable source (although I have scoured many academic databases for it). After extensive searching, I have only been able to find the paper posted on two fringe websites (ufoevidence.org and another site reposting it from the "Paranormal & UFO Information Network," pufoin.com). The website most people cite when promoting this quote is that of a certain St. Catherine of Siena parish (where Dr. Thigpen worked; so one is inclined to assume he simply posted it there); that website, however, does not cite the source of the quote, therefore it is doubtless simply an uncredited reposting of the same material. Here is what the paper I found declares:

> From St. Fr. Pio, the following dialogue is documented and officially published by the Cappuchin [sic] Order:
> Question: *Father, some claim that there are creatures of God on other planets, too.* Answer [allegedly from Padre Pio]: What else? Do you think they don't exist and that God's omnipotence is limited to this small planet Earth? What else? Do you think there are no other beings who love the Lord?
> Another question: *Father, I think the Earth is nothing compared to other planets and stars.* Answer [allegedly from Padre Pio]: Exactly! Yes, and we Earthlings are nothing, too. The Lord certainly did not limit His glory to this small Earth. On other planets other beings exist who did not sin and fall as we did. (Don Nello Castello: Così parlò Padre Pio; Vicenza, 1974).

While the first claim included here from Balducci—i.e., that the dialogue is "documented and officially published" by St. Pio's order—is often made by others (who are doubtless simply deferring to Balducci's assertion), it is unclear what he means by this. The book's publisher is listed as being an Italian hospital, not the Capuchin order, and I have not been able to find any mention of the book on any lists of Capuchin publications. Indeed, the book itself appears virtually impossible to find, and it is highly unlikely that anyone now reiterating this alleged conversation of St. Pio has himself read it recorded in this book. I am not claiming the book does not contain the quote. My point is only that when *no one* reiterating this claim has access to the book from which it derives, we are completely detached from context and from the ability to assess this claim with respect to other claims made in the same book (which is always an important task, especially for controversial remarks).

Instead, whenever this quote is being relayed today, it is almost certainly being taken from a fringe Ufology website, which itself is purportedly quoting a paper written by Balducci, which itself claims to quote this 1974 book, which itself is allegedly recounting a conversation Padre Pio had, but which does not even indicate who had this supposed conversation.

We are, therefore, so many degrees removed from reality here that no one should give any credence whatsoever to this account *unless and until* it can be proven who exactly is the person who had this alleged conversation with the saint, so that this person can be consulted to verify its authenticity. Without knowing who the person is and having a verification from that person himself or herself, we are just dealing with the typical type of hearsay that has already attributed innumerable completely bogus quotes to Padre Pio. Indeed, this saint has been the object of more false attributions than just about any saint in recent history.

If Padre Pio really did believe in aliens, and even insisted upon their existence, then we should grant the ET promoters one thing—that would indeed be quite noteworthy (even though, in this case, St. Pio would simply be mistaken). Therefore, such an attribution would need to be definitively established before any discerning reader would lend it credibility. Yet we are left with only the flimsiest evidence one could imagine; no better than any mere rumor.

Padre Pio gave personal spiritual direction to thousands of individuals who frequently spoke (and still speak) of what he told them. They do so publicly and with their faces and real names attached. They can be contacted (or at least have been contacted) to verify the veracity of the quotes they attributed to him if these quotes were especially consequential. Where is the same dynamic seen with Padre Pio's alleged alien belief? The answer is that it is nowhere. *No one* has gone on record and asserted that Padre Pio told him that he believed in aliens. If Padre Pio really believed in aliens and was so emphatic about that belief, as this quote indicates, then why would he only share that with a single person (who, conveniently for the ET promoters, we cannot identify) in a private conversation?

In his book, Dr. Thigpen speculates that extraterrestrials may have been a part of St. Pio's "**divinely inspired knowledge**."[444] But consider how abysmally this great saint would have failed to act upon such a momentous and groundbreaking "revelation" as that if, despite countless opportunities to relay it in a manner we could actually trust, he only managed to once sneak it into a private conversation with one person. While entertaining such a speculation as that, one might as well also accuse this extraordinary mystic saint of being an insufferably apathetic coward and sluggard.

Let us contrast this to another quote *correctly* attributed to Padre Pio, but which some attempted to dispute: his repeated endorsement of the Servant of God Luisa Piccarreta. There, we are not left with hearsay; we have written affirmations of the endorsement, we have multiple identified individuals who relayed it, and we have all of these accounts contained in the official biography of Luisa, published by the Vatican in 2016 (for details, see www.SunOfMyWill.com). Even then, many people opposed the attribution—and one cannot blame them for wanting to be sure of such a thing (*even though it is not remarkable; other Italian saints of that time who knew Luisa or knew of her, such as St. Hannibal di Francis and even Pope St. Pius X, also endorsed her*) before granting it credibility. In this case, however, we do have such surety. In the case of Padre Pio supposedly believing in aliens, we haven't the faintest hint of credibility.[445]

Another reason to dismiss this quote is the *type* of alien belief being asserted within it. Among Catholic ET promoters, there are varying degrees of impiety found within their premises. On the one hand, there are those who take the "least impious" (but still extremely wrong and dangerous) approach to their ET belief: they still regard earth as the spiritual center of the universe, they still regard human beings as the ultimate recipients of God's intervention into the universe, and therefore they believe that "aliens" are in dire need of hearing the Gospel from us and being evangelized. On the other—exceedingly impious—extreme, there are those who blasphemously posit multiple Incarnations of God or who (like Msgr. Balducci) regard the earth and earthlings as pathetically spiritually "unevolved;" the very "worst" of God's creation, in dire need of salvation from the "aliens." And it is this latter type of particularly evil alien belief that the quote in question attributes to Padre Pio. It depicts the questioner saying he or she regards Earth as "**nothing compared to other planets**," and Padre Pio supposedly responding, "**exactly**!", and declaring that, "***we earthlings are nothing,* too**"!

But as any Christian knows, *this* is the planet in which God Himself chose to become incarnate! *This* is the planet that will host Judgment Day. *This* is the planet where God's *only* true Church exists. Whoever would nevertheless posit that this planet is "nothing" compared to planets with alien civilizations is guilty of espousing a gravely impious and remarkably erroneous brand of alien belief. Moreover, *this* is the planet in which the Mother of God was Immaculately Conceived. She (according to this bogus quote), being an "earthling," is a mere "nothing." Yet we know—dogmatically—that she is not only the greatest creature in the universe but also the greatest possible creature; she is the Queen of all.

We can be quite sure that Padre Pio would never say such absurd things. This quote, alleging St. Pio's alien belief, is—like countless other fabrications attributed to him—not worth the paper on which it is written. (Perhaps that is why the book containing it has long been impossible to find—one wonders if those who know the real backstory of this false attribution demanded that the publisher take it out of print.)

***

Let us, however, pretend that this quote really is relaying a conversation held with Padre Pio and that the saint really did say these things. As we noted, all this would mean is that he was wrong—as *all* saints are on *many* things.

Padre Pio was an astonishingly holy saint. But he was also a simple man who trusted those whom one was generally expected to trust. He died in the year 1968—well into the UFO craze, and well into the period of time Pope St. Paul VI spoke of with the "smoke of Satan" entering the Church of God thanks to "pagan prophets of science." (See Part Four.) Men in the Vatican were becoming giddy for extraterrestrials, as the Great Deception was firmly establishing itself in the very place Satan ultimately wants it enshrined: Rome. If Padre Pio believed in aliens due to the assurances of clergymen in the Roman hierarchy who insisted such belief was practically obligatory, then he would not be the only exceedingly holy person who was misled by such false claims.

We also do not know when this supposed conversation with Padre Pio purportedly took place. If we pretend it is true and that it did happen before 1960, then it would also possible that Padre Pio believed in aliens due to his being influenced by Maria Valtorta's writings (these writings speak of "inhabited worlds" other than earth; we will consider them in the next section). Indeed, it is well known that he had read them. However, towards the end of 1959, the Holy Office (Congregation for the Doctrine of the Faith) condemned this mystic's writings and in the beginning of 1960, Pope St. John XXIII ordered this condemnation to be published. If Padre Pio asserted something before 1960 that he gleaned from those writings, he certainly would not have asserted it again after 1960. But again, most importantly: we have no reliable evidence of alien belief actually being supported by this great saint. The entire corpus of reliable accounts we have from him is utterly devoid of any openness to, much less advocacy of, ET belief.

***

In addition to *Così Parlò Padre Pio*, one more book is sometimes mentioned as bolstering the claim that Padre Pio believed in aliens (when, in fact, it only mitigates that very claim): *La Mia Vita Vicino a Padre Pio*, by Ms. Cleonice Morcaldi. Although Dr. Thigpen's own 2022 book does not cite or even mention it, he did discuss it in a 2023 letter written to a Catholic journalist, which was published to the latter's website[446] and received widespread promulgation. In that letter Thigpen appeared to concede—despite his "*considerable effort...with the help of some providential connections of a friend in Italy with persons who were personally acquainted with the source*"—that even the book he did cite (*Così Parlò Padre Pio*) does *not* indicate who it was that allegedly heard Padre Pio endorse belief in aliens, thereby confirming that we are dealing with mere hearsay.*

Unfortunately, other publications have falsely claimed that the author of that book—Fr. Nello Castello—*was* relaying *his own* direct account of Padre Pio's words. For example, the 2017 book, *Padre Pio: Heavenly Facts and Words of Wisdom*, by Giuseppe Caccioppoli, makes this claim. It is possible that Dr. Thigpen derived some of the errors in the forthcoming quote from that book's erroneous references. With respect to *La Mia Vita Vicino a Padre Pio,* Thigpen claims, in his letter to the journalist:

> This conclusion may be borne out by a second source for the quote, *La mia vita a vicino Padre Pio: Diario Intimo Spirituale* ("My Life Near Padre Pio: An Intimate Spiritual Diary) by Cleonice Morcaldi ... It was published much more recently, in 2020, and again, an English translation is not yet available. ... The quote appears on page 85 of the book. We must note that even though St. Pio's words are the same in both passages, the words of the questions put to him vary slightly between these two books... these may in fact be accounts of the same dialogue, with either Morcaldi or Castello paraphrasing, or perhaps remembering imperfectly, the question as Morcaldi asked it or as Castello heard it reported.

---

* In the letter, Thigpen acknowledges "The context of the quote in the book [*Così Parlò Padre Pio*] suggests that [its author] was reporting an exchange of the saint with a [unidentified] third party."

> ... I think it reasonable, then, to accept the testimony of these two individuals that St. Pio did in fact believe that intelligent extraterrestrial creatures exist and that at least some of them have not fallen the way our human race did.

There are several errors in Thigpen's letter. First, on a more mundane level, he is wrong about the book's publication date and the page of the reference (it was published in 1997, not 2020, and the relevant quote is on page 59, not page 85: www.DSDOConnor.com/Pio). Most importantly, however, is the fact that Thigpen completely misrepresents the book's content. It does *not* recount the same words that the *Cosi Parlo* book attributes to Padre Pio—*not even close.* The only thing contained in this 1997 book that is in any way relevant to the extraterrestrial question is the following brief exchange, which I here present in its entirety and without abridgement:

> —When I was told that the planets are inhabited, my faith was shaken.
> —*And what? Don't you wish there were other beings? That God's omnipotence had been limited to this little planet of ours?*
> —I am full of doubts! I'm afraid I no longer have faith.
> —*But rest assured. The Lord shines in your soul**

At this point, Padre Pio and Ms. Morcaldi immediately moved on to other matters (directly before this exchange, they had merely been discussing fear, love, and miracles, in terms entirely unrelated to inhabited planets). Notably absent are any of the blasphemous claims that the *Così Parlò Padre Pio* book attributes to St. Pio (i.e., Pio agreeing that aliens exist and claiming that earthlings are "nothing," and earth is "nothing" compared to aliens).

As we can see, in this book, Padre Pio does *not* affirm that he believes in aliens. He is simply trying to help one of his spiritual daughters whose faith had been shaken by those in the Church claiming aliens exist. Instead of launching into a theological or scientific treatise to assure her those people were wrong, he responds in his usual way; not so much intellectually resolving the confusion, but instead seeking to heal the wound that brought it about. Obviously, an ET promoter would take even this exchange as supposed "proof" that St. Pio believed in aliens. But an honest assessment of his response, which is nothing but a few rhetorical questions, yields anything but that conclusion. Padre Pio was known to respond in enigmatic ways to various questions and concerns; this would simply be one example of that approach. Perhaps he could see, in Morcaldi's soul (he could often read souls), that the easiest way to bolster her Faith was not to dispute aliens, but to ask questions which might be taken as implying that aliens would be no affront to God's Omnipotence. (Recall

---

* In the original Italian: "*Quando mi han detto che i pianeti sono abitati, la mia fede si è scossa. E che? Non vorresti che ci fossero altri esseri? Che l'onnipotenza di Dio si fosse limitata a questo nostro piccolo pianeta? Sono piena di dubbi! Temo di non avere più fede. Ma sta' tranquilla. Il Signore risplende nell'anima tua*"

that, even from the first pages of the book now before you, we have conceded that aliens are entirely "possible" *in accordance with God's Omnipotence.* It is not that they "could not exist," rather, it is that the most faithful approach to Scripture, Magisterium, Sacred Tradition, etc., assures us that they *do not* exist.)

Imagine an analogous hypothetical scenario. Suppose Morcaldi had instead said to Padre Pio, *"When I was told that everyone without exception went to Heaven, my faith was shaken."* (Here, she would have been merely relaying being told the heresy of Universalism, which also became popular during the 20th century.) The saint could have responded by recounting the many Scripture verses and Magisterial teachings from which we can clearly infer this is not the case. Or he could have just said *"And what? Don't you wish that everyone was saved? That God's omnipotence had been limited to exclude some from salvation?"* This would not have been an endorsement of the heresy of Universalism; it would merely have been an encouragement to Morcaldi to not let her faith become shaken even in light of this heresy's proposal.

Note as well that when Morcaldi shared that she was afraid she no longer had faith, Padre Pio did not respond by insisting that aliens exist or even that her Catholic Faith was reconcilable with aliens. Quite the opposite, he assured this woman (*who just indicated to him that she felt Catholicism was irreconcilable with aliens!*) not merely that she had faith, but that "**the Lord shines in your soul**"! This is remarkable. It is even possible that St. Pio was testing her with his rhetorical questions, and in her refusal to take them as an indication aliens exist, she passed this test.

***

We have now seen—laid out clearly before our eyes without obfuscation—the relevant selections from the books that are the *only two* ultimate sources for the innumerable claims now circulating on the internet with respect to Padre Pio and aliens. What emerges from their contrast is deeply telling. It is precisely the book that does *not* indicate whom Padre Pio was speaking to that attributes the blasphemous ET-belief claims to the saint. The book that *does* indicate who was speaking with him recounts the conversation (which was likely the same one) being devoid of any claims from the saint that he believed in aliens! It is not difficult to determine which is more worthy of our trust.

In his letter quoted above, Dr. Thigpen claims, *"I think it reasonable, then, to accept the testimony of these two individuals that St. Pio did in fact believe that intelligent extraterrestrial creatures exist."* In fact, we do not have a *single* individual giving "testimony" that Padre Pio believed in aliens, much less two testimonies! We have one author, Fr. Costello, relaying an alleged private conversation without disclosing the person it involved. That is not a "testimony," that is hearsay. We have another author, Ms. Morcaldi, recounting (again, likely the same) conversation, devoid of any claim that Padre Pio believed in aliens.*

Here is the more likely reality: Morcaldi, in her own book, recounting *her own dialogues* with Padre Pio, was seeking to gently rebuke Fr. Costello's false account of the conversation, which was embellished with an outlandish addition that did not actually take place. Note that Costello's book (*Così Parlò Padre Pio*) was published well before Morcaldi's book. Therefore, Morcaldi was doubtless aware of this false attribution to the saint based on her own conversation with him. Perhaps her accurate recounting of the same conversation in her own book was her way of correcting Costello's account.

***

Let us conclude, however, by pretending that Costello's account was accurate. Even then, we have no way of assessing what exactly Padre Pio meant. That would have been the only time he ever so much as mentioned this matter. (This, recall, is another sure testimony to the quote's fraudulent nature—if that was his view, how could he have never found a *single* other opportunity to say it except extremely briefly in one private conversation?). I will readily concede that the most immediate way to understand those words would be in reference to aliens (hence my previous observation that such a reference would be nothing short of blasphemous).

But it is also quite possible that such words as those were not references to aliens at all. From that single, isolated, private and informal remark, we could not even be certain Pio was not simply referring to *angels* having various interactions throughout the universe (which, as we will shortly see, is also how many of her devotees interpret Valtorta's messages on this matter—messages St. Pio read). Never does even Costello's attribution show Padre Pio clarifying that he is referring to *material* beings (what we mean today by "aliens"); all it refers to are "creatures of God" who "did not sin and fall as we did." This could just as easily refer to unfallen angels (i.e., angels properly so-called, as opposed to demons) assigned to glorify God through their interactions on other planets.

Therefore, even if we pretended Costello's account was accurate, an (honest) ET promoter is still left needing to admit one thing: without any other words whatsoever—spoken or written—from Padre Pio (or from anyone among the thousands he conversed with who can be consulted on his

---

* Thigpen does discuss the possibility that two separate conversations were being recounted in the two books. But we have no reason to believe that without knowing whom the other one took place with. He claims it is likely St. Pio would have simply said identical things in both conversations. I disagree. This saint did not regurgitate memorized responses. Each thing he said was beautifully crafted for the sake of the person to whom he was speaking.

words) on this matter, we have no way of accurately gauging and clarifying what his views actually were. Costello's account would be at best "interesting."

What About Pope Sts. John Paul II and Paul VI?

Moving on to the next saint who Catholic ET promoters insist believed in aliens, we should address their claims about Pope John Paul II. Here, we have significantly less to consider, as we are only dealing with one alleged report given by one newspaper in the year 1999 which claimed to recount one brief exchange the Pope had with a small child.

Here as with the ostensible Padre Pio quote, the only source we have to draw from is the paper (published on two fringe Ufology websites) from Msgr. Balducci. Although I have read many references to the alleged quote, tracing back the trail of citations always leads back to Balducci. Here is the purported quote, as described in Dr. Thigpen's book:

> Finally of note in this regard is a remark by the popular Polish Pope Saint John Paul II (1920–2005). According to a report of his visit to the parish of Sant'Innocenzo I Papa e San Guido Vescovo in Rome on November 28, 1999, the pope had a brief but significant exchange with a child who was attending the event. When the little one asked him, "Holy Father, are there any aliens?" the saint did not respond, "We don't know," or even "If they exist, then ..." Instead, he replied simply, "Always remember: They are children of God as we are." [447]

At no point does Dr. Thigpen (or any other author I have read who relays this quote) indicate where exactly this "report" was published or by whom. There is, however, an actual report of this visit on the Vatican's official website,[448] and nowhere within it is there any mention of this exchange (or anything about aliens). Moreover, I have not even been able to find this "report" described within Balducci's own papers. Dr. Thigpen cites a document by Balducci posted on the "Scribd" website. However, the document he cites says nothing about this matter. Nevertheless, I will assume Thigpen simply accidentally cited the wrong thing, and that he did indeed read this quote within something Balducci wrote somewhere. Regardless of that assumption, we have no grounds whatsoever for believing this event took place. No one knows *anything* about this "report," so we cannot even *begin* to attempt to verify it.

Even here, we should consider the proper understanding of this encounter, if we pretend that it did happen. The Pope would have been answering an impromptu question from a small child. The Pope likely would have wanted the child to simply understand that every rational creature is a child of God. Alternatively, perhaps he was even "playing along," like an adult might do if asked by a child about Santa Claus, or with a child's imaginary friend, or with the fictional plotline of one of his favorite stories.

Ultimately, we must consider how bizarre it would be for so prolific an author and speaker as John Paul II/Karol Wojtyla, if he did believe in aliens, to be incapable of finding a *single* opportunity to clearly address it; instead choosing to relay this remarkable (remarkably problematic, that is) view only by way of a random remark to a small child. This, despite publishing tens of thousands of pages worth of material (between his own writings and his talks, homilies, etc.), all of which *can* validly be attributed to him.

Clearly, to attempt to draw meaningful conclusions from this supposed encounter, relayed in a "report" that evidently is nowhere to be found, is not merely to build a castle on the sand—it is to attempt to build one floating midair. Yet Dr. Thigpen exercises some elaborate imaginative powers here to squeeze out of this myth an argument for extraterrestrials. In recent podcasts, he has even attempted to use this particular "encounter" with the Pope to outright dismiss all considerations of Paragraph 356 of the Catechism with respect to aliens. Instead of trusting the word of the Catechism, he trusts his interpretation of the non-existent reports of this likely non-existent encounter: he insists that if anyone understood the Catechism, it was John Paul II, and if he was okay with aliens, we likewise must assume the Catechism presents no problems for belief in extraterrestrials. (In fact, as we saw in Part Two, the Catechism is entirely unambiguous in ruling out aliens, with language so clear that no one may interpret them away with sophistical acrobatics.) The bankruptcy of such approaches as these, regularly employed by Catholic ET promoters, testifies to the bankruptcy of their thesis. They cannot dispute that the Catechism (and other authoritative texts and demonstrative arguments) rules out aliens, therefore they resort to condemning as "fundamentalists" or "proof texters" (as Dr. Thigpen regularly does) those who acknowledge and submit to the Catechism's teachings on this topic.

***

Pope St. Paul VI and Aliens

The other saint Dr. Thigpen defers to in supposed support of alien belief is Pope St. Paul VI. Thigpen writes:

> According to a report by Reginaldo Francisco, the French Catholic philosopher and theologian Jean Guitton once had a conversation with Pope Saint Paul VI (1897–1978) in which they discussed ETI. The pope found the possibility of extraterrestrials to be reasonable and could see how "the universal Church" would in that case include more than the human race[449]

We are not even dealing with a quote here, only a general description of an alleged conversation, so very little could be made of this *even if* we could have confidence in what Jean Guitton relayed. All we have is one man's claim that from a conversation he had, Paul VI found some possibility "reasonable."

Dr. Thigpen cites Thomas O'Meara for this claim. O'Meara, in turn, cites an author by the name of Francesco Bertola. Bertola, in turn, is apparently citing Reginaldo Francisco. And Reginaldo Francisco, in turn, is reporting on something that allegedly transpired with Jean Guitton. And Jean Guitton is the one we are told is relaying the gist of this supposed conversation. Here as usual with claims such as these in support of ET belief, we are playing the game of telephone with several layers of removal from reality and no realistic way of knowing what actually transpired. If one is willing to believe all claims of that nature when they pertain to things allegedly said by Popes, he would have stopped being Catholic long ago.

Note that we are not even presented with a claim that the Pope *believed* in aliens, but only that he supposedly said such belief could be "reasonable" in some conversation. It is unlikely that Paul VI said even that, but if he did, he was simply mistaken, as popes often are in their personal opinions. If would not have been that sainted Pope's only mistake.

***

Dr. Thigpen also cites other saints in supposed support of his thesis, when in fact their quotations have no bearing whatsoever on it. For example, he quotes St. John Chrysostom's teaching that "with God, nothing is difficult... with God it is easy to make worlds without number and end." Obviously, there is no grounds here for supposing that Chrysostom believed God actually did do this, or might have. As we will see in a forthcoming appendix, this is a theological point on God's Omnipotence, not an encouragement to speculate about aliens. St. John Chrysostom was a Father of the Church, and whoever is interested in seeing how the teachings of the Fathers rule out aliens should consult Part Two of this book.

What About Garabandal, Maria Valtorta, and Medjugorje?

Maria Valtorta was a lay Italian author who died in the year 1961 and published the famous *Poem of the Man-God*. A number of passages within her over ten-thousand-pages-worth of writings contain alleged revelations from Jesus and Mary referring to "inhabited worlds," and thus she is sometimes deferred to by ET promoters in support of their thesis.

Valtorta's writings, however, were effectively condemned by the Church in 1959 and placed on the Index of Prohibited Books. Unlike other mystics whose writings were similarly dealt with (e.g. St. Faustina and the Servant of God Luisa Piccarreta), there has been no comparable walking back of those ecclesiastical censures against Valtorta. Also unlike Luisa (who only had an individual translation of a tiny fraction of her works placed on the Index, with all the rest untouched; dozens even with *Imprimaturs*, and who has since been declared a Servant of God, among many other verifications of authenticity), the entirety of Valtorta's main work itself was condemned and there has been no progress on a cause of Beatification.

This does not necessarily mean Valtorta's writings are all false; the Index, of course, was abrogated in 1966, and the Church could well in the future grant them ecclesial approbations or open Valtorta's cause. What is certain, however, is that there are at least some errors in her writings, and therefore they are not all supernatural in origin. For example, they speak theologically erroneously about the Fall of Man, claiming (allegedly from Jesus Himself) that even before Eve ate the fruit, her "flesh was aroused" by Satan "caressing" Eve. This, however, is impossible, as such arousal would be a result of concupiscence, which was *only* a *result* of the Fall. Before the Fall, only purely intellectual fault could have occurred within Adam and Eve—illicit fleshly arousal was absolutely impossible. Moreover, since the 1959 condemnation and on two separate occasions, Pope Bendict XVI (as Cardinal Ratzinger) appeared to discourage the *Poem of the Man God*.[450]

My purpose here is not to condemn Valtorta or her writings. I have heard testimonies of those positively affected by them, and I am in no place to dispute those good fruits. My knowledge of her messages is not deep, and I do not intend to even weigh in on the debate now raging about them, much less issue a judgment of my own. My intent is only to note one conclusion we all (including Valtorta's most zealous devotees) should draw from what we can easily glean: Valtorta's writings cannot be deferred to in seeking to settle a controversial matter such as this—especially when we have private revelations that are far more reliable (not to mention Scripture, Magisterium, and Sacred Tradition) which expressly and repeatedly rule out aliens.

Without going into great detail, I will also add that some devotees of Valtorta insist that even those passages which speak of "inhabited planets" do not actually refer to extraterrestrials. They insist, rather, that these selections refer to the interactions of angels with the heavenly bodies, irrational (but animate) creatures scattered about the cosmos, or a poetic way of referring to the inanimate structures throughout the galaxies that each, in their own way (not rationally, though), testify to the glory of God—only personified in the mystical language employed within Valtorta's writings. If indeed the pertinent passages in Valtorta are authentic mysticism, then these interpretations are certainly the correct ones.

***

The apparitions of the Blessed Virgin Mary to four girls at Garabandal, Spain, took place in the 1960s. While I do believe in them (I will, of course, submit to any forthcoming Church decrees), it is important to note that they have received "non constat" declarations from the Church—that is, "**it cannot be said to be** supernatural in origin." Although this may sound like a formal condemnation to those unacquainted with the nature of ecclesial rulings on apparitions, it is actually quite distinct from a condemnation, i.e., a "constat de non," which indicates "**it can be said to be non**-supernatural in origin." Essentially, the Church has (thus far) stated it cannot decide that Garabandal is supernatural (authentic) and it cannot decide that Garabandal is non-supernatural (inauthentic). Accordingly, the faithful are free to discern the apparitions on their own and follow their consciences on the matter.

One thing, however, is clear from Garabandal's ecclesial status: as with Valtorta, Garabandal should not be deferred to in seeking to settle controversial theological matters. Garabandal, like most apparitions, exhorts us to prayer, conversion, repentance, etc., and it also prophesies extraordinary events—such as Chastisements, the Warning (or Illumination of Conscience), and a great Miracle. There is no theological difficulty with (much less error within) any of these exhortations or prophecies, therefore there is little reason to be incredulous regarding them if heeding these messages helps one's spiritual life.

The question of extraterrestrials, though, does not factor into the apparitions' core messages at all, and may be entirely made up. Here, we are dealing only with a single alleged third hand account of one friend who told Conchita (one of the seers) to ask the Virgin Mary, "are there intelligent beings in outer space?", and we are told that the answer was simply "yes," and that a follow up question was allegedly answered: "They are like men, tainted alike by sin, but also redeemed by Christ just like men."

I have not been able to find this supposed dialogue recorded in any of the reliable books on Garabandal. For example, the 662-page authoritative text on the apparitions, *She Went in Haste to the Mountain*, has absolutely no mention of it. Every other book on Garabandal I have been able to find is equally devoid of any reference to this supposed exchange. Some experts in Garabandal who have largely dedicated their lives to promoting it have even resolutely insisted that this attribution is utterly false, and that no such message about aliens is contained anywhere in relation to Garabandal or in Conchita's writings or sayings. One Garabandal promoter wrote:

> **I can assure you aliens have not on any occasion been recorded as a topic of discussion in any reputable book or discourse that included verifiable testimony from any of the Seers simply because the subject matter between Our Holy Mother and the children does not exist. It's a lie** from [name redacted], as are many [claims]...[451]

The insistence from promoters such as the one quoted above is likely correct, especially when we consider that Conchita is still alive. She has had several decades to confirm this claim about aliens, and never once has, despite its prominence. Any such claim about extraterrestrials is entirely absent from those interviews of Conchita we actually have recordings of or from which we have trustworthy transcripts.

But let us suppose that this really was something that Conchita relayed. Even then, we must note that such claims made in interviews with Conchita in relation to Garabandal have already been proven false, therefore we know that we cannot necessarily place too much credence in them. For example, a blind man named Joey Lomangino was (based on what was relayed in one of these interviews regarding a prophecy allegedly given by Our Lady to Conchita)—supposed to miraculously receive his eyesight back at the prophesied Great Miracle. As one author noted:

> On March 19th, 1964, **Conchita wrote to Joey to say that Our Lady had just told her that "you shall see on the very day of the Miracle".** This prophecy became very widely known. Devotees of Garabandal understood it to mean that Joey would be present at the village for the Miracle and would have his physical sight restored. Fifty years later, however, on June 18th 2014, Joey died in New York, surrounded by his loving family.[452]

Many attempts by Garabandal devotees have been made to explain this prophetic miss, but none are as honest as simply admitting that this was a failed prophecy. This does not mean that Garabandal is an inauthentic apparition. It simply means we cannot assume that every letter or interview in relation to it making a claim about what the Virgin Mary allegedly said is in fact an accurate representation of what the Virgin Mary truly said. This was not the only prophetic failure from Garabandal, though. Even Padre Pio was supposed to be present for the Miracle—he died 55 years ago, and the Miracle has not even happened yet. This, too, is explained away by some devotees, insisting he "will be there" because he is in Heaven; but that is simply not what the prophecy indicated.

Even authentic apparitions can be a mixture of truth and falsity. In consideration of this reality, some approved apparitions sometimes only see a fraction of their messages approved by the Church. The Devil is an opportunist, and he despises apparitions of his adversary, the Virgin, more than almost anything else. When he sees that Our Lady is appearing somewhere, we can be assured that he does not rest in seeking to inject himself into the phenomenon somehow; wherever a door may be left open to his entry.

Consequently, we must always read all private revelations—even unquestionably authentic ones—through the lens of Scripture and Magisterium. Only Public Revelation (the Bible) is directly authored by the Holy Spirit. All private revelations are received according to the mode of the receiver (i.e., the seer), and this seer could also easily, entirely innocently and inadvertently, add his or her own subjective thoughts into the message, confusing their own imagination with what Heaven directly stated.

I conclude by reiterating that I do believe in Garabandal—though I am not claiming *certainty* in its authenticity, and I will submit to any decrees the Church might promulgate in the future. I do not believe that Conchita actually relayed this teaching on aliens from Our Lady, but I am certain that even if she did, she simply misunderstood the Blessed Virgin, mistook her own thoughts for the Blessed Virgin's words, or even was deceived by the Devil pretending to give a message from Mary (even exceedingly holy people and authentic seers can be deceived at times). While the main thrust of any authentic private revelation is certainly likewise authentic, obscure details may not be.

***

On the question of the apparitions of Our Lady at Medjugorje (in Bosnia) and extraterrestrials, we are confronted with almost no material. While those who claim that private revelations given through Garabandal or Maria Valtorta endorsed alien belief are deeply mistaken, they are at least operating on the basis of *something*. But whoever claims that Our Lady endorsed aliens at Medjugorje is simply outright lying. Such a man has revealed he is willing to misrepresent even the Blessed Virgin herself.

Some sources allege that one of the Medjugorje seers, Marija, asked the Virgin, "is there life on other planets?", and that the response was supposedly, "it is not time for you to know this now." First, it must be noted that this exchange is not contained *anywhere* in the over 40 years of messages reported in relation to these apparitions (messages now totaling well over one hundred thousand words). It is only something that some writers have alleged was relayed informally by Marija.

More important, however, is the recognition that even if this alleged quote is authentic, it contains no indication whatsoever that aliens exist. The alleged response from the Virgin Mary does not say what the ET promoters pretend it does. They treat this quote as if it was akin to the Virgin signaling, with a smirk and a wink, that aliens exist. In fact, the quote does not say or imply that "aliens exist, *but it is not yet time for us to know about them.*"

It says almost the opposite: that it is not the time for *that question itself* to be answered by her. Now, if indeed the ET Deception is the Great Deception—which is a major thesis of this book—then it would be perfectly sensible that God would not allow Our Lady to directly and explicitly settle the question in the world's most popular ongoing apparition. Perhaps that would risk depriving The Test of its value. Alternatively, the exchange may be comparable to a mother being asked, by her very young children, "Is it true that babies are brought by a stork?" The answer, of course, is "no." But as a small child is unprepared for "the talk" on how babies come about, the mother may prefer to simply respond that it is not yet the time for the child to know about the answer to that question. Perhaps if this conversation really occurred, Marija herself was, for whatever reason, not prepared to hear at that moment that aliens do not exist.

In a tragic irony, therefore, those Medjugorje promoters who also promote belief in extraterrestrials are bluntly violating Our Lady's desires here (if this exchange really happened) by presenting this quote as a justification for their ET promotion. If the quote is authentic, it implicitly instructs them *not* to insist upon the very views they propagate!

Let us also recall that the private revelations of Maria Simma (reviewed in Part Two) explicitly declare that there are no aliens, and that any supposed ET encounter is a Satanic ploy. Simma's revelations, however, are deeply connected to Medjugorje. Moreover, even the most renowned promoters of Medjugorje heartily endorse Simma, including Fr. Slavko himself. It would be strange to believe in the authenticity of Medjugorje but not Maria Simma. And it would be incoherent to believe in the authenticity of Maria Simma while also believing in (much less promoting) extraterrestrials.

Finally, if this exchange between Marija and Our Lady is authentic, it repudiates all claims that aliens are now among us (which, recall, is an almost universal claim among ET promoters). If aliens are already here, interacting with thousands if not millions of people, constantly buzzing our skies, leaving wreckages and corpses, etc., then it would obviously be nonsensical for Our Lady to say that it is *not time to know* about them. An ET promoter who claims aliens are already here, but who also promotes Medjugorje and believes in this exchange, is essentially leading a double life.

What About St. Jerome and the Satyr?

"Satyrs" are well-known entities in ancient Greek Paganism and other false religions. They were often regarded as numbering among the "daimones," an umbrella term that was used for certain supposed beings who stand "between gods and men," and "bring the prayers of men to the gods." St. Augustine famously refuted this demonic mythology in *City of God*. The truth in brief, is that "daimones" or "daimons" are either demons or fictions. Every early Christian would have been well aware of such things and likewise aware of their decidedly false or demonic nature.

The norm that Satyrs are demons may have exceptions (i.e., the term could have been used for certain deformed humans, a possibility we will consider presently), but the norm itself is not and was not controversial. Dr. Paul Thigpen nonetheless argues that Christianity must be fine with the idea of non-human intelligent incarnate creatures because of an account St. Jerome wrote about St. Anthony's travels in the desert, and the latter's encounter with one such creature that claimed it was a "satyr." (To this list of supposed non-human, non-angelic intelligences he adds nymphs, fairies, pixies, leprechauns, elves, dwarfs, trolls, brownies, menehune, and stick people. While any Christian should know these beings are either fictional or simply guises worn by demons, Thigpen argues they are real—but non-demonic, non-human, and non-angelic—and that they likewise prove his point about NHI.) Dr. Thigpen writes:

> Satyrs are one of many creatures portrayed by the ancients but now considered mythical. ...Jerome reported that the satyr was a manlike creature, but with "a hooked snout, horned forehead, and extremities like goats' feet." When Anthony asked him who he was, the rather friendly satyr replied: "*I am a mortal being and one of those inhabitants of the desert whom the Gentiles deluded by various forms of error worship under the names of Fauns, Satyrs, and Incubi. I am sent to represent my tribe.*" Then he entreated Anthony to pray for him, because his fellows had heard that Christ had come to Earth and that the gospel was being proclaimed throughout the world. Anthony shed tears of joy and marveled that "beasts speak of Christ." Then the satyr departed quickly. ... Though the satyr was not extraterrestrial (today he might be designated "other terrestrial" or "ultraterrestrial"), he represented a form of non-human, non-angelic intelligence. And Saint Jerome believed that such creatures actually existed... Our point here is not to claim that satyrs are real. Our point is that Saint Jerome apparently had no problem believing in the existence of non-human, non-angelic intelligences. ... if such a brilliant, devout, and well-catechized Catholic Christian [as Jerome] saw no conflict between his faith and the existence of intelligent creatures neither human nor angelic, we need not fear that such an openness is somehow foolish or heretical.[453]

Dr. Thigpen's argument above, however, consists of an extraction of only those excerpts which appear to support his thesis (while ignoring those which refute it), a misinterpretation of what St. Jerome actually wrote, and a contradiction of his (Thigpen's) own argument for the orthodoxy of belief in aliens. Let us consider each of these flaws below.

First, Thigpen ignores the sentences *immediately* preceding the ones he quotes. There, St. Jerome describes yet another *demon* that Anthony encountered; this time, in the form of a centaur. Jerome relays:

> All at once he [Anthony] beholds a creature of mingled shape, **half horse half man, called by the poets Hippocentaur**. At the sight of this he arms himself by making on his forehead the sign of salvation, and then exclaims, "Holloa! Where in these parts is a servant of God living?" The monster after gnashing out some kind of outlandish utterance, in words broken rather than spoken through his bristling lips, **at length finds a friendly mode of communication, and extending his right hand points out the way desired**. ... But **whether the devil took this shape to terrify him, or whether it be that the desert which is known to abound in monstrous animals engenders that kind of creature also, we cannot decide**.

Again, this is what comes *immediately* before Jerome's description of Anthony's encounter with the "satyr." Consequently, no one who is actually reading Jerome's account would fail to have on the forefront of his mind the consideration that these beings Anthony was here encountering may be either demons assuming a deceptive form, or "monstrous **animals**" of some mysterious sort. There is no consideration whatsoever that these creatures are anything but *animals* or *demons*. The fact that this "centaur" even "utters words" and manages to engage in "a friendly mode of communication" does not shake St. Jerome's conviction that this is no child of God; no creature of another species than us having reason—i.e., it was (in our contemporary terms) certainly not an NHI (non-human, non-angelic intelligence), nor was it (as Thigpen asserts with respect to the "Satyr") an indication that Jerome found the idea of such things acceptable. Recall, as we saw in Part Two, that Jerome emphatically rejected the ET belief of Origen, and it is disingenuous to use any writings from this saint to argue for a belief he condemned as heretical.

As we saw with Balaam's Donkey, even an animal can be compelled to "utter words" by God (which does not indicate that the animal itself is rational), and a demon can also do the same using an animal as an instrument (e.g., the serpent in Genesis 3). Note that Jerome's reference to the thing as "half horse half man" is only a description of its "mingled **shape**," not its nature. Half "man" is certainly not what this thing *was*. Jerome is certain it was either a demonic apparition, or a "monstrous animal" of some sort; he simply does not know which. (I am sure we can safely conclude it was a demon.)

Immediately after describing this encounter, Jerome proceeds to describe Anthony's encounter with the "Satyr." Here, we again have multiple possible interpretations of what transpired, none of which support Thigpen's thesis. The description Jerome provides of the "Satyr" is much more similar to a normal human being than the centaur. It simply has a deformed nose, forehead, and feet. It could even have been a member of a particular race of humans who suffer from various deformities. Recall the teachings of St. Augustine we considered in Part Two:

> At Hippo-Diarrhytus there is a man whose hands are crescent-shaped, and have only two fingers each, and his feet similarly formed. **If there were a race like him, it would be added to the history of the curious and wonderful. Shall we therefore deny that this man is descended from that one man [Adam] who was first created?** ... Some years ago, quite within my own memory, a man was born in the East, double in his upper, but single in his lower half—having two heads, two chests, four hands, but one body and two feet like an ordinary man; and he lived so long that many had an opportunity of seeing him. But who could enumerate all the human births that have differed widely from their ascertained parents? As, therefore, **no one will deny that these are all descended from that one man, so all the races which are reported to have diverged in bodily appearance from the usual course which nature generally or almost universally preserves, <u>if they are embraced in that definition of man as rational and mortal animals, unquestionably trace their pedigree to that one first father of all</u>.** We are supposing these stories about various races who differ from one another and

> from us to be true; but possibly they are not: for if we were not aware that apes, and monkeys, and sphinxes are not men, but beasts, those historians would possibly describe them as races of men, and flaunt with impunity their false and vainglorious discoveries. But supposing they are men of whom these marvels are recorded, what if God has seen fit to create some races in this way, that we might not suppose that the monstrous births which appear among ourselves are the failures of that wisdom whereby He fashions the human nature, as we speak of the failure of a less perfect workman? Accordingly, it ought not to seem absurd to us, that as in individual races there are monstrous births, so in the whole race there are monstrous races. Wherefore, to conclude this question cautiously and guardedly, either these things which have been told of some races have no existence at all; or if they do exist, they are not human races [i.e., are mere animals without reason]; or if they are human [i.e., mortal, rational], they are descended from Adam. (St. Augustine. *City of God*. Book XVI. Ch. 8.)

Rightly does St. Augustine categorically rule out the very *possibility* of a race of rational mortal creatures who are not also, like us, descendants of Adam and Eve. He emphasizes that if some creature is a "rational and mortal animal," it is "**unquestionably**" a human being; a child of Adam.

The contrast between Jerome's adjacent descriptions of Anthony's encounters with the centaur and the satyr is deeply telling, and it directly refutes Dr. Thigpen's thesis. It is *precisely because* the centaur could not possibly be regarded as a human (no degree of deformation in a human birth or a human race could assume the form of a half-horse, "half-man") that Jerome is certain it was either a mere animal or a demonic apparition. In other words, it is *precisely because* Jerome realizes there are no "intelligent creatures neither human nor angelic" (Thigpen, Ch. 10) that he realizes he can discern possibilities for the satyr that were not possible for the centaur. Jerome presupposes the *opposite* of the very conclusion Thigpen tries to extract from Jerome!

Nevertheless, reasons remain to consider that this "satyr" which Anthony encountered could simply have been another demonic apparition. Thigpen claims that the "satyr" simply "departed quickly." In fact, Jerome writes: "[Anthony] had not finished speaking when, as if on wings, the wild creature fled away." Such a manner of travel would not appear natural to a creature with two legs, as this Satyr is described. A critic may say that a demon would not speak the way the Satyr did—beseeching prayers, referring to the Gentiles as deluded into erroneous worship, and referring to "your Lord and ours." But this is begging the question (i.e., circular reasoning). Demons constantly deceive and try to appear as if they were pious creatures, in order to seduce men. This is not merely *generally* true, it was a constant experience of St. Anthony *himself*. As Anthony noted, recounted in the work written of him by St. Athanasius:

> **...[Demons] are treacherous, and are ready to change themselves into**

all forms and assume all appearances. Very often also without appearing they imitate the music of harp and voice, and **recall the words of Scripture**. Sometimes, too, while we are reading they immediately repeat many times, like an echo, what is read. **They arouse us from our sleep to prayers**... At another time **they assume the appearance of monks and feign the speech of holy men,** that by their similarity they may deceive and thus drag their victims where they will.[454]

Note that the Satyr did not utter specific words that would be categorically outside of the willingness of demons to employ. For example, it did not specifically adore Jesus Christ by name, or make the sign of the cross on itself. It only referred to the "Lord" and asked for prayers. Such words are easily within the scope of what a demon might be willing to say in order to deceive. (Adoring the name of Jesus—confessing with faith that He is God come in the Flesh—on the other hand, would entail too much of a torment for them, even as a means to the end of deceiving a soul.)

Granted, Jerome does then speak of "a **man** of that kind" being brought alive to Alexandria during the time of Constantine, and thus exhorts, "let no one scruple to believe this incident." This might incline one toward the former interpretation (i.e., the "Satyr" as simply a deformed human). But Jerome does *not* insist that this was the case with the particular Satyr in question; only that he has heard of *another* case of a Satyr-like individual being seen in Alexandria and Antioch. Yet, Thigpen argues, "Jerome thus left no doubt that he believed the creature was real and the incident truly took place." But we cannot, from Jerome's claim, draw conclusions about the particular "Satyr" now under consideration. Jerome only says that the truth of the Satyr incident "is supported" by what allegedly once happened in Alexandria. Nevertheless, we should not rule out the possibility. A human sufficiently deformed to resemble a "Satyr" is not at all unpalatable. Even Socrates was said to look very much like a Satyr (cf. *Symposium*). Consider that we have *no* reliable accounts of entire groups of "Satyrs" being proven to be truly incarnate beings. We only see accounts of *one* individual "Satyr's" corpse (i.e., a deformed human's corpse) being brought before the Emperor. Even if, however, there truly was a whole race of "Satyrs" (which seems highly unlikely), the proper interpretation of that situation would be the one given above by St. Augustine, who insisted that any rational, mortal creature is "**unquestionably**" a man—a descendant of Adam.

A third possibility is that this "Satyr" simply was a strange animal which was miraculously or demonically given the power of speech. This interpretation appears supported by Jerome's account of Anthony's own words, wherein he says "*Woe to you, Alexandria, who instead of God worships monsters... What will you say now?* ***Beasts*** *speak of Christ, and you instead of God worship monsters.*" Anthony would never refer to this satyr as a "beast" if it was a rational creature as men are.

The final possibility is the obvious one—the one that almost everyone would prefer today, but which I did not want to pounce upon immediately lest I be mistaken for an incredulous "de-mystifier" who simply will not believe anything extraordinary and desires to render all such claims boring and ordinary! It is quite possible that this encounter simply did not happen. St. Jerome might have misunderstood what was reported to him (recall that this account is not in St. Anthony's own words), or the portions of text in question could be apocryphal additions, or the passage might be intended to be understood in a more legendary than literal fashion. The latter is what scholars tend to prefer (though I am not necessarily condoning their take). Theologian Fr. John Gavin even regards the whole text as essentially similar, in motivation and method, to the *Chronicles of Narnia*, writing:

> ...the popular elements of the story were certainly meant to attract a wider audience. **[Jerome] clearly drew upon pre-existing stories and legends surrounding the titular saint and presented them in a form that would both entertain and inspire**. It has been noted, for example, that Jerome borrows images of the "weird"—bizarre, striking examples of the supernatural and magic found in ancient romances—**in order to embellish his tales and enchant his readers.** ... In the wilderness Antony encounters two beasts that epitomized savagery for the ancient world: the centaur and the faun, symbolic of humanity's bestial tendencies and unfettered passions ... Yet, in his meetings with these hybrids Antony is shocked to discover a transformation in their characters ... The prophecy of Isaiah regarding the defeat of Babylon and the establishment of a new order is fulfilled before Anthony's eyes: "*But wild beasts will lie down there and its [Babylon's] houses will be full of howling creatures; there ostriches will dwell, and there satyrs will dance*" (Is. 13:21). All has been redeemed in Christ ... Antony was the witness of a new heaven and new earth in the making ... Despite the temporal and cultural divide, Jerome's fanciful Life of Paul the Hermit and Lewis's enchanting [Narnia] share a common vision of the Christian struggle in a creation groaning for redemption. In both worlds, Christ or Aslan recover a paradise that had been long subjected to corrupt, demonic despots.[455]

In other words, under Fr. Gavin's reading, St. Jerome simply provided a legend that symbolized the Triumph of Christ even in the order of creation. Jerome knew that all his readers were aware of the presence of beings like centaurs and satyrs in Pagan myths, and to refer to even these being conquered by grace provides an inspiring story. Yet, Catholic dogma of course holds that no demon can ever repent, therefore as most historical references to "Satyrs" and such are clearly references to demons (this fact is uncontroversial in Catholic thought), we must carefully reserve any story about their "conversion" to the status of mere myth.

***

Whichever of those four interpretations one chooses – the "Satyr" as a deformed man, a demonic apparition, an animal, or a mere legend not intended as nonfictional – one thing remains certain: it was *not* a "non-human, non-angelic intelligence."

Despite immense amounts of Scripture, Magisterium, and Tradition (which we reviewed in Parts One and Two) indicating there are no "intelligent creatures neither human nor angelic," Thigpen asserts that there are. In this context, he does so solely on the basis of this one brief paragraph from Jerome discussing an alleged encounter of Anthony's, which certainly is irrelevant to his claim. (He provides no other foundations for this claim in the argument he makes in that chapter, and he even brings up the Satyr again in another chapter to attempt to justify the orthodoxy of other NHI claims.) From this basis *alone*, he declares, "we need not fear that such an openness is somehow foolish or heretical." But he has only succeeded in demonstrating that such an openness is precisely that: utterly foolish.

In conclusion, we must recall that the entire defense that Catholic ET promoters like Dr. Thigpen employ to portray their thesis as orthodox is that the various Magisterial documents (which teach that *only* man is capable of knowing and loving God) *only apply to earth*. (As if the force of Magisterial truths runs up against some impenetrable barrier somewhere in the stratosphere.)

We already saw, in Part Two, how this restriction is false (*the Catechism, and other Magisterial documents, do not say only earth is being referred to – they say "all" is being referred to, and the word "all" is unambiguous*), and self-contradictory (*the ET promoters' whole point is that "aliens" are actually on earth!*). Yet we should also note that even this attempt to phrase ET belief in an orthodox manner itself completely undermines their "Satyr" thesis. There are no "Satyrs" (if by that one means non-angelic, non-demonic, non-human intelligent creatures), but if there were, they would obviously be just as *earthly* as we are. Therefore, they are ruled out by Church teaching *even as* the ET promoters interpret it.

Dr. Thigpen says that, "*Our point here is not to claim that satyrs are real. Our point is that Saint Jerome apparently had no problem believing in the existence of non-human, non-angelic intelligences. ... [therefore] we need not fear that such an openness is somehow foolish or heretical.*" But this caveat does not give him the ability to have his cake and eat it too. Does he, or does he not, stand by his interpretation of paragraph 365 of the Catechism (and other similar Magisterial teachings)? If he does, he must concede that *his own interpretation* of Jerome only describes this saint as succumbing to unorthodoxy. If, instead, he stands by his interpretation of Jerome, then he is undermining his own insistence about what the Catechism "really" means. One thing is certain: he cannot have it both ways.

In still another manner, however, Thigpen's argument seeks to have it both ways. He and many other Catholic ET promoters insist that the various condemnations of ET belief one can find throughout Church History are actually just *"object[ions] to the idea that* ***the human race*** *is not all one family, descended from the same first parents."*[456] And they are right, Polygenism is a heresy. But what, then, of the Satyr? While the Satyr which Anthony encountered is referred to as a "beast," St. Jerome specifically referred to the individual Satyr brought to Alexandria as "**a man**." Thigpen inserts a bracketed remark where he includes that quote, instructing us to interpret the word, "man," as simply, "creature." But that is not what Jerome said. Whatever deformed individual was brought to Alexandria was, simply, *a man*. Yet Thigpen would have us believe in NHI because of this account, although the text itself repudiates his interpretation. As, therefore, this individual "Satyr" was indeed "a man," Thigpen is (by claiming that it was *not*, but was rather some other type of creature) contradicting the very defense of ET belief he offers elsewhere to try to rescue it from various condemnations by saints and popes. He is implying that "men" exist who are not like us, but rather originate from other first parents.

There is no way to rescue the NHI Deception from censure by Catholic orthodoxy. Whenever one tries to defend it in one context, he only—in the very act of doing so—illustrates how thoroughly it succumbs to contradicting yet another Truth of the Faith.

(*Note that I am only focusing on Dr. Thigpen's argument here because he is the most prominent author to recently make it. Many others have similarly argued, and what is considered above addresses their claims as well.*)

What About Bl. Emmerich's Revelations on the Moon?

Bl. Emmerich's holiness and orthodoxy is beyond reproach, and her mysticism is surely authentic. Unfortunately, however, the books attributed to her suffer from several compounding problems which prevent us from regarding each passage contained therein as necessarily reflecting the reality of what God actually showed the mystic. First, Emmerich was not *dictating messages* received from Jesus, but rather was *describing visions* she interiorly saw, and she would even at times admit that she was not sure if she was describing them accurately. Second, and most importantly, Emmerich did not write down the revelations herself. Her visions were recorded only during the last several years of her life by a certain Clemens Brentano—a prominent secular poet in the German Romanticism movement—who visited her and listened to her recount them. More problematic still, he did not speak her dialect, and his notes were often imperfect or even entirely lacking. Those situations required him to use only his memory of the conversations with Emmerich to later recreate them on paper. He even edited that final product years later, leaving us with little ability to know what came from him and what came from Emmerich herself.

None of this deprives of value the volumes we have from Emmerich. It simply means that we cannot approach each passage therein with the same degree of confidence we can heed the revelations of some other mystics.* Instead, potentially problematic elements in the volumes attributed to Emmerich should simply be left aside if they cannot be found confirmed by other, more reliable, recordings of revelations given to authentic mystics. Precisely such a problematic element is used by one of today's popular Catholic ET promoters as a defense of his thesis, though in his book on the topic, he abridges out the portions of the quote that most clearly illustrate its failings. He quotes Emmerich (as reported by Brentano) as follows:

> She saw on the moon "many human figures flying from light into darkness as if hiding their shame, as if their conscience were in a bad state. ... I never saw any worship offered to God on the moon. ... The souls that I see hiding in darkness seem to be without suffering or joy, as if imprisoned till the Day of Judgement."[457]

Firstly, the most appropriate interpretation of this passage is to see it as referring to either purging souls, damned souls, or perhaps even souls consigned to some form of "limbo" until the end of time, for those who wish to posit such a place. Indeed, Heaven and hell are not only necessarily described as physical "places." They can be considered *states of being*, and just as purging souls or even damned souls are known to appear on earth (even at times being called "ghosts"), there is nothing to prevent them from having interactions on the moon, either. I do not intend to present that as a likely scenario; my point is only that the quote above should not be taken as a reference to aliens. Indeed, it specifically says that "human figures" are being discussed. Obviously, it is not referring to human bodies (such could not exist on the moon), therefore it must be taken as a reference to the other aspect of the human person: the soul.

It may, however, be more appropriate to simply leave aside this particular passage from Emmerich. In the portions of the quote above that the author left out, Emmerich is claimed by Brentano to have described:

---

* For example, in Part Two, we considered the revelations to the Servant of God Luisa Piccarreta. Those messages were all written down, directly by Luisa herself, and mostly consisted in a simple word-for-word transcription of what Jesus told her in revelations directly prior to her writing them down. She spent forty years writing out these revelations. Each message even bears the very day, month, and year, on which it was received. Moreover, all the messages were received under the most intense scrutiny and guidance of Archbishop-appointed priest spiritual directors, and they were immediately reviewed by Church-appointed ecclesial censors. Since Luisa's own time, they have been stored securely in the Church's keeping. (Photocopies of her original handwritten notebooks can readily be had.) The confidence we can have in them can only be described as immense.

> In other parts [of the moon] are fields and thickets in which animals roam ... The soil is yellow and stony; the vegetation like pith, fungi, or mushrooms.[458]

Indeed, there are no mushrooms on the moon, much less fields in which animals roam. Even if Brentano accurately recounted what Emmerich did tell him, Emmerich was not being given a vision of the moon.

The same author also quotes another passage where Emmerich allegedly describes "**planetary spirits... fallen spirits, but not devils**." However, this is simply a reference to some other class of demons than whichever one Emmerich had in mind by referring to "devils." As the quote itself notes, "spirits" are being referred to, *not* incarnate creatures (i.e., not "aliens"). Just as there is a hierarchy of angels in nine choirs, so too there is a ranking of fallen angels. Perhaps we could speculate that these "fallen planetary spirits" are those (fallen) angels whom, originally, God destined to be guardian angels, but relinquished this mission upon rebelling with Lucifer.

What About C.S. Lewis and His "Space Trilogy"?

The renowned 20th century Christian apologist and author, Clive Staples Lewis, wrote many beautiful works and provided powerful defenses of Christianity. He also believed in aliens, even writing a lengthy trilogy of novels (the "Space Trilogy," consisting of *Out of the Silent Planet, Perelandra,* and *That Hideous Strength*), largely centered around theological and philosophical explorations of aliens living on Mars and Venus. This setting enabled him to explore what an unfallen rational (incarnate) creature might behave like, along with other interesting themes. Many of these explorations proved edifying. When, however, we consider Lewis' own real-life views on the matter of aliens, we can only wonder what his stance would have been had he lived several years longer and witnessed the discovery that Mars was devoid of all life (much less intelligent life).

I have long benefited from the works of Lewis, and I highly recommend them. That said, he is a far cry from being a source Catholics should consult in settling delicate theological and philosophical matters. From his reversion back to Christianity (from atheism), all the way to his death, he remained a staunch Protestant. As such, he had little comprehension of many of the resources any Catholic can draw from to easily dismiss the possibility of aliens (e.g., Catholic Mariology, Christology, Eschatology, Magisterium, Sacred Tradition, the *sensus fidelium*, and Ecclesiology—see Part Two). He likewise died before the ET craze of the 20th century had fully revealed—by its fruits—just how diabolical to the core it was and is.

Although all of this greatly mitigates the gravity of Lewis' belief in aliens, it does not entirely exonerate him, either. As we saw in Part One, Scripture itself clearly enough rules out extraterrestrials. Unfortunately, Lewis let wild speculations get the better of him on this point. But it was not only this point which his overly "open" theological posture led him to posit absurdities. As we have noted, when one begins to question what Genesis reveals about human nature (supposing it is not—when Scripture clearly and repeatedly indicates it is—*unique*), that attitude cannot be neatly contained to only generate one or two errors; it inevitably spreads. Naturally, one who wonders, *"perhaps if Genesis simply excluded mention of other material beings made in His Image, it also excluded mention of other genders beyond male and female."* Indeed, Lewis also posited the possibility of not only more than two genders, but a full seven of them! In his Space Trilogy, he wrote:

> Ransom knew ... that celestial spirit who now flashed between them : vigilant Malacandra, captain of a cold orb, whom men call Mars and Mavors, and Tyr who put his hand in the wolf-mouth. ... he warned Merlin that now the time was coming when he must play the man. The three gods who had already met in the Blue Room were less unlike humanity than the two whom they still awaited. **In Viritrilbia and Venus and Malacandra were represented those two of the Seven genders** which bear a certain analogy to the biological sexes, and can therefore be in some measure understood by men. **It would not be so with those who were now preparing to descend. These also doubtless had their genders, but we have no clue to them**. These would be mightier energies : ancient eldils, steersmen of giant worlds which have never from the beginning been subdued to the sweet humiliations of organic life.[459]

Just as Lewis, we can be sure, never would have written that if he had seen what would come, in the 21st century, with transgender ideology, so too I am sure he never would have written in support of extraterrestrials if he saw what belief in them would seduce men into in the decades following his death.

C.S. Lewis was a wonderful novelist and a powerful Christian Apologist. But he was also deeply mistaken on many points. His belief in extraterrestrials was just one such mistake. His expositions of evolution in *Mere Christianity* smack of Fr. Teilhard's errors and New Age theory. His discourse on the "narrowing down" of evil in *That Hideous Strength* is deeply misguided. His ruminations on hell and purgatory in *The Great Divorce* are often interesting but also deeply theologically flawed. In *The Last Battle* he describes Heaven and hell as the same place (only received differently)—a common theme in Modernist thought but repudiated by Catholic teaching. In another work he even suggests that the past can be changed (which, as we saw in Part Five, not even God can make happen), and in many other places he speaks deeply erroneously about the Church, the Blessed Virgin, and other topics one could not expect a non-Catholic to expound upon accurately. I encourage anyone who appreciates his writings to continue to benefit from the good that Lewis entrusted to us, but also to seek out a foundation of fully reliable theology and philosophy elsewhere.

What About the New Baltimore Catechism #2 and Other Texts With Imprimaturs?

Recall, as noted from even the very introduction of this book, that God "could" have created innumerable inhabited worlds—He simply *did not do so* (and we can conclude that He did not do so from a faithful approach to Scripture, Tradition, Magisterium, and more). Nevertheless, it remains technically accurate to say it is "possible" that this is the case, in one restricted sense of the word (i.e., His *Omnipotence allows* for such a thing). Various texts prefer, when the extraterrestrial question arises, to simply relay this observation and nothing more. Obviously, I believe such an approach is imprudent and dangerous. But it is not erroneous, either.

The revised 1969 edition of the Baltimore Catechism #2 took this approach. Within Lesson 5, Question 51 reads:

> Is it possible that there are intelligent beings created by God on other planets of the universe? Yes; it is possible that there are intelligent beings created by God on other planets of the universe, because God's power is unlimited.

Before saying anything else, I want to affirm the great value of the Baltimore Catechism; it is what my wife and I use to catechize our own children, and I highly recommend it. But it is quite unfortunate that this paragraph was added. As far as I can tell, no other versions or revisions of the Baltimore Catechism—all the way back to 1885 (when, as is mentioned in Part Two, the ET debate was already raging)—contained it; only this space age revision has this teaching, and after this revision, no more editions were released.

Note that this text does not say aliens exist, or that they are likely to exist, or even that positing their existence is harmonious with Sacred Tradition or in accordance with Scripture or Magisterium. It simply says their existence is "possible" due only to the fact that "God's power is unlimited." Ultimately, this is little more than a re-phrasing of saints like John Chrysostom, who spoke of how God's Omnipotence means he "could have created innumerable worlds." Even great Catholic authors like him have long discussed what is possible *in the strict sense* that it is not outside of God's unlimited power. And this is all the Baltimore Catechism is saying with respect to aliens. It could have simply said, "Yes, aliens are possible." Instead, it clarifies that it is only intending to observe a logical consequence of God's Omnipotence, not relay a thesis that is harmonious with the Faith.

This attribute of God has is important to recognize so that we do not misunderstand His all-powerfulness. But it is equally important to recognize what God has chosen not to do. For example, Aquinas, by this same token, said that God could have assumed not just one nature (Jesus Christ), but *all* natures; i.e., it is possible due to God's Omnipotence that we could all literally be the Word of God Himself. Yet, to actually propose this would obviously be absurd. It would violate Scripture, Tradition, and Magisterium, in a thousand ways. Christianity *cannot* be reconciled with such Pantheistic premises. Similarly (though, admittedly, not as severely), Christianity is at odds with the notion of extraterrestrials, even though they are "possible" merely from the perspective of God's "unlimited power."

In Part Two, we reviewed the Catholic scholar Dr. Marie George's extensive research into this theme in the writings of the Fathers of the Church. Her observations on their teachings and the contemporary ET promoters' (mis)use of them, applies just as well to the question at hand. She writes:

> ... **nothing in tradition supports the notion that a plurality of inhabitable planets exists** ... **A careless reading of certain patristic authors might lead one to think that they endorse pluralism [i.e., alien belief], when they are simply affirming that God is able to make many worlds.** For example, St. John Chrysostom (345-407) says: "*For with God nothing is difficult ... it is easy [for Him] to make worlds without number and end...*" **Chrysostom here is only affirming God's power to make many worlds; he is not making a case for the actual existence of many worlds**. Athanasius (297-373), St. Basil (329-379) and St. Bonaventure (1217-1274) also affirm that **God is capable of creating many worlds, but do not adopt the position that God actually did so.** ... **all [Church Fathers] who do consider the many-earths question, even if only implicitly, all give a negative answer** ... every church Father and Doctor who paid some sort of attention to some version of many earths, always rejected the notion, with the single exception of Origen [whom the Church condemned as a heretic for this very reason].[460]

***

Even, however, if some local Catechism *did* condone alien belief (and this one does not come so much as close to doing that), such a teaching would have no value when compared to the Magisterial texts which can only be properly interpreted as ruling out alien belief (see Part Two). A text may well have an *Imprimatur* (as, for example, the Baltimore Catechism does), but this does not render it Magisterial. Such "local" Catechisms as these are usually very helpful, but they carry *no* doctrinal authority of their own.

On the other hand, the *Catechism of the Catholic Church* (which *does* rule out aliens, but was not published at the time this Baltimore Catechism revision was written) has great Magisterial weight. It is not a local Catechism. It is *the universal* Catechism. The Apostolic Constitution, *Fidei Depositum,* which issued it, was promulgated by Pope St. John Paul II in 1992, who, by way of a "declaration," explicitly granted it doctrinal value (cf., §IV). No Catholic may treat its authority like that of other Catechisms; i.e., as a glorified index of teachings, wherein only the documents cited can be said to carry the Magisterial weight. The only other Catechism with similar weight is the Roman Catechism (the Catechism of the Council of Trent).

As we have noted throughout this book, alien belief is not formally heretical. It is simply false (and its defense invariably includes formal heresies). It is, moreover, easy for a discerning Christian to see its falsity. However, since it is not formally heretical, there is nothing to prevent an *Imprimatur* being granted to a text that promotes it. Such ecclesiastical approbations are not endorsements of the veracity of the claims made within the texts they apply to; they are only affirmations that, in the opinion of the one bestowing them, the texts contain no formal heresies.

Therefore, it does not matter how many books may exist, with *Imprimaturs*, which are open to or even promoting of belief in extraterrestrials. The position remains not only false, but false in such a way that a sincere Catholic approach to the Faith can conclude, with certainty, that it is false.

Why Is the Virgin Mary Called "Queen of the Universe" If There Are No Aliens?

Jesus is indeed the King of the Universe, and the Blessed Virgin is the Queen of the Universe. These titles have long been established in Sacred Tradition; they have nothing to do with the notion of rational creatures dwelling throughout the galaxies, nor do they even implicitly give grounds for such speculations.

In Catholic theology, "the universe" simply refers to all that God has made. The Blessed Virgin is its Queen because she, as the Mother of Jesus and the Spouse of the Holy Spirit, is the Queen of all Creation—which includes all the angels and all the other saints, each of whom she surpasses by far. Never in Catholic teaching or tradition has this title been taken as an implication that other inhabited planets exist.

Situating Christian truths within the context of the entire "universe" has always been a fixture of the teachings of the saints. Yet, as we saw in Part Two, speculations about extraterrestrials only began with the "Enlightenment." Clearly, Sacred Tradition sees no bridge from one to the other; only modernists invented that notion. As the *New Catholic Encyclopedia*'s entry on the *Order of the Universe* explains:

> The universe is here taken to mean the totality of created beings, both material and spiritual. The order of the universe is the complex of relationships joining them to one another and to God. ... Although the doctrine of the order of the universe was **explained most fully by St. Thomas Aquinas in the 13th century, its roots go back 2,000 years before this to two widely separated cultures of the 6th century B.C.** [viz., ancient Greek and Jewish thought] ... For subsequent Christian writers

God's work as an ordered universe is a frequent theme. Clement of Rome (c. A.D. 97) exhorts the disobedient Christians at Corinth to submission by proposing to them the divinely established order of the universe ... Lactantius in the early 4th century saw the beauty and order of the universe as manifesting to all the existence of God ... St. Augustine urged the goodness and beauty of the whole created universe against the Manichaean doctrine of the evil of matter ... Boethius taught a universal order of providence, embracing all things and drawing good even from evil ... St. John Damascene, summing up the traditions of Eastern Christianity, taught that the ordered unity of the universe, made up of various and opposing parts, offers manifest proof of the omnipotent power of the Creator, by whose will the cosmos holds together ... all the great commentators on the Sentences [of Peter Lombard; i.e., the medieval scholastics] treat at this point the question of the universe and its perfection: St. Albert The Great, St. Bonaventure, St. Thomas Aquinas, Peter of Tarentaise (Bl. Innocent V), Richard Of Middleton, Giles Of Rome, Durandus Of Saint-Pourçain, And Denis The Carthusian ... St. Thomas uses the doctrine of the order of the universe to clarify more than 70 different questions in the Summa theologiae ... Since the order of the universe is the complete plan of God for communicating His life and goodness, and includes both the natural disposition of things and the supernatural economy of grace in Christ, the universe as such is God's greatest created manifestation of Himself and can serve to illuminate almost every truth of faith. ... [Since they] are more fully understood when considered as parts of a whole to which they belong ... Finally, other truths about creatures ... can be integrated into [doctrine on the Order of the Universe] and thereby illuminated. For example, the solidarity of all men, implied in the doctrines of original sin and redemption, can best be grasped as an aspect of the solidarity of the whole universe. **Mary as Mother of the Head of all creation is Queen of the universe**. Sacred history is the movement of the universe to its final perfection. **The Church especially can be more fully appreciated. For the Church on earth is the essential anticipation and seed of the Church in heaven, the city of the blessed, which is the ultimate perfection of the universe**. This makes clear the connection between Christ's headship of creation and of the Church, which St. Paul is concerned to emphasize (Col 1.15–20). The whole structure of the Church, its channels of authority in carrying on the mission it bears from Christ, its visible signs of grace by which Christ's intention to redeem and sanctify is efficaciously applied to the world, its sacrifice in which Christ the Head unites all things to Himself as priest and victim in the movement of history toward God—this structure is set at the heart of the universe, the one supreme work of God.

The lengthy quote above was called for to illustrate the beauty of Sacred Tradition's expositions on the Order of the Universe—a beauty perversely disfigured by belief in extraterrestrials. The entire theology of this venerable Tradition is robbed of its core principles when one throws alien belief into the mix; just as moral theology is ruined when one proposes that intrinsic evils may be licit depending upon circumstances, and Eucharistic theology is destroyed when one pretends the Blessed Sacrament is a mere symbol.

As we can see, expounding upon Christian doctrine in light of the Order of the entire Universe has been a constant theme from the beginning of the Church. Countless saints (far more than those noted above) did so, yet not one of them did so in such a way as to give grounds for speculating that this Universal Order allows for rational beings dwelling on other planets.

In fact, the first major departure from the unanimous consensus of the Fathers (and all the saints following them) on the nature of the Universal Order is seen in the writings of Fr. Pierre Teilhard de Chardin during the 20th century. He insisted that we must no longer regard the Order of the Universe as being God's deliberate story, mediated through His miraculous interventions, and centralized on the great events of Salvation History on earth—*from Original Sin to the Protoevangelium; from the Prophets to Christ; from the Incarnation to the Passion, Death, and Resurrection of Jesus; from the founding of the Church to its consummation at the End of Time with Christ's Second Coming in the flesh, etc.*—but rather the unfolding of the Deistic process of Darwinian "evolution" being drawn towards some eventual "omega point." This heretical notion, in turn, formed the basis for much contemporary Catholic ET promotion.

The *man*, Jesus Christ—and our awaiting of His Coming in Glory—for de Chardin (and those of his mindset—i.e., Fr. Richard Rohr, whom we considered in Part One), is insignificant. Instead, Fr. De Chardin taught that there could be innumerable other Incarnations throughout the galaxies, and that any notion of "earth's Salvation History" being universal is absurd. As we saw in Part Four, de Chardin's teachings are nothing but a "synthesis of all heresies;" their motivation, content, and legacy is thoroughly (and diabolically) rotten.

On the particular question of Jesus and Mary's titles, however—here as with many other ET Deceptions—it appears that the activism of Msgr. Corrado Balducci was pivotal in fostering the expectation that, whenever the Church speaks of the Virgin as Queen of the Universe, and Jesus as King of the Universe, this is actually a subtle indication that alien belief is being promoted. This is, of course, as much drivel. But with these assurances, Balducci inspired certain Ufologists such as Jaime Maussan (who, as we saw in Part Four, is a flagrant charlatan) to regard their patently anti-Christian ET-based teachings as "in keeping with the times," and seduced them to suppose that they "will soon be vindicated by the Vatican." That some Catholic ET promoters use this absurd notion as a justification for their alien belief promulgation is only a testimony to how low they have sunk in advocating for their thesis.

In fact, the Blessed Virgin has been referred to as "Queen of the Universe" long before belief in extraterrestrials began infiltrating even the Vatican itself in the 1960s.

> **O Queen of the universe**, and most bountiful sovereign! thou art the great advocate of sinners, the sure port of those who have suffered shipwreck... (Prayer of St. Ephrem. Born 309 A.D.)
> ... as long as the world should last, [the Blessed Virgin] should obtain all that She would ever ask for her clients; that the greatest sinners, if they availed themselves of her intercession, should find salvation; that in the new Church and law of the Gospel She should be the Co-operatrix and Teacher of salvation with Christ her most holy Son. This was to be her privilege **especially after His Ascension into Heaven, when She should remain, as Queen of the universe, as the representative and instrument of the Divine power on earth**. (Venerable Mary of Agreda. †1665 A.D. *The Mystical City of God*. The Presentation of the Infant Jesus in the Temple.)
> Therefore we behold her taken up from this valley of tears into the heavenly Jerusalem, amid choirs of Angels. And we honour her, glorified above all the Saints, **crowned with stars by her Divine Son and seated at His side the sovereign Queen of the universe**. (Pope Leo XIII. *Iucunda Semper Expectatione*. §4. 1894 A.D.) This is most fitting for a method of venerating the Virgin, who is rightly styled the Mystical Rose of Paradise, and who, as Queen of the universe, shines therein with a crown of stars. (Pope Leo XIII. *Fidentem Piumque Animum*. §2. 1896 A.D.)

Naturally, references to Jesus Christ as the King of the Universe are even more constant in Catholic tradition, back to the early times of the Church; therefore, for the sake of space we will not catalogue them here. Yet they too equally demonstrate the futility of supposing that references to His (or Mary's) dominion over "the universe" is some stealth, Gnostic acknowledgement of aliens. Let us, therefore, be on guard against all Gnosticism. Whenever a Catholic theologian (no matter what letters precede or follow his name, and no matter what "credentials" he boasts) proposes that various truths of the Faith (which we have always known the true meaning of), are actually surreptitious revelations of extraterrestrials, we can be sure such an individual is (whether he recognizes this or not) a deceiver. The holiness of the Church will indeed grow until the end of time. But the foundations of the Faith must never be "re-read" or "reformulated"—as even the most supposedly "orthodox minded" of Catholic ET promoters concede would be necessary in light of their insistence aliens exist. We can only ever build upon the foundation that Public Revelation and Sacred Tradition has given us. We can *never* modify that foundation, and we can *never* build a new one.

> **Brothers and sisters: You are God's building. According to the grace**

of God given to me, like a wise master builder I laid a foundation, and another is building upon it. But each one must be careful how he builds upon it, for no one can lay a foundation other than the one that is there, namely, Jesus Christ. (1 Corinthians 3:9-11)

***

This point compels me to share some personal reflections, with which we will conclude this book.

37. A Personal Reflection on My Calling

Fighting against ET promotion and other related sci-fi deceptions was not exactly a task I grew up longing to undertake, nor is it even now my life's mission. It is a particular task—but one to which I believe God has called me.

However, my mission remains, above all, the Faith: doing my best to be a good Catholic Christian while striving to evangelize others accordingly, and, more specifically, proclaiming the Divine Mercy (particularly as revealed by Jesus to St. Faustina) and the Divine Will (particularly as revealed by Jesus to the Servant of God Luisa Piccarreta, but also other mystics). The emergence of this new "particular task" of zealously warning the Faithful against diabolical sci-fi deceptions has been put before me especially since the year 2020, and this has compelled me to pause and ponder why I am someone whom God has asked to argue against the ET Deception.

The conclusion I have come to is this: despite my unworthiness, I am a man who no one could accuse of simply being "*a rigid Pharisee who limits God and will immediately commence a knee-jerk-rejection of anything that is new.*" The reason is simple: my mission—the revelations of Jesus to St. Faustina, the Servant of God Luisa Piccarreta, Blessed Conchita, Blessed Dina Belanger, and many other mystics of the 20th century—constitutes announcing the most astounding news one can possibly imagine. Any "rigid Pharisee" would, by definition, categorically reject (or at least ignore) the message of these mystics. Yet, their message is my life's task. While I deserve many criticisms, one of the few I do not deserve is being labeled a "God-limiter."

These private revelations all remain thoroughly *private*—they do not add anything to the Deposit of Faith, and they stand in perfect harmony with the almost 2,000 years of organic growth of Sacred Tradition that led up to them. But they nevertheless reveal truths as astounding as one could licitly entertain while still fully abiding by Catholic orthodoxy. They promise a "new and Divine holiness," of "Living in the Divine Will," which surpasses even the holiness of the great saints of earlier centuries, and is now available for the asking. Anyone who remains in a state of grace, continues to pursue the "ordinary" means of sanctification, and is interiorly disposed to receive so great a gift, may receive it by simply asking for it. These revelations moreover promise that the time will soon come when this great holiness of God's Will shall triumph over the earth, so that the People of God may be truly prepared for the great Wedding Feast that is Heaven, which shall commence for the whole Church upon the General Resurrection and the Last Judgment. In other words, they promise that the Our Father prayer means exactly what it says, and that it soon will be fulfilled—once enough people are longing for it, striving for it, and asking for it to reign.

> In union with Christ take your stand as suppliants before the Heavenly Father and allow that prayer to rise to Him from your lips again and again ... '... Thy will be done on earth, as it is in heaven!' Only then shall we be influenced solely by the honor of God and by zeal to give Him greater glory, when we **earnestly desire the restoration of His Kingdom—the Kingdom of justice, of love, and of peace—throughout all the world**." (Venerable Pope Pius XII)[461]

All of this, however, may elicit a question from some: *"If you are so open to this astounding development, Daniel, why not also be open to aliens? Couldn't that also simply be some new and extraordinary truth God has reserved for our times?"* The answer is, *absolutely not.*

The revelations of Jesus to the 20th century mystics on Living in the Divine Will and hastening its Reign on earth stand as diametrically opposed to the notion that extraterrestrials exist (and are already here, or are coming soon to "intervene and save us") as a Satanic ritual stands opposite the Holy Sacrifice of the Mass. And wherever Satanism resembles something holy it only does so incredibly superficially, and only while grotesquely perverting it. Let us consider this fact in the next section, after recalling, from Part Four, what Venerable Fulton Sheen prophesied:

> "Progress [, they say,] is automatic thanks to science—education and evolution, which will one day make man a kind of a god as H.G. Wells said, with his feet on the earth and his hands among the stars. ... **The anti-Christ will not be so called, otherwise he would have no followers ... He will come disguised** ... He will write books on the new idea of God to suit the way people live; induce faith in astrology so as to make not the will but the stars responsible for sins; he will explain guilt away psychologically ... he will foster science but only to have armament makers use one marvel of science to destroy another ... he will invoke religion to destroy religion; he will even speak of Christ and say that he was the greatest man who ever lived ... Because his religion will be brotherhood without the fatherhood of God, he will deceive even the elect. **He will set up a counter-Church which will be the ape of the Church because, he the devil, is the ape of God. It will have all the notes and characteristics of the Church, but in reverse and emptied of its divine content. It will be a mystical body of the anti-Christ that will in all externals resemble the mystical body of Christ**. ... [Today, many Christians] read the same novels as modern pagans, educate their children in the same godless way...allow pagan practices ... Since the amalgamation of the Christian and the pagan spirit has set in, since the gold is married with an alloy, the entirety must be thrust into the furnace that the dross may be burned away. The value of the trial will be to set us apart ... There are Times of Troubles and it is not so much a Third World War that is to be feared, as the rebirth of Leviathan, the coming of the Day of the Beast..." —Archbishop Fulton Sheen[462]

The ET Deception: Diabolical Aping of God's Authentic Calls to the Church Today

> "Even Satan disguises himself as an angel of light."
> —2 Corinthians 11:14
>
> "The serpent poured water like a river out of his mouth after the woman, to sweep her away with the flood." —Revelation 12:15

The Devil always apes the things of God. We know this about him, but we must also bear in mind that he knows the prophecies just as we do—or, rather, he knows them better. He knows he will soon be cast back into hell—his kingdom on earth decimated—when the Our Father prayer is fulfilled. This is why he has been hell-bent on preventing the revelations heralding its fulfillment from being disseminated within the Church. But he has not been successful. The Church has now so vindicated and approved the various mystics and revelations that speak of this Gift and this Reign (see my 2021 book, *Thy Will Be Done*), that no sincere Catholic can any longer doubt their authenticity. All that remains is those who know about this astounding news doing everything they can to proclaim it from the rooftops.

> ... **If the Divine Fiat is known, the kingdom of the enemy is over. Here is all his rage.** But the Lord will win, because it is divine decree that His Kingdom will come upon earth. It is a matter of time, but He will make His way; He lacks neither power nor wisdom to dispose the circumstances. But I tell you: whatever you can do [to make the Divine Will known]—do it. (Letter of the Servant of God Luisa Piccarreta to "Irene." December 5, 1939)

While the Devil will doubtless continue his labors to put roadblocks before such dissemination within the Church, his larger plans lie elsewhere. If he cannot succeed in preventing this propagation, what could be more effective than announcing his own Satanic counterfeit, in an effort to seduce souls to place their hopes in that instead of in the Triumph of Christ?

And this is the crux of the matter. Everywhere in ET promotion, we see the diabolical inversion of what God has promised to the authentic mystics (not to mention within Scripture and Magisterium, and throughout Sacred Tradition). ET belief's promise of a techno-utopia is the Anti-Era. Its promise of scientific and even existential enlightenment is the Anti-Gift. Its "revelations from aliens" is the Anti-Mysticism. It's "ontological shock" is the diabolical aping of the enrapturing beauty of the words of Jesus.

Let us consider just one of the many mystics Jesus has chosen to announce His messages today. As I wrote in Chapter Eight of *Thy Will Be Done*:

> To Concepción Cabrera de Armida—now known as *Blessed* Conchita

(she died in 1937 and was Beatified in 2019)—the Gift is revealed in unmistakable clarity. ... The theologian commissioned by the Church to examine all of Conchita's writings during her cause of Beatification wrote that her "doctrine is completely sound and Catholic," but went on to offer a rare admission for a scholar in his position: "I must confess that when I read these pages I received great spiritual benefit and **often felt enveloped by a holy fear, as if by the presence of God who was speaking.**"[463] When someone, so experienced with reading spiritual treatises as a theologian appointed by the Church to scrutinize a mystic's cause, speaks so profoundly about a given work, we can rest assured that something Divine is at play, and we can rest doubly assured of the same when the mystic herself is later beatified. Conchita produced thousands of pages of writings, and their predominant theme teaches that there is a new sanctity, available for the asking, which far surpasses the greatest possible sanctity of the previous era. Confirming this analysis are the works of Father Marie-Michel Philipon ... A towering theologian whose writings are cited multiple times in the *New Catholic Encyclopedia,* and who proved the prophetic nature of his intuitions by advocating for St. Elizabeth of the Trinity's daring spirituality before she was even declared a Servant of God, Fr. Philipon sums up Conchita's spirituality in the following passage: "*A theologian must above all pose this question to himself: "What then did God intend to bring about through His humble servant [Conchita] for the benefit of His entire Church?" **The greatest degree of Holiness is attainable for everyone** ...] **We are incontestably in a new era of spirituality.***"[464]

Conchita herself, however, was told by Jesus:

May the whole world have recourse to this Holy Spirit since the day of His reign has arrived. This last stage of the world belongs very specially to Him that He be honored and exalted ... **peace will come along with a moral and spiritual reaction, greater than the evil by which the world is tormented ... He will come, I will send Him again clearly manifest in His effects, which will astonish the world** and impel the Church to holiness ... I want to return to the world in My priests. **I want to renew the world** of souls by making Myself seen in My priests.[465] **The restoration will be universal, not limited to some places or nations** ... **This world needs to be regenerated, spiritualized and saved.** ...[I want] **to return to earth in [My] priests in order to bring about a new era of salvation and sanctification in the world** ... After so many centuries, which are like a day for Me, I want to perfect this unity in My Church.[466] **The Trinity awaits this profound renewal, and already sees it, feels it, cherishes it and blesses it.**[467] Then all those wills, many haughty, others independent, arrogant and rebellious will finally be united, humiliated and conquered by love ... and they will form only one desire, only one will with Mine, in the Unity of the Trinity. The day when this happens will be a triumph for My beloved Church.[468]

Blessed Conchita, like all the 20th century mystics to whom Jesus spoke on this theme, is assured by Him that the entire world will soon be transformed by a new outpouring of God's grace. It will certainly not involve Christ's *physical* (visible) coming to earth—that can only occur at the very end of time—but rather a *Eucharistic* Reign of His *Will* (i.e., "through the ministry of priests"). This Reign, therefore, is entirely dependent upon traditional Catholic teaching on holiness. But as modern ears—even within the Church—largely do not want to hear about holiness, the Devil sees his opportunity. He can promise a "new era," and a total "transformation," but without all that "baggage" of Christian dogma, prayer, and morality. And he can do so, more effectively than with any other method, through modern man's giddy anticipation of intervention from "extraterrestrials."

Let us, therefore, summarize in one table the radical difference between the private revelations on Living in the Divine Will and hastening its Reign on earth on the one hand, and on the other, the ET Deception which fosters expectation of imminent contact with and intervention from "aliens."

Living in the Divine Will & Hastening Its Reign on Earth	**Believing in Aliens & Seeking Enlightenment from Them**
Core truth of the Faith from the very beginning (e.g., Matthew 6:10, Luke 22:42, Hebrews 10, Matthew 12:50, Matthew 7:21, Romans 8:19, 2 Timothy 4:1, John 12:32, Revelation 1:7, etc.)	Completely absent from the foundation of the Faith in Scripture; even refuted by many Biblical passages. Repudiated not only by the New Testament, but also the Old.
Key theme of Sacred Tradition's development throughout the centuries; the saints (as Church History progressed) spoke ever more boldly on it: the Fathers, St. Maximus, St. Bernard, St. Francis de Sales, St. Thérèse of Lisieux, etc.	Repudiated by Sacred Tradition. Rejected by all the Fathers of the Church, and not condoned by a single saint. Absent from all pre-Enlightenment Christian writers except ones condemned by the Church for that very proposition.[469]
Verified by an explosion of authentic private revelations: Servant of God Luisa Piccarreta, Bl. Conchita, St. Faustina, St. Maximilian Kolbe, Servant of God Archbishop Luis Martinez, Bl. Dina Belanger, etc.	Not contained in a single authentic private revelation, despite an immense number of such revelations in the last hundred years. (It is, however, contained in many patently false "revelations.")
Promoted in many Magisterial teachings: e.g., *Annum Sacrum* (Leo XIII) *E Supremi* (Pius X), *Quas Primas* & *Miserentissimus Redemptor*, (Pius XI), address on the "New and Divine Holiness"[470] (John Paul II), etc.	Condemned in a number of Magisterial teachings (e.g. the Catechism §395, Pope Zachary, Pope Pius II, and implicitly by Pope Pius XII and Leo XIII). Moreover, no Magisterial teachings even give any basis for speculating about this point.

Generates an enormous outpouring of good fruits: vocations, growth in holiness, works of mercy, veritable miracles, new religious orders, etc.	Generates an avalanche of thoroughly rotten fruits, with no good ones to speak of (see Part Four).
In Sum: this development stands in perfect harmony with Sacred Tradition just as the blooming of the flower and the generation of fruit stands in perfect harmony with a plant's growth.	In Sum: this development stands in diametric opposition to the entirety of Sacred Tradition just as Transgenderism only perverts the entire Christian understanding of human nature.

At this point, the question we introduced above—"*If one is open to the astounding developments on the Gift and the Era, shouldn't he also be open to aliens?*"—has been definitively answered in the negative. Whoever cannot distinguish the two notions might also be incapable of distinguishing a heap of rotting garbage from a breathtakingly beautiful work of art. (In fact, many today cannot do so.) Let us, however, compare the trash heap and the work of art in one concrete example.

It is difficult to think of a prominent Catholic author whose message is more diametrically opposed to the one I present than Fr. Richard Rohr. We considered his teachings in Part One, and they can be summarized as follows: *The Church just never got it. For 2,000 years Catholics have been fundamentally deluded as to what Jesus really came to earth to accomplish and teach. But finally, today, due to advances in evolution and science and enlightenment and understanding of other religions and rejecting the view that man is unique (and that earth's Salvation History is supreme)* ***and realizing there are aliens,*** *we are finally able to get it; we are able to finally grasp that we need to focus less on Jesus and more on 'the cosmic Christ.'*

The message I promote, pertaining to the Gift and the Era is the precise opposite of this modernist, New Age, "cosmic Christ"-based message Fr. Rohr promotes to accommodate ET belief. (Although, in truth, the Gift is far bolder than even Fr. Rohr's "most daring" propositions.) For my insistence is as follows: the Church *always* "got it." Jesus made the essence of His mission on earth superabundantly clear, and Sacred Tradition's development, the lives of the Saints, the Magisterium, the mysticism, the Liturgy, etc., of the following twenty centuries, have *always* faithfully and truthfully testified to this with ever ascending degrees of effectiveness in sanctification. Our task now, moreover, is to be far *more* devoted to Jesus—far *more* focused on Him—than ever before; not to divert attention *away* from Him for the sake of some "new understanding" of a "cosmic Christ."

We have at long last arrived at the time when the fruit of that same plant—Sacred Tradition—which has always been beautifully and organically given growth by the Holy Spirit is now ready to be picked. The picking of that fruit consists in none other than the accomplishment of the Will of God on earth as in Heaven. "*All things find their perfection in returning to their origin,*" as St. Thomas Aquinas observed, and just as the form of the fruit is contained within the plant's own seed, whereas new seeds only emerge once that fruit is fully formed, so the essence of our mission now consists in the complete explication of those greatest of all words, which are at once a prayer, a command, and—yes—a prophecy: "**Thy will be done on earth as it is in heaven**." (Matthew 6:10)

Continuing the analogy, the approach of Fr. Rohr and his ilk would have us believe we've simply been looking at the wrong plant the whole time; or would encourage us to ignore the plant and its fruit, and instead drive to the store to buy an artificial one and a piece of candy.

This 2,000-year preparation (or, rather, 6,000-year) can likewise be compared to a stunning classical masterpiece nearing its crescendo. Fr. Rohr's message, on the other hand, essentially compares Sacred Tradition to a poorly trained middle school band unbearably hacking away at their instruments for what seems like an eternity, until a conductor (Fr. Rohr) finally arrives to teach them a few things. Never trust a Catholic author whose view of our venerable Sacred Tradition is so dim.

Yet it is precisely this dim view of Public Revelation and Sacred Tradition that is inextricable from the propositions of the ET promoters. They do not openly phrase their thesis in these terms, but it remains so that they are accusing the Holy Spirit of contradicting the promise of Christ by, for two thousand years, abysmally failing to guide the Church "to all truth" (John 16:13)—by failing to reveal ETs in Scripture, the Fathers, the Doctors, the Saints, the Liturgy, private revelation, or *anywhere* else we know to look for His guidance. What is more, these ET promoters indicate that, this whole time, the Holy Spirit stood by idly and allowed those world religions with the most anti-Christian of teachings—Hinduism and Buddhism—to become the *de facto* heroes of faith; and the most patently false of "private revelations" (e.g. Islam, Seventh Day Adventism, Mormonism, Scientology, *Urantia*, and on the list goes) to become the *de facto* heroes of prophecy. For it is these false (and even diabolical) sources, not Christianity, which have always taught the universe is filled with inhabited planets. Any belief in ETs always carries—if not explicitly stated then at least inescapably latent within itself—the supposition that all these evils and errors have always been the *real* protagonists of Salvation History; with Catholicism as understood by the saints being the real antagonists of the same.

There comes a point when one must begin sincerely pondering if a certain attitude becomes tantamount to making an accusation against the Holy Spirit which we must never even *risk* making. Jesus said:

> He who is not with me is against me, and he who does not gather with me scatters. Therefore I tell you, every sin and blasphemy will be forgiven men, but the blasphemy against the Spirit will not be forgiven. And whoever says a word against the Son of man will be forgiven; **but whoever speaks against the Holy Spirit will not be forgiven, either in**

> **this age or in the age to come. Either make the tree good, and its fruit good; or make the tree bad, and its fruit bad; for the tree is known by its fruit**. (Matthew 12:30-33)

Now, Jesus will *always* forgive you if you are sorry for your sins. My aim is not to induce anyone to despair; that would only itself be another temptation from the Devil. My aim is only to ensure we understand how serious it is that we never succumb to doubting, explicitly or implicitly, the power of the Holy Spirit.

For the Holy Spirit is *not* inept. He is the Third Person of the Eternal Trinity, and He is the very soul of the Church—the *Catholic* Church. We cannot even begin to comprehend how perfectly He has been in charge of everything that has transpired during the Church's History—nor how perfectly He is in charge of what is yet to come. Let us trust in Him, never doubting His Omnipotence or Goodness in what has happened in the past, what is happening now, or what will happen in the future.

> "The Holy Spirit is at work with the Father and the Son from the beginning to the completion of the plan for our salvation. But in these "end times," ushered in by the Son's redeeming Incarnation, the Spirit is revealed and given, recognized and welcomed as a person. Now can this divine plan, accomplished in Christ, the firstborn and head of the new creation, be embodied in mankind by the outpouring of the Spirit..." - *Catechism of the Catholic Church*, §686

> "Let it suffice to state that, **as Christ is the Head of the Church, so is the Holy Ghost her soul.** ... This being so, **no further and fuller "manifestation and revelation of the Divine Spirit" may be imagined or expected**; for that **which now takes place in the Church is the most perfect possible,** and will last until that day when the Church herself, having passed through her militant career, shall be taken up into the joy of the saints triumphing in heaven." —Leo XIII. *Divinum illud munus,* §6

> "Sanctify your whole Church in every people and nation; pour out, we pray, the gifts of the holy spirit across the face of the earth; and, **with the divine grace that was at work when the Gospel was first proclaimed, fill now once more the hearts of believers."** —Collect for the Feast of Pentecost. Roman Missal

38. Endnotes

---

[1] Daniel O'Connor's Blog. August, 2022. "All the Devil Wants is a Little Dialogue." https://dsdoconnor.com/2022/08/22/all-the-devil-wants-is-a-little-dialogue/
[2] Marie George. *Christianity and Extraterrestrials?: A Catholic Perspective.* iUniverse. 2005. Ch. 4
[3] Andrew Davison. *Astrobiology and Christian Doctrine.* Cambridge University Press. 2023. Page 99, 109
[4] Outreach: "An LGBTQ Catholic Resource" Richard J. Clifford, S.J.: Using "Male and female he created them" to adjudicate gender controversies is "thoroughly misguided" https://outreach.faith/2023/06/richard-j-clifford-s-j-using-male-and-female-he-created-them-to-adjudicate-gender-identity-controversies-is-thoroughly-misguided
[5] Fr. Thomas Weinandy. *Of Jesus and Aliens.* The Catholic Thing. July 2023. https://www.thecatholicthing.org/2023/07/16/of-jesus-and-aliens/
[6] Hugh Owen. "Would Extraterrestrial Intelligent Life Redound to the Glory of God?" The Kolbe Center. December, 2021. https://www.kolbecenter.org/would-extraterrestrial-intelligent-life-redound-to-the-glory-of-god/
[7] Michael Hichborn. "UFOs and Catholic Cosmology" Lepanto Institute. https://www.lepantoin.org/wp/ufos/
[8] Fr. Thomas Weinandy. *Of Jesus and Aliens.* The Catholic Thing. July 2023. https://www.thecatholicthing.org/2023/07/16/of-jesus-and-aliens/
[9] Douglas Burton-Christie. Spiritus: A Journal of Christian Spirituality 2.1 (2002) vii-viii. Johns Hopkins University Press.
[10] Religion & Ethics Newsweekly. Richard Rohr. November 2011. PBS. https://www.pbs.org/wnet/religionandethics/2011/11/11/november-11-2011-richard-rohr/9902/
[11] Statement from Fr. Richard Rohr, OFM after meeting Pope Francis. Center for Action and Contemplation. July 2022. https://cac.org/news/statement-from-fr-richard-rohr-ofm-after-meeting-pope-francis/
[12] "*Richard Rohr on THE UNIVERSAL CHRIST – September 16th, 2018*" YouTube, Center for Action and Contemplation. https://youtu.be/KD7B3wr3xeY
[13] *Ibid.*
[14] Romano Guardini. *The Lord.* Part II. Chapter VI.
[15] Hugh Owen. "Would Extraterrestrial Intelligent Life Redound to the Glory of God?" The Kolbe Center. December 2021. https://www.kolbecenter.org/would-extraterrestrial-intelligent-life-redound-to-the-glory-of-god/
[16] Voyager 1 Tracker. NASA. https://voyager.jpl.nasa.gov/
[17] Paul Thigpen. *Extraterrestrial Intelligence and the Catholic Faith.* TAN. 2022. Ch. 14
[18] Andrew Davison. *Astrobiology and Christian Doctrine.* Cambridge University Press. 2023. Page 352
[19] John Paul II. General Audience. April 22, 1998. https://www.vatican.va/jubilee_2000/magazine/documents/ju_mag_01101998_p-27_en.html
[20] Cardinal Joseph Ratzinger. Congregation For The Doctrine Of The Faith. Declaration, "Dominus Iesus": On The Unicity And Salvific Universality Of Jesus Christ And The Church. August, 2000. https://www.vatican.va/roman_curia/congregations/cfaith/documents/rc_con_cfaith_doc_20000806_dominus-iesus_en.html
[21] Paul Thigpen. *Extraterrestrial Intelligence and the Catholic Faith.* TAN. 2022. Ch. 14.
[22] Dr. Robert Sungenis. *Review of Extraterrestrial Intelligence and the Catholic Church: Are We Alone in the Universe with God and the Angels?*

[23] Fr. Thomas Weinandy. *Of Jesus and Aliens*. The Catholic Thing. July 2023. https://www.thecatholicthing.org/2023/07/16/of-jesus-and-aliens/
[24] Christopher Fisher & David Fergusson. *Karl Rahner and the Extra-Terrestrial Intelligence Question*. Heythrop Journal. Volume 47. P.275-290 (2006).
[25] The Traditional Latin Mass, still said throughout the world to this day, maintains this tradition.
[26] Cf. The Traditional "Act of Faith."
[27] Responsum of the Congregation for the Doctrine of the Faith to a dubium regarding the blessing of the unions of persons of the same sex, March 2021 https://press.vatican.va/content/salastampa/en/bollettino/pubblico/2021/03/15/210315b.html
[28] Fr. Maximilian Mary Dean. *A Primer on the Absolute Primacy of Christ: Blessed John Duns Scotus and the Franciscan Thesis*. January 2006. Conclusion.
[29] Paul Thigpen. *Extraterrestrial Intelligence and the Catholic Faith*. TAN. 2022. Ch. 2
[30] Communion and Stewardship: "Human Persons Created in the Image of God." International Theological Commission. September 2004. Vatican.va. Ch. 1
[31] Andrew Davison. *Astrobiology and Christian Doctrine*. Cambridge University Press. 2023. Pages 156-157, 170
[32] E.J. Dionne Jr. "For Jet-Age Pope: Angels, Devil and Indulgences" The New York Times. July 1986. https://www.nytimes.com/1986/07/18/world/for-jet-age-pope-angels-devil-and-indulgences.html
[33] Thaddeus Baklinski. "Catholic University to Give Award to Goddess-Worshipping Theologian." LifeSiteNews. September 2012. https://www.lifesitenews.com/news/catholic-university-to-give-award-to-goddess-worshipping-theologian/
[34] Elizabeth Johnson. "Interpret: As with the Bible, so too with church teaching on homosexuality." Outreach. September 2023. https://outreach.faith/2023/09/interpret-as-with-the-bible-so-too-with-church-teaching-on-homosexuality/
[35] Ibid.
[36] Ibid.
[37] Andrew Davison. *Astrobiology and Christian Doctrine*. Cambridge University Press. 2023. Page 346-347
[38] Paul Thigpen. *Extraterrestrial Intelligence and the Catholic Faith*. TAN. 2022. Ch. 14
[39] Decrees of the First Vatican Council. Chapter 2.9
[40] Council of Trent. Decree Concerning the Edition, and the Use, of the Sacred Books
[41] Hugh Owen. "Would Extraterrestrial Intelligent Life Redound to the Glory of God?" The Kolbe Center. December, 2021. https://www.kolbecenter.org/would-extraterrestrial-intelligent-life-redound-to-the-glory-of-god/
[42] Quote from: John Carey, PhD. *Ireland and the Antipodes: The Heterodoxy of Virgil of Salzburg*. Speculum, Vol. 64, No. 1 (Jan., 1989), pp. 1-10
[43] Alberto Martinez. *Burned Alive: Bruno, Galileo and the Inquisition*. Reaktion Books. 2018. Page 241
[44] Paul Thigpen. *Extraterrestrial Intelligence and the Catholic Faith*. TAN. 2022. Ch. 2
[45] Cum sicut accepimus. Denzinger 1362-1365. P. 351. 43rd Edition. English Translation, Ignatius Press, 2012.
[46] Paul Thigpen. *Extraterrestrial Intelligence and the Catholic Faith*. TAN. 2022. Ch. 2
[47] Fr. Reginald Garrigou-Lagrange. On Divine Revelation: The Teaching of the Catholic Faith. Translated by Matthew Minerd. Emmaus Academic. 2022.
[48] Address of His Holiness Benedict XVI to the ITC on the Occasion of Its Annual Plenary Assembly. December 7, 2012.

[49] "Sensus Fidei In the Life of the Church." 2014. International Theological Commission.
[50] Joel Parkyn. *Exotheology: Theological Explorations of Intelligent Extraterrestrial Life.* Pickwick Publications. 2021.Introduction. (Selected Excerpts)
[51] Ibid. Page 412.
[52] Cf. G.S. Kirk & J.E. Raven. *Presocratic Philosophers.* Cambridge University Press, 1984. §564
[53] Charles L. Harper, Jr. *God, Science, and Humility: Ten Scientists Consider Humility Theology.* Page 112.
[54] Michael Crowe. *Extraterrestrial Life Debate, Antiquity to 1915: A Source Book.* University of Notre Dame Press. 2008. Part One.
[55] Ibid.
[56] Ibid.
[57] Paul Thigpen. *Extraterrestrial Intelligence and the Catholic Faith.* TAN. 2022. Ch. 1
[58] Marie George. *Christianity and Extraterrestrials?: A Catholic Perspective.* iUniverse. 2005. Ch. 4
[59] Ibid.
[60] Ibid.
[61] Michael Crowe. *Extraterrestrial Life Debate, Antiquity to 1915: A Source Book.* University of Notre Dame Press. 2008.. Preface.
[62] Joel Parkyn. *Exotheology: Theological Explorations of Intelligent Extraterrestrial Life.* Pickwick Publications. 2021.Page 130
[63] Ibid. Page 105.
[64] Ibid.
[65] Kirschner, Stefan, "Nicole Oresme", The Stanford Encyclopedia of Philosophy (Fall 2021 Edition), Edward N. Zalta (ed.)
[66] Nicole Oresme. *Le Livre du ciel et du monde.* Book I, Chapter 24, 36b-39c. Quoted in Michael Crowe's *The Extraterrestrial Life Debate, 1750-1900.* Dover Publications. 2011. Chapter 1.
[67] "On the Uniqueness of the World." Vanderbilt University. https://www.vanderbilt.edu/AnS/physics/astrocourses/ast203/med_univ_unique.html
[68] Pierre Duhem. Quoted in Roger Ariew, *Medieval Cosmology.* Part V. Chapter 13. "The Plurality of Worlds in Fifteenth-Century Cosmology."
[69] Michael Crowe. *The Extraterrestrial Life Debate, 1750-1900.* Dover Publications. 2011. Part One.
[70] Ibid.
[71] Ibid.
[72] Joel Parkyn. *Exotheology: Theological Explorations of Intelligent Extraterrestrial Life.* Pickwick Publications. 2021. Page 119
[73] Henrik Bogdan and Martin Starr. *Aleister Crowley and Western Esotericism.* Oxford University Press. 2012. Page 183.
[74] Miller, Clyde Lee, "Cusanus, Nicolaus [Nicolas of Cusa]", The Stanford Encyclopedia of Philosophy (Winter 2021 Edition), Edward N. Zalta. Note: the full quote claims that few later thinkers even "understood" Cusa. Indeed, a number of Cusa's teachings would require much difficulty to "understand"—e.g., his astronomical views—not, however, his teaching on aliens. We can be sure that these views did not merely "fail to be understood," rather, they were simply entirely non influential since they were, rightly, not taken seriously by the Christians of that era.
[75] Alberto Martinez. "Was Giordano Bruno Burned at the Stake for Believing in Exoplanets?" March 2018. Scientific American.

[76] *Letter from Cardinal Angelo Sodano on the Occasion of a Congress of Studies on the Personality of Giordano Bruno*. February 14, 2000. Vatican.va
[77] Marie George. *Christianity and Extraterrestrials?: A Catholic Perspective.* iUniverse. 2005. Ch. 4
[78] Alberto Martinez. Burned Alive: Bruno, Galileo and the Inquisition. Reaktion Books. 2018. Chapter One.
[79] Andrew Davison. *Astrobiology and Christian Doctrine.* Cambridge University Press. 2023. Page 37
[80] Pope Pius X. *Pascendi Dominici Gregi,* §39
[81] Michael Crowe. *The Extraterrestrial Life Debate, 1750-1900.* Dover Publications. 2011. Part 3.
[82] Ibid.
[83] Ibid. Part 1.
[84] Ibid.
[85] Ibid. Part 3.
[86] Ibid.
[87] Ibid.
[88] Ibid.
[89] Ibid. Part 1.
[90] Ibid. Part 2.
[91] Ibid. Fr. Burque, however, also noted that, hypothetically, if aliens were proved to exist, it would have no negative effect on Catholicism; and for this simple observation, some wrongly cite him as a pluralist.
[92] Ibid. Part 3.
[93] Ibid.
[94] Ibid.
[95] Ibid.
[96] Ibid.
[97] Michael Crowe. *Extraterrestrial Life Debate, Antiquity to 1915: A Source Book.* University of Notre Dame Press. 2008. Part Three
[98] Michael Crowe. *The Extraterrestrial Life Debate, 1750-1900.* Dover Publications. 2011. Part 2.
[99] Ibid.
[100] Ibid.
[101] Michael Crowe. *Extraterrestrial Life Debate, Antiquity to 1915: A Source Book.* University of Notre Dame Press. 2008. Part Three.
[102] Ibid.
[103] Cathy Gutierrez. *The Occult in Nineteenth-Century America. Contexts and Consequences:* New Studies in Religion and History. The Davies Group, 2005. Introduction
[104] https://web.archive.org/web/20090326183109/http://shell.cas.usf.edu/~alevine/pasteur.pdf
[105] Sarah Willburn, Tatiana Kontou. *The Ashgate Research Companion to Nineteenth-Century Spiritualism and the Occult.* Routledge. 2017. Foreword.
[106] Ibid.
[107] Ibid. Ch. 6
[108] St Francis de Sales. *The Saint Francis de Sales Collection [15 Books]* (p. 487). Catholic Way Publishing.
[109] St. Alphonsus Liguori. *The Saint Alphonsus de Liguori Collection [30 Books]* (p. 625). Catholic Way Publishing.
[110] Note: the last clause is indeed St. Hannibal's own; he includes those words in the

original text. However, they are part of the abridged portion of what it is included in *The Sun of My Will*

[111] Carl E. Schmöger. The Life and Revelations of Anne Catherine Emmerich: Book 2. TAN. 2014. "Feast of the Guardian Angels (1820)"

[112] *The Revelations of St. Birgitta of Sweden*. Volume 4. Oxford University Press. 2015. Translated by Denis Searby. Book VIII. Page 100. §67-71

[113] Liber Caelestis. Book IV. Ch. 67. Oxford University Press. 2008

[114] Venerable Mary of Agreda. *The Mystical City of God*. Translation by Fr. George Blatter. Veritatis Splendor Publications. 2013.

[115] Eltz, Nicky. *Get Us Out Of Here*. Preface.

[116] Ibid. Ch. 7

[117] Ibid.

[118] Fr. Stanley Jaki. *A Late Awakening and Other Essays*. Real View Books. 2006. Page 103

[119] Hugh Ross. *Lights in the Sky & Little Green Men: A Rational Christian Look at UFOs and Extraterrestrials*. Reasons to Believe. 2002. Appendix B.

[120] Michael Crowe. *The Extraterrestrial Life Debate, 1750-1900*. Dover Publications. 2011. Part 3.

[121] Suzanne Goldenberg. Planet Earth is home to 8.7 million species, scientists estimate. The Guardian. August 2011. https://www.theguardian.com/environment/2011/aug/23/species-earth-estimate-scientists

[122] Mark Pagel. *The Oxford Encyclopedia of Evolution*. Oxford University Press. 2012. Page 138.

[123] Doug Gross, CNN.com September 26th, 2011.

[124] Michael Crowe. *Extraterrestrial Life Debate, Antiquity to 1915: A Source Book*. University of Notre Dame Press. 2008. Conclusion.

[125] Cf., Simo Knuuttila. *Reforging the Great Chain of Being: Studies in the History of Modal Theories*. Springer. 2013. Page 3.

[126] *New Catholic Encyclopedia*. FINITE BING.

[127] Arthur Lovejoy. *The Great Chain of Being: A Study of the History of an Idea*. Harvard University Press. 1976. Pages 116-118

[128] https://www.peterkreeft.com/topics-more/pillars_kant.htm

[129] Fr. Stanley Jaki. *A Late Awakening and Other Essays*. Real View Books. 2006. "Christ, Extraterrestrial, and the Devil."

[130] Arthur Lovejoy. *The Great Chain of Being: A Study of the History of an Idea*. Harvard University Press. 1976. Page 140

[131] Ibid., Page 155

[132] Hugh Ross. *Why the Universe Is the Way It Is*. Baker Books. 2008. Chapter 6.

[133] Michael Crowe. *The Extraterrestrial Life Debate, 1750-1900*. Dover Publications. 2011. Chapter 11.

[134] Michael Crowe. *Extraterrestrial Life Debate, Antiquity to 1915: A Source Book*. University of Notre Dame Press. 2008. Part 3.

[135] Ibid.

[136] Ibid.

[137] This Day In History: "The Great Moon Hoax" is published in the "New York Sun". History.com. https://www.history.com/this-day-in-history/the-great-moon-hoax

[138] Michael Crowe. The Extraterrestrial Life Debate, 1750-1900. Dover Publications. 2011. Chapter 4.

[139] Ibid.

[140] Ibid.

[141] Ibid.
[142] Marc Seifer. *Wizard: The Life and Times of Nikola Tesla: Biography of a Genius*. Citadel. 2016. Page 209
[143] Ibid. Ch. 17
[144] Patrick Moore, translator. *Camille Flammarion's the Planet Mars*. Springer. 1980. Translator's Preface
[145] Michael Crowe. *The Extraterrestrial Life Debate, 1750-1900*. Dover Publications. 2011. Part 3.
[146] *Cammille Flammarion's The Planet Mars*. Editor's Preface.
[147] Camille Flammarion, Popular Astronomy. 1894. Quoted in Crossley, Robert. The Massachusetts Review , Autumn, 2000, Vol. 41, No. 3 pp. 297-318
[148] "FLAMMARION PREDICTS TALKING WITH MARS; He Says 'Psychic Waves' Will Be Developed to the Point of Overcoming Space." The New York Times. December 1923. https://www.nytimes.com/1923/12/12/archives/flammarion-predicts-talking-with-mars-he-says-psychic-waves-will-be.html
[149] Michael Crowe. *The Extraterrestrial Life Debate, 1750-1900*. Dover Publications. 2011. Part 3.
[150] Quoted in Ibid.
[151] George Basalla. Civilized *Life in the Universe: Scientists on Intelligent Extraterrestrials*. Oxford University Press. 2008. Page 58.
[152] Ibid.
[153] Ibid.
[154] Ibid. Chapter 5.
[155] Marc Seifer. *Wizard: The Life and Times of Nikola Tesla: Biography of a Genius*. Citadel. 2016. Ch. 17
[156] Ibid.
[157] Ibid.
[158] Ibid.
[159] Ibid.
[160] Ibid. Chapter 48
[161] Ibid. Chapter 46
[162] Ibid.
[163] Ibid.
[164] Keay Davidson. *Carl Sagan: A Life.* Trade Paper Press. 2000. Page 91
[165] Sagan & Swan's Voyager Mars Landing Sites (1965). Wired Magazine. https://www.wired.com/2013/02/sagan-swans-voyager-mars-landing-sites-1965/
[166] https://www.wired.com/2010/07/0714first-mars-closeup-photo/
[167] https://www.newspapers.com/newspage/435402308/ , https://web.archive.org/web/20160805020812/http:/pqasb.pqarchiver.com/washingtonpost_historical/doc/148085303.html , https://www.nytimes.com/1976/07/18/archives/the-genesis-strategy-a-chilling-prospect.html
[168] Mattias Desmet. *The Psychology of Totalitarianism.* Chelsea Green Publishing. 2022. Chapter 1.
[169] Congressional Report. UNIDENTIFIED AERIAL PHENOMENA. May 17, 2022. U.S. House of Representatives, Permanent Select Committee on Intelligence, Subcommittee on Counterterrorism, Counterintelligence, and Counterproliferation, Washington, D.C.
https://www.congress.gov/117/meeting/house/114761/documents/HHRG-117-IG05-Transcript-20220517.pdf
[170] https://imagine.gsfc.nasa.gov/features/cosmic/nearest_galaxy_info.html

[171] DOE Explains...Relativity. Office of Science. Energy.gov. https://www.energy.gov/science/doe-explainsrelativity
[172] Milton Rothman. *A Physicist's Guide to Skepticism: Applying Laws of Physics to Faster-Than-Light Travel, Psychic Phenomena, Telepathy, Time Travel, UFOs, and Other Pseudoscientific Claims*. Prometheus. 1988. Chapter 4.
[173] Barry Markovksy. (Edited by Michael Shermer.) The Skeptic Encyclopedia of Pseudoscience. ABC-CLIO. 2002. "UFOs."
[174] Ed Regis. *Interstellar Travel as Delusional Fantasy* [Excerpt]. Scientific American. October 2015. https://www.scientificamerican.com/article/interstellar-travel-as-delusional-fantasy-excerpt/
[175] Paul Sutter. *Is Interstellar Travel Really Possible?* Discovery.com June 2021. https://www.discovery.com/space/is-interstellar-travel-really-possible-
[176] Hugh Ross. *Lights in the Sky & Little Green Men: A Rational Christian Look at UFOs and Extraterrestrials*. Reasons to Believe. 2002. Chapter 5.
[177] Therefore, the so-called "Zoo Hypothesis" will not work.
[178] Stephen Webb. *If the Universe Is Teeming with Aliens ... WHERE IS EVERYBODY?: Seventy-Five Solutions to the Fermi Paradox and the Problem of Extraterrestrial Life*. Springer. 2015. Chapter 1
[179] Stephen Webb. *If the Universe Is Teeming with Aliens ... WHERE IS EVERYBODY?: Fifty Solutions to the Fermi Paradox*. Springer. 2002. Chapter 6
[180] Milton Rothman. *A Physicist's Guide to Skepticism: Applying Laws of Physics to Faster-Than-Light Travel, Psychic Phenomena, Telepathy, Time Travel, UFOs, and Other Pseudoscientific Claims*. Prometheus. 1988. Chapter 6.
[181] John Alexander. *UFOs: Myths, Conspiracies, and Realities*. St. Martin's Griffin. 2012. Chapter 11.
[182] Ibid.
[183] Jason Lisle. *The Physics of Einstein: Black holes, time travel, distant starlight, E=mc2*. Biblical Science Institute. 2018. Page 197
[184]https://web.archive.org/web/20060928234930/http://nai.arc.nasa.gov/astrobio/astrobio_detail.cfm?ID=1538
[185] Jacques Vallée. *REVELATIONS: Alien Contact and Human Deception*. Anomalist Books. 2008. Conclusion.
[186] Ibid.
[187] Philip Jaekl, "What is behind the decline in UFO Sightings?" The Guardian. September, 2018. https://www.theguardian.com/world/2018/sep/21/what-is-behind-the-decline-in-ufo-sightings
[188] Ibid.
[189] Matt Moffett. "Tale of Stinky Extraterrestrials Stirs Up UFO Crowd in Brazil" The Wall Street Journal. June 1996. https://www.wsj.com/articles/SB835915673862027500
[190] Timothy Dailey, PhD. *The Paranormal Conspiracy*. Ch. 4
[191] https://studyfinds.org/americans-security-cameras-study/
[192] Hugh Ross. *Lights in the Sky & Little Green Men: A Rational Christian Look at UFOs and Extraterrestrials*. Reasons to Believe. 2002. Ch. 16
[193] Jacques Vallée. *REVELATIONS: Alien Contact and Human Deception*. Anomalist Books. 2008. Introduction
[194] John Horgan. "Is speculation in multiverses as immoral as speculation in subprime mortgages?" Scientific American. January 2011 https://blogs.scientificamerican.com/cross-check/is-speculation-in-multiverses-as-immoral-as-speculation-in-subprime-mortgages/

[195] "Russian Orthodox Church equates aliens with demons." Interfax. April 202 https://interfax.com/newsroom/top-stories/68479/
[196] Fr. Stanley Jaki. *A Late Awakening and Other Essays*. Real View Books. 2006. Page 101.
[197] Fr. Spyridon Bailey. *The UFO Deception: An Orthodox Christian Perspective*. FeedARead.com 2021. Pages 157-164, excerpts
[198] "Bad Boys for Life," 2020.
[199] Charles Fraune. *Slaying Dragons II - The Rise of the Occult: What Exorcists & Former Occultists Want You to Know*. Slaying Dragons Press. 2022. Ch. 13
[200] Gary Bates. *Alien Intrusion*. Creation Book Publishers. 2010. Page 243.
[201] Ibid. 282-284
[202] Fr. Chad Ripperger. *Dominion: The Nature of Diabolic Warfare*. 2022. Pages 411-412
[203] Whitley Strieber. *Them*. Walker & Collier, Inc. 2023. Ch. 15
[204] Ibid
[205] https://www.unknowncountry.com/insight/my-catholic-struggle-by-whitley-strieber/
[206] Whitley Strieber. *Them*. Walker & Collier, Inc. 2023. Page 7.
[207] Fr. Chad Ripperger. *Dominion: The Nature of Diabolic Warfare*. 2022. Page 228
[208] Whitley Strieber. *Them*. Walker & Collier, Inc. 2023. Page 253.
[209] Fr. Chad Ripperger. *Dominion: The Nature of Diabolic Warfare*. 2022. Pages 411-413
[210] Whitley Strieber. Foreword for Vallée's *DIMENSIONS*
[211] Charles Upton. *The System of Antichrist: Truth & Falsehood in Postmodernism & the New Age*. Sophia Perennis. 2001. Page 463
[212] Jacques Vallée. *DIMENSIONS: A Casebook of Alien Contact*. Anomalist Books. 2008. Part Two. Ch. 7
[213] Ibid. Ch 5
[214] Fr. Spyridon Bailey. *The UFO Deception: An Orthodox Christian Perspective*. FeedARead.com 2021. Ch 11, 12, 13, 15 (excerpts)
[215] Keay Davidson. *Carl Sagan: A Life*. Trade Paper Press. 2000. Preface.
[216] Ibid.
[217] Carl Sagan. *The Demon-Haunted World*. Random House Publishing Group. 1997.
[218] https://apps.dtic.mil/sti/pdfs/AD0688332.pdf
[219] https://religiousdemonology.com/basics
[220] *Shamanic Initiations, Alien Abduction Phenomena, and the Return of the Archetypal Feminine: An Experiential Distillation* Tiffany Vance-Huffman Naropa University January 2023.
[221] Hugh Ross. *Lights in the Sky & Little Green Men: A Rational Christian Look at UFOs and Extraterrestrials*. Reasons to Believe. 2002. Chapter 16.
[222] http://www.alienresistance.org/satanic-ritual-abuse-sra-and-alien-abduction-comparison/
[223] https://www.piercingthecosmicveil.com/frequently-asked-questions
[224] http://www.alienresistance.org/ufo-alien-deception/alienabductions-stop-in-the-name-jesus-christ/
[225] Jacques Vallée. *REVELATIONS: Alien Contact and Human Deception*. Anomalist Books. 2008 Appendix.
[226] Jacques Vallée. *DIMENSIONS: A Casebook of Alien Contact*. Anomalist Books. 2008. Part One. Ch. 2
[227] Jim Marrs. *Alien Agenda: Investigating the Extraterrestrial Presence Among Us*. William Morrow Paperbacks. 2000. Page 350
[228] R.L. Dione. *God Drives a Flying Saucer*. Bantam. 1973. Ch. 6, 7, and 8. Excerpts.

[229]Jesus Christ The Bearer Of The Water Of Life: A Christian reflection on the "New Age." Pontifical Council For Culture; Pontifical Council For Interreligious Dialogue. Vatican.va. 2003. https://www.vatican.va/roman_curia/pontifical_councils/interelg/documents/rc_pc_interelg_doc_20030203_new-age_en.html
[230] Ibid.
[231] https://religiondispatches.org/hell-in-a-cell-the-popes-exorcist-reflects-the-growing-belief-that-cocksure-men-will-save-us-in-the-battle-of-good-v-evil/
[232] Joseph Laycock. (Volume edited by Ben Zeller.) *Handbook of UFO Religions.* Brill Handbooks on Contemporary Religion, Volume: 20. Brill. 2021. Page 105
[233] Ben Zeller. *Handbook of UFO Religions.* Brill Handbooks on Contemporary Religion, Volume: 20. Brill. 2021. Introduction.
[234] David Wilkinson. *Science, Religion, and the Search for Extraterrestrial Intelligence.* Oxford University Press. 2013. Pages 177-178
[235] Adam Lusher. "Meeting extraterrestrials: Should we contact aliens?" Independent UK. July 2015. https://www.independent.co.uk/news/science/meeting-extraterrestrials-should-we-contact-aliens-10420032.html
[236] Michael Ricciardelli. "Professor Named One of Five Catholic Scientists that 'Shaped our Understanding of the World'" June 2018. Seton Hall University. https://www.shu.edu/arts-sciences/news/father-stanley-jaki-a-great-mind-that-shaped-the-world.html
[237] Fr. Stanley Jaki. *A Late Awakening and Other Essays.* Real View Books. 2006. Page 101.
[238] "*The UFO Rabbit Hole Podcast.*" February 24th, 2023, on Twitter.
[239] Ted Peters. *UFOs: The Religious Dimension.* CrossCurrents. Fall 1977. Vol. 27. No. 3. Pp. 261-278. Wiley.
[240] Robert Hermann. *God, Science, and Humility: Ten Scientists Consider Humility Theology.* Templeton Press. 2000. Page 97
[241] John Updike. *Pigeon Feathers.* Page 118-119.
[242] Gary Bates. *Alien Intrusion.* Creation Book Publishers. 2010. Pages 54-55
[243] H.G. Wells. "The War That Will End War," The Daily News. August 14, 1914
[244] "Hiccups from Outer Space" Russell Davies, reviewing Close Encounters of the Third Kind in The Observer, March 19, 1978. Quoted in *Dimensions,* Jacques Vallée.
[245] Entry on CINEMA. 1993.
[246] The Telegraph Reporters. "Stanley Kubrick explains the ending of 2001: A Space Odyssey in newly discovered interview." July 2018. https://www.telegraph.co.uk/films/2018/07/09/stanley-kubrick-finally-explains-ending-2001-space-odyssey-unearthed/
[247] https://www.krusch.com/kubrick/Q12.html
[248] *The Encyclopedia of Science Fiction.* 1993. "Close Encounters of the Third Kind" entry
[249] Charles Upton. *The Alien Disclosure Deception: The Metaphysics of Social Engineering.* Sophia Perennis. 2021.
[250] Jacques Vallée. *DIMENSIONS: A Casebook of Alien Contact.* Anomalist Books. 2008. Part Three. Chapter 8.
[251] John Baxter. *Steven Spielberg: The Unauthorised Biography.* Harper Collins. 1998.
[252] Fr. Spyridon Bailey. *The UFO Deception: An Orthodox Christian Perspective.* FeedARead.com 2021. Chapter 16
[253] Adam Daniel. *A Critical Companion to Steven Spielberg.* Lexington Books. 2019. Chapter 3.
[254] Michael Brown. *Where the Cross Stands.* Spiritdaily Publishing. 2017. Chapter 21
[255] David Weintraub. *Religions and Extraterrestrial Life: How Will We Deal With It?*

(Springer Praxis Books). Springer. 2014.
256 Fr. Stanley Jaki. *A Late Awakening and Other Essays.* Real View Books. 2006. Page 105.
257 "Swiss bishop: 'Synodal' church is a 'protestantized' rejection of the Catholic faith" LifeSiteNews. July 2023. https://www.lifesitenews.com/opinion/swiss-bishop-synodal-church-is-a-protestantized-rejection-of-the-catholic-faith/
258 https://onepeterfive.com/teilhard-chardin-vii-architect/ Note: This is just one of a multitude of authors who has published this quote attributed to Pope Pius XII. Many others have done the same for decades. However, I have struggled to identify the primary source. I nevertheless preserve the quote here—with, albeit, this disclaimer—in view of its clear accuracy and its harmony with what Pius XII did write, elsewhere, on the same themes promoted by de Chardin (e.g., in *Humani Generis.*) Until the original source of the quote can be verified, however, it should not be regarded as certain.
259 Quoted in: Wolfgang Smith. *Teilhardism and the New Religion.* TAN Books. 2009. Chapter X
260 "The Teilhard de Chardin Project" https://teilhard.com/2013/09/12/the-teilhard-de-chardin-project-coming-april-2015/
261 https://getpocket.com/explore/item/how-will-our-religions-handle-the-discovery-of-alien-life?utm_source=pocket-newtab
262 Teilhard Pierre de Chardin. *Fall, Redemption, and geocentrism.* 1969
263 Cardinal Gerhard Müller. Meeting of the Superiors of the Congregation for the Doctrine of the Faith
with the Presidency of the Leadership Conference of Women Religious (LCWR). April 30, 2014 https://www.vatican.va/roman_curia/congregations/cfaith/muller/rc_con_cfaith_doc_20140430_muller-lcwr_en.html
264 Robert Hermann. *God, Science, and Humility: Ten Scientists Consider Humility Theology.* Templeton Press. 2000. Page 41-42
265 Paul Thigpen. *Extraterrestrial Intelligence and the Catholic Faith.* TAN. 2022. Ch. 8
266 Joel Parkyn. *Exotheology: Theological Explorations of Intelligent Extraterrestrial Life.* Pickwick Publications. 2021. Page 141.
267 Entry on "Cosmic Consciousness"
268 Paola Harris. *UFOs: How Does One Speak to A Ball of Light?* 2012. Section Two.
269 Ibid
270 Fr. Stanley Jaki. *A Late Awakening and Other Essays.* Real View Books. 2006. Page 104.
271 Fr. Thomas Weinandy. *Of Jesus and Aliens.* The Catholic Thing. July 2023. https://www.thecatholicthing.org/2023/07/16/of-jesus-and-aliens/
272 Brenda Denzler. *The Lure of the Edge: Scientific Passions, Religious Beliefs, and the Pursuit of UFOs.* University of California Press. 2003. Footnote 119
273 Steven Greer. *Disclosure.* 2013. Section I. §2
274 Paola Harris. *UFOs: How Does One Speak to a Ball of Light?* Section Three.
275 https://dsdoconnor.com/maussan/
276 Alberto Martinez. *Burned Alive: Bruno, Galileo and the Inquisition.* Reaktion Books. 2018. Page 244
277 https://paolaharris.com/latest-news-paola-harris/historical-inteview-monsignore-corrado-balducci-with-paola-harris
278 Quoted in, Charles Upton. *The Alien Disclosure Deception: The Metaphysics of Social Engineering.* Sophia Perennis. 2021. Part II. Addendum
279 Charles Upton. *The System of Antichrist: Truth & Falsehood in Postmodernism & the*

New Age. Sophia Perennis. 2001.
[280] John Thavis. *The Vatican Prophecies: Investigating Supernatural Signs, Apparitions, and Miracles in the Modern Age*. Viking. 2015. Chapter Six.
[281] Fr. Spyridon Bailey. *The UFO Deception: An Orthodox Christian Perspective*. Feed-ARead.com 2021.
[282] John Thavis. *The Vatican Prophecies: Investigating Supernatural Signs, Apparitions, and Miracles in the Modern Age*. Viking. 2015. Chapter Six.
[283] Claire Giangrave. "Could Catholicism handle the discovery of extraterrestrial life?" Crux. February 2017. https://cruxnow.com/global-church/2017/02/catholicism-handle-discovery-extraterrestrial-life
[284] Timothy Dailey. *The Paranormal Conspiracy: The Truth about Ghosts, Aliens and Mysterious Beings*. Chosen Books. 2015. Chapter 1.
[285] Quoted in Michael Crowe. *Extraterrestrial Life Debate, Antiquity to 1915: A Source Book*. University of Notre Dame Press. 2008. Part Four.
[286] Jorg Matthias Determann. *Islam, Science Fiction and Extraterrestrial Life: The Culture of Astrobiology in the Muslim World*. Bloomsbury. 2020. Page 10-11
[287] David Weintraub. *Religions and Extraterrestrial Life: How Will We Deal With It?* Springer. 2014. Page 166
[288] https://getpocket.com/explore/item/how-will-our-religions-handle-the-discovery-of-alien-life?utm_source=pocket-newtab
[289] David Weintraub. *Religions and Extraterrestrial Life: How Will We Deal With It?* (Springer Praxis Books). Springer. 2014. Chapter 17
[290] Ibid.
[291] Ibid.
[292] Ibid. Chapter 16
[293] Ibid. Chapter 19
[294] Ibid. Chapter 18
[295] Walter Martin. *The Kingdom of the Occult*. Thomas Nelson Publishers. 2008. Page 191.
[296] Ibid.
[297] Christopher Partridge. *The Occult World* (Routledge Worlds). Routledge. 2016. Page 150
[298] https://getpocket.com/explore/item/how-will-our-religions-handle-the-discovery-of-alien-life?utm_source=pocket-newtab
[299] Michael Crowe. *The Extraterrestrial Life Debate, 1750-1900*. Dover Publications. 2011. Chapter 5.
[300] Ibid.
[301] Ben Zeller. *Handbook of UFO Religions*. Brill Handbooks on Contemporary Religion, Volume: 20. Brill. 2021.page 23
[302] George Chryssides (Edited by Ben Zeller.) *Handbook of UFO Religions*. Brill Handbooks on Contemporary Religion, Volume: 20. Brill. 2021. Chapter 17
[303] Ibid.
[304] Ibid.
[305] Ben Zeller. *Heaven's Gate: America's UFO Religion*. NYU Press. 2014. Page 102
[306] Christopher Partridge. *UFO Religions*. Routledge. 2003. Part 2. Chapter 2.
[307] Ibid.
[308] Ibid.
[309] David Wilkinson. *Science, Religion, and the Search for Extraterrestrial Intelligence*. Oxford University Press. 2013. Chapter 1.
[310] Gary Bates. *Alien Intrusion*. Creation Book Publishers. 2010. Pages 303-304

[311] Henrik Bogdan. *Aleister Crowley and Western Esotericism.* Oxford University Press. 2012. Page 273.
[312] Timothy Dailey. *The Paranormal Conspiracy: The Truth about Ghosts, Aliens and Mysterious Beings.* Chosen Books. 2015. Chapter 10.
[313] Gregory Reece. *UFO Religions: Inside Flying Saucer Cults and Culture.* I.B. Tauris Publishers. 2007. Pages 184-185
[314] Gary Bates. *Alien Intrusion.* Creation Book Publishers. 2010. Pages 301-303
[315] Ibid.
[316] https://youtu.be/qjG-Wz2aZME
[317] https://www.aetherius.org/
[318] "Talking to Aliens Is Their Religion." The New York Times. August 2020. https://www.nytimes.com/2020/08/18/opinion/gods-from-space-aetherius.html
[319] https://www.aetherius.org/oldest-international-ufo-organisation-validated-by-recent-government-admissions/
[320] Hugh Ross. *Lights in the Sky & Little Green Men: A Rational Christian Look at UFOs and Extraterrestrials.* Reasons to Believe. 2002. Chapter 14.
[321] Jorg Matthias Determann. *Islam, Science Fiction and Extraterrestrial Life: The Culture of Astrobiology in the Muslim World.* Bloomsbury. 2020. Pages 113-114
[322] Gregg Tomusko. *The Catholic Church and The Urantia Book.* 2023. Pages 28-29
[323] Ibid. page 89
[324] Ibid. Page 98
[325] https://www.medjugorje.ws/en/articles/marija-pavlovic-lunetti-tomislav-vlasic-caritas-of-birmingham-friend-of-medjugorje-terry-colafrancesco/
[326] Ibid.
[327] TOWARDS THE NEW CREATION: official website of the Church of Jesus Christ of the Universe https://towardsthenewcreation.com/
[328] Ibid.
[329] Voice and Echo of the Divine Messengers. "Apparitions of Christ Jesus." https://www.mensajerosdivinos.org/en/aparicion-de-cristo/saturday-august-15-2020
[330] Ibid. "Messages of the Virgin Mary." https://www.mensajerosdivinos.org/en/mensaje-de-la-virgen-maria/wednesday-december-25-2019-0
[331] Ibid. "Apparitions of Christ Jesus." https://www.mensajerosdivinos.org/en/mensaje-de-cristo-jesus/saturday-december-28-2019
[332] Ibid. "Messages of the Virgin Mary." https://www.mensajerosdivinos.org/en/mensaje-de-la-virgen-maria/thursday-february-25-2016
[333] https://www.mensajerosdivinos.org/en/tag/11408
[334] https://www.mensajerosdivinos.org/en/tag/14577
[335] https://www.redalyc.org/journal/2433/243364810005/html/#fn4
[336] Ibid.
[337] https://www.mensajerosdivinos.org/en/mensaje-de-san-jose/monday-january-18-2016
[338] Joel Achenbach. "The Outre Limits." The Washington Post. March 19, 1997. https://www.washingtonpost.com/archive/lifestyle/1997/03/19/the-outre-limits/0bc6c9d1-4022-4baf-afbf-06e41e23239c/
[339] en.thbongiovannifamily.it
[340] Ibid.
[341] Rory Carol. "Written in blood." The Guardian. June 2002. https://www.theguardian.com/media/2002/jun/17/mondaymediasection.italy
[342] St. Athanasius. *Life of St. Anthony.* https://www.newadvent.org/fathers/2811.htm

[343] "The battle for souls -The mystic saints vs. the demons " https://www.mysticsofthechurch.com/2013/12/the-battle-for-souls-mystic-saints-vs.html
[344] St. Alphonsus Liguori. *Uniformity with God's Will*. Chapter 2.
[345] Dr. Ingrid Merkel & Allen Debus. *Hermeticism and the Renaissance*. Page 116.
[346] Quoted from Ibid. page 134-135
[347] Fr. Chad Ripperger. *Dominion: The Nature of Diabolic Warfare*. 2022. Pages 100-101
[348] Ibid. Pages 382-383
[349] Ibid. Page 22
[350] Fr. Jordan Aumann. *Spiritual Theology*. Chapter 14.
[351] Ibid.
[352] Ben Zeller. *Handbook of UFO Religions*. Brill Handbooks on Contemporary Religion, Volume: 20. Brill. 2021. Introduction.
[353] Jacques Vallée. *REVELATIONS: Alien Contact and Human Deception*. Anomalist Books. 2008. Conclusion.
[354] Gregory Kanon. *The Great UFO Hoax: The Final Solution to the UFO Mystery*. Galde Press, Inc. 1997. Foreword
[355] Fr. Stanley Jaki. *A Late Awakening and Other Essays*. Real View Books. 2006. Pages 104-105
[356] https://www.shu.edu/arts-sciences/news/father-stanley-jaki-a-great-mind-that-shaped-the-world.html
[357] https://www.nytimes.com/2009/04/13/nyregion/13jaki.html
[358] St. Augustine. *City of God*. Book 20. Chapter 19
[359] Ibid.
[360] Fr. Jordan Aumann. *Spiritual Theology*. Part II, Ch. 7
[361] Pope Paul VI. "Confronting The Devil's Power" General Audience, November 15, 1972.
[362] Joe Tremblay. The 100 year test. Catholic News Agency. February 2013 https://www.catholicnewsagency.com/column/52453/the-100-year-test
[363] "The Terrifying Vision That Led Pope Leo XIII To Write The Saint Michael Prayer " https://ucatholic.com/vision-of-pope-leo
[364] Ibid.
[365] Christopher Partridge. *Alien demonology: The Christian roots of the malevolent extraterrestrial in UFO religions and abduction spiritualities*. Religion, 34:3, 163-189, DOI: 10.1016/j.religion.2004.04.014
[366] http://www.catholicapologetics.info/catholicteaching/privaterevelation/lasalet.html
[367] https://the-american-catholic.com/2017/02/26/fulton-sheen-on-the-anti-christ/
[368] Jan Faye. *Niels Bohr and the Philosophy of Physics*. Bloomsbury Academic. 2014. Page 134-135.
[369] Ibid.
[370] George Musser. "The Biologist Blowing Our Minds." Nautilus. June 2023. https://nautil.us/the-biologist-blowing-our-minds-323905/
[371] https://twitter.com/drmichaellevin/status/1637449677028093953
[372] Stanley Jaki. *Brain, Mind and Computers*. Introduction
[373] https://dsdoconnor.com/2022/08/22/all-the-devil-wants-is-a-little-dialogue/
[374] Darren Orf. "AI Has Suddenly Evolved to Achieve Theory of Mind." Popular Mechanics. February 2023. https://www.popularmechanics.com/technology/robots/a42958546/artificial-intelligence-theory-of-mind-chatgpt/
[375] Jim McDermott. "I asked A.I. to write homilies for Ash Wednesday-and the results

were wild." America Magazine. February 2023. https://www.americamagazine.org/faith/2023/02/22/homily-ash-wednesday-244788
[376] *The Making of Star Wars: The Empire Strikes Back (Enhanced Edition).* J. W. Rinzler. 2013. Page 25.
[377] Dean Kowalski. *Steven Spielberg and Philosophy: We're Gonna Need a Bigger Book* (The Philosophy of Popular Culture). University Press of Kentucky. 2011. Pages 89-90
[378] George Mejia channel. "Bicentennial Man Final Scene." Uploaded August 2014. https://youtu.be/6K2J3D0hTKY
[379] Even the administrator of the YouTube channel has no control or power over this (a fact I can testify to as a YouTube channel owner myself).
[380] Gary Bates. *Alien Intrusion.* Creation Book Publishers. 2010. Chapter 2.
[381] By implying that our own spiritual faculties are only material; no categorically different than any computer.
[382] Yuval Noah Harari YouTube Channel. "Humanity is not that simple | Yuval Noah Harari & Pedro Pinto." Uploaded June 2023. https://youtu.be/4hIlDiVDww4
[383] https://twitter.com/lexfridman/status/1653051310034305025
[384] "Tamagotchi kids: could the future of parenthood be having virtual children in the metaverse?" The Guardian. May 2022. https://www.theguardian.com/technology/2022/may/31/tamagotchi-kids-future-parenthood-virutal-children-metaverse
[385] Douglas Busvine. "Collective consciousness to replace God - author Dan Brown." Reuters. October 2017. https://www.yahoo.com/news/collective-consciousness-replace-god-author-dan-brown-120033225.html
[386] John Brandon. "An AI god will emerge by 2042 and write its own bible. Will you worship it?" VentureBeat. October 2017. https://venturebeat.com/ai/an-ai-god-will-emerge-by-2042-and-write-its-own-bible-will-you-worship-it/
[387] Spencer Van Dyk. "'I warned you guys in 1984,' 'Terminator' filmmaker James Cameron says of AI's risks to humanity." CTV News. July 2023. https://www.ctvnews.ca/sci-tech/i-warned-you-guys-in-1984-terminator-filmmaker-james-cameron-says-of-ai-s-risks-to-humanity-1.6484546
[388] https://twitter.com/elonmusk/status/1699440845890494582
[389] Walter Isaacson. "Inside Elon Musk's Struggle for the Future of AI." TIME Magazine. September 2023. https://time.com/6310076/elon-musk-ai-walter-isaacson-biography/
[390] Ibid.
[391] Javier David. "Rise of the machines! Musk warns of 'summoning the demon' with AI: Report." CNBC. October 2014. https://www.cnbc.com/2014/10/25/teslas-musk-ai-is-like-summoning-the-demon-washington-post.html
[392] *The Life and Revelations of Anne Catherine Emmerich.* Carl E. Schmoger, C.SS.R. TAN. 2012. Volume II. Ch.3
[393] Christopher Partridge. *The Occult World* (Routledge Worlds). Routledge. 2016. Page 202.
[394] Samuel E Loewenstamm. "The Making and Destruction of the Golden Calf." Biblica, vol. 48, no. 4, 1967. Pages 481–490.
[395] https://youtu.be/cFIKpoIt4aE
[396] Contra-macroevolution
[397] World Economic Forum. "A cyber-attack with COVID-like characteristics?" https://www.weforum.org/videos/a-cyber-attack-with-covid-like-characteristics
[398] https://youtu.be/cDybeNbFJXE
[399] Paul Thigpen. *Extraterrestrial Intelligence and the Catholic Faith.* TAN. 2022. What About UFOs?

[400] Milton Rothman. *A Physicist's Guide to Skepticism: Applying Laws of Physics to Faster-Than-Light Travel, Psychic Phenomena, Telepathy, Time Travel, UFOs, and Other Pseudo-scientific Claims.* Prometheus. 1988.
[401] "Happy the elephant is not a person, a court rules." NPR/Associated Press. June 2022. https://www.npr.org/2022/06/14/1105031075/bronx-zoo-elephant-not-person-court-rules
[402] https://pawfecthouse.com/collections/gifts-for-pet-lovers/products/remember-when-visiting-our-house-personalized-decorative-mat
[403] https://www.mensajerosdivinos.org/en/blog/revelations-divine-messengers-about-kingdoms-nature-part-3-animal-kingdom
[404] NR Staff. "Stupid Pet Tricks." National Review. September 2003. https://www.nationalreview.com/2003/09/stupid-pet-tricks/
[405] http://sonyafitzpatrick.com/
[406] https://www.ecatholic2000.com/cts/untitled-115.shtml
[407] Sophie Bushwick. "How Scientists Are Using AI to Talk to Animals." Scientific American. February 2023. https://www.scientificamerican.com/article/how-scientists-are-using-ai-to-talk-to-animals/
[408] Peter Kreft. *Summa Philosophica.* St. Augustine's Press. 2012. Page 108
[409] https://youtu.be/foahTqz7On4
[410] Jeffrey Kluger. "Koko the Gorilla Wasn't Human, But She Taught Us So Much About Ourselves." TIME Magazine. June 2018 https://time.com/5318710/koko-gorilla-life/
[411] Stephen Anderson. *Doctor Dolittle's Delusion: Animals and the Uniqueness of Human Language.* Yale University Press. 2004. Chapter 11.
[412] Kennedy Hall. "Dr. Robert Malone: World Economic Forum plans to 'hack' human beings are a fantasy." LifeSiteNews. June 2022.
https://www.lifesitenews.com/blogs/dr-robert-malone-world-economic-forum-plans-to-hack-human-beings-are-a-fantasy/
[413] Rich McCormick. "Odds are we're living in a simulation, says Elon Musk." The Verge. June 2016. https://www.theverge.com/2016/6/2/11837874/elon-musk-says-odds-living-in-simulation
[414] https://dsdoconnor.com/tyson/
[415] St. Louis de Montfort. "Prayer for Missionaries." https://www.montfort.org.uk/Writings/PM.php
[416] St. Louis de Montfort, *True Devotion to Mary*, paragraphs 46-48.
[417] *Le Pelerinage de Lourdes.* Encyclical of Pope Pius XII Warning Against Materialism on the Centenary of the Apparitions at Lourdes. July 2, 1957
[418] Pope Pius XII. Encyclical, *Fidei Donum.* April 21, 1957
[419] General Audience of John Paul II. "May Your Kingdom Come" https://www.vatican.va/content/john-paul-ii/en/audiences/2002/documents/hf_jp-ii_aud_20021106.html November 6, 2002
[420] Pope John Paul II. Easter Address. March 10th, 1986
[421] Address of Pope John Paul II to the Rogationist Fathers. § 6. May 16, 1997. For more context and analysis of this quote, please see Chapter 12 of *Thy Will Be Done* (2021)
[422] Cf. *Summa Contra Gentiles.* Book II. Chapter 46, §5
[423] Letter of the Servant of God Luisa Piccarreta to Federico Abresch
[424] Letter of the Servant of God Luisa Piccarreta to "Irene." December 5, 1939
[425] Pope Francis. Morning Meditation in the Chapel of the Domus Sanctae Marthae. https://www.vatican.va/content/francesco/en/cotidie/2014/documents/papa-

francesco-cotidie_20140512_ostiaries.html
426 Elizabeth Dias. "For Pope Francis, It's About More than Martians." TIME Magazine. May 2014. https://time.com/99616/for-pope-francis-its-about-more-than-martians/
427 Elise Harris. "Do aliens exist? Pope Francis tackles this (and other things) in new interview." Catholic News Agency. October 2015. https://www.catholicnewsagency.com/news/32820/do-aliens-exist-pope-francis-tackles-this-and-other-things-in-new-interview
428 Pope Francis. Apostolic Letter, Sublimitas Et Miseria Hominis, On The Fourth Centenary Of The Birth Of Blaise Pascal https://www.vatican.va/content/francesco/en/apost_letters/documents/20230619-sublimitas-et-miseria-hominis.html
429 Simon Caldwell. "Pope Benedict predicted gender ideology would be final rebellion against God" The Catholic Herald. May 2023. https://catholicherald.co.uk/pope-benedict-predicted-gender-ideology-would-be-final-rebellion-against-god/
430 Frances Kennedy. "Rome warns the clergy not to get too familiar with the Devil." Independent UK. September 2000. https://www.independent.co.uk/news/world/europe/rome-warns-the-clergy-not-to-get-too-familiar-with-the-devil-699589.html
431 Msgr. Corrado Balducci. *The Devil "Alive and Active in Our World."* Alba House. 1990. Page 126.
432 https://angelusnews.com/arts-culture/leon-bloy/
433 Fr. Chad Ripperger. *Dominion: The Nature of Diabolic Warfare.* 2022.
434 Pope John Paul II. Homily at the Beatification Of Francisco And Jacinta Marto. Shepherds Of Fatima. May 13, 2000 https://www.vatican.va/content/john-paul-ii/en/travels/2000/documents/hf_jp-ii_hom_20000513_beatification-fatima.html
435 https://www.ecatholic2000.com/haydock/ntcomment278.shtml
436 Ibid.
437 Ibid.
438 http://newtheologicalmovement.blogspot.com/2012/10/did-st-raphael-lie-when-he-said-i-am.html
439 https://isidore.co/aquinas/english/QDdeAnima.htm
440 Ibid.
441 St. Thomas Aquinas. *De Anima.* Article 8.
442 Ibid.
443 i.e., in accordance with the just demands of nature, which, in a sense, He is "required" to grant.
444 St. Thomas Aquinas. *De Anima.* Article 8.
445 Recall, as well, that the revelations of Jesus to Luisa repeatedly rule out the possibility of aliens—see Part Two.
446https://spiritdaily.org/blog/mail/mailbag-scholar-documents-padre-pios-comments-on-extraterrestrial-life
447 Paul Thigpen. *Extraterrestrial Intelligence and the Catholic Faith.* TAN. 2022. Ch. 8
448 https://www.vatican.va/content/john-paul-ii/it/speeches/1999/november/documents/hf_jp-ii_spe_19991128_parrocchia-santi-innocenzo-guido.html
449 Paul Thigpen. *Extraterrestrial Intelligence and the Catholic Faith.* TAN. 2022. Ch. 8
450 https://ruor.uottawa.ca/bitstream/10393/37164/4/Anthony%20PILLARI.pdf
451 https://garabandalnews.org/2018/06/10/garabandal-why-2018/
452 https://catholicstand.com/20-20-vision-of-garabandal-with-marc-conza/
453 Paul Thigpen. *Extraterrestrial Intelligence and the Catholic Faith.* TAN. 2022. Ch. 10

[454] St. Athanasius. *Life of St. Anthony*. https://www.newadvent.org/fathers/2811.htm
[455] Gavin, John. "St. Jerome's Narnia: transformation and asceticism in the desert and beyond the wardrobe." *Mythlore*, vol. 33, no. 2, spring-summer 2015, pp. 113+
[456] Paul Thigpen. *Extraterrestrial Intelligence and the Catholic Faith*. TAN. 2022. Ch. 1
[457] Paul Thigpen. *Extraterrestrial Intelligence and the Catholic Faith*. TAN. 2022. Ch. 7
[458] *The Life And Revelations Of Anne Catherine Emmerich*. Volume One. Page 208
[459] C.S. Lewis. *That Hideous Strength*. Chapter 15.
[460] Marie George. *Christianity and Extraterrestrials?: A Catholic Perspective*. iUniverse. 2005. Chapter 4.
[461] *Fidei Donum*. April 21, 1957
[462] https://the-american-catholic.com/2017/02/26/fulton-sheen-on-the-anti-christ/
[463] Juan Gutierrez Gonzales, M.Sp.S. *Priests of Christ*. Pious Society of St. Paul, Inc. 2015. Theological Introduction.
[464] Fr. Marie-Michel Philipon. *Conchita: A Mother's Spiritual Diary*. Conclusion.
[465] Ibid.
[466] Juan Gutierrez Gonzales, M.Sp.S. *Priests of Christ*. Pious Society of St. Paul, Inc. 2015. Theological Introduction. Imprimatur from. Domenico Di Raimondo Romo, M.Sp.S. Pages 64-65
[467] Ibid. Pages 341-342
[468] Ibid.
[469] The only exception to this appears to be Nicholas of Cusa. To understand how his contribution to the matter, see Part Two.
[470] Address to the Rogationist Fathers. May 16, 1997

Jesus, I Trust in You

THY WILL BE DONE

†

Our Father, Who art in Heaven,
Hallowed be Thy Name. Thy Kingdom come.
Thy Will be done, on earth as it is in Heaven.
Give us this day our daily bread.
And forgive us our trespasses, as we forgive those who trespass against us. And lead us not into temptation,
but deliver us from evil. Amen.

✡✡✡

Hail Mary, full of grace, the Lord is with thee.
Blessed art thou among women,
and blessed is the fruit of thy womb, Jesus.
Holy Mary, Mother of God, pray for us sinners,
now and at the hour of our death. Amen.

✡✡✡

Glory be to the Father, and to the Son
and to the Holy Spirit,
as it was in the beginning, is now, and ever shall be,
world without end. Amen.

✡✡✡

Saint Michael the Archangel, defend us in battle. Be our protection against the wickedness and snares of the Devil; May God rebuke him, we humbly pray; And do thou, O Prince of the Heavenly Host, by the power of God, cast into hell Satan and all evil spirits who prowl about the world seeking the ruin of souls.
Amen.

About the Author

Daniel O'Connor is an adjunct professor of philosophy and religion at a State University of New York Community College, where he has taught for seven years. For over a decade serving as an educator, he is honored to have instructed thousands of students in courses on philosophy, existentialism, Catholic catechesis, comparative religion, mathematics, physics, and more. Originally a mechanical engineer, Daniel's first job after graduating RPI (Rensselaer) had him running high-tech experiments at the GE Global Research headquarters aimed at achieving breakthroughs in carbon-nanotube-based quantum electron emissions. There, he ran a test resulting in a world record, but realized—after defending the right to life on a radio show debate later that same day—that he could do infinitely more good for the world by speaking up for the truth than by contributing to the world's technological advancement. After a powerful GE manager informed Daniel he must promise to never again speak about religion at work, Daniel quit on the spot. In 2013, Daniel obtained a master's degree in Philosophical Theology from a Catholic college and seminary in Connecticut, and has been teaching ever since. He has thus far completed several years of post-master's studies towards his PhD in Philosophy at the University at Albany. Daniel is the author of several books, including *Thy Will Be Done*. He writes for his personal website (www.DSDOConnor.com) where his books, talks, videos, and other works may be found. Daniel lives in New York with his wife, Regina, and their five children, Joseph, David, Mary, Luisa, and John Paul.

***

Have you found this book helpful?

Kindly consider leaving a review for it on Amazon (simply search for this book's title and author on Amazon.com, or find it by going directly to amazon.com/Daniel-OConnor/e/B00UA0DJ4O or www.OnlyManBearsHisImage.com.) Each review posted helps this book to be introduced to more people.